SPC
Calculations for Control Limits

Notation:

UCL—Upper Control Limit
LCL—Lower Control Limit
CL —Center Line
n —Sample Size
PCR—Process Capability Ratio
$\hat{\sigma}$ —Process Standard Deviation

$\bar{x}$ —Average of Measurements
$\bar{\bar{x}}$ —Average of Averages
R —Range
$\bar{R}$ —Average of Ranges
USL—Upper Specification Limit
LSL—Lower Specification Limit

Variables Data ($\bar{x}$ and R Control Charts)

$\bar{x}$ Control Chart

$\text{UCL} = \bar{\bar{x}} + A_2\bar{R}$

$\text{LCL} = \bar{\bar{x}} - A_2\bar{R}$

$\text{CL} = \bar{\bar{x}}$

R Control Chart

$\text{UCL} = \bar{R}\, D_4$

$\text{LCL} = \bar{R}\, D_3$

$\text{CL} = \bar{R}$

Capability Study

$C_p = (\text{USL} - \text{LSL})/(6\,\hat{\sigma})$; where $\hat{\sigma} = \bar{R}/d_2$

n	A_2	D_3	D_4	d_2
2	1.880	0.000	3.267	1.128
3	1.023	0.000	2.574	1.693
4	0.729	0.000	2.282	2.059
5	0.577	0.000	2.114	2.326
6	0.483	0.000	2.004	2.534
7	0.419	0.076	1.924	2.704
8	0.373	0.136	1.864	2.847
9	0.337	0.184	1.816	2.970
10	0.308	0.223	1.777	3.078

Attribute Data (p, np, c, and u Control Charts)

Control Chart Formulas

	p (fraction)	np (number of nonconforming)	c (count of nonconformances)	u (count of nonconformances/unit)
CL	$\bar{p}$	$n\bar{p}$	$\bar{c}$	$\bar{u}$
UCL	$\bar{p}+3\sqrt{\frac{\bar{p}(1-\bar{p})}{n}}$	$n\bar{p}+3\sqrt{n\bar{p}(1-\bar{p})}$	$\bar{c}+3\sqrt{\bar{c}}$	$\bar{u}+3\sqrt{\frac{\bar{u}}{n}}$
LCL	$\bar{p}-3\sqrt{\frac{\bar{p}(1-\bar{p})}{n}}$	$n\bar{p}-3\sqrt{n\bar{p}(1-\bar{p})}$	$\bar{c}-3\sqrt{\bar{c}}$	$\bar{u}-3\sqrt{\frac{\bar{u}}{n}}$
Notes	If n varies, use $\bar{n}$ or individual n_i	n must be a constant	n must be a constant	If n varies, use $\bar{n}$ or individual n_i

Guide to Univariate Process Monitoring and Control

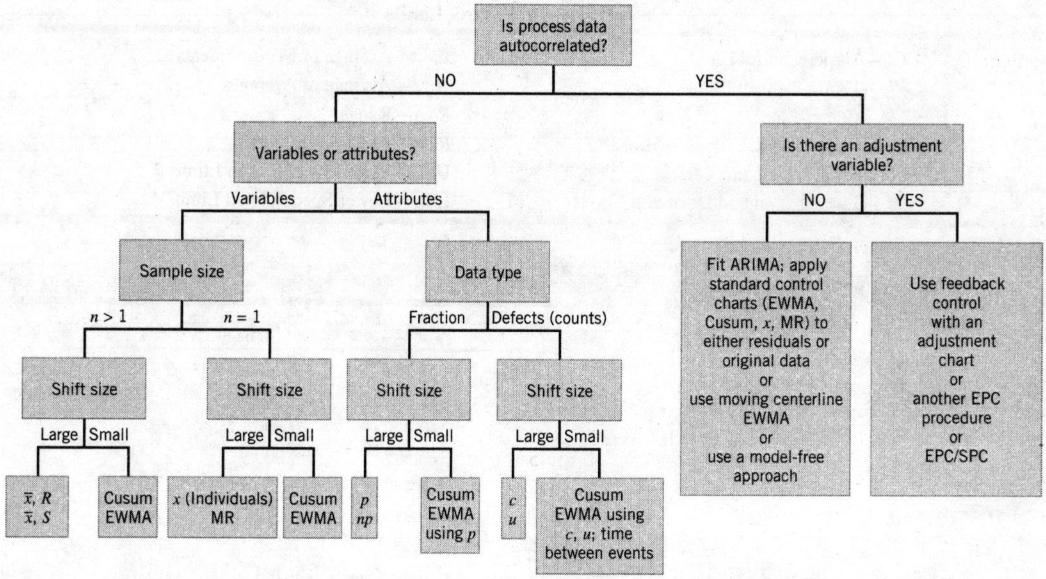

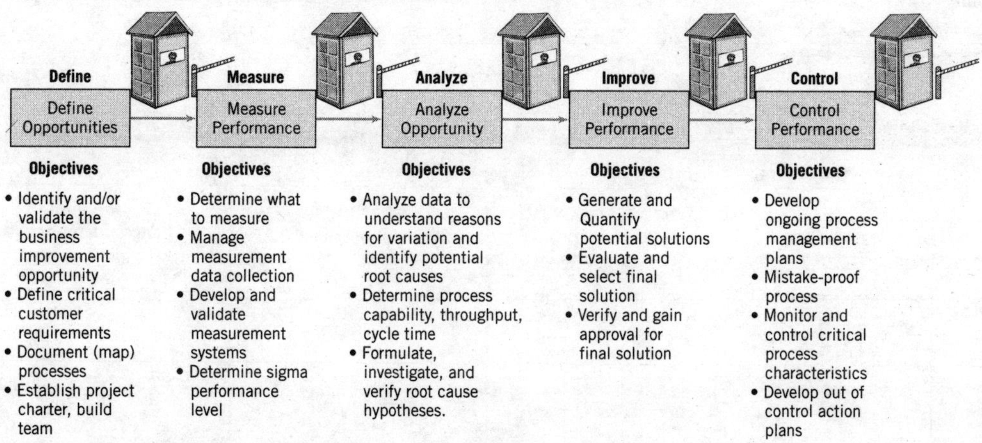

The DMAIC Process

Sixth Edition

Statistical Quality Control: A Modern Introduction

International Student Version

DOUGLAS C. MONTGOMERY
Arizona State University

WILEY-
INDIA

Statistical Quality Control: A Modern Introduction
Sixth Edition

Authorized reprint by Wiley India Pvt. Ltd., 4436/7, Ansari Road, Daryaganj, New Delhi – 110002.

Cover Image: Getty Images/iStockphoto

Reprint: 2018

Printed at: Nisha Enterprises.

ISBN: 978-81-265-2506-5

About the Author

Douglas C. Montgomery is Regents' Professor of Industrial Engineering and Statistics and the Arizona State University Foundation Professor of Engineering. He received his B.S., M.S., and Ph.D. degrees from Virginia Polytechnic Institute, all in engineering. From 1969 to 1984 he was a faculty member of the School of Industrial & Systems Engineering at the Georgia Institute of Technology; from 1984 to 1988 he was at the University of Washington, where he held the John M. Fluke Distinguished Chair of Manufacturing Engineering, was Professor of Mechanical Engineering, and was Director of the Program in Industrial Engineering.

Dr. Montgomery has research and teaching interests in engineering statistics including statistical quality-control techniques, design of experiments, regression analysis and empirical model building, and the application of operations research methodology to problems in manufacturing systems. He has authored and coauthored more than 190 technical papers in these fields and is the author of twelve other books. Dr. Montgomery is a Fellow of the American Society for Quality, a Fellow of the American Statistical Association, a Fellow of the Royal Statistical Society, a Fellow of the Institute of Industrial Engineers, an elected member of the International Statistical Institute, and an elected Academican of the International Academy of Quality. He is a Shewhart Medalist of the American Society for Quality, and he also has received the Brumbaugh Award, the Lloyd S. Nelson Award, the William G. Hunter Award, and two Shewell Awards from the ASQ. He is a recipient of the Ellis R. Ott Award. He is a former editor of the *Journal of Quality Technology,* is one of the current chief editors of *Quality and Reliability Engineering International,* and serves on the editorial boards of several journals.

Preface

Introduction

This book is about the use of modern statistical methods for quality control and improvement. It provides comprehensive coverage of the subject from basic principles to state-of-the-art concepts and applications. The objective is to give the reader a sound understanding of the principles and the basis for applying them in a variety of situations. Although statistical techniques are emphasized throughout, the book has a strong engineering and management orientation. Extensive knowledge of statistics is not a prerequisite for using this book. Readers whose background includes a basic course in statistical methods will find much of the material in this book easily accessible.

Audience

The book is an outgrowth of more than 35 years of teaching, research, and consulting in the application of statistical methods for industrial problems. It is designed as a textbook for students enrolled in colleges and universities, who are studying engineering, statistics, management, and related fields and are taking a first course in statistical quality control. The basic quality-control course is often taught at the junior or senior level. All of the standard topics for this course are covered in detail. Some more advanced material is also available in the book, and this could be used with advanced undergraduates who have had some previous exposure to the basics or in a course aimed at graduate students. I have also used the text materials extensively in programs for professional practitioners, including quality and reliability engineers, manufacturing and development engineers, product designers, managers, procurement specialists, marketing personnel, technicians and laboratory analysts, inspectors, and operators. Many professionals have also used the material for self-study.

Chapter Organization and Topical Coverage

The book contains five parts. Part I is introductory. The first chapter is an introduction to the philosophy and basic concepts of quality improvement. It notes that quality has become a major business strategy and that organizations that successfully improve quality can increase their productivity, enhance their market penetration, and achieve greater profitability and a strong competitive advantage. Some of the managerial and implementation aspects of quality improvement are included. Chapter 2 describes DMAIC, an acronym for define, measure, analyze, improve, and control. The DMAIC process is an excellent framework to use in conducting quality improvement projects. DMAIC often is associated with six-sigma, but regardless of the approach taken by an organization strategically, DMAIC is an excellent tactical tool for quality professionals to employ.

Part II is a description of statistical methods useful in quality improvement. Topics include sampling and descriptive statistics, the basic notions of probability and probability distributions, point and interval estimation of parameters, and statistical hypothesis testing. These topics are usually covered in a basic course in statistical methods; however, their presentation in this text is from the quality-engineering viewpoint. My experience has been that even readers with a strong statistical background will find the approach to this material useful and somewhat different from a standard statistics textbook.

Part III contains four chapters covering the basic methods of statistical process control (SPC) and methods for process capability analysis. Even though several SPC problem-solving tools are discussed (including Pareto charts and cause-and-effect diagrams, for example), the primary focus in this section is on the Shewhart control chart. The Shewhart control chart certainly is not new, but its use in modern-day business and industry is of tremendous value.

There are four chapters in Part IV that present more advanced SPC methods. Included are the cumulative sum and exponentially weighted moving average control charts (Chapter 9), several important univariate control charts such as procedures for short production runs, autocorrelated data, and multiple stream processes (Chapter 10), multivariate process monitoring and control (Chapter 11), and feedback adjustment techniques (Chapter 12). Some of this material is at a higher level than Part III, but much of it is accessible by advanced undergraduates or first-year graduate students. This material forms the basis of a second course in statistical quality control and improvement for this audience.

Part V contains two chapters that show how statistically designed experiments can be used for process design, development, and improvement. Chapter 13 presents the fundamental concepts of designed experiments and introduces factorial and fractional factorial designs, with particular emphasis on the two-level system of designs. These designs are used extensively in the industry for factor screening and process characterization. Although the treatment of the subject is not extensive and is no substitute for a formal course in experimental design, it will enable the reader to appreciate more sophisticated examples of experimental design. Chapter 14 introduces response surface methods and designs, illustrates evolutionary operation (EVOP) for process monitoring, and shows how statistically designed experiments can be used for process robustness studies. Chapters 13 and 14 emphasize the important interrelationship between statistical process control and experimental design for process improvement.

Two chapters deal with acceptance sampling in Part VI. The focus is on lot-by-lot acceptance sampling, although there is some discussion of continuous sampling and MIL STD 1235C in Chapter 14. Other sampling topics presented include various aspects of the design of acceptance-sampling plans, a discussion of MIL STD 105E, MIL STD 414 (and their civilian counterparts, ANSI/ASQC ZI.4 and ANSI/ASQC ZI.9), and other techniques such as chain sampling and skip-lot sampling.

Throughout the book, guidelines are given for selecting the proper type of statistical technique to use in a wide variety of situations. Additionally, extensive references to journal articles and other technical literature should assist the reader in applying the methods described. I also have showed how the different techniques presented are used in the DMAIC process.

Supporting Text Materials

Supplemental Text Material

I have written a set of supplemental materials to augment many of the chapters in the book. The supplemental material contains topics that could not easily fit into a chapter without seriously disrupting the flow. The topics are shown in the Table of Contents for the book and in the individual chapter outlines. Some of this material consists of proofs or derivations, new topics of a (sometimes) more advanced nature, supporting details concerning remarks or concepts presented in the text, and answers to frequently asked questions. The supplemental material provides an interesting set of accompanying readings for anyone curious about the field. It is available at www.wiley.com/college/montgomery

Instructor's Materials

The instructor's section of the textbook Web site contains the following:

1. Solutions to the text problems
2. The supplemental text material described above
3. A set of Microsoft® PowerPoint® slides for the basic SPC course
4. Data sets from the book, in electronic form
5. Image Gallery, illustrations from the book in electronic format

The instructor's section is for instructor use only and is password-protected. Visit the Instructor Companion Site portion of the Web site by going to www.wiley.com or call your Wiley representative to register for a password.

The World Wide Web Page

The Web page for the book is accessible through the Wiley home page. It contains the supplemental text material and the data sets in electronic form. It will also be used to post items of interest to text users. Go to www.wiley.com.

ACKNOWLEDGMENTS

Many people have generously contributed their time and knowledge of statistics and quality improvement to this book. I would like to thank Dr. Bill Woodall, Dr. Doug Hawkins, Dr. Joe Sullivan, Dr. George Runger, Dr. Bert Keats, Dr. Bob Hogg, Mr. Eric Ziegel, Dr. Joe Pignatiello, Dr. John Ramberg, Dr. Ernie Saniga, Dr. Enrique Del Castillo, Dr. Sarah Streett, and Dr. Jim Alloway for their thorough and insightful comments on this and previous editions. They generously shared many of their ideas and teaching experiences with me, leading to substantial improvements in the book.

Over the years since the first edition was published, I have received assistance and ideas from a great many other people. A complete list of colleagues with whom I have interacted would be impossible to enumerate. However, some of the major contributors and their professional affiliations are as follows: Dr. Mary R. Anderson-Rowland, Dr. Dwayne A. Rollier, Dr. Norma F. Hubele, and Dr. Murat Kulahci, Arizona State University; Mr. Seymour M. Selig, formerly of the Office of Naval Research; Dr. Lynwood A. Johnson, Dr. Russell G. Heikes, Dr. David E. Fyffe, and Dr. H. M. Wadsworth, Jr., Georgia Institute of Technology; Dr. Sharad Prabhu and Dr. Robert Rodriguez, SAS Institute; Dr. Scott Kowalski, Minitab; Dr. Richard L. Storch and Dr. Christina M. Mastrangelo, University of Washington; Dr. Cynthia A. Lowry, formerly of Texas Christian University; Dr. Smiley Cheng, Dr. John Brewster, Dr. Brian Macpherson, and Dr. Fred Spiring, the University of Manitoba; Dr. Joseph D. Moder, University of Miami; Dr. Frank B. Alt, University of Maryland; Dr. Kenneth E. Case, Oklahoma State University; Dr. Daniel R. McCarville, Dr. Lisa Custer, Dr. Pat Spagon, and Mr. Robert Stuart, all formerly of Motorola; Dr. Richard Post, Intel Corporation; Dr. Dale Sevier, San Diego State University; Mr. John A. Butora, Mr. Leon V. Mason, Mr. Lloyd K. Collins, Mr. Dana D. Lesher, Mr. Roy E. Dent, Mr. Mark Fazey, Ms. Kathy Schuster, Mr. Dan Fritze, Dr. J. S. Gardiner, Mr. Ariel Rosentrater, Mr. Lolly Marwah, Mr. Ed Schleicher, Mr. Amiin Weiner, and Ms. Elaine Baechtle, IBM; Mr. Thomas C. Bingham, Mr. K. Dick Vaughn, Mr. Robert LeDoux, Mr. John Black, Mr. Jack Wires, Dr. Julian Anderson, Mr. Richard Alkire, and Mr. Chase Nielsen, the Boeing Company; Ms. Karen Madison, Mr. Don Walton, and Mr. Mike Goza, Alcoa; Mr. Harry Peterson-Nedry, Ridgecrest Vineyards and The Chehalem Group; Dr. Russell A. Boyles, formerly of Precision Castparts Corporation; Dr. Sadre Khalessi and Mr. Franz Wagner, Signetics Corporation;

Mr. Larry Newton and Mr. C. T. Howlett, Georgia Pacific Corporation; Mr. Robert V. Baxley, Monsanto Chemicals; Dr. Craig Fox, Dr. Thomas L. Sadosky, Mr. James F. Walker, and Mr. John Belvins, the Coca-Cola Company; Mr. Bill Wagner and Mr. Al Pariseau, Litton Industries; Mr. John M. Fluke, Jr., John Fluke Manufacturing Company; Dr. Paul Tobias, formerly of IBM and Semitech; Dr. William DuMouchel and Ms. Janet Olson, BBN Software Products Corporation. I would also like to acknowledge the many contributions of my late partner in Statistical Productivity Consultants, Mr. Sumner S. Averett. All of these individuals and many others have contributed to my knowledge of the quality improvement field.

Other acknowledgments go to the editorial and production staff at Wiley, particularly Ms. Charity Robey and Mr. Wayne Anderson, with whom I worked for many years, and Ms. Jenny Welter; they have had much patience with me over the years and have contributed greatly toward the success of this book. Dr. Cheryl L. Jennings made many valuable contributions by her careful checking of the manuscript and proof materials. I also thank Dr. Gary Hogg and Dr. Ron Askin, former and current chairs of the Department of Industrial Engineering at Arizona State University, for their support and for providing a terrific environment in which to teach and conduct research.

I thank the various professional societies and publishers who have given permission to reproduce their materials in my text. Permission credit is acknowledged at appropriate places in this book.

I am also indebted to the many organizations that have sponsored my research and my graduate students for a number of years, including the member companies of the National Science Foundation/Industry/University Cooperative Research Center in Quality and Reliability Engineering at Arizona State University, the Office of Naval Research, the National Science Foundation, the Semiconductor Research Corporation, the Aluminum Company of America, and the IBM Corporation. Finally, I would like to thank the many users of the previous editions of this book, including students, practicing professionals, and my academic colleagues. Many of the changes and improvements in this edition of the book are the direct result of your feedback.

DOUGLAS C. MONTGOMERY
Tempe, Arizona

Contents

PART 1

Introduction

Controlling and improving quality has become an important business strategy for many organizations; manufacturers, distributors, transportation companies, financial services organizations; health care providers, and government agencies. Quality is a competitive advantage. A business that can delight customers by improving and controlling quality can dominate its competitors. This book is about the technical methods for achieving success in quality control and improvement, and offers guidance on how to successfully implement these methods.

Part 1 contains two chapters. Chapter 1 contains the basic definitions of quality and quality improvement, provides a brief overview of the tools and methods discussed in greater detail in subsequent parts of the book, and discusses the management systems for quality improvement. Chapter 2 is devoted to the DMAIC (define, measure, analyze, improve, and control) problem-solving process, which is an excellent framework for implementing quality improvement. We also show how the methods discussed in the book are used in DMAIC.

1 Modern Quality Management and Improvement

CHAPTER OUTLINE

CHAPTER OVERVIEW AND LEARNING OBJECTIVES

This book is about the use of statistical methods and other problem-solving techniques to improve the **quality** of the products used by our society. These products consist of **manufactured goods** such as automobiles, computers, and clothing, as well as **services** such as the generation and distribution of electrical energy, public transportation, banking, retailing, and health care. Quality improvement methods can be applied to any area within a company or organization, including manufacturing, process development, engineering design, finance and accounting, marketing, distribution and logistics, customer service, and field service of products. This text presents the technical tools that are needed to achieve quality improvement in these organizations.

In this chapter we give the basic definitions of quality, quality improvement, and other quality engineering terminology. We also discuss the historical development of quality improvement methodology and overview the statistical tools essential for modern professional practice. A brief discussion of some management and business aspects for implementing quality improvement is also given.

After careful study of this chapter you should be able to do the following:

1. Define and discuss quality and quality improvement
2. Discuss the different dimensions of quality
3. Discuss the evolution of modern quality improvement methods
4. Discuss the role that variability and statistical methods play in controlling and improving quality
5. Describe the quality management philosophies of W. Edwards Deming, Joseph M. Juran, and Armand V. Feigenbaum
6. Discuss total quality management, the Malcolm Baldrige National Quality Award, six-sigma, and quality systems and standards
7. Explain the links between quality and productivity and between quality and cost
8. Discuss product liability
9. Discuss the three functions: quality planning, quality assurance, and quality control and improvement

1.1 The Meaning of Quality and Quality Improvement

We may define **quality** in many ways. Most people have a conceptual understanding of quality as relating to one or more desirable characteristics that a product or service should possess. Although this conceptual understanding is certainly a useful starting point, we will give a more precise and useful definition.

Quality has become one of the most important consumer decision factors in the selection among competing products and services. The phenomenon is widespread, regardless of whether the consumer is an individual, an industrial organization, a retail store, a bank or financial institution, or a military defense program. Consequently, understanding and improving quality are key factors leading to business success, growth, and enhanced competitiveness. There is a substantial return on investment from improved quality and from successfully employing quality as an integral part of overall business strategy. In this section we provide operational definitions of quality and quality improvement. We begin with a brief discussion of the different dimensions of quality and some basic terminology.

1.1.1 Dimensions of Quality

The quality of a product can be described and evaluated in several ways. It is often very important to differentiate these different **dimensions of quality.** Garvin (1987) provides an excellent discussion of eight components or dimensions of quality. We summarize his key points concerning these dimensions of quality as follows:

1. **Performance** (Will the product do the intended job?) Potential customers usually evaluate a product to determine if it will perform certain specific functions and determine how well it performs them. For example, you could evaluate spreadsheet software packages for a PC to determine which data manipulation operations they perform. You may discover that one outperforms another with respect to the execution speed.

2. **Reliability** (How often does the product fail?) Complex products, such as many appliances, automobiles, or airplanes, will usually require some repair over their service life. For example, you should expect that an automobile will require occasional repair, but if the car requires frequent repair, we say that it is unreliable. There are many industries in which the customer's view of quality is greatly impacted by the reliability dimension of quality.
3. **Durability** (How long does the product last?) This is the effective service life of the product. Customers obviously want products that perform satisfactorily over a long period of time. The automobile and major appliance industries are examples of businesses where this dimension of quality is very important to most customers.
4. **Serviceability** (How easy is it to repair the product?) There are many industries in which the customer's view of quality is directly influenced by how quickly and economically a repair or routine maintenance activity can be accomplished. Examples include the appliance and automobile industries and many types of service industries (how long did it take a credit card company to correct an error in your bill?).
5. **Aesthetics** (What does the product look like?) This is the visual appeal of the product, often taking into account factors such as style, color, shape, packaging alternatives, tactile characteristics, and other sensory features. For example, soft-drink beverage manufacturers have relied on the visual appeal of their packaging to differentiate their product from other competitors.
6. **Features** (What does the product do?) Usually, customers associate high quality with products that have added features; that is, those that have features beyond the basic performance of the competition. For example, you might consider a spreadsheet software package to be of superior quality if it had built-in statistical analysis features while its competitors did not.
7. **Perceived Quality** (What is the reputation of the company or its product?) In many cases, customers rely on the past reputation of the company concerning quality of its products. This reputation is directly influenced by failures of the product that are highly visible to the public or that require product recalls, and by how the customer is treated when a quality-related problem with the product is reported. Perceived quality, customer loyalty, and repeated business are closely interconnected. For example, if you make regular business trips using a particular airline, and the flight almost always arrives on time and the airline company does not lose or damage your luggage, you will probably prefer to fly on that carrier instead of its competitors.
8. **Conformance to Standards** (Is the product made exactly as the designer intended?) We usually think of a high-quality product as one that exactly meets the requirements placed on it. For example, how well does the hood fit on a new car? Is it perfectly flush with the fender height, and is the gap exactly the same on all sides? Manufactured parts that do not exactly meet the designer's requirements can cause significant quality problems when they are used as the components of a more complex assembly. An automobile consists of several thousand parts. If each one is just slightly too big or too small, many of the components will not fit together properly, and the vehicle (or its major subsystems) may not perform as the designer intended.

We see from the foregoing discussion that quality is indeed a multifaceted entity. Consequently, a simple answer to questions such as "What is quality?" or "What is quality improvement?" is not easy. The **traditional** definition of quality is based on the viewpoint that products and services must meet the requirements of those who use them.

Definition

Quality means fitness for use.

There are two general aspects of fitness for use: **quality of design** and **quality of conformance.** All goods and services are produced in various grades or levels of quality. These variations in grades or levels of quality are intentional, and, consequently, the appropriate technical term is quality of design. For example, all automobiles have as their basic objective providing safe transportation for the consumer. However, automobiles differ with respect to size, appointments, appearance, and performance. These differences are the result of intentional design differences among the types of automobiles. These design differences include the types of materials used in construction, specifications on the components, reliability obtained through engineering development of engines and drive trains, and other accessories or equipment.

The quality of conformance is how well the product conforms to the specifications required by the design. Quality of conformance is influenced by a number of factors, including the choice of manufacturing processes, the training and supervision of the workforce, the types of process controls, tests, and inspection activities that are employed, the extent to which these procedures are followed, and the motivation of the workforce to achieve quality.

Unfortunately, this definition has become associated more with the conformance aspect of quality than with design. This is in part due to the lack of formal education most designers and engineers receive in quality engineering methodology. This also leads to much less focus on the customer and more of a "conformance-to-specifications" approach to quality, regardless of whether the product, even when produced to standards, was actually "fit-for-use" by the customer. Also, there is still a widespread belief that quality is a problem that can be dealt with solely in manufacturing, or that the only way quality can be improved is by "gold-plating" the product.

We prefer a **modern** definition of quality:

Definition

Quality is inversely proportional to variability.

Note that this definition implies that if variability[1] in the important characteristics of a product decreases, the quality of the product increases.

As an example of the operational effectiveness of this definition, a few years ago, one of the automobile companies in the United States performed a comparative study of a transmission that was manufactured in a domestic plant and by a Japanese supplier. An analysis of warranty claims and repair costs indicated that there was a striking difference between the two sources of production, with the Japanese-produced transmission having much lower costs, as shown in Fig. 1.1. As part of the study to discover the cause of this difference in cost and performance, the company selected random samples of transmissions from each plant, disassembled them, and measured several critical quality characteristics.

[1] We are referring to unwanted or harmful variability. There are situations in which variability is actually good. As my good friend Bob Hogg has pointed out, "I really like Chinese food, but I don't want to eat it every night."

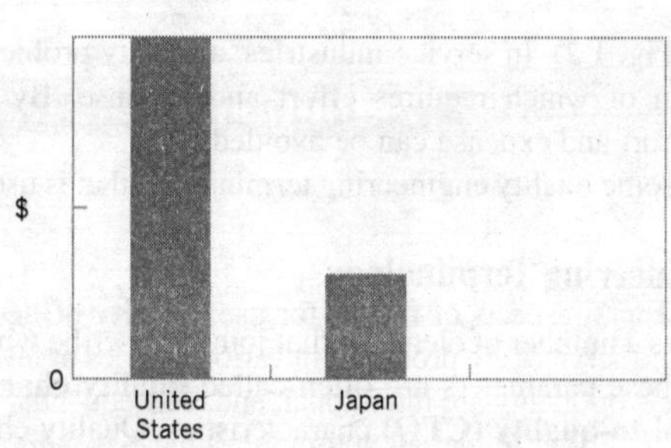

FIGURE 1.1 Warranty costs for transmissions.

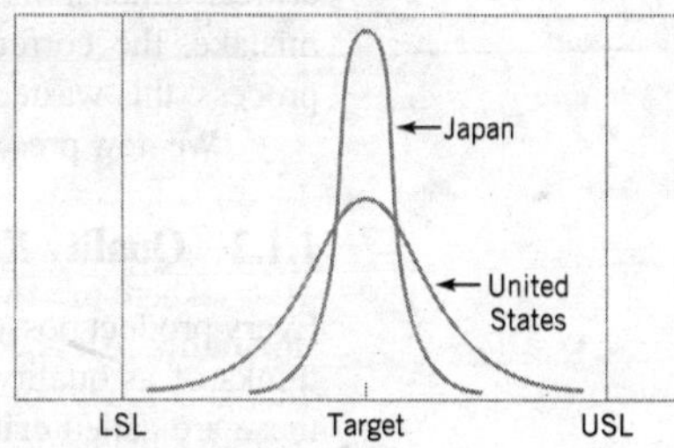

FIGURE 1.2 Distributions of critical dimensions for transmissions.

Figure 1.2 is generally representative of the results of this study. Note that both distributions of critical dimensions are centered at the desired or target value. However, the distribution of the critical characteristics for the transmissions manufactured in the United States takes up about 75% of the width of the specifications, implying that very few nonconforming units would be produced. In fact, the plant was producing at a quality level that was quite good, based on the generally accepted view of quality within the company. In contrast, the Japanese plant produced transmissions for which the same critical characteristics take up only about 25% of the specification band. As a result, there is considerably less variability in the critical quality characteristics of the Japanese-built transmissions in comparison to those built in the United States.

This is a very important finding. Jack Welch, the retired chief executive officer of General Electric, has observed that your customer doesn't see the mean of your process (the target in Fig. 1.2), he only sees the variability around that target that you have not removed. In almost all cases, this variability has significant customer impact.

There are two obvious questions here: Why did the Japanese do this? How did they do this? The answer to the "why" question is obvious from examination of Fig. 1.1. Reduced variability has directly translated into lower costs (the Japanese fully understood the point made by Welch). Furthermore, the Japanese-built transmissions shifted gears more smoothly, ran more quietly, and were generally perceived by the customer as superior to those built domestically. Fewer repairs and warranty claims means less **rework** and the reduction of wasted time, effort, and money. Thus, quality truly is inversely proportional to variability. Furthermore, it can be communicated very precisely in a language that everyone (particularly managers and executives) understands—namely, money.

How did the Japanese do this? The answer lies in the systematic and effective use of the methods described in this book. It also leads to the following definition of **quality improvement.**

Definition

Quality improvement is the reduction of variability in processes and products.

Excessive variability in process performance often results in **waste.** For example, consider the wasted money, time, and effort that is associated with the repairs represented in Fig. 1.1. Therefore, an alternate and frequently very useful definition is that quality improvement is the **reduction of waste.** This definition is particularly effective in **service industries,** where there may not be as many things that can be directly measured (like the transmission critical dimensions in Fig. 1.2). In service industries, a quality problem may be an error or a mistake, the correction of which requires effort and expense. By improving the service process, this wasted effort and expense can be avoided.

We now present some quality engineering terminology that is used throughout the book.

1.1.2 Quality Engineering Terminology

Every product possesses a number of elements that jointly describe what the user or consumer thinks of as quality. These parameters are often called **quality characteristics.** Sometimes these are called **critical-to-quality (CTQ)** characteristics. Quality characteristics may be of several types:

1. **Physical:** length, weight, voltage, viscosity
2. **Sensory:** taste, appearance, color
3. **Time Orientation:** reliability, durability, serviceability

Note that the different types of quality characteristics can relate directly or indirectly to the dimensions of quality discussed in the previous section.

Quality engineering is the set of operational, managerial, and engineering activities that a company uses to ensure that the quality characteristics of a product are at the nominal or required levels and that the variability around these desired levels is minimum. The techniques discussed in the book form much of the basic methodology used by engineers and other technical professionals to achieve these goals.

Most organizations find it difficult (and expensive) to provide the customer with products that have quality characteristics that are always identical from unit to unit, or are at levels that match customer expectations. A major reason for this is **variability.** There is a certain amount of variability in every product; consequently, no two products are ever identical. For example, the thickness of the blades on a jet turbine engine impeller is not identical even on the same impeller. Blade thickness will also differ between impellers. If this variation in blade thickness is small, then it may have no impact on the customer. However, if the variation is large, then the customer may perceive the unit to be undesirable and unacceptable. Sources of this variability include differences in materials, differences in the performance and operation of the manufacturing equipment, and differences in the way the operators perform their tasks. This line of thinking led to the previous definition of quality improvement.

Since variability can only be described in statistical terms, **statistical methods** play a central role in quality improvement efforts. In the application of statistical methods to quality engineering, it is fairly typical to classify data on quality characteristics as either **attributes** or **variables** data. Variables data are usually continuous measurements, such as length, voltage, or viscosity. Attributes data, on the other hand, are usually discrete data, often taking the form of counts. Such as the number of loan applications that could not be properly processed because of missing required information, or the number of emergency room arrivals that have to wait more than 30 minutes to receive medical attention. We will describe statistical-based quality engineering tools for dealing with both types of data.

Quality characteristics are often evaluated relative to **specifications.** For a manufactured product, the specifications are the desired measurements for the quality characteristics of the components and subassemblies that make up the product, as well as the desired values for the quality characteristics in the final product. For example, the diameter of a shaft used in an automobile transmission cannot be too large or it will not fit into the mating bearing, nor can it be too small, resulting in a loose fit, causing vibration, wear, and early failure of the assembly. In the service industries, specifications are typically in terms of the maximum amount of time to process an order or to provide a particular service.

A value of a measurement that corresponds to the desired value for that quality characteristic is called the **nominal** or **target value** for that characteristic. These target values are usually bounded by a range of values that, most typically, we believe will be sufficiently close to the target so as to not impact the function or performance of the product if the quality characteristic is in that range. The largest allowable value for a quality characteristic is called the **upper specification limit (USL),** and the smallest allowable value for a quality characteristic is called the **lower specification limit (LSL).** Some quality characteristics have specification limits on only one side of the target. For example, the compressive strength of a component used in an automobile bumper likely has a target value and a lower specification limit, but not an upper specification limit.

Specifications are usually the result of the engineering design process for the product. Traditionally, design engineers have arrived at a product design configuration through the use of engineering science principles, which often results in the designer specifying the target values for the critical design parameters. Then prototype construction and testing follow. This testing is often done in a very unstructured manner, without the use of statistically based experimental design procedures, and without much interaction with or knowledge of the manufacturing processes that must produce the component parts and final product. However, through this general procedure, the specification limits are usually determined by the design engineer. Then the final product is released to manufacturing. We refer to this as the **over-the-wall** approach to design.

Problems in product quality usually are greater when the over-the-wall approach to design is used. In this approach, specifications are often set without regard to the inherent variability that exists in materials, processes, and other parts of the system, which results in components or products that are nonconforming; that is, **nonconforming products** are those that fail to meet one or more of its specifications. A specific type of failure is called a **nonconformity.** A nonconforming product is not necessarily unfit for use; for example, a detergent may have a concentration of active ingredients that is below the lower specification limit, but it may still perform acceptably if the customer uses a greater amount of the product. A nonconforming product is considered **defective** if it has one or more **defects,** which are nonconformities that are serious enough to significantly affect the safe or effective use of the product. Obviously, failure on the part of a company to improve its manufacturing processes can also cause nonconformities and defects.

The over-the-wall design process has been the subject of much attention in the past 25 years. CAD/CAM systems have done much to automate the design process and to more effectively translate specifications into manufacturing activities and processes. Design for manufacturability and assembly has emerged as an important part of overcoming the inherent problems with the over-the-wall approach to design, and most engineers receive some background on those areas today as part of their formal education. The recent emphasis on **concurrent engineering** has stressed a team approach to design, with specialists in manufacturing, quality engineering, and other disciplines working together with the product designer at the earliest stages of the product design process. Furthermore, the effective use of the quality improvement methodology in this book, at all levels of the process used in technology commercialization and product realization, including product design, development, manufacturing, distribution, and customer support, plays a crucial role in quality improvement.

1.2 A Brief History of Quality Control and Improvement

Quality always has been an integral part of virtually all products and services. However, our awareness of its importance and the introduction of formal methods for quality control and improvement have been an evolutionary development. Table 1.1 presents a timeline of some

■ TABLE 1.1
A Timeline of Quality Methods

1700–1900	Quality is largely determined by the efforts of an individual craftsman.
	Eli Whitney introduces standardized, interchangeable parts to simplify assembly.
1875	Frederick W. Taylor introduces "Scientific Management" principles to divide work into smaller, more easily accomplished units—the first approach to dealing with more complex products and processes. The focus was on productivity. Later contributors were Frank Gilbreth and Henry Gantt.
1900–1930	Henry Ford—the assembly line—further refinement of work methods to improve productivity and quality; Ford developed mistake-proof assembly concepts, self-checking, and in-process inspection.
1901	First standards laboratories established in Great Britain.
1907–1908	AT&T begins systematic inspection and testing of products and materials.
1908	W. S. Gosset (writing as "Student") introduces the *t*-distribution—results from his work on quality control at Guinness Brewery.
1915–1919	WWI—British government begins a supplier certification program.
1919	Technical Inspection Association is formed in England; this later becomes the Institute of Quality Assurance.
1920s	AT&T Bell Laboratories forms a quality department—emphasizing quality, inspection and test, and product reliability.
	B. P. Dudding at General Electric in England uses statistical methods to control the quality of electric lamps.
1922–1923	R. A. Fisher publishes series of fundamental papers on designed experiments and their application to the agricultural sciences.
1924	W. A. Shewhart introduces the control chart concept in a Bell Laboratories technical memorandum.
1928	Acceptance sampling methodology is developed and refined by H. F. Dodge and H. G. Romig at Bell Labs.
1931	W. A. Shewhart publishes *Economic Control of Quality of Manufactured Product*—outlining statistical methods for use in production and control chart methods.
1932	W. A. Shewhart gives lectures on statistical methods in production and control charts at the University of London.
1932–1933	British textile and woolen industry and German chemical industry begin use of designed experiments for product/process development.
1933	The Royal Statistical Society forms the Industrial and Agricultural Research Section.
1938	W. E. Deming invites Shewhart to present seminars on control charts at the U.S. Department of Agriculture Graduate School.
1940	The U.S. War Department publishes a guide for using control charts to analyze process data.
1940–1943	Bell Labs develop the forerunners of the military standard sampling plans for the U.S. Army.
1942	In Great Britain, the Ministry of Supply Advising Service on Statistical Methods and Quality Control is formed.
1942–1946	Training courses on statistical quality control are given to industry; more than 15 quality societies are formed in North America.
1944	*Industrial Quality Control* begins publication.
1946	The American Society for Quality Control (ASQC) is formed as the merger of various quality societies.
	The International Standards Organization (ISO) is founded.
	Deming is invited to Japan by the Economic and Scientific Services Section of the U.S. War Department to help occupation forces in rebuilding Japanese industry.
	The Japanese Union of Scientists and Engineers (JUSE) is formed.
1946–1949	Deming is invited to give statistical quality control seminars to Japanese industry.
1948	G. Taguchi begins study and application of experimental design.
1950	Deming begins education of Japanese industrial managers; statistical quality control methods begin to be widely taught in Japan.
	K. Ishikawa introduces the cause-and-effect diagram.
1950s	Classic texts on statistical quality control by Eugene Grant and A. J. Duncan appear.
1951	A. V. Feigenbaum publishes the first edition of his book, *Total Quality Control*.
	JUSE establishes the Deming Prize for significant achievement in quality control and quality methodology.

(*continued*)

1951+	G. E. P. Box and K. B. Wilson publish fundamental work on using designed experiments and response surface methodology for process optimization; focus is on chemical industry. Applications of designed experiments in the chemical industry grow steadily after this.
1954	Joseph M. Juran is invited by the Japanese to lecture on quality management and improvement.
	British statistician E. S. Page introduces the cumulative sum (CUSUM) control chart.
1957	J. M. Juran and F. M. Gryna's *Quality Control Handbook* is first published.
1959	*Technometrics* (a journal of statistics for the physical, chemical, and engineering sciences) is established; J. Stuart Hunter is the founding editor.
	S. Roberts introduces the exponentially weighted moving average (EWMA) control chart. The U.S. manned spaceflight program makes industry aware of the need for reliable products; the field of reliability engineering grows from this starting point.
1960	G. E. P. Box and J. S. Hunter write fundamental papers on 2^{k-p} factorial designs.
	The quality control circle concept is introduced in Japan by K. Ishikawa.
1961	National Council for Quality and Productivity is formed in Great Britain as part of the British Productivity Council.
1960s	Courses in statistical quality control become widespread in industrial engineering academic programs.
	Zero defects (ZD) programs are introduced in certain U.S. industries.
1969	*Industrial Quality Control* ceases publication, replaced by *Quality Progress* and the *Journal of Quality Technology* (Lloyd S. Nelson is the founding editor of *JQT*).
1970s	In Great Britain, the NCQP and the Institute of Quality Assurance merge to form the British Quality Association.
1975–1978	Books on designed experiments oriented toward engineers and scientists begin to appear.
	Interest in quality circles begins in North America—this grows into the total quality management (TQM) movement.
1980s	Experimental design methods are introduced to and adopted by a wider group of organizations, including electronics, aerospace, semiconductor, and the automotive industries.
	The works of Taguchi on designed experiments first appear in the United States.
1984	The American Statistical Association (ASA) establishes the Ad Hoc Committee on Quality and Productivity; this later becomes a full section of the ASA.
	The journal *Quality and Reliability Engineering International* appears.
1986	Box and others visit Japan, noting the extensive use of designed experiments and other statistical methods.
1987	ISO publishes the first quality systems standard.
	Motorola's six-sigma initiative begins.
1988	The Malcolm Baldrige National Quality Award is established by the U.S. Congress.
	The European Foundation for Quality Management is founded; this organization administers the European Quality Award.
1989	The journal *Quality Engineering* appears.
1990s	ISO 9000 certification activities increase in U.S. industry; applicants for the Baldrige award grow steadily; many states sponsor quality awards based on the Baldrige criteria.
1995	Many undergraduate engineering programs require formal courses in statistical techniques, focusing on basic methods for process characterization and improvement.
1997	Motorola's six-sigma approach spreads to other industries.
1998	The American Society for Quality Control becomes the American Society for Quality (see www.asq.org), attempting to indicate the broader aspects of the quality improvement field.
2000s	ISO 9000:2000 standard is issued. Supply-chain management and supplier quality become even more critical factors in business success. Quality improvement activities expand beyond the traditional industrial setting into many other areas including financial services, health care, insurance, and utilities.

of the important milestones in this evolutionary process. We will briefly discuss some of the events on this timeline.

Frederick W. Taylor introduced some principles of scientific management as mass production industries began to develop prior to 1900. Taylor pioneered dividing work into tasks so that the product could be manufactured and assembled more easily. His work led to substantial improvements in productivity. Also, because of standardized production and assembly methods, the quality of manufactured goods was positively impacted as well. However, along with the standardization of work methods came the concept of work standards—a standard time to accomplish the work, or a specified number of units that must be produced per period. Frank Gilbreth and others extended this concept to the study of motion and work design. Much of this had a positive impact on productivity, but it often did not sufficiently emphasize the quality aspect of work. Furthermore, if carried to extremes, work standards have the risk of halting innovation and continuous improvement, which we recognize today as being a vital aspect of all work activities.

Statistical methods and their application in quality improvement have had a long history. In 1924, Walter A. Shewhart of the Bell Telephone Laboratories developed the statistical control chart concept, which is often considered the formal beginning of statistical quality control. Toward the end of the 1920s, Harold F. Dodge and Harry G. Romig, both of Bell Telephone Laboratories, developed statistically based acceptance sampling as an alternative to 100% inspection. By the middle of the 1930s, statistical quality-control methods were in wide use at Western Electric, the manufacturing arm of the Bell System. However, the value of statistical quality control was not widely recognized by industry.

World War II saw a greatly expanded use and acceptance of statistical quality-control concepts in manufacturing industries. Wartime experience made it apparent that statistical techniques were necessary to control and improve product quality. The American Society for Quality Control was formed in 1946. This organization promotes the use of quality improvement techniques for all types of products and services. It offers a number of conferences, technical publications, and training programs in quality assurance. The 1950s and 1960s saw the emergence of reliability engineering, the introduction of several important textbooks on statistical quality control, and the viewpoint that quality is a way of managing the organization.

In the 1950s, designed experiments for product and process improvement were first introduced in the United States. The initial applications were in the chemical industry. These methods were widely exploited in the chemical industry, and they are often cited as one of the primary reasons that the U.S. chemical industry is one of the most competitive in the world and has lost little business to foreign companies. The spread of these methods outside the chemical industry was relatively slow until the late 1970s or early 1980s, when many Western companies discovered that their Japanese competitors had been systematically using designed experiments since the 1960s for process improvement, new process development, evaluation of new product designs, improvement of reliability and field performance of products, and many other aspects of product design, including selection of component and system tolerances. This discovery sparked further interest in statistically designed experiments and resulted in extensive efforts to introduce the methodology in engineering and development organizations in industry, as well as in academic engineering curricula.

Since 1980, there has been a profound growth in the use of statistical methods for quality and overall business improvement in the United States. This has been motivated, in part, by the widespread loss of business and markets suffered by many domestic companies that began during the 1970s. For example, the U.S. automobile industry was nearly destroyed by foreign competition during this period. One domestic automobile company estimated its operating losses at nearly $1 million *per hour* in 1980. The adoption and use of statistical methods have played a central role in the re-emergence of U.S. industry. Various management systems have also emerged as frameworks in which to implement quality improvement. In the next two sections we briefly discuss the statistical methods that are the central focus of this book and give an overview of some key aspects of quality management.

1.3 Statistical Methods for Quality Control and Improvement

This textbook concentrates on statistical and engineering technology useful in quality improvement. Specifically, we focus on three major areas: **statistical process control, design of experiments,** and (to a lesser extent) **acceptance sampling.** In addition to these techniques, a number of other statistical and analytical tools are useful in analyzing quality problems and improving the performance of processes. The role of some of these tools is illustrated in Fig. 1.3, which presents a **process** as a system with a set of inputs and an output. In the case of a manufacturing process, the controllable input factors $x_1, x_2, \ldots, x_p$ are process variable such as temperatures, pressures, feed rates, and other process variables. The inputs $z_1, z_2, \ldots, z_q$ are uncontrollable (or difficult to control) inputs, such as environmental factors or properties of raw materials provided by an external supplier. The production process transforms the input raw materials, component parts, and subassemblies into a finished product that has several quality characteristics. The output variable y is a quality characteristic, that is, a measure of process and product quality. This model can also be used to represent **non-manufacturing** or **service processes.** For example, consider a process in a financial institution that processes automobile loan applications. The inputs are the loan applications, which contain information about the customer and his/her credit history, the type of car to be purchased, its price, and the loan amount. The controllable factors are the type of training that the loan officer receives, the specific rules and policies that the bank imposed on these loans, and the number of people working as loan officers at each time period. The uncontrollable factors include prevailing interest rates, the amount of capital available for these types of loans in each time period, and the number of loan applications that require processing each period. The output quality characteristics include whether or not the loan is funded, the number of funded loans that are actually accepted by the applicant, and the cycle time; that is, the length of time that the customer waits until a decision on his/her loan application is made. In service systems, cycle time is often a very important CTQ.

A **control chart** is one of the primary techniques of **statistical process control (SPC).** A typical control chart is shown in Fig. 1.4. This chart plots the averages of measurements of a quality characteristic in samples taken from the process versus time (or the sample number). The chart has a center line (CL) and upper and lower control limits (UCL and LCL in Fig. 1.4). The center line represents where this process characteristic should fall if there are no unusual sources of variability present. The control limits are determined from some simple statistical considerations that we will discuss in Chapters 4, 5, and 6. Classically, control

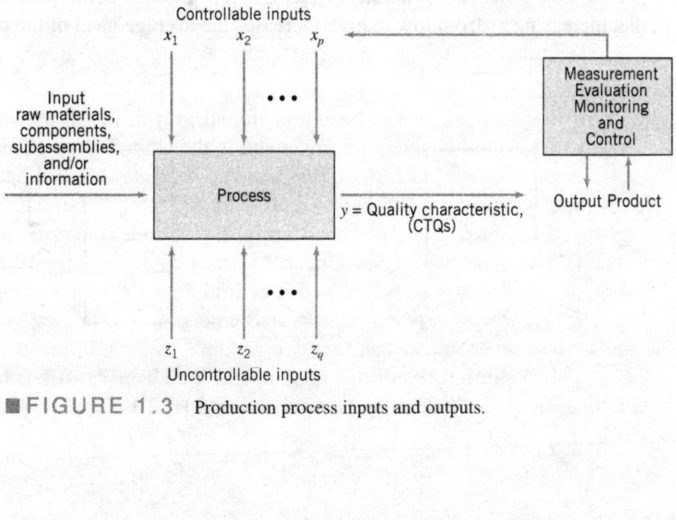

■ FIGURE 1.3 Production process inputs and outputs.

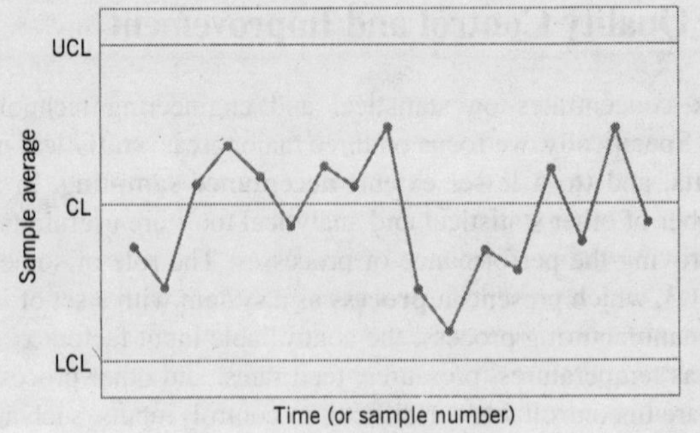

■ FIGURE 1.4 A typical control chart.

charts are applied to the output variable(s) in a system such as in Fig. 1.4. However, in some cases they can be usefully applied to the inputs as well.

The control chart is a very useful **process monitoring technique;** when unusual sources of variability are present, sample averages will plot outside the control limits. This is a signal that some investigation of the process should be made and corrective action to remove these unusual sources of variability taken. Systematic use of a control chart is an excellent way to reduce variability.

A **designed experiment** is extremely helpful in discovering the key variables influencing the quality characteristics of interest in the process. A designed experiment is an approach to systematically varying the controllable input factors in the process and determining the effect these factors have on the output product parameters. Statistically designed experiments are invaluable in reducing the variability in the quality characteristics and in determining the levels of the controllable variables that optimize process performance. Often significant breakthroughs in process performance and product quality also result from using designed experiments.

One major type of designed experiment is the **factorial design,** in which factors are varied together in such a way that all possible combinations of factor levels are tested. Figure 1.5 shows two possible factorial designs for the process in Fig. 1.3, for the cases of $p = 2$ and $p = 3$ controllable factors. In Fig. 1.5*a,* the factors have two levels, low and high, and the four possible test combinations in this factorial experiment form the corners of a square. In Fig. 1.5*b,* there are three factors each at two levels, giving an experiment with eight test combinations arranged at the corners of a cube. The distributions at the corners of the cube represent the process performance at each combination of the controllable factors x_1, x_2, and x_3. It is clear that some combinations of factor levels produce better results than others. For example, increasing x_1 from low to high increases the average level of the process output and could

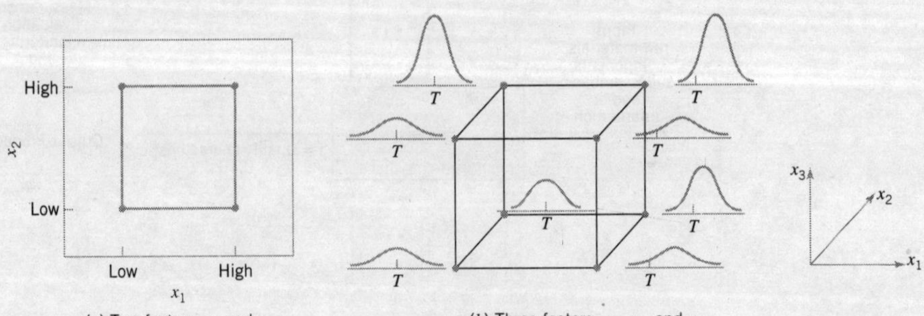

(*a*) Two factors, x_1 and x_2

(*b*) Three factors, x_1, x_2, and x_3

■ FIGURE 1.5 Factorial designs for the process in Fig. 1.3.

shift it off the target value (T). Furthermore, process variability seems to be substantially reduced when we operate the process along the back edge of the cube, where x_2 and x_3 are at their high levels.

Designed experiments are a major **off-line** quality-control tool, because they are often used during development activities and the early stages of manufacturing, rather than as a routine **on-line** or **in-process** procedure. They play a crucial role in reducing variability.

Once we have identified a list of important variables that affect the process output, it is usually necessary to model the relationship between the influential input variables and the output quality characteristics. Statistical techniques useful in constructing such models include regression analysis and time series analysis. Detailed discussions of designed experiments, regression analysis, and time series modeling are in Montgomery (2005), Montgomery, Peck, and Vining (2006), and Box, Jenkins, and Reinsel (1994).

When the important variables have been identified and the nature of the relationship between the important variables and the process output has been quantified, then an on-line statistical process-control technique for monitoring and surveillance of the process can be employed with considerable effectiveness. Techniques such as control charts can be used to monitor the process output and detect when changes in the inputs are required to bring the process back to an in-control state. The models that relate the influential inputs to process outputs help determine the nature and magnitude of the adjustments required. In many processes, once the dynamic nature of the relationships between the inputs and the outputs are understood, it may be possible to routinely adjust the process so that future values of the product characteristics will be approximately on target. This routine adjustment is often called **engineering control, automatic control,** or **feedback control.** We will briefly discuss these types of process control schemes in Chapter 11 and illustrate how statistical process control (or **SPC**) methods can be successfully integrated into a manufacturing system in which engineering control is in use.

The third area of quality control and improvement that we discuss is **acceptance sampling.** This is closely connected with inspection and testing of product, which is one of the earliest aspects of quality control, dating back to long before statistical methodology was developed for quality improvement. Inspection can occur at many points in a process. Acceptance sampling, defined as the inspection and classification of a sample of units selected at random from a larger batch or lot and the ultimate decision about disposition of the lot, usually occurs at two points: incoming raw materials or components, or final production.

Several different variations of acceptance sampling are shown in Fig. 1.6. In Fig. 1.6*a*, the inspection operation is performed immediately following production, before the product is shipped to the customer. This is usually called **outgoing inspection.** Figure 1.6*b* illustrates **incoming inspection;** that is, a situation in which lots of batches of product are sampled as they are received from the supplier. Various lot-dispositioning decisions are illustrated in Fig. 1.6*c*.

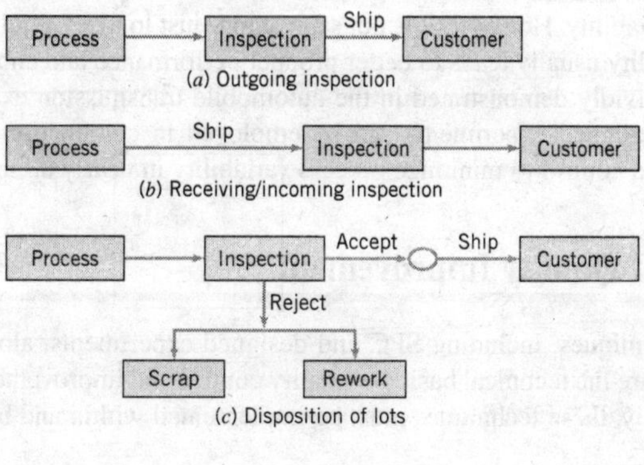

■ **FIGURE 1.6** Variations of acceptance sampling.

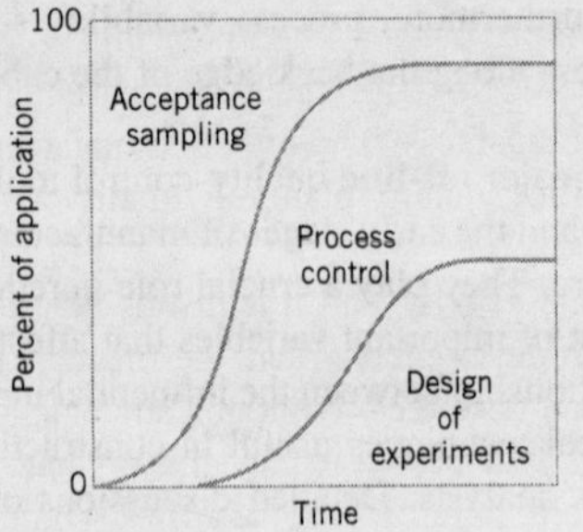

■ FIGURE 1.7 Phase diagram of the use of quality-engineering methods.

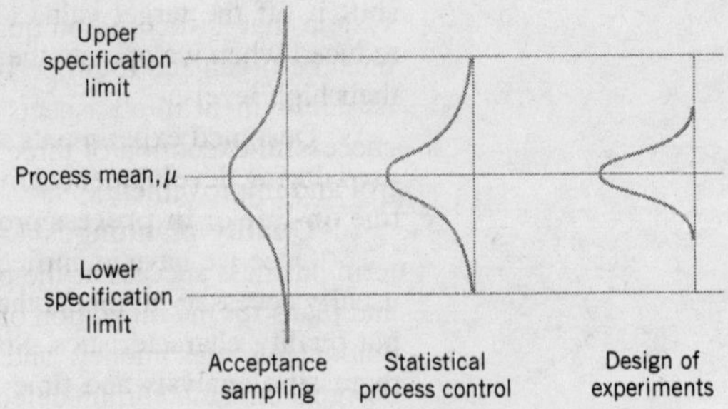

■ FIGURE 1.8 Application of quality-engineering techniques and the systematic reduction of process variability.

Sampled lots may either be accepted or rejected. Items in a rejected lot are typically either scrapped or recycled, or they may be reworked or replaced with good units. This latter case is often called **rectifying inspection.**

Modern quality assurance systems usually place less emphasis on acceptance sampling and attempt to make statistical process control and designed experiments the focus of their efforts. Acceptance sampling tends to reinforce the conformance-to-specification view of quality and does not have any feedback into either the production process or engineering design or development that would necessarily lead to quality improvement.

Figure 1.7 shows the typical evolution in the use of these techniques in most organizations. At the lowest level of maturity, management may be completely unaware of quality issues, and there is likely to be no effective organized quality improvement effort. Frequently there will be some modest applications of acceptance-sampling and inspection methods, usually for incoming parts and materials. The first activity as maturity increases is to intensify the use of sampling inspection. The use of sampling will increase until it is realized that quality cannot be inspected or tested into the product.

At that point, the organization usually begins to focus on process improvement. Statistical process control and experimental design potentially have major impacts on manufacturing, product design activities, and process development. The systematic introduction of these methods usually marks the start of substantial quality, cost, and productivity improvements in the organization. At the highest levels of maturity, companies use designed experiments and statistical process control methods intensively and make relatively modest use of acceptance sampling.

The primary **objective** of quality engineering efforts is the **systematic reduction of variability** in the key quality characteristics of the product. Figure 1.8 shows how this happens over time. In the early stages, when acceptance sampling is the major technique in use, process "fallout," or units that do not conform to the specifications, constitute a high percentage of the process output. The introduction of statistical process control will stabilize the process and reduce the variability. However, it is not satisfactory just to meet requirements—further reduction of variability usually leads to better product performance and enhanced competitive position, as was vividly demonstrated in the automobile transmission example discussed earlier. Statistically designed experiments can be employed in conjunction with statistical process monitoring and control to minimize process variability in nearly all industrial settings.

1.4 Management Aspects of Quality Improvement

Statistical techniques, including SPC and designed experiments, along with other problem-solving tools are the technical basis for quality control and improvement. However, to be used most effectively, these techniques must be implemented within and be part of a management system that is focused on quality improvement. The management system of an organization must be organized to properly direct the overall quality improvement philosophy and ensure its deployment in all aspects of the business. The effective management of quality involves successful execution of three activities: quality planning, quality assurance, and quality control and improvement.

Quality planning is a strategic activity, and it is just as vital to an organization's long-term business success as the product development plan, the financial plan, the marketing plan, and plans for the utilization of human resources. Without a strategic quality plan, an enormous amount of time, money, and effort will be wasted by the organization dealing with faulty designs, manufacturing defects, field failures, and customer complaints. Quality planning involves identifying customers, both external and those that operate internal to the business, and identifying their needs [this is sometimes called listening to the **voice of the customer (VOC)**]. Then products or services that meet or exceed customer expectations must be developed. The eight dimensions of quality discussed in Section 1.1.1 are an important part of this effort. The organization must then determine how these products and services will be realized. Planning for quality improvement on a specific, systematic basis is also a vital part of this process.

Quality assurance is the set of activities that ensures the quality levels of products and services are properly maintained and that supplier and customer quality issues are properly resolved. Documentation of the quality system is an important component. Quality system documentation involves four components: policy, procedures, work instructions and specifications, and records. Policy generally deals with what is to be done and why, while procedures focus on the methods and personnel that will implement policy. Work instructions and specifications are usually product-, department-, tool-, or machine-oriented. Records are a way of documenting the policies, procedures, and work instructions that have been followed. Records are also used to track specific units or batches of product, so that it can be determined exactly how they were produced. Records are often vital in providing data for dealing with customer complaints, corrective actions, and, if necessary, product recalls. Development, maintenance, and control of documentation are important quality assurance functions. One example of document control is ensuring that specifications and work instructions developed for operating personnel reflect the latest design and engineering changes.

Quality control and improvement involve the set of activities used to ensure that the products and services meet requirements and are improved on a continuous basis. Since variability is often a major source of poor quality, statistical techniques, including SPC and designed experiments, are the major tools of quality control and improvement. Quality improvement is often done on a project-by-project basis and involves teams led by personnel with specialized knowledge of statistical methods and experience in applying them. Projects should be selected so that they have significant business impact and are linked with the overall business goals for quality identified during the planning process. The techniques in this book are integral to successful quality control and improvement.

The next section provides a brief overview of some of the key elements of quality management. We discuss some of the important quality philosophies; quality systems and standards; the link between quality and productivity and quality and cost; economic and legal implications of quality; and some aspects of implementation. The three aspects of quality planning, quality assurance, and quality control and improvement will be woven into the discussion.

1.4.1 Quality Philosophy and Management Strategies

Many people have contributed to the statistical methodology of quality improvement. However, in terms of implementation and management philosophy, three individuals emerge as the leaders: W. E. Deming, J. M. Juran, and A. V. Feigenbaum. We now briefly discuss the approaches and philosophy of those leaders in quality management.

W. Edwards Deming. W. Edwards Deming was educated in engineering and physics at the University of Wyoming and Yale University. He worked for Western Electric and was influenced greatly by Walter A. Shewhart, the developer of the control chart. After leaving Western Electric, Deming held government jobs with the U.S. Department of Agriculture and the Bureau of the Census. During World War II, Deming worked for the War Department and the Census Bureau. Following the war, he became a consultant to Japanese industries and convinced their top management of the power of statistical methods and the importance of quality as a competitive weapon. This commitment to and use of statistical methods has been a key element in the expansion of Japan's industry and economy. The Japanese Union of Scientists and Engineers created the Deming Prize for quality improvement in his honor. Until his death in 1994, Deming was an active consultant and speaker; he was an inspirational force for quality improvement in this country and around the world. He firmly believed that the responsibility for quality rests with management; that is, most of the opportunities for quality improvement require management action, and very few opportunities lie at the workforce or operator level. Deming was a harsh critic of many American management practices.

The Deming philosophy is an important framework for implementing quality and productivity improvement. This philosophy is summarized in his 14 points for management. We now give a brief statement and discussion of **Deming's 14 points:**

1. **Create a constancy of purpose focused on the improvement of products and services.** Deming was very critical of the short-term thinking of American management, which tends to be driven by quarterly business results and doesn't always focus on strategies that benefit the organization in the long run. Management should constantly try to improve product design and performance. This must include investment in research, development, and innovation will have long-term payback to the organization.
2. **Adopt a new philosophy that recognizes we are in a different economic era.** Reject poor workmanship, defective products, or bad service. It costs as much to produce a defective unit as it does to produce a good one (and sometimes more). The cost of dealing with scrap, rework, and other losses created by defectives is an enormous drain on company resources.
3. **Do not rely on mass inspection to "control" quality.** All inspection can do is sort out defectives, and at that point it is too late—the organization already has paid to produce those defectives. Inspection typically occurs too late in the process, it is expensive, and it is often ineffective. Quality results from prevention of defectives through process improvement, not inspection.
4. **Do not award business to suppliers on the basis of price alone, but also consider quality.** Price is a meaningful measure of a supplier's product only if it is considered in relation to a measure of quality. In other words, the total cost of the item must be considered, not just the purchase price. When quality is considered, the lowest bidder frequently is not the low-cost supplier. Preference should be given to suppliers who use modern methods of quality improvement in their business and who can demonstrate process control and capability. An adversarial relationship with suppliers is harmful. It is important to build effective, long-term relationships.
5. **Focus on continuous improvement.** Constantly try to improve the production and service system. Involve the workforce in these activities and make use of statistical methods, particularly the statistically based problem-solving tools discussed in this book.
6. **Practice modern training methods and invest in on-the-job training for all employees.** Everyone should be trained in the technical aspects of their job, and in modern

quality- and productivity-improvement methods as well. The training should encourage all employees to practice these methods every day. Too often, employees are not encouraged to use the results of training, and management often believes employees do not need training or already should be able to practice the methods. Many organizations devote little or no effort to training.

7. **Improve leadership, and practice modern supervision methods.** Supervision should not consist merely of passive surveillance of workers but should be focused on helping the employees improve the system in which they work. The number one goal of supervision should be to improve the work system and the product.
8. **Drive out fear.** Many workers are afraid to ask questions, report problems, or point out conditions that are barriers to quality and effective production. In many organizations the economic loss associated with fear is large; only management can eliminate fear.
9. **Break down the barriers between functional areas of the business.** Teamwork among different organizational units is essential for effective quality and productivity improvement to take place.
10. **Eliminate targets, slogans, and numerical goals for the workforce.** A target such as "zero defects" is useless without a plan for the achievement of this objective. In fact, these slogans and "programs" are usually counterproductive. Work to improve the system and provide information on that.
11. **Eliminate numerical quotas and work standards.** These standards have historically been set without regard to quality. Work standards are often symptoms of management's inability to understand the work process and to provide an effective management system focused on improving this process.
12. **Remove the barriers that discourage employees from doing their jobs.** Management must listen to employee suggestions, comments, and complaints. The person who is doing the job knows the most about it and usually has valuable ideas about how to make the process work more effectively. The workforce is an important participant in the business, and not just an opponent in collective bargaining.
13. **Institute an ongoing program of education for all employees.** Education in simple, powerful statistical techniques should be mandatory for all employees. Use of the basic SPC problem-solving tools, particularly the control chart, should become widespread in the business. As these charts become widespread and as employees understand their uses, they will be more likely to look for the causes of poor quality and to identify process improvements. Education is a way of making everyone partners in the quality improvement process.
14. **Create a structure in top management that will vigorously advocate the first 13 points.** This structure must be driven from the very top of the organization. It must also include concurrent education/training activities and expedite application of the training to achieve improved business results. Everyone in the organization must know that continuous improvement is a common goal.

As we read Deming's 14 points we notice that there is a strong emphasis on **organizational change.** Also, the role of management in guiding this change process is of dominating importance. However, what should be changed, and how should this change process be started? For example, if we want to improve the yield of a semiconductor manufacturing process, what should we do? It is in this area that statistical methods come into play most frequently. To improve the semiconductor process, we must determine which controllable factors in the process influence the number of defective units produced. To answer this question, we must collect data on the process and see how the system reacts

■ TABLE 1.2
Deming's Seven Deadly Diseases of Management

1. Lack of constancy of purpose
2. Emphasis on short-term profits
3. Evaluation of performance, merit rating, and annual reviews of performance
4. Mobility of top management
5. Running a company on visible figures alone
6. Excessive medical costs
7. Excessive legal damage awards

to change in the process variables. Then actions to improve the process can be designed and implemented. Statistical methods, such as designed experiments and control charts, can contribute to these activities.

Deming frequently wrote and spoke about the **seven deadly diseases of management,** listed in Table 1.2. He believed that each disease was a barrier to the effective implementation of his philosophy. The first, lack of constancy of purpose, relates to the first of Deming's 14 points. Continuous improvement of products, processes, and services gives assurance to all stakeholders in the enterprise (employees, executives, investors, suppliers) that dividends and increases in the value of the business will continue to grow.

The second disease, too much emphasis on short-term profits, might make the "numbers" look good, but if this is achieved by reducing research and development investment, by eliminating employees' training, and by not deploying quality improvement activities, then irreparable long-term damage to the business is the ultimate result. Concerning the third disease, Deming believed that performance evaluation encouraged short-term performance, rivalries and fear, and discouraged effective teamwork. Performance reviews can leave employees bitter and discouraged, and they may feel unfairly treated, especially if they are working in an organization where their performance is impacted by system forces that are flawed and out of their control.

The fourth disease, management mobility, refers to the widespread practice of job-hopping; that is, a manger spending very little time in the business function for which he or she is responsible. This often results in key decisions being made by someone who really doesn't understand the business. Managers often spend more time thinking about their next career move than about their current job and how to do it better. Frequent reorganizing and shifting management responsibilities is a barrier to constancy of purpose and often is a waste of resources that should be devoted to improving products and services. Bringing in a new chief executive officer to improve quarterly profits often leads to a business strategy that leaves a path of destruction throughout the business.

The fifth disease, management by visible figures alone (such as the number of defects, customer complaints, and quarterly profits) suggests that the really important factors that determine long-term organizational success are unknown and unknowable. As some evidence of this, of the 100 largest companies in 1900, only 16 still exist today, and of the 25 largest companies in 1900, only two are still among the top 25. Obviously, some visible figures are important; for example, suppliers and employees must be paid on time and the bank accounts must be managed. However, if visible figures alone were key determinates of success, it's likely that many more of the companies of 1900 still would be in business.

Deming's cautions about excessive medical expenses—his sixth deadly disease—are certainly prophetic: Health care costs may be the most important issue facing many sectors of business in the United States toady. For example, the medical costs for current and

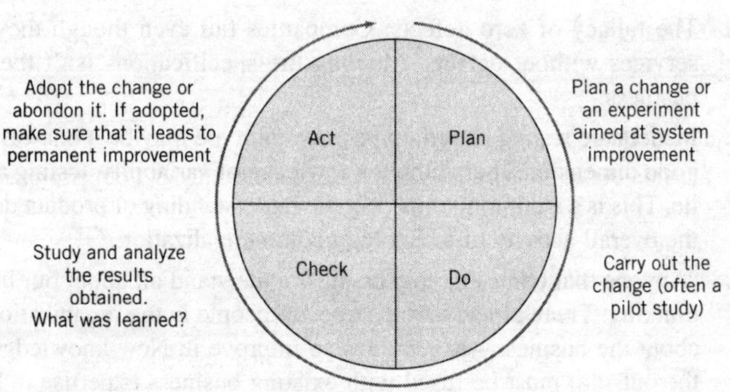

■ **FIGURE 1.9** The Shewhart cycle.

retired employees of United States automobile manufacturers General Motors, Ford, and Chrysler currently is estimated to be between $1200 and $1600 per vehicle, contrasted with $250 to $350 per vehicle for Toyota and Honda, two Japanese automobile manufacturers with extensive North American manufacturing and assembly operations. The seventh disease, liability and excessive damage awards, is also a major issue facing many organizations. Deming was fond of observing that the United States had more lawyers per capita than any other nation. He believed that government intervention likely would be necessary to provide effective long-term solutions to the medical cost and excessive liability awards problems.

Deming recommended the **Shewhart cycle,** shown in Figure 1.9, as a model to guide improvement. The four steps, **Plan-Do-Check-Act,** are often called the **PDCA cycle.** Sometimes the **Check** step is called **Study,** and the cycle becomes the **PDSA cycle.** In **Plan,** we propose a change in the system that is aimed at improvement. In **Do,** we carry out the change, usually on a small or pilot scale to ensure that we learn the results that will be obtained. **Check** consists of analyzing the results of the change to determine what has been learned about the changes that were carried out. In **Act,** we either adopt the change or, if it was unsuccessful, abandon it. The process is almost always iterative, and may require several cycles for solving complex problems.

In addition to the Deming's 14 points and his seven deadly diseases of management, Deming wrote and lectured about an extensive collection of **obstacles to success.** Some of these include:

1. The belief that automation, computers, and new machinery will solve problems.
2. Searching for examples—trying to copy existing solutions.
3. The "our problems are different" excuse and not realizing that the principles that will solve them are universal.
4. Obsolete schools, particularly business schools, where graduates have not been taught how to successfully run businesses.
5. Poor teaching of statistical methods in industry: Teaching tools without a framework for using them is going to be unsuccessful.
6. Reliance on inspection to produce quality.
7. Reliance on the "quality control department" to take care of all quality problems.
8. Blaming the workforce for problems.
9. False starts, such as broad teaching of statistical methods without a plan as to how to use them, quality circles, employee suggestion systems, and other forms of "instant pudding."

10. The fallacy of zero defects: Companies fail even though they produce products and services without defects. Meeting the specifications isn't the complete story in any business.

11. Inadequate testing of prototypes: A prototype may be a one-off article, with artificially good dimensions, but without knowledge of variability, testing a prototype tells very little. This is a symptom of inadequate understanding of product design, development, and the overall activity of technology commercialization.

12. "Anyone that comes to help us must understand all about our business." This is bizarre thinking: There already are competent people in the organization who know everything about the business—except how to improve it. New knowledge and ideas (often from the outside) must be fused with existing business expertise to bring about change and improvement.

Joseph M. Juran. Juran was born in 1904. He is one of the founding fathers of the quality-control and improvement field. He worked for Walter A. Shewhart at AT&T Bell Laboratories and was at the leading edge of quality improvement throughout his career. Juran became the chief industrial engineer at Western Electric (part of the Bell System). He was an assistant administrator for the Lend-Lease Administration during World War II and played an important role in simplifying the administrative and paper work processes of that agency. After the war, he became the head of the Department of Administrative Engineering at New York University. He was invited to speak to Japanese industry leaders as they began their industrial transformation in the early 1950s. He also created an active consulting practice (the Juran Institute) and lectured widely through the American Management Association. He was the co-author (with Frank M. Gryna) of the *Quality Control Handbook,* a standard reference for quality methods and improvement since its initial publication in 1957.

The Juran quality management philosophy focuses on three components: **planning**, **control**, and **improvement**. These are known as the **Juran Trilogy.** As we have noted previously, planning involves identifying external customers and determining their needs. Then products or services that meet these customer needs are designed and/or developed, and the processes for producing these products or services are then developed. The planning process should also involve planning for quality improvement on a regular (typically annual) basis. Control is employed by the operating forces of the business to ensure that the product or service meets the requirements. SPC is one of the primary tools of control. Improvement aims to achieve performance and quality levels that are higher than current levels. Juran emphasizes that improvement must be on a project-by-project basis. These projects are typically identified at the planning stage of the trilogy. Improvement can either be continuous (or incremental) or by breakthrough. Typically, a breakthrough improvement is the result of studying the process and identifying a set of changes that result in a large, relatively rapid improvement in performance. Designed experiments are an important tool that can be used to achieve breakthrough.

Armand V. Feigenbaum. Feigenbaum first introduced the concept of companywide quality control in his historic book *Total Quality Control* (first published in 1951). This book influenced much of the early philosophy of quality management in Japan in the early 1950s. In fact, many Japanese companies used the term "total quality control" to describe their efforts. He proposed a three-step approach to improving quality: quality leadership, quality technology, and organizational commitment. By **quality technology,** Feigenbaum means statistical methods and other technical and engineering methods, such as the ones discussed in this book.

Feigenbaum is concerned with organizational structure and a systems approach to improving quality. He proposed a 19-step improvement process, of which use of statistical methods was step 17. He initially suggested that much of the technical capability be concentrated in a specialized department. This is in contrast to the more modern view that knowledge and use of statistical tools need to be widespread. However, the organizational aspects of Feigenbaum's work are important, as quality improvement does not usually spring forth as a "grass roots" activity; it requires a lot of management commitment to make it work.

The brief descriptions of the philosophies of Deming, Juran, and Feigenbaum have highlighted both the common aspects and differences of their viewpoints. In this author's opinion, there are more similarities than differences among them, and the similarities are what is important. All three of these pioneers stress the importance of quality as an essential competitive weapon, the important role that management must play in implementing quality improvement, and the importance of statistical methods and techniques in the "quality transformation" of an organization.

Total Quality Management. **Total quality management (TQM)** is a strategy for implementing and managing quality improvement activities on an organizationwide basis. TQM began in the early 1980s, with the philosophies of Deming and Juran as the focal point. It evolved into a broader spectrum of concepts and ideas, involving participative organizations and work culture, customer focus, supplier quality improvement, integration of the quality system with business goals, and many other activities to focus all elements of the organization around the quality improvement goal. Typically, organizations that have implemented a TQM approach to quality improvement have quality councils or high-level teams that deal with strategic quality initiatives, workforce-level teams that focus on routine production or business activities, and cross-functional teams that address specific quality improvement issues.

TQM has only had moderate success for a variety of reasons, but frequently because there is insufficient effort devoted to widespread utilization of the technical tools of variability reduction. Many organizations saw the mission of TQM as one of training. Consequently, many TQM efforts engaged in widespread training of the workforce in the philosophy of quality improvement and a few basic methods. This training was usually placed in the hands of human resources departments, and much of it was ineffective. The trainers often had no real idea about *what* methods should be taught, and success was usually measured by the percentage of the workforce that had been "trained," not by whether any measurable impact on business results had been achieved. Some general reasons for the lack of conspicuous success of TQM include (1) lack of topdown, high-level **management commitment and involvement;** (2) inadequate use of statistical methods and insufficient recognition of variability reduction as a prime objective; (3) general as opposed to specific business-results-oriented objectives; and (4) too much emphasis on widespread **training** as opposed to focused technical **education.**

Another reason for the erratic success of TQM is that many managers and executives have regarded it as just another "program" to improve quality. During the 1950s and 1960s, programs such as **Zero Defects** and **Value Engineering** abounded, but they had little real impact on quality and productivity improvement. During the heyday of TQM in the 1980s, another popular program was the **Quality is Free** initiative, in which management worked on identifying the cost of quality (or the cost of nonquality, as the Quality is Free devotees so cleverly put it). Indeed, identification of quality costs can be very useful (we discuss quality costs in Section 1.4.3), but the Quality is Free practitioners often had no idea about what to do to actually improve many types of complex industrial processes. In fact, the leaders of this initiative had no knowledge about statistical methodology and completely failed to understand its role in quality improvement. When TQM is wrapped around an ineffective program such as this, disaster is often the result.

Quality Systems and Standards. The International Standards Organization (founded in 1946 in Geneva, Switzerland), known as ISO, has developed a series of standards for quality systems. The first standards were issued in 1987. The current version of the standard is known as the ISO 9000 series. It is a generic standard, broadly applicable to any type of organization, and it is often used to demonstrate a supplier's ability to control its processes. The three standards of ISO 9000 are:

> ISO 9000:2000 Quality Management System—Fundamentals and Vocabulary
> ISO 9001:2000 Quality Management System—Requirements
> ISO 9004:2000 Quality Management System—Guidelines for Performance Improvement

ISO 9000 is also an American National Standards Institute and an ASQ standard.

The ISO 9001:2000 standard has eight clauses: (1) Scope, (2) Normative References, (3) Definitions, (4) Quality Management Systems, (5) Management Responsibility, (6) Resource Management, (7) Product (or Service) Realization, and (8) Measurement, Analysis, and Improvement. Clauses 4 through 8 are the most important, and their key components and requirements are shown in Table 1.3. To become certified under the ISO standard, a company must select a **registrar** and prepare for a **certification audit** by this registrar. There is no single independent authority that licenses, regulates, monitors, or qualifies registrars. As we will discuss later, this is a serious problem with the ISO system. Preparing for the certification audit involves many activities, including (usually) an initial or phase I audit that checks the present quality management system against the standard. This is usually followed by establishing teams to ensure that all components of the key clause are developed and implemented, training of personnel, developing applicable documentation, and developing and installing all new components of the quality system that may be required. Then the certification audit takes place. If the company is certified, then periodic **surveillance audits** by the registrar continue, usually on an annual (or perhaps six-month) schedule.

Many organizations have required their suppliers to become certified under ISO 9000, or one of the standards that are more industry-specific. Examples of these industry-specific quality system standards are AS 9100 for the aerospace industry; ISO/TS 16949 and QS 9000 for the automotive industry; and TL 9000 for the telecommunications industry. Many components of these standards are very similar to those of ISO 9000.

Much of the focus of ISO 9000 (and of the industry-specific standards) is on formal documentation of the quality system; that is, on **quality assurance** activities. Organizations usually must make extensive efforts to bring their documentation into line with the requirements of the standards; this is the Achilles' heel of ISO 9000 and other related or derivative standards. There is far too much effort devoted to documentation, paperwork, and bookkeeping and not nearly enough to actually reducing variability and improving processes and products. Furthermore, many of the third-party registrars, auditors, and consultants that work in this area are not sufficiently educated or experienced enough in the **technical** tools required for **quality improvement** or how these tools should be deployed. They are all too often unaware of what constitutes modern engineering and statistical practice, and usually are familiar with only the most elementary techniques. Therefore, they concentrate largely on the documentation, record keeping, and paperwork aspects of certification.

There is also evidence that ISO certification or certification under one of the other industry-specific standards does little to prevent poor quality products from being designed, manufactured, and delivered to the customer. For example, in 1999–2000, there were numerous incidents of rollover accidents involving Ford Explorer vehicles equipped with Bridgestone/Firestone tires. There were nearly 300 deaths in the United States alone attributed to these accidents, which led to a recall by Bridgestone/Firestone of approximately 6.5 million tires. Apparently, many of the tires involved in these incidents were manufactured at the Bridgestone/Firestone plant in Decatur, Illinois. In an article on this story in *Time* magazine (September 18, 2000), there was a photograph (p. 38) of the sign at the entrance of the Decatur plant which stated that the plant was "QS 9000 Certified" and "ISO 14001 Certified" (ISO 14001 is an environmental standard).

■ **TABLE 1.3**
ISO 9001:2000 Requirements

4.0	**Quality Management System**
4.1	General Requirements
	The organization shall establish, document, implement, and maintain a quality management system and continually improve its effectiveness in accordance with the requirements of the international standard.
4.2	Documentation Requirements
	Quality management system documentation will include a quality policy and quality objectives; a quality manual; documented procedures; documents to ensure effective planning, operation, and control of processes; and records required by the international standard.
5.0	**Management System**
5.1	Management Commitment
	a. Communication of meeting customer, statutory, and regulatory requirements
	b. Establishing a quality policy
	c. Establishing quality objectives
	d. Conducting management reviews
	e. Ensuring that resources are available
5.2	Top management shall ensure that customer requirements are determined and are met with the aim of enhancing customer satisfaction.
5.3	Management shall establish a quality policy.
5.4	Management shall ensure that quality objectives shall be established. Management shall ensure that planning occurs for the quality management system.
5.5	Management shall ensure that responsibilities and authorities are defined and communicated.
5.6	Management shall review the quality management system at regular intervals.
6.0	**Resource Management**
6.1	The organization shall determine and provide needed resources.
6.2	Workers will be provided necessary education, training, skills, and experience.
6.3	The organization shall determine, provide, and maintain the infrastructure needed to achieve conformity to product requirements.
6.4	The organization shall determine and manage the work environment needed to achieve conformity to product requirements.
7.0	**Product or Service Realization**
7.1	The organization shall plan and develop processes needed for product or service realization.
7.2	The organization shall determine requirements as specified by customers.
7.3	The organization shall plan and control the design and development for its products or services.
7.4	The organization shall ensure that purchased material or product conforms to specified purchase requirements.
7.5	The organization shall plan and carry out production and service under controlled conditions.
7.6	The organization shall determine the monitoring and measurements to be undertaken and the monitoring and measuring devices needed to provide evidence of conformity of products or services to determined requirements.
8.0	**Measurement, Analysis, and Improvement**
8.1	The organization shall plan and implement the monitoring, measurement, analysis, and improvement process for continual improvement and conformity to requirements.
8.2	The organization shall monitor information relating to customer perceptions.
8.3	The organization shall ensure that product that does not conform to requirements is identified and controlled to prevent its unintended use or delivery.
8.4	The organization shall determine, collect, and analyze data to demonstrate the suitability and effectiveness of the quality management system, including
	a. Customer satisfaction
	b. Conformance data
	c. Trend data
	d. Supplier data
8.5	The organization shall continually improve the effectiveness of the quality management system.

Adapted from the ISO 9001:2000 Standard, International Standards Organization, Geneva, Switzerland, 2003.

Although the assignable causes underlying these incidents have not been fully discovered, there are clear indicators that despite quality systems certification, Bridgestone/Firestone experienced significant quality problems. ISO certification alone is no guarantee that good quality products are being designed, manufactured, and delivered to the customer. Relying on ISO certification is a strategic management mistake.

It has been estimated that ISO certification activities are approximately a *$40 billion annual business,* worldwide. Much of this money flows to the registrars, auditors, and consultants. This amount does not include all of the internal costs incurred by organizations to achieve registration, such as the thousands of hours of engineering and management effort, travel, internal training, and internal auditing. It is not clear whether any significant fraction of this expenditure has made its way to the bottom line of the registered organizations. Furthermore, there is no assurance that certification has any real impact on quality (as in the Bridgestone/Firestone tire incidents). Many quality engineering authorities believe that ISO certification is largely a waste of effort. Often, organizations would be far better off to "just say no to ISO" and spend a small fraction of that $40 billion on their quality systems and another larger fraction on meaningful variability reduction efforts, develop their own internal (or perhaps industry-based) quality standards, rigorously enforce them, and pocket the difference.

The Malcolm Baldrige National Quality Award. The Malcolm Baldrige National Quality Award (MBNQA) was created by the U.S. Congress in 1987. It is given annually to recognize U.S. organizations for performance excellence. Awards are given to organizations in five categories: manufacturing, service, small business, health care, and education. Three awards may be given each year in each category. Many organizations compete for the awards, and many companies use the performance excellence criteria for self-assessment. The award is administered by NIST (the National Institute of Standards and Technology).

The performance excellence criteria and their interrelationships are shown in Fig. 1.10. The point values for these criteria in the MBNQA are shown in Table 1.4. The criteria are directed towards results, where results are a composite of customer satisfaction and retention, market share and new market development, product/service quality, productivity and operational effectiveness, human resources development, supplier performance, and public/corporate citizenship. The criteria are nonprescriptive. That is, the focus is on results, not the use of specific procedures or tools.

The MBNQA process is shown in Fig. 1.11. An applicant sends the completed application to NIST. This application is then subjected to a first-round review by a team of Baldrige

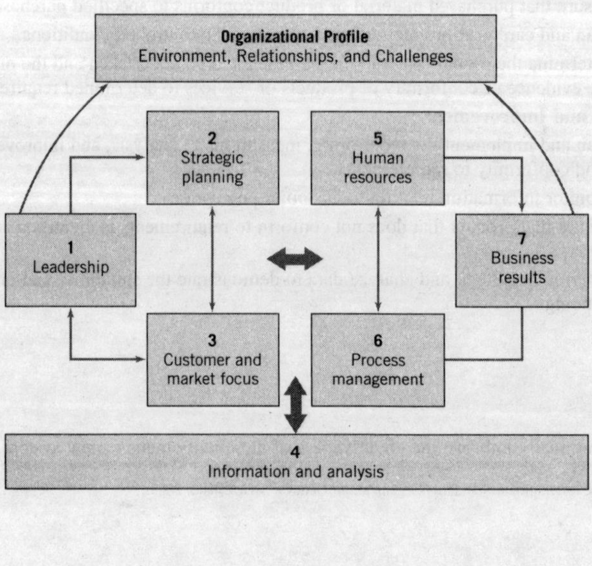

■ **FIGURE 1.10** The structure of the MBNQA performance excellence criteria. (Source: Foundation for the Malcolm Baldrige National Quality Award, 2002 Criteria for Performance Excellence.)

TABLE 1.4
Performance Excellence Categories and Point Values

	Category / Item	Item Points	Category Points
1	**Leadership**		**120**
	1.1 Leadership System	80	
	1.2 Company Responsibility and Citizenship	40	
2	**Strategic Planning**		**85**
	2.1 Strategy Development Process	40	
	2.2 Company Strategy	45	
3	**Customer and Market Focus**		**85**
	3.1 Customer and Market Knowledge	40	
	3.2 Customer Satisfaction and Relationship Enhancement	45	
4	**Information and Analysis**		**90**
	4.1 Measurement and Analysis of Performance	50	
	4.2 Information Management	40	
5	**Human Resource Focus**		**85**
	5.1 Work Systems	35	
	5.2 Employee Education, Training, and Development	25	
	5.3 Employee Well-Being and Satisfaction	25	
6	**Process Management**		**85**
	6.1 Management of Product and Service Processes	45	
	6.2 Management of Business Processes	25	
	6.3 Management of Support Processes	15	
7	**Business Results**		**450**
	7.1 Customer Results	125	
	7.2 Financial and Market Results	125	
	7.3 Human Resource Results	80	
	7.4 Organizational Results	120	
	Total Points		**1,000**

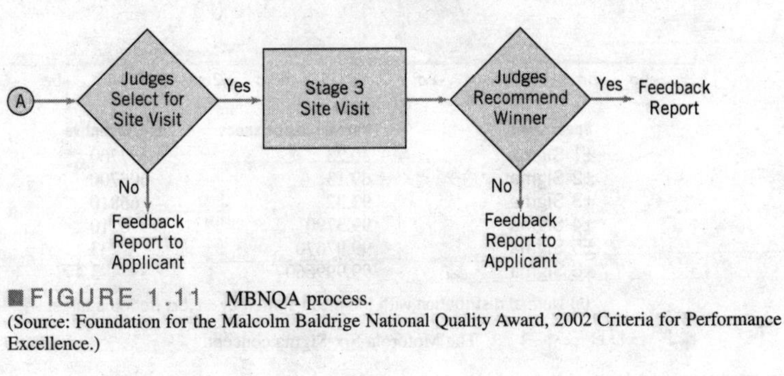

FIGURE 1.11 MBNQA process.
(Source: Foundation for the Malcolm Baldrige National Quality Award, 2002 Criteria for Performance Excellence.)

examiners. The board of Baldrige examiners consists of highly qualified volunteers from a variety of fields. Judges evaluate the scoring on the application to determine if the applicant will continue to **consensus.** During the consensus phase, a group of examiners who scored the original application determines a consensus score for each of the items. Once consensus is reached and a consensus report written, judges then make a site-visit determination. A site visit typically is a one-week visit by a team of four to six examiners who produce a site-visit report. The site-visit reports are used by the judges as the basis of determining the final MBNQA winners.

As shown in Fig. 1.10, feedback reports are provided to the applicant at up to three stages of the MBNQA process. Many organizations have found these reports very helpful and use them as the basis of planning for overall improvement of the organization and for driving improvement in business results.

Six-Sigma. Products with many components typically have many opportunities for failure or defects to occur. Motorola developed the **Six-Sigma program** in the late 1980s as a response to the demand for their products. The focus of six-sigma is reducing variability in key product quality characteristics to the level at which failure or defects are extremely unlikely.

Figure 1.12*a* shows a normal probability distribution as a model for a quality characteristic with the specification limits at three standard deviations on either side of the mean.

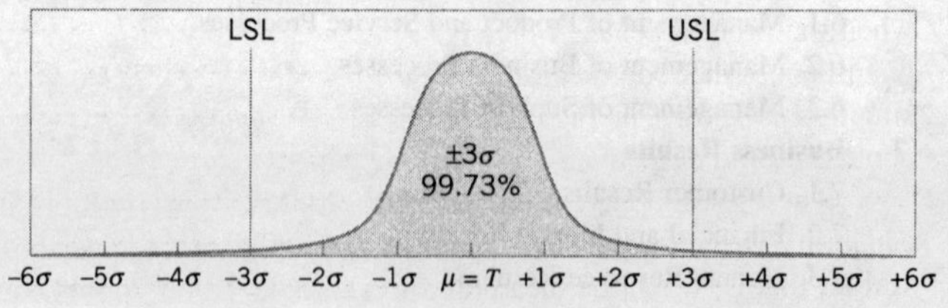

Spec. Limit	Percent Inside Specs	ppm Defective
±1 Sigma	68.27	317300
±2 Sigma	95.45	45500
±3 Sigma	99.73	2700
±4 Sigma	99.9937	63
±5 Sigma	99.999943	0.57
±6 Sigma	99.9999998	0.002

(*a*) Normal distribution centered at the target (*T*)

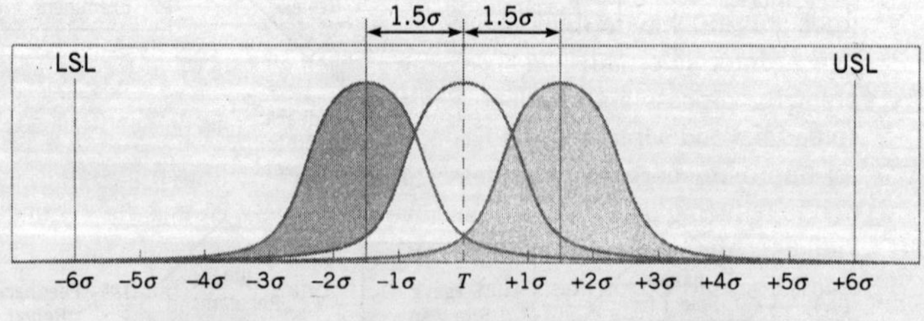

Spec. Limit	Percent inside specs	ppm Defective
±1 Sigma	30.23	697700
±2 Sigma	69.13	608700
±3 Sigma	93.32	66810
±4 Sigma	99.3790	6210
±5 Sigma	99.97670	233
±6 Sigma	99.999660	3.4

(*b*) Normal distribution with the mean shifted by ±1.5σ from the target

■ FIGURE 1.12 The Motorola Six-Sigma concept.

Now it turns out that in this situation the probability of producing a product within these specifications is 0.9973, which corresponds to 2700 parts per million (ppm) defective. This is referred to as **three-sigma quality performance,** and it actually sounds pretty good. However, suppose we have a product that consists of an assembly of 100 independent components or parts and all 100 of these parts must be nondefective for the product to function satisfactorily. The probability that any specific unit of product is nondefective is

$$0.9973 \times 0.9973 \times \ldots \times 0.9973 = (0.9973)^{100} = 0.7631$$

That is, about 23.7% of the products produced under three-sigma quality will be defective. This is not an acceptable situation, because many products used by today's society are made up of many components. Even a relatively simple service activity, such as a visit by a family of four to a fast-food restaurant, can involve the assembly of several dozen components. A typical automobile has about 100,000 components and an airplane has between one and two million!

The Motorola six-sigma concept is to reduce the variability in the process so that the specification limits are at least six standard deviations from the mean. Then, as shown in Fig. 1.12*a*, there will only be about 2 parts per *billion* defective. Under **six-sigma quality,** the probability that any specific unit of the hypothetical product above is nondefective is 0.9999998, or 0.2 ppm, a much better situation.

When the six-sigma concept was initially developed, an assumption was made that when the process reached the six-sigma quality level, the process mean was still subject to disturbances that could cause it to shift by as much as 1.5 standard deviations off target. This situation is shown in Fig. 1.12*b*. Under this scenario, a six-sigma process would produce about 3.4 ppm defective.

There is an apparent inconsistency in this. As we will discuss in Chapter 8 on process capability, we can only make predictions about process performance when the process is **stable;** that is, when the mean (and standard deviation, too) is **constant.** If the mean is drifting around, and ends up as much as 1.5 standard deviations off target, a prediction of 3.4 ppm defective may not be very reliable, because the mean might shift by *more* than the "allowed" 1.5 standard deviations. Process **performance** isn't predictable unless the process **behavior** is stable.

However, no process or system is ever truly stable, and even in the best of situations, disturbances occur. These disturbances can result in the process mean shifting off-target, an increase in the process standard deviation, or both. The concept of a six-sigma process is one way to **model** this behavior. Like all models, it's probably not exactly right, but it has proven to be a useful way to think about process performance.

Motorola established six-sigma as both an objective for the corporation and as a focal point for process and product quality improvement efforts. In recent years, six-sigma has spread beyond Motorola and has come to encompass much more. It has become a program for improving corporate **business performance** by both improving quality and paying attention to reducing costs. Companies involved in a six-sigma effort utilize specially trained individuals, called Green Belts (GBs), Black Belts (BBs), and Master Black Belts (MBBs) lead teams focused on projects that have both quality and business (economic) impacts for the organization. The "belts" have specialized training and education on statistical methods and the quality and process improvement tools in this textbook that equips them to function as team leaders, facilitators, and problem solvers. Typical six-sigma projects are four to six months in duration and are selected for their potential impact in the business. The paper by Hoerl (2001) describes the components of a typical BB education program. Six-sigma uses a specific five-step problem-solving approach: Define, Measure, Analyze, Improve, and Control (DMAIC). The DMAIC framework utilizes control charts, designed experiments, process capability analysis, measurement systems capability studies, and many other basic statistical tools. The DMAIC approach is an extremely effective framework for improving processes. In Chapter 2, we will give a fuller presentation of DMAIC.

The goals of six-sigma, a 3.4 ppm defect level, may seem artificially or arbitrarily high, but it is easy to demonstrate that even the delivery of relatively simple products or services at high levels of quality can lead to the need for six-sigma thinking. For example, consider the visit to a fast-food restaurant mentioned above. The customer orders a typical meal: a hamburger (bun, meat, special sauce, cheese, pickle, onion, lettuce, and tomato), fries, and a soft drink. This product has ten components. Is 99% good quality satisfactory? If we assume that all ten components are independent, the probability of a good meal is

$$P\{\text{Single meal good}\} = (0.99)^{10} = 0.9044$$

which looks pretty good. There is better than a 90% chance that the customer experience will be satisfactory. Now suppose that the customer is a family of four. Again, assuming independence, the probability that all four meals are good is

$$P\{\text{All meal good}\} = (0.9044)^4 = 0.6690.$$

This isn't so nice. The chances are only about two out of three that all of the family meals are good. Now suppose that this hypothetical family of four visits this restaurant once a month (this is about all their cardiovascular systems can stand!). The probability that all visits result in good meals for everybody is

$$P\{\text{All visits during the year good}\} = (0.6690)^{12} = 0.0080.$$

This is obviously unacceptable. So, even in a very simple service system involving a relatively simple product, very high levels of quality and service are required to produce the desired high-quality experience for the customer.

Business organizations have been very quick to understand the potential benefits of six-sigma and to adopt the principles and methods. Between 1987 and 1993, Motorola reduced defectivity on its products by approximately 1300%. This success led to many organizations adopting the approach. Since its origins, there have been three generations of six-sigma implementations. **Generation I** six-sigma focused on defect elimination and basic variability reduction. Motorola is often held up as an exemplar of Generation I six-sigma. In **Generation II** six-sigma, the emphasis on variability and defect reduction remained, but now there was a strong effort to tie these efforts to projects and activities that improved business performance through cost reduction. General Electric is often cited as the leader of the Generation II phase of six-sigma.

In **Generation III,** six-sigma has the additional focus of creating value throughout the organization and for its stakeholders (owners, employees, customers, suppliers, and society at large). Creating value can take many forms: increasing stock prices and dividends, job retention or expansion, expanding markets for company products/services, developing new products/services that reach new and broader markets, and increasing the levels of customer satisfaction throughout the range of products and services offered.

Many different kinds of businesses have embraced six-sigma and made it part of the culture of doing business. Consider the following statement from Jim Owens, chairman of heavy equipment manufacturer Caterpillar, Inc., who wrote in the 2005 annual company report:

> ". . . I believe that our people and world-class six-sigma deployment distinguish Caterpillar from the crowd. What an incredible success story six-sigma has been for Caterpillar! It is the way we do business—how we manage quality, eliminate waste, reduce costs, create new products and services, develop future leaders, and help the company grow profitably. We continue to find new ways to apply the methodology to tackle business challenges. Our leadership team is committed to encoding six-sigma into Caterpillar's "DNA" and extending its deployment to our dealers and suppliers—more than 500 of whom have already embraced the six-sigma way of doing business."

At the annual meeting of Bank of America in 2004, chief executive officer Kenneth D. Lewis told the attendees that the company had record earnings in 2003, had significantly improved the customer experience, and had raised its community development funding target to $750 billion over ten years. "Simply put, Bank of America has been making it happen," Lewis said. "And we've been doing it by following a disciplined, customer-focused and organic growth strategy." Citing the companywide use of six-sigma techniques for process improvement, he noted that in fewer than three years, Bank of America had "saved millions of dollars in expenses, cut cycle times in numerous areas of the company by half or more, and reduced the number of processing errors."

These are strong endorsements of six-sigma from two highly recognized business leaders that lead two very different types of organizations, manufacturing and financial services. Caterpillar and Bank of America are good examples of Generation III six-sigma companies, because their implementations are focused on value creation for all stakeholders in the broad sense. Note Lewis's emphasis on reducing cycle times and reducing processing errors (items that will greatly improve customer satisfaction), and Owens's remarks on extending six-sigma to suppliers and dealers—the entire supply chain. Six-sigma has spread well beyond its manufacturing origins into areas including health care, many types of service business, and government/public service (the U.S. Navy has a strong and very successful six-sigma program). The reason for the success of six-sigma in organizations outside the traditional manufacturing sphere is that variability is everywhere, and where there is variability, there is an opportunity to improve business results. Some examples of situations where a six-sigma program can be applied to reduce variability, eliminate defects, and improve business performance include:

- Meeting delivery schedule and delivery accuracy targets
- Eliminating rework in preparing budgets and other financial documents
- Proportion of repeat visitors to an e-commerce Website, or proportion of visitors that make a purchase
- Minimizing cycle time or reducing customer waiting time in any service system
- Reducing average and variability in days outstanding of accounts receivable
- Optimizing payment of outstanding accounts
- Minimizing stock-out or lost sales in supply chain management
- Minimizing costs of public accountants, legal services, and other consultants
- Inventory management (both finished goods and work-in-process)
- Improving forecasting accuracy and timing
- Improving audit processes
- Closing financial books, improving accuracy of journal entry and posting (a 3 to 4% error rate is fairly typical)
- Reducing variability in cash flow
- Improving payroll accuracy
- Improving purchase order accuracy and reducing rework of purchase orders

The structure of a six-sigma organization is shown in Figure 1.13. The lines in this figure identify the key links among the functional units. The **leadership team** is the executive responsible for that business unit and appropriate members of his/her staff and direct reports. This person has overall responsibility for approving the improvement projects undertaken by the six-sigma teams. Each project has a **champion,** a business leader whose job is to facilitate project identification and selection, identify black belts and other team members who are necessary for successful project completion, remove barriers to project completion, make

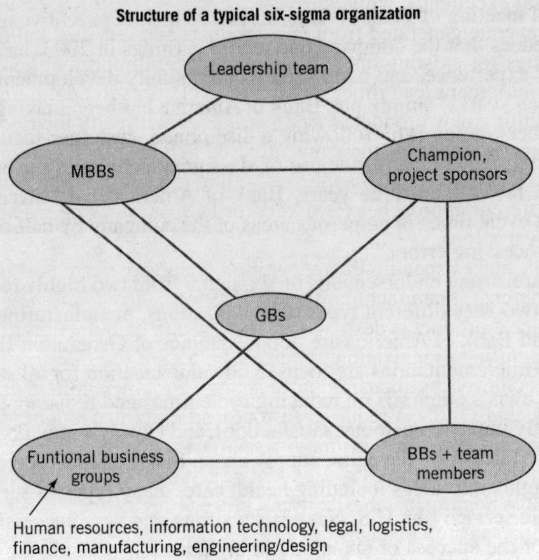

■ **FIGURE 1.13** The structure of a six-sigma organization (Adapted from R. D. Snee and R. W. Hoerl, *Six-Sigma Beyond the Factory Floor*, Upper Saddle River, NJ: Pearson Prentice Hall, 2005).

sure that the resources required for project completion are available, and conduct regular meetings with the team or the Black Belt to ensure that progress is being made and the project is on schedule. The champion role is not full time, and champions often have several projects under their supervision. Black Belts are team leaders that are involved in the actual project completion activities. Team members often spend 25% of their time on the project, and may be drawn from different areas of the business, depending on project requirements. Green Belts typically have less training and experience in six-sigma tools and approaches than the Black Belts, and may lead projects of their own under the direction of a champion or Black Belt, or they may be part of a Black Belt–led team. A Master Black Belt is a technical leader, and may work with the champion and the leadership team in project identification and selection, project reviews, consulting with Black Belts on technical issues, and training of Green Belts and Black Belts. Typically, the Black Belt and Master Black Belt roles are full time.

In recent years, two other tool sets have become identified with six-sigma, **lean systems,** and **design for six-sigma (DFSS)**. Many organizations regularly use one or both of these approaches as an integral part of their six-sigma implementation.

Design for six-sigma is an approach for taking the variability reduction and process improvement philosophy of six-sigma upstream from manufacturing or production into the design process, where new products (or services or service processes) are designed and developed. Broadly speaking, DFSS is a structured and disciplined methodology for the efficient commercialization of technology that results in new products, services, or processes. By a product, we mean anything that is sold to a consumer for use; by a service, we mean an activity that provides value or benefit to the consumer. DFSS spans the entire development process from the identification of customer needs to the final launch of the new product or service. Customer input is obtained through **voice of the customer (VOC)** activities designed to determine what the customer really wants, to set priorities based on actual customer wants, and to determine if the business can meet those needs at a competitive price that will enable it to make a profit. VOC data is usually obtained by customer interviews, by a direct interaction with and observation of the customer, through focus groups, by surveys, and by analysis of customer satisfaction data. The purpose is to develop a set of critical to quality requirements for the product or service. Traditionally, six-sigma is used to achieve

operational excellence, while DFSS is focused on improving business results by increasing the sales revenue generated from new products and services and finding new applications or opportunities for existing ones. In many cases, an important gain from DFSS is the reduction of development lead time; that is, the cycle time to commercialize new technology and get the resulting new products to market. DFSS is directly focused on increasing value in the organization. Many of the tools that are used in operational six-sigma are also used in DFSS. The DMAIC process is also applicable, although some organizations and practitioners have slightly different approaches (DMADV, or Define, Measure, Analyze, Design, and Verify, is a popular variation).

DFSS makes specific the recognition that every design decision is a business decision, and that the cost, manufacturability, and performance of the product are determined during design. Once a product is designed and released to manufacturing, it is almost impossible for the manufacturing organization to make it better. Furthermore, overall business improvement cannot be achieved by focusing on reducing variability in manufacturing alone (operational six-sigma), and DFSS is required to focus on customer requirements while simultaneously keeping process capability in mind. Specifically, matching the capability of the production system and the requirements at each stage or level of the design process (refer to Figure 1.14) is essential. When mismatches between process capabilities and design requirements are discovered, either design changes or different production alternatives are considered to resolve the conflicts. Throughout the DFSS process, it is important that the following points be kept in mind:

- Is the product concept well identified?
- Are customers real?
- Will customers buy this product?
- Can the company make this product at competitive cost?
- Are the financial returns acceptable?
- Does this product fit with the overall business strategy?
- Is the risk assessment acceptable?
- Can the company make this product better than the competition?
- Can product reliability, maintainability goals be met?
- Has a plan for transfer to manufacturing been developed and verified?

Lean systems are designed to eliminate waste. By waste, we mean unnecessarily long cycle times, or waiting times between value-added work activities. Waste can also include rework (doing something over again to eliminate defects introduced the first time) or scrap.

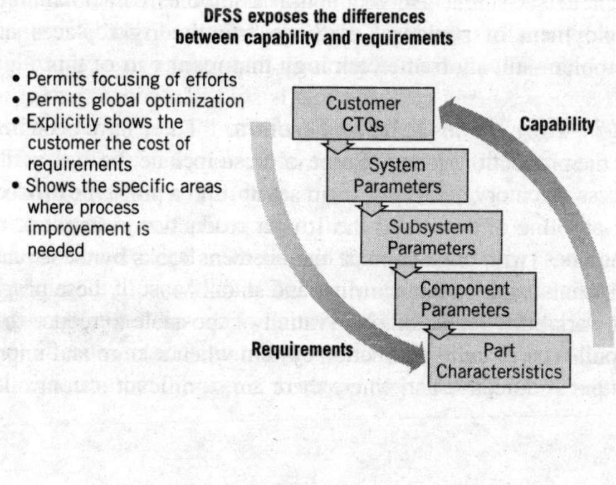

■ FIGURE 1.14 Matching product requirements and production capability in DFSS.

Rework and scrap are often the result of excess variability, so there is an obvious connection between six-sigma and lean. An important metric in lean is the process cycle efficiency (PCE) defined as

$$\text{Process cycle efficiency} = \frac{\text{Value-add time}}{\text{Process cycle time}}$$

where the value-add time is the amount of time actually spent in the process that transforms the form, fit, or function of the product or service that results in something for which the customer is willing to pay. PCE is a direct measure of how efficiently the process is converting the work that is in-process into completed products or services. Process cycle time is also related to the amount of work that is in-process through **Little's Law:**

$$\text{Process cycle time} = \frac{\text{Work-in-process}}{\text{Average completion rate}}$$

The average completion rate is a measure of capacity; that is, it is the output of a process over a defined time period. For example, consider a mortgage refinance operation at a bank. If the average completion rate for submitted applications is 100 completions per day, and there are 1,500 applications waiting for processing, the process cycle time is

$$\text{Process cycle time} = \frac{1500}{100} = 15 \text{ days}$$

Often the cycle time can be reduced by eliminating waste and inefficiency in the process, resulting in an increase in the completion rate.

Lean also makes use of many tools of industrial engineering and operations research. One of the most important of these is **discrete-event simulation;** in which a computer model of the system is built and used to quantify the impact of changes to the system that improve its performance. Simulation models are often very good predictors of the performance of a new or redesigned system. Both manufacturing and service organizations can greatly benefit by using simulation models to study the performance of their processes.

Ideally, six-sigma/DMAIC, DFSS, and lean tools are used simultaneously and harmoniously in an organization to achieve high levels of process performance and significant business improvement. Figure 1.15 highlights many of the important complimentary aspects of these three sets of tools.

Six-sigma (often combined with DFSS and Lean) has been much more successful than its predecessors, notably TQM. The project-by-project approach and the focus on obtaining improvement in bottom-line business results has been instrumental in obtaining management commitment to six-sigma. Another major component in obtaining success is driving the proper deployment of statistical methods into the right places in the organization. The DMAIC problem-solving framework is an important part of this.

Just-in-Time, Poka-Yoke, and Others. There have been many initiatives devoted to improving the production system. Some of these include the Just-in-Time approach emphasizing in-process inventory reduction, rapid set-up, and a pull-type production system; Poka-Yoke or mistake-proofing of processes; the Toyota production system and other Japanese manufacturing techniques (with once-popular management books by those names); reengineering; theory of constraints; agile manufacturing; and so on. Most of these programs devote far too little attention to variability reduction. It's virtually impossible to reduce the in-process inventory or operate a pull-type or agile production system when a large and unpredictable fraction of the process output is defective and where there are significant uncontrolled sources of variability.

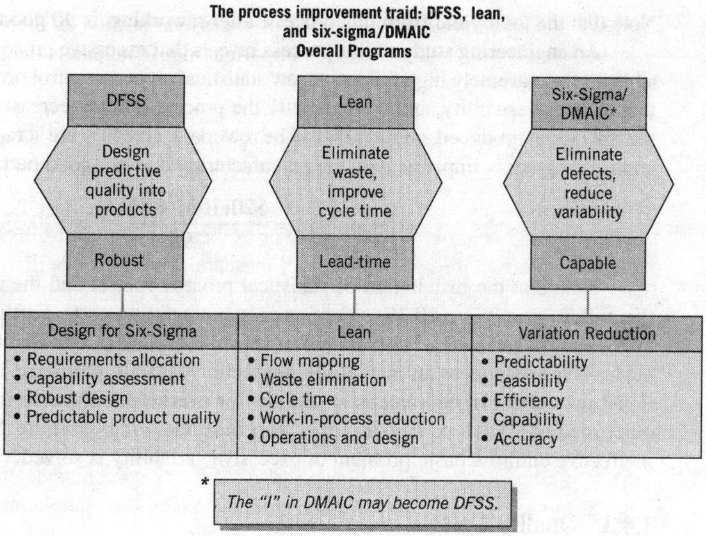

■ FIGURE 1.15 Six-sigma/DMAIC, lean, and DFSS: How they fit together.

Such efforts will not achieve their full potential without a major focus on statistical methods for process improvement and variability reduction to accompany them.

1.4.2 The Link Between Quality and Productivity

Producing high-quality products in the modern industrial environment is not easy. A significant aspect of the problem is the rapid evolution of technology. The past 20 years have seen an explosion of technology in such diverse fields as electronics, metallurgy, ceramics, composite materials, biotechnology, and the chemical and pharmaceutical sciences, which has resulted in many new products and services. For example, in the electronics field the development of the integrated circuit has revolutionized the design and manufacture of computers and many electronic office products. Basic integrated circuit technology has been supplanted by large-scale integration (LSI) and very large-scale integration (VLSI) technology, with corresponding developments in semiconductor design and manufacturing. When technological advances occur rapidly and when the new technologies are used quickly to exploit competitive advantages, the problems of designing and manufacturing products of superior quality are greatly complicated.

Often, too little attention is paid to achieving all dimensions of an optimal process: economy, efficiency, productivity, and quality. Effective quality improvement can be instrumental in increasing productivity and reducing cost. To illustrate, consider the manufacture of a mechanical component used in a copier machine. The parts are manufactured in a machining process at a rate of approximately 100 parts per day. For various reasons, the process is operating at a first-pass yield of about 75%. (That is, about 75% of the process output conforms to specifications, and about 25% of the output is nonconforming.) About 60% of the fallout (the 25% nonconforming) can be reworked into an acceptable product, and the rest must be scrapped. The direct manufacturing cost through this stage of production per part is approximately \$20. Parts that can be reworked incur an additional processing charge of \$4. Therefore, the manufacturing cost per good part produced is

$$\text{Cost/good part} = \frac{\$20(100) + \$4(15)}{90} = \$22.89$$

Note that the total yield from this process, after reworking, is 90 good parts per day.

An engineering study of this process reveals that excessive process variability is responsible for the extremely high fallout. A new statistical process-control procedure is implemented that reduces variability, and consequently the process fallout decreases from 25% to 5%. Of the 5% fallout produced, about 60% can be reworked, and 40% are scrapped. After the process-control program is implemented, the manufacturing cost per good part produced is

$$\text{Cost/good part} = \frac{\$20(100) + \$4(3)}{98} = \$20.53$$

Note that the installation of statistical process control and the reduction of variability that follows result in a 10.3% reduction in manufacturing costs. Furthermore, productivity is up by almost 10%; 98 good parts are produced each day as opposed to 90 good parts previously. This amounts to an increase in production capacity of almost 10%, without any additional investment in equipment, workforce, or overhead. Efforts to improve this process by other methods (such as Just-in-Time, lean manufacturing, etc.) are likely to be completely ineffective until the basic problem of excessive variability is solved.

1.4.3 Quality Costs

Financial controls are an important part of business management. These financial controls involve a comparison of actual and budgeted costs, along with analysis and action on the differences between actual and budget. It is customary to apply these financial controls on a department or functional level. For many years, there was no direct effort to measure or account for the costs of the quality function. However, many organizations now formally evaluate the cost associated with quality. There are several reasons why the cost of quality should be explicitly considered in an organization. These include the following:

1. The increase in the cost of quality because of the increase in the complexity of manufactured products associated with advances in technology
2. Increasing awareness of life-cycle costs, including maintenance, spare parts, and the cost of field failures
3. Quality engineers and managers can most effectively communicate quality issues in a way that management understands.

As a result, quality costs have emerged as a financial control tool for management and as an aid in identifying opportunities for reducing quality costs.

Generally speaking, quality costs are those categories of costs that are associated with producing, identifying, avoiding, or repairing products that do not meet requirements. Many manufacturing and service organizations use four categories of quality costs: prevention costs, appraisal costs, internal failure costs, and external failure costs. These cost categories are shown in Table 1.5. We now discuss these categories in more detail.

Prevention Costs. Prevention costs are those costs associated with efforts in design and manufacturing that are directed toward the prevention of nonconformance. Broadly speaking, prevention costs are all costs incurred in an effort to "make it right the first time." The important subcategories of prevention costs follow.

Quality planning and engineering. Costs associated with the creation of the overall quality plan, the inspection plan, the reliability plan, the data system, and all specialized plans and activities of the quality-assurance function; the preparation of manuals and procedures used to communicate the quality plan; and the costs of auditing the system.

New products review. Costs of the preparation of bid proposals, the evaluation of new designs from a quality viewpoint, the preparation of tests and experimental programs to

■ TABLE 1.5
Quality Costs

Prevention Costs	Internal Failure Costs
Quality planning and engineering	Scrap
New products review	Rework
Product/process design	Retest
Process control	Failure analysis
Burn-in	Downtime
Training	Yield losses
Quality data acquisition and analysis	Downgrading (off-specing)
Appraisal Costs	**External Failure Costs**
Inspection and test of incoming material	Complaint adjustment
Product inspection and test	Returned product/material
Materials and services consumed	Warranty charges
Maintaining accuracy of test equipment	Liability costs
	Indirect costs

evaluate the performance of new products, and other quality activities during the development and preproduction stages of new products or designs.

Product/process design. Costs incurred during the design of the product or the selection of the production processes that are intended to improve the overall quality of the product. For example, an organization may decide to make a particular circuit component redundant because this will increase the reliability of the product by increasing the mean time between failures. Alternatively, it may decide to manufacture a component using process A rather than process B, because process A is capable of producing the product at tighter tolerances, which will result in fewer assembly and manufacturing problems. This may include a vendor's process, so the cost of dealing with other than the lowest bidder may also be a prevention cost.

Process control. The cost of process-control techniques, such as control charts, that monitor the manufacturing process in an effort to reduce variation and build quality into the product.

Burn-in. The cost of preshipment operation of the product to prevent early-life failures in the field.

Training. The cost of developing, preparing, implementing, operating, and maintaining formal training programs for quality.

Quality data acquisition and analysis. The cost of running the quality data system to acquire data on product and process performance; also the cost of analyzing these data to identify problems. It includes the work of summarizing and publishing quality information for management.

Appraisal Costs. Appraisal costs are those costs associated with measuring, evaluating, or auditing products, components, and purchased materials to ensure conformance to the standards that have been imposed. These costs are incurred to determine the condition of the product from a quality viewpoint and ensure that it conforms to specifications. The major subcategories follow.

Inspection and test of incoming material. Costs associated with the inspection and testing of all material. This subcategory includes receiving inspection and test; inspection, test, and evaluation at the vendor's facility; and a periodic audit of the quality-assurance system. This could also include intraplant vendors.

Product inspection and test. The cost of checking the conformance of the product throughout its various stages of manufacturing, including final acceptance testing, packing and shipping checks, and any test done at the customer's facilities prior to turning the product over to the customer. This also includes life testing, environmental testing, and reliability testing.

Materials and services consumed. The cost of material and products consumed in a destructive test or devalued by reliability tests.

Maintaining accuracy of test equipment. The cost of operating a system that keeps the measuring instruments and equipment in calibration.

Internal Failure Costs. Internal failure costs are incurred when products, components, materials, and services fail to meet quality requirements, and this failure is discovered prior to delivery of the product to the customer. These costs would disappear if there were no defects in the product. The major subcategories of internal failure costs follow.

Scrap. The net loss of labor, material, and overhead resulting from defective product that cannot economically be repaired or used.

Rework. The cost of correcting nonconforming units so that they meet specifications. In some manufacturing operations rework costs include additional operations or steps in the manufacturing process that are created to solve either chronic defects or sporadic defects.

Retest. The cost of reinspection and retesting of products that have undergone rework or other modifications.

Failure analysis. The cost incurred to determine the causes of product failures.

Downtime. The cost of idle production facilities that results from nonconformance to requirements. The production line may be down because of nonconforming raw materials supplied by a supplier, which went undiscovered in receiving inspection.

Yield losses. The cost of process yields that are lower than might be attainable by improved controls (for example, soft-drink containers that are overfilled because of excessive variability in the filling equipment).

Downgrading/off-specing. The price differential between the normal selling price and any selling price that might be obtained for a product that does not meet the customer's requirements. Downgrading is a common practice in the textile, apparel goods, and electronics industries. The problem with downgrading is that products sold do not recover the full contribution margin to profit and overhead as do products that conform to the usual specifications.

External Failure Costs. External failure costs occur when the product does not perform satisfactorily after it is delivered to the customer. These costs would also disappear if every unit of product conformed to requirements. Subcategories of external failure costs follow.

Complaint adjustment. All costs of investigation and adjustment of justified complaints attributable to the nonconforming product.

Returned product/material. All costs associated with receipt, handling, and replacement of the nonconforming product or material that is returned from the field.

Warranty charges. All costs involved in service to customers under warranty contracts.

Liability costs. Costs or awards incurred from product liability litigation.

Indirect costs. In addition to direct operating costs of external failures, there are a significant number of indirect costs. These are incurred because of customer dissatisfaction with the level of quality of the delivered product. Indirect costs may reflect the customer's attitude toward the company. They include the costs of loss of business reputation, loss of future business, and loss of market share that inevitably results from delivering products and services that do not conform to the customer's expectations regarding fitness for use.

The Analysis and Use of Quality Costs. How large are quality costs? The answer, of course, depends on the type of organization and the success of their quality improvement effort. In some organizations quality costs are 4% or 5% of sales, whereas in others they can be as high as 35% or 40% of sales. Obviously, the cost of quality will be very different for a high-technology computer manufacturer than for a typical service industry, such as a department store or hotel chain. In most organizations, however, quality costs are higher than necessary, and management should make continuing efforts to appraise, analyze, and reduce these costs.

The usefulness of quality costs stems from the **leverage effect;** that is, dollars invested in prevention and appraisal have a payoff in reducing dollars incurred in internal and external failures that exceeds the original investment. For example, a dollar invested in prevention may return $10 or $100 (or more) in savings from reduced internal and external failures.

Quality-cost analyses have as their principal objective cost reduction through identification of improvement opportunities. This is often done with a **Pareto analysis.** The Pareto analysis consists of identifying quality costs by category, or by product, or by type of defect or nonconformity. For example, inspection of the quality-cost information in Table 1.6 concerning defects or nonconformities in the assembly of electronic components onto printed circuit boards reveals that insufficient solder is the highest quality cost incurred in this operation. Insufficient solder accounts for 42% of the total defects in this particular type of board and for almost 52% of the total scrap and rework costs. If the wave solder process can be improved, then there will be dramatic reductions in the cost of quality.

How much reduction in quality costs is possible? Although the cost of quality in many organizations can be significantly reduced, it is unrealistic to expect it can be reduced to zero. Before that level of performance is reached, the incremental costs of prevention and appraisal will rise more rapidly than the resulting cost reductions. However, paying attention to quality costs in conjunction with a focused effort on variability reduction has the capability of reducing quality costs by 50% or 60% provided that no organized effort has previously existed. This cost reduction also follows the Pareto principle; that is, most of the cost reductions will come from attacking the few problems that are responsible for the majority of quality costs.

In analyzing quality costs and in formulating plans for reducing the cost of quality, it is important to note the role of prevention and appraisal. Many organizations devote far too much effort to appraisal and not enough to prevention. This is an easy mistake for an organization to make, because appraisal costs are often budget line items in manufacturing. On the

■ **TABLE 1.6**
Monthly Quality-Costs Information for Assembly of Printed Circuit Boards

Type of Defect	Percent of Total Defects	Scrap and Rework Costs
Insufficient solder	42%	$37,500.00 (52%)
Misaligned components	21	12,000.00
Defective components	15	8,000.00
Missing components	10	5,100.00
Cold solder joints	7	5,000.00
All other causes	5	4,600.00
Totals	100%	$72,200.00

other hand, prevention costs may not be routinely budgeted items. It is not unusual to find in the early stages of a quality-cost program that appraisal costs are eight or ten times the magnitude of prevention costs. This is probably an unreasonable ratio, as dollars spent in prevention have a much greater payback than do dollars spent in appraisal.

Generating the quality-cost figures is not always easy, because most quality-cost categories are not a direct component in the accounting records of the organization. Consequently, it may be difficult to obtain extremely accurate information on the costs incurred with respect to the various categories. The organization's accounting system can provide information on those quality-cost categories that coincide with the usual business accounts, such as, for example, product testing and evaluation. In addition, many companies will have detailed information on various categories of failure cost. The information for cost categories for which exact accounting information is not available should be generated by using estimates, or, in some cases, by creating special monitoring and surveillance procedures to accumulate those costs over the study period.

The reporting of quality costs is usually done on a basis that permits straightforward evaluation by management. Managers want quality costs expressed in an index that compares quality cost with the opportunity for quality cost. Consequently, the usual method of reporting quality costs is in the form of a ratio, where the numerator is quality-cost dollars and the denominator is some measure of activity, such as (1) hours of direct production labor, (2) dollars of direct production labor, (3) dollars of processing costs, (4) dollars of manufacturing cost, (5) dollars of sales, or (6) units of product.

Upper management may want a standard against which to compare the current quality-cost figures. It is difficult to obtain absolute standards and almost as difficult to obtain quality-cost levels of other companies in the same industry. Therefore, the usual approach is to compare current performance with past performance so that, in effect, quality-cost programs report variances from past performance. These trend analyses are primarily a device for detecting departures from standard and for bringing them to the attention of the appropriate managers. They are not necessarily in and of themselves a device for ensuring quality improvements.

This brings us to an interesting observation: Some quality-cost collection and analysis efforts fail. That is, a number of companies have started quality-cost analysis activities, used them for some time, and then abandoned the programs as ineffective. There are several reasons why this occurs. Chief among these is failure to use quality-cost information as a mechanism for generating improvement opportunities. If we use quality cost information as a scorekeeping tool only, and do not make conscious efforts to identify problem areas and develop improved operating procedures and processes, then the programs will not be totally successful.

Another reason why quality-cost collection and analysis doesn't lead to useful results is that managers become preoccupied with perfection in the cost figures. Overemphasis in treating quality costs as part of the accounting systems rather than as a management control tool is a serious mistake. This approach greatly increases the amount of time required to develop the cost data, analyze them, and identify opportunities for quality improvements. As the time required to generate and analyze the data increases, management becomes more impatient and less convinced of the effectiveness of the activity. Any program that appears to management as going nowhere is likely to be abandoned.

A final reason for the failure of a quality-cost program is that management often underestimates the depth and extent of the commitment to prevention that must be made. The author has had numerous opportunities to examine quality cost data in many companies. In companies without effective quality improvement programs, the dollars allocated to prevention rarely exceed 1% to 2% of revenue. This must be increased to a threshold of about 5% to 6% of revenue, and these additional prevention dollars must be spent largely on the technical methods of quality improvement, and not on establishing programs such as TQM, Zero Defects, or other similar activities. If management is persistent in this effort, then the cost of quality will decrease substantially. These cost savings will typically begin to occur in one to two years, although it could be longer in some companies.

1.4.4 Legal Aspects of Quality

Consumerism and product liability are important reasons why quality assurance is an important business strategy. Consumerism is in part due to the seemingly large number of failures in the field of consumer products and the perception that service quality is declining. Highly visible field failures often prompt the questions of whether today's products are as good as their predecessors and whether manufacturers are really interested in quality. The answer to both of these questions is yes. Manufacturers are always vitally concerned about field failures because of heavy external failure costs and the related threat to their competitive position. Consequently, most producers have made product improvements directed toward reducing field failures. For example, solid-state and integrated-circuit technology has greatly reduced the failure of electronic equipment that once depended on the electron tube. Virtually every product line of today is superior to that of yesterday.

Consumer dissatisfaction and the general feeling that today's products are inferior to their predecessors arise from other phenomena. One of these is the explosion in the number of products. For example, a 1% field-failure rate for a consumer appliance with a production volume of 50,000 units per year means 500 field failures. However, if the production rate is 500,000 units per year and the field-failure rate remains the same, then 5,000 units will fail in the field. This is equivalent, in the total number of dissatisfied customers, to a 10% failure rate at the lower production level. Increasing production volume increases the **liability exposure** of the manufacturer. Even in situations in which the failure rate declines, if the production volume increases more rapidly than the decrease in failure rate, the total number of customers who experience failures will still increase.

A second aspect of the problem is that consumer tolerance for minor defects and aesthetic problems has decreased considerably, so that blemishes, surface-finish defects, noises, and appearance problems that were once tolerated now attract attention and result in adverse consumer reaction. Finally, the competitiveness of the marketplace forces many manufacturers to introduce new designs before they are fully evaluated and tested in order to remain competitive. These "early releases" of unproved designs are a major reason for new product quality failures. Eventually, these design problems are corrected, but the high failure rate connected with new products often supports the belief that today's quality is inferior to that of yesterday.

Product liability is a major social, market, and economic force. The legal obligation of manufacturers and sellers to compensate for injury or damage caused by defective products is not a recent phenomenon. The concept of product liability has been in existence for many years, but its emphasis has changed recently. The first major product liability case occurred in 1916 and was tried before the New York Court of Appeals. The court held that an automobile manufacturer had a product liability obligation to a car buyer, even though the sales contract was between the buyer and a third party—namely, a car dealer. The direction of the law has always been that manufacturers or sellers are likely to incur a liability when they have been unreasonably careless or negligent in what they have designed, or produced, or how they have produced it. In recent years, the courts have placed a more stringent rule in effect called **strict liability.** Two principles are characteristic of strict liability. The first is a strong responsibility for both manufacturer and merchandiser, requiring immediate responsiveness to unsatisfactory quality through product service, repair, or replacement of defective product. This extends into the period of actual use by the consumer. By producing a product, the manufacturer and seller must accept responsibility for the ultimate use of that product—not only for its performance, but also for its environmental effects, the safety aspects of its use, and so forth.

The second principle involves advertising and promotion of the product. Under strict product liability all advertising statements must be supportable by valid company quality or certification data, comparable to that now maintained for product identification under regulations for such products as automobiles.

These two strict product liability principles result in strong pressure on manufacturers, distributors, and merchants to develop and maintain a high degree of factually based evidence concerning the performance and safety of their products. This evidence must cover not only the quality of the product as it is delivered to the consumer, but also its durability or reliability, its protection from possible side effects or environmental hazards, and its safety aspects in actual use. A strong quality-assurance program can help management in ensuring that this information will be available, if needed.

1.4.5 Implementing Quality Improvement

In the past few sections we have discussed the philosophy of quality improvement, the link between quality and productivity, and both economic and legal implications of quality. These are important aspects of the management of quality within an organization. There are certain other aspects of the overall management of quality that warrant some attention.

Management must recognize that quality is a multifaceted entity, incorporating the eight dimensions we discussed in Section 1.1.1. For convenient reference, Table 1.7 summarizes these quality dimensions.

A critical part of the **strategic management of quality** within any business is the recognition of these dimensions by management and the selection of dimensions along which the business will compete. It will be very difficult to compete against companies that can successfully accomplish this part of the strategy.

A good example is the Japanese dominance of the videocassette recorder (VCR) market. The Japanese did not invent the VCR; the first units for home use were designed and produced in Europe and North America. However, the early VCRs produced by these companies were very unreliable and frequently had high levels of manufacturing defects. When the Japanese entered the market, they elected to compete along the dimensions of reliability and conformance to standards (no defects). This strategy allowed them to quickly dominate the market. In subsequent years, they expanded the dimensions of quality to include added features, improved performance, easier serviceability, improved aesthetics, and so forth. They have used total quality as a competitive weapon to raise the entry barrier to this market so high that it is virtually impossible for a new competitor to enter.

Management must do this type of strategic thinking about quality. It is not necessary that the product be superior in all dimensions of quality, but management must **select and develop** the "niches" of quality along which the company can successfully compete. Typically, these dimensions will be those that the competition has forgotten or ignored. The American automobile industry has been severely impacted by foreign competitors who expertly practiced this strategy.

The critical role of **suppliers** in quality management must not be forgotten. In fact, supplier selection and **supply chain management** may be the most critical aspects of successful

■ TABLE 1.7

The Eight Dimensions of Quality from Section 1.1.1

1. Performance	5. Aesthetics
2. Reliability	6. Features
3. Durability	7. Perceived quality
4. Serviceability	8. Conformance to standards

quality management in industries such as automotive, aerospace, and electronics, where a very high percentage of the parts in the end item are manufactured by outside suppliers. Many companies have instituted formal supplier quality-improvement programs as part of their own **internal** quality-improvement efforts. Selection of suppliers based on **quality, schedule,** and **cost,** rather than on cost alone, is also a vital strategic management decision that can have a long-term significant impact on overall competitiveness.

It is also critical that management recognize that quality improvement must be a total, company-wide activity, and that every organizational unit *must* actively participate. Obtaining this participation is the responsibility of (and a significant challenge to) senior management. What is the role of the quality-assurance organization in this effect? The responsibility of quality assurance is to assist management in providing quality assurance for the companies' products. Specifically, the quality-assurance function is a technology warehouse that contains the skills and resources necessary to generate products of acceptable quality in the marketplace. Quality management also has the responsibility for evaluating and using quality-cost information for identifying improvement opportunities in the system, and for making these opportunities known to higher management. It is important to note, however, that the **quality function is not responsible for quality.** After all, the quality organization does not design, manufacture, distribute, or service the product. Thus, the responsibility for quality is distributed throughout the entire organization.

The philosophy of Deming, Juran, and Feigenbaum implies that responsibility for quality spans the entire organization. However, there is a danger that if we adopt the philosophy that "quality is everybody's job," then quality will become nobody's job. This is why quality planning and analysis are important. Because quality improvement activities are so broad, successful efforts require, as an initial step, top management commitment. This commitment involves emphasis on the importance of quality, identification of the respective quality responsibilities of the various organizational units, and explicit accountability for quality improvement of all managers and employees in the company.

Finally, strategic management of quality in an organization must involve all three components discussed earlier: **quality planning**, **quality assurance**, and **quality control and improvement**. Furthermore, *all* of the individuals in the organization must have an understanding of the basic tools of quality improvement. Central among these tools are the elementary statistical concepts that form the basis of process control and that are used for the analysis of process data. It is increasingly important that everyone in an organization, from top management to operating personnel, have an awareness of basic statistical methods and of how these methods are useful in manufacturing, engineering design, and development and in the general business environment. Certain individuals must have higher levels of skills; for example, those engineers and managers in the quality-assurance function would generally be experts in one or more areas of process control, reliability engineering, design of experiments, or engineering data analysis. However, the key point is the philosophy that statistical methodology is a language of communication about problems that enables management to mobilize resources rapidly and to efficiently develop solutions to such problems. Because six-sigma incorporates most of the elements for success that we have identified, it has proven to be a very effective framework for implementing quality improvement.

Important Terms and Concepts

Acceptance sampling
Appraisal costs
Critical-to-quality (CTQ)
Deming's 14 points
Designed experiments
Dimensions of quality
Fitness for use
Internal and external failure costs

ISI 9000:2000
The Juran Trilogy
The Malcolm Baldrige National Quality Award
Nonconforming product or service
Prevention costs
Product liability
Quality assurance
Quality characteristics
Quality control and improvement
Quality engineering
Quality of conformance
Quality of design
Quality planning
Quality systems and standards
Six-Sigma
Specifications
Statistical process control (SPC)
Total quality management (TQM)
Variability

Discussion Questions and Exercises

1.1. Briefly discuss the eight dimensions of quality. Does this improve our understanding of quality?

1.2. Select a specific product or service, and discuss how the eight dimensions of quality impact its overall acceptance by consumers.

1.3. Why is it difficult to define quality?

1.4. What are the three primary technical tools used for quality control and improvement?

1.5. Distinguish among quality planning, quality assurance, and quality control and improvement.

1.6. Can an understanding of the multidimensional nature of quality lead to improved product design or better service?

1.7. Explain why it is necessary to consider variability around the mean or nominal dimension as a measure of quality.

1.8. What are the internal customers of a business? Why are they important from a quality perspective?

1.9. Is there a difference between quality for a manufactured product and quality for a service? Give some specific examples.

1.10. Compare and contrast Deming's and Juran's philosophies of quality.

1.11. What is the Malcolm Baldrige National Quality Award? Who is eligible for the award?

1.12. What is meant by the cost of quality?

1.13. Discuss the statement, "Quality is the responsibility of the quality assurance organization."

1.14. What are the three components of the ISO 9000:2000 standard?

1.15. Who was Walter A. Shewhart?

1.16. What would motivate a business to compete for the Malcolm Baldrige National Quality Award?

1.17. Most of the quality management literature states that without top management leadership, quality improvement will not occur. Do you agree or disagree with this statement? Discuss why.

1.18. Are internal failure costs more or less important than external failure costs?

1.19. What is a six-sigma process?

1.20. Suppose you had the opportunity to improve quality in a hospital. Which areas of the hospital would you look to as opportunities for quality improvement? What metrics would you use as measures of quality?

1.21. Reconsider the fast-food restaurant visit discussed in the chapter. What would be the results for the family of four on each visit and annually if the probability of good quality on each meal component was increased to 0.999?

1.22. Reconsider the fast-food restaurant visit discussed in the chapter. What levels of quality would you consider acceptable for the family of four on each visit and annually? What probability of good quality on each meal component would be required in order to achieve these targets?

1.23. Hundreds of companies and organizations have won the Baldrige Award. Collect information on at least two winners. What success have they had since receiving the award?

2 The DMAIC Problem Solving Process

Chapter Outline

Chapter Overview and Learning Objectives

Quality and process improvement occurs most effectively on a project-by-project basis. DMAIC (typically pronounced "duh-MAY-ick") is a structured five-step problem-solving procedure that can be used to successfully complete projects by proceeding through and implementing solutions that are designed to solve root causes of quality and process problems, and to establish best practices to ensure that the solutions are permanent and can be replicated in other relevant business operations. This chapter explains the DMAIC procedure and introduces many of the tools used in each step. Many of the DMAIC tools are discussed in greater detail in subsequent textbook chapters and references to those chapters are provided. Examples of projects that utilize DMAIC also are presented.

After careful study of this chapter, you should be able to do the following:

1. Understand the importance of selecting good projects for improvement activities.
2. Explain the five steps of DMAIC: Define, Measure, Analyze, Improve, and Control.
3. Explain the purpose of tollgate reviews.
4. Understand the decision-making requirements of the tollgate review for each DMAIC step.
5. Know when and when not to use DMAIC.
6. Understand how DMAIC fits into the framework of the six-sigma philosophy.

2.1 Overview of DMAIC

DMAIC is a structured problem-solving procedure widely used in quality and process improvement. It is often associated with six-sigma activities, and almost all implementations of six-sigma use the **DMAIC problem solving process** for project management and completion. However, DMAIC is not necessarily formally tied to six-sigma, and can be used regardless of

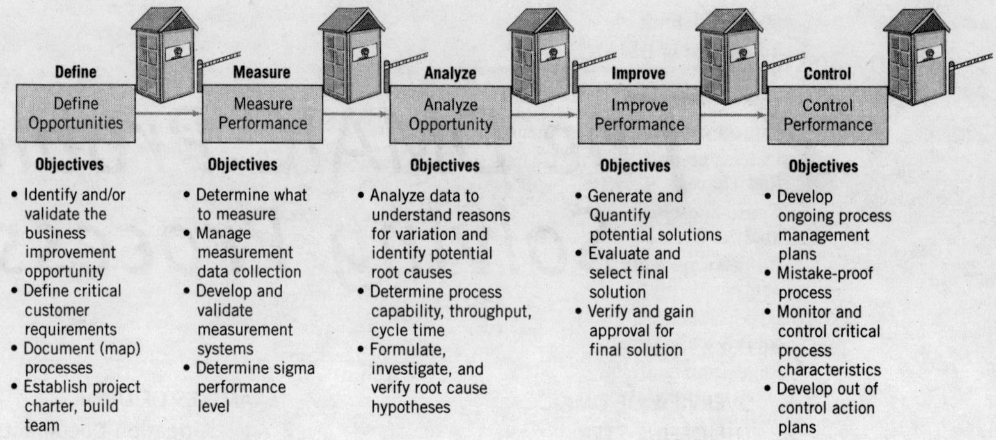

■ FIGURE 2.1 The DMAIC problem solving process.

an organization's use of six-sigma. It is a very general procedure. For example, lean projects that focus on cycle time reduction, throughput improvement, and waste elimination can be easily and efficiently conducted using DMAIC.

The letters DMAIC form an acronym for the five steps, **Define, Measure, Analyze, Improve,** and **Control**. These steps are illustrated graphically in Figure 2.1. Notice that there are **"tollgates"** between each of the major steps in DMAIC. At a tollgate, a project team presents its work to managers and "owners" of the process. In a six-sigma organization, the tollgate participants also would include the project champion, master black belts, and other black belts not working directly on the project. Tollgates are where the project is reviewed to ensure that it is on track and they provide a continuing opportunity to evaluate whether the team can successfully complete the project on schedule. Tollgates also present an opportunity to provide guidance regarding the use of specific technical tools and other information about the problem. Organization problems and other barriers to success—and strategies for dealing with them—also often are identified during tollgate reviews. Tollgates are critical to the overall problem-solving process. It is important that these reviews be conducted very soon after the team completes each step.

The DMAIC structure encourages creative thinking about the problem and its solution within the definition of the original product, process, or service. When the process is operating so badly that it is necessary to abandon the original process and start over, or if it is determined that a new product or service is required, then the improve step of DMAIC actually becomes a **design** step. In a six-sigma organization, that probably means that a Design for Six-Sigma (DFSS) effort is required. (See Chapter 1 for a discussion of DFSS.)

One of the reasons that DMAIC is so successful is that it focuses on the effective use of a relatively small set of tools. Table 2.1 shows the tools, along with the DMAIC steps where they are most likely to be used, and where the tools are discussed and or illustrated in this textbook. [Other tools, or variations of the ones shown here, are used occasionally in DMAIC. Some books on six-sigma give useful overviews of many of these other tools; for example, see George (2002) and Snee and Hoerl (2005).]

Projects are an essential aspect of quality and process improvement. Projects are an integral component of six-sigma, but quality and business improvement via projects traces its origins back to Juran, who always urged a project-by-project approach to improving quality. Selecting, managing, and completing projects successfully is critical in deploying any systematic business improvement effort, not just six-sigma.

■ TABLE 2.1
Tools Used in DMAIC

Tool	Define	Measure	Analyze	Improve	Control
Project charter	Chapter 2				
Process maps & flow charts	Chapter 2	Chapter 5			
Cause-and-effect analysis		Chapter 5			
Process capability analysis		Chapters 6, 8			
Hypothesis tests, confidence intervals			Chapter 4		
Regression analysis, other multivariate methods			Chapter 4		
Gauge R&R		Chapter 8			
Failure mode & effects analysis			Chapter 2		
Designed experiments			Chapters 13, 14	Chapters 13, 14	
SPC and process control plans		Chapters 5, 6, 7, 9, 10, 11, 12	Chapters 5, 6, 7, 9, 10, 11, 12		Chapters 5, 6, 7, 9, 10, 11, 12

A project should represent a potential **breakthrough** in the sense that it will result in a major improvement in the product or service. Project impact should be evaluated in terms of its financial benefit to the business, as measured and evaluated by the finance or accounting unit; this helps ensure more objective project evaluations. Obviously, projects with high potential impact are most desirable. This **financial systems integration** is standard practice in six-sigma and should be a part of any DMAIC project, even if the organization isn't currently engaged in a six-sigma deployment.

The **value opportunity** of projects must be clearly identified and projects must be well aligned with corporate business objectives at all levels. At the highest (corporate) level, the stockholders, top executives, members of the board of directors, and business analysts who guide investors typically are interested in return on equity, return on invested capital, stock price, dividends, earnings, earnings per share of stock, growth in operating income, sales growth, generation of new designs, products and patents, and development of future business leaders. At the business unit or operations level, managers and executives are interested in factory metrics such as yield, cycle time and throughput, profit and loss optimization, customer satisfaction, delivery and due-date performance, cost reduction, safety of employees and customers, efficient use of assets, new product introduction, sales and marketing effectiveness, development of people, and supply chain performance (cost, quality, service). Aligning projects with both business-unit goals and corporate-level metrics helps ensure that the best projects are considered for selection.

The first types of projects that companies usually undertake are designed to demonstrate the potential success of an overall improvement effort. These projects often focus on the areas of the business that are full of opportunities, but they also often are driven by current problems. Issues that are identified by customers or from customer satisfaction (or dissatisfaction) feedback, such as analysis of field failures and customer returns, sometimes are the source of these projects.

Such initial opportunistic projects often are successful, but they typically are not the basis for long-term success; most easy opportunities soon are exhausted. A different approach to project definition and selection needs to evolve. One widely used approach is basing projects on strategic business objectives. In this approach, defining the key set of critical business processes and the metrics that drive them is the first step toward successful project development. Linking those processes together to form an integrated view of the business then follows. Projects that focus on the key business metrics and strategic objectives, as well as the interfaces among critical business processes, are likely to have significant value to the company. The only risks here are that the projects may be very large, and still may focus only on some narrow aspect of the business, which may reduce the organization's overall exposure to the improvement process and reduce or delay its impact. A good project selection and management system prevents such problems from occurring. Many companies have set up formal project selection committees and conducted regular meetings between customers and the project selection committees to help meet that goal. Ideally, projects are strategic and well aligned with corporate metrics, and are not local (tactical). Local projects often are reduced to firefighting, their solutions rarely are broadly implemented in other parts of the business, and too often the solutions aren't permanent; within a year or two, the same old problems reoccur. Some companies use a **dashboard** system—which graphically tracks trends and results—to effectively facilitate the project selection and management process.

Project selection is probably the most important part of any business improvement process. Projects should be able to be completed within a reasonable time frame and should have real impact on key business metrics. This means that a lot of thought must go into defining the organization's key business processes, understanding their interrelationships, and developing appropriate performance measures.

What should be considered when evaluating proposed projects? Suppose that a company is operating at the 4σ level (that is, about 6,210 ppm defective, assuming the 1.5σ shift in the mean that is customary with six-sigma applications). This is actually reasonably good performance, and many of today's organizations have achieved the 4–4.5σ level of performance for many of their key business processes. The objective is to achieve the 6σ performance level (3.4 ppm). What implications does this have for project selection criteria? Suppose that the criterion is a 25% annual improvement in quality level. Then to reach the six-sigma performance level, it will take x years, where x is the solution to

$$3.4 = 6210(1 - 0.25)^x$$

It turns out that x is about 34 years. Clearly, a goal of improving performance by 25% annually isn't going to work—no organization will wait for 34 years to achieve its goal. Quality improvement is a never-ending process, but no management team that understands how to do the above arithmetic will support such a program.

Raising the annual project goal to 50% helps a lot, reducing x to about 11 years, a much more realistic time frame. If the business objective is to be a six-sigma organization in five years, then the annual project improvement goal should be about 75%.

These calculations are the reasons why many quality-improvement authorities urge organizations to concentrate their efforts on projects that have real impact and high payback to the organization. By that they usually mean projects that achieve at least a 50% annual return in terms of quality improvement.

Is this level of improvement possible? The answer is yes, and many companies have achieved this rate of improvement. For example, Motorola's annual improvement rate exceeded 65% during the first few years of their six-sigma initiative. To do this consistently, however, companies most devote considerable effort to project definition, management, execution, and implementation. It's also why the best possible people in the organization should be involved in these activities.

2.2 The Define Step

The objective of the define step of DMAIC is to identify the project opportunity and to verify or validate that it represents legitimate breakthrough potential. A project must be important to customers (voice of the customer) and important to the business. Stakeholders who work in the process and its downstream customers need to agree on the potential usefulness of the project.

One of the first items that must be completed in the define step is a **project charter.** This is a short document (typically about two pages) that contains a description of the project and its scope, the start and the anticipated completion dates, an initial description of both primary and secondary metrics that will be used to measure success and how those metrics align with business unit and corporate goals, the potential benefits to the customer, the potential financial benefits to the organization, milestones that should be accomplished during the project, the team members and their roles, and any additional resources that are likely to be needed to complete the project. Figure 2.2 shows a project charter for a customer product return process. Typically, the project sponsor (or champion in a six-sigma implementation) plays a significant role in developing the project charter, and may use a draft charter as a basis for organizing the team and assigning responsibility for project completion. Generally, a team should be able to complete a project charter in two to four working days; if it takes longer, the scope of the project may be too big. The charter should also identify the customer's *critical-to-quality characteristics (CTQs)* that are impacted by the project.

Graphic aids are also useful in the define step; the most common ones used include process maps and flow charts, value stream maps (see Chapter 5), and the SIPOC diagram. Flow charts and value stream maps provide much visual detail and facilitate understanding about what needs to be changed in a process. The **SIPOC diagram** is a high-level map of a process. *SIPOC* is an acronym for *S*uppliers, *I*nput, *P*rocess, *O*utput, and *C*ustomers, defined as:

1. The **suppliers** are those who provide the information, material, or other items that are worked on in the process.
2. The **input** is the information or material provided.
3. The **process** is the set of steps actually required to do the work.

<table>
<tr><td>Business Case
• This project supports the business quality goals, namely a) reduce customer resolution cycle time by x% and b) improve customer satisfaction by y%.</td><td>Opportunity Statement
• An opportunity exists to close the gap between our customer expectations and our actual performance by reducing the cycle time of the customer return process.</td></tr>
<tr><td>Goal Statement
• Reduce the overall response cycle time for returned product from our customers by x% year to year.</td><td>Project Scope
• Overall response cycle time is measured from the receipt of a product return to the time that either the customer has the product replaced or the customer is reimbursed.</td></tr>
<tr><td>Project Plan
• Activity — Start — End
Define — 6/04 — 6/30
Measure — 6/18 — 7/30
Analyze — 7/15 — 8/30
Improve — 8/15 — 9/30
Control — 9/15 — 10/30
Track Benefits — 11/01</td><td>Team
• Team Sponsor
• Team Leader
• Team Members</td></tr>
</table>

■ **FIGURE 2.2** A project charter for a customer returns process.

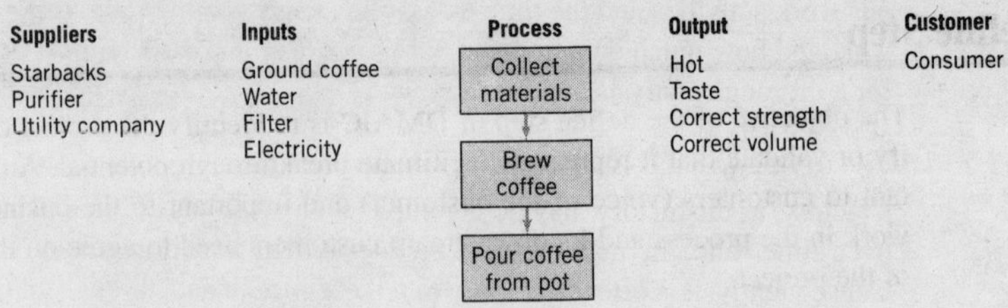

■ FIGURE 2.3 A SIPOC diagram.

4. The **output** is the product, service, or information sent to the customer.
5. The **customer** is either the external customer or the next step in the internal business.

SIPOC diagrams give a simple overview of a process and are useful for understanding and visualizing basic process elements. They are especially useful in the nonmanufacturing setting and in service systems in general, where the idea of a process or process thinking is often hard to understand. That is, people who work in banks, financial institutions, hospitals, accounting firms, e-commerce, government agencies, and most transactional/service organizations don't always see what they do as being part of a process. Constructing a process map can be an eye-opening experience, as it often reveals aspects of the process that people were not aware of or didn't fully understand.

Figure 2.3 is a SIPOC diagram developed by a company for their internal coffee service process. The team was asked to reduce the number of defects and errors in the process and the cycle time to prepare the coffee. The first step they performed was to create the SIPOC diagram to identify the basic elements of the process that they were planning to improve.

The team also will need to prepare an action plan for moving forward to the other DMAIC steps. This will include individual work assignments and tentative completion dates. Particular attention should be paid to the measure step as it will be performed next.

Finally, the team should prepare for the define step tollgate review, which should focus on the following:

1. Does the problem statement focus on symptoms, and not on possible causes or solutions?
2. Are all the key stakeholders identified?
3. What evidence is there to confirm the value opportunity represented by this project?
4. Has the scope of the project been verified to ensure that it is neither too small nor too large?
5. Has a SIPOC diagram or other high-level process map been completed?
6. Have any obvious barriers or obstacles to successful completion of the project been ignored?
7. Is the team's action plan for the measure step of DMAIC reasonable?

2.3 The Measure Step

The purpose of the measure step is to evaluate and understand the current state of the process. This involves collecting data on measures of quality, cost, and throughput/cycle time. It is important to develop a list of all of the **key process input variables** (sometimes abbreviated KPIV) and the **key process output variables (KPOV).** The KPIV and KPOV may have been identified at least tentatively during the define step, but they must be completely defined and measured during the measure step. Important factors may be the time spent to perform various work activities and the time that work spends waiting for additional processing. Deciding what and how much data to collect are important tasks; there must be sufficient data to allow for a thorough analysis and understanding of current process performance with respect to the key metrics.

Data may be collected by examining historical records, but this may not always be satisfactory, as the history may be incomplete, the methods of record keeping may have changed over time, and, in many cases, the desired information never may have been retained. Consequently, it is often necessary to collect current data through an observational study. This may be done by collecting process data over a continuous period of time (such as every hour for two weeks) or it may be done by sampling from the relevant data streams. When there are many human elements in the system, work sampling may be useful. This form of sampling involves observing workers at random times and classifying their activity at that time into appropriate categories. In transactional and service businesses, it may be necessary to develop appropriate measurements and a measurement system for recording the information that are specific to the organization. This again points out a major difference between manufacturing and services: Measurement systems and data on system performance often exist in manufacturing, as the necessity for the data is usually more obvious in manufacturing than in services.

The data that are collected are used as the basis for determining the current state or **baseline performance** of the process. Additionally, the **capability** of the measurement system should be evaluated. This may be done using a formal gauge capability study (called *gauge repeatability* and *reproducibility,* or *gauge R & R,* discussed in Chapter 8.) At this point, it is also a good idea to begin to divide the process cycle time into value-added and non-value-added activities and to calculate estimates of process cycle efficiency and process cycle time, a appropriate (see Chapter 1).

The data collected during the Measure Step may be displayed in various ways such as histograms, stem-and-leaf diagrams, run charts, scatted diagrams, and Pareto charts. Chapters 3 and 4 provide information on these techniques.

At the end of the Measure Step, the team should update the project charter (if necessary), re-examine the project goals and scope, and re-evaluate team makeup. They may consider expanding the team to include members of downstream or upstream business units if the Measure activities indicate that these individuals will be valuable in subsequent DMAIC steps. Any issues or concerns that may impact project success need to be documented and shared with the process owner or project sponsor. In some cases, the team may be able to make quick, immediate recommendations for improvement, such as the elimination of an obvious non-value-added step or removing a source of unwanted variability.

Finally, it is necessary to prepare for the measure step tollgate review. Issues and expectations that will be addressed during this tollgate include the following:

1. There must be a comprehensive process flow chart or value stream map. All major process steps and activities must be identified, along with suppliers and customers. If appropriate, areas where queues and work-in-process accumulate should be identified and queue lengths, waiting times, and work-in-process levels reported.
2. A list of KPIVs and KPOVs must be provided, along with identification of how the KPOVs related to customer satisfaction or the customers CTQs.
3. Measurement systems capability must be documented.
4. Any assumptions that were made during data collection must be noted.
5. The team should be able to respond to requests such as, "Explain where that data came from," and questions such as, "How did you decide what data to collect?" "How valid is your measurement system?" and "Did you collect enough data to provide a reasonable picture of process performance?"

2.4 The Analyze Step

In the analyze step, the objective is to use the data from the measure step to begin to determine the cause-and-effect relationships in the process and to understand the different sources of variability. In other words, in the analyze step we want to determine the potential causes of the defects, quality problems, customer issues, cycle time and throughput problems, or waste and inefficiency that motivated the project. It is important to separate the sources of variability into **common causes** and **assignable causes.** We discuss these sources of variability in Chapter 4 but, generally speaking, common causes are sources of variability that are embedded in the system or process itself, while assignable causes usually arise from an external source. Removing a common cause of variability usually means changing the process, while removing an assignable cause usually involves eliminating that specific problem. A common cause of variability might be inadequate training of personnel processing insurance claims, while an assignable cause might be a tool failure on a machine.

There are many tools that are potentially useful in the Analyze Step. Among these are **control charts,** which are useful in separating common cause variability from assignable cause variability; statistical **hypothesis testing** and **confidence interval** estimation, which can be used to determine if different conditions of operation produce statistically significantly different results and to provide information about the accuracy with which parameters of interest have been estimated; and **regression analysis,** which allows models relating outcome variables of interest to independent input variables to be built. (Chapter 4 contains a discussion of hypothesis tests, confidence intervals, and regression. Chapter 5 introduces control charts, which are very powerful tools with many applications. Many chapters in Parts III and IV of the book discuss different types and applications of control charts.)

Discrete-event computer simulation is another powerful tool useful in the Analyze Step. It is particularly useful in service and transactional businesses, although its use is not confined to those types of operations. For example, there have been many successful applications of discrete-event simulation in studying scheduling problems in factories to improve cycle time and throughput performance. In a discrete-event simulation model, a computer model simulates a process in an organization. For example, a computer model could simulate what happens when a home mortgage loan application enters a bank. Each loan application is a discrete event. The arrival rates, processing times, and even the routing of the applications through the bank's process are random variables. The specific realizations of these random variables influence the backlogs or queues of applications that accumulate at the different processing steps.

Other random variables can be defined to model the effect of incomplete applications, erroneous information and other types of errors and defects, and delays in obtaining information from outside sources, such as credit histories. By running the simulation model for many loans, reliable estimates of cycle time, throughput, and other quantities of interest can be obtained.

Failure modes and effects analysis (FMEA) is another useful tool during the analyze stage. FMEA is used to prioritize the different potential sources of variability, failures, errors, or defects in a product or process relative to three criteria:

1. The likelihood that something will go wrong (ranked on a 1 to 10 scale with 1 = not likely and 10 = almost certain).
2. The ability to detect a failure, defect or error (ranked on a 1 to 10 scale with 1 = very likely to detect and 10 = very unlikely to detect).
3. The severity of a failure, defect or error (ranked on a 1 to 10 scale with 1 = little impact and 10 = extreme impact, including extreme financial loss, injury, or loss of life).

The three scores for each potential source of variability, failure, error or defect are multiplied together to obtain a **risk priority number (RPN).** Sources of variability or failures with the highest RPNs are the focus for further process improvement or redesign efforts.

The analyze tools are used with historical data or data that was collected in the measure step. This data is often very useful in providing clues about potential causes of the problems that the process is experiencing. Sometimes these clues can lead to breakthroughs and actually identify specific improvements. In most cases, however, the purpose of the analyze step is to explore and understand tentative relationships between and among process variables and to develop insight about potential process improvements. A list of specific opportunities and root causes that are targeted for action in the improve step should be developed. Improvement strategies will be further developed and actually tested in the improve step.

In preparing for the analyze tollgate review, the team should consider the following issues and potential questions:

1. What opportunities are going to be targeted for investigation in the improve step?
2. What data and analysis supports that investigating the targeted opportunities and improving/eliminating them will have the desired outcome on the KPOVs and customer CTQs that were the original focus of the project?
3. Are there other opportunities that are not going to be further evaluated? If so, why?
4. Is the project still on track with respect to time and anticipated outcomes? Are any additional resources required at this time?

2.5 The Improve Step

In the measure and analyze steps, the team focused on deciding which KPIVs and KPOVs to study, what data to collect, how to analyze and display the data, identified potential sources of variability, and determined how to interpret the data they obtained. In the improve step, they turn to creative thinking about the specific changes that can be made in the process and other things that can be done to have the desired impact on process performance.

A broad range of tools can be used in the improve step. Redesigning the process to improve work flow and reduce bottlenecks and work-in-process will make extensive use of flow charts and/or value stream maps. Sometimes **mistake-proofing** (designing an operation so that it can be done only one way—the right way) an operation will be useful. Designed experiments are probably the most important statistical tool in the improve step. Designed experiments can be applied either to an actual physical process or to a computer simulation model of that process, and can be used both for determining which factors influence the outcome of a process and for determining the optimal combination of factor settings. (Designed experiments are discussed in detail in Part V.)

The objectives of the improve step are to develop a solution to the problem and to **pilot test** the solution. The pilot test is a form of **confirmation experiment:** it evaluates and documents the solution and confirms the solution attains the project goals. This may be an iterative activity, with the original solution being refined, revised, and improved several times as a result of the pilot test's outcome.

The tollgate review for the improve step should involve the following:

1. Adequate documentation of how the problem solution was obtained.
2. Documentation on alternative solutions that were considered.
3. Complete results of the pilot test, including data displays, analysis, experiments, and simulation analyses.

4. Plans to implement the pilot test results on a full-scale basis. This should include dealing with any regulatory requirements (FDA, OSHA, legal, for example), personnel concerns (such as additional training requirements), or impact on other business standard practices.
5. Analysis of any risks of implementing the solution, and appropriate risk-management plans.

2.6 The Control Step

The objectives of the control step are to complete all remaining work on the project and to hand off the improved process to the process owner along with a **process control plan** and other necessary procedures to ensure that the gains from the project will be institutionalized. That is, the goal is to ensure that the gains are of help in the process and, if possible, the improvements will be implemented in other similar processes in the business.

The process owner should be provided with before and after data on key process metrics, operations and training documents, and updated current process maps. The process control plan should be a system for monitoring the solution that has been implemented, including methods and metrics for periodic auditing. Control charts are an important statistical tool used in the control step of DMAIC; many process control plans involve control charts on critical process metrics.

The transition plan for the process owner should include a validation check several months after project completion. It is important to ensure that the original results are still in place and stable so that the positive financial impact will be sustained. It is not unusual to find that something has gone wrong in the transition to the improved process. The ability to respond rapidly to unanticipated failures should be factored into the plan.

The tollgate review for the control step typically includes the following issues:

1. Data illustrating that the before and after results are in line with the project charter should be available. (Were the original objectives accomplished?)
2. Is the process control plan complete? Are procedures to monitor the process, such as control charts, in place?
3. Is all essential documentation for the process owner complete?
4. A summary of lessons learned from the project should be available.
5. A list of opportunities that were not pursued in the project should be prepared. This can be used to develop future projects; it is very important to maintain an inventory of good potential projects to keep the improvement process going.
6. A list of opportunities to use the results of the project in other parts of the business should be prepared.

2.7 Examples of DMAIC

2.7.1 Litigation Documents

Litigation usually creates a very large number of documents. These can be internal work papers, consultants' reports, affidavits, court filings, documents obtained via subpoena, and papers from many other sources. In some cases, there can be hundreds of thousands of documents and millions of pages. DMAIC was applied in the corporate legal department of DuPont, led by DuPont lawyer, Julie Mazza, who spoke about the project at an American Society for Quality meeting [Mazza (2000)]. The case is also discussed in Snee and Hoerl (2005). The objective was to develop an efficient process to allow timely access to needed documents with minimal errors. Document management is extremely important in litigation;

it also can be time-consuming and expensive. The process was usually manual, so it was subject to human error, with lost or incorrect documents fairly common problems. In the specific case presented by Mazza, there was an electronic data base that listed and classified all of the documents, but the documents themselves were in hard copy form.

Define. The DuPont legal function and the specific legal team involved in this specific litigation were the customers for this process. Rapid and error-free access to needed documents was essential. For example, if a request for a document could not be answered in 30 days, the legal team would have to file a request for an extension with the court. Such extensions add cost, time, and detract from the credibility of the legal team. A project team consisting of process owners, legal subject-matter experts, clerks, an information systems specialist, and Mazza (who was also a black belt in Dupont's six-sigma program) was formed. The team decided to focus on CTQs involving reduction of cycle time, reduction of errors, elimination of non-value-added process activities, and reduction of costs. They began by mapping the entire document-production process, including defining the steps performed by DuPont legal, outside counsel, and the outside documents-management company. This process map was instrumental in identifying non-value-added activities.

Measure. In the measure step, the team formally measured the degree to which the CTQs were being met by reviewing data in the electronic data base; obtaining actual invoices; reviewing copying and other labor charges, the costs of data entry, and the charges for shipping, court fees for filing for extensions; and studying how frequently individual documents in the data base were being handled. It was difficult to accurately measure the frequency of handling. Many of the cost categories contained non-value-added costs because of errors, such as having to copy a different document because the wrong document had been pulled and copied. Another error was allowing a confidential document to be copied.

Analyze. The team worked with the data obtained during the measure step and the knowledge of team members to identify many of the underlying causes and cost exposures. A failure modes and effects analysis highlighted many of the most important issues that needed to be addressed to improve the system. The team also interviewed many of the people who worked in the process to better understand how they actually did the work and the problems they encountered. This is often very important in nonmanufacturing and service organizations because these types of operations can have a much greater human factor. Some of the root causes of problems they uncovered were:

1. A high turnover rate for the contractor's clerks
2. Inadequate training
3. Inattention to the job, causes by clerks feeling they had no ownership in the process
4. The large volume of documents

The team concluded that many of the problems in the system were the result of a manual document-handling system.

Improve. To improve the process, the team proposed a digital scanning system for the documents. This solution had been considered previously, but always had been discarded because of cost. However, the team had done a very thorough job of identifying the real costs of the manual system and the inability of a manual system to ever really improve the situation. The better information produced during the measure and analyze steps allowed the team to successfully propose a digital scanning system that the company accepted.

The team worked with DuPont's information technology group to identify an appropriate system, get the system in place, and to scan all of the documents. They remapped the new process and, on the basis of a pilot study, estimated that the unit cost of processing a page of a document would be reduced by about 50%, which would result in about $1.13 million in savings. About 70% of the non-value-added activities in the process were eliminated. After the new system was implemented, it was proposed for use in all of the DuPont legal functions; the total savings were estimated at about $10 million.

Control. The control plan involved designing the new system to automatically track and report the estimated costs per document. The system also tracked performance on other critical CTQs and reported the information to users of the process. Invoices from contactors also were forwarded to the process owners as a mechanism for monitoring ongoing costs. Explanations about how the new system worked and necessary training were provided for all those who used the system. Extremely successful, the new system provided significant cost savings, improvement in cycle time, and reduction of many frequently occurring errors.

2.7.2 Improving On-Time Delivery

A key customer contacted a machine tool manufacturer about poor recent performance they had experienced regarding on-time delivery of the product. On-time deliveries were at 85%, instead of the desired target value of 100%, and the customer could choose to exercise a penalty clause to reduce by up to 15% of the price of each tool, or about a $60,000 loss for the manufacturer. The customer was also concerned about the manufacturer's factory capacity and its capability to meet their production schedule in the future. The customer represented about $8 million of business volume for the immediate future—the manufacturer needed a revised business process to resolve the problem or the customer might consider seeking a second source supplier for the critical tool.

A team was formed to determine the root causes of the delivery problem and implement a solution. One team member was a project engineer who was sent to a supplier factory, with the purpose to work closely with the supplier, to examine all the processes used in manufacturing of the tool, and to identify any gaps in the processes that affected delivery. Some of the supplier's processes might need improvement.

Define. The objective of the project was to achieve 100% on-time delivery. The customer had a concern regarding on-time delivery capability, and a late deliveries penalty clause could be applied to current and future shipments at a cost to the manufacturer. Late deliveries also would jeopardize the customer's production schedule, and without an improved process to eliminate the on-time delivery issue, the customer might consider finding a second source for the tool. The manufacturer could potentially lose as much as half of the business from the customer, in addition to incurring the 15% penalty costs. The manufacturer also would experience a delay in collecting the 80% equipment payment customarily made upon shipment.

The potential savings for meeting the on-time delivery requirement was $300,000 per quarter. Maintaining a satisfied customer also was critical.

Measure. The contractual lead time for delivery of the tool was eight weeks. That is, the tool must be ready for shipment eight weeks upon receipt of the purchase order. The CTQ for this process was to meet the target contractual lead time. Figure 2.4 shows the process map for the existing process, from purchase order receipt to shipment. The contractual lead time could be met only when there was no excursion or variation in the process. Some historical data on this process was available, and additional data was collected over approximately a two-month period.

Analyze. Based on the data collected from the measure step, the team concluded that problems areas came from:

1. Supplier quality issues: Parts failed prematurely. This caused delay in equipment final testing due to trouble shooting or waiting for replacement parts.

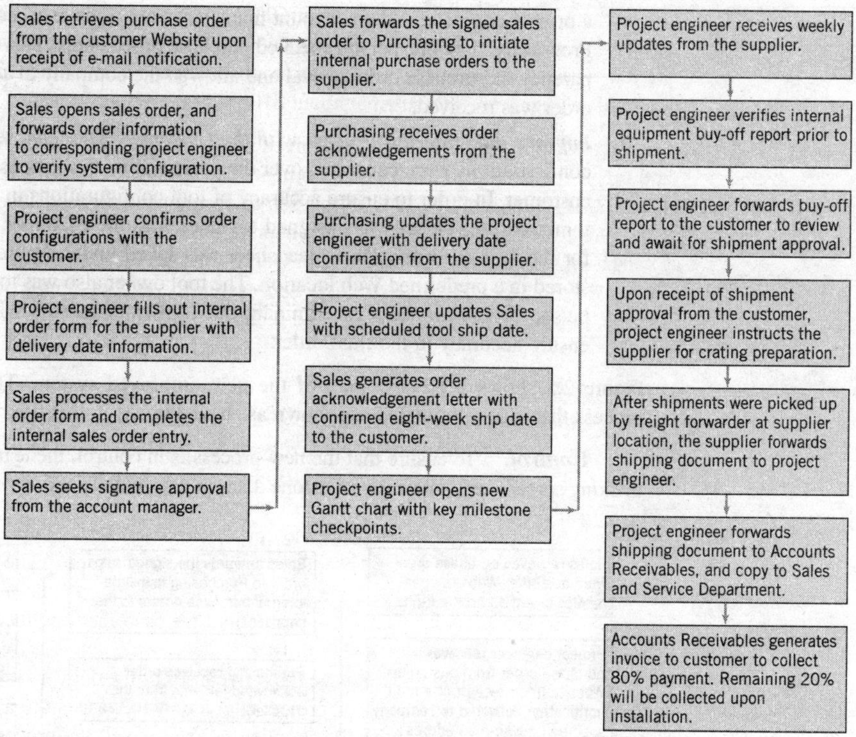

■ FIGURE 2.4 The original process map.

2. Purchase order process delay: Purchase orders were not processed promptly, resulting in delayed internal project start dates.
3. Delay in customer confirmation: It took up to three days to confirm the final equipment configuration with the customer. This delayed most of the early manufacturing steps and complicated production scheduling.
4. Incorrect tool configuration orders: There were many processes on the customer side, leading to frequent confusion when the customer placed the order and often resulting in an incorrect tool configuration. This caused rework at the mid-stream of the manufacturing cycle, and contributed greatly to the delivery delay problem.

Improve. In order to meet the eight-week contractual lead time, the team knew that it was necessary to eliminate any possible process variation, starting from receipt of the purchase order to shipment of the equipment. Three major corrective actions were taken:

1. *Supplier Quality Control and Improvement:* An internal buy-off checklist for the supplier was implemented that contained all required testing of components and subsystems that had to be completed prior to shipment. This action was taken to minimize part failures both in manufacturing and final test as well as in the field. The supplier agreed to provide consigned critical spare parts to the manufacturer so that it could save on shipping time for replacement parts if part failures were encountered during manufacturing and final testing.
2. *Improve the Internal Purchase Order Process:* A common e-mail address was established to receive all purchase order notifications. Three people (a sales support engineer,

a project engineer, and an account manager) were to have access to the e-mail account. Previously, only one person checked purchase order status. This step enhanced the transparency of purchase order arrival and allowed the company to act promptly when a new order was received.

3. *Improve the Ordering Process with the Customer:* The team realized that various tool configurations were generated over the years due to new process requirements from the customer. In order to ensure accuracy of tool configurations in a purchase order, a customized spreadsheet was designed together with the customer to identify the key data for the tool on order. The spreadsheet was saved under a purchase order number and stored in a predefined Web location. The tool owner also was to take ownership of what he/she ordered to help to eliminate the confirmation step with the customer and to ensure accuracy in the final order.

Figure 2.5 shows a process map of the new, improved system. The steps in the original process that were eliminated are shown as shaded boxes in this figure.

Control. To ensure that the new process is in control, the team revised the production tracking spreadsheet with firm milestone dates and provided a more visual format. An updating

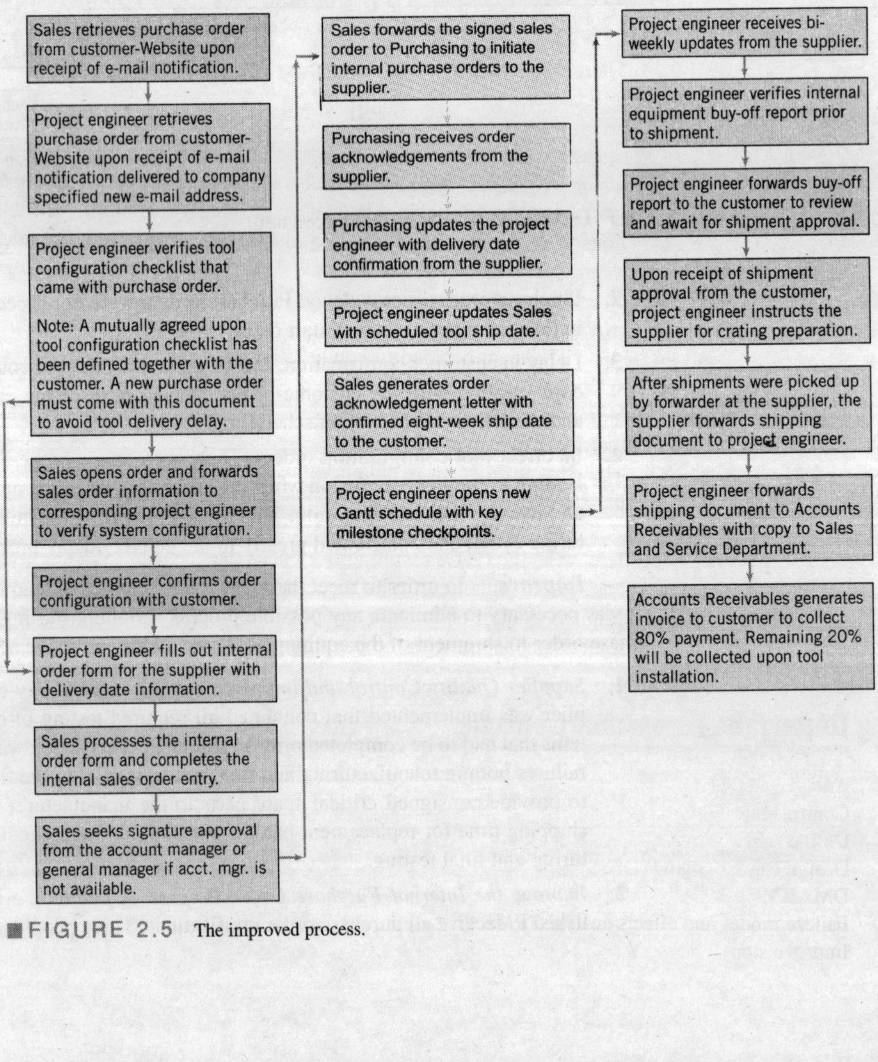

■ FIGURE 2.5 The improved process.

procedure was provided on a biweekly basis by the factory to reflect up-to-date information. The project engineer would be able to monitor the progress of each tool on order and take action accordingly should any unplanned deviation from the schedule occur.

After implementing the new process, including the new production tracking procedure, the manufacturer was able to ship tools with 100% on-time delivery. The cost savings were more than $300,000 each quarter. Equally important, the customer was satisfied, and continued to remain confidence manufacturer's in the capability and capacity.

2.7.3 Improving Service Quality in a Bank

Kovach (2007) describes how the DMAIC problem solving process can be used to improve service quality for a banking process. During the define and measure phases of this project, the team identified several CTQs to be improved:

1. Speed of service
2. Consistent service
3. An easy-to-use process
4. A pleasant environment
5. Knowledgeable staff

There were many factors that could be investigated to improve these CTQs. The team decided to focus on two areas of improvement: improved teller and customer work stations and new training for the staff. In the improve stage, they decided to use a designed experiment to investigate the effects of these two factors on the CTQs. Four different branches were selected in which to conduct the experiment. Notice that this is a **physical experiment,** not an experiment with a computer simulation model of the branch operations. New teller and customer work stations were designed and installed in two of the branches. The team designed a new training program and delivered it to the staff at two of the branches, one with the new work stations and one without the new facilities. (This was a two-factor factorial experiment, with each of the two factors having two levels. We discuss these types of experiments extensively in this book.)

The team decided to conduct the experiment for 30 working days. Each day was considered to be a block (as we will discuss in later chapters, blocking is a design technique for eliminating the effects of nuisance factors on the experimental results; here the nuisance factors were transaction types, volumes, and different customers at each of the four branches). The response data was obtained by asking customers to complete a survey instrument that registered their degree of satisfaction with the previously identified CTQs.

The results of the experiment demonstrated that there was a statistically significant difference in the CTQs resulting from both the new work stations and the new training, with the best results obtained from the combination of the new work stations and the new training. Implementation of the new stations and training was expected to significantly improve customer satisfaction with the banking process across the bank's branches.

Important Terms and Concepts

Analyze step
Control step
Define step
Design for Six-Sigma (DFSS)
DMAIC
Failure modes and effects analysis (FMEA)
Improve step
Key process input variables (KPIV)
Key process output variables (KPOV)
Measure step
Project charter
SIPOC diagram
Six-Sigma
Tollgate

Discussion Questions and Exercises

2.1. Discuss the similarities between the Shewhart cycle and DMAIC.

2.2. Explain the importance of tollgates in the DMAIC Problem Solving process.

2.3. Is there a point at which seeking further improvement in quality and productivity isn't economically advisable? Discuss your answer.

2.4. One of the objectives of the control plan in DMAIC is to "hold the gain." What does this mean?

2.5. Why are designed experiments most useful in the improve step of DMAIC?

2.6. An important part of a project is to identify the key process input variables (KPIV) and key process output variables (KPOV). Suppose that you are in charge of a hospital emergency room. Discuss the KPIVs and KPOVs for this business. How do they relate to possible customer CTQs?

2.7. An important part of a project is to identify the key process input variables (KPIV) and key process output variables (KPOV). Suppose that you are the owner/manager of a small business that provides mailboxes, copy services, and mailing services. Discuss the KPIVs and KPOVs for this business. How do they relate to possible customer CTQs?

2.8. Suppose that during the analyze phase an obvious solution is discovered. Should that solution be immediately implemented and the remaining steps of DMAIC abandoned? Discuss your answer.

2.9. Explain why it is important to separate sources of variability into special or assignable causes and common or chance causes.

2.10. Consider improving service quality in a restaurant. What are the KPIVs and KPOVs that you should consider? How do these relate to likely customer CTQs?

2.11. Suppose that your business is operating at the three-sigma quality level. If projects have an average improvement rate of 50% annually, how many years will it take to achieve six-sigma quality?

2.12. Discuss why, in general, determining what to measure and how to make measurements is more difficult in service processes and transactional businesses than in manufacturing.

2.13. Suppose that you want to improve the process of loading passengers onto an airplane. Would a discrete-event simulation model of this process be useful? What data would have to be collected to build this model?

2.14. Suppose that you manage an airline reservation system and want to improve service quality. What are the important CTQs for this process? What are the KPIVs and KPOVs? How do these relate to the customer CTQs that you have identified?

2.15. It has been estimated that safe aircraft carrier landings operate at about the 5σ level. What level of ppm defective does this imply?

2.16. What information would you have to collect in order to build a discrete-event simulation model of a retail branch-banking operation? Discuss how this model could be used to determine appropriate staffing levels for the bank.

PART 2

Statistical Methods Useful in Quality Control and Improvement

Statistics is a collection of techniques useful for making decisions about a process or population based on an analysis of the information contained in a sample from that population. Statistical methods play a vital role in quality control and improvement. They provide the principal means by which a product is sampled, tested, and evaluated, and the information in those data is used to control and improve the process and the product. Furthermore, statistics is the language in which development engineers, manufacturing, procurement, management, and other functional components of the business communicate about quality.

This part contains two chapters. Chapter 3 gives a brief introduction to **descriptive statistics**, showing how simple graphical and numerical techniques can be used to summarize the information in sample data. The use of **probability distributions** to model the behavior of product parameters in a process or lot is then discussed. Chapter 4 presents techniques of **statistical inference**—that is, how the information contained in a sample can be used to draw conclusions about the population from which the sample was drawn.

3 Statistical Models for Quality Control and Improvement

Chapter Outline

The supplemental material is on the textbook website www.wiley.com/college/montgomery.

Chapter Overview and Learning Objectives

This textbook is about the use of statistical methodology in quality control and improvement. This chapter has two objectives. First, we show how simple tools of descriptive statistics can be used to express variation quantitatively in a quality characteristic when a **sample** of data on this characteristic is available. Generally, the sample is just a subset of data taken from some larger population or process. The second objective is to introduce **probability distributions** and show how they provide a tool for modeling or describing the quality characteristics of a process.

After careful study of this chapter you should be able to do the following:

1. Construct and interpret visual data displays, including the stem-and-leaf plot, the histogram, and the box plot
2. Compute and interpret the sample mean, the sample variance, the sample standard deviation, and the sample range
3. Explain the concepts of a random variable and a probability distribution
4. Understand and interpret the mean, variance, and standard deviation of a probability distribution
5. Determine probabilities from probability distributions
6. Understand the assumptions for each of the discrete probability distributions presented
7. Understand the assumptions for each of the continuous probability distributions presented
8. Select an appropriate probability distribution for use in specific applications
9. Use probability plots
10. Use approximations for some hypergeometric and binomial distributions

3.1 Describing Variation

3.1.1 The Stem-and-Leaf Plot

No two units of product produced by a process are identical. Some **variation** is inevitable. As examples, the net content of a can of soft drink varies slightly from can to can, and the output voltage of a power supply is not exactly the same from one unit to the next. **Statistics** is the science of analyzing data and drawing conclusions, taking variation in the data into account.

There are several graphical methods that are very useful for summarizing and presenting data. One of the most useful graphical techniques is the **stem-and-leaf display.**

Suppose that the data are represented by $x_1, x_2, \ldots, x_n$ and that each number x_i consists of at least two digits. To construct a stem-and-leaf plot, we divide each number x_i into two parts: a stem, consisting of one or more of the leading digits; and a leaf, consisting of the remaining digits. For example, if the data consist of percent defective information between 0 and 100 on lots of semiconductor wafers, then we can divide the value 76 into the stem 7 and the leaf 6. In general, we should choose relatively few stems in comparison with the number of observations. It is usually best to choose between 5 and 20 stems. Once a set of stems has been chosen, they are listed along the left-hand margin of the display, and beside each stem all leaves corresponding to the observed data values are listed in the order in which they are encountered in the data set.

EXAMPLE 3.1 Health Insurance Claims

ta in Table 3.1 are a sample of the cycle time in days to process and pay employee health insurance claims in a large com-
onstruct a stem-and-leaf plot for these data.

SOLUTION

To construct the stem-and-leaf plot, we could select the values 1, 2, 3, 4, and 5 as the stems. However, this would result in all 40 data values being compacted into only five stems, the minimum number that is usually recommended. An alternative would be to split each stem into a lower and an upper half, with the leaves 0–4 being assigned to the lower portion of the stem and the leaves 5–9 being assigned to the upper portion. Figure 3.1 is the stem-and-leaf plot generated by Minitab, and it uses the stem-splitting strategy. The column to the left of the stems gives a cumulative count of the number of observations that are at or below that stem for the smaller stems, and at or above that stem for the larger stems. For the middle stem, the number in parentheses indicates the number of observations included in that stem. Inspection of the plot reveals that the distribution of the number of days to process and pay an employee health insurance claim has an approximately symmetric shape, with a single peak. The stem-and-leaf display allows us to quickly determine some important features of the data that are not obvious from the data table. For example, Fig. 3.1 gives a visual impression of shape, spread or variability, and the central tendency or middle of the data (which is close to 35).

■ **TABLE 3.1**

Cycle Time in Days to Pay Employee Health Insurance Claims

Claim	Days	Claim	Days	Claim	Days	Claim	Days
1	48	11	35	21	37	31	16
2	41	12	34	22	43	32	22
3	35	13	36	23	17	33	33
4	36	14	42	24	26	34	30
5	37	15	43	25	28	35	24
6	26	16	36	26	27	36	23
7	36	17	56	27	45	37	22
8	46	18	32	28	33	38	30
9	35	19	46	29	22	39	31
10	47	20	30	30	27	40	17

Stem-and-Leaf Display: Days

```
Stem-and-leaf of Days
N = 40
Leaf Unit = 1.0
  3   1  677
  8   2  22234
 13   2  66778
(8)   3  00012334
 19   3  555666677
 10   4  1233
  6   4  56678
  1   5
  1   5  6
```

■ **FIGURE 3.1** Stem-and-left plot for the health insurance claim data.

The version of the stem-and-leaf plot produced by Minitab is sometimes called an **ordered stem-and-leaf plot,** because the leaves are arranged by magnitude. This version of the display makes it very easy to find **percentiles** of the data. Generally, the 100 kth percentile is a value such that at least 100 k% of the data values are at or below this value and at least 100 $(1 - k)$% of the data values are at or above this value.

The **fiftieth percentile** of the data distribution is called the **sample median** $\tilde{x}$. The median can be thought of as the data value that exactly divides the sample in half, with half of the observations smaller than the median and half of them larger.

If n, the number of observations, is odd, finding the median is easy. First sort the observations in ascending order (or rank the data from smallest observation to largest observation). Then the median will be the observation in rank position $[(n - 1)/2 + 1]$ on this list. If n is even, the median is the average of the $(n/2)$st and $(n/2 + 1)$st ranked observations. Since in our example $n = 40$ is an even number, the median is the average of the two observations with rank 20 and 21, or

$$\tilde{x} = \frac{33 + 34}{2} = 33.5$$

The **tenth percentile** is the observation with rank $(0.1)(40) + 0.5 = 4.5$ (halfway between the fourth and fifth observation), or $(22 + 22)/2 = 22$. The **first quartile** is the observation

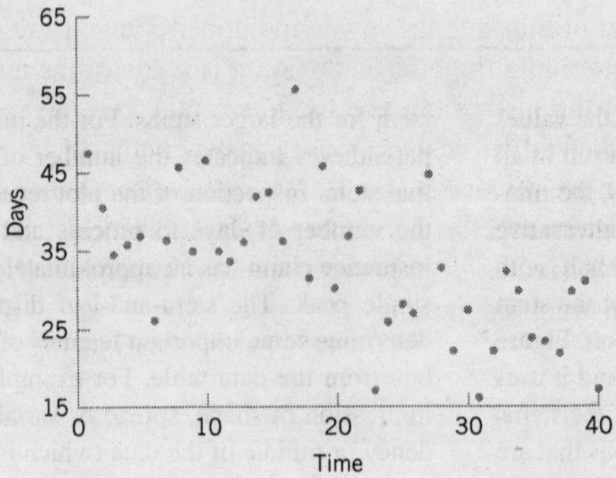

■ FIGURE 3.2 A time series plot of the health insurance data in Table 3.1.

with rank (0.25)(40) + 0.5 = 10.5 (halfway between the tenth and eleventh observation) or (26 + 27)/2 = 26.5, and the **third quartile** is the observation with rank (0.75)(40) + 0.5 = 30.5 (halfway between the thirtieth and thirty-first observation), or (37 + 41) = 39. The first and third quartiles are occasionally denoted by the symbols Q1 and Q3, respectively, and the **interquartile range** IQR = Q3 − Q1 is occasionally used as a measure of variability. For the insurance claim data the interquartile range is IQR = Q3 − Q1 = 39 − 26.5 = 12.5.

Finally, although the stem-and-leaf display is an excellent way to visually show the variability in data, it does not take the **time order** of the observations into account. Time is often a very important factor that contributes to variability in quality improvement problems. We could, of course, simply plot the data values versus time; such a graph is called a **time series plot** or a **run chart.**

Suppose that the cycle time to process and pay employee health insurance claims in Table 3.1 are shown in time sequence. Figure 3.2 shows the time series plot of the data. We used Minitab to construct this plot (called a **marginal plot**) and requested a dot plot of the data to be constructed in the *y*-axis margin. This display clearly indicates that time is an important source of variability in this process. More specifically, the processing cycle time for the first 20 claims is substantially longer than the cycle time for the last 20 claims. Something may have changed in the process (or have been deliberately changed by operating personnel) that is responsible for the cycle time improvement. Later in this book we formally introduce the control chart as a graphical technique for monitoring processes such as this one, and for producing a statistically based signal when a process change occurs.

3.1.2 The Histogram

A **histogram** is a more compact summary of data than a stem-and-leaf plot. To construct a histogram for continuous data, we must divide the range of the data into intervals, which are usually called **class intervals, cells,** or **bins.** If possible, the bins should be of equal width to enhance the visual information in the histogram. Some judgment must be used in selecting the number of bins so that a reasonable display can be developed. The number of bins depends on the number of observations and the amount of scatter or dispersion in the data. A histogram that uses either too few or too many bins will not be informative. We usually find that between 5 and 20 bins is satisfactory in most cases and that the number of bins should increase with *n*. Choosing the number of bins approximately equal to the square root of the number of observations often works well in practice.[1]

[1]There is no universal agreement about how to select the number of bins for a histogram. Some basic statistics textbooks suggest using Sturges's rule, which sets the number of bins $h = 1 + \log_2 n$, where n is the sample size. There are many variations of Sturges's rule. Computer software packages use many different algorithms to determine the number and width of bins, and some of them may not be based on Sturges's rule.

Once the number of bins and the lower and upper boundary of each bin has been determined, the data are sorted into the bins and a count is made of the number of observations in each bin. To construct the histogram, use the horizontal axis to represent the measurement scale for the data and the vertical scale to represent the counts, or **frequencies.** Sometimes the frequencies in each bin are divided by the total number of observations (n), and then the vertical scale of the histogram represents **relative frequencies.** Rectangles are drawn over each bin and the height of each rectangle is proportional to frequency (or relative frequency). Most statistics packages construct histograms.

EXAMPLE 3.2 Metal Thickness in Silicon Wafers

Table 3.2 presents the thickness of a metal layer on 100 silicon wafers resulting from a chemical vapor deposition (CVD) process in a semiconductor plant. Construct a histogram for these data.

■ TABLE 3.2
Layer Thickness (Å) on Semiconductor Wafers

438	450	487	451	452	441	444	461	432	471
413	450	430	437	465	444	471	453	431	458
444	450	446	444	466	458	471	452	455	445
468	459	450	453	473	454	458	438	447	463
445	466	456	434	471	437	459	445	454	423
472	470	433	454	464	443	449	435	435	451
474	457	455	448	478	465	462	454	425	440
454	441	459	435	446	435	460	428	449	442
455	450	423	432	459	444	445	454	449	441
449	445	455	441	464	457	437	434	452	439

SOLUTION

Because the data set contains 100 observations and $\sqrt{100} = 10$, we suspect that about 10 bins will provide a satisfactory histogram. We constructed the histogram using the Minitab option that allows the user to specify the number of bins. The resulting Minitab histogram is shown in Fig. 3.3. Notice that the midpoint of the first bin is 415Å, and that the histogram only has eight bins that contain a nonzero frequency. A histogram, like a stem-and-leaf plot, gives a visual impression of the shape of the distribution of the measurements, as well as some information about the inherent variability in the data. Note the reasonably symmetric or bell-shaped distribution of the metal thickness data.

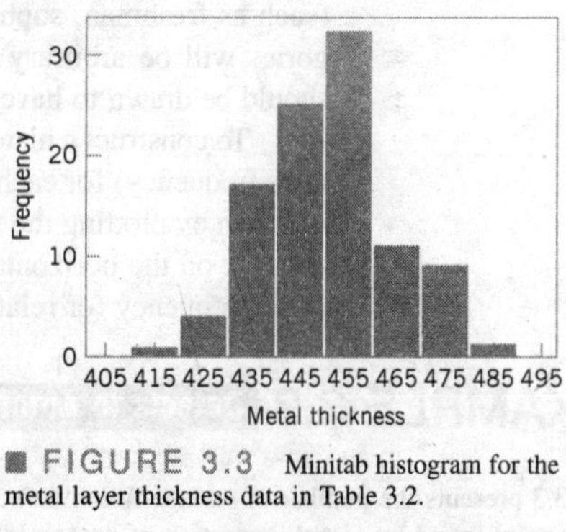

■ **FIGURE 3.3** Minitab histogram for the metal layer thickness data in Table 3.2.

Most computer packages have a default setting for the number of bins. Figure 3.4 is the Minitab histogram obtained with the default setting, which leads to a histogram with 15 bins. Histograms can be relatively sensitive to the choice of the number and width of the bins. For small data sets, histograms may change dramatically in appearance if the number and/or width of the bins changes. For this reason, we prefer to think of the histogram as a technique best suited for **larger data sets** containing, say, 75 to 100 or more observations. Because the number of observations in the layer thickness is moderately large (n = 100), the choice of

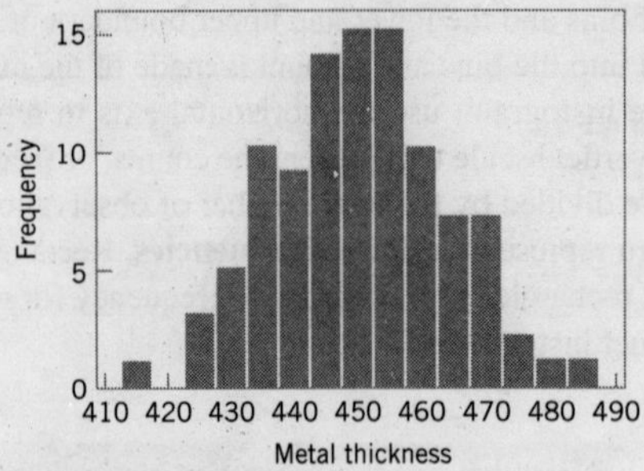

■ FIGURE 3.4 Minitab histogram with 15 bins for the metal layer thickness data.

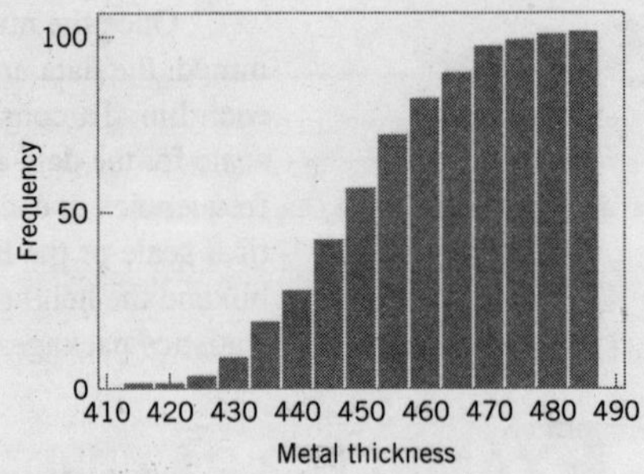

■ FIGURE 3.5 A cumulative frequency plot of the metal thickness data from Minitab.

the number of bins is not especially important, and the histograms in Figs. 3.3 and 3.4 convey very similar information.

Notice that in passing from the original data or a stem-and-leaf plot to a histogram, we have in a sense lost some information because the original observations are not preserved on the display. However, this loss in information is usually small compared with the conciseness and ease of interpretation of the histogram, particularly in large samples.

Histograms are always easier to interpret if the bins are of equal width. If the bins are of unequal width, it is customary to draw rectangles whose areas (as opposed to heights) are proportional to the number of observations in the bins.

Figure 3.5 shows a variation of the histogram available in Minitab (i.e., the **cumulative frequency plot**). In this plot, the height of each bar represents the number of observations that are less than or equal to the upper limit of the bin. Cumulative frequencies are often very useful in data interpretation. For example, we can read directly from Fig. 3.5 that about 75 of the 100 wafers have a metal layer thickness that is less than 460Å.

Frequency distributions and histograms can also be used with qualitative, categorical, or count (discrete) data. In some applications, there will be a natural ordering of the categories (such as freshman, sophomore, junior, and senior), whereas in others the order of the categories will be arbitrary (such as male and female). When using categorical data, the bars should be drawn to have equal width.

To construct a histogram for discrete or count data, first determine the frequency (or relative frequency) for each value of x. Each of the x values corresponds to a bin. The histogram is drawn by plotting the frequencies (or relative frequencies) on the vertical scale and the values of x on the horizontal scale. Then above each value of x, draw a rectangle whose height is the frequency (or relative frequency) corresponding to that value.

EXAMPLE 3.3 Defects in Automobile Hoods

Table 3.3 presents the number of surface finish defects in the primer paint found by visual inspection of automobile hoods that were painted by a new experimental painting process. Construct a histogram for these data.

■ TABLE 3.3
Surface Finish Defects in Painted Automobile Hoods

6	1	5	7	8	6	0	2	4	2
5	2	4	4	1	4	1	7	2	3
4	3	3	3	6	3	2	3	4	5
5	2	3	4	4	4	2	3	5	7
5	4	5	5	4	5	3	3	3	12

SOLUTION

Figure 3.6 is the histogram of the defects. Notice that the number of defects is a discrete variable. From either the histogram or the tabulated data we can determine

$$\text{Proportions of hoods with at least 3 defects} = \frac{39}{50} = 0.78$$

and

$$\text{Proportions of hoods with between 0 and 2 defects} = \frac{11}{50} = 0.22$$

These proportions are examples of relative frequencies.

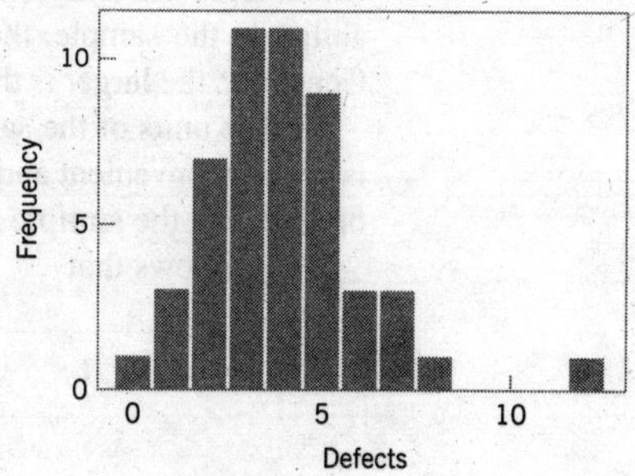

■ **FIGURE 3.6** Histogram of the number of defects in painted automobile hoods (Table 3.3).

3.1.3 Numerical Summary of Data

The stem-and-leaf plot and the histogram provide a visual display of three properties of sample data: the shape of the distribution of the data, the central tendency in the data, and the scatter or variability in the data. It is also helpful to use numerical measures of central tendency and scatter.

Suppose that $x_1, x_2, \ldots, x_n$ are the observations in a sample. The most important measure of central tendency in the sample is the **sample average,**

$$\bar{x} = \frac{x_1 + x_2 + \cdots + x_n}{n} = \frac{\sum_{i=1}^{n} x_i}{n} \tag{3.1}$$

Note that the sample average $\bar{x}$ is simply the arithmetic mean of the n observations. The sample average for the metal thickness data in Table 3.2 is

$$\bar{x} = \frac{\sum_{i=1}^{100} x_i}{100} = \frac{45.001}{100} = 450.01 \text{Å}$$

Refer to Fig. 3.3 and note that the sample average is the point at which the histogram exactly "balances." Thus, the sample average represents the center of mass of the sample data.

The variability in the sample data is measured by the **sample variance,**

$$s^2 = \frac{\sum_{i=1}^{n} (x_i - \bar{x})^2}{n-1} \tag{3.2}$$

Note that the sample variance is simply the sum of the squared deviations of each observation from the sample average $\bar{x}$, divided by the sample size minus one. If there is no variability in the sample, then each sample observation $x_i = \bar{x}$, and the sample variance $s^2 = 0$. Generally, the larger is the sample variance s^2, the greater is the variability in the sample data.

The units of the sample variance s^2 are the square of the original units of the data. This is often inconvenient and awkward to interpret, and so we usually prefer to use the square root of s^2, called the **sample standard deviation** ***s***, as a measure of variability.

It follows that

$$s = \sqrt{\frac{\sum_{i=1}^{n} (x_i - \bar{x})^2}{n-1}} \tag{3.3}$$

The primary advantage of the sample standard deviation is that it is expressed in the original units of measurement. For the metal thickness data, we find that

$$s^2 = 180.2928 \text{ Å}^2$$

and

$$s = 13.43 \text{ Å}$$

To more easily see how the standard deviation describes variability, consider the two samples shown here:

Sample 1	Sample 2
$x_1 = 1$	$x_1 = 1$
$x_2 = 3$	$x_2 = 5$
$x_3 = 5$	$x_3 = 9$
$\bar{x} = 3$	$\bar{x} = 5$

Obviously, sample 2 has greater variability than sample 1. This is reflected in the standard deviation, which for sample 1 is

$$s = \sqrt{\frac{\sum_{i=1}^{3} (x_i - \bar{x})^2}{2}} = \sqrt{\frac{(1-3)^2 + (3-3)^2 + (5-3)^2}{2}} = \sqrt{4} = 2$$

and for sample 2 is

$$s = \sqrt{\frac{\sum_{i=1}^{3} (x_i - \bar{x})^2}{2}} = \sqrt{\frac{(1-5)^2 + (5-5)^2 + (9-5)^2}{2}} = \sqrt{16} = 4$$

Thus, the larger variability in sample 2 is reflected by its larger standard deviation. Now consider a third sample, say

Sample 3
$x_1 = 101$
$x_2 = 103$
$x_3 = 105$
$\bar{x} = 103$

The standard deviation for this third sample is $s = 2$, which is identical to the standard deviation of sample 1. Comparing the two samples, we see that both samples have identical variability or scatter about the average, and this is why they have the same standard deviations. This leads to an important point: **The standard deviation does not reflect the magnitude of the sample data, only the scatter about the average.**

Hand-held calculators are frequently used for calculating the sample average and standard deviation. Note that equations (3.2) and (3.3) are not very efficient computationally, because every number must be entered into the calculator twice. A more efficient formula is

$$s = \sqrt{\frac{\sum_{i=1}^{n} x_i^2 - \frac{\left(\sum_{i=1}^{n} x_i\right)^2}{n}}{n-1}} \tag{3.4}$$

In using equation (3.4), each number would only have to be entered once, provided that $\Sigma_{i=1}^{n} x_i$ and $\Sigma_{i=1}^{n} x_i^2$ could be simultaneously accumulated in the calculator. Many inexpensive hand-held calculators perform this function and have automatic calculation of $\bar{x}$ and s.

3.1.4 The Box Plot

The stem-and-leaf display and the histogram provide a visual impression about a data set, whereas the sample average and standard deviation provide quantitative information about specific features of the data. The **box plot** is a graphical display that simultaneously displays several important features of the data, such as location or central tendency, spread or variability, departure from symmetry, and identification of observations that lie unusually far from the bulk of the data (these observations are often called "outliers").

A box plot displays the three quartiles, the minimum, and the maximum of the data on a rectangular box, aligned either horizontally or vertically. The box encloses the interquartile range with the left (or lower) line at the first quartile Q1 and the right (or upper) line at the third quartile Q3. A line is drawn through the box at the second quartile (which is the fiftieth percentile or the median) Q2 = $\tilde{x}$. A line at either end extends to the extreme values. These lines are usually called **whiskers.** Some authors refer to the box plot as the **box and whisker plot.** In some computer programs, the whiskers only extend a distance of 1.5 (Q3 – Q1) from the ends of the box, at most, and observations beyond these limits are flagged as potential outliers. This variation of the basic procedure is called a **modified box plot.**

EXAMPLE 3.4 Hole Diameter

The data in Table 3.4 are diameters (in mm) of holes in a group of 12 wing leading edge ribs for a commercial transport airplane. Construct and interpret a box plot of those data.

TABLE 3.4
Hole Diameters (in mm) in Wing Leading Edge Ribs

120.5	120.4	120.7
120.9	120.2	121.1
120.3	120.1	120.9
121.3	120.5	120.8

(continued)

SOLUTION

The box plot is shown in Fig. 3.7. Note that the median of the sample is halfway between the sixth and seventh rank-ordered observation, or (120.5 + 120.7)/2 = 120.6, and that the quartiles are Q1 = 120.35 and Q3 = 120.9. The box plot indicates that the hole diameter distribution is not exactly symmetric around a central value, because the left and right whiskers and the left and right boxes around the median are not the same lengths.

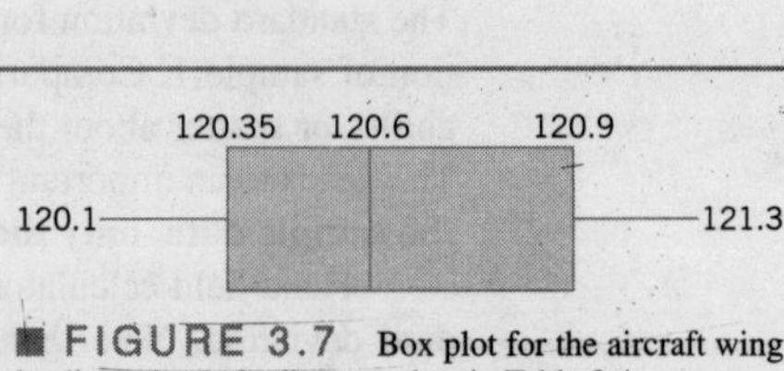

■ FIGURE 3.7 Box plot for the aircraft wing leading edge hole diameter data in Table 3.4.

Box plots are very useful in graphical comparisons among data sets, because they have visual impact and are easy to understand. For example, Fig. 3.8 shows the comparative box plots for a manufacturing quality index on products at three manufacturing plants. Inspection of this display reveals that there is too much variability at plant 2 and that plants 2 and 3 need to raise their quality index performance.

3.1.5 Probability Distributions

The histogram (or stem-and-leaf plot, or box plot) is used to describe *sample* data. A **sample** is a collection of measurements selected from some larger source or **population.** For example, the measurements on layer thickness in Table 3.2 are obtained from a sample of wafers selected from the manufacturing process. The population in this example is the collection of all layer thicknesses produced by that process. By using statistical methods, we may be able to analyze the sample layer thickness data and draw certain conclusions about the process that manufactures the wafers.

A **probability distribution** is a mathematical model that relates the value of the variable with the probability of occurrence of that value in the population. In other words, we might visualize layer thickness as a **random variable,** because it takes on different values in the population according to some random mechanism, and then the probability distribution of layer thickness describes the probability of occurrence of any value of layer thickness in the population. There are two types of probability distributions.

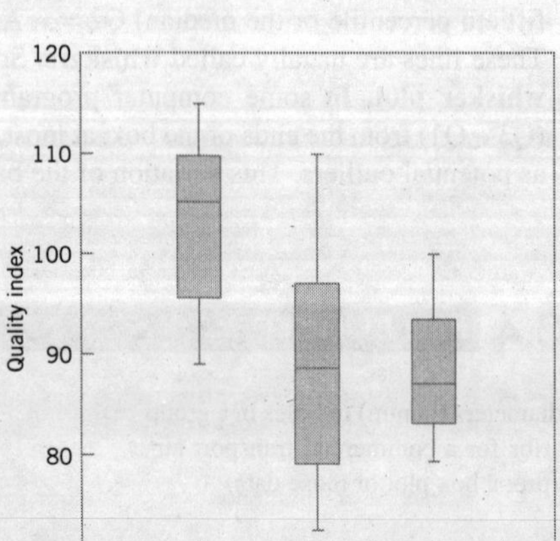

■ FIGURE 3.8 Comparative box plots of a quality index for products produced at three plants.

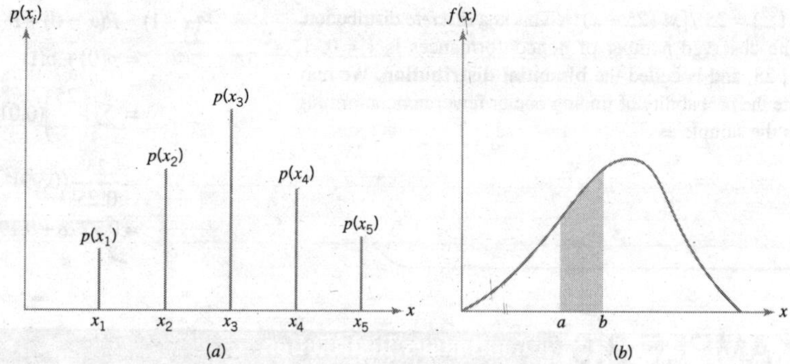

FIGURE 3.9 Probability distributions. (*a*) Discrete case. (*b*) Continuous case.

Definition

1. **Continuous distributions.** When the variable being measured is expressed on a continuous scale, its probability distribution is called a *continuous distribution.* The probability distribution of metal layer thickness is continuous.
2. **Discrete distributions.** When the parameter being measured can only take on certain values, such as the integers 0, 1, 2, . . . , the probability distribution is called a *discrete distribution.* For example, the distribution of the number of nonconformities or defects in printed circuit boards would be a discrete distribution.

Examples of discrete and continuous probability distributions are shown in Figs. 3.9*a* and 3.9*b*, respectively. The appearance of a discrete distribution is that of a series of vertical "spikes," with the height of each spike proportional to the probability. We write the probability that the random variable x takes on the specific value x_i as

$$P\{x = x_i\} = p(x_i)$$

The appearance of a continuous distribution is that of a smooth curve, with the area under the curve equal to probability, so that the probability that x lies in the interval from a to b is written as

$$P\{a \le x \le b\} = \int_a^b f(x)dx$$

EXAMPLE 3.5 A Discrete Distribution

A manufacturing process produces thousands of semiconductor chips per day. On the average, 1% of these chips do not conform to specifications. Every hour, an inspector selects a random sample of 25 chips and classifies each chip in the sample as conforming or nonconforming. If we let x be the random variable representing the number of nonconforming chips in the sample, then the probability distribution of x is

$$p(x) = \binom{25}{x}(0.01)^x(0.99)^{25-x} \qquad x = 0,1,2,\ldots,25$$

(continued)

where $\binom{25}{x} = 25!/[x!\,(25-x)!]$. This is a *discrete* distribution, since the observed number of nonconformances is $x = 0, 1, 2, \ldots, 25$, and is called the **binomial distribution.** We may calculate the probability of finding one or fewer nonconforming parts in the sample as

$$\begin{aligned} P(x \le 1) &= P(x=0) + P(x=1) \\ &= p(0) + p(1) \\ &= \sum_{x=0}^{1} \binom{25}{x} (0.01)^x (0.99)^{25-x} \\ &= \frac{25!}{0!\,25!}(0.99)^{25}(0.01)^0 + \frac{25!}{1!\,24!}(0.99)^{24}(0.01)^1 \\ &= 0.7778 + 0.1964 = 0.9742 \end{aligned}$$

EXAMPLE 3.6 A Continuous Distribution

Suppose that x is a random variable that represents the actual contents in ounces of a 1-1b bag of coffee beans. The probability distribution of x is assumed to be

$$f(x) = \frac{1}{1.5} \qquad 15.5 \le x \le 17.0$$

This is a *continuous* distribution, since the range of x is the interval [15.5, 17.0]. This distribution is called the **uniform distribution,** and it is shown graphically in Fig. 3.10. Note that the area under the function $f(x)$ corresponds to probability, so that the probability of a bag containing less than 16.0 oz is

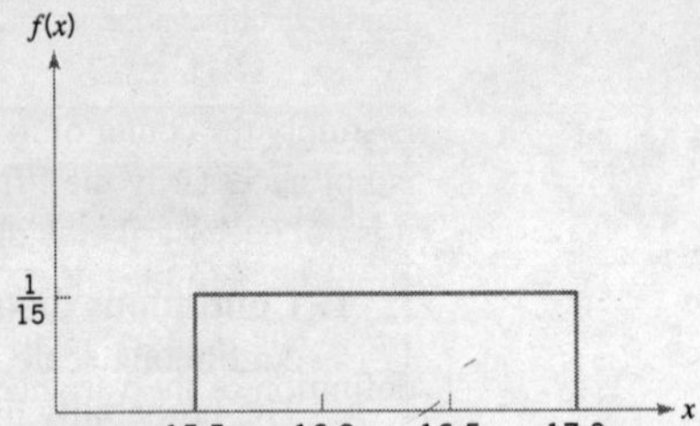

■ **FIGURE 3.10** The uniform distribution for Example 3.6.

$$P\{x \le 16.0\} = \int_{15.5}^{16.0} f(x)dx = \int_{15.5}^{16.0} \frac{1}{1.5}dx$$

$$= \left.\frac{x}{1.5}\right|_{15.5}^{16.0} = \frac{16.0-15.5}{1.5} = 0.3333$$

This follows intuitively from inspection of Fig. 3.9.

In Sections 3.2 and 3.3 we present several useful discrete and continuous distributions.

The **mean** μ of a probability distribution is a measure of the **central tendency** in the distribution, or its **location.** The mean is defined as

$$\mu = \begin{cases} \int_{-\infty}^{\infty} x f(x)\, dx, x \text{ continuous} & (3.5a) \\ \sum_{i=1}^{\infty} x_i p(x_i), x \text{ discrete} & (3.5b) \end{cases}$$

For the case of a discrete random variable with exactly N equally likely values [that is, $p(x_i) = 1/N$], then equation 3.5b reduces to

$$\mu = \frac{\sum_{i=1}^{N} x_i}{N}$$

Note the similarity of this last expression to the sample average $\bar{x}$ defined in equation 3.1. The mean is the point at which the distribution exactly "balances" (see Fig. 3.11). Thus, the mean

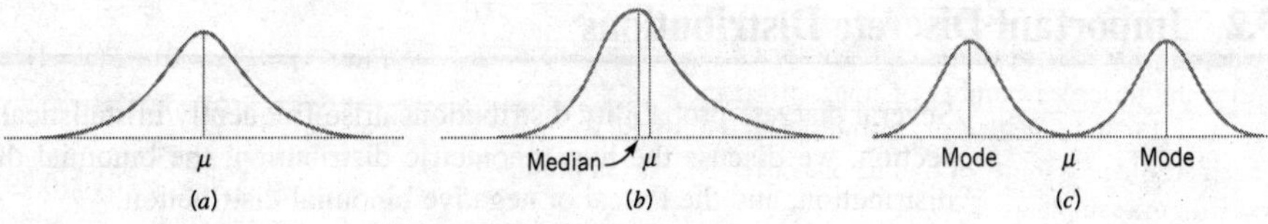

■ FIGURE 3.11 The mean of a distribution.

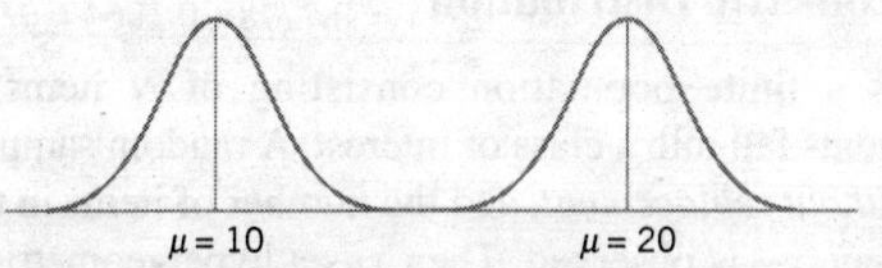

■ FIGURE 3.12 Two probability distributions with different means.

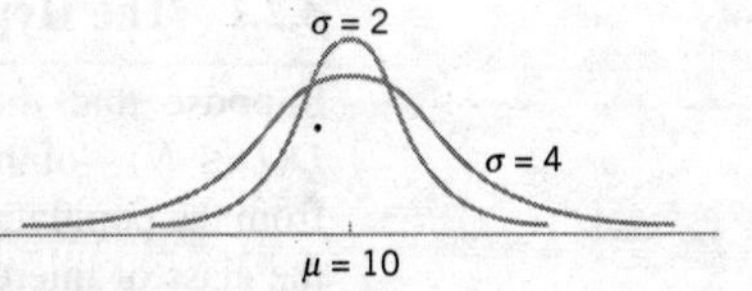

■ FIGURE 3.13 Two probability distributions with the same mean but different standard deviations.

is simply the center of mass of the probability distribution. Note from Fig. 3.11*b* that the mean is not necessarily the fiftieth percentile of the distribution (the **median**), and from Fig. 3.11c it is not necessarily the most likely value of the variable (which is called the **mode**). The mean simply determines the **location** of the distribution, as shown in Fig. 3.12.

The scatter, spread, or variability in a distribution is expressed by the **variance** σ^2. The definition of the variance is

$$\sigma^2 = \begin{cases} \int_{-\infty}^{\infty} (x-\mu)^2 f(x)dx, x \text{ continuous} & (3.6a) \\ \sum_{i=1}^{\infty} (x_i - \mu)^2 p(x_i), x \text{ discrete} & (3.6b) \end{cases}$$

when the random variable is discrete with N equally likely values, then equation (3.6b) becomes

$$\sigma^2 = \frac{\sum_{i=1}^{N} (x_i - \mu)^2}{N}$$

and we observe that in this case the variance is the average squared distance of each member of the population from the mean. Note the similarity to the sample variance s^2, defined in equation 3.2. If $\sigma^2 = 0$, there is no variability in the population. As the variability increases, the variance σ^2 increases. The variance is expressed in the square of the units of the original variable. For example, if we are measuring voltages, the units of the variance are (volts)^2. Thus, it is customary to work with the square root of the variance, called the **standard deviation** σ. It follows that

$$\sigma = \sqrt{\sigma^2} = \sqrt{\frac{\sum_{i=1}^{N} (x_i - \mu)^2}{N}} \qquad (3.7)$$

The standard deviation is a measure of spread or scatter in the population expressed in the original units. Two distributions with the same mean but different standard deviations are shown in Fig. 3.13.

3.2 Important Discrete Distributions

Several discrete probability distributions arise frequently in statistical quality control. In this section, we discuss the hypergeometric distribution, the binomial distribution, the Poisson distribution, and the Pascal or negative binomial distribution.

3.2.1 The Hypergeometric Distribution

Suppose that there is a finite population consisting of N items. Some number—say, $D(D \le N)$—of these items fall into a class of interest. A random sample of n items is selected from the population *without replacement*, and the number of items in the sample that fall into the class of interest—say, x—is observed. Then x is a hypergeometric random variable with the probability distribution defined as follows.

Definition

The **hypergeometric probability distribution** is

$$p(x) = \frac{\binom{D}{x}\binom{N-D}{n-x}}{\binom{N}{n}} \qquad x = 0,1,2,\ldots,\min(n,D) \tag{3.8}$$

The mean and variance of the distribution are

$$\mu = \frac{nD}{N} \tag{3.9}$$

and

$$\sigma^2 = \frac{nD}{N}\left(1-\frac{D}{N}\right)\left(\frac{N-n}{N-1}\right) \tag{3.10}$$

In the above definition, the quantity

$$\binom{a}{b} = \frac{a!}{b!(a-b)!}$$

is the number of combinations of a items taken b at a time.

The hypergeometric distribution is the appropriate probability model for selecting a random sample of n items without replacement from a lot of N items of which D are nonconforming or defective. By a random sample, we mean a sample that has been selected in such a way that all possible samples have an equal chance of being chosen. In these applications, x usually represents the number of nonconforming items found in the sample. For example, suppose that a lot contains 100 items, 5 of which do not conform to requirements. If 10 items are selected at random without replacement, then the probability of finding one or fewer nonconforming items in the sample is

$$P\{x \le 1\} = P\{x = 0\} + P\{x = 1\}$$

$$= \frac{\binom{5}{0}\binom{95}{10}}{\binom{100}{10}} + \frac{\binom{5}{1}\binom{95}{9}}{\binom{100}{10}} = 0.92314$$

In Chapter 15 we show how probability models such as this can be used to design acceptance-sampling procedures.

Some computer programs can perform these calculations. The display below is the output from Minitab for calculating cumulative hypergeometric probabilities with $N = 100$, $D = 5$ (note that Minitab uses the symbol M instead of D, and $n = 5$). Minitab will also calculate the individual probabilities for each value of x.

Cumulative Distribution Function

Hypergeometric with N = 100, M = 5, and n = 10

x	P(X <= x)	x	P(X <= x)
0	0.58375	6	1.00000
1	0.92314	7	1.00000
2	0.99336	8	1.00000
3	0.99975	9	1.00000
4	1.00000	10	1.00000
5	1.00000		

3.2.2 The Binomial Distribution

Consider a process that consists of a sequence of n independent trials. By independent trials, we mean that the outcome of each trial does not depend in any way on the outcome of previous trials. When the outcome of each trial is either a "success" or a "failure," the trials are called **Bernoulli trials.** If the probability of "success" on any trial—say, p—is constant, then the number of "successes" x in n Bernoulli trials has the **binomial distribution** with parameters n and p, defined as follows.

Definition

The **binomial distribution** with parameters $n \ge 0$ and $0 < p < 1$ is

$$p(x) = \binom{n}{x} p^x (1-p)^{n-x} \qquad x = 0, 1, \ldots, n \tag{3.11}$$

The mean and variance of the binomial distribution are

$$\mu = np \tag{3.12}$$

and

$$\sigma^2 = np(1-p) \tag{3.13}$$

The binomial distribution is used frequently in quality engineering. It is the appropriate probability model for sampling from an infinitely large population, where p represents the fraction of defective or nonconforming items in the population. In these applications, x usually represents the number of nonconforming items found in a random sample of n items. For example, if $p = 0.10$ and $n = 15$, then the probability of obtaining x nonconforming items is computed from equation 3.11 as follows:

Probability Density Function

Binomial with n = 15 and p = 0.1

x	P(X = x)	x	P(X = x)
0	0.205891	6	0.001939
1	0.343152	7	0.000277
2	0.266896	8	0.000031
3	0.128505	9	0.000003
4	0.042835	10	0.000000
5	0.010471		

Minitab was used to perform these calculations. Notice that for all values of x that lie between $10 \leq x \leq 15$ the probability of finding x "successes" in 15 trials is zero.

Several binomial distributions are shown graphically in Fig. 3.14. The shape of those examples is typical of all binomial distributions. For a fixed n, the distribution becomes more symmetric as p increases from 0 to 0.5 or decreases from 1 to 0.5. For a fixed p, the distribution becomes more symmetric as n increases.

A random variable that arises frequently in statistical quality control is

$$\hat{p} = \frac{x}{n} \tag{3.14}$$

where x has a binomial distribution with parameters n and p. Often $\hat{p}$ is the ratio of the observed number of defective or nonconforming items in a sample (x) to the sample size (n)

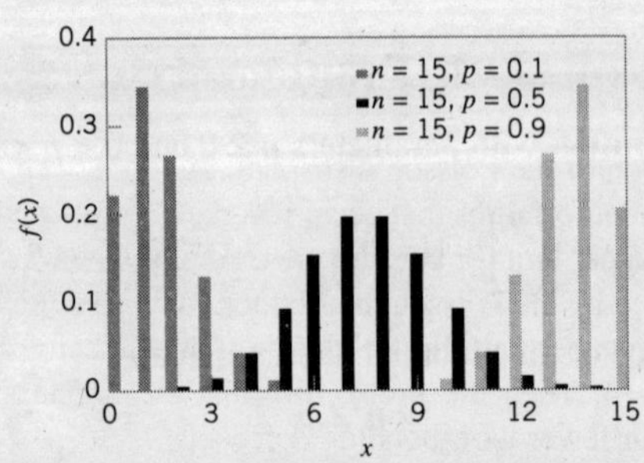

(*a*) Binomial distributions for different values of p with $n = 15$.

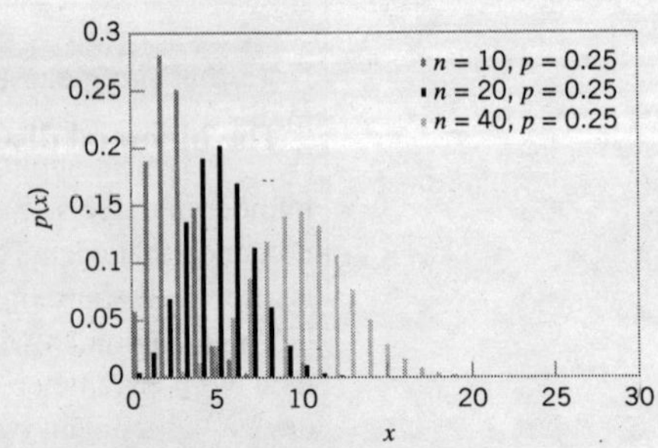

(*b*) Binomial distributions for different values of n with $p = 0.25$.

■ FIGURE 3.14 Binomial distributions for selected values of n and p.

and this is usually called the **sample fraction defective** or **sample fraction nonconforming.** The " ^ " symbol is used to indicate that $\hat{p}$ is an estimate of the true, unknown value of the binomial parameter p. The probability distribution of $\hat{p}$ is obtained from the binomial, since

$$P\{\hat{p} \le a\} = P\left\{\frac{x}{n} \le a\right\} = p\{x \le na\} = \sum_{x=0}^{[na]} \binom{n}{x} p^x (1-p)^{n-x}$$

where $[na]$ denotes the largest integer less than or equal to na. It is easy to show that the mean of $\hat{p}$ is p and that the variance of $\hat{p}$ is

$$\sigma_{\hat{p}}^2 = \frac{p(1-p)}{n}$$

3.2.3 The Poisson Distribution

A useful discrete distribution in statistical quality control is the Poisson distribution, defined as follows.

Definition

The **Poisson distribution** is

$$p(x) = \frac{e^{-\lambda} \lambda^x}{x!} \qquad x = 0, 1, \ldots \tag{3.15}$$

where the parameter $\lambda > 0$. The **mean** and **variance** of the Poisson distribution are

$$\mu = \lambda \tag{3.16}$$

and

$$\sigma^2 = \lambda \tag{3.17}$$

Note that the mean and variance of the Poisson distribution are both equal to the parameter λ.

A typical application of the Poisson distribution in quality control is as a model of the number of defects or nonconformities that occur in a unit of product. In fact, any random phenomenon that occurs on a per unit (or per unit area, per unit volume, per unit time, etc.) basis is often well approximated by the Poisson distribution. As an example, suppose that the number of wire-bonding defects per unit that occur in a semiconductor device is Poisson distributed with parameter $\lambda = 4$. Then the probability that a randomly selected semiconductor device will contain two or fewer wire-bonding defects is

$$P\{x \le 2\} = \sum_{x=0}^{2} \frac{e^{-4} 4^x}{x!} = 0.018316 + 0.073263 + 0.146525 = 0.238104$$

Minitab can perform these calculations. Using the Poisson distribution with the mean = 4 results in:

Probability Density Function

Poisson with mean = 4

x	P(X = x)
0	0.018316
1	0.073263
2	0.146525

Several Poisson distributions are shown in Fig. 3.15. Note that the distribution is *skewed;* that is, it has a long tail to the right. As the parameter λ becomes larger, the Poisson distribution becomes symmetric in appearance.

It is possible to derive the Poisson distribution as a limiting form of the binomial distribution. That is, in a binomial distribution with parameters n and p, if we let n approach infinity and p approach zero in such a way that $np = \lambda$ is a constant, then the Poisson distribution results. It is also possible to derive the Poisson distribution using a pure probability argument. [For more information about the Poisson distribution, see Hines, Montgomery, Goldsman, and Borror (2004); Montgomery and Runger (2007); and the supplemental text material.]

3.2.4 The Pascal and Related Distributions

The Pascal distribution, like the binomial distribution, has its basis in Bernoulli trials. Consider a sequence of independent trials, each with probability of success p, and let x denote the trial on which the rth success occurs. Then x is a Pascal random variable with probability distribution defined as follows.

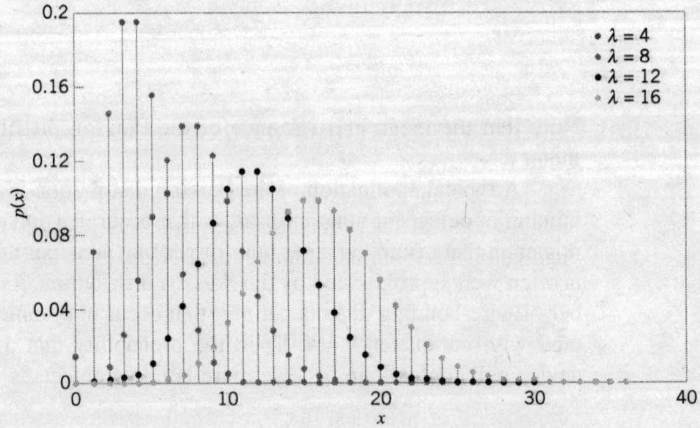

■ FIGURE 3.15 Poisson probability distributions for selected values of λ.

Definition

The **Pascal distribution** is

$$p(x) = \binom{x-1}{r-1} p^r (1-p)^{x-r} \qquad x = r, r+1, r+2, \ldots \tag{3.18}$$

where $r \geq 1$ is an integer. The ***mean*** and ***variance*** of the Pascal distribution are

$$\mu = \frac{r}{p} \tag{3.19}$$

and

$$\sigma^2 = \frac{r(1-p)}{p^2} \tag{3.20}$$

respectively.

Two special cases of the Pascal distribution are of interest. The first of these occurs when $r > 0$ and is not necessarily an integer. The resulting distribution is called the **negative binomial distribution.** It is relatively standard to refer to equation (3.18) as the negative binomial distribution, even when r is an integer. The negative binomial distribution, like the Poisson distribution, is sometimes useful as the underlying statistical model for various types of "count" data, such as the occurrence of nonconformities in a unit of product (see Section 7.3.1). There is an important duality between the binomial and negative binomial distributions. In the binomial distribution, we fix the sample size (number of Bernoulli trials) and observe the number of successes; in the negative binomial distribution, we fix the number of successes and observe the sample size (number of Bernoulli trials) required to achieve them. This concept is particularly important in various kinds of sampling problems.

The other special case of the Pascal distribution is if $r = 1$, in which case we have the **geometric distribution.** It is the distribution of the number of Bernoulli trials until the *first* success.

3.3 Important Continuous Distributions

In this section we discuss several continuous distributions that are important in statistical quality control. These include the normal distribution, the lognormal distribution, the exponential distribution, the gamma distribution, and the Weibull distribution.

3.3.1 The Normal Distribution

The normal distribution is probably the most important distribution in both the theory and application of statistics. If x is a normal random variable, then the probability distribution of x is defined as follows.

Definition

The **normal distribution** is

$$f(x) = \frac{1}{\sigma\sqrt{2\pi}} e^{-\frac{1}{2}\left(\frac{x-\mu}{\sigma}\right)^2} \qquad -\infty < x < \infty \tag{3.21}$$

The mean of the normal distribution is μ $(-\infty < \mu < \infty)$ and the variance is $\sigma^2 > 0$.

The normal distribution is used so much that we frequently employ a special notation, $x \sim N(\mu, \sigma^2)$, to imply that x is normally distributed with mean μ and variance σ^2. The visual appearance of the normal distribution is a symmetric, unimodal or **bell-shaped** curve and is shown in Fig. 3.16.

There is a simple interpretation of the standard deviation σ of a normal distribution, which is illustrated in Fig. 3.17. Note that 68.26% of the population values fall between the limits defined by the mean plus and minus one standard deviation ($\mu \pm 1\sigma$); 95.46% of the values fall between the limits defined by the mean plus and minus two standard deviations ($\mu \pm 2\sigma$); and 99.73% of the population values fall within the limits defined by the mean plus and minus three standard deviations ($\mu \pm 3\sigma$). Thus, the standard deviation measures the distance on the horizontal scale associated with the 68.26%, 95.46%, and 99.73% containment limits. It is common practice to round these percentages to 68%, 95%, and 99.7%.

The cumulative normal distribution is defined as the probability that the normal random variable x is less than or equal to some value a, or

$$P\{x \le a\} = F(a) = \int_{-\infty}^{a} \frac{1}{\sigma\sqrt{2\pi}} e^{-\frac{1}{2}\left(\frac{x-\mu}{\sigma}\right)^2} dx \tag{3.22}$$

This integral cannot be evaluated in closed form. However, by using the change of variable

$$z = \frac{x-\mu}{\sigma} \tag{3.23}$$

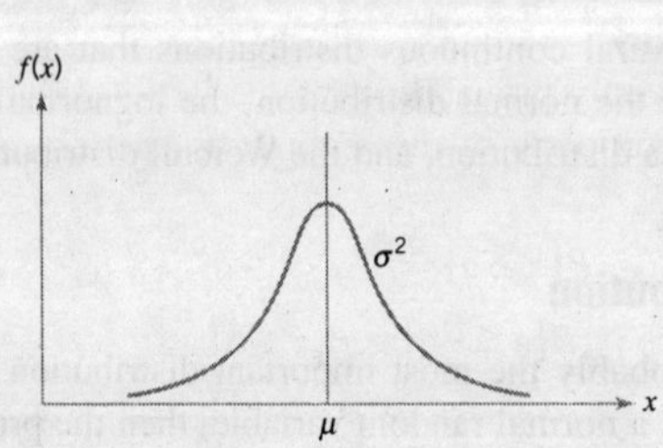

■ FIGURE 3.16 The normal distribution.

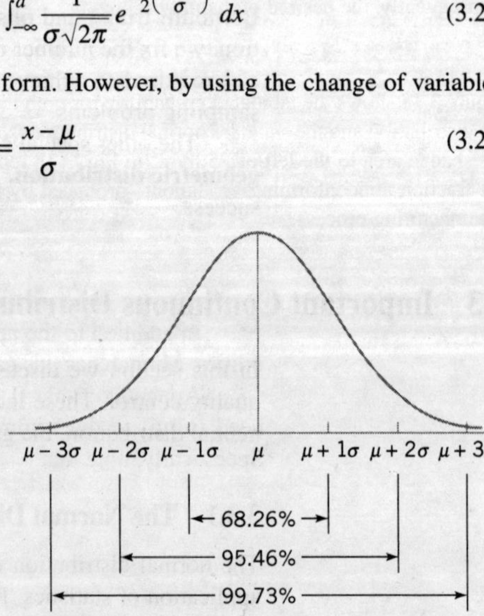

■ FIGURE 3.17 Areas under the normal distribution.

the evaluation can be made independent of μ and σ^2. That is,

$$P\{x \le a\} = P\left\{z \le \frac{a-\mu}{\sigma}\right\} \equiv \Phi\left(\frac{a-\mu}{\sigma}\right)$$

where $\Phi(\cdot)$ is the cumulative distribution function of the **standard normal distribution** (mean = 0, standard deviation = 1). A table of the cumulative standard normal distribution is given in Appendix Table II. The transformation (3.23) is usually called **standardization,** because it converts a $N(\mu, \sigma^2)$ random variable into an $N(0, 1)$ random variable.

EXAMPLE 3.7 Tensile Strength of Paper

The tensile strength of paper used to make grocery bags is an important quality characteristic. It is known that the strength—say, x—is normally distributed with mean $\mu = 40$ lb/in^2 and standard deviation $\sigma = 2$ lb/in^2, denoted $x \sim N(40, 2^2)$. The purchaser of the bags requires them to have a strength of at least 35 lb/in^2. Calculate the probability that bags produced from this paper will meet or exceed the specification.

SOLUTION

The probability that a bag produced from this paper will meet or exceed the specification is $P\{x \ge 35\}$. Note that

$$P\{x \ge 35\} = 1 - P\{x \le 35\}$$

To evaluate this probability from the standard normal tables, we standardize the point 35 and find

$$P\{x \le 35\} = P\left\{z \le \frac{35-40}{2}\right\} =$$

$$P\{z \le -2.5\} = \Phi(-2.5) = 0.0062$$

Consequently, the desired probability is

$$P\{x \ge 35\} = 1 - P\{x \le 35\} = 1 - 0.0062 = 0.9938$$

Figure 3.18 shows the tabulated probability for both the $N(40, 2^2)$ distribution and the standard normal distribution. Note that the shaded area to the left of 35 lb/in^2 in Fig. 3.18 represents the fraction nonconforming or "fallout" produced by the bag manufacturing process.

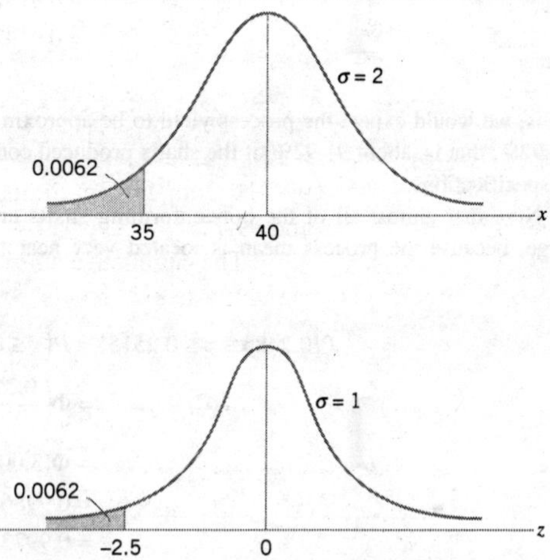

■ FIGURE 3.18 Calculation of $P\{x \le 35\}$ in Example 3.7.

In addition to the appendix table, many computer programs can calculate normal probabilities. Minitab has this capability.

Appendix Table II gives only probabilities to the left of positive values of z. We will need to utilize the symmetry property of the normal distribution to evaluate probabilities. Specifically, note that

$$P\{x \ge a\} = 1 - P\{x \le a\} \tag{3.24}$$

$$P\{x \le -a\} = P\{x \le a\} \tag{3.25}$$

and

$$P\{x \ge -a\} = P\{x \le a\} \tag{3.26}$$

It is helpful in problem solution to draw a graph of the distribution, as in Fig. 3.18.

EXAMPLE 3.8 Shaft Diameters

The diameter of a metal shaft used in a disk-drive unit is normally distributed with mean 0.2508 in. and standard deviation 0.0005 in. The specifications on the shaft have been established as 0.2500 ± 0.0015 in. What fraction of the shafts produced conform to specifications?

SOLUTION

The appropriate normal distribution is shown in Fig. 3.19. Note that

$$\begin{aligned} P\{0.2485 \le x \le 0.2515\} &= P\{x \le 0.2515\} - P\{x \le 0.2485\} \\ &= \Phi\left(\frac{0.2515 - 0.2508}{0.0005}\right) - \Phi\left(\frac{0.2485 - 0.2508}{0.0005}\right) \\ &= \Phi(1.40) - \Phi(-4.60) \\ &= 0.9192 - 0.0000 \\ &= 0.9192 \end{aligned}$$

Thus, we would expect the process yield to be approximately 91.92%; that is, about 91.92% of the shafts produced conform to specifications.

Note that almost all of the nonconforming shafts are too large, because the process mean is located very near to the upper specification limit. Suppose that we can **recenter** the manufacturing process, perhaps by adjusting the machine, so that the process mean is exactly equal to the nominal value of 0.2500. Then we have

$$\begin{aligned} P\{0.2485 \le x \le 0.2515\} &= P\{x \le 0.2515\} - P\{x \le 0.2485\} \\ &= \Phi\left(\frac{0.2515 - 0.2500}{0.0005}\right) - \Phi\left(\frac{0.2485 - 0.2500}{0.0005}\right) \\ &= \Phi(3.00) - \Phi(-3.00) \\ &= 0.99865 - 0.00135 \\ &= 0.9973 \end{aligned}$$

By recentering the process we have increased the yield of the process to approximately 99.73%.

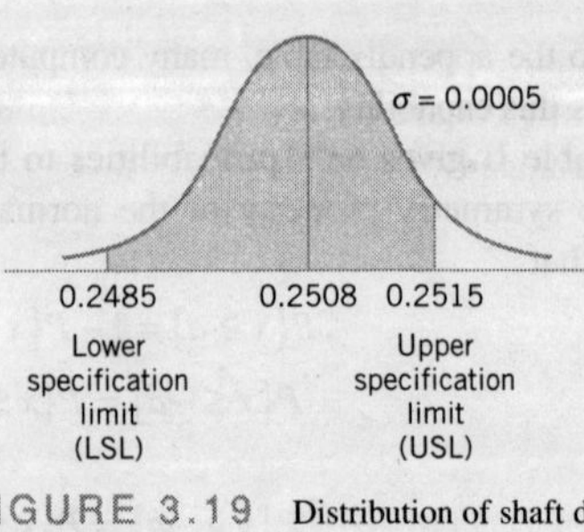

■ FIGURE 3.19 Distribution of shaft diameters, Example 3.8.

EXAMPLE 3.9 Another Use of the Standard Normal Table

Sometimes instead of finding the probability associated with a particular value of a normal random variable, we find it necessary to do the opposite—find a particular value of a normal random variable that results in a given probability. For example, suppose that $x \sim N(10, 9)$. Find the value of x—say, a—such that $P\{x > a\} = 0.05$.

SOLUTION

From the problem statement, we have

$$P\{x > a\} = P\left\{z > \frac{a-10}{3}\right\} = 0.05$$

or

$$P\left\{z \le \frac{a-10}{3}\right\} = 0.95$$

From Appendix Table II, we have $P\{z \le 1.645\} = 0.95$, so

$$\frac{a-10}{3} = 1.645$$

or

$$a = 10 + 3(1.645) = 14.935$$

The normal distribution has many useful properties. One of these is relative to **linear combinations** of normally and independently distributed random variables. If $x_1, x_2 \ldots, x_n$ are normally and independently distributed random variables with means $\mu_1, \mu_2, \ldots, \mu_n$ and variances $\sigma_1^2, \sigma_2^2, \ldots, \sigma_n^2$, respectively, then the distribution of

$$y = a_1x_1 + a_2x_2 + \cdots + a_nx_n$$

is normal with mean

$$\mu_y = a_1\mu_1 + a_2\mu_2 + \cdots + a_n\mu_n \tag{3.27}$$

and variance

$$\sigma_y^2 = a_1^2\sigma_1^2 + a_2^2\sigma_2^2 + \cdots + a_n^2\sigma_n^2 \tag{3.28}$$

where $a_1, a_2, \ldots, a_n$ are constants.

The Central Limit Theorem. The normal distribution is often assumed as the appropriate probability model for a random variable. Later on, we will discuss how to check the validity of this assumption; however, the central limit theorem is often a justification of approximate normality.

Definition

The Central Limit Theorem if $x_1, x_2, \ldots, x_n$ are independent random variables with mean μ_i and variance σ_i^2, and if $y = x_1 + x_2 + \cdots + x_n$, then the distribution of

$$\frac{y - \sum_{i=1}^{n}\mu_i}{\sqrt{\sum_{i=1}^{n}\sigma_i^2}}$$

approaches the $N(0, 1)$ distribution as n approaches infinity.

The central limit theorem implies that the sum of n independently distributed random variables is approximately normal, regardless of the distributions of the individual variables. The approximation improves as n increases. In many cases the approximation will be good for small n—say, $n < 10$—whereas in some cases we may require very large n—say, $n > 100$—for the approximation to be satisfactory. In general, if the x_i are identically distributed, and the distribution of each x_i does not depart radically from the normal, then the central limit theorem works quite well for $n \geq 3$ or 4. These conditions are met frequently in quality-engineering problems.

3.3.2 The Lognormal Distribution

Variables in a system sometimes follow an exponential relationship, say $x = \exp(w)$. If the exponent is a random variable, say w, $x = \exp(w)$ is a random variable and the distribution of x is of interest. An important special case occurs when w has a normal distribution. In that case, the distribution of x is called a **lognormal distribution.** The name follows from the transformation $\ln(x) = w$. That is, the natural logarithm of x is normally distributed.

Probabilities for x are obtained from the transformation to w, but we need to recognize that the range of x is $(0, \infty)$. Suppose that w is normally distributed with mean θ and variance ω^2; then the cumulative distribution function for x is

$$F(a) = P[x \leq a] = P[\exp(w) \leq a] = P[w \leq \ln(a)]$$

$$= P\left[z \leq \frac{\ln(a) - \theta}{\omega}\right] = \Phi\left[\frac{\ln(a) - \theta}{\omega}\right]$$

for $x > 0$, where z is a standard normal random variable. Therefore, Appendix Table II can be used to determine the probability. Also, $f(x) = 0$, for $x \leq 0$. The lognormal random variable is always nonnegative.

The lognormal distribution is defined as follows.

Definition

Let w have a normal distribution mean θ and variance ω^2; then $x = \exp(w)$ is a **lognormal random variable,** and the lognormal distribution is

$$f(x) = \frac{1}{x\omega\sqrt{2\pi}} \exp\left[-\frac{(\ln(x) - \theta)^2}{2\omega^2}\right] \quad 0 < x < \infty \tag{3.29}$$

The mean and variance of x are

$$\mu = e^{\theta + \omega^2/2} \quad \text{and} \quad \sigma^2 = e^{2\theta + \omega^2}\left(e^{\omega^2} - 1\right) \tag{3.30}$$

The parameters of a lognormal distribution are θ and ω^2, but care is needed to interpret that these are the mean and variance of the normal random variable w. The mean and variance of x are the functions of these parameters shown in equation (3.30). Figure 3.20 illustrates lognormal distributions for selected values of the parameters.

The lifetime of a product that degrades over time is often modeled by a lognormal random variable. For example, this is a common distribution for the lifetime of a semiconductor laser. Other continuous distributions can also be used in this type of application. However, because the lognormal distribution is derived from a simple exponential function of a normal random variable, it is easy to understand and easy to evaluate probabilities.

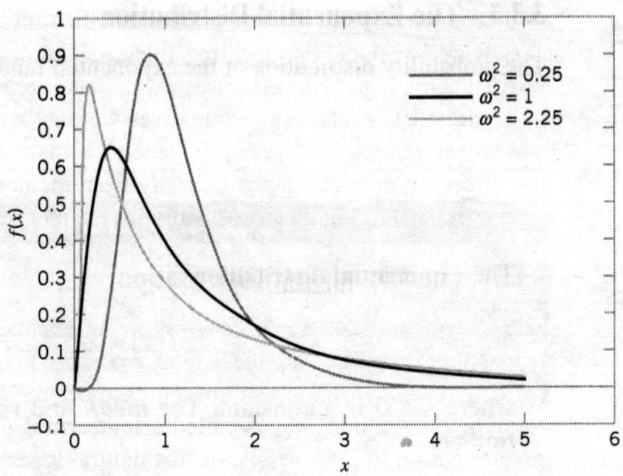

■ FIGURE 3.20 Lognormal probability density functions with $\theta = 0$ for selected values of ω^2.

EXAMPLE 3.10 Medical Laser Lifetime

The lifetime of a medical laser used in ophthalmic surgery has a lognormal distribution with $\theta = 6$ and $\omega = 1.2$ hours. What is the probability the lifetime exceeds 500 hours?

SOLUTION

From the cumulative distribution function for the lognormal random variable

$$P(x > 500) = 1 - P[\exp(w) \le 500] = 1 - P[w \le \ln(500)]$$

$$= \Phi\left(\frac{\ln(500) - 6}{1.2}\right) = 1 - \Phi(0.1788)$$

$$= 1 - 0.5710 = 0.4290$$

What lifetime is exceeded by 99% of lasers? Now the question is to determine a such that $P(x > a) = 0.99$. Therefore,

$$P(x > a) = P[\exp(w) > a] = P[w > \ln(a)]$$

$$= 1 - \Phi\left(\frac{\ln(a) - 6}{1.2}\right) = 0.99$$

From Appendix Table II, $1 - \Phi(a) = 0.99$ when $a = -2.33$. Therefore,

$$\frac{\ln(a) - 6}{1.2} = -2.33 \quad \text{and} \quad a = \exp(3.204) = 24.63 \text{ hours}$$

Determine the mean and standard deviation of lifetime. Now,

$$\mu = e^{\theta + \omega^2/2} = \exp(6 + 0.72) = 828.82 \text{ hours}$$

$$\sigma^2 = e^{2\theta + \omega^2}\left(e^{\omega^2} - 1\right) = \exp(12 + 1.44)[\exp(1.44) - 1]$$

$$= 2{,}212{,}419.85$$

so the standard deviation of the lifetime is 1487.42 hours. Notice that the standard deviation of the lifetime is large relative to the mean.

3.3.3 The Exponential Distribution

The probability distribution of the exponential random variable is defined as follows.

Definition

The **exponential distribution** is

$$f(x) = \lambda e^{-\lambda x} \qquad x \geq 0 \tag{3.31}$$

where $\lambda > 0$ is a constant. The ***mean*** and ***variance*** of the exponential distribution are

$$\mu = \frac{1}{\lambda} \tag{3.32}$$

and

$$\sigma^2 = \frac{1}{\lambda^2} \tag{3.33}$$

respectively.

Several exponential distributions are shown in Fig. 3.21.

The cumulative exponential distribution is

$$\begin{aligned} F(a) &= P\{x \leq a\} \\ &= \int_0^a \lambda e^{-\lambda t} dt \\ &= 1 - e^{-\lambda a} \qquad a \geq 0 \end{aligned} \tag{3.34}$$

Figure 3.22 illustrates the exponential cumulative distribution function.

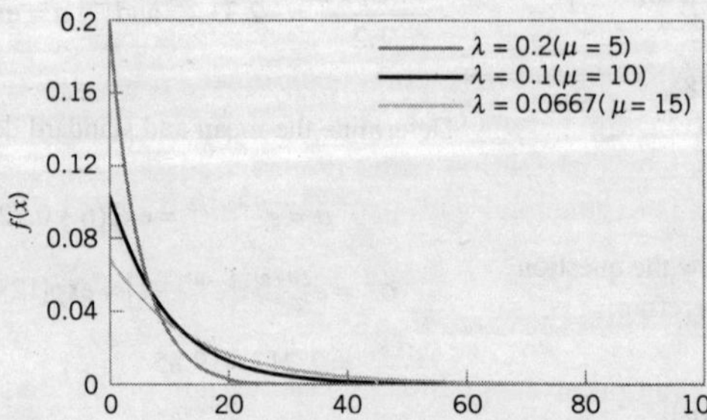

■ FIGURE 3.21 Exponential distributions for selected values of λ.

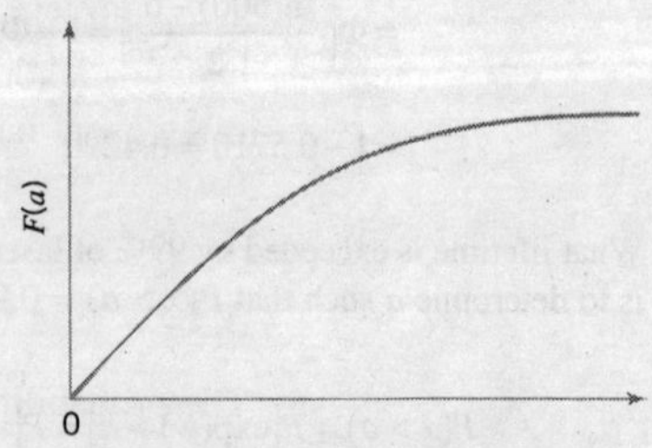

■ FIGURE 3.22 The cumulative exponential distribution function.

The exponential distribution is widely used in the field of **reliability engineering** as a model of the time to failure of a component or system. In these applications, the parameter λ is called the **failure rate** of the system, and the mean of the distribution $1/\lambda$ is called the **mean time to failure.**[2] For example, suppose that an electronic component in an airborne radar system has a useful life described by an exponential distribution with failure rate 10^{-4}/h; that is, $\lambda = 10^{-4}$. The mean time to failure for this component is $1/\lambda = 10^4 = 10{,}000$ h. If we wanted to determine the probability that this component would fail before its expected life, we would evaluate

$$P\left\{x \le \frac{1}{\lambda}\right\} = \int_0^{1/\lambda} \lambda e^{-\lambda t}\,dt = 1 - e^{-1} = 0.63212$$

This result holds regardless of the value of λ; that is, the probability that a value of an exponential random variable will be less than its mean is 0.63212. This happens, of course, because the distribution is not symmetric.

There is an important relationship between the exponential and Poisson distributions. If we consider the Poisson distribution as a model of the number of occurrences of some event in the interval $(0, t]$, then from equation 3.15 we have

$$p(x) = \frac{e^{-\lambda t}(\lambda t)^x}{x!}$$

Now $x = 0$ implies that there are no occurrences of the event in $(0, t]$, and $P\{x = 0\} = p(0) = e^{-\lambda t}$. We may think of $p(0)$ as the probability that the interval to the first occurrence is greater than t, or

$$P\{y > t\} = p(0) = e^{-\lambda t}$$

where y is the random variable denoting the interval to the first occurrence. Since

$$F(t) = P\{y \le t\} = 1 - e^{-\lambda t}$$

and using the fact that $f(y) = dF(y)/dy$, we have

$$f(y) = \lambda e^{-\lambda y} \tag{3.35}$$

as the distribution of the interval to the first occurrence. We recognize equation (3.35) as an exponential distribution with parameter λ. Therefore, we see that if the number of occurrences of an event has a Poisson distribution with parameter λ, then the distribution of the interval *between* occurrences is exponential with parameter λ.

3.3.4 The Gamma Distribution

The probability distribution of the gamma random variable is defined as follows.

[2]See the supplemental text material for more information.

Definition

The **gamma distribution** is

$$f(x) = \frac{\lambda}{\Gamma(r)}(\lambda x)^{r-1} e^{-\lambda x} \qquad x \geq 0 \tag{3.36}$$

with **shape parameter** $r > 0$ and **scale parameter** $\lambda > 0$. The **mean** and **variance** of the gamma distribution are

$$\mu = \frac{r}{\lambda} \tag{3.37}$$

and

$$\sigma^2 = \frac{r}{\lambda^2} \tag{3.38}$$

respectively.[3]

Several gamma distributions are shown in Fig. 3.23. Note that if $r = 1$, the gamma distribution reduces to the exponential distribution with parameter λ (Section 3.3.3). The gamma distribution can assume many different shapes, depending on the values chosen for r and λ. This makes it useful as a model for a wide variety of continuous random variables.

If the parameter r is an integer, then the gamma distribution is the sum of r independently and identically distributed exponential distributions, each with parameter λ. That is, if $x_1, x_2, \ldots, x_r$ are exponential with parameter λ and independent, then

$$y = x_1 + x_2 + \cdots + x_r$$

is distributed as gamma with parameters r and λ. There are a number of important applications of this result.

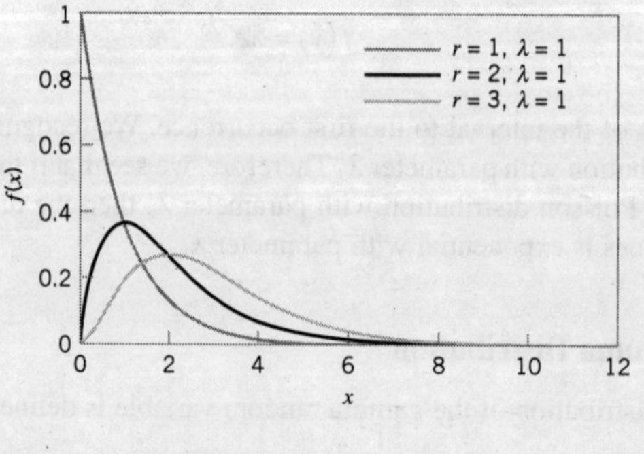

■ FIGURE 3.23 Gamma distributions for selected values or r and $\lambda = 1$.

[3] $\Gamma(r)$ in the denominator of equation 3.36 is the gamma function, defined as $\Gamma(r) = \int_0^\infty x^{r-1} e^{-x} dx$, $r > 0$. If r is a positive integer, then $\Gamma(r) = (r-1)!$

EXAMPLE 3.11 A Standby Redundant System

Consider the system shown in Fig. 3.24. This is called a **standby redundant system,** because while component 1 is on, component 2 is off, and when component 1 fails, the switch automatically turns component 2 on. If each component has a life described by an exponential distribution with $\lambda = 10^{-4}$/h, say, then the system life is gamma distributed with parameters $r = 2$ and $\lambda = 10^{-4}$. Thus, the mean time to failure is $\mu = r/\lambda = 2/10^{-4} = 2 \times 10^4$ h.

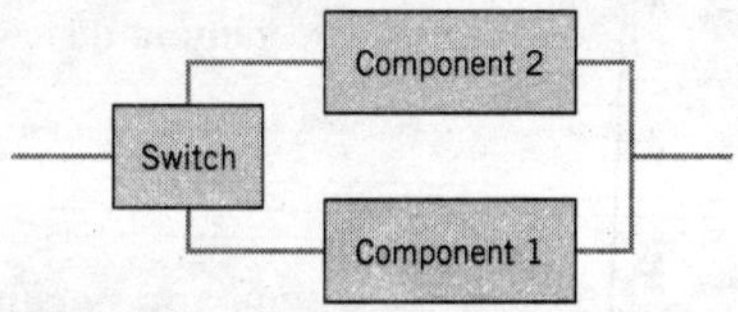

■ **FIGURE 3.24** The standby redundant system for Example 3.11.

The cumulative gamma distribution is

$$F(a) = 1 - \int_a^\infty \frac{\lambda}{\Gamma(r)} (\lambda t)^{r-1} e^{-\lambda t} dt \tag{3.39}$$

If r is an integer, then equation 3.39 becomes

$$F(a) = 1 - \sum_{k=0}^{r-1} e^{-\lambda a} \frac{(\lambda a)^k}{k!} \tag{3.40}$$

Consequently, the cumulative gamma distribution can be evaluated as the sum of r Poisson terms with parameter λa. This result is not too surprising, if we consider the Poisson distribution as a model of the number of occurrences of an event in a fixed interval, and the gamma distribution as the model of the portion of the interval required to obtain a specific number of occurrences.

3.3.5 The Weibull Distribution

The Weibull distribution is defined as follows.

Definition

The **Weibull distribution** is

$$f(x) = \frac{\beta}{\theta}\left(\frac{x}{\theta}\right)^{\beta-1} \exp\left[-\left(\frac{x}{\theta}\right)^{\beta}\right] \qquad x \ge 0 \tag{3.41}$$

where $\theta > 0$ is the **scale parameter,** and $\beta > 0$ is the **shape parameter.** The **mean** and **variance** of the Weibull distribution are

$$\mu = \theta \Gamma\left(1 + \frac{1}{\beta}\right) \tag{3.42}$$

and

$$\sigma^2 = \theta^2 \left[\Gamma\left(1 + \frac{2}{\beta}\right) - \left\{\Gamma\left(1 + \frac{1}{\beta}\right)\right\}^2\right] \tag{3.43}$$

respectively.

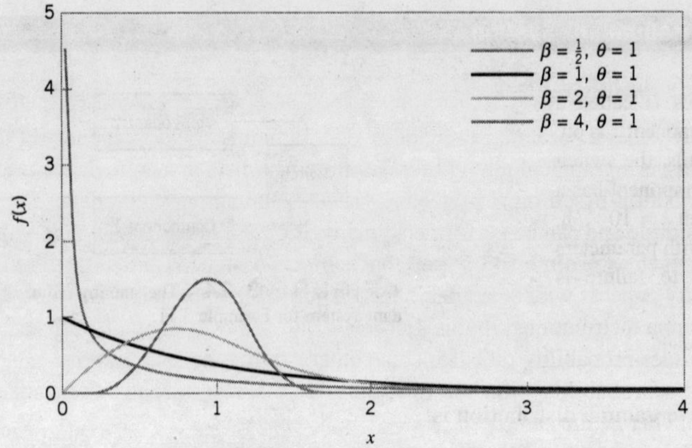

■ FIGURE 3.25 Weibull distributions for selected values of the shape parameter β and scale parameter $\theta = 1$.

The Weibull distribution is very flexible, and by appropriate selection of the parameters θ and β, the distribution can assume a wide variety of shapes. Several Weibull distributions are shown in Fig. 3.25 for $\theta = 1$ and $\beta = 1/2$, 1, 2, and 4. Note that when $\beta = 1$, the Weibull distribution reduces to the exponential distribution with mean $1/\theta$. The cumulative Weibull distribution is

$$F(a) = 1 - \exp\left[-\left(\frac{a}{\theta}\right)^{\beta}\right] \tag{3.44}$$

The Weibull distribution has been used extensively in reliability engineering as a model of time to failure for electrical and mechanical components and systems. Examples of situations in which the Weibull has been used include electronic devices such as memory elements, mechanical components such as bearings, and structural elements in aircraft and automobiles.[4]

EXAMPLE 3.12 Time to Failure for Electronic Components

The time to failure for an electronic component used in a flat panel display unit is satisfactorily modeled by a Weibull distribution with $\beta = \frac{1}{2}$ and $\theta = 5000$. Find the mean time to failure and the fraction of components that are expected to survive beyond 20,000 hours.

SOLUTION

The mean time to failure is

$$\mu = \theta\Gamma\left(1 + \frac{1}{\beta}\right) = 5000\Gamma\left(1 + \frac{1}{\frac{1}{2}}\right)$$

$$= 5000\Gamma(3) = 10{,}000 \text{ hours}$$

The fraction of components expected to survive a = 20,000 hours is

$$1 - F(a) = \exp\left[-\left(\frac{a}{\theta}\right)^{\beta}\right]$$

or

$$1 - F(20{,}000) = \exp\left[-\left(\frac{20{,}000}{5{,}000}\right)^{\frac{1}{2}}\right]$$

$$= e^{-2}$$

$$= 0.1353$$

That is, all but about 13.53% of the subassemblies will fail by 20,000 hours.

[4]See the supplemental text material for more information.

3.4 Probability Plots

3.4.1 Normal Probability Plots

How do we know whether a particular probability distribution is a reasonable model for data? **Probability plotting** is a graphical method for determining whether sample data conform to a hypothesized distribution based on a subjective visual examination of the data. The general procedure is very simple and can be performed quickly. Probability plotting typically uses special graph paper, known as **probability paper,** that has been designed for the hypothesized distribution. Probability paper is widely available for the normal, lognormal, Weibull, and various chi-square and gamma distributions. In this section we illustrate the **normal probability plot.** Section 3.4.2 discusses probability plots for some other continuous distributions.

To construct a probability plot, the observations in the sample are first ranked from smallest to largest. That is, the sample $x_1, x_2, \ldots, x_n$ is arranged as $x_{(1)}, x_{(2)}, \ldots, x_{(n)}$, where $x_{(1)}$ is the smallest observation, $x_{(2)}$ is the second smallest observation, and so forth, with $x_{(n)}$ the largest. The ordered observations $x_{(j)}$ are then plotted against their observed cumulative frequency $(j - 0.5)/n$ [or $100\,(j - 0.5)/n$] on the appropriate probability paper. If the hypothesized distribution adequately describes the data, the plotted points will fall approximately along a straight line; if the plotted points deviate significantly and systematically from a straight line, the hypothesized model is not appropriate. Usually, the determination of whether or not the data plot as a straight line is subjective. The procedure is illustrated in the following example.

EXAMPLE 3.13 A Normal Probability Plot

Observations on the road octane number of ten gasoline blends are as follows: 88.9, 87.0, 90.0, 88.2, 87.2, 87.4, 87.8, 89.7, 86.0, and 89.6. We hypothesize that octane number is adequately modeled by a normal distribution. Is this a reasonable assumption?

SOLUTION

To use probability plotting to investigate this hypothesis, first arrange the observations in ascending order and calculate their cumulative frequencies $(j - 0.5)/10$ as shown in the following table.

j	$x_{(j)}$	$(j-0.5)/10$
1	86.0	0.05
2	87.0	0.15
3	87.2	0.25
4	87.4	0.35
5	87.8	0.45
6	88.2	0.55
7	88.9	0.65
8	89.6	0.75
9	89.7	0.85
10	90.0	0.95

The pairs of values $x_{(j)}$ and $(j - 0.5)/10$ are now plotted on normal probability paper. This plot is shown in Fig. 3.26. Most normal probability paper plots $100(j - 0.5)/n$ on the left vertical scale (and some also plot $100[1 - (j - 0.5)/n]$ on the right vertical scale), with the variable value plotted on the horizontal scale. A straight line, chosen subjectively as a "best fit" line, has been drawn through the plotted points. In drawing the straight line, you should be influenced more by the points near the middle of the plot than by the extreme points. A good rule of thumb is to draw the line approximately between the twenty-fifth and seventy-fifth percentile points. This is how the line in Fig. 3.26 was determined. In assessing the systematic deviation of the points from the straight line, imagine a fat pencil lying along the line. If all the points are covered by this imaginary pencil, a normal distribution adequately describes the data. Because the points in Fig. 3.26 would pass the fat pencil test, we conclude that the normal distribution is an appropriate model for the road octane number data.

(continued)

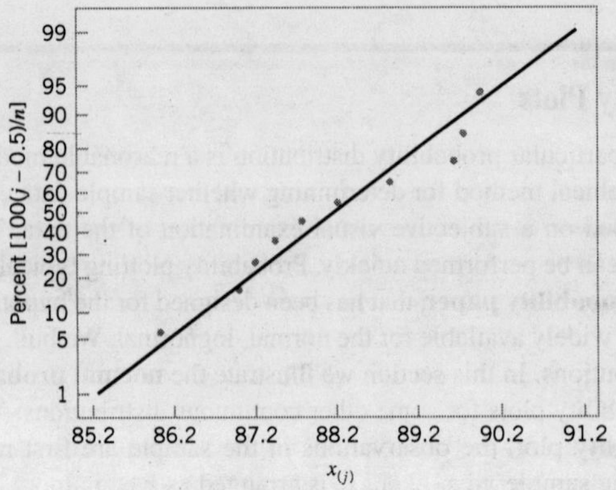

■ FIGURE 3.26 Normal probability plot of the road octane number data.

A normal probability plot can also be constructed on ordinary graph paper by plotting the standardized normal scores z_j against $x_{(j)}$, where the standardized normal scores satisfy

$$\frac{j-0.5}{n} = P\left(Z \le z_j\right) = \Phi\left(z_j\right)$$

For example, if $(j-0.5)/n = 0.05$, $\Phi(z_j) = 0.05$ implies that $z_j = -1.64$. To illustrate, consider the data from the previous example. In the following table we show the standardized normal scores in the last column.

Figure 3.27 presents the plot of z_j versus $x_{(j)}$. This normal probability plot is equivalent to the one in Fig. 3.26. We can obtain an estimate of the mean and standard deviation directly from a normal probability plot. The mean is estimated as the fiftieth percentile. From Fig. 3.25, we would estimate the mean road octane number as 88.2. The standard deviation is proportional to the slope of the straight line on the plot, and one standard deviation is the difference between the eighty-fourth and fiftieth percentiles. In Fig. 3.26, the eighty-fourth percentile is about 90, and the estimate of the standard deviation is $90 - 88.2 = 1.8$.

A very important application of normal probability plotting is in **verification of assumptions** when using statistical inference procedures that require the normality assumption. This will be illustrated subsequently.

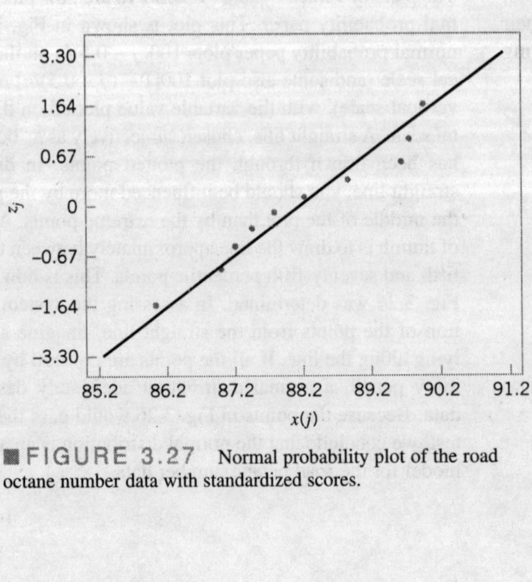

■ FIGURE 3.27 Normal probability plot of the road octane number data with standardized scores.

j	$x_{(j)}$	$(j-0.5)/10$	z_j
1	86.0	0.05	−1.64
2	87.0	0.15	−1.04
3	87.2	0.25	−0.67
4	87.4	0.35	−0.39
5	87.8	0.45	−0.13
6	88.2	0.55	0.13
7	88.9	0.65	0.39
8	89.6	0.75	0.67
9	89.7	0.85	1.04
10	90.0	0.95	1.64

■ **TABLE 3.5**
Aluminum Contamination (ppm)

30	30	60	63	70	79	87
90	101	102	115	118	119	119
120	125	140	145	172	182	
183	191	222	244	291	511	

From "The Lognormal Distribution for Modeling Quality Data When the Mean Is Near Zero," *Journal of Quality Technology*, 1990, pp. 105–110.

3.4.2 Other Probability Plots

Probability plots are extremely useful and are often the first technique used when we need to determine which probability distribution is likely to provide a reasonable model for data. In using probability plots, usually the distribution is chosen by subjective assessment of the probability plot. More formal statistical **goodness-of-fit** tests can also be used in conjunction with probability plotting.

To illustrate how probability plotting can be useful in determining the appropriate distribution for data, consider the data on aluminum contamination (ppm) in plastic shown in Table 3.5. Figure 3.28 presents several probability plots of this data, constructed using Minitab. Figure 3.28*a* is a normal probability plot. Notice how the data in the tails of the plot

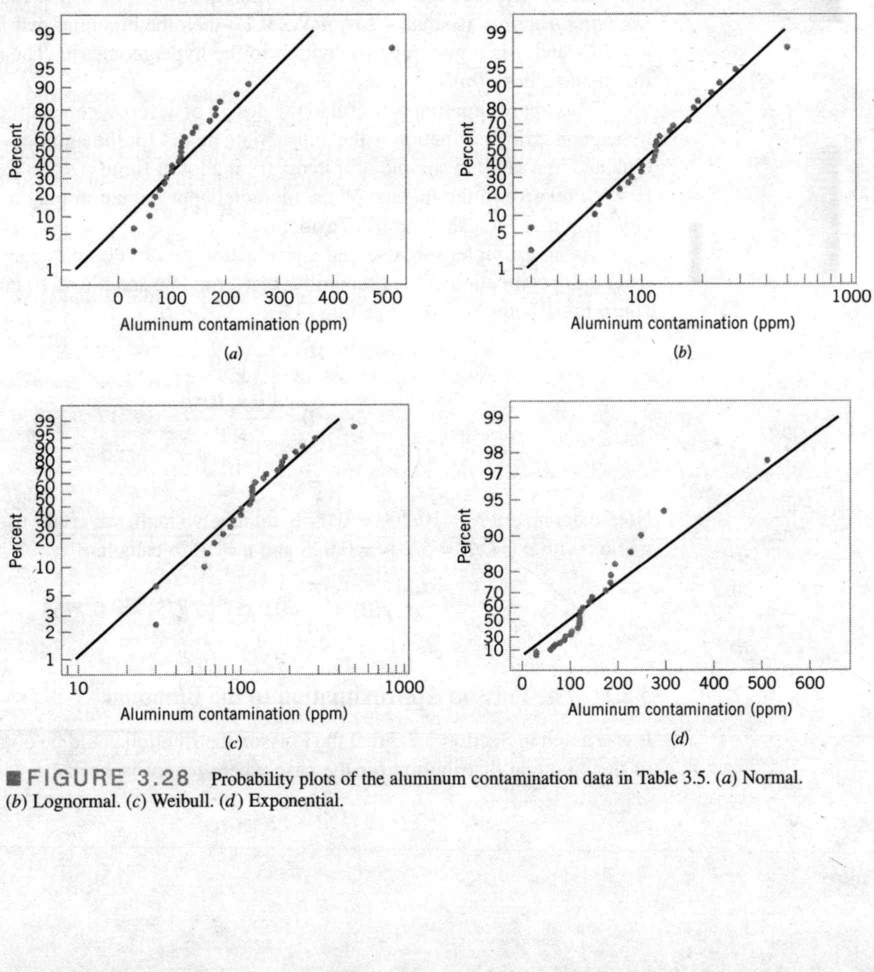

■ **FIGURE 3.28** Probability plots of the aluminum contamination data in Table 3.5. (*a*) Normal. (*b*) Lognormal. (*c*) Weibull. (*d*) Exponential.

bend away from the straight line; this is an indication that the normal distribution is not a good model for the data. Figure 3.28*b* is a lognormal probability plot of the data. The data fall much closer to the straight line in this plot, particularly the observations in the tails, suggesting that the lognormal distribution is more likely to provide a reasonable model for the data than is the normal distribution.

Finally, Fig. 3.28*c* and 3.28*d* are Weibull and exponential probability plots for the data. The observations in these plots are not very close to the straight line, suggesting that neither the Weibull nor the exponential is a very good model for the data. Therefore, based on the four probability plots that we have constructed, the lognormal distribution appears to be the most appropriate choice as a model for the aluminum contamination data.

3.5 Some Useful Approximations

In certain quality control problems, it is sometimes useful to approximate one probability distribution with another. This is particularly helpful in situations where the original distribution is difficult to manipulate analytically. In this section, we present three such approximations: (1) the binomial approximation to the hypergeometric, (2) the Poisson approximation to the binomial, and (3) the normal approximation to the binomial.

3.5.1 The Binomial Approximation to the Hypergeometric

Consider the hypergeometric distribution in equation (3.8). If the ratio n/N (often called the *sampling fraction*) is small—say, $n/N \leq 0.1$—then the binomial distribution with parameters $p = D/N$ and n is a good approximation to the hypergeometric. The approximation is better for small values of n/N.

This approximation is useful in the design of acceptance-sampling plans. Recall that the hypergeometric distribution is the appropriate model for the number of nonconforming items obtained in a random sample of n items from a lot of finite size N. Thus, if the sample size n is small relative to the lot size N, the binomial approximation may be employed, which usually simplifies the calculations considerably.

As an example, suppose that a production lot of 200 units contains 5 units that do not meet the specifications. The probability that a random sample of 10 units will contain no nonconforming items is, from equation (3.8),

$$p(0) = \frac{\binom{5}{0}\binom{195}{10}}{\binom{200}{10}} = 0.7717$$

Note that since $n/N = 10/200 = 0.05$ is relatively small, we could use the binomial approximation with $p = D/N = 5/200 = 0.025$ and $n = 10$ to calculate

$$p(0) = \binom{5}{0}(0.025)^0(0.975)^{10} = 0.7763$$

3.5.2 The Poisson Approximation to the Binomial

It was noted in Section 3.2.3 that the Poisson distribution could be obtained as a limiting form of the binomial distribution for the case where p approaches zero and n approaches infinity with $\lambda = np$ constant. This implies that, for small p and large n, the Poisson distribution with $\lambda = np$ may be used to approximate the binomial distribution. The approximation is usually good for large n and if $p < 0.1$. The larger is the value of n and the smaller is the value of p, the better is the approximation.

3.5.3 The Normal Approximation to the Binomial

In Section 3.2.2 we defined the binomial distribution as the sum of a sequence of n Bernoulli trials, each with probability of success p. If the number of trials n is large, then we may use the central limit theorem to justify the normal distribution with mean np and variance $np(1-p)$ as an approximation to the binomial. That is,

$$P\{x=a\} = \binom{n}{a} p^a (1-p)^{n-a}$$

$$= \frac{1}{\sqrt{2\pi np(1-p)}} e^{-\frac{1}{2}\left[(a-np)^2/np(1-p)\right]}$$

Since the binomial distribution is discrete and the normal distribution is continuous, it is common practice to use *continuity corrections* in the approximation, so that

$$P\{x=a\} \cong \Phi\left(\frac{a+\frac{1}{2}-np}{\sqrt{np(1-p)}}\right) - \Phi\left(\frac{a-\frac{1}{2}-np}{\sqrt{np(1-p)}}\right)$$

where Φ denotes the standard normal cumulative distribution function. Other types of probability statements are evaluated similarly, such as

$$P\{a \le x \le b\} \cong \Phi\left(\frac{b+\frac{1}{2}-np}{\sqrt{np(1-p)}}\right) - \Phi\left(\frac{a-\frac{1}{2}-np}{\sqrt{np(1-p)}}\right)$$

The normal approximation to the binomial is known to be satisfactory for p of approximately 1/2 and $n > 10$. For other values of p, larger values of n are required. In general, the approximation is not adequate for $p < 1/(n+1)$ or $p > n/(n+1)$, or for values of the random variable outside an interval six standard deviations wide centered about the mean (i.e., the interval $np \pm 3\sqrt{(np(1-p))}$.

We may also use the normal approximation for the random variable $\hat{p} = x/n$—that is, the sample fraction defective of Section 3.2.2. The random variable $\hat{p}$ is approximately normally distributed with mean p and variance $p(1-p)/n$, so that

$$P\{u \le \hat{p} \le v\} \cong \Phi\left(\frac{v-p}{\sqrt{p(1-p)/n}}\right) - \Phi\left(\frac{u-p}{\sqrt{p(1-p)/n}}\right)$$

Since the normal will serve as an approximation to the binomial, and since the binomial and Poisson distributions are closely connected, it seems logical that the normal may serve to approximate the Poisson. This is indeed the case, and if the mean λ of the Poisson distribution is large (say, at least 15), then the normal distribution with $\mu = \lambda$ and $\sigma^2 = \lambda$ is a satisfactory approximation.

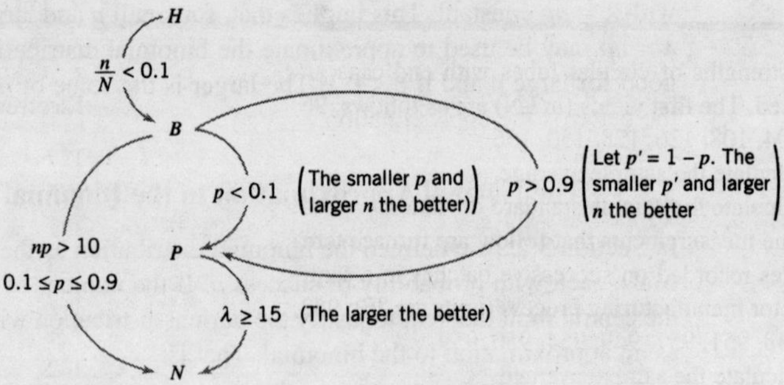

■ FIGURE 3.29 Approximations to probability distributions.

3.5.4 Comments on Approximations

A summary of the approximations discussed above is presented in Fig. 3.29. In this figure, H, B, P, and N represent the hypergeometric, binomial, Poisson, and normal distributions, respectively. The widespread availability of modern microcomputers, good statistics software packages, and hand-held calculators has made reliance on these approximations largely unnecessary, but there are situations in which they are useful, particularly in the application of the popular three-sigma limit control charts.

Important Terms and Concepts

Approximations to probability distributions
Binomial distribution
Box plot
Central limit theorem
Continuous distribution
Control limit theorem
Descriptive statistics
Discrete distribution
Exponential distribution
Gamma distribution
Geometric distribution
Histogram
Hypergeometric probability distribution
Interquartile range
Lognormal distribution
Mean of a distribution
Median
Negative binomial distribution
Normal distribution
Normal probability plot
Pascal distribution
Percentile
Poisson distribution
Population
Probability distribution
Probability plotting
Quartile
Random variable
Run chart
Sample
Sample average
Sample standard deviation
Sample variance
Standard deviation
Standard normal distribution
Statistics
Stem-and-leaf display
Time series plot
Uniform distribution
Variance of a distribution
Weibull distribution

Exercises

3.1. Yield strengths of circular tubes with end caps are measured. The first yields (in kN) are as follows: 96, 102, 104, 108, 126, 128, 150, 156
(a) Calculate the sample average.
(b) Calculate the sample standard deviation.

3.2. The nine measurements that follow are furnace temperatures recorded on successive batches in a semiconductor manufacturing process (units are °F): 953, 955, 948, 951, 957, 949, 954, 950, 959
(a) Calculate the sample average.
(b) Calculate the sample standard deviation.

3.3. Consider the furnace temperature data in Exercise 3.2.
(a) Find the sample median of these data.
(b) How much could the largest temperature measurement increase without changing the sample median?

3.4. The content of liquid detergent bottles is being analyzed. Twelve bottles, randomly selected from the process, are measured, and the results are as follows (in fluid ounces): 16.05, 16.03, 16.02, 16.04, 16.05, 16.01, 16.02, 16.02, 16.03, 16.01, 16.00, 16.07
(a) Calculate the sample average.
(b) Calculate the sample standard deviation.

3.5. The data shown in Table 3E.1 are chemical process yield readings on successive days (read down, then across). Construct a histogram for these data. Comment on the shape of the histogram. Does it resemble any of the distributions that we have discussed in this chapter?

■ **TABLE 3E.1**
Process Yield

94.1	87.3	94.1	92.4	84.6	85.4
93.2	84.1	92.1	90.6	83.6	86.6
90.6	90.1	96.4	89.1	85.4	91.7
91.4	95.2	88.2	88.8	89.7	87.5
88.2	86.1	86.4	86.4	87.6	84.2
86.1	94.3	85.0	85.1	85.1	85.1
95.1	93.2	84.9	84.0	89.6	90.5
90.0	86.7	87.3	93.7	90.0	95.6
92.4	83.0	89.6	87.7	90.1	88.3
87.3	95.3	90.3	90.6	94.3	84.1
86.6	94.1	93.1	89.4	97.3	83.7
91.2	97.8	94.6	88.6	96.8	82.9
86.1	93.1	96.3	84.1	94.4	87.3
90.4	86.4	94.7	82.6	96.1	86.4
89.1	87.6	91.1	83.1	98.0	84.5

■ **TABLE 3E.2**
Electronic Component Failure Time

127	124	121	118
125	123	136	131
131	120	140	125
124	119	137	133
129	128	125	141
121	133	124	125
142	137	128	140
151	124	129	131
160	142	130	129
125	123	122	126

3.6. Consider the chemical process yield data in Exercise 3.5. Calculate the sample average and standard deviation.

3.7. Consider the chemical process yield data in Exercise 3.5. Construct a stem-and-leaf plot for the data and compare it with the histogram from Exercise 3.5. Which display provides more information about the process?

3.8. The time to failure in hours of an electronic component subjected to an accelerated life test is shown in Table 3E.2. To accelerate the failure test, the units were tested at an elevated temperature (read down, then across).
(a) Calculate the sample average and standard deviation.
(b) Construct a histogram.
(c) Construct a stem-and-leaf plot.
(d) Find the sample median and the lower and upper quartiles.

3.9. An article in *Quality Engineering* (Vol. 4, 1992, pp. 487–495) presents viscosity data from a batch chemical process. A sample of these data is presented in Table 3E.3 on the next page (read down, then across).
(a) Construct a stem-and-leaf display for the viscosity data.
(b) Construct a frequency distribution and histogram.
(c) Convert the stem-and-leaf plot in part (a) into an ordered stem-and-leaf plot. Use this graph to assist in locating the median and the upper and lower quartiles of the viscosity data.
(d) What are the ninetieth and tenth percentiles of viscosity?

■ TABLE 3E.3
Viscosity

13.3	14.9	15.8	16.0
14.5	13.7	13.7	14.9
15.3	15.2	15.1	13.6
15.3	14.5	13.4	15.3
14.3	15.3	14.1	14.3
14.8	15.6	14.8	15.6
15.2	15.8	14.3	16.1
14.5	13.3	14.3	13.9
14.6	14.1	16.4	15.2
14.1	15.4	16.9	14.4
14.3	15.2	14.2	14.0
16.1	15.2	16.9	14.4
13.1	15.9	14.9	13.7
15.5	16.5	15.2	13.8
12.6	14.8	14.4	15.6
14.6	15.1	15.2	14.5
14.3	17.0	14.6	12.8
15.4	14.9	16.4	16.1
15.2	14.8	14.2	16.6
16.8	14.0	15.7	15.6

3.10. Construct and interpret a normal probability plot of the volumes of the liquid detergent bottles in Exercise 3.4.

3.11. Construct a normal probability plot of the chemical process yield data in Exercise 3.5. Does the assumption that process yield is well modeled by a normal distribution seem reasonable?

3.12. Construct a normal probability plot of the failure time data in Exercise 3.8. Does the assumption that failure time for this component is well modeled by a normal distribution seem reasonable?

3.13. Consider the viscosity data in Exercise 3.9. Construct a normal probability plot, a lognormal probability plot, and a Weibull probability plot for these data. Based on the plots, which distribution seems to be the best model for the viscosity data?

3.14. An important quality characteristic of water is the concentration of suspended solid material (in ppm). Table 3E.4 contains 40 measurements on suspended solids for a certain lake. Construct a normal probability plot, a lognormal probability plot, and a Weibull probability plot for these data. Based on the plots, which distribution seems to be the best model for the concentration of suspended solids?

3.15. Consider the concentration of suspended solids from Exercise 3.14. Assume that reading across then down gives the data in time order. Construct and interpret a time-series plot.

■ TABLE 3E.4
Concentration of Suspended Solids (ppm)

0.78	9.59	2.26	8.13	3.16
4.33	11.70	0.22	125.93	1.30
0.15	0.20	0.29	13.72	0.96
0.29	2.93	3.65	3.47	1.73
14.21	1.79	0.54	14.81	0.68
0.09	5.81	5.17	21.01	0.41
4.75	2.82	1.30	4.57	74.74
0.78	1.94	3.52	20.10	4.98

■ TABLE 3E.5
Cycles to Failure of Test Coupons

8078	1891	13912	3407	6168
15504	1893	12551	6861	1334
9438	6227	2562	2074	6770
7971	17081	9245	19041	21997

3.16. Table 3E.5 contains 20 observations on cycles to failure of aluminum test coupons subjected to repeated alternating stress of 15,000 psi at 20 cycles per second. Construct a normal probability plot, a lognormal probability plot, and a Weibull probability plot for these data. Based on the plots, which distribution seems to be the best model for the cycles to failure for this material?

3.17. Reconsider the yield data in Exercise 3.5. Construct a time-series plot for these data. Interpret the plot.

3.18. Consider the viscosity data in Exercise 3.9. Assume that reading down then across gives the data in time order. Construct and interpret a time-series plot.

3.19. Construct a box plot for the data in Exercise 3.4.

3.20. The probability distribution of the discrete random variable x is $p(x) = kr^x$, $0 < r < 1$. Find the appropriate value for k if $x = 0, 1, \ldots$.

3.21. The probability distribution of x is $f(x) = ke^{-x}$, $0 \le x \le \infty$. Find the appropriate value of k. Find the mean and variance of x.

3.22. Suppose that two fair dice are tossed and the random variable observed—say, x—is the sum of the two up faces. Describe the sample space of this experiment, and determine the probability distribution of x.

3.23. Find the mean and variance of the random variable in Exercise 3.22.

3.24. A manufacturer of electronic calculators offers a one-year warranty. If the calculator fails for any reason during this period, it is replaced. The time to failure is well modeled by the following probability distribution:

$$f(x) = 0.125e^{-0.125x} \quad x > 0$$

(a) What percentage of the calculators will fail within the warranty period?
(b) The manufacturing cost of a calculator is \$50, and the profit per sale is \$25. What is the effect of warranty replacement on profit?

3.25. The random variable x takes on the values 1, 2, or 3 with probabilities $(1 + 3k)/3$, $(1 + 2k)/3$, and $(0.5 + 5k)/3$, respectively.
(a) Find the appropriate value of k.
(b) Find the mean and variance of x.
(c) Find the cumulative distribution function.

3.26. A mechatronic assembly is subjected to a final functional test. Suppose that defects occur at random in these assemblies, and that defects occur according to a Poisson distribution with parameter $\lambda = 0.02$.
(a) What is the probability that an assembly will have exactly one defect?
(b) What is the probability that an assembly will have one or more defects?
(c) Suppose that you improve the process so that the occurrence rate of defects is cut in half to $\lambda = 0.01$. What effect does this have on the probability that an assembly will have one or more defects?

3.27. A production process operates with 1% nonconforming output. Every hour a sample of 25 units of product is taken, and the number of nonconforming units counted. If one or more nonconforming units are found, the process is stopped and the quality control technician must search for the cause of nonconforming production. Evaluate the performance of this decision rule.

3.28. **Continuation of Exercise 3.27.** Consider the decision rule described in Exercise 3.27. Suppose that the process suddenly deteriorates to 4% nonconforming output. How many samples, on average, will be required to detect this?

3.29. A sample of 100 units is selected from a production process that is 1% nonconforming. What is the probability that $\hat{p}$ will exceed the true fraction nonconforming by k standard deviations, where $k = 1, 2$, and 3?

3.30. A random sample of 50 units is drawn from a production process every half hour. The fraction of nonconforming product manufactured is 0.02. What is the probability that $\hat{p} \leq 0.04$ if the fraction nonconforming really is 0.02?

3.31. A lot of size $N = 30$ contains three nonconforming units. What is the probability that a sample of five units selected at random contains exactly one nonconforming unit? What is the probability that it contains one or more nonconformances?

3.32. An electronic component for a medical X-ray unit is produced in lots of size $N = 25$. An acceptance testing procedure is used by the purchaser to protect against lots that contain too many nonconforming components. The procedure consists of selecting five components at random from the lot (without replacement) and testing them. If none of the components is nonconforming, the lot is accepted.
(a) If the lot contains two nonconforming components, what is the probability of lot acceptance?
(b) Calculate the desired probability in (a) using the binomial approximation. Is this approximation satisfactory? Why or why not?
(c) Suppose the lot size was $N = 150$. Would the binomial approximation be satisfactory in this case?
(d) Suppose that the purchaser will reject the lot with the decision rule of finding one or more nonconforming components in a sample of size n, and wants the lot to be rejected with probability at least 0.95 if the lot contains five or more nonconforming components. How large should the sample size n be?

3.33. The billing department of a major credit card company attempts to control errors (clerical, data transmission, etc.) on customers' bills. Suppose that errors occur according to a Poisson distribution with parameter $\lambda = 0.01$. What is the probability that a customer's bill selected at random will contain one error?

3.34. Glass bottles are formed by pouring molten glass into a mold. The molten glass is prepared in a furnace lined with firebrick. As the firebrick wears, small pieces of brick are mixed into the molten glass and finally appear as defects (called "stones") in the bottle. If we can assume that stones occur randomly at the rate of 0.00001 per bottle, what is the probability that a bottle selected at random will contain at least one such defect?

3.35. Surface-finish defects in a small electric appliance occur at random with a mean rate of 0.1 defects per unit. Find the probability that a randomly selected unit will contain at least one surface-finish defect.

3.36. A production process operates in one of two states: the in-control state, in which most of the units produced conform to specifications, and an out-of-control state, in which most of the units produced are defective. The process will shift from the in-control to the out-of-control state at random. Every hour, a quality control technician checks the process, and if it is in the out-of-control state, the technician detects this with probability p. Assume that when the process shifts out of control it does so immediately following a check by the inspector, and once a shift has occurred, the process cannot automatically correct itself. If t denotes the number of periods the process remains out of control following a shift before detection, find the probability distribution of t. Find the mean number of periods the process will remain in the out-of-control state.

3.37. The life of an automotive battery is normally distributed with mean 900 days and standard deviation 35 days. What fraction of these batteries would be expected to survive beyond 1,000 days?

3.38. If x is normally distributed with mean μ and standard deviation four, and given that the probability that x is less than 32 is 0.0228, find the value of μ.

3.39. The tensile strength of a metal part is normally distributed with mean 40 lb and standard deviation 5 lb. If 50,000 parts are produced, how many would you expect to fail to meet a minimum specification limit of 35 lb tensile strength? How many would have a tensile strength in excess of 48 lb?

3.40. The output voltage of a power supply is normally distributed with mean 5 V and standard deviation 0.02 V. If the lower and upper specifications for voltage are 4.95 V and 5.05 V, respectively, what is the probability that a power supply selected at random will conform to the specifications on voltage?

3.41. **Continuation of Exercise 3.40.** Reconsider the power supply manufacturing process in Exercise 3-40. Suppose we wanted to improve the process. Can shifting the mean reduce the number of nonconforming units produced? How much would the process variability need to be reduced in order to have all but one out of 1000 units conform to the specifications?

3.42. A lightbulb has a normally distributed light output with mean 5,000 end foot-candles and standard deviation of 50 end foot-candles. Find a lower specification limit such that only 0.5% of the bulbs will not exceed this limit.

3.43. A quality characteristic of a product is normally distributed with mean μ and standard deviation one. Specifications on the characteristic are $6 \le x \le 8$. A unit that falls within specifications on this quality characteristic results in a profit of C_0. However, if $x < 6$, the profit is $-C_1$, whereas if $x > 8$, the profit is $-C_2$. Find the value of μ that maximizes the expected profit.

3.44. The specifications on an electronic component in a target-acquisition system are that its life must be between 5,000 and 10,000 h. The life is normally distributed with mean 7,500 h. The manufacturer realizes a price of $10 per unit produced; however, defective units must be replaced at a cost of $5 to the manufacturer. Two different manufacturing processes can be used, both of which have the same mean life. However, the standard deviation of life for process 1 is 1000 h, whereas for process 2 it is only 500 h. Production costs for process 2 are twice those for process 1. What value of production costs will determine the selection between processes 1 and 2?

3.45. Derive the mean and variance of the Poisson distribution.

3.46. Derive the mean and variance of the exponential distribution.

3.47. Derive the mean and variance of the binomial distribution.

4 Statistical Inference in Quality Control and Improvement

CHAPTER OUTLINE

The supplemental material is on the textbook website www.wiley.com/college/montgomery.

Chapter Overview and Learning Objectives

In the previous chapter we discussed the use of probability distributions in modeling or describing the output of a process. In all the examples presented, we assumed that the parameters of the probability distribution, and, hence, the parameters of the process, were known. This is usually a very unrealistic assumption. For example, in using the binomial distribution to model the number of nonconforming units found in sampling from a production process we assumed that the parameter p of the binomial distribution was known. The physical interpretation of p is that it is the true fraction of nonconforming units produced by the process. It is impossible to know this exactly in a real production process. Furthermore, if we did know the true value of p and it was relatively constant over time, we could argue that formal process monitoring and control procedures were unnecessary, provided p was "acceptably" small.

In general, the parameters of a process are unknown; furthermore, they can usually change over time. Therefore, we need to develop procedures to estimate the parameters of probability distributions and solve other inference or decision-oriented problems relative to them. The standard statistical techniques of parameter estimation and hypothesis testing are useful in this respect. These techniques are the underlying basis for much of the methodology of statistical quality control. In this chapter, we present some of the elementary results of statistical inference, indicating its usefulness in quality improvement problems. Key topics include point and confidence interval estimation of means, variances, and binomial parameters, hypothesis testing on means, variances, and binomial parameters, and the use of normal probability plots.

After careful study of this chapter you should be able to do the following:

1. Explain the concept of random sampling
2. Explain the concept of a sampling distribution
3. Explain the general concept of estimating the parameters of a population or probability distribution
4. Know how to explain the precision with which a parameter is estimated
5. Construct and interpret confidence intervals on a single mean and on the difference in two means
6. Construct and interpret confidence intervals on a single variance or the ratio of two variances
7. Construct and interpret confidence intervals on a single proportion and on the difference in two proportions
8. Test hypotheses on a single mean and on the difference in two means
9. Test hypotheses on a single variance and on the ratio of two variances
10. Test hypotheses on a single proportion and on the difference in two proportions
11. Use the P-value approach for hypothesis testing
12. Understand how the analysis of variance (ANOVA) is used to test hypotheses about the equality of more than two means
13. Understand how to fit and interpret linear regression models

4.1 Statistics and Sampling Distributions

The objective of statistical inference is to draw conclusions or make decisions about a population based on a sample selected from the population. Frequently, we will assume that *random samples* are used in the analysis. The word "random" is often applied to any method or sample selection that lacks systematic direction. We will define a sample—say, $x_1, x_2, \ldots, x_n$—as

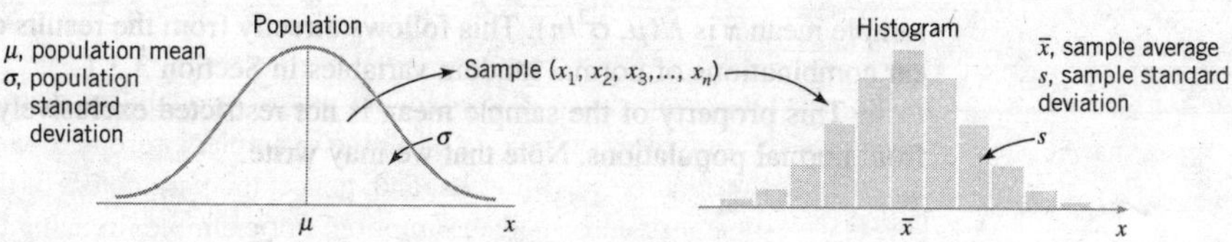

■ FIGURE 4.1 Relationship between a population and a sample.

a **random sample** of size n if it is selected so that the observations $\{x_i\}$ are independently and identically distributed. This definition is suitable for random samples drawn from infinite populations or from finite populations where sampling is performed with *replacement.* In sampling *without replacement* from a finite population of N items we say that a sample of n items is a random sample if each of the $\binom{N}{n}$ possible samples has an equal probability of being chosen. Figure 4.1 illustrates the relationship between the population and the sample.

Although most of the methods we will study assume that random sampling has been used, there are several other sampling strategies that are occasionally useful in quality control. Care must be exercised to use a method of analysis that is consistent with the sampling design; inference techniques intended for random samples can lead to serious errors when applied to data obtained from other sampling techniques.

Statistical inference uses quantities computed from the observations in the sample. A **statistic** is defined as any function of the sample data that does not contain unknown parameters. For example, let $x_1, x_2, \ldots, x_n$ represent the observations in a sample. Then the sample mean

$$\bar{x} = \frac{\sum_{i=1}^{n} x_i}{n} \tag{4.1}$$

the sample variance

$$s^2 = \frac{\sum_{i=1}^{n} (x_i - \bar{x})^2}{n-1} \tag{4.2}$$

and the sample standard deviation

$$s = \sqrt{\frac{\sum_{i=1}^{n} (x_i - \bar{x})^2}{n-1}} \tag{4.3}$$

are statistics. The statistics $\bar{x}$ and s (or s^2) describe the central tendency and variability, respectively, of the sample.

If we know the probability distribution of the population from which the sample was taken, we can often determine the probability distribution of various statistics computed from the sample data. The probability distribution of a statistic is called a **sampling distribution.** We now present the sampling distributions associated with three common sampling situations.

4.1.1 Sampling from a Normal Distribution

Suppose that x is a normally distributed random variable with mean μ and variance σ^2. If $x_1, x_2, \ldots, x_n$ is a random sample of size n from this process, then the distribution of the sample mean $\bar{x}$ is $N(\mu, \sigma^2/n)$. This follows directly from the results on the distribution of linear combinations of normal random variables in Section 3.3.1.

This property of the sample mean is not restricted exclusively to the case of sampling from normal populations. Note that we may write

$$\left(\frac{\bar{x}-\mu}{\sigma}\right)\sqrt{n} = \frac{\sum_{i=1}^{n} x_i - n\mu}{\sigma\sqrt{n}}$$

From the central limit theorem we know that, regardless of the distribution of the population, the distribution of $\Sigma_{i=1}^{n} x_i$ is approximately normal with mean $n\mu$ and variance $n\sigma^2$. Therefore, regardless of the distribution of the population, the sampling distribution of the sample mean is approximately

$$\bar{x} \sim N\left(\mu, \frac{\sigma^2}{n}\right)$$

An important sampling distribution defined in terms of the normal distribution is the **chi-square** or **χ^2 distribution.** If $x_1, x_2, \ldots, x_n$ are normally and independently distributed random variables with mean zero and variance one, then the random variable

$$y = x_1^2 + x_2^2 + \cdots + x_n^2$$

is distributed as chi-square with n degrees of freedom. The chi-square probability distribution with n degrees of freedom is

$$f(y) = \frac{1}{2^{n/2}\Gamma\left(\frac{n}{2}\right)} y^{(n/2)-1} e^{-y/2} \qquad y > 0 \tag{4.4}$$

Several chi-square distributions are shown in Fig. 4.2. The distribution is skewed with mean $\mu = n$ and variance $\sigma^2 = 2n$. A table of the percentage points of the chi-square distribution is given in Appendix Table III.

To illustrate the use of the chi-square distribution, suppose that $x_1, x_2, \ldots, x_n$ is a random sample from an $N(\mu, \sigma^2)$ distribution. Then the random variable

$$y = \frac{\sum_{i=1}^{n} (x_1 - \bar{x})^2}{\sigma^2} \tag{4.5}$$

has a chi-square distribution with $n - 1$ degrees of freedom. However, using equation (4.2), which defines the sample variance, we may rewrite equation 4.5 as

$$y = \frac{(n-1)s^2}{\sigma^2}$$

That is, the sampling distribution of $(n-1)s^2/\sigma^2$ is χ^2_{n-1} when sampling from a normal distribution.

Another useful sampling distribution is the ***t* distribution.** If x is a standard normal random variable and if y is a chi-square random variable with k degrees of freedom, and if x and y are independent, then the random variable

$$t = \frac{x}{\sqrt{y/k}} \tag{4.6}$$

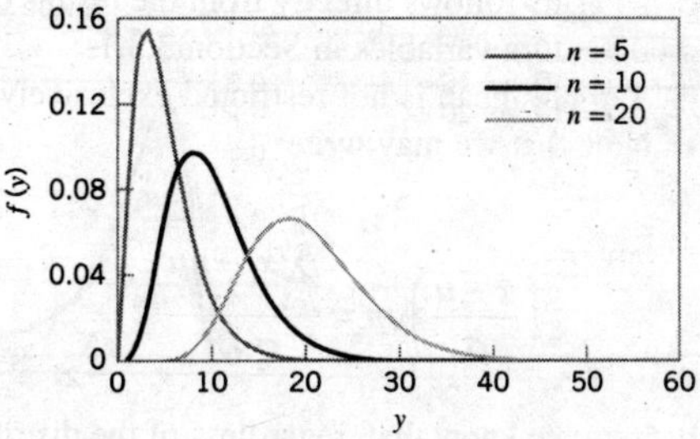

FIGURE 4.2 Chi-square distribution for selected values of n (number of degrees of freedom).

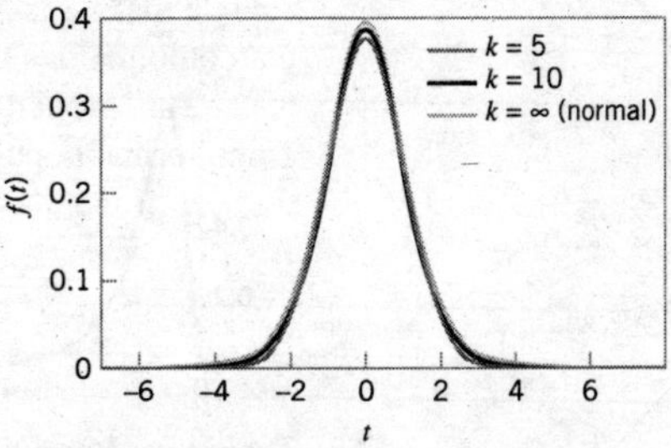

FIGURE 4.3 The t distribution for selected values of k (number of degrees of freedom).

is distributed as t with k degrees of freedom. The probability distribution of t is

$$f(t) = \frac{\Gamma[(k+1)/2]}{\sqrt{k\pi}\,\Gamma(k/2)}\left(\frac{t^2}{k}+1\right)^{-(k+1)/2} \qquad -\infty < t < \infty \tag{4.7}$$

and the mean and variance of t are $\mu = 0$ and $\sigma^2 = k/(k-2)$ for $k > 2$, respectively. The degrees of freedom for t are the degrees of freedom associated with the chi-square random variable in the denominator of equation (4.6). Several t distributions are shown in Fig. 4.3. Note that if $k = \infty$, the t distribution reduces to the standard normal distribution. A table of percentage points of the t distribution is given in Appendix Table IV.

As an example of a random variable that is distributed as t, suppose that $x_1, x_2, \ldots, x_n$ is a random sample from the $N(\mu, \sigma^2)$ distribution. If $\bar{x}$ and s^2 are computed from this sample, then

$$\frac{\bar{x}-\mu}{s/\sqrt{n}} = \frac{\dfrac{\bar{x}-\mu}{\sigma/\sqrt{n}}}{s/\sigma} \sim \frac{N(0,1)}{\sqrt{\chi^2_{n-1}/(n-1)}}$$

using the fact that $(n-1)s^2/\sigma^2 \sim \chi^2_{n-1}$. Now, $\bar{x}$ and s^2 are independent, so the random variable

$$\frac{\bar{x}-\mu}{s/\sqrt{n}} \tag{4.8}$$

has a t distribution with $n-1$ degrees of freedom.

The last sampling distribution based on the normal process that we will consider is the ***F* distribution.** If w and y are two independent chi-square random variables with u and v degrees of freedom, respectively, then the ratio

$$F_{u,v} = \frac{w/u}{y/v} \tag{4.9}$$

is distributed as F with u numerator degrees of freedom and v denominator degrees of freedom. If x is an F random variable with u numerator and v denominator degrees of freedom, then the distribution is

$$f(x) = \frac{\Gamma\left(\dfrac{u+v}{2}\right)\left(\dfrac{u}{v}\right)^{u/2}}{\Gamma\left(\dfrac{u}{2}\right)\Gamma\left(\dfrac{v}{2}\right)} \frac{x^{(u/2)-1}}{\left[\left(\dfrac{u}{v}\right)x+1\right]^{(u+v)/2}} \qquad 0 < x < \infty \tag{4.10}$$

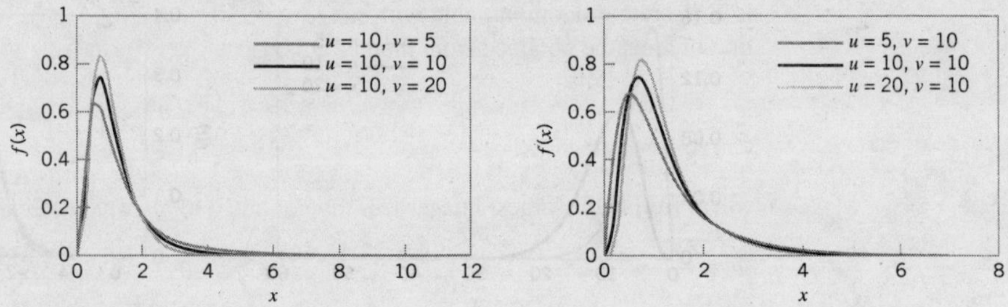

■ FIGURE 4.4 The F distribution for selected values of u (numerator degrees of freedom) and v (denominator degrees of freedom).

Several F distributions are shown in Fig. 4.4. A table of percentage points of the F distribution is given in Appendix Table V.

As an example of a random variable that is distributed as F, suppose we have two independent normal processes—say, $x_1 \sim N(\mu_1, \sigma_1^2)$, and $x_2 \sim N(\mu_2, \sigma_2^2)$. Let $x_{11}, x_{12}, \ldots, x_{1n_1}$ be a random sample of n_1 observations from the first normal process and $x_{21}, x_{22}, \ldots, x_{2n_2}$ be a random sample of size n_2 from the second. If s_1^2 and s_2^2 are the sample variances, then the ratio

$$\frac{s_1^2/\sigma_1^2}{s_2^2/\sigma_2^2} \sim F_{n_1-1,\, n_2-1}$$

This follows directly from the sampling distribution of s^2 discussed previously. The F distribution will be used in making inferences about the variances of two normal distributions.

4.1.2 Sampling from a Bernoulli Distribution

In this section, we discuss the sampling distributions of statistics associated with the Bernoulli distribution. The random variable x with probability function

$$p(x) = \begin{cases} p & x = 1 \\ (1-p) = q & x = 0 \end{cases}$$

is called a **Bernoulli random variable.** That is, x takes on the value 1 with probability p and the value 0 with probability $1 - p = q$. A realization of this random variable is often called a **Bernoulli trial.** The sequence of Bernoulli trials $x_1, x_2, \ldots,$ is a Bernoulli process. The outcome $x = 1$ is often called "success," and the outcome $x = 0$ is often called "failure."

Suppose that a random sample of n observations—say, $x_1, x_2, \ldots, x_n$—is taken from a Bernoulli process with constant probability of success p. Then the sum of the sample observations

$$x = x_1 + x_2 + \cdots + x_n \tag{4.11}$$

has a binomial distribution with parameters n and p. Furthermore, since each x_i is either 0 or 1, the sample mean

$$\bar{x} = \frac{1}{n}\sum_{i=1}^{n} x_i \tag{4.12}$$

is a discrete random variable with range space $\{0, 1/n, 2/n, \ldots, (n-1)/n, 1\}$. The distribution of $\bar{x}$ can be obtained from the binomial since

$$P\{\bar{x} \le a\} = P\{x \le an\} = \sum_{k=0}^{[an]} \binom{n}{k} p^k (1-p)^{n-k}$$

where $[an]$ is the largest integer less than or equal to an. The mean and variance of $\bar{x}$ are

$$\mu_{\bar{x}} = p$$

and

$$\sigma_{\bar{x}}^2 = \frac{p(1-p)}{n}$$

respectively. This same result was given previously in Section 3.2.2, where the random variable $\hat{p}$ (often called the sample fraction nonconforming) was introduced.

4.1.3 Sampling from a Poisson Distribution

The Poisson distribution was introduced in Section 3.2.3. Consider a random sample of size n from a Poisson distribution with parameter λ—say, $x_1, x_2, \ldots, x_n$. The distribution of the sample sum

$$x = x_1 + x_2 + \cdots + x_n \tag{4.13}$$

is also Poisson with parameter $n\lambda$. More generally, the sum of n independent Poisson random variables is distributed Poisson with parameter equal to the sum of the individual Poisson parameters.

Now consider the distribution of the sample mean

$$\bar{x} = \frac{1}{n}\sum_{i=1}^{n} x_i \tag{4.14}$$

This is a discrete random variable that takes on the values $\{0, 1/n, 2/n, \ldots\}$, and with probability distribution found from

$$P\{\bar{x} \le a\} = P\{x \le an\} = \sum_{k=0}^{[an]} \frac{e^{-n\lambda}(n\lambda)^k}{k!} \tag{4.15}$$

where $[an]$ is the largest integer less than or equal to an. The mean and variance of $\bar{x}$ are

$$\mu_{\bar{x}} = \lambda$$

and

$$\sigma_{\bar{x}}^2 = \frac{\lambda}{n}$$

respectively.

Sometimes more general linear combinations of Poisson random variables are used in quality-engineering work. For example, consider the linear combination

$$L = a_1 x_1 + a_2 x_2 + \cdots + a_m x_m = \sum_{i=1}^{m} a_i x_i \tag{4.16}$$

where the $\{x_i\}$ are independent Poisson random variables each having parameter $\{\lambda_i\}$ respectively, and the $\{a_i\}$ are constants. This type of function occurs in situations where a unit of product can have m different types of defects or nonconformities (each modeled with a Poisson distribution with parameter λ_i) and the function used for quality monitoring purposes is a linear combination of the number of observed nonconformities of each type. The constants $\{a_i\}$ in equation (4.16) might be chosen to weight some types of nonconformities more heavily than others. For example, functional defects on a unit would receive heavier weight than appearance flaws. These schemes are sometimes called **demerit** procedures (see Section 7.3.3). In general, the distribution of L is not Poisson unless all $a_i = 1$ in equation (4.16); that is, sums of independent Poisson random variables are Poisson distributed, but more general linear combinations are not.

4.2 Point Estimation of Process Parameters

A random variable is characterized or described by its probability distribution. This distribution is described by its **parameters.** For example, the mean μ and variance σ^2 of the normal distribution (equation 3.21) are its parameters, whereas λ is the parameter of the Poisson distribution (equation 3.15). In statistical quality control, the probability distribution is used to describe or model some quality characteristic, such as a critical dimension of a product or the fraction defective of the manufacturing process. Therefore, we are interested in making inferences about the parameters of probability distributions. Since the parameters are generally unknown, we require procedures to estimate them from sample data.

We may define an estimator of an unknown parameter as a statistic that corresponds to the parameter. A particular numerical value of an estimator, computed from sample data, is called an **estimate.** A **point estimator** is a statistic that produces a single numerical value as the estimate of the unknown parameter. To illustrate, consider the random variable x with probability distribution $f(x)$ shown in Fig. 4.1 on p. 105. Suppose that the mean μ and variance σ^2 of this distribution are both unknown. If a random sample of n observations is taken, then the **sample mean** $\bar{x}$ and **sample variance** s^2 are point estimators of the **population mean** μ and **population variance** σ^2, respectively. Suppose that this distribution represents a process producing bearings and the random variable x is the inside diameter. We want to obtain point estimates of the mean and variance of the inside diameter of bearings produced by this process. We could measure the inside diameters of a random sample of $n = 20$ bearings (say). Then the sample mean and sample variance could be computed. If this yields $\bar{x} = 1.495$ and $s^2 = 0.001$, then the point estimate of μ is $\hat{\mu} = \bar{x} = 1.495$ and the point estimate of σ^2 is $\hat{\sigma}^2 = s^2 = 0.001$. Recall that the "^" symbol is used to denote an estimate of a parameter.

The mean and variance of a distribution are not necessarily the parameters of the distribution. For example, the parameter of the Poisson distribution is λ, while its mean and variance are $\mu = \lambda$ and $\sigma^2 = \lambda$ (*both* the mean *and* variance are λ), and the parameters of the binomial distribution are n and p, while its mean and variance are $\mu = np$ and $\sigma^2 = np(1 - p)$, respectively. We may show that a good point estimator of the parameter λ of a Poisson distribution is

$$\hat{\lambda} = \frac{1}{n}\sum_{i=1}^{n} x_i = \bar{x}$$

and that a good point estimator of the parameter p of a binomial distribution is

$$\hat{p} = \frac{1}{n}\sum_{i=1}^{n} x_i = \bar{x}$$

for fixed n. In the binomial distribution the observations in the random sample $\{x_i\}$ are either 1 or 0, corresponding to "success" and "failure," respectively.

A number of important properties are required of good point estimators. Two of the most important of these properties are the following:

1. The point estimator should be **unbiased.** That is, the expected value of the point estimator should be the parameter being estimated.
2. The point estimator should have **minimum variance.** Any point estimator is a random variable. Thus, a minimum variance point estimator should have a variance that is smaller than the variance of any other point estimator of that parameter.

The *sample* mean and variance $\bar{x}$ and s^2 are unbiased estimators of the *population* mean and variance μ and σ^2, respectively. That is,

$$E(\bar{x}) = \mu \quad \text{and} \quad E\left(s^2\right) = \sigma^2$$

where the operator E is simply the expected value operator, a shorthand way of writing the process of finding the mean of a random variable. (See the supplemental material for this chapter for more information about mathematical expectation.)

The sample standard deviation s is *not* an unbiased estimator of the population standard deviation σ. It can be shown that

$$\begin{aligned} E(s) &= \left(\frac{2}{n-1}\right)^{1/2} \frac{\Gamma(n/2)}{\Gamma[(n-1)/2]}\sigma \\ &= c_4\sigma \end{aligned} \tag{4.17}$$

Appendix Table VI gives values of c_4 for sample sizes $2 \le n \le 25$. We can obtain an unbiased estimate of the standard deviation from

$$\hat{\sigma} = \frac{s}{c_4} \tag{4.18}$$

In many applications of statistics to quality-engineering problems, it is convenient to estimate the standard deviation by the **range method.** Let $x_1, x_2, \ldots, x_n$ be a random sample of n observations from a normal distribution with mean μ and variance σ^2. The **range** of the sample is

$$\begin{aligned} R &= \max\left(x_i\right) - \min\left(x_i\right) \\ &= x_{\max} - x_{\min} \end{aligned} \tag{4.19}$$

That is, the range R is simply the difference between the largest and smallest sample observations. The random variable $W = R/\sigma$ is called the **relative range.** The distribution of W has been well studied. The mean of W is a constant d_2 that depends on the size of the sample. That is, $E(W) = d_2$. Therefore, an unbiased estimator of the standard deviation σ of a normal distribution is

$$\hat{\sigma} = \frac{R}{d_2} \tag{4.20}$$

Values of d_2 for sample sizes $2 \le n \le 25$ are given in Appendix Table VI.

Using the range to estimate σ dates from the earliest days of statistical quality control, and it was popular because it is very simple to calculate. With modern calculators and computers, this isn't a major consideration today. Generally, the "quadratic estimator" based on s is preferable. However, if the sample size n is relatively small, the range method actually works very well. The relative efficiency of the range method compared to s is shown here for various sample sizes:

Sample Size n	Relative Efficiency
2	1.000
3	0.992
4	0.975
5	0.955
6	0.930
10	0.850

For moderate values of n—say, $n \geq 10$—the range loses efficiency rapidly, as it ignores all of the information in the sample between the extremes. However, for small sample sizes—say, $n \leq 6$—it works very well and is entirely satisfactory. We will use the range method to estimate the standard deviation for certain types of control charts in Chapter 6. The **supplemental text material** contains more information about using the range to estimate variability. Also see Woodall and Montgomery (2000–01).

4.3 Statistical Inference for a Single Sample

The techniques of statistical inference can be classified into two broad categories: **parameter estimation** and **hypothesis testing.** We have already briefly introduced the general idea of **point estimation** of process parameters.

A **statistical hypothesis** is a statement about the values of the parameters of a probability distribution. For example, suppose we think that the mean inside diameter of a bearing is 1.500 in. We may express this statement in a formal manner as

$$\begin{aligned} H_0&: \ \mu = 1.500 \\ H_1&: \ \mu \neq 1.500 \end{aligned} \tag{4.21}$$

The statement $H_0: \mu = 1.500$ in equation (4.21) is called the **null hypothesis,** and $H_1: \mu \neq 1.500$ is called the **alternative hypothesis.** In our example, H_1 specifies values of the mean diameter that are either greater than 1.500 or less than 1.500, and is called a **two-sided alternative hypothesis.** Depending on the problem, various one-sided alternative hypotheses may be appropriate.

Hypothesis testing procedures are quite useful in many types of statistical quality-control problems. They also form the mathematical basis for most of the statistical process-control techniques to be described in Parts III and IV of this textbook. An important part of any hypothesis testing problem is determining the parameter values specified in the null and alternative hypotheses. Generally, this is done in one of three ways. First, the values may result from past evidence or knowledge. This happens frequently in statistical quality control, where we use past information to specify values for a parameter corresponding to a state of control, and then periodically test the hypothesis that the parameter value has not changed. Second, the values may result from some theory or model of the process. Finally, the values chosen for the parameter may be the result of contractual or design specifications, a situation that occurs frequently. Statistical hypothesis testing procedures may be used to check the conformity of the process parameters to their specified values, or to assist in modifying the process until the desired values are obtained.

To test a hypothesis, we take a random sample from the population under study, compute an appropriate **test statistic,** and then either reject or fail to reject the null hypothesis H_0. The set of values of the test statistic leading to rejection of H_0 is called the **critical region** or **rejection region** for the test.

Two kinds of errors may be committed when testing hypotheses. If the null hypothesis is rejected when it is true, then a **type I error** has occurred. If the null hypothesis is not rejected when it is false, then a **type II error** has been made. The probabilities of these two types of errors are denoted as

$$\alpha = P\{\text{type I error}\} = P\{\text{reject } H_0 | H_0 \text{ is true}\}$$

$$\beta = P\{\text{type II error}\} = P\{\text{fail to reject } H_0 | H_0 \text{ is false}\}$$

Sometimes it is more convenient to work with the **power of a statistical test,** where

$$\text{Power} = 1 - \beta = P\{\text{reject } H_0 | H_0 \text{ is false}\}$$

Thus, the power is the probability of *correctly* rejecting H_0. In quality control work, α is sometimes called the **producer's risk,** because it denotes the probability that a good lot will be rejected, or the probability that a process producing acceptable values of a particular quality characteristic will be rejected as performing unsatisfactorily. In addition, β is sometimes called the **consumer's risk,** because it denotes the probability of accepting a lot of poor quality, or allowing a process that is operating in an unsatisfactory manner relative to some quality characteristic to continue in operation.

The general procedure in hypothesis testing is to specify a value of the probability of type I error α, and then to design a test procedure so that a small value of the probability of type II error β is obtained. Thus, we can directly control or choose the α risk. The β risk is generally a function of sample size and is controlled indirectly. The larger is the sample size(s) used in the test, the smaller is the β risk.

In this section we will review hypothesis testing procedures when a **single sample** of n observations has been taken from the process. We will also show how the information about the values of the process parameters that is in this sample can be expressed in terms of an interval estimate called a **confidence interval.** In Section 4.4 we will consider statistical inference for two samples from two possibly different processes.

4.3.1 Inference on the Mean of a Population, Variance Known

Hypothesis Testing. Suppose that x is a random variable with unknown mean μ and known variance σ^2. We wish to test the hypothesis that the mean is equal to a standard value—say, μ_0. The hypothesis may be formally stated as

$$\begin{aligned} H_0&: \mu = \mu_0 \\ H_1&: \mu \neq \mu_0 \end{aligned} \tag{4.22}$$

The procedure for testing this hypothesis is to take a random sample of n observations on the random variable x, compute the test statistic

$$Z_0 = \frac{\bar{x} - \mu_0}{\sigma/\sqrt{n}} \tag{4.23}$$

and reject H_0 if $|Z_0| > Z_{\alpha/2}$ where $Z_{\alpha/2}$ is the upper $\alpha/2$ percentage point of the standard normal distribution. This procedure is sometimes called the one-sample *Z-test.*

We may give an intuitive justification of this test procedure. From the central limit theorem, we know that the sample mean $\bar{x}$ is distributed approximately $N(\mu, \sigma^2/n)$. Now if H_0: $\mu = \mu_0$ is true, then the test statistic Z_0 is distributed approximately $N(0, 1)$; consequently, we would expect $100(1 - \alpha)\%$ of the values of Z_0 to fall between $-Z_{\alpha/2}$ and $Z_{\alpha/2}$. A sample producing a value of Z_0 outside of these limits would be unusual if the null hypothesis were true and is evidence that H_0: $\mu = \mu_0$ should be rejected. Note that α is the probability of type I error for the test, and the intervals $(Z_{\alpha/2}, \infty)$ and $(-\infty, -Z_{\alpha/2})$ form the critical region for the test. The standard normal distribution is called the **reference distribution** for the Z-test.

In some situations we may wish to reject H_0 only if the true mean is larger than μ_0. Thus, the **one-sided** alternative hypothesis is H_1: $\mu > \mu_0$, and we would reject H_0: $\mu = \mu_0$ only if $Z_0 > Z_\alpha$. If rejection is desired only when $\mu < \mu_0$, then the alternative hypothesis is H_1: $\mu < \mu_0$, and we reject H_0 only if $Z_0 < -Z_\alpha$.

EXAMPLE 4.1 Computer Response Time

The response time of a distributed computer system is an important quality characteristic. The system manager wants to know whether the mean response time to a specific type of command exceeds 75 millisec. From previous experience, he knows that the standard deviation of response time is 8 millisec. Use a type I error of $\alpha = 0.05$.

SOLUTION

The appropriate hypotheses are

$$H_0: \mu = 75$$
$$H_1: \mu > 75$$

The command is executed 25 times and the response time for each trial is recorded. We assume that these observations can be considered as a random sample of the response times. The sample average response time is $\bar{x} = 79.25$ millisec. The value of the test statistic is

$$Z_0 = \frac{\bar{x} - \mu_0}{\sigma/\sqrt{n}} = \frac{79.25 - 75}{8/\sqrt{25}} = 2.66$$

Because we specified a type I error of $\alpha = 0.05$ and the test is one-sided, then from Appendix Table II we find $Z_\alpha = Z_{0.05} = 1.645$. Therefore, we reject H_0: $\mu = 75$ and conclude that the mean response time exceeds 75 millisec.

Minitab will perform the one-sample Z-test. The Minitab output for Example 4.1 is shown in the following boxed display.

One-Sample Z

```
Test of mu = 75 vs > 75
The assumed standard deviation = 8

                             95% Lower
 N    Mean    SE Mean        Bound      Z       P
25   79.25       1.60        76.62   2.66   0.004
```

Minitab also can calculate **confidence intervals** for parameters. We will now introduce the confidence interval and explain its interpretation and application.

Confidence Intervals. An interval estimate of a parameter is the interval between two statistics that includes the true value of the parameter with some probability. For example, to construct an interval estimator of the mean μ, we must find two statistics L and U such that

$$P\{L \le \mu \le U\} = 1 - \alpha \tag{4.24}$$

The resulting interval

$$L \le \mu \le U$$

is called a **100(1 − α)% confidence interval (CI)** for the unknown mean μ. L and U are called the lower and upper confidence limits, respectively, and $1 - \alpha$ is called the **confidence coefficient.** Sometimes the half-interval width $U - \mu$ or $\mu - L$ is called the **accuracy** of the confidence interval. The interpretation of a CI is that if a large number of such intervals are constructed, each resulting from a random sample, then $100(1 - \alpha)\%$ of these intervals will contain the true value of μ. Thus, confidence intervals have a frequency interpretation.

The CI (4.24) might be more properly called a **two-sided** confidence interval, as it specifies both a lower and an upper bound on μ. Sometimes in quality-control applications, a **one-sided** confidence bound might be more appropriate. A one-sided lower $100(1 - \alpha)\%$ confidence bound on μ would be given by

$$L \le \mu \tag{4.25}$$

where L, the lower confidence bound, is chosen so that

$$P\{L \le \mu\} = 1 - \alpha \tag{4.26}$$

A one-sided upper $100(1 - \alpha)\%$ confidence bound on μ would be

$$\mu \le U \tag{4.27}$$

where U, the upper confidence bound, is chosen so that

$$P\{\mu \le U\} = 1 - \alpha \tag{4.28}$$

Confidence Interval on the Mean with Variance Known. Consider the random variable x, with unknown mean μ and known variance σ^2. Suppose a random sample of n observations is taken—say, $x_1, x_2, \ldots, x_n$—and $\bar{x}$ is computed. Then the $100(1 - \alpha)\%$ two-sided CI on μ is

$$\bar{x} - Z_{\alpha/2}\frac{\sigma}{\sqrt{n}} \le \mu \le \bar{x} + Z_{\alpha/2}\frac{\sigma}{\sqrt{n}} \tag{4.29}$$

where $Z_{\alpha/2}$ is the percentage point of the $N(0, 1)$ distribution such that $P\{z \ge Z_{\alpha/2}\} = \alpha/2$.

Note that x is distributed approximately $N(\mu, \sigma^2/n)$ regardless of the distribution of x, from the central limit theorem. Consequently, equation (4.29) is an approximate $100(1 - \alpha)\%$ confidence interval for μ regardless of the distribution of x. If x is distributed $N(\mu, \sigma^2)$, then equation (4.29) is an exact $100(1 - \alpha)\%$ CI. Furthermore, a $100(1 - \alpha)\%$ upper confidence bound on μ is

$$\mu \le \bar{x} + Z_{\alpha}\frac{\sigma}{\sqrt{n}} \tag{4.30}$$

whereas a $100(1-\alpha)\%$ lower confidence bound on μ is

$$\bar{x} - Z_\alpha \frac{\sigma}{\sqrt{n}} \le \mu \tag{4.31}$$

EXAMPLE 4.2 Computer Response Time

Reconsider the computer response time scenario from Example 4.1. Since $\bar{x} = 79.25$ millisec, we know that a reasonable point estimate of the mean response time is $\hat{\mu} = \bar{x} = 79.25$ millisec. Find a 95% two-sided confidence interval.

SOLUTION

From equation 4.29 we can compute

$$\bar{x} - Z_{\alpha/2}\frac{\sigma}{\sqrt{n}} \le \mu \le \bar{x} + Z_{\alpha/2}\frac{\sigma}{\sqrt{n}}$$

$$79.25 - 1.96\frac{8}{\sqrt{25}} \le \mu \le 79.25 + 1.96\frac{8}{\sqrt{25}}$$

$$76.114 \le \mu \le 82.386$$

Another way to express this result is that our estimate of mean response time is 79.25 millisec ± 3.136 millisec with 95% confidence.

In the original Example 4.1, the alternative hypothesis was one-sided. In these situations, some analysts prefer to calculate a one-sided confidence bound. The Minitab output for Example 4.1 on p. 114 provider a 95% *lower confidence bound* on μ, which is computed from equation 4.31 as 76.62.

Notice that the CI from Minitab does *not* include the value $\mu = 75$. Furthermore, in Example 4.1 the hypothesis H_0: $\mu = 75$ was rejected at $\alpha = 0.05$. This is not a coincidence. In general, the test of significance for a parameter at level of significance α will lead to rejection of H_0 if, and only if, the parameter value specific in H_0 is not included in the $100(1-\alpha)\%$ confidence interval.

4.3.2 The Use of *P*-Values for Hypothesis Testing

The traditional way to report the results of a hypothesis test is to state that the null hypothesis was or was not rejected at a specified α-value or **level of significance.** This is often called *fixed significance level testing.* For example, in the previous computer response time problem, we can say that H_0: $\mu = 75$ was rejected at the 0.05 level of significance. This statement of conclusions is often inadequate, because it gives the analyst no idea about whether the computed value of the test statistic was just barely in the rejection region or very far into this region. Furthermore, stating the results this way imposes the predefined level of significance on other users of the information. This approach may be unsatisfactory, as some decision makers might be uncomfortable with the risks implied by $\alpha = 0.05$.

To avoid these difficulties the ***P*-value approach** has been adopted widely in practice. The *P*-value is the probability that the test statistic will take on a value that is at least as extreme as the observed value of the statistic when the null hypothesis H_0 is true. Thus, a *P*-value conveys much information about the weight of evidence against H_0, and so a decision maker can draw a conclusion at *any* specified level of significance. We now give a formal definition of a *P*-value.

Definition

The ***P*-value** is the smallest level of significance that would lead to rejection of the null hypothesis H_0.

It is customary to call the test statistic (and the data) significant when the null hypothesis H_0 is rejected; therefore, we may think of the *P*-value as the smallest level α at which the data are significant. Once the *P*-value is known, the decision maker can determine for himself or herself how significant the data are without the data analyst formally imposing a preselected level of significance.

For the normal distribution tests discussed above, it is relatively easy to compute the *P*-value. If Z_0 is the computed value of the test statistic, then the *P*-value is

$$P = \begin{cases} 2\left[1-\Phi\left(\left|Z_0\right|\right)\right] & \text{for a two-tailed test:} \quad H_0\colon\ \mu=\mu_0 \quad H_1\colon\ \mu\neq\mu_0 \\ 1-\Phi\left(Z_0\right) & \text{for an upper-tailed test:} \quad H_0\colon\ \mu=\mu_0 \quad H_1\colon\ \mu>\mu_0 \\ \Phi\left(Z_0\right) & \text{for a lower-tailed test:} \quad H_0\colon\ \mu=\mu_0 \quad H_1\colon\ \mu<\mu_0 \end{cases}$$

Here, $\Phi(Z)$ is the standard normal cumulative distribution function defined in Chapter 3. To illustrate this, consider the computer response time problem in Example 4.1. The computed value of the test statistic is $Z_0 = 2.66$ and since the alternative hypothesis is one-tailed, the *P*-value is

$$P = 1-\Phi(2.66) = 0.0039$$

Thus, H_0: $\mu = 75$ would be rejected at any level of significance $\alpha \geq P = 0.0039$. For example, H_0 would be rejected if $\alpha = 0.01$, but it would not be rejected if $\alpha = 0.001$.

It is not always easy to compute the exact *P*-value for a test. However, most modern computer programs for statistical analysis report *P*-values, and they can be obtained using some hand-held calculators. Notice that Minitab reported a *P*-value for Example 4.1 (the reported value was 0.004). It is also possible to use the statistical tables in the Appendix to approximate the *P*-value in some cases.

4.3.3 Inference on the Mean of a Normal Distribution, Variance Unknown

Hypothesis Testing. Suppose that x is a normal random variable with unknown mean μ and unknown variance σ^2. We wish to test the hypothesis that the mean equals a standard value μ_0; that is,

$$\begin{aligned} H_0\colon\ \mu &= \mu_0 \\ H_1\colon\ \mu &\neq \mu_0 \end{aligned} \tag{4.32}$$

Note that this problem is similar to that of Section 4.3.1, except that now the variance is unknown. Because the variance is unknown, we must make the additional assumption that the random variable is normally distributed. The normality assumption is needed to formally develop the statistical test, but moderate departures from normality will not seriously affect the results.

As σ^2 is unknown, it may be estimated by s^2. If we replace σ in equation 4.23 by s, we have the **test statistic**

$$t_0 = \frac{\bar{x} - \mu_0}{s/\sqrt{n}} \tag{4.33}$$

The **reference distribution** for this test statistic is the t distribution with $n - 1$ degrees of freedom. For a fixed significance level test, the null hypothesis H_0: $\mu = \mu_0$ will be rejected if $|(t_0)| > t_{\alpha/2,n-1}$, where $t_{\alpha/2,n-1}$ denotes the upper $\alpha/2$ percentage point of the t distribution with $n - 1$ degrees of freedom. The critical regions for the one-sided alternative hypotheses are as follows: if H_1: $\mu_1 > \mu_0$, reject H_0 if $t_0 > t_{\alpha,n-1}$, and if H_1: $\mu_1 < \mu_0$, reject H_0 if $t_0 < -t_{\alpha,n-1}$. One could also compute the P-value for a t-test. Most computer software packages report the P-value along with the computed value of t_0.

EXAMPLE 4.3 Rubberized Asphalt

Rubber can be added to asphalt to reduce road noise when the material is used as pavement. Table 4.1 shows the stabilized viscosity (cP) of 15 specimens of asphalt paving material. To be suitable for the intended pavement application, the mean stabilized viscosity should be equal to 3200. Test this hypothesis using $\alpha = 0.05$. Based on experience we are willing to initially assume that stabilized viscosity is normally distributed.

■ **TABLE 4.1**
Stabilized Viscosity of Rubberized Asphalt

Specimen	Stabilized Viscosity
1	3193
2	3124
3	3153
4	3145
5	3093
6	3466
7	3355
8	2979
9	3182
10	3227
11	3256
12	3332
13	3204
14	3282
15	3170

SOLUTION

The appropriate hypotheses are

$$H_0: \mu = 3200$$
$$H_1: \mu \neq 3200$$

The sample mean and sample standard deviation are

$$\bar{x} = \frac{1}{15}\sum_{i=1}^{15} x_i = \frac{48{,}161}{15} = 3210.73$$

$$s = \sqrt{\frac{\sum_{i=1}^{15} x_i^2 - \frac{\left(\sum_{i=1}^{15} x_i\right)^2}{15}}{15-1}} = \sqrt{\frac{154{,}825{,}783 - \frac{(48{,}161)^2}{15}}{14}} = 117.61$$

and the test statistic is

$$t_0 = \frac{\bar{x} - \mu_0}{s/\sqrt{n}} = \frac{3210.73 - 3200}{117.61/\sqrt{15}} = 0.35$$

Since the calculated value of the test statistic does not exceed $t_{0.025,\,14} = 2.145$ or $-t_{0.025,\,14} = -2.145$, we cannot reject the null hypothesis. Therefore, there is no strong evidence to conclude that the mean stabilized viscosity is different from 3200 cP.

The assumption of normality for the t-test can be checked by constructing a normal probability plot of the stabilized viscosity data. Figure 4.5 shows the normal probability plot. Because the observations lie along the straight line, there is no problem with the normality assumption.

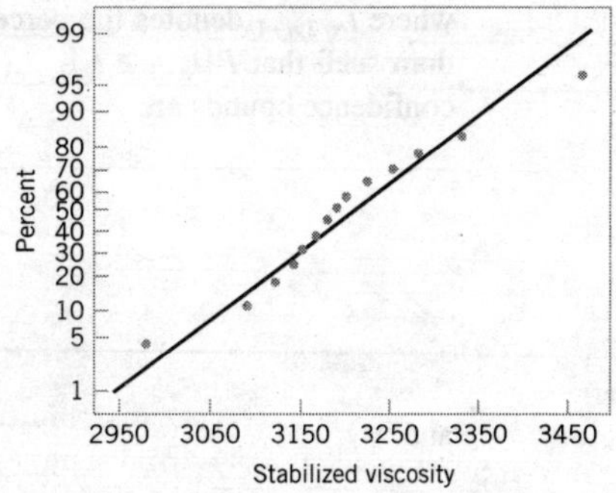

■ FIGURE 4.5 Normal probability plot of the stabilized viscosity data.

Minitab can conduct the one-sample t-test. The output from this software package is shown in the following display:

One-Sample T: Example 4.3

```
Test of mu = 3200 vs mu not = 3200

Variable         N      Mean     StDev   SE Mean
Example 4.3     15    3210.7     117.6      30.4

Variable             95.0% CI          T        P
Example 4.3    (3145.6, 3275.9)     0.35    0.729
```

Notice that Minitab computes both the test statistic and a 95% confidence interval for the mean stabilized viscosity. We will give the confidence interval formula below; however, recalling the discussion about the connection between hypothesis tests and confidence intervals at the conclusion of Example 4.3, we observe that because the 95% confidence interval includes the value 3200, we would be unable to reject the null hypothesis H_0: $\mu = 3200$. Note that Minitab also reports a P-value for the t-test.

Confidence Interval on the Mean of a Normal Distribution with Variance Unknown. Suppose that x is a normal random variable with unknown mean μ and unknown variance σ^2. From a random sample of n observations the sample mean $\bar{x}$ and sample variance s^2 are computed. Then a $100(1-\alpha)\%$ two-sided CI on the true mean is

$$\bar{x} - t_{\alpha/2,n-1}\frac{s}{\sqrt{n}} \le \mu \le \bar{x} + t_{\alpha/2,n-1}\frac{s}{\sqrt{n}} \tag{4.34}$$

where $t_{\alpha/2,n-1}$ denotes the percentage point of the t distribution with $n - 1$ degrees of freedom such that $P\{t_{n-1} \geq t_{\alpha/2,\, n-1}\} = \alpha/2$. The corresponding upper and lower $100(1 - \alpha)\%$ confidence bounds are

$$\mu \leq \bar{x} + t_{\alpha,n-1}\frac{s}{\sqrt{n}} \tag{4.35}$$

and

$$\bar{x} - t_{\alpha,n-1}\frac{s}{\sqrt{n}} \leq \mu \tag{4.36}$$

respectively.

EXAMPLE 4.4 Rubberized Viscosity

Reconsider the stabilized viscosity data from Example 4.3. Find a 95% confidence interval on the mean stabilized viscosity.

SOLUTION

Using equation 4.34, we can find the 95% CI on the mean stabilized viscosity as follows:

$$\bar{x} - t_{\alpha/2,n-1}\frac{s}{\sqrt{n}} \leq \mu \leq \bar{x} + t_{\alpha/2,n-1}\frac{s}{\sqrt{n}}$$

$$3210.73 - 2.145\frac{117.61}{\sqrt{15}} \leq \mu \leq 3210.73 + 2.145\frac{117.61}{\sqrt{15}}$$

$$3145.59 \leq \mu \leq 3275.87$$

Another way to express this result is that our estimate of the mean stabilized viscosity is 3210.73 ± 65.14 cP with 95% confidence. This confidence interval was reported by Minitab in the box on page 118.

The manufacturer may only be concerned about stabilized viscosity values that are too low and consequently may be interested in a one-sided confidence bound. The 95% lower confidence bound on mean stabilized viscosity is found from equation 4.36, using $t_{0.05,\,14} = 1.761$ as

$$3210.73 - 1.761\frac{117.61}{\sqrt{15}} \leq \mu$$

or

$$3157.25 \leq \mu$$

4.3.4 Inference on the Variance of a Normal Distribution

Hypothesis Testing. We now review hypothesis testing on the variance of a normal distribution. Whereas tests on means are relatively insensitive to the normality assumption, test procedures for variances are not.

Suppose we wish to test the hypothesis that the variance of a normal distribution equals a constant—say, σ_0^2. The hypotheses are

$$\begin{aligned} H_0&: \ \sigma^2 = \sigma_0^2 \\ H_1&: \ \sigma^2 \neq \sigma_0^2 \end{aligned} \tag{4.37}$$

The test statistic for this hypothesis is

$$\chi_0^2 = \frac{(n-1)s^2}{\sigma_0^2} \tag{4.38}$$

where s^2 is the sample variance computed from a random sample of n observations. For a fixed significance level test, the null hypothesis is rejected if $\chi_0^2 > \chi_{\alpha/2,n-1}^2$ or if $\chi_0^2 < \chi_{1-\alpha/2,n-1}^2$ where $\chi_{\alpha/2,n-1}^2$ and $\chi_{1-\alpha/2,n-1}^2$ are the upper $\alpha/2$ and lower $1 - (\alpha/2)$ percentage points of the chi-square distribution with $n - 1$ degrees of freedom. If a one-sided alternative is specified—say, $H_1: \sigma^2 < \sigma_0^2$, then we would reject if $\chi_0^2 < \chi_{1-\alpha,n-1}^2$. For the other one-sided alternative $H_1: \sigma^2 > \sigma_0^2$, reject if $\chi_0^2 > \chi_{\alpha,n-1}^2$.

This test is very useful in many quality-improvement applications. For example, consider a normal random variable with mean μ and variance σ^2. If σ^2 is less than or equal to some value—say, σ_0^2—then the natural inherent variability of the process will be well within the design requirements, and, consequently, almost all of the production will conform to specifications. However, if σ^2 exceeds σ_0^2, then the natural variability in the process will exceed the specification limits, resulting in a high percentage of nonconforming production or "fallout." In other words, **process capability** is directly related to **process variability.** Equations (4.37) and (4.38) may be used to analyze various other similar situations, and as we will see subsequently, they form the basis for a monitoring or control procedure for process variability.

Confidence Interval on the Variance of a Normal Distribution. Suppose that x is a normal random variable with unknown mean μ and unknown variance σ^2. Let the sample variance s^2 be computed from a random sample of n observations. Then a $100(1 - \alpha)\%$ two-sided CI on the variance is

$$\frac{(n-1)s^2}{\chi_{\alpha/2,n-1}^2} \leq \sigma^2 \leq \frac{(n-1)s^2}{\chi_{1-\alpha/2,n-1}^2} \tag{4.39}$$

where $\chi_{\alpha/2,n-1}^2$ denotes the percentage point of the chi-square distribution such that $P\{\chi_{n-1}^2 \geq \chi_{\alpha/2,n-1}^2\} = \alpha/2$. A CI or the standard deviation can be found by taking the square root throughout in equation (4.39).

If one-sided confidence bounds are desired, they may be obtained from equation (4.39) by using only the upper (or lower) limit with the probability level increased from $\alpha/2$ to α. That is, the upper and lower $100(1 - \alpha)\%$ confidence bounds are

$$\sigma^2 \leq \frac{(n-1)s^2}{\chi_{1-\alpha,n-1}^2} \tag{4.40}$$

and

$$\frac{(n-1)s^2}{\chi^2_{\alpha,n-1}} \le \sigma^2 \tag{4.41}$$

respectively.

We may use the stabilized viscosity data from Example 4.3 to demonstrate the computation of a 95% (say) confidence interval on σ^2. Note that for the data in Table 4.1, we have $s = 117.61$ and $s^2 = 13{,}832.11$. From Appendix Table III, we find that $\chi^2_{0.025,14} = 26.12$ and $\chi^2_{0.975,14} = 5.63$. Therefore, from equation 4.39 we find the 95% two-sided confidence interval on σ^2 as

$$\frac{(14)13{,}832.11}{26.12} \le \sigma^2 \le \frac{(14)13{,}832.11}{5.63}$$

which reduces to $7413.84 \le \sigma^2 \le 34{,}396.01$ The confidence interval on the standard deviation is

$$86.10 \le \sigma \le 185.46$$

4.3.5 Inference on a Population Proportion

Hypothesis Testing. Suppose we wish to test the hypothesis that the proportion p of a population equals a standard value—say, p_0. The test we will describe is based on the normal approximation to the binomial. If a random sample of n items is taken from the population and x items in the sample belong to the class associated with p, then to test

$$\begin{aligned} H_0&: \ p = p_0 \\ H_1&: \ p \ne p_0 \end{aligned} \tag{4.42}$$

we use the statistic

$$Z_0 = \begin{cases} \dfrac{(x+0.5) - np_0}{\sqrt{np_0(1-p_0)}} & \text{if } x < np_0 \\ \dfrac{(x-0.5) - np_0}{\sqrt{np_0(1-p_0)}} & \text{if } x > np_0 \end{cases} \tag{4.43}$$

For a fixed significance level test, the null hypothesis H_0: $p = p_0$ is rejected if $|Z_0| > Z_{\alpha/2}$. The one-sided alternative hypotheses are treated similarly. A P-value approach also can be used. Since this is a Z-test, the P-values are calculated just as in the Z-test for the mean.

EXAMPLE 4.5 A Forging Process

A foundry produces steel forgings used in automobile manufacturing. We wish to test the hypothesis that the fraction conforming or fallout from this process is 10%. In a random sample of 250 forgings, 41 were found to be nonconforming. What are your conclusions using $\alpha = 0.05$?

SOLUTION

To test

$$H_0: \; p = 0.1$$
$$H_1: \; p \neq 0.1$$

we calculate the test statistic

$$Z_0 = \frac{(x - 0.5) - np_0}{\sqrt{np_0(1 - p_0)}} = \frac{(41 - 0.5) - (250)(0.1)}{\sqrt{250(0.1)(1 - 0.1)}} = 3.27$$

Using $\alpha = 0.05$ we find $Z_{0.025} = 1.96$, and therefore H_0: $p = 0.1$ is rejected (the P-value here is $P = 0.00108$). That is, the process fraction nonconforming or fallout is not equal to 10%.

As noted above, this test is based as the normal approximation to the binomial. When this is the appropriate, three is an exact test available. For details, see Montgomery and Runger (2007).

Confidence Intervals on a Population Proportion. It is frequently necessary to construct $100(1 - \alpha)\%$ CIs on a population proportion p. This parameter frequently corresponds to a lot or process fraction nonconforming. Now p is only one of the parameters of a binomial distribution, and we usually assume that the other binomial parameter n is known. If a random sample of n observations from the population has been taken, and x "nonconforming" observations have been found in this sample, then the unbiased point estimator of p is $\hat{p} = x/n$.

There are several approaches to constructing the CI on p. If n is large and $p \geq 0.1$ (say), then the normal approximation to the binomial can be used, resulting in the $100(1 - \alpha)\%$ confidence interval:

$$\hat{p} - Z_{\alpha/2}\sqrt{\frac{\hat{p}(1 - \hat{p})}{n}} \leq p \leq \hat{p} + Z_{\alpha/2}\sqrt{\frac{\hat{p}(1 - \hat{p})}{n}} \tag{4.44}$$

If n is small, then the binomial distribution should be used to establish the confidence interval on p. If n is large but p is small, then the Poisson approximation to the binomial is useful in constructing confidence intervals. Examples of these latter two procedures are given by Duncan (1986).

EXAMPLE 4.6 Mortgage Applications

In a random sample of 80 home mortgage applications processed by an automated decision system, 15 of the applications were not approved. The point estimate of the fraction that was not approved is

$$\hat{p} = \frac{15}{80} = 0.1875$$

Assuming that the normal approximation to the binomial is appropriate, find a 95% confidence interval on the fraction of nonconforming mortgage applications in the process.

(continued)

SOLUTION

The desired confidence interval is found from equation 4.44 as

$$0.1875 - 1.96\sqrt{\frac{0.1875(0.8125)}{80}} \le p \le 0.1875 + 1.96\sqrt{\frac{0.1875(0.8125)}{80}}$$

which reduces to

$$0.1020 \le p \le 0.2730$$

4.3.6 The Probability of Type II Error and Sample Size Decisions

In most hypothesis testing situations, it is important to determine the probability of type II error associated with the test. Equivalently, we may elect to evaluate the power of the test. To illustrate how this may be done, we will find the probability of type II error associated with the test of

$$H_0\colon\ \mu = \mu_0$$
$$H_1\colon\ \mu \ne \mu_0$$

where the variance σ^2 is known. The test procedure was discussed in Section 4.3.1.

The test statistic for this hypothesis is

$$Z_0 = \frac{\bar{x} - \mu_0}{\sigma/\sqrt{n}}$$

and under the null hypothesis the distribution of Z_0 is $N(0, 1)$. To find the probability of type II error, we must assume that the null hypothesis H_0: $\mu = \mu_0$ is false and then find the distribution of Z_0. Suppose that the mean of the distribution is really $\mu_1 = \mu_0 + \delta$, where $\delta > 0$. Thus, the alternative hypothesis H_1: $\mu \ne \mu_0$ is true, and under this assumption the distribution of the test statistic Z_0 is

$$Z_0 \sim N\left(\frac{\delta\sqrt{n}}{\sigma}, 1\right) \tag{4.45}$$

The distribution of the test statistic Z_0 under both hypotheses H_0 and H_1 is shown in Fig. 4.6. We note that the probability of type II error is the probability that Z_0 will fall between $-Z_{\alpha/2}$ and $Z_{\alpha/2}$ given that the alternative hypothesis H_1 is true. To evaluate this probability, we must find $F(Z_{\alpha/2}) - F(-Z_{\alpha/2})$, where F denotes the cumulative distribution function of the $N(\delta\sqrt{n}/\sigma, 1)$ distribution. In terms of the standard normal cumulative distribution, we then have

$$\beta = \Phi\left(Z_{\alpha/2} - \frac{\delta\sqrt{n}}{\sigma}\right) - \Phi\left(-Z_{\alpha/2} - \frac{\delta\sqrt{n}}{\sigma}\right) \tag{4.46}$$

as the probability of type II error. This equation will also work when $\delta < 0$.

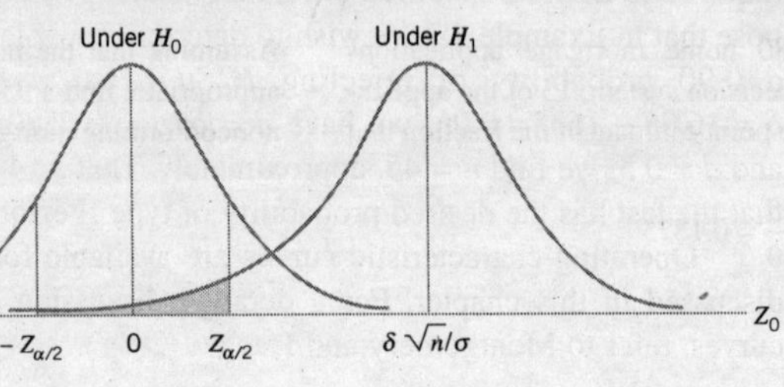

■ FIGURE 4.6 The distribution of Z_0 under H_0 and H_1.

EXAMPLE 4.7 Finding the Power of a Test

The mean contents of coffee cans filled on a particular production line are being studied. Standards specify that the mean contents must be 16.0 oz, and from past experience it is known that the standard deviation of the can contents is 0.1 oz. The hypotheses are

$$H_0: \mu = 16.0$$
$$H_1: \mu \neq 16.0$$

A random sample of nine cans is to be used, and the type I error probability is specified as $\alpha = 0.05$. Therefore, the test statistic is

$$Z_0 = \frac{\bar{x} - 16.0}{0.1\sqrt{9}}$$

and H_0 is rejected if $|Z_0| > Z_{0.025} = 1.96$. Find the probability of type II error and the power of the test, if the true mean contents are $\mu_1 = 16.1$ oz.

SOLUTION

Since we are given that $\delta = \mu_1 - \mu_0 = 16.1 - 16.0 = 0.1$, we have

$$\begin{aligned}\beta &= \Phi\left(Z_{\alpha/2} - \frac{\delta\sqrt{n}}{\sigma}\right) - \Phi\left(-Z_{\alpha/2} - \frac{\delta\sqrt{n}}{\sigma}\right)\\ &= \Phi\left(1.96 - \frac{(0.1)(3)}{0.1}\right) - \Phi\left(-1.96 - \frac{(0.1)(3)}{0.1}\right)\\ &= \Phi(-1.04) - \Phi(-4.96)\\ &= 0.1492\end{aligned}$$

That is, the probability that we will incorrectly fail to reject H_0 if the true mean contents are 16.1 oz is 0.1492. Equivalently, we can say that the power of the test is $1 - \beta = 1 - 0.1492 = 0.8508$.

We note from examining equation 4.46 and Fig. 4.6 that β is a function of n, δ, and α. It is customary to plot curves illustrating the relationship between these parameters. Such a set of curves is shown in Fig. 4.7 for $\alpha = 0.05$. Graphs such as these are usually called **operating-characteristic (OC) curves.** The parameter on the vertical axis of these curves is β, and the parameter on the horizontal axis is $d = |\delta|/\sigma$. From examining the operating-characteristic curves, we see that

1. The further the true mean μ_1 is from the hypothesized value μ_0 (i.e., the larger the value of δ), the smaller is the probability of type II error for a given n and α. That is, for a specified sample size and α, the test will detect large differences more easily than small ones.
2. As the sample size n increases, the probability of type II error gets smaller for a specified δ and α. That is, to detect a specified difference we may make the test more powerful by increasing the sample size.

Operating-characteristic curves are useful in determining how large a sample is required to detect a specified difference with a particular probability. As an illustration, suppose that in Example 4.7 we wish to determine how large a sample will be necessary to have a 0.90 probability of rejecting H_0: $\mu = 16.0$ if the true mean is $\mu = 16.05$. Since $\delta = 16.05 - 16.0 = 0.05$, we have $d = |\delta|/\sigma = |0.05|/0.1 = 0.5$. From Fig. 4.7 with $\beta = 0.10$ and $d = 0.5$, we find $n = 45$, approximately. That is, 45 observations must be taken to ensure that the test has the desired probability of type II error.

Operating-characteristic curves are available for most of the standard statistical tests discussed in this chapter. For a detailed discussion of the use of operating-characteristic curves, refer to Montgomery and Runger (2007).

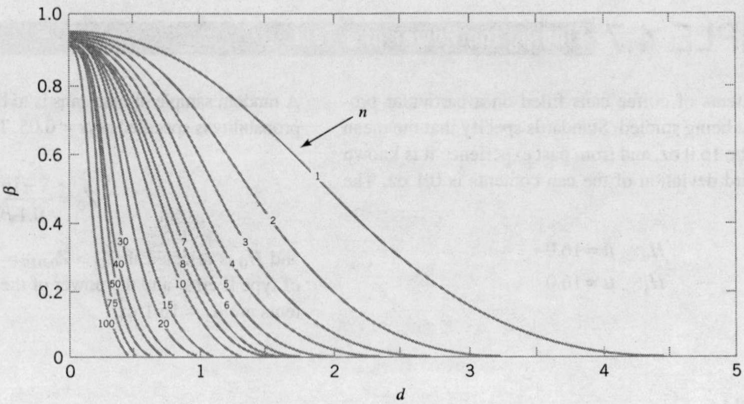

■ FIGURE 4.7 Operating-characteristic curves for the two-sided normal test with $\alpha = 0.05$. (Reproduced with permission from C. L. Ferris, F. E. Grubbs, and C. L. Weaver, "Operating Characteristic Curves for the Common Statistical Tests of Significance," *Annals of Mathematical Statistics*, June 1946.)

Minitab can also perform power and sample size calculations for several hypothesis testing problems. The following Minitab display reproduces the power calculations from the coffee can–filling problem in Example 4.7.

Power and Sample Size

```
1-Sample Z Test
Testing mean = null (versus not = null)
Calculating power for mean = null + difference
Alpha = 0.05 Sigma = 0.1
                  Sample
Difference          Size     Power
       0.1             9    0.8508
```

The following display shows several sample size and power calculations based on the rubberized asphalt problem in Example 4.3.

Power and Sample Size

```
1-Sample t Test
Testing mean = null (versus not = null)
Calculating power for mean = null + difference
Alpha = 0.05 Sigma = 117.61
                Sample
Difference        Size     Power
        50          15    0.3354
```

```
1-Sample t Test
Testing mean = null (versus not = null)
Calculating power for mean = null + difference
Alpha = 0.05 Sigma = 117.61

              Sample   Target   Actual
Difference      Size    Power    Power
        50        46   0.8000   0.8055

1-Sample t Test
Testing mean = null (versus not = null)
Calculating power for mean = null + difference
Alpha = 0.05 Sigma = 117.61

              Sample
Difference      Size    Power
       100        15   0.8644
```

In the first portion of the display, Minitab calculates the power of the test in Example 4.3, assuming that the engineer would wish to reject the null hypothesis if the true mean stabilized viscosity differed from 3200 by as much as 50, using $s = 117.61$ as an estimate of the true standard deviation. The power is 0.3354, which is low. The next calculation determines the sample size that would be required to produce a power of 0.8, a much better value. Minitab reports that a considerably larger sample size, $n = 46$, would be required. The final calculation determines the power with $n = 15$ if a larger difference between the true mean stabilized viscosity and the hypothesized value is of interest. For a difference of 100, Minitab reports the power to be 0.8644.

4.4 Statistical Inference for Two Samples

The previous section presented hypothesis tests and confidence intervals for a single population parameter (the mean μ, the variance σ^2, or a proportion p). This section extends those results to the case of two independent populations.

The general situation is shown in Fig. 4.8. Population 1 has mean μ_1 and variance σ_1^2, whereas population 2 has mean μ_2 and variance σ_2^2. Inferences will be based on two random

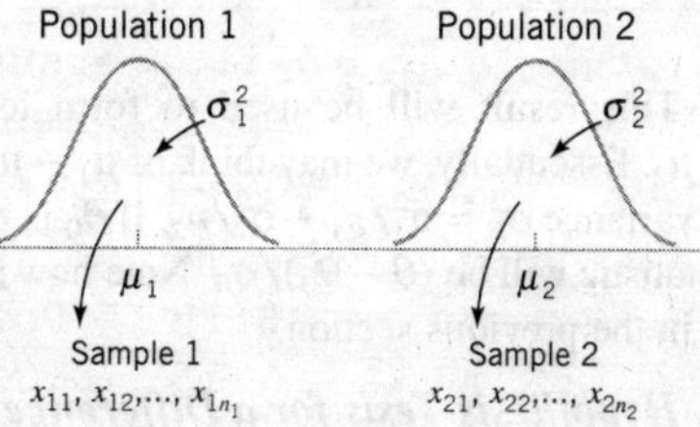

FIGURE 4.8 Two independent populations

samples of sizes n_1 and n_2, respectively. That is, $x_{11}, x_{12}, \ldots, x_{1n_1}$ is a random sample of n_1 observations from population 1, and $x_{21}, x_{22}, \ldots, x_{2n_2}$ is a random sample of n_2 observations from population 2.

4.4.1 Inference for a Difference in Means, Variances Known

In this section we consider statistical inferences on the difference in means $\mu_1 - \mu_2$ of the populations shown in Fig. 4.8, where the variances σ_1^2 and σ_2^2 are known. The assumptions for this section are summarized here.

Assumptions

1. $x_{11}, x_{12}, \ldots, x_{1n_1}$ is a random sample from population 1.
2. $x_{21}, x_{22}, \ldots, x_{2n_2}$ is a random sample from population 2.
3. The two populations represented by x_1 and x_2 are independent.
4. Both populations are normal, or if they are not normal, the conditions of the central limit theorem apply.

A logical point estimator of $\mu_1 - \mu_2$ is the difference in sample means $\bar{x}_1 - \bar{x}_2$. Based on the properties of expected values, we have

$$E(\bar{x}_1 - \bar{x}_2) = E(\bar{x}_1) - E(\bar{x}_2) = \mu_1 - \mu_2$$

and the variance of $\bar{x}_1 - \bar{x}_2$ is

$$V(\bar{x}_1 - \bar{x}_2) = V(\bar{x}_1) + V(\bar{x}_2) = \frac{\sigma_1^2}{n_1} + \frac{\sigma_2^2}{n_2}$$

Based on the assumptions and the preceding results, we may state the following.

The quantity

$$Z = \frac{\bar{x}_1 - \bar{x}_2 - (\mu_1 - \mu_2)}{\sqrt{\dfrac{\sigma_1^2}{n_1} + \dfrac{\sigma_2^2}{n_2}}} \tag{4.47}$$

has an $N(0, 1)$ distribution.

This result will be used to form tests of hypotheses and confidence intervals on $\mu_1 - \mu_2$. Essentially, we may think of $\mu_1 - \mu_2$ as a parameter θ, and its estimator is $\hat{\theta} = \bar{x}_1 - \bar{x}_2$ with variance $\sigma_{\hat{\theta}}^2 = \sigma_1^2/n_1 + \sigma_2^2/n_2$. If θ_0 is the null hypothesis value specified for θ, then the test statistic will be $(\theta - \theta_0)/\sigma_{\hat{\theta}}$ Note how similar this is to the test statistic for a single mean used in the previous section.

Hypothesis Tests for a Difference in Means, Variances Known. We now consider hypothesis testing on the difference in the means $\mu_1 - \mu_2$ of the two populations in

Fig. 4.8. Suppose we are interested in testing that the difference in means $\mu_1 - \mu_2$ is equal to a specified value Δ_0. Thus, the null hypothesis will be stated as H_0: $\mu_1 - \mu_2 = \Delta_0$. Obviously, in many cases, we will specify $\Delta_0 = 0$ so that we are testing the equality of two means (i.e., H_0: $\mu_1 = \mu_2$). The appropriate test statistic would be found by replacing $\mu_1 - \mu_2$ in equation 4.47 with Δ_0, and this test statistic would have a standard normal distribution under H_0. Suppose that the alternative hypothesis is H_1: $\mu_1 - \mu_2 \neq \Delta_0$. Now, a sample value of $\bar{x}_1 - \bar{x}_2$ that is considerably different from Δ_0 is evidence that H_1 is true. Because Z has the $N(0, 1)$ distribution when H_0 is true, we would take $-Z_{\alpha/2}$ and $Z_{\alpha/2}$ as the boundaries of the critical region just as we did in the single sample hypothesis testing problem of Section 4.3.1. This would give a test with level of significance α. Critical regions for the one-sided alternatives would be located similarly. A P-value approach can also be used. Formally, we summarize these results here.

Testing Hypotheses on $\mu_1 - \mu_2$, Variances Known

Null hypothesis: H_0: $\mu_1 - \mu_2 = \Delta_0$

$$\text{Test statistic:} \quad Z_0 = \frac{\bar{x}_1 - \bar{x}_2 - \Delta_0}{\sqrt{\dfrac{\sigma_1^2}{n_1} + \dfrac{\sigma_2^2}{n_2}}} \tag{4.48}$$

Alternative Hypotheses	Fixed Significance Level Rejection Criterion	P-value
H_1: $\mu_1 - \mu_2 \neq \Delta_0$	$Z_0 < -Z_{\alpha/2}$ or $Z_0 > Z_{\alpha/2}$	$P = 2[1 - (\Phi\lvert Z_0\rvert)]$
H_1: $\mu_1 - \mu_2 > \Delta_0$	$Z_0 > Z_\alpha$	$P = 1 - \Phi(Z_0)$
H_1: $\mu_1 - \mu_2 < \Delta_0$	$Z_0 < -Z_\alpha$	$P = \Phi(Z_0)$

EXAMPLE 4.8 Comparing Paint Formulations

A product developer is interested in reducing the drying time of a primer paint. Two formulations of the paint are tested; formulation 1 is the standard chemistry, and formulation 2 has a new drying ingredient that should reduce the drying time. From experience, it is known that the standard deviation of drying time is eight minutes, and this inherent variability should be unaffected by the addition of the new ingredient. Ten specimens are painted with formulation 1, and another 10 specimens are painted with formulation 2; the 20 specimens are painted in random order. The two sample average drying times are $\bar{x}_1 = 121$ min and $\bar{x}_2 = 112$ min, respectively. What conclusions can the product developer draw about the effectiveness of the new ingredient, using $\alpha = 0.05$?

SOLUTION

The hypotheses of interest here are

$$H_0: \mu_1 - \mu_2 = 0$$
$$H_1: \mu_1 - \mu_2 > 0$$

or equivalently,

$$H_0: \mu_1 = \mu_2$$
$$H_1: \mu_1 > \mu_2$$

(continued)

Now since $\bar{x}_1 = 121$ min and $\bar{x}_2 = 112$ min, the test statistic is

$$Z_0 = \frac{121 - 112}{\sqrt{\frac{(8)^2}{10} + \frac{(8)^2}{10}}} = 2.52$$

Because the test statistic $Z_0 = 2.52 > Z_{0.05} = 1.645$, we reject H_0: $\mu_1 = \mu_2$ at the $\alpha = 0.05$ level and conclude that adding the new ingredient to the paint significantly reduces the drying time. Alternatively, we can find the P-value for this test as

$$P\text{-value} = 1 - \Phi(2.52) = 0.0059$$

Therefore, H_0: $\mu_1 = \mu_2$ would be rejected at any significance level $\alpha \geq 0.0059$.

Confidence Interval on a Difference in Means, Variances Known. The $100(1 - \alpha)\%$ CI on the difference in two means $\mu_1 - \mu_2$ when the variances are known can be found directly from results given previously in this section. Recall that $x_{11}, x_{12}, \ldots, x_{1n_1}$, is a random sample of n_1 observations from the first population and $x_{21}, x_{22}, \ldots, x_{2n_2}$ is a random sample of n_2 observations from the second population. If $\bar{x}_1$ and $\bar{x}_2$ are the means of these two samples, then a $100(1 - \alpha)\%$ confidence interval on the difference in means $\mu_1 - \mu_2$ is given by the following.

$$\bar{x}_1 - \bar{x}_2 - Z_{\alpha/2}\sqrt{\frac{\sigma_1^2}{n_1} + \frac{\sigma_2^2}{n_2}} \leq \mu_1 - \mu_2 \leq \bar{x}_1 - \bar{x}_2 + Z_{\alpha/2}\sqrt{\frac{\sigma_1^2}{n_1} + \frac{\sigma_2^2}{n_2}} \tag{4.49}$$

This is a two-sided CI. One-sided confidence bounds can be obtained by using the approach illustrated in Section 4.3 for the single-sample case.

4.4.2 Inference for a Difference in Means of Two Normal Distributions, Variances Unknown

We now extend the results of the previous section to the difference in means of the two distributions in Fig. 4.8 when the variances of both distributions σ_1^2 and σ_2^2 are unknown. If the sample sizes n_1 and n_2 exceed 30, then the normal distribution procedures in Section 4.4.1 could be used. However, when small samples are taken, we will assume that the populations are normally distributed and base our hypotheses tests and confidence intervals on the t distribution. This nicely parallels the case of inference on the mean of a single sample with unknown variance.

Hypotheses Tests for the Difference in Means. We now consider tests of hypotheses on the difference in means $\mu_1 - \mu_2$ of two normal distributions where the variances σ_1^2 and σ_2^2 are unknown. A t-statistic will be used to test these hypotheses. As noted above, the normality assumption is required to develop the test procedure, but moderate departures from normality do not adversely affect the procedure. Two different situations must be treated. In the first case, we assume that the variances of the two normal distributions are unknown but equal; that is, $\sigma_1^2 = \sigma_2^2 = \sigma^2$. In the second, we assume that σ_1^2 and σ_2^2 are unknown and not necessarily equal.

Case 1: $\sigma_1^2 = \sigma_2^2 = \sigma^2$. Suppose we have two independent normal populations with unknown means μ_1 and μ_2, and unknown but equal variances, $\sigma_1^2 = \sigma_2^2 = \sigma^2$. We wish to test

$$\begin{aligned} H_0&: \ \mu_1 - \mu_2 = \Delta_0 \\ H_1&: \ \mu_1 - \mu_2 \neq \Delta_0 \end{aligned} \tag{4.50}$$

Let $x_{11}, x_{12}, \ldots, x_{1n_1}$ be a random sample of n_1 observations from the first population and $x_{21}, x_{22}, \ldots, x_{2n_2}$ be a random sample of n_2 observations from the second population. Let $\bar{x}_1, \bar{x}_2, s_1^2, s_2^2$ be the sample means and sample variances, respectively. Now the expected value of the difference in sample means $\bar{x}_1 - \bar{x}_2$ is $E(\bar{x}_1 - \bar{x}_2) = \mu_1 - \mu_2$, so $\bar{x}_1 - \bar{x}_2$ is an unbiased estimator of the difference in means. The variance of $\bar{x}_1 - \bar{x}_2$ is

$$V(\bar{x}_1 - \bar{x}_2) = \frac{\sigma^2}{n_1} + \frac{\sigma^2}{n_2} = \sigma^2\left(\frac{1}{n_1} + \frac{1}{n_2}\right)$$

It seems reasonable to combine the two sample variances s_1^2 and s_2^2 to form an estimator of σ^2. The **pooled estimator** of σ^2 is defined as follows.

The **pooled estimator** of σ^2, denoted by s_p^2, is defined by

$$s_p^2 = \frac{(n_1 - 1)s_1^2 + (n_2 - 1)s_2^2}{n_1 + n_2 - 2} \tag{4.51}$$

It is easy to see that the pooled estimator s_p^2 can be written as

$$\begin{aligned} s_p^2 &= \frac{n_1 - 1}{n_1 + n_2 - 2} s_1^2 + \frac{n_2 - 1}{n_1 + n_2 - 2} s_2^2 \\ &= w s_1^2 + (1 - w) s_2^2 \end{aligned}$$

where $0 < w \le 1$. Thus s_p^2 is a **weighted average** of the two sample variances s_1^2 and s_2^2, where the weights w and $1 - w$ depend on the two sample sizes n_1 and n_2. Obviously, if $n_1 = n_2 = n$, then $w = 0.5$ and s_p^2 is simply the arithmetic average of s_1^2 and s_2^2. If $n_1 = 10$ and $n_2 = 20$ (say), then $w = 0.32$ and $1 - w = 0.68$. The first sample contributes $n_1 - 1$ degrees of freedom to s_p^2 and the second sample contributes $n_2 - 1$ degrees of freedom. Therefore, s_p^2 has $n_1 + n_2 - 2$ degrees of freedom.

Now we know that

$$z = \frac{\bar{x}_1 - \bar{x}_2 - (\mu_1 - \mu_2)}{\sigma\sqrt{\dfrac{1}{n_1} + \dfrac{1}{n_2}}}$$

has a $N(0, 1)$ distribution. Replacing σ by s_p gives the following.

Given the assumptions of this section, the quantity

$$t = \frac{\bar{x}_1 - \bar{x}_2 - (\mu_1 - \mu_2)}{s_p\sqrt{\dfrac{1}{n_1} + \dfrac{1}{n_2}}} \tag{4.52}$$

has a t distribution with $n_1 + n_2 - 2$ degrees of freedom.

The use of this information to test the hypotheses in equation (4.50) is now straightforward: Simply replace $\mu_1 - \mu_2$ by Δ_0, and the resulting **test statistic** has a t distribution with $n_1 + n_2 - 2$ degrees of freedom under H_0: $\mu_1 - \mu_2 = \Delta_0$. The location of the critical region for both two-sided and one-sided alternatives parallels those in the one-sample case. This procedure is usually called the pooled t-test.

The Two-Sample Pooled *t*-Test[1]

Null hypothesis: $H_0: \mu_1 - \mu_2 = \Delta_0$

Test statistic:
$$t_0 = \frac{\bar{x}_1 - \bar{x}_2 - \Delta_0}{s_p\sqrt{\dfrac{1}{n_1} + \dfrac{1}{n_2}}} \tag{4.53}$$

Alternative Hypotheses	Fixed Significance Level Rejection Criterion	*P*-Value
$H_1: \mu_1 - \mu_2 \neq \Delta_0$	$t_0 > t_{\alpha/2, n_1+n_2-2}$ or $t_0 < -t_{\alpha/2, n_1+n_2-2}$	P = Sum of the probability above t_0 and below t_0
$H_1: \mu_1 - \mu_2 > \Delta_0$	$t_0 > t_{\alpha, n_1+n_2-2}$	P = Probability above t_0
$H_1: \mu_1 - \mu_2 < \Delta_0$	$t_0 < -t_{\alpha, n_1+n_2-2}$	P = Probability below t_0

EXAMPLE 4.9 Comparing Mean Yields

Two catalysts are being analyzed to determine how they affect the mean yield of a chemical process. Specifically, catalyst 1 is currently in use, but catalyst 2 is acceptable. Since catalyst 2 is cheaper, it should be adopted, providing it does not change the process yield. An experiment is run in the pilot plant and results in the data shown in Table 4.2. Is there any difference between the mean yields? Use $\alpha = 0.05$ and assume equal variances.

■ **TABLE 4.2**
Catalyst Yield Data, Example 4.9

Observation Number	Catalyst 1	Catalyst 2
1	91.50	89.19
2	94.18	90.95
3	92.18	90.46
4	95.39	93.21
5	91.79	97.19
6	89.07	97.04
7	94.72	91.07
8	89.21	92.75
	$\bar{x}_1 = 92.255$	$\bar{x}_2 = 92.733$
	$s_1 = 2.39$	$s_2 = 2.98$

SOLUTION

The hypotheses are

$$H_0: \mu_1 = \mu_2$$
$$H_1: \mu_1 \neq \mu_2$$

From Table 4.2 we have $\bar{x}_1 = 92.255$, $s_1 = 2.39$, $n_1 = 8$, $\bar{x}_2 = 92.733$, $s_2 = 2.98$, and $n_2 = 8$. Therefore,

$$s_p^2 = \frac{(n_1 - 1)s_1^2 + (n_2 - 1)s_2^2}{n_1 + n_2 - 2} = \frac{(7)(2.39)^2 + (7)(2.98)^2}{8 + 8 - 2} = 7.30$$

$$s_p = \sqrt{7.30} = 2.70$$

[1] Although we have given the development of this procedure for the case where the sample sizes could be different, there is an advantage to using equal sample sizes $n_1 = n_2 = n$. When the sample sizes are the same from both populations, the t-test is very robust to the assumption of equal variances.

and

$$t_0 = \frac{\bar{x}_1 - \bar{x}_2}{2.70\sqrt{\frac{1}{n_1} + \frac{1}{n_2}}} = \frac{92.255 - 92.733}{2.70\sqrt{\frac{1}{8} + \frac{1}{8}}} = -0.35$$

Because $t_{0.025,14} = -2.145$, and $-2.145 < -0.35 < 2.145$, the null hypothesis cannot be rejected. That is, at the 0.05 level of significance, we do not have strong evidence to conclude that catalyst 2 results in a mean yield that differs from the mean yield when catalyst 1 is used.

Figure 4.9 shows comparative box plots for the yield data for the two types of catalysts. These comparative box plots indicate that there is no obvious difference in the median of the two samples, although the second sample has a slightly larger sample dispersion or variance. There are no exact rules for comparing two samples with box plots; their primary value is in the visual impression they provide as a tool for explaining the results of a hypothesis test, as well as in verification of assumptions.

Figure 4.10 presents a Minitab normal probability plot of the two samples of yield data. Note that both samples plot approximately along straight lines, and the straight lines for each sample have similar slopes. (Recall that the slope of the line is proportional to the standard deviation.) Therefore, we conclude that the normality and equal variances assumptions are reasonable.

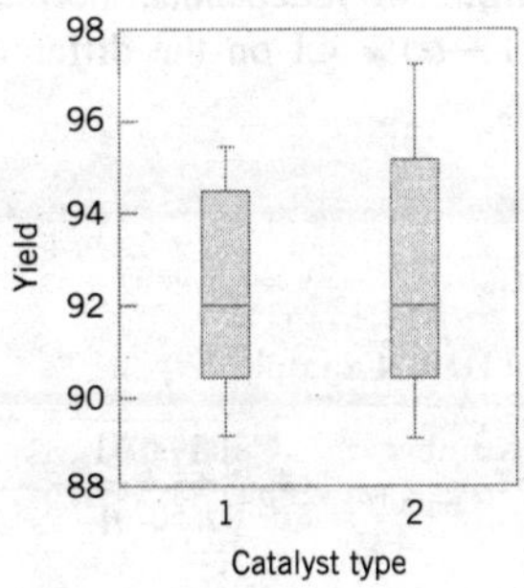

■ FIGURE 4.9 Comparative box plots for the catalyst yield data.

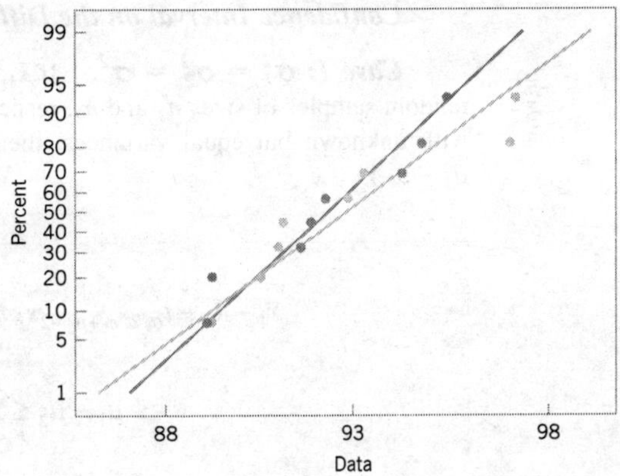

■ FIGURE 4.10 Minitab normal probability plot of the catalyst yield-data.

A P-value could also be used for decision making in this example. The actual value is $P = 0.7289$. (This value was obtained from a hand-held calculator.) Therefore, since the P-value exceeds $\alpha = 0.05$, the null hypothesis cannot be rejected.

Case 2: $\sigma_1^2 \neq \sigma_2^2$. In some situations, we cannot reasonably assume that the unknown variances σ_1^2 and σ_2^2 are equal. There is not an exact t-statistic available for testing H_0: $\mu_1 - \mu_2 = \Delta_0$ in this case. However, if H_0: $\mu_1 - \mu_2 = \Delta_0$ is true, then the statistic

$$t_0^* = \frac{\bar{x}_1 - \bar{x}_2 - \Delta_0}{\sqrt{\frac{s_1^2}{n_1} + \frac{s_2^2}{n_2}}} \tag{4.54}$$

is distributed approximately as t with degrees of freedom given by

$$v = \frac{\left(\frac{s_1^2}{n_1} + \frac{s_2^2}{n_2}\right)^2}{\frac{\left(s_1^2/n_1\right)^2}{n_1 - 1} + \frac{\left(s_2^2/n_2\right)^2}{n_2 - 1}} - 2 \tag{4.55}$$

Therefore, if $\sigma_1^2 \neq \sigma_2^2$, the hypotheses on differences in the means of two normal distributions are tested as in the equal variances case, except that t_0^* is used as the test statistic and $n_1 + n_2 - 2$ is replaced by v in determining the degrees of freedom for the test.

Confidence Interval on the Difference on Means, Variances Unknown.

Case 1: $\boldsymbol{\sigma_1^2 = \sigma_2^2 = \sigma^2}$. If $\bar{x}_1$, $\bar{x}_2$, s_1^2, and s_2^2 are the means and variances of two random samples of sizes n_1 and n_2, respectively, from two independent normal populations with unknown but equal variances, then a $100(1 - \alpha)\%$ CI on the difference in means $\mu_1 - \mu_2$ is

$$\bar{x}_1 - \bar{x}_2 - t_{\alpha/2,\, n_1+n_2-2}\, s_p \sqrt{\frac{1}{n_1} + \frac{1}{n_2}} \le \mu_1 - \mu_2 \le \bar{x}_1 - \bar{x}_2 + t_{\alpha/2,\, n_1+n_2-2}\, s_p \sqrt{\frac{1}{n_1} + \frac{1}{n_2}} \tag{4.56}$$

where $s_p = \sqrt{[(n_1 - 1)s_1^2 + (n_2 - 1)s_2^2]/(n_1 + n_2 - 2)}$ is the pooled estimate of the common population standard deviation, and $t_{\alpha/2, n_1+n_2-2}$ is the upper $\alpha/2$ percentage point of the t distribution with $n_1 + n_2 - 2$ degrees of freedom.

Case 2: $\boldsymbol{\sigma_1^2 \neq \sigma_2^2}$. If $\bar{x}_1$, $\bar{x}_2$, s_1^2, and s_2^2 are the means and variances of two random samples of sizes n_1 and n_2, respectively, from two independent normal populations with unknown and unequal variances, then an approximate $100(1 - \alpha)\%$ CI on the difference in means $\mu_1 - \mu_2$ is

$$\bar{x}_1 - \bar{x}_2 - t_{\alpha/2,\, v} \sqrt{\frac{s_1^2}{n_1} + \frac{s_2^2}{n_2}} \le \mu_1 - \mu_2 \le \bar{x}_1 - \bar{x}_2 + t_{\alpha/2,\, v} \sqrt{\frac{s_1^2}{n_1} + \frac{s_2^2}{n_2}} \tag{4.57}$$

where v is given by equation 4.55 and $t_{\alpha/2,v}$ is the upper $\alpha/2$ percentage point of the t distribution with v degrees of freedom.

EXAMPLE 4.10 Doped Versus Undoped Cement

An article in the journal *Hazardous Waste and Hazardous Materials* (Vol. 6, 1989) reported the results of an analysis of the weight of calcium in standard cement and cement doped with lead. Reduced levels of calcium would indicate that the hydration mechanism in the cement is blocked and would allow water to attack various locations in the cement structure. Ten samples of standard cement had an average weight percent calcium of $\bar{x}_1 = 90.0$, with a sample standard deviation of $s_1 = 5.0$, and 15 samples of the lead-doped cement had an average weight percent calcium of $\bar{x}_2 = 87.0$, with a sample standard deviation of $s_2 = 4.0$. Is there evidence to support a claim that doping the cement with lead changes the mean weight of calcium in the cement?

SOLUTION

We will assume that weight percent calcium is normally distributed and find a 95% confidence interval on the difference in means, $\mu_1 - \mu_2$, for the two types of cement. Furthermore, we will assume that both normal populations have the same standard deviation.

The pooled estimate of the common standard deviation is found using equation 4.51 as follows:

$$s_p^2 = \frac{(n_1-1)s_1^2 + (n_2-1)s_2^2}{n_1+n_2-2} = \frac{(9)(5.0)^2 + 14(4.0)^2}{10+15-2} = 19.52$$

Therefore, the pooled standard deviation estimate is $s_p = \sqrt{19.52} = 4.4$. The 95% CI is found using equation 4.56:

$$\bar{x}_1 - \bar{x}_2 - t_{0.025,23}s_p\sqrt{\frac{1}{n_1}+\frac{1}{n_2}} \le \mu_1 - \mu_2 \le \bar{x}_1 - \bar{x}_2 + t_{0.025,23}s_p\sqrt{\frac{1}{n_1}+\frac{1}{n_2}}$$

or upon substituting the sample values and using $t_{0.025,23} = 2.069$,

$$90.0 - 87.0 - 2.069(4.4)\sqrt{\frac{1}{10}+\frac{1}{15}} \le \mu_1 - \mu_2 \le 90.0 - 87.0 + 2.069(4.4)\sqrt{\frac{1}{10}+\frac{1}{15}}$$

which reduces to

$$-0.72 \le \mu_1 - \mu_2 \le 6.72$$

Note that the 95% CI includes zero; therefore, at this level of confidence we cannot conclude that there is a difference in the means. Put another way, there is no evidence that doping the cement with lead affected the mean weight percent of calcium; therefore, we cannot claim that the presence of lead affects this aspect of the hydration mechanism at the 95% level of confidence.

Computer Solution. Two-sample statistical tests can be performed using most statistics software packages. The following display presents the output from the Minitab two-sample *t*-test routine for the catalyst yield data in Example 4.9.

Two-Sample *t*-test and CI: Catalyst 1, Catalyst 2

```
Two-sample T for Catalyst 1 vs Catalyst 2
              N    Mean   StDev   SE Mean
Catalyst 1    8   92.26    2.39      0.84
Catalyst 2    8   92.73    2.98       1.1
Difference = mu Catalyst 1 - mu Catalyst 2
Estimate for difference: -0.48
95% CI for difference: -(3.39, 2.44)
t-test of difference = 0 (vs not = ): T-value = -0.35
  P-Value = 0.729 DF = 14
```

The output includes summary statistics for each sample, confidence intervals on the difference in means, and the hypothesis testing results. This analysis was performed assuming equal variances. Minitab has an option to perform the analysis assuming unequal variances. The confidence levels and α-value may be specified by the user. The hypothesis testing procedure indicates that we cannot reject the hypothesis that the mean yields are equal, which agrees with the conclusions we reached originally in Example 4.9.

Minitab will also perform power and sample size calculations for the two-sample pooled t-test. The following display from Minitab illustrates some calculations for the catalyst yield problem in Example 4.9.

Power and Sample Size

```
2-Sample t Test

Testing mean 1 = mean 2 (versus not = )
Calculating power for mean 1 = mean 2 + difference
Alpha = 0.05 Sigma = 2.7

            Sample
Difference   Size      Power
2              8      0.2816

2-Sample t Test

Testing mean 1 = mean 2 (versus not = )
Calculating power for mean 1 = mean 2 + difference
Alpha = 0.05 Sigma = 2.7

             Sample                     Actual
Difference    Size    Target Power      Power
2              27        0.7500         0.7615
```

In the first part of the display, Minitab calculates the power of the test in Example 4.9 assuming that we want to reject the null hypothesis if the true mean difference in yields for the two catalysts were as large as 2, using the pooled estimate of the standard deviation $s_p = 2.70$. For the sample size of $n_1 = n_2 = 8$ for each catalyst, the power is reported as 0.2816, which is quite low. The next calculation determines the sample size that would be required to produce a power of 0.75, a much better value. Minitab reports that a considerably larger sample size for each catalyst type, $n_1 = n_2 = 27$, would be required.

Paired Data. It should be emphasized that we have assumed that the two samples used in the above tests are independent. In some applications, *paired* data are encountered. Observations in an experiment are often paired to prevent extraneous factors from inflating the estimate of the variance; hence, this method can be used to improve the precision of comparisons between means. For a further discussion of paired data, see Montgomery and Runger (2007). The analysis of such a situation is illustrated in the following example.

EXAMPLE 4.11 The Paired *t*-Test

Two different types of machines are used to measure the tensile strength of synthetic fiber. We wish to determine whether or not the two machines yield the same average tensile strength values. Eight specimens of fiber are randomly selected, and one strength measurement is made using each machine on each specimen. The coded data are shown in Table 4.3.

The data in this experiment have been paired to prevent the difference between fiber specimens (which could be substantial) from affecting the test on the difference between machines. The test procedure consists of obtaining the differences of the pair of observations on each of the n specimens—say, $d_j = x_{1j} - x_{2j}, j = 1, 2, \ldots, n$—and then testing the hypothesis that the mean of the difference μ_d is zero. Note that testing H_0: $\mu_d = 0$ is equivalent to testing H_0: $\mu_1 = \mu_2$; furthermore, the test on μ_d is simply the one-sample t-test discussed in Section 4.3.3. The test statistic is

$$t_0 = \frac{\bar{d}}{s_d/\sqrt{n}}$$

where

$$\bar{d} = \frac{1}{n}\sum_{j=1}^{n} d_j$$

and

$$s_d^2 = \frac{\sum_{j=1}^{n}(d_j - \bar{d})^2}{n-1} = \frac{\sum_{j=1}^{n} d_j^2 - \frac{\left(\sum_{j=1}^{n} d_j\right)^2}{n}}{n-1}$$

and H_0: $\mu_d = 0$ is rejected if $|t_0| > t_{\alpha/2,n-1}$.

In our example we find that

$$\bar{d} = \frac{1}{n}\sum_{j=1}^{n} d_j = \frac{1}{8}(-11) = -1.38$$

$$s_d^2 = \frac{\sum_{j=1}^{n} d_j^2 - \frac{\left(\sum_{j=1}^{n} d_j\right)^2}{n}}{n-1} = \frac{65 - \frac{(-11)^2}{8}}{7} = 7.13$$

Therefore, the test statistic is

$$t_0 = \frac{\bar{d}}{s_d/\sqrt{n}} = \frac{-1.38}{2.67/\sqrt{8}} = -1.46$$

Choosing $\alpha = 0.05$ results in $t_{0.025,7} = 2.365$, and we conclude that there is no strong evidence to indicate that the two machines differ in their mean tensile strength measurements (the P-value is $P = 0.18$).

TABLE 4.3
Paired Tensile Strength Data for Example 4.11

Specimen	Machine 1	Machine 2	Difference
1	74	78	−4
2	76	79	−3
3	74	75	−1
4	69	66	3
5	58	63	−5
6	71	70	1
7	66	66	0
8	65	67	−2

4.4.3 Inference on the Variances of Two Normal Distributions

Hypothesis Testing. Consider testing the hypothesis that the variances of two independent normal distributions are equal. If random samples of sizes n_1 and n_2 are taken from populations 1 and 2, respectively, then the test statistic for

$$H_0: \sigma_1^2 = \sigma_2^2$$
$$H_1: \sigma_1^2 \neq \sigma_2^2$$

is simply the ratio of the two sample variances,

$$F_0 = \frac{s_1^2}{s_2^2} \tag{4.58}$$

We would reject H_0 if $F_0 > F_{\alpha/2,n_1-1,n_2-1}$ or if $F_0 < F_{1-(\alpha/2),n_1-1,n_2-1}$, where $F_{(\alpha/2),n_1-1,n_2-1}$ and $F_{1-(\alpha/2),n_1-1,n_2-1}$ denote the upper $\alpha/2$ and lower $1-(\alpha/2)$ percentage points of the F distribution with n_1-1 and n_2-1 degrees of freedom, respectively. The following display summarizes the test procedures for the one-sided alternative hypotheses.

Testing Hypotheses on $\sigma_1^2 = \sigma_2^2$ from Normal Distributions

Null hypothesis: H_0: $\sigma_1^2 = \sigma_2^2$

Alternative Hypotheses	Test Statistics	Rejection Criterion
H_1: $\sigma_1^2 < \sigma_2^2$	$F_0 = \dfrac{s_2^2}{s_1^2}$	$F_0 > F_{\alpha,n_2-1,n_1-1}$
H_1: $\sigma_1^2 > \sigma_2^2$	$F_0 = \dfrac{s_1^2}{s_2^2}$	$F_0 > F_{\alpha,n_1-1,n_2-1}$

Confidence Interval on the Ratio of the Variances of Two Normal Distributions. Suppose that $x_1 \sim N(\mu_1, \sigma_1^2)$ and $x_2 \sim N(\mu_2, \sigma_2^2$, where μ_1, and σ_2^2 are unknown, and we wish to construct a $100(1-\alpha)\%$ confidence interval on σ_1^2/σ_2^2. If s_1^2 and s_2^2 are the sample variances, computed from random samples of n_1 and n_2 observations, respectively, then the $100(1-\alpha)\%$ two-sided CI is

$$\frac{s_1^2}{s_2^2} F_{1-\alpha/2,n_2-1,n_1-1} \le \frac{\sigma_1^2}{\sigma_2^2} \le \frac{s_1^2}{s_2^2} F_{\alpha/2,n_2-1,n_1-1} \tag{4.59}$$

where $F_{\alpha/2,u,v}$ is the percentage point of the F distribution with u and v degrees of freedom such that $P\{F_{u,v} \ge F_{\alpha/2,u,v}\} = \alpha/2$. The corresponding upper and lower confidence bounds are

$$\frac{\sigma_1^2}{\sigma_2^2} \le \frac{s_1^2}{s_2^2} F_{\alpha,n_2-1,n_1-1} \tag{4.60}$$

and

$$\frac{s_1^2}{s_2^2} F_{1-\alpha,n_2-1,n_1-1} \le \frac{\sigma_1^2}{\sigma_2^2} \tag{4.61}$$

respectively.[2]

[2]Appendix Table V gives only upper tail points of F; that is, $F_{\alpha,u,v}$ Lower tail points $F_{1-\alpha,u,v}$ may be found using the relationship $F_{1-\alpha,u,v} = 1/F_{\alpha,u,v}$.

4.4.4 Inference on Two Population Proportions

We now consider the case where there are two binomial parameters of interest—say, p_1 and p_2—and we wish to draw inferences about these proportions. We will present large-sample hypothesis testing and confidence interval procedures based on the normal approximation to the binomial.

Large-Sample Test for H_0: $p_1 = p_2$. Suppose that the two independent random samples of sizes n_1 and n_2 are taken from two populations, and let x_1 and x_2 represent the number of observations that belong to the class of interest in samples 1 and 2, respectively. Furthermore, suppose that the normal approximation to the binomial is applied to each population, so that the estimators of the population proportions $\hat{p}_1 = x_1/n_1$ and $\hat{p}_2 = x_2/n_2$ and have approximate normal distributions. We are interested in testing the hypotheses

$$H_0: \ p_1 = p_2$$
$$H_1: \ p_1 \neq p_2$$

The statistic

$$Z = \frac{\hat{p}_1 - \hat{p}_2 - (p_1 - p_2)}{\sqrt{\dfrac{p_1(1-p_1)}{n_1} + \dfrac{p_2(1-p_2)}{n_2}}} \tag{4.62}$$

is distributed approximately as standard normal and is the basis of a test for H_0: $p_1 = p_2$. Specifically, if the null hypothesis H_0: $p_1 = p_2$ is true, then using the fact that $p_1 = p_2 = p$, the random variable

$$Z = \frac{\hat{p}_1 - \hat{p}_2}{\sqrt{p(1-p)\left(\dfrac{1}{n_1} + \dfrac{1}{n_2}\right)}}$$

is distributed approximately $N(0, 1)$. An estimator of the common parameter p is

$$\hat{p} = \frac{x_1 + x_2}{n_1 + n_2}$$

The test statistic for H_0: $p_1 = p_2$ is then

$$Z_0 = \frac{\hat{p}_1 - \hat{p}_2}{\sqrt{\hat{p}(1-\hat{p})\left(\dfrac{1}{n_1} + \dfrac{1}{n_2}\right)}}$$

This leads to the test procedures described here.

Testing Hypothesis on Two Population Proportions

Null hypothesis: H_0: $p_1 = p_2$

Test statistic:
$$Z_0 = \frac{\hat{p}_1 - \hat{p}_2}{\sqrt{\hat{p}(1-\hat{p})\left(\dfrac{1}{n_1} + \dfrac{1}{n_2}\right)}} \tag{4.63}$$

Alternative Hypotheses	Fixed Significance Level Rejection Criterion	*P*-value
$H_1: p_1 \neq p_2$	$Z_0 > Z_{\alpha/2}$ or $Z_0 < -Z_{\alpha/2}$	$P = 2[1 - \Phi(\lvert Z_0 \rvert)]$
$H_1: p_1 > p_2$	$Z_0 > Z_\alpha$	$P = 1 - \Phi(Z_0)$
$H_1: p_1 < p_2$	$Z_0 < -Z_\alpha$	$P = \Phi(Z_0)$

Confidence Interval on the Difference in Two Population Proportions. If there are two population proportions of interest—say, p_1 and p_2—it is possible to construct a $100(1 - \alpha)\%$ CI on their difference. The CI is as follows.

$$\hat{p}_1 - \hat{p}_2 - Z_{\alpha/2}\sqrt{\frac{\hat{p}_1(1-\hat{p}_1)}{n_1} + \frac{\hat{p}_2(1-\hat{p}_2)}{n_2}} \leq p_1 - p_2$$
$$\leq \hat{p}_1 - \hat{p}_2 + Z_{\alpha/2}\sqrt{\frac{\hat{p}_1(1-\hat{p}_1)}{n_1} + \frac{\hat{p}_2(1-\hat{p}_2)}{n_2}} \quad (4.64)$$

This result is based on the normal approximation to the **binomial distribution**.

4.5 What If There Are More Than Two Populations? The Analysis of Variance

As this chapter has illustrated, testing and experimentation are a natural part of the engineering analysis process and arise often in quality control and improvement problems. Suppose, for example, that an engineer is investigating the effect of different heat-treating methods on the mean hardness of a steel alloy. The experiment would consist of testing several specimens of alloy using each of the proposed heat-treating methods and then measuring the hardness of each specimen. The data from this experiment could be used to determine which heat-treating method should be used to provide maximum mean hardness.

If there are only two heat-treating methods of interest, this experiment could be designed and analyzed using the two-sample *t*-test presented in this chapter. That is, the experimenter has a single **factor** of interest—heat-treating methods—and there are only two **levels** of the factor.

Many single-factor experiments require that more than two levels of the factor be considered. For example, the engineer may want to investigate five different heat-treating methods. In this chapter we show how the **analysis of variance** (ANOVA) can be used for comparing means when there are more than two levels of a single factor. We will also discuss **randomization** of the experimental runs and the important role this concept plays in the overall experimentation strategy. In Part IV, we will discuss how to design and analyze experiments with several factors.

4.5.1 An Example

A manufacturer of paper used for making grocery bags is interested in improving the tensile strength of the product. Product engineering thinks that tensile strength is a function of the hardwood concentration in the pulp and that the range of hardwood concentrations of practical

■ TABLE 4.4
Tensile Strength of Paper (psi)

Hardwood Concentration (%)	Observations 1	2	3	4	5	6	Totals	Averages
5	7	8	15	11	9	10	60	10.00
10	12	17	13	18	19	15	94	15.67
15	14	18	19	17	16	18	102	17.00
20	19	25	22	23	18	20	127	21.17
							383	15.96

interest is between 5% and 20%. A team of engineers responsible for the study decides to investigate four levels of hardwood concentration: 5%, 10%, 15%, and 20%. They decide to make up six test specimens at each concentration level, using a pilot plant. All 24 specimens are tested on a laboratory tensile tester, in random order. The data from this experiment are shown in Table 4.4.

This is an example of a completely randomized single-factor experiment with four levels of the factor. The levels of the factor are sometimes called **treatments,** and each treatment has six observations or **replicates.** The role of **randomization** in this experiment is extremely important. By randomizing the order of the 24 runs, the effect of any nuisance variable that

■ FIGURE 4.11 (*a*) Box plots of hardwood concentration data. (*b*) Display of the model in equation 4.65 for the completely randomized single-factor experiment.

may influence the observed tensile strength is approximately balanced out. For example, suppose that there is a warm-up effect on the tensile testing machine; that is, the longer the machine is on, the greater the observed tensile strength. If all 24 runs are made in order of increasing hardwood concentration (that is, all six 5% concentration specimens are tested first, followed by all six 10% concentration specimens, etc.), then any observed differences in tensile strength could also be due to the warm-up effect.

It is important to graphically analyze the data from a designed experiment. Figure 4.11*a* presents box plots of tensile strength at the four hardwood concentration levels. This figure indicates that changing the hardwood concentration has an effect on tensile strength; specifically, higher hardwood concentrations produce higher observed tensile strength. Furthermore, the distribution of tensile strength at a particular hardwood level is reasonably symmetric, and the variability in tensile strength does not change dramatically as the hardwood concentration changes.

Graphical interpretation of the data is always useful. Box plots show the variability of the observations *within* a treatment (factor level) and the variability *between* treatments. We now discuss how the data from a single-factor randomized experiment can be analyzed statistically.

4.5.2 The Analysis of Variance

Suppose we have a different levels of a single factor that we wish to compare. Sometimes, each factor level is called a treatment, a very general term that can be traced to the early applications of experimental design methodology in the agricultural sciences. The response for each of the a treatments is a random variable. The observed data would appear as shown in Table 4.5. An entry in Table 4.5—say, y_{ij}—represents the jth observation taken under treatment i. We initially consider the case in which there are an equal number of observations, n, on each treatment.

We may describe the observations in Table 4.5 by the **linear statistical model**

$$y_{ij} = \mu + \tau_i + \varepsilon_{ij} \begin{cases} i = 1, 2, \ldots, a \\ j = 1, 2, \ldots, n \end{cases} \tag{4.65}$$

where y_{ij} is a random variable denoting the (ij)th observation, μ is a parameter common to all treatments called the **overall mean,** τ_i is a parameter associated with the ith treatment called the ith *treatment effect,* and ε_{ij} is a random error component. Note that the model could have been written as

$$y_{ij} = \mu_i + \varepsilon_{ij} \begin{cases} i = 1, 2, \ldots, a \\ j = 1, 2, \ldots, n \end{cases}$$

■ **TABLE 4.5**
Typical Data for a Single-Factor Experiment

Treatment	Observations				Totals	Averages
1	y_{11}	y_{12}	...	y_{1n}	$y_{1\cdot}$	$\bar{y}_{1\cdot}$
2	y_{21}	y_{22}	...	y_{2n}	$y_{2\cdot}$	$\bar{y}_{2\cdot}$
.	.	.	...	.	.	.
.	.	.	...	.	.	.
.	.	.	...	.	.	.
a	y_{a1}	y_{a2}	...	y_{an}	$y_{a\cdot}$	$\bar{y}_{a\cdot}$
					$y_{\cdot\cdot}$	$\bar{y}_{\cdot\cdot}$

where $\mu_i = \mu + \tau_i$ is the mean of the ith treatment. In this form of the model, we see that each treatment defines a population that has mean μ_i, consisting of the overall mean μ plus an effect τ_i that is due to that particular treatment. We will assume that the errors ε_{ij} are normally and independently distributed with mean zero and variance σ^2. Therefore, each treatment can be thought of as a normal population with mean μ_i and variance σ^2. See Fig. 4.11*b*.

Equation (4.65) is the underlying model for a single-factor experiment. Furthermore, since we require that the observations are taken in random order and that the environment (often called the experimental units) in which the treatments are used is as uniform as possible, this design is called a **completely randomized experimental design.**

We now present the analysis of variance for testing the equality of a population means. This is called a **fixed effects model analysis of variance (ANOVA)**. However, the ANOVA is a far more useful and general technique; it will be used extensively in Chapters 13 and 14. In this section we show how it can be used to test for equality of treatment effects. The treatment effects τ_i are usually defined as deviations from the overall mean μ, so that

$$\sum_{i=1}^{a} \tau_i = 0 \tag{4.66}$$

Let $\bar{y}_{i.}$ represent the total of the observations under the ith treatment and $\bar{y}_{i\cdot}$ represent the average of the observations under the ith treatment. Similarly, let $y_{..}$ represent the grand total of all observations and $\bar{y}_{..}$ represent the grand mean of all observations. Expressed mathematically,

$$y_{i\cdot} = \sum_{j=1}^{n} y_{ij} \qquad \bar{y}_{i\cdot} = y_{i\cdot}/n \quad i = 1,2,\ldots,a$$
$$y_{..} = \sum_{i=1}^{a}\sum_{j=1}^{n} y_{ij} \quad \bar{y}_{..} = y_{..}/N \tag{4.67}$$

where $N = an$ is the total number of observations. Thus, the "dot" subscript notation implies summation over the subscript that it replaces.

We are interested in testing the equality of the a treatment means $\mu_1, \mu_2, \ldots, \mu_a$. Using equation (4.66), we find that this is equivalent to testing the hypotheses

$$\begin{aligned} H_0&: \ \tau_1 = \tau_2 = \cdots = \tau_a = 0 \\ H_1&: \ \tau_i \neq 0 \ \text{ for at least one } i \end{aligned} \tag{4.68}$$

Thus, if the null hypothesis is true, each observation consists of the overall mean μ plus a realization of the random error component ε_{ij}. This is equivalent to saying that all N observations are taken from a normal distribution with mean μ and variance σ^2. Therefore, if the null hypothesis is true, changing the levels of the factor has no effect on the mean response.

The ANOVA partitions the total variability in the sample data into two component parts. Then, the test of the hypothesis in equation 4.68 is based on a comparison of two independent estimates of the population variance. The total variability in the data is described by the **total sum of squares**

$$SS_T = \sum_{i=1}^{a}\sum_{j=1}^{n}\left(y_{ij} - \bar{y}_{..}\right)^2$$

The basic ANOVA partition of the total sum of squares is given in the following definition.

The sum of squares identity is

$$\sum_{i=1}^{a}\sum_{j=1}^{n}\left(y_{ij}-\bar{y}_{..}\right)^2 = n\sum_{i=1}^{a}\left(\bar{y}_{i.}-\bar{y}_{..}\right)^2 + \sum_{i=1}^{a}\sum_{j=1}^{n}\left(y_{ij}-\bar{y}_{i.}\right)^2 \tag{4.69}$$

The proof of this identity is straightforward. Note that we may write

$$\sum_{i=1}^{a}\sum_{j=1}^{n}\left(y_{ij}-\bar{y}_{..}\right)^2 = \sum_{i=1}^{a}\sum_{j=1}^{n}\left[\left(\bar{y}_{i.}-\bar{y}_{..}\right)+\left(y_{ij}-\bar{y}_{i.}\right)\right]^2$$

or

$$\sum_{i=1}^{a}\sum_{j=1}^{n}\left(y_{ij}-\bar{y}_{..}\right)^2 = n\sum_{i=1}^{a}\left(\bar{y}_{i.}-\bar{y}_{..}\right)^2 + \sum_{i=1}^{a}\sum_{j=1}^{n}\left(y_{ij}-\bar{y}_{i.}\right)^2 + 2\sum_{i=1}^{a}\sum_{j=1}^{n}\left(\bar{y}_{i.}-\bar{y}_{..}\right)\left(y_{ij}-\bar{y}_{i.}\right) \tag{4.70}$$

Note that the cross-product term in equation 4.70 is zero, since

$$\sum_{j=1}^{n}\left(y_{ij}-\bar{y}_{i.}\right) = y_{i.} - n\bar{y}_{i.} = y_{i.} - n\left(y_{i.}/n\right) = 0$$

Therefore, we have shown that equation 4.70 will reduce to equation (4.69).

The identity in equation (4.69) shows that the total variability in the data, measured by the total sum of squares, can be partitioned into a sum of squares of differences between treatment means and the grand mean and a sum of squares of differences of observations within a treatment from the treatment mean. Differences between observed treatment means and the grand mean measure the differences between treatments, whereas differences of observations within a treatment from the treatment mean can be due only to random error. Therefore, we write equation (4.69) symbolically as

$$SS_T = SS_{\text{Treatments}} + SS_E \tag{4.71}$$

where

$$SS_T = \sum_{i=1}^{a}\sum_{j=1}^{n}\left(y_{ij}-\bar{y}_{..}\right)^2 = \text{total sum of squares}$$

$$SS_{\text{Treatments}} = n\sum_{i=1}^{a}\left(\bar{y}_{i.}-\bar{y}_{..}\right)^2 = \text{treatment sum of squares}$$

and

$$SS_E = \sum_{i=1}^{a}\sum_{j=1}^{n}\left(y_{ij}-\bar{y}_{j.}\right)^2 = \text{error sum of squares}$$

We can gain considerable insight into how the ANOVA works by examining the expected values of $SS_{\text{Treatments}}$ and SS_E. This will lead us to an appropriate statistic for testing the hypothesis of no differences among treatment means (or $\tau_i = 0$).

The expected value of the treatment sum of squares is

$$E(SS_{\text{Treatments}}) = (a-1)\sigma^2 + n\sum_{i=1}^{a}\tau_i^2$$

Now if the null hypothesis in equation (4.68) is true, each τ_i is equal to zero and

$$E\left(\frac{SS_{\text{Treatments}}}{a-1}\right) = \sigma^2$$

If the alternative hypothesis is true, then

$$E\left(\frac{SS_{\text{Treatments}}}{a-1}\right) = \sigma^2 + \frac{n\sum_{i=1}^{a}\tau_i^2}{a-1}$$

The ratio $MS_{\text{Treatments}} = SS_{\text{Treatments}}/(a-1)$ is called the **mean square for treatments.** Thus, if H_0 is true, $MS_{\text{Treatments}}$ is an unbiased estimator of σ^2 whereas if H_1 is true, $MS_{\text{Treatments}}$ estimates σ^2 plus a positive term that incorporates variation due to the systematic difference in treatment means. (Refer to the supplemental material for this chapter for the proofs of these two statements.)

We can also show that the expected value of the error sum of squares is $E(SS_E) = a(n-1)\sigma^2$. Therefore, the **error mean square** $MS_E = SS_E/[a(n-1)]$ is an unbiased estimator of σ^2 regardless of whether or not H_0 is true.

The **error mean square**

$$MS_E = \frac{SS_E}{a(n-1)}$$

is an unbiased estimator of σ^2.

There is also a partition of the number of degrees of freedom that corresponds to the sum of squares identity in equation (4.69). That is, there are $an = N$ observations; thus, SS_T has $an - 1$ degrees of freedom. There are a levels of the factor, so $SS_{\text{Treatments}}$ has $a - 1$ degrees of freedom. Finally, within any treatment there are n replicates providing $n - 1$ degrees of freedom with which to estimate the experimental error. Since there are a treatments, we have $a(n - 1)$ degrees of freedom for error. Therefore, the degrees of freedom partition is

$$an - 1 = a - 1 + a(n-1)$$

Now assume that each of the a populations can be modeled as a normal distribution. Using this assumption we can show that if the null hypothesis H_0 is true, the ratio

$$F_0 = \frac{SS_{\text{Treatments}}/(a-1)}{SS_E/[a(n-1)]} = \frac{MS_{\text{Treatments}}}{MS_E} \tag{4.72}$$

has an F distribution with $a - 1$ and $a(n - 1)$ degrees of freedom. Furthermore, from the expected mean squares, we know that MS_E is an unbiased estimator of σ^2. Also, under the null hypothesis, $MS_{\text{Treatments}}$ is an unbiased estimator of σ^2. However, if the null hypothesis is false, then the expected value of $MS_{\text{Treatments}}$ is greater than σ^2. Therefore, under the alternative hypothesis, the expected value of the numerator of the test statistic (equation 4.72) is greater than the expected value of the denominator. Consequently, we should reject H_0 if the statistic is large. This implies an upper-tail, one-tail critical region. Therefore, we would reject H_0 if $F_0 > F_{\alpha,a-1,a(n-1)}$ where F_0 is computed from equation (4.72). A P-value approach can also be used, with the P-value equal to the probability above F_0 in the $F_{a-1,a(n-1)}$ distribution.

Efficient computational formulas for the sums of squares may be obtained by expanding and simplifying the definitions of $SS_{\text{Treatments}}$ and SS_T. This yields the following results.

Definition

The sums of squares computing formulas for the analysis of variance with equal sample sizes in each treatment are

$$SS_T = \sum_{i=1}^{a}\sum_{j=1}^{n} y_{ij}^2 - \frac{y_{..}^2}{N} \tag{4.73}$$

and

$$SS_{\text{Treatments}} = \sum_{i=1}^{a} \frac{y_{i.}^2}{n} - \frac{y_{..}^2}{N} \tag{4.74}$$

The error sum of squares is obtained by subtraction as

$$SS_E = SS_T - SS_{\text{Treatments}} \tag{4.75}$$

The computations for this test procedure are usually summarized in tabular form as shown in Table 4.6. This is called an **analysis of variance** (or **ANOVA**) table.

■ **TABLE 4.6**
The Analysis of Variance for a Single-Factor Experiment

Source of Variation	Sum of Squares	Degrees of Freedom	Mean Square	F_0
Treatments	$SS_{\text{Treatments}}$	$a - 1$	$MS_{\text{Treatments}}$	$\frac{MS_{\text{Treatments}}}{MS_E}$
Error	SS_E	$a(n - 1)$	MS_E	
Total	SS_T	$an - 1$		

EXAMPLE 4.12 The Paper Tensile Strength Experiment

Consider the paper tensile strength experiment described in Section 4.5.1. Use the analysis of variance to test the hypothesis that different hardwood concentrations do not affect the mean tensile strength of the paper.

SOLUTION

The hypotheses are

$$H_0: \quad \tau_1 = \tau_2 = \tau_3 = \tau_4 = 0$$
$$H_1: \quad \tau_i \neq 0 \text{ for at least one } i$$

We will use $\alpha = 0.01$. The sums of squares for the ANOVA are computed from equations 4.73, 4.74, and 4.75 as follows:

$$SS_T = \sum_{i=1}^{4}\sum_{j=1}^{6} y_{ij}^2 - \frac{y_{..}^2}{N}$$
$$= (7)^2 + (8)^2 + \cdots + (20)^2 - \frac{(383)^2}{24} = 512.96$$

$$SS_{\text{Treatments}} = \sum_{i=1}^{4} \frac{y_{i.}^2}{n} - \frac{y_{..}^2}{N}$$
$$= \frac{(60)^2 + (94)^2 + (102)^2 + (127)^2}{6} - \frac{(383)^2}{24} = 382.79$$

$$SS_E = SS_T - SS_{\text{Treatments}}$$
$$= 512.96 - 382.79 = 130.17$$

We usually do not perform these calculations by hand. The ANOVA from Minitab is presented in Table 4.7. Since $F_{0.01,3,20} = 4.94$, we reject H_0 and conclude that hardwood concentration in the pulp significantly affects the strength of the paper. Note that the computer output reports a P-value for the test statistic $F = 19.61$ in Table 4.7 of zero. This is a truncated value; the actual P-value is $P = 3.59 \times 10^{-6}$. However, since the P-value is considerably smaller than $\alpha = 0.01$, we have strong evidence to conclude that H_0 is not true. Note that Minitab also provides some summary information about each level of hardwood concentration, including the confidence interval on each mean.

■ TABLE 4.7
Minitab Analysis of Variance Output for the Paper Tensile Strength Experiment

```
                     One-Way Analysis of Variance

Analysis of Variance
Source     DF       SS        MS        F        P
Factor      3   382.79    127.60    19.61    0.000
Error      20   130.17      6.51
Total      23   512.96
                                     Individual 95% CIs For Mean
                                     Based on Pooled StDev
Level       N      Mean     StDev    —+———————+———————+———————+
5           6    10.000     2.828    (—*—)
10          6    15.667     2.805               (—*—)
15          6    17.000     1.789                  (—*—)
20          6    21.167     2.639                        (—*—)
                                     —+———————+———————+———————+
Pooled StDev = 2.551                 10.0    15.0    20.0    25.0
```

Note that the ANOVA tells us whether there is a difference among means. It does not tell us which means differ. If the analysis of variance indicates that there is a statistically significant difference among means, there is a simple graphical procedure that can be used to isolate the specific differences. Suppose that $\bar{y}_{1.}, \bar{y}_{2.}, \ldots, \bar{y}_{a.}$ are the observed averages for these factor levels. Each treatment average has standard deviation $\sigma/\sqrt{n}$, where σ is the standard deviation of an individual observation. If all treatment means are equal, the observed means $\bar{y}_{i.}$ would behave as if they were a set of observations drawn at random from a normal distribution with mean μ and standard deviation $\sigma/\sqrt{n}$.

Visualize this normal distribution capable of being slid along an axis below which the treatment means $\bar{y}_{1.}, \bar{y}_{2.}, \ldots, \bar{y}_{a.}$ are plotted. If all treatment means are equal, there should be some position for this distribution that makes it obvious that the $\bar{y}_{i.}$ values were drawn from the same distribution. If this is not the case, then the $\bar{y}_{i.}$ values that do not appear to have been drawn from this distribution are associated with treatments that produce different mean responses.

The only flaw in this logic is that σ is unknown. However, we can use $\sqrt{MS_E}$ from the analysis of variance to estimate σ. This implies that a t distribution should be used instead of the normal in making the plot, but since the t looks so much like the normal, sketching a normal curve that is approximately $6\sqrt{MS_E/n}$ units wide will usually work very well.

Figure 4.12 shows this arrangement for the hardwood concentration experiment in Section 4.5.1. The standard deviation of this normal distribution is

$$\sqrt{MS_E/n} = \sqrt{6.51/6} = 1.04$$

If we visualize sliding this distribution along the horizontal axis, we note that there is no location for the distribution that would suggest that all four observations (the plotted means) are typical, randomly selected values from that distribution. This, of course, should be expected, because the analysis of variance has indicated that the means differ, and the display in Fig. 4.12 is simply a graphical representation of the analysis of variance results. The figure does indicate that treatment 4 (20% hardwood) produces paper with higher mean tensile strength than do the other treatments, and treatment 1 (5% hardwood) results in lower mean tensile strength than do the other treatments. The means of treatments 2 and 3 (10 and 15% hardwood, respectively) do not differ.

This simple procedure is a rough but very useful and effective technique for comparing means following an analysis of variance. However, there are many other more formal ways to do this. For more details on these procedures, see Montgomery (2005).

4.5.3 Checking Assumptions: Residual Analysis

The analysis of variance assumes that the model errors (and as a result, the observations) are normally and independently distributed with the same variance in each factor level. These

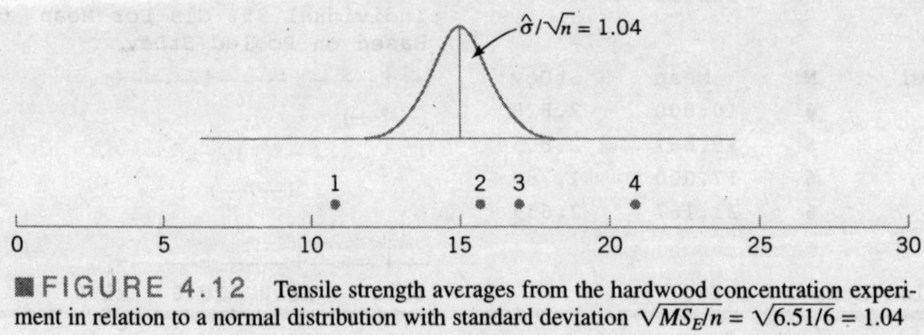

■ FIGURE 4.12 Tensile strength averages from the hardwood concentration experiment in relation to a normal distribution with standard deviation $\sqrt{MS_E/n} = \sqrt{6.51/6} = 1.04$

■ TABLE 4.8
Residuals for the Hardwood Experiment

Hardwood Concentration	Residuals					
5%	−3.00	−2.00	5.00	1.00	−1.00	0.00
10%	−3.67	1.33	−2.67	2.33	+3.33	−0.67
15%	−3.00	1.00	2.00	0.00	−1.00	1.00
20%	−2.17	3.83	0.83	1.83	−3.17	−1.17

assumptions can be checked by examining the residuals. We define a residual as the difference between the actual observation y_{ij} and the value $\hat{y}_{ij}$ that would be obtained from a least squares fit of the underlying analysis of variance model to the sample data. For the type of experimental design in this situation, the value $\hat{y}_{ij}$ is the factor-level mean $\bar{y}_{i.}$. Therefore, the residual is $e_{ij} = y_{ij} - \bar{y}_{i.}$; that is, the difference between an observation and the corresponding factor-level mean. The residuals for the hardwood percentage experiment are shown in Table 4.8.

The normality assumption can be checked by constructing a normal probability plot of the residuals. To check the assumption of equal variances at each factor level, plot the residuals against the factor levels and compare the spread in the residuals. It is also useful to plot the residuals against $\bar{y}_{i.}$ (sometimes called the **fitted value**); the variability in the residuals should not depend in any way on the value of $y_{i.}$. When a pattern appears in these plots, it usually suggests the need for data **transformation**—that is, analyzing the data in a different metric. For example, if the variability in the residuals increases with $\bar{y}_{i.}$, then a transformation such as $\log y$ or $\sqrt{y}$ should be considered. In some problems the dependency of residual scatter on y_i is very important information. It may be desirable to select the factor level that results in maximum mean response; however, this level may also cause more variation in response from run to run.

The independence assumption can be checked by plotting the residuals against the run order in which the experiment was performed. A pattern in this plot, such as sequences of positive and negative residuals, may indicate that the observations are not independent. This suggests that run order is important or that variables that change over time are important and have not been included in the experimental design.

A normal probability plot of the residuals from the hardwood concentration experiment is shown in Fig. 4.13. Figures 4.14 and 4.15 present the residuals plotted against the

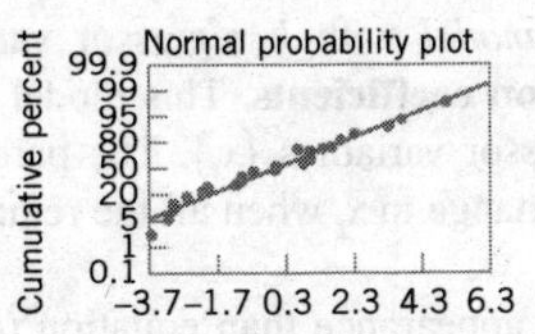

■ FIGURE 4.13 Normal probability plot of residuals from the hardwood concentration experiment.

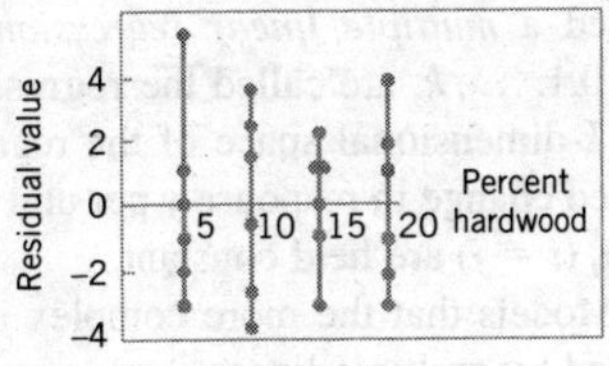

■ FIGURE 4.14 Plot of residuals versus factor levels.

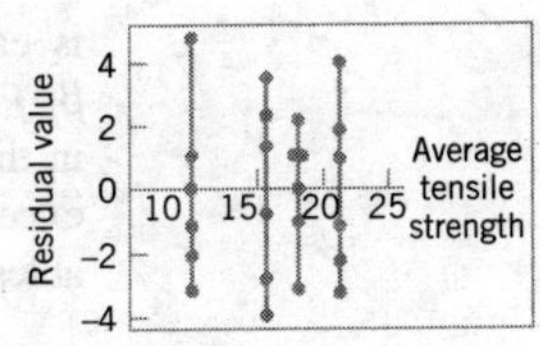

■ FIGURE 4.15 Plot of residuals verus $\bar{y}_i$.

factor levels and the fitted value $\bar{y}_i$. These plots do not reveal any model inadequacy or unusual problem with the assumptions.

4.6 Linear Regression Models

In many problems, two or more variables are related and it is of interest to model and explore this relationship. For example, in a chemical process the yield of product is related to the operating temperature. The chemical engineer may want to build a model relating yield to temperature and then use the model for prediction, process optimization, or process control.

In general, suppose that there is a single **dependent variable** or **response** y that depends on k **independent** or **repressor variables,** for example, $x_1, x_2, \ldots, x_k$ The relationship between these variables is characterized by a mathematical model called a **regression model.** The regression model is fit to a set of sample data. In some instances, the experimenter knows the exact form of the true functional relationship between y and $x_1, x_2, \ldots, x_k$. However, in most cases, the true functional relationship is unknown, and the experimenter chooses an appropriate function to approximate the true model. Low-order polynomial models are widely used as approximating functions.

There are many applications of regression models on quality and process implement. In this section, we present some aspects of fitting these models. More complete presentations of regression are available in Montgomery, Peck, and Vining (2006).

As an example of a linear regression model, suppose that we wish to develop an empirical model relating the viscosity of a polymer to the temperature and the catalyst feed rate. A model that might describe this relationship is

$$y = \beta_0 + \beta_1 x_1 + \beta_2 x_2 + \varepsilon \tag{4.76}$$

where y represents the viscosity, x_1 represents the temperature, and x_2 represents the catalyst feed rate. This is a **multiple linear regression model** with two independent variables. We often call the independent variables **predictor variables** or **regressors.** The term *linear* is used because Equation 4.76 is a linear function of the unknown parameter β_0, β_1, and β_2. The model describes a plane in the two-dimensional x_1, x_2, space. The parameter β_0 defines the intercept of the plane. We sometimes call β_1 and β_2 *partial regression coefficients* because β_1 measures the expected change in y per unit change in x_1 when x_2 is held constant and β_2 measures the expected change in y per unit change in x_2 when x_1 is held constant.

In general, the response variable y may be related to k regressor variables. The model

$$y = \beta_0 + \beta_1 x_1 + \beta_2 x_2 + \cdots + \beta_k x_k + \varepsilon \tag{4.77}$$

is called a *multiple linear regression model* with k regressor variables. The parameters $\beta_j, j = 0,1, \ldots, k$, are called the **regression coefficients.** This model describes a hyper plane in the k-dimensional space of the regressor variables $\{x_j\}$. The parameter β_j represents the expected change in response y per unit change in x_j when all the remaining independent variables x_i $(i \neq j)$ are held constant.

Models that the more complex in appearance than equation (4.77) may often still be analyzed by multiple linear regression techniques. For example, consider adding an interaction term to the first-order model in two variables, say

$$y = \beta_0 + \beta_1 x_1 + \beta_2 x_2 + \beta_{12} x_1 x_2 + \varepsilon \tag{4.78}$$

If we let $x_3 = x_1x_2$ and $\beta_3 = \beta_{12}$, then equation (4.78) can be written as

$$y = \beta_0 + \beta_1x_1 + \beta_2x_2 + \beta_3x_3 + \varepsilon \tag{4.79}$$

which is a standard multiple linear regression model with three regressors. As another example, consider the second-order **response surface model** in two variables:

$$y = \beta_0 + \beta_1x_1 + \beta_2x_x + \beta_{11}x_1^2 + \beta_{22}x_2^2 + \beta_{12}x_1x_2 + \varepsilon \tag{4.80}$$

If we let $x_3 = x_1^2$, $x_4 = x_2^2$, $x_5 = x_1x_2$, $\beta_3 = \beta_{11}$, $\beta_4 = \beta_{22}$, and $\beta_5 = \beta_{12}$, then this becomes

$$y = \beta_0 + \beta_1x_1 + \beta_2x_2 + \beta_3x_3 + \beta_4x_4 + \beta_5x_5 = \varepsilon \tag{4.81}$$

which is a linear regression model. In general, any regression model that is linear in the parameters (the βs) is a linear regression model, regardless of the shape of the responses surface that it generates.

In this section, we will summarize methods for estimating the parameters in multiple linear regression models. This is often called **model fitting.** We will also discuss methods for testing hypotheses and constructing confidence intervals for these models as well as for checking the adequacy of the model fit. For more complete presentations of regression, refer to Montgomery, Peck, and Vining (2006).

4.6.1 Estimation of the Parameters in Linear Regression Models

The method of **least squares** is typically used to **estimate** the regression coefficients in a multiple linear regression model. Suppose that $n > k$ observations on the response variable are available, say $y_1, y_2, \ldots, y_n$. Along with each observed response y_i, we will have an observation on each regressor variable and let x_{ij} denote the ith observation or level of variable x_j. The date will appear as in Table 4.9. We assume that the error term ε in the model has $E(\varepsilon) = 0$ and $V(\varepsilon) = \sigma^2$ and that the $\{\varepsilon_i\}$ are uncorrelated random variables.

We may write the model equation [equation (4.77)] in terms of the observations in Table 4.9 as

$$\begin{aligned} y_i &= \beta_0 + \beta_1x_{i1} + \beta_2x_{i2} + \cdots + \beta_kx_{ik} + \varepsilon_i \\ &= \beta_0 + \sum_{j=1}^{k} \beta_jx_{ij} + \varepsilon_i \quad i = 1, 2, \ldots, n \end{aligned} \tag{4.82}$$

■ **TABLE 4.9**
Data for Multiple Linear Regression

y	x_1	x_2	...	x_k
y_1	x_{11}	x_{12}	...	x_{1k}
y_2	x_{21}	x_{22}	...	x_{2k}
$\vdots$	$\vdots$	$\vdots$		$\vdots$
y_n	x_{n1}	x_{n2}		x_{nk}

The method of least squares chooses the βs in equation (4.82) so that the sum of the squares of the errors, ε_i, is minimized. The least squares function is

$$L = \sum_{i=1}^{n} \varepsilon_i^2 = \sum_{i=1}^{n} \left(y_i - \beta_0 - \sum_{j=1}^{k} \beta_j x_{ij} \right)^2 \tag{4.83}$$

The function L is to be minimized with respect to $\beta_0, \beta_1, \ldots, \beta_k$. The least squares estimators, say $\beta_0, \beta_1, \ldots, \beta_k$, must satisfy

$$\left. \frac{\partial L}{\partial \beta_0} \right|_{\hat{\beta}_0, \hat{\beta}_1, \ldots, \hat{\beta}_k} = -2 \sum_{i=1}^{n} \left(y_i - \hat{\beta}_0 - \sum_{j=1}^{k} \hat{\beta}_j x_{ij} \right) = 0 \tag{4.84a}$$

and

$$\left. \frac{\partial L}{\partial \beta_j} \right|_{\hat{\beta}_0, \hat{\beta}_1, \ldots, \hat{\beta}_k} = -2 \sum_{i=1}^{n} \left(y_i - \hat{\beta}_0 - \sum_{j=1}^{k} \hat{\beta}_j x_{ij} \right) x_{ij} = 0 \quad j = 1, 2, \ldots, k \tag{4.84b}$$

Simplifying Equation 4.84 we obtain

$$\begin{aligned}
n\hat{\beta}_0 + \hat{\beta}_i \sum_{i=1}^{n} x_{i1} + \hat{\beta}_2 \sum_{i=1}^{n} x_{i2} + \cdots + \hat{\beta}_k \sum_{i=1}^{n} x_{ik} &= \sum_{i=1}^{n} y_i \\
\hat{\beta}_0 \sum_{i=1}^{n} x_{i1} + \hat{\beta}_1 \sum_{i=1}^{n} x_{i1}^2 \square + \hat{\beta}_2 \sum_{i=1}^{n} x_{i1} x_{i2} + \cdots + \hat{\beta}_k \sum_{i=1}^{n} x_{i1} x_{ik} &= \sum_{i=1}^{n} x_{i1} y_i \\
\vdots \qquad \qquad \vdots \qquad \qquad \vdots \qquad \qquad \vdots \qquad &\qquad \vdots \\
\hat{\beta}_0 \sum_{i=1}^{n} x_{ik} + \hat{\beta}_1 \sum_{i=1}^{n} x_{ik} x_{i1} + \hat{\beta}_2 \sum_{i=1}^{n} x_{ik} x_{i2} + \cdots + \hat{\beta}_k \sum_{i=1}^{n} x_{ik}^2 &= \sum_{i=1}^{n} x_{ik} y_i
\end{aligned} \tag{4.85}$$

These equations are called the **least squares normal equations.** Note that there are $p = k + 1$ normal equations, one for each of the unknown regression coefficients. The solution to the normal equations will be the least squares estimators of the regression coefficients $\hat{\beta}_0, \hat{\beta}_1, \ldots, \hat{\beta}_k$.

It is simpler to solve the normal equations if they are expressed in matrix notation. We now give a matrix development of the normal equations that parallels the development of equation (4.85). The model in terms of the observations, equation (4.82) may be written in matrix notation as

$$\mathbf{y} = \mathbf{X}\boldsymbol{\beta} + \boldsymbol{\varepsilon}$$

where

$$\mathbf{y} = \begin{bmatrix} y_1 \\ y_2 \\ \vdots \\ y_n \end{bmatrix}, \quad \mathbf{X} = \begin{bmatrix} 1 & x_{11} & x_{12} & \cdots & x_{1k} \\ 1 & x_{21} & x_{22} & \cdots & x_{2k} \\ \vdots & \vdots & \vdots & & \vdots \\ 1 & x_{n1} & x_{n2} & \cdots & x_{nk} \end{bmatrix}, \quad \boldsymbol{\beta} = \begin{bmatrix} \beta_0 \\ \beta_1 \\ \vdots \\ \beta_k \end{bmatrix}, \quad \text{and} \quad \boldsymbol{\varepsilon} = \begin{bmatrix} \varepsilon_1 \\ \varepsilon_2 \\ \vdots \\ \varepsilon_n \end{bmatrix}$$

In general, $\mathbf{y}$ is an $(n \times 1)$ vector of the observations, $\mathbf{X}$ is an $(n \times p)$ matrix of the levels of the independent variables, $\boldsymbol{\beta}$ is a $(p \times 1)$ vector of the regression coefficients, and $\boldsymbol{\varepsilon}$ is an $(n \times 1)$ vector of random errors.

We wish to find the vector of least squares estimators, $\hat{\boldsymbol{\beta}}$, that minimizes

$$L = \sum_{i=1}^{n} \varepsilon_i^2 = \boldsymbol{\varepsilon}'\boldsymbol{\varepsilon} = (\mathbf{y} - \mathbf{X}\boldsymbol{\beta})'(\mathbf{y} - \mathbf{X}\boldsymbol{\beta})$$

Note that L may be expressed as

$$\begin{aligned} L &= \mathbf{y}'\mathbf{y} - \boldsymbol{\beta}'\mathbf{X}'\mathbf{y} - \mathbf{y}'\mathbf{X}\boldsymbol{\beta} + \boldsymbol{\beta}'\mathbf{X}'\mathbf{X}\boldsymbol{\beta} \\ &= \mathbf{y}'\mathbf{y} - 2\boldsymbol{\beta}'\mathbf{X}'\mathbf{y} + \boldsymbol{\beta}'\mathbf{X}'\mathbf{X}\boldsymbol{\beta} \end{aligned} \tag{4.86}$$

because $\boldsymbol{\beta}'\mathbf{X}'\mathbf{y}$ is a (1×1) matrix, or a scalar, and its transpose $(\boldsymbol{\beta}'\mathbf{X}'\mathbf{y})' = \mathbf{y}'\mathbf{X}\boldsymbol{\beta}$ is the same scalar. The least squares estimators must satisfy

$$\left.\frac{\partial L}{\partial \boldsymbol{\beta}}\right|_{\hat{\boldsymbol{\beta}}} = -2\mathbf{X}'\mathbf{y} + 2\mathbf{X}'\mathbf{X}\hat{\boldsymbol{\beta}} = \mathbf{0}$$

which simplifies to

$$\mathbf{X}'\mathbf{X}\hat{\boldsymbol{\beta}} = \mathbf{X}'\mathbf{y} \tag{4.87}$$

Equation (4.87) is the matrix form of the least squares normal equations. It is identical to equation (4.85). To solve the normal equations, multiply both sides of equation (4.87) by the inverse of $\mathbf{X}'\mathbf{X}$. Thus, the least squares estimator of $\boldsymbol{\beta}$ is

$$\hat{\boldsymbol{\beta}} = (\mathbf{X}'\mathbf{X})^{-1}\mathbf{X}'\mathbf{y} \tag{4.88}$$

It is easy to see that the matrix form for the normal equations is identical to the scalar form. Writing out equation (4.87) in detail, we obtain

$$\begin{bmatrix} n & \sum_{i=1}^{n} x_{i1} & \sum_{i=1}^{n} x_{i2} & \cdots & \sum_{i=1}^{n} x_{ik} \\ \sum_{i=1}^{n} x_{i1} & \sum_{i=1}^{n} x_{i1}^2 & \sum_{i=1}^{n} x_{i1}x_{i2} & \cdots & \sum_{i=1}^{n} x_{i1}x_{ik} \\ \vdots & \vdots & \vdots & & \vdots \\ \sum_{i=1}^{n} x_{ik} & \sum_{i=1}^{n} x_{ik}x_{i1} & \sum_{i=1}^{n} x_{ik}x_{i2} & \cdots & \sum_{i=1}^{n} x_{ik}^2 \end{bmatrix} \begin{bmatrix} \hat{\beta}_0 \\ \hat{\beta}_1 \\ \vdots \\ \hat{\beta}_k \end{bmatrix} = \begin{bmatrix} \sum_{i=1}^{n} y_i \\ \sum_{i=1}^{n} x_{i1}y_i \\ \vdots \\ \sum_{i=1}^{n} x_{ik}y_i \end{bmatrix}$$

If the indicated matrix multiplication is performed, the scalar form of the normal equations [i.e., equation (4.85)] will result. In this form it is easy to see that $\mathbf{X}'\mathbf{X}$ is a $(p \times p)$ symmetric matrix and $\mathbf{X}'\mathbf{y}$ is a $(p \times 1)$ column vector. Note the special structure of the $\mathbf{X}'\mathbf{X}$ matrix. The diagonal elements of $\mathbf{X}'\mathbf{X}$ are the sums of squares of the elements in the columns of $\mathbf{X}$, and the off-diagonal elements are the sums of cross-products of the elements in the columns of $\mathbf{X}$. Furthermore, note that the elements of $\mathbf{X}'\mathbf{y}$ are the sums of cross-products of the columns of $\mathbf{X}$ and the observations $\{y_i\}$.

The fitted regression model is

$$\hat{\mathbf{y}} = \mathbf{X}\hat{\boldsymbol{\beta}} \tag{4.89}$$

In scalar notation, the fitted model is

$$\hat{y}_i = \hat{\beta}_0 + \sum_{j=1}^{k} \hat{\beta}_j x_{ij} \quad i = 1, 2, \ldots, n$$

The difference between the actual observation y_i and the corresponding fitted value $\hat{y}_i$ is the **residual,** say $e_i = y_i - \hat{y}_i$. The $(n \times 1)$ vector of residuals is denoted by

$$\mathbf{e} = \mathbf{y} - \hat{\mathbf{y}} \tag{4.90}$$

Estimating σ^2. It is also usually necessary to estimate σ^2. To develop an estimator of this parameter, consider the sum of squares of the residuals, say

$$SS_E = \sum_{i=1}^{n} (y_i - \hat{y}_i)^2 = \sum_{i=1}^{n} e_i^2 = \mathbf{e}'\mathbf{e}$$

Substituting $\mathbf{e} = \mathbf{y} - \hat{\mathbf{y}} = \mathbf{y} - \mathbf{X}\hat{\boldsymbol{\beta}}$, we have

$$\begin{aligned} SS_E &= (\mathbf{y} - \mathbf{X}\hat{\boldsymbol{\beta}})'(\mathbf{y} - \mathbf{X}\hat{\boldsymbol{\beta}}) \\ &= \mathbf{y}'\mathbf{y} - \hat{\boldsymbol{\beta}}'\mathbf{X}'\mathbf{y} - \mathbf{y}'\mathbf{X}\hat{\boldsymbol{\beta}} + \hat{\boldsymbol{\beta}}'\mathbf{X}'\mathbf{X}\hat{\boldsymbol{\beta}} \\ &= \mathbf{y}'\mathbf{y} - 2\hat{\boldsymbol{\beta}}'\mathbf{X}'\mathbf{y} + \hat{\boldsymbol{\beta}}'\mathbf{X}'\mathbf{X}\hat{\boldsymbol{\beta}} \end{aligned}$$

Because $\mathbf{X}'\mathbf{X}\hat{\boldsymbol{\beta}} = \mathbf{X}'\mathbf{y}$, this last equation becomes

$$SS_E = \mathbf{y}'\mathbf{y} - \hat{\boldsymbol{\beta}}'\mathbf{X}'\mathbf{y} \tag{4.91}$$

Equation (4.91) is called the **error** or **residual sum of squares,** and it has $n - p$ degrees of freedom associated with it. It can be shown that

$$E(SS_E) = \sigma^2(n - p)$$

so an unbiased estimator of σ^2 is given by

$$\hat{\sigma}^2 = \frac{SS_E}{n - p} \tag{4.92}$$

Properties of the Estimators. The method of least squares produces an unbiased estimator of the parameter $\boldsymbol{\beta}$ in the linear regression model. This may be easily demonstrated by taking the expected value of $\hat{\boldsymbol{\beta}}$ as follows:

$$\begin{aligned} E(\hat{\boldsymbol{\beta}}) &= E\left[(\mathbf{X}'\mathbf{X})^{-1}\mathbf{X}'\mathbf{y}\right] = E\left[(\mathbf{X}'\mathbf{X})^{-1}\mathbf{X}'(\mathbf{X}\boldsymbol{\beta} + \boldsymbol{\varepsilon})\right] \\ &= E\left[(\mathbf{X}'\mathbf{X})^{-1}\mathbf{X}'\mathbf{X}\boldsymbol{\beta} + (\mathbf{X}'\mathbf{X})^{-1}\mathbf{X}'\boldsymbol{\varepsilon}\right] = \boldsymbol{\beta} \end{aligned}$$

because $E(\boldsymbol{\varepsilon}) = \mathbf{0}$ and $(\mathbf{X}'\mathbf{X})^{-1}\mathbf{X}'\mathbf{X} = \mathbf{I}$. Thus, $\hat{\boldsymbol{\beta}}$ is an unbiased estimator of $\boldsymbol{\beta}$.

The variance property of $\hat{\boldsymbol{\beta}}$ is expressed in the **covariance matrix**:

$$\text{Cov}(\hat{\boldsymbol{\beta}}) \equiv E\{[\hat{\boldsymbol{\beta}} - E(\hat{\boldsymbol{\beta}})][\hat{\boldsymbol{\beta}} - E(\hat{\boldsymbol{\beta}})]'\} \tag{4.93}$$

which is just a symmetric matrix whose ith main diagonal element is the variance of the individual regression coefficient $\hat{\beta}_i$ and whose (ij)th element is the covariance between $\hat{\beta}_i$ and $\hat{\beta}_j$. The covariance matrix of $\hat{\boldsymbol{\beta}}$ is

$$\text{Cov}(\hat{\boldsymbol{\beta}}) = \sigma^2(\mathbf{X}'\mathbf{X})^{-1} \tag{4.94}$$

EXAMPLE 4.13 Fitting a Linear Regression Model

Sixteen observations on the operating cost of a branch office of a finance company (y) and two predictor variables—number of new loan applications (x_1) and number of loans outstanding (x_2)—are shown in Table 4.10. Fit a multiple linear regression model

$$y = \beta_0 + \beta_1 x_1 + \beta_2 x_2 + \varepsilon$$

to these data.

■ TABLE 4.10
Consumers Finance Data for Example 4.13

Observation	New Applications (x_1)	Number of Loans Outstanding (x_2)	Cost
1	80	8	2256
2	93	9	2340
3	100	10	2426
4	82	12	2293
5	90	11	2330
6	99	8	2368
7	81	8	2250
8	96	10	2409
9	94	12	2364
10	93	11	2379
11	97	13	2440
12	95	11	2364
13	100	8	2404
14	85	12	2317
15	86	9	2309
16	87	12	2328

SOLUTION

The **X** matrix and **y** vector are

$$\mathbf{X} = \begin{bmatrix} 1 & 80 & 8 \\ 1 & 93 & 9 \\ 1 & 100 & 10 \\ 1 & 82 & 12 \\ 1 & 90 & 11 \\ 1 & 99 & 8 \\ 1 & 81 & 8 \\ 1 & 96 & 10 \\ 1 & 94 & 12 \\ 1 & 93 & 11 \\ 1 & 97 & 13 \\ 1 & 95 & 11 \\ 1 & 100 & 8 \\ 1 & 85 & 12 \\ 1 & 86 & 9 \\ 1 & 87 & 12 \end{bmatrix} \quad \mathbf{y} = \begin{bmatrix} 2256 \\ 2340 \\ 2426 \\ 2293 \\ 2330 \\ 2368 \\ 2250 \\ 2409 \\ 2364 \\ 2379 \\ 2440 \\ 2364 \\ 2404 \\ 2317 \\ 2309 \\ 2328 \end{bmatrix}$$

The $\mathbf{X}'\mathbf{X}$ matrix is

$$\mathbf{X}'\mathbf{X} = \begin{bmatrix} 1 & 1 & \cdots & 1 \\ 80 & 93 & \cdots & 87 \\ 8 & 9 & \cdots & 12 \end{bmatrix} \begin{bmatrix} 1 & 80 & 8 \\ 1 & 93 & 9 \\ \vdots & \vdots & \vdots \\ 1 & 87 & 12 \end{bmatrix} = \begin{bmatrix} 16 & 1458 & 164 \\ 1458 & 133{,}560 & 14{,}946 \\ 164 & 14{,}946 & 1{,}726 \end{bmatrix}$$

and the $\mathbf{X}'\mathbf{y}$ vector is

$$\mathbf{X}'\mathbf{y} = \begin{bmatrix} 1 & 1 & \cdots & 1 \\ 80 & 93 & \cdots & 87 \\ 8 & 9 & \cdots & 12 \end{bmatrix} \begin{bmatrix} 2256 \\ 2340 \\ \vdots \\ 2328 \end{bmatrix} = \begin{bmatrix} 37{,}577 \\ 3{,}429{,}550 \\ 385{,}562 \end{bmatrix}$$

The least squares estimate of $\boldsymbol{\beta}$ is

$$\hat{\boldsymbol{\beta}} = (\mathbf{X}'\mathbf{X})^{-1}\mathbf{X}'\mathbf{y}$$

(continued)

■ **TABLE 4.11**
Predicted Values, Residuals, and Other Diagnostics from Example 4.13

Observation i	y_i	Predicted Value $\hat{y}_i$	Residual e_i	h_{ii}	Studentized Residual	D_i	*R*-Student
1	2256	2244.5	11.5	0.350	0.87	0.137	0.87
2	2340	2352.1	−12.1	0.102	−0.78	0.023	−0.77
3	2426	2414.1	11.9	0.177	0.80	0.046	0.79
4	2293	2294.0	−1.0	0.251	−0.07	0.001	−0.07
5	2330	2346.4	−16.4	0.077	−1.05	0.030	−1.05
6	2368	2389.3	−21.3	0.265	−1.52	0.277	−1.61
7	2250	2252.1	−2.1	0.319	−0.15	0.004	−0.15
8	2409	2383.6	25.4	0.098	1.64	0.097	1.76
9	2364	2385.5	−21.5	0.142	−1.42	0.111	−1.48
10	2379	2369.3	9.7	0.080	0.62	0.011	0.60
11	2440	2416.9	23.1	0.278	1.66	0.354	1.80
12	2364	2384.5	−20.5	0.096	−1.32	0.062	−1.36
13	2404	2396.9	7.1	0.289	0.52	0.036	0.50
14	2317	2316.9	0.1	0.185	0.01	0.000	<0.01
15	2309	2298.8	10.2	0.134	0.67	0.023	0.66
16	2328	2332.1	−4.1	0.156	−0.28	0.005	−0.27

or

$$\hat{\boldsymbol{\beta}} = \begin{bmatrix} 14.176004 & -0.129746 & -0.223453 \\ -0.129746 & 1.429184 \times 10^{-3} & -4.763947 \times 10^{-5} \\ -0.223453 & -4,763947 \times 10^{-5} & 2.222381 \times 10^{-2} \end{bmatrix} \begin{bmatrix} 37,577 \\ 3,429,550 \\ 385,562 \end{bmatrix}$$

$$= \begin{bmatrix} 1566.07777 \\ 7.62129 \\ 8.58485 \end{bmatrix}$$

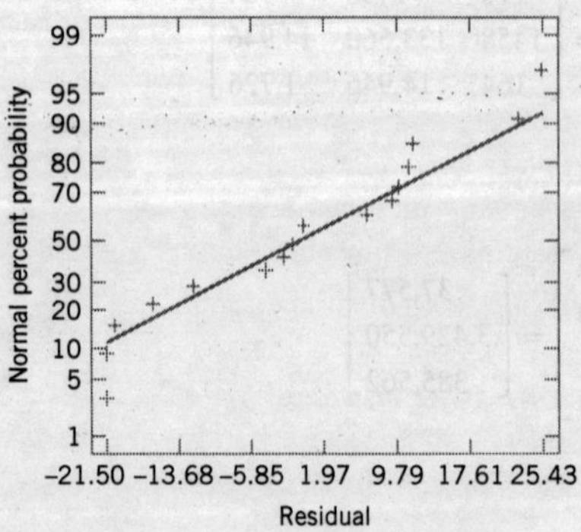

■ **FIGURE 4.16** Normal probability plot of residuals, Example 4.13.

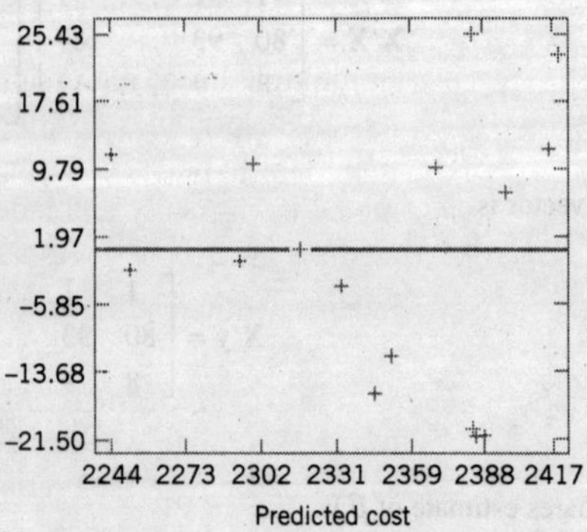

■ **FIGURE 4.17** Plot of residuals versus predicted cost, Example 4.13.

The least squares fit, with the regression coefficients reported to two decimal places, is

$$\hat{y} = 1566.08 + 7.62x_1 + 8.58x_2$$

The first three columns of Table 4.11 present the actual observations y_i, the predicted or fitted values $\hat{y}_i$, and the residuals. Figure 4.16 is a normal probability plot of the residuals. Plots of the residuals versus the predicted values $\hat{y}_i$ and versus the two variables x_1 and x_2 are shown in Figures 4.17, 4.18, and 4.19, respectively. Just as in ANOVA, residual plotting is an integral part of regression model building. These plots indicate that variance of the observed cost tends to increase with the magnitude of cost. Figure 4.18 suggests that the variability in cost may be increasing as the number of new applications increases.

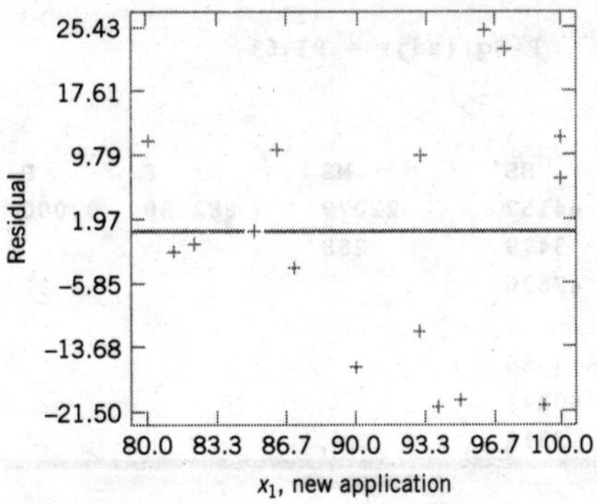

■ FIGURE 4.18 Plot of residuals versus x_1 (new applications), Example 4.13.

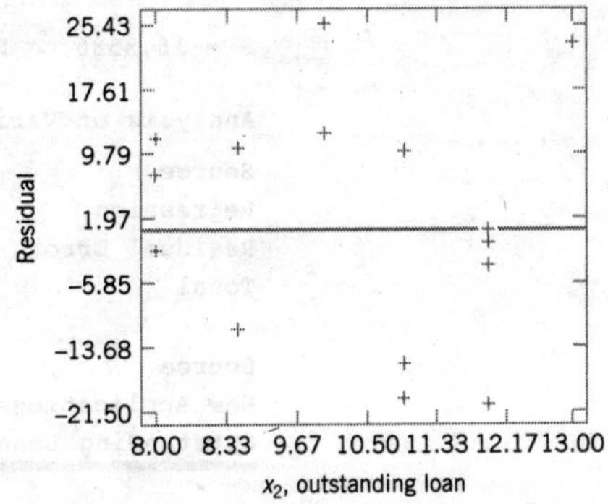

■ FIGURE 4.19 Plot of residuals versus x_2 (outstanding loan), Example 4.13.

Using the Computer. Regression model fitting is almost always done using a statistical software package. Table 4.12 shows some of the output obtained when Minitab is used to fit the consumer finance regression model in Example 4.13. In subsequent sections, we will discuss the analysis of variance and t-test information in Table 4.12 and will show how these quantities were computed.

4.6.2 Hypothesis Testing in Multiple Regression

In multiple linear regression problems, certain tests of hypotheses about the model parameters are helpful in measuring the usefulness of the model. In this section, we describe several important hypothesis-testing procedures. These procedures require that the errors ε_i in the model be normally and independently distributed with mean zero and variance σ^2, abbreviated $\varepsilon \sim \text{NID}(0, \sigma^2)$. As a result of this assumption, the observations y_i are normally and independently distributed with mean $\beta_0 + \sum_{j=1}^{k} \beta_j x_{ij}$ and variance σ^2.

Test for Significance of Regression. The test for significance of regression is a test to determine whether a linear relationship exists between the response variable y and a subset of the regressor variables $x_1, x_2, \ldots, x_k$. The appropriate hypotheses are

$$\begin{aligned} H_0&: \beta_1 = \beta_2 = \cdots = \beta_k = 0 \\ H_1&: \beta_j \neq 0 \quad \text{for at least one } j \end{aligned} \tag{4.95}$$

■ **TABLE 4.12**
Minitab Output for the Consumer Finance Regression Model, Example 4.13

Regression Analysis: Cost versus New Applications, Outstanding Loans

```
The regression equation is
Cost = 1566 + 7.62 New Applications + 8.58 Outstanding Loans

Predictor              Coef     SE Coef        T        P
Constant            1566.08       61.59    25.43    0.000
New Applications     7.6213      0.6184    12.32    0.000
Outstanding Loans     8.585       2.439     3.52    0.004

S = 16.3586     R-Sq = 92.7%     R-Sq (adj) = 91.6%

Analysis of Variance
Source             DF        SS        MS        F        P
Regression          2     44157     22079    82.50    0.000
Residual Error     13      3479       268
Total              15     47636

Source             DF    Seq SS
New Applications    1     40841
Outstanding Loans   1      3316
```

Rejection of H_0 in equation (4.95) implies that at least one of the regressor variables $x_1, x_2, \ldots, x_k$ contributes significantly to the model. The test procedure involves an analysis of variance partitioning of the total sum of squares SS_T into a sum of squares due to the model (or to regression) and a sum of squares due to residual (or error), say

$$SS_T = SS_R + SS_E \tag{4.96}$$

Now if the null hypothesis H_0: $\beta_1 = \beta_2 = \cdots = \beta_k = 0$ is true, then SS_R/σ^2 is distributed as χ^2_k, where the number of degrees of freedom for χ^2 is equal to the number of regressor variables in the model. Also, we can show that SS_E/σ^2 is distributed as χ^2_{n-k-1} and that SS_E and SS_R are independent. The test procedure for H_0: $\beta_1 = \beta_2 = \cdots = \beta_k = 0$ is to compute

$$F_0 = \frac{SS_R/k}{SS_E/(n-k-1)} = \frac{MS_R}{MS_E} \tag{4.97}$$

and to reject H_0 if F_0 exceeds $F_{\alpha,k,n-k-1}$. Alternatively, we could use the *P*-value approach to hypothesis testing and, thus, reject H_0 if the *P*-value for the statistic F_0 is less than α. The test is usually summarized in an analysis of variance table such as Table 4.13.

■ **TABLE 4.13**
Analysis of Variance for Significance of Regression in Multiple Regression

Source of Variation	Sum of Squares	Degrees of Freedom	Mean Square	F_0
Regression	SS_R	k	MS_R	MS_R/MS_E
Error or residual	SS_E	$n-k-1$	MS_E	
Total	SS_T	$n-1$		

A computational formula for SS_R may be found easily. We have derived a computational formula for SS_E in equation (4.91)—that is,

$$SS_E = \mathbf{y}'\mathbf{y} - \hat{\boldsymbol{\beta}}'\mathbf{X}'\mathbf{y}$$

Now, because $SS_T = \sum_{i=1}^{n} y_i^2 - (\sum_{i=1}^{n} y_i)^2/n = \mathbf{y}'\mathbf{y} - (\sum_{i=1}^{n} y_i)^2/n$, we may rewrite the foregoing equation as

$$SS_E = \mathbf{y}'\mathbf{y} - \frac{\left(\sum_{i=1}^{n} y_i\right)^2}{n} - \left[\hat{\boldsymbol{\beta}}'\mathbf{X}'\mathbf{y} - \frac{\left(\sum_{i=1}^{n} y_i\right)^2}{n}\right]$$

or

$$SS_E = SS_T - SS_R$$

Therefore, the regression sum of squares is

$$SS_R = \hat{\boldsymbol{\beta}}'\mathbf{X}'\mathbf{y} - \frac{\left(\sum_{i=1}^{n} y_i\right)^2}{n} \tag{4.98}$$

and the error sum of squares is

$$SS_E = \mathbf{y}'\mathbf{y} - \hat{\boldsymbol{\beta}}'\mathbf{X}'\mathbf{y} \tag{4.99}$$

and the total sum of squares is

$$SS_T = \mathbf{y}'\mathbf{y} - \frac{\left(\sum_{i=1}^{n} y_i\right)^2}{n} \tag{4.100}$$

These computations are almost always performed with regression software. For instance, Table 4.12 shows some of the output from Minitab for the consumer finance regression model in Example 4.13. The lower portion in this display is the analysis of variance for the model. The test of significance of regression in this example involves the hypotheses

$$H_0\colon \beta_1 = \beta_2 = 0$$
$$H_1\colon \beta_j \neq 0 \quad \text{for at least one } j$$

The P-value in Table 4.13 for the F statistic [equation (4.97)] is very small, so we would conclude that at least one of the two variables—new applications (x_1) and outstanding loans (x_2)—has a nonzero regression coefficient.

Table 4.13 also reports the coefficient to multiple determination R^2, where

$$R^2 = \frac{SS_R}{SS_T} = 1 - \frac{SS_E}{SS_T} \tag{4.101}$$

The statistic R^2 is a measure of the amount of reduction in the variability of y obtained by using the regressor variables $x_1, x_2, \ldots, x_k$ in the model. However, a large value of R^2 does not necessarily imply that the regression model is a good one. Adding a variable to the model will always increase R^2, regardless of whether the additional variable is statistically significant or not. Thus, it is possible for models that have large values of R^2 to yield poor predictions of new observations or estimates of the mean response.

Because R^2 always increases as we add terms to the model, some regression model builders prefer to use an **adjusted R² statistic** defined as

$$R^2_{\text{adj}} = 1 - \frac{SS_E/(n-p)}{SS_T/(n-1)} = 1 - \left(\frac{n-1}{n-p}\right)(1-R^2) \tag{4.102}$$

In general, the adjusted R^2 statistic will not always increase as variables are added to the model. In fact, if unnecessary terms are added, the value of R^2_{adj} will often decrease.

For example, consider the consumer finance regression model. The adjusted R^2 for the model is shown in Table 4.12. It is computed as

$$\begin{aligned} R^2_{\text{adj}} &= 1 - \left(\frac{n-1}{n-p}\right)(1-R^2) \\ &= 1 - \left(\frac{15}{13}\right)(1-0.92697) = 0.915735 \end{aligned}$$

which is very close to the ordinary R^2. When R^2 and R^2_{adj} differ dramatically, there is a good chance that nonsignificant terms have been included in the model.

Tests on Individual Regression Coefficients and Groups of Coefficients. We are frequently interested in testing hypotheses on the individual regression coefficients. Such tests would be useful in determining the value of each regressor variable in the regression model. For example, the model might be more effective with the inclusion of additional variables or perhaps with the deletion of one or more of the variables already in the model.

Adding a variable to the regression model always causes the sum of squares for regression to increase and the error sum of squares to decrease. We must decide whether the increase in the regression sum of squares is sufficient to warrant using the additional variable in the model. Furthermore, adding an unimportant variable to the model can actually increase the mean square error, thereby decreasing the usefulness of the model.

The hypotheses for testing the significance of any individual regression coefficient, say β_j, are

$$\begin{aligned} H_0&: \beta_j = 0 \\ H_1&: \beta_j \neq 0 \end{aligned}$$

If $H_0: \beta_j = 0$ is not rejected, then this indicates that x_j can be deleted from the model. The test statistic for this hypothesis is

$$t_0 = \frac{\hat{\beta}_j}{\sqrt{\hat{\sigma}^2 C_{jj}}} \tag{4.103}$$

where C_{jj} is the diagonal element of $(\mathbf{X}'\mathbf{X})^{-1}$ corresponding to $\hat{\beta}_j$. The null hypothesis $H_0: \beta_j = 0$ is rejected if $|t_0| > t_{\alpha/2, n-k-1}$. Note that this is really a partial or marginal test because the regression coefficient $\hat{\beta}_j$ depends on all the other regressor variables x_i $(i \neq j)$ that are in the model.

The denominator of equation (4.103), $\sqrt{\hat{\sigma}^2 C_{jj}}$, is often called the **standard error** of the regression coefficient $\hat{\beta}_j$. That is,

$$se(\hat{\beta}_j) = \sqrt{\hat{\sigma}^2 C_{jj}} \tag{4.104}$$

Therefore, an equivalent way to write the test statistic in equation (4.103) is

$$t_0 = \frac{\hat{\beta}_j}{se(\hat{\beta}_j)} \tag{4.105}$$

Most regression computer programs provide the t-test for each model parameter. For example, consider Table 4.12, which contains the Minitab output for Example 4.13. The upper portion of this table gives the least squares estimate of each parameter, the standard error, the t-statistic, and the corresponding P-value. We would conclude that both variables, new applications and outstanding loans, contribute significantly to the model.

We may also directly examine the contribution to the regression sum of squares for a particular variable, say x_j, given that other variables x_i $(i \neq j)$ are included in the model. The procedure for doing this is the general regression significance test or, as it is often called, the **extra sum of squares method.** This procedure can also be used to investigate the contribution of a *subset* of the regressor variables to the model. Consider the regression model with k regressor variables:

$$\mathbf{y} = \mathbf{X}\boldsymbol{\beta} + \boldsymbol{\varepsilon}$$

where $\mathbf{y}$ is $(n \times 1)$, $\mathbf{X}$ is $(n \times p)$, $\boldsymbol{\beta}$ is $(p \times 1)$, $\boldsymbol{\varepsilon}$ is $(n \times 1)$, and $p = k + 1$. We would like to determine if the subset of regressor variables $x_1, x_2, \ldots, x_r (r < k)$ contribute significantly to the regression model. Let the vector of regression coefficients be partitioned as follows:

$$\boldsymbol{\beta} = \begin{bmatrix} \boldsymbol{\beta}_1 \\ \boldsymbol{\beta}_2 \end{bmatrix}$$

where $\boldsymbol{\beta}_1$ is $(r \times 1)$ and $\boldsymbol{\beta}_2$ is $[(p - r) \times 1]$. We wish to test the hypotheses

$$\begin{aligned} H_0&: \boldsymbol{\beta}_1 = \mathbf{0} \\ H_1&: \boldsymbol{\beta}_1 \neq \mathbf{0} \end{aligned} \tag{4.106}$$

The model may be written as

$$\mathbf{y} = \mathbf{X}\boldsymbol{\beta} + \varepsilon = \mathbf{X}_1\boldsymbol{\beta}_1 + \mathbf{X}_2\boldsymbol{\beta}_2 + \varepsilon \tag{4.107}$$

where $\mathbf{X}_1$ represents the columns of $\mathbf{X}$ associated with $\boldsymbol{\beta}_1$ and $\mathbf{X}_2$ represents the columns of $\mathbf{X}$ associated with $\boldsymbol{\beta}_2$.

For the **full model** (including both $\boldsymbol{\beta}_1$ and $\boldsymbol{\beta}_2$), we know that $\hat{\boldsymbol{\beta}} = (\mathbf{X}'\mathbf{X})^{-1}\mathbf{X}'\mathbf{y}$. Also, the regression such of squares for all variables including the intercept is

$$SS_R(\boldsymbol{\beta}) = \hat{\boldsymbol{\beta}}'\mathbf{X}'\mathbf{y} \qquad (p \text{ degrees of freedom})$$

and

$$MS_E = \frac{\mathbf{y}'\mathbf{y} - \hat{\boldsymbol{\beta}}\mathbf{X}'\mathbf{y}}{n - p}$$

$SS_R(\boldsymbol{\beta})$ is called the regression sum of squares due to $\boldsymbol{\beta}$. To find the contribution of the terms in $\boldsymbol{\beta}_1$ to the regression, we fit the model assuming the null hypothesis $H_0: \boldsymbol{\beta}_1 = \mathbf{0}$ to be true. The **reduced model** is found from equation (4.107) with $\boldsymbol{\beta}_1 = \mathbf{0}$:

$$\mathbf{y} = \mathbf{X}_2\boldsymbol{\beta}_2 + \varepsilon \tag{4.108}$$

The least squares estimator of $\boldsymbol{\beta}_2$ is $\hat{\boldsymbol{\beta}}_2 = (\mathbf{X}'_2\mathbf{X}_2)^{-1}\mathbf{X}'_2\mathbf{y}$, and

$$SS_R(\boldsymbol{\beta}_2) = \hat{\boldsymbol{\beta}}'_2\mathbf{X}'_2\mathbf{y} \qquad (p - r \text{ degrees of freedom}) \tag{4.109}$$

The regression sum of squares due to $\boldsymbol{\beta}_1$ given that $\boldsymbol{\beta}_2$ is already in the model is

$$SS_R(\boldsymbol{\beta}_1|\boldsymbol{\beta}_2) = SS_R(\boldsymbol{\beta}) - SS_R(\boldsymbol{\beta}_2) \tag{4.110}$$

This sum of squares has r degrees of freedom. It is the "extra sum of squares" due to $\boldsymbol{\beta}_1$. Note that $SS_R(\boldsymbol{\beta}_1|\boldsymbol{\beta}_2)$ is the increase in the regression sum of squares due to including the variables $x_1, x_2, \ldots, x_r$ in the model.

Now, $SS_R(\boldsymbol{\beta}_1|\boldsymbol{\beta}_2)$ is independent of MS_E, and the null hypothesis $\boldsymbol{\beta}_1 = \mathbf{0}$ may be tested by the statistic

$$F_0 = \frac{SS_R(\boldsymbol{\beta}_1|\boldsymbol{\beta}_2)/r}{MS_E} \tag{4.111}$$

If $F_0 > F_{\alpha,r,n-p}$, we reject H_0, concluding that at least one of the parameters in $\boldsymbol{\beta}_1$ is not zero, and, consequently, at least one of the variables $x_1, x_2, \ldots, x_r$ in $\mathbf{X}_1$ contributes significantly to the regression model. Some authors call the test in equation (4.111) a **partial *F*-test.**

The partial *F*-test is very useful. We can use it to measure the contribution of x_j as if it were the last variable added to the model by computing

$$SS_R(\beta_j|\beta_0, \beta_1, \ldots, \beta_{j-1}, \beta_{j+1}, \ldots, \beta_k)$$

This is the increase in the regression sum of squares due to adding x_j to a model that already includes $x_1, \ldots, x_{j-1}, x_{j+1}, \ldots, x_k$. Note that the partial *F*-test on a single variable x_j is equivalent to the *t*-test in equation (4.103). However, the partial *F*-test is a more general procedure in that we can measure the effect of sets of variables.

EXAMPLE 4.14 The Extra Sum of Squares Method

Consider the consumer finance data in Example 4.13. Evaluate the contribution of x_2 (outstanding loans) to the model.

SOLUTION

The hypotheses we wish to test are

$$H_0\colon \beta_2 = 0$$
$$H_1\colon \beta_2 \neq 0$$

This will require the extra sum of squares due to β_2, or

$$\begin{aligned} SS_R(\beta_2|\beta_1, \beta_0) &= SS_R(\beta_0, \beta_1, \beta_2) - SS_R(\beta_0, \beta_1) \\ &= SS_R(\beta_1, \beta_2|\beta_0) - SS_R(\beta_2|\beta_0) \end{aligned}$$

Now from Table 4.12, where we tested for significance of regression, we have

$$SS_R(\beta_1, \beta_2|\beta_0) = 44{,}157.1$$

which was called the model sum of squares in the table. This sum of squares has two degrees of freedom.

The reduced model is

$$y = \beta_0 + \beta_1 x_1 + \varepsilon$$

The least squares fit for this model is

$$\hat{y} = 1652.3955 + 7.6397x_1$$

and the regression sum of squares for this model (with one degree of freedom) is

$$SS_R(\beta_1|\beta_0) = 40{,}840.8$$

Note that $SS_R(\beta_1|\beta_0)$ is shown at the bottom of the Minitab output in Table 4.12 under the heading "Seq SS." Therefore,

$$\begin{aligned} SS_R(\beta_2|\beta_0, \beta_1) &= 44{,}157.1 - 40{,}840.8 \\ &= 3316.3 \end{aligned}$$

with $2 - 1 = 1$ degree of freedom. This is the increase in the regression sum of squares that results from adding x_2 to model already containing x_1, and it is shown at the bottom of the Minitab output in Table 4.12. To test $H_0\colon \beta_2 = 0$, from the test statistic we obtain

$$F_0 = \frac{SS_R(\beta_2|\beta_0, \beta_1)/1}{MS_E} = \frac{3316.3/1}{267.604} = 12.3926$$

Note that MS_E from the full model (Table 4.12) is used in the denominator of F_0. Now, because $F_{0.05,1,13} = 4.67$, we would reject $H_0\colon \beta_2 = 0$ and conclude that x_2 (outstanding loans) contributes significantly to the model.

Because this partial *F*-test involves only a single regressor, it is equivalent to the *t*-test because the square of a *t* random variable with v degrees of freedom is an *F* random variable with 1 and v degrees of freedom. To see this, note from Table 4.12 that the *t*-statistic for $H_0\colon \beta_2 = 0$ resulted in $t_0 = 3.5203$ and that $t_0^2 = (3.5203)^2 = 12.3925 \simeq F_0$.

4.6.3 Confidence Intervals in Multiple Regression

It is often necessary to construct confidence interval estimates for the regression coefficients $\{\beta_j\}$ and for other quantities of interest from the regression model. The development of a procedure for obtaining these CIs requires that we assume the errors $\{\varepsilon_i\}$ to be normally and independently distributed with mean zero and variance σ^2, the same assumption made in the section on hypothesis testing in Section 4.6.2

Confidence Intervals on the Individual Regression Coefficients. Because the least squares estimator $\hat{\boldsymbol{\beta}}$ is a linear combination of the observations, it follows that $\hat{\boldsymbol{\beta}}$ is normally distributed with mean vector $\boldsymbol{\beta}$ and covariance matrix $\sigma^2(\mathbf{X}'\mathbf{X})^{-1}$. Then each of the statistics

$$\frac{\hat{\beta}_j - \beta_j}{\sqrt{\hat{\sigma}^2 C_{jj}}} \qquad j = 0, 1, \ldots, k \tag{4.112}$$

is distributed as t with $n - p$ degrees of freedom, where C_{jj} is the (jj)th element of the $(\mathbf{X}'\mathbf{X})^{-1}$ matrix, and $\hat{\sigma}^2$ is the estimate of the error variance, obtained from equation (4.92). Therefore, a $100(1 - \alpha)$ percent CI for the regression coefficient β_j, $j = 0, 1, \ldots, k$, is

$$\hat{\beta}_j - t_{\alpha/2,n-p}\sqrt{\hat{\sigma}^2 C_{jj}} \le \beta_j \le \hat{\beta}_j + t_{\alpha/2,n-p}\sqrt{\hat{\sigma}^2 C_{jj}} \tag{4.113}$$

Note that this CI could also be written as

$$\hat{\beta}_j - t_{\alpha/2,n-p}se(\hat{\beta}_j) \le \beta_j \le \hat{\beta}_j + t_{\alpha/2,n-p}se(\hat{\beta}_j)$$

because $se(\hat{\beta}_j) = \sqrt{\hat{\sigma}^2 C_{jj}}$.

EXAMPLE 4.15 A Confidence Interval on a Regression Coefficient

Construct a 95% confidence interval for the parameter β_1 in Example 4.13.

SOLUTION

The estimate of β_1 is $\hat{\beta}_1 = 7.62129$, and because $\hat{\sigma}^2 = 267.604$ and $C_{11} = 1.429184 \times 10^{-3}$, we find that

$$\hat{\beta}_1 - t_{0.025,13}\sqrt{\hat{\sigma}^2 C_{11}} \le \beta_1 \le \hat{\beta}_1 + t_{0.025,13}\sqrt{\hat{\sigma}^2 C_{11}}$$
$$7.62129 - 2.16\sqrt{(267.604)(1.429184 \times 10^{-3})} \le \beta_1$$
$$\le 7.62129 + 2.16\sqrt{(267.604)(1.429184 \times 10^{-3})}$$
$$7.62129 - 2.16(0.6184) \le \beta_1 \le 7.62129 + 2.16(0.6184)$$

and the 95% confidence interval on β_1 is

$$6.2855 \le \beta_1 \le 8.9570$$

Confidence Interval on the Mean Response. We may also obtain a confidence interval on the mean response at a particular point, say, $x_{01}, x_{02}, \ldots, x_{0k}$. We first define the vector

$$\mathbf{x}_0 = \begin{bmatrix} 1 \\ x_{01} \\ x_{02} \\ \vdots \\ x_{0k} \end{bmatrix}$$

The mean response at this point is

$$\mu_{y|\mathbf{x}_0} = \beta_0 + \beta_1 x_{01} + \beta_2 x_{02} + \cdots + \beta_k x_{0k} = \mathbf{x}_0'\boldsymbol{\beta}$$

The estimated mean response at this point is

$$\hat{y}(\mathbf{x}_0) = \mathbf{x}_0'\hat{\boldsymbol{\beta}} \tag{4.114}$$

This estimator is unbiased because $E[\hat{y}(\mathbf{x}_0)] = E(\mathbf{x}_0'\hat{\boldsymbol{\beta}}) = \mathbf{x}_0'\boldsymbol{\beta} = \mu_{y|\mathbf{x}_0}$, and the variance of $\hat{y}(\mathbf{x}_0)$ is

$$V[\hat{y}(\mathbf{x}_0)] = \sigma^2\mathbf{x}_0'(\mathbf{X}'\mathbf{X})^{-1}\mathbf{x}_0 \tag{4.115}$$

Therefore, a $100(1-\alpha)$ percent CI on the mean response at the point $x_{01}, x_{02}, \ldots, x_{0k}$ is

$$\hat{y}(\mathbf{x}_0) - t_{\alpha/2,n-p}\sqrt{\hat{\sigma}^2\mathbf{x}_0'(\mathbf{X}'\mathbf{X})^{-1}\mathbf{x}_0} \le \mu_{y|\mathbf{x}_0} \le y(\mathbf{x}_0) + t_{\alpha/2,n-p}\sqrt{\hat{\sigma}^2\mathbf{x}_0'(\mathbf{X}'\mathbf{X})^{-1}\mathbf{x}_0} \tag{4.116}$$

Minitab will calculate the CI in equation (4.116) for points of interest. For example, suppose that for the consumer finance regression model we are interested in finding an estimate of the mean cost and the associated 95% CI at two points: (1) New Applications = 85 and Outstanding Loans = 10, and (2) New Applications = 95 and Outstanding Loans = 12. Minitab reports the point estimates and the 95% CI calculated from equation (4.116) in Table 4.14.

When there are 85 new applications and 10 outstanding loans, the point estimate of cost is 2299.74, and the 95% CI is (2287.63, 2311.84), and when there are 95 new applications and 12 outstanding loans, the point estimate of cost is 2293.12, and the 95% CI is (2379.37, 2406.87). Notice that the lengths of the two confidence intervals are different. The length of the CI on the mean response depend on not only the level of confidence that is specified and the estimate of σ^2, but on the **location** of the point of interest. As the distance of the point from the center of the region of the predictor variables increases, the length of the confidence interval increases. Because the second point is further from the center of the region of the predictors, the second CI is longer than the first.

4.6.4 Prediction of New Response Observations

A regression model can be used to predict future observations on the response y corresponding to particular values of the regressor variables, say $x_{01}, x_{02}, \ldots, x_{0k}$. If $\mathbf{x}_0' = [1, x_{01}, x_{02}, \ldots, x_{0k}]$, then a point estimate for the future observation y_0 at the point $x_{01}, x_{02}, \ldots, x_{0k}$ is computed from equation (4.114):

$$\hat{y}(\mathbf{x}_0) = \mathbf{x}_0'\hat{\boldsymbol{\beta}}$$

■ **TABLE 4.14**
Minitab Output

```
Predicted Values for New Observations

New
Obs       Fit    SE Fit        95% CI                  95% PI
  1   2299.74      5.60   (2287.63, 2311.84)   (2262.38,  2337.09)
  2   2393.12      6.36   (2379.37, 2406.87)   (2355.20,  2431.04)

Values of Predictors for New Observations

New               New   Outstanding
Obs      Applications         Loans
  1              85.0          10.0
  2              95.0          12.0
```

A 100(1 − α) percent **prediction interval** (PI) for this future observation is

$$\hat{y}(\mathbf{x}_0) - t_{\alpha/2,n-p}\sqrt{\hat{\sigma}^2(1 + \mathbf{x}_0'(\mathbf{X}'\mathbf{X})^{-1}\mathbf{x}_0)} \le y_0 \le \hat{y}(\mathbf{x}_0) + t_{\alpha/2,n-p}\sqrt{\hat{\sigma}^2(1 + \mathbf{x}_0'(\mathbf{X}'\mathbf{X})^{-1}\mathbf{x}_0)} \quad (4.117)$$

In predicting new observations and in estimating the mean response at a given point $x_{01}, x_{02}, \ldots, x_{0k}$, we must be careful about extrapolating beyond the region containing the original observations. It is very possible that a model that fits well in the region of the original data will no longer fit well outside of that region.

The Minitab output in Table 4.14 shows the 95% prediction intervals on cost for the consumer finance regression model at the two points considered previously: (1) New Applications = 85 and Outstanding Loans = 10, and (2) New Applications = 95 and Outstanding Loans = 12. The predicted value of the future observation is exactly equal to the estimate of the mean at the point of interest. Notice that the prediction intervals are longer that the corresponding confidence intervals. You should be able to see why this happens from examining equations (4.116) and (4.117). The prediction intervals also get longer as the point where the prediction is made moves further away from the center of the predictor variable region.

4.6.5 Regression Model Diagnostics

As we emphasized in analysis of variance, **model adequacy checking** is an important part of the data analysis procedure. This is equally important in building regression models, and as we illustrated in Example 4.13, **residual plots** should always be examined for a regression model. In general, it is always necessary (1) to examine the fitted model to ensure that it provides an adequate approximation to the true system, and (2) to verify that none of the least squares regression assumptions are violated. The regression model will probably give poor or misleading results unless it is an adequate fit.

In addition to residual plots, other model diagnostics are frequently useful in regression. This section briefly summarizes some of these procedures. For more complete presentations, see Montgomery, Peck, and Vining (2006) and Myers (1990).

Scaled Residuals and PRESS. Many model builders prefer to work with **scaled residuals** in contrast to the ordinary least squares residuals. These scaled residuals often convey more information than do the ordinary residuals.

One type of scaled residual is the **standardized residual:**

$$d_i = \frac{e_i}{\hat{\sigma}} \qquad i = 1, 2, \ldots, n \quad (4.118)$$

where we generally use $\hat{\sigma} = \sqrt{MS_E}$ in the computation. These standardized residuals have mean zero and approximately unit variance; consequently, they are useful in looking for **outliers**. Most of the standardized residuals should lie in the interval $-3 \le d_i \le 3$, and any observation with a standardized residual outside of this interval is potentially unusual with respect to its observed response. These outliers should be carefully examined because they may represent something as simple as a data-recording error or something of more serious concern, such as a region of the regressor variable space where the fitted model is a poor approximation to the true response surface.

The standardizing process in equation (4.118) scales the residuals by dividing them by their approximate average standard deviation. In some data sets, residuals may have standard deviations that differ greatly. We now present a scaling that takes this into account.

The vector of fitted values $\hat{y}_i$ corresponding to the observed values y_i is

$$\begin{aligned}\hat{\mathbf{y}} &= \mathbf{X}\\ &= \mathbf{X}(\mathbf{X}'\mathbf{X})^{-1}\mathbf{X}'\mathbf{y}\\ &= \mathbf{Hy}\end{aligned} \tag{4.119}$$

The $n \times n$ matrix $\mathbf{H} = \mathbf{X}(\mathbf{X}'\mathbf{X})^{-1}\mathbf{X}'$ is usually called the "hat" matrix because it maps the vector of observed values into a vector of fitted values. The hat matrix and its properties play a central role in regression analysis.

The residuals from the fitted model may be conveniently written in matrix notation as

$$\mathbf{e} = \mathbf{y} - \hat{\mathbf{y}}$$

and it turns out that the covariance matrix of the residuals is

$$\text{Cov}(\mathbf{e}) = \sigma^2(\mathbf{I} - \mathbf{H}) \tag{4.120}$$

The matrix $\mathbf{I} - \mathbf{H}$ is generally not diagonal, so the residuals have different variances and they are correlated.

Thus, the variance of the ith residual is

$$V(e_i) = \sigma^2(1 - h_{ii}) \tag{4.121}$$

where h_{ii} is the ith diagonal element of $\mathbf{H}$. Because $0 \le h_{ii} \le 1$, using the residual mean square MS_E to estimate the variance of the residuals actually overestimates $V(e_i)$. Furthermore, because h_{ii} is a measure of the location of the ith point in x space, the variance of e_i depends on where the point x_i lies. Generally, residuals near the center of the x space have larger variance than do residuals at more remote locations. Violations of model assumptions are more likely at remote points, and these violations may be hard to detect from inspection of e_i (or d_i) because their residuals will usually be smaller.

We recommend taking this inequality of variance into account when scaling the residuals. We suggest plotting the **studentized residuals:**

$$r_i = \frac{e_i}{\sqrt{\hat{\sigma}^2(1 - h_{ii})}} \qquad i = 1, 2, \ldots, n \tag{4.122}$$

with $\hat{\sigma}^2 = MS_E$ instead of e_i (or d_i). The studentized residuals have constant variance $V(r_i) = 1$ regardless of the location of $\mathbf{x}_i$ when the form of the model is correct. In many situations the variance of the residuals stabilizes, particularly for large data sets. In these cases, there may be little difference between the standardized and studentized residuals. Thus standardized and studentized residuals often convey equivalent information. However, because any point with a large residual and a large h_{ii} is potentially highly influential on the least squares fit, examination of the studentized residuals is generally recommended. Table 4.11 displays the hat diagonals h_{ii} and the studentized residuals for the consumer finance regression model in Example 4.13.

The prediction error sum of squares (PRESS) provides a useful residual scaling. To calculate PRESS, we select an observation—for example, i. We fit the regression model to the remaining $n - 1$ observations and use this equation to predict the withheld observation y_i. Denoting this predicted value $\hat{y}_{(i)}$, we may find the prediction error for point i as $e_{(i)} = y_i - \hat{y}_{(i)}$. The prediction error is often called the ith PRESS residual. This procedure is repeated for each observation $i = 1, 2, \ldots, n$, producing a set of n PRESS residuals $e_{(1)}, e_{(2)}, \ldots, e_{(n)}$. Then the PRESS statistic is defined as the sum of squares of the n PRESS residuals as in

$$\text{PRESS} = \sum_{i=1}^{n} e_{(i)}^2 = \sum_{i=1}^{n} [y_i - \hat{y}_{(i)}]^2 \tag{4.123}$$

Thus, PRESS uses each possible subset of $n - 1$ observations as an estimation data set, and every observation in turn is used to form a prediction data set.

It would initially seem that calculating PRESS requires fitting n different regressions. However, it is possible to calculate PRESS from the results of a single least squares fit to all n observations. It turns out that the ith PRESS residual is

$$e_{(i)} = \frac{e_i}{1 - h_{ii}} \tag{4.124}$$

Thus, because PRESS is just the sum of the squares of the PRESS residuals, a simple computing formula is

$$\text{PRESS} = \sum_{i=1}^{n} \left(\frac{e_i}{1 - h_{ii}} \right)^2 \tag{4.125}$$

From equation (4.124) it is easy to see that the PRESS residual is just the ordinary residual weighted according to the diagonal elements of the hat matrix h_{ii}. Data points for which h_{ii} are large will have large PRESS residuals. These observations will generally be *high influence* points. Generally, a large difference between the ordinary residual and the PRESS residuals will indicate a point where the model fits the data well, but a model built without that point predicts poorly. In the next section we will discuss some other measures of influence.

Finally, we note that PRESS can be used to compute an approximate R^2 for prediction, say

$$R^2_{\text{Prediction}} = 1 - \frac{\text{PRESS}}{SS_T} \tag{4.126}$$

This statistic gives some indication of the predictive capability of the regression model. For the consumer finance regression model from Example 4.13, we can compute the PRESS residuals using the ordinary residuals and the values of h_{ii} found in Table 4.11. The corresponding value of the PRESS statistic is PRESS = 5207.7. Then

$$\begin{aligned} R^2_{\text{Prediction}} &= 1 - \frac{\text{PRESS}}{SS_T} \\ &= 1 - \frac{5207.7}{47{,}635.9} = 0.8907 \end{aligned}$$

Therefore, we could expect this model to "explain" about 89% of the variability in predicting new observations, as compared to the approximately 93% of the variability in the original data explained by the least squares fit. The overall predictive capability of the model based on this criterion seems very satisfactory.

The studentized residual r_i discussed above is often considered an outlier diagnostic. It is customary to use MS_E as an estimate of σ^2 in computing r_i. This is referred to as internal scaling of the residual because MS_E is an internally generated estimate of σ^2 obtained from fitting the model to all n observations. Another approach would be to use an estimate of σ^2 based on a data set with the ith observation removed. We denote the estimate of σ^2 so obtained by $S^2_{(i)}$. We can show that

$$S^2_{(i)} = \frac{(n - p)MS_E - e_i^2/(1 - h_{ii})}{n - p - 1} \tag{4.127}$$

The estimate of σ^2 in equation (4.127) is used instead of MS_E to produce an externally studentized residual, usually called R-student, given by

$$t_i = \frac{e_i}{\sqrt{S^2_{(i)}(1 - h_{ii})}} \qquad i = 1, 2, \ldots, n \tag{4.128}$$

In many situations, t_i will differ little from the studentized residual r_i. However, if the ith observation is influential, then $S^2_{(i)}$ can differ significantly from MS_E, and thus the R-student will be more sensitive to this point. Furthermore, under the standard assumptions, t_i has a t_{n-p-1} distribution. Thus R-student offers a more formal procedure for outlier detection via hypothesis testing. Table 4.11 displays the values of R-student for the consumer finance regression model in Example 4.13. None of those values is unusually large.

Influence Diagnostics. We occasionally find that a small subset of the data exerts a disproportionate influence on the fitted regression model. That is, parameter estimates or predictions may depend more on the influential subset than on the majority of the data. We would like to locate these influential points and assess their impact on the model. If these influential points are "bad" values, they should be eliminated. On the other hand, there may be nothing wrong with these points. But if they control key model properties, we would like to know it because it could affect the use of the model. In this section, we describe and illustrate some useful measures of influence.

The disposition of points in x space is important in determining model properties. In particular, remote observations potentially have disproportionate leverage on the parameter estimates, predicted values, and the usual summary statistics.

The hat matrix $\mathbf{H} = \mathbf{X}(\mathbf{X}'\mathbf{X})^{-1}\mathbf{X}'$ is very useful in identifying influential observations. As noted earlier, $\mathbf{H}$ determines the variances and covariances of $\hat{\mathbf{y}}$ and $\mathbf{e}$ because $V(\hat{\mathbf{y}}) = \sigma^2\mathbf{H}$ and $V(\mathbf{e}) = \sigma^2(\mathbf{I} - \mathbf{H})$. The elements h_{ij} of $\mathbf{H}$ may be interpreted as the amount of leverage exerted by y_j on $\hat{y}_i$. Thus, inspection of the elements of $\mathbf{H}$ can reveal points that are potentially influential by virtue of their location in x space. Attention is usually focused on the diagonal elements h_{ii}. Because $\Sigma_{i=1}^{n} h_{ii} = \text{rank}(\mathbf{H}) = \text{rank}(\mathbf{X}) = p$, the average size of the diagonal element of the $\mathbf{H}$ matrix is p/n. As a rough guideline, then, if a diagonal element h_{ii} is greater than $2p/n$, observation i is a high leverage point. To apply this to the consumer finance regression model in Example 4.13, note that $2p/n = 2(3)/16 = 0.375$. Table 4.11 gives the hat diagonals h_{ii} for the first-order model; because none of the h_{ii} exceeds 0.375, we would conclude that there are no leverage points in these data.

The hat diagonals will identify points that are potentially influential due to their location in x space. It is desirable to consider both the location of the point and the response variable in measuring influence. Cook (1977, 1979) has suggested using a measure of the squared distance between the least squares estimate based on all n points $\hat{\boldsymbol{\beta}}$ and the estimate obtained by deleting the i point, say $\hat{\boldsymbol{\beta}}_{(i)}$. This distance measure can be expressed as

$$D_1 = \frac{(\hat{\boldsymbol{\beta}}_{(i)} - \hat{\boldsymbol{\beta}})'\mathbf{X}'\mathbf{X}(\hat{\boldsymbol{\beta}}_{(i)} - \hat{\boldsymbol{\beta}})}{pMS_E} \qquad i = 1, 2, \ldots, n \tag{4.129}$$

A reasonable cutoff for D_i is unity. That is, we usually consider observations for which $D_i > 1$ to be influential.

The D_i statistic is actually calculated from

$$D_i = \frac{r_i^2}{P}\frac{V[\hat{y}(x_i)]}{V(e_i)} = \frac{r_i^2}{p}\frac{h_{ii}}{(1 - h_{ii})} \qquad i = 1, 2, \ldots, n \tag{4.130}$$

Note that, apart from the constant p, D_i is the product of the square of the ith studentized residual and $h_{ii}/(1 - h_{ii})$. This ratio can be shown to be the distance from the vector $\mathbf{x}_i$ to the centroid of the remaining data. Thus, D_i is made up of a component that reflects how well the model fits the ith observation y_i and a component that measures how far that point is from the rest of the data. Either component (or both) may contribute to a large value of D_i.

Table 4.11 presents the values of D_i for the regression model fit to the consumer finance data in Example 4.13. None of these values of D_i exceeds 1, so there is no strong evidence of influential observations in these data.

Important Terms and Concepts

Alternative hypothesis
Analysis of variance (ANOVA)
Binomial distribution
Checking assumptions for statistical inference procedures
Chi-square distribution
Confidence interval
Confidence intervals on means, known variance(s)
Confidence intervals on means, unknown variance(s)
Confidence intervals on proportions
Confidence intervals on the variance of a normal distribution
Confidence intervals on the variances of two normal distributions
Critical region for a test statistic
F-distribution
Hypothesis testing
Least square estimator
Linear statistical model
Minimum variance estimator
Null hypothesis
P-value
P-value approach
Parameters of a distribution
Point estimator
Poisson distribution
Pooled estimator
Power of a statistical test
Random sample
Regression model
Residual analysis
Sampling distribution
Scaled residuals
Statistic
t-distribution
Test statistic
Tests of hypotheses on means, known variance(s)
Tests of hypotheses on means, unknown variance(s)
Tests of hypotheses on proportions
Tests of hypotheses on the variance of a normal distribution
Tests of hypotheses on the variances of two normal distributions
Type I error
Type II error
Unbiased estimator

Exercises

4.1. The diameters of aluminum alloy rods produced on an extrusion machine are known to have a standard deviation of 0.0001 in. A random sample of 25 rods has an average diameter of 0.5046 in.

(a) Test the hypothesis that mean rod diameter is 0.5025 in. Assume a two-sided alternative and use $\alpha = 0.05$.

(b) Find the *P*-value for this test.

(c) Construct a 95% two-sided confidence interval on the mean rod diameter.

4.2. The service life of a battery used in a cardiac pacemaker is assumed to be normally distributed. A random sample of 10 batteries is subjected to an accelerated life test by running them continuously at an elevated temperature until failure, and the following lifetimes (in hours) are obtained: 25.5, 26.1, 26.8, 23.2, 24.2, 28.4, 25.0, 27.8, 27.3, and 25.7.

(a) The manufacturer wants to be certain that the mean battery life exceeds 25 h. What conclusions can be drawn from these data (use $\alpha = 0.05$)?

(b) Construct a 90% two-sided confidence interval on mean life in the accelerated test.

(c) Construct a normal probability plot of the battery life data. What conclusions can you draw?

4.3. Using the data from Exercise 4.2, construct a 95% lower confidence interval on mean battery life. Why would the manufacturer be interested in a one-sided confidence interval?

4.4. The inside diameters of bearings used in an aircraft landing gear assembly are known to have a standard deviation of $\sigma = 0.002$ cm. A random sample of 15 bearings has an average inside diameter of 8.2535 cm.

(a) Test the hypothesis that the mean inside bearing diameter is 8.25 cm. Use a two-sided alternative and $\alpha = 0.05$.

(b) Find the *P*-value for this test.

(c) Construct a 95% two-sided confidence interval on mean bearing diameter.

4.5. A machine is used to fill containers with a liquid product. Fill volume can be assumed to be normally distributed. A random sample of 10 containers is selected, and the net contents (oz) are as follows: 12.03, 12.01, 12.04, 12.02, 12.05, 11.98, 11.96, 12.02, 12.05, and 11.99.

(a) Suppose that the manufacturer wants to be sure that the mean net contents exceeds 12 oz. What conclusions can be drawn from the data (use $\alpha = 0.01$)?

(b) Construct a 95% two-sided confidence interval on the mean fill volume.

(c) Does the assumption of normality seem appropriate for the fill volume data?

4.6. The tensile strength of a fiber used in manufacturing cloth is of interest to the purchaser. Previous experience indicates that the standard deviation of tensile strength is 2 psi. A random sample of eight fiber specimens is selected, and the average tensile strength is found to be 127 psi.

(a) Test the hypothesis that the mean tensile strength equals 125 psi versus the alternative that the mean exceeds 125 psi. Use $\alpha = 0.05$.

(b) What is the *P*-value for this test?

(c) Discuss why a one-sided alternative was chosen in part (a).

(d) Construct a 95% lower confidence interval on the mean tensile strength.

4.7. Ferric chloride is used as a flux in some types of extraction metallurgy processes. This material is shipped in containers, and the container weight varies. It is important to obtain an accurate estimate of mean container weight. Suppose that from long experience a reliable value for the standard deviation of flux container weight is determined to be 4 lb. How large a sample would be required to construct a 95% two-sided confidence interval on the mean that has a total width of 1 lb?

4.8. The output voltage of a power supply is assumed to be normally distributed. Sixteen observations taken at random on voltage are as follows: 10.35, 9.30, 10.00, 9.96, 11.65, 12.00, 11.25, 9.58, 11.54, 9.95, 10.28, 8.37, 10.44, 9.25, 9.38, and 10.85.

(a) Test the hypothesis that the mean voltage equals 12 V against a two-sided alternative using $\alpha = 0.05$.

(b) Construct a 95% two-sided confidence interval on μ.

(c) Test the hypothesis that $\sigma^2 = 11$ using $\alpha = 0.05$.

(d) Construct a 95% two-sided confidence interval on σ.

(e) Construct a 95% upper confidence interval on σ.

(f) Does the assumption of normality seem reasonable for the output voltage?

4.9. Two different hardening processes, (1) saltwater quenching and (2) oil quenching, are used on samples of a particular type of metal alloy. The results are shown in Table 4E.1. Assume that hardness is normally distributed.

■ **TABLE 4E.1**
Hardness Data for Exercise 4.9

Saltwater Quench	Oil Quench
145	152
150	150
153	147
148	155
141	140
152	146
146	158
154	152
139	151
148	143

(a) Test the hypothesis that the mean hardness for the saltwater quenching process equals the mean hardness for the oil quenching process. Use $\alpha = 0.05$ and assume equal variances.

(b) Assuming that the variances σ_1^2 and σ_2^2 are equal, construct a 95% confidence interval on the difference in mean hardness.

(c) Construct a 95% confidence interval on the ratio σ_1^2/σ_2^2. Does the assumption made earlier of equal variances seem reasonable?

(d) Does the assumption of normality seem appropriate for these data?

4.10. Two machines are used for filling glass bottles with a soft-drink beverage. The filling processes have known standard deviations $\sigma_1 = 0.010$ liter and $\sigma_2 = 0.015$ liter, respectively. A random sample of $n_1 = 25$ bottles from machine 1 and $n_2 = 20$ bottles from machine 2 results in average net contents of $\bar{x}_1 = 2.04$ liters and $\bar{x}_2 = 2.07$ liters.

(a) Test the hypothesis that both machines fill to the same net contents, using $\alpha = 0.05$. What are your conclusions?

(b) Find the *P*-value for this test.

(c) Construct a 95% confidence interval on the difference in mean fill volume.

4.11. Suppose that $x_1 \sim N(\mu_1, \sigma_1^2)$ and $x_2 \sim N(\mu_2, \sigma_2^2)$, and that x_1 and x_2 are independent. Develop a procedure for constructing a $100(1 - \alpha)\%$ confidence interval on $\mu_1 - \mu_2$, assuming that σ_1^2 and σ_2^2 are unknown and cannot be assumed equal.

4.12. Two quality control technicians measured the surface finish of a metal part, obtaining the data in Table 4E.2. Assume that the measurements are normally distributed.

(a) Test the hypothesis that the mean surface finish measurements made by the two technicians are equal. Use $\alpha = 0.05$, and assume equal variances.

■ **TABLE 4E.2**

Surface Finish Data for Exercise 4.12.

Technician 1	Technician 2
1.45	1.54
1.37	1.41
1.21	1.56
1.54	1.37
1.48	1.20
1.29	1.31
1.34	1.27
	1.35

(b) What are the practical implications of the test in part (a)? Discuss what practical conclusions you would draw if the null hypothesis were rejected.
(c) Assuming that the variances are equal, construct a 95% confidence interval on the mean difference in surface-finish measurements.
(d) Test the hypothesis that the variances of the measurements made by the two technicians are equal. Use $\alpha = 0.05$. What are the practical implications if the null hypothesis is rejected?
(e) Construct a 95% confidence interval estimate of the ratio of the variances of technician measurement error.
(f) Construct a 95% confidence interval on the variance of measurement error for technician 2.
(g) Does the normality assumption seem reasonable for the data?

4.13. A new purification unit is installed in a chemical process. Before its installation, a random sample yielded the following data about the percentage of impurity: $\bar{x}_1 = 9.85$, $s_1^2 = 6.79$, and $n_1 = 10$. After installation, a random sample resulted in $\bar{x}_2 = 8.08$, $s_2^2 = 6.18$, and $n_2 = 8$.
(a) Can you conclude that the two variances are equal? Use $\alpha = 0.05$.
(b) Can you conclude that the new purification device has reduced the mean percentage of impurity? Use $\alpha = 0.05$.

4.14. The diameter of a metal rod is measured by 12 inspectors, each using both a micrometer caliper and a vernier caliper. The results are shown in Table 4E.3. Is there a difference between the mean measurements produced by the two types of caliper? Use $\alpha = 0.01$.

4.15. A random sample of 500 connecting rod pins contains 65 nonconforming units. Estimate the process fraction nonconforming.
(a) Test the hypothesis that the true fraction defective in this process is 0.08. Use $\alpha = 0.05$.

■ **TABLE 4E.3**

Measurements Made by the Inspectors

Inspector	Micrometer Caliper	Vernier Caliper
1	0.150	0.151
2	0.151	0.150
3	0.151	0.151
4	0.152	0.150
5	0.151	0.151
6	0.150	0.151
7	0.151	0.153
8	0.153	0.155
9	0.152	0.154
10	0.151	0.151
11	0.151	0.150
12	0.151	0.152

(b) Find the *P*-value for this test.
(c) Construct a 95% upper confidence interval on the true process fraction nonconforming.

4.16. Two processes are used to produce forgings used in an aircraft wing assembly. Of 200 forgings selected from process 1, 10 do not conform to the strength specifications, whereas of 300 forgings selected from process 2, 20 are nonconforming.
(a) Estimate the fraction nonconforming for each process.
(b) Test the hypothesis that the two processes have identical fractions nonconforming. Use $\alpha = 0.05$.
(c) Construct a 90% confidence interval on the difference in fraction nonconforming between the two processes.

4.17. Two different types of glass bottles are suitable for use by a soft-drink beverage bottler. The internal pressure strength of the bottle is an important quality characteristic. It is known that $\sigma_1 = \sigma_2 = 3.0$ psi. From a random sample of $n_1 = n_2 = 16$ bottles, the mean pressure strengths are observed to be $\bar{x}_1 = 175.8$ psi and $\bar{x}_2 = 181.3$ psi. The company will not use bottle design 2 unless its pressure strength exceeds that of bottle design 1 by at least 5 psi. Based on the sample data, should they use bottle design 2 if we use $\alpha = 0.05$? What is the *P*-value for this test?

4.18. Suppose we wish to test the hypotheses

$$H_0: \mu = 15$$
$$H_1: \mu \neq 15$$

where we know that $\sigma^2 = 9.0$. If the true mean is really 20, what sample size must be used to ensure that the probability of type II error is no greater than 0.10? Assume that $\alpha = 0.05$.

4.19. **Sample size allocation.** Suppose we are testing the hypotheses

$$H_0: \mu_1 = \mu_2$$
$$H_1: \mu_1 \neq \mu_2$$

where σ_1^2 and σ_2^2 are known. Resources are limited, and consequently the total sample size $n_1 + n_2 = N$. How should we allocate the N observations between the two populations to obtain the most powerful test?

4.20. An experiment was conducted to investigate the filling capability of packaging equipment at a winery in Newberg, Oregon. Twenty bottles of Pinot Gris were randomly selected and the fill volume (in ml) measured. Assume that fill volume has a normal distribution. The data are as follows: 753, 751, 752, 753, 753, 753, 752, 753, 754, 754, 752, 751, 752, 750, 753, 755, 753, 756, 751, and 750.

(a) Do the data support the claim that the standard deviation of fill volume is less than 1 ml? Use $\alpha = 0.05$.

(b) Find a 95% two-sided confidence interval on the standard deviation of fill volume.

(c) Does it seem reasonable to assume that fill volume has a normal distribution?

4.21. Develop a test for the hypotheses

$$H_0: \mu_1 = 2\mu_2$$
$$H_1: \mu_1 \neq 2\,\mu_2$$

where σ_1^2 and σ_2^2 are known.

4.22. Consider the hypotheses

$$H_0: \quad \mu = \mu_0$$
$$H_1: \quad \mu \neq \mu_0$$

where σ^2 is known. Derive a general expression for determining the sample size for detecting a true mean of $\mu_1 \neq \mu_0$ with probability $1 - \beta$ if the type I error is α.

4.23. Nonconformities occur in glass bottles according to a Poisson distribution. A random sample of 100 bottles contains a total of 11 nonconformities.

(a) Develop a procedure for testing the hypothesis that the mean of a Poisson distribution λ equals a specified value λ_0. Hint: Use the normal approximation to the Poisson.

(b) Use the results of part (a) to test the hypothesis that the mean occurrence rate of nonconformities is $\lambda = 0.15$. Use $\alpha = 0.01$.

4.24. An in-line tester is used to evaluate the electrical function of printed circuit boards. This machine counts the number of defects observed on each board. A random sample of 1000 boards contains a total of 688 defects. Is it reasonable to conclude that the mean occurrence rate of defects is $\lambda = 1$? Use the results of part (a) of Exercise 4.23 and assume that $\alpha = 0.05$.

■ **TABLE 4E.4**
Uniformity Data for the Experiment in Exercise 4.26

Wafer Position	Uniformity		
1	2.76	5.67	4.49
2	1.43	1.70	2.19
3	2.34	1.97	1.47
4	0.94	1.36	1.65

4.25. An inspector counts the surface-finish defects in dishwashers. A random sample of five dishwashers contains three such defects. Is there reason to conclude that the mean occurrence rate of surface-finish defects per dishwasher exceeds 0.5? Use the results of part (a) of Exercise 4.23 and assume that $\alpha = 0.05$.

4.26. An article in the *Journal of the Electrochemical Society* (Vol. 139, No. 2, 1992, pp. 524–532) describes an experiment to investigate the low-pressure vapor deposition of polysilicon. The experiment was carried out in a large-capacity reactor at SEMATECH in Austin, Texas. The reactor has several wafer positions, and four of these positions are selected at random. The response variable is film thickness uniformity. Three replicates of the experiment were run, and the data are shown in Table 4E.4.

(a) Is there a difference in the wafer positions? Use the analysis of variance and $\alpha = 0.05$.

(b) Estimate the variability due to wafer positions.

(c) Estimate the random error component.

(d) Analyze the residuals from this experiment and comment on model adequacy.

4.27. An article in *Environmental International* (Vol. 18, No. 4, 1992) describes an experiment in which the amount of radon released in showers was investigated. Radon-enriched water was used in the experiment, and six different orifice diameters were tested in shower heads. The data from the experiment are shown in Table 4E.5.

■ **TABLE 4E.5**
Radon Data for the Experiment in Exercise 4.27

Orifice Diameter	Radon Released (%)			
0.37	80	83	83	85
0.51	75	75	79	79
0.71	74	73	76	77
1.02	67	72	74	74
1.40	62	62	67	69
1.99	60	61	64	66

■ TABLE 4E.6
Baked Density Data for Exercise 4.28

Temperature (°C)	Density					
500	41.8	41.9	41.7	41.6	41.5	41.7
525	41.4	41.3	41.7	41.6	41.7	41.8
550	41.2	41.0	41.6	41.9	41.7	41.3
575	41.0	40.6	41.8	41.2	41.9	41.5

(a) Does the size of the orifice affect the mean percentage of radon released? Use the analysis of variance and $\alpha = 0.05$.
(b) Analyze the results from this experiment.

4.28. An aluminum producer manufactures carbon anodes and bakes them in a ring furnace prior to use in the smelting operation. The baked density of the anode is an important quality characteristic, as it may affect anode life. One of the process engineers suspects that firing temperature in the ring furnace affects baked anode density. An experiment was run at four different temperature levels, and six anodes were baked at each temperature level. The data from the experiment are shown in Table 4E.6.
(a) Does firing temperature in the ring furnace affect mean baked anode density?
(b) Find the residuals for this experiment and plot them on a normal probability scale. Comment on the plot.
(c) What firing temperature would you recommend using?

4.29. Plot the residuals from Exercise 4.28 against the firing temperatures. Is there any indication that variability in baked anode density depends on the firing temperature? What firing temperature would you recommend using?

4.30. An article in the *ACI Materials Journal* (Vol. 84, 1987, pp. 213–216) describes several experiments investigating the rodding of concrete to remove entrapped air. A 3-in. diameter cylinder was used, and the number of times this rod was used is the design variable. The resulting compressive strength of the concrete specimen is the response. The data are shown in Table 4E.7.

■ TABLE 4E.7
Compressive Strength Data for Exercise 4.30

Rodding Level	Compressive Strength		
10	1530	1530	1440
15	1610	1650	1500
20	1560	1730	1530
25	1500	1490	1510

(a) Is there any difference in compressive strength due to the rodding level? Answer this question by using the analysis of variance with $\alpha = 0.05$.
(b) Construct box plots of compressive strength by rodding level. Provide a practical interpretation of these plots.
(c) Construct a normal probability plot of the residuals from this experiment. Does the assumption of a normal distribution for compressive strength seem reasonable?

4.31. Compare the mean compressive strength at each rodding level from Exercise 4.30 with a scaled *t* distribution. What conclusions would you draw from this plot?

4.32. An article in *Solid State Technology* (May 1987) describes an experiment to determine the effect of C_2F_6 flow rate on etch uniformity on a silicon wafer used in integrated-circuit manufacturing. Three flow rates are tested, and the resulting uniformity (in percent) is observed for six test units at each flow rate. The data are shown in Table 4E.8.
(a) Does C_2F_6 flow rate affect etch uniformity? Answer this question by using an analysis of variance with $\alpha = 0.05$.
(b) Construct a box plot of the etch uniformity data. Use this plot, together with the analysis of variance results, to determine which gas flow rate would be best in terms of etch uniformity (a small percentage is best).
(c) Plot the residuals versus predicted C_2F_6 flow. Interpret this plot.
(d) Does the normality assumption seem reasonable in this problem?

4.33. Compare the mean etch uniformity values at each of the C_2F_6 flow rates from Exercise 4.32 with a scaled *t* distribution. Does this analysis indicate that there are differences in mean etch uniformity at the different flow rates? Which flows produce different results?

4.34. A plant distills liquid air to produce oxygen, nitrogen, and argon. The percentage of impurity in the oxygen is though to be linearly related to the amount of impurities in the air as measured by the "pollution

■ TABLE 4E.8
Uniformity Data for Exercise 4.32

C_2F_6 Flow (SCCM)	Observations					
	1	2	3	4	5	6
125	2.7	2.6	4.6	3.2	3.0	3.8
160	4.6	4.9	5.0	4.2	3.6	4.2
200	4.6	2.9	3.4	3.5	4.1	5.1

count" in parts per million (ppm). A sample of plant operating data is shown below:

Purity (%)	93.3	92.0	92.4	91.7	94.0	94.6	93.6	
Pollution count (ppm)		1.10	1.45	1.36	1.59	1.08	0.75	1.20
Purity (%)	93.1	93.2	92.9	92.2	91.3	90.1	91.6	91.9
Pollution count (ppm)	0.99	0.83	1.22	1.47	1.81	2.03	1.75	1.68

(a) Fit a linear regression model to the data.
(b) Test for significance of regression.
(c) Find a 95% confidence interval on β_1.

4.35. The tensile strength of a paper product is related to the amount of hardwood in the pulp. Ten samples are produced in the pilot plant, and the data obtained are shown in the Table 4E.9.
(a) Fit a linear regression model relating strength to percent hardwood.
(b) Test the model in part (a) for significance of regression.
(c) Find a 95% confidence interval on the parameter β_1.

4.36. Plot the residuals from Problem 4.34 and comment on model adequacy.

4.37. Plot the residuals from Problem 4.35 and comment on model adequacy.

4.38. The brake horsepower developed by an automobile engine on a dynomometer is thought to be a function of the engine speed in revolutions per minute (rpm), the road octane number of the fuel, and the engine compression. An experiment is run in the laboratory and the data are drawn in Table 4E.10:
(a) Fit a multiple regression model to these data.
(b) Test for significance of regression, What conclusions can you draw?
(c) Based on t-tests, do you need all three regressor variables in the model?

■ **TABLE 4E.9**
Tensile Strength Data for Exercise 4.35

Strength	Percent Hardwood	Strength	Percent Hardwood
160	10	181	20
171	15	188	25
175	15	193	25
182	20	195	28
184	20	200	30

■ **TABLE 4E.10**
Automobile Engine Data for Exercise 4.38

Brake Horsepower	rpm	Road Octane Number	Compression
225	2000	90	100
212	1800	94	95
229	2400	88	110
222	1900	91	96
219	1600	86	100
278	2500	96	110
246	3000	94	98
237	3200	90	100
233	2800	88	105
224	3400	86	97
223	1800	90	100
230	2500	89	104

4.39. Analyze the residuals from the regression model in Exercise 4.38. Comment on model adequacy.

4.40. Suppose that you are testing H_1: $\mu = \mu_0$ versus H_1: $\mu > \mu_0$ with a sample size of 15. Use the table of the t distribution percentage points to find lower and upper bounds on the P-value for the following observed values of the test statistic:
(a) $t_0 = 2.30$ (b) $t_0 = 3.41$
(c) $t_0 = 1.98$ (d) $t_0 = 1.55$

4.41. Consider the Minitab output shown below.

Test and CI for One Proportion

```
Test of p = 0.3 vs p not = 0.3

Sample   X    N    Sample p          95% CI            Z-Value    P-Value
1        98   300  0.326667   (0.273596, 0.379737)     1.01       0.313
```

(a) Is this a one-sided or two-sided test?
(b) Can the null hypothesis be rejected at the 0.05 level?
(c) Construct an approximate 90% CI for p.
(d) What is the P-value if the alternative hypothesis is H_1: $p > 0.3$?

4.42. Consider the Minitab output below.

```
One-Sample Z

Test of mu = 30 vs not = 30
The assumed standard deviation = 1.3

 N    Mean   SE Mean       95% CI          Z  P
15  31.400     0.336  (30.742, 32.058)  ?  ?
```

(a) Fill in the missing values. What conclusions would you draw?
(b) Is this a one-sided or two-sided test?
(c) Use the output and a normal table to find a 95% CI on the mean.
(d) How was the SE mean calculated?
(e) What is the P-value if the alternative hypothesis is H_1: $\mu > 30$?

4.43. Consider the Minitab output below.

```
One-Sample T

Test of mu = 95 vs not = 95

 N   Mean StDev SE Mean       95% CI          T      P
20 94.580    ?    0.671  (93.176, 95.984)  ?  0.539
```

(a) Fill in the missing values. Can the null hypothesis be rejected at the 0.05 level? Why?
(b) Is this a one-sided or two-sided test?
(c) How many degress of freedom are there on the t-test statistic?
(d) Use the output and a normal table to find a 95% CI on the mean.
(e) Suppose that the hypotheses had been H_1: $\mu = 90$ versus H_1: $\mu > 90$. What conclusions would you have drawn?

4.44. Consider the Minitab output below.

```
Test and CI for Two Proportions

Sample    X     N   Sample p
1       185   300   0.616667
2       301     ?   0.602000

Defference = p (1) - p (2)
Estimate for difference: ?
95% CI for difference:   (-0.0551024, 0.0844357)
Test for difference = 0 (vs not = 0): Z = ? P-value = 0.680
```

(a) Fill in the missing values.
(b) Is this a one-sided or two-sided test?
(c) What is the P-value if the alternative hypothesis is H_1: $p_1 = p_2$ versus H_1: $p_1 > p_2$?
(d) Construct an approximate 90% CI for the difference in the two proportions.

4.45. Consider the Minitab output shown below.

```
Two-Sample T-Test and CI

Sample   N    Mean   StDev   SE Mean
1       15   50.20    1.75      0.45
2       15   51.98    2.15      0.56

Difference = mu (1) - mu (2)
Estimate for difference: ?
95% CI for difference: (-3.246, -0.314)
T-Test of difference = 0 (vs not =): T-Value =-2.49   P-Value = 0.019   DF = ?
Both use Pooled StDev = 1.9602
```

(a) Fill in the missing values.

(b) Can the null hypothesis be rejected at a the 0.05 level? Why?

(c) Use the output and the t-table to find a 99% CI on the difference in means.

(d) Suppose that the alternative hypothesis was H_1: $\mu_1 = \mu_2$ versus H_1: $\mu_1 > \mu_2$. What is the P-value? What conclusions would you draw?

4.46. Consider a one-way or single-factor ANOVA with four treatments and five replications. Use the table of the F distribution percentage points to find lower and upper bounds on the P-value for the following observed values of the test statistic:

(a) $F_0 = 2.50$ (b) $F_0 = 3.75$
(c) $F_0 = 5.98$ (d) $F_0 = 1.90$

4.47. Consider the Minitab ANOVA output below. Fill in the blanks. You may give bounds on the P-value. What conclusions can you draw based on the information in this display?

One-way ANOVA

Source	DF	SS	MS	F	P
Factor	3	54.91	?	?	?
Error	?	19.77	?		
Total	15	74.67			

S = 1.283 R-Sq = 73.53% R-Sq(adj) = 66.91%

PART 3

Basic Methods of Statistical Process Control and Capability Analysis

It is impossible to inspect or test quality into a product; the product must be built right the first time. This implies that the manufacturing process must be stable and that all individuals involved with the process (including operators, engineers, quality-assurance personnel, and management) must continuously seek to improve process performance and reduce variability in key parameters. On-line **statistical process control** (SPC) is a primary tool for achieving this objective. Control charts are the simplest type of on-line statistical process-control procedure. Chapters 5 through 8 present many of the basic SPC techniques, concentrating primarily on the type of control chart proposed by Walter A. Shewhart and called the **Shewhart control chart.**

Chapter 5 is an introduction to the general methodology of statistical process control. This chapter describes several fundamental SPC problem-solving tools, including an introduction to the Shewhart control chart. A discussion of how to implement SPC is given, along with some comments on deploying SPC in nonmanufacturing environments. Chapter 6 introduces Shewhart control charts for measurement data, sometimes called **variables control charts.** The $\bar{x}$ and R control charts are discussed in detail, along with several important variations of these charts. Chapter 7 presents Shewhart control charts for **attribute data,** such as a fraction defective or nonconforming, nonconformities (defects), or nonconformities per unit of product. Chapter 8 explores **process capability analysis;** that is, how control charts and other statistical techniques can be used to estimate the natural capability of a process and to determine how it will perform relative to specifications on the product. Some aspects of setting specifications and tolerances, including the tolerance "stack-up" problem, are also presented.

Throughout this section we stress the three fundamental uses of a control chart:

1. Reduction of process variability
2. Monitoring and surveillance of a process
3. Estimation of product or process parameters

5 How SPC Works

CHAPTER OUTLINE

The supplemental material is on the textbook Website www.wiley.com/college/montgomery.

CHAPTER OVERVIEW AND LEARNING OBJECTIVES

This chapter has three objectives. The first is to present the basic statistical control process (SPC) problem-solving tools, called the magnificent seven, and to illustrate how these tools form a cohesive, practical framework for quality improvement. These tools form an important basic approach to both reducing variability and monitoring the performance of a process, and are widely used in both the analyze and control steps of DMAIC. The second objective is to describe the statistical basis of the Shewhart control chart. The reader will see how decisions about sample size, sampling interval, and placement of control limits affect the performance of a control chart. Other key concepts include the idea of rational subgroups, interpretation of control chart signals and patterns, and the average run length as a measure of control chart performance. The third objective is to discuss and illustrate some practical issues in the implementation of SPC.

After careful study of this chapter you should be able to do the following:

1. Understand chance and assignable causes of variability in a process
2. Explain the statistical basis of the Shewhart control chart, including choice of sample size, control limits, and sampling interval
3. Explain the rational subgroup concept
4. Understand the basic tools of SPC: the histogram or stem-and-leaf plot, the check sheet, the Pareto chart, the cause-and-effect diagram, the defect concentration diagram, the scatter diagram, and the control chart
5. Explain phase I and phase II use of control charts
6. Explain how average run length is used as a performance measure for a control chart
7. Explain how sensitizing rules and pattern recognition are used in conjunction with control charts

5.1 Introduction

If a product is to meet or exceed customer expectations, generally it should be produced by a process that is stable or repeatable. More precisely, the process must be capable of operating with little variability around the target or nominal dimensions of the product's quality characteristics. **Statistical process control (SPC)** is a powerful collection of problem-solving tools useful in achieving process stability and improving capability through the reduction of variability.

SPC is one of the greatest technological developments of the twentieth century because it is based on sound underlying principles, is easy to use, has significant impact, and can be applied to any process. Its seven major tools are

1. Histogram or stem-and-leaf plot
2. Check sheet
3. Pareto chart
4. Cause-and-effect diagram
5. Defect concentration diagram
6. Scatter diagram
7. Control chart

Although these tools, often called **"the magnificent seven,"** are an important part of SPC, they comprise only its technical aspects. The proper deployment of SPC helps create an environment in which all individuals in an organization seek continuous improvement in quality and productivity. This environment is best developed when management becomes involved in the process. Once this environment is established, routine application of the magnificent seven becomes part of the usual manner of doing business, and the organization is well on its way to achieving its quality improvement objectives.

Of the seven tools, the Shewhart control chart is probably the most technically sophisticated. It was developed in the 1920s by Walter A. Shewhart of the Bell Telephone

Laboratories. To understand the statistical concepts that form the basis of SPC, we must first describe Shewhart's theory of variability.

5.2 Chance and Assignable Causes of Quality Variation

In any production process, regardless of how well designed or carefully maintained it is, a certain amount of inherent or natural variability will always exist. This natural variability or "background noise" is the cumulative effect of many small, essentially unavoidable causes. In the framework of statistical quality control, this natural variability is often called a "stable system of chance causes." A process that is operating with only **chance causes of variation** present is said to be **in statistical control**. In other words, the chance causes are an inherent part of the process.

Other kinds of variability may occasionally be present in the output of a process. This variability in key quality characteristics usually arises from three sources: improperly adjusted or controlled machines, operator errors, or defective raw material. Such variability is generally large when compared to the background noise, and it usually represents an unacceptable level of process performance. We refer to these sources of variability that are not part of the chance cause pattern as **assignable causes of variation**. A process that is operating in the presence of assignable causes is said to be an **out-of-control process.**[1]

These chance and assignable causes of variation are illustrated in Fig. 5.1. Until time t_1 the process shown in this figure is in control; that is, only chance causes of variation are present. As a result, both the mean and standard deviation of the process are at their in-control values (say, μ_0 and σ_0). At time t_1 an assignable cause occurs. As shown in Fig. 5.1, the effect of this assignable cause is to shift the process mean to a new value $\mu_1 > \mu_0$. At time t_2 another assignable cause occurs, resulting in $\mu = \mu_0$, but now the process standard deviation has shifted to a larger value $\sigma_1 > \sigma_0$. At time t_3 there is another assignable cause present, resulting in both the process mean and standard deviation taking on out-of-control values. From time t_1 forward, the presence of assignable causes has resulted in an out-of-control process.

Processes will often operate in the in-control state for relatively long periods of time. However, no process is truly stable forever, and, eventually, assignable causes will occur, seemingly at random, resulting in a shift to an out-of-control state where a larger proportion of the process output does not conform to requirements. For example, note from Fig. 5.1 that when the process is in control, most of the production will fall between the lower and upper specification limits (LSL and USL, respectively). When the process is out of control, a higher proportion of the process lies outside of these specifications.

A major objective of statistical process control is to quickly detect the occurrence of assignable causes of process shifts so that investigation of the process and corrective action may be undertaken before many nonconforming units are manufactured. The **control chart** is an on-line process-monitoring technique widely used for this purpose. Control charts may also be used to estimate the parameters of a production process, and, through this information, to determine process capability. The control chart may also provide information useful in improving the process. Finally, remember that the eventual goal of statistical process control is the **elimination of variability in the process.** It may not be possible to completely eliminate variability, but the control chart is an effective tool in reducing variability as much as possible.

We now present the statistical concepts that form the basis of control charts. Chapters 6 and 7 develop the details of construction and use of the standard types of control charts.

[1]The terminology **chance** and **assignable causes** was developed by Shewhart. Today, some writers use the terminology **common cause** instead of **chance cause** and **special cause** instead of **assignable cause.**

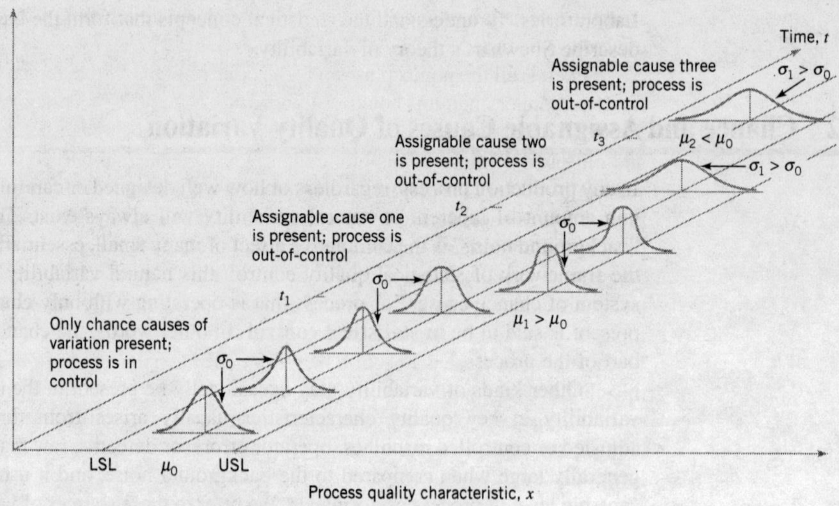

■ FIGURE 5.1 Chance and assignable causes of variation.

5.3 Statistical Basis of the Control Chart

5.3.1 Basic Principles

A typical control chart is shown in Fig. 5.2. The control chart is a graphical display of a quality characteristic that has been measured or computed from a sample versus the sample number or time. The chart contains a **center line** that represents the average value of the quality characteristic corresponding to the in-control state. (That is, only chance causes are present.) Two other horizontal lines, called the **upper control limit** (UCL) and the **lower control limit** (LCL), are also shown on the chart. These control limits are chosen so that if the process is in control, nearly all of the sample points will fall between them. As long as the points plot within the control limits, the process is assumed to be in control, and no action is necessary. However, a point that plots outside of the control limits is interpreted as evidence that the process is out of control, and investigation and corrective action are required to find and eliminate the assignable cause or causes responsible for this behavior. It is customary to connect the sample points on the control chart with

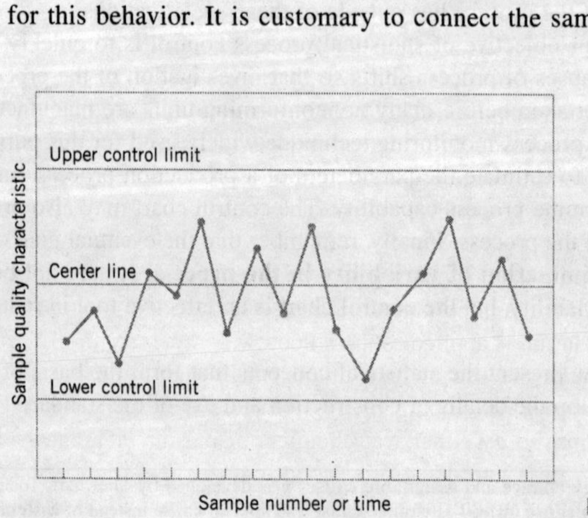

■ FIGURE 5.2 A typical control chart.

straight-line segments, so that it is easier to visualize how the sequence of points has evolved over time.

Even if all the points plot inside the control limits, if they behave in a systematic or nonrandom manner, then this could be an indication that the process is out of control. For example, if 18 of the last 20 points plotted above the center line but below the upper control limit and only two of these points plotted below the center line but above the lower control limit, we would be very suspicious that something was wrong. If the process is in control, all the plotted points should have an essentially random pattern. Methods for looking for sequences or nonrandom patterns can be applied to control charts as an aid in detecting out-of-control conditions. Usually, there is a reason why a particular nonrandom pattern appears on a control chart, and if it can be found and eliminated, process performance can be improved. This topic is discussed further in Sections 5.3.5 and 6.2.4.

There is a close connection between control charts and **hypothesis testing.** To illustrate this connection, suppose that the vertical axis in Fig. 5.2 is the sample average $\bar{x}$. Now, if the current value of $\bar{x}$ plots between the control limits, we conclude that the process mean is in control; that is, it is equal to some value μ_0. On the other hand, if $\bar{x}$ exceeds either control limit, we conclude that the process mean is out of control; that is, it is equal to some value $\mu_1 \neq \mu_0$. In a sense, then, the control chart is a test of the hypothesis that the process is in a state of statistical control. A point plotting within the control limits is equivalent to failing to reject the hypothesis of statistical control, and a point plotting outside the control limits is equivalent to rejecting the hypothesis of statistical control.

The hypothesis testing framework is useful in many ways, but there are some differences in viewpoint between control charts and hypothesis tests. For example, when testing statistical hypotheses, we usually check the validity of assumptions, whereas control charts are used to detect departures from an assumed state of statistical control. In general, we should not worry too much about assumptions such as the form of the distribution or independence when we are applying control charts to a process to reduce variability and achieve statistical control. Furthermore, an assignable cause can result in many different types of shifts in the process parameters. For example, the mean could shift instantaneously to a new value and remain there (this is sometimes called a **sustained shift**); or it could shift abruptly; but the assignable cause could be short-lived and the mean could then return to its nominal or in-control value; or the assignable cause could result in a steady drift or trend in the value of the mean. Only the sustained shift fits nicely within the usual statistical hypothesis testing model.

One place where the hypothesis testing framework is useful is in analyzing the **performance** of a control chart. For example, we may think of the probability of type I error of the control chart (concluding the process is out of control when it is really in control) and the probability of type II error of the control chart (concluding the process is in control when it is really out of control). It is occasionally helpful to use the operating-characteristic curve of a control chart to display its probability of type II error. This would be an indication of the ability of the control chart to detect process shifts of different magnitudes. This can be of value in determining which type of control chart to apply in certain situations. For more discussion of hypothesis testing, the role of statistical theory, and control charts, see Woodall (2000).

To illustrate the preceding ideas, we give an example of a control chart. In semiconductor manufacturing, an important fabrication step is photolithography, in which a light-sensitive photoresist material is applied to the silicon wafer, the circuit pattern is exposed on the resist typically through the use of high-intensity UV light, and the unwanted resist material is removed through a developing process. After the resist pattern is defined, the underlying material is removed by either wet chemical or plasma etching. It is fairly typical to follow development with a hard-bake process to increase resist adherence and etch resistance. An important quality characteristic in hard bake is the flow width of the resist, a measure of how

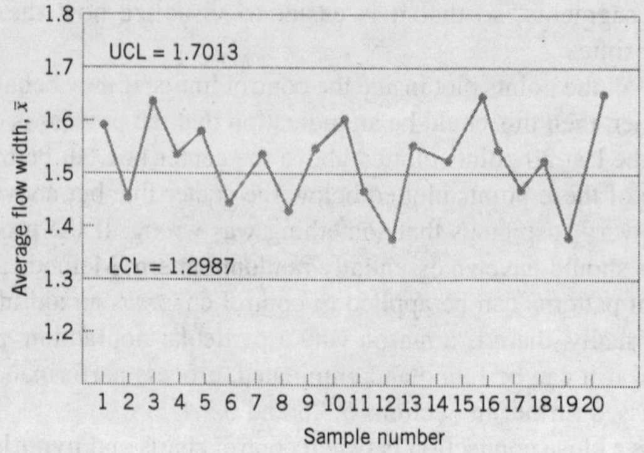

■ **FIGURE 5.3** $\bar{x}$ control chart for flow width.

much it expands due to the baking process. Suppose that flow width can be controlled at a mean of 1.5 microns, and it is known that the standard deviation of flow width is 0.15 microns. A control chart for the average flow width is shown in Fig. 5.3. Every hour, a sample of five wafers is taken, the average flow width ($\bar{x}$) computed, and $\bar{x}$ plotted on the chart. Because this control chart utilizes the sample average $\bar{x}$ to monitor the process mean, it is usually called an $\bar{x}$ control chart. Note that all of the plotted points fall inside the control limits, so the chart indicates that the process is considered to be in statistical control.

To assist in understanding the statistical basis of this control chart, consider how the control limits were determined. The process mean is 1.5 microns, and the process standard deviation is $\sigma = 0.15$ microns. Now if samples of size $n = 5$ are taken, the standard deviation of the sample average $\bar{x}$ is

$$\sigma_{\bar{x}} = \frac{\sigma}{\sqrt{n}} = \frac{0.15}{\sqrt{5}} = 0.0671$$

Therefore, if the process is in control with a mean flow width of 1.5 microns, then by using the central limit theorem to assume that $\bar{x}$ is approximately normally distributed, we would expect $100(1-\alpha)\%$ of the sample means $\bar{x}$ to fall between $1.5 + Z_{\alpha/2}(0.0671)$ and $1.5 - Z_{\alpha/2}(0.0671)$. We will arbitrarily choose the constant $Z_{\alpha/2}$ to be 3, so that the upper and lower control limits become

$$\text{UCL} = 1.5 + 3(0.0671) = 1.7013$$

and

$$\text{LCL} = 1.5 - 3(0.0671) = 1.2987$$

as shown on the control chart. These are typically called **three-sigma control limits.**[2] The width of the control limits is inversely proportional to the sample size n for a given multiple of sigma. Note that choosing the control limits is equivalent to setting up the critical region for testing the hypothesis

$$H_0: \quad \mu = 1.5$$
$$H_1: \quad \mu \neq 1.5$$

where $\sigma = 0.15$ is known. Essentially, the control chart tests this hypothesis repeatedly at different points in time. The situation is illustrated graphically in Fig. 5.4.

---

[2]Note that "sigma" refers to the standard deviation of the statistic plotted on the chart (i.e., $\sigma_{\bar{x}}$), *not* the standard deviation of the quality characteristic.

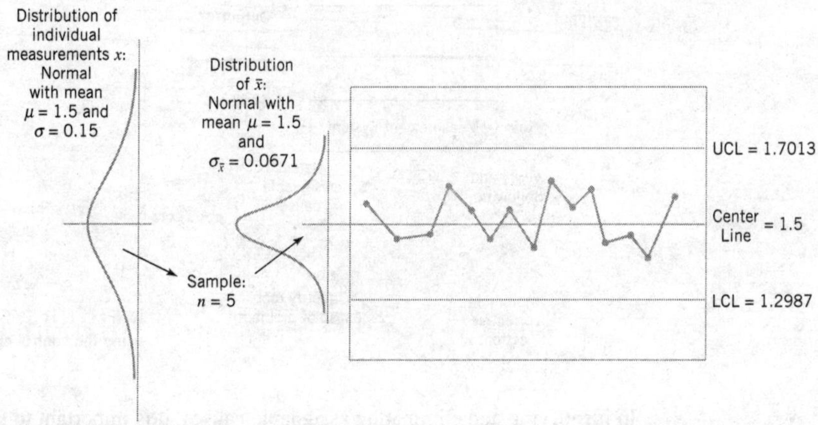

FIGURE 5.4 How the control chart works.

We may give a general **model** for a control chart. Let w be a sample statistic that measures some quality characteristic of interest, and suppose that the mean of w is μ_w and the standard deviation of w is σ_w. Then the center line, the upper control limit, and the lower control limit become

$$\begin{aligned} \text{UCL} &= \mu_w + L\sigma_w \\ \text{Center line} &= \mu_w \\ \text{LCL} &= \mu_w - L\sigma_w \end{aligned} \tag{5.1}$$

where L is the "distance" of the control limits from the center line, expressed in standard deviation units. This general theory of control charts was first proposed by Walter A. Shewhart, and control charts developed according to these principles are often called **Shewhart control charts**.

The control chart is a device for describing in a precise manner exactly what is meant by statistical control; as such, it may be used in a variety of ways. In many applications, it is used for on-line process surveillance. That is, sample data are collected and used to construct the control chart, and if the sample values of $\bar{x}$ (say) fall within the control limits and do not exhibit any systematic pattern, we say the process is in control at the level indicated by the chart. Note that we may be interested here in determining *both* whether the past data came from a process that was in control and whether future samples from this process indicate statistical control.

The most important use of a control chart is to **improve** the process. We have found that, generally,

1. Most processes do not operate in a state of statistical control, and
2. Consequently, the routine and attentive use of control charts will identify assignable causes. If these causes can be eliminated from the process, variability will be reduced and the process will be improved.

This process improvement activity using the control chart is illustrated in Fig. 5.5. Note that

3. The control chart will only **detect** assignable causes. Management, operator, and engineering **action** will usually be necessary to eliminate the assignable causes.

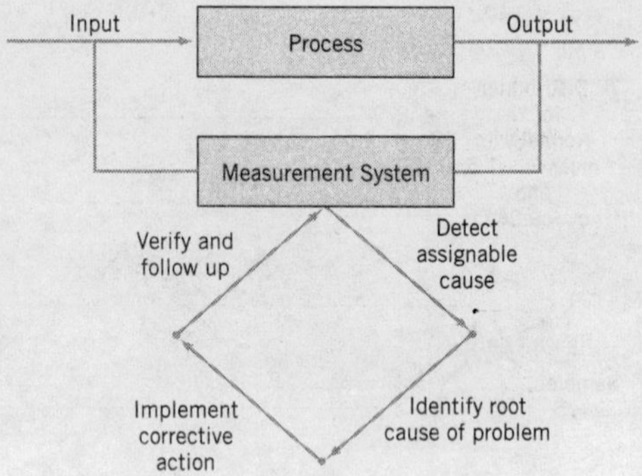

■ **FIGURE 5.5** Process improvement using the control chart.

In identifying and eliminating assignable causes, it is important to find the **root cause** of the problem and to attack it. A cosmetic solution will not result in any real, long-term process improvement. Developing an effective system for corrective action is an essential component of an effective SPC implementation.

A very important part of the corrective action process associated with control chart usage is the **out-of-control-action plan (OCAP)**. An OCAP is a flow chart or text-based description of the sequence of activities that must take place following the occurrence of an *activating event*. These are usually out-of-control signals from the control chart. The OCAP consists of *checkpoints*, which are potential assignable causes, and *terminators*, which are actions taken to resolve the out-of-control condition, preferably by eliminating the assignable cause. It is very important that the OCAP specify as complete a set as possible of checkpoints and terminators, and that these be arranged in an order that facilitates process diagnostic activities. Often, analysis of prior failure modes of the process and/or product can be helpful in designing this aspect of the OCAP. Furthermore, an OCAP is a *living document* in the sense that it will be modified over time as more knowledge and understanding of the process is gained. Consequently, when a control chart is introduced, an initial OCAP should accompany it. Control charts without an OCAP are not likely to be useful as a process improvement tool.

The OCAP for the hard-bake process is shown in Fig. 5.6. This process has two controllable variables, temperature and time. In this process, the mean flow width is monitored with an $\bar{x}$ control chart, and the process variability is monitored with a control chart for the range, or an R chart. Notice that if the R chart exhibits an out-of-control signal, operating personnel are directed to contact process engineering immediately. If the $\bar{x}$ control chart exhibits an out-of-control signal, operators are directed to check process settings and calibration and then make adjustments to temperature in an effort to bring the process back into a state of control. If these adjustments are unsuccessful, process engineering personnel are contacted.

We may also use the control chart as an **estimating device.** That is, from a control chart that exhibits statistical control, we may estimate certain process parameters, such as the mean, standard deviation, fraction nonconforming or fallout, and so forth. These estimates may then be used to determine the **capability** of the process to produce acceptable products. Such **process-capability studies** have considerable impact on many management decision problems that occur over the product cycle, including make or buy decisions, plant and process improvements that reduce process variability, and contractual agreements with customers or vendors regarding product quality.

Control charts may be classified into two general types. If the quality characteristic can be measured and expressed as a number on some continuous scale of measurement, it is usually called a **variable.** In such cases, it is convenient to describe the quality characteristic with a measure of central tendency and a measure of variability. Control charts for central tendency

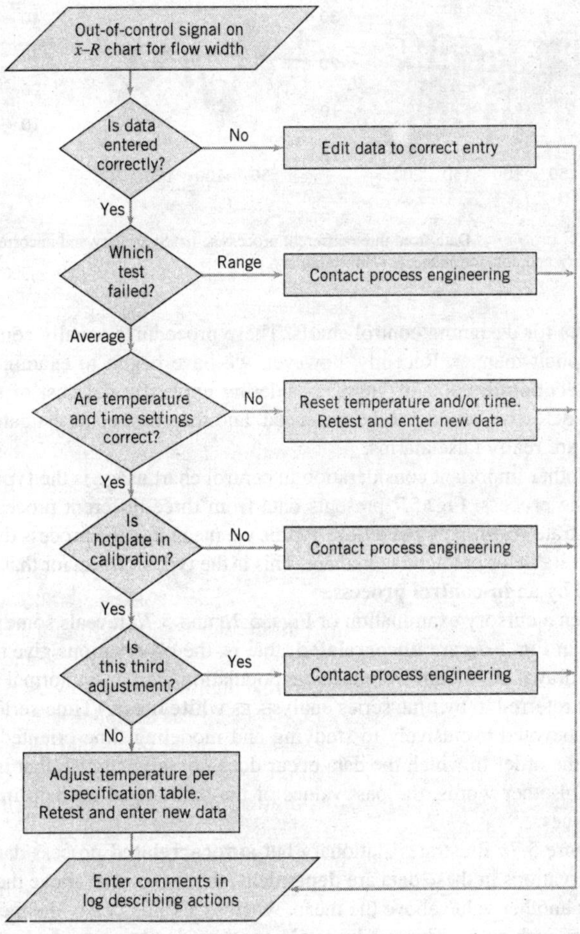

■ **FIGURE 5.6** The out-of-control-action plan (OCAP) for the hard-bake process.

and variability are collectively called **variables control charts.** The $\bar{x}$ chart is the most widely used chart for controlling central tendency, whereas charts based on either the sample range or the sample standard deviation are used to control process variability. Control charts for variables are discussed in Chapter 6. Many quality characteristics are not measured on a continuous scale or even a quantitative scale. In these cases, we may judge each unit of product as either conforming or nonconforming on the basis of whether or not it possesses certain attributes, or we may count the number of nonconformities (defects) appearing on a unit of product. Control charts for such quality characteristics are called **attributes control charts** and are discussed in Chapter 7.

An important factor in control chart use is the **design of the control chart.** By this we mean the selection of the sample size, control limits, and frequency of sampling. For example, in the $\bar{x}$ chart of Fig. 5.3, we specified a sample size of five measurements, three-sigma control limits, and the sampling frequency to be every hour. In most quality-control problems, it is customary to design the control chart using primarily statistical considerations. For example, we know that increasing the sample size will decrease the probability of type II error, thus enhancing the chart's ability to detect an out-of-control state, and so forth. The use of statistical criteria such as these along with industrial experience has led to general guidelines and

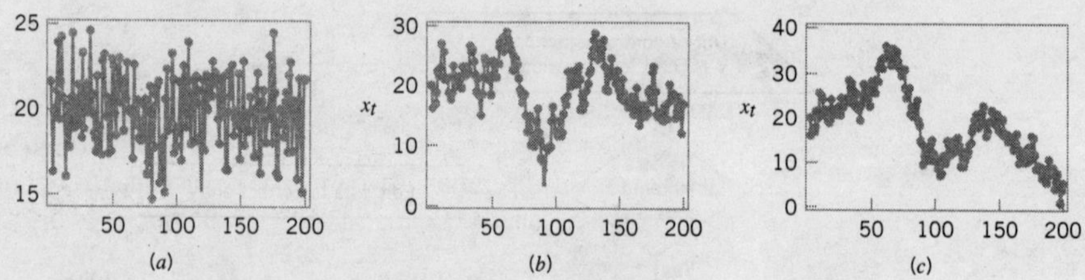

■ **FIGURE 5.7** Data from three different processes. (*a*) Stationary and uncorrelated (white noise). (*b*) Stationary and autocorrelated. (*c*) Nonstationary.

procedures for designing control charts. These procedures usually consider cost factors only in an implicit manner. Recently, however, we have begun to examine control chart design from an **economic** point of view, considering explicitly the cost of sampling, losses from allowing defective product to be produced, and the costs of investigating out-of-control signals that are really false alarms.

Another important consideration in control chart usage is the **type of variability** exhibited by the process. Fig. 5.7 presents data from three different processes. Figures 5.7*a* and 5.7*b* illustrate **stationary behavior.** By this we mean that the process data vary around a fixed mean in a stable or predictable manner. This is the type of behavior that Shewhart implied was produced by an **in-control process**.

Even a cursory examination of Figs. 5.7*a* and 5.7*b* reveals some important differences. The data in Fig. 5.7*a* are **uncorrelated;** that is, the observations give the appearance of having been drawn at random from a stable population, perhaps a normal distribution. This type of data is referred to by time series analysts as **white noise.** (Time-series analysis is a field of statistics devoted exclusively to studying and modeling time-oriented data.) In this type of process, the order in which the data occur does not tell us much that is useful to analyze the process. In other words, the past values of the data are of no help in predicting any of the future values.

Figure 5.7*b* illustrates stationary but **autocorrelated** process data. Notice that successive observations in these data are **dependent;** that is, a value above the mean tends to be followed by another value above the mean, whereas a value below the mean is usually followed by another such value. This produces a data series that has a tendency to move in moderately long "runs" on either side of the mean.

Figure 5.7*c* illustrates **nonstationary** variation. This type of process data occurs frequently in the chemical and process industries. Note that the process is very unstable in that it drifts or "wanders about" without any sense of a stable or fixed mean. In many industrial settings, we stabilize this type of behavior by using **engineering process control,** (such as **feedback control**). This approach to process control is required when there are factors that affect the process that cannot be stabilized, such as environmental variables or properties of raw materials. When the control scheme is effective, the process output will *not* look like Fig. 5.7*c,* but will resemble either Fig. 5.7*a* or 5.7*b.*

Shewhart control charts are most effective when the in-control process data look like Fig. 5.7*a.* By this we mean that the charts can be designed so that their performance is predictable and reasonable to the user, and that they are effective in reliably detecting out-of-control conditions. Most of our discussion of control charts in this chapter and in Chapters 6 and 7 will assume that the in-control process data are stationary and uncorrelated.

With some modifications, Shewhart control charts and other types of control charts can be applied to autocorrelated data. We discuss this in more detail in Part IV of the book. We also discuss feedback control and the use of SPC in systems where feedback control is employed in Part IV.

Control charts have had a long history of use in U.S. industries and in many offshore industries as well. There are at least five reasons for their popularity.

1. **Control charts are a proven technique for improving productivity.** A successful control chart program will reduce scrap and rework, which are the primary productivity killers in *any* operation. If you reduce scrap and rework, then productivity increases, cost decreases, and production capacity (measured in the number of *good* parts per hour) increases.
2. **Control charts are effective in defect prevention.** The control chart helps keep the process in control, which is consistent with the "do it right the first time" philosophy. It is never cheaper to sort out "good" units from "bad" units later on than it is to build it right initially. If you do not have effective process control, you are paying someone to make a nonconforming product.
3. **Control charts prevent unnecessary process adjustment.** A control chart can distinguish between background noise and abnormal variation; no other device including a human operator is as effective in making this distinction. If process operators adjust the process based on periodic tests unrelated to a control chart program, they will often overreact to the background noise and make unneeded adjustments. Such unnecessary adjustments can actually result in a deterioration of process performance. In other words, the control chart is consistent with the "if it isn't broken, don't fix it" philosophy.
4. **Control charts provide diagnostic information.** Frequently, the pattern of points on the control chart will contain information of diagnostic value to an experienced operator or engineer. This information allows the implementation of a change in the process that improves its performance.
5. **Control charts provide information about process capability.** The control chart provides information about the value of important process parameters and their stability over time. This allows an estimate of process capability to be made. This information is of tremendous use to product and process designers.

Control charts are among the most important management control tools; they are as important as cost controls and material controls. Modern computer technology has made it easy to implement control charts in *any* type of process, as data collection and analysis can be performed on a microcomputer or a local area network terminal in real-time, on-line at the work center. Some additional guidelines for implementing a control chart program are given at the end of Chapter 7.

5.3.2 Choice of Control Limits

Specifying the **control limits** is one of the critical decisions that must be made in designing a control chart. By moving the control limits farther from the center line, we decrease the risk of a type I error—that is, the risk of a point falling beyond the control limits, indicating an out-of-control condition when no assignable cause is present. However, widening the control limits will also increase the risk of a type II error—that is, the risk of a point falling between the control limits when the process is really out of control. If we move the control limits closer to the center line, the opposite effect is obtained: The risk of type I error is increased, while the risk of type II error is decreased.

For the $\bar{x}$ chart shown in Fig. 5.3, where three-sigma control limits were used, if we assume that the flow width is normally distributed, we find from the standard normal table that the probability of type I error is 0.0027. That is, an incorrect out-of-control signal or false alarm will be generated in only 27 out of 10,000 points. Furthermore, the probability that a point taken when the process is in control will exceed the three-sigma limits in one direction only is 0.00135. Instead of specifying the control limit as a multiple of the standard deviation of $\bar{x}$, we could have directly chosen the type I error probability and calculated the corresponding control limit. For example, if we specified a 0.001 type I error probability in one direction, then the appropriate multiple of the standard deviation would be 3.09. The control limits for the $\bar{x}$ chart would then be

$$\text{UCL} = 1.5 + 3.09(0.0671) = 1.7073$$
$$\text{LCL} = 1.5 - 3.09(0.0671) = 1.2927$$

These control limits are usually called **0.001 probability limits,** although they should logically be called 0.002 probability limits, because the total risk of making a type I error is 0.002. There is only a slight difference between the two limits.

Regardless of the distribution of the quality characteristic, it is standard practice in the United States to determine the control limits as a multiple of the standard deviation of the statistic plotted on the chart. The multiple usually chosen is three; hence, three-sigma limits are customarily employed on control charts, regardless of the type of chart employed. In the United Kingdom and parts of Western Europe, probability limits are used, with the standard probability level in each direction being 0.001.

We typically justify the use of three-sigma control limits on the basis that they give good results in practice. Moreover, in many cases, the true distribution of the quality characteristic is not known well enough to compute exact probability limits. If the distribution of the quality characteristic is reasonably approximated by the normal distribution, then there will be little difference between three-sigma and 0.001 probability limits.

Two Limits on Control Charts. Some analysts suggest using two sets of limits on control charts, such as those shown in Fig. 5.8. The outer limits—say, at three-sigma—are the usual **action limits**; that is, when a point plots outside of this limit, a search for an assignable cause is made and corrective action is taken if necessary. The inner limits, usually at two-sigma, are called **warning limits**. In Fig. 5.8, we have shown the three-sigma upper and lower control limits for the $\bar{x}$ chart for flow width. The upper and lower warning limits are located at

$$\text{UWL} = 1.5 + 2(0.0671) = 1.6342$$
$$\text{LWL} = 1.5 - 2(0.0671) = 1.3658$$

When probability limits are used, the action limits are generally 0.001 limits and the warning limits are 0.025 limits.

If one or more points fall between the warning limits and the control limits, or very close to the warning limit, we should be suspicious that the process may not be operating properly. One possible action to take when this occurs is to increase the sampling frequency and/or the sample size so that more information about the process can be obtained quickly. Process control schemes that change the sample size and/or the sampling frequency depending on the position of the current sample value are called **adaptive** or **variable sampling interval** (or **variable sample size,** etc.) schemes. These techniques have been used in practice for many years and have recently been studied extensively by researchers in the field. We will discuss this technique again in Part IV of this book.

The use of warning limits can increase the **sensitivity** of the control chart; that is, it can allow the control chart to signal a shift in the process more quickly. One of their disadvantages is that they may be confusing to operating personnel. This is not usually a serious objection, however, and many practitioners use warning limits routinely on control charts. A more serious objection is that although the use of warning limits can improve the sensitivity of the chart, they also result in an increased risk of false alarms. We will discuss the use of sensitizing rules (such as warning limits) more thoroughly in Section 5.3.6.

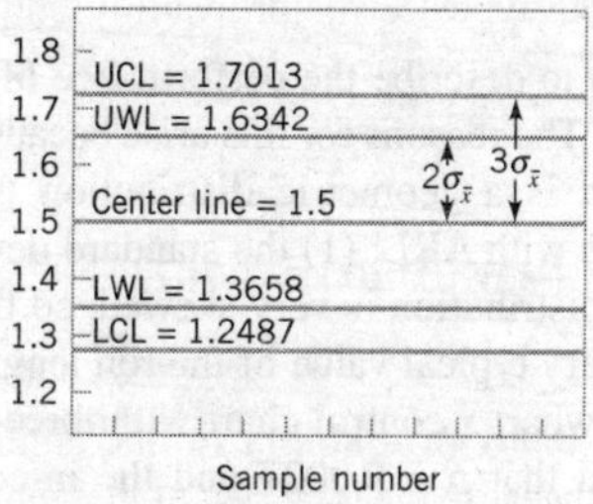

■ FIGURE 5.8 An $\bar{x}$ chart with two-sigma and three-sigma warning limits.

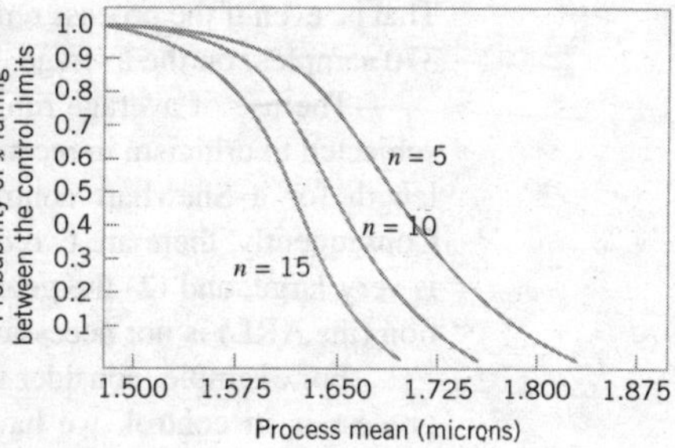

■ FIGURE 5.9 Operating-characteristic curves for an $\bar{x}$ chart.

5.3.3 Sample Size and Sampling Frequency

In designing a control chart, we must specify both the **sample size** and the **frequency of sampling**. In general, larger samples will make it easier to detect small shifts in the process. This is demonstrated in Fig. 5.9, where we have plotted the operating-characteristic curve for the $\bar{x}$ chart in Fig. 5.3 for various sample sizes. Note that the probability of detecting a shift from 1.500 microns to 1.650 microns (for example) increases as the sample size n increases. When choosing the sample size, we must keep in mind the size of the shift that we are trying to detect. If the process shift is relatively large, then we use smaller sample sizes than those that would be employed if the shift of interest were relatively small.

We must also determine the frequency of sampling. The most desirable situation from the point of view of detecting shifts would be to take large samples very frequently; however, this is usually not economically feasible. The general problem is one of **allocating sampling effort.** That is, either we take small samples at short intervals or larger samples at longer intervals. Current industry practice tends to favor smaller, more frequent samples, particularly in high-volume manufacturing processes, or where a great many types of assignable causes can occur. Furthermore, as automatic sensing and measurement technology develops, it is becoming possible to greatly increase sampling frequencies. Ultimately, every unit can be tested as it is manufactured. Automatic measurement systems and microcomputers with SPC software applied at the work center for real-time, on-line process control is an effective way to apply statistical process control.

Another way to evaluate the decisions regarding sample size and sampling frequency is through the **average run length (ARL)** of the control chart. Essentially, the ARL is the average number of points that must be plotted before a point indicates an out-of-control condition. If the process observations are uncorrelated, then for any Shewhart control chart, the ARL can be calculated easily from

$$\text{ARL} = \frac{1}{p} \tag{5.2}$$

where p is the probability that any point exceeds the control limits. This equation can be used to evaluate the performance of the control chart.

To illustrate, for the $\bar{x}$ chart with three-sigma limits, $p = 0.0027$ is the probability that a single point falls outside the limits when the process is in control. Therefore, the average run length of the $\bar{x}$ chart when the process is in control (called ARL_0) is

$$\text{ARL}_0 = \frac{1}{p} = \frac{1}{0.0027} = 370$$

That is, even if the process remains in control, an out-of-control signal will be generated every 370 samples, on the average.

The use of average run lengths to describe the performance of control charts has been subjected to criticism in recent years. The reasons for this arise because the distribution of run length for a Shewhart control chart is a geometric distribution (refer to Section 3.2.4). Consequently, there are two concerns with ARL: (1) the standard deviation of the run length is very large, and (2) the geometric distribution is very skewed, so the mean of the distribution (the ARL) is not necessarily a very typical value of the run length.

For example, consider the Shewhart $\bar{x}$ control chart with three-sigma limits. When the process is in control, we have noted that $p = 0.0027$ and the in-control ARL_0 is $ARL_0 = 1/p = 1/0.0027 = 370$. This is the mean of the geometric distribution. Now the standard deviation of the geometric distribution is

$$\sqrt{(1-p)}/p = \sqrt{(1-0.0027)}/0.0027 \cong 370$$

That is, the standard deviation of the geometric distribution in this case is approximately equal to its mean. As a result, the actual ARL_0 observed in practice for the Shewhart $\bar{x}$ control chart will likely vary considerably. Furthermore, for the geometric distribution with $p = 0.0027$, the tenth and fiftieth percentiles of the distribution are 38 and 256, respectively. This means that approximately 10% of the time the in-control run length will be less than or equal to 38 samples and 50% of the time it will be less than or equal to 256 samples. This occurs because the geometric distribution with $p = 0.0027$ is quite skewed to the right. For this reason, some analysts like to report percentiles of the run length distribution instead of just the ARL.

It is also occasionally convenient to express the performance of the control chart in terms of its **average time to signal (ATS)**. If samples are taken at fixed intervals of time that are h hours apart, then

$$ATS = ARL h \qquad (5.3)$$

Consider the hard-bake process discussed earlier, and suppose we are sampling every hour. Equation (5.3) indicates that we will have a **false alarm** about every 370 hours on the average.

Now consider how the control chart performs in detecting shifts in the mean. Suppose we are using a sample size of $n = 5$ and that when the process goes out of control the mean shifts to 1.725 microns. From the operating characteristic curve in Fig. 5.9 we find that if the process mean is 1.725 microns, the probability of $\bar{x}$ falling between the control limits is approximately 0.35. Therefore, p in equation (5.2) is 0.35, and the out-of-control ARL (called ARL_1) is

$$ARL_1 = \frac{1}{p} = \frac{1}{0.35} = 2.86$$

That is, the control chart will require 2.86 samples to detect the process shift, on the average, and since the time interval between samples is $h = 1$ hour, the average time required to detect this shift is

$$ATS = ARL_1 h = 2.86\,(1) = 2.86 \text{ hours}$$

Suppose that this is unacceptable, because production of wafers with mean flow width of 1.725 microns results in excessive scrap costs and can result in further upstream manufacturing problems. How can we reduce the time needed to detect the out-of-control condition? One method is to sample more frequently. For example, if we sample every half hour, then the average time to signal for this scheme is $ATS = ARL_1\ h = 2.86(\frac{1}{2}) = 1.43$; that is, only

1.43 hours will elapse (on the average) between the shift and its detection. The second possibility is to increase the sample size. For example, if we use $n = 10$, then Fig. 5.9 shows that the probability of $\bar{x}$ falling between the control limits when the process mean is 1.725 microns is approximately 0.1, so that $p = 0.9$, and from equation (5.2) the out-of-control ARL or ARL_1 is

$$ARL_1 = \frac{1}{p} = \frac{1}{0.9} = 1.11$$

and, if we sample every hour, the average time to signal is

$$ATS = ARL_1 h = 1.11(1) = 1.11 \text{ hours}$$

Thus, the larger sample size would allow the shift to be detected more quickly than with the smaller one.

To answer the question of sampling frequency more precisely, we must take several factors into account, including the cost of sampling, the losses associated with allowing the process to operate out of control, the rate of production, and the probabilities with which various types of process shifts occur. We discuss various methods for selecting an appropriate sample size and sampling frequency for a control chart in the next four chapters.

5.3.4 Rational Subgroups

A fundamental idea in the use of control charts is the collection of sample data according to what Shewhart called the **rational subgroup** concept. To illustrate this concept, suppose that we are using an $\bar{x}$ control chart to detect changes in the process mean. Then the rational subgroup concept means that subgroups or samples should be selected so that if assignable causes are present, the chance for differences *between* subgroups will be maximized, while the chance for differences due to these assignable causes *within* a subgroup will be minimized.

When control charts are applied to production processes, the time order of production is a logical basis for rational subgrouping. Even though time order is preserved, it is still possible to form subgroups erroneously. If some of the observations in the sample are taken at the end of one shift and the remaining observations are taken at the start of the next shift, then any differences between shifts might not be detected. Time order is frequently a good basis for forming subgroups because it allows us to detect assignable causes that occur over time.

Two general approaches to constructing rational subgroups are used. In the first approach, each sample consists of units that were produced at the same time (or as closely together as possible). Ideally, we would like to take **consecutive** units of production. This approach is used when the primary purpose of the control chart is to detect process shifts. It minimizes the chance of variability due to assignable causes *within* a sample, and it maximizes the chance of variability *between* samples if assignable causes are present. It also provides a better estimate of the standard deviation of the process in the case of variables control charts. This approach to rational subgrouping essentially gives a snapshot of the process at each point in time where a sample is collected.

Figure 5.10 illustrates this type of sampling strategy. In Fig. 5.10*a* we show a process for which the mean experiences a series of sustained shifts, and the corresponding observations obtained from this process at the points in time along the horizontal axis, assuming that five consecutive units are selected. Figure 5.10*b* shows the $\bar{x}$ **control chart** and an ***R* chart** (or **range chart**) for these data. The center line and control limits on the *R* chart are constructed using the range of each sample in the upper part of the figure (details will be given in Chapter 6). Note that although the process mean is shifting, the process variability is stable. Furthermore, the within-sample measure of variability is used to construct the control

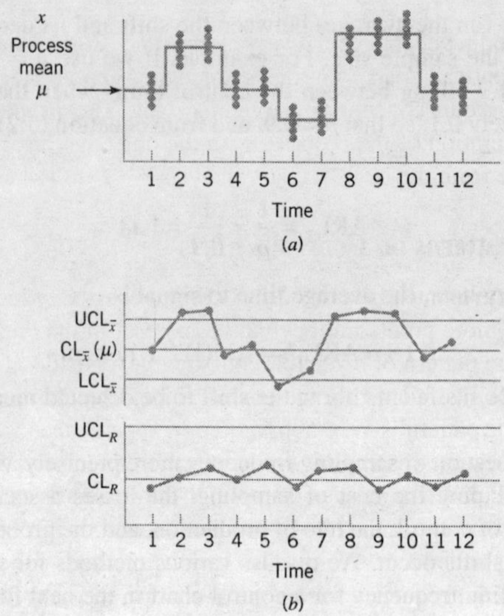

■ **FIGURE 5.10** The snapshot approach to rational subgroups. (*a*) Behavior of the process mean. (*b*) Corresponding $\bar{x}$ and R control charts.

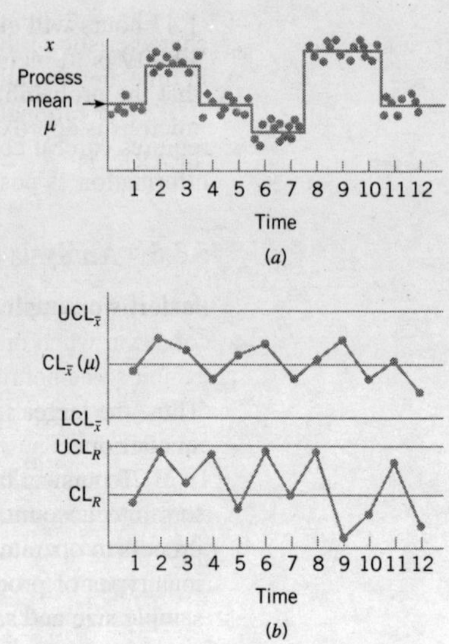

■ **FIGURE 5.11** The random sample approach to rational subgroups. (*a*) Behavior of the process mean. (*b*) Corresponding $\bar{x}$ and R control charts.

limits on the $\bar{x}$ chart. Note that the $\bar{x}$ chart in Fig. 5.10*b* has points out of control corresponding to the shifts in the process mean.

In the second approach, each sample consists of units of product that are representative of *all* units that have been produced since the last sample was taken. Essentially, each subgroup is a **random sample of all process output over the sampling interval.** This method of rational subgrouping is often used when the control chart is employed to make decisions about the acceptance of all units of product that have been produced since the last sample. In fact, if the process shifts to an out-of-control state and then back in control again *between* samples, it is sometimes argued that the snapshot method of rational subgrouping will be ineffective against these types of shifts, and so the random sample method must be used.

When the rational subgroup is a random sample of all units produced over the sampling interval, considerable care must be taken in interpreting the control charts. If the process mean drifts between several levels during the interval between samples, this may cause the range of the observations within the sample to be relatively large, resulting in wider limits on the $\bar{x}$ chart. This scenario is illustrated in Fig. 5.11. In fact, **we can often make any process appear to be in statistical control just by stretching out the interval between observations in the sample.** It is also possible for shifts in the process average to cause points on a control chart for the range or standard deviation to plot out of control, even though there has been no shift in process variability.

There are other bases for forming rational subgroups. For example, suppose a process consists of several machines that pool their output into a common stream. If we sample from this common stream of output, it will be very difficult to detect whether any of the machines are out of control. A logical approach to rational subgrouping here is to apply control chart techniques to the output for each individual machine. Sometimes this concept needs to be applied to different heads on the same machine, different work stations, different operators, and so forth. In many situations, the rational subgroup will consist of a single observation. This situation occurs frequently in the chemical and process industries where the quality characteristic of the product changes relatively slowly and samples taken very close together in time are virtually identical, apart from measurement or analytical error.

The rational subgroup concept is very important. The proper selection of samples requires careful consideration of the process, with the objective of obtaining as much useful information as possible from the control chart analysis.

5.3.5 Analysis of Patterns on Control Charts

Patterns on control charts must be assessed. A control chart may indicate an out-of-control condition when one or more points fall beyond the control limits or when the plotted points exhibit some nonrandom pattern of behavior. For example, consider the $\bar{x}$ chart shown in Fig. 5.12. Although all 25 points fall within the control limits, the points do not indicate statistical control because their pattern is very nonrandom in appearance. Specifically, we note that 19 of 25 points plot below the center line, while only 6 of them plot above. If the points truly are random, we should expect a more even distribution above and below the center line. We also observe that following the fourth point, five points in a row increase in magnitude. This arrangement of points is called a ***run.*** Since the observations are increasing, we could call this a *run up.* Similarly, a sequence of decreasing points is called a *run down.* This control chart has an unusually long run up (beginning with the fourth point) and an unusually long run down (beginning with the eighteenth point).

In general, we define a run as a sequence of observations of the same type. In addition to runs up and runs down, we could define the types of observations as those above and below the center line, respectively, so that two points in a row above the center line would be a run of length 2.

A run of length 8 or more points has a very low probability of occurrence in a random sample of points. Consequently, any type of run of length 8 or more is often taken as a signal of an out-of-control condition. For example, eight consecutive points on one side of the center line may indicate that the process is out of control.

Although runs are an important measure of nonrandom behavior on a control chart, other types of patterns may also indicate an out-of-control condition. For example, consider the $\bar{x}$ chart in Fig. 5.13. Note that the plotted sample averages exhibit a cyclic behavior, yet they all fall within the control limits. Such a pattern may indicate a problem with the process such as operator fatigue, raw material deliveries, heat or stress buildup, and so forth. Although the process is not really out of control, the yield may be improved by elimination or reduction of the sources of variability causing this cyclic behavior (see Fig. 5.14).

The problem is one of **pattern recognition**—that is, recognizing systematic or nonrandom patterns on the control chart and identifying the reason for this behavior. The ability to interpret a particular pattern in terms of assignable causes requires experience and knowledge

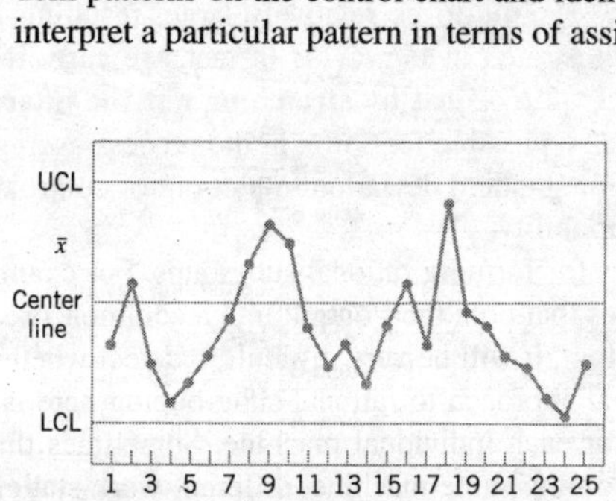

FIGURE 5.12 An $\bar{x}$ control chart.

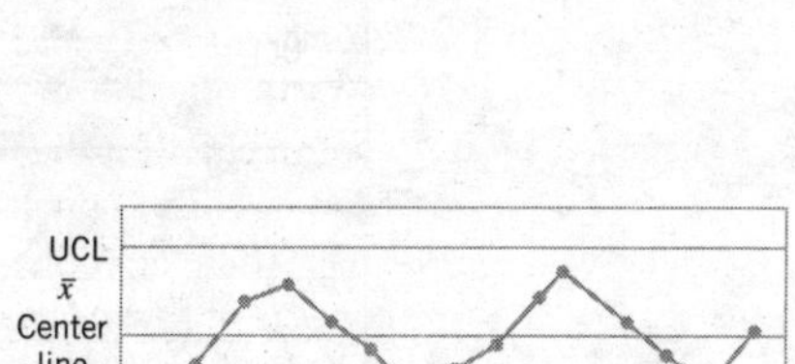

FIGURE 5.13 An $\bar{x}$ chart with a cyclic pattern.

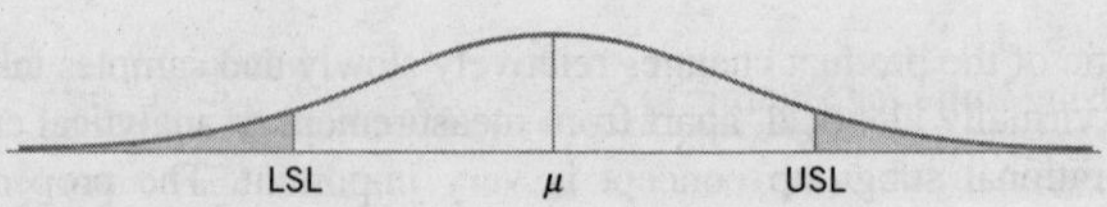

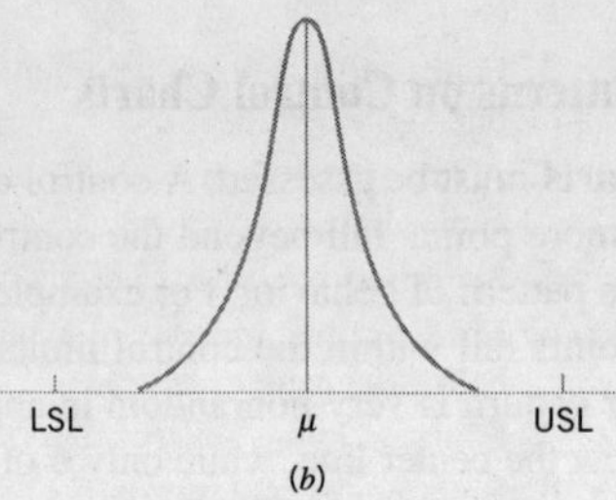

■ **FIGURE 5.14** (*a*) Variability with the cyclic pattern. (*b*) Variability with the cyclic pattern eliminated.

of the process. That is, we must not only know the statistical principles of control charts, but we must also have a good understanding of the process. We discuss the interpretation of patterns on control charts in more detail in Chapter 6.

The Western Electric Handbook (1956) suggests a set of decision rules for detecting nonrandom patterns on control charts. Specifically, it suggests concluding that the process is out of control if either

1. One point plots outside the three-sigma control limits,
2. Two out of three consecutive points plot beyond the two-sigma warning limits,
3. Four out of five consecutive points plot at a distance of one-sigma or beyond from the center line, or
4. Eight consecutive points plot on one side of the center line.

Those rules apply to one side of the center line at a time. Therefore, a point above the *upper* warning limit followed immediately by a point below the *lower* warning limit would not signal an out-of-control alarm. These are often used in practice for enhancing the sensitivity of control charts. That is, the use of these rules can allow smaller process shifts to be detected more quickly than would be the case if our only criterion was the usual three-sigma control limit violation.

Figure 5.15 shows an $\bar{x}$ control chart with the one-sigma, two-sigma, and three-sigma limits used in the Western Electric procedure. Note that these limits partition the control chart

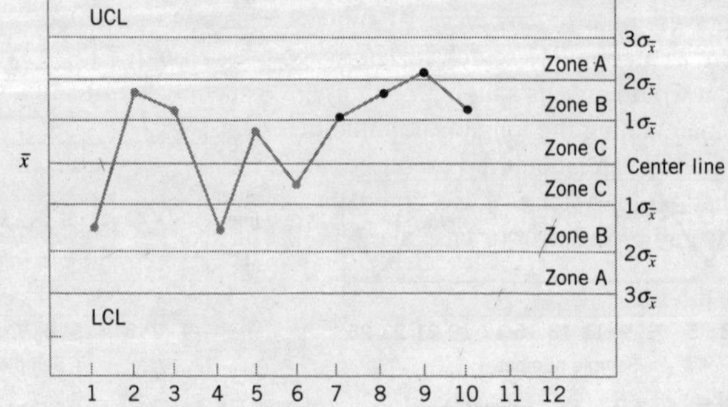

■ **FIGURE 5.15** The Western Electric or zone rules, with the last four points showing a violation of rule 3.

■ **TABLE 5.1**
Some Sensitizing Rules for Shewhart Control Charts

Standard Action Signal:		
	1. One or more points outside of the control limits.	Western Electric Rules
	2. Two of three consecutive points outside the two-sigma warning limits but still inside the control limits.	Western Electric Rules
	3. Four of five consecutive points beyond the one-sigma limits.	Western Electric Rules
	4. A run of eight consecutive points on one side of the center line.	Western Electric Rules
	5. Six points in a row steadily increasing or decreasing.	
	6. Fifteen points in a row in zone C (both above and below the center line).	
	7. Fourteen points in a row alternating up and down.	
	8. Eight points in a row on both sides of the center line with none in zone C.	
	9. An unusual or nonrandom pattern in the data.	
	10. One or more points near a warning or control limit.	

into three zones (A, B, and C) on each side of the center line. Consequently, the Western Electric rules are sometimes called the **zone rules** for control charts. Note that the last four points fall in zone B or beyond. Thus, since four of five consecutive points exceed the one-sigma limit, the Western Electric procedure will conclude that the pattern is nonrandom and the process is out of control.

5.3.6 Discussion of Sensitizing Rules for Control Charts

As may be gathered from earlier sections, several criteria may be applied simultaneously to a control chart to determine whether the process is out of control. The basic criterion is one or more points outside of the control limits. The supplementary criteria are sometimes used to increase the **sensitivity** of the control charts to a small process shift so that we may respond more quickly to the assignable cause. Some of the **sensitizing rules for control charts** that are widely used in practice are shown in Table 5.1. For a good discussion of some of these rules, see Nelson (1984). Frequently, we will inspect the control chart and conclude that the process is out of control if any one or more of the criteria in Table 5.1 are met.

When several of these sensitizing rules are applied simultaneously, we often use a **graduated response** to out-of-control signals. For example, if a point exceeded a control limit, we would immediately begin to search for the assignable cause, but if one or two consecutive points exceeded only the two-sigma warning limit, we might increase the frequency of sampling from every hour to say, every 10 minutes. This **adaptive sampling response** might not be as severe as a complete search for an assignable cause, but if the process were really out of control, it would give us a high probability of detecting this situation more quickly than we would by maintaining the longer sampling interval.

In general, care should be exercised when using several decision rules simultaneously. Suppose that the analyst uses k decision rules and that criterion i has type I error probability α_i. Then the overall type I error or false alarm probability for the decision based on all k tests is

$$\alpha = 1 - \prod_{i=1}^{k}(1-\alpha_i) \tag{5.4}$$

provided that all k decision rules are independent. However, the independence assumption is not valid with the usual sensitizing rules. Furthermore, the value of α_i is not always clearly defined for the sensitizing rules, because these rules involve several observations.

Champ and Woodall (1987) investigated the average run length performance for the Shewhart control chart with various sensitizing rules. They found that the use of these rules does improve the ability of the control chart to detect smaller shifts, but the in-control average run length can be substantially degraded. For example, assuming independent process data and using a Shewhart control chart with the Western Electric rules results in an in-control ARL of 91.25, in contrast to 370 for the Shewhart control chart alone.

Some of the individual Western Electric rules are particularly troublesome. An illustration is the rule of several (usually seven or eight) consecutive points which either increase or decrease. This rule is very ineffective in detecting a trend, the situation for which it was designed. It does, however, greatly increase the false alarm rate. See Davis and Woodall (1988) for more details.

5.3.7 Phase I and Phase II of Control Chart Application

Standard control chart usage involves **phase I and phase II applications**, with two different and distinct objectives. In phase I, a set of process data is gathered and analyzed all at once in a **retrospective** analysis, constructing **trial control limits** to determine if the process has been in control over the period of time where the data were collected, and to see if reliable control limits can be established to monitor future production. This is typically the first thing that is done when control charts are applied to any process. Control charts in phase I primarily assist operating personnel in bringing the process into a state of statistical control. Phase II begins after we have a "clean" set of process data gathered under stable conditions and representative of in-control process performance. In phase II, we use the control chart to **monitor** the process by comparing the sample statistic for each successive sample as it is drawn from the process to the control limits.

Thus, in phase I we are comparing a collection of, say, m points to a set of control limits computed from those points. Typically $m = 20$ or 25 subgroups are used in phase I. It is fairly typical in phase I to assume that the process is initially out of control, so the objective of the analyst is to bring the process into a state of statistical control. Control limits are calculated based on the m subgroups and the data plotted on the control charts. Points that are outside the control limits are investigated, looking for potential assignable causes. Any assignable causes that are identified are worked on by engineering and operating personnel in an effort to eliminate them. Points outside the control limits are then excluded and a new set of revised control limits calculated. Then new data are collected and compared to these revised limits. Sometimes this type of analysis will require several cycles in which the control chart is employed, assignable causes are detected and corrected, revised control limits are calculated, and the out-of-control action plan is updated and expanded. Eventually the process is stabilized, and a clean set of data that represents in-control process performance is obtained for use in phase II.

Generally, Shewhart control charts are very effective in phase I because they are easy to construct and interpret, and because they are effective in detecting both large, sustained shifts in the process parameters and outliers (single excursions that may have resulted from assignable causes of short duration), measurement errors, data recording and/or transmission errors, and the like. Furthermore, patterns on Shewhart control charts often are easy to interpret and have direct physical meaning. The sensitizing rules discussed in the previous sections are also easy to apply to Shewhart charts. (This is an optional feature in most SPC software.) The types of assignable causes that usually occur in phase I result in fairly large process shifts—exactly the scenario in which the Shewhart control chart is most effective. Average run length is not usually a reasonable performance measure for phase I; we are typically more interested in the probability that an assignable cause will be detected than in the occurrence of false alarms. For good discussions of phase I control chart usage and related matters, see the papers by Woodall (2000), Borror and Champ (2001), Boyles (2000), and Champ and Chou (2003), and the standard ANSI/ASQC B1–133–1996 Quality Control Chart Methodologies (this can be downloaded at e-standards.asq.org).

In phase II, we usually assume that the process is reasonably stable. Often, the assignable causes that occur in phase II result in smaller process shifts, because (it is hoped) most of the really ugly sources of variability have been systematically removed during phase I. Our emphasis is now on **process monitoring,** not on bringing an unruly process into control. Average run length is a valid basis for evaluating the performance of a control chart in phase II. Shewhart control charts are much less likely to be effective in phase II because they are not very sensitive to small to moderate size process shifts; that is, their ARL performance is relatively poor. Attempts to solve this problem by employing sensitizing rules such as those discussed in the previous section are likely to be unsatisfactory, because the use of these supplemental sensitizing rules increases the false alarm rate of the Shewhart control chart. [Recall the discussion of the Champ and Woodall (1987) paper in the previous section.] The routine use of sensitizing rules to detect small shifts or to react more quickly to assignable causes in phase II should be discouraged. The cumulative sum and EWMA control charts discussed in Chapter 9 are much more likely to be effective in phase II.

5.4 The Rest of the Magnificent Seven

Although the control chart is a very powerful problem-solving and process-improvement tool, it is most effective when its use is fully integrated into a comprehensive SPC program. The seven major SPC problem-solving tools should be widely taught throughout the organization and used routinely to identify improvement opportunities and to assist in reducing variability and eliminating waste. They can be used in several ways throughout the DMAIC problem-solving process. The magnificent seven, introduced in Section 5.1, are listed again here for convenience:

1. Histogram or stem-and-leaf plot
2. Check sheet
3. Pareto chart
4. Cause-and-effect diagram
5. Defect concentration diagram
6. Scatter diagram
7. Control chart

We introduced the histogram and the stem-and-leaf plot in Chapter 3, and discussed the control chart in Section 5.3. In this section, we illustrate the rest of the tools.

Check Sheet. In the early stages of process improvement, it will often become necessary to collect either historical or current operating data about the process under investigation. This is a common activity in the measure step of DMAIC. A **check sheet** can be very useful in this data collection activity. The check sheet shown in Fig. 5.16 was developed by an aerospace firm engineer who was investigating defects that occurred on one of the firm's tanks. The engineer designed the check sheet to help summarize all the

CHECK SHEET
DEFECT DATA FOR 2002–2003 YTD

Part No.: TAX-41
Location: Bellevue
Study Date: 6/5/03
Analyst: TCB

	2002												2003					
Defect	1	2	3	4	5	6	7	8	9	10	11	12	1	2	3	4	5	Total
Parts damaged		1		3	1	2		1		10	3		2	2	7	2		34
Machining problems			3	3				1	8		3		8	3				29
Supplied parts rusted			1	1		2	9											13
Masking insufficient		3	6	4	3	1												17
Misaligned weld	2																	2
Processing out of order	2															2		4
Wrong part issued		1						2										3
Unfinished fairing			3															3
Adhesive failure				1							1		2			1	1	6
Powdery alodine					1													1
Paint out of limits						1								1				2
Paint damaged by etching			1															1
Film on parts						3		1	1									5
Primer cans damaged								1										1
Voids in casting									1	1								2
Delaminated composite										2								2
Incorrect dimensions											13	7	13	1		1	1	36
Improper test procedure										1								1
Salt-spray failure													2			2		4
TOTAL	4	5	14	12	5	9	9	6	10	14	20	7	27	7	7	6	2	166

■ **FIGURE 5.16** A check sheet to record defects on a tank used in an aerospace application.

historical defect data available on the tanks. Because only a few tanks were manufactured each month, it seemed appropriate to summarize the data monthly and to identify as many different types of defects as possible. The **time-oriented summary** is particularly valuable in looking for **trends** or other meaningful patterns. For example, if many defects occur during the summer, one possible cause that might be the use of temporary workers during a heavy vacation period.

When designing a check sheet, it is important to clearly specify the type of data to be collected, the part or operation number, the date, the analyst, and any other information useful in diagnosing the cause of poor performance. If the check sheet is the basis for performing further calculations or is used as a worksheet for data entry into a computer, then it is important to be sure that the check sheet will be adequate for this purpose. In some cases, a trial run to validate the check sheet layout and design may be helpful.

Pareto Chart. The **Pareto chart** is simply a frequency distribution (or histogram) of attribute data arranged by category. Pareto charts are often used in both the

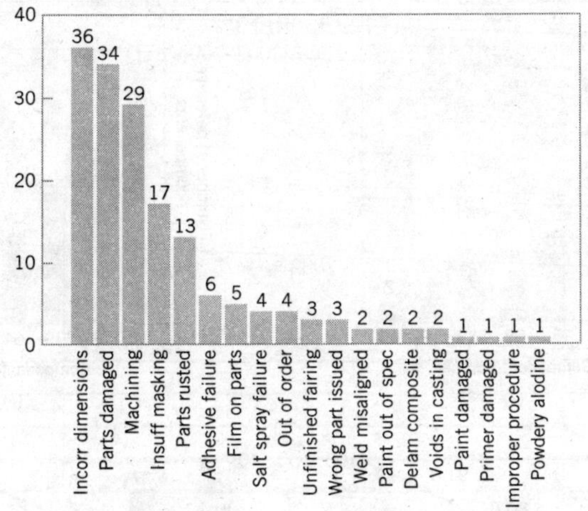

■ **FIGURE 5.17** Pareto chart of the tank defect data.

measure and analyze steps of DMAIC. To illustrate a Pareto chart, consider the tank defect data presented in Fig. 5.16. Plotting the total frequency of occurrence of each defect type (the last column of the table in Fig. 5.16) against the various defect types will produce Fig. 5.17, which is called a Pareto chart.[3] Through this chart, the user can quickly and visually identify the most frequently occurring types of defects. For example, Fig. 5.17 indicates that incorrect dimensions, parts damaged, and machining are the most commonly encountered defects. Thus the causes of these defect types probably should be identified and attacked first.

Note that the Pareto chart does not automatically identify the most *important* defects, but only the most *frequent.* For example, in Fig. 5.17 casting voids occur very infrequently (2 of 166 defects, or 1.2%). However, voids could result in scrapping the tank, a potentially large cost exposure—perhaps so large that casting voids should be elevated to a major defect category. When the list of defects contains a mixture of those that might have extremely serious consequences and others of much less importance, one of two methods can be used:

1. Use a weighting scheme to modify the frequency counts. Weighting schemes for defects are discussed in Chapter 7.
2. Accompany the *frequency* **Pareto chart** analysis with a **cost** or *exposure Pareto chart.*

There are many variations of the basic Pareto chart. Figure 5.18*a* shows a Pareto chart applied to an electronics assembly process using surface-mount components. The vertical axis is the percentage of components incorrectly located, and the horizontal axis is the component number, a code that locates the device on the printed circuit board. Note that locations 27 and 39 account for 70% of the errors. This may be the result of the *type* or *size* of components at these locations, or of *where* these locations are on the board layout. Figure 5.18*b* presents another Pareto chart from the electronics industry. The vertical axis is the number of defective components, and the horizontal axis is the component number. Note that each vertical bar has been broken down by supplier to produce a *stacked Pareto chart.* This

[3]The name *Pareto chart* is derived from Italian economist Vilfredo Pareto (1848–1923), who theorized that in certain economies the majority of the wealth was held by a disproportionately small segment of the population. Quality engineers have observed that defects usually follow a similar Pareto distribution.

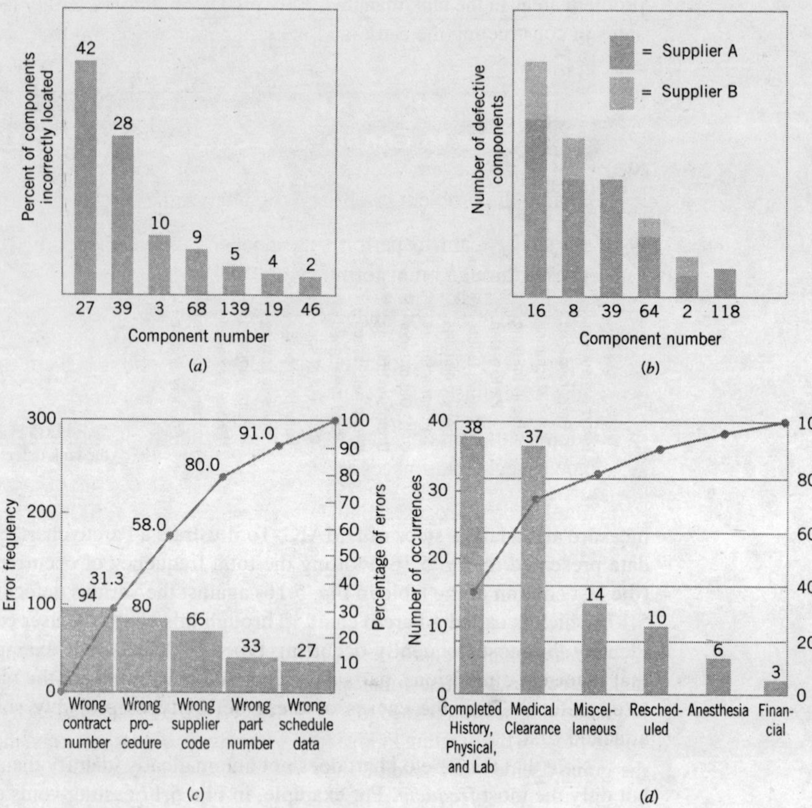

■ **FIGURE 5.18** Examples of Pareto charts.

analysis clearly indicates that supplier A provides a disproportionately large share of the defective components.

Pareto charts are widely used in **nonmanufacturing applications** of quality improvement methods. A Pareto chart used by a quality improvement team in a procurement organization is shown in Fig. 5.18*c*. The team was investigating errors on purchase orders in an effort to reduce the organization's number of purchase order changes. (Each change typically cost between \$100 and \$500, and the organization issued several hundred purchase order changes each month.) This Pareto chart has two scales: one for the actual error frequency and another for the percentage of errors. Figure 5.18*d* presents a Pareto chart constructed by a quality improvement team in a hospital to reflect the reasons for cancellation of scheduled outpatient surgery.

In general, the Pareto chart is one of the most useful of the magnificent seven. Its applications to quality improvement are limited only by the ingenuity of the analyst.

Cause-and-Effect Diagram. Once a defect, error, or problem has been identified and isolated for further study, we must begin to analyze potential causes of this undesirable effect. In situations where causes are not obvious (sometimes they are), the **cause-and-effect diagram** is a formal tool frequently useful in unlayering potential causes. The cause-and-effect diagram is very useful in the analyze and improve steps of DMAIC. The cause-and-effect diagram constructed by a quality improvement team assigned to identify potential problem areas in the tank manufacturing process mentioned earlier is shown in Fig. 5.19. The steps in constructing the cause-and-effect diagram are as follows:

How to Construct a Cause-and-Effect Diagram

1. Define the problem or effect to be analyzed.
2. Form the team to perform the analysis. Often the team will uncover potential causes through brainstorming.
3. Draw the effect box and the center line.
4. Specify the major potential cause categories and join them as boxes connected to the center line.
5. Identify the possible causes and classify them into the categories in step 4. Create new categories, if necessary.
6. Rank order the causes to identify those that seem most likely to impact the problem.
7. Take corrective action.

In analyzing the tank defect problem, the team elected to lay out the major categories of tank defects as machines, materials, methods, personnel, measurement, and environment. A brainstorming session ensued to identify the various subcauses in each of these major categories and to prepare the diagram in Fig. 5.19. Then through discussion and the process of elimination, the group decided that materials and methods contained the most likely cause categories.

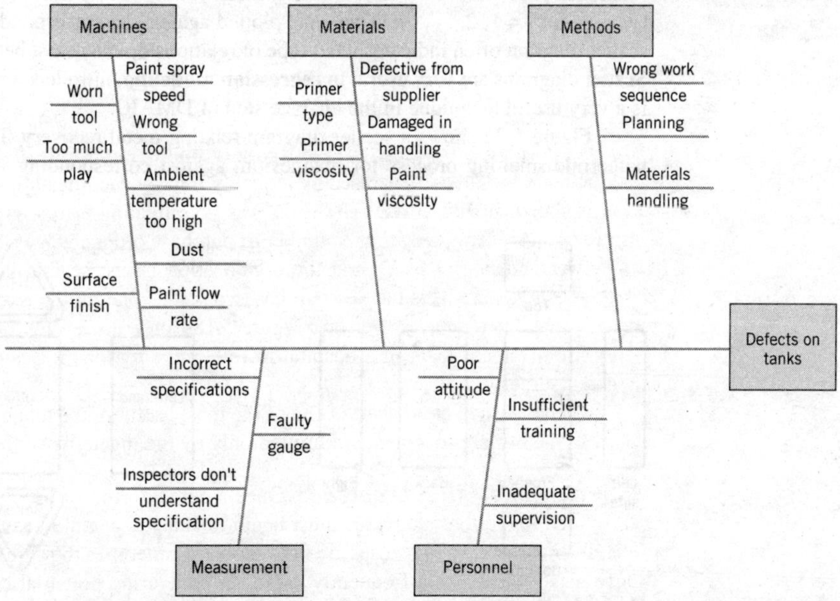

■ FIGURE 5.19 Cause-and-effect diagram for the tank defect problem.

Cause-and-effect analysis is an extremely powerful tool. A highly detailed cause-and-effect diagram can serve as an effective troubleshooting aid. Furthermore, the construction of a cause-and-effect diagram as a **team experience** tends to get people involved in attacking a problem rather than in affixing blame.

Defect Concentration Diagram. A **defect concentration diagram** is a picture of the unit, showing all relevant views. Then the various types of defects are drawn on the picture, and the diagram is analyzed to determine whether the **location** of the defects on the unit conveys any useful information about the potential causes of the defects. Defect concentration diagrams are very useful in the analyze step of DMAIC.

Figure 5.20 presents a defect concentration diagram for the final assembly stage of a refrigerator manufacturing process. Surface-finish defects are identified by the dark shaded areas on the refrigerator. From inspection of the diagram it seems clear that materials handling is responsible for the majority of these defects. The unit is being moved by securing a belt around the middle, and this belt is either too loose or tight, worn out, made of abrasive material, or too narrow. Furthermore, when the unit is moved the corners are being damaged. It is possible that worker fatigue is a factor. In any event, proper work methods and improved materials handling will likely improve this process dramatically.

Figure 5.21 shows the defect concentration diagram for the tank problem mentioned earlier. Note that this diagram shows several different broad categories of defects, each identified with a specific code. Often different colors are used to indicate different types of defects.

When defect data are portrayed on a defect concentration diagram over a sufficient number of units, patterns frequently emerge, and the location of these patterns often contains much information about the causes of the defects. We have found defect concentration diagrams to be important problem-solving tools in many industries, including plating, painting and coating, casting and foundry operations, machining, and electronics assembly.

Scatter Diagram. The **scatter diagram** is a useful plot for identifying a potential relationship between two variables. Data are collected in pairs on the two variables—say, (y_i, x_i)—for $i = 1, 2, \ldots, n$. Then y_i is plotted against the corresponding x_i. The shape of the scatter diagram often indicates what type of relationship may exist between the two variables. Scatter diagrams are very useful in **regression modeling,** introduced in Chapter 3. Regression is a very useful technique in the analyze step of DMAIC.

Figure 5.22 shows a scatter diagram relating metal recovery (in percent) from a magnathermic smelting process for magnesium against corresponding values of the amount of

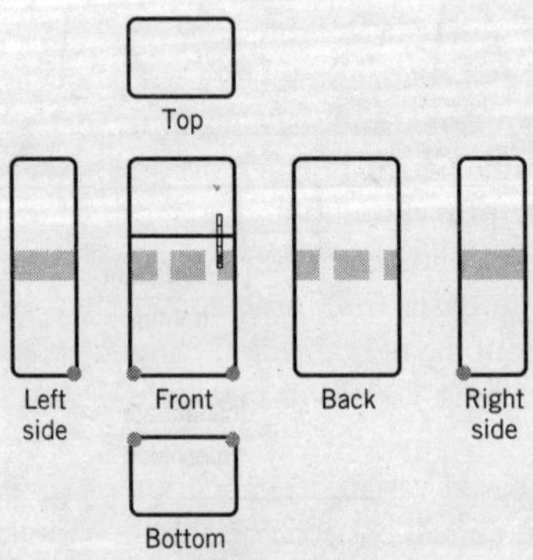

■ FIGURE 5.20 Surface-finish defects on a refrigerator.

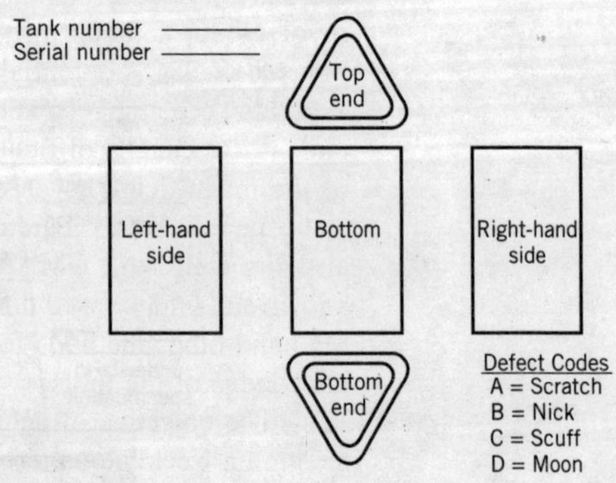

■ FIGURE 5.21 Defect concentration diagram for the tank.

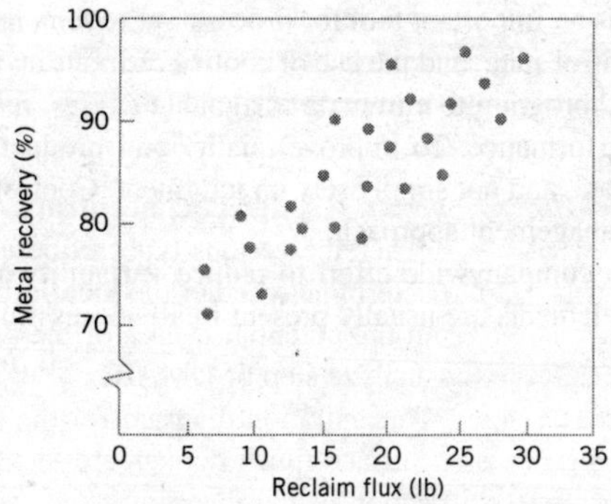

■ **FIGURE 5.22** A scatter diagram.

reclaim flux added to the crucible. The scatter diagram indicates a strong **positive correlation** between metal recovery and flux amount; that is, as the amount of flux added is increased, the metal recovery also increases. It is tempting to conclude that the relationship is one based on cause and effect: By increasing the amount of reclaim flux used, we can always ensure high metal recovery. This thinking is potentially dangerous, because ***correlation does*** *not necessarily imply* **causality.** This apparent relationship could be caused by something quite different. For example, both variables could be related to a third one, such as the temperature of the metal prior to the reclaim pouring operation, and this relationship could be responsible for what we see in Fig. 5.22. If higher temperatures lead to higher metal recovery and the practice is to add reclaim flux in proportion to temperature, adding more flux when the process is running at low temperature will do nothing to enhance yield. The scatter diagram is useful for identifying **potential relationships. Designed experiments** [see Montgomery (2005)] **must be used to verify causality.**

5.5 Implementing SPC in a Quality Improvement Program

The methods of statistical process control can provide significant payback to those companies that can successfully implement them. Although SPC seems to be a collection of statistically based problem-solving tools, there is more to the successful use of SPC than learning and using these tools. SPC is most effective when it is integrated into an overall, companywide quality improvement program. It can be implemented using the DMAIC approach. Indeed, the basic SPC tools are an integral part of DMAIC. **Management involvement** and **commitment** to the quality improvement process are the most vital components of SPC's potential success. Management is a role model, and others in the organization look to management for guidance and as an example. A team approach is also important, as it is usually difficult for one person alone to introduce process improvements. Many of the magnificent seven are helpful in building an improvement team, including cause-and-effect diagrams, Pareto charts, and defect concentration diagrams. This team approach also fits well with DMAIC. The basic SPC problem-solving tools must become widely known and widely used throughout the organization. Ongoing education of personnel about SPC and other methods for reducing variability are necessary to achieve this widespread knowledge of the tools.

The objective of an SPC-based variability reduction program is continuous improvement on a weekly, quarterly, and annual basis. SPC is not a one-time program to be applied when the business is in trouble and later abandoned. Quality improvement that is focused on reduction of variability must become part of the culture of the organization.

The control chart is an important tool for process improvement. Processes do not naturally operate in an in-control state, and the use of control charts is an important step that must be taken early in an SPC program to eliminate assignable causes, reduce process variability, and stabilize process performance. To improve quality and productivity, we must begin to manage with facts and data, and not simply rely on judgment. Control charts are an important part of this change in management approach.

In implementing a companywide effort to reduce variability and improve quality, we have found that several elements are usually present in all successful efforts. These elements are as follows:

Elements of a Successful SPC Program

1. Management leadership
2. A team approach, focusing on project-oriented applications
3. Education of employees at all levels
4. Emphasis on reducing variability
5. Measuring success in quantitative (economic) terms
6. A mechanism for communicating successful results throughout the organization

We cannot overemphasize the importance of **management leadership** and the **team/project approach.** Successful quality improvement is a "top-down" management-driven activity. It is also important to measure progress and success in quantitative (economic) terms and to spread knowledge of this success throughout the organization. When successful improvements are communicated throughout the company, this can provide motivation and incentive to improve other processes and to make continuous improvement a usual part of the way of doing business.

5.6 An Application of SPC

In this section, we give an account of how SPC methods were used to improve quality and productivity in a copper plating operation at a printed circuit board fabrication facility. This process was characterized by high levels of defects such as brittle copper and copper voids and by long cycle time. The long cycle time was particularly troublesome, as it had led to an extensive work backlog and was a major contributor to poor conformance to the factory production schedule.

Management chose this process area for an initial implementation of SPC. The DMAIC approach was used. An improvement team was formed, consisting of the plating tank operator, the manufacturing engineer responsible for the process, and a quality engineer. All members of the team had been exposed to DMAIC and the magnificent seven in a company-sponsored seminar. During the define step, it was decided to concentrate on reducing the flow time through the process, as the missed delivery targets were considered to be the most serious obstacle to improving productivity. The team quickly determined (during the measure step)

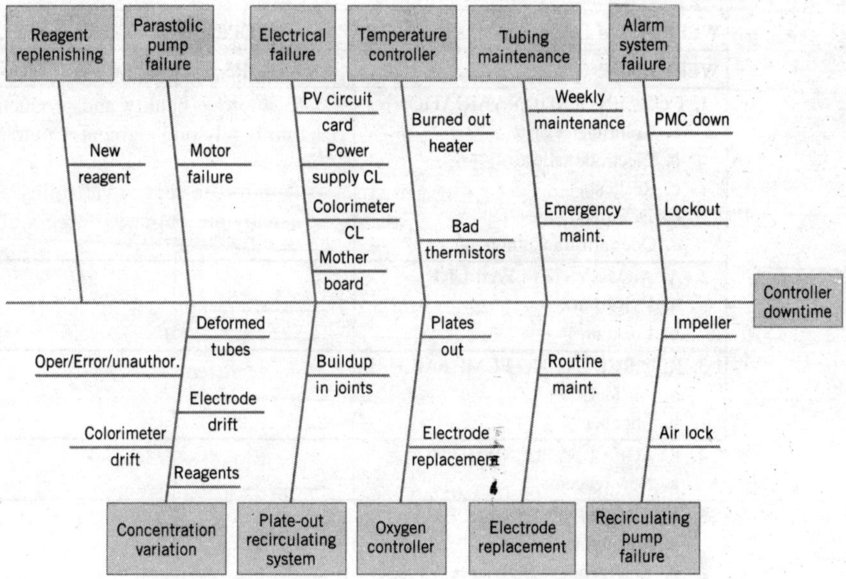

■ **FIGURE 5.23** Cause-and-effect diagram for controller downtime.

that excessive downtime on the controller that regulated the copper concentration in the plating tank was a major factor in the excessive flow time; controller downtime translated directly into lost production.

As part of the analyze step, the team decided to use a cause-and-effect analysis to begin to isolate the potential causes of controller downtime. Figure 5.23 shows the cause-and-effect diagram that was produced during a brainstorming session. The team was able to quickly identify 11 major potential causes of controller downtime. However, when they examined the equipment logbook to make a more definitive diagnosis of the causes of downtime based on actual process performance, the results were disappointing. The logbook contained little useful information about causes of downtime; instead, it contained only a chronological record of when the machine was up and when it was down.

The team then decided that it would be necessary to collect valid data about the causes of controller downtime. They designed the check sheet shown in Fig. 5.24 as a supplemental page for the logbook. The team agreed that whenever the equipment was down, one team member would assume responsibility for filling out the check sheet. Note that the major causes of controller downtime identified on the cause-and-effect diagram were used to structure the headings and subheadings on the check sheet. The team agreed that data would be collected over a four- to six-week period.

As more reliable data concerning the causes of controller downtime became available, the team was able to analyze it using other SPC techniques. Figure 5.25 presents the Pareto analysis of the controller failure data produced during the six-week study of the process. Note that concentration variation is a major cause of downtime. Actually, the situation is probably more complex than it appears. The third largest category of downtime causes is reagent replenishment. Frequently, the reagent in the colorimeter on the controller is replenished because concentration has varied so far outside the process specifications that reagent replenishment and colorimeter recalibration is the only step that can be used to bring the process back on line. Therefore, it is possible that up to 50% of the downtime associated with controller failures can be attributed to concentration variation.

WEEKLY TALLY	OPERATOR ________		
WEEK ENDING ________	ERRORS	DESCRIPTION	ACTION
1. CONCENTRATION VARIATION			
a. Colorimeter drift	________		
b. Electrode failure	________		
c. Reagents	________		
d. Deformed tubes	________		
e. Oper/error/unauthorized	________		
2. ALARM SYSTEM FAILURE			
a. PMC down	________		
b. Lockout	________		
3. RECIRCULATING PUMP FAILURE			
a. Air lock	________		
b. Impeller	________		
4. REAGENT REPLENISHING			
a. New reagent	________		
5. TUBING MAINTENANCE			
a. Weekly maintenance	________		
b. Emergency maintenance	________		
6. ELECTRODE REPLACEMENT			
a. Routine maintenance	________		
7. TEMPERATURE CONTROLLER			
a. Burned out heater	________		
b. Bad thermistors	________		
8. OXYGEN CONTROLLER			
a. Plates out	________		
b. Electrode replacement	________		
9. PARASTOLIC PUMP FAILURE			
a. Motor failure	________		
10. ELECTRICAL FAILURE			
a. PV circuit card	________		
b. Power supply CL	________		
c. Colorimeter CL	________		
d. Motherboard	________		
11. PLATE-OUT RECIRCULATING			
a. Buildup at joints	________		
TOTAL COUNT			

■ FIGURE 5.24 Check sheet for logbook.

Figure 5.26 presents a Pareto analysis of only the concentration variation data. From this diagram we know that colorimeter drift and problems with reagents are major causes of concentration variation. This information led the manufacturing engineer on the team to conclude that rebuilding the colorimeter would be an important step in improving the process.

During the time that these process data were collected, the team decided to run statistical control charts on the process. The information collected to this point about process performance was the basis for constructing the initial OCAPs (out-of-control-action plans) for these control charts. These control charts and their OCAP, would also be useful in the

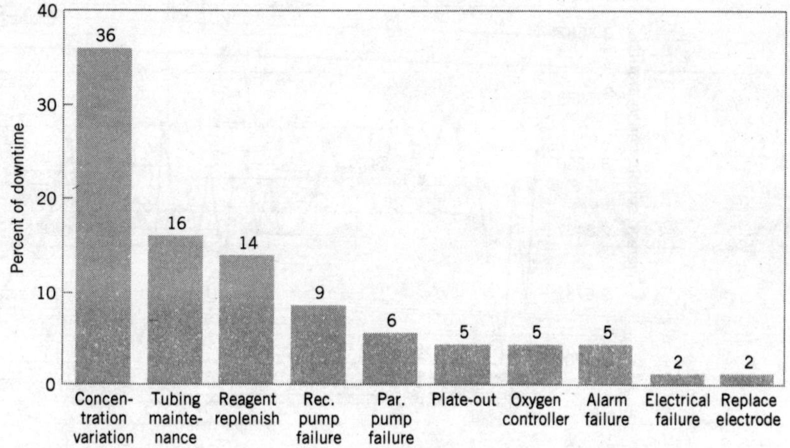

■ **FIGURE 5.25** Pareto analysis of controller failures.

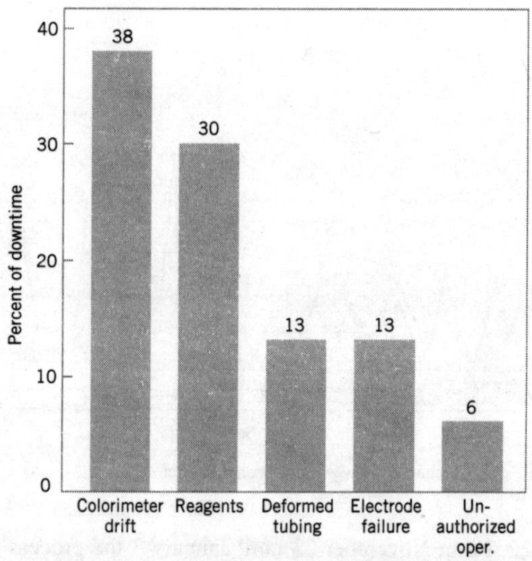

■ **FIGURE 5.26** Pareto analysis of concentration variation.

control step of DMAIC. Copper concentration is measured in this process manually three times per day. Figure 5.27 presents the $\bar{x}$ control chart for average daily copper concentration; that is, each point plotted in the figure is a daily average. The chart shows the center line and three-sigma statistical control limits. (We will discuss the construction of these limits in more detail in the next few chapters.) Note that there are a number of points outside the control limits, indicating that assignable causes are present in the process. Figure 5.28 presents the range or R chart for daily copper concentration. On this chart, R represents the difference between the maximum and minimum copper concentration readings in a day. Note that the R chart also exhibits a lack of statistical control. In particular, the second half of the R chart appears much more unstable than the first half. Examining the dates along the horizontal axis, the team noted that severe variation in average daily copper concentration only appeared after January 3. The last observations on copper concentration had been taken

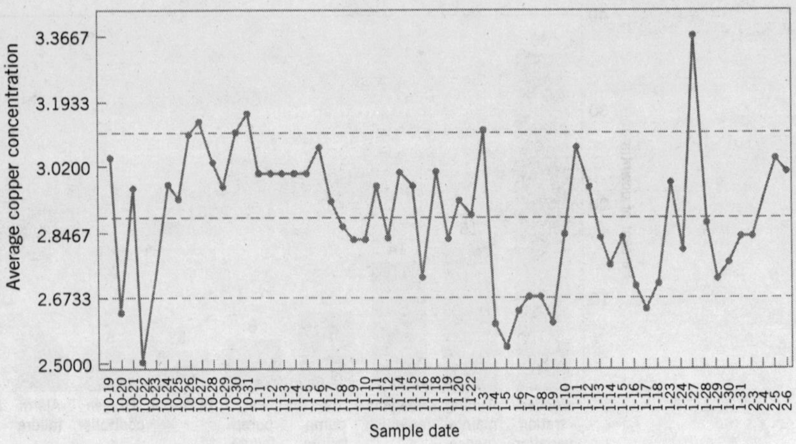

■ **FIGURE 5.27** $\bar{x}$ chart for the average daily copper concentration.

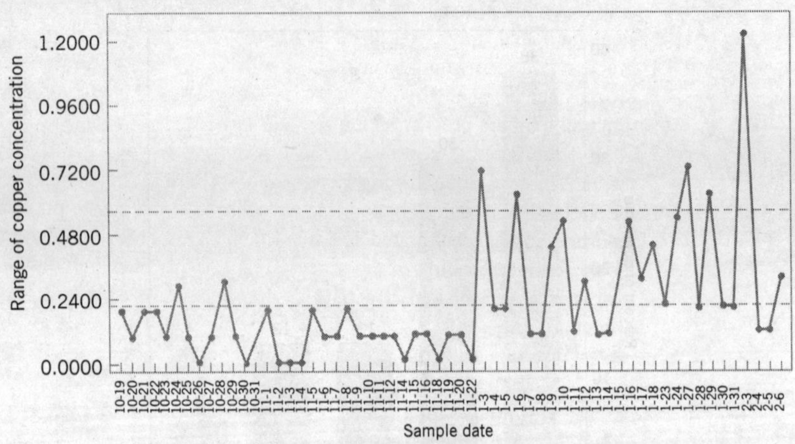

■ **FIGURE 5.28** *R* chart for daily copper concentration.

on November 22. From November 23 until January 3 the process had been in a shutdown mode because of holidays. Apparently, when the process was restarted, substantial deterioration in controller/colorimeter performance had occurred. This hastened engineering's decision to rebuild the colorimeter.

Figure 5.29 presents a **tolerance diagram** of daily copper concentration readings. In this figure, each day's copper concentration readings are plotted, and the extremes are connected with a vertical line. In some cases, more than one observation is plotted at a single position, so a numeral is used to indicate the number of observations plotted at each particular point. The center line on this chart is the process average over the time period studied, and the upper and lower limits are the specification limits on copper concentration. Every instance in which a point is outside the specification limits would correspond to nonscheduled downtime on the process. Several things are evident from examining the tolerance diagram. First, the process average is significantly different from the nominal specification on copper concentration (the midpoint of the upper and lower tolerance band). This implies that the calibration of the colorimeter may be inadequate. That is, we are literally aiming at the wrong target. Second, we

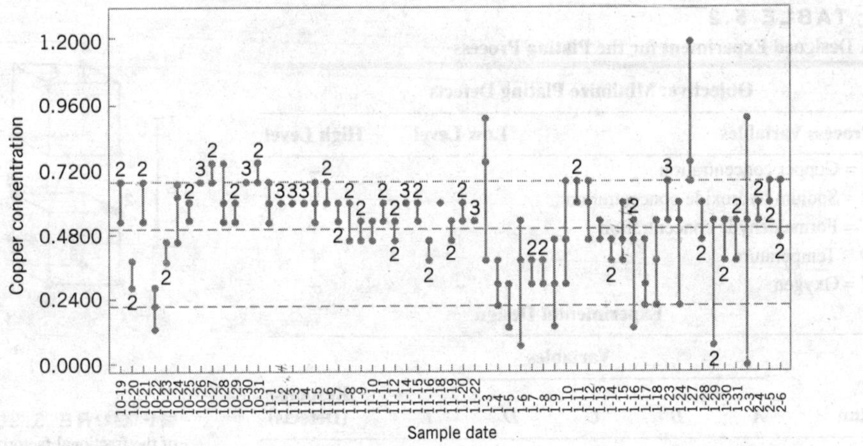

FIGURE 5.29 Tolerance diagram of daily copper concentration.

note that there is considerably more variation in the daily copper concentration readings after January 3 than there was prior to shutdown. Finally, if we could reduce variation in the process to a level roughly consistent with that observed prior to shutdown and correct the process centering, many of the points outside specifications would not have occurred, and downtime on the process should be reduced.

To initiate the improve step, the team first decided to rebuild the colorimeter and controller. This was done in early February. The result of this maintenance activity was to restore the variability in daily copper concentration readings to the pre-shutdown level. The rebuilt colorimeter was recalibrated and subsequently was able to hold the correct target. This recentering and recalibration of the process reduced the downtime on the controller from approximately 60% to less than 20%. At this point, the process was capable of meeting the required production rate.

Once this aspect of process performance was improved, the team directed its efforts to reducing the number of defective units produced by the process. Generally, as noted earlier, defects fell into two major categories: brittle copper and copper voids. The team decided that, although control charts and statistical process-control techniques could be applied to this problem, the use of a **designed experiment** might lead to a more rapid solution. As noted in Chapter 1, the objective of a designed experiment is to generate information that will allow us to understand and model the relationship between the process variables and measures of the process performance.

The designed experiment for the plating process is shown in Table 5.2 and Fig. 5.30. The objective of this experiment was to provide information that would be useful in minimizing plating defects. The process variables considered in the experiment were copper concentration, sodium hydroxide concentration, formaldehyde concentration, temperature, and oxygen. A low level and high level, represented symbolically by the minus and plus signs in Table 5.2, were chosen for each process variable. The team initially considered a **factorial experiment**—that is, an experimental design in which all possible combinations of these factor levels would be run. This design would have required 32 runs—that is, a run at each of the 32 corners of the cubes in Fig. 5.30. Since this is too many runs, a **fractional factorial design** that used only 16 runs was ultimately selected. This fractional factorial design is shown in the bottom half of Table 5.2 and geometrically in Fig. 5.30. In this experimental design, each row of the table is a run on the process. The combination of minus and plus signs in each column of that row determines the low and high levels of the five process

■ **TABLE 5.2**
A Designed Experiment for the Plating Process

Objective: Minimize Plating Defects

Process Variables	Low Level	High Level
A = Copper concentration	−	+
B = Sodium hydroxide concentration	−	+
C = Formaldehyde concentration	−	+
D = Temperature	−	+
E = Oxygen	−	+

Experimental Design

Run	Variables A	B	C	D	E	Response (Defects)
1	−	−	−	−	+	
2	+	−	−	−	−	
3	−	+	−	−	−	
4	+	+	−	−	+	
5	−	−	+	−	−	
6	+	−	+	−	+	
7	−	+	+	−	+	
8	+	+	+	−	−	
9	−	−	−	+	−	
10	+	−	−	+	+	
11	−	+	−	+	+	
12	+	+	−	+	−	
13	−	−	+	+	+	
14	+	−	+	+	−	
15	−	+	+	+	−	
16	+	+	+	+	+	

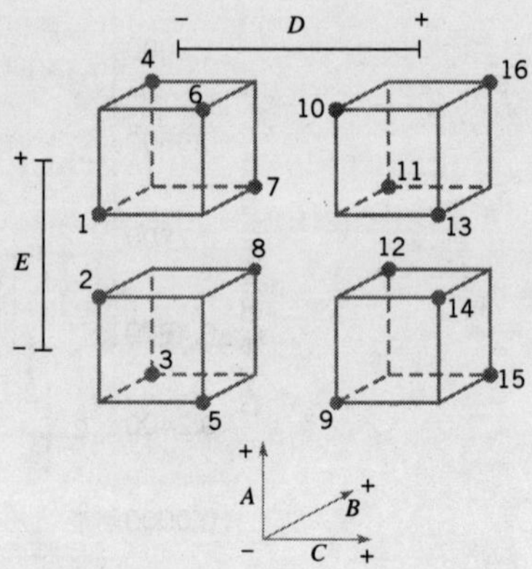

■ **FIGURE 5.30** A geometric view of the fractional factorial design for the plating process experiment.

variables to be used during that run. For example, in run 1 copper concentration, sodium hydroxide concentration, formaldehyde concentration, and temperature are run at the low level and oxygen is run at the high level. The process would be run at each of the 16 sets of conditions described by the design (for reasons to be discussed later, the runs would not be made in the order shown in Table 5.2), and a response variable—an observed number of plating defects—would be recorded for each run. Then these data could be analyzed using simple statistical techniques to determine which factors have a significant influence on plating defects, whether or not any of the factors jointly influence the occurrence of defects, and whether it is possible to adjust these variables to new levels that will reduce plating defects below their current level. Although a complete discussion of design of experiments is beyond the scope of this text, we will present examples of designed experiments for improving process performance in Part V.

After the team conducted the experiment shown in Table 5.2 and analyzed the resulting process data, they determined that several of the process variables that they identified for the study were important and had significant impact on the occurrence of plating defects. They were able to adjust these factors to new levels, and as a result, plating defects were reduced by approximately a factor of 10. Therefore, at the conclusion of the team's initial effort at applying SPC to the plating process, it had made substantial improvements in product cycle time through the process and had taken a major step in improving the process capability.

5.7 Applications of Statistical Process Control and Quality Improvement Tools in Transactional and Service Businesses

This book presents the underlying principles of SPC. Many of the examples used to reinforce these principles are in an industrial, product-oriented framework. There have been many successful applications of SPC methods in the manufacturing environment. However, the principles themselves are general; there are many applications of SPC techniques and other quality engineering and statistical tools in nonmanufacturing settings, including transactional and service businesses.

These nonmanufacturing applications do not differ substantially from the more usual industrial applications. As an example, the control chart for fraction nonconforming (which is discussed in Chapter 7) could be applied to reducing billing errors in a bank credit card operation as easily as it could be used to reduce the fraction of nonconforming printed circuit boards produced in an electronics plant. The $\bar{x}$ and R charts discussed in this chapter and applied to the hard-bake process could be used to monitor and control the flow time of accounts payable through a finance function. Transactional and service industry applications of SPC and related methodology sometimes require ingenuity beyond that normally required for the more typical manufacturing applications. There seems to be two primary reasons for this difference:

1. Most transactional and service businesses do not have a natural measurement system that allows the analyst to easily define quality.
2. The system that is to be improved is usually fairly obvious in a manufacturing setting, whereas the observability of the process in a nonmanufacturing setting may be fairly low.

For example, if we are trying to improve the performance of a personal computer assembly line, then it is likely that the line will be contained within one facility and the activities of the system will be readily observable. However, if we are trying to improve the business performance of a financial services organization, then the observability of the process may be low. The actual activities of the process may be performed by a group of people who work in different locations, and the operation steps or workflow sequence may be difficult to observe. Furthermore, the lack of a quantitative and objective measurement system in most nonmanufacturing processes complicates the problem.

The key to applying statistical process-control and other related methods in a nonmanufacturing environment is to focus initial efforts on resolving these two issues. We have found that once the system is adequately defined and a valid measurement system has been developed, most of the SPC tools discussed in this chapter can easily be applied to a wide variety of nonmanufacturing operations including finance, marketing, material and procurement, customer support, field service, engineering development and design, and software development and programming.

Flow charts, operation process charts, and **value stream mapping** are particularly useful in developing process definition and process understanding. A flow chart is simply a chronological sequence of process steps or work flow. Sometimes flow charting is called **process mapping.** Flow charts or process maps must be constructed in sufficient detail to identify **value-added** versus **non-value-added** work activity in the process.

Most nonmanufacturing processes have scrap, rework, and other **non-value-added operations,** such as unnecessary work steps and choke points or bottlenecks. A systematic analysis of these processes can often eliminate many of these non-value-added activities. The flow chart is helpful in visualizing and defining the process so that non-value-added activities can be identified. Some ways to remove non-value-added activities and simplify the process are summarized in the following box:

Ways to Eliminate Non-value-Added Activities

1. Rearrange the sequence of worksteps
2. Rearrange the physical location of the operator in the system
3. Change work methods
4. Change the type of equipment used in the process
5. Redesign forms and documents for more efficient use
6. Improve operator training
7. Improve supervision
8. Identify more clearly the function of the process to all employees
9. Try to eliminate unnecessary steps
10. Try to consolidate process steps

Figure 5.31 is an example of a flow chart for a process in a service industry. It was constructed by a process improvement team in an accounting firm that was studying the process of preparing Form 1040 income tax returns; this particular flow chart documents only one particular subprocess, that of assembling final tax documents. This flow chart was constructed as part of the define step of DMAIC. Note the high level of detail in the flow chart to assist the team find waste or non-value-added activities. In this example, the team used special symbols in their flow chart. Specifically, they used the **operation process chart** symbols shown as follows:

Operation Process Chart Symbols

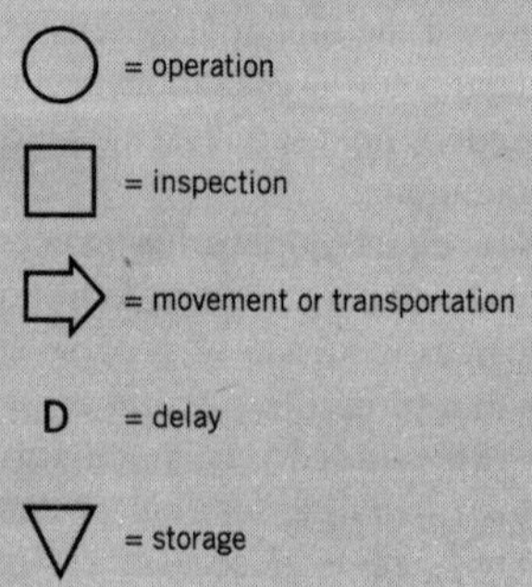

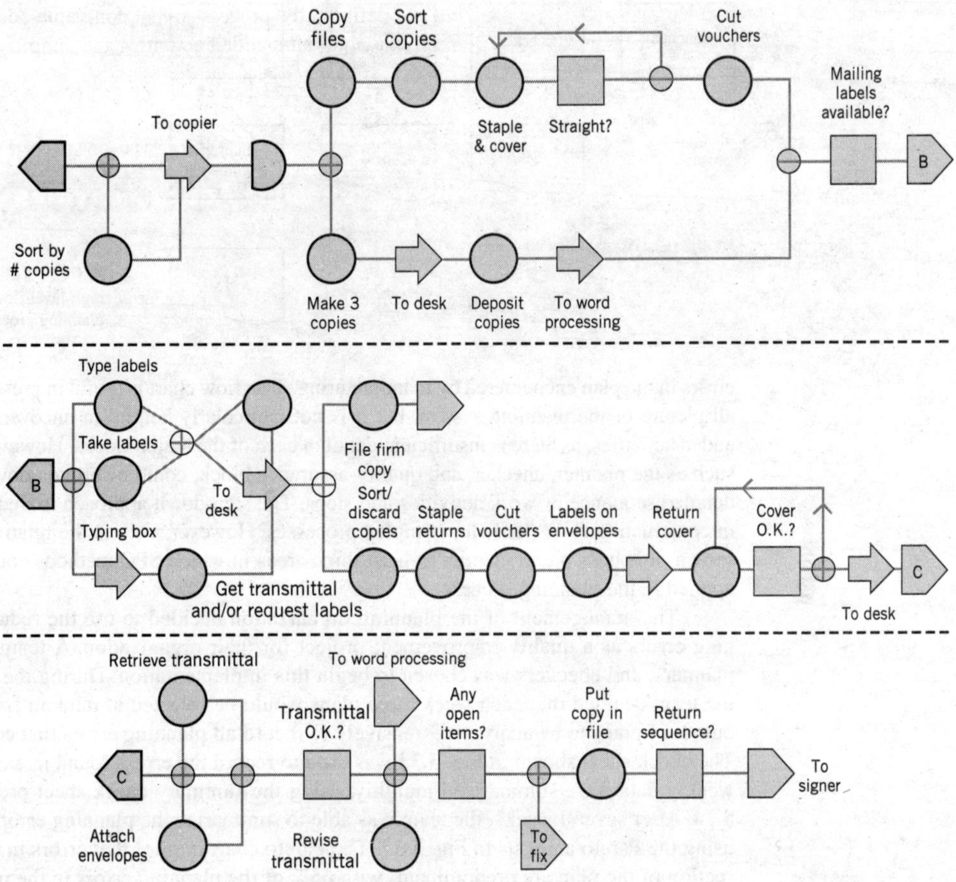

■ **FIGURE 5.31** Flow chart of the assembly portion of the Form 1040 tax return process.

We have found that these symbols are very useful in helping team members identify improvement opportunities. For example, delays, most inspections, and many movements usually represent non-value-added activities. The accounting firm was able to use quality improvement methods and the DMAIC approach successfully in their Form 1040 process, reducing the tax document preparation cycle time (and work content) by about 25%, and reducing the cycle time for preparing the client bill from over 60 days to zero (that's right, zero!). The client's bill is now included with his or her tax return.

As another illustration, consider an example of applying quality improvement methods in a planning organization. This planning organization, part of a large aerospace manufacturing concern, produces the plans and documents that accompany each job to the factory floor. The plans are quite extensive, often several hundred pages long. Errors in the planning process can have a major impact on the factory floor, contributing to scrap and rework, lost production time, overtime, missed delivery schedules, and many other problems.

Figure 5.32 presents a high-level flow chart of this planning process. After plans are produced, they are sent to a checker who tries to identify obvious errors and defects in the plans. The plans are also reviewed by a quality-assurance organization to ensure that process specifications are being met and that the final product will conform to engineering standards. Then the plans are sent to the shop, where a liaison engineering organization deals with any

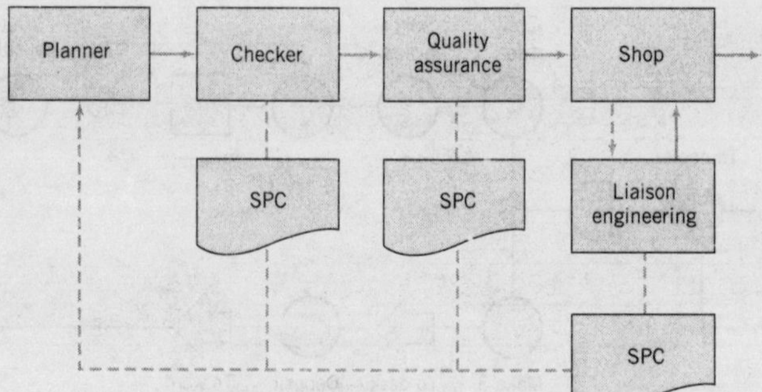

■ **FIGURE 5.32** A high-level flow chart of the planning process.

errors in the plan encountered by manufacturing. This flow chart is useful in presenting an overall picture of the planning system, but it is not particularly helpful in uncovering non-value-added activities, as there is insufficient detail in each of the major blocks. However, each block, such as the planner, checker, and quality-assurance block, could be broken down into a more detailed sequence of work activities and steps. The step-down approach is frequently helpful in constructing flow charts for complex processes. However, even at the relatively high level shown, it is possible to identify at least three areas in which SPC methods could be usefully applied in the planning process.

The management of the planning organization decided to use the reduction of planning errors as a quality improvement project for their organization. A team of managers, planners, and checkers was chosen to begin this implementation. During the measure step, the team decided that each week three plans would be selected at random from the week's output of plans to be analyzed extensively to record all planning errors that could be found. The check sheet shown in Fig. 5.33 was used to record the errors found in each plan. These weekly data were summarized monthly, using the summary check sheet presented in Fig. 5.34. After several weeks, the team was able to summarize the planning error data obtained using the Pareto analysis in Fig. 5.35. The Pareto chart implies that errors in the operations section of the plan are predominant, with 65% of the planning errors in the operations section. Figure 5.36 presents a further Pareto analysis of the operations section errors, showing that omitted operations and process specifications are the major contributors to the problem.

The team decided that many of the operations errors were occurring because planners were not sufficiently familiar with the manufacturing operations and the process specifications that were currently in place. To improve the process, a program was undertaken to refamiliarize planners with the details of factory floor operations and to provide more feedback on the type of planning errors actually experienced. Figure 5.37 presents a run chart of the planning errors per operation for 25 consecutive weeks. Note that there is a general tendency for the planning errors per operation to decline over the first half of the study period. This decline may be due partly to the increased training and supervision activities for the planners and partly to the additional feedback given regarding the types of planning errors that were occurring. The team also recommended that substantial changes be made in the work methods used to prepare plans. Rather than having an individual planner with overall responsibility for the operations section, it recommended that this task become a team activity so that knowledge and experience regarding the interface between factor and planning operations could be shared in an effort to further improve the process.

The planning organization began to use other SPC tools as part of their quality improvement effort. For example, note that the run chart in Fig. 5.37 could be converted to a Shewhart control chart with the addition of a center line and appropriate control limits. Once the planners

DATA SHEET			
P/N ______________			
	ERRORS	DESCRIPTION	ACTION
1. HEADER SECT.			
a. PART NO.			
b. ITEM			
c. MODEL			
2. DWG/DOC SECT.			
3. COMPONENT PART SECT.			
a. PROCUREMENT CODES			
b. STAGING			
c. MOA (#SIGNS)			
4. MOTE SECT.			
5. MATERIAL SECT.			
a. MCC CODE (NON MP&R)			
6. OPERATION SECT.			
a. ISSUE STORE(S)			
b. EQUIPMENT USAGE			
c. OPC FWC MNEMONICS			
d. SEQUENCING			
e. OPER'S OMITTED			
f. PROCESS SPECS			
g. END ROUTE STORE			
h. WELD GRID			
7. TOOL/SHOP AIDS ORDERS			
8. CAR/SHOP STOCK PREP.			
REMARKS:			
		CHECKER ______________	
NO. OF OPERATIONS ______________		DATE ______________	

FIGURE 5.33 The check sheet for the planning example.

were exposed to the concepts of SPC, control charts came into use in the organization and proved effective in identifying assignable causes; that is, periods of time in which the error rates produced by the system were higher than those that could be justified by chance cause alone. It is its ability to differentiate between assignable and chance causes that makes the control chart so indispensable. Management must react differently to an assignable cause than it does to a chance or random cause. Assignable causes are due to phenomena external to the system, and they must be tracked down and their root causes eliminated. Chance or random causes are part of the system itself. They can only be reduced or eliminated by making changes in how the system operates. This may mean changes in work methods and procedures, improved levels of operator training, different types of equipment and facilities, or improved input materials, all of which are the responsibility of management. In the planning process, many of the common causes identified were related to the experience, training, and supervision of the individual planners, as well as poor input information from design and development engineering. These common causes were systematically removed from the

Monthly Data Summary					
1. HEADER SECT.					
a. PART NO.					
b. ITEM					
c. MODEL					
2. DWG/DOC SECT.					
3. COMPONENT PART SECT.					
a. PROCUREMENT CODES					
b. STAGING					
c. MOA (#SIGNS)					
4. MOTE SECT.					
5. MATERIAL SECT.					
a. MCC CODE (NON MP&R)					
6. OPERATION SECT.					
a. ISSUE STORE(S)					
b. EQUIPMENT USAGE					
c. OPC FWC MNEMONICS					
d. SEQUENCING					
e. OPER'S OMITTED					
f. PROCESS SPECS					
g. END ROUTE STORE					
h. WELD GRID					
7. TOOL/SHOP AIDS ORDERS					
TOTAL NUMBER ERRORS					
TOTAL OPERATIONS CHECKED					
WEEK ENDING					

■ **FIGURE 5.34** The summary check sheet.

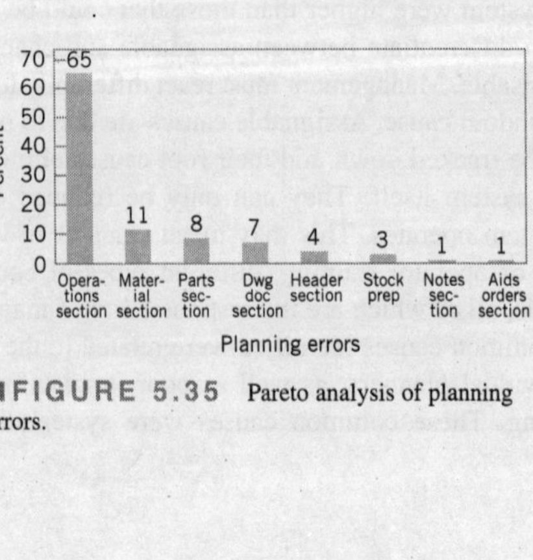

■ **FIGURE 5.35** Pareto analysis of planning errors.

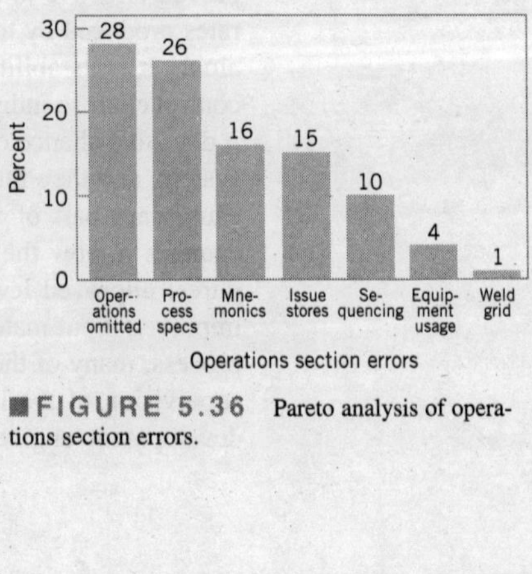

■ **FIGURE 5.36** Pareto analysis of operations section errors.

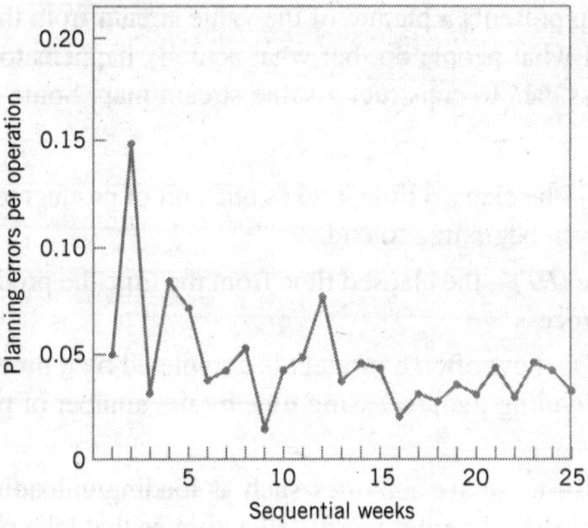

■ **FIGURE 5.37** A run chart of planning errors.

process, and the long-term impact of the SPC implementation in this organization was to reduce planning errors to a level of less than one planning error per 1000 operations.

Value stream mapping is another way to see the flow of material and information in a process. A value stream map is much like a flow chart, but it usually incorporates other information about the activities that are occurring at each step in the process and the information that is required or generated. It is a big picture tool that helps an improvement team focus on optimizing the entire process, without focusing too narrowly on only one process activity or step which could lead to suboptimal solutions.

Like a flow chart or operations process chart, a value stream map usually is constructed using special symbols. The box below presents the symbols usually employed on value stream maps.

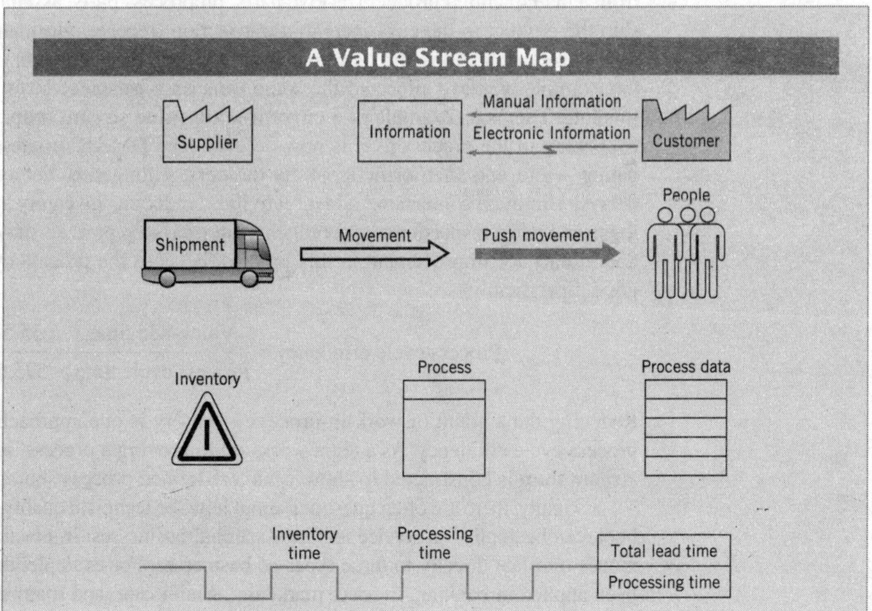

The value stream map presents a picture of the value stream from the product's viewpoint: It is not a flow chart of what people do, but what actually happens to the product. It is necessary to collect process data to construct a value stream map. Some of the data typically collected includes:

1. *Lead time (LT)*—the elapsed time it takes one unit of product to move through the entire value stream from beginning to end.
2. *Processing time (PT)*—the elapsed time from the time the product enters a process until it leaves that process.
3. *Cycle time (CT)*—how often a product is completed by a process. Cycle time is a rate, calculated by dividing the processing time by the number of people or machines doing the work.
4. *Setup time (ST)*—these are activities such as loading/unloading, machine preparation, testing, and trial runs. In other words, all activities that take place between completing a good product until starting to work on the next unit or batch of product.
5. *Available time (AT)*—the time each day that the value stream can operate if there is product to work on.
6. *Uptime (UT)*—the percent of time the process actually operates as compared to the available time or planned operating time.
7. *Pack size*—the quantity of product required by the customer for shipment.
8. *Batch size*—the quantity of product worked on and moved at one time.
9. *Queue time*—the time a product spends waiting for processing.
10. *Work-in-process (WIP)*—product that is being processed but is not yet complete.
11. *Information flows*—schedules, forecasts, and other information that tells each process what to do next.

Figure 5.38 shows an example of a value stream map that could be almost anything from a manufactured product (receive parts, preprocess parts, assemble the product, pack and ship the product to the customer) to a transaction (receive information, preprocess information, make calculations and decision, inform customer of decision or results). Notice that in the example we have allocated the setup time on a per-piece basis and included that in the timeline. This is an example of a **current-state value stream map.** That is, it shows what is happening in the process as it is now defined. The DMAIC process can be useful in eliminating waste and inefficiencies in the process, eliminating defects and rework, reducing delays, eliminating nonvalue-added activities, reducing inventory (WIP, unnecessary backlogs), reducing inspections, and reducing unnecessary product movement. There is a lot of opportunity for improvement in this process, because the process cycle efficiency isn't very good. Specifically,

$$\text{Process cycle efficiency} = \frac{\text{Value-add time}}{\text{Process cycle time}} = \frac{35.5}{575.5} = 0.0617$$

Reducing the amount of work-in-process inventory is one approach that would improve the process cycle efficiency. As a team works on improving a process, often a **future-state value stream map** is constructed to show what a redefined process should look like.

Finally, there are often questions about how the technical quality improvement tools in this book can be applied in service and transactional businesses. In practice, almost all of the techniques translate directly to these types of businesses. For example, designed experiments have been applied in banking, finance, marketing, health care, and many other service/transactional businesses. Designed experiments can be used in any application where we can manipulate the

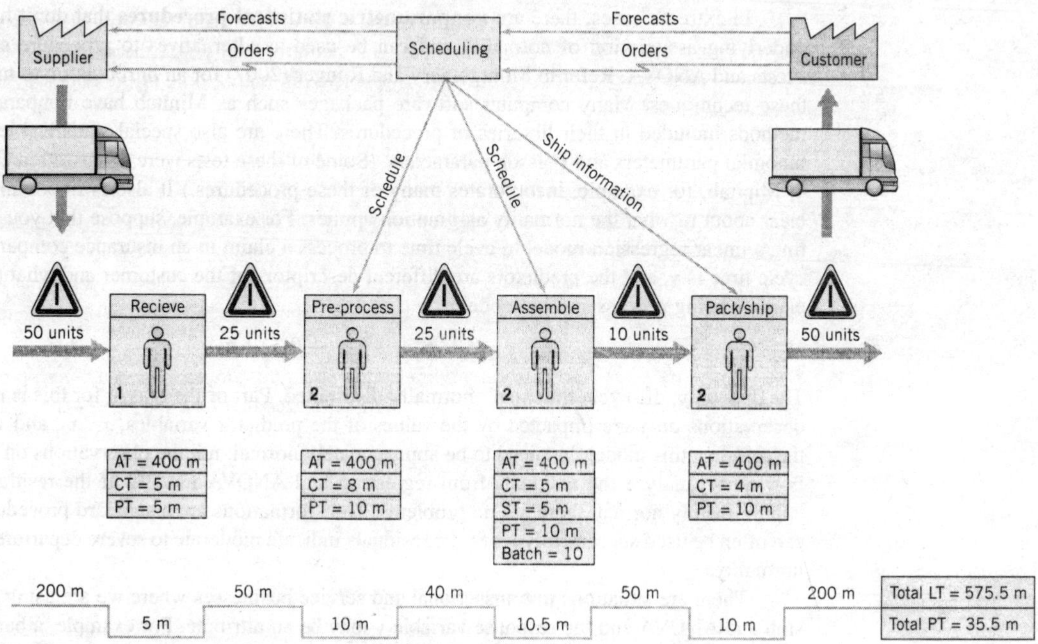

■ FIGURE 5.38 A value stream map.

decision variables in the process. Sometimes we will use a **simulation model** of the process to facilitate conducting the experiment. Similarly, control charts have many applications in the service economy, as will be illustrated in this book. It is a big mistake to assume that these techniques are not applicable just because you are not working in a manufacturing environment.

Still, one difference in the service economy is that you are more likely to encounter attribute data. Manufacturing often has lots of continuous measurement data, and it is often safe to assume that these data are at least approximately normally distributed. However, in service and transactional processes, more of the data that you will use in quality improvement projects is either proportion defective, percent good, or counts of errors or defects. In Chapter 7, we discuss control charting procedures for dealing with attribute data. These control charts have many applications in the service economy. However, even some of the continuous data encountered in service and transactional businesses, such as cycle time, may not be normally distributed.

Let's talk about the normality assumption. It turns out that many statistical procedures (such as the *t*-tests and ANOVA from Chapter 4) are very insensitive to the normality assumption. That is, moderate departures from normality have little impact on their effectiveness. There are some procedures that are fairly sensitive to normality, such as tests on variances, this book carefully identifies such procedures. One alternative to dealing with moderate to severe non-normality is to **transform** the original data (say, by taking logarithms) to produce a new set of data whose distribution is closer to normal. A disadvantage of this is that nontechnical people often don't understand data transformation and are not comfortable with data presented in an unfamiliar scale. One way to deal with this is to perform the statistical analysis using the transformed data, but to present results (graphs, for example) with the data in the original units.

In extreme cases, there are **nonparametric statistical procedures** that don't have an underlying assumption of normality and can be used as alternatives to procedure such as *t*-tests and ANOVA. Refer to Montgomery and Runger (2007) for an introduction to many of these techniques. Many computer software packages such as Minitab have nonparametric methods included in their libraries of procedures. There are also special statistical tests for binomial parameters and Poisson parameters. (Some of these tests were discussed in Chapter 4; Minitab, for example, incorporates many of these procedures.) It also is important to be clear about to what the normality assumption applies. For example, suppose that you are fitting a linear regression model to cycle time to process a claim in an insurance company. The cycle time is y, and the predictors are different descriptors of the customer and what type of claim is being processed. The model is

$$y = \beta_0 + \beta_1 x_1 + \beta_2 x_2 + \beta_3 x_3 + \varepsilon$$

The data on y, the cycle time, isn't normally distributed. Part of the reason for this is that the observations on y are impacted by the values of the predictor variables, x_1, x_2, and x_3. It is the errors in this model that need to be approximately normal, not the observations on y. That is why we analyze the residuals from regression and ANOVA models. If the residuals are approximately normal, there are no problems. Transformations are a standard procedure that can often be used successfully when the residuals indicate moderate to severe departures from normality.

There are situations in transactional and service businesses where we are using regression and ANOVA and the response variable y may be an attribute. For example, a bank may want to predict the proportion of mortgage applications that are actually funded. This is a measure of yield in their process. Yield probably follows a binomial distribution. Most likely, yield isn't well approximated by a normal distribution, and a standard linear regression model wouldn't be satisfactory. However, there are modeling techniques based on **generalized linear models** that handle many of these cases. For example, **logistic regression** can be used with binomial data and Poisson regression can be used with many kinds of count data. Montgomery, Peck, and Vining (2006) contains information on applying these techniques. Logistic regression is available in Minitab and JMP software provides routines for both logistic and Poisson regression.

Important Terms and Concepts

Action limits
Assignable causes of variation
Average run length (ARL)
Average time to signal
Cause-and-effect diagram
Chance causes of variation
Check sheet
Control chart
Control limits
Defect concentration diagram
Designed experiments
Flow charts, operations process charts, and value stream mapping
Factorial experiment
In-control process
Magnificent seven
Out-of-control-action plan (OCAP)
Out-of-control process
Pareto chart
Patterns on control charts
Phase I and phase II applications
Rational subgroups
Sample size for control charts
Sampling frequency for control charts
Scatter diagram
Sensitizing rules for control charts
Shewhart control charts
Statistical control of a process
Statistical process control (SPC)
Three-sigma control limits
Warning limits

Exercises

5.1. What is meant by the statement that a process is in a state of statistical control?

5.2. Discuss type I and type II errors relative to the control chart. What practical implication in terms of process operation do these two types of errors have?

5.3. If a process is in a state of statistical control, does it necessarily follow that all or nearly all of the units of product produced will be within the specification limits?

5.4. What are chance and assignable causes of variability? What part do they play in the operation and interpretation of a Shewhart control chart?

5.5. Discuss the relationship between a control chart and statistical hypothesis testing.

5.6. What are warning limits on a control chart? How can they be used?

5.7. Discuss the logic underlying the use of three-sigma limits on Shewhart control charts. How will the chart respond if narrower limits are chosen? How will it respond if wider limits are chosen?

5.8. What information is provided by the operating characteristic curve of a control chart?

5.9. Consider the control chart shown here. Does the pattern appear random?

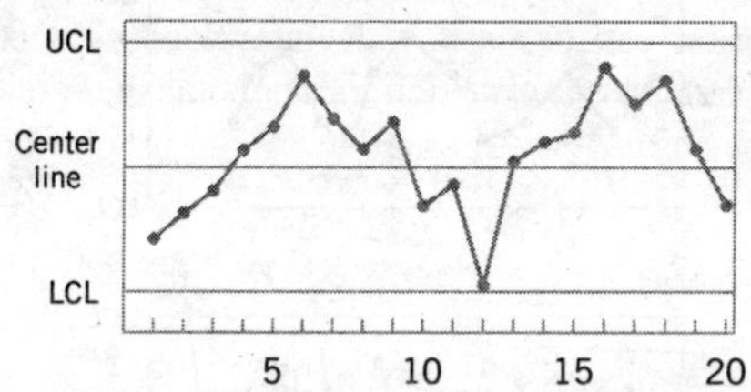

5.10. Consider the control chart shown here. Does the pattern appear random?

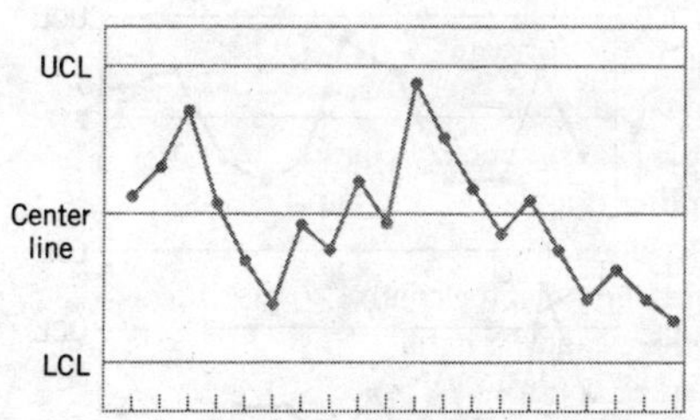

5.11. A manufacturing process produces 500 parts per hour. A sample part is selected about every half-hour, and after five parts are obtained, the average of these five measurements is plotted on an $\bar{x}$ control chart.

(a) Is this an appropriate sampling scheme if the assignable cause in the process results in an instantaneous upward shift in the mean that is of very short duration?

(b) If your answer is no, propose an alternative procedure.

5.12. A molding process uses a five-cavity mold for a part used in an automotive assembly. The wall thickness of the part is the critical quality characteristic. It has been suggested to use $\bar{x}$ and R charts to monitor this process, and to use as the subgroup or sample all five parts that result from a single "shot" of the machine. What do you think of this sampling strategy? What impact does it have on the ability of the charts to detect assignable causes?

5.13. Consider the sampling scheme proposed in Exercise 5.11. Is this scheme appropriate if the assignable cause results in a slow, prolonged upward drift in the mean? If your answer is no, propose an alternative procedure.

5.14. Is the average run length performance of a control chart a more meaningful measure of performance than the type I and type II error probabilities? What information does ARL convey that the statistical error probabilities do not?

5.15. When taking samples or subgroups from a process, do you want assignable causes occurring within the subgroups or between them? Fully explain your answer.

5.16. Discuss the rational subgroup concept. What part does it play in control chart analysis?

5.17. Sketch warning limits on the control chart in Exercise 5.9. Do these limits indicate any potential out-of-control conditions?

5.18. Apply the Western Electric rules to the control chart presented in Exercise 5.9. Would these rules result in any out-of-control signals?

5.19. Consider the control chart shown in Exercise 5.10. Would the use of warning limits reveal any potential out-of-control conditions?

5.20. Apply the Western Electric rules to the control chart in Exercise 5.10. Are any of the criteria for declaring the process out of control satisfied?

5.21. How do the costs of sampling, the costs of producing an excessive number of defective units, and the costs of searching for assignable causes impact on the choice of parameters of a control chart?

5.22. If the time order of production has not been recorded in a set of data from a process, is it possible to detect the presence of assignable causes?

5.23. Consider the time-varying process behavior shown below. Match each of these several patterns of process performance to the corresponding $\bar{x}$ and R charts shown in figures (a) to (e) below.

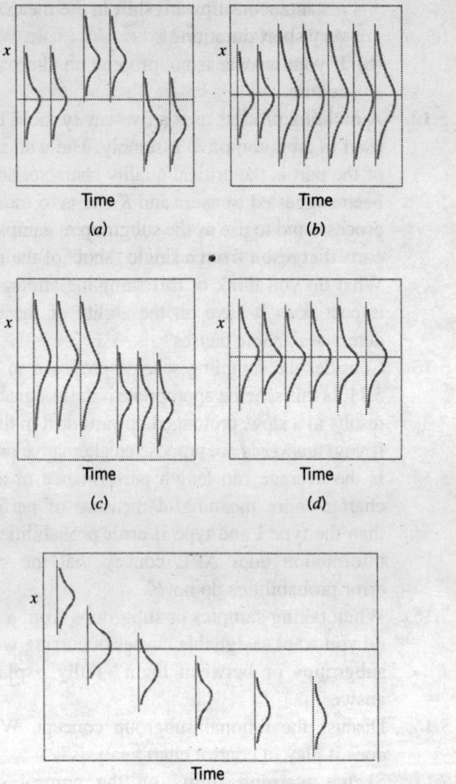

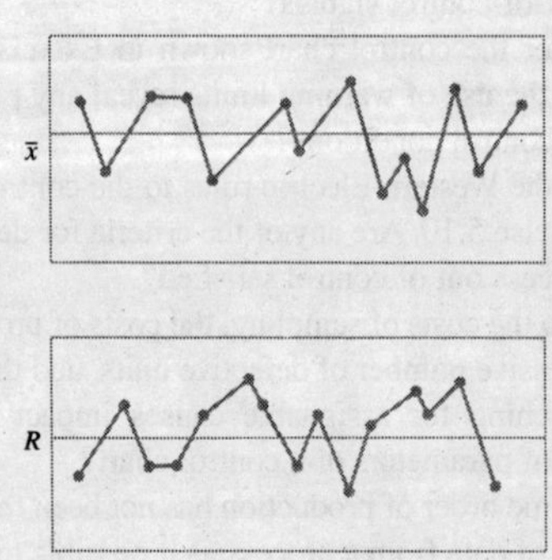

(1)

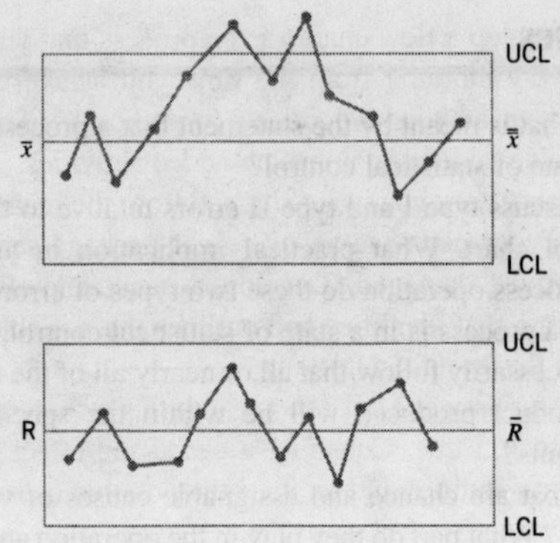

(2)

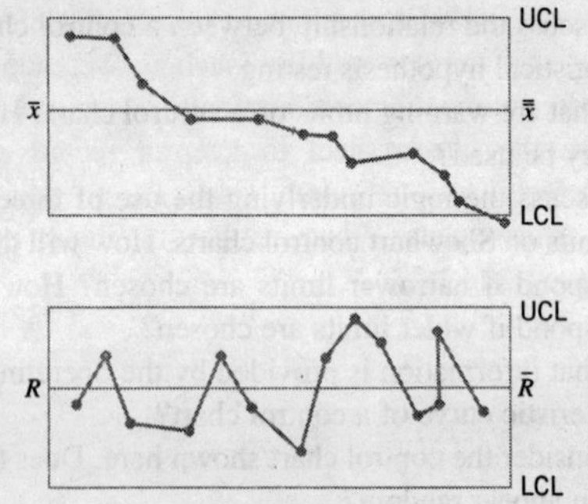

(3)

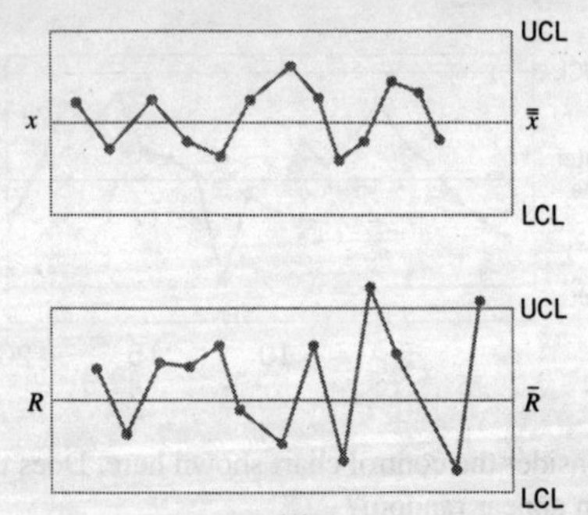

(4)

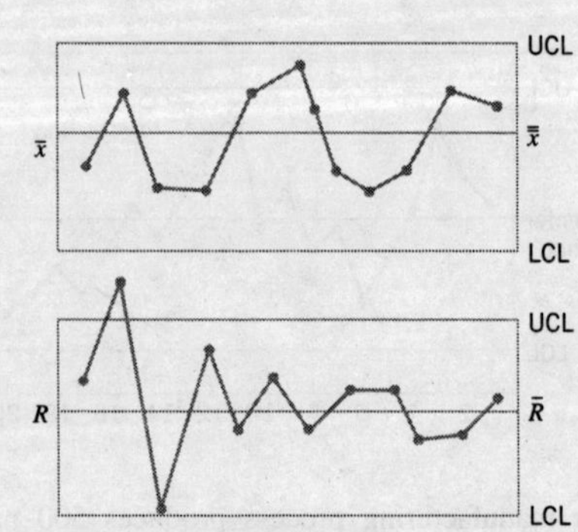

(5)

5.24. Develop a flow chart for the process that you follow every morning from the time you awake until you arrive at your workplace (or school). Identify the value-added and nonvalue-added activities.

5.25. Laboratory glassware shipped from the manufacturer to your plant via an overnight package service has arrived damaged. Develop a cause-and-effect diagram that identifies and outlines the possible causes of this event.

5.26. A car has gone out of control during a snowstorm and struck a tree. Construct a cause-and-effect diagram that identifies and outlines the possible causes of the accident.

5.27. The magnificent seven can be used in our personal lives. Develop a check sheet to record "defects" you have in your personal life (such as overeating, being rude, not meeting commitments, missing class, etc.). Use the check sheet to keep a record of these "defects" for one month. Use a Pareto chart to analyze these data. What are the underlying causes of these "defects"?

5.28. A process is normally distributed and in control, with known mean and variance, and the usual three-sigma limits are used on the $\bar{x}$ control chart, so that the probability of a single point plotting outside the control limits when the process is in control is 0.0027. Suppose that this chart is being used in phase I and the averages from a set of m samples or subgroups from this process is plotted on this chart. What is the probability that at least one of the averages will plot outside the control limits when $m = 5$? Repeat these calculations for the cases where $m = 10$, $m = 20$, $m = 30$, and $m = 50$. Discuss the results that you have obtained.

5.29. Reconsider the situation in Exercise 5.28. Suppose that the process mean and variance were unknown and had to be estimated from the data available from the m subgroups. What complications would this introduce in the calculations that you performed in Exercise 5.28?

6 Variables Control Charts

CHAPTER OUTLINE

The supplemental material is on the textbook Website www.wiley.com/college/montgomery.

CHAPTER OVERVIEW AND LEARNING OBJECTIVES

A quality characteristic that is measured on a numerical scale is called a **variable.** Examples include dimensions such as length or width, temperature, and volume. This chapter presents Shewhart control charts for these types of quality characteristics. The $\bar{x}$ and R control charts are widely used to monitor the mean and variability of variables. Several variations of the $\bar{x}$ and R charts are also given, including a procedure to adapt them to individual measurements. The chapter concludes with typical applications of variables control charts.

After careful study of this chapter you should be able to do the following:

1. Understand the statistical basis of Shewhart variables control charts
2. Know how to design variables control charts
3. Know how to set up and use $\bar{x}$ and R control charts
4. Know how to estimate process capability from the control chart information
5. Know how to interpret patterns on $\bar{x}$ and R control charts
6. Know how to set up and use $\bar{x}$ and s or s^2 control charts
7. Know how to set up and use control charts for individual measurements
8. Understand the importance of the normality assumption for individuals control charts and know how to check this assumption
9. Understand the rational subgroup concept for variables control charts
10. Determine the average run length for variables control charts

6.1 Introduction

Many quality characteristics can be expressed in terms of a **numerical measurement.** For example, the diameter of a bearing could be measured with a micrometer and expressed in millimeters. A single measurable quality characteristic, such as a dimension, weight, or volume, is called a **variable.** Variables control charts are used extensively. Control charts are one of the primary tools used in the analize and control steps of DMAIC.

When dealing with a quality characteristic that is a variable, it is usually necessary to monitor both the mean value of the quality characteristic and its variability. Control of the process average or mean quality level is usually done with the control chart for means, or the **$\bar{x}$ control chart.** Process variability can be monitored with either a control chart for the standard deviation, called the ***s* control chart,** or a control chart for the range, called an ***R* control chart.** The R chart is more widely used. Usually, separate $\bar{x}$ and R charts are maintained for each quality characteristic of interest. (However, if the quality characteristics are closely related, this can sometimes cause misleading results; refer to Chapter 12 of Part IV.) The $\bar{x}$ and R (or s) charts are among the most important and useful on-line statistical process monitoring and control techniques.

It is important to maintain control over both the process mean and process variability. Figure 6.1 illustrates the output of a production process. In Fig. 6.1*a* both the mean μ and standard deviation σ are in control at their nominal values (say, μ_0 and σ_0); consequently, most of the process output falls within the specification limits. However, in Fig. 6.1*b* the mean has shifted to a value $\mu_1 > \mu_0$, resulting in a higher fraction of nonconforming product. In Fig. 6.1*c* the process standard deviation has shifted to a value $\sigma_1 > \sigma_0$. This also results in higher process fallout, even though the process mean is still at the nominal value.

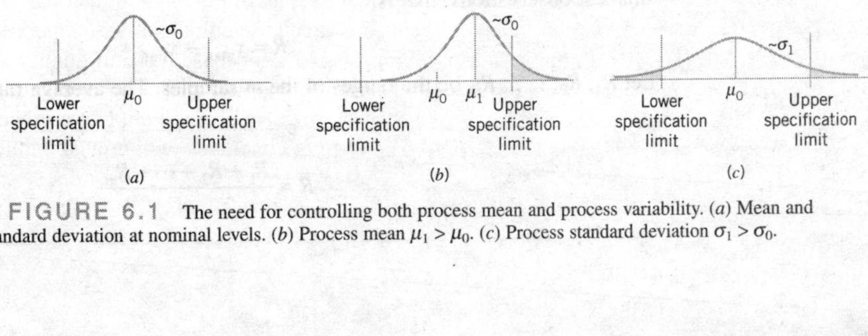

■ FIGURE 6.1 The need for controlling both process mean and process variability. (*a*) Mean and standard deviation at nominal levels. (*b*) Process mean $\mu_1 > \mu_0$. (*c*) Process standard deviation $\sigma_1 > \sigma_0$.

6.2 Control Charts for $\bar{x}$ and R

6.2.1 Statistical Basis of the Charts

Suppose that a quality characteristic is normally distributed with mean μ and standard deviation σ, where both μ and σ are known. If $x_1, x_2, \ldots, x_n$ is a sample of size n, then the average of this sample is

$$\bar{x} = \frac{x_1 + x_2 + \cdots + x_n}{n}$$

and we know that $\bar{x}$ is normally distributed with mean μ and standard deviation $\sigma_{\bar{x}} = \sigma/\sqrt{n}$. Furthermore, the probability is $1 - \alpha$ that any sample mean will fall between

$$\mu + Z_{\alpha/2}\sigma_{\bar{x}} = \mu + Z_{\alpha/2}\frac{\sigma}{\sqrt{n}} \quad \text{and} \quad \mu - Z_{\alpha/2}\sigma_{\bar{x}} = \mu - Z_{\alpha/2}\frac{\sigma}{\sqrt{n}} \tag{6.1}$$

Therefore, if μ and σ are known, equation (6.1) could be used as upper and lower control limits on a control chart for sample means. As noted in Chapter 5, it is customary to replace $Z_{\alpha/2}$ by 3, so that three-sigma limits are employed. If a sample mean falls outside of these limits, it is an indication that the process mean is no longer equal to μ.

We have assumed that the distribution of the quality characteristic is normal. However, the above results are still approximately correct even if the underlying distribution is nonnormal, because of the central limit theorem. We discuss the effect of the normality assumption on variables control charts in Section 6.2.5.

In practice, we usually will not know μ and σ. Therefore, they must be estimated from preliminary samples or subgroups taken when the process is thought to be in control. These estimates should usually be based on at least 20 to 25 samples. Suppose that m samples are available, each containing n observations on the quality characteristic. Typically, n will be small, often either 4, 5, or 6. These small sample sizes usually result from the construction of rational subgroups and from the fact that the sampling and inspection costs associated with variables measurements are usually relatively large. Let $\bar{x}_1, \bar{x}_2, \ldots, \bar{x}_m$ be the average of each sample. Then the best estimator of μ, the process average, is the grand average—say,

$$\bar{\bar{x}} = \frac{\bar{x}_1 + \bar{x}_2 + \cdots + \bar{x}_m}{m} \tag{6.2}$$

Thus, $\bar{\bar{x}}$ would be used as the center line on the $\bar{x}$ chart.

To construct the control limits, we need an estimate of the standard deviation σ. Recall from Chapter 4 (Section 4.2) that we may estimate σ from either the standard deviations or the ranges of the m samples. For the present, we will use the range method. If $x_1, x_2, \ldots, x_n$ is a sample of size n, then the range of the sample is the difference between the largest and smallest observations; that is,

$$R = x_{\max} - x_{\min}$$

Let $R_1, R_2, \ldots, R_m$ be the ranges of the m samples. The average range is

$$\bar{R} = \frac{R_1 + R_2 + \cdots + R_m}{m} \tag{6.3}$$

We may now give the formulas for constructing the control limits on the $\bar{x}$ chart. They are as follows:

Control Limits for the $\bar{x}$ Chart

$$\begin{aligned} UCL &= \bar{\bar{x}} + A_2\bar{R} \\ \text{Center line} &= \bar{\bar{x}} \\ LCL &= \bar{\bar{x}} - A_2\bar{R} \end{aligned} \tag{6.4}$$

The constant A_2 is tabulated for various sample sizes in Appendix Table VI.

Process variability may be monitored by plotting values of the sample range R on a control chart. The center line and control limits of the R chart are as follows:

Control Limits for the R Chart

$$\begin{aligned} UCL &= D_4\bar{R} \\ \text{Center line} &= \bar{R} \\ LCL &= D_3\bar{R} \end{aligned} \tag{6.5}$$

The constants D_3 and D_4 are tabulated for various values of n in Appendix Table VI.

Development of Equations (6.4) and (6.5). The development of the equations for computing the control limits on the $\bar{x}$ and R control charts is relatively easy. In Chapter 4 (Section 4.2) we observed that there is a well-known relationship between the range of a sample from a normal distribution and the standard deviation of that distribution. The random variable $W = R/\sigma$ is called the **relative range.** The parameters of the distribution of W are a function of the sample size n. The mean of W is d_2. Consequently, an estimator of σ is $\hat{\sigma} = R/d_2$. Values of d_2 for various sample sizes are given in Appendix Table VI. Therefore, if $\bar{R}$ is the average range of the m preliminary samples, we may use

$$\hat{\sigma} = \frac{\bar{R}}{d_2} \tag{6.6}$$

to estimate σ. This is an unbiased estimator of σ.

If we use $\bar{\bar{x}}$ as an estimator of μ and $\bar{R}/d_2$ as an estimator of σ, then the parameters of the $\bar{x}$ chart are

$$\begin{aligned} \text{UCL} &= \bar{\bar{x}} + \frac{3}{d_2\sqrt{n}}\bar{R} \\ \text{Center line} &= \bar{\bar{x}} \\ \text{LCL} &= \bar{\bar{x}} - \frac{3}{d_2\sqrt{n}}\bar{R} \end{aligned} \tag{6.7}$$

If we define

$$A_2 = \frac{3}{d_2\sqrt{n}} \tag{6.8}$$

then equation (6.7) reduces to equation (6.4).

Now consider the R chart. The center line will be $\bar{R}$. To determine the control limits, we need an estimate of σ_R. Assuming that the quality characteristic is normally distributed, $\hat{\sigma}_R$ can be found from the distribution of the relative range $W = R/\sigma$. The standard deviation of W, say d_3, is a known function of n. Thus, since

$$R = W\sigma$$

the standard deviation of R is

$$\sigma_R = d_3\sigma$$

Since σ is unknown, we may estimate σ_R by

$$\hat{\sigma}_R = d_3\frac{\bar{R}}{d_2} \tag{6.9}$$

Consequently, the parameters of the R chart with the usual three-sigma control limits are

$$\begin{aligned} \text{UCL} &= \bar{R} + 3\hat{\sigma}_R = \bar{R} + 3d_3\frac{\bar{R}}{d_2} \\ \text{Center line} &= \bar{R} \\ \text{LCL} &= \bar{R} - 3\hat{\sigma}_R = \bar{R} - 3d_3\frac{\bar{R}}{d_2} \end{aligned} \tag{6.10}$$

If we let

$$D_3 = 1 - 3\frac{d_3}{d_2} \quad \text{and} \quad D_4 = 1 + 3\frac{d_3}{d_2}$$

equation (6.10) reduces to equation (6.5).

Phase I Application of $\bar{x}$ and R Charts. In **phase I control chart usage,** when preliminary samples are used to construct $\bar{x}$ and R control charts, it is customary to treat the control limits obtained from equations (6.4) and (6.5) as **trial control limits.** They allow us to determine whether the process was in control when the m initial samples were selected. To determine whether the process was in control when the preliminary samples were collected, plot the values of $\bar{x}$ and R from each sample on the charts and analyze the resulting display. If all points plot inside the control limits and no systematic behavior is evident, we conclude that the process was in control in the past, and the trial control limits are suitable for controlling current or future production. It is highly desirable to have 20–25 samples or subgroups of size n (typically n is between 3 and 5) to compute the trial control limits. We can, of course, work with fewer data but the control limits are not as reliable.

Suppose that one or more of the values of either $\bar{x}$ or R plot out of control when compared to the trial control limits. Clearly, if control limits for current or future production are to be meaningful, they must be based on data from a process that is in control. Therefore, when the hypothesis of past control is rejected, it is necessary to **revise** the trial control limits. This is done by examining each of the out-of-control points, looking for an assignable cause. If an assignable cause is found, the point is discarded and the trial control limits are recalculated, using only the remaining points. Then these remaining points are reexamined for control. (Note that points that were in control initially may now be out of control, because the new trial control limits will generally be tighter than the old ones.) This process is continued until all points plot in control, at which point the trial control limits are adopted for current use.

In some cases, it may not be possible to find an assignable cause for a point that plots out of control. There are two courses of action open to us. The first of these is to eliminate the point, just as if an assignable cause had been found. There is no analytical justification for choosing this action, other than that points that are outside of the control limits are likely to have been drawn from a probability distribution characteristic of an out-of-control state. The alternative is to retain the point (or points) considering the trial control limits as appropriate for current control. Of course, if the point really does represent an out-of-control condition, the resulting control limits will be too wide. However, if there are only one or two such points, this will not distort the control chart significantly. If future samples still indicate control, then the unexplained points can probably be safely dropped.

Occasionally, when the initial sample values of $\bar{x}$ and R are plotted against the trial control limits, many points will plot out of control. Clearly, if we arbitrarily drop the out-of-control points, we will have an unsatisfactory situation, as few data will remain with which we can recompute reliable control limits. We also suspect that this approach would ignore much useful information in the data. On the other hand, searching for an assignable cause for *each* out-of-control point is unlikely to be successful. We have found that when many of the initial samples plot out of control against the trial limits, it is better to concentrate on **the patterns on control charts** formed by these points. Such a pattern will almost always exist. Usually, the assignable cause associated with the pattern of out-of-control points is fairly easy to identify. Removal of this process problem usually results in a major process improvement.

6.2.2 Development and Use of $\bar{x}$ and R Charts

In the previous section we presented the statistical background for $\bar{x}$ and R control charts. We now illustrate the construction and application of these charts. We also discuss some guidelines for using these charts in practice.

EXAMPLE 6.1 $\bar{x}$ and R Charts for a Manufacturing Process

A hard-bake process (see Section 5.3.1) is used in conjunction with photolithography in semiconductor manufacturing. We wish to establish statistical control of the flow width of the resist in this process using $\bar{x}$ and R charts. Twenty-five samples, each of size five wafers, have been taken when we think the process is in control. The interval of time between samples or subgroups is one hour. The flow width measurement data (in microns) from these samples are shown in Table 6.1.

(continued)

■ **TABLE 6.1**
Flow Width Measurements (microns) for the Hard-Bake Process

Sample Number	Wafers 1	2	3	4	5	$\bar{x}_i$	R_i
1	1.3235	1.4128	1.6744	1.4573	1.6914	1.5119	0.3679
2	1.4314	1.3592	1.6075	1.4666	1.6109	1.4951	0.2517
3	1.4284	1.4871	1.4932	1.4324	1.5674	1.4817	0.1390
4	1.5028	1.6352	1.3841	1.2831	1.5507	1.4712	0.3521
5	1.5604	1.2735	1.5265	1.4363	1.6441	1.4882	0.3706
6	1.5955	1.5451	1.3574	1.3281	1.4198	1.4492	0.2674
7	1.6274	1.5064	1.8366	1.4177	1.5144	1.5805	0.4189
8	1.4190	1.4303	1.6637	1.6067	1.5519	1.5343	0.2447
9	1.3884	1.7277	1.5355	1.5176	1.3688	1.5076	0.3589
10	1.4039	1.6697	1.5089	1.4627	1.5220	1.5134	0.2658
11	1.4158	1.7667	1.4278	1.5928	1.4181	1.5242	0.3509
12	1.5821	1.3355	1.5777	1.3908	1.7559	1.5284	0.4204
13	1.2856	1.4106	1.4447	1.6398	1.1928	1.3947	0.4470
14	1.4951	1.4036	1.5893	1.6458	1.4969	1.5261	0.2422
15	1.3589	1.2863	1.5996	1.2497	1.5471	1.4083	0.3499
16	1.5747	1.5301	1.5171	1.1839	1.8662	1.5344	0.6823
17	1.3680	1.7269	1.3957	1.5014	1.4449	1.4874	0.3589
18	1.4163	1.3864	1.3057	1.6210	1.5573	1.4573	0.3153
19	1.5796	1.4185	1.6541	1.5116	1.7247	1.5777	0.3062
20	1.7106	1.4412	1.2361	1.3820	1.7601	1.5060	0.5240
21	1.4371	1.5051	1.3485	1.5670	1.4880	1.4691	0.2185
22	1.4738	1.5936	1.6583	1.4973	1.4720	1.5390	0.1863
23	1.5917	1.4333	1.5551	1.5295	1.6866	1.5592	0.2533
24	1.6399	1.5243	1.5705	1.5563	1.5530	1.5688	0.1156
25	1.5797	1.3663	1.6240	1.3732	1.6887	1.5264	0.3224
					$\Sigma\bar{x}_i$ =	37.6400	$\Sigma R_i = 8.1302$
					$\bar{\bar{x}}$ =	1.5056	$\bar{R} = 0.32521$

SOLUTION

When setting up $\bar{x}$ and R control charts, it is best to begin with the R chart. Because the control limits on the $\bar{x}$ chart depend on the process variability, unless process variability is in control, these limits will not have much meaning. Using the data in Table 6.1, we find that the center line for the R chart is

$$\bar{R} = \frac{\sum_{i=1}^{25} R_i}{25} = \frac{8.1302}{25} = 0.32521$$

For samples of $n = 5$, we find from Appendix Table VI that $D_3 = 0$ and $D_4 = 2.114$. Therefore, the control limits for the R chart are, using equation (6.5),

$$\text{LCL} = \bar{R}D_3 = 0.32521(0) = 0$$

$$\text{UCL} = \bar{R}D_4 = 0.32521(2.114) = 0.68749$$

The R chart is shown in Fig. 6.2*b*. Both control charts in Fig. 6.2 were constructed by Minitab. Note that the UCL for the R chart is reported as 0.6876, because Minitab uses more decimal places in the calculation than we did. When the 25 sample ranges are plotted on the R chart in Fig. 6.2*b* there is no indication of an out-of-control condition.

Since the R chart indicates that process variability is in control, we may now construct the $\bar{x}$ chart. The center line is

$$\bar{\bar{x}} = \frac{\sum_{i=1}^{25} \bar{x}_i}{25} = \frac{37.6400}{25} = 1.5056$$

To find the control limits on the $\bar{x}$ chart, we use $A_2 = 0.577$ from Appendix Table VI for samples of size $n = 5$ and equation (6.4) to find

$$\text{UCL} = \bar{\bar{x}} + A_2\bar{R} = 1.5056 + (0.577)(0.32521) = 1.69325$$

and

$$\text{LCL} = \bar{\bar{x}} - A_2\bar{R} = 1.5056 - (0.577)(0.32521) = 1.31795$$

The $\bar{x}$ chart is shown in Fig. 6.2*a*. When the preliminary sample averages are plotted on this chart, no indication of an out-of-control condition is observed. Therefore, since both the $\bar{x}$ and R charts exhibit control, we would conclude that the process is in control at the stated levels and adopt the trial control limits for use in phase II, where monitoring of future production is of interest.

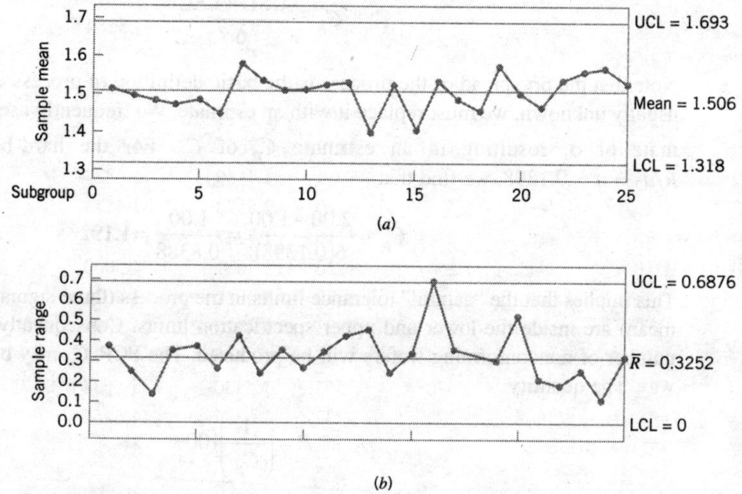

■ **FIGURE 6.2** $\bar{x}$ and R charts (from Minitab) for flow width in the hard-bake process.

Estimating Process Capability. The $\bar{x}$ and R charts provide information about the performance or **process capability** of the process. From the $\bar{x}$ chart, we may estimate the mean flow width of the resist in the hard-bake process as $\bar{\bar{x}} = 1.5056$ microns. The process standard deviation may be estimated using equation (6.6); that is,

$$\hat{\sigma} = \frac{\bar{R}}{d_2} = \frac{0.32521}{2.326} = 0.1398 \text{ microns}$$

where the value of d_2 for samples of size five is found in Appendix Table VI. The specification limits on flow width are 1.50 ± 0.50 microns. The control chart data may be used to describe the capability of the process to produce wafers relative to these specifications. Assuming that flow width is a normally distributed random variable, with mean 1.5056 and standard deviation 0.1398, we may estimate the fraction of nonconforming wafers produced as

$$\begin{aligned} p &= P\{x < 1.00\} + P\{x > 2.00\} \\ &= \Phi\left(\frac{1.00 - 1.5056}{0.1398}\right) + 1 - \Phi\left(\frac{2.00 - 1.5056}{0.1398}\right) \\ &= \Phi(-3.61660) + 1 - \Phi(3.53648) \\ &\simeq 0.00015 + 1 - 0.99980 \\ &\simeq 0.00035 \end{aligned}$$

That is, about 0.035 percent [350 parts per million (ppm)] of the wafers produced will be outside of the specifications.

Another way to express process capability is in terms of the **process capability ratio (PCR) C_p**, which for a quality characteristic with both upper and lower specification limits (USL and LSL, respectively) is

$$C_p = \frac{\text{USL} - \text{LSL}}{6\sigma} \tag{6.11}$$

Note that the 6σ spread of the process is the basic definition of process capability. Since σ is usually unknown, we must replace it with an estimate. We frequently use $\hat{\sigma} = \overline{R}/d_2$ as an estimate of σ, resulting in an estimate $\hat{C}_p$ of C_p. For the hard-bake process, since $\overline{R}/d_2 = \hat{\sigma} = 0.1398$, we find that

$$\hat{C}_p = \frac{2.00 - 1.00}{6(0.1398)} = \frac{1.00}{0.8388} = 1.192$$

This implies that the "natural" tolerance limits in the process (three-sigma above and below the mean) are inside the lower and upper specification limits. Consequently, a moderately small number of nonconforming wafers will be produced. The PCR C_p may be interpreted another way. The quantity

$$P = \left(\frac{1}{C_p}\right)100\%$$

is simply the percentage of the specification band that the process uses up. For the hard-bake process an estimate of P is

$$\hat{P} = \left(\frac{1}{\hat{C}_p}\right)100\% = \left(\frac{1}{1.192}\right)100\% = 83.89$$

That is, the process uses up about 84% of the specification band.

Figure 6.3 illustrates three cases of interest relative to the PCR C_p and process specifications. In Fig. 6.3*a* the PCR C_p is greater than unity. This means that the process uses up much less than 100% of the tolerance band. Consequently, relatively few non-conforming units

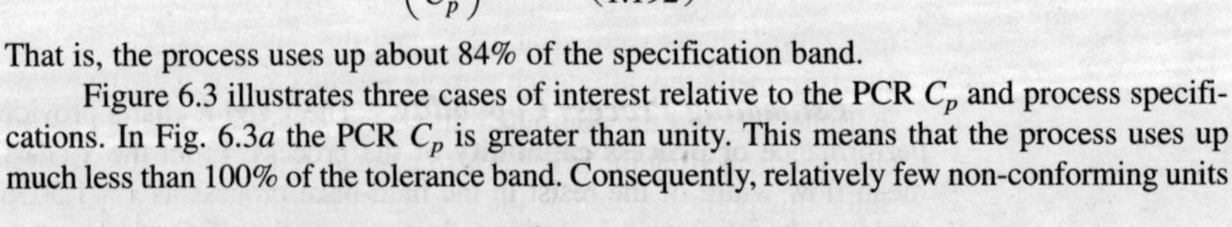

■ FIGURE 6.3 Process fallout and the process capability ratio C_p.

will be produced by this process. Figure 6.3*b* shows a process for which the PCR $C_p = 1$; that is, the process uses up all the tolerance band. For a normal distribution this would imply about 0.27% (or 2700 ppm) nonconforming units. Finally, Fig. 6.3*c* presents a process for which the PCR $C_p < 1$; that is, the process uses up more than 100% of the tolerance band. In this case the process is very yield-sensitive, and a large number of nonconforming units will be produced.

Note that all the cases in Fig. 6.3 assume that the process is centered at the midpoint of the specification band. In many situations this will not be the case, and as we will see in Chapter 8 (which is devoted to a more extensive treatment of process capability analysis), some modification of the PCR C_p is necessary to describe this situation adequately.

Revision of Control Limits and Center Lines. The effective use of any control chart will require **periodic revision** of the control limits and center lines. Some practitioners establish regular periods for review and revision of control chart limits, such as every week, every month, or every 25, 50, or 100 samples. When revising control limits, remember that it is highly desirable to use at least 25 samples or subgroups (some authorities recommend 200–300 individual observations) in computing control limits.

Sometimes the user will replace the center line of the $\bar{x}$ chart with a **target value,** say $\bar{\bar{x}}_0$. If the R chart exhibits control, this can be helpful in shifting the process average to the desired value, particularly in processes where the mean may be changed by a fairly simple adjustment of a manipulatable variable in the process. If the mean is not easily influenced by a simple process adjustment, then it is likely to be a complex and unknown function of several process variables and a target value $\bar{\bar{x}}_0$ may not be helpful, as use of that value could result in many points outside the control limits. In such cases, we would not necessarily know whether the point was really associated with an assignable cause or whether it plotted outside the limits because of a poor choice for the center line.

When the R chart is out of control, we often eliminate the out-of-control points and recompute a revised value of $\bar{R}$. This value is then used to determine new limits and center line on the R chart and new limits on the $\bar{x}$ chart. This will tighten the limits on both charts, making them consistent with a process standard deviation σ consistent with use of the *revised* $\bar{R}$ in the relationship $\bar{R}/d_2$. This estimate of σ could be used as the basis of a preliminary analysis of process capability.

Phase II Operation of the $\bar{x}$ and R Charts. Once a set of reliable control limits is established, we use the control chart for monitoring future production. This is called **phase II control chart usage.**

Twenty additional samples of wafers from the hard-bake process were collected after the control charts were established and the sample values of $\bar{x}$ and R plotted on the control charts immediately after each sample was taken. The data from these new samples are shown in Table 6.2, and the continuations of the $\bar{x}$ and R charts are shown in Fig. 6.4. The control charts indicate that the process is in control, until the $\bar{x}$-value from the 43rd sample is plotted. Since this point (as well as the $\bar{x}$-value from sample 45) plots above the upper control limit, we would suspect that an assignable cause has occurred at or before that time. The general pattern of points on the $\bar{x}$ chart from about subgroup 38 onward is indicative of a shift in the process mean.

Once the control chart is established and is being used in on-line process monitoring, one is often tempted to use the sensitizing rules (or Western Electric rules) discussed in Chapter 5 (Section 5.3.6) to speed up shift detection. Here, for example, the use of such rules would likely result in the shift being detected around sample 40. However, recall the discussion from Section 5.3.3 in which we discouraged the routine use of these sensitizing rules

■ **TABLE 6.2**
Additional Samples for Example 6.1

Sample Number	Wafers 1	2	3	4	5	$\bar{x}_i$	R_i
26	1.4483	1.5458	1.4538	1.4303	1.6206	1.4998	0.1903
27	1.5435	1.6899	1.5830	1.3358	1.4187	1.5142	0.3541
28	1.5175	1.3446	1.4723	1.6657	1.6661	1.5332	0.3215
29	1.5454	1.0931	1.4072	1.5039	1.5264	1.4152	0.4523
30	1.4418	1.5059	1.5124	1.4620	1.6263	1.5097	0.1845
31	1.4301	1.2725	1.5945	1.5397	1.5252	1.4724	0.3220
32	1.4981	1.4506	1.6174	1.5837	1.4962	1.5292	0.1668
33	1.3009	1.5060	1.6231	1.5831	1.6454	1.5317	0.3445
34	1.4132	1.4603	1.5808	1.7111	1.7313	1.5793	0.3181
35	1.3817	1.3135	1.4953	1.4894	1.4596	1.4279	0.1818
36	1.5765	1.7014	1.4026	1.2773	1.4541	1.4824	0.4241
37	1.4936	1.4373	1.5139	1.4808	1.5293	1.4910	0.0920
38	1.5729	1.6738	1.5048	1.5651	1.7473	1.6128	0.2425
39	1.8089	1.5513	1.8250	1.4389	1.6558	1.6560	0.3861
40	1.6236	1.5393	1.6738	1.8698	1.5036	1.6420	0.3662
41	1.4120	1.7931	1.7345	1.6391	1.7791	1.6716	0.3811
42	1.7372	1.5663	1.4910	1.7809	1.5504	1.6252	0.2899
43	1.5971	1.7394	1.6832	1.6677	1.7974	1.6970	0.2003
44	1.4295	1.6536	1.9134	1.7272	1.4370	1.6321	0.4839
45	1.6217	1.8220	1.7915	1.6744	1.9404	1.7700	0.3187

for on-line monitoring of a stable process because they greatly increase the occurrence of false alarms.

In examining control chart data, it is sometimes helpful to construct a run chart of the individual observations in each sample. This chart is sometimes called a **tier chart** or **tolerance diagram.** This may reveal some pattern in the data, or it may show that a particular

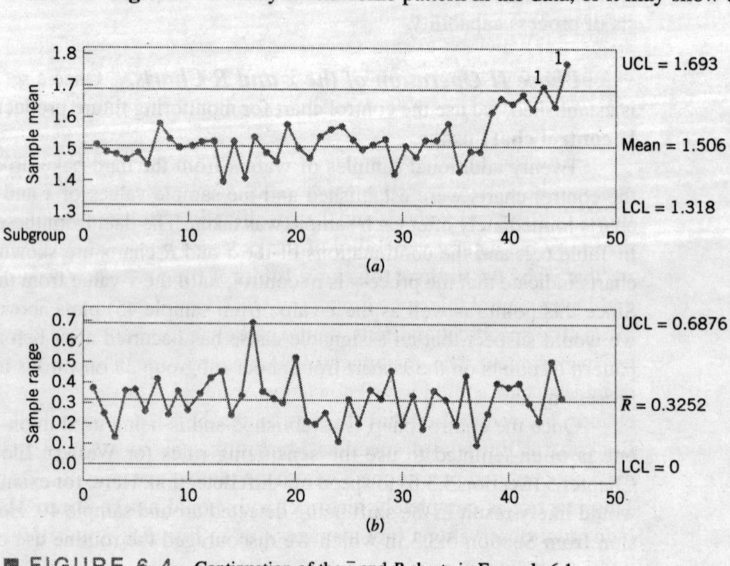

■ **FIGURE 6.4** Continuation of the $\bar{x}$ and R charts in Example 6.1.

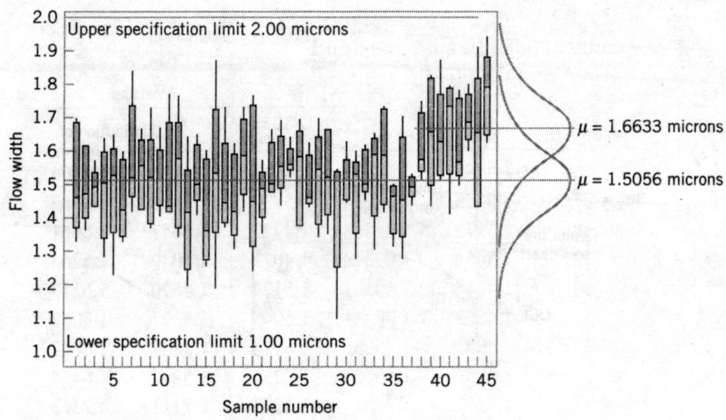

■ **FIGURE 6.5** Tier chart constructed using the Minitab box plot procedure for the flow width data.

value of $\bar{x}$ or R was produced by one or two unusual observations in the sample. A box plot is usually a very simple way to construct the tier diagram.

A tier chart of the flow width data observations is shown in Fig. 6.5. This chart does not indicate that the out-of-control signals were generated by unusual individual observations, but instead, they probably resulted from a shift in the mean around the time that sample 38 was taken. The average of the averages of samples 38 through 45 is 1.6633 microns. The specification limits of 1.50 ± 0.50 microns are plotted in Fig. 6.5, along with a sketch of the normal distribution that represents process output when the process mean equals the in-control value 1.5056 microns. A sketch of the normal distribution representing process output at the new apparent mean diameter of 1.6633 microns is also shown in Fig. 6.5. It is obvious that a much higher percentage of nonconforming wafers will be produced at this new mean flow rate. Since the process is out of control, a search for the cause of this shift in the mean must be conducted. The out-of-control-action plan (**OCAP**) for this control chart, shown in Fig. 5.6, would play a key role in these activities by directing operating personnel through a series of sequential activities to find the assignable cause. Often additional input and support from engineers, management, and the quality engineering staff is necessary to find and eliminate assignable causes.

Control Limits, Specification Limits, and Natural Tolerance Limits. A point that should be emphasized is that there is no connection or relationship between the **control limits** on the $\bar{x}$ and R charts and the **specification limits** on the process. The control limits are driven by the natural variability of the process (measured by the process standard deviation σ), that is, by the **natural tolerance limits of the process.** It is customary to define the upper and lower natural tolerance limits, say UNTL and LNTL, as 3σ above and below the process mean. The specification limits, on the other hand, are determined externally. They may be set by management, the manufacturing engineers, the customer, or by product developers/designers. One should have knowledge of inherent process variability when setting specifications, but **remember that there is no mathematical or statistical relationship between the control limits and specification limits.** The situation is summarized in Fig. 6.6. We have encountered practitioners who have plotted specification limits on the $\bar{x}$ control chart. This practice is completely incorrect and should not be done. When dealing with plots of *individual* observations (not averages), as in Fig. 6.5, it is helpful to plot the specification limits on that chart.

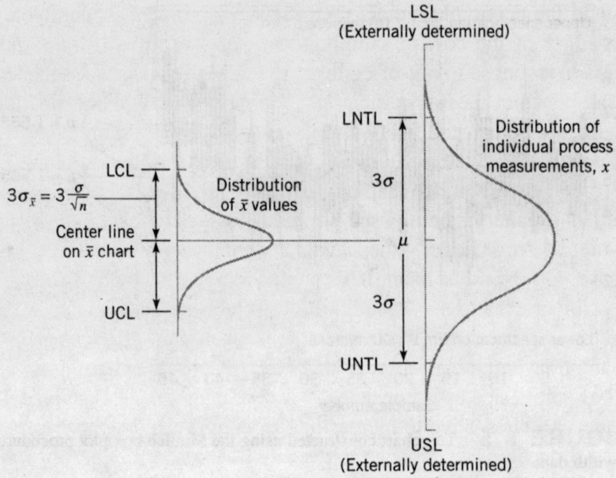

■ FIGURE 6.6 Relationship of natural tolerance limits, control limits, and specification limits.

Rational Subgroups. **Rational subgroups** play an important role in the use of $\bar{x}$ and R control charts. Defining a rational subgroup in practice may be easier with a clear understanding of the functions of the two types of control charts. The $\bar{x}$ chart monitors the average quality level in the process. Therefore, samples should be selected in such a way that maximizes the chances for shifts in the process average to occur between samples, and thus to show up as out-of-control points on the $\bar{x}$ chart. The R chart, on the other hand, measures the variability *within* a sample. Therefore, samples should be selected so that variability within samples measures only chance or random causes. Another way of saying this is that the $\bar{x}$ chart monitors **between-sample variability** (variability in the process over time), and the R chart measures **within-sample variability** (the instantaneous process variability at a given time).

An important aspect of this is evident from carefully examining how the control limits for the $\bar{x}$ and R charts are determined from past data. The estimate of the process standard deviation σ used in constructing the control limits is calculated from the variability **within** each sample (i.e., from the individual sample ranges). Consequently, the estimate of σ reflects only **within-sample variability.** It is not correct to estimate σ based on the usual quadratic estimator—say,

$$s = \sqrt{\frac{\sum_{i=1}^{m}\sum_{j=1}^{n}\left(x_{ij} - \bar{\bar{x}}\right)^2}{mn - 1}}$$

where x_{ij} is the jth observation in the ith sample, because if the sample *means* differ, then this will cause s to be too large. Consequently, σ will be overestimated. Pooling all of the preliminary data in this manner to estimate σ is not a good practice because it potentially combines *both between*-sample and *within*-sample variability. The control limits must be based on only **within-sample variability.** Refer to the supplemental text material for more details.

Guidelines for the Design of the Control Chart. To design the $\bar{x}$ and R charts, we must specify the sample size, control limit width, and frequency of sampling to be used. It is not possible to give an exact solution to the problem of control chart design, unless the analyst has detailed information about both the statistical characteristics of the control chart tests and the economic factors that affect the problem. A complete solution of the problem knowledges of the cost of sampling, the costs of investigating and possibly correcting the process in response to out-of-control signals, and the costs associated with producing a product that does not meet specifications. Given this kind of information, an economic decision model could be constructed to allow economically optimum control chart design. In Chapter 10 (Section 10.6) we briefly discuss this approach to the problem. However, it is possible to give some general guidelines now that will aid in control chart design.

If the $\bar{x}$ chart is being used primarily to detect moderate to large process shifts—say, on the order of 2σ or larger—then relatively small samples of size $n = 4$, 5, or 6 are reasonably effective. On the other hand, if we are trying to detect small shifts, then larger sample sizes of possibly $n = 15$ to $n = 25$ are needed. When smaller samples are used, there is less risk of a process shift occurring while a sample is taken. If a shift does occur while a sample is taken, the sample average can obscure this effect. Consequently, this is an argument for using as small a sample size as is consistent with the magnitude of the process shift that one is trying to detect. An alternative to increasing the sample size is to use warning limits and other sensitizing procedures to enhance the ability of the control chart to detect small process shifts. However, as we discussed in Chapter 5, we do not favor the routine use of these sensitizing rules. If you are interested in small shifts, use the CUSUM or EWMA charts in Chapter 9.

The R chart is relatively insensitive to shifts in the process standard deviation for small samples. For example, samples of size $n = 5$ have only about a 40% chance of detecting on the first sample a shift in the process standard deviation from σ to 2σ. Larger samples would seem to be more effective, but we also know that the range method for estimating the standard deviation drops dramatically in efficiency as n increases. Consequently, for large n—say, $n > 10$ or 12—it is probably best to use a control chart for s or s^2 instead of the R chart. Details of the construction of these charts are shown in Sections 6.3.1 and 6.3.2.

From a statistical point of view, the operating-characteristic curves of the $\bar{x}$ and R charts can be helpful in choosing the sample size. They provide a feel for the magnitude of process shift that will be detected with a stated probability for any sample size n. These operating-characteristic curves are discussed in Section 6.2.6.

The problem of choosing the sample size and the frequency of sampling is one of **allocating sampling effort.** Generally, the decision maker will have only a limited number of resources to allocate to the inspection process. The available strategies will usually be either to take small, frequent samples or to take larger samples less frequently. For example, the choice may be between samples of size 5 every half hour or samples of size 20 every two hours. It is impossible to say which strategy is best in all cases, but current industry practice favors small, frequent samples. The general belief is that if the interval between samples is too great, too much defective product will be produced before another opportunity to detect the process shift occurs. From economic considerations, if the cost associated with producing defective items is high, smaller, more frequent samples are better than larger, less frequent ones. Variable sample interval and variable sample size schemes could, of course, be used. Refer to Chapter 10.

The rate of production also influences the choice of sample size and sampling frequency. If the rate of production is high—say, 50,000 units per hour—then more frequent sampling is called for than if the production rate is extremely slow. At high rates of production, many nonconforming units of product will be produced in a very short time when process shifts occur. Furthermore, at high production rates, it is sometimes possible to obtain fairly large samples economically. For example, if we produce 50,000 units per hour, it does not take an appreciable difference in time to collect a sample of size 20 compared to a sample of size 5. If per unit inspection and testing costs are not excessive, high-speed production processes are often monitored with moderately large sample sizes.

The use of three-sigma control limits on the $\bar{x}$ and R control charts is a widespread practice. There are situations, however, when departures from this customary choice of control limits are helpful. For example, if false alarms or type I errors (when an out-of-control signal is generated when the process is really in control) are very expensive to investigate, then it may be best to use wider control limits than three-sigma—perhaps as wide as 3.5-sigma. However, if the process is such that out-of-control signals are quickly and easily investigated with a minimum of lost time and cost, then narrower control limits, perhaps at 2.5-sigma, are appropriate.

Changing Sample Size on the $\bar{x}$ and R Charts. We have presented the development of $\bar{x}$ and R charts assuming that the sample size n is constant from sample to sample. However, there are situations in which the sample size n is not constant. One situation is that of **variable sample size on control charts;** that is, each sample may consist of a different number of observations. The $\bar{x}$ and R charts are generally not used in this case because they lead to a changing center line on the R chart, which is difficult to interpret for many users. The $\bar{x}$ and s charts in Section 6.3.2 would be preferable in this case.

Another situation is that of making a **permanent** (or **semipermanent**) **change** in the sample size because of cost or because the process has exhibited good stability and fewer resources are being allocated for process monitoring. In this case, it is easy to recompute the new control limits directly from the old ones without collecting additional samples based on the new sample size. Let

$$\bar{R}_{\text{old}} = \text{average range for the old sample size}$$
$$\bar{R}_{\text{new}} = \text{average range for the new sample size}$$
$$n_{\text{old}} = \text{old sample size}$$
$$n_{\text{new}} = \text{new sample size}$$
$$d_2(\text{old}) = \text{factor } d_2 \text{ for the old sample size}$$
$$d_2(\text{new}) = \text{factor } d_2 \text{ for the new sample size}$$

For the $\bar{x}$ chart the new control limits are

$$\begin{aligned} \text{UCL} &= \bar{\bar{x}} + A_2\left[\frac{d_2(\text{new})}{d_2(\text{old})}\right]\bar{R}_{\text{old}} \\ \text{LCL} &= \bar{\bar{x}} - A_2\left[\frac{d_2(\text{new})}{d_2(\text{old})}\right]\bar{R}_{\text{old}} \end{aligned} \tag{6.12}$$

where the center line $\bar{\bar{x}}$ is unchanged and the factor A_2 is selected for the *new* sample size. For the R chart, the new parameters are

$$\begin{aligned} \text{UCL} &= D_4\left[\frac{d_2(\text{new})}{d_2(\text{old})}\right]\bar{R}_{\text{old}} \\ \text{CL} = \bar{R}_{\text{new}} &= \left[\frac{d_2(\text{new})}{d_2(\text{old})}\right]\bar{R}_{\text{old}} \\ \text{LCL} &= \max\left\{0, D_3\left[\frac{d_2(\text{new})}{d_2(\text{old})}\right]\bar{R}_{\text{old}}\right\} \end{aligned} \tag{6.13}$$

where D_3 and D_4 are selected for the *new* sample size.

EXAMPLE 6.2 Changing Sample Size

To illustrate the above procedure, consider the $\bar{x}$ and R charts developed for the hard-bake process in Example 6.1. These charts were based on a sample size of five wafers. Suppose that since the process exhibits good control, the process engineering personnel want to reduce the sample size to three wafers. Set up the new control charts.

SOLUTION

From Example 6.1, we know that

$$n_{\text{old}} = 5 \quad \bar{R}_{\text{old}} = 0.32521$$

and from Appendix Table VI we have

$$d_2(\text{old}) = 2.326 \quad d_2(\text{new}) = 1.693$$

Therefore, the new control limits on the $\bar{x}$ chart are found from equation (6.12) as

$$\begin{aligned} \text{UCL} &= \bar{\bar{x}} + A_2\left[\frac{d_2(\text{new})}{d_2(\text{old})}\right]\bar{R}_{\text{old}} \\ &= 1.5056 + (1.023)\left[\frac{1.693}{2.326}\right](0.32521) \\ &= 1.5056 + 0.2422 = 1.7478 \end{aligned}$$

and

$$\begin{aligned} \text{LCL} &= \bar{\bar{x}} - A_2\left[\frac{d_2(\text{new})}{d_2(\text{old})}\right]\bar{R}_{\text{old}} \\ &= 1.5056 - (1.023)\left[\frac{1.693}{2.326}\right](0.32521) \\ &= 1.5056 - 0.2422 = 1.2634 \end{aligned}$$

For the R chart, the new parameters are given by equation (6.13):

$$\begin{aligned} \text{UCL} &= D_4\left[\frac{d_2(\text{new})}{d_2(\text{old})}\right]\bar{R}_{\text{old}} \\ &= (2.574)\left[\frac{1.693}{2.326}\right](0.32521) \\ &= 0.6093 \end{aligned}$$

$$\begin{aligned} \text{CL} = \bar{R}_{\text{new}} &= \left[\frac{d_2(\text{new})}{d_2(\text{old})}\right]\bar{R}_{\text{old}} \\ &= \left[\frac{1.693}{2.326}\right](0.32521) \\ &= 0.2367 \end{aligned}$$

$$\begin{aligned} \text{LCL} &= \max\left\{0, D_3\left[\frac{d_2(\text{new})}{d_2(\text{old})}\right]\bar{R}_{\text{old}}\right\} \\ &= 0 \end{aligned}$$

Figure 6.7 shows the new control limits. Note that the effect of reducing the sample size is to *increase* the width of the limits on the $\bar{x}$ chart (because $\sigma/\sqrt{n}$ is smaller when $n = 5$ than when $n = 3$) and to *lower* the center line and the upper control limit on the R chart (because the expected range from a sample of $n = 3$ is smaller than the expected range from a sample of $n = 5$).

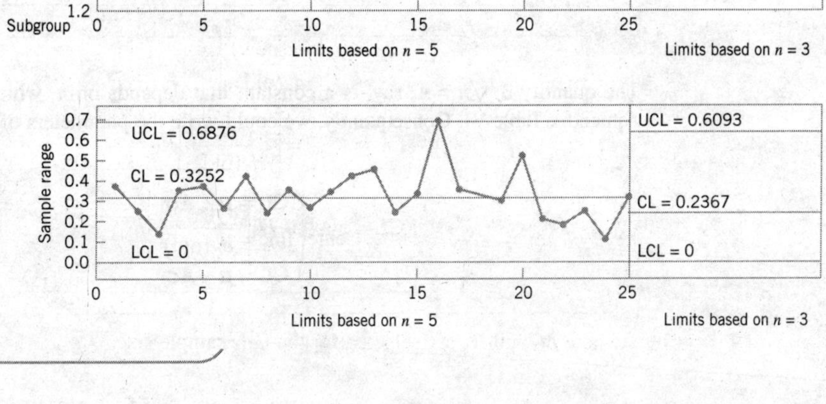

■ **Figure 6.7** Recalculated control limits for the hard-bake process in Example 6.1 to reflect changing the sample size from $n = 5$ to $n = 3$.

Probability Limits on the $\bar{x}$ and R Charts. It is customary to express the control limits on the $\bar{x}$ and R charts as a multiple of the standard deviation of the statistic plotted on the charts. If the multiple chosen is k, then the limits are referred to as k-sigma limits, the usual choice being $k = 3$. As mentioned in Chapter 5, however, it is also possible to define the control limits by specifying the type I error level for the test. These are called **probability limits for control charts** and are used extensively in the United Kingdom and some parts of Western Europe.

It is easy to choose probability limits for the $\bar{x}$ chart. Since $\bar{x}$ is approximately normally distributed, we may obtain a desired type I error of α by choosing the multiple of sigma for the control limit as $k = Z_{\alpha/2}$, where $Z_{\alpha/2}$ is the upper $\alpha/2$ percentage point of the standard normal distribution. Note that the usual **three-sigma control limits** imply that the type I error probability is $\alpha = 0.0027$. If we choose $\alpha = 0.002$, for example, as most writers who recommend probability limits do, then $Z_{\alpha/2} = Z_{0.001} = 3.09$. Consequently, there is very little difference between such control limits and three-sigma control limits.

We may also construct R charts using probability limits. If $\alpha = 0.002$, the 0.001 and 0.999 percentage points of the distribution of the relative range $W = R/\sigma$ are required. These points obviously depend on the subgroup size n. Denoting these points by $W_{0.001}(n)$ and $W_{0.999}(n)$, and estimating σ by $\bar{R}/d_2$, we would have the 0.001 and 0.999 limits for R as $W_{0.001}(n)(\bar{R}/d_2)$ and $W_{0.999}(n)(\bar{R}/d_2)$. If we let $D_{0.001} = W_{0.001}(n)/d_2$ and $D_{0.999} = W_{0.999}(n)/d_2$, then the probability limits for the R chart are

$$\text{UCL} = D_{0.999}\bar{R}$$
$$\text{LCL} = D_{0.001}\bar{R}$$

Tables of pairs of values $(D_{0.001}, D_{0.999})$, $(D_{0.005}, D_{0.995})$, and $(D_{0.025}, D_{0.975})$ for $2 \le n \le 10$ are in Grant and Leavenworth (1980). These control limits will not differ substantially from the customary three-sigma limits. However, for sample sizes $3 \le n \le 6$, they will produce a positive lower control limit for the R chart whereas the conventional three-sigma limits do not.

6.2.3 Charts Based on Standard Values

When it is possible to specify standard values for the process mean and standard deviation, we may use these standards to establish the control charts for $\bar{x}$ and R without analysis of past data. Suppose that the standards given are μ and σ. Then the parameters of the $\bar{x}$ chart are

$$\begin{aligned} \text{UCL} &= \mu + 3\frac{\sigma}{\sqrt{n}} \\ \text{Center line} &= \mu \\ \text{LCL} &= \mu - 3\frac{\sigma}{\sqrt{n}} \end{aligned} \tag{6.14}$$

The quantity $3/\sqrt{n} = A$, say, is a constant that depends on n, which has been tabulated in Appendix Table VI. Consequently, we could write the parameters of the $\bar{x}$ chart as

$$\begin{aligned} \text{UCL} &= \mu + A\sigma \\ \text{Center line} &= \mu \\ \text{LCL} &= \mu - A\sigma \end{aligned} \tag{6.15}$$

To construct the R chart with a standard value of σ, recall that $\sigma = R/d_2$, where d_2 is the mean of the distribution of the relative range. Furthermore, the standard deviation of R is $\sigma_R = d_3\sigma$, where d_3 is the standard deviation of the distribution of the relative range. Therefore, the parameters of the control chart are

$$\begin{aligned} \text{UCL} &= d_2\sigma + 3d_3\sigma \\ \text{Center line} &= d_2\sigma \\ \text{LCL} &= d_2\sigma - 3d_3\sigma \end{aligned} \tag{6.16}$$

It is customary to define the constants

$$D_1 = d_2 - 3d_3$$
$$D_2 = d_2 + 3d_3$$

These constants are tabulated in Appendix Table VI. Thus, the parameters of the R chart with standard σ given are

$$\begin{aligned} \text{UCL} &= D_2\sigma \\ \text{Center line} &= d_2\sigma \\ \text{LCL} &= D_1\sigma \end{aligned} \tag{6.17}$$

One must exercise considerable care when standard values of μ and σ are given. It may be that these standards are not really applicable to the process, and as a result, the $\bar{x}$ and R charts will produce many out-of-control signals relative to the specified standards. If the process is really in control at some *other* mean and standard deviation, then the analyst may spend considerable effort looking for assignable causes that do not exist. Standard values of σ seem to give more trouble than standard values of μ. In processes where the mean of the quality characteristic is controlled by adjustments to the machine, standard or target values of μ are sometimes helpful in achieving management goals with respect to process performance.

6.2.4 Interpretation of $\bar{x}$ and R Charts

We have noted previously that a control chart can indicate an out-of-control condition even though no single point plots outside the control limits, if the pattern of the plotted points exhibits nonrandom or systematic behavior. In many cases, the pattern of the plotted points will provide useful diagnostic information on the process, and this information can be used to make process modifications that reduce variability (the goal of statistical process control). Furthermore, these patterns occur fairly often in phase I (retrospective study of past data), and their elimination is frequently crucial in bringing a process into control.

In this section, we briefly discuss **interpretation of control charts,** focusing on some of the more common patterns that appear on $\bar{x}$ and R charts and some of the process characteristics that may produce the patterns. To effectively interpret $\bar{x}$ and R charts, the analyst must be familiar with both the statistical principles underlying the control chart and the process itself. Additional information on the interpretation of patterns on control charts is in the Western Electric *Statistical Quality Control Handbook* (1956, pp. 149–183).

In interpreting patterns on the $\bar{x}$ chart, we must first determine whether or not the R chart is in control. Some assignable causes show up on *both* the $\bar{x}$ and R charts. If both the $\bar{x}$ and R charts exhibit a nonrandom pattern, the best strategy is to eliminate the R chart assignable causes first. In many cases, this will automatically eliminate the nonrandom pattern on the $\bar{x}$ chart. Never attempt to interpret the $\bar{x}$ chart when the R chart indicates an out-of-control condition.

Cyclic patterns occasionally appear on the control chart. A typical example is shown in Fig. 6.8. Such a pattern on the $\bar{x}$ chart may result from systematic environmental changes such as temperature, operator fatigue, regular rotation of operators and/or machines, or fluctuation in voltage or pressure or some other variable in the production equipment. R charts will sometimes reveal cycles because of maintenance schedules, operator fatigue, or tool wear resulting in excessive variability. In one study in which this author was involved, systematic variability in the fill volume of a metal container was caused by the on–off cycle of a compressor in the filling machine.

A **mixture** is indicated when the plotted points tend to fall near or slightly outside the control limits, with relatively few points near the center line, as shown in Fig. 6.9. A mixture pattern is generated by two (or more) overlapping distributions generating the process output. The probability distributions that could be associated with the mixture pattern in Fig. 6.9 are shown on the right-hand side of that figure. The severity of the mixture pattern depends on the extent to which the distributions overlap. Sometimes mixtures result from "overcontrol," where the operators make process adjustments too often, responding to random variation in the output rather than systematic causes. A mixture pattern can also occur when output product from several sources (such as parallel machines) is fed into a common stream which is then sampled for process monitoring purposes.

A **shift in process level** is illustrated in Fig. 6.10. These shifts may result from the introduction of new workers; changes in methods, raw materials, or machines; a change in the inspection method or standards; or a change in either the skill, attentiveness, or motivation of the operators. Sometimes an improvement in process performance is noted following introduction of a control chart program, simply because of motivational factors influencing the workers.

A **trend,** or continuous movement in one direction, is shown on the control chart in Fig. 6.11. Trends are usually due to a gradual wearing out or deterioration of a tool or some other critical process component. In chemical processes they often occur because of settling

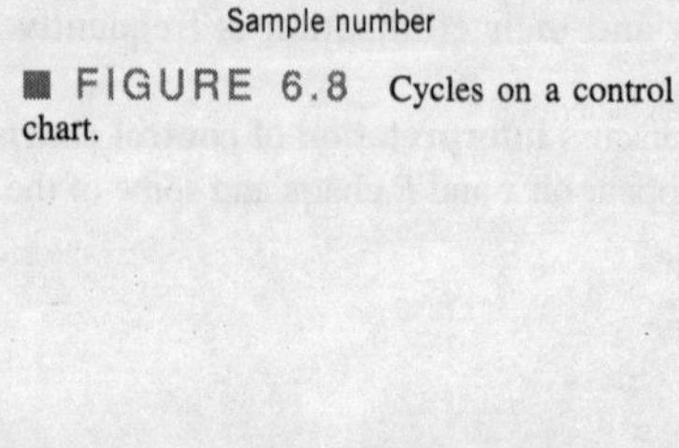

■ FIGURE 6.8 Cycles on a control chart.

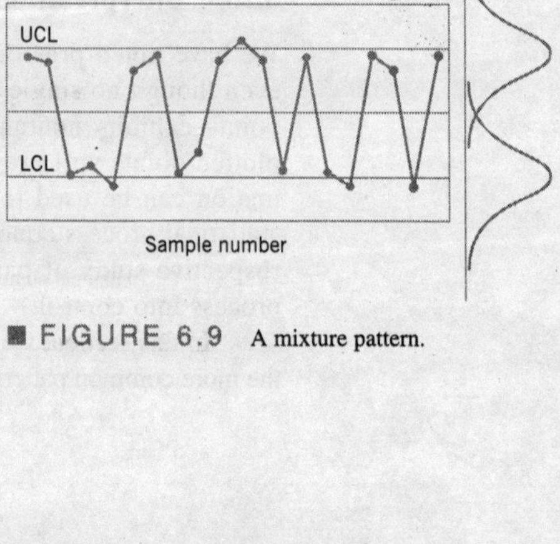

■ FIGURE 6.9 A mixture pattern.

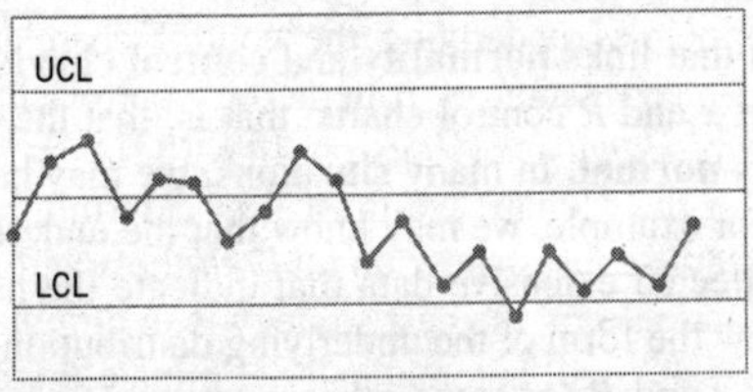

■ FIGURE 6.10 A shift in process level.

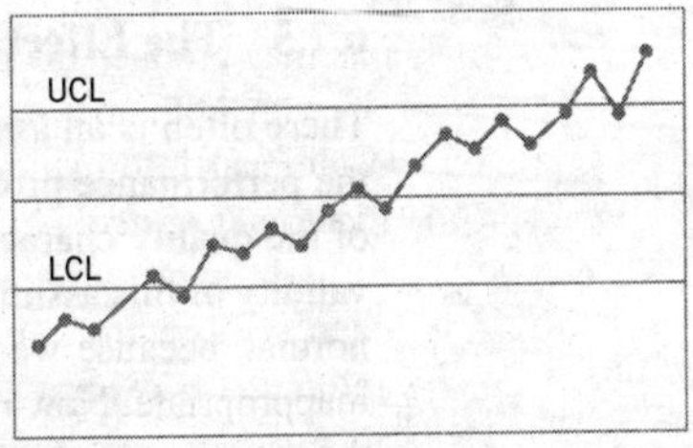

■ FIGURE 6.11 A trend in process level.

or separation of the components of a mixture. They can also result from human causes, such as operator fatigue or the presence of supervision. Finally, trends can result from seasonal influences, such as temperature. When trends are due to tool wear or other systematic causes of deterioration, this may be directly incorporated into the control chart model. A device useful for monitoring and analyzing processes with trends is the **regression control chart** [see Mandel (1969)]. The **modified control chart**, discussed in Chapter 9, is also used when the process exhibits tool wear.

Stratification, or a tendency for the points to cluster artificially around the center line, is illustrated in Fig. 6.12. We note that there is a marked lack of natural variability in the observed pattern. One potential cause of stratification is incorrect calculation of control limits. This pattern may also result when the sampling process collects one or more units from several different underlying distributions within each subgroup. For example, suppose that a sample of size 5 is obtained by taking one observation from each of five parallel processes. If the largest and smallest units in each sample are relatively far apart because they come from two different distributions, then R will be incorrectly inflated, causing the limits on the $\bar{x}$ chart to be too wide. In this case R incorrectly measures the variability *between* the different underlying distributions, in addition to the chance cause variation that it is intended to measure.

In interpreting patterns on the $\bar{x}$ and R charts, one should consider the two charts jointly. If the underlying distribution is normal, then the random variables $\bar{x}$ and R computed from the same sample are statistically independent. Therefore, $\bar{x}$ and R should behave independently on the control chart. If there is correlation between the $\bar{x}$ and R values—that is, if the points on the two charts "follow" each other—then this indicates that the underlying distribution is skewed. If specifications have been determined assuming normality, then those analyses may be in error.

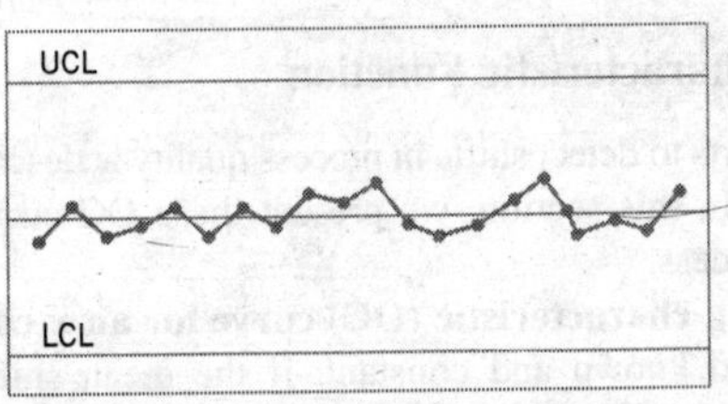

■ FIGURE 6.12 A stratification pattern.

6.2.5 The Effect of Non-normality on $\bar{x}$ and R Charts

There often is an assumption that links **normality** and **control charts** in the development of the performance properties of $\bar{x}$ and R control charts; that is, that the underlying distribution of the quality characteristic is **normal.** In many situations, we may have reason to doubt the validity of this assumption. For example, we may know that the underlying distribution is not normal, because we have collected extensive data that indicate the normality assumption is inappropriate. Now if we know the form of the underlying distribution, it is possible to derive the sampling distributions of $\bar{x}$ and R (or some other measure of process variability) and to obtain exact probability limits for the control charts. This approach could be difficult in some cases, and most analysts would probably prefer to use the standard approach based on the normality assumption if they believed that the effect of departure from this assumption was not serious. However, we may know nothing about the form of the underlying distribution, and then our only choice may be to use the normal theory results. Obviously, in either case, we would be interested in knowing the effect of departures from normality on the usual control charts for $\bar{x}$ and R.

Several authors have investigated the effect of departures from normality on control charts. Burr (1967) notes that the usual normal theory control limit constants are very robust to the normality assumption and can be employed unless the population is extremely non-normal. Schilling and Nelson (1976), Chan, Hapuarachchi, and Macpherson (1988), and Yourstone and Zimmer (1992) have also studied the effect of non-normality on the control limits of the $\bar{x}$ chart. Schilling and Nelson investigated the uniform, right triangular, gamma (with $\lambda = 1$ and $r = \frac{1}{2}$, 1, 2, 3, and 4), and two bimodal distributions formed as mixtures of two normal distributions. Their study indicates that, in most cases, samples of size 4 or 5 are sufficient to ensure reasonable robustness to the normality assumption.

The worst cases observed were for small values of r in the gamma distribution [$r = \frac{1}{2}$ and $r = 1$ (the exponential distribution)]. For example, they report the actual α-risk to be 0.014 or less if $n \geq 4$ for the gamma distribution with $r = \frac{1}{2}$, as opposed to a theoretical value of 0.0027 for the normal distribution.

While the use of three-sigma control limits on the $\bar{x}$ chart will produce an α-risk of 0.0027 if the underlying distribution is normal, the same is not true for the R chart. The sampling distribution of R is not symmetric, even when sampling from the normal distribution, and the long tail of the distribution is on the high or positive side. Thus, symmetric three-sigma limits are only an approximation, and the α-risk on such an R chart is *not* 0.0027. (In fact, for $n = 4$, it is $\alpha = 0.00461$.) Furthermore, the R chart is more sensitive to departures from normality than the $\bar{x}$ chart.

Once again, it is important to remember the role of theory and assumptions such as normality and independence. These are fundamental to the study of the performance of the $\bar{x}$ control chart which is very useful for assessing its suitability for phase II, but plays a much less important role in phase I. In fact, these considerations are not a primary concern in phase I.

6.2.6 The Operating-Characteristic Function

The ability of the $\bar{x}$ and R charts to detect shifts in process quality is described by their operating-characteristic (OC) curves. In this section, we present these OC curves for charts used for phase II monitoring of a process.

Consider the **operating-characteristic (OC) curve for an $\bar{x}$ control chart.** The standard deviation σ is assumed known and constant. If the mean shifts from the in-control value—say, μ_0—to another value $\mu_1 = \mu_0 + k\sigma$, the probability of *not* detecting this shift on the first subsequent sample or the β-risk is

$$\beta = P\{\text{LCL} \leq \bar{x} \leq \text{UCL} \mid \mu = \mu_1 = \mu_0 + k\sigma\} \tag{6.18}$$

Since $\bar{x} \sim N(\mu, \sigma^2/n)$, and the upper and lower control limits are UCL $= \mu_0 + L\sigma/\sqrt{n}$ and LCL $= \mu_0 - L\sigma/\sqrt{n}$, we may write equation (6.18) as

$$\beta = \Phi\left[\frac{\text{UCL} - (\mu_0 + k\sigma)}{\sigma/\sqrt{n}}\right] - \Phi\left[\frac{\text{LCL} - (\mu_0 + k\sigma)}{\sigma/\sqrt{n}}\right]$$

$$= \Phi\left[\frac{\mu_0 + L\sigma/\sqrt{n} - (\mu_0 + k\sigma)}{\sigma/\sqrt{n}}\right] - \Phi\left[\frac{\mu_0 - L\sigma/\sqrt{n} - (\mu_0 + k\sigma)}{\sigma/\sqrt{n}}\right]$$

where Φ denotes the standard normal cumulative distribution function. This reduces to

$$\beta = \Phi\left(L - k\sqrt{n}\right) - \Phi\left(-L - k\sqrt{n}\right) \tag{6.19}$$

To illustrate the use of equation (6.19), suppose that we are using an $\bar{x}$ chart with $L = 3$ (the usual three-sigma limits), the sample size $n = 5$, and we wish to determine the probability of detecting a shift to $\mu_1 = \mu_0 + 2\sigma$ on the first sample following the shift. Then, since $L = 3$, $k = 2$, and $n = 5$, we have

$$\beta = \Phi\left[3 - 2\sqrt{5}\right] - \Phi\left[-3 - 2\sqrt{5}\right]$$
$$= \Phi(-1.47) - \Phi(-7.37)$$
$$\cong 0.0708$$

This is the β-risk, or the probability of not detecting such a shift. The probability that such a shift *will* be detected on the first subsequent sample is $1 - \beta = 1 - 0.0708 = 0.9292$.

To construct the OC curve for the $\bar{x}$ chart, plot the β-risk against the magnitude of the shift we wish to detect expressed in standard deviation units for various sample sizes n. These probabilities may be evaluated directly from equation (6.19). This OC curve is shown in Fig. 6.13 for the case of three-sigma limits ($L = 3$).

Figure 6.13 indicates that for the typical sample sizes 4, 5, and 6, the $\bar{x}$ chart is not particularly effective in detecting a small shift—say, those on the order of 1.5σ or less—on the first sample following the shift. For example, if the shift is 1.0σ and $n = 5$, then from Fig. 6.13, we have $\beta = 0.75$, approximately. Thus, the probability that the shift will be detected on the first sample is only $1 - \beta = 0.25$. However, the probability that the shift is detected on

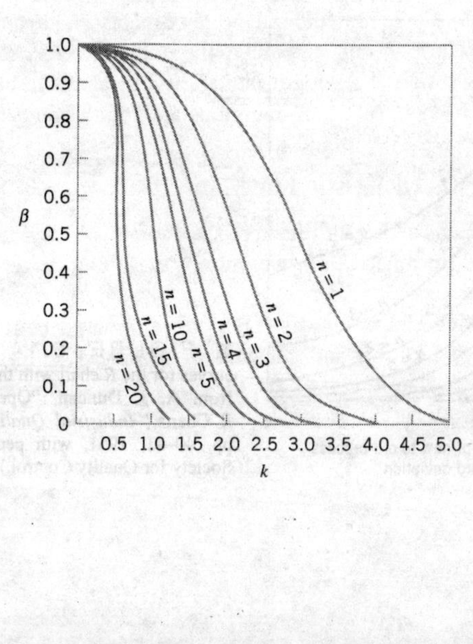

■ FIGURE 6.13 Operating-characteristic curves for the $\bar{x}$ chart with three-sigma limits. $\beta = P$ (not detecting a shift of $k\sigma$ in the mean on the first sample following the shift).

the second sample is $\beta(1-\beta) = 0.75(0.25) = 0.19$, whereas the probability that it is detected on the third sample is $\beta^2(1-\beta) = (0.75^2)0.25 = 0.14$. Thus, the probability that the shift will be detected on the rth subsequent sample is simply $1-\beta$ times the probability of not detecting the shift on each of the initial $r-1$ samples, or

$$\beta^{r-1}(1-\beta)$$

In general, the expected number of samples taken before the shift is detected is simply the **average run length,** or

$$\text{ARL} = \sum_{r=1}^{\infty} r\beta^{r-1}(1-\beta) = \frac{1}{1-\beta}$$

Therefore, in our example, we have

$$\text{ARL} = \frac{1}{1-\beta} = \frac{1}{0.25} = 4$$

In other words, the expected number of samples taken to detect a shift of 1.0σ with $n = 5$ is four.

The above discussion provides a supportive argument for the use of small sample sizes on the $\bar{x}$ chart. Even though small sample sizes often result in a relatively large β-risk, because samples are collected and tested periodically, there is a very good chance that the shift will be detected reasonably quickly, although perhaps not on the first sample following the shift.

To construct the OC curve for the R chart, the distribution of the relative range $W = R/\sigma$ is employed. Suppose that the in-control value of the standard deviation is σ_0. Then the OC curve plots the probability of not detecting a shift to a new value of σ—say, $\sigma_1 > \sigma_0$—on the first sample following the shift. Figure 6.14 presents the OC curve, in which β is plotted against $\lambda = \sigma_1/\sigma_0$ (the ratio of new to old process standard deviation) for various values of n.

From examining Fig. 6.14, we observe that the R chart is not very effective in detecting process shifts for small sample sizes. For example, if the process standard deviation doubles (i.e., $\lambda = \sigma_1/\sigma_0 = 2$), which is a fairly large shift, then samples of size 5 have only about a 40% chance of detecting this shift on each subsequent sample. Most quality engineers believe that the R chart is insensitive to small or moderate shifts for the usual subgroup sizes of $n = 4$, 5, or 6. If $n > 10$ or 12, the s chart discussed in Section 6.3.1 should generally be used instead of the R chart.

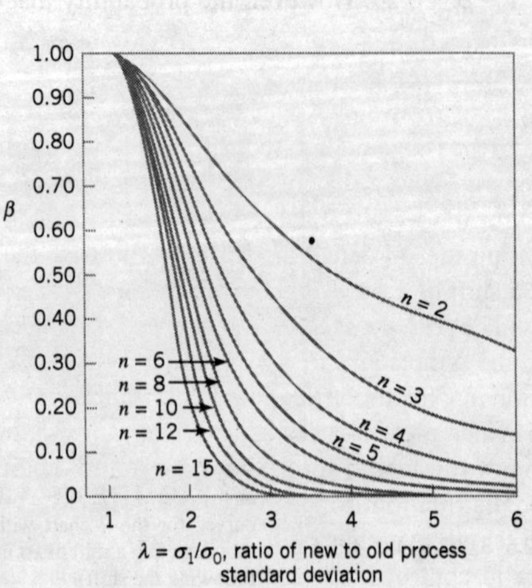

■ FIGURE 6.14 Operating-characteristic curves for the R chart with three-sigma limits. (Adapted from A. J. Duncan, "Operating Characteristics of R Charts," *Industrial Quality Control*, vol. 7, no. 5, pp. 40–41, 1951, with permission of the American Society for Quality Control.)

The OC curves in Figs. 6.13 and 6.14 assume that the $\bar{x}$ and R charts are used for on-line process monitoring; that is, phase II process monitoring. It is occasionally useful to study the statistical performance of a chart used to analyze past data (phase I). This can give some indication of how the number of preliminary subgroups used to establish the control chart affects the chart's ability to detect out-of-control conditions that existed when the data were collected. It is from such analytical studies, as well as practical experience, that the recommendation to use at least 20 to 25 preliminary subgroups in establishing $\bar{x}$ and R charts has evolved.

6.2.7 The Average Run Length for the $\bar{x}$ Chart

For any **Shewhart control chart,** we have noted previously that the ARL can be expressed as

$$\text{ARL} = \frac{1}{P(\text{one point plots out of control})}$$

or

$$\text{ARL}_0 = \frac{1}{\alpha} \tag{6.20}$$

for the in-control ARL and

$$\text{ARL}_1 = \frac{1}{1-\beta} \tag{6.21}$$

for the out-of-control ARL. These results are actually rather intuitive. If the observations plotted on the control chart are independent, then the number of points that must be plotted until the first point exceeds a control limit is a geometric random variable with parameter p (see Chapter 3). The mean of this geometric distribution is simply $1/p$, the average run length.

Since it is relatively easy to develop a general expression for β for the $\bar{x}$ control chart to detect a shift in the mean of $k\sigma$ [see equation (6.19)], then it is not difficult to construct a set of ARL curves for the $\bar{x}$ chart. Figure 6.15 presents these ARL curves for sample sizes of $n =$ 1, 2, 3, 4, 5, 7, 9, and 16 for the $\bar{x}$ control chart, where the ARL is in terms of the expected number of *samples* taken in order to detect the shift. To illustrate the use of Fig. 6.15, note that if we wish to detect a shift of 1.5σ using a sample size of $n = 3$, then the average number of samples required will be $\text{ARL}_1 = 3$. Note also that we could reduce the ARL_1 to approximately 1 if we increased the sample size to $n = 16$.

Recall our discussion in Chapter 5 (Section 5.3.3) indicating that ARLs are subject to some criticism as performance measures for control charts. We noted there (and above as well) that the distribution of run length for a Shewhart control chart is geometric and that this can be a very skewed distribution, so the average (that is, the ARL) may not be the best measure of a typical run length. Another issue concerning ARL relates to the fact that the computations for a specific control chart are usually based on **estimates** of the process

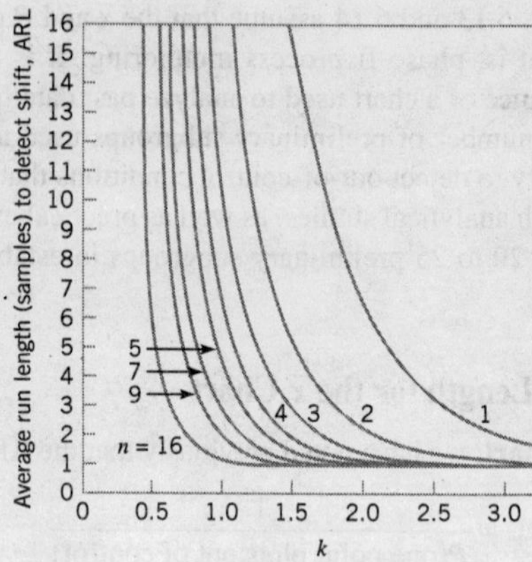

■ **FIGURE 6.15** Average run length (samples) for the $\bar{x}$ chart with three-sigma limits, where the process mean shifts by $k\sigma$. (Adapted from *Modern Methods for Quality Control and Improvement*, by H. M. Wadsworth, K. S. Stephens, and A. B. Godfrey, 2nd edition, John Wiley & Sons, 2002.)

parameters. This results in inflation of both ARL_0 and ARL_1. For example, suppose that the center line of the chart is estimated perfectly, but the process standard deviation is overestimated by 10%. This would result in $ARL_0 = 517$, considerably longer than the nominal or "theoretical" value of 370. With a normally distributed process, we are just as likely to underestimate the process standard deviation by 10%, and this would result in $ARL_0 = 268$, a value considerably shorter than 370. The average is $(268 + 517)/2 = 392.5$, suggesting that errors in estimating the process standard deviation result in ARLs that are overestimated. There is a very comprehensive literature review and discussion of this topic in the paper by Jensen et al. (2006).

Two other performance measures based on ARL are sometimes of interest. The average time to signal is the number of time periods that occur until a signal is generated on the control chart. If samples are taken at equally spaced intervals of time h, then the **average time to signal** or the ATS is

$$\text{ATS} = \text{ARL}\, h \tag{6.22}$$

It may also be useful to express the ARL in terms of the expected number of individual *units* sampled—say, I—rather than the number of samples taken to detect a shift. If the sample size is n, the relationship between I and ARL is

$$I = n\, \text{ARL} \tag{6.23}$$

Figure 6.16 presents a set of curves that plot the expected number of individual units I that must be sampled for the $\bar{x}$ chart to detect a shift of $k\sigma$. To illustrate the use of the curve, note that to detect a shift of 1.5σ, an $\bar{x}$ chart with $n = 16$ will require that approximately 16 units be sampled, whereas if the sample size is $n = 3$, only about 9 units will be required, on the average.

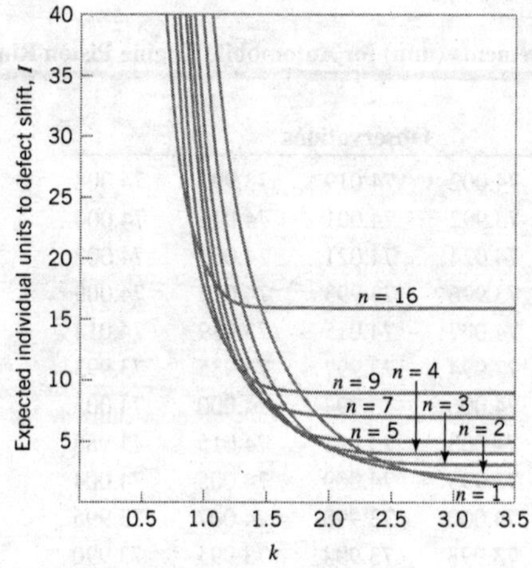

■ **FIGURE 6.16** Average run length (individual units) for the $\bar{x}$ chart with three-sigma limits, where the process mean shifts by $k\sigma$. (Adapted from *Modern Methods for Quality Control and Improvement*, by H. M. Wadsworth, K. S. Stephens, and A. B. Godfrey, 2nd edition, John Wiley & Sons, 2002.)

6.3 Control Charts for $\bar{x}$ and s

Although $\bar{x}$ and R charts are widely used, it is occasionally desirable to estimate the process standard deviation directly instead of indirectly through the use of the range R. This leads to control charts for $\bar{x}$ and s, where s is the sample standard deviation.[1] Generally, $\bar{x}$ and s charts are preferable to their more familiar counterparts, $\bar{x}$ and R charts, when either

1. The sample size n is moderately large—say, $n > 10$ or 12. (Recall that the range method for estimating σ loses statistical efficiency for moderate to large samples.)
2. The sample size n is variable.

In this section, we illustrate the construction and operation of $\bar{x}$ and s control charts. We also show how to deal with variable sample size and discuss an alternative to the s chart.

6.3.1 Construction and Operation of $\bar{x}$ and s Charts

Setting up and operating control charts for $\bar{x}$ and s requires about the same sequence of steps as those for $\bar{x}$ and R charts, except that for each sample we must calculate the sample average $\bar{x}$ and the sample standard deviation s. Table 6.3 presents the inside diameter measurements of forged automobile engine piston rings. Each sample or subgroup consists of five piston rings. We have calculated the sample average and sample standard deviation for each of the 25 samples. We will use these data to illustrate the construction and operation of $\bar{x}$ and s charts.

If σ^2 is the unknown variance of a probability distribution, then an unbiased estimator of σ^2 is the sample variance

$$s^2 = \frac{\sum_{i=1}^{n}(x_i - \bar{x})^2}{n-1}$$

[1]Some authors refer to the s chart as the σ chart.

■ **TABLE 6.3**
Inside Diameter Measurements (mm) for Automobile Engine Piston Rings

Sample Number	Observations					$\bar{x}_i$	s_i
1	74.030	74.002	74.019	73.992	74.008	74.010	0.0148
2	73.995	73.992	74.001	74.011	74.004	74.001	0.0075
3	73.988	74.024	74.021	74.005	74.002	74.008	0.0147
4	74.002	73.996	73.993	74.015	74.009	74.003	0.0091
5	73.992	74.007	74.015	73.989	74.014	74.003	0.0122
6	74.009	73.994	73.997	73.985	73.993	73.996	0.0087
7	73.995	74.006	73.994	74.000	74.005	74.000	0.0055
8	73.985	74.003	73.993	74.015	73.988	73.997	0.0123
9	74.008	73.995	74.009	74.005	74.004	74.004	0.0055
10	73.998	74.000	73.990	74.007	73.995	73.998	0.0063
11	73.994	73.998	73.994	73.995	73.990	73.994	0.0029
12	74.004	74.000	74.007	74.000	73.996	74.001	0.0042
13	73.983	74.002	73.998	73.997	74.012	73.998	0.0105
14	74.006	73.967	73.994	74.000	73.984	73.990	0.0153
15	74.012	74.014	73.998	73.999	74.007	74.006	0.0073
16	74.000	73.984	74.005	73.998	73.996	73.997	0.0078
17	73.994	74.012	73.986	74.005	74.007	74.001	0.0106
18	74.006	74.010	74.018	74.003	74.000	74.007	0.0070
19	73.984	74.002	74.003	74.005	73.997	73.998	0.0085
20	74.000	74.010	74.013	74.020	74.003	74.009	0.0080
21	73.982	74.001	74.015	74.005	73.996	74.000	0.0122
22	74.004	73.999	73.990	74.006	74.009	74.002	0.0074
23	74.010	73.989	73.990	74.009	74.014	74.002	0.0119
24	74.015	74.008	73.993	74.000	74.010	74.005	0.0087
25	73.982	73.984	73.995	74.017	74.013	73.998	0.0162
						$\Sigma =$ 1850.028	0.2351
						$\bar{\bar{x}} =$ 74.001	$\bar{s} = 0.0094$

However, the sample standard deviation s is *not* an unbiased estimator of σ. In Chapter 4 (Section 4.2) we observed that if the underlying distribution is normal, then s actually estimates $c_4\sigma$, where c_4 is a constant that depends on the sample size n. Furthermore, the standard deviation of s is $\sigma\sqrt{1 - c_4^2}$. This information can be used to establish control charts on $\bar{x}$ and s.

Consider the case where a standard value is given for σ. Since $E(s) = c_4\sigma$, the center line for the chart is $c_4\sigma$. The three-sigma control limits for s are then

$$\text{UCL} = c_4\sigma + 3\sigma\sqrt{1-c_4^2}$$
$$\text{LCL} = c_4\sigma - 3\sigma\sqrt{1-c_4^2}$$

It is customary to define the two constants

$$B_5 = c_4 - 3\sqrt{1-c_4^2} \quad \text{and} \quad B_6 = c_4 + 3\sqrt{1-c_4^2} \tag{6.24}$$

Consequently, the parameters of the s chart with a standard value for σ given become

$$\begin{aligned} \text{UCL} &= B_6\sigma \\ \text{Center line} &= c_4\sigma \\ \text{LCL} &= B_5\sigma \end{aligned} \tag{6.25}$$

Values of B_5 and B_6 are tabulated for various sample sizes in Appendix Table VI. The parameters of the corresponding $\bar{x}$ chart are given in equation (6.15), Section 6.2.3.

If no standard is given for σ, then it must be estimated by analyzing past data. Suppose that m preliminary samples are available, each of size n, and let s_i be the standard deviation of the ith sample. The average of the m standard deviations is

$$\bar{s} = \frac{1}{m}\sum_{i=1}^{m} s_i$$

The statistic $\bar{s}/c_4$ is an unbiased estimator of σ. Therefore, the parameters of the s chart would be

$$\begin{aligned} \text{UCL} &= \bar{s} + 3\frac{\bar{s}}{c_4}\sqrt{1-c_4^2} \\ \text{Center line} &= \bar{s} \\ \text{LCL} &= \bar{s} - 3\frac{\bar{s}}{c_4}\sqrt{1-c_4^2} \end{aligned}$$

We usually define the constants

$$B_3 = 1 - \frac{3}{c_4}\sqrt{1-c_4^2} \quad \text{and} \quad B_4 = 1 + \frac{3}{c_4}\sqrt{1-c_4^2} \tag{6.26}$$

Consequently, we may write the parameters of the s chart as

$$\begin{aligned} \text{UCL} &= B_4\bar{s} \\ \text{Center line} &= \bar{s} \\ \text{LCL} &= B_3\bar{s} \end{aligned} \tag{6.27}$$

Note that $B_4 = B_6/c_4$ and $B_3 = B_5/c_4$.

When $\bar{s}/c_4$ is used to estimate σ, we may define the control limits on the corresponding $\bar{x}$ chart as

$$\begin{aligned} \text{UCL} &= \bar{\bar{x}} + \frac{3\bar{s}}{c_4\sqrt{n}} \\ \text{Center line} &= \bar{\bar{x}} \\ \text{LCL} &= \bar{\bar{x}} - \frac{3\bar{s}}{c_4\sqrt{n}} \end{aligned}$$

Let the constant $A_3 = 3/(c_4\sqrt{n})$. Then the $\bar{x}$ chart parameters become

$$\begin{aligned} \text{UCL} &= \bar{\bar{x}} + A_3\bar{s} \\ \text{Center line} &= \bar{\bar{x}} \\ \text{LCL} &= \bar{\bar{x}} - A_3\bar{s} \end{aligned} \tag{6.28}$$

The constants B_3, B_4, and A_3 for construction of $\bar{x}$ and s charts from past data are listed in Appendix Table VI for various sample sizes.

Note that we have assumed that the sample standard deviation is defined as

$$s = \sqrt{\frac{\sum_{i=1}^{n}(x_i - \bar{x})^2}{n-1}} \tag{6.29}$$

Some authors define s with n in the denominator of equation (6.29) instead of $n - 1$. When this is the case, the definitions of the constants c_4, B_3, B_4, and A_3 are altered. The corresponding constants based on the use of n in calculating s are called c_2, B_1, B_2, and A_1, respectively. See Bowker and Lieberman (1972) for their definitions.

Traditionally, quality engineers have preferred the R chart to the s chart because of the simplicity of calculating R from each sample. The availability of hand-held calculators with automatic calculation of s and computers at workstations to implement control charts on site have eliminated any computational difficulty.

EXAMPLE 6.3 $\bar{x}$ and s Charts for the Piston Ring Data

Construct and interpret $\bar{x}$ and s charts using the piston ring inside diameter measurements in Table 6.3.

SOLUTION

The grand average and the average standard deviation are

$$\bar{\bar{x}} = \frac{1}{25}\sum_{i=1}^{25}\bar{x}_i = \frac{1}{25}(1850.028) = 74.001$$

and

$$\bar{s} = \frac{1}{25}\sum_{i=1}^{25}s_i = \frac{1}{25}(0.2351) = 0.0094$$

respectively. Consequently, the parameters for the $\bar{x}$ chart are

$$\begin{aligned} \text{UCL} &= \bar{\bar{x}} + A_3\bar{s} = 74.001 + (1.427)(0.0094) = 74.014 \\ \text{CL} &= \bar{\bar{x}} = 74.001 \\ \text{LCL} &= \bar{\bar{x}} - A_3\bar{s} = 74.001 - (1.427)(0.0094) = 73.988 \end{aligned}$$

and for the s chart

$$\begin{aligned} \text{UCL} &= B_4\bar{s} = (2.089)(0.0094) = 0.0196 \\ \text{CL} &= \bar{s} = 0.0094 \\ \text{LCL} &= B_3\bar{s} = (0)(0.0094) = 0 \end{aligned}$$

The control charts are shown in Fig. 6.17. There is no indication that the process is out of control, so those limits could be adopted for phase II monitoring of the process.

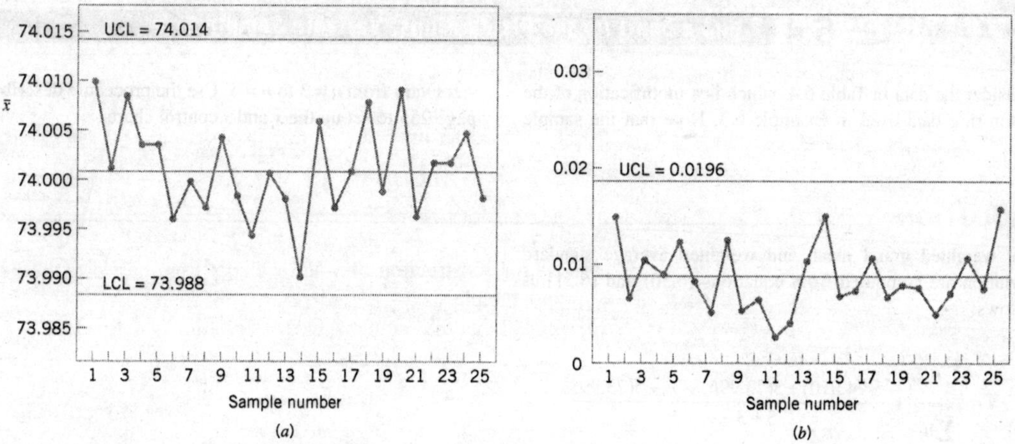

■ FIGURE 6.17 The $\bar{x}$ and s control charts for Example 6.3. (*a*) The $\bar{x}$ chart with control limits based on $\bar{s}$. (*b*) The s control chart.

Estimation of σ. We can estimate the process standard deviation using the fact that s/c_4 is an unbiased estimate of σ. Therefore, since $c_4 = 0.9400$ for samples of size 5, our estimate of the process standard deviation is

$$\hat{\sigma} = \frac{\bar{s}}{c_4} = \frac{0.0094}{0.9400} = 0.01$$

6.3.2 The $\bar{x}$ and s Control Charts with Variable Sample Size

The $\bar{x}$ and s control charts are relatively easy to apply in cases where the sample sizes are variable. In this case, we should use a weighted average approach in calculating $\bar{\bar{x}}$ and $\bar{s}$. If n_i is the number of observations in the ith sample, then use

$$\bar{\bar{x}} = \frac{\sum_{i=1}^{m} n_i \bar{x}_i}{\sum_{i=1}^{m} n_i} \tag{6.30}$$

and

$$\bar{s} = \left[\frac{\sum_{i=1}^{m} (n_i - 1) s_i^2}{\sum_{i=1}^{m} n_i - m} \right]^{1/2} \tag{6.31}$$

as the center lines on the $\bar{x}$ and s control charts, respectively. The control limits would be calculated from equations (6.27) and (6.28), respectively, but the constants A_3, B_3, and B_4 will depend on the sample size used in each individual subgroup.

EXAMPLE 6.4 $\bar{x}$ and s Chart for the Piston Rings, Variable Sample Size

Consider the data in Table 6.4, which is a modification of the piston-ring data used in Example 6.3. Note that the sample sizes vary from $n = 3$ to $n = 5$. Use the procedure described on page 255 to set up the $\bar{x}$ and s control charts.

SOLUTION

The weighted grand mean and weighted average standard deviation are computed from equations (6.30) and (6.31) as follows:

$$\bar{\bar{x}} = \frac{\sum_{i=1}^{25} n_i \bar{x}_i}{\sum_{i=1}^{25} n_i} = \frac{5(74.010)+3(73.996)+\cdots+5(73.998)}{5+3+\cdots+5}$$

$$= \frac{8362.075}{113} = 74.001$$

■ **TABLE 6.4**

Inside Diameter Measurements (mm) on Automobile Engine Piston Rings

Sample Number	Observations					$\bar{x}_i$	s_i
1	74.030	74.002	74.019	73.992	74.008	74.010	0.0148
2	73.995	73.992	74.001			73.996	0.0046
3	73.988	74.024	74.021	74.005	74.002	74.008	0.0147
4	74.002	73.996	73.993	74.015	74.009	74.003	0.0091
5	73.992	74.007	74.015	73.989	74.014	74.003	0.0122
6	74.009	73.994	73.997	73.985		73.996	0.0099
7	73.995	74.006	73.994	74.000		73.999	0.0055
8	73.985	74.003	73.993	74.015	73.988	73.997	0.0123
9	74.008	73.995	74.009	74.005		74.004	0.0064
10	73.998	74.000	73.990	74.007	73.995	73.998	0.0063
11	73.994	73.998	73.994	73.995	73.990	73.994	0.0029
12	74.004	74.000	74.007	74.000	73.996	74.001	0.0042
13	73.983	74.002	73.998			73.994	0.0100
14	74.006	73.967	73.994	74.000	73.984	73.990	0.0153
15	74.012	74.014	73.998			74.008	0.0087
16	74.000	73.984	74.005	73.998	73.996	73.997	0.0078
17	73.994	74.012	73.986	74.005		73.999	0.0115
18	74.006	74.010	74.018	74.003	74.000	74.007	0.0070
19	73.984	74.002	74.003	74.005	73.997	73.998	0.0085
20	74.000	74.010	74.013			74.008	0.0068
21	73.982	74.001	74.015	74.005	73.996	74.000	0.0122
22	74.004	73.999	73.990	74.006	74.009	74.002	0.0074
23	74.010	73.989	73.990	74.009	74.014	74.002	0.0119
24	74.015	74.008	73.993	74.000	74.010	74.005	0.0087
25	73.982	73.984	73.995	74.017	74.013	73.998	0.0162

and

$$\bar{s} = \left[\frac{\sum_{i=1}^{25} (n_i - 1)s_i^2}{\sum_{i=1}^{25} n_i - 25} \right]^{1/2} = \left[\frac{4(0.0148)^2 + 2(0.0046)^2 + \cdots + 4(0.0162)^2}{5+3+\cdots+5-25} \right]^{1/2}$$

$$= \left[\frac{0.009324}{88} \right]^{1/2} = 0.0103$$

Therefore, the center line of the $\bar{x}$ chart is $\bar{\bar{x}} = 74.001$, and the center line of the s chart is $\bar{s} = 0.0103$. The control limits may now be easily calculated. To illustrate, consider the first sample. The limits for the $\bar{x}$ chart are

$$\text{UCL} = 74.001 + (1.427)(0.0103) = 74.016$$
$$\text{CL} = 74.001$$
$$\text{LCL} = 74.001 - (1.427)(0.0103) = 73.986$$

The control limits for the s chart are

$$\text{UCL} = (2.089)(0.0103) = 0.022$$
$$\text{CL} = 0.0103$$
$$\text{LCL} = 0(0.0103) = 0$$

Note that we have used the values of A_3, B_3, and B_4 for $n_1 = 5$. The limits for the second sample would use the values of these constants for $n_2 = 3$. The control limit calculations for all 25 samples are summarized in Table 6.5. The control charts are plotted in Fig. 6.18.

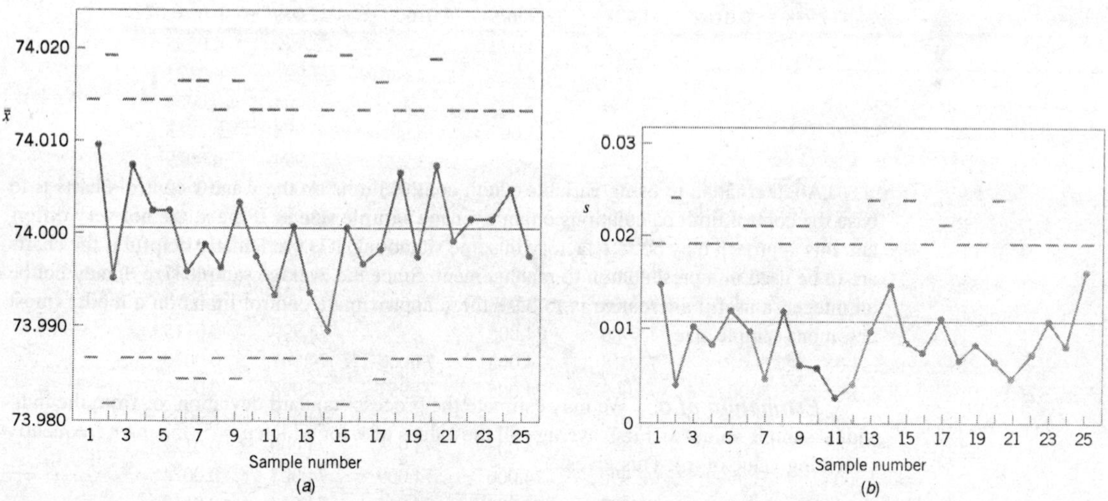

FIGURE 6.18 The (a) $\bar{x}$ and (b) s control charts for piston-ring data with variable sample size, Example 6.4.

(continued)

■ TABLE 6.5
Computation of Control Limits for $\bar{x}$ and s Charts with Variable Sample Size

					$\bar{x}$ Chart				*s* Chart	
Sample	n	$\bar{x}$	s	A_3	LCL	UCL	B_3	B_4	LCL	UCL
1	5	74.010	0.0148	1.427	73.986	74.016	0	2.089	0	0.022
2	3	73.996	0.0046	1.954	73.981	74.021	0	2.568	0	0.026
3	5	74.008	0.0147	1.427	73.986	74.016	0	2.089	0	0.022
4	5	74.003	0.0091	1.427	73.986	74.016	0	2.089	0	0.022
5	5	74.003	0.0122	1.427	73.986	74.016	0	2.089	0	0.022
6	4	73.996	0.0099	1.628	73.984	74.018	0	2.266	0	0.023
7	4	73.999	0.0055	1.628	73.984	74.018	0	2.266	0	0.023
8	5	73.997	0.0123	1.427	73.986	74.016	0	2.089	0	0.022
9	4	74.004	0.0064	1.628	73.984	74.018	0	2.266	0	0.023
10	5	73.998	0.0063	1.427	73.986	74.016	0	2.089	0	0.022
11	5	73.994	0.0029	1.427	73.986	74.016	0	2.089	0	0.022
12	5	74.001	0.0042	1.427	73.986	74.016	0	2.089	0	0.022
13	3	73.994	0.0100	1.954	73.981	74.021	0	2.568	0	0.026
14	5	73.990	0.0153	1.427	73.986	74.016	0	2.089	0	0.022
15	3	74.008	0.0087	1.954	73.981	74.021	0	2.568	0	0.026
16	5	73.997	0.0078	1.427	73.986	74.016	0	2.089	0	0.022
17	4	73.999	0.0115	1.628	73.984	74.018	0	2.226	0	0.023
18	5	74.007	0.0070	1.427	73.986	74.016	0	2.089	0	0.022
19	5	73.998	0.0085	1.427	73.986	74.016	0	2.089	0	0.022
20	3	74.008	0.0068	1.954	73.981	74.021	0	2.568	0	0.026
21	5	74.000	0.0122	1.427	73.986	74.016	0	2.089	0	0.022
22	5	74.002	0.0074	1.427	73.986	74.016	0	2.089	0	0.022
23	5	74.002	0.0119	1.427	73.986	74.016	0	2.089	0	0.022
24	5	74.005	0.0087	1.427	73.986	74.016	0	2.089	0	0.022
25	5	73.998	0.0162	1.427	73.986	74.016	0	2.089	0	0.022

An alternative to using variable-width control limits on the $\bar{x}$ and s control charts is to base the control limit calculations on an **average sample size $\bar{n}$.** If the n_i are not very different, this approach may be satisfactory in some situations; it is particularly helpful if the charts are to be used in a presentation to management. Since the average sample size n_i may not be an integer, a useful alternative is to base these approximate control limits on a modal (most common) sample size.

Estimation of σ. We may estimate the process standard deviation, σ, from the individual sample values s_i. First, average all the values of s_i for which $n_i = 5$ (the most frequently occurring value of n_i). This gives

$$\bar{s} = \frac{0.1715}{17} = 0.0101$$

The estimate of the process σ is then

$$\hat{\sigma} = \frac{\bar{s}}{c_4} = \frac{0.0101}{0.9400} = 0.01$$

where the value of c_4 used is for samples of size $n = 5$.

6.3.3 The s^2 Control Chart

Most quality engineers use either the R chart or the s chart to monitor process variability, with s preferable to R for moderate to large sample sizes. Some practitioners recommend a control chart based directly on the sample variance s^2, the **s^2 control chart.** The parameters for the s^2 control chart are

$$\begin{aligned} \text{UCL} &= \frac{\bar{s}^2}{n-1}\chi^2_{\alpha/2,n-1} \\ \text{Center line} &= \bar{s}^2 \\ \text{LCL} &= \frac{\bar{s}^2}{n-1}\chi^2_{1-(\alpha/2),n-1} \end{aligned} \tag{6.32}$$

where $\chi^2_{\alpha/2,}$ and $\chi^2_{(\alpha/2),n-1}$ denote the upper and lower $\alpha/2$ percentage points of the chi-square distribution with $n - 1$ degrees of freedom, and $\bar{s}^2$ is an average sample variance obtained from the analysis of preliminary data. A standard value σ^2 could be used in equation (6.32) instead of $\bar{s}^2$ if one were available. Note that this control chart is defined with probability limits.

6.4 The Shewhart Control Chart for Individual Measurements

There are many situations in which the sample size used for process monitoring is $n = 1$; that is, the sample consists of an individual unit. Some examples of these situations are as follows:

1. Automated inspection and measurement technology is used, and every unit manufactured is analyzed so there is no basis for rational subgrouping.
2. Data comes available relatively slowly, and it is inconvenient to allow sample sizes of $n > 1$ to accumulate before analysis. The long interval between observations will cause problems with rational subgrouping. This occurs frequently in both manufacturing and nonmanufacturing situations.
3. Repeat measurements on the process differ only because of laboratory or analysis error, as in many chemical processes.
4. Multiple measurements are taken on the same unit of product, such as measuring oxide thickness at several different locations on a wafer in semiconductor manufacturing.
5. In process plants, such as papermaking, measurements on some parameter such as coating thickness *across* the roll will differ very little and produce a standard deviation that is much too small if the objective is to control coating thickness *along* the roll.

In such situations, the **control chart for individual units** is useful. (The cumulative sum and exponentially weighted moving-average control charts discussed in Chapter 9 will be a better alternative in phase II or when the magnitude of the shift in process mean that is of interest is small.) In many applications of the *individuals control chart*, we use the *moving range* two successive observations as the basis of estimating the process variability. The moving range is defined as

$$\text{MR}_i = |x_i - x_{i-1}|$$

It is also possible to establish a **moving range control chart.** The procedure is illustrated in the following example.

EXAMPLE 6.5 Loan Processing Costs

The mortgage loan processing unit of a bank monitors the costs of processing loan applications. The quantity tracked is the average weekly processing costs, obtained by dividing total weekly costs by the number of loans processed during the week. The processing costs for the most recent 20 weeks are shown in Table 6.6. Set up individual and moving range control charts for these data.

SOLUTION

To set up the control chart for individual observations, note that the sample average cost of the 20 observations is $\bar{x} = 300.5$ and that the average of the moving ranges of two observations is $\overline{\text{MR}} = 7.79$. To set up the moving range chart, we use $D_3 = 0$ and $D_4 = 3.267$ for $n = 2$. Therefore, the moving range chart has center line $\overline{\text{MR}} = 7.79$, LCL = 0, and $\text{UCL} = D_4\overline{\text{MR}} = (3.267)7.79 = 25.45$. The control chart (from Minitab) is shown in Fig. 6.19*b*. Notice that no points are out of control.

For the control chart for individual measurements, the parameters are

$$\begin{aligned} \text{UCL} &= \bar{x} + 3\frac{\overline{\text{MR}}}{d_2} \\ \text{Center line} &= \bar{x} \\ \text{LCL} &= \bar{x} - 3\frac{\overline{\text{MR}}}{d_2} \end{aligned} \qquad (6.33)$$

■ **TABLE 6.6**
Costs of Processing Mortgage Loan Applications

Weeks	Cost x	Moving Range MR
1	310	
2	288	22
3	297	9
4	298	1
5	307	9
6	303	4
7	294	9
8	297	3
9	308	11
10	306	2
11	294	12
12	299	5
13	297	2
14	299	2
15	314	15
16	295	19
17	293	2
18	306	13
19	301	5
20	304	3
	$\bar{x} = 300.5$	$\overline{\text{MR}} = 7.79$

If a moving range of $n = 2$ observations is used, then $d_2 = 1.128$. For the data in Table 6.6, we have

$$\text{UCL} = \bar{x} + 3\frac{\overline{\text{MR}}}{d_2} = 300.5 + 3\frac{7.79}{1.128} = 321.22$$

$$\text{Center line} = \bar{x} = 34.088$$

$$\text{LCL} = \bar{x} - 3\frac{\overline{\text{MR}}}{d_2} = 300.5 - 3\frac{7.79}{1.128} = 279.78$$

The control chart for individual cost values is shown in Fig. 6.19*a*. There are no out of control observations on the individuals control chart.

The interpretation of the individuals control chart is very similar to the interpretation of the ordinary $\bar{x}$ control chart. A shift in the process mean will result in a single point or a series of points that plot outside the control limits on the control chart for individuals. Sometimes a point will plot outside the control limits on both the individuals chart and the moving range chart. This will often occur because a large value of x will also lead to a large value of the moving range for that sample. This is very typical behavior for the individuals and moving range control charts. It is most likely an indication that the mean is out of control and not an indication that both the mean and the variance of the process are out of control.

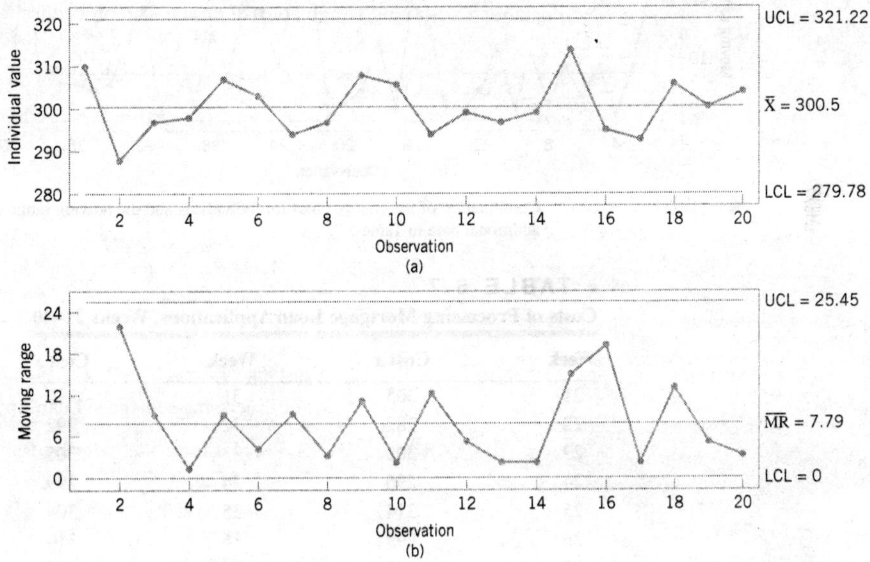

■ FIGURE 6.19 Control charts for (*a*) individual observations on cost and for (*b*) the moving range.

Phase II Operation and Interpretation of the Charts. Table 6.7 contains data on mortgage application processing costs for weeks 21–40. These data are plotted in Fig. 6.20 on the continuation of the control chart for individuals and the moving range control chart developed in Example 6.5. As this figure makes clear, an upward shift in cost has occurred around week 39, since there is an obvious "shift in process level" pattern on the chart for individuals followed by another out-of-control signal at week 40. Note that the moving range chart also reacts to this level shift with a single large spike at week 39. This spike on the moving range chart is sometimes helpful in identifying exactly where a process shift in the mean has occurred. Clearly one should look for possible assignable causes around week 39. Possible causes could include an unusual number of applications requiring additional manual underwriting work, or possibly new underwriters working in the process, or possibly temporary underwriters replacing regular employees taking vacations.

Some care should be exercised in interpreting patterns on the moving range chart. The moving ranges are correlated, and this correlation may often induce a pattern of runs or cycles

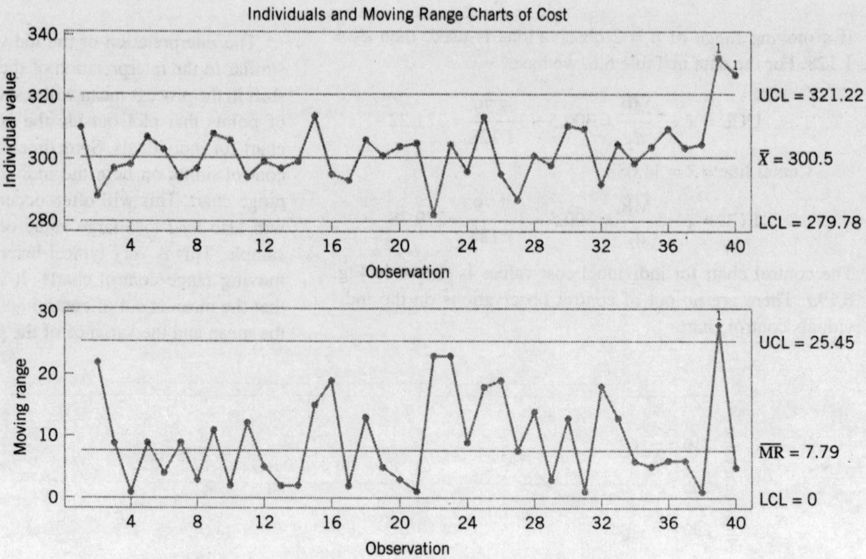

■ FIGURE 6.20 Continuation of the control chart for individuals and the moving range using the additional data in Table 6.7.

■ TABLE 6.7
Costs of Processing Mortgage Loan Applications, Weeks 21–40

Week	Cost x	Week	Cost x
21	305	31	310
22	282	32	292
23	305	33	305
24	296	34	299
25	314	35	304
26	295	36	310
27	287	37	304
28	301	38	305
29	298	39	333
30	311	40	328

on the chart. Such a pattern is evident on the moving range chart in Fig. 6.21. The individual measurements on the x chart are assumed to be uncorrelated, however, and any apparent pattern on this chart should be carefully investigated.

Some authorities have recommended not constructing and plotting the moving range chart. They point out (correctly, we add) that the moving range chart cannot really provide useful information about a shift in process variability. For example, see Rigdon, Cruthis, and Champ (1994). In effect, shifts in the process mean also show up on the moving range chart. Our feeling is that as long as the analyst is careful in interpretation and relies primarily on the individuals chart, little trouble will ensue from plotting both charts.

Average Run Lengths. Crowder (1987b) has studied the average run length of the combined control chart for individuals and moving range chart. He produces ARLs for various settings of the control limits and shifts in the process mean and standard deviation. In general, his work shows that the ARL_0 of the combined procedure will generally be much less than the ARL_0 of a standard Shewhart control chart when the process is in control (recall that ARL_0 for a

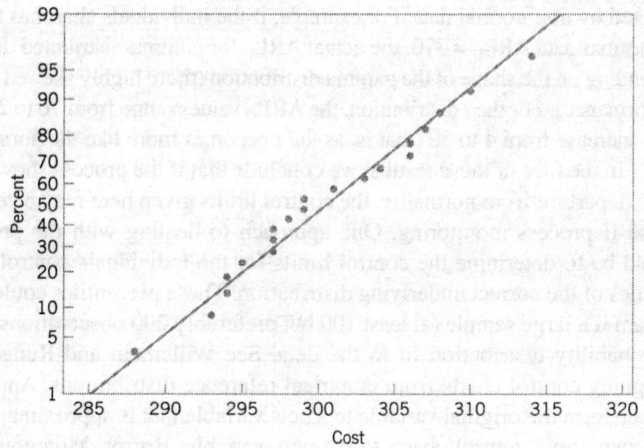

■ FIGURE 6.21 Normal probability plot of the mortgage application processing cost data from Table 6.6, Example 6.5.

Shewhart chart is 370 samples), if we use the conventional three-sigma limits on the charts. In general, results closer to the Shewhart in-control ARL are obtained if we use three-sigma limits on the chart for individuals and compute the upper control limit on the moving range chart from

$$\text{UCL} = D\overline{MR}$$

where the constant D should be chosen such that $4 \le D \le 5$.

One can get a very good idea about the ability of the individuals control chart to detect process shifts by looking at the OC curves in Fig. 6.13 or the ARL curves in Fig. 6.15. For an individuals control chart with three-sigma limits, we can compute the following:

Size of Shift	β	ARL_1
1σ	0.9772	43.96
2σ	0.8413	6.30
3σ	0.5000	2.00

Note that the ability of the individuals control chart to detect small shifts is very poor. For instance, consider a continuous chemical process in which samples are taken every hour. If a shift in the process mean of about one standard deviation occurs, the information above tells us that it will take about 44 samples, on the average, to detect the shift. This is nearly two full days of continuous production in the out-of-control state, a situation that has potentially devastating economic consequences. This limits the usefulness of the individuals control chart in phase II process monitoring.

Some individuals have suggested that control limits narrower than three-sigma be used on the chart for individuals to enhance its ability to detect small process shifts. This is a dangerous suggestion, as narrower limits will dramatically reduce the value of ARL_0 and increase the occurrence of false alarms to the point where the charts are ignored and hence become useless. If we are interested in detecting small shifts in phase II, then the correct approach is to use either the cumulative sum control chart or the exponentially weighted moving average control chart (see Chapter 9).

Normality. Our discussion in this section has made an assumption that the observations follow a normal distribution. Borror, Montgomery, and Runger (1999) have studied the phase II performance of the Shewhart control chart for individuals when the process data are not normal. They investigated various gamma distributions to represent skewed process data and t distributions to represent symmetric normal-like data. They found that the in-control ARL is dramatically affected by non-normal data. For example, if the individuals chart has three-sigma limits so that for normal data $ARL_0 = 370$, the actual ARL_0 for gamma-distributed data is between 45 and 97, depending on the shape of the gamma distribution (more highly skewed distributions yield poorer performance). For the t distribution, the ARL_0 values range from 76 to 283 as the degrees of freedom increase from 4 to 50 (that is, as the t becomes more like the normal distribution).

In the face of these results, we conclude that if the process shows evidence of even moderate departure from normality, the control limits given here may be entirely inappropriate for phase II process monitoring. One approach to dealing with the problem of non-normality would be to determine the control limits for the individuals control chart based on the percentiles of the correct underlying distribution. These percentiles could be obtained from a histogram if a large sample (at least 100 but preferably 200 observations) were available, or from a probability distribution fit to the data. See Willemain and Runger (1996) for details on designing control charts from empirical reference distributions. Another approach would be to transform the original variable to a new variable that is approximately normally distributed, and then apply control charts to the new variable. Borror, Montgomery, and Runger (1999) show how a properly designed EWMA control chart is very insensitive to the normality assumption. This approach will be discussed in Chapter 9.

It is important to check the normality assumption when using the control chart for individuals. A simple way to do this is with the normal probability plot. Figure 6.21 is the normal probability plot for the mortgage application processing cost data in Table 6.6. There is no obvious problem with the normality assumption in these data. However, remember that the normal probability plot is but a **crude check** of the normality assumption and the individuals control chart is very sensitive to non-normality. Furthermore, mean shifts could show up as a problem with normality on the normal probability plot. Process stability is needed to properly interpret the plot. We suggest that the Shewhart individuals chart be used with extreme caution, particularly in phase II process monitoring.

EXAMPLE 6.6 The Use of Transformations

Table 6.8 presents consecutive measurements on the resistivity of 25 silicon wafers after an epitaxial layer is deposited in a single-wafer deposition process. Construct an individuals control chart for this process.

TABLE 6.8
Resistivity Data for Example 6.6

Sample, i	Resistivity (x_i)	ln (x_i)	MR	Sample, i	Resistivity (x_i)	ln (x_i)	MR
1	216	5.37528		14	242	5.48894	0.23791
2	290	5.66988	0.29460	15	168	5.12396	0.36498
3	236	5.46383	0.20605	16	360	5.88610	0.76214
4	228	5.42935	0.03448	17	226	5.42053	0.46557
5	244	5.49717	0.06782	18	253	5.53339	0.11286
6	210	5.34711	0.15006	19	380	5.94017	0.40678
7	139	4.93447	0.41264	20	131	4.87520	1.06497
8	310	5.73657	0.80210	21	173	5.15329	0.27809
9	240	5.48064	0.25593	22	224	5.41165	0.25836
10	211	5.35186	0.12878	23	195	5.27300	0.13865
11	175	5.16479	0.18707	24	199	5.29330	0.02030
12	447	6.10256	0.93777	25	226	5.42053	0.12723
13	307	5.72685	0.37571				
						$\overline{\ln (x_i)} = 5.44402$	$\overline{MR} = 0.33712$

SOLUTION

A normal probability plot of the resistivity measurements is shown in Fig. 6.22. This plot was constructed by Minitab, which fits the line to the points by least squares (not the best method). It is clear from inspection of the normal probability plot that the normality assumption for resistivity is at best questionable, so it would be dangerous to apply an individuals control chart to the original process data.

Figure 6.22 indicates that the distribution of resistivity has a long tail to the right, and consequently we would expect the log transformation (or a similar transformation) to produce a distribution that is closer to normal. The natural log of resistivity is shown in column three of Table 6.8, and the normal probability plot of the natural log of resistivity is shown in Fig. 6.23. Clearly the log transformation has resulted in a new variable that is more nearly approximated by a normal distribution than were the original resistivity measurements.

The last column of Table 6.8 shows the moving ranges of the natural log of resistivity. Figure 6.24 presents the individuals and moving range control charts for the natural log of resistivity. Note that there is no indication of an out-of-control process.

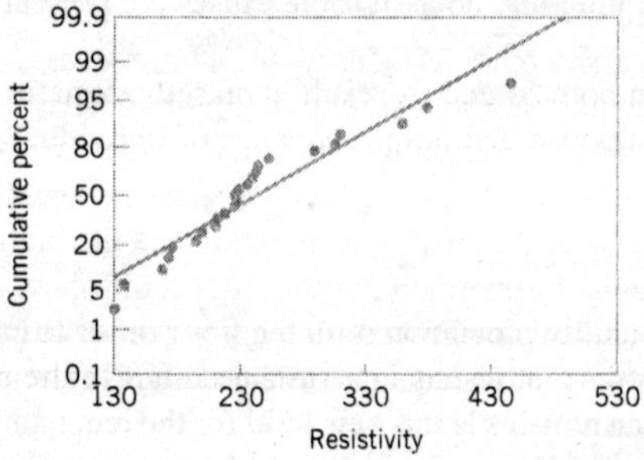

■ FIGURE 6.22 Normal probability plot of resistivity.

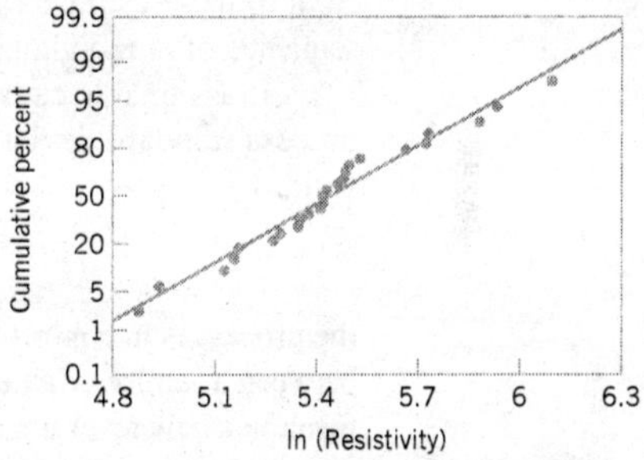

■ FIGURE 6.23 Normal probability plot of ln (resistivity).

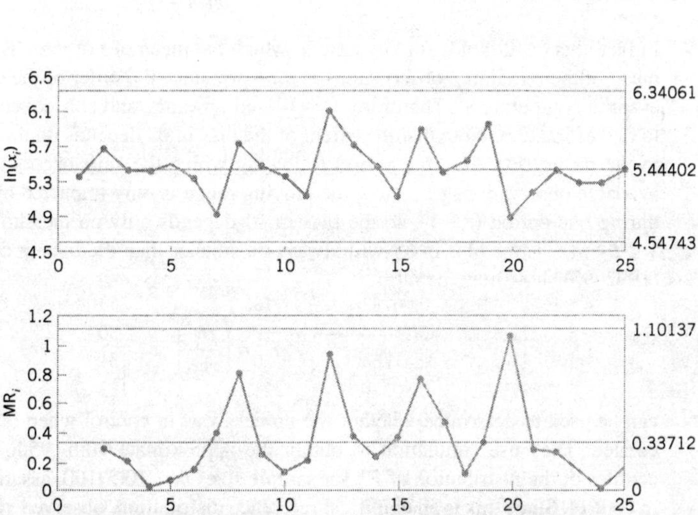

■ FIGURE 6.24 Individuals and moving range control charts on ln (resistivity), Example 6.6

More about Estimating σ. Very often in practice we use moving ranges in estimating σ for the individuals control chart. Recall that moving ranges are defined as $MR_i = |(x_i - x_{i-1})|$, $i = 2, 3 \ldots, m$. More properly, this statistic should be called a moving range of **span two** since the number of observations used to calculate the range in the moving window could be increased. The most common estimator is the one we used in Example 6.5, based on the **average moving range** $\overline{MR} = \sum_{i=2}^{m} MR_i/(m-1)$ and can be written as

$$\hat{\sigma}_1 = 0.8865\overline{MR}$$

where the constant 0.8865 is the reciprocal of d_2 for samples of size 2. For in-control processes, Cryer and Ryan (1990), among others, have pointed out that a more efficient estimator is one based on the sample standard deviation

$$\hat{\sigma}_2 = \frac{s}{c_4}$$

Both of these estimators are unbiased, assuming that no assignable causes are present in the sequence of m individual observations.

If assignable causes are present, then both $\hat{\sigma}_1$ and $\hat{\sigma}_2$ result in biased estimates of the process standard deviation. To illustrate, suppose that in the sequence of individual observations

$$x_1, x_2, \ldots, x_t, x_{t+1}, \ldots, x_m$$

the process is in control with mean μ_0 and standard deviation σ for the first t observations, but between x_t and x_{t+1} an assignable cause occurs that results in a sustained shift in the process mean to a new level $\mu = \mu_0 + \delta\sigma$ and the mean remains at this new level for the remaining sample observations $x_t + 1, \ldots, x_m$. Under these conditions, Woodall and Montgomery (2000–01) show that

$$E\left(s^2\right) = \sigma^2 + \frac{t(m-1)}{m(m-1)}(\delta\sigma)^2$$

In fact, this result holds for any case in which the mean of t of the observations is μ_0 and the mean of the remaining observations is $\mu_0 + \delta\sigma$, since the order of the observations is not relevant in computing s^2. Therefore, s^2 is biased upwards, and consequently $\hat{\sigma}_2 = S/c_4$ will tend to overestimate σ. Note that the extent of the bias in $\hat{\sigma}_2$ depends on the magnitude of the shift in the mean ($\delta\sigma$), the time period following which the shift occurs (t), and the number of available observations (m). Now the moving range is only impacted by the shift in the mean during one period ($t + 1$), so the bias in $\hat{\sigma}_1$ depends only on the shift magnitude and m. If $1 < t < m - 1$, the bias in $\hat{\sigma}_1$ will always be smaller than the bias in $\hat{\sigma}_2$. Cruthis and Rigdon (1992–93) show how the ratio

$$F^* = \left(\frac{\hat{\sigma}_1}{\hat{\sigma}_2}\right)^2$$

can be used to determine whether the process was in control when both estimates were calculated. They use simulation to obtain the approximate 90th, 95th, 99th, and 99.9th percentiles of the distribution of F^* for sample sizes $m = 10(5)100$, assuming that the process is in control. Since this is an empirical reference distribution, observed values of F^* that exceed one of these percentiles is an indication that the process was not in control over the time period during which the m observations were collected.

One way to reduce or possibly eliminate the bias in estimating σ when a sustained shift in the mean is present is to base the estimator on the **median** of the moving ranges of span two, as suggested by Clifford (1959) and Bryce, Gaudard, and Joiner (1997–98). This estimator is

$$\hat{\sigma}_3 = 1.047\overline{\text{MR}}$$

where $\overline{\text{MR}}$ is the median of the span-two moving ranges, and 1.047 is the reciprocal of the control chart constant d_4 for subgroups of size two defined such that $E(\tilde{R}) = d_4\sigma$ and $\tilde{R}$ is the median range. A table of d_4 values is in Wadsworth, Stephens, and Godfrey (2002). Essentially, only one of the span-two moving ranges should be affected by the sustained shift, and this single large moving range will have little impact on the value of the median moving range, certainly much less impact than it will have on the average moving range. Constructing an individuals control chart using the median moving range to estimate σ is an option in Minitab.

Now suppose that the assignable cause affects a single observation rather than causing a sustained shift in the mean. If there is a single observation that has mean $\mu_0 + \delta\sigma$, then

$$E\left(s^2\right) = \sigma^2 + \frac{1}{m}(\delta\sigma)^2$$

and this observation will affect two of the span-two moving ranges. If there are two adjacent such observations, then

$$E\left(s^2\right) = \sigma^2 + \frac{2(m-2)}{m(m-1)}(\delta\sigma)^2$$

and two of the span-two moving ranges will be affected by the out-of-control observations. Thus, when the assignable cause affects one or only a few adjacent observations, we expect the bias in s^2 to be smaller than when a sustained shift occurs. However, if an assignable cause producing a sustained shift in the mean occurs either very early in the sequence of observations or very late, it will produce much the same effect as an assignable cause affecting only one or a few adjacent points.

Some authors have suggested basing the estimate of σ on moving ranges of span greater than two, and some computer programs for control charts offer this as an option. It is easy to show that this will always lead to potentially increased bias in the estimate of σ when assignable causes are present. Note that if one uses a span-three moving range and there is a single observation whose mean is affected by the assignable cause, then this single observation will affect up to three of the moving ranges. Thus, a span-three moving range will result in more bias in the estimate of σ than will the moving range of span two. Furthermore, two span-three moving ranges will be affected by a sustained shift. In general, if one uses a span-w moving range and there is a single observation whose mean is affected by the assignable cause, up to w of these moving ranges will be impacted by this observation. Furthermore, if there is a sustained shift in the mean, up to $w - 1$ of the moving ranges will be affected by the shift in the mean. Consequently, increasing the span of a moving average beyond two results in increasing the bias in the estimate of σ if assignable causes that either produce sustained shifts in the process mean or that affect the mean of a single observation (or a few adjacent ones) are present. In fact, Wetherill and Brown (1991) advise plotting the estimate of σ versus the span of the moving average used to obtain the estimate. A sharply rising curve indicates the presence of assignable causes. For more discussion of using ranges to estimate process variability, see Woodall and Montgomery (2000–01).

■ TABLE 6.9
Formulas for Control Charts, Standards Given

Chart	Center Line	Control Limits
$\bar{x}$ (μ and σ given)	μ	$\mu \pm A\sigma$
R (σ given)	$d_2\sigma$	UCL $= D_2\sigma$, LCL $= D_1\sigma$
s (σ given)	$c_4\sigma$	UCL $= B_6\sigma$, LCL $= B_5\sigma$

■ TABLE 6.10
Formulas for Control Charts, Control Limits Based on Past Data (No Standards Given)

Chart	Center Line	Control Limits
$\bar{x}$ (using R)	$\bar{\bar{x}}$	$\bar{\bar{x}} \pm A_2\bar{R}$
$\bar{x}$ (using s)	$\bar{\bar{x}}$	$\bar{\bar{x}} \pm A_3 S$
R	$\bar{R}$	UCL $= D_4\bar{R}$, LCL $= D_3\bar{R}$
s	$\bar{s}$	UCL $= B_4\bar{s}$, LCL $= B_3\bar{s}$

6.5 Summary of Procedures for $\bar{x}$, R, And s Charts

It is convenient to summarize in one place the various computational formulas for the major types of variables control charts discussed in this chapter. Table 6.9 summarizes the formulas for $\bar{x}$, R, and s charts when standard values for μ and σ are given. Table 6.10 provides the corresponding summary when no standard values are given and trial control limits must be established from analysis of past data. The constants given for the s chart assume that $n - 1$ is used in the denominator of s. All constants are tabulated for various sample sizes in Appendix Table VI.

6.6 Applications of Variables Control Charts

There are many interesting applications of variables control charts. In this section, a few of them will be described to give additional insights into how the control chart works, as well as ideas for further applications.

EXAMPLE 6.7 Using Control Charts to Improve Suppliers' Processes

A large aerospace manufacturer purchased an aircraft component from two suppliers. These components frequently exhibited excessive variability on a key dimension that made it impossible to assemble them into the final product. This problem always resulted in expensive rework costs and occasionally caused delays in finishing the assembly of an airplane.

The materials receiving group performed 100% inspection of these parts in an effort to improve the situation. They maintained $\bar{x}$ and R charts on the dimension of interest for both suppliers. They found that the fraction of nonconforming units was about the same for both suppliers, but for very different reasons. Supplier A could produce parts with mean dimension equal to the required value, but the process was out of statistical control. Supplier B could maintain good statistical control and, in general, produced a part that exhibited considerably less variability than parts from supplier A, but its process was centered so far off the nominal required dimension that many parts were out of specification.

This situation convinced the procurement organization to work with both suppliers, persuading supplier A to implement SPC and to begin working at continuous improvement, and assisting supplier B to find out why his process was consistently centered incorrectly. Supplier B's problem was ultimately tracked to some incorrect code in an NC (numerical-controlled) machine, and the use of SPC at supplier A resulted in considerable reduction in variability over a six-month period. As a result of these actions, the problem with these parts was essentially eliminated.

EXAMPLE 6.8 Using SPC to Purchase a Machine Tool

An article in *Manufacturing Engineering* ("Picking a Marvel at Deere," January 1989, pp. 74–77) describes how the John Deere Company uses SPC methods to help choose production equipment. When a machine tool is purchased, it must go through the company capability demonstration prior to shipment to demonstrate that the tool has the ability to meet or exceed the established performance criteria. The procedure was applied to a programmable controlled bandsaw. The bandsaw supplier cut 45 pieces that were analyzed using $\bar{x}$ and R charts to demonstrate statistical control and to provide the basis for process capability analysis. The saw proved capable, and the supplier learned many useful things about the performance of his equipment. Control and capability tests such as this one are a basic part of the equipment selection and acquisition process in many companies.

EXAMPLE 6.9 SPC Implementation in a Short-Run Job-Shop

One of the more interesting aspects of SPC is the successful implementation of control charts in a job-shop manufacturing environment. Most job-shops are characterized by short production runs, and many of these shops produce parts on production runs of fewer than 50 units. This situation can make the routine use of control charts appear to be somewhat of a challenge, as not enough units are produced in any one batch to establish the control limits.

This problem can usually be easily solved. Since statistical process-control methods are most frequently applied to a characteristic of a product, we can extend SPC to the job-shop environment by focusing on the **process characteristic** in each unit of product. To illustrate, consider a drilling operation in a job-shop. The operator drills holes of various sizes in each part passing through the machine center. Some parts require one hole, and others several holes of different sizes. It is almost impossible to construct an $\bar{x}$ and R chart on hole diameter, since each part is potentially different. The correct approach is to focus on the characteristic of interest in the *process*. In this case, the manufacturer is interested in drilling holes that have the correct diameter, and therefore wants to reduce the variability in hole diameter as much as possible. This may be accomplished by control charting the *deviation* of the actual hole diameter from the nominal diameter. Depending on the process production rate and the mix of parts produced, either a control chart for individuals with a moving range control chart or a conventional $\bar{x}$ and R chart can be used. In these applications, it is usually important to mark the start of each lot or to batch carefully on the control chart, so that if changing the size, position, or number of holes drilled on each part affects the process the resulting pattern on the control charts will be easy to interpret.

EXAMPLE 6.10 Use of $\bar{x}$ and R Charts in Transactional and Service Businesses

Variables control charts have found frequent application in both manufacturing and nonmanufacturing settings. A fairly widespread but erroneous notion about these charts is that they do not apply to the nonmanufacturing environment because the "product is different." Actually, if we can make measurements on the product that are reflective of quality, function, or performance, then the *nature* of the product has no bearing on the general applicability of control charts. There are, however, two commonly encountered differences between manufacturing and transactional/service business situations: (1) In the nonmanufacturing environment, specification limits rarely apply to the product, so the notion of process capability is often undefined; and (2) more imagination may be required to select the proper variable or variables for measurement.

One application of $\bar{x}$ and R control charts in a transactional business environment involved the efforts of a finance group to reduce the time required to process its accounts payable. The division of the company in which the problem occurred had recently experienced a considerable increase in business volume, and along with this expansion came a gradual lengthening of the time the finance department needed to process check requests. As a result, many suppliers were being paid beyond the normal 30-day period, and the company was failing to capture the discounts available from its suppliers for prompt payment. The quality-improvement team assigned to this project used the flow time through the finance department as the variable for control chart analysis. Five completed check requests were selected each day, and the average and range of flow time were plotted on $\bar{x}$ and R charts. Although management and operating personnel had addressed this problem before, the use of $\bar{x}$ and R charts was responsible for substantial improvements. Within nine months, the finance department had reduced the percentage of invoices paid late from over 90% to under 3%, resulting in an annual savings of several hundred thousand dollars in realized discounts to the company.

EXAMPLE 6.11 The Need for Care in Selecting Rational Subgroups

Figure 6.25*a* shows a casting used in a gas turbine jet aircraft engine. This part is typical of those produced by both casting and machining processes for use in gas turbine engines and auxiliary power units in the aerospace industry—cylindrical parts created by rotating the cross section around a central axis. The vane height on this part is a critical quality characteristic.

Data on vane heights are collected by randomly selecting five vanes on each casting produced. Initially, the company constructed $\bar{x}$ and *s* control charts on these data to control and improve the process. This usually produced many out-of-control points on the $\bar{x}$ chart, with an occasional out-of-control point on the *s* chart. Figure 6.26 shows typical $\bar{x}$ and *s* charts for 20 castings. A more careful analysis of the control-charting procedure revealed that the chief problem was the use of the five measurements on a single part as a rational subgroup, and that the out-of-control conditions on the $\bar{x}$ chart did not provide a valid basis for corrective action.

Remember that the control chart for $\bar{x}$ deals with the issue of whether or not the between-sample variability is consistent with the within-sample variability. In this case it is not: The vanes on a single casting are formed together in a common wax mold assembly. It is likely that the vane heights on a specific casting will be very similar, and it is reasonable to believe that there will be more variation in average vane height between the castings.

This situation was handled by using the *s* chart in the ordinary way to measure variation in vane height. However, as this

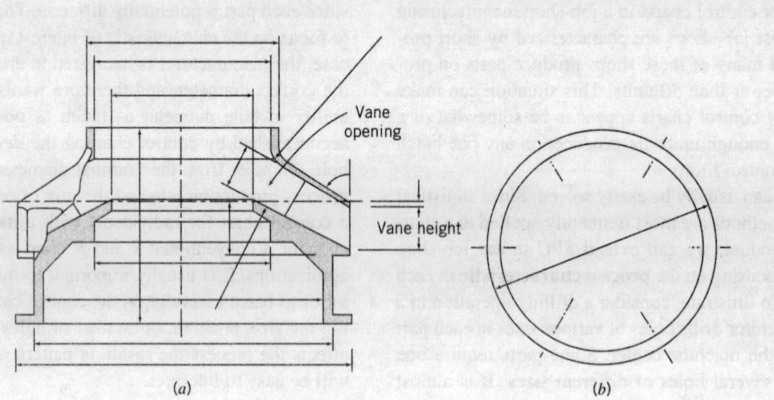

■ FIGURE 6.25 An aerospace casting.

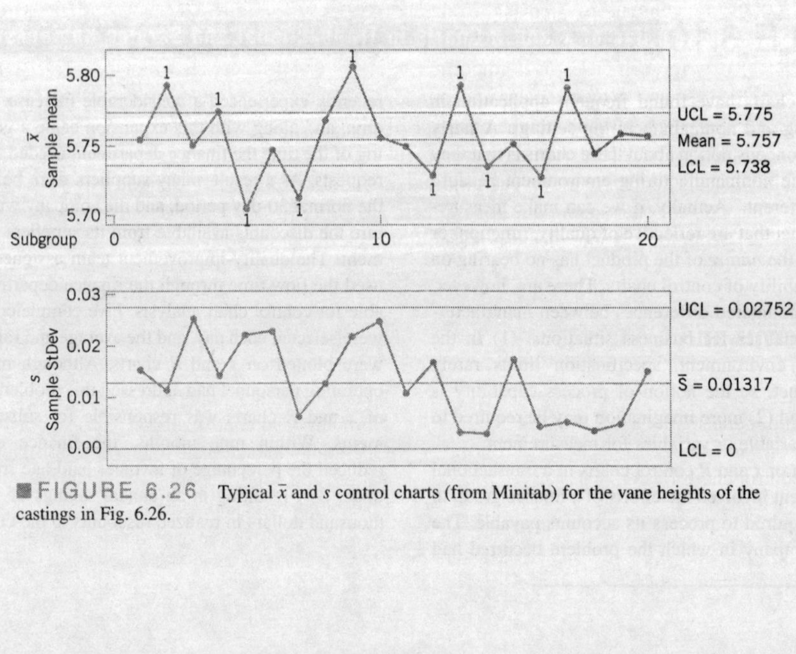

■ FIGURE 6.26 Typical $\bar{x}$ and *s* control charts (from Minitab) for the vane heights of the castings in Fig. 6.26.

standard deviation is clearly too small to provide a valid basis for control of $\bar{x}$, the quality engineer at the company decided to treat the average vane height on each casting as an *individual measurement* and to control average vane height by using a control chart for individuals with a moving range chart. This solution worked extremely well in practice, and the group of three control charts provided an excellent basis for process improvement.

Figure 6.27 shows this set of three control charts as generated by Minitab. The Minitab package generates these charts automatically, referring to them as "between/within" control charts. Note that the individuals chart exhibits control, whereas the $\bar{x}$ chart in Fig. 6.26 did not. Essentially, the moving range of the average vane heights provides a much more reasonable estimate of the variability in height **between parts.** The *s* chart can be thought of as a measure of the variability in vane height on a single casting. We want this variability to be as small as possible, so that all vanes on the same part will be nearly identical. The paper by Woodall and Thomas (1995) is a good reference on this general subject.

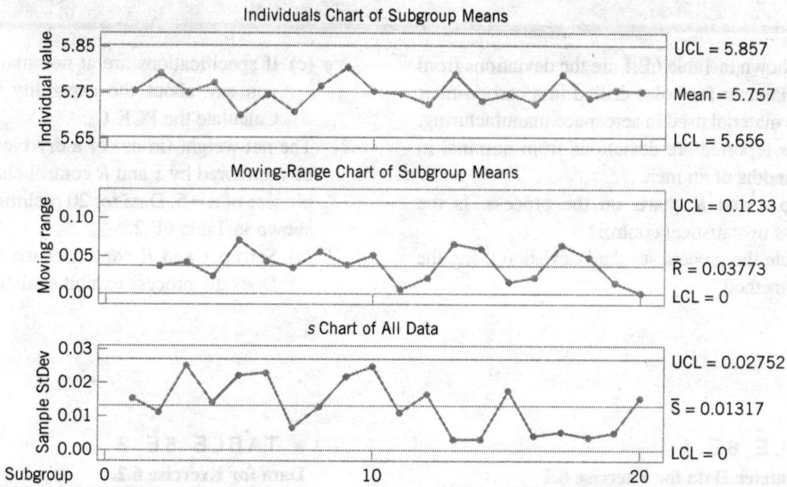

■ FIGURE 6.27 Individuals, moving-range, and *s* control charts for the vane heights of the castings in Fig. 6.25.

Situations such as the one described in Example 6.11 occur frequently in the application of control charts. For example, there are many similar problems in the semiconductor industry. In such cases, it is important to study carefully the behavior of the variables being measured and to have a clear understanding of the purpose of the control charts. For instance, if the variation in vane height on a specific casting were completely unrelated, using the average height as an individual measurement could be very inappropriate. It would be necessary to (1) use a control chart on each individual vane included in the sample, (2) investigate the use of a control chart technique for multistream processes, or (3) use some multivariate control chart technique. Some of these possibilities are discussed in the chapters in Part IV of the text.

Important Terms and Concepts

Average run length
Control chart for individuals units
Control limits
Interpretation of control charts
Moving-range control chart
Natural tolerance limits of a process
Normality and control charts
Operating-characteristic (OC) curve for the $\bar{x}$ control chart
Patterns on control charts
Phase I control chart usage

Phase II control chart usage
Probability limits for control charts
Process capability
Process capability ratio (PCR) C_p
R control chart
Rational subgroups
s control chart
s^2 control chart
Shewhart control charts
Specification limits
Three-sigma control limits
Tier chart or tolerance diagram
Trial control limits
Variable sample size on control charts
Variables control charts
$\bar{x}$ control chart

Exercises

6.1. The data shown in Table 6E.1 are the deviations from nominal diameter for holes drilled in a carbon-fiber composite material used in aerospace manufacturing. The values reported are deviations from nominal in ten-thousandths of an inch.

(a) Set up $\bar{x}$ and R charts on the process. Is the process in statistical control?

(b) Estimate the process standard deviation using the range method.

(c) If specifications are at nominal ±100, what can you say about the capability of this process? Calculate the PCR C_p.

6.2. The net weight (in oz) of a dry bleach product is to be monitored by $\bar{x}$ and R control charts using a sample size of $n = 5$. Data for 20 preliminary samples are shown in Table 6E.2.

(a) Set up $\bar{x}$ and R control charts using these data. Does the process exhibit statistical control?

■ **TABLE 6E.1**
Hole Diameter Data for Exercise 6.1

Sample Number	x_1	x_2	x_3	x_4	x_5
1	−30	+50	−20	+10	+30
2	0	+50	−60	−20	+30
3	−50	+10	+20	+30	+20
4	−10	−10	+30	−20	+50
5	+20	−40	+50	+20	+10
6	0	0	+40	−40	+20
7	0	0	+20	−20	−10
8	+70	−30	+30	−10	0
9	0	0	+20	−20	+10
10	+10	+20	+30	+10	+50
11	+40	0	+20	0	+20
12	+30	+20	+30	+10	+40
13	+30	−30	0	+10	+10
14	+30	−10	+50	−10	−30
15	+10	−10	+50	+40	0
16	0	0	+30	−10	0
17	+20	+20	+30	+30	−20
18	+10	−20	+50	+30	+10
19	+50	−10	+40	+20	0
20	+50	0	0	+30	+10

■ **TABLE 6E.2**
Data for Exercise 6.2.

Sample Number	x_1	x_2	x_3	x_4	x_5
1	15.8	16.3	16.2	16.1	16.6
2	16.3	15.9	15.9	16.2	16.4
3	16.1	16.2	16.5	16.4	16.3
4	16.3	16.2	15.9	16.4	16.2
5	16.1	16.1	16.4	16.5	16.0
6	16.1	15.8	16.7	16.6	16.4
7	16.1	16.3	16.5	16.1	16.5
8	16.2	16.1	16.2	16.1	16.3
9	16.3	16.2	16.4	16.3	16.5
10	16.6	16.3	16.4	16.1	16.5
11	16.2	16.4	15.9	16.3	16.4
12	15.9	16.6	16.7	16.2	16.5
13	16.4	16.1	16.6	16.4	16.1
14	16.5	16.3	16.2	16.3	16.4
15	16.4	16.1	16.3	16.2	16.2
16	16.0	16.2	16.3	16.3	16.2
17	16.4	16.2	16.4	16.3	16.2
18	16.0	16.2	16.4	16.5	16.1
19	16.4	16.0	16.3	16.4	16.4
20	16.4	16.4	16.5	16.0	15.8

TABLE 6E.3
Bearing Diameter Data

Sample Number	$\bar{x}$	R	Sample Number	$\bar{x}$	R
1	34.5	3	13	35.4	8
2	34.2	4	14	34.0	6
3	31.6	4	15	37.1	5
4	31.5	4	16	34.9	7
5	35.0	5	17	33.5	4
6	34.1	6	18	31.7	3
7	32.6	4	19	34.0	8
8	33.8	3	20	35.1	4
9	34.8	7	21	33.7	2
10	33.6	8	22	32.8	1
11	31.9	3	23	33.5	3
12	38.6	9	24	34.2	2

(b) Estimate the process mean and standard deviation.

(c) Does fill weight seem to follow a normal distribution?

(d) If the specifications are at 16.2 ± 0.5, what conclusions would you draw about process capability?

(e) What fraction of containers produced by this process is likely to be below the lower specification limit of 15.7 oz?

6.3. The data shown in Table 6E.3 are $\bar{x}$ and R values for 24 samples of size $n = 5$ taken from a process producing bearings. The measurements are made on the inside diameter of the bearing, with only the last three decimals recorded (i.e., 34.5 should be 0.50345).

(a) Set up $\bar{x}$ and R charts on this process. Does the process seem to be in statistical control? If necessary, revise the trial control limits.

(b) If specifications on this diameter are 0.5030 ± 0.0010, find the percentage of nonconforming bearings produced by this process. Assume that diameter is normally distributed.

6.4. A high-voltage power supply should have a nominal output voltage of 350 V. A sample of four units is selected each day and tested for process-control purposes. The data shown in Table 6E.4 give the difference between the observed reading on each unit and the nominal voltage times ten; that is,

x_i = (observed voltage on unit i - 350)10

(a) Set up $\bar{x}$ and R charts on this process. Is the process in statistical control?

TABLE 6E.4
Voltage Data for Exercise 6.4.

Sample Number	x_1	x_2	x_3	x_4
1	6	9	10	15
2	10	4	6	11
3	7	8	10	5
4	8	9	6	13
5	9	10	7	13
6	12	11	10	10
7	16	10	8	9
8	7	5	10	4
9	9	7	8	12
10	15	16	10	13
11	8	12	14	16
12	6	13	9	11
13	16	9	13	15
14	7	13	10	12
15	11	7	10	16
16	15	10	11	14
17	9	8	12	10
18	15	7	10	11
19	8	6	9	12
20	13	14	11	15

(b) If specifications are at $350 \text{ V} \pm 5 \text{ V}$, what can you say about process capability?

(c) Is there evidence to support the claim that voltage is normally distributed?

6.5. Rework Exercise 6.1 using the s chart.

6.6. Rework Exercise 6.4 using the s chart.

6.7. The fill volume of soft-drink beverage bottles is an important quality characteristic. The volume is measured (approximately) by placing a gauge over the crown and comparing the height of the liquid in the neck of the bottle against a coded scale. On this scale, a reading of zero corresponds to the correct fill height. Fifteen samples of size $n = 10$ have been analyzed, and the fill heights are shown in Table 6E.5.

(a) Set up $\bar{x}$ and s control charts on this process. Does the process exhibit statistical control? If necessary, construct revised control limits.

(b) Set up an R chart, and compare with the s chart in part (a).

■ **TABLE 6E.5**
Fill Height Data for Exercise 6.7

Sample Number	x_1	x_2	x_3	x_4	x_5	x_6	x_7	x_8	x_9	x_{10}
1	2.5	0.5	2.0	−1.0	1.0	−1.0	0.5	1.5	0.5	−1.5
2	0.0	0.0	0.5	1.0	1.5	1.0	−1.0	1.0	1.5	−1.0
3	1.5	1.0	1.0	−1.0	0.0	−1.5	−1.0	−1.0	1.0	−1.0
4	0.0	0.5	−2.0	0.0	−1.0	1.5	−1.5	0.0	−2.0	−1.5
5	0.0	0.0	0.0	−0.5	0.5	1.0	−0.5	−0.5	0.0	0.0
6	1.0	−0.5	0.0	0.0	0.0	0.5	−1.0	1.0	−2.0	1.0
7	1.0	−1.0	−1.0	−1.0	0.0	1.5	0.0	1.0	0.0	0.0
8	0.0	−1.5	−0.5	1.5	0.0	0.0	0.0	−1.0	0.5	−0.5
9	−2.0	−1.5	1.5	1.5	0.0	0.0	0.5	1.0	0.0	1.0
10	−0.5	3.5	0.0	−1.0	−1.5	−1.5	−1.0	−1.0	1.0	0.5
11	0.0	1.5	0.0	0.0	2.0	−1.5	0.5	−0.5	2.0	−1.0
12	0.0	−2.0	−0.5	0.0	−0.5	2.0	1.5	0.0	0.5	−1.0
13	−1.0	−0.5	−0.5	−1.0	0.0	0.5	0.5	−1.5	−1.0	−1.0
14	0.5	1.0	−1.0	−0.5	−2.0	−1.0	−1.5	0.0	1.5	1.5
15	1.0	0.0	1.5	1.5	1.0	−1.0	0.0	1.0	−2.0	−1.5

(c) Set up an s^2 chart and compare with the s chart in part (a).

6.8. Samples of $n = 6$ items each are taken from a process at regular intervals. A quality characteristic is measured, and $\bar{x}$ and R values are calculated for each sample. After 50 samples, we have

$$\sum_{i=1}^{50} \bar{x}_i = 2000 \quad \text{and} \quad \sum_{i=1}^{50} R_i = 200$$

Assume that the quality characteristic is normally distributed.

(a) Compute control limits for the $\bar{x}$ and R control charts.

(b) All points on both control charts fall between the control limits computed in part (a). What are the natural tolerance limits of the process?

(c) If the specification limits are 41 ± 5.0, what are your conclusions regarding the ability of the process to produce items within these specifications?

(d) Assuming that if an item exceeds the upper specification limit it can be reworked, and if it is below the lower specification limit it must be scrapped, what percent scrap and rework is the process producing?

(e) Make suggestions as to how the process performance could be improved.

6.9. Control charts on $\bar{x}$ and s are to be maintained on the torque readings of a bearing used in a wingflap actuator assembly. Samples of size $n = 10$ are to be used, and we know from past experience that when the process is in control, bearing torque has a normal distribution with mean $\mu = 80$ inch-pounds and standard deviation $\sigma = 10$ inch-pounds. Find the center line and control limits for these control charts.

6.10. Consider the piston ring data shown in Table 6E.1. Assume that the specifications on this component are $74.000 + 0.05$ mm.

(a) Set up $\bar{x}$ and R control charts on this process. Is the process in statistical control?

(b) Note that the control limits on the $\bar{x}$ chart in part (a) are identical to the control limits on the $\bar{x}$ chart in Example 6.1, where the limits were based on s. Will this always happen?

(c) Estimate process capability for the piston-ring process. Estimate the percentage of piston rings produced that will be outside of the specification.

6.11. Table 6E.6 shows 15 additional samples for the piston ring process (Table 6E.1), taken after the initial control charts were established. Plot these data on the $\bar{x}$ and R chart developed in Exercise 6.10. Is the process in control?

■ **TABLE 6E.6**
Piston Ring Diameter Data for Exercise 6.11

Sample Number, i	Observations					$\bar{x}_i$	R_i
26	74.012	74.015	74.030	73.986	74.000	74.009	0.044
27	73.995	74.010	73.990	74.015	74.001	74.002	0.025
28	73.987	73.999	73.985	74.000	73.990	73.992	0.015
29	74.008	74.010	74.003	73.991	74.006	74.004	0.019
30	74.003	74.000	74.001	73.986	73.997	73.997	0.017
31	73.994	74.003	74.015	74.020	74.004	74.007	0.026
32	74.008	74.002	74.018	73.995	74.005	74.006	0.023
33	74.001	74.004	73.990	73.996	73.998	73.998	0.014
34	74.015	74.000	74.016	74.025	74.000	74.011	0.025
35	74.030	74.005	74.000	74.016	74.012	74.013	0.030
36	74.001	73.990	73.995	74.010	74.024	74.004	0.034
37	74.015	74.020	74.024	74.005	74.019	74.017	0.019
38	74.035	74.010	74.012	74.015	74.026	74.020	0.025
39	74.017	74.013	74.036	74.025	74.026	74.023	0.023
40	74.010	74.005	74.029	74.000	74.020	74.013	0.029

6.12. Consider the $\bar{x}$ and R charts you established in Exercise 6.3 using $n = 5$.

(a) Suppose that you wished to continue charting this quality characteristic using $\bar{x}$ and R charts based on a sample size of $n = 3$. What limits would be used on the $\bar{x}$ and R charts?

(b) What would be the impact of the decision you made in part (a) on the ability of the $\bar{x}$ chart to detect a 2σ shift in the mean?

(c) Suppose you wished to continue charting this quality characteristic using $\bar{x}$ and R charts based on a sample size of $n = 8$. What limits would be used on the $\bar{x}$ and R charts?

(d) What is the impact of using $n = 8$ on the ability of the $\bar{x}$ chart to detect a 2σ shift in the mean?

6.13. Parts manufactured by an injection molding process are subjected to a compressive strength test. Twenty samples of five parts each are collected, and the compressive strengths (in psi) are shown in Table 6E.7.

TABLE 6E.7
Strength Data for Exercise 6.13

Sample Number	x_1	x_2	x_3	x_4	x_5	$\bar{x}$	R
1	83.0	81.2	78.7	75.7	77.0	79.1	7.3
2	88.6	78.3	78.8	71.0	84.2	80.2	17.6
3	85.7	75.8	84.3	75.2	81.0	80.4	10.4
4	80.8	74.4	82.5	74.1	75.7	77.5	8.4
5	83.4	78.4	82.6	78.2	78.9	80.3	5.2
6	75.3	79.9	87.3	89.7	81.8	82.8	14.5
7	74.5	78.0	80.8	73.4	79.7	77.3	7.4
8	79.2	84.4	81.5	86.0	74.5	81.1	11.4
9	80.5	86.2	76.2	64.1	80.2	81.4	9.9
10	75.7	75.2	71.1	82.1	74.3	75.7	10.9
11	80.0	81.5	78.4	73.8	78.1	78.4	7.7
12	80.6	81.8	79.3	73.8	81.7	79.4	8.0
13	82.7	81.3	79.1	82.0	79.5	80.9	3.6
14	79.2	74.9	78.6	77.7	75.3	77.1	4.3
15	85.5	82.1	82.8	73.4	71.7	79.1	13.8
16	78.8	79.6	80.2	79.1	80.8	79.7	2.0
17	82.1	78.2	75.5	78.2	82.1	79.2	6.6
18	84.5	76.9	83.5	81.2	79.2	81.1	7.6
19	79.0	77.8	81.2	84.4	81.6	80.8	6.6
20	84.5	73.1	78.6	78.7	80.6	79.1	11.4

TABLE 6E.8
New Data for Exercise 6.13, part (b)

Sample Number	x_1	x_2	x_3	x_4	x_5	$\bar{x}$	R
1	68.9	81.5	78.2	80.8	81.5	78.2	12.6
2	69.8	68.6	80.4	84.3	83.9	77.4	15.7
3	78.5	85.2	78.4	80.3	81.7	80.8	6.8
4	76.9	86.1	86.9	94.4	83.9	85.6	17.5
5	93.6	81.6	87.8	79.6	71.0	82.7	22.5
6	65.5	86.8	72.4	82.6	71.4	75.9	21.3
7	78.1	65.7	83.7	93.7	93.4	82.9	27.9
8	74.9	72.6	81.6	87.2	72.7	77.8	14.6
9	78.1	77.1	67.0	75.7	76.8	74.9	11.0
10	78.7	85.4	77.7	90.7	76.7	81.9	14.0
11	85.0	60.2	68.5	71.1	82.4	73.4	24.9
12	86.4	79.2	79.8	86.0	75.4	81.3	10.9
13	78.5	99.0	78.3	71.4	81.8	81.7	27.6
14	68.8	62.0	82.0	77.5	76.1	73.3	19.9
15	83.0	83.7	73.1	82.2	95.3	83.5	22.2

(a) Establish $\bar{x}$ and R control charts for compressive strength using these data. Is the process in statistical control?

(b) After establishing the control charts in part (a), 15 new subgroups were collected and the compressive strengths are shown in Table 6E.8. Plot the $\bar{x}$ and R values against the control units from part (a) and draw conclusions.

6.14. Reconsider the data presented in Exercise 6.13.

(a) Rework both parts (a) and (b) of Exercise 6.13 using the $\bar{x}$ and s charts.

(b) Does the s chart detect the shift in process variability more quickly than the R chart did originally in part (b) of Exercise 6.13?

6.15. Samples of $n = 4$ items are taken from a process at regular intervals. A normally distributed quality characteristic is measured and $\bar{x}$ and s values are calculated for each sample. After 50 subgroups have been analyzed, we have

$$\sum_{i=1}^{50} \bar{x}_i = 1000 \quad \text{and} \quad \sum_{i=1}^{50} s_i = 72$$

(a) Compute the control limit for the $\bar{x}$ and s control charts.
(b) Assume that all points on both charts plot within the control limits. What are the natural tolerance limits of the process?
(c) If the specification limits are 19 ± 4.0, what are your conclusions regarding the ability of the process to produce items conforming to specifications?
(d) Assuming that if an item exceeds the upper specification limit it can be reworked, and if it is below the lower specification limit it must be scrapped, what percent scrap and rework is the process now producing?
(e) If the process were centered at μ = 19.0, what would be the effect on percent scrap and rework?

6.16. Consider the $\bar{x}$ and R chart that you established in Exercise 6.10 for the piston ring process. Suppose that you want to continue control charting piston ring diameter using n = 3. What limits would be used on the $\bar{x}$ and R chart?

6.17. Samples of size n = 5 are collected from a process every half hour. After 50 samples have been collected, we calculate $\bar{\bar{x}} = 20.0$ and $\bar{s} = 1.5$. Assume that both charts exhibit control and that the quality characteristic is normally distributed.
(a) Estimate the process standard deviation.
(b) Find the control limits on the $\bar{x}$ and s charts.
(c) If the process mean shifts to 22, what is the probability of concluding that the process is still in control?

6.18. Samples of size n = 5 are taken from a manufacturing process every hour. A quality characteristic is measured, and $\bar{x}$ and R are computed for each sample. After 25 samples have been analyzed, we have

$$\sum_{i=1}^{25} \bar{x}_i = 662.50 \quad \text{and} \quad \sum_{i=1}^{25} R_i = 9.00$$

The quality characteristic is normally distributed.
(a) Find the control limits for the $\bar{x}$ and R charts.
(b) Assume that both charts exhibit control. If the specifications are 26.40 ± 0.50, estimate the fraction nonconforming.
(c) If the mean of the process were 26.40, what fraction nonconforming would result?

6.19. Control charts for $\bar{x}$ and R are maintained for an important quality characteristic. The sample size is n = 7; $\bar{x}$ and R are computed for each sample. After 35 samples, we have found that

$$\sum_{i=1}^{35} \bar{x}_i = 7805 \quad \text{and} \quad \sum_{i=1}^{35} R_i = 1200$$

(a) Set up $\bar{x}$ and R charts using these data.
(b) Assuming that both charts exhibit control, estimate the process mean and standard deviation.
(c) If the quality characteristic is normally distributed and if the specifications are 220 ± 35, can the process meet the specifications? Estimate the fraction nonconforming.
(d) Assuming the variance to remain constant, state where the process mean should be located to minimize the fraction nonconforming. What would be the value of the fraction nonconforming under these conditions?

6.20. A process is to be monitored with standard values $\mu = 10$ and $\sigma = 2.5$. The sample size is $n = 2$.
(a) Find the center line and control limits for the $\bar{x}$ chart.
(b) Find the center line and control limits for the R chart.
(c) Find the center line and control limits for the s chart.

6.21. A critical dimension of a machined part has specifications 100 ± 10. Control chart analysis indicates that the process is in control with $\bar{\bar{x}} = 104$ and $\bar{R} = 9.30$. The control charts use samples of size $n = 5$. If we assume that the characteristic is normally distributed, can the mean be located (by adjusting the tool position) so that all output meets specifications? What is the present capability of the process?

6.22. An $\bar{x}$ chart is used to control the mean of a normally distributed quality characteristic. It is known that $\sigma = 6.0$ and $n = 4$. The center line = 200, UCL = 209, and LCL = 191. If the process mean shifts to 188, find the probability that this shift is detected on the first subsequent sample.

6.23. A TiW layer is deposited on a substrate using a sputtering tool. Table 6E.9 contains layer thickness measurements (in Angstroms) on 20 subgroups of four substrates.

■ **TABLE 6E.9**
Layer Thickness Data for Exercise 6.23

Subgroup	x_1	x_2	x_3	x_4
1	459	449	435	450
2	443	440	442	442
3	457	444	449	444
4	469	463	453	438
5	443	457	445	454
6	444	456	456	457
7	445	449	450	445
8	446	455	449	452
9	444	452	457	440
10	432	463	463	443
11	445	452	453	438
12	456	457	436	457
13	459	445	441	447
14	441	465	438	450
15	460	453	457	438
16	453	444	451	435
17	451	460	450	457
18	422	431	437	429
19	444	446	448	467
20	450	450	454	454

(a) Set up and R control charts on this process. Is the process in control? Revise the control limits as necessary.
(b) Estimate the mean and standard deviation of the process.
(c) Is the layer thickness normally distributed?
(d) If the specifications are at 450 ± 30, estimate the process capability.

6.24. Continuation of Exercise 6.23. Table 6E.9 contains 10 new subgroups of thickness data. Plot this data on the control charts constructed in Exercise 6.23 (a). Is the process in statistical control?

6.25. Continuation of Exercise 6.10. Suppose that following the construction of the $\bar{x}$ and R control charts in Exercise 6.23, the process engineers decided to change the subgroup size to $n = 2$. Table 6E.11 contains 10 new subgroups of thickness data. Plot this data on the control charts from Exercise 6.23 (a) based on the new subgroup size. Is the process in statistical control?

■ **TABLE 6E.10**
Additional Thickness Data for Exercise 6.24.

Subgroup	x_1	x_2	x_3	x_4
21	454	449	443	461
22	449	441	444	455
23	442	442	442	450
24	443	452	438	430
25	446	459	457	457
26	454	448	445	462
27	458	449	453	438
28	450	449	445	451
29	443	440	443	451
30	457	450	452	437

■ **TABLE 6E.11**
Additional Thickness Data for Exercise 6.25.

Subgroup	x_1	x_2
21	454	449
22	449	441
23	442	442
24	443	452
25	446	459
26	454	448
27	458	449
28	450	449
29	443	440
30	457	450

6.26. Rework Exercises 6.23 and 6.24 using $\bar{x}$ and s control charts.

6.27. Control charts on $\bar{x}$ and R for samples of size $n = 5$ are to be maintained on the tensile strength in pounds of a yarn. To start the charts, 30 samples were selected, and the mean and range of each computed. This yields

$$\sum_{i=1}^{30} \bar{x}_i = 607.8 \quad \text{and} \quad \sum_{i=1}^{30} R_i = 144$$

(a) Compute the center line and control limits for the $\bar{x}$ and R control charts.

(b) Suppose both charts exhibit control. There is a single lower specification limit of 16 lb. If strength is normally distributed, what fraction of yarn would fail to meet specifications?

6.28. The data in Table 6E.12 were collected from a process manufacturing power supplies. The variable of interest is output voltage, and $n = 5$.

(a) Compute center lines and control limits suitable for controlling future production.

(b) Assume that the quality characteristic is normally distributed. Estimate the process standard deviation.

(c) What are the apparent three-sigma natural tolerance limits of the process?

(d) What would be your estimate of the process fraction nonconforming if the specifications on the characteristic were 103 ± 4?

(e) What approaches to reducing the fraction nonconforming can you suggest?

6.29. Control charts for $\bar{x}$ and R are to be established to control the tensile strength of a metal part. Assume that tensile strength is normally distributed. Thirty samples of size $n = 6$ parts are collected over a period of time with the following results:

$$\sum_{i=1}^{30} \bar{x}_i = 6000 \quad \text{and} \quad \sum_{i=1}^{30} R_i = 150$$

(a) Calculate control limits for $\bar{x}$ and R.

(b) Both charts exhibit control. The specifications on tensile strength are 200 ± 5. What are your conclusions regarding process capability?

(c) For the above $\bar{x}$ chart, find the β-risk when the true process mean is 199.

6.30. An $\bar{x}$ chart has a center line of 100, uses three-sigma control limits, and is based on a sample size of four. The process standard deviation is known to be six. If the process mean shifts from 100 to 92, what is the probability of detecting this shift on the first sample following the shift?

6.31. Specifications on a cigar lighter detent are 0.3220 and 0.3200 in. Samples of size 5 are taken every 45 min with the results shown in Table 6E.13 (measured as deviations from 0.3210 in 0.0001 in.).

■ **TABLE 6E.12**
Voltage Data for Exercise 6.28.

Sample Number	$\bar{x}$	R	Sample Number	$\bar{x}$	R
1	103	4	11	105	4
2	102	5	12	103	2
3	104	2	13	102	3
4	105	11	14	105	4
5	104	4	15	104	5
6	106	3	16	105	3
7	102	7	17	106	5
8	105	2	18	102	2
9	106	4	19	105	4
10	104	3	20	103	2

■ **TABLE 6E.13**
Data for Exercise 6.31.

Sample Number	x_1	x_2	x_3	x_4	x_5
1	1	9	6	9	6
2	9	4	3	0	3
3	0	9	0	3	2
4	1	1	0	2	1
5	−3	0	−1	0	−4
6	−7	2	0	0	2
7	−3	−1	−1	0	−2
8	0	−2	−3	−3	−2
9	2	0	−1	−3	−1
10	0	2	−1	−1	2
11	−3	−2	−1	−1	2
12	−16	2	0	−4	−1
13	−6	−3	0	0	−8
14	−3	−5	5	0	5
15	−1	−1	−1	−2	−1

■ TABLE 6E.14
New Data for Exercise 6.32

Sample Number	x_1	x_2	x_3	x_4	x_5
16	2	10	9	6	5
17	1	9	5	9	4
18	0	9	8	2	5
19	−3	0	5	1	4
20	2	10	9	3	1
21	−5	4	0	6	−1
22	0	2	−5	4	6
23	10	0	3	1	5
24	−1	2	5	6	−3
25	0	−1	2	5	−2

(a) Set up an R chart and examine the process for statistical control.

(b) What parameters would you recommend for an R chart for on-line control?

(c) Estimate the standard deviation of the process.

(d) What is the process capability?

6.32. **Continuation of Exercise 6.31.** Reconsider the data from Exercise 6.31 and establish $\bar{x}$ and R charts with appropriate trial control limits. Revise these trial limits as necessary to produce a set of control charts for monitoring future production. Suppose that the new data in Table 6E.14 are observed.

(a) Plot these new observations on the control chart. What conclusions can you draw about process stability?

(b) Use all 25 observations to revise the control limits for the $\bar{x}$ and R charts. What conclusions can you draw now about the process?

6.33. Control charts for $\bar{x}$ and R are maintained on the tensile strength of a metal fastener. After 30 samples of size $n = 6$ are analyzed, we find that

$$\sum_{i=1}^{30} \bar{x}_i = 12{,}870 \quad \text{and} \quad \sum_{i=1}^{30} R_i = 1350$$

(a) Compute control limits on the R chart.

(b) Assuming that the R chart exhibits control, estimate the parameters μ and σ.

(c) If the process output is normally distributed, and if the specifications are 440 ± 40, can the process meet the specifications? Estimate the fraction nonconforming.

(d) If the variance remains constant, where should the mean be located to minimize the fraction nonconforming?

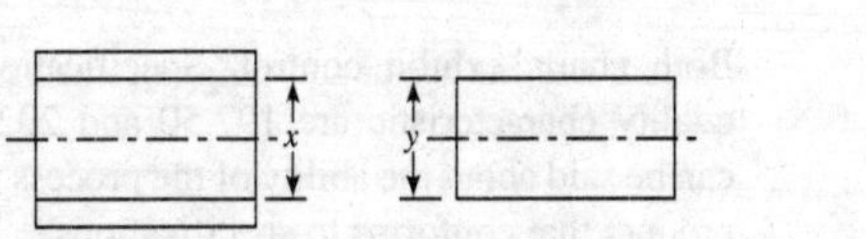

■ FIGURE 6.28 Parts for Exercise 6.34.

6.34. Two parts are assembled as shown in Figure 6.28. Assume that the dimensions x and y are normally distributed with means μ_x and μ_y and standard deviations σ_x and σ_y, respectively. The parts are produced on different machines and are assembled at random. Control charts are maintained on each dimension for the range of each sample ($n = 5$). Both range charts are in control.

(a) Given that for 20 samples on the range chart controlling x and 10 samples on the range chart controlling y, we have

$$\sum_{i=1}^{20} R_{x_i} = 18.608 \quad \text{and} \quad \sum_{i=1}^{10} R_{y_i} = 6.978$$

Estimate σ_x and σ_y.

(b) If it is desired that the probability of a smaller clearance (i.e., $x - y$) than 0.09 should be 0.006, what distance between the average dimensions (i.e., $\mu_x - \mu_y$) should be specified?

6.35. An $\bar{x}$ chart on a normally distributed quality characteristic is to be established with the standard values $\mu = 100$, $\sigma = 8$, and $n = 4$. Find the following:

(a) The two-sigma control limits.

(b) The 0.005 probability limits.

6.36. Control charts for $\bar{x}$ and s with $n = 4$ are maintained on a quality characteristic. The parameters of these charts are as follows:

$\bar{x}$ Chart	s Chart
UCL = 201.88	UCL = 2.266
Center line = 200.00	Center line = 1.000
LCL = 198.12	LCL = 0

Both charts exhibit control. Specifications on the quality characteristic are 197.50 and 202.50. What can be said about the ability of the process to produce product that conforms to specifications?

6.37. Thirty samples each of size 7 have been collected to establish control over a process. The following data were collected:

$$\sum_{i=1}^{30} \bar{x}_i = 2700 \quad \text{and} \quad \sum_{i=1}^{30} R_i = 120$$

(a) Calculate trial control limits for the two charts.

(b) On the assumption that the R chart is in control, estimate the process standard deviation.

(c) Suppose an s chart were desired. What would be the appropriate control limits and center line?

6.38. An $\bar{x}$ chart is to be established based on the standard values $\mu = 600$ and $\sigma = 12$, with $n = 9$. The control limits are to be based on an α-risk of 0.01. What are the appropriate control limits?

6.39. Specifications on a normally distributed dimension are 600 ± 20. $\bar{x}$ and R charts are maintained on this dimension and have been in control over a long period of time. The parameters of these control charts are as follows ($n = 9$).

$\bar{x}$ Chart	s Chart
UCL = 616	UCL = 32.36
Center line = 610	Center line = 17.82
LCL = 604	LCL = 3.28

(a) What are your conclusions regarding the capability of the process to produce items within specifications?

(b) Construct an OC curve for the $\bar{x}$ chart assuming that σ is constant.

6.40. Statistical monitoring of a quality characteristic uses both an $\bar{x}$ and an s chart. The charts are to be based on the standard values $\mu = 200$ and $\sigma = 10$, with $n = 4$.

(a) Find three-sigma control limits for the s chart.

(b) Find a center line and control limits for the $\bar{x}$ chart such that the probability of a type I error is 0.05.

6.41. An $\bar{x}$ chart with three-sigma limits has parameters as follows:

UCL = 104
Center line = 100
LCL = 96
$n = 5$

Suppose the process quality characteristic being controlled is normally distributed with a true mean of 98 and a standard deviation of 8. What is the probability that the control chart would exhibit lack of control by at least the third point plotted?

6.42. Consider the $\bar{x}$ chart defined in Exercise 6.41. Find the ARL_1 for the chart.

6.43. $\bar{x}$ and R charts with $n = 4$ are used to monitor a normally distributed quality characteristic. The control chart parameters are

$\bar{x}$ Chart	R Chart
UCL = 815	UCL = 46.98
Center line = 800	Center line = 20.59
LCL = 785	LCL = 0

Both charts exhibit control. What is the probability that a shift in the process mean to 790 will be detected on the first sample following the shift?

6.44. Consider the $\bar{x}$ chart in Exercise 6.43. Find the average run length for the chart.

6.45. One-pound coffee cans are filled by a machine, sealed, and then weighed automatically. After adjusting for the weight of the can, any package that weighs less than 16 oz is cut out of the conveyor. The weights of 25 successive cans are shown in Table 6E.14. Set up a moving range control chart and a control chart for individuals. Estimate the mean and standard deviation of the amount of coffee packed in each can. Is it reasonable to assume that can weight is normally distributed? If the process remains in control at this level, what percentage of cans will be underfilled?

6.46. Control charts for $\bar{x}$ and s have been maintained on a process and have exhibited statistical control. The

■ TABLE 6E.14
Can Weight Data for Exercise 6.45

Can Number	Weight	Can Number	Weight
1	16.11	14	16.12
2	16.08	15	16.10
3	16.12	16	16.08
4	16.10	17	16.13
5	16.10	18	16.15
6	16.11	19	16.12
7	16.12	20	16.10
8	16.09	21	16.08
9	16.12	22	16.07
10	16.10	23	16.11
11	16.09	24	16.13
12	16.07	25	16.10
13	16.13		

sample size is $n = 6$. The control chart parameters are as follows:

$\bar{x}$ Chart	s Chart
UCL = 708.20	UCL = 3.420
Center line = 706.00	Center line = 1.738
LCL = 703.80	LCL = 0.052

(a) Estimate the mean and standard deviation of the process.
(b) Estimate the natural tolerance limits for the process.
(c) Assume that the process output is well modeled by a normal distribution. If specifications are 703 and 709, estimate the fraction nonconforming.
(d) Suppose the process mean shifts to 702.00 while the standard deviation remains constant. What is the probability of an out-of-control signal occurring on the first sample following the shift?
(e) For the shift in part (d), what is the probability of detecting the shift by at least the third subsequent sample?

6.47. A normally distributed quality characteristic is monitored through use of an $\bar{x}$ and an R chart. These charts have the following parameters ($n = 4$):

$\bar{x}$ Chart	R Chart
UCL = 626.0	UCL = 18.795
Center line = 620.0	Center line = 8.236
LCL = 614.0	LCL = 0

Both charts exhibit control.
(a) What is the estimated standard deviation of the process?
(b) Suppose an s chart were to be substituted for the R chart. What would be the appropriate parameters of the s chart?
(c) If specifications on the product were 610 ± 15, what would be your estimate of the process fraction nonconforming?
(d) What could be done to reduce this fraction nonconforming?
(e) What is the probability of detecting a shift in the process mean to 610 on the first sample following the shift (σ remains constant)?
(f) What is the probability of detecting the shift in part (e) by at least the third sample after the shift occurs?

6.48. Control charts for $\bar{x}$ and R are in use with the following parameters:

$\bar{x}$ Chart	R Chart
UCL = 363.0	UCL = 16.18
Center line = 360.0	Center line = 8.91
LCL = 357.0	LCL = 1.64

The sample size is $n = 9$. Both charts exhibit control. The quality characteristic is normally distributed.
(a) What is the α-risk associated with the $\bar{x}$ chart?
(b) Specifications on this quality characteristic are 358 ± 6. What are your conclusions regarding the ability of the process to produce items within specifications?

(c) Suppose the mean shifts to 357. What is the probability that the shift will not be detected on the first sample following the shift?

(d) What would be the appropriate control limits for the $\bar{x}$ chart if the type I error probability were to be 0.01?

6.49. The following $\bar{x}$ and s charts based on $n = 4$ have shown statistical control:

$\bar{x}$ Chart	s Chart
UCL = 710	UCL = 18.08
Center line = 700	Center line = 7.979
LCL = 690	LCL = 0

(a) Estimate the process parameters μ and σ.

(b) If the specifications are at 705 ± 15, and the process output is normally distributed, estimate the fraction nonconforming.

(c) For the $\bar{x}$ chart, find the probability of a type I error, assuming σ is constant.

(d) Suppose the process mean shifts to 693 and the standard deviation simultaneously shifts to 12. Find the probability of detecting this shift on the $\bar{x}$ chart on the first subsequent sample.

(e) For the shift of part (d), find the average run length.

6.50. The viscosity of a polymer is measured hourly. Measurements for the last twenty hours are shown in Table 6E.15.

■ **TABLE 6E.15**
Viscosity Data for Exercise 6.50

Test	Viscosity	Test	Viscosity
1	2838	11	3174
2	2785	12	3102
3	3058	13	2762
4	3064	14	2975
5	2996	15	2719
6	2882	16	2861
7	2878	17	2797
8	2920	18	3078
9	3050	19	2964
10	2870	20	2805

(a) Does viscosity follow a normal distribution?

(b) Set up a control chart on viscosity and a moving range chart. Does the process exhibit statistical control?

(c) Estimate the process mean and standard deviation.

6.51. **Continuation of Exercise 6.50.** The next five measurements on viscosity are 3163, 3199, 3054, 3147, and 3156. Do these measurements indicate that the process is in statistical control?

6.52. Thirty observations on concentration (in g/l) of the active ingredient in a liquid cleaner produced in a continuous chemical process are shown in Table 6E.16.

■ **TABLE 6E.16**
Data for Exercise 6E.52

Observation	Concentration	Observation	Concentration
1	60.4	16	99.9
2	69.5	17	59.3
3	78.4	18	60.0
4	72.8	19	74.7
5	78.2	20	75.8
6	78.7	21	76.6
7	56.9	22	68.4
8	78.4	23	83.1
9	79.6	24	61.1
10	100.8	25	54.9
11	99.6	26	69.1
12	64.9	27	67.5
13	75.5	28	69.2
14	70.4	29	87.2
15	68.1	30	73.0

(a) A normal probability plot of the concentration data is shown in Figure 6.29. The straight line was fit by eye to pass approximately through the twentieth and eightieth percentiles. Does the normality assumption seem reasonable here?

(b) Set up an individuals and moving range control chart for the concentration data. Interpret the charts.

(c) Construct a normal probability plot for the natural log of concentration. Is the transformed variable normally distributed?

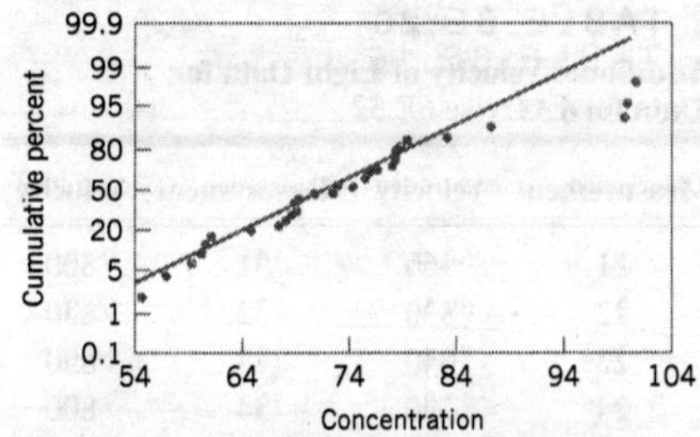

FIGURE 6.29 Normal Probability Plot of the Concentration Data for Exercise 6.52.

(d) Repeat part (b), using the natural log of concentration as the charted variable. Comment on any differences in the charts you note in comparison to those constructed in part (b).

6.53. (a) Thirty observations on the oxide thickness of individual silicon wafers are shown in Table 6E.17. Use these data to set up a control chart on oxide thickness and a moving range chart. Does the process exhibit statistical control? Does oxide thickness follow a normal distribution?

TABLE 6E.17
Data for Exercise 6.53

Wafer	Oxide Thickness	Wafer	Oxide Thickness
1	45.4	16	58.4
2	48.6	17	51.0
3	49.5	18	41.2
4	44.0	19	47.1
5	50.9	20	45.7
6	55.2	21	60.6
7	45.5	22	51.0
8	52.8	23	53.0
9	45.3	24	56.0
10	46.3	25	47.2
11	53.9	26	48.0
12	49.8	27	55.9
13	46.9	28	50.0
14	49.8	29	47.9
15	45.1	30	53.4

(b) Following the establishment of the control charts in part (a), ten new wafers were observed. The oxide thickness measurements are as follows:

Wafer	Oxide Thickness	Wafer	Oxide Thickness
1	54.3	6	51.5
2	57.5	7	58.4
3	64.8	8	67.5
4	62.1	9	61.1
5	59.6	10	63.3

Plot these observations against the control limits determined in part (a). Is the process in control?

(c) Suppose the assignable cause responsible for the out-of-control signal in part (b) is discovered and removed from the process. Twenty additional wafers are subsequently sampled. Plot the oxide thickness against the part (a) control limits. What conclusions can you draw? The new data are shown in Table 6E.18.

6.54. The uniformity of a silicon wafer following an etching process is determined by measuring the layer thickness at several locations and expressing unifor-

TABLE 6E.18
Additional Data for Exercise 6.53, part (c)

Wafer	Oxide Thickness	Wafer	Oxide Thickness
1	43.4	11	50.0
2	46.7	12	61.2
3	44.8	13	46.9
4	51.3	14	44.9
5	49.2	15	46.2
6	46.5	16	53.3
7	48.4	17	44.1
8	50.1	18	47.4
9	53.7	19	51.3
10	45.6	20	42.5

■ **TABLE 6E.19**

Uniformity Data for Exercise 6.54

Wafer	Uniformity	Wafer	Uniformity
1	11	16	15
2	16	17	16
3	22	18	12
4	14	19	11
5	34	20	18
6	22	21	14
7	13	22	13
8	11	23	18
9	6	24	12
10	11	25	13
11	11	26	12
12	23	27	15
13	14	28	21
14	12	29	21
15	7	30	14

mity as the range of the thicknesses. Table 6E.19 presents uniformity determinations for 30 consecutive wafers processed through the etching tool.

(a) Is there evidence that uniformity is normally distributed? If not, find a suitable transformation for the data.

(b) Construct a control chart for individuals and a moving range control chart for uniformity for the etching process. Is the process in statistical control?

6.55. Continuation of Exercise 6.56. Michelson actually made 100 measurements on the velocity of light in five trials of 20 observations each. The second set of 20 measurements is shown in Table 6E.20.

(a) Plot these new measurements on the control charts constructed in Exercise 6.56. Are these new measurements in statistical control? Give a practical interpretation of the control charts.

(b) Is there evidence that the variability in the measurements has decreased between trial 1 and trial 2?

6.56. In 1879, A. A. Michelson measured the velocity of light in air using a modification of a method proposed by the French physicist Foucauld. Twenty of

■ **TABLE 6E.20**

Additional Velocity of Light Data for Exercise 6.55.

Measurement	Velocity	Measurement	Velocity
21	960	31	800
22	830	32	830
23	940	33	850
24	790	34	800
25	960	35	880
26	810	36	790
27	940	37	900
28	880	38	760
29	880	39	840
30	880	40	800

■ **TABLE 6E.21**

Velocity of Light Data for Exercise 6E.56

Measurement	Velocity	Measurement	Velocity
1	850	11	850
2	1000	12	810
3	740	13	950
4	980	14	1000
5	900	15	980
6	930	16	1000
7	1070	17	980
8	650	18	960
9	930	19	880
10	760	20	960

these measurements are in Table 6E.21 (the value reported is in kilometers per second and has 299,000 subtracted from it). Use these data to set up an individuals and a moving range control chart. Is there some evidence that the measurements of the velocity of light are normally distributed? Do the measurements exhibit statistical control? Revise the control limits if necessary.

6.57. Reconsider the situation in Exercise 6.45. Construct an individuals control chart using the median of the span-two moving ranges to estimate variability.

■ TABLE 6E.22
Data for Exercise 6.59

Observation	x	Observation	x
1	10.07	14	9.58
2	10.47	15	8.80
3	9.45	16	12.94
4	9.44	17	10.78
5	8.99	18	11.26
6	7.74	19	9.48
7	10.63	20	11.28
8	9.78	21	12.54
9	9.37	22	11.48
10	9.95	23	13.26
11	12.04	24	11.10
12	10.93	25	10.82
13	11.54		

Compare this control chart to the one constructed in Exercise 6.45 and discuss.

6.58. Reconsider the polymer viscosity data in Exercise 6.50. Use the median of the span-two moving ranges to estimate σ and set up the individuals control chart. Compare this chart to the one originally constructed using the average moving range method to estimate σ.

6.59. Consider the individuals measurement data shown in Table 6E.22.
(a) Estimate σ using the average of the moving ranges of span two.
(b) Estimate σ using s/c_4.
(c) Estimate σ using the median of the span-two moving ranges.
(d) Estimate σ using the average of the moving ranges of span 3, 4, . . . , 20.
(e) Discuss the results you have obtained.

6.60. **Continuation of Exercise 6.53.** Use all 60 observations on oxide thickness.
(a) Set up an individuals control chart with σ estimated by the average moving range method.
(b) Set up an individuals control chart with σ estimated by the median moving range method.
(c) Compare and discuss the two control charts.

■ TABLE 6E.23
Vane Heights for Exercise 6.61.

Casting	Vane 1	Vane 2	Vane 3	Vane 4	Vane 5
1	5.77799	5.74907	5.76672	5.74836	5.74122
2	5.79090	5.78043	5.79163	5.79393	5.81158
3	5.77314	5.71216	5.74810	5.77292	5.75591
4	5.77030	5.75903	5.77157	5.79687	5.78063
5	5.72047	5.68587	5.73302	5.70472	5.68116
6	5.77265	5.76426	5.74373	5.71338	5.74765
7	5.70581	5.70835	5.71866	5.71252	5.72089
8	5.76466	5.78766	5.76115	5.77523	5.75590
9	5.79397	5.83308	5.77902	5.81122	5.82335
10	5.78671	5.76411	5.75941	5.75619	5.71787
11	5.75352	5.74144	5.74109	5.76817	5.75019
12	5.72787	5.70716	5.75349	5.72389	5.73488
13	5.79707	5.79231	5.79022	5.79694	5.79805
14	5.73765	5.73615	5.73249	5.74006	5.73265
15	5.72477	5.76565	5.76963	5.74993	5.75196
16	5.73199	5.72926	5.72963	5.72259	5.73513
17	5.79166	5.79516	5.79903	5.78548	5.79826
18	5.74973	5.74863	5.73994	5.74405	5.74682
19	5.76449	5.75632	5.76197	5.76684	5.75474
20	5.75168	5.75579	5.73979	5.77963	5.76933

6.61. The vane heights for 20 of the castings from Fig. 6.25 are shown in Table 6E.23. Construct the "between/within" control charts for these process data using a range chart to monitor the within-castings vane height. Compare these to the control charts shown in Fig. 6.27.

6.62. The diameter of the casting in Fig. 6.25 is also an important quality characteristic. A coordinate measuring machine is used to measure the diameter of each casting at five different locations. Data for 20 castings are shown in the Table 6E.24.
(a) Set up $\bar{x}$ and R charts for this process, assuming the measurements on each casting form a rational subgroup.
(b) Discuss the charts you have constructed in part (a).
(c) Construct "between/within" charts for this process.

■ **TABLE 6E.24**
Diameter Data for Exercise 6.62.

	Diameter				
Casting	**1**	**2**	**3**	**4**	**5**
1	11.7629	11.7403	11.7511	11.7474	11.7374
2	11.8122	11.7506	11.7787	11.7736	11.8412
3	11.7742	11.7114	11.7530	11.7532	11.7773
4	11.7833	11.7311	11.7777	11.8108	11.7804
5	11.7134	11.6870	11.7305	11.7419	11.6642
6	11.7925	11.7611	11.7588	11.7012	11.7611
7	11.6916	11.7205	11.6958	11.7440	11.7062
8	11.7109	11.7832	11.7496	11.7496	11.7318
9	11.7984	11.8887	11.7729	11.8485	11.8416
10	11.7914	11.7613	11.7356	11.7628	11.7070
11	11.7260	11.7329	11.7424	11.7645	11.7571
12	11.7202	11.7537	11.7328	11.7582	11.7265
13	11.8356	11.7971	11.8023	11.7802	11.7903
14	11.7069	11.7112	11.7492	11.7329	11.7289
15	11.7116	11.7978	11.7982	11.7429	11.7154
16	11.7165	11.7284	11.7571	11.7597	11.7317
17	11.8022	11.8127	11.7864	11.7917	11.8167
18	11.7775	11.7372	11.7241	11.7773	11.7543
19	11.7753	11.7870	11.7574	11.7620	11.7673
20	11.7572	11.7626	11.7523	11.7395	11.7884

(d) Do you believe that the charts in part (c) are more informative than those in part (a)? Discuss why.

(e) Provide a practical interpretation of the "within" chart.

6.63. In the semiconductor industry, the production of microcircuits involves many steps. The wafer fabrication process typically builds these microcircuits on silicon wafers, and there are many microcircuits per wafer. Each production lot consists of between 16 and 48 wafers. Some processing steps treat each wafer separately, so that the batch size for that step is one wafer. It is usually necessary to estimate several components of variation: within-wafer, between-wafer, between-lot, and the total variation.

(a) Suppose that one wafer is randomly selected from each lot and that a single measurement on a critical dimension of interest is taken. Which components of variation could be estimated with these data? What type of control charts would you recommend?

(b) Suppose that each wafer is tested at five fixed locations (say, the center and four points at the circumference). The average and range of these within-wafer measurements are $\bar{x}_{WW}$ and R_{WW}, respectively. What components of variability are estimated using control charts based on these data?

(c) Suppose that one measurement point on each wafer is selected and that this measurement is recorded for five consecutive wafers. The average and range of these between-wafer measurements are $\bar{x}_{BW}$ and R_{BW}, respectively. What components of variability are estimated using control charts based on these data? Would it be necessary to run separate $\bar{x}$ and R charts for all five locations on the wafer?

(d) Consider the question in part (c). How would your answer change if the test sites on each wafer were randomly selected and varied from wafer to wafer?

(e) What type of control charts and rational subgroup scheme would you recommend to control the batch-to-batch variability?

6.64. Consider the situation described in Exercise 6.63. A critical dimension (measured in μm) is of interest to the process engineer. Suppose that five fixed positions are used on each wafer (position 1 is the center) and that two consecutive wafers are selected from each batch. The data that result from several batches are shown in Table 6E.25.

(a) What can you say about overall process capability?

(b) Can you construct control charts that allow within-wafer variability to be evaluated?

(c) What control charts would you establish to evaluate variability between wafers? Set up these charts and use them to draw conclusions about the process.

(d) What control charts would you use to evaluate lot-to-lot variability? Set up these charts and use them to draw conclusions about lot-to-lot variability.

■ **TABLE 6E.25**
Data for Exercise 6.64

Lot Number	Wafer Number	Position 1	2	3	4	5	Lot Number	Wafer Number	Position 1	2	3	4	5
1	1	2.15	2.13	2.08	2.12	2.10	11	1	2.15	2.13	2.14	2.09	2.08
	2	2.13	2.10	2.04	2.08	2.05		2	2.11	2.13	2.10	2.14	2.10
2	1	2.02	2.01	2.06	2.05	2.08	12	1	2.03	2.06	2.05	2.01	2.00
	2	2.03	2.09	2.07	2.06	2.04		2	2.04	2.08	2.03	2.10	2.07
3	1	2.13	2.12	2.10	2.11	2.08	13	1	2.05	2.03	2.05	2.09	2.08
	2	2.03	2.08	2.03	2.09	2.07		2	2.08	2.01	2.03	2.04	2.10
4	1	2.04	2.01	2.10	2.11	2.09	14	1	2.08	2.04	2.05	2.01	2.08
	2	2.07	2.14	2.12	2.08	2.09		2	2.09	2.11	2.06	2.04	2.05
5	1	2.16	2.17	2.13	2.18	2.10	15	1	2.14	2.13	2.10	2.10	2.08
	2	2.17	2.13	2.10	2.09	2.13		2	2.13	2.10	2.09	2.13	2.15
6	1	2.04	2.06	1.97	2.10	2.08	16	1	2.06	2.08	2.05	2.03	2.09
	2	2.03	2.10	2.05	2.07	2.04		2	2.03	2.01	1.99	2.06	2.05
7	1	2.04	2.02	2.01	2.00	2.05	17	1	2.05	2.03	2.08	2.01	2.04
	2	2.06	2.04	2.03	2.08	2.10		2	2.06	2.05	2.03	2.05	2.00
8	1	2.13	2.10	2.10	2.15	2.13	18	1	2.03	2.08	2.04	2.00	2.03
	2	2.10	2.09	2.13	2.14	2.11		2	2.04	2.03	2.05	2.01	2.04
9	1	1.95	2.03	2.08	2.07	2.08	19	1	2.16	2.13	2.10	2.13	2.12
	2	2.01	2.03	2.06	2.05	2.04		2	2.13	2.15	2.18	2.19	2.13
10	1	2.04	2.08	2.09	2.10	2.01	20	1	2.06	2.03	2.04	2.09	2.10
	2	2.06	2.04	2.07	2.04	2.01		2	2.01	1.98	2.05	2.08	2.06

7 Attributes Control Charts

CHAPTER OUTLINE

The supplemental material is on the textbook Website www.wiley.com/college/montgomery.

CHAPTER OVERVIEW AND LEARNING OBJECTIVES

Many quality characteristics cannot be conveniently represented numerically. In such cases, we usually classify each item inspected as either conforming or nonconforming to the specifications on that quality characteristic. The terminology **defective** or **nondefective** is often used to identify these two classifications of product. More recently, the terminology **conforming** and **nonconforming** has become popular. Quality characteristics of this type are called **attributes.** Some examples of quality characteristics that are attributes are the proportion of warped automobile engine connecting rods in a day's production, the number of nonfunctional semiconductor chips on a wafer, the number of errors or mistakes made in completing a loan application, and the number of medical errors made in a hospital.

This chapter presents three widely used attributes control charts. The first of these relates to the fraction of nonconforming or defective product produced by a manufacturing process, and is called the **control chart for fraction nonconforming,** or p chart. In some situations it is more convenient to deal with the number of **defects** or **nonconformities** observed rather than the fraction nonconforming. The second type of control chart that we study, called the **control chart for nonconformities,** or the *c* chart, is designed to deal with this case. Finally, we present a **control chart for nonconformities per unit,** or the *u* chart, which is useful in situations where the average number of nonconformities per unit is a more convenient basis for process control. An excellent supplement to this chapter is the paper by Woodall (1997) that summarizes over 250 papers on attributes control charts and provides a comprehensive bibliography. The chapter concludes with some guidelines for implementing control charts.

After careful study of this chapter you should be able to do the following:

1. Understand the statistical basis of attributes control charts
2. Know how to design attributes control charts
3. Know how to set up and use the *p* chart for fraction nonconforming
4. Know how to set up and use the *np* control chart for the number of nonconforming items
5. Know how to set up and use the *c* control chart for defects
6. Know how to set up and use the *u* control chart for defects per unit
7. Use attributes control charts with variable sample size
8. Understand the advantages and disadvantages of attributes versus variables control charts
9. Understand the rational subgroup concept for attributes control charts
10. Determine the average run length for attributes control charts

7.1 Introduction

In Chapter 6, we introduced control charts for quality characteristics that are expressed as variables. Although these control charts enjoy widespread application they are not universally applicable because not all quality characteristics can be expressed with variables data. For example, consider a glass container for a liquid product. Suppose we examine a container and classify it into one of the two categories called *conforming* or *nonconforming,* depending on whether the container meets the requirements on one or more quality characteristics. This is an example of **attributes data,** and a control chart for the fraction of nonconforming containers could be established (we show how to do this in Section 7.2). Alternatively, in some processes we may examine a unit of product and count defects or nonconformities on the unit. These types of data are widely encountered in the semiconductor industry, for example. In Section 7.3 we show how to establish control charts for counts, or for the average number of counts per unit.

Attributes charts are generally not as informative as variables charts because there is typically more information in a numerical measurement than in merely classifying a unit as conforming or nonconforming. However, attribute charts do have important applications. They are particularly useful in service industries and in nonmanufacturing quality-improvement efforts because so many of the quality characteristics found in these environments are not easily measured on a numerical scale.

7.2 The Control Chart for Fraction Nonconforming

The **fraction nonconforming** is defined as the ratio of the number of nonconforming items in a population to the total number of items in that population. The items may have *several* quality characteristics that are examined simultaneously by the inspector. If the item does not conform to standard on one or more of these characteristics, it is classified as nonconforming.

We usually express the fraction nonconforming as a decimal, although occasionally the percent nonconforming (which is simply 100% times the fraction nonconforming) is used. When demonstrating or displaying the control chart to production personnel or presenting results to management, the percent nonconforming is often used, as it has more intuitive appeal. Although it is customary to work with fraction nonconforming, we could also analyze the fraction conforming just as easily, resulting in a control chart on **process yield.** For example, many manufacturing organizations operate a yield-management system at each stage of their manufacturing process, with the first-pass yield tracked on a control chart.

The statistical principles underlying the control chart for fraction nonconforming are based on the binomial distribution. Suppose the production process is operating in a stable manner, such that the probability that any unit will not conform to specifications is p, and that successive units produced are independent. Then each unit produced is a realization of a Bernoulli random variable with parameter p. If a random sample of n units of product is selected, and if D is the number of units of product that are nonconforming, then D has a binomial distribution with parameters n and p; that is,

$$P\{D=x\}=\binom{n}{x}p^x(1-p)^{n-x} \qquad x=0,\ 1,\ \ldots,\ n \tag{7.1}$$

From Section 3.2.2 we know that the mean and variance of the random variable D are np and $np(1-p)$, respectively.

The **sample fraction nonconforming** is defined as the ratio of the number of nonconforming units in the sample D to the sample size n; that is,

$$\hat{p}=\frac{D}{n} \tag{7.2}$$

As noted in Section 3.2.2, the distribution of the random variable $\hat{p}$ can be obtained from the binomial. Furthermore, the mean and variance of $\hat{p}$ are

$$\mu_{\hat{p}}=p \tag{7.3}$$

and

$$\sigma_{\hat{p}}^2=\frac{p(1-p)}{n} \tag{7.4}$$

respectively. We will now see how this theory can be applied to the development of a control chart for fraction nonconforming. Because the chart monitors the process fraction nonconforming p, it is also called the p chart.

7.2.1 Development and Operation of the Control Chart

In Chapter 5, we discussed the general statistical principles on which the Shewhart control chart is based. If w is a statistic that measures a quality characteristic, and if the mean of w is μ_w and the variance of w is σ_w^2, then the general model for the Shewhart control chart is as follows:

$$\begin{aligned} \text{UCL} &= \mu_w + L\sigma_w \\ \text{Center line} &= \mu_w \\ \text{LCL} &= \mu_w - L\sigma_w \end{aligned} \tag{7.5}$$

where L is the distance of the control limits from the center line, in multiples of the standard deviation of w. It is customary to choose $L = 3$.

Suppose that the true fraction nonconforming p in the production process is known or is a specified **standard value.** Then from equation (7.5), the center line and control limits of the fraction nonconforming control chart would be as follows:

Fraction Nonconforming Control Chart: Standard Given

$$\begin{aligned} \text{UCL} &= p + 3\sqrt{\frac{p(1-p)}{n}} \\ \text{Center line} &= p \\ \text{LCL} &= p - 3\sqrt{\frac{p(1-p)}{n}} \end{aligned} \tag{7.6}$$

Depending on the values of p and n, sometimes the lower control limit LCL < 0. In these cases, we customarily set LCL = 0 and assume that the control chart only has an upper control limit. The actual operation of this chart would consist of taking subsequent samples of n units, computing the sample fraction nonconforming $\hat{p}$, and plotting the statistic $\hat{p}$ on the chart. As long as $\hat{p}$ remains within the control limits and the sequence of plotted points does not exhibit any systematic nonrandom pattern, we can conclude that the process is in control at the level p. If a point plots outside of the control limits, or if a nonrandom pattern in the plotted points is observed, we can conclude that the process fraction nonconforming has most likely shifted to a new level and the process is out of control.

When the process fraction nonconforming p is not known, then it must be estimated from observed data. The usual procedure is to select m preliminary samples, each of size n. As a general rule, m should be at least 20 or 25. Then if there are D_i nonconforming units in sample i, we compute the fraction nonconforming in the ith sample as

$$\hat{p}_i = \frac{D_i}{n} \qquad i = 1, 2, \ldots, m$$

and the average of these individual sample fractions nonconforming is

$$\bar{p} = \frac{\sum_{i=1}^{m} D_i}{mn} = \frac{\sum_{i=1}^{m} \hat{p}_i}{m} \tag{7.7}$$

The statistic $\bar{p}$ estimates the unknown fraction nonconforming p. The center line and control limits of the control chart for fraction nonconforming are computed as follows:

Fraction Nonconforming Control Chart: No Standard Given

$$\begin{aligned} \text{UCL} &= \bar{p} + 3\sqrt{\frac{\bar{p}(1-\bar{p})}{n}} \\ \text{Center line} &= \bar{p} \\ \text{LCL} &= \bar{p} - 3\sqrt{\frac{\bar{p}(1-\bar{p})}{n}} \end{aligned} \tag{7.8}$$

This control chart is also often called the *p-chart*.

The control limits defined in equation (7.8) should be regarded as **trial control limits.** The sample values of $\hat{p}_i$ from the preliminary subgroups should be plotted against the trial limits to test whether the process was in control when the preliminary data were collected. This is the usual phase I aspect of control chart usage. Any points that exceed the trial control limits should be investigated. If assignable causes for these points are discovered, they should be discarded and new trial control limits determined. Refer to the discussion of trial control limits for the $\bar{x}$ and R charts in Chapter 6.

If the control chart is based on a known or standard value for the fraction nonconforming p, then the calculation of trial control limits is generally unnecessary. However, one should be cautious when working with a standard value for p. Since in practice the true value of p would rarely be known with certainty, we would usually be given a standard value of p that represents a desired or **target value** for the process fraction nonconforming. If this is the case, and future samples indicate an out-of-control condition, we must determine whether the process is out of control at the *target p* but in control at some *other* value of p. For example, suppose we specify a target value of $p = 0.01$, but the process is really in control at a larger value of fraction nonconforming—say, $p = 0.05$. Using the control chart based on $p = 0.01$, we see that many of the points will plot above the upper control limit, indicating an out-of-control condition. However, the process is really out of control only with respect to the target $p = 0.01$. Sometimes it may be possible to "improve" the level of quality by using target values, or to bring a process into control at a particular level of quality performance. In processes where the fraction nonconforming can be controlled by relatively simple process adjustments, target values of p may be useful.

EXAMPLE 7.1 Construction and Operation of a Fraction Nonconforming Control Chart

Frozen orange juice concentrate is packed in 6-oz cardboard cans. These cans are formed on a machine by spinning them from cardboard stock and attaching a metal bottom panel. By inspection of a can, we may determine whether, when filled, it could possibly leak either on the side seam or around the bottom joint. Such a nonconforming can has an improper seal on either the side seam or the bottom panel. Set up a control chart to improve the fraction of nonconforming cans produced by this machine.

SOLUTION

To establish the control chart, 30 samples of $n = 50$ cans each were selected at half-hour intervals over a three-shift period in which the machine was in continuous operation. The data are shown in Table 7.1.

We construct a phase I control chart using this preliminary data to determine if the process was in control when these data were collected. Since the 30 samples contain $\sum_{i=1}^{30} D_i = 347$ nonconforming cans, we find from equation (7.7),

$$\bar{p} = \frac{\sum_{i=1}^{m} D_i}{mn} = \frac{347}{(30)(50)} = 0.2313$$

Using $\bar{p}$ as an estimate of the true process fraction nonconforming, we can now calculate the upper and lower control limits as

$$\bar{p} \pm 3\sqrt{\frac{\bar{p}(1-\bar{p})}{n}} = 0.2313 \pm 3\sqrt{\frac{0.2313(0.7687)}{50}}$$
$$= 0.2313 \pm 3(0.0596)$$
$$= 0.2313 \pm 0.1789$$

Therefore,

$$\text{UCL} = \bar{p} + 3\sqrt{\frac{\bar{p}(1-\bar{p})}{n}} = 0.2313 + 0.1789 = 0.4102$$

and

$$\text{LCL} = \bar{p} - 3\sqrt{\frac{\bar{p}(1-\bar{p})}{n}} = 0.2313 - 0.1789 = 0.0524$$

■ TABLE 7.1
Data for Trial Control Limits, Example 7.1, Sample Size $n = 50$

Sample Number	Number of Nonconforming Cans, D_i	Sample Fraction Nonconforming, $\hat{p}_i$	Sample Number	Number of Nonconforming Cans, D_i	Sample Fraction Nonconforming, $\hat{p}_i$
1	12	0.24	17	10	0.20
2	15	0.30	18	5	0.10
3	8	0.16	19	13	0.26
4	10	0.20	20	11	0.22
5	4	0.08	21	20	0.40
6	7	0.14	22	18	0.36
7	16	0.32	23	24	0.48
8	9	0.18	24	15	0.30
9	14	0.28	25	9	0.18
10	10	0.20	26	12	0.24
11	5	0.10	27	7	0.14
12	6	0.12	28	13	0.26
13	17	0.34	29	9	0.18
14	12	0.24	30	6	0.12
15	22	0.44		347	$\overline{p} = 0.2313$
16	8	0.16			

The control chart with center line at $\overline{p} = 0.2313$ and the above upper and lower control limits is shown in Fig. 7.1. The sample fraction nonconforming from each preliminary sample is plotted on this chart. We note that two points, those from samples 15 and 23, plot above the upper control limit, so the process is not in control. These points must be investigated to see whether an assignable cause can be determined.

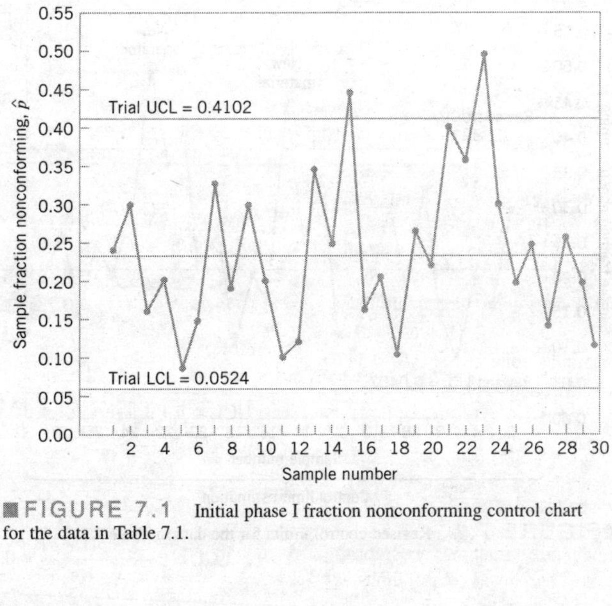

■ FIGURE 7.1 Initial phase I fraction nonconforming control chart for the data in Table 7.1.

(continued)

Analysis of the data from sample 15 indicates that a new batch of cardboard stock was put into production during that half-hour period. The introduction of new batches of raw material sometimes causes irregular production performance, and it is reasonable to believe that this has occurred here. Furthermore, during the half-hour period in which sample 23 was obtained, a relatively inexperienced operator had been temporarily assigned to the machine, and this could account for the high fraction nonconforming obtained from that sample. Consequently, samples 15 and 23 are eliminated, and the new center line and revised control limits are calculated as

$$\bar{p} = \frac{301}{(28)(50)} = 0.2150$$

$$\text{UCL} = \bar{p} + 3\sqrt{\frac{\bar{p}(1-\bar{p})}{n}} = 0.2150 + 3\sqrt{\frac{0.2150(0.7850)}{50}} = 0.3893$$

$$\text{LCL} = \bar{p} - 3\sqrt{\frac{\bar{p}(1-\bar{p})}{n}} = 0.2150 - 3\sqrt{\frac{0.2150(0.7850)}{50}} = 0.0407$$

The revised center line and control limits are shown on the control chart in Fig. 7.2. Note that we have not dropped samples 15 and 23 from the chart, but they have been excluded from the control limit calculations, and we have noted this directly on the control chart. This annotation of the control chart to indicate unusual points, process adjustments, or the type of investigation made at a particular point in time forms a useful record for future process analysis and should become a standard practice in control chart usage.

Note also that the fraction nonconforming from sample 21 now exceeds the upper control limit. However, analysis of the data does not produce any reasonable or logical assignable cause for this, and we decide to retain the point. Therefore, we conclude that the new control limits in Fig. 7.2 can be used for future samples. Thus, we have concluded the control limit estimation phase (phase I) of control chart usage.

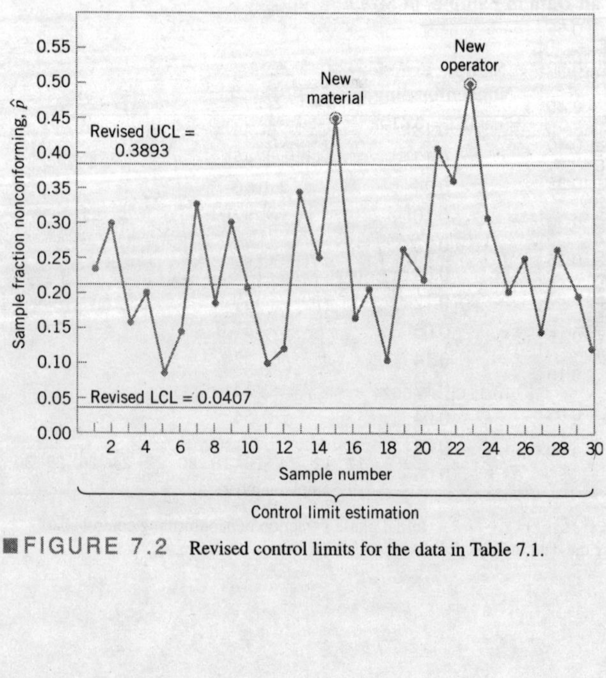

■ FIGURE 7.2 Revised control limits for the data in Table 7.1.

Sometimes examination of control chart data reveals information that affects other points that are not necessarily outside the control limits. For example, if we had found that the temporary operator working when sample 23 was obtained was actually working during the entire two-hour period in which samples 21–24 were obtained, then we should discard all four samples, even if only sample 21 exceeded the control limits, on the grounds that this inexperienced operator probably had some adverse influence on the fraction nonconforming during the entire period.

Before we conclude that the process is in control at this level, we could examine the remaining 28 samples for runs and other nonrandom patterns. The largest run is one of length 5 above the center line, and there are no obvious patterns present in the data. There is no strong evidence of anything other than a random pattern of variation about the center line.

We conclude that the process is in control at the level p = 0.2150 and that the revised control limits should be adopted for monitoring current production. However, we note that although the process is in control, the fraction nonconforming is much too high. That is, the process is operating in a stable manner, and no unusual **operator-controllable** problems are present. It is unlikely that the process quality can be improved by action at the workforce level. The nonconforming cans produced are **management controllable** because an intervention by management in the process will be required to improve performance. Plant management agrees with this observation and directs that, in addition to implementing the control chart program, the engineering staff should analyze the process in an effort to improve the process yield. This study indicates that several adjustments can be made on the machine that should improve its performance.

During the next three shifts following the machine adjustments and the introduction of the control chart, an additional 24 samples of n = 50 observations each are collected. These data are shown in Table 7.2, and the sample fractions nonconforming are plotted on the control chart in Fig. 7.3.

From an examination of Fig. 7.3, our immediate impression is that the process is now operating at a new quality level that is substantially better than the center line level of $\overline{p}$ = 0.2150. One point, that from sample 41, is below the lower control limit. No assignable cause for this out-of-control signal can be determined. The only logical reasons for this ostensible change in process performance are the machine adjustments made by the engineering staff and, possibly, the operators themselves. It is not unusual to find that process performance improves following the introduction of formal statistical process-control procedures, often because the operators are more aware of process quality and because the control chart provides a continuing visual display of process performance.

We may formally test the hypothesis that the process fraction nonconforming in this current three-shift period differs

■ **TABLE 7.2**

Orange Juice Concentrate Can Data in Samples of Size n = 50

Sample Number	Number of Nonconforming Cans, D_i	Sample Fraction Nonconforming, $\hat{p}_i$	Sample Number	Number of Nonconforming Cans, D_i	Sample Fraction Nonconforming, $\hat{p}_i$
31	9	0.18	44	6	0.12
32	6	0.12	45	5	0.10
33	12	0.24	46	4	0.08
34	5	0.10	47	8	0.16
35	6	0.12	48	5	0.10
36	4	0.08	49	6	0.12
37	6	0.12	50	7	0.14
38	3	0.06	51	5	0.10
39	7	0.14	52	6	0.12
40	6	0.12	53	3	0.06
41	2	0.04	54	5	0.10
42	4	0.08		133	$\overline{p}$ = 0.1108
43	3	0.06			

(continued)

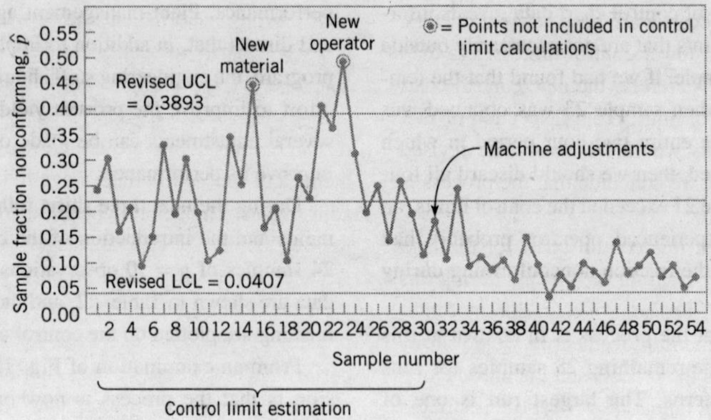

■ FIGURE 7.3 Continuation of the fraction nonconforming control chart, Example 7.1.

from the process fraction nonconforming in the preliminary data, using the procedure given in Section 4.3.4. The hypotheses are

$$H_0: \quad p_1 = p_2$$
$$H_1: \quad p_1 > p_2$$

where p_1 is the process fraction nonconforming from the preliminary data and p_2 is the process fraction nonconforming in the current period. We may estimate p_1 by $\hat{p}_1 = \overline{p} = 0.2150$, and p_2 by

$$\hat{p}_2 = \frac{\sum_{i=31}^{54} D_i}{(50)(24)} = \frac{133}{1200} = 0.1108$$

The (approximate) test statistic for the above hypothesis is, from equation (4.63),

$$Z_0 = \frac{\hat{p}_1 - \hat{p}_2}{\sqrt{\hat{p}(1-\hat{p})\left(\frac{1}{n_1} + \frac{1}{n_2}\right)}}$$

where

$$\hat{p} = \frac{n_1\hat{p}_1 + n_2\hat{p}_2}{n_1 + n_2}$$

In our example, we have

$$\hat{p} = \frac{(1400)(0.2150) + (1200)(0.1108)}{1400 + 1200} = 0.1669$$

and

$$Z_0 = \frac{0.2150 - 0.1108}{\sqrt{(0.1669)(0.8331)\left(\frac{1}{1400} + \frac{1}{1200}\right)}} = 7.10$$

Comparing this to the upper 0.05 point of the standard normal distribution, we find that $Z_0 = 7.10 > Z_{0.05} = 1.645$. Consequently, we reject H_0 and conclude that there has been a significant decrease in the process fallout.

Based on the apparently successful process adjustments, it seems logical to revise the control limits again, using only the most recent samples (numbers 31–54). This results in the new control chart parameters:

$$\text{Center line} = \overline{p} = 0.1108$$

$$\text{UCL} = \overline{p} + 3\sqrt{\frac{\overline{p}(1-\overline{p})}{n}} = 0.1108 + 3\sqrt{\frac{(0.1108)(0.8892)}{50}} = 0.2440$$

$$\text{LCL} = \overline{p} - 3\sqrt{\frac{\overline{p}(1-\overline{p})}{n}} = 0.1108 - 3\sqrt{\frac{(0.1108)(0.8892)}{50}} = -0.0224 = 0$$

Figure 7.4 shows the control chart with these new parameters. Note that since the calculated lower control limit is less than zero, we have set LCL = 0. Therefore, the new control chart will have only an upper control limit. From inspection of Fig. 7.4, we see that all the points would fall inside the revised upper control limit; therefore, we conclude that the process is in control at this new level.

The continued operation of this control chart for the next five shifts is shown in Fig. 7.5. Data for the process during this period are shown in Table 7.3. The control chart does not indicate lack of control. Despite the improvement in yield following the engineering changes in the process and the introduction of the control chart, the process fallout of $\overline{p} = 0.1108$ is still too high. Further analysis and action will be required to improve the yield. These management interventions may be further adjustments to the machine. **Statistically designed experiments** (see Part IV) are an appropriate way to determine which machine adjustments are critical to further process improvement, and the appropriate magnitude and direction of these adjustments. The control chart should be continued during the period in which the adjustments are made. By marking the time scale of the control chart *when* a process change is made, the control chart becomes a **logbook** in which the timing of process interventions and their subsequent effect on process performance are easily seen. This logbook aspect of control chart usage is extremely important.

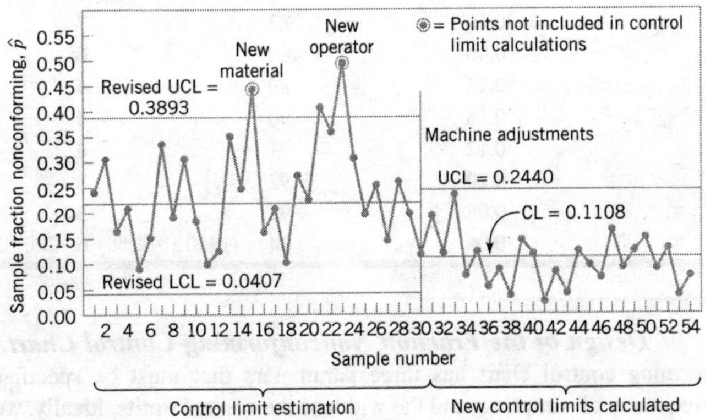

■ **FIGURE 7.4** New control limits on the fraction nonconforming control chart, Example 7.1.

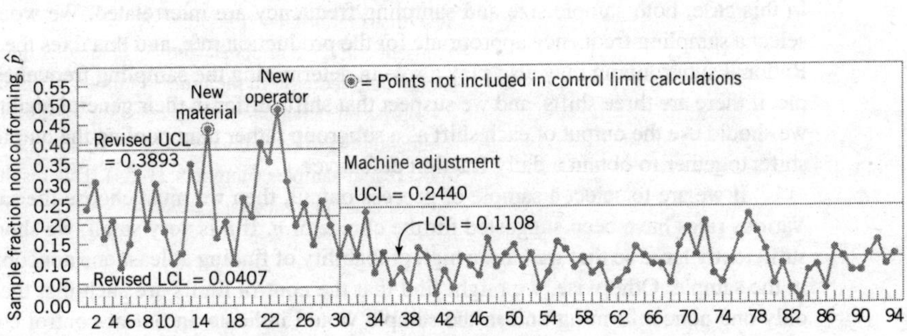

■ **FIGURE 7.5** Completed fraction nonconforming control chart, Example 7.1.

(continued)

■ TABLE 7.3
New Data for the Fraction Nonconforming Control Chart in Fig. 7.5, $n = 50$

Sample Number	Number of Nonconforming Cans, D_i	Sample Fraction Nonconforming, $\hat{p}_i$	Sample Number	Number of Nonconforming Cans, D_i	Sample Fraction Nonconforming, $\hat{p}_i$
55	8	0.16	75	5	0.10
56	7	0.14	76	8	0.16
57	5	0.10	77	11	0.22
58	6	0.12	78	9	0.18
59	4	0.08	79	7	0.14
60	5	0.10	80	3	0.06
61	2	0.04	81	5	0.10
62	3	0.06	82	2	0.04
63	4	0.08	83	1	0.02
64	7	0.14	84	4	0.08
65	6	0.12	85	5	0.10
66	5	0.10	86	3	0.06
67	5	0.10	87	7	0.14
68	3	0.06	88	6	0.12
69	7	0.14	89	4	0.08
70	9	0.18	90	4	0.08
71	6	0.12	91	6	0.12
72	10	0.20	92	8	0.16
73	4	0.08	93	5	0.10
74	3	0.06	94	6	0.12

Design of the Fraction Nonconforming Control Chart. The fraction nonconforming control chart has three parameters that must be specified: the sample size, the frequency of sampling, and the width of the control limits. Ideally, we should have some general guidelines for selecting those parameters.

It is relatively common to base a control chart for fraction nonconforming on 100% inspection of *all* process output over some convenient period of time, such as a shift or a day. In this case, both sample size and sampling frequency are interrelated. We would generally select a sampling frequency appropriate for the production rate, and this fixes the sample size. Rational subgrouping may also play a role in determining the sampling frequency. For example, if there are three shifts, and we suspect that shifts differ in their general quality level, then we should use the output of each shift as a subgroup rather than pooling the output of all three shifts together to obtain a daily fraction defective.

If we are to select a sample of process output, then we must choose the sample size n. Various rules have been suggested for the choice of n. If p is very small, we should choose n sufficiently large so that we have a high probability of finding at least one nonconforming unit in the sample. Otherwise, we might find that the control limits are such that the presence of only one nonconforming unit in the sample would indicate an out-of-control condition. For example, if $p = 0.01$ and $n = 8$, we find that the upper control limit is

$$\text{UCL} = p + 3\sqrt{\frac{p(1-p)}{n}} = 0.01 + 3\sqrt{\frac{(0.01)(0.99)}{8}} = 0.1155$$

If there is one nonconforming unit in the sample, then $\hat{p} = \frac{1}{8} = 0.1250$, and we can conclude that the process is out of control. Since for any $p > 0$ there is a positive probability of producing *some* defectives, it is unreasonable in many cases to conclude that the process is out of control on observing a single nonconforming item.

To avoid this pitfall, we can choose the sample size n so that the probability of finding at least one nonconforming unit per sample is at least γ. For example, suppose that $p = 0.01$, and we want the probability of at least one nonconforming unit in the sample to be at least 0.95. If D denotes the number of nonconforming units, then we want to find n such that $P\{D \geq 1\} \geq 0.95$. Using the Poisson approximation to the binomial, we find from the cumulative Poisson table that $\lambda = np$ must exceed 3.00. Consequently, since $p = 0.01$, this implies that the sample size should be 300.

Duncan (1986) has suggested that the sample size should be large enough that we have approximately a 50% chance of detecting a process shift of some specified amount. For example, suppose that $p = 0.01$, and we want the probability of detecting a shift to $p = 0.05$ to be 0.50. Assuming that the normal approximation to the binomial applies, we should choose n so that the upper control limit exactly coincides with the fraction nonconforming in the out-of-control state.[1] If δ is the magnitude of the process shift, then n must satisfy

$$\delta = L\sqrt{\frac{p(1-p)}{n}} \tag{7.9}$$

Therefore,

$$n = \left(\frac{L}{\delta}\right)^2 p(1-p) \tag{7.10}$$

In our example, $p = 0.01$, $\delta = 0.05 - 0.01 = 0.04$, and if three-sigma limits are used, then from equation (7.10),

$$n = \left(\frac{3}{0.04}\right)^2 (0.01)(0.99) = 56$$

If the in-control value of the fraction nonconforming is small, another useful criterion is to choose n large enough so that the control chart will have a positive lower control limit. This ensures that we will have a mechanism to force us to investigate one or more samples that contain an unusually small number of nonconforming items. Since we wish to have

$$\text{LCL} = p - L\sqrt{\frac{p(1-p)}{n}} > 0 \tag{7.11}$$

this implies that

$$n > \frac{(1-p)}{p} L^2 \tag{7.12}$$

For example, if $p = 0.05$ and three-sigma limits are used, the sample size must be

$$n > \frac{0.95}{0.05}(3)^2 = 171$$

Thus, if $n \geq 172$ units, the control chart will have a positive lower control limit.

[1] If $\hat{p}$ is approximately normal, then the probability that $\hat{p}$ exceeds the UCL is 0.50 if the UCL equals the out-of-control fraction nonconforming p, due to the symmetry of the normal distribution. See Section 3.4.3 for a discussion of the normal approximation to the binomial.

Three-sigma control limits are usually employed on the control chart for fraction nonconforming on the grounds that they have worked well in practice. As discussed in Section 5.3.2, narrower control limits would make the control chart more sensitive to small shifts in p but at the expense of more frequent "false alarms." Occasionally, we have seen narrower limits used in an effort to *force* improvement in process quality. Care must be exercised in this, however, as too many false alarms will destroy the operating personnel's confidence in the control chart program.

We should note that the fraction nonconforming control chart is not a universal model for *all* data on fraction nonconforming. It is based on the binomial probability model; that is, the probability of occurrence of a nonconforming unit is *constant,* and successive units of production are *independent.* In processes where nonconforming units are clustered together, or where the probability of a unit being nonconforming depends on whether or not previous units were nonconforming, the fraction nonconforming control chart is often of little use. In such cases, it is necessary to develop a control chart based on the correct probability model.

Interpretation of Points on the Control Chart for Fraction Nonconforming. Example 7.1 illustrated how points that plot beyond the control limits are treated, both in establishing the control chart and during its routine operation. Care must be exercised in interpreting points that plot *below* the lower control limit. These points often do not represent a real improvement in process quality. Frequently, they are caused by errors in the inspection process resulting from inadequately trained or inexperienced inspectors or from improperly calibrated test and inspection equipment. We have also seen cases in which inspectors deliberately passed nonconforming units or reported fictitious data. The analyst must keep these warnings in mind when looking for assignable causes if points plot below the lower control limits. Not all downward shifts in p are attributable to improved quality.

The* np *Control Chart. It is also possible to base a control chart on the number nonconforming rather than the fraction nonconforming. This is often called an **number nonconforming (*np*) control chart.** The parameters of this chart are as follows.

The *np* Control Chart

$$\begin{aligned} \text{UCL} &= np + 3\sqrt{np(1-p)} \\ \text{Center line} &= np \\ \text{LCL} &= np - 3\sqrt{np(1-p)} \end{aligned} \tag{7.13}$$

If a standard value for p is unavailable, then $\bar{p}$ can be used to estimate p. Many nonstatistically trained personnel find the np chart easier to interpret than the usual fraction nonconforming control chart.

EXAMPLE 7.2 An *np* Control Chart

Set up an np control chart for the orange juice concentrate can process in Example 7.1.

Using the data in Table 7.1, we found that

$$\bar{p} = 0.2313 \qquad n = 50$$

SOLUTION

Therefore, the parameters of the *np* control chart would be

$$\text{UCL} = n\bar{p} + 3\sqrt{n\bar{p}(1-\bar{p})} = 50(0.2313) + 3\sqrt{(50)(0.2313)(0.7687)} = 20.510$$

$$\text{Center line} = n\bar{p} = 50(0.2313) = 11.565$$

$$\text{LCL} = n\bar{p} - 3\sqrt{n\bar{p}(1-\bar{p})} = 50(0.2313) - 3\sqrt{(50)(0.2313)(0.7687)} = 2.620$$

Now in practice, the number of nonconforming units in each sample is plotted on the *np* control chart, and the number of nonconforming units is an integer. Thus, if 20 units are nonconforming the process is in control, but if 21 occur the process is out of control. Similarly, there are three nonconforming units in the sample and the process is in control, but two nonconforming units would imply an out-of-control process. Some practitioners prefer to use integer values for control limits on the *np* chart instead of their decimal fraction counterparts. In this example we could choose 2 and 21 as the LCL and UCL, respectively, and the process would be considered out of control if a sample value of *np* plotted at or beyond the control limits.

7.2.2 Variable Sample Size

In some applications of the control chart for fraction nonconforming, the sample is a 100% inspection of process output over some period of time. Since different numbers of units could be produced in each period, the control chart would then have a variable sample size. There are three approaches to constructing and operating a control chart with a variable sample size.

Variable-Width Control Limits. The first and perhaps the most simple approach is to determine control limits for each individual sample that are based on the specific sample size. That is, if the *i*th sample is of size n_i, then the upper and lower control limits are $\bar{p} \pm 3\sqrt{\bar{p}(1-\bar{p})/n_i}$. Note that the width of the control limits is inversely proportional to the square root of the sample size.

To illustrate this approach, consider the data in Table 7.4. These data came from the purchasing group of a large aerospace company. This group issues purchase orders to the company's suppliers. The sample sizes in Table 7.4 are the total number of purchase orders issued each week. Obviously, this is not constant. A nonconforming unit is a purchase order with an error. Among the most common errors are specifying incorrect part numbers, wrong delivery dates, and wrong supplier information. Any of these mistakes can result in a purchase order change, which takes time and resources and may result in delayed delivery of material.

For the 25 samples, we calculate

$$\bar{p} = \frac{\sum_{i=1}^{25} D_i}{\sum_{i=1}^{25} n_i} = \frac{234}{2450} = 0.096$$

Consequently, the center line is at 0.096, and the control limits are

$$\text{UCL} = \bar{p} + 3\hat{\sigma}_{\hat{p}} = 0.096 + 3\sqrt{\frac{(0.096)(0.904)}{n_i}}$$

and

$$\text{LCL} = \bar{p} - 3\hat{\sigma}_{\hat{p}} = 0.096 - 3\sqrt{\frac{(0.096)(0.904)}{n_i}}$$

■ TABLE 7.4

Purchase Order Data for a Control Chart for Fraction Nonconforming with Variable Sample Size

Sample Number, i	Sample Size, n_i	Number of Nonconforming Units, D_i	Sample Fraction Nonconforming, $\hat{p}_i = D_i/n_i$	Standard Deviation $\hat{\sigma}_{\hat{p}} = \sqrt{\frac{(0.096)(0.904)}{n_i}}$	Control Limits LCL	Control Limits UCL
1	100	12	0.120	0.029	0.009	0.183
2	80	8	0.100	0.033	0	0.195
3	80	6	0.075	0.033	0	0.195
4	100	9	0.090	0.029	0.009	0.183
5	110	10	0.091	0.028	0.012	0.180
6	110	12	0.109	0.028	0.012	0.180
7	100	11	0.110	0.029	0.009	0.183
8	100	16	0.160	0.029	0.009	0.183
9	90	10	0.110	0.031	0.003	0.189
10	90	6	0.067	0.031	0.003	0.189
11	110	20	0.182	0.028	0.012	0.180
12	120	15	0.125	0.027	0.015	0.177
13	120	9	0.075	0.027	0.015	0.177
14	120	8	0.067	0.027	0.015	0.177
15	110	6	0.055	0.028	0.012	0.180
16	80	8	0.100	0.033	0	0.195
17	80	10	0.125	0.033	0	0.195
18	80	7	0.088	0.033	0	0.195
19	90	5	0.056	0.031	0.003	0.189
20	100	8	0.080	0.029	0.009	0.183
21	100	5	0.050	0.029	0.009	0.183
22	100	8	0.080	0.029	0.009	0.183
23	100	10	0.100	0.029	0.009	0.183
24	90	6	0.067	0.031	0.003	0.189
25	90	9	0.100	0.031	0.003	0.189
	2450	234	2.383			

where $\hat{\sigma}_{\hat{p}}$ is the estimate of the standard deviation of the sample fraction nonconforming $\hat{p}$. The calculations to determine the control limits are displayed in the last three columns of Table 7.4. The manually constructed control chart is plotted in Fig. 7.6.

Many popular quality control computer programs will handle the variable sample size case. Figure 7.7 presents the computer-generated control chart corresponding to Fig. 7.6. This control chart was obtained using Minitab.

Control Limits Based on an Average Sample Size. The second approach is to base the control chart on an *average* **sample size,** resulting in an **approximate set of control limits.** This assumes that future sample sizes will not differ greatly from those previously observed. If this approach is used, the control limits will be *constant,* and the resulting control chart will not look as formidable to operating personnel as the control chart with variable limits. However, if there is an unusually large variation in the size of a particular sample or if a point plots near the approximate control limits, then the *exact* control limits for that point

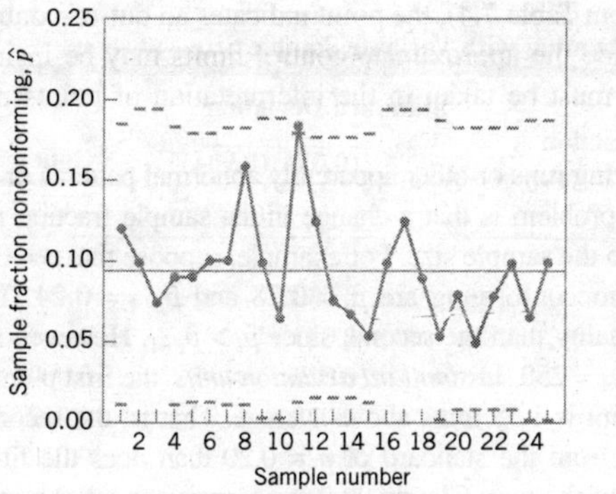

FIGURE 7.6 Control chart for fraction nonconforming with variable sample size.

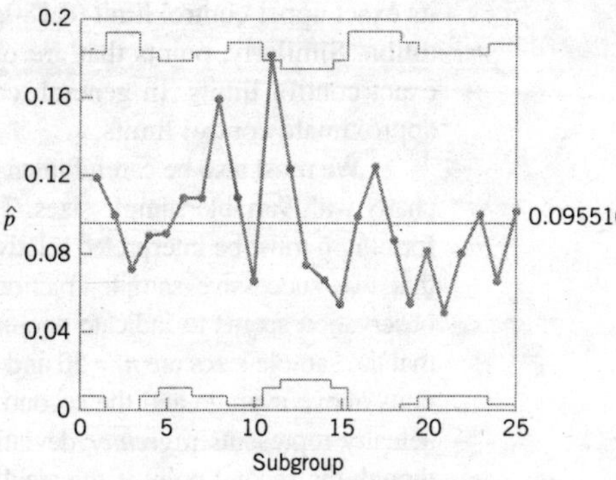

FIGURE 7.7 Control chart for fraction nonconforming with variable sample size using Minitab.

should be determined and the point examined relative to that value. For the purchase order data in Table 7.4, we find that the average sample size is

$$\bar{n} = \frac{\sum_{i=1}^{25} n_i}{25} = \frac{2450}{25} = 98$$

Therefore, the approximate control limits are

$$\text{UCL} = \bar{p} + 3\sqrt{\frac{\bar{p}(1-\bar{p})}{\bar{n}}} = 0.096 + 3\sqrt{\frac{(0.096)(0.904)}{98}} = 0.185$$

and

$$\text{LCL} = \bar{p} - \sqrt{\frac{\bar{p}(1-\bar{p})}{\bar{n}}} = 0.096 - 3\sqrt{\frac{(0.096)(0.904)}{98}} = 0.007$$

The resulting control chart is shown in Fig. 7.8. Note that $\hat{p}$ for sample 11 plots close to the approximate upper control limit, yet it appears to be in control. However, when compared to

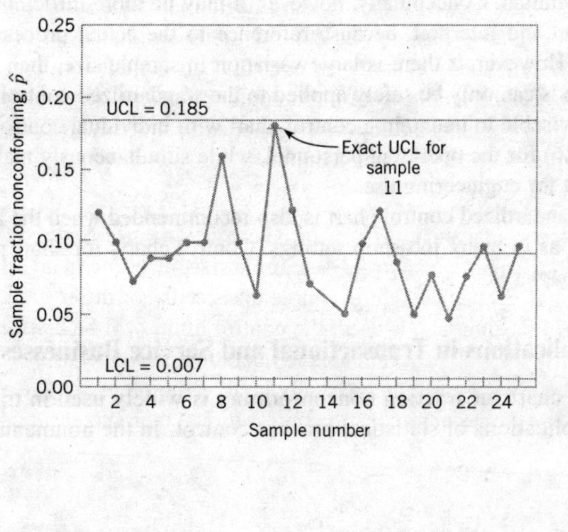

FIGURE 7.8 Control chart for fraction nonconforming based on average sample size.

its exact upper control limit (0.180, from Table 7.4), the point indicates an out-of-control condition. Similarly, points that are outside the approximate control limits may be inside their exact control limits. In general, care must be taken in the interpretation of points near the approximate control limits.

We must also be careful in analyzing runs or other apparently abnormal patterns on control charts with variable sample sizes. The problem is that a change in the sample fraction nonconforming $\hat{p}$ must be interpreted relative to the sample size. For example, suppose that $p = 0.20$ and that two successive sample fractions nonconforming are $\hat{p}_t = 0.28$ and $\hat{p}_{i+1} = 0.24$. The first observation seems to indicate poorer quality than the second, since $\hat{p}_i > \hat{p}_{i+1}$. However, suppose that the sample sizes are $n_i = 50$ and $n_{i+1} = 250$. In *standard deviation units,* the first point is 1.41 units above average and the second point is 1.58 units above average. That is, the second point actually represents a *greater* deviation from the standard of $p = 0.20$ than does the first, even though the second point is the smaller of the two. Clearly, looking for runs or other nonrandom patterns is virtually meaningless here.

The Standardized Control Chart. The third approach to dealing with variable sample size is to use a **standardized control chart,** where the points are plotted in standard deviation units. Such a control chart has the center line at zero, and upper and lower control limits of +3 and −3, respectively. The variable plotted on the chart is

$$Z_i = \frac{\hat{p}_i - p}{\sqrt{\dfrac{p(1-p)}{n_i}}} \tag{7.14}$$

where p (or $\bar{p}$ if no standard is given) is the process fraction nonconforming in the in-control state. The standardized control chart for the purchase order data in Table 7.4 is shown in Fig. 7.9. The calculations associated with this control chart are shown in Table 7.5. Tests for runs and pattern-recognition methods could safely be applied to this chart, because the relative changes from one point to another are all expressed in terms of the same units of measurement.

The standardized control chart is no more difficult to construct or maintain than either of the other two procedures discussed in this section. In fact, many quality control software packages either automatically execute this as a standard feature or can be programmed to plot a standardized control chart. For example, the version of Fig. 7.9 shown in Fig. 7.10 was created using Minitab. Conceptually, however, it may be more difficult for operating personnel to understand and interpret, because reference to the actual process fraction defective has been "lost." However, if there is large variation in sample size, then runs and pattern-recognition methods can only be safely applied to the standardized control chart. In such a case, it might be advisable to maintain a control chart with individual control limits for each sample (as in Fig. 7.6) for the operating personnel, while simultaneously maintaining a standardized control chart for engineering use.

The standardized control chart is also recommended when the length of the production run is short, as in many job-shop settings. Control charts for short production runs are discussed in Chapter 9.

7.2.3 Applications in Transactional and Service Businesses

The control chart for fraction nonconforming is widely used in transactional and service industry applications of statistical process control. In the nonmanufacturing environment,

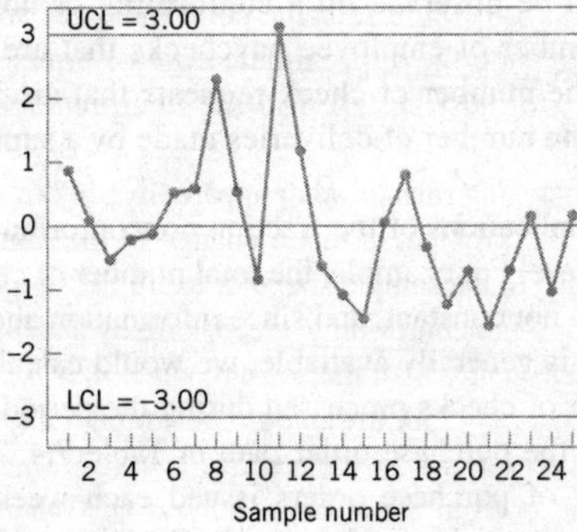

■ FIGURE 7.9 Standardized control chart for fraction nonconforming.

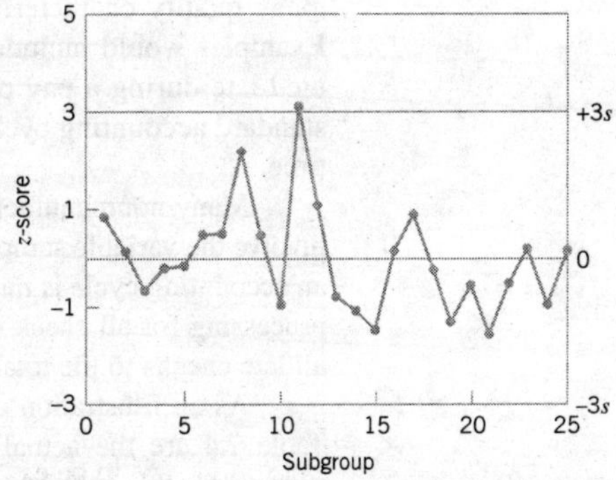

■ FIGURE 7.10 Standardized control chart from Minitab for fraction nonconforming, Table 7.4.

■ **TABLE 7.5**
Calculations for the Standardized Control Chart in Fig. 7.9, $\hat{p} = 0.096$

Sample Number, i	Sample Size, n_i	Number of Nonconforming Units, D_i	Sample Fraction Nonconforming, $\hat{p}_i = D_i/n_i$	Standard Deviation $\hat{\sigma}_p = \sqrt{\frac{(0.096)(0.904)}{n_i}}$	$z_i = \frac{\hat{p}_i - \bar{p}}{\sqrt{\frac{(0.096)(0.904)}{n_i}}}$
1	100	12	0.120	0.029	0.83
2	80	8	0.100	0.033	0.12
3	80	6	0.075	0.033	–0.64
4	100	9	0.090	0.029	–0.21
5	110	10	0.091	0.028	–0.18
6	110	12	0.109	0.028	0.46
7	100	11	0.110	0.029	0.48
8	100	16	0.160	0.029	2.21
9	90	10	0.110	0.031	0.45
10	90	6	0.067	0.031	–0.94
11	110	20	0.182	0.028	3.07
12	120	15	0.125	0.027	1.07
13	120	9	0.075	0.027	–0.78
14	120	8	0.067	0.027	–1.07
15	110	6	0.055	0.028	–1.46
16	80	8	0.100	0.033	0.12
17	80	10	0.125	0.033	0.88
18	80	7	0.088	0.033	–0.24
19	90	5	0.056	0.031	–1.29
20	100	8	0.080	0.029	–0.55
21	100	5	0.050	0.029	–1.59
22	100	8	0.080	0.029	–0.55
23	100	10	0.100	0.029	0.14
24	90	6	0.067	0.031	–0.94
25	90	9	0.100	0.031	0.13

many quality characteristics can be observed on a conforming or nonconforming basis. Examples would include the number of employee paychecks that are in error or distributed late during a pay period, the number of check requests that are not paid within the standard accounting cycle, and the number of deliveries made by a supplier that are not on time.

Many nonmanufacturing applications of the fraction nonconforming control chart will involve the variable sample size case. For example, the total number of check requests during an accounting cycle is most likely not constant, and since information about the timeliness of processing for all check requests is generally available, we would calculate $\hat{p}$ as the ratio of all late checks to the total number of checks processed during the period.

As an illustration consider the purchase order data in Table 7.4. The sample sizes in Table 7.4 are the actual number of purchase orders issued each week. It would be very unusual for this to be exactly the same from week to week. Consequently, a fraction nonconforming control chart with variable sample size was an ideal approach for this situation. The use of this control chart was a key initial step in identifying many of the root causes of the errors on purchase orders and in developing the corrective actions necessary to improve the process.

7.2.4 The Operating-Characteristic Function and Average Run Length Calculations

The operating-characteristic (or OC) function of the fraction nonconforming control chart is a graphical display of the probability of incorrectly accepting the hypothesis of statistical control (i.e., a type II or β-error) against the process fraction nonconforming. The OC curve provides a measure of the **sensitivity** of the control chart—that is, its ability to detect a shift in the process fraction nonconforming from the nominal value $\bar{p}$ to some other value p. The probability of type II error for the fraction nonconforming control chart may be computed from

$$\begin{aligned}\beta &= P\{\hat{p} < \text{UCL}|p\} - P\{\hat{p} \le \text{LCL}|p\} \\ &= P\{D < n\text{UCL}|p\} - P\{D \le n\text{LCL}|p\}\end{aligned} \tag{7.15}$$

Since D is a binomial random variable with parameters n and p, the β-error defined in equation (7.15) can be obtained from the cumulative binomial distribution. Note that when the LCL is negative, the second term on the right-hand side of equation (7.15) should be dropped.

Table 7.6 illustrates the calculations required to generate the OC curve for a control chart for fraction nonconforming with parameters $n = 50$, LCL = 0.0303, and UCL = 0.3697. Using these parameters, equation (7.15) becomes

$$\begin{aligned}\beta &= P\{D < (50)(0.3697)|p\} - P\{D \le (50)(0.0303)|p\} \\ &= P\{D < 18.49|p\} - P\{D \le 1.52|p\}\end{aligned}$$

However, since D must be an integer, we find that

$$\beta = P\{D \le 18|p\} - P\{D \le 1|p\}$$

The OC curve is plotted in Fig. 7.11.

■ TABLE 7.6

Calculations[a] for Constructing the OC Curve for a Control Chart for Fraction Nonconforming with $n = 50$, LCL = 0.0303, and UCL = 0.3697

p	$P\{D \le 18 \mid p\}$	$P\{D \le 1 \mid p\}$	$\beta = P\{D \le 18 \mid p\} - P\{D \le 1 \mid p\}$
0.01	1.0000	0.9106	0.0894
0.03	1.0000	0.5553	0.4447
0.05	1.0000	0.2794	0.7206
0.10	1.0000	0.0338	0.9662
0.15	0.9999	0.0029	0.9970
0.20	0.9975	0.0002	0.9973
0.25	0.9713	0.0000	0.9713
0.30	0.8594	0.0000	0.8594
0.35	0.6216	0.0000	0.6216
0.40	0.3356	0.0000	0.3356
0.45	0.1273	0.0000	0.1273
0.50	0.0325	0.0000	0.0325
0.55	0.0053	0.0000	0.0053

[a]The probabilities in this table were found by evaluating the cumulative binomial distribution. For small p ($p < 0.1$, say) the Poisson approximation could be used, and for larger values of p the normal approximation could be used.

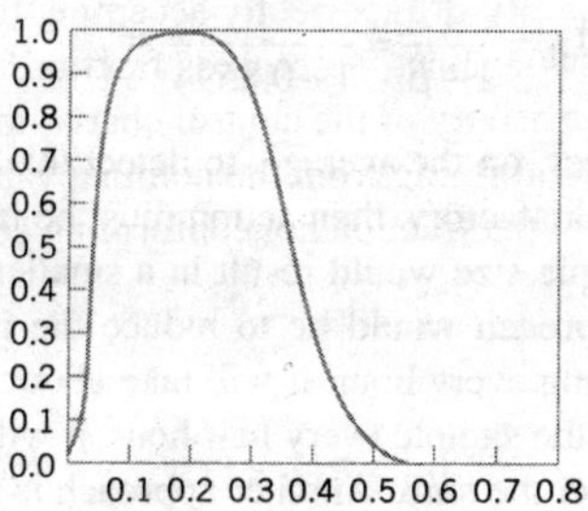

■ FIGURE 7.11 Operating-characteristic curve for the fraction nonconforming control chart with $\bar{p} = 0.20$, LCL = 0.0303, and UCL = 0.3697.

We may also calculate average run lengths (ARLs) for the fraction nonconforming control chart. Recall from Chapter 5 that for uncorrelated process data the ARL for any Shewhart control chart can be written as

$$\text{ARL} = \frac{1}{P(\text{sample point plots out of control})}$$

Thus, if the process is in control, ARL_0 is

$$\text{ARL}_0 = \frac{1}{\alpha}$$

and if it is out of control, then

$$ARL_1 = \frac{1}{1-\beta}$$

These probabilities (α, β) can be calculated directly from the binomial distribution or read from an OC curve.

To illustrate, consider the control chart for fraction nonconforming used in the OC curve calculations in Table 7.6. This chart has parameters $n = 50$, UCL = 0.3697, LCL = 0.0303, and the center line is $\bar{p} = 0.20$. From Table 7.6 (or the OC curve in Fig. 7.11) we find that if the process is in control with $p = \bar{p}$, the probability of a point plotting in control is 0.9973. Thus, in this case $\alpha = 1 - \beta = 0.0027$, and the value of ARL_0 is

$$ARL_0 = \frac{1}{\alpha} = \frac{1}{0.0027} \simeq 370$$

Therefore, if the process is really in control, we will experience a false out-of-control signal about every 370 samples. (This will be approximately true, in general, for any Shewhart control chart with three-sigma limits.) This in-control ARL_0 is generally considered to be satisfactorily large. Now suppose that the process shifts out of control to $p = 0.3$. Table 7.6 indicates that if $p = 0.3$, then $\beta = 0.8594$. Therefore, the value of ARL_1 is

$$ARL_1 = \frac{1}{1-\beta} = \frac{1}{1-0.8594} \simeq 7$$

and it will take about seven samples, on the average, to detect this shift with a point outside of the control limits. If this is unsatisfactory, then action must be taken to reduce the out-of-control ARL_1. Increasing the sample size would result in a smaller value of β and a shorter out-of-control ARL_1. Another approach would be to reduce the interval *between* samples. That is, if we are currently sampling every hour, it will take about seven hours, on the average, to detect the shift. If we take the sample every half hour, it will require only three and a half hours, on the average, to detect the shift. Another approach is to use a control chart that is more responsive to small shifts, such as the cumulative sum charts in Chapter 9.

7.3 Control Charts for Nonconformities (Defects)

A nonconforming item is a unit of product that does not satisfy one or more of the specifications for that product. Each specific point at which a specification is not satisfied results in a **defect** or **nonconformity.** Consequently, a nonconforming item will contain at least one nonconformity. However, depending on their nature and severity, it is quite possible for a unit to contain several nonconformities and *not* be classified as nonconforming. As an example, suppose we are manufacturing personal computers. Each unit could have one or more very minor flaws in the cabinet finish, and since these flaws do not seriously affect the unit's functional operation, it could be classified as conforming. However, if there are too many of these flaws, the personal computer should be classified as nonconforming, since the flaws would be very noticeable to the customer and might affect the sale of the unit. There are many practical situations in which we prefer to work directly with the number of defects or nonconformities rather than the fraction nonconforming. These include the number of defective welds in 100 m of oil pipeline, the number of broken rivets in an aircraft wing, the number of functional defects in an electronic logic device, the number of errors on a document, and so forth.

It is possible to develop control charts for either the **total number of nonconformities** in a unit or the **average number of nonconformities per unit.** These control charts usually assume that the occurrence of nonconformities in samples of constant size is well modeled by the Poisson distribution. Essentially, this requires that the number of opportunities or potential locations for nonconformities be infinitely large and that the probability of occurrence of a nonconformity at any location be small and constant. Furthermore, the **inspection unit** must be the same for each sample. That is, each inspection unit must always represent an identical **area of opportunity** for the occurrence of nonconformities. In addition, we can count nonconformities of several different types on one unit, as long as the above conditions are satisfied for each class of nonconformity.

In most practical situations, these conditions will not be satisfied exactly. The number of opportunities for the occurrence of nonconformities may be finite, or the probability of occurrence of nonconformities may not be constant. As long as these departures from the assumptions are not severe, the Poisson model will usually work reasonably well. There are cases, however, in which the Poisson model is completely inappropriate. These situations are discussed in more detail at the end of Section 7.3.1.

7.3.1 Procedures with Constant Sample Size

Consider the occurrence of nonconformities in an inspection unit of product. In most cases, the inspection unit will be a single unit of product, although this is not necessarily always so. The inspection unit is simply an entity for which it is convenient to keep records. It could be a group of 5 units of product, 10 units of product, and so on. Suppose that defects or nonconformities occur in this inspection unit according to the Poisson distribution; that is,

$$p(x) = \frac{e^{-c}c^x}{x!} \qquad x = 0, 1, 2, \ldots$$

where x is the number of nonconformities and $c > 0$ is the parameter of the Poisson distribution. From Section 3.2.3 we recall that both the mean and variance of the Poisson distribution are the parameter c. Therefore, a **control chart for nonconformities, or c chart** with three-sigma limits would be defined as follows,[2]

Control Chart for Nonconformities: Standard Given

$$\begin{aligned} \text{UCL} &= c + 3\sqrt{c} \\ \text{Center line} &= c \\ \text{LCL} &= c - 3\sqrt{c} \end{aligned} \qquad (7.16)$$

assuming that a standard value for c is available. Should these calculations yield a negative value for the LCL, set LCL = 0.

If no standard is given, then c may be estimated as the observed average number of nonconformities in a preliminary sample of inspection units—say, $\bar{c}$. In this case, the control chart has parameters defined as follows.

[2]The α-risk for three-sigma limits is not equally allocated above the UCL and below the LCL, because the Poisson distribution is asymmetric. Some authors recommend the use of probability limits for this chart, particularly when c is small.

Control Chart for Nonconformities: No Standard Given

$$\begin{aligned} \text{UCL} &= \bar{c} + 3\sqrt{\bar{c}} \\ \text{Center line} &= \bar{c} \\ \text{LCL} &= \bar{c} - 3\sqrt{\bar{c}} \end{aligned} \tag{7.17}$$

When no standard is given, the control limits in equation (7.17) should be regarded as *trial* control limits, and the preliminary samples examined for lack of control in the usual phase I analysis. The control chart for nonconformities is also sometimes called the *c* chart.

EXAMPLE 7.3 Nonconformities in Printed Circuit Boards

Table 7.7 presents the number of nonconformities observed in 26 successive samples of 100 printed circuit boards. Note that, for reasons of convenience, the inspection unit is defined as 100 boards. Set up a *c* chart for these data.

■ **TABLE 7.7**
Data on the Number of Nonconformities in Samples of 100 Printed Circuit Boards

Sample Number	Number of Nonconformities	Sample Number	Number of Nonconformities
1	21	14	19
2	24	15	10
3	16	16	17
4	12	17	13
5	15	18	22
6	5	19	18
7	28	20	39
8	20	21	30
9	31	22	24
10	25	23	16
11	20	24	19
12	24	25	17
13	16	26	15

SOLUTION

Since the 26 samples contain 516 total nonconformities, we estimate *c* by

$$\bar{c} = \frac{516}{26} = 19.85$$

Therefore, the trial control limits are given by

$$\begin{aligned} \text{UCL} &= \bar{c} + 3\sqrt{\bar{c}} = 19.85 + 3\sqrt{19.85} = 33.22 \\ \text{Center line} &= \bar{c} = 19.85 \\ \text{LCL} &= \bar{c} - 3\sqrt{\bar{c}} = 19.85 - 3\sqrt{19.85} = 6.48 \end{aligned}$$

The control chart is shown in Fig. 7.12. The number of observed nonconformities from the preliminary samples is plotted on this chart. Two points plot outside the control limits, samples 6 and 20. Investigation of sample 6 revealed that a new inspector had examined the boards in this sample and that he did not recognize several of the types of nonconformities that could have been present. Furthermore, the unusually large number of nonconformities in sample 20 resulted from a temperature control problem in the wave soldering machine, which was subsequently repaired. Therefore, it seems reasonable to exclude these two

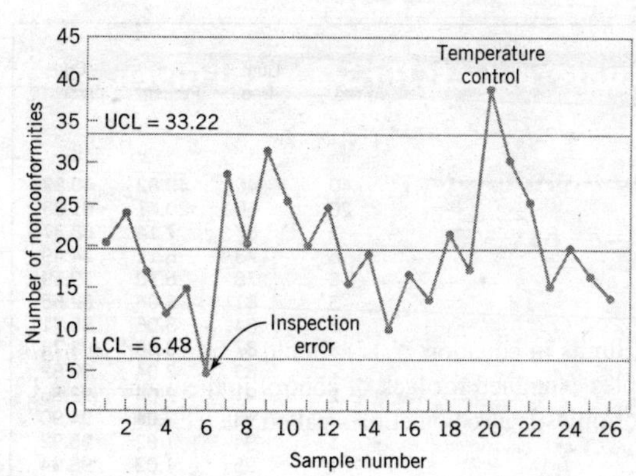

FIGURE 7.12 Control chart for nonconformities for Example 7.3.

samples and revise the trial control limits. The estimate of c is now computed as

$$\bar{c} = \frac{472}{24} = 19.67$$

and the revised control limits are

$$\text{UCL} = \bar{c} + 3\sqrt{\bar{c}} = 19.67 + 3\sqrt{19.67} = 32.97$$

$$\text{Center line} = \bar{c} = 19.67$$

$$\text{LCL} = \bar{c} - 3\sqrt{\bar{c}} = 19.67 - 3\sqrt{19.67} = 6.36$$

These become the standard values against which production in the next period can be compared.

Twenty new samples, each consisting of one inspection unit (i.e., 100 boards), are subsequently collected. The number of nonconformities in each sample is noted and recorded in Table 7.8. These points are plotted on the control chart in Fig. 7.13. No lack of control is indicated; however, the number of nonconformities per board is still unacceptably high. Further action is necessary to improve the process.

TABLE 7.8
Additional Data for the Control Chart for Nonconformities, Example 7.3

Sample Number	Number of Nonconformities	Sample Number	Number of Nonconformities
27	16	37	18
28	18	38	21
29	12	39	16
30	15	40	22
31	24	41	19
32	21	42	12
33	28	43	14
34	20	44	9
35	25	45	16
36	19	46	21

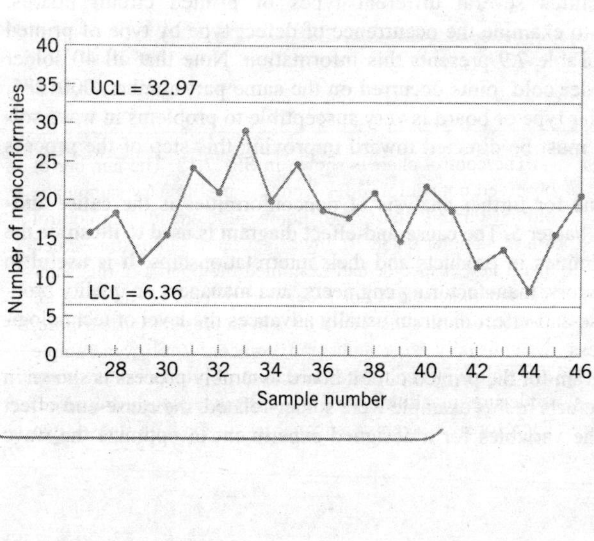

FIGURE 7.13 Continuation of the control chart for nonconformities. Example 7.3.

Defect code		Freq.	Cum. freq.	Percent	Cum. percent
Sold. Insufficie	**	40	40	40.82	40.82
Sold.cold joint	********************	20	60	20.41	61.23
Sold. opens/dewe	*******	7	67	7.14	68.37
Comp. improper 1	******	6	73	6.12	74.49
Sold. splatter/w	*****	5	78	5.10	79.59
Tst. mark ec mark	***	3	81	3.06	82.65
Tst. mark white m	***	3	84	3.06	85.71
Raw cd shroud re	***	3	87	3.06	88.78
Comp. extra part	**	2	89	2.04	90.82
Comp. damaged	**	2	91	2.04	92.86
Comp. missing	**	2	93	2.04	94.90
Wire incorrect s	*	1	94	1.02	95.92
Stamping oper id	*	1	95	1.02	96.94
Stamping missing	*	1	96	1.02	97.96
Sold. short	*	1	97	1.02	98.98
Raw cd damaged	*	1	98	1.02	100.00
	1 10 20 30 40 Number of defects				

■ FIGURE 7.14 Pareto analysis of nonconformities for the printed circuit board process.

Further Analysis of Nonconformities. Defect or nonconformity data are always more informative than fraction nonconforming, because there will usually be several different *types* of nonconformities. By analyzing the nonconformities by type, we can often gain considerable insight into their cause. This can be of considerable assistance in developing the **out-of-control-action plans** (OCAPs) that must accompany control charts.

For example, in the printed circuit board process, there are sixteen different types of defects. Defect data for 500 boards are plotted on a Pareto chart in Fig. 7.14. Note that over 60% of the total number of defects is due to *two defect types:* solder insufficiency and solder cold joints. This points to further problems with the wave soldering process. If these problems can be isolated and eliminated, there will be a dramatic increase in process yield. Notice that the nonconformities follow the Pareto distribution; that is, most of the defects are attributable to a few (in this case, two) defect types.

This process manufactures several different types of printed circuit boards. Therefore, it may be helpful to examine the occurrence of defect type by type of printed circuit board (part number). Table 7.9 presents this information. Note that all 40 solder insufficiencies and all 20 solder cold joints occurred on the same part number, 0001285. This implies that this particular type of board is very susceptible to problems in wave soldering, and special attention must be directed toward improving this step of the process for this part number.

Another useful technique for further analysis of nonconformities is the **cause-and-effect diagram** discussed in Chapter 5. The cause-and-effect diagram is used to illustrate the various sources of nonconformities in products and their interrelationships. It is useful in focusing the attention of operators, manufacturing engineers, and managers on quality problems. Developing a good cause-and-effect diagram usually advances the level of technological understanding of the process.

A cause-and-effect diagram for the printed circuit board assembly process is shown in Fig. 7.15. Since most of the defects in this example were solder-related, the cause-and-effect diagram could help choose the variables for a designed experiment to optimize the wave

■ **TABLE 7.9**
Table of Defects Classified by Part Number and Defect Code

Part Number / Frequency / Percent / Row Percent / Column Percent	Component Component Missing	Damaged (NO)	Code Component Extra Part	Component Improper I	Raw Raw Card Shroud RE	Card Damaged	Solder Short	Solder Solder Opens/DEWE	Cold Joint
0001285	1	0	0	0	0	1	0	5	20
	1.02	0.00	0.00	0.00	0.00	1.02	0.00	5.10	20.41
	1.41	0.00	0.00	0.00	0.00	1.41	0.00	7.04	28.17
	50.00	0.00	0.00	0.00	0.00	100.00	0.00	71.43	100.00
0001481	1	2	2	6	3	0	1	2	0
	1.02	2.04	6.12	3.06	0.00	0.00	1.02	2.04	0.00
	3.70	7.41	22.22	11.11	0.00	0.00	3.70	7.41	0.00
	50.00	100.00	100.00	100.00	100.00	0.00	100.00	28.57	0.00
0006429	0	0	0	0	0	0	0	0	0
	0.00	0.00	0.00	0.00	0.00	0.00	0.00	0.00	0.00
	0.00	0.00	0.00	0.00	0.00	0.00	0.00	0.00	0.00
	0.00	0.00	0.00	0.00	0.00	0.00	0.00	0.00	0.00
Total	2	2	2	6	3	1	1	7	20
	2.04	2.04	2.04	6.12	3.06	1.02	1.02	7.14	20.41

Part Number / Frequency / Percent / Row Percent / Column Percent	Solder Insufficiencies	Solder Splatter	Code Stamping Missing	Test Stamping Operator ID	Test Mark White M	Wire Mark EC Mark	Incorrect 5	Good Unit(s)	Total
0001285	40	0	0	0	2	1	1	0	71
	40.82	0.00	0.00	0.00	2.04	1.02	1.02	0.00	72.45
	56.32	0.00	0.00	0.00	2.82	1.41	1.41	0.00	
	100.00	0.00	0.00	0.00	66.67	33.33	100.00	0.00	
0001481	0	5	1	1	1	2	0	0	27
	0.00	5.10	1.02	1.02	1.02	2.04	0.00	0.00	27.55
	0.00	18.52	3.70	3.70	3.70	7.41	0.00	0.00	
	0.00	100.00	100.00	100.00	33.33	66.67	0.00	0.00	
0006429	0	0	0	0	0	0	0	0	0
	0.00	0.00	0.00	0.00	0.00	0.00	0.00	0.00	0.00
	0.00	0.00	0.00	0.00	0.00	0.00	0.00	0.00	
	0.00	0.00	0.00	0.00	0.00	0.00	0.00	0.00	
Total	40	5	1	1	3	3	1	0	98
	40.82	5.10	1.02	1.02	3.06	3.06	1.02	0.00	100.00

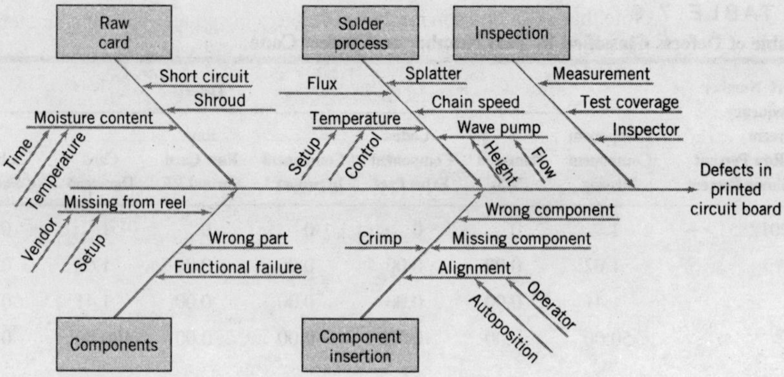

■ FIGURE 7.15 Cause-and-effect diagram.

soldering process. There are several ways to draw the diagram. This one focuses on the three main generic sources of nonconformities: materials, operators, and equipment. Another useful approach is to organize the diagram according to the flow of material through the process.

Choice of Sample Size: The* u *Chart. Example 7.3 illustrates a control chart for nonconformities with the sample size exactly equal to one inspection unit. The inspection unit is chosen for operational or data-collection simplicity. However, there is no reason why the sample size must be restricted to one inspection unit. In fact, we would often prefer to use *several* inspection units in the sample, thereby increasing the area of opportunity for the occurrence of nonconformities. The sample size should be chosen according to statistical considerations, such as specifying a sample size large enough to ensure a positive lower control limit or to obtain a particular probability of detecting a process shift. Alternatively, economic factors could enter into sample-size determination.

Suppose we decide to base the control chart on a sample size of n inspection units. Note that n does not have to be an integer. To illustrate this, suppose that in Example 7.3 we were to specify a subgroup size of $n = 2.5$ inspection units. Then the sample size becomes $(2.5)(100) = 250$ boards. There are two general approaches to constructing the revised chart once a new sample size has been selected. One approach is simply to redefine a new inspection unit that is equal to n times the old inspection unit. In this case, the center line on the new control chart is $n\bar{c}$ and the control limits are located at $n\bar{c} \pm 3\sqrt{n\bar{c}}$, where $\bar{c}$ is the observed mean number of nonconformities in the *original* inspection unit. Suppose that in Example 7.3, after revising the trial control limits, we decided to use a sample size of $n = 2.5$ inspection units. Then the center line would have been located at $n\bar{c} = (2.5)(19.67) = 49.18$ and the control limits would have been $49.18 \pm 3\sqrt{49.18}$ or LCL = 28.14 and UCL = 70.22.

The second approach involves setting up a control chart based on the average number of nonconformities per inspection unit. If we find x *total* nonconformities in a sample of n inspection units, then the *average* number of nonconformities per inspection unit is

$$u = \frac{x}{n} \tag{7.18}$$

Note that x is a Poisson random variable; consequently, the parameters of the control chart for the average number of nonconformities per unit are as follows,

Control Chart for Average Number of Nonconformities per Unit

$$\begin{aligned} \text{UCL} &= \bar{u} + 3\sqrt{\frac{\bar{u}}{n}} \\ \text{Center line} &= \bar{u} \\ \text{LCL} &= \bar{u} - 3\sqrt{\frac{\bar{u}}{n}} \end{aligned} \tag{7.19}$$

where $\bar{u}$ represents the observed average number of nonconformities per unit in a preliminary set of data. Control limits found from equation (7.19) would be regarded as trial control limits. This per-unit chart often is called the **control chart for nonconformities, or *u* chart.**

EXAMPLE 7.4 Control Charts in Supply Chain Operations

A supply chain engineering group monitors shipments of materials through the company distribution network. Errors on either the delivered material or the accompanying documentation are tracked on a weekly basis. Fifty randomly selected shipments are examined and the errors recorded. Data for twenty weeks are shown in Table 7.10. Set up a u control chart to monitor this process.

SOLUTION

From the data in Table 7.10, we estimate the number of errors (nonconformities) per unit (shipment) to be:

$$\bar{u} = \frac{\sum_{i=1}^{20} u_i}{20} = \frac{1.48}{20} = 0.0740$$

Therefore, the parameters of the control chart are

$$\text{UCL} = \bar{u} + 3\sqrt{\frac{\bar{u}}{n}} = 0.0740 + 3\sqrt{\frac{0.0740}{50}} = 0.1894$$

$$\text{Center line} = \bar{u} = 1.93$$

$$\text{LCL} = \bar{u} - 3\sqrt{\frac{\bar{u}}{n}} = 0.0740 - 3\sqrt{\frac{0.0740}{50}} = -0.0414$$

Since the LCL < 0, we would set LCL = 0 for the u chart. The control chart is shown in Fig. 7.16. The preliminary data do not exhibit lack of statistical control; therefore, the trial control limits given here would be adopted for phase II monitoring of future operations. Once again, note that, although the process is in control, the average number of errors per shipment is high. Action should be taken to improve the supply chain system.

(continued)

■ **TABLE 7.10**
Data on Number of Shipping Errors in a Supply Chain Network

Sample Number (week), i	Sample Size, n	Total Number of Errors (Nonconformities), x_i	Average Number of Errors (Nonconformities) per Unit, $u_i = x_i/n$
1	50	2	0.04
2	50	3	0.06
3	50	8	0.16
4	50	1	0.02
5	50	1	0.02
6	50	4	0.08
7	50	1	0.02
8	50	4	0.08
9	50	5	0.10
10	50	1	0.02
11	50	8	0.16
12	50	2	0.04
13	50	4	0.08
14	50	3	0.06
15	50	4	0.08
16	50	1	0.02
17	50	8	0.16
18	50	3	0.06
19	50	7	0.14
20	50	4	0.08
		74	1.48

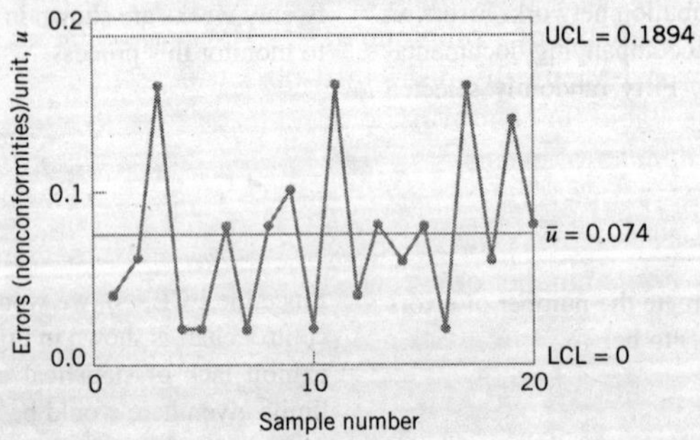

■ **FIGURE 7.16** The control chart for nonconformities per unit from Minitab for Example 7.4.

Alternative Probability Models for Count Data. Most applications of the c chart assume that the Poisson distribution is the correct probability model underlying the process. However, it is not the only distribution that could be utilized as a model of "count" or nonconformities per unit-type data. Various types of phenomena can produce distributions of defects that are not well modeled by the Poisson distribution. In the Poisson distribution, the mean and the variance are equal. When the sample data indicate that the sample variance is substantially different from the mean, the Poisson assumption is likely to be inappropriate.

The situation where the Poisson assumption is likely to be inappropriate is when nonconformities tend to occur in **clusters;** that is, if there is one nonconformity in some part of a product, then it is likely that there will be others. Note that there are at least two random processes at work here: one generating the number and location of clusters, and the second generating the number of nonconformities within each cluster. If the number of clusters has a Poisson distribution and the number of nonconformities within each cluster has a common distribution (say, f), then the total number of nonconformities has a **compound Poisson distribution.** Many types of compound or generalized distributions could be used as a model for count-type data. As an illustration, if the number of clusters has a Poisson distribution and the number of nonconformities within each cluster is also Poisson, then Neyman's type-A distribution models the total number of nonconformities. Alternatively, if the cluster distribution is gamma and the number of nonconformities within each cluster is Poisson, the negative binomial distribution results. Johnson and Kotz (1969) give a good summary of these and also discuss other discrete distributions that could be useful in modeling count-type data.

Mixtures of various types of nonconformities can lead to situations in which the total number of nonconformities is not adequately modeled by the Poisson distribution. Similar situations occur when the count data have either too many or too few zeros. A good discussion of this general problem is the paper by Jackson (1972). The use of the negative binomial distribution to model count data in inspection units of varying size has been studied by Sheaffer and Leavenworth (1976). The dissertation by Gardiner (1987) describes the use of various discrete distributions to model the occurrence of defects in integrated circuits.

As we noted in Section 3.2.4, the geometric distribution can also be useful as a model for count or "event" data. Kaminski et al. (1992) have proposed control charts for counts based on the geometric distribution. The probability model that they use for the geometric distribution is

$$p(x) = p(1-p)^{x-a} \text{ for } x = a, a+1, a+2, \ldots$$

where a is the known minimum possible number of events. Suppose that the data from the process is available as a subgroup of size n, say $x_1, x_2, \ldots. x_n$. These observations are independently and identically distributed observations from a geometric distribution when the process is stable (in control). The two statistics that can be used to form a control chart are the ***total*** number of events

$$T = x_1 + x_2 + \ldots + x_n$$

and the ***average*** number of events

$$\bar{x} = \frac{x_1 + x_2 + \ldots + x_n}{n}$$

It turns out that the sum of independently and identically distributed geometric random variables is a negative binomial random variable. This would be useful information in constructing OC curves or calculating ARLs for the control charts for T or $\bar{x}$.

The mean and variance of the total number of events T are

$$\mu_T = n\left(\frac{1-p}{p} + a\right)$$

and

$$\sigma_T^2 = \frac{n(1-p)}{p^2}$$

and the mean and variance of the average number of events are

$$\mu_{\bar{x}} = \frac{1-p}{p} + a$$

and

$$\sigma_{\bar{x}}^2 = \frac{1-p}{np^2}$$

Consequently, the control charts can be constructed in the usual manner for Shewhart charts. Kaminski et al. (1992) refer to the control chart for the total number of events as a "*g* chart" and the control chart for the average number of events as an "*h* chart." The center lines and control limits for each chart are shown in the following display.

g and *h* Control Charts, Standards Given

	Total number of events chart, *g* chart	Average number of events chart, *h* chart
Upper control limit (UCL)	$n\left(\frac{1-p}{p}+a\right)+L\sqrt{\frac{n(1-p)}{p^2}}$	$\frac{1-p}{p}+a+L\sqrt{\frac{1-p}{np^2}}$
Center line (CL)	$n\left(\frac{1-p}{p}+a\right)$	$\frac{1-p}{p}+a$
Lower control limit (LCL)	$n\left(\frac{1-p}{p}+a\right)-L\sqrt{\frac{n(1-p)}{p^2}}$	$\frac{1-p}{p}+a-L\sqrt{\frac{1-p}{np^2}}$

While we have assumed that a is known, in most situations the parameter p will likely be unknown. The estimator for p is

$$\hat{p} = \frac{1}{\bar{\bar{x}} - a + 1}$$

where $\bar{\bar{x}}$ is the average of all of the count data. Suppose that there are m subgroups available, each of size n, and let the total number of events in each subgroup be $t_1, t_2, \ldots, t_m$. The average number of events per subgroup is

$$\bar{t} = \frac{t_1 + t_2 + \cdots + t_m}{m}$$

Therefore,

$$\bar{\bar{x}} = \frac{\bar{t}}{n} = \frac{1-\hat{p}}{\hat{p}} + a$$

and

$$\frac{1-\hat{p}}{\hat{p}^2} = \left(\frac{\bar{t}}{n} - a\right)\left(\frac{\bar{t}}{n} - a + 1\right)$$

The center line and control limits for the g chart and the h chart based on an estimate of p are shown below.

g and h Control Charts, No Standards Given

	Total number of events chart, g chart	Average number of events chart, h chart
Upper control limit (UCL)	$\bar{t} + L\sqrt{n\left(\frac{\bar{t}}{n} - a\right)\left(\frac{\bar{t}}{n} - a + 1\right)}$	$\frac{\bar{t}}{n} + \frac{L}{\sqrt{n}}\sqrt{\left(\frac{\bar{t}}{n} - a\right)\left(\frac{\bar{t}}{n} - a + 1\right)}$
Center line (CL)	$\bar{t}$	$\frac{\bar{t}}{n}$
Lower control limit (LCL)	$\bar{t} - L\sqrt{n\left(\frac{\bar{t}}{n} - a\right)\left(\frac{\bar{t}}{n} - a + 1\right)}$	$\frac{\bar{t}}{n} - \frac{L}{\sqrt{n}}\sqrt{\left(\frac{\bar{t}}{n} - a\right)\left(\frac{\bar{t}}{n} - a + 1\right)}$

7.3.2 Procedures with Variable Sample Size

Control charts for nonconformities are occasionally formed using 100% inspection of the product. When this method of sampling is used, the number of inspection units in a sample will usually not be constant. For example, the inspection of rolls of cloth or paper often leads to a situation in which the size of the sample varies, because not all rolls are exactly the same length or width. If a control chart for nonconformities (c chart) is used in this situation, both the center line and the control limits will vary with the sample size. Such a control chart would be very difficult to interpret. The correct procedure is to use a control chart for nonconformities per unit (u chart). This chart will have a constant center line; however, the control limits will vary inversely with the square root of the sample size n.

EXAMPLE 7.5 Constructing a u chart

In a textile finishing plant, dyed cloth is inspected for the occurrence of defects per 50 square meters. The data on ten rolls of cloth are shown in Table 7.11. Use these data to set up a control chart for nonconformities per unit.

■ **TABLE 7.11**
Occurrence of Nonconformities in Dyed Cloth

Roll Number	Number of Square Meters	Total Number of Nonconformities	Number of Inspection Units in Roll, n	Number of Nonconformities per Inspection Unit
1	500	14	10.0	1.40
2	400	12	8.0	1.50
3	650	20	13.0	1.54
4	500	11	10.0	1.10
5	475	7	9.5	0.74
6	500	10	10.0	1.00
7	600	21	12.0	1.75
8	525	16	10.5	1.52
9	600	19	12.0	1.58
10	625	23	12.5	1.84
		153	107.50	

(continued)

SOLUTION

The center line of the chart should be the average number of nonconformities per inspection unit—that is, the average number of nonconformities per 50 square meters, computed as

$$\bar{u} = \frac{153}{107.5} = 1.42$$

Note that $\bar{u}$ is the ratio of the total number of observed nonconformities to the total number of inspection units.

The control limits on this chart are computed from equation (7.19) with n replaced by n_i. The width of the control limits will vary inversely with n_i, the number of inspection units in the roll. The calculations for the control limits are displayed in Table 7.12. Figure 7.17 plots the control chart constructed by Minitab.

■ **TABLE 7.12**
Calculation of Control Limits, Example 7.5

Roll Number, i	n_i	UCL = $\bar{u} + 3\sqrt{\bar{u}/n_i}$	LCL = $\bar{u} - 3\sqrt{\bar{u}/n_i}$
1	10.0	2.55	0.29
2	8.0	2.68	0.16
3	13.0	2.41	0.43
4	10.0	2.55	0.29
5	9.5	2.58	0.26
6	10.0	2.55	0.29
7	12.0	2.45	0.39
8	10.5	2.52	0.32
9	12.0	2.45	0.39
10	12.5	2.43	0.41

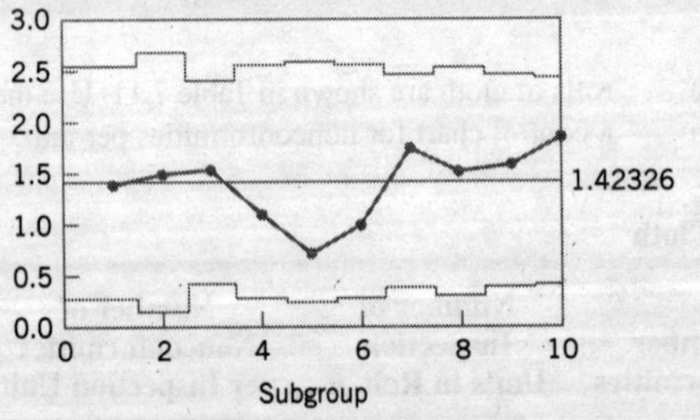

■ **FIGURE 7.17** Computer-generated (Minitab) control chart for Example 7.5.

As noted previously, the u chart should always be used when the sample size is variable. The most common implementation involves variable control limits, as illustrated in Example 7.5. There are, however, two other possible approaches:

1. Use control limits based on an average sample size

$$\bar{n} = \sum_{i=1}^{m} n_i / m$$

2. Use a standardized control chart (this is the preferred option). This second alternative would involve plotting a standardized statistic

$$Z_i = \frac{u_i - \bar{u}}{\sqrt{\frac{\bar{u}}{n_i}}} \tag{7.20}$$

on a control chart with LCL = −3 and UCL = +3 and the center line at zero. This chart is appropriate if tests for runs and other pattern-recognition methods are to be used in conjunction with the chart. Figure 7.18 shows the standardized version of the control chart in Example 7.5. This standardized control chart could also be useful in the short production run situation (see Chapter 10, Section 10.1).

7.3.3 Demerit Systems

With complex products such as automobiles, computers, or major appliances, we usually find that many different types of nonconformities or defects can occur. Not all of these types of defects are equally important. A unit of product having one very serious defect would probably be classified as nonconforming to requirements, but a unit having several minor defects might not necessarily be nonconforming. In such situations, we need a method to classify nonconformities or defects according to severity and to weight the various types of defects in a reasonable manner. **Demerit systems for attribute data** can be of value in these situations.

One possible demerit scheme is defined as follows.

Class A Defects—Very Serious. The unit is either completely unfit for service, or will fail in service in such a manner that cannot be easily corrected in the field, or will cause personal injury or property damage.

Class B Defects—Serious. The unit will possibly suffer a Class A operating failure, or will certainly cause somewhat less serious operating problems, or will certainly have reduced life or increased maintenance cost.

Class C Defects—Moderately Serious. The unit will possibly fail in service, or cause trouble that is less serious than operating failure, or possibly have reduced life or increased maintenance costs, or have a major defect in finish, appearance, or quality of work.

Class D Defects—Minor. The unit will not fail in service but has minor defects in finish, appearance, or quality of work.

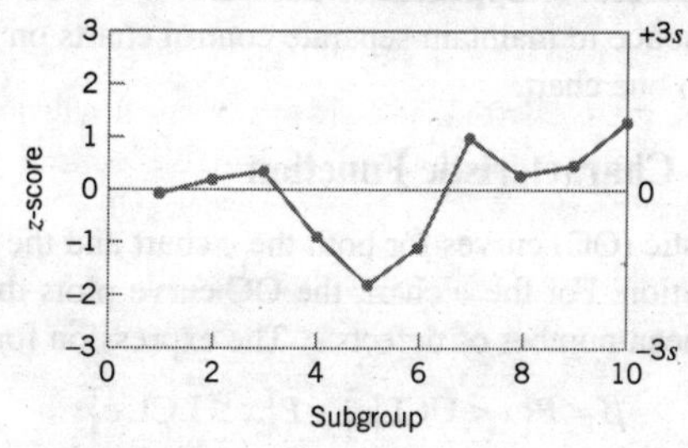

■ FIGURE 7.18 Standardized control chart for nonconformities per unit, Example 7.5.

Let c_{iA}, c_{iB}, c_{iC}, and c_{iD} represent the number of Class A, Class B, Class C, and Class D defects, respectively, in the ith inspection unit. We assume that each class of defect is independent, and the occurrence of defects in each class is well modeled by a Poisson distribution. Then we define the number of **demerits** in the inspection unit as

$$d_i = 100c_{iA} + 50c_{iB} + 10c_{iC} + c_{iD} \tag{7.21}$$

The demerit weights of Class A—100, Class B—50, Class C—10, and Class D—1 are used fairly widely in practice. However, any reasonable set of weights appropriate for a specific problem may also be used.

Suppose that a sample of n inspection units is used. Then the number of demerits per unit is

$$u_i = \frac{D}{n} \tag{7.22}$$

where $D = \sum_{i=1}^{n} d_i$ is the total number of demerits in all n inspection units. Since u_i is a linear combination of independent Poisson random variables, the statistics u_i could be plotted on a control chart with the following parameters:

$$\begin{aligned} \text{UCL} &= \bar{u} + 3\hat{\sigma}_u \\ \text{Center line} &= \bar{u} \\ \text{LCL} &= \bar{u} - 3\hat{\sigma}_u \end{aligned} \tag{7.23}$$

where

$$\bar{u} = 100\bar{u}_A + 50\bar{u}_B + 10\bar{u}_C + \bar{u}_D \tag{7.24}$$

and

$$\hat{\sigma}_u = \left[\frac{(100)^2\bar{u}_A + (50)^2\bar{u}_B + (10)^2\bar{u}_C + \bar{u}_D}{n}\right]^{1/2} \tag{7.25}$$

In the preceding equations, $\bar{u}_A$, $\bar{u}_B$, $\bar{u}_C$, and $\bar{u}_D$ represent the average number of Class A, Class B, Class C, and Class D defects per unit. The values of $\bar{u}_A$, $\bar{u}_B$, $\bar{u}_C$, and $\bar{u}_D$ are obtained from the analysis of preliminary data, taken when the process is supposedly operating in control. Standard values for u_A, u_B, u_C, and u_D may also be used, if they are available.

Jones, Woodall, and Conerly (1999) provide a very thorough discussion of demerit-based control charts. They show how probability-based limits can be computed as alternatives to the traditional three-sigma limits used above. They also show that, in general, the probability limits give superior performance. They are, however, more complicated to compute.

Many variations of this idea are possible. For example, we can classify nonconformities as either **functional defects** or **appearance defects** if a two-class system is preferred. It is also fairly common practice to maintain separate control charts on each defect class rather than combining them into one chart.

7.3.4 The Operating-Characteristic Function

The operating-characteristic (OC) curves for both the c chart and the u chart can be obtained from the Poisson distribution. For the c chart, the OC curve plots the probability of type II error β against the true mean number of defects c. The expression for β is

$$\beta = P\{x < \text{UCL}|c\} - P\{x \le \text{LCL}|c\} \tag{7.26}$$

■ **TABLE 7.13**
Calculation of the OC Curve for a c Chart with UCL = 33.22 and LCL = 6.48

c	$P\{x \le 33\|c\}$	$P\{x \le 6\|c\}$	$\beta = P\{x \le 33\|c\} - P\{x \le 6\|c\}$
1	1.000	0.999	0.001
3	1.000	0.966	0.034
5	1.000	0.762	0.238
7	1.000	0.450	0.550
10	1.000	0.130	0.870
15	0.999	0.008	0.991
20	0.997	0.000	0.997
25	0.950	0.000	0.950
30	0.744	0.000	0.744
33	0.546	0.000	0.546
35	0.410	0.000	0.410
40	0.151	0.000	0.151
45	0.038	0.000	0.038

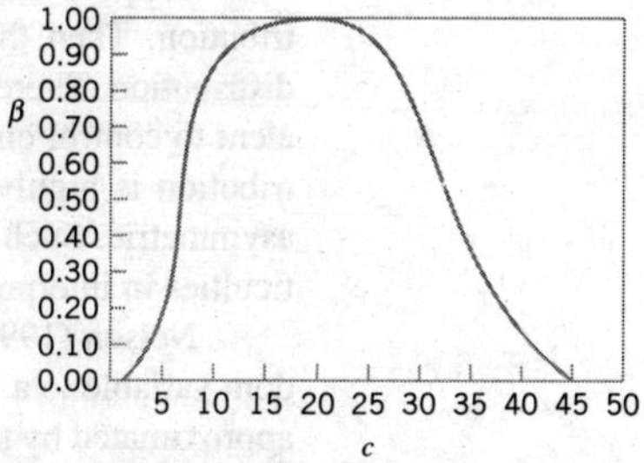

■ **FIGURE 7.19** OC curve of a c chart with LCL = 6.48 and UCL = 33.22.

where x is a Poisson random variable with parameter c. Note that if the LCL < 0 the second term on the right-hand side of equation (7.26) should be dropped.

We will generate the OC curve for the c chart in Example 7.3. For this example, since the LCL = 6.48 and the UCL = 33.22, equation (7.26) becomes

$$\beta = P\{x < 33.22|c\} - P\{x \le 6.48|c\}$$

Since the number of nonconformities must be integer, this is equivalent to

$$\beta = P\{x \le 33|c\} - P\{x \le 6|c\}$$

These probabilities are evaluated in Table 7.13. The OC curve is shown in Fig. 7.19.

For the u chart, we may generate the OC curve from

$$\begin{aligned}\beta &= P\{x < \text{UCL}|u\} - P\{x \le \text{LCL}|u\} \\ &= P\{c < n\text{UCL}|u\} - P\{c \le n\text{LCL}|u\} \\ &= P\{n\text{LCL} < x \le n\text{UCL}|u\} \\ &= \sum_{x=\langle n\text{LCL}\rangle}^{[n\text{UCL}]} \frac{e^{-nu}(nu)^x}{x!}\end{aligned} \tag{7.27}$$

where $\langle n\text{LCL}\rangle$ denotes the smallest integer greater than or equal to nLCL and $[n\text{UCL}]$ denotes the largest integer less than or equal to nUCL. The limits on the summation in equation (7.26) follow from the fact that the total number of nonconformities observed in a sample of n inspection units must be an integer. Note that n need not be an integer.

7.3.5 Dealing with Low Defect Levels

When defect levels or in general, ***count rates***, in a process become very low—say, under 1000 occurrences per million—there will be very long periods of time between the occurrence of a nonconforming unit. In these situations, many samples will have zero defects, and a control chart with the statistic consistently plotting at zero will be relatively uninformative. Thus, conventional c and u charts become ineffective as count rates are driven into the low parts per million (ppm) range.

One way to deal with this problem is adopt a **time between occurrence control chart,** which charts a new variable: the time between the successive occurrences of the count. The time-between-events control chart has been very effective as a process-control procedure for processes with low defect levels.

Suppose that defects or counts or "events" of interest occur according to a Poisson distribution. Then the probability distribution of the time between events is the exponential distribution. Therefore, constructing a time-between-events control chart is essentially equivalent to control charting an exponentially distributed variable. However, the exponential distribution is highly skewed, and as a result, the corresponding control chart would be very asymmetric. Such a control chart would certainly look unusual, and might present some difficulties in interpretation for operating personnel.

Nelson (1994) has suggested solving this problem by transforming the exponential random variable to a Weibull random variable such that the resulting Weibull distribution is well approximated by the normal distribution. If y represents the original exponential random variable, the appropriate transformation is

$$x = y^{1/3.6} = y^{0.2777} \tag{7.28}$$

One would now construct a control chart on x, assuming that x follows a normal distribution.

EXAMPLE 7.6

A chemical engineer wants to set up a control chart for monitoring the occurrence of failures of an important valve. She has decided to use the number of hours between failures as the variable to monitor. Table 7.14 shows the number of hours between failures for the last twenty failures of this valve. Figure 7.20 is a normal probability plot of the time between failures.

SOLUTION

Set up a time-between-events control chart for this process. Clearly, time between failures is not normally distributed. Table 7.14 also shows the values of the transformed time between events, computed from equation (7.27). Figure 7.21 is a normal probability plot of the transformed time between failures. Note that the plot indicates that the distribution of this transformed variable is well approximated by the normal.

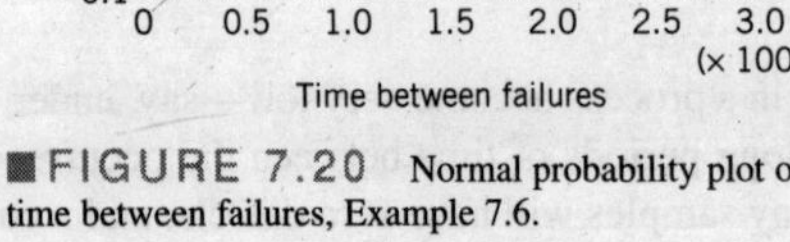

■ FIGURE 7.20 Normal probability plot of time between failures, Example 7.6.

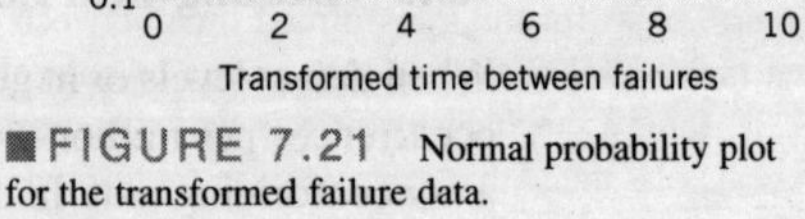

■ FIGURE 7.21 Normal probability plot for the transformed failure data.

■ **TABLE 7.14**
Time between Failure Data, Example 7.6

Failure	Time between Failures, y (hr)	Transformed Value of Time between Failures, $x = y^{0.2777}$
1	286	4.80986
2	948	6.70903
3	536	5.72650
4	124	3.81367
5	816	6.43541
6	729	6.23705
7	4	1.46958
8	143	3.96768
9	431	5.39007
10	8	1.78151
11	2837	9.09619
12	596	5.89774
13	81	3.38833
14	227	4.51095
15	603	5.91690
16	492	5.59189
17	1199	7.16124
18	1214	7.18601
19	2831	9.09083
20	96	3.55203

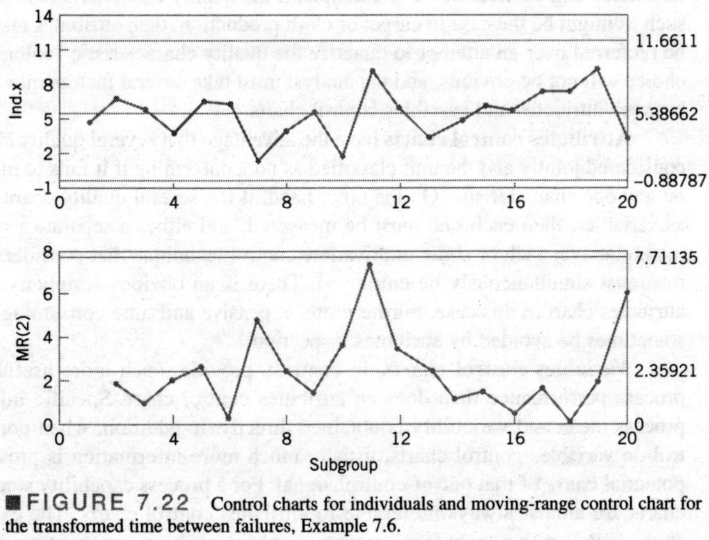

■ **FIGURE 7.22** Control charts for individuals and moving-range control chart for the transformed time between failures, Example 7.6.

Figure 7.22 is a control chart for individuals and a moving range control chart for the transformed time between failures. Note that the control charts indicate a state of control, implying that the failure mechanism for this valve is constant. If a process change is made that improves the failure rate (such as a different type of maintenance action), then we would expect to see the mean time between failures get longer. This would result in points plotting above the upper control limit on the individuals control chart in Fig. 7.22.

The previous example illustrated the use of the individuals control chart with time-between-events data. In many cases, the cusum and EWMA control charts in Chapter 4 would be better alternatives, because they are more effective in detecting small shifts in the mean.

Kittlitz (1999) has also investigated transforming the exponential distribution for control charting purposes. He notes that a log transformation will stabilize the variance of the exponential distribution, but produces a rather negatively skewed distribution. Kittlitz suggests using the transformation $x = y^{0.25}$, noting that it is very similar to Nelson's recommendation and it is also very easy to compute (simply push the square root key on the calculator twice!).

7.3.6 Nonmanufacturing Applications

The c chart and u chart are widely used in transactional and service business applications of statistical process control. In effect, we can treat **errors** in those environments the same as we treat defects or nonconformities in the manufacturing world. To give just a few examples, we can plot errors on engineering drawings, errors on plans and documents, and errors in computer software as c or u charts. An example using u charts to monitor errors in computer software during product development is given in Gardiner and Montgomery (1987).

7.4 Choice Between Attributes and Variables Control Charts

In many applications, the analyst will have to choose between using a variables control chart, such as the $\bar{x}$ and R charts, and an attributes control chart, such as the p chart. In some cases, the choice will be clear-cut. For example, if the quality characteristic is the color of the item, such as might be the case in carpet or cloth production, then attributes inspection would often be preferred over an attempt to quantify the quality characteristic "color." In other cases, the choice will not be obvious, and the analyst must take several factors into account in choosing between attributes and variables control charts.

Attributes control charts have the advantage that several quality characteristics can be considered jointly and the unit classified as nonconforming if it fails to meet the specification on any one characteristic. On the other hand, if the several quality characteristics are treated as variables, then each one must be measured, and either a separate $\bar{x}$ and R chart must be maintained on each or some multivariate control technique that considers all the characteristics must simultaneously be employed. There is an obvious simplicity associated with the attributes chart in this case. Furthermore, expensive and time-consuming measurements may sometimes be avoided by attributes inspection.

Variables control charts, in contrast, provide much more useful information about process performance than does an attributes control chart. Specific information about the process mean and variability is obtained directly. In addition, when points plot out of control on variables control charts, usually much more information is provided relative to the potential *cause* of that out-of-control signal. For a process capability study, variables control charts are almost always preferable to attributes control charts. The exceptions to this are studies relative to nonconformities produced by machines or operators in which there are a very limited number of sources of nonconformities, or studies directly concerned with process yields and fallouts.

Perhaps the most important advantage of the $\bar{x}$ and R control charts is that they often provide an indication of impending trouble and allow operating personnel to take corrective action *before* any defectives are actually produced. Thus, $\bar{x}$ and R charts are *leading indicators* of trouble, whereas p charts (or c and u charts) will not react unless the process has already changed

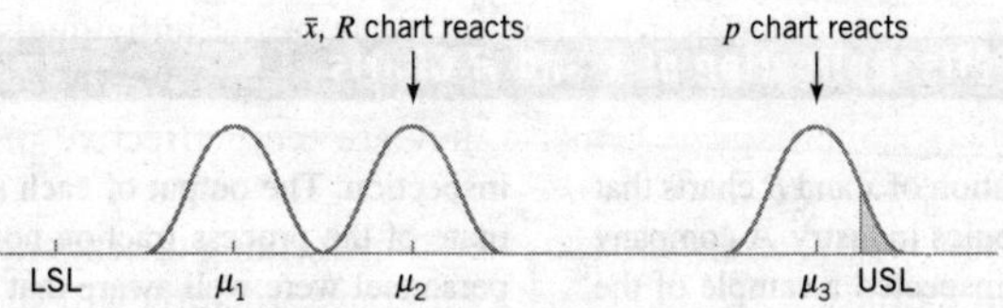

■ **FIGURE 7.23** Why the $\bar{x}$ and R charts can warn of impending trouble.

so that *more* nonconforming units are being produced. This increased efficiency of the $\bar{x}$ and R charts is much more pronounced when p is small, but less so when p is close to 0.5.

To illustrate, consider the production process depicted in Fig. 7.23. When the process mean is at μ_1, few nonconforming units are produced. Suppose the process mean begins to shift upward. By the time it has reached μ_2, the $\bar{x}$ and R charts will have reacted to the change in the mean by generating a strong nonrandom pattern and possibly several out-of-control points. However, a p chart would not react until the mean had shifted all the way to μ_3, or until the actual number of nonconforming units produced had increased. Thus, the $\bar{x}$ and R charts are more powerful control tools than the p chart.

For a specified level of protection against process shifts, variables control charts usually require a much smaller sample size than does the corresponding attributes control chart. Thus, although variables-type inspection is usually more expensive and time-consuming on a per unit basis than attributes inspection, many fewer units must be examined. This is an important consideration, particularly in cases where inspection is destructive (such as opening a can to measure the volume of product within or to test chemical properties of the product). The following example demonstrates the economic advantage of variables control charts.

EXAMPLE 7.7 The Advantage of Variables Control Chart

The nominal value of the mean of a quality characteristic is 50, and the standard deviation is 2. The process is controlled by an $\bar{x}$ chart. Specification limits on the process are established at ± three-sigma, such that the lower specification limit is 44 and the upper specification limit is 56. When the process is in control at the nominal level of 50, the fraction of nonconforming product produced, assuming that the quality characteristic is normally distributed, is 0.0027. Suppose that the process mean were to shift to 52. The fraction of nonconforming product produced following the shift is approximately 0.0228. Suppose that we want the probability of detecting this shift on the first subsequent sample to be 0.50. Find the appropriate sample size for the $\bar{x}$ chart and compare it to the sample size for a p chart that has the same probability of detecting the shift.

SOLUTION

The sample size on the $\bar{x}$ chart must be large enough for the upper three-sigma control limit to be 52. This implies that

$$50 + \frac{3(2)}{\sqrt{n}} = 52$$

or $n = 9$. If a p chart is used, then we may find the required sample size to give the same probability of detecting the shift from equation (7.10), that is,

$$n = \left(\frac{L}{\delta}\right)^2 p(1-p)$$

where $L = 3$ is the width of the control limits, $p = 0.0027$ is the in-control fraction nonconforming, and $\delta = 0.0228 - 0.0027 = 0.0201$ is the magnitude of the shift. Consequently, we find

$$n = (3/0.0201)^2(0.0027)(0.9973) = 59.98$$

or $n \simeq 60$ would be required for the p chart. Unless the cost of measurements inspection is more than seven times as costly as attributes inspection, the $\bar{x}$ chart is less expensive to operate.

Generally speaking, variables control charts are preferable to attributes. However, this logic can be carried to an illogical extreme, as shown in Example 7.8.

EXAMPLE 7.8 A Misapplication of $\bar{x}$ and R Charts

This example illustrates a misapplication of $\bar{x}$ and R charts that the author encountered in the electronics industry. A company manufacturing a box-level product inspected a sample of the production units several times each shift using attributes inspection. The output of each sample inspection was an estimate of the process fraction nonconforming $\hat{p}_i$. The company personnel were well aware that attributes data did not contain as much information about the process as variables data, and

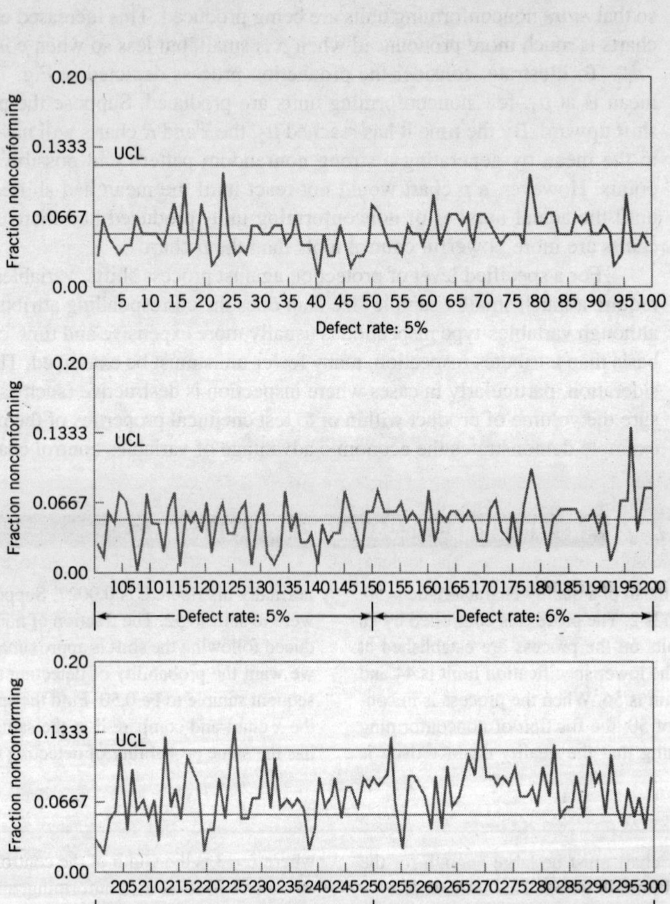

■ FIGURE 7.24 Fraction nonconforming control chart for Example 7.8.

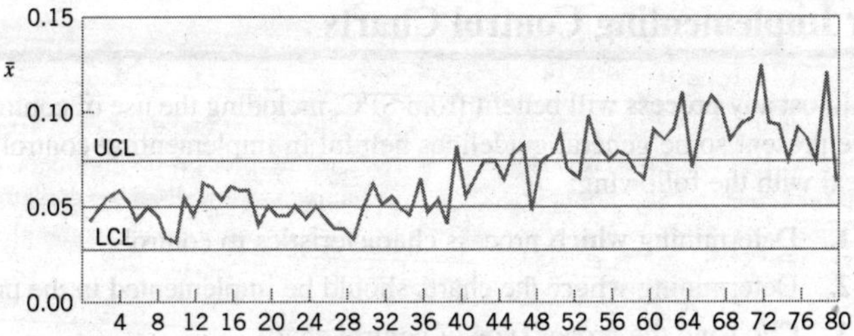

FIGURE 7-25 $\bar{x}$ chart for Example 7.8.

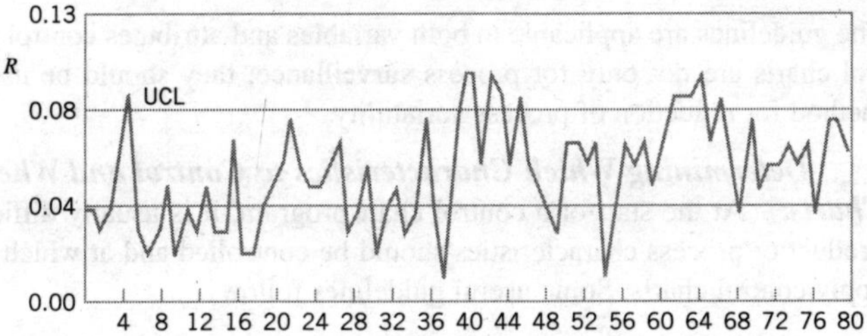

FIGURE 7.26 R chart for Example 7.8.

were exploring ways to get more useful information about their process. A consultant to the company (*not* the author) had suggested that they could achieve this objective by converting their fraction nonconforming data into $\bar{x}$ and R charts. To do so, each group of five successive values of $\hat{p}_i$ was treated as if it were a sample of five *variables* measurements; then the average and range were computed as

$$\bar{x} = \frac{1}{5}\sum_{i=1}^{5} \hat{p}_i$$

and

$$R = \max(\hat{p}_i) - \min(\hat{p}_i)$$

and these values were plotted on $\bar{x}$ and R charts. The consultant claimed that this procedure would provide more information than the fraction nonconforming control chart.

This suggestion was incorrect. If the inspection process actually produces attributes data governed by the binomial distribution with fixed n, then the sample fraction nonconforming contains *all* the information in the sample (this is an application of the concept of minimal sufficient statistics) and forming two new functions of $\hat{p}_i$ will not provide any additional information.

To illustrate this idea, consider the control chart for fraction nonconforming in Fig. 7.24. This chart was produced by drawing 100 samples (each of size 200) from a process for which $p = 0.05$ and by using these data to compute the control limits. Then the sample draws were continued until sample 150, where the population fraction nonconforming was increased to $p = 0.06$. At each subsequent 50-sample interval, the value of p was increased by 0.01. Note that the control chart reacts to the shift in p at sample number 196. Figures 7.25 and 7.26 present the $\bar{x}$ and R charts obtained by subgrouping the sample values of $\hat{p}_i$ as suggested above. The first twenty of those subgroups were used to compute the center line and control limits on the $\bar{x}$ and R charts. Note that the $\bar{x}$ chart reacts to the shift in $\hat{p}$ at about subgroup number 40. (This would correspond to *original* samples 196–200.) This result is to be expected, as the $\bar{x}$ chart is really monitoring the fraction nonconforming p. The R chart in Fig. 7.26 is misleading, however. One subgroup within the original set used to construct the control limits is out of control. (This is a false alarm, since $p = 0.05$ for all 100 original samples.) Furthermore, the out-of-control points beginning at about subgroup 40 do not contribute any additional useful information about the process because when $\hat{p}$ shifts from 0.05 to 0.06 (say), the standard deviation of p will *automatically* increase. Therefore, in this case there is no added benefit to the user from $\bar{x}$ and R charts.

This is not to say that the conventional fraction nonconforming control chart based on the binomial probability distribution is the right control chart for all fraction nonconforming data, just as the c chart (based on the Poisson distribution) is not always the right control chart for defect data. If the variability in $\hat{p}_i$ from sample to sample is greater than that which could plausibly be explained by the binomial model, then the analyst should determine the *correct* underlying probability model and base the control chart on that distribution.

7.5 Guidelines for Implementing Control Charts

Almost any process will benefit from SPC, including the use of control charts. In this section, we present some general guidelines helpful in implementing control charts. Specifically, we deal with the following:

1. Determining **which** process characteristics to control
2. Determining **where** the charts should be implemented in the process
3. Choosing the proper **type** of control charts
4. Taking **actions** to improve processes as the result of SPC/control chart analysis
5. Selecting data-collection systems and computer software

The guidelines are applicable to both variables and attributes control charts. Remember, control charts are not only for process surveillance; they should be used as an active, on-line method for reduction of process variability.

Determining Which Characteristics to Control and Where to Put the Control Charts. At the start of a control chart program, it is usually difficult to determine which product or process characteristics should be controlled and at which points in the process to apply control charts. Some useful guidelines follow.

1. At the beginning, control charts should be applied to any product characteristics or manufacturing operations believed to be important. The charts will provide immediate feedback as to whether they are actually needed.
2. The control charts found to be unnecessary should be removed, and others that engineering and operator judgment indicates may be required should be added. More control charts will usually be employed until the process has stabilized.
3. Information on the number and types of control charts on the process should be kept current. It is best to keep separate records on the variables and attributes charts. In general, after the control charts are first installed, the number of control charts tends to increase rather steadily. After that, it will usually decrease. When the process stabilizes, we typically find that it has the same number of charts from one year to the next. However, they are not necessarily the same charts.
4. If control charts are being used effectively and if new knowledge is being gained about the key process variables, we should find that the number of $\bar{x}$ and R charts increases and the number of attributes control charts decreases.
5. At the beginning of a control chart program there will usually be more attributes control charts, applied to semifinished or finished units near the *end* of the manufacturing process. As we learn more about the process, these charts will be replaced with $\bar{x}$ and R charts applied *earlier* in the process to the critical parameters and operations that result in nonconformities in the finished product. Generally, **the earlier that process control can be established, the better.** In a complex assembly process, this may imply that process controls need to be implemented at the vendor or supplier level.
6. Control charts are an on-line, process-monitoring procedure. They should be implemented and maintained as close to the work center as possible, so that feedback will be rapid. Furthermore, the process operators and process engineering should have direct responsibility for collecting the process data, maintaining the charts, and interpreting the results. The operators and engineers have the detailed knowledge of the process required to correct process upsets and use the control chart to improve process performance.

Microcomputers can speed up the feedback and should be an integral part of any modern, on-line, process-control procedure.

7. The out-of-control-action plan (OCAP) is a vital part of the control chart. Operating and engineering personnel should strive to keep OCAPs up-to-date and valid.

Choosing the Proper Type of Control Chart.

A. $\overline{x}$ and R (or $\overline{x}$ and s) charts. Consider using variables control charts in these situations:

1. A new process is coming on stream, or a new product is being manufactured by an existing process.
2. The process has been in operation for some time, but it is chronically in trouble or unable to hold the specified tolerances.
3. The process is in trouble, and the control chart can be useful for diagnostic purposes (troubleshooting).
4. Destructive testing (or other expensive testing procedures) is required.
5. It is desirable to reduce acceptance-sampling or other downstream testing to a minimum when the process can be operated in control.
6. Attributes control charts have been used, but the process is either out of control or in control but the yield is unacceptable.
7. There are very tight specifications, overlapping assembly tolerances, or other difficult manufacturing problems.
8. The operator must decide whether or not to adjust the process, or when a setup must be evaluated.
9. A change in product specifications is desired.
10. Process stability and capability must be continually demonstrated, such as in regulated industries.

B. Attributes Charts (*p* charts, *c* charts, and *u* charts). Consider using attributes control charts in these situations:

1. Operators control the assignable causes, and it is necessary to reduce process fallout.
2. The process is a complex assembly operation and product quality is measured in terms of the occurrence of nonconformities, successful or unsuccessful product function, and so forth. (Examples include computers, office automation equipment, automobiles, and the major subsystems of these products.)
3. Process control is necessary, but measurement data cannot be obtained.
4. A historical summary of process performance is necessary. Attributes control charts, such as *p* charts, *c* charts, and *u* charts, are very effective for summarizing information about the process for management review.
5. Remember that attributes charts are generally inferior to charts for variables. Always use $\overline{x}$ and R or $\overline{x}$ and s charts whenever possible.

C. Control Charts for Individuals. Consider using the control chart for individuals in conjunction with a moving-range chart in these situations:

1. It is inconvenient or impossible to obtain more than one measurement per sample, or repeat measurements will only differ by laboratory or analysis error. Examples often occur in chemical processes.

2. Automated testing and inspection technology allow measurement of every unit produced. In these cases, also consider the cumulative sum control chart and the exponentially weighted moving average control chart discussed in Chapter 9.
3. The data become available very slowly, and waiting for a larger sample will be impractical or make the control procedure too slow to react to problems. This often happens in nonproduct situations; for example, accounting data may become available only monthly.
4. Generally, once we are in phase II, individuals charts have poor performance in shift detection and can be very sensitive to departures from normality. Always use the EWMA and CUSUM charts of Chapter 9 in phase II instead of individuals charts whenever possible.

Actions Taken to Improve the Process. Process improvement is the primary objective of statistical process control. The application of control charts will give information on two key aspects of the process: statistical control and capability. Figure 7.27 shows the possible states in which the process may exist with respect to these two issues. Technically speaking, the capability of a process cannot be adequately assessed until statistical control has been established, but we will use a less precise definition of capability that is just a qualitative assessment of whether or not the level of nonconforming units produced is low enough to warrant no immediate *additional* effort to further improve the process.

Figure 7.27 gives the answers to two questions: "Is the process in control?" and "Is the process capable?" (in the sense of the previous paragraph). Each of the four cells in the figure contains some recommended courses of action that depend on the answers to these two questions. The box in the northwest corner is the ideal state: the process is in statistical control and exhibits adequate capability for present business objectives. In this case, SPC methods are valuable for process monitoring and for warning against the occurrence of any new assignable causes that could cause slippage in performance. The northeast corner implies that the process exhibits statistical control but has poor capability. Perhaps the PCR is lower than the value required by the customer, or there is sufficient variability remaining to result in excessive scrap or rework. In this case, SPC methods may be useful for process diagnosis and improvement, primarily through the recognition of *patterns* on the control chart, but the control charts will not produce very many out-of-control signals. It will usually be necessary to intervene actively in the process to improve it. Experimental design methods are helpful in this regard [see Montgomery (2005)]. Usually, it is also helpful to reconsider the

		IS THE PROCESS CAPABLE? Yes	No
IS THE PROCESS IN CONTROL?	Yes	SPC	SPC Experimental design Investigate specifications Change process
	No	SPC	SPC Experimental design Investigate specifications Change process

■ FIGURE 7.27 Actions taken to improve a process.

specifications: They may have been set at levels tighter than necessary to achieve function or performance from the part. As a last resort, we may have to consider changing the process; that is, investigating or developing new technology that has less variability with respect to this quality characteristic than the existing process.

The lower two boxes in Fig. 7.27 deal with the case of an out-of-control process. The southeast corner presents the case of a process that is out of control and not capable. (Remember our nontechnical use of the term *capability.*) The actions recommended here are identical to those for the box in the northeast corner, except that SPC would be expected to yield fairly rapid results now, because the control charts should be identifying the presence of assignable causes. The other methods of attack will warrant consideration and use in many cases, however. Finally, the southwest corner treats the case of a process that exhibits lack of statistical control but does not produce a meaningful number of defectives because the specifications are very wide. SPC methods should still be used to establish control and reduce variability in this case, for the following reasons:

1. Specifications can change without notice.
2. The customer may require both **control** and **capability.**
3. The fact that the process experiences assignable causes implies that unknown forces are at work; these unknown forces could result in poor capability in the near future.

Selection of Data-Collection Systems and Computer Software. The past few years have produced an explosion of quality control software and electronic data-collection devices. Some SPC consultants recommended against using the computer, noting that it is unnecessary, since most applications of SPC in Japan emphasized the *manual* use of control charts. If the Japanese were successful in the 1960s and 1970s using manual control charting methods, then does the computer truly have a useful role in SPC?

The answer to this question is yes, for several reasons:

1. Although it can be helpful to begin with manual methods of control charting at the start of an SPC implementation, it is necessary to move successful applications to the computer very soon. The computer is a great productivity improvement device. We don't drive cars with the passenger safety systems of the 1960s and we don't fly airplanes with 1960s avionics technology. We shouldn't use 1960s technology with control charts either.
2. The computer will enable the SPC data to become part of the companywide manufacturing database, and in that form, the data will be useful (and hence more likely to be used) to everyone—management, engineering, marketing, and so on, *not* only manufacturing and quality.
3. A computer-based SPC system can provide more information than any manual system. It permits the user to monitor many quality characteristics and to provide automatic signaling of assignable causes.

What type of software should be used? That is a difficult question to answer, because all applications have unique requirements and the capability of the software is constantly changing. However, several features are necessary for successful results:

1. The software should be capable of stand-alone operation on a personal computer, on a multiterminal local area network, or on a multiterminal minicomputer-host system. SPC packages that are exclusively tied to a large mainframe system are frequently not very useful because they usually cannot produce control charts and other routine reports in a timely manner.

2. The system must be user-friendly. If operating personnel are to use the system, it must have limited options, be easy to use, provide adequate error correction opportunities, and contain many on-line help features. It should ideally be possible to tailor or customize the system for each application, although this installation activity may have to be carried out by engineering/technical personnel.
3. The system should provide display of control charts for at least the last 25 samples. Ideally, the length of record displayed should be controlled by the user. Printed output should be immediately available on either a line printer or a plotter.
4. File storage should be sufficient to accommodate a reasonable amount of process history. Editing and updating files should be straightforward. Provisions to transfer data to other storage media or to transfer the data to a master manufacturing database is critical.
5. The system should be able to handle multiple files simultaneously. Only rarely does a process have only one quality characteristic that needs to be examined.
6. The user should be able to calculate control limits from any subset of the data on the file. The user should have the capability to input center lines and control limits directly.
7. The system should be able to accept a variety of inputs, including manual data entry, input from an electronic instrument, or input from another computer or instrument controller. It is important to have the capability for real-time process monitoring, or to be able to transfer data from a real-time data acquisition system.
8. The system should support other statistical applications, including as a minimum histograms and computation of process capability indices.
9. Service and support from the software supplier after purchase is always an important factor in deciding which software package to use.

The purchase price of commercially available software varies widely. Obviously, the total cost of software is very different from the purchase price. In many cases, a $500 SPC package is really a $10,000 package when we take into account the total costs of making the package work correctly in the intended application. It is also relatively easy to establish control charts with most of the popular spreadsheet software packages. However, it may be difficult to integrate those spreadsheet control charts into the overall manufacturing database or other business systems.

Important Terms and Concepts

Attribute data
Average run length for attribute control charts
Cause-and-effect diagram
Choice between attributes and variables data
Control chart for defects or nonconformities per unit or *u* chart
Control chart for fraction nonconforming or *p* chart
Control chart for nonconformities or *c* chart
Control chart for number nonconforming or *np* chart
Defect
Defective
Demerit systems for attribute data
Design of attributes control charts
Fraction defective
Fraction nonconforming
Nonconformity
Operating characteristic curve for the *c* and *u* charts
Operating characteristic curve for the *p* chart
Pareto chart
Standardized control charts
Time between occurrence control charts
Variable sample size for attributes control chart

Exercises

7.1. The data in Table 7E.1 represent the results of inspecting all units of a personal computer produced for the past ten days. Does the process appear to be in control?

7.2. A process that produces titanium forgings for automobile turbocharger wheels is to be controlled through use of a fraction nonconforming chart. Initially, one sample of size 150 is taken each day for twenty days, and the results shown in Table 7E.4 are observed.
(a) Establish a control chart to monitor future production.
(b) What is the smallest sample size that could be used for this process and still give a positive lower control limit on the chart?

7.3. The data in Table 7E.3 give the number of nonconforming bearing and seal assemblies in samples of size 100. Construct a fraction nonconforming control chart for these data. If any points plot out of control, assume that assignable causes can be found and determine the revised control limits.

7.4. The number of nonconforming switches in samples of size 150 are shown in Table 7E.4. Construct a fraction nonconforming control chart for these data. Does the process appear to be in control? If not,

■ **TABLE 7E.1**
Personal Computer Inspecting Results

Day	Units Inspected	Nonconforming Units	Fraction Nonconforming
1	80	4	0.050
2	110	7	0.064
3	90	5	0.056
4	75	8	0.107
5	130	6	0.046
6	120	6	0.050
7	70	4	0.057
8	125	5	0.040
9	105	8	0.076
10	95	7	0.074

■ **TABLE 7E.2**
Nonconforming Unit Data for Exercise 7.2

Day	Nonconforming Units	Day	Nonconforming Units
1	3	11	2
2	2	12	4
3	4	13	1
4	2	14	3
5	5	15	6
6	2	16	0
7	1	17	1
8	2	18	2
9	0	19	3
10	5	20	2

■ **TABLE 7E.3**
Data for Exercise 7.3

Sample Number	Number of Nonconforming Assemblies	Sample Number	Number of Nonconforming Assemblies
1	7	11	6
2	4	12	15
3	1	13	0
4	3	14	9
5	6	15	5
6	8	16	1
7	10	17	4
8	5	18	5
9	2	19	7
10	7	20	12

■ **TABLE 7E.4**
Number of Nonconforming Switches

Sample Number	Number of Nonconforming Switches	Sample Number	Number of Nonconforming Switches
1	8	11	6
2	1	12	0
3	3	13	4
4	0	14	0
5	2	15	3
6	4	16	1
7	0	17	15
8	1	18	2
9	10	19	3
10	6	20	0

■ TABLE 7E.5
Data for Exercise 7.5

Day	Number of Nonconforming Units
1	3
2	4
3	3
4	2
5	6
6	12
7	5
8	1
9	2
10	2

assume that assignable causes can be found for all points outside the control limits and calculate the revised control limits.

7.5. Based on the data in Table 7E.5 if an np chart is to be established, what would you recommend as the center line and control limits? Assume that $n = 500$.

7.6. Diodes used on printed circuit boards are produced in lots of size 1000. We wish to control the process producing these diodes by taking samples of size 64 from each lot. If the nominal value of the fraction nonconforming is $p = 0.10$, determine the parameters of the appropriate control chart. To what level must the fraction nonconforming increase to make the β-risk equal to 0.50? What is the minimum sample size that would give a positive lower control limit for this chart?

7.7. A control chart indicates that the current process fraction nonconforming is 0.02. If fifty items are inspected each day, what is the probability of detecting a shift in the fraction nonconforming to 0.04 on the first day after the shift? By the end of the third day following the shift?

7.8. A control chart for the number of nonconforming piston rings is maintained on a forging process with $np = 16.0$. A sample of size 100 is taken each day and analyzed.

(a) What is the probability that a shift in the process average to $np = 20.0$ will be detected on the first day following the shift? What is the probability that the shift will be detected by at least the end of the third day?

(b) Find the smallest sample size that will give a positive lower control limit.

7.9. A process is controlled with a fraction nonconforming control chart with three-sigma limits, $n = 100$, UCL = 0.161, center line = 0.080, and LCL = 0.

(a) Find the equivalent control chart for the number nonconforming.

(b) Use the Poisson approximation to the binomial to find the probability of a type I error.

(c) Use the correct approximation to find the probability of a type II error if the process fraction nonconforming shifts to 0.2.

(d) What is the probability of detecting the shift in part (c) by at most the fourth sample after the shift?

7.10. A control chart for the fraction nonconforming is to be established using a center line of $p = 0.10$. What sample size is required if we wish to detect a shift in the process fraction nonconforming to 0.20 with probability 0.50?

7.11. A control chart for fraction nonconforming indicates that the current process average is 0.03. The sample size is constant at 200 units.

(a) Find the three-sigma control limits for the control chart.

(b) What is the probability that a shift in the process average to 0.08 will be detected on the first subsequent sample? What is the probability that this shift will be detected at least by the fourth sample following the shift?

7.12. In designing a fraction nonconforming chart with center line at $p = 0.20$ and three-sigma control limits, what is the sample size required to yield a positive lower control limit? What is the value of n necessary to give a probability of 0.50 of detecting a shift in the process to 0.26?

7.13. A control chart is used to control the fraction nonconforming for a plastic part manufactured in an injection molding process. Ten subgroups yield the data in Table 7E.6

(a) Set up a control chart for the number nonconforming in samples of $n = 100$.

(b) For the chart established in part (a), what is the probability of detecting a shift in the process

■ TABLE 7E.6
Nonconforming Unit Data for Exercise 7.13

Sample Number	Sample Size	Number Nonconforming
1	100	10
2	100	15
3	100	31
4	100	18
5	100	24
6	100	12
7	100	23
8	100	15
9	100	8
10	100	8

fraction nonconforming to 0.30 on the first sample after the shift has occurred?

7.14. (a) A control chart for the number nonconforming is to be established, based on samples of size 400. To start the control chart, thirty samples were selected and the number nonconforming in each sample determined, yielding $\Sigma_{i=1}^{30} D_i = 1200$. What are the parameters of the *np* chart?

(b) Suppose the process average fraction nonconforming shifted to 0.15. What is the probability that the shift would be detected on the first subsequent sample?

7.15. A process is being controlled with a fraction nonconforming control chart. The process average has been shown to be 0.07. Three-sigma control limits are used, and the procedure calls for taking daily samples of 400 items.

(a) Calculate the upper and lower control limits.

(b) If the process average should suddenly shift to 0.10, what is the probability that the shift would be detected on the first subsequent sample?

(c) What is the probability that the shift in part (b) would be detected on the first or second sample taken after the shift?

7.16. A fraction nonconforming control chart with center line 0.10, UCL = 0.19, and LCL = 0.01 is used to control a process.

(a) If three-sigma limits are used, find the sample size for the control chart.

(b) Use the Poisson approximation to the binomial to find the probability of type I error.

(c) Use the Poisson approximation to the binomial to find the probability of type II error if the process fraction defective is actually $p = 0.20$.

7.17. Consider the control chart designed in Exercise 7.14. Find the average run length to detect a shift to a fraction nonconforming of 0.15.

7.18. Consider the control chart in Exercise 7.16. Find the average run length if the process fraction nonconforming shifts to 0.20.

7.19. A fraction nonconforming control chart has center line 0.01, UCL = 0.0399, LCL = 0, and $n = 100$. If three-sigma limits are used, find the smallest sample size that would yield a positive lower control limit.

7.20. Why is the *np* chart not appropriate with variable sample size?

7.21. A maintenance group improves the effectiveness of its repair work by monitoring the number of maintenance requests that require a second call to complete the repair. Twenty weeks of data are shown in Table 7E.7.

(a) Find trial control limits for this process.

(b) Design a control chart for controlling future production.

■ TABLE 7E.7
Data for Exercise 7.21

Week	Total Requests	Second Visit Required	Week	Total Requests	Second Visit Required
1	200	6	11	100	1
2	250	8	12	100	0
3	250	9	13	100	1
4	250	7	14	200	4
5	200	3	15	200	5
6	200	4	16	200	3
7	150	2	17	200	10
8	150	1	18	200	4
9	150	0	19	250	7
10	150	2	20	250	6

7.22. Analyze the data in Exercise 7.21 using an average sample size.

7.23. Construct a standardized control chart for the data in Exercise 7.21.

7.24. **Continuation of Exercise 7.21.** Note that in Exercise 7.21 there are only four different sample sizes; $n = 100$, 150, 200, and 250. Prepare a control chart that has a set of limits for each possible sample size and show how it could be used as an alternative to the variable-width control limit method used in Exercise 7.21. How easy would this method be to use in practice?

7.25. A fraction nonconforming control chart is to be established with a center line of 0.01 and two-sigma control limits.

(a) How large should the sample size be if the lower control limit is to be nonzero?

(b) How large should the sample size be if we wish the probability of detecting a shift to 0.04 to be 0.50?

7.26. A fraction nonconforming control chart with $n = 400$ has the following parameters:

$$\text{UCL} = 0.0809$$
$$\text{Center line} = 0.0500$$
$$\text{LCL} = 0.0191$$

(a) Find the width of the control limits in standard deviation units.

(b) What would be the corresponding parameters for an equivalent control chart based on the number nonconforming?

(c) What is the probability that a shift in the process fraction nonconforming to 0.0300 will be detected on the first sample following the shift?

7.27. A fraction nonconforming control chart with $n = 400$ has the following parameters:

$$\text{UCL} = 0.0962$$
$$\text{Center line} = 0.0500$$
$$\text{LCL} = 0.0038$$

(a) Find the width of the control limits in standard deviation units.

(b) Suppose the process fraction nonconforming shifts to 0.15. What is the probability of detecting the shift on the first subsequent sample?

7.28. The following fraction nonconforming control chart with $n = 100$ is used to control a process:

$$\text{UCL} = 0.0750$$
$$\text{Center line} = 0.0400$$
$$\text{LCL} = 0.0050$$

(a) Use the Poisson approximation to the binomial to find the probability of a type I error.

(b) Use the Poisson approximation to the binomial to find the probability of a type II error, if the true process fraction nonconforming is 0.0600.

(c) Draw the OC curve for this control chart.

(d) Find the ARL when the process is in control and the ARL when the process fraction nonconforming is 0.0600.

7.29. Construct a standardized control chart for the data in Exercise 7.1.

7.30. Consider the fraction nonconforming control chart in Exercise 7.2. Find the equivalent *np* chart.

7.31. Consider an *np* chart with *k*-sigma control limits. Derive a general formula for determining the minimum sample size to ensure that the chart has a positive lower control limit.

7.32. A paper mill uses a control chart to monitor the imperfection in finished rolls of paper. Production output is inspected for twenty days, and the resulting data are shown here. Use these data to set up a control chart for nonconformities per roll of paper. Does the process appear to be in statistical control? What center line and control limits would you recommend for controlling current production?

7.33. **Continuation of Exercise 7.32.** Consider the papermaking process in Exercise 7.32. Set up a *u* chart based on an average sample size to control this process.

7.34. **Continuation of Exercise 7.32.** Consider the papermaking process in Exercise 7.32. Set up a standardized *u* chart for this process.

7.35. The data in Table 7E.9 represent the number of nonconformities per 1000 meters in telephone cable. From analysis of these data, would you conclude that the process is in statistical control? What control procedure would you recommend for future production?

TABLE 7E.8
Data on Imperfections in Rolls of Paper

Day	Number of Rolls Produced	Total Number of Imperfections	Day	Number of Rolls Produced	Total Number of Imperfections
1	18	12	11	18	18
2	18	14	12	18	14
3	24	20	13	18	9
4	22	18	14	20	10
5	22	15	15	20	14
6	22	12	16	20	13
7	20	11	17	24	16
8	20	15	18	24	18
9	20	12	19	22	20
10	20	10	20	21	17

TABLE 7E.9
Telephone Cable Data for Exercise 7.35

Sample Number	Number of Nonconformities	Sample Number	Number of Nonconformities
1	1	12	6
2	1	13	9
3	3	14	11
4	7	15	15
5	8	16	8
6	10	17	3
7	5	18	6
8	13	19	7
9	0	20	4
10	19	21	9
11	24	22	20

7.36. The number of nonconformities found on final inspection of a tape deck is shown in Table 7E.10. Can you conclude that the process is in statistical control? What center line and control limits would you recommend for controlling future production?

TABLE 7E.10
Data on Nonconformities in Tape Decks

Deck Number	Number of Nonconformities	Deck Number	Number of Nonconformities
2412	0	2421	1
2413	1	2422	0
2414	1	2423	3
2415	0	2424	2
2416	2	2425	5
2417	1	2426	1
2418	1	2427	2
2419	3	2428	1
2420	2	2429	1

7.37. Consider the data in Exercise 7.35. Suppose a new inspection unit is defined as 2500 m of wire.

(a) What are the center line and control limits for a control chart for monitoring future production based on the total number of nonconformities in the new inspection unit?

(b) What are the center line and control limits for a control chart for average nonconformities per unit used to monitor future production?

7.38. Consider the data in Exercise 7.36. Suppose we wish to define a new inspection unit of four tape decks.

(a) What are the center line and control limits for a control chart for monitoring future production based on the total number of defects in the new inspection unit?

(b) What are the center line and control limits for a control chart for nonconformities per unit used to monitor future production?

7.39. An automobile manufacturer wishes to control the number of nonconformities in a subassembly area producing manual transmissions. The inspection unit is defined as four transmissions, and data from sixteen samples (each of size 4) are shown in Table 7E.11.

(a) Set up a control chart for nonconformities per unit.

■ TABLE 7E.11
Data for Exercise 7.39

Sample Number	Number of Nonconformities	Sample Number	Number of Nonconformities
1	1	9	2
2	3	10	1
3	2	11	0
4	1	12	2
5	0	13	1
6	2	14	1
7	1	15	2
8	5	16	3

(b) Do these data come from a controlled process? If not, assume that assignable causes can be found for all out-of-control points and calculate the revised control chart parameters.

(c) Suppose the inspection unit is redefined as eight transmissions. Design an appropriate control chart for monitoring future production.

7.40. The number of workmanship nonconformities observed in the final inspection of disk-drive assemblies has been tabulated as shown in Table 7E.12. Does the process appear to be in control?

■ TABLE 7E.12
Data for Exercise 7.40

Day	Number of Assemblies Inspected	Total Number of Imperfections	Day	Number of Assemblies Inspected	Total Number of Imperfections
1	2	10	6	4	24
2	4	30	7	2	15
3	2	18	8	4	26
4	1	10	9	3	21
5	3	20	10	1	8

7.41. Find the three-sigma control limits for
(a) a c chart with process average equal to nine nonconformities.
(b) a u chart with $c = 16$ and $n = 4$.

7.42. Find the three-sigma control limits for
(a) a c chart with process average equal to four nonconformities.
(b) a u chart with $c = 4$ and $n = 4$.

7.43. Find 0.900 and 0.100 probability limits for a c chart when the process average is equal to sixteen nonconformities.

7.44. Find 0.975 and 0.025 probability limits for a control chart for nonconformities when $c = 7.6$.

7.45. A control chart for nonconformities per unit uses 0.95 and 0.05 probability limits. The center line is at $u = 1.4$. Determine the control limits if the sample size is $n = 10$.

7.46. Find 0.980 and 0.020 probability limits for a control chart for nonconformities per unit when $u = 6.0$ and $n = 3$.

7.47. A control chart for nonconformities is to be constructed with $c = 2.0$, LCL = 0, and UCL such that the probability of a point plotting outside control limits when $c = 2.0$ is only 0.005.
(a) Find the UCL.
(b) What is the type I error probability if the process is assumed to be out of control only when two consecutive points fall outside the control limits?

7.48. Assembled portable television sets are subjected to a final inspection for surface defects. A total procedure is established based on the requirement that if the average number of nonconformities per unit is 4.0, the probability of concluding that the process is in control will be 0.99. There is to be no lower control limit. What is the appropriate type of control chart and what is the required upper control limit?

7.49. A textile mill wishes to establish a control procedure on flaws in towels it manufactures. Using an inspection unit of 50 units, past inspection data show that 100 previous inspection units had 850 total flaws. What type of control chart is appropriate? Design the control chart such that it has two-sided probability control limits of $\alpha = 0.06$, approximately. Give the center line and control limits.

7.50. A control chart is to be established on a process producing refrigerators. The inspection unit is one refrigerator, and a common chart for nonconformities is to be used. As preliminary data, 16 nonconformities were counted in inspecting 30 refrigerators.
(a) What are the three-sigma control limits?
(b) What is the α-risk for this control chart?
(c) What is the β-risk if the average number of defects is actually two (i.e., if $c = 2.0$)?
(d) Find the average run length if the average number of defects is actually two.

7.51. The manufacturer wishes to set up a control chart at the final inspection station for a gas water heater. Defects in workmanship and visual quality features are checked in this inspection. For the past 22 working days, 176 water heaters were inspected and a total of 924 nonconformities reported.
(a) What type of control chart would you recommend here and how would you use it?
(b) Using two water heaters as the inspection unit, calculate the center line and control limits that are consistent with the past 22 days of inspection data.
(c) What is the probability of type I error for the control chart in part (b)?

7.52. Consider the situation described in Exercise 7.50.
(a) Find two-sigma control limits and compare these with the control limits found in part (a) of Exercise 7.50.
(b) Find the α-risk for the control chart with two-sigma control limits and compare with the results of part (b) of Exercise 7.50.
(c) Find the β-risk for $c = 2.0$ for the chart with two-sigma control limits and compare with the results of part (c) of Exercise 7.50.
(d) Find the ARL if $c = 2.0$ and compare with the ARL found in part (d) of Exercise 7.50.

7.53. Suppose that we wish to design a control chart for nonconformities per unit with L-sigma limits. Find the minimum sample size that would result in a positive lower control limit for this chart.

7.54. A control chart for nonconformities is maintained on a process producing desk calculators. The inspection unit is defined as two calculators. The average number of nonconformities per machine when the process is in control is estimated to be two.
(a) Find the appropriate three-sigma control limits for this size inspection unit.
(b) What is the probability of type I error for this control chart?

7.55. A production line assembles electric clocks. The average number of nonconformities per clock is estimated to be 0.75. The quality engineer wishes to establish a c chart for this operation, using an inspection unit of six clocks. Find the three-sigma limits for this chart.

7.56. What practical difficulties could be encountered in monitoring time-between-events data?

7.57. Suggest at least two nonmanufacturing scenarios in which attributes control charts could be useful for process monitoring.

7.58. A paper by R. N. Rodriguez ("Health Care Applications of Statistical Process Control: Examples Using the SAS® System," *SAS Users Group International: Proceedings of the 21st Annual Conference*, 1996) illustrated several informative applications of control charts to the health care environment. One of these showed how a control chart was employed to analyze the number of office visits by health care plan members. The data for clinic E are shown in Table 7E.13 (see next page).
The variable NVISITE is the number of visits to clinic E each month, and MMSE is the number of members enrolled in the health care plan each month, in units of member months. DAYS is the number of days in each month. The variable NYRSE converts MMSE to units of thousand members per year, and is computed as follows: NYRSE = MMSE(Days/30)/12000. NYRSE represents the "area of opportunity." The variable PHASE separates the data into two time periods.
(a) Use the data from P 1 to construct a control chart for monitoring the rate of office visits performed at clinic E. Does this chart exhibit control?

■ TABLE 7E.13
Data for Exercise 7.56

Month	Phase	NVISITE	NYRSE	Days	MMSE
Jan. 94	1	1421	0.66099	31	7676
Feb. 94	1	1303	0.59718	28	7678
Mar. 94	1	1569	0.66219	31	7690
Apr. 94	1	1576	0.64608	30	7753
May 94	1	1567	0.66779	31	7755
Jun. 94	1	1450	0.65575	30	7869
July 94	1	1532	0.68105	31	7909
Aug. 94	1	1694	0.68820	31	7992
Sep. 94	2	1721	0.66717	30	8006
Oct. 94	2	1762	0.69612	31	8084
Nov. 94	2	1853	0.68233	30	8188
Dec. 94	2	1770	0.70809	31	8223
Jan. 95	2	2024	0.78215	31	9083
Feb. 95	2	1975	0.70684	28	9088
Mar. 95	2	2097	0.78947	31	9168

■ TABLE 7E.14
Data for Exercise 7.59

Month	NSCANB	MMSB	Days	NYRSB
Jan. 94	50	26838	31	2.31105
Feb. 94	44	26903	28	2.09246
March 94	71	26895	31	2.31596
Apr. 94	53	26289	30	2.19075
May 94	53	26149	31	2.25172
Jun. 94	40	26185	30	2.18208
July 94	41	26142	31	2.25112
Aug. 94	57	26092	31	2.24681
Sept. 94	49	25958	30	2.16317
Oct. 94	63	25957	31	2.23519
Nov. 94	64	25920	30	2.16000
Dec. 94	62	25907	31	2.23088
Jan. 95	67	26754	31	2.30382
Feb. 95	58	26696	28	2.07636
March 95	89	26565	31	2.28754

(b) Plot the data from P 2 on the chart constructed in part (a). Is there a difference in the two phases?

(c) Consider only the P 2 data. Do these data exhibit control?

7.59. A paper by R. N. Rodriguez ("Health Care Applications of Statistical Process Control: Examples Using the SAS® System," *SAS Users Group International: Proceedings of the 21st Annual Conference,* 1996) illustrated several informative applications of control charts to the health care environment. One of these showed how a control chart was employed to analyze the rate of CAT scans performed each month at a clinic. The data used in this example are shown in Table 7E.14. NSCANB is the number of CAT scans performed each month and MMSB is the number of members enrolled in the health care plan each month, in units of member months. DAYS is the number of days in each month. The variable NYRSB converts MMSB to units of thousand members per year, and is computed as follows: NYRSB = MMSB(Days/30)/12000. NYRSB represents the "area of opportunity." Construct an appropriate control chart to monitor the rate at which CAT scans are performed at this clinic.

7.60. Kaminski et al. (1992) present data on the number of orders per truck at a distribution center. Some of this data is shown in Table 7E.15.

(a) Set up a c chart for the number of orders per truck. Is the process in control?

(b) Set up a t chart for the number of orders per truck, assuming a geometric distribution with $a = 1$. Is the process in control?

(c) Discuss the findings from parts (a) and (b). Is the Poisson distribution a good model for these data? Is there evidence of this in the data?

■ **TABLE 7E.15**
Number of Orders per Truck for Exercise 7.60

Truck	No. of Orders	Truck	No. of Orders	Truck	No. of Orders	Truck	No. of Orders
1		9		17		25	
2		10		18		26	
3		11		19		27	
4		12		20		28	
5		13		21		29	
6		14		22		30	
7		15		23		31	
8		16		24		32	

■ **TABLE 7E.16**
Customer Error Data for Exercise 7.61

Day	Record 1	Record 2	Record 3	Record 4	Record 5
1	8	7	1	11	17
2	11	1	11	2	9
3	1	1	8	2	5
4	3	2	5	1	4
5	3	2	13	6	5
6	6	3	3	3	1
7	8	8	2	1	5
8	4	10	2	6	4
9	1	6	1	3	2
10	15	1	3	2	8
11	1	7	13	5	1
12	6	7	9	3	1
13	7	6	3	3	1
14	2	9	3	8	7
15	6	14	7	1	8
16	2	9	4	2	1
17	11	1	1	3	2
18	5	5	19	1	3
19	6	15	5	6	6
20	2	7	9	2	8
21	7	5	6	14	10
22	4	3	8	1	2
23	4	1	4	20	5
24	15	2	7	10	17
25	2	15	3	11	2

7.61. The data in Table 7E.16 are the number of information errors found in customer records in a marketing company database. Five records were sampled each day.

(a) Set up a *c* chart for the total number of errors. Is the process in control?

(b) Set up a *t* chart for the total number of errors, assuming a geometric distribution with $a = 1$. Is the process in control?

(c) Discuss the findings from parts (a) and (b). Is the Poisson distribution a good model for the customer error data? Is there evidence of this in the data?

8 Determining Process and Measurement Systems Capability

Chapter Outline

The supplemental material is on the textbook Website www.wiley.com/college/montgomery.

Chapter Overview and Learning Objectives

In Chapter 6, we formally introduced the concept of process capability, or how the inherent variability in a process compares with the specifications or requirements for the product. Process capability analysis is an important tool in the DMAIC process, with application in both the analyze and improve steps. This chapter provides more extensive discussion of process capability, including several ways to study or analyze the capability of a process. We believe that the control chart is a simple and effective process capability analysis technique. We also extend the presentation of process capability ratios that we began in Chapter 6, showing how to interpret these ratios and discussing their potential dangers. The chapter also contains information on evaluating measurement system performance, illustrating graphical methods, as well as techniques based on the analysis of variance. Measurement systems analysis is used extensively in DMAIC, principally during the measure step. We also discuss setting specifications on individual discrete parts or components and estimating the natural tolerance limits of a process.

After careful study of this chapter you should be able to do the following:

1. Investigate and analyze process capability using control charts, histograms, and probability plots
2. Understand the difference between process capability and process potential
3. Calculate and properly interpret process capability ratios
4. Understand the role of the normal distribution in interpreting most process capability ratios
5. Calculate confidence intervals on process capability ratios
6. Know how to conduct and analyze a measurement systems capability (or gauge R & R) experiment
7. Know how to estimate the components of variability in a measurement system
8. Know how to set specifications on components in a system involving interaction components to ensure that overall system requirements are met
9. Estimate the natural limits of a process from a sample of data from that process

8.1 Introduction

Statistical techniques can be helpful throughout the product cycle, including development activities prior to manufacturing, in quantifying process variability, in analyzing this variability relative to product requirements or specifications, and in assisting development and manufacturing in eliminating or greatly reducing this variability. This general activity is called **process capability analysis.**

Process capability refers to the **uniformity** of the process. Obviously, the variability of critical-to-quality characteristics in the process is a measure of the uniformity of output. There are two ways to think of this variability:

1. The natural or inherent variability in a critical-to-quality characteristic at a specified time; that is, "instantaneous" variability
2. The variability in a critical-to-quality characteristic over time

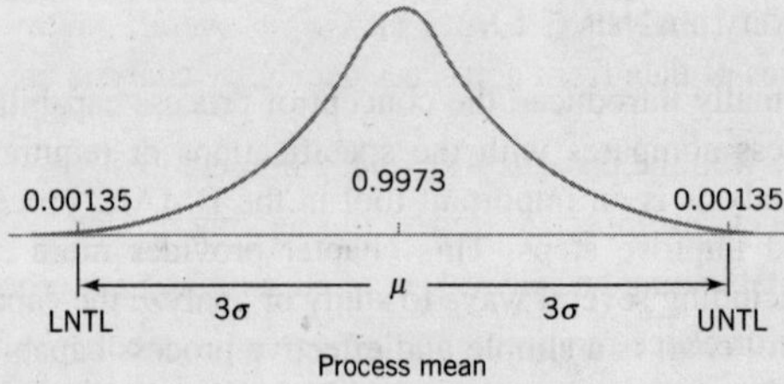

■ **FIGURE 8.1** Upper and lower natural tolerance limits in the normal distribution.

We present methods for investigating and assessing both aspects of process capability. Determining process capability is an important part of the DMAIC process. It is used primarily in the analyze step, but it also can be useful in other steps, such as improve.

It is customary to take the six-sigma spread in the distribution of the product quality characteristic as a measure of process capability. Figure 8.1 shows a process for which the quality characteristic has a normal distribution with mean μ and standard deviation σ. The upper and lower **natural tolerance limits of the process** fall at $\mu + 3\sigma$ and $\mu - 3\sigma$, respectively; that is,

$$\text{UNTL} = \mu + 3\sigma$$
$$\text{LNTL} = \mu - 3\sigma$$

For a normal distribution, the natural tolerance limits include 99.73% of the variable, or put another way, only 0.27% of the process output will fall outside the natural tolerance limits. Two points should be remembered:

1. 0.27% outside the natural tolerances sounds small, but this corresponds to 2700 nonconforming parts per million.
2. If the distribution of process output is non-normal, then the percentage of output falling outside $\mu \pm 3\sigma$ may differ considerably from 0.27%.

We define **process capability analysis** as a formal study to estimate **process capability.** The estimate of process capability may be in the form of a probability distribution having a specified shape, center (mean), and spread (standard deviation). For example, we may determine that the process output is normally distributed with mean $\mu = 1.0$ cm and standard deviation $\sigma = 0.001$ cm. In this sense, a process capability analysis may be performed **without regard to specifications on the quality characteristic.** Alternatively, we may express process capability as a percentage outside of specifications. However, specifications are not *necessary* to process capability analysis.

A process capability study usually measures functional parameters or critical-to-quality characteristics on the product, not the process itself. When the analyst can directly observe the process and can control or monitor the data-collection activity, the study is a true process capability study, because by controlling the data collection and knowing the time sequence of the data, inferences can be made about the stability of the process over time. However, when we have available only sample units of product, perhaps obtained from the supplier, and there is no direct observation of the process or time history of production, then the study is more properly called **product characterization.** In a product characterization study we can only estimate the distribution of the product quality characteristic or the process yield (fraction conforming to specifications); we can say nothing about the dynamic behavior of the process or its state of statistical control.

Process capability analysis is a vital part of an overall quality-improvement program. Among the major uses of data from a process capability analysis are the following:

1. Predicting how well the process will hold the tolerances
2. Assisting product developers/designers in selecting or modifying a process
3. Assisting in establishing an interval between sampling for process monitoring
4. Specifying performance requirements for new equipment
5. Selecting between competing suppliers and other aspects of supply chain management
6. Planning the sequence of production processes when there is an interactive effect of processes on tolerances
7. Reducing the variability in a process

Thus, process capability analysis is a technique that has application in many segments of the product cycle, including product and process design, supply chain management, production or manufacturing planning, and manufacturing.

Three primary techniques are used in process capability analysis: **histograms** or **probability plots, control charts,** and **designed experiments.** We will discuss and illustrate each of these methods in the next three sections. We will also discuss the process capability ratio (PCR) introduced in Chapter 6 and some useful variations of this ratio.

8.2 Process Capability Analysis Using a Histogram or a Probability Plot

8.2.1 Using the Histogram

The histogram can be helpful in estimating process capability. Alternatively, a stem-and-leaf plot may be substituted for the histogram. At least 100 or more observations should be available for the histogram (or the stem-and-leaf plot) to be moderately stable so that a reasonably reliable estimate of process capability may be obtained. If the quality engineer has access to the process and can control the data-collection effort, the following steps should be followed prior to data collection:

1. Choose the machine or machines to be used. If the results based on one (or a few) machines are to be extended to a larger population of machines, the machine selected should be representative of those in the population. Furthermore, if the machine has multiple workstations or heads, it may be important to collect the data so that head-to-head variability can be isolated. This may imply that designed experiments should be used.
2. Select the process operating conditions. Carefully define conditions, such as cutting speeds, feed rates, and temperatures, for future reference. It may be important to study the effects of varying these factors on process capability.
3. Select a representative operator. In some studies, it may be important to estimate *operator* variability. In these cases, the operators should be selected at random from the population of operators.
4. Carefully monitor the data-collection process, and record the time order in which each unit is produced.

The histogram, along with the sample average $\bar{x}$ and sample standard deviation s, provides information about process capability. You may wish to review the guidelines for constructing histograms in Chapter 3.

EXAMPLE 8.1 Estimating Process Capability with a Histogram

Figure 8.2 presents a histogram of the bursting strength of 100 glass containers. The data are shown in Table 8.1. What is the capability of the process?

SOLUTION

Analysis of the 100 observations gives

$$\bar{x} = 264.06 \qquad s = 32.02$$

Consequently, the process capability would be estimated as

$$\bar{x} \pm 3s$$

or

$$264.06 \pm 3(32.02) \simeq 264 \pm 96 \text{ psi}$$

Furthermore, the shape of the histogram implies that the distribution of bursting strength is approximately normal. Thus, we can estimate that approximately 99.73% of the bottles manufactured by this process will burst between 168 and 360 psi. Note that we can estimate process capability *independent of the specifications on bursting strength.*

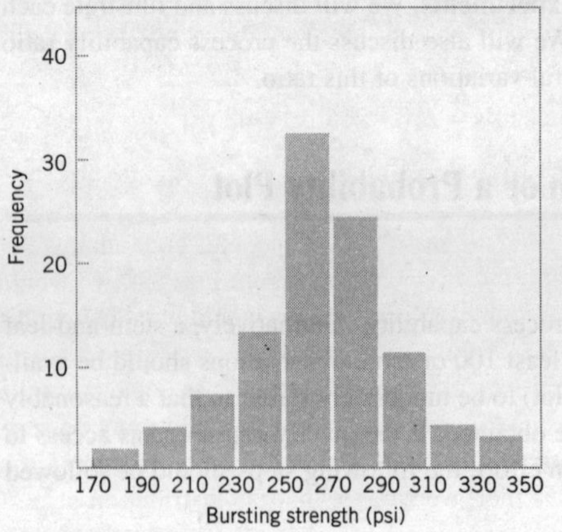

■ FIGURE 8.2 Histogram for the bursting-strength data.

■ TABLE 8.1
Bursting Strengths for 100 Glass Containers

265	197	346	280	265	200	221	265	261	278
205	286	317	242	254	235	176	262	248	250
263	274	242	260	281	246	248	271	260	265
307	243	258	321	294	328	263	245	274	270
220	231	276	228	223	296	231	301	337	298
268	267	300	250	260	276	334	280	250	257
260	281	208	299	308	264	280	274	278	210
234	265	187	258	235	269	265	253	254	280
299	214	264	267	283	235	272	287	274	269
215	318	271	293	277	290	283	258	275	251

An advantage of using the histogram to estimate process capability is that it gives an immediate, visual impression of process performance. It may also immediately show the reason for poor process performance. For example, Fig. 8.3*a* shows a process with adequate potential capability, but the process target is poorly located, whereas Fig. 8.3*b* shows a process with poor capability resulting from excess variability.

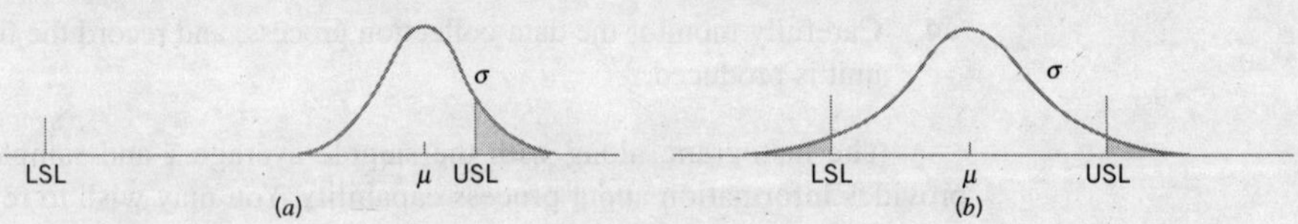

■ FIGURE 8.3 Some reasons for poor process capability. (*a*) Poor process centering. (*b*) Excess process variability.

8.2.2 Probability Plotting

Probability plotting is an alternative to the histogram that can be used to determine the shape, center, and spread of the distribution. It has the advantage that it is unnecessary to divide the range of the variable into class intervals, and it often produces reasonable results for moderately small samples (which the histogram will not). Generally, a probability plot is a graph of the ranked data versus the sample cumulative frequency on special paper with a vertical scale chosen so that the cumulative distribution of the assumed type is a straight line. In Chapter 3 we discussed and illustrated **normal probability plots.** These plots are very useful in process capability studies.

To illustrate the use of a normal probability plot in a process capability study, consider the following 20 observations on glass container bursting strength: 197, 200, 215, 221, 231, 242, 245, 258, 265, 265, 271, 275, 277, 278, 280, 283, 290, 301, 318, and 346. Figure 8.4 is the normal probability plot of strength. Note that the data lie nearly along a straight line, implying that the distribution of bursting strength is normal. Recall from Chapter 4 that the mean of the normal distribution is the fiftieth percentile, which we may estimate from Fig. 8.4 as approximately 265 psi, and the standard deviation of the distribution is the *slope* of the straight line. It is convenient to estimate the standard deviation as the difference between the eighty-fourth and the fiftieth percentiles. For the strength data shown above and using Fig. 8.4, we find that

$$\hat{\sigma} = \text{84th percentile} - \text{50th percentile} = 298 - 265 \text{ psi} = 33 \text{ psi}$$

Note that $\hat{\mu} = 265$ psi and $\hat{\sigma} = 33$ psi are not far from the sample average $\bar{x} = 264.06$ and standard deviation $s = 32.02$.

The normal probability plot can also be used to estimate process yields and fallouts. For example, the specification on container strength is LSL = 200 psi. From Fig. 8.4, we would estimate that about 5% of the containers manufactured by this process would burst below this limit.

Care should be exercised in using probability plots. If the data do not come from the assumed distribution, inferences about process capability drawn from the plot may be seriously in error. Figure 8.5 presents a normal probability plot of times to failure (in hours) of a valve in a chemical plant. From examining this plot, we can see that the distribution of failure time is not normal.

An obvious disadvantage of probability plotting is that it is not an objective procedure. It is possible for two analysts to arrive at different conclusions using the same data. For this reason, it is often desirable to supplement probability plots with more formal statistically

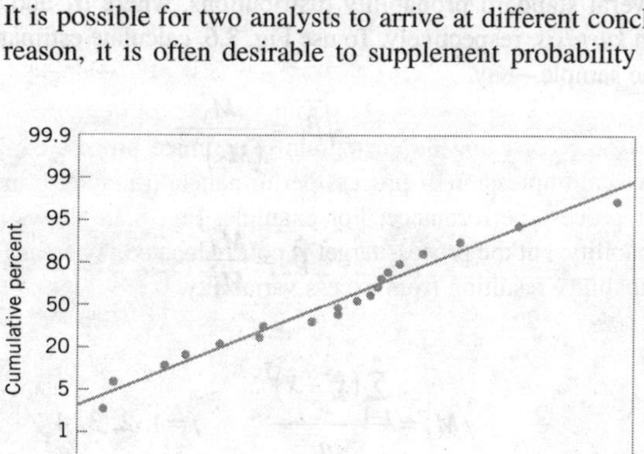

■ **FIGURE 8.4** Normal probability plot of the container-strength data.

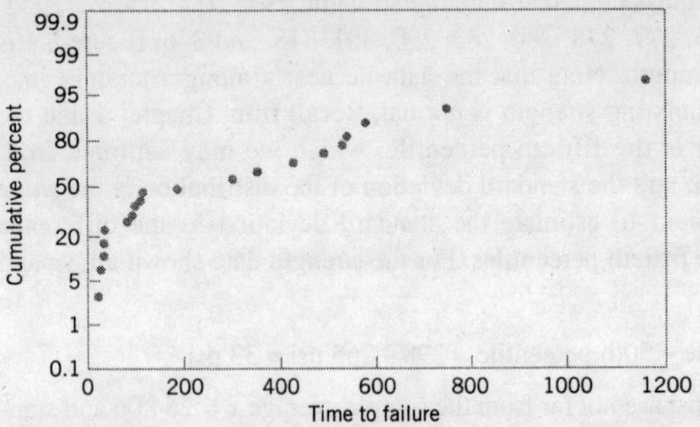

■ FIGURE 8.5 Normal probability plot of time to failure of a valve.

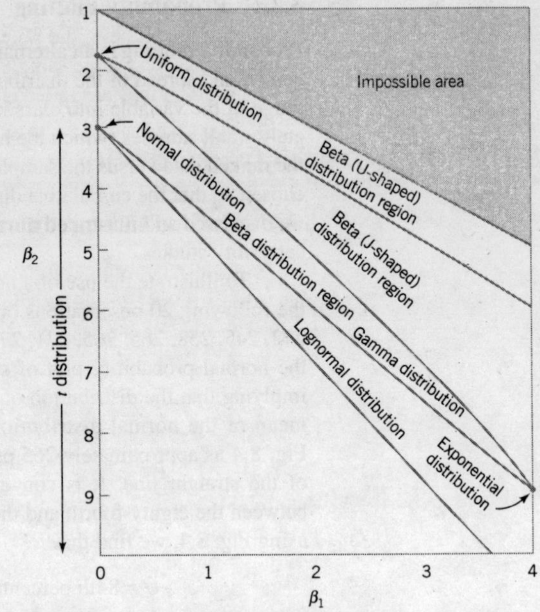

■ FIGURE 8.6 Regions in the β_1, β_2 plane for various distributions. (From *Statistical Models in Engineering* by G. J. Hahn and S. S. Shapiro, John Wiley: New York, 1967.)

based goodness-of-fit tests. A good introduction to these tests is in Shapiro (1980). Augmenting the interpretation of a normal probability plot with the Shapiro-Wilk test for normality can make the procedure much more powerful and objective.

Choosing the distribution to fit the data is also an important step in probability plotting. Sometimes we can use our knowledge of the physical phenomena or past experience to suggest the choice of distribution. In other situations, the display in Fig. 8.6 may be useful in selecting a distribution that describes the data. This figure shows the regions in the β_1, β_2 plane for several standard probability distributions, where β_1 and β_2 are the measures of *skewness* and *kurtosis*, respectively. To use Fig. 8.6, calculate estimates of skewness and kurtosis from the sample—say,

$$\sqrt{\hat{\beta}_1} = \frac{M_3}{(M_2)^{3/2}} \tag{8.1}$$

and

$$\hat{\beta}_2 = \frac{M_4}{M_2^2} \tag{8.2}$$

where

$$M_j = \frac{\sum_{i=1}^{n}(x_i - \bar{x})^j}{n} \qquad j = 1, 2, 3, 4 \tag{8.3}$$

and plot the point $(\hat{\beta}_1, \hat{\beta}_2)$ on the graph. If the plotted point falls close to a point, line, or region that corresponds to one of the distributions in the figure, then this distribution is a logical choice to use as a model for the data. If the point falls in regions of the β_1, β_2 plane where *none* of the distributions seems appropriate, other, more general probability distributions, such as the Johnson or Pearson families of distributions, may be required. A note of caution should be sounded here; the skewness and kurtosis statistics are not reliable unless they are computed from very large samples. Procedures similar to that in Fig. 8.6 for fitting these distributions and graphs are in Hahn and Shapiro (1967).

8.3 Process Capability Ratios

8.3.1 Use and Interpretation of C_p

It is frequently convenient to have a simple, quantitative way to express process capability. One way to do so is through the **process capability ratio (PCR) C_p** first introduced in Chapter 6. Recall that

$$C_p = \frac{\text{USL} - \text{LSL}}{6\sigma} \tag{8.4}$$

where USL and LSL are the upper and lower specification limits, respectively. C_p and other process capability ratios are used extensively in industry. They are also widely *misused.* We will point out some of the more common abuses of process capability ratios. An excellent recent book on process capability ratios that is highly recommended is Kotz and Lovelace (1998). There is also extensive technical literature on process capability analysis and process capability ratios. The review paper by Kotz and Johnson (2002) and the bibliography by Spiring, Leong, Cheng, and Yeung (2003) are excellent sources.

In a practical application, the process standard deviation σ is almost always unknown and must be replaced by an estimate σ. To estimate σ we typically use either the *sample standard deviation s* or $\overline{R}/d_2$ (when variables control charts are used in the capability study). This results in an estimate of C_p—say,

$$\hat{C}_p = \frac{\text{USL} - \text{LSL}}{6\hat{\sigma}} \tag{8.5}$$

To illustrate the calculation of C_p, recall the semiconductor hard-bake process first analyzed in Example 6.1 using $\overline{x}$ and R charts. The specifications on flow width are USL = 1.00 microns and LSL = 2.00 microns, and from the R chart we estimated $\sigma = \overline{R}/d_2 = 0.1398$. Thus, our estimate of the PCR C_p is

$$\hat{C}_p = \frac{\text{USL} - \text{LSL}}{6\hat{\sigma}} = \frac{2.00 - 1.00}{6(0.1398)} = 1.192$$

In Chapter 6, we assumed that flow width is approximately normally distributed (a reasonable assumption, based on the histogram in Fig. 8.7) and the cumulative normal distribution table in the Appendix was used to estimate that the process produces approximately 350 ppm (parts per million) defective.

The PCR C_p in equation (8.4) has a useful practical interpretation—namely,

$$P = \left(\frac{1}{C_p}\right)100 \tag{8.6}$$

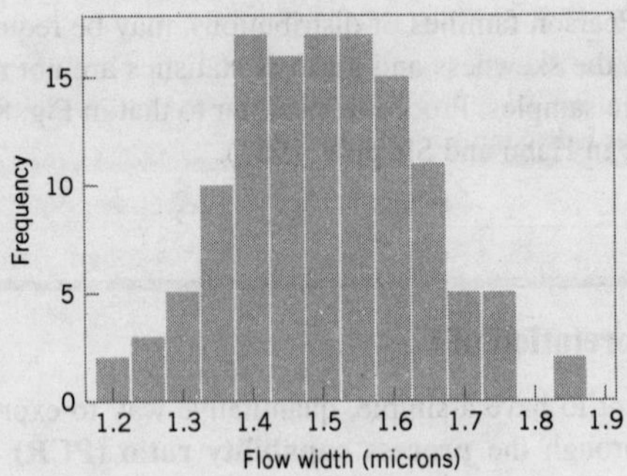

■ FIGURE 8.7 Histogram of flow width from Example 6.1.

is the percentage of the specification band used up by the process. The hard-bake process uses

$$P = \left(\frac{1}{1.192}\right)100 = 83.89$$

percent of the specification band.

Equations (8.4) and (8.5) assume that the process has both upper and lower specification limits. For one-sided specifications, **one-sided process-capability ratios** are used. One-sided PCRs are defined as follows.

$$C_{pu} = \frac{\text{USL} - \mu}{3\sigma} \quad \text{(upper specification only)} \tag{8.7}$$

$$C_{pl} = \frac{\mu - \text{LSL}}{3\sigma} \quad \text{(lower specification only)} \tag{8.8}$$

Estimates $\hat{C}_{pu}$ and $\hat{C}_{pl}$ would be obtained by replacing μ and σ in equations (8.7) and (8.8) by estimates $\hat{\mu}$ and $\hat{\sigma}$, respectively.

EXAMPLE 8.2 One-Sided Process-Capability Ratios

Construct a one-sided process-capability ratio for the container bursting-strength data in Example 8.1. Suppose that the lower specification limit on bursting strength is 200 psi.

SOLUTION

We will use $\bar{x} = 264$ and $s = 32$ as estimates of μ and σ, respectively, and the resulting estimate of the one-sided lower process-capability ratio is

$$\hat{C}_{pl} = \frac{\hat{\mu} - \text{LSL}}{3\hat{\sigma}} = \frac{264 - 200}{3(32)} = 0.67$$

The fraction of defective containers produced by this process is estimated by finding the area to the left of $Z = (\text{LSL} - \mu)/\sigma = (200 - 264)/32 = -2$ under the standard normal distribution. The estimated fallout is about 2.28% defective, or about 22,800 nonconforming containers per million. Note that if the normal distribution were an inappropriate model for strength, then this last calculation would have to be performed using the appropriate probability distribution.

■ TABLE 8.2

Values of the Process Capability Ratio (C_p) and Associated Process Fallout for a Normally Distributed Process (in Defective ppm) That Is in Statistical Control

	Process Fallout (in defective ppm)	
PCR	**One-Sided Specifications**	**Two-Sided Specifications**
0.25	226,628	453,255
0.50	66,807	133,614
0.60	35,931	71,861
0.70	17,865	35,729
0.80	8,198	16,395
0.90	3,467	6,934
1.00	1,350	2,700
1.10	484	967
1.20	159	318
1.30	48	96
1.40	14	27
1.50	4	7
1.60	1	2
1.70	0.17	0.34
1.80	0.03	0.06
2.00	0.0009	0.0018

The process capability ratio is a measure of the ability of the process to manufacture product that meets the specifications. Table 8.2 presents several values of the PCR C_p along with the associated values of process fallout, expressed in defective parts or nonconforming units of product per million (ppm). To illustrate the use of Table 8.2, notice that a PCR for a normally distributed stable process of $C_p = 1.00$ implies a fallout rate of 2700 ppm for two-sided specifications, whereas a PCR of $C_p = 1.50$ for this process implies a fallout rate of 4 ppm for one-sided specifications.

The ppm quantities in Table 8.2 were calculated using the following **important assumptions:**

1. The quality characteristic has a normal distribution.
2. The process is in statistical control.
3. In the case of two-sided specifications, the process mean is centered between the lower and upper specification limits.

These assumptions are absolutely **critical** to the **accuracy** and **validity** of the reported numbers, and if they are not valid, then the reported quantities may be seriously in error. For example, Somerville and Montgomery (1996) report an extensive investigation of the errors in using the normality assumption to make inferences about the ppm level of a process when in fact the underlying distribution is non-normal. They investigated various non-normal distributions and observed that errors of several orders of magnitude can result in predicting ppm by erroneously making the normality assumption. Even when using a *t* distribution with as many as 30 degrees of freedom, substantial errors result. Thus even though a *t* distribution

■ TABLE 8.3
Recommended Minimum Values of the Process Capability Ratio

	Two-Sided Specifications	One-Sided Specifications
Existing processes	1.33	1.25
New processes	1.50	1.45
Safety, strength, or critical parameter, existing process	1.50	1.45
Safety, strength, or critical parameter, new process	1.67	1.60

with 30 degrees of freedom is symmetrical and almost visually indistinguishable from the normal, the longer and heavier tails of the *t* distribution make a significant difference when estimating the ppm. Consequently, symmetry in the distribution of process output alone is insufficient to ensure that any PCR will provide a reliable prediction of process ppm. We will discuss the non-normality issue in more detail in Section 8.3.3.

Stability or **statistical control** of the process is also **essential** to the correct interpretation of any PCR. Unfortunately, it is fairly common practice to compute a PCR from a sample of historical process data without any consideration of whether or not the process is in statistical control. If the process is not in control, then of course its parameters are unstable, and the value of these parameters in the future is uncertain. Thus the predictive aspects of the PCR regarding process ppm performance are lost.

Finally, remember that what we actually observe in practice is an **estimate** of the PCR. This estimate is subject to error in estimation, since it depends on sample statistics. English and Taylor (1993) report that large errors in estimating PCRs from sample data can occur, so the estimate one actually has at hand may not be very reliable. It is always a good idea to report the estimate of any PCR in terms of a **confidence interval.** We will show how to do this for some of the commonly used PCRs in Section 8.3.5.

Table 8.3 presents some recommended **guidelines for minimum values** of the PCR. The bottle-strength characteristic is a parameter closely related to the safety of the product; bottles with inadequate pressure strength may fail and injure consumers. This implies that the PCR should be at least 1.45. Perhaps one way the PCR could be improved would be by increasing the mean strength of the containers—say, by pouring more glass in the mold.

We point out that the values in Table 8.3 are only **minimums.** In recent years, many companies have adopted criteria for evaluating their processes that include process capability objectives that are more stringent than those of Table 8.3. For example, a six-sigma company would require that when the process mean is in control, it will not be closer than six standard deviations from the nearest specification limit. This, in effect, requires that the minimum acceptable value of the process capability ratio will be at least 2.0.

8.3.2 Process Capability Ratio for an Off-Center Process

The process capability ratio C_p does not take into account *where* the process mean is located relative to the specifications. C_p simply measures the spread of the specifications relative to the six-sigma spread in the process. For example, the top two normal distributions in Fig. 8.8 both have $C_p = 2.0$, but the process in panel (*b*) of the figure clearly has lower capability than the process in panel (*a*) because it is not operating at the midpoint of the interval between the specifications.

This situation may be more accurately reflected by defining a new process capability ratio—**PRC C_{pk}**—that takes process centering into account. This quantity is

$$C_{pk} = \min\left(C_{pu}, C_{pl}\right) \tag{8.9}$$

Note that C_{pk} is simply the one-sided PCR for the specification limit nearest to the process average. For the process shown in Fig. 8.8*b*, we would have

$$\begin{aligned} C_{pk} &= \min\left(C_{pu}, C_{pl}\right) \\ &= \min\left(C_{pu} = \frac{\text{USL} - \mu}{3\sigma}, C_{pl} = \frac{\mu - \text{LSL}}{3\sigma}\right) \\ &= \min\left(C_{pu} = \frac{62-53}{3(2)} = 1.5, C_{pl} = \frac{53-38}{3(2)} = 2.5\right) \\ &= 1.5 \end{aligned}$$

Generally, if $C_p = C_{pk}$, the process is centered at the midpoint of the specifications, and when $C_{pk} < C_p$ the process is off-center.

The magnitude of C_{pk} relative to C_p is a direct measure of how off-center the process is operating. Several commonly encountered cases are illustrated in Fig. 8.8. Note in panel (*c*) of Fig. 8.8 that $C_{pk} = 1.0$ while $C_p = 2.0$. One can use Table 8.2 to get a quick estimate of potential improvement that would be possible by centering the process. If we take $C_p = 1.0$ in Table 8.2 and read the fallout from the one-sided specifications column, we can estimate the *actual* fallout as 1350 ppm. However, if we can center the process, then $C_p = 2.0$ can be achieved, and Table 8.2 (using $C_p = 2.0$ and two-sided specifications) suggests that the *potential*

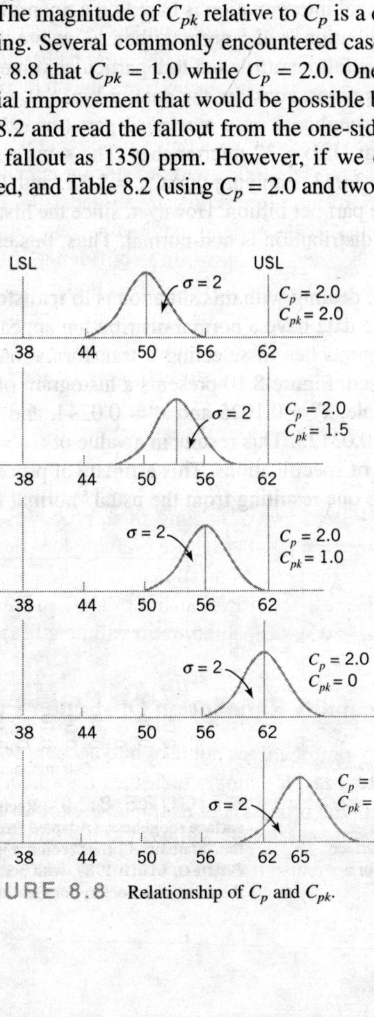

■ FIGURE 8.8 Relationship of C_p and C_{pk}.

fallout is 0.0018 ppm, an improvement of several orders of magnitude in process performance. Thus, we usually say that C_p measures **potential capability** in the process, whereas C_{pk} measures **actual capability.**

Panel (*d*) of Fig. 8.8 illustrates the case in which the process mean is exactly equal to one of the specification limits, leading to $C_{pk} = 0$. As panel (*e*) illustrates, when $C_{pk} < 0$ the implication is that the process mean lies outside the specifications. Clearly, if $C_{pk} < -1$, the entire process lies outside the specification limits. Some authors define C_{pk} to be nonnegative, so that values less than zero are defined as zero.

Many quality-engineering authorities have advised against the **routine use** of process capability ratios such as C_p and C_{pk} (or the others discussed later in this section) on the grounds that they are an oversimplification of a complex phenomenon. Certainly, any statistic that combines information about both location (the mean and process centering) and variability and that requires the assumption of normality for its meaningful interpretation is likely to be misused (or abused). Furthermore, as we will see, point estimates of process capability ratios are virtually useless if they are computed from small samples. Clearly, these ratios need to be used and interpreted very carefully.

8.3.3 Normality and the Process Capability Ratio

An important assumption underlying our discussion of process capability and the ratios C_p and C_{pk} is that their usual interpretation is based on a **normal distribution** of process output. If the underlying distribution is non-normal, then as we previously cautioned, the statements about expected process fallout attributed to a particular value of C_p or C_{pk} may be in error.

To illustrate this point, consider the data in Fig. 8.9, which is a histogram of 80 measurements of surface roughness on a machined part (measured in microinches). The upper specification limit is at USL = 32 microinches. The sample average and standard deviation are $\bar{x} = 10.44$ and $S = 3.053$, implying that $\hat{C}_{pu} = 2.35$, and Table 8.2 would suggest that the fallout is less than one part per billion. However, since the histogram is highly skewed, we are fairly certain that the distribution is non-normal. Thus, this estimate of capability is unlikely to be correct.

One approach to dealing with this situation is to **transform the data** so that in the new, transformed metric the data have a normal distribution appearance. There are various graphical and analytical approaches to selecting a transformation. In this example, a reciprocal transformation was used. Figure 8.10 presents a histogram of the reciprocal values $x^* = 1/x$. In the transformed scale, $\bar{x}^* = 0.1025$ and $s^* = 0.0244$, and the original upper specification limit becomes $1/32 = 0.03125$. This results in a value of $\hat{C}_{pl} = 0.97$, which implies that about 1350 ppm are outside of specifications. This estimate of process performance is clearly much more realistic than the one resulting from the usual "normal theory" assumption.

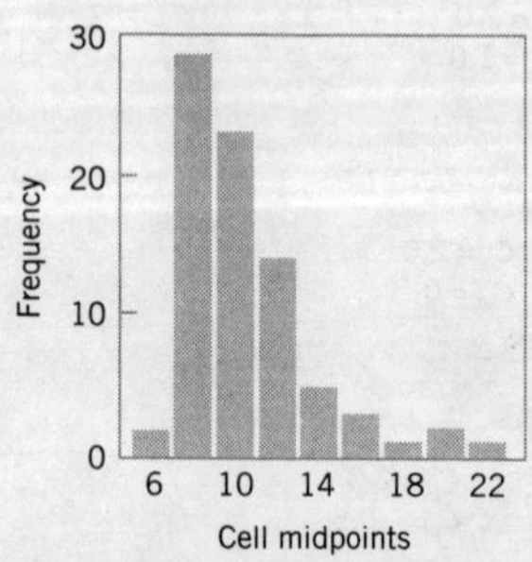

■ FIGURE 8.9 Surface roughness in microinches for a machined part.

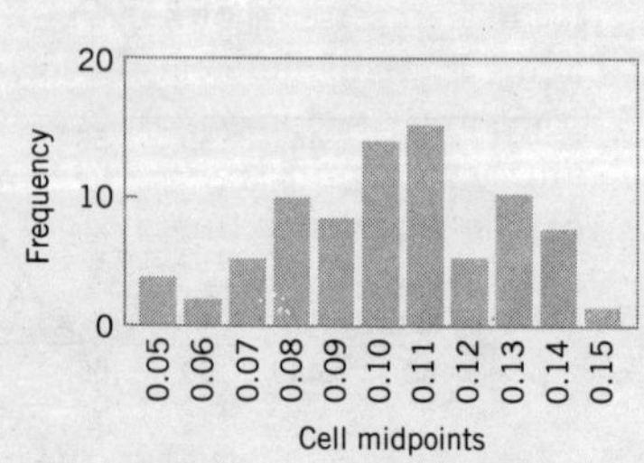

■ FIGURE 8.10 Reciprocals of surface roughness. (Adapted from data in the "Statistics Corner" column in *Quality Progress,* March 1989, with permission of the American Society for Quality Control.)

Other approaches have been considered in dealing with non-normal data. There have been various attempts to extend the definitions of the standard capability indices to the case of non-normal distributions. Luceño (1996) introduced the index C_{pc}, defined as

$$C_{pc} = \frac{\text{USL} - \text{LSL}}{6\sqrt{\dfrac{\pi}{2}}E|X - T|} \tag{8.10}$$

where the process target value $T = \frac{1}{2}(\text{USL} + \text{LSL})$. Luceño uses the second subscript in C_{pc} to stand for *confidence,* and he stresses that the confidence intervals based on C_{pc} are reliable; of course, this statement should be interpreted cautiously. The author has also used the constant $6\sqrt{\pi/2} = 7.52$ in the denominator, to make it equal to 6σ when the underlying distribution is normal. We will give the confidence interval for C_{pc} in Section 8.3.5.

There have also been attempts to modify the usual capability indices so that they are appropriate for two **general families** of distributions, the Pearson and Johnson families. This would make PCRs broadly applicable for both normal and non-normal distributions. Good discussions of these approaches are in Rodriguez (1992) and Kotz and Lovelace (1998).

The general idea is to use appropriate **quantiles** of the process distribution—say, $x_{0.00135}$ and $x_{0.99865}$—to define a quantile-based PCR—say,

$$C_p(q) = \frac{\text{USL} - \text{LSL}}{x_{0.99865} - x_{0.00135}} \tag{8.11}$$

Now since in the normal distribution $x_{0.00135} = \mu - 3\sigma$ and $x_{0.99865} = \mu + 3\sigma$, we see that in the case of a normal distribution $C_p(q)$ reduces to C_p. Clements (1989) proposed a method for determining the quantiles based on the Pearson family of distributions. In general, however, we could fit *any* distribution to the process data, determine its quantiles $x_{0.99865}$ and $x_{0.00135}$, and apply equation (8.11). Refer to Kotz and Lovelace (1998) for more information.

8.3.4 More about Process Centering

The process capability ratio C_{pk} was initially developed because C_p does not adequately deal with the case of a process with mean μ that is not centered between the specification limits. However, C_{pk} alone is still an inadequate measure of process centering. For example, consider the two processes shown in Fig. 8.11. Both processes A and B have $C_{pk} = 1.0$, yet their centering is clearly different. To characterize process centering satisfactorily, C_{pk} must be compared to C_p. For process A, $C_{pk} = C_p = 1.0$, implying that the process is centered, whereas for process B, $C_p = 2.0 > C_{pk} = 1.0$, implying that the process is off-center. For any fixed value of μ in the interval from LSL to USL, C_{pk} depends inversely on σ and becomes large as σ

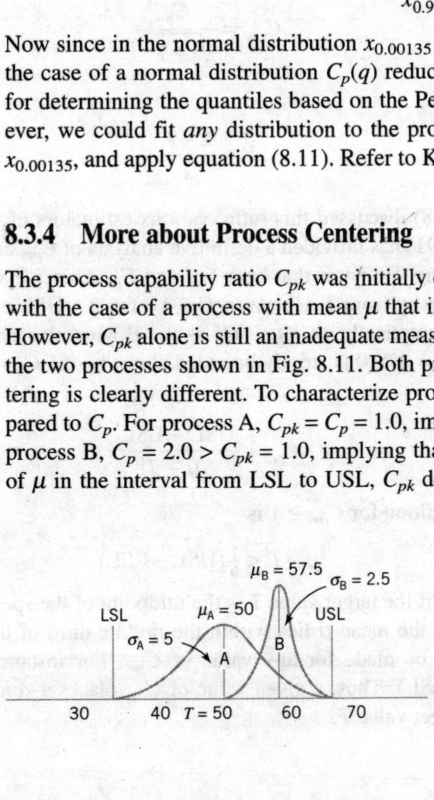

■ FIGURE 8.11 Two processes with $C_{pk} = 1.0$.

approaches zero. This characteristic can make C_{pk} unsuitable as a measure of centering. That is, a large value of C_{pk} does not really tell us anything about the location of the mean in the interval from LSL to USL.

One way to address this difficulty is to use a process capability ratio that is a better indicator of centering. PCR C_{pm} is one such ratio,

$$C_{pm} = \frac{\text{USL} - \text{LSL}}{6\tau} \tag{8.12}$$

and τ is the square root of expected squared deviation from target $T = \frac{1}{2}(\text{USL} + \text{LSL})$,

$$\begin{aligned}\tau^2 &= E\left[(x-T)^2\right] \\ &= E\left[(x-\mu)^2\right] + (\mu - T)^2 \\ &= \sigma^2 + (\mu - T)^2\end{aligned}$$

Thus, equation (8.12) can be written as

$$C_{pm} = \frac{\text{USL} - \text{LSL}}{6\sqrt{\sigma^2 + (\mu - T)^2}} = \frac{C_p}{\sqrt{1+\xi^2}} \tag{8.13}$$

where

$$\xi = \frac{\mu - T}{\sigma} \tag{8.14}$$

A logical way to estimate C_{pm} is by

$$\hat{C}_{pm} = \frac{\hat{C}_p}{\sqrt{1+V^2}} \tag{8.15}$$

where

$$V = \frac{\bar{x} - T}{s} \tag{8.16}$$

Chan et al. (1988) discussed this ratio, various estimators of C_{pm}, and their sampling properties. Boyles (1991) has provided a definitive analysis of C_{pm} and its usefulness in measuring process centering. He notes that both C_{pk} and C_{pm} coincide with C_p when $\mu = T$ and decrease as μ moves away from T. However, $C_{pk} < 0$ for $\mu >$ USL or $\mu <$ LSL, whereas C_{pm} approaches zero asymptotically as $|(\mu - T)| \to \infty$. Boyles also shows that the C_{pm} of a process with $|(\mu - T)| = \Delta > 0$ is strictly bounded above by the C_p value of a process with $\sigma = \Delta$. That is,

$$C_{pm} < \frac{\text{USL} - \text{LSL}}{6|\mu - T|} \tag{8.17}$$

Thus, a necessary condition for $C_{pm} \geq 1$ is

$$|\mu - T| < \tfrac{1}{6}(\text{USL} - \text{LSL})$$

This statistic says that if the target value T is the midpoint of the specifications, a C_{pm} of one or greater implies that the mean μ lies within the middle third of the specification band. A similar statement can be made for any value of C_{pm}. For instance, $C_{pm} \geq \frac{4}{3}$ implies that $|(\mu - T)| < \frac{1}{8}(\text{USL} - \text{LSL})$. Thus, a given value of C_{pm} places a constraint on the difference between μ and the target value T.

EXAMPLE 8.3 Process Centering

To illustrate the use of C_{pm}, consider the two processes A and B in Fig. 8.11. For process A we find that

$$C_{pm} = \frac{C_p}{\sqrt{1+\xi^2}} = \frac{1.0}{\sqrt{1+0}} = 1.0$$

since process A is centered at the target value $T = 50$. Note that $C_{pm} = C_{pk}$ for process A. Now consider process B:

$$C_{pm} = \frac{C_p}{\sqrt{1+\xi^2}} = \frac{2}{\sqrt{1+(3)^2}} = 0.63$$

If we use equation (8.17), this is equivalent to saying that the process mean lies approximately within the middle half of the specification range. Visual examination of Fig. 8.11 reveals this to be the case.

Pearn et al. (1992) proposed the process capability ratio

$$C_{pkm} = \frac{C_{pk}}{\sqrt{1+\left(\frac{\mu - T}{\sigma}\right)^2}} = \frac{C_{pk}}{\sqrt{1+\xi^2}} \tag{8.18}$$

This is sometimes called a "third generation" process capability ratio, since it is constructed from the "second generation" ratios C_{pk} and C_{pm} in the same way that they were generated from the "first generation" ratio C_p. The motivation of this new ratio is increased sensitivity to departures of the process mean μ from the desired target T. For more details, see Kotz and Lovelace (1998).

8.3.5 Confidence Intervals and Tests on Process Capability Ratios

Confidence Intervals on Process Capability Ratios. Much of the industrial use of process capability ratios focuses on computing and interpreting the **point estimate** of the desired quantity. It is easy to forget that $\hat{C}_p$ or $\hat{C}_{pk}$ (for examples) are simply point estimates, and, as such, are subject to statistical fluctuation. An alternative that should become standard practice is to report **confidence intervals for process capability ratios.**

It is easy to find a confidence interval for the "first generation" ratio C_p. If we replace σ by s in the equation for C_p, we produce the usual point estimator $\hat{C}_p$. If the quality characteristic follows a normal distribution, then a $100(1 - \alpha)\%$ confidence interval on C_p is obtained from

$$\frac{\text{USL} - \text{LSL}}{6s}\sqrt{\frac{\chi^2_{1-\alpha/2,n-1}}{n-1}} \le C_p \le \frac{\text{USL} - \text{LSL}}{6s}\sqrt{\frac{\chi^2_{\alpha/2,n-1}}{n-1}} \tag{8.19}$$

or

$$\hat{C}_p\sqrt{\frac{\chi^2_{1-\alpha/2,n-1}}{n-1}} \le C_p \le \hat{C}_p\sqrt{\frac{\chi^2_{\alpha/2,n-1}}{n-1}} \tag{8.20}$$

where $\chi^2_{1-\alpha/2,n-1}$ and $\chi^2_{\alpha/2,n-1}$ are the lower $\alpha/2$ and upper $\alpha/2$ percentage points of the chi-square distribution with $n - 1$ degrees of freedom. These percentage points are tabulated in Appendix Table III.

EXAMPLE 8.4 A Confidence Interval in C_p

Suppose that a stable process has upper and lower specifications at USL = 62 and LSL = 38. A sample of size $n = 20$ from this process reveals that the process mean is centered approximately at the midpoint of the specification interval and that the sample standard deviation $s = 1.75$. Find a 95% confidence interval on C_p.

SOLUTION

A point estimate of C_p is

$$\hat{C}_p = \frac{\text{USL} - \text{LSL}}{6s} = \frac{62 - 38}{6(1.75)} = 2.29$$

The 95% confidence interval on C_p is found from equation (8.20) as follows:

$$\hat{C}_p \sqrt{\frac{\chi^2_{1-0.025,n-1}}{n-1}} \le C_p \le \hat{C}_p \sqrt{\frac{\chi^2_{0.025,n-1}}{n-1}}$$

$$2.29\sqrt{\frac{8.91}{19}} \le C_p \le 2.29\sqrt{\frac{32.85}{19}}$$

$$1.57 \le C_p \le 3.01$$

where $\chi^2_{0.975,19} = 8.91$ and $\chi^2_{0.025,19} = 32.85$ were taken from Appendix Table III.

The confidence interval on C_p in Example 8.4 is relatively wide because the sample standard deviation s exhibits considerable fluctuation in small to moderately large samples. This means, in effect, that confidence intervals on C_p based on small samples will be wide.

Note also that the confidence interval uses s rather than $\overline{R}/d_2$ to estimate σ. This further emphasizes that the process must be **in statistical control** for PCRs to have any real meaning. If the process is not in control, s and $\overline{R}/d_2$ could be very different, leading to very different values of the PCR.

For more complicated ratios such as C_{pk} and C_{pm}, various authors have developed approximate confidence intervals; for example, see Zhang, Stenbeck, and Wardrop (1990), Bissell (1990), Kushler and Hurley (1992), and Pearn et al. (1992). If the quality characteristic is normally distributed, then an approximate $100(1 - \alpha)\%$ confidence interval on C_{pk} is given as follows.

$$\hat{C}_{pk}\left[1 - Z_{\alpha/2}\sqrt{\frac{1}{9n\hat{C}_{pk}^2} + \frac{1}{2(n-1)}}\right] \le C_{pk} \le \hat{C}_{pk}\left[1 + Z_{\alpha/2}\sqrt{\frac{1}{9n\hat{C}_{pk}^2} + \frac{1}{2(n-1)}}\right] \tag{8.21}$$

Kotz and Lovelace (1998) give an extensive summary of confidence intervals for various PCRs.

EXAMPLE 8.5 A Confidence Interval in C_{pk}

A sample of size $n = 20$ from a stable process is used to estimate C_{pk}, with the result that $\hat{C}_{pk} = 1.33$. Find an approximate 95% confidence interval on C_{pk}.

SOLUTION

Using equation (8.21), an approximate 95% confidence interval on C_{pk} is

$$\hat{C}_{pk}\left[1 - Z_{\alpha/2}\sqrt{\frac{1}{9n\hat{C}_{pk}^2} + \frac{1}{2(n-1)}}\right] \le C_{pk} \le \hat{C}_{pk}\left[1 + Z_{\alpha/2}\sqrt{\frac{1}{9n\hat{C}_{pk}^2} + \frac{1}{2(n-1)}}\right]$$

$$1.33\left[1 - 1.96\sqrt{\frac{1}{9(20)(1.33)^2} + \frac{1}{2(19)}}\right] \le C_{pk} \le 1.33\left[1 + 1.96\sqrt{\frac{1}{9(20)(1.33)^2} + \frac{1}{2(19)}}\right]$$

or

$$0.88 \le C_{pk} \le 1.78$$

This is an extremely wide confidence interval. Based on the sample data, the ratio C_{pk} could be less than 1 (a very bad situation), or it could be as large as 1.78 (a very good situation). Thus, we have learned very little about actual process capability, because C_{pk} is very imprecisely estimated. The reason for this, of course, is that a very small sample ($n = 20$) has been used.

For non-normal data, the PCR C_{pc} developed by Luceño (1996) can be employed. Recall that C_{pc} was defined in equation (8.10). Luceño developed the confidence interval for C_{pc} as follows: First, evaluate $|(x - T)|$, whose expected value is estimated by

$$\bar{c} = \frac{1}{n}\sum_{i=1}^{n}|x_i - T|$$

leading to the estimator

$$\hat{C}_{pc} = \frac{\text{USL} - \text{LSL}}{6\sqrt{\frac{\pi}{2}}\,\bar{c}}$$

A $100(1 - \alpha)\%$ confidence interval for $E|(x - T)|$ is given as

$$\bar{c} \pm t_{\alpha/2,n-1}\frac{s_c}{\sqrt{n}}$$

where

$$s_c^2 = \frac{1}{n-1}\sum_{i=1}^{n}\left(|x_i - T| - \bar{c}\right)^2 = \frac{1}{n-1}\left(\sum_{i=1}^{n}|x_i - T|^2 - n\bar{c}^2\right)$$

Therefore, a $100(1-\alpha)\%$ confidence interval for C_{pc} is given by

$$\frac{\hat{C}_{pc}}{1+t_{\alpha/2,n-1}\left[s_c/\left(\bar{c}\sqrt{n}\right)\right]} \le C_{pc} \le \frac{\hat{C}_{pc}}{1-t_{\alpha/2,n-1}\left[s_c/\left(\bar{c}\sqrt{n}\right)\right]} \quad (8.22)$$

Testing Hypotheses about PCRs. A practice that is becoming increasingly common in industry is to require a supplier to **demonstrate** process capability as part of the contractual agreement. Thus, it is frequently necessary to demonstrate that the process capability ratio C_p meets or exceeds some particular target value—say, C_{p0}. This problem may be formulated as a hypothesis testing problem

$$H_0: \quad C_p = C_{p0} \text{ (or the process is not capable)}$$
$$H_1: \quad C_p \ge C_{p0} \text{ (or the process is capable)}$$

We would like to reject H_0 (recall that in statistical hypothesis testing rejection of H_0 is always a strong conclusion), thereby demonstrating that the process is capable. We can formulate the statistical test in terms of $\hat{C}_p$, so that we will reject H_0 if $\hat{C}_p$ exceeds a critical value C.

Kane (1986) has investigated this test, and provides a table of sample sizes and critical values for C to assist in testing process capability. We may define C_p(High) as a process capability that we would like to accept with probability $1-\alpha$ and C_p(Low) as a process capability that we would like to reject with probability $1-\beta$. Table 8.4 gives values of $C_p(\text{High})/C_p(\text{Low})$ and $C/C_p(\text{Low})$ for varying sample sizes and $\alpha=\beta=0.05$ or $\alpha=\beta=0.10$. Example 8.6 illustrates the use of this table.

EXAMPLE 8.6 Supplier Qualification

A customer has told his supplier that, in order to qualify for business with his company, the supplier must demonstrate that his process capability exceeds $C_p = 1.33$. Thus, the supplier is interested in establishing a procedure to test the hypotheses

$$H_0: \quad C_p = 1.33$$
$$H_1: \quad C_p > 1.33$$

The supplier wants to be sure that if the process capability is below 1.33 there will be a high probability of detecting this (say, 0.90), whereas if the process capability exceeds 1.66 there will be a high probability of judging the process capable (again, say, 0.90). This would imply that $C_p(\text{Low}) = 1.33$, $C_p(\text{High}) = 1.66$, and $\alpha=\beta=0.10$. To find the sample size and critical value for C from Table 8.4, compute

$$\frac{C_p(\text{High})}{C_p(\text{Low})} = \frac{1.66}{1.33} = 1.25$$

■ **TABLE 8.4**
Sample Size and Critical Value Determination for Testing H_0: $C_p = C_{p0}$

	(a) $\alpha=\beta=0.10$		(b) $\alpha=\beta=0.05$	
Sample Size, n	**C_p(High)/ C_p(Low)**	**C/C_p(Low)**	**C_p(High)/ C_p(Low)**	**C/C_p(Low)**
10	1.88	1.27	2.26	1.37
20	1.53	1.20	1.73	1.26
30	1.41	1.16	1.55	1.21
40	1.34	1.14	1.46	1.18
50	1.30	1.13	1.40	1.16
60	1.27	1.11	1.36	1.15
70	1.25	1.10	1.33	1.14
80	1.23	1.10	1.30	1.13
90	1.21	1.10	1.28	1.12
100	1.20	1.09	1.26	1.11

Source: Adapted from Kane (1986), with permission of the American Society for Quality Control.

and enter the table value in panel (*a*) where $\alpha = \beta = 0.10$. This yields

$$n = 70$$

and

$$C/C_p(\text{Low}) = 1.10$$

from which we calculate

$$C = C_p(\text{Low})1.10 = 1.33(1.10) = 1.46$$

Thus, to demonstrate capability, the supplier must take a sample of $n = 70$ parts, and the sample process capability ratio $\hat{C}_p$ must exceed $C \le 1.46$.

This example shows that, in order to demonstrate that process capability is at least equal to 1.33, the *observed sample* $\hat{C}_p$ will have to exceed 1.33 by a considerable amount. This illustrates that some common industrial practices may be questionable statistically. For example, it is fairly common practice to accept the process as capable at the level $C_p \ge 1.33$ if the *sample* $\hat{C}_p \ge 1.33$ based on a sample size of $30 \le n \le 50$ parts. Clearly, this procedure does not account for sampling variation in the estimate of σ, and larger values of n and/or higher acceptable values of $\hat{C}_p$ may be necessary in practice.

Process Performance Indices. In 1991, the Automotive Industry Action Group (AIAG) was formed and consists of representatives of the "big three" (Ford, General Motors, and Chrysler) and the American Society for Quality Control (now the American Society for Quality). One of their objectives was to standardize the reporting requirements from suppliers and in general of their industry. The AIAG recommends using the process capability indices C_p and C_{pk} when the process is in control, with the process standard deviation estimated by $\hat{\sigma} = \overline{R}/d_2$. When the process is *not* in control, the AIAG recommends using **process performance indices P_p and P_{pk}**, where, for example,

$$\hat{P}_p = \frac{\text{USL} - \text{LSL}}{6s}$$

and s is the usual sample standard deviation $s = \sqrt{\sum_{i=1}^{n}(x_i - \overline{x})^2/(n-1)}$. Even the American National Standards Institute in ANSI Standard Z1 on Process Capability Analysis (1996) states that P_p and P_{pk} should be used when the process is not in control.

Now it is clear that when the process is normally distributed and in control, $\hat{P}_p$ is essentially $\hat{C}_p$ and $\hat{P}_{pk}$ is essentially $\hat{C}_{pk}$ because for a stable process the difference between s and $\hat{\sigma} = \overline{R}/d_2$ is minimal. However, please note that if the process is **not** in control, the indices P_p and P_{pk} have no meaningful interpretation relative to process capability, because they cannot **predict** process performance. Furthermore, their statistical properties are not determinable, and so no valid inference can be made regarding their true (or population) values. Also, P_p and P_{pk} provide no motivation or incentive to the companies that use them to bring their processes into control.

Kotz and Lovelace (1998) strongly recommend **against** the use of P_p and P_{pk}, indicating that these indices are actually a step **backward** in quantifying process capability. They refer to the mandated use of P_p and P_{pk} through quality standards or industry guidelines as undiluted "statistical terrorism" (i.e., the use or misuse of statistical methods along with threats and/or intimidation to achieve a business objective).

This author agrees completely with Kotz and Lovelace. The process performance indices P_p and P_{pk} are actually more than a step backward. **They are a waste of engineering and management effort—they tell you nothing.** Unless the process is stable (in control), no index is going to carry useful predictive information about process capability or convey any information about future performance. Instead of imposing the use of meaningless indices, organizations should devote effort to developing and implementing an effective process characterization, control, and improvement plan. This is a much more reasonable and effective approach to process improvement.

8.4 Process Capability Analysis Using a Control Chart

Histograms, probability plots, and process capability ratios summarize the performance of the process. They do not necessarily display the **potential capability** of the process because they do not address the issue of **statistical control,** or show systematic patterns in process output that, if eliminated, would reduce the variability in the quality characteristic. Control charts are very effective in this regard. The control chart should be regarded as the primary technique of process capability analysis.

Both attributes and variables control charts can be used in process capability analysis. The $\bar{x}$ and R charts should be used whenever possible, because of the greater power and better information they provide relative to attributes charts. However, both p charts and c (or u) charts are useful in analyzing process capability. Techniques for constructing and using these charts are given in Chapters 6 and 7. Remember that to use the p chart there must be specifications on the product characteristics. The $\bar{x}$ and R charts allow us to study processes without regard to specifications.

The $\bar{x}$ and R control charts allow both the instantaneous variability (short-term process capability) and variability across time (long-term process capability) to be analyzed. It is particularly helpful if the data for a process capability study are collected in two to three different time periods (such as different shifts, different days, etc.).

Table 8.5 presents the container bursting-strength data in 20 samples of five observations each. The calculations for the $\bar{x}$ and R charts are summarized here:

$\bar{x}$ Chart

$$\text{Center line} = \bar{\bar{x}} = 264.06$$

$$\text{UCL} = \bar{\bar{x}} + A_2\bar{R} = 264.06 + (0.577)(77.3) = 308.66$$

$$\text{LCL} = \bar{\bar{x}} - A_2\bar{R} = 264.06 - (0.577)(77.3) = 219.46$$

R Chart

$$\text{Center line} = \bar{R} = 77.3$$

$$\text{UCL} = D_4\bar{R} = (2.115)(77.3) = 163.49$$

$$\text{LCL} = D_3\bar{R} = (0)(77.3) = 0$$

Figure 8.12 presents the $\bar{x}$ and R charts for the 20 samples in Table 8.5. Both charts exhibit statistical control. The process parameters may be estimated from the control chart as

$$\hat{\mu} = \bar{\bar{x}} = 264.06$$

$$\hat{\sigma} = \frac{\bar{R}}{d_2} = \frac{77.3}{2.326} = 33.23$$

■ TABLE 8.5
Glass Container Strength Data (psi)

Sample	Data					$\bar{x}$	R
1	265	205	263	307	220	252.0	102
2	268	260	234	299	215	255.2	84
3	197	286	274	243	231	246.2	89
4	267	281	265	214	318	269.0	104
5	346	317	242	258	276	287.8	104
6	300	208	187	264	271	246.0	113
7	280	242	260	321	228	266.2	93
8	250	299	258	267	293	273.4	49
9	265	254	281	294	223	263.4	71
10	260	308	235	283	277	272.6	73
11	200	235	246	328	296	261.0	128
12	276	264	269	235	290	266.8	55
13	221	176	248	263	231	227.8	87
14	334	280	265	272	283	286.8	69
15	265	262	271	245	301	268.8	56
16	280	274	253	287	258	270.4	34
17	261	248	260	274	337	276.0	89
18	250	278	254	274	275	266.2	28
19	278	250	265	270	298	272.2	48
20	257	210	280	269	251	253.4	70
						$\bar{\bar{x}} = 264.06$	$\bar{R} = 77.3$

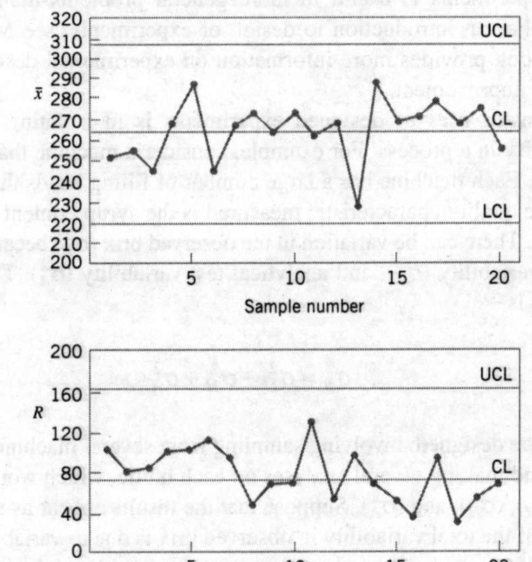

■ FIGURE 8.12 $\bar{x}$ and R charts for the bottle-strength data.

Thus, the one-sided lower process capability ratio is estimated by

$$\hat{C}_{pl} = \frac{\mu - \text{LSL}}{3\hat{\sigma}} = \frac{264.06 - 200}{3(33.23)} = 0.64$$

Clearly, since strength is a safety-related parameter, the process capability is inadequate.

This example illustrates a process that is in control but operating at an unacceptable level. There is no evidence to indicate that the production of nonconforming units is **operator-controllable.** Engineering and/or management intervention will be required either to improve the process or to change the requirements if the quality problems with the bottles are to be solved. The objective of these interventions is to increase the process capability ratio to at least a minimum acceptable level. The control chart can be used as a monitoring device or logbook to show the effect of changes in the process on process performance.

Sometimes the process capability analysis indicates an out-of-control process. It is **unsafe** to estimate process capability in such cases. The process must be stable in order to produce a reliable estimate of process capability. When the process is out of control in the early stages of process capability analysis, the first objective is finding and eliminating the assignable causes in order to bring the process into an in-control state.

8.5 Process Capability Analysis Using Designed Experiments

A designed experiment is a systematic approach to varying the input **controllable** variables in the process and analyzing the effects of these process variables on the output. Designed experiments are also useful in discovering *which* set of process variables is influential on the output, and at what levels these variables should be held to optimize process performance. Thus, design of experiments is useful in more general problems than merely estimating process capability. For an introduction to design of experiments, see Montgomery (2005). Part V of this textbook provides more information on experimental design methods and on their use in process improvement.

One of the major uses of designed experiments is in isolating and estimating the **sources of variability** in a process. For example, consider a machine that fills bottles with a soft-drink beverage. Each machine has a large number of filling heads that must be independently adjusted. The quality characteristic measured is the syrup content (in degrees brix) of the finished product. There can be variation in the observed brix (σ_B^2) because of machine variability (σ_M^2), head variability (σ_H^2), and analytical test variability (σ_A^2). The variability in the observed brix value is

$$\sigma_B^2 = \sigma_M^2 + \sigma_H^2 + \sigma_A^2$$

An experiment can be designed, involving sampling from several machines and several heads on each machine, and making several analyses on each bottle, which would allow estimation of the variances (σ_M^2), (σ_H^2), and (σ_A^2). Suppose that the results appear as in Fig. 8.13. Since a substantial portion of the total variability in observed brix is due to variability between heads, this indicates that the process can perhaps best be improved by reducing the head-to-head variability. This could be done by more careful setup or by more careful control of the operation of the machine.

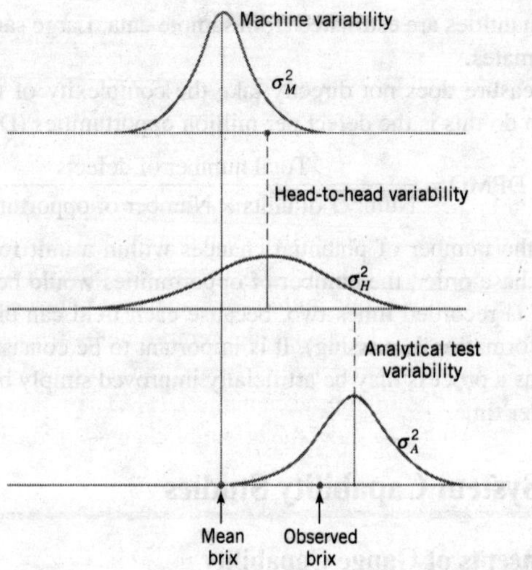

■ **FIGURE 8.13** Sources of variability in the bottling line example.

8.6 Process Capability Analysis with Attribute Data

Often process performance is measured in terms of **attribute** data; that is, nonconforming units or defectives, or nonconformities or defects. When a fraction nonconforming is the measure of performance, it is typical to use the parts per million (ppm) defective as a measure of process capability. In some organizations, this ppm defective is converted to an equivalent sigma level. For example, a process producing 2700 ppm defective would be equivalent to a three-sigma process (without the "usual" 1.5 σ shift in the mean that many six-sigma organizations employ in the calculations taken into account).

When dealing with nonconformities or defects, a defects per unit (DPU) statistic is often used as a measure of capability, where

$$\text{DPU} = \frac{\text{Total number of defects}}{\text{Total number of units}}$$

Here the unit is something that is delivered to a customer and can be evaluated or judged as to its suitability. Some examples include:

1. An invoice
2. A shipment
3. A customer order
4. An enquiry or call

The defects or nonconformities are anything that does not meet the customer requirements, such as:

1. An error on an invoice
2. An incorrect or incomplete shipment
3. An incorrect or incomplete customer order
4. A call that is not satisfactorily completed

Obviously, these quantities are estimated from sample data. Large samples need to be used to obtain reliable estimates.

The DPU measure does not directly take the complexity of the unit into account. A widely used way to do this is the defect per million opportunities (DPMO) measure

$$\text{DPMO} = \frac{\text{Total number of defects}}{\text{Number of units} \times \text{Number of opportunities}}$$

Opportunities are the number of potential chances within a unit for a defect to occur. For example, on a purchase order, the number of opportunities would be the number of fields in which information is recorded times two, because each field can either be filled out incorrectly or blank (information is missing). It is important to be consistent about how opportunities are defined, as a process may be artificially improved simply by increasing the number of opportunities over time.

8.7 Gauge and Measurement System Capability Studies

8.7.1 Basic Concepts of Gauge Capability

Determining the capability of the measurement system is an important aspect of many quality and process improvement activities. Generally, in any activity involving measurements, some of the observed variability will be inherent in the units or items that are being measured, and some of the variability will result from the measurement system that is used. The measurement system will consist (minimally) of an instrument or gauge, and it often has other components, such as the operator(s) that uses it and the conditions or different points in time under which the instrument is used. There may also be other factors that impact measurement system performance, such as setup or calibration activities. The purpose of most measurement systems capability studies is to:

1. Determine how much of the total observed variability is due to the gauge or instrument
2. Isolate the components of variability in the measurement system
3. Assess whether the instrument or gauge is capable (that is, is it suitable for the intended application)

Measurements are a significant component of any quality system. Measurement is an integral component of the DMAIC problem-solving process, but it's even more important than that. An ineffective measurement system can dramatically impact business performance because it leads to uninformed (and usually bad) decision making.

In this section we will introduce the two R's of measurement systems capability: **repeatability** (do we get the same observed value if we measure the same unit several times under identical conditions), and **reproducibility** (how much difference in observed values do we experience when units are measured under different conditions, such as different operators, time periods, and so forth).

These quantities answer only indirectly the fundamental question: Is the system able to distinguish between good and bad units? That is, what is the probability that a good unit is judged to be defective and, conversely, that a bad unit is passed along to the customer as good? These misclassification probabilities are fairly easy to calculate from the results of a standard measurement systems capability study, and give reliable, useful, and easy-to-understand information about measurement systems performance.

In addition to repeatability and reproducibility, there are other important aspects of measurement systems capability. The **linearity** of a measurement system reflects the differences in observed accuracy and/or precision experienced over the range of measurements made by the system. A simple linear regression model is often used to describe this feature.

Problems with linearity are often the result of calibration and maintenance issues. **Stability,** or different levels of variability in different operating regimes, can result from warm-up effects, environmental factors, inconsistent operator performance, and inadequate standard operating procedure. **Bias** reflects the difference between observed measurements and a "true" value obtained from a master or gold standard, or from a different measurement technique known to produce accurate values.

It is very difficult to monitor, control, improve, or effectively manage a process with an inadequate measurement system. It's somewhat analogous to navigating a ship through fog without radar—eventually you are going to hit the iceberg! Even if no catastrophe occurs, you always are going to be wasting time and money looking for problems where none exist and dealing with unhappy customers who received defective product. Because excessive measurement variability becomes part of overall product variability, it also negatively impacts many other process improvement activities, such as leading to larger sample sizes in comparative or observational studies, more replication in designed experiments aimed at process improvement, and more extensive product testing.

To introduce some of the basic ideas of measurement systems analysis (MSA) consider a simple but reasonable model for measurement system capability studies

$$y = x + \varepsilon \tag{8.23}$$

where y is the total observed measurement, x is the true value of the measurement on a unit of product, and ε is the measurement error. We will assume that x and ε are normally and independently distributed random variables with means μ and 0 and variances (σ_P^2) and (σ_{Gauge}^2), respectively. **The variance of the total observed measurement, y, is then**

$$\sigma_{\text{Total}}^2 = \sigma_P^2 + \sigma_{\text{Gauge}}^2 \tag{8.24}$$

Control charts and other statistical methods can be used to separate these components of variance, as well as to give an assessment of gauge capability.

EXAMPLE 8.7 Measuring Gauge Capability

An instrument is to be used as part of a proposed SPC implementation. The quality-improvement team involved in designing the SPC system would like to get an assessment of gauge capability. Twenty units of the product are obtained, and the **process operator** who will actually take the measurements for the control chart uses the instrument to measure each unit of product twice. The data are shown in Table 8.6.

SOLUTION

Figure 8.14 shows the $\bar{x}$ and R charts for these data. Note that the $\bar{x}$ chart exhibits many out-of-control points. This is to be expected, because in this situation the $\bar{x}$ chart has an interpretation that is somewhat different from the usual interpretation. The $\bar{x}$ chart in this example shows the **discriminating power** of the instrument—literally, the ability of the gauge to distinguish between units of product. The R chart directly shows the magnitude of measurement error, or the gauge capability. The R values represent the difference between measurements made on the same unit using the same instrument. In this example, the R chart is in control. This indicates that the operator is having no difficulty in making consistent measurements. Out-of-control points on the R chart could indicate that the operator is having difficulty using the instrument.

The standard deviation of measurement error, σ_{Gauge}, can be estimated as follows:

$$\hat{\sigma}_{\text{Gauge}} = \frac{\bar{R}}{d_2} = \frac{1.0}{1.128} = 0.887$$

The distribution of measurement error is usually well approximated by the normal. Thus, $\hat{\sigma}_{\text{Guage}}$ is a good estimate of gauge capability.

(continued)

■ **TABLE 8.6**
Parts Measurement Data

Part Number	Measurements 1	2	$\bar{x}$	R
1	21	20	20.5	1
2	24	23	23.5	1
3	20	21	20.5	1
4	27	27	27.0	0
5	19	18	18.5	1
6	23	21	22.0	2
7	22	21	21.5	1
8	19	17	18.0	2
9	24	23	23.5	1
10	25	23	24.0	2
11	21	20	20.5	1
12	18	19	18.5	1
13	23	25	24.0	2
14	24	24	24.0	0
15	29	30	29.5	1
16	26	26	26.0	0
17	20	20	20.0	0
18	19	21	20.0	2
19	25	26	25.5	1
20	19	19	19.0	0
			$\bar{\bar{x}} = 22.3$	$\bar{R} = 1.0$

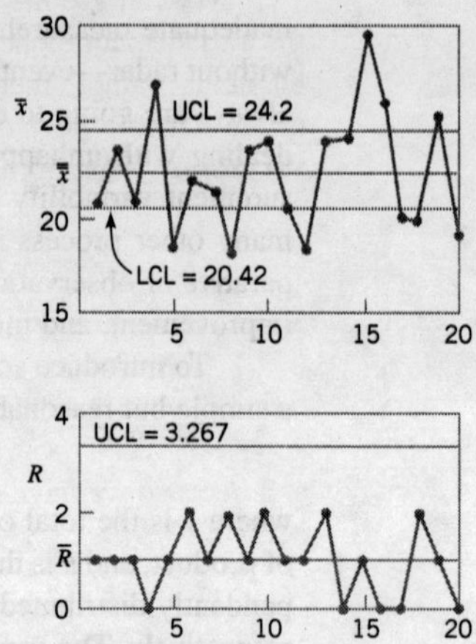

■ **FIGURE 8.14** Control charts for the gauge capability analysis in Example 8.7.

It is a fairly common (but not necessarily good) practice to compare the estimate of gauge capability to the width of the specifications or the tolerance band (USL − LSL) for the part that is being measured. The ratio of $k\hat{\sigma}_{\text{Gauge}}$ to the total tolerance band is often called the **precision-to-tolerance (*P/T*) ratio:**

$$P/T = \frac{k\hat{\sigma}_{\text{Guage}}}{\text{USL} - \text{LSL}} \tag{8.25}$$

In equation (8.25), popular choices for the constant k are $k = 5.15$ and $k = 6$. The value $k = 5.15$ corresponds to the limiting value of the number of standard deviations between bounds of a 95% tolerance interval that contains at least 99% of a normal population, and $k = 6$ corresponds to the number of standard deviations between the usual natural tolerance limits of a normal population.

The part used in Example 8.7 has USL = 60 and LSL = 5. Therefore, taking $k = 6$ in equation (8.25), an estimate of the *P/T* ratio is

$$P/T = \frac{6(0.887)}{60 - 5} = \frac{5.32}{55} = 0.097$$

Values of the estimated ratio P/T of 0.1 or less often are taken to imply adequate gauge capability. This is based on the generally used rule that requires a measurement device to be calibrated in units one-tenth as large as the accuracy required in the final measurement. However, we should use **caution** in accepting this general rule of thumb in all cases. A gauge must be sufficiently capable to measure product accurately enough and precisely enough so that the analyst can make the correct decision. This may not necessarily require that $P/T \leq 0.1$.

We can use the data from the gauge capability experiment in Example 8.7 to estimate the variance components in equation (8.24) associated with total observed variability. From the actual sample measurements in Table 8.6, we can calculate $s = 3.17$. This is an estimate of the standard deviation of **total variability,** including both **product variability** and **gauge variability.** Therefore,

$$\hat{\sigma}^2_{\text{Total}} = s^2 = (3.17)^2 = 10.05$$

Since from equation (8.24) we have

$$\sigma^2_{\text{Total}} = \sigma^2_P + \sigma^2_{\text{Gauge}}$$

and because we have an estimate of $\hat{\sigma}^2_{\text{Gauge}} = (0.887)^2 = 0.79$, we can obtain an estimate of σ^2_P as

$$\hat{\sigma}^2_P = \hat{\sigma}^2_{\text{Total}} - \hat{\sigma}^2_{\text{Gauge}} = 10.05 - 0.79 = 9.26$$

Therefore, an estimate of the standard deviation of the product characteristic is

$$\hat{\sigma}_p = \sqrt{9.26} = 3.04$$

There are other measures of gauge capability that have been proposed. One of these is the ratio of process (part) variability to total variability:

$$\rho_P = \frac{\sigma^2_P}{\sigma^2_{\text{Total}}} \tag{8.26}$$

and another is the ratio of measurement system variability to total variability:

$$\rho_M = \frac{\sigma^2_{\text{Gauge}}}{\sigma^2_{\text{Total}}} \tag{8.27}$$

Obviously, $\rho_P = 1 - \rho_M$. For the situation in Example 8.7 we can calculate an estimate of ρ_M as follows:

$$\hat{\rho}_M = \frac{\hat{\sigma}^2_{\text{Gauge}}}{\hat{\sigma}^2_{\text{Total}}} = \frac{0.79}{10.05} = 0.0786$$

Thus the variance of the measuring instrument contributes about 7.86% of the total observed variance of the measurements.

Another measure of measurement system adequacy is defined by the AIAG (1995) [note that there is also on updated edition of this manual, AIAG (2002)] as the **signal-to-noise ratio (*SNR*)**:

$$SNR = \sqrt{\frac{2\rho_P}{1 - \rho_P}} \tag{8.28}$$

AIAG defined the *SNR* as the number of distinct levels or categories that can be reliably obtained from the measurements. A value of five or greater is recommended, and a value of less than two indicates inadequate gauge capability. For Example 8.7 we have $\hat{\rho}_M = 0.0786$, and using $\hat{\rho}_P = 1 - \hat{\rho}_M$ we find that $\hat{\rho}_P = 1 - \hat{\rho}_M = 1 - 0.0786 = 0.9214$, so an estimate of the *SNR* in equation (8.28) is

$$SNR = \sqrt{\frac{2\hat{\rho}_P}{1 - \hat{\rho}_P}} = \sqrt{\frac{2(0.9214)}{1 - 0.9214}} = 4.84$$

Therefore, the gauge in Example 8.7 would not meet the suggested requirement of an *SNR* of at least five. However, this requirement on the *SNR* is somewhat arbitrary. Another measure of gauge capability is the **discrimination ratio *(DR)***

$$DR = \frac{1 + \rho_P}{1 - \rho_P} \tag{8.29}$$

Some authors have suggested that for a gauge to be capable the *DR* must exceed four. This is a very arbitrary requirement. For the situation in Example 8.7, we would calculate an estimate of the discrimination ratio as

$$\widehat{DR} = \frac{1 + \rho_P}{1 - \rho_P} = \frac{1 + 0.9214}{1 - 0.9214} = 24.45$$

Clearly by this measure, the gauge is capable.

Finally, in this section we have focused primarily on instrument or **gauge precision**, not **gauge accuracy**. These two concepts are illustrated in Fig. 8.15. In this figure, the bull's-eye of the target is considered to be the true value of the measured characteristic, or μ the mean of

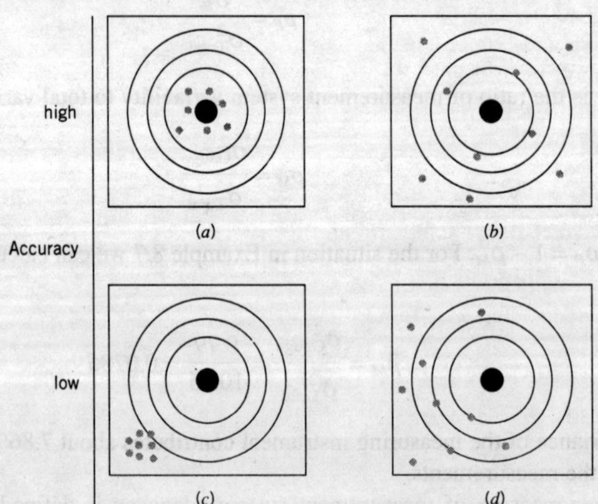

■ **FIGURE 8.15** The concepts of accuracy and precision. (*a*) The gauge is accurate and precise. (*b*) The gauge is accurate but not precise. (*c*) The gauge is not accurate but it is precise. (*d*) The gauge is neither accurate nor precise.

x in equation (8.23). Accuracy refers to the ability of the instrument to measure the true value correctly on average, whereas precision is a measure of the inherent variability in the measurement system. Evaluating the accuracy of a gauge or measurement system often requires the use of a standard, for which the true value of the measured characteristic is known. Often the accuracy feature of an instrument can be modified by making adjustments to the instrument or by the use of a properly constructed calibration curve.

It is also possible to design measurement systems capability studies to investigate two components of measurement error, commonly called the **repeatability** and the **reproducibility** of the gauge. We define reproducibility as the variability due to different operators using the gauge (or different time periods, or different environments, or in general, different conditions) and repeatability as reflecting the basic inherent precision of the gauge itself. That is,

$$\sigma^2_{\text{Measurement Error}} = \sigma^2_{\text{Gauge}} = \sigma^2_{\text{Repeatability}} + \sigma^2_{\text{Reproducibility}} \tag{8.30}$$

The experiment used to measure the components of σ^2_{Gauge} is usually called a gauge R & R study, for the two components of σ^2_{Gauge}. We now show how to analyze **gauge R & R experiments**.

8.7.2 The Analysis of Variance Method

An example of a gauge R & R study, taken from the paper by Houf and Berman (1988) is shown in Table 8.7. The data are measurements on thermal impedance (in degrees C per Watt × 100) on a power module for an induction motor starter. There are 10 parts, 3 operators, and 3 measurements per part. The gauge R & R study is a designed experiment. Specifically, it is a **factorial experiment**, so-called because each inspector or "operator" measures all of the parts.

The analysis of variance introduced in Chapter 9 can be extended to analyze the data from a gauge R & R experiment and to estimate the appropriate components of measurement systems variability. We give only an introduction to the procedure here; for more details, see Montgomery (2005), Montgomery and Runger (1993a,b), Borror, Montgomery, and Runger (1997), Burdick and Larson (1997), the review paper by Burdick, Borror, and Montgomery (2003), the book by Burdick, Borror, and Montgomery (2005), and the supplemental text material for this chapter.

TABLE 8.7

Thermal Impedance Data (°C/W × 100) for the Gauge R & R Experiment

Part	Inspector 1			Inspector 2			Inspector 3		
Number	Test 1	Test 2	Test 3	Test 1	Test 2	Test 3	Test 1	Test 2	Test 3
1	37	38	37	41	41	40	41	42	41
2	42	41	43	42	42	42	43	42	43
3	30	31	31	31	31	31	29	30	28
4	42	43	42	43	43	43	42	42	42
5	28	30	29	29	30	29	31	29	29
6	42	42	43	45	45	45	44	46	45
7	25	26	27	28	28	30	29	27	27
8	40	40	40	43	42	42	43	43	41
9	25	25	25	27	29	28	26	26	26
10	35	34	34	35	35	34	35	34	35

If there are *a* randomly selected parts and *b* randomly selected operators, and each operator measures every part *n* times, then the measurements (i = part, j = operator, k = measurement) could be represented by the model

$$y_{ijk} = \mu + P_i + O_j + (PO)_{ij} + \varepsilon_{ijk} \begin{cases} i = 1, 2, \ldots, p \\ j = 1, 2, \ldots, o \\ k = 1, 2, \ldots, n \end{cases}$$

where the model parameters P_i, O_j, $(PO)_{ij}$, and ε_{ijk} are all independent random variables that represent the effects of parts, operators, the interaction or joint effects of parts and operators, and random error. This is a **random effects model analysis of variance (ANOVA).** It is also sometimes called the standard model for a gauge R & R experiment. We assume that the random variables P_i, O_j, $(PO)_{ij}$, and ε_{ijk} are normally distributed with mean zero and variances given by $V(P_i) = \sigma_P^2$, $V(O_j) = \sigma_O^2$, $V[(PO)_{ij}] = \sigma_{PO}^2$, and $V(\varepsilon_{ijk}) = \sigma^2$. Therefore, the variance of any observation is

$$V(y_{ijk}) = \sigma_P^2 + \sigma_O^2 + \sigma_{PO}^2 + \sigma^2 \tag{8.31}$$

and σ_P^2, σ_O^2, σ_{PO}^2, and σ^2 are the **variance components.** We want to estimate the variance components.

Analysis of variance methods can be used to estimate the variance components. The procedure involves partitioning the total variability in the measurements into the following component parts:

$$SS_{\text{Total}} = SS_{\text{Parts}} + SS_{\text{Operators}} + SS_{P \times O} + SS_{\text{Error}} \tag{8.32}$$

where, as in Chapter 4, the notation *SS* represents a sum of squares. Although these sums of squares could be computed manually,[1] in practice we always use a computer software package to perform this task. Each sum of squares on the right-hand side of equation (8.32) is divided by its degrees of freedom to produce mean squares:

$$MS_P = \frac{SS_{\text{Parts}}}{p-1}$$

$$MS_O = \frac{SS_{\text{Operators}}}{o-1}$$

$$MS_{PO} = \frac{SS_{P \times O}}{(p-1)(o-1)}$$

$$MS_E = \frac{SS_{\text{Error}}}{po(n-1)}$$

We can show that the expected values of the mean squares are as follows:

$$E(MS_P) = \sigma^2 + n\sigma_{PO}^2 + bn\sigma_P^2$$

$$E(MS_O) = \sigma^2 + n\sigma_{PO}^2 + an\sigma_O^2$$

$$E(MS_{PO}) = \sigma^2 + n\sigma_{PO}^2$$

[1]The experimental structure here is that of a factorial design. See Chapter 13 and the supplemental text material for more details about the analysis of variance, including computing.

and

$$E(MS_E) = \sigma^2$$

The variance components may be estimated by equating the calculated numerical values of the mean squares from an analysis of variance computer program to their expected values and solving for the variance components. This yields

$$\hat{\sigma}^2 = MS_E$$
$$\hat{\sigma}^2_{PO} = \frac{MS_{PO} - MS_E}{n}$$
$$\hat{\sigma}^2_{O} = \frac{MS_O - MS_{PO}}{pn} \tag{8.33}$$
$$\hat{\sigma}^2_{P} = \frac{MS_P - MS_{PO}}{on}$$

Table 8.8 shows the analysis of variance for this experiment. The computations were performed using the Balanced ANOVA routine in Minitab. Based on the P-values, we conclude that the effect of parts is large, operators may have a small effect, and there is no significant part-operator interaction. We may use equation (8.33) to estimate the variance components as follows:

$$\hat{\sigma}^2_P = \frac{437.33 - 2.70}{(3)(3)} = 48.29$$

$$\hat{\sigma}^2_O = \frac{19.63 - 2.70}{(10)(3)} = 0.56$$

$$\hat{\sigma}^2_{PO} = \frac{2.70 - 0.51}{3} = 0.73$$

■ **TABLE 8.8**

ANOVA: Thermal Impedance versus Part Number, Operator

```
Factor          Type     Levels          Values
Part Num random              10          1      2      3      4      5      6      7
                                         8      9     10
Operator random               3          1      2      3
Analysis of Variance for Thermal
Source                      DF           SS          MS          F          P
Part Num                     9      3935.96      437.33     162.27      0.000
Operator                     2        39.27       19.63       7.28      0.005
Part Num*Operator           18        48.51        2.70       5.27      0.000
Error                       60        30.67        0.51
Total                       89      4054.40

Source                Variance     Error  Expected Mean Square for Each
                      component    term   Term (using unrestricted model)
 1 Part Num           48.2926      3      (4) + 3(3) + 9(1)
 2 Operator           0.5646       3      (4) + 3(3) + 30(2)
 3 Part Num*Operator  0.7280       4      (4) + 3(3)
 4 Error              0.5111              (4)
```

and

$$\hat{\sigma}^2 = 0.51$$

Note that these estimates also appear at the bottom of the Minitab output.

Occasionally we will find that the estimate of one of the variance components will be negative. This is certainly not reasonable, since by definition variances are nonnegative. Unfortunately, negative estimates of variance components can result when we use the analysis of variance method of estimation (this is considered one of its drawbacks). There are a variety of ways to deal with this. One possibility is to assume that the negative estimate means that the variance component is really zero and just set it to zero, leaving the other nonnegative estimates unchanged. Another approach is to estimate the variance components with a method that assures nonnegative estimates. Finally, when negative estimates of variance components occur, they are usually accompanied by nonsignificant model sources of variability. For example, if $\hat{\sigma}_{PO}$ is negative, it will usually be because the interaction source of variability is nonsignificant. We should take this as evidence that σ^2_{PO} really is zero, that there is no interaction effect, and fit a **reduced model** of the form

$$y_{ijk} = \mu + P_i + O_j + \varepsilon_{ijk}$$

that does not include the interaction term. This is a relatively easy approach and one that often works nearly as well as more sophisticated methods.

Typically we think of σ^2 as the **repeatability** variance component, and the gauge **reproducibility** as the sum of the operator and the part × operator variance components,

$$\sigma^2_{\text{Reproducibility}} = \sigma^2_O + \sigma^2_{PO}$$

Therefore

$$\sigma^2_{\text{Gauge}} = \sigma^2_{\text{Reproducibility}} + \sigma^2_{\text{Repeatability}}$$

and the estimate for our example is

$$\begin{aligned}\hat{\sigma}^2_{\text{Gauge}} &= \hat{\sigma}^2 + \hat{\sigma}^2_O + \hat{\sigma}^2_{PO} \\ &= 0.51 + 0.56 + 0.73 \\ &= 1.80\end{aligned}$$

The lower and upper specifications on this power module are LSL = 18 and USL = 58. Therefore the *P/T* ratio for the gauge is estimated as

$$P/T = \frac{6\hat{\sigma}_{\text{Gauge}}}{\text{USL} - \text{LSL}} = \frac{6(1.34)}{58 - 18} = 0.27$$

By the standard measures of gauge capability, this gauge would not be considered capable because the estimate of the *P/T* ratio exceeds 0.10.

8.7.3 Confidence Intervals in Gauge R & R Studies

The gauge R & R study and the ANOVA procedure described in the previous section resulted in point estimates of the experimental model variance components and for σ^2_{Gauge}, $\sigma^2_{\text{Repeatability}}$, and $\sigma^2_{\text{Reproducibility}}$. It can be very informative to obtain **confidence intervals for**

gauge R & R studies. Confidence intervals in measurement systems capability studies are discussed in Montgomery (2001), Montgomery and Runger (1993a,b), Borror, Montgomery, and Runger (1997), Burdick and Larson (1997), the review paper by Burdick, Borror, and Montgomery (2003) and the book by Burdick, Borror, and Montgomery (2005). Among the different methods for obtaining these confidence intervals, the modified large sample (MLS) method produces good results and is relatively easy to implement for the standard gauge capability experiment described in Section 8.7.2, where both parts and operators are considered to be random factors. Other methods for constructing confidence intervals and computer programs to implement these methods are in Burdick, Borror, and Montgomery (2005).

Table 8.9 contains the MLS confidence interval equations for the parameters that are usually of interest in a measurement systems capability study. Definitions of the quantities used in Table 8.9 are in Table 8.10. References for all of the confidence interval equations in Table 8.9 are in Burdick, Borror, and Montgomery (2003). Note that the percentage point of the F distribution defined in Table 8.10 as $F_{\alpha,df,\infty} = \chi^2_{\alpha,df}$.

The last column in Table 8.9 contains the 95% confidence intervals for each parameter, and the last column of Table 8.10 shows the numerical values of the quantities used in computing the 95% confidence intervals. All of the confidence intervals in Table 8.9 are fairly wide because there are only three operators, and this results in only two degrees of freedom to estimate the operator effect. Therefore, this will have an impact on length of any confidence interval for any parameter that is a function of σ_o^2. This suggests that to obtain narrower confidence intervals in a gauge R & R study, it will be necessary to increase the number of operators. Since it is fairly standard practice to use only two or three operators in these studies, this implies that one needs to carefully consider the consequences of applying a standard design to estimate gauge capability.

8.7.4 False Defectives and Passed Defectives

In previous sections we have introduced several ways to summarize the capability of a gauge or instrument, including the P/T ratio [equation (8.25)], the signal-to-noise ratio SNR [equation (8.28)],

■ **TABLE 8.9**
100(1 – α)% MLS Confidence Intervals for the Standard Gauge R & R Experiment

Parameter	Lower Bound	Upper Bound	Example 95% Interval
σ_p^2	$\hat{\sigma}_P^2 - \frac{\sqrt{V_{LP}}}{on}$	$\hat{\sigma}_P^2 + \frac{\sqrt{V_{UP}}}{on}$	[22.69; 161.64]
σ_{Gauge}^2	$\hat{\sigma}_{\text{Gauge}}^2 - \frac{\sqrt{V_{LM}}}{pn}$	$\hat{\sigma}_{\text{Gauge}}^2 + \frac{\sqrt{V_{UM}}}{pn}$	[1.20; 27.02]
σ_{Total}^2	$\hat{\sigma}_{\text{Total}}^2 - \frac{\sqrt{V_{LT}}}{pon}$	$\hat{\sigma}_{\text{Total}}^2 + \frac{\sqrt{V_{UT}}}{pon}$	[24.48; 166.23]
ρ_p	$L_P = \frac{pL^*}{pL^* + o}$	$U_P = \frac{pU^*}{pU^* + o}$	[0.628; 0.991]
ρ_m	$1 - U_P$	$1 - L_P$	[0.009; 0.372]

■ **TABLE 8.10**
Definition of Terms in Table 8.9

Term	Definition	Value in Example
V_{LP}	$G_1^2 MS_P^2 + H_3^2 MS_{PO}^2 + G_{13} MS_P$	53,076.17
V_{UP}	$H_1^2 MS_P^2 + G_3^2 MS_{PO}^2 + H_{13} MS_P^2 MS_{PO}$	1,040,643.4
V_{LM}	$G_2^2 MS_O^2 + G_3^2 (p-1)^2 MS_{PO}^2 + G_4^2 p^2 (n-1)^2 MS_E^2$	321.282
V_{UM}	$H_2^2 MS_O^2 + H_3^2 (p-1)^2 MS_{PO}^2 + H_4^2 p^2 (n-1)^2 MS_E^2$	572,150.12
V_{LT}	$G_1^2 p^2 MS_P^2 + G_2^2 o^2 MS_O^2 + G_3^2 (po-p-o)^2 MS_{PO}^2 + G_4^2 (po)^2 (n-1)^2 MS_E^2$	5,311,676.7
V_{UT}	$H_1^2 p^2 MS_P^2 + H_2^2 o^2 MS_O^2 + H_3^2 (po-p-o)^2 MS_{PO}^2 + H_4^2 (po)^2 (n-1)^2 MS_E^2$	109,230,276
G_1	$1 - 1/F_{1-\alpha/2:p-1,\infty}$	0.5269
G_2	$1 - 1/F_{1-\alpha/2:o-1,\infty}$	0.7289
G_3	$1 - 1/F_{1-\alpha/2:(p-1)(o-1),\infty}$	0.4290
G_4	$1 - 1/F_{1-\alpha/2:po(n-1),\infty}$	0.2797
H_1	$1/F_{\alpha/2:p-1,\infty} - 1$	2.3329
H_2	$1/F_{\alpha/2:o-1,\infty} - 1$	38.4979
H_3	$1/F_{\alpha/2:(p-1)(o-1),\infty} - 1$	1.1869
H_4	$1/F_{\alpha/2:po(n-1),\infty} - 1$	0.4821
G_{13}	$\dfrac{\left(F_{1-\alpha/2:p-1,(p-1)(o-1)} - 1\right)^2 - G_1^2 F_{1-\alpha/2:p-1,(p-1)(o-1)}^2 - H_3^2}{F_{1-\alpha/2:p-1,(p-1)(o-1)}}$	−0.0236
H_{13}	$\dfrac{\left(1 - F_{\alpha/2:p-1,(p-1)(o-1)}\right)^2 - H_1^2 F_{\alpha/2:p-1,(p-1)(o-1)}^2 - G_3^2}{F_{\alpha/2:p-1,(p-1)(o-1)}}$	−0.1800
L^*	$\dfrac{MS_P - F_{1-\alpha/2:p-1,(p-1)(o-1)} MS_{PO}}{p(n-1)F_{1-\alpha/2:p-1,\infty} MS_E + F_{1-\alpha/2:p-1,o-1} MS_O + (p-1)F_{1-\alpha/2:p-1,\infty} MS_{PO}}$	0.5075
U^*	$\dfrac{MS_P - F_{\alpha/2:p-1,(p-1)(o-1)} MS_{PO}}{p(n-1)F_{\alpha/2:p-1,\infty} MS_E + F_{\alpha/2:p-1,o-1} MS_O + (p-1)F_{\alpha/2:p-1,\infty} MS_{PO}}$	31.6827

the discrimination ratio DR [equation (8.29)], and ρ_P and ρ_M [equations (8.26) and (8.27)]. None of these quantities really describe the capability of the gauge in any sense that is directly interpretable. The effective capability of a measuring system is best described in terms of how well it discriminates between good and bad parts. Consider the model first proposed in equation (8.23):

$$y = x + \varepsilon$$

where y is the total observed measurement, x is the true value of the measurement, and e is the measurement error. The random variables x and ε are normally and independently distributed random variables with means μ and 0 and variances σ_P^2 and σ_{Gauge}^2, respectively. The joint probability density function of y and x, say $f(y, x)$, is bivariate normal with mean vector $[\mu, \mu]'$ and covariance matrix

$$\begin{bmatrix} \sigma_{\text{Total}}^2 & \sigma_P^2 \\ \sigma_P^2 & \sigma_P^2 \end{bmatrix}$$

A unit of product or part is in conformance to the specifications if

$$\text{LSL} '' x '' \text{USL} \tag{8.34}$$

and the measurement system will "pass" a unit as a nondefective if

$$\text{LSL} '' y '' \text{USL} \tag{8.35}$$

If equation (8.34) is true but equation (8.35) is false, a conforming part has been incorrectly failed. Alternatively, if (8.34) is false but equation (8.35) is true, a nonconforming part has been incorrectly passed. Sometimes this is called a missed fault. A very useful way to describe the capability of a measurement system is in terms of **producer's risk** and **consumer's risk.** The producer's risk δ is defined as the conditional probability that a measurement system will fail a part when the part conforms to the specifications (this is also called a false failure). The consumer's risk β is defined as the conditional probability that a measurement system will pass a part when the part does not conform to the specifications (this is the missed fault described above).

Expressions are available for computing the two conditional probabilities:

$$\delta = \frac{\displaystyle\int_{\text{LSL}}^{\text{USL}}\int_{-\infty}^{\text{LSL}} f(y, x)dydx + \int_{\text{LSL}}^{\text{USL}}\int_{\text{USL}}^{\infty} f(y, x)dydx}{\displaystyle\int_{\text{LSL}}^{\text{USL}} f(x)dx} \tag{8.36}$$

and

$$\beta = \frac{\displaystyle\int_{-\infty}^{\text{LSL}}\int_{\text{LSL}}^{\text{USL}} f(y, x)dydx + \int_{\text{USL}}^{\infty}\int_{\text{LSL}}^{\text{USL}} f(y, x)dydx}{\displaystyle 1 - \int_{\text{LSL}}^{\text{USL}} f(x)dx} \tag{8.37}$$

where $f(x)$ represents the marginal probability density function for x which is normal with mean μ and variance σ_P^2. Figure 8.16 shows the regions of false failures (FF) and missed faults

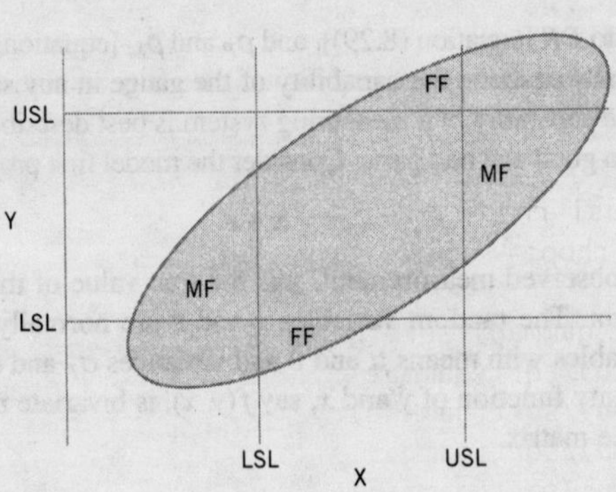

■ FIGURE 8.16 Missed fault (MF) and false failures (FF) regions of a measurement system shown on a bivariate normal distribution contour. [From Burdick, Borror, and Montgomery (2003).]

(MF) on a density contour of the bivariate normal distribution. Thus, equations (8.36) and (8.37) can be used to compute δ and β for given values of μ, σ_P^2, σ_{Total}^2, LSL, and USL. The SAS code to perform this computation is shown in Table 8.11.

In practice, we don't know the true values of μ, σ_P^2, and σ_{Total}^2. If one uses only point estimates, the calculation does not account for the uncertainty in the estimates. It would be very helpful to provide confidence intervals for these parameters in the calculation of δ and β. One way to do this is to compute δ and β under different scenarios suggested by the confidence intervals on the variance components. For example, a pessimistic scenario might consider the worst possible performance for the measurement system, and the worst possible capability for the manufacturing process. To do this, set σ_P^2 equal to the upper bound of the confidence interval for σ_P^2 and solve for the value of σ_{Total}^2 that provides the lower bound on ρ_P. Conversely, one might consider an optimistic scenario with the best possible performance for the measurement system combined with the best process capability. For some other suggestions, see Burdick, Borror, and Montgomery (2003).

Table 8.12 shows the calculation of the producer's risk (δ) and the consumer's risk (β) using equations (8.36) and (8.37) under the two scenarios discussed above. The scenario labeled "Pessimistic" is computed assuming the worst possible performance for both the production process and the measurement system. This is done by computing δ and β using the upper bound on σ_P^2 and the lower bound on ρ_P. We used the sample mean 35.8 for the value of μ, the computed confidence bounds in Table 8.10, and solved for σ_{Total}^2 using the relationship $\sigma_{\text{Total}}^2 = \sigma_P^2/\rho_P$. The SAS code shown in Table 8.11 was used to make this calculation. The scenario labeled "Optimistic" uses the best condition for both the process and the measurement system. In particular, we use the lower bound of σ_P^2 and the upper bound of ρ_P. As with the first scenario, we use the point estimate $\hat{\mu} = 35.8$. Notice that the range for the producer's risk is from 0.002% to 15.2% and for the consumer's risk is from 12.3% to 31.0%. Those are very wide intervals, due mostly to the small number of operators used in this particular gauge R & R experiment.

Burdick, Park, Montgomery, and Borror (2005) present another method for obtaining confidence intervals for the misclassification rates δ and β based on the generalized inference approach. See Tsui and Weerahandi (1989) and Weerahandi (1993) for a discussion of generalized inference. This is a computer-intensive approach and requires specialized software. Refer to Burdick, Borror, and Montgomery (2005).

■ TABLE 8.11

SAS Code for Computing Measurement System Misclassification Probabilities δ and β [From Burdick, Borror, and Montgomery (2003)]

```
data misclass;
input mu lsl usl rhop gammap;
gammat=gammap/rhop;
cov=gammap;
corr=cov/(sqrt(gammap)*sqrt(gammat));
uslstdy=(usl-mu)/sqrt(gammat);
uslstdx=(usl-mu)/sqrt(gammap);
lslstdy=(lsl-mu)/sqrt(gammat);
lslstdx=(lsl-mu)/sqrt(gammap);

ff1=probbnrm(uslstdx, lslstdy, corr)-
probbnrm (lslstdx, lslstdy, corr);
ff2=probnorm(uslstdx)-probbnrm(uslstdx, uslstdy, corr);
mf1=probbnrm(lslstdx, uslstdy, corr)-
probbnrm(lslstdx, lslstdy, corr);
mf2=probnorm(uslstdy)-probbnrm(uslstdx, uslstdy, corr);
delta=(ff1+ff2)/(probnorm(uslstdx)-
probnorm(lslstdx));
beta=(mf1+mf2)/(1-(probnorm(uslstdx)-
probnorm(lslstdx));

keep mu lsl usl rhop gammap gammat delta beta;
datalines;
35.8 18 58 .628 161.64
;
proc print data=misclass;
run;
```

Note: In the input statement, rhop is ρ_P and gamma p is σ_P^2.

8.7.5 Attribute Gauge Capability

In previous sections we have assumed that the measurements are numerical, such as physical dimensions, or properties that can be expressed on a numerical scale. There are many situations where the output of a gauge is an attribute, such as pass/fail. Nominal or ordinal data is also relatively common. Attribute gauge capabilities can be conducted in many of these situations.

A very common situation is to determine if operating personnel consistently make the same decisions regarding the units that they are inspecting or analyzing. For example,

■ TABLE 8.12

Measurement System Error Rates for Two Scenarios

Scenario	σ_P^2	ρ_P	δ	β
Pessimistic	161.64	0.628	15.2%	31.0%
Optimistic	22.69	0.991	0.002%	12.3%

■ TABLE 8.13

Loan Evaluation Data for Attribute Gauge Capability Analysis

Application	Classification	Sue1	Sue2	Fred1	Fred2	John1	John2
1	Fund-1	Fund-3	Fund-3	Fund-2	Fund-2	Fund-1	Fund-3
2	Fund-3	Fund-3	Fund-3	Fund-3	Fund-3	Fund-3	Fund-1
3	Fund-1	Fund-3	Fund-3	Fund-2	Fund-2	Fund-1	Fund-1
4	Fund-1	Fund-1	Fund-1	Fund-2	Fund-1	Fund-1	Fund-1
5	Fund-2	Fund-1	Fund-2	Fund-2	Fund-2	Fund-2	Fund-1
6	Fund-3	Fund-3	Fund-3	Fund-1	Fund-3	Fund-3	Fund-1
7	Fund-3	Fund-3	Fund-3	Fund-3	Fund-3	Fund-3	Fund-3
8	Fund-3	Fund-3	Fund-3	Fund-1	Fund-3	Fund-3	Fund-3
9	Fund-1	Fund-3	Fund-3	Fund-1	Fund-1	Fund-1	Fund-1
10	Fund-2	Fund-1	Fund-2	Fund-2	Fund-2	Fund-2	Fund-1
11	Decline	Decline	Decline	Fund-3	Fund-3	Decline	Decline
12	Fund-2	Fund-3	Fund-1	Fund-2	Fund-2	Fund-2	Fund-2
13	Fund-2	Fund-2	Fund-2	Fund-2	Fund-2	Fund-2	Fund-1
14	Fund-2	Fund-2	Fund-2	Fund-2	Fund-2	Fund-2	Fund-2
15	Fund-1	Fund-1	Fund-1	Fund-1	Fund-1	Fund-1	Fund-1
16	Fund-2	Fund-2	Fund-2	Fund-2	Fund-2	Fund-2	Fund-1
17	Fund-3	Decline	Fund-3	Fund-1	Fund-1	Fund-3	Fund-3
18	Fund-3	Fund-3	Fund-1	Fund-3	Fund-3	Fund-3	Fund-1
19	Decline	Fund-3	Fund-3	Fund-3	Decline	Decline	Decline
20	Fund-1	Fund-1	Fund-1	Fund-1	Fund-1	Fund-1	Fund-1
21	Fund-2	Fund-2	Fund-2	Fund-1	Fund-2	Fund-2	Fund-1
22	Fund-2	Fund-1	Fund-2	Fund-2	Fund-2	Fund-2	Fund-2
23	Fund-1	Fund-1	Fund-1	Fund-1	Fund-1	Fund-1	Fund-1
24	Fund-3	Decline	Fund-3	Fund-1	Fund-2	Fund-3	Fund-1
25	Fund-3	Fund-3	Fund-3	Fund-3	Fund-3	Fund-3	Fund-3
26	Fund-3	Fund-3	Fund-3	Fund-3	Fund-3	Fund-3	Fund-1
27	Fund-2	Fund-2	Fund-2	Fund-2	Fund-1	Fund-2	Fund-2
28	Decline	Decline	Decline	Fund-3	Decline	Decline	Decline
29	Decline	Decline	Decline	Fund-3	Decline	Decline	Fund-3
30	Fund-2	Fund-2	Fund-2	Fund-2	Fund-2	Fund-2	Fund-2

consider a bank that uses manual underwriting to analyze mortgage loan applications. Each underwriter must use the information supplied by the applicant and other external information such as credit history to classify the application into one of four categories; decline or do not fund, fund-1, fund-2, and fund-3. The fund-2 and fund-3 categories are applicants that are considered low-risk loans while fund-1 is a higher risk applicant. Suppose that 30 applications are selected and evaluated by a panel of senior underwriters who arrive at a consensus evaluation for each application, then three different underwriters (Sue, Fred, and John) are asked to evaluate each application twice. The applications are "blinded" (customer names, addresses and other identifying information removed) and the two evaluations are performed several days apart. The data are shown in Table 8.13. The column labeled "classification" in this table is the consensus decision reached by the panel of senior underwriters.

The attribute gauge capability analysis in this situation would determine the proportion of time that the underwriter agrees with him/herself in evaluating the loan application. This is a measure of repeatability. We would also be interested in the proportion of time that the underwriter agrees with the correct classification. This is a measure of bias.

■ TABLE 8.14
Minitab Attribute Agreement Analysis for the Loan Evaluation Data in Table 8.13

Attribute Agreement Analysis for Sue1, Sue2, Fred1, Fred2, John1, John2

Within Appraisers

Assessment Agreement

Appraiser	# Inspected	# Matched	Percent	95% CI
Sue	30	23	76.67	(57.72, 90.07)
Fred	30	21	70.00	(50.60, 85.27)
John	30	18	60.00	(40.60, 77.34)

Matched: Appraiser agrees with him/herself across trials.

Each Appraiser vs Standard

Assessment Agreement

Appraiser	# Inspected	# Matched	Percent	95% CI
Sue	30	19	63.33	(43.86, 80.07)
Fred	30	17	56.67	(37.43, 74.54)
John	30	18	60.00	(40.60, 77.34)

Matched: Appraiser's assessment across trials agrees with the known standard.

Between Appraisers

Assessment Agreement

# Inspected	# Matched	Percent	95% CI
30	7	23.33	(9.93, 42.28)

Matched: All appraisers' assessments agree with each other.

All Appraisers vs Standard

Assessment Agreement

# Inspected	# Matched	Percent	95% CI
30	7	23.33	(9.93, 42.28)

Matched: All appraisers' assessments agree with the known standard.

Using Minitab to calculate the percentages of agreement (the Attribute Agreement Analysis routine in Minitab v15) results in the output shown in Table 8.14. Notice that Minitab also calculates and displays confidence intervals on the percent match. Figure 8.17 presents graphs of the confidence intervals for the percentages within underwriters (a measure of how well the underwriters agree with themselves across trials) and for the percentage of times the underwriters agree with the standard (correct) answer. Generally, while there is considerable subjectivity in interpreting the results of attribute gauge capability studies, there is not great agreement in this study. More training may be needed to ensure that underwriters produce more consistent and correct decision for mortgage loan applications.

Good references to other approaches for conducting attribute gauge capability studies are Boyles (2001), De Mast and Van Wieringen (2004) (2007), and Van Wieringen (2003).

8.8 Setting Specification Limits on Discrete Components

It is often necessary to use information from a process capability study to set specifications on discrete parts or components that interact with other components to form the final product. This is particularly important in complex assemblies to prevent **tolerance stack-up problems** where there are many interacting dimensions. This section discusses some aspects of

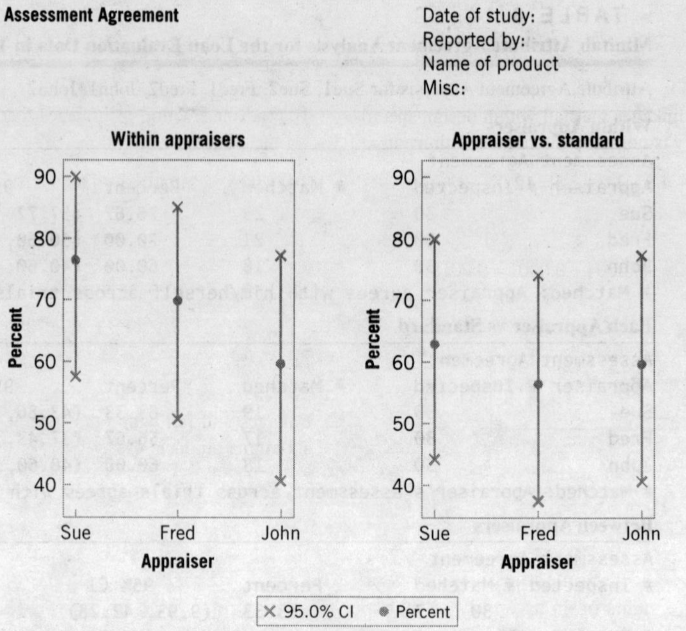

■ FIGURE 8.17 Confidence intervals for the attribute agreement analysis.

setting specifications on components to ensure that the final product meets specifications. Some of these concepts are an integral part of design for six-sigma (DFSS).

8.8.1 Linear Combinations

In many cases, the dimension of an item is a linear combination of the dimensions of the component parts. That is, if the dimensions of the components are $x_1, x_2, \ldots, x_n$, then the dimension of the final assembly is

$$y = a_1x_1 + a_2x_2 + \cdots + a_nx_n \tag{8.38}$$

where the a_c are constants.

If the x_i are normally and independently distributed with mean μ_i and variance σ_i^2, then y is normally distributed with mean $\mu_y = \Sigma_{n=1}^{i} a_i\mu_i$ and variance $\sigma_y^2 = \Sigma_{n=1}^{i} a_i^2\,\sigma_i^2$. Therefore, if μ_i and σ_i^2 are known for each component, the fraction of assembled items falling outside the specifications can be determined.

EXAMPLE 8.8 Meeting Customer Specifications

A linkage consists of four components as shown in Fig. 8.18. The lengths of x_1, x_2, x_3, and x_4 are known to be $x_1 \sim N(2.0, 0.0004)$, $x_2 \sim N(4.5, 0.0009)$, $x_3 \sim N(3.0, 0.0004)$, and $x_4 \sim N(2.5, 0.0001)$. The lengths of the components can be assumed independent, because they are produced on different machines. All lengths are in inches. Determine the proportion of linkages that meet the customer specification on overall length of 12 ± 0.10.

SOLUTION

To find the fraction of linkages that fall within design specification limits, note that y is normally distributed with mean

$$\mu_y = 2.0 + 4.5 + 3.0 + 2.5 = 12.0$$

and variance

$$\sigma_y^2 = 0.0004 + 0.0009 + 0.0004 + 0.0001 = 0.0018$$

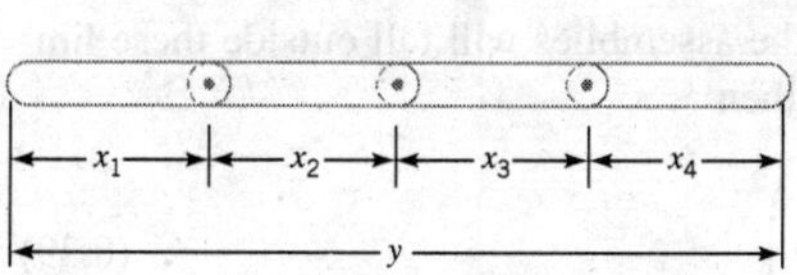

FIGURE 8.18 A linkage assembly with four components.

To find the fraction of linkages that are within specification, we must evaluate

$$\begin{aligned} P\{11.90 \le y \le 12.10\} &= P\{y \le 12.10\} - P\{y \le 11.90\} \\ &= \Phi\left(\frac{12.10 - 12.00}{\sqrt{0.0018}}\right) - \Phi\left(\frac{11.90 - 12.00}{\sqrt{0.0018}}\right) \\ &= \Phi(2.36) - \Phi(-2.36) \\ &= 0.99086 - 0.00914 \\ &= 0.98172 \end{aligned}$$

Therefore, we conclude that 98.172% of the assembled linkages will fall within the specification limits. This is not a six-sigma product.

Sometimes it is necessary to determine specification limits on the individual components of an assembly so that specification limits on the final assembly will be satisfied. This is demonstrated in Example 8.9.

EXAMPLE 8.9 Designing a Six-Sigma Product

Consider the assembly shown in Fig. 8.19. Suppose that the specifications on this assembly are 6.00 ± 0.06 in. Let each component x_1, x_2, and x_3 be normally and independently distributed with means $\mu_1 = 1.00$ in., $\mu_2 = 3.00$ in., and $\mu_3 = 2.00$ in., respectively. Suppose that we want the specification limits to fall inside the natural tolerance limits of the process for the final assembly so that $C_p = 2.0$, approximately, for the final assembly. This is a six-sigma product, resulting in about 3.4 defective assemblies per million.

The length of the final assembly is normally distributed. Furthermore, if as a six-sigma product, this implies that the natural tolerance limits must be located at $\mu \pm 6\sigma_y$. Now $\mu_y = \mu_1 + \mu_2 + \mu_3 = 1.00 + 3.00 + 2.00 = 6.00$, so the process is centered at the nominal value. Therefore, the maximum possible value of σ_y that would yield an acceptable product is

$$\sigma_y = \frac{0.06}{6} = 0.010$$

That is, if $\sigma_y \le 0.010$, then the number of nonconforming assemblies produced will be acceptable.

Now let us see how this affects the specifications on the individual components. The variance of the length of the final assembly is

$$\sigma_y^2 = \sigma_1^2 + \sigma_2^2 + \sigma_3^2 \le (0.010)^2 = 0.0001$$

Suppose that the variances of the component lengths are all equal; that is, $\sigma_1^2 = \sigma_2^2 = \sigma_3^2 = \sigma^2$ (say). Then

$$\sigma_y^2 = 3\sigma^2$$

and the maximum possible value for the variance of the length of any component is

$$\sigma^2 = \frac{\sigma_y^2}{3} = \frac{0.0001}{3} = 0.000033$$

Effectively, if $\sigma^2 \le 0.000033$ for each component, then the natural tolerance limits for the final assembly will be inside the specification limits such that $C_p = 2.0$.

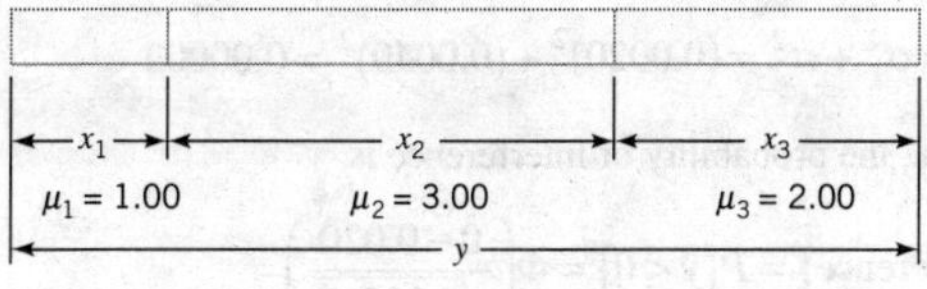

FIGURE 8.19 Assembly for Example 8.9.

(continued)

This can be translated into specification limits on the individual components. If we assume that the natural tolerance limits and the specification limits for the components are to coincide exactly, then the specification limits for each component are as follows:

$$x_1: \quad 1.00 \pm 3.00\sqrt{(0.000033)} = 1.00 \pm 0.01732$$
$$x_2: \quad 3.00 \pm 3.00\sqrt{(0.000033)} = 3.00 \pm 0.01732$$
$$x_3: \quad 2.00 \pm 3.00\sqrt{(0.000033)} = 2.00 \pm 0.01732$$

It is possible to give a general solution to the problem in Example 8.9. Let the assembly consist of n components having common variance σ^2. If the natural tolerances of the assembly are defined so that no more than $\alpha\%$ of the assemblies will fall outside these limits, and $2W$ is the width of the specification limits, then

$$\sigma_y^{2*} = \left(\frac{W}{Z_{\alpha/2}}\right)^2 \tag{8.39}$$

is the maximum possible value for the variance of the final assembly that will permit the natural tolerance limits and the specification limits to coincide. Consequently, the maximum permissible value of the variance for the individual components is

$$\sigma^{2*} = \frac{\sigma_y^{2*}}{n} \tag{8.40}$$

EXAMPLE 8.10 Assembly of a Shaft and a Bearing

A shaft is to be assembled into a bearing. The internal diameter of the bearing is a normal random variable—say, x_1—with mean $\mu_1 = 1.500$ in. and standard deviation $\sigma_1 = 0.0020$ in. The external diameter of the shaft—say, x_2—is normally distributed with mean $\mu_2 = 1.480$ in. and standard deviation $\sigma_2 = 0.0040$ in. The assembly is shown in Fig. 8.20.

When the two parts are assembled, interference will occur if the shaft diameter is larger than the bearing diameter—that is, if

$$y = x_1 - x_2 < 0$$

Note that the distribution of y is normal with mean

$$\mu_y = \mu_1 - \mu_2 = 1.500 - 1.480 = 0.020$$

and variance

$$\sigma_y^2 = \sigma_1^2 + \sigma_2^2 = (0.0020)^2 + (0.0040)^2 = 0.00002$$

Therefore, the probability of interference is

$$P\{\text{interference}\} = P\{y < 0\} = \Phi\left(\frac{0 - 0.020}{\sqrt{0.00002}}\right) =$$
$$\Phi(-4.47) = 0.000004 \text{ (4 ppm)}$$

which indicates that very few assemblies will have interference. This is essentially a six-sigma design.

In problems of this type, we occasionally define a minimum clearance—say, C—such that

$$P\{\text{clearance} < C\} = \alpha$$

Thus, C becomes the natural tolerance for the assembly and can be compared with the design specification. In our example, if we establish $\alpha = 0.0001$ (i.e., only 1 out of 10,000 assemblies or 100 ppm will have clearance less than or equal to C), then we have

$$\frac{C - \mu_y}{\sigma_y} = -Z_{0.0001}$$

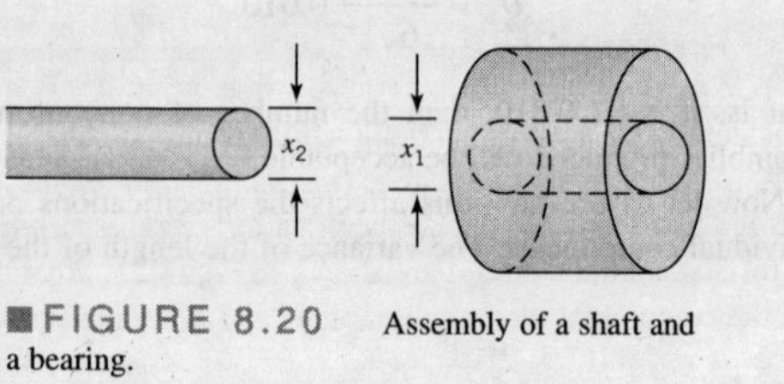

■ FIGURE 8.20 Assembly of a shaft and a bearing.

or

$$\frac{C - 0.020}{\sqrt{0.00002}} = -3.71$$

which implies that $C = 0.020 - (3.71)\sqrt{0.00002} = 0.0034$. That is, only 1 out of 10,000 assemblies will have clearance less than 0.0034 in.

8.8.2 Nonlinear Combinations

In some problems, the dimension of interest may be a **nonlinear function** of the n component dimensions $x_1, x_2, \ldots x_n$—say,

$$y = g(x_1, x_2, \ldots, x_n) \tag{8.41}$$

In problems of this type, the usual approach is to approximate the nonlinear function g by a linear function of the x_i in the region of interest. If $\mu_1, \mu_2, \ldots \mu_n$ are the nominal dimensions associated with the components $x_1, x_2, \ldots x_n$, then by expanding the right-hand side of equation (8.41) in a Taylor series about $\mu_1, \mu_2, \ldots \mu_n$, we obtain

$$\begin{aligned} y &= g(x_1, x_2, \ldots, x_n) \\ &= g(\mu_1, \mu_2, \ldots, \mu_n) + \sum_{i=1}^{n} (x_i - \mu_i) \frac{\partial g}{\partial x_i}\bigg|_{\mu_1, \mu_2, \ldots, \mu_n} + R \end{aligned} \tag{8.42}$$

where R represents the higher-order terms. Neglecting the terms of higher order, we can apply the expected value and variance operators to obtain

$$\mu_y \simeq g(\mu_1, \mu_2, \ldots, \mu_n) \tag{8.43}$$

and

$$\sigma_y^2 \simeq \sum_{i=1}^{n} \left(\frac{\partial g}{\partial x_i}\bigg|_{\mu_1, \mu_2, \ldots, \mu_n} \right)^2 \sigma_i^2 \tag{8.44}$$

This procedure to find an approximate mean and variance of a nonlinear combination of random variables is sometimes called the **delta method.** Equation (8.44) is often called the **transmission of error formula.**

The following example illustrates how these results are useful in tolerance problems.

EXAMPLE 8.11 A Product with Nonlinear Dimensions

Consider the simple DC circuit components shown in Fig. 8.21. Suppose that the voltage across the points (a, b) is required to be 100 ± 2 V. The specifications on the current and the resistance in the circuit are shown in Fig. 8.21. We assume that the component random variables I and R are normally and independently distributed with means equal to their nominal values.

From Ohm's law, we know that the voltage is

$$V = IR$$

(continued)

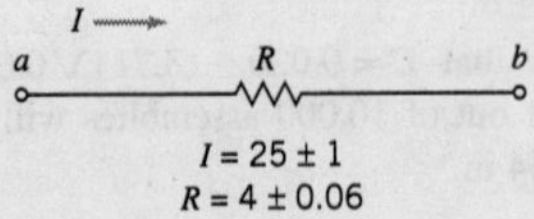

■ FIGURE 8.21
Electrical circuit for Example 8.11.

Since this involves a nonlinear combination, we expand V in a Taylor series about mean current μ_I and mean resistance μ_R, yielding

$$V \simeq \mu_I \mu_R + (I - \mu_I)\mu_R + (R - \mu_R)\mu_I$$

neglecting the terms of higher order. Now the mean and variance of voltage are

$$\mu_V \simeq \mu_I \mu_R$$

and

$$\sigma_V^2 \simeq \mu_R^2 \sigma_I^2 + \mu_I^2 \sigma_R^2$$

approximately, where σ_I^2 and σ_R^2 are the variances of I and R, respectively.

Now suppose that I and R are centered at their nominal values and that the natural tolerance limits are defined so that $\alpha = 0.0027$ is the fraction of values of each component falling outside these limits. Assume also that the specification limits are exactly equal to the natural tolerance limits. For the current I we have $I = 25 \pm 1$ A. That is, $24 \le I \le 26$ A correspond to the natural tolerance limits *and* the specifications. Since $I \sim N(25, \sigma_I^2)$, and since $Z_{\alpha/2} = Z_{0.00135} = 3.00$, we have

$$\frac{26 - 25}{\sigma_I} = 3.00$$

or $\sigma_I = 0.33$. For the resistance, we have $R = 4 \pm 0.06$ ohm as the specification limits *and* the natural tolerance limits. Thus,

$$\frac{4.06 - 4.00}{\sigma_R} = 3.00$$

and $\sigma_R = 0.02$. Note that σ_I and σ_R are the largest possible values of the component standard deviations consistent with the natural tolerance limits falling inside or equal to the specification limits.

Using these results, and if we assume that the voltage V is approximately normally distributed, then

$$\mu_V \simeq \mu_I \mu_R = (25)(4) = 100 \text{ V}$$

and

$$\sigma_V^2 \simeq \mu_R^2 \sigma_I^2 + \mu_I^2 \sigma_R^2 = (4)^2(0.33)^2 + (25)^2(0.02)^2 = 1.99$$

approximately. Thus $\sigma_V = \sqrt{1.99} = 1.41$. Therefore, the probability that the voltage will fall within the design specifications is

$$\begin{aligned} P\{98 \le V \le 102\} &= P\{V \le 102\} - P\{V \le 98\} \\ &= \Phi\left(\frac{102 - 100}{1.41}\right) - \Phi\left(\frac{98 - 100}{1.41}\right) \\ &= \Phi(1.42) - \Phi(-1.42) \\ &= 0.92219 - 0.07781 \\ &= 0.84438 \end{aligned}$$

That is, only 84% of the observed output voltages will fall within the design specifications. Note that the natural tolerance limits or process capability for the output voltage is

$$\mu_V \pm 3.00\sigma_V$$

or

$$100 \pm 4.23 \text{ V}$$

In this problem the process capability ratio is

$$C_p = \frac{\text{USL} - \text{LSL}}{6\sigma} = \frac{102 - 98}{6(1.41)} = 0.47$$

Note that, although the individual current and resistance variations are not excessive relative to their specifications, because of tolerance stack-up problems, they interact to produce a circuit whose performance relative to the voltage specifications is very poor.

8.9 Estimating the Natural Tolerance Limits of a Process

In many types of production processes, it is customary to think of the natural tolerance limits as those limits that contain a certain fraction—say, $1 - \alpha$—of the distribution. In this section we present some approaches to estimating the natural tolerance limits of a process.

If the underlying distribution of the quality characteristic and its parameters are known—say, on the basis of long experience—then the tolerance limits may be readily established. For example, in Section 8.7, we studied several problems involving tolerances where the quality characteristic was normally distributed with known mean μ and known variance σ^2. If in this case we define the tolerance limits as those limits that contain $100(1-\alpha)\%$ of the distribution of this quality characteristic, then these limits are simply $\mu \pm Z_{\alpha/2}\sigma$. If $\alpha = 0.05$ (say), then the tolerance limits are given by $\mu \pm 1.96\sigma$.

In most practical problems, both the form of the distribution and its parameters will be unknown. However, the parameters may usually be estimated from sample data. In certain cases, then, it is possible to estimate the tolerance limits of the process by use of these sample statistics. We will discuss two procedures for estimating natural tolerance limits, one for those situations in which the normality assumption is reasonable, and a nonparametric approach useful in cases where the normality assumption is inappropriate.

The estimation of the natural tolerance limits of a process is an important problem with many significant practical implications. As noted previously, unless the product specifications exactly coincide with or exceed the natural tolerance limits of the process (PCR ≥ 1), an extremely high percentage of the production will be outside specifications, resulting in a high loss or rework rate.

8.9.1 Tolerance Limits Based on the Normal Distribution

Suppose a random variable x is normally distributed with mean μ and variance σ^2, both unknown. From a random sample of n observations, the sample mean $\bar{x}$ and sample variance s^2 may be computed. A logical procedure for estimating the natural tolerance limits $\mu \pm Z_{\alpha/2}\sigma$ is to replace μ by $\bar{x}$ and σ by s, yielding

$$\bar{x} \pm Z_{\alpha/2}s \tag{8.45}$$

Since $\bar{x}$ and s are only *estimates* and not the *true* parameter values, we cannot say that the above interval always contains $100(1-\alpha)\%$ of the distribution. However, one may determine a constant K, such that in a large number of samples a fraction γ of the intervals $\bar{x} \pm Ks$ will include at least $100(1-\alpha)\%$ of the distribution. Values of K for $2 \le n \le 1000$, $\gamma = 0.90, 0.95, 0.99$, and $\alpha = 0.10, 0.05$, and 0.01 are given in Appendix Table VII.

EXAMPLE 8.12 Constructing a Tolerance Interval

The manufacturer of a solid-fuel rocket propellant is interested in finding the tolerance limits of the process such that 95% of the burning rates will lie within these limits with probability 0.99. It is known from previous experience that the burning rate is normally distributed. A random sample of 25 observations shows that the sample mean and variance of burning rate are $\bar{x} = 40.75$ and $s^2 = 1.87$, respectively. Since $\alpha = 0.05$, $\gamma = 0.99$, and $n = 25$, we find $K = 2.972$ from Appendix Table VII. Therefore, the required tolerance limits are found as $\bar{x} \pm 2.972s = 40.75 \pm (2.972)(1.37) = 40.75 \pm 4.07 = [36.68, 44.82]$.

We note that there is a fundamental difference between confidence limits and tolerance limits. **Confidence limits** are used to provide an interval estimate of the parameter of a distribution, whereas **tolerance limits** are used to indicate the limits between which we can expect to find a specified proportion of a population. Note that as n approaches infinity, the length of a confidence interval approaches zero, while the tolerance limits approach the corresponding value for the population. Thus, in Appendix Table VII, as n approaches infinity for $\alpha = 0.05$, say, K approaches 1.96.

It is also possible to specify one-sided tolerance limits based on the normal distribution. That is, we may wish to state that with probability γ at least $100(1-\alpha)\%$ of the distribution is greater than the lower tolerance limit $\bar{x} - Ks$ or less than the upper tolerance limit $\bar{x} + Ks$. Values of K for these one-sided tolerance limits for $2 \le n \le 1000$, $\gamma = 0.90, 0.95, 0.99$, and $\alpha = 0.10, 0.05$, and 0.01 are given in Appendix Table VIII.

8.9.2 Nonparametric Tolerance Limits

It is possible to construct **nonparametric** (or ***distribution-free***) **tolerance limits** that are valid for any continuous probability distribution. These intervals are based on the distribution of the extreme values (largest and smallest sample observation) in a sample from an arbitrary continuous distribution. For two-sided tolerance limits, the number of observations that must be taken to ensure that with probability γ at least $100(1-\alpha)\%$ of the distribution will lie between the largest and smallest observations obtained in the sample is

$$n \simeq \frac{1}{2} + \left(\frac{2-\alpha}{\alpha}\right)\frac{\chi^2_{1-\gamma,4}}{4}$$

approximately. Thus, to be 99% certain that at least 95% of the population will be included between the sample extreme values, we have $\alpha = 0.05$, $\gamma = 0.99$, and consequently,

$$n \simeq \frac{1}{2} + \left(\frac{1.95}{0.05}\right)\frac{13.28}{4} = 130$$

For one-sided nonparametric tolerance limits such that with probability γ at least $100(1-\alpha)\%$ of the population exceeds the smallest sample value (or is less than the largest sample value), we must take a sample of

$$n = \frac{\log(1-\gamma)}{\log(1-\alpha)}$$

observations. Thus, the upper nonparametric tolerance limit that contains at least 90% of the population with probability at least 0.95 ($\alpha = 0.10$ and $\gamma = 0.95$) is the largest observation in a sample of

$$n = \frac{\log(1-\gamma)}{\log(1-\alpha)} = \frac{\log(0.05)}{\log(0.90)} = 28$$

observations.

In general, nonparametric tolerance limits have limited practical value, because to construct suitable intervals that contain a relatively large fraction of the distribution with high probability, large samples are required. In some cases, the sample sizes required may be so large as to prohibit their use. If one can specify the *form* of the distribution, it is possible for a given sample size to construct tolerance intervals that are narrower than those obtained from the nonparametric approach.

Important Terms and Concepts

ANOVA approach to a gauge R & R experiment
Components of gauge error
Components of measurement error
Confidence intervals for gauge R & R studies
Confidence intervals on process capability ratios
Consumer's risk or missed fault for a gauge
Control charts and process capability analysis
Delta method

Discrimination ratio (*DR*) for a gauge
Estimating variance components
Factorial experiment
Gauge R & R experiment
Graphical methods for process capability analysis
Measurement systems capability analysis
Natural tolerance limits for a normal distribution
Natural tolerance limits of a process
Nonparametric tolerance limits
Normal distribution and process capability ratios
One-sided process-capability ratios
PCR C_p
PCR C_{pk}
PCR C_{pm}
Precision and accuracy of a gauge
Precision-to-tolerence (P/T) ratio
Process capability
Process capability analysis
Process performance indices P_p and P_{pk}
Producer's risk or false failure for a gauge
Product characterization
Random effects model ANOVA
Signal-to-noise ratio (*SNR*) for a gauge
Tolerance stack-up problems
Transmission of error formula

Exercises

8.1. Estimate process capability using $\bar{x}$ and *R* charts for the power supply voltage data in Exercise 6.4. If specifications are at 350 ± 5 V, calculate C_p, C_{pk}, and C_{pkm}. Interpret these capability ratios.

8.2. Consider the hole diameter data in Exercise 6.1. Estimate process capability using $\bar{x}$ and *R* charts. If specifications are at 0 ± 0.01, calculate C_p, C_{pk}, and C_{pkm}. Interpret these ratios.

8.3. Perform a process capability analysis using $\bar{x}$ and *R* charts for the data in Exercise 6.3.

8.4. Consider the two processes shown in Table 8E.1 (the sample size $n = 5$):
Specifications are at 100 ± 10. Calculate C_p, C_{pk}, and C_{pm} and interpret these ratios. Which process would you prefer to use?

8.5. A process is in statistical control with $\bar{\bar{x}} = 199$ and $\bar{R} = 3.5$. The control chart uses a sample size of $n = 4$. Specifications are at 200 ± 8. The quality characteristic is normally distributed.
(a) Estimate the potential capability of the process.
(b) Estimate the actual process capability.
(c) How much improvement could be made in process performance if the mean could be centered at the nominal value?

8.6. Suppose that 20 of the parts manufactured by the processes in Exercise 8.4 were assembled so that their dimensions were additive; that is,

$$x = x_1 + x_2 + \cdots + x_{20}$$

Specifications on *x* are 2000 ± 200. Would you prefer to produce the parts using process A or process B? Why? Do the capability ratios computed in Exercise 8.4 provide any guidance for process selection?

8.7. A process is in control with $\bar{\bar{x}} = 100$, $\bar{s} = 1.05$, and $n = 5$. The process specifications are at 95 ± 10. The quality characteristic has a normal distribution.
(a) Estimate the potential capability.
(b) Estimate the actual capability.
(c) How much could the fallout in the process be reduced if the process were corrected to operate at the nominal specification?

8.8. A process is in statistical control with $\bar{\bar{x}} = 39.7$ and $\bar{R} = 2.5$. The control chart uses a sample size of $n = 2$. Specifications are at 40 ± 5. The quality characteristic is normally distributed.
(a) Estimate the potential capability of the process.
(b) Estimate the actual process capability.
(c) Calculate and compare the PCRs C_{pkm} and C_{pkm}.
(d) How much improvement could be made in process performance if the mean could be centered at the nominal value?

8.9. The length of time required to reimburse employee expense claims is a characteristic that can be used to

■ **TABLE 8E.1**
Process Data for Exercise 8.4

Process A	Process B
$\bar{\bar{x}}_A = 100$	$\bar{\bar{x}}_B = 105$
$\bar{S}_A = 3$	$\bar{S}_B = 1$

■ TABLE 8E.2

Days to Par Expense Claims

5	5	16	17	14	12
8	13	6	12	11	10
18	18	13	12	19	14
17	16	11	22	13	16
10	18	12	12	12	14

describe the performance of the process. Table 8E.2 gives the cycle times (in days) of 30 randomly selected employee expense claims. Estimate the capability of this process.

8.10. The failure time in hours of 10 LSI memory devices follows: 1210, 1275, 1400, 1695, 1900, 2105, 2230, 2250, 2500, and 2625. Plot the data on normal probability paper and, if appropriate, estimate process capability. Is it safe to estimate the proportion of circuits that fail below 1200 h?

8.11. The height of the disk used in a computer disk drive assembly is a critical quality characteristic. Table 8E.3 gives the heights (in mm) of 25 disks randomly selected from the manufacturing process. Prepare a normal probability plot of the disk height data and estimate process capability.

8.12. The weights of nominal 1-kg containers of a concentrated chemical ingredient are shown in Table 8E.4. Prepare a normal probability plot of the data and estimate process capability.

8.13. Consider the package weight data in Exercise 8.12. Suppose there is a lower specification at 0.985 kg. Calculate an appropriate process capability ratio for this material. What percentage of the packages produced by this process is estimated to be below the specification limit?

■ TABLE 8E.3

Disk Height Data for Exercise 8.11

20.0106	20.0090	20.0067	19.9772	20.0001
19.9940	19.9876	20.0042	19.9986	19.9958
20.0075	20.0018	20.0059	19.9975	20.0089
20.0045	19.9891	19.9956	19.9884	20.0154
20.0056	19.9831	20.0040	20.0006	20.0047

■ TABLE 8E.4

Weights of Containers

0.9475	0.9775	0.9965	1.0075	1.0180
0.9705	0.9860	0.9975	1.0100	1.0200
0.9770	0.9960	1.0050	1.0175	1.0250

■ TABLE 8E.5

Response Time Data for Exercise 8.14

80	102	86	94	86	106	105	110	127	97
110	104	97	128	98	84	97	87	99	94
105	104	84	77	125	85	80	104	103	109
115	89	100	96	96	87	106	100	102	93

8.14. An electric utility tracks the response time to customer-reported outages. The data in Table 8E.5 are a random sample of 40 of the response times (in minutes) for one operating division of this utility during a single month.
(a) Estimate the capability of the utility's process for responding to customer-reported outages.
(b) The utility wants to achieve a 90% response rate in under two hours, as response to emergency outages is an important measure of customer satisfaction. What is the capability of the process with respect to this objective?

8.15. A company has been asked by an important customer to demonstrate that its process capability ratio C_p exceeds 1.33. It has taken a sample of 50 parts and obtained the point estimate $\hat{C}_p = 1.52$. Assume that the quality characteristic follows a normal distribution. Can the company demonstrate that C_p exceeds 1.33 at the 95% level of confidence? What level of confidence would give a one-sided lower confidence limit on C_p that exceeds 1.33?

8.16. A normally distributed process has specifications of LSL = 75 and USL = 85 on the output. A random sample of 25 parts indicates that the process is centered at the middle of the specification band and the standard deviation is $s = 1.5$.
(a) Find a point estimate of C_p.
(b) Find a 95% confidence interval on C_p. Comment on the width of this interval.

8.17. The molecular weight of a particular polymer should fall between 2100 and 2350. Fifty samples of this material were analyzed with the results $\bar{x} = 2275$ and $s = 60$. Assume that molecular weight is normally distributed.
(a) Calculate a point estimate of C_{pk}.
(b) Find a 95% confidence interval on C_{pk}.

8.18. Suppose that a quality characteristic has a normal distribution with specification limits at USL = 100 and LSL = 90. A random sample of 30 parts results in $\bar{x} = 97$ and $s = 1.6$.
(a) Calculate a point estimate of C_{pk}.
(b) Find a 95% confidence interval on C_{pk}.

TABLE 8E.6
Measurement Data for Exercise 8.20

Part Number	Measurements 1	Measurements 2	Part Number	Measurements 1	Measurements 2
1	20	20	9	20	20
2	19	20	10	23	22
3	21	21	11	28	22
4	24	20	12	19	25
5	21	21	13	21	20
6	25	26	14	20	21
7	18	17	15	18	18
8	16	15			

8.19. Consider a simplified version of equation (8.19):

$$\hat{C}_{pk}\left[1-Z_{\alpha/2}\sqrt{\frac{1}{2(n-1)}}\right] \le C_{pk} \le \hat{C}_{pk}\left[1+Z_{\alpha/2}\sqrt{\frac{1}{2(n-1)}}\right]$$

Note that this was obtained by assuming that the term $9n$ in equation (8.19) will probably be large. Rework Exercise 8.18 using this equation and compare your answer to the original answer obtained from equation (8.19). How good is the approximation suggested in this problem?

8.20. The data in Table 8E.6 were taken by one operator during a gauge capability study.
(a) Estimate gauge capability.
(b) Does the control chart analysis of these data indicate any potential problem in using the gauge?

8.21. In a study to isolate both gauge repeatability and gauge reproducibility, two operators use the same gauge to measure 10 parts three times each. The data are shown in Table 8E.7.
(a) Estimate gauge repeatability and reproducibility.
(b) Estimate the standard deviation of measurement error.
(c) If the specifications are at 50 ± 10, what can you say about gauge capability?

8.22. Ten parts are measured three times by the same operator in a gauge capability study. The data are shown in Table 8E.8.
(a) Describe the measurement error that results from the use of this gauge.
(b) Estimate total variability and product variability.
(c) What percentage of total variability is due to the gauge?

TABLE 8E.7
Measurement Data for Exercise 8.21

Part Number	Operator 1 Measurements 1	2	3	Operator 2 Measurements 1	2	3
1	50	49	50	50	48	51
2	52	52	51	51	51	51
3	53	50	50	54	52	51
4	49	51	50	48	50	51
5	48	49	48	48	49	48
6	52	50	50	52	50	50
7	51	51	51	51	50	50
8	52	50	49	53	48	50
9	50	51	50	51	48	49
10	47	46	49	46	47	48

TABLE 8E.8
Measurement Data for Exercise 8.22

Part Number	Measurements 1	2	3
1	100	101	100
2	95	93	97
3	101	103	100
4	96	95	97
5	98	98	96
6	99	98	98
7	95	97	98
8	100	99	98
9	100	100	97
10	100	98	99

(d) If specifications on the part are at 100 ± 15, find the *P/T* ratio for this gauge. Comment on the adequacy of the gauge.

8.23. An operator–instrument combination is known to test parts with an average error of zero; however, the standard deviation of measurement error is estimated to be 3. Samples from a controlled process were analyzed, and the total variability was estimated to be $\hat{\sigma} = 5$. What is the true process standard deviation?

8.24. Consider the situation in Example 8.8. A new gauge is being evaluated for this process. The same operator measures the same 20 parts twice using the new gauge and obtains the data shown in Table 8E.9 on the next page.
(a) What can you say about the performance of the new gauge relative to the old one?

■ **TABLE 8E.9**
Measurement Data for Exercise 8.24

Part Number	Measurements 1	Measurements 2	Part Number	Measurements 1	Measurements 2
1	19	23	11	20	25
2	22	28	12	16	15
3	19	24	13	25	24
4	28	23	14	24	22
5	16	19	15	31	27
6	20	19	16	24	23
7	21	24	17	20	24
8	17	15	18	17	19
9	24	26	19	25	23
10	25	23	20	17	16

(b) If specifications are at 25 ± 15, what is the *P/T* ratio for the new gauge?

8.25. A measurement systems experiment involving 20 parts, three operators, and two measurements per part is shown in the Table 8E.10.

■ **TABLE 8E.10**
Measurement Data for Exercise 8.25

Part Number	Operator 1 Measurements 1	Operator 1 Measurements 2	Operator 2 Measurements 1	Operator 2 Measurements 2	Operator 3 Measurements 1	Operator 3 Measurements 2
1	21	20	20	20	19	21
2	24	23	24	24	23	24
3	20	21	19	21	20	22
4	27	27	28	26	27	28
5	19	18	19	18	18	21
6	23	21	24	21	23	22
7	22	21	22	24	22	20
8	19	17	18	20	19	18
9	24	23	25	23	24	24
10	25	23	26	25	24	25
11	21	20	20	20	21	20
12	18	19	17	19	18	19
13	23	25	25	25	25	25
14	24	24	23	25	24	25
15	29	30	30	28	31	30
16	26	26	25	26	25	27
17	20	20	19	20	20	20
18	19	21	19	19	21	23
19	25	26	25	24	25	25
20	19	19	18	17	19	17

(a) Estimate the repeatability and reproducibility of the gauge.

(b) What is the estimate of total gauge variability?

(c) If the product specifications are at LSL = 6 and USL = 60, what can you say about gauge capability?

8.26. Reconsider the gauge R & R experiment in Exercise 8.25. Calculate the quantities *SNR* and *DR* for this gauge. Discuss what information these measures provide about the capability of the gauge.

8.27. The surface tension of a chemical product, measured on a coded scale, is given by the relationship

$$s = (3 + 0.05x)^2$$

where x is a component of the product with probability distribution

$$f(x) = \frac{1}{26}(5x - 2) \qquad 2 \le x \le 4$$

Find the mean and variance of s.

8.28. A product is packaged by filling a container completely full. This container is shaped as shown in the figure. The process that produces these containers is examined, and the following information collected on the three critical dimensions:

Variable	Mean	Variance
L—Length	6.0	0.01
H—Height	3.0	0.01
W—Width	4.0	0.01

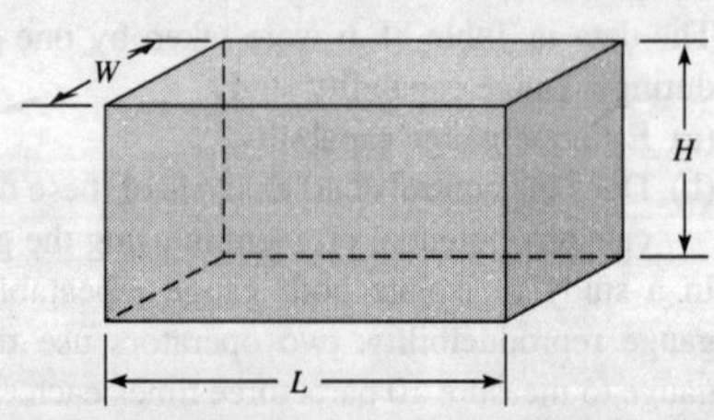

Assuming the variables to be independent, what are approximate values for the mean and variance of container volume?

8.29. Two parts are assembled as shown in the figure. The distributions of x_1 and x_2 are normal, with $\mu_1 = 20$, $\sigma_1 = 0.3$, $\mu_2 = 19.6$, and $\sigma_2 = 0.4$. The specifications of the clearance between the mating parts are 0.5 ± 0.4. What fraction of assemblies will fail to meet specifications if assembly is at random?

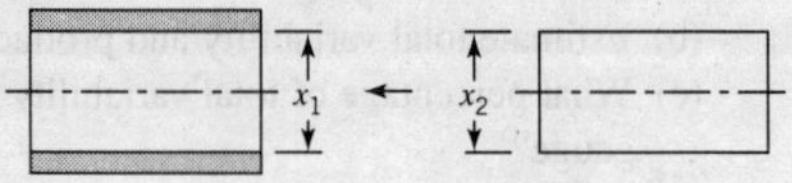

8.30. Three parts are assembled in series so that their critical dimensions x_1, x_2, and x_3 add. The dimensions of each part are normally distributed with the following parameters: $\mu_1 = 100$, $\sigma_1 = 4$, $\mu_2 = 75$, $\sigma_2 = 4$, $\mu_3 = 75$, and $\sigma_3 = 2$. What is the probability that an assembly chosen at random will have a combined dimension in excess of 262?

8.31. A rectangular piece of metal of width W and length L is cut from a plate of thickness T. If W, L, and T are independent random variables with means and standard deviations as given here and the density of the metal is 0.08 g/cm³, what would be the estimated mean and standard deviation of the weights of pieces produced by this process?

Variable	Mean	Standard Deviation
W	10 cm	0.2 cm
L	20 cm	0.3 cm
T	3 cm	0.1 cm

8.32. Two mating parts have critical dimensions x_1 and x_2 as shown in the figure. Assume that x_1 and x_2 are normally distributed with means μ_1 and μ_2 and standard deviations $\sigma_1 = 0.400$ and $\sigma_2 = 0.300$. If it is desired that the probability of a smaller clearance (i.e., $x_1 - x_2$) than 0.09 should be 0.006, what distance between the average dimension of the two parts (i.e., $\mu_1 - \mu_2$) should be specified by the designer?

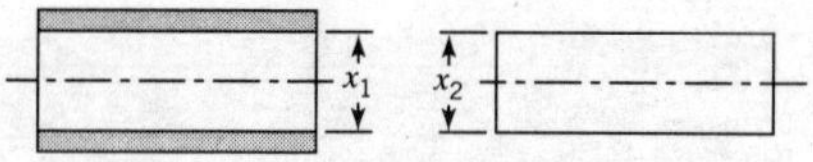

8.33. An assembly of two parts is formed by fitting a shaft into a bearing. It is known that the inside diameters of bearings are normally distributed with mean 2.010 cm and standard deviation 0.002 cm, and that the outside diameters of the shafts are normally distributed with mean 2.004 cm and standard deviation 0.001 cm. Determine the distribution of clearance between the parts if random assembly is used. What is the probability that the clearance is positive?

8.34. Two resistors are connected to a battery as shown in the figure. Find approximate expressions for the mean and variance of the resulting current (I). E, R_1, and R_2 are random variables with means μ_E, μ_{R1}, μ_{R2}, and variances σ_E^2, σ_{R1}^2, and σ_{R2}^2, respectively.

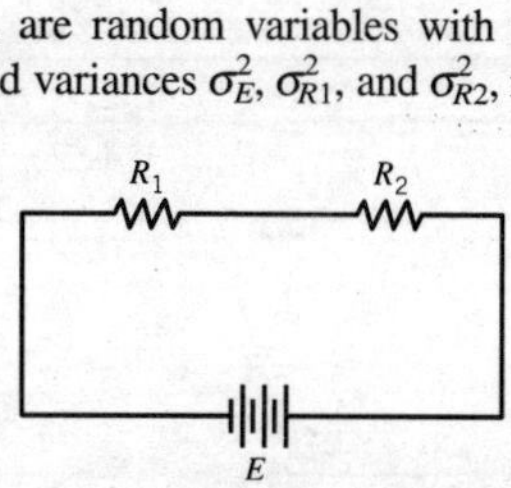

8.35. A sample of 25 measurements on a normally distributed quality characteristic has a mean of 85 and a standard deviation of 1. Using a confidence probability of 0.95, find a value such that 90% of the future measurements on this quality characteristic will lie above it.

8.36. A sample of 10 items from a normal population had a mean of 300 and a standard deviation of 10. Using these data, estimate a value for the random variable such that the probability is 0.95 that 90% of the measurements on this random variable will lie below the value.

8.37. We wish to estimate a two-sided natural tolerance interval that will include 99% of the values of a random variable with probability 0.80. If nothing is known about the distribution of the random variable, how large should the sample be?

8.38. Find the sample size required to construct an upper nonparametric tolerance limit that contains at least 95% of the population with probability at least 0.95. How would this limit actually be computed from sample data?

8.39. How large a sample is required to obtain a natural tolerance interval that has probability 0.90 of containing 95% of the distribution? After the data are collected, how would you construct the interval?

8.40. A random sample of $n = 40$ pipe sections resulted in a mean wall thickness of 0.1264 in. and a standard deviation of 0.0003 in. We assume that wall thickness is normally distributed.

(a) Between what limits can we say with 95% confidence that 95% of the wall thicknesses should fall?

(b) Construct a 95% confidence interval on the true mean thickness. Explain the difference between this interval and the one constructed in part (a).

mean and variance of the resulting current (I). E, R, and r are random variables with means μ_E, μ_R, μ_r and variances σ_E^2, σ_R^2 and σ_r^2, respectively.

[illegible] A sample of 25 measurements on a normally distributed quality characteristic has a mean of 85 and a standard deviation of 1. Using a confidence probability of 0.95, find a value such that 90% of the future measurements on this quality characteristic will lie above it.

[illegible] A sample of 10 items from a normal population had a mean of 300 and a standard deviation of 10. Using these data, estimate a value for the random variable such that the probability is 0.95 that 90% of the measurements on this random variable will lie below the value.

[illegible] We wish to estimate a two-sided natural tolerance interval that will include 99% of the values of a random variable with probability 0.80. If nothing is known about the distribution of the random variable, how large should the sample be?

[illegible] Find the sample size required to construct an upper nonparametric tolerance limit that will contain at least 95% of the population with probability at least 0.95. How would this limit actually be computed from sample data?

[illegible] How large a sample is required to obtain a natural tolerance interval that has probability 0.99 of containing 95% of the distribution? After the data are collected, how would you construct the interval?

[illegible] A random sample of n weld pipe sections resulted in a mean wall thickness of 0.1264 in. and a standard deviation of 0.0003 in. We assume that wall thickness is normally distributed.

(a) Between what limits can we say with 95% confidence that 99% of the wall thicknesses should fall?

(b) Construct a 95% confidence interval on the mean thickness. Explain the difference between this interval and the one constructed in part (a).

[illegible] Three parts are assembled in series so that their critical dimensions x_1, x_2, and x_3 add. The dimensions of each part are normally distributed with the following parameters: $\mu_1 = 100$, $\sigma_1 = 4$, $\mu_2 = 75$, $\sigma_2 = 4$, $\mu_3 = 75$, and $\sigma_3 = 2$. What is the probability that an assembly chosen at random will have a combined dimension in excess of 262?

[illegible] A rectangular piece of metal of width W and length L is cut from a plate of thickness T. If W, L, and T are independent random variables with means and standard deviations as given here and the density of the metal is 0.08 g/cm³, what would be the estimated mean and standard deviation of the weights of pieces produced by this process?

Variable	Mean	Standard Deviation
W	10 cm	0.2 cm
L	20 cm	0.1 cm
T	[illegible] cm	0.[illegible] cm

[illegible] Two mating parts have critical dimensions x_1 and x_2 as shown in the figure. Assume that x_1 and x_2 are normally distributed with means μ_1 and μ_2 and standard deviations $\sigma_1 = 0.400$ and $\sigma_2 = 0.300$. If it is desired that the probability of a smaller clearance (i.e., $x_1 - x_2$) than 0.09 should be 0.006, what distance between the average dimension of the two parts (i.e., $\mu_1 - \mu_2$) should be specified by the designer?

[illegible] An assembly of two parts is formed by fitting a shaft into a bearing. It is known that the inside diameters of bearings are normally distributed with mean 2.010 cm and standard deviation 0.002 cm, and that the outside diameters of the shafts are normally distributed with mean 2.004 cm and standard deviation 0.001 cm. Determine the distribution of clearance between the parts if random assembly is used. What is the probability that the clearance is positive?

[illegible] Two resistors are connected to a battery as shown in the figure. Find approximate expressions for the

PART 4

Other Statistical Process-Monitoring and Control Techniques

Part III focused on the basic methods of statistical process-control and capability analysis. Many of these techniques, such as the Shewhart control charts, have been in use for well over 75 years. However, the increasing emphasis on variability reduction, yield enhancement, and process improvement along with the success of the basic methods has led to the development of many new techniques for statistical process monitoring and control. This part contains four chapters describing some of these techniques. Chapter 9 presents the cumulative sum (cusum) control chart and the exponentially weighted moving average (EWMA) control chart. These procedures are not really new, since they date from the 1950s, but they are generally considered somewhat more advanced techniques than the Shewhart charts. As we will see, the cusum and the EWMA offer considerable performance improvement relative to Shewhart charts. Cusum and EWMA control charts are very useful in phase II process-monitoring situations. Chapter 10 is a survey of several univariate process control techniques, including methods for short production runs and monitoring techniques suitable for processes in which the data are autocorrelated. Chapter 11 is an introduction to multivariate process monitoring and control, techniques that are applicable when there are two or more related process variables that are of interest. Chapter 12 presents techniques for process control by feedback adjustment. In these systems the output quality characteristic of interest is influenced by a manipulatable process variable, and we use the deviation of the current output from its desired or target value to determine how much adjustment to make so that the next observation will be on target. These feedback control schemes are also called engineering process control, and they are widely used in the chemical and process industries.

Some of the topics presented in this part may require more statistical and mathematical background than the material in Part III. Two very useful references to accompany this section are the panel discussion on statistical process monitoring and control that appeared in the *Journal of Quality Technology* in 1997 [see Montgomery and Woodall (1997)] and the paper on research issues in SPC in the *Journal of Quality Technology* in 1999 [see Woodall and Montgomery (1999)].

9 Time-Weighted Control Charts

CHAPTER OUTLINE

The supplemental material is on the textbook Website www.wiley.com/college/montgomery.

Chapter Overview and Learning Objectives

Chapters 5, 6, and 7 have concentrated on basic SPC methods. The control charts featured in these chapters are predominantly **Shewhart control charts.** These charts are extremely useful in phase I implementation of SPC, where the process is likely to be out of control and experiencing assignable causes that result in large shifts in the monitored parameters. Shewhart charts are also very useful in the diagnostic aspects of bringing an unruly process into statistical control, because the patterns on these charts often provide guidance regarding the nature of the assignable cause.

A major disadvantage of a Shewhart control chart is that it uses only the information about the process contained in the last sample observation and it ignores any information given by the entire sequence of points. This feature makes the Shewhart control chart relatively insensitive to small process shifts, say, on the order of about 1.5σ or less. This potentially makes Shewhart control charts less useful in phase II monitoring problems, where the process tends to operate in control, reliable estimates of the process parameters (such as the mean and standard deviation) are available, and assignable causes do not typically result in large process upsets or disturbances. Of course, other criteria, such as warning limits and other sensitizing rules, can be applied to Shewhart control charts in phase II to improve their performance against small shifts. However, the use of these procedures reduces the simplicity and ease of interpretation of the Shewhart control chart, and as we have previously observed, they also dramatically reduce the average run length of the chart when the process is actually in control. This can be very undesirable in phase II process monitoring.

Two very effective alternatives to the Shewhart control chart may be used when small process shifts are of interest: the **cumulative sum (cusum) control chart**, and the **exponentially weighted moving average (EWMA) control chart.** Cusum and EWMA control charts are excellent alternatives to the Shewhart control chart for phase II process monitoring situations. These control charts are the subject of this chapter.

After careful study of this chapter you should be able to do the following:

1. Set up and use cusum control charts for monitoring the process mean
2. Design a cusum control chart for the mean to obtain specific ARL performance
3. Incorporate a fast initial response feature into the cusum control chart
4. Use a combined Shewhart-cusum monitoring scheme
5. Set up and use EWMA control charts for monitoring the process mean
6. Design an EWMA control chart for the mean to obtain specific ARL performance
7. Understand why the EWMA control chart is robust to the assumption of normality
8. Understand the performance advantage of cusum and EWMA control charts relative to Shewhart control charts
9. Set up and use a control chart based on an ordinary (unweighted) moving average

9.1 The Cumulative Sum Control Chart

9.1.1 Basic Principles: The Cusum Control Chart for Monitoring the Process Mean

Consider the data in Table 9.1, column (a). The first 20 of these observations were drawn at random from a normal distribution with mean $\mu = 10$ and standard deviation $\sigma = 1$. These observations have been plotted on a Shewhart control chart in Fig. 9.1. The center line and

TABLE 9.1
Data for the Cusum Example

Sample, i	(a) x_i	(b) $x_i - 10$	(c) $C_i = (x_i - 10) + C_{i-1}$
1	9.45	−0.55	−0.55
2	7.99	−2.01	−2.56
3	9.29	−0.71	−3.27
4	11.66	1.66	−1.61
5	12.16	2.16	0.55
6	10.18	0.18	0.73
7	8.04	−1.96	−1.23
8	11.46	1.46	0.23
9	9.20	−0.80	−0.57
10	10.34	0.34	−0.23
11	9.03	−0.97	−1.20
12	11.47	1.47	0.27
13	10.51	0.51	0.78
14	9.40	−0.60	0.18
15	10.08	0.08	0.26
16	9.37	−0.63	−0.37
17	10.62	0.62	0.25
18	10.31	0.31	0.56
19	8.52	−1.48	−0.92
20	10.84	0.84	−0.08
21	10.90	0.90	0.82
22	9.33	−0.67	0.15
23	12.29	2.29	2.44
24	11.50	1.50	3.94
25	10.60	0.60	4.54
26	11.08	1.08	5.62
27	10.38	0.38	6.00
28	11.62	1.62	7.62
29	11.31	1.31	8.93
30	10.52	0.52	9.45

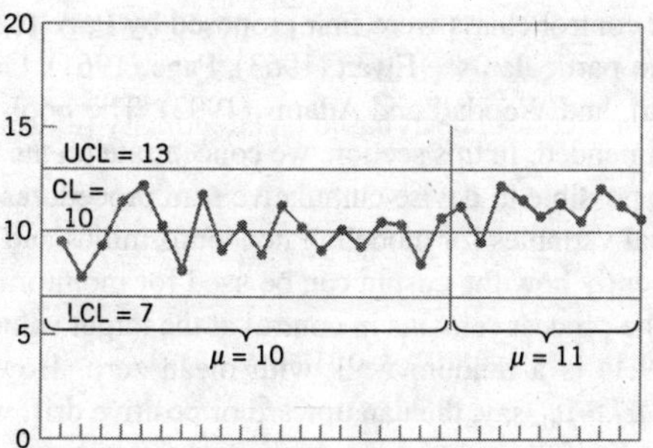

FIGURE 9.1 A Shewhart control chart for the data in Table 9.1.

three-sigma control limits on this chart are at

$$\text{UCL} = 13$$
$$\text{Center line} = 10$$
$$\text{LCL} = 7$$

Note that all 20 observations plot in control.

The last 10 observations in column (a) of Table 9.1 were drawn from a normal distribution with mean $\mu = 11$ and standard deviation $\sigma = 1$. Consequently, we can think of these last 10 observations as having been drawn from the process when it is out of control—that is, after the process has experienced a shift in the mean of 1σ. These last 10 observations are also plotted on the control chart in Fig. 9.1. None of these points plots outside the control limits, so we have no strong evidence that the process is out of control. Note that there is an indication of a shift in process level for the last 10 points, because all but one of the points plot above the center line. However, if we rely on the traditional signal of an out-of-control process, one or more points beyond a three-sigma control limit, then the Shewhart control chart has failed to detect the shift.

The reason for this failure, of course, is the relatively small magnitude of the shift. The Shewhart chart for averages is very effective if the magnitude of the shift is 1.5σ to 2σ or larger. For smaller shifts, it is not as effective. The cumulative sum (or cusum) control chart is a good alternative when small shifts are important.

The cusum chart directly incorporates all the information in the sequence of sample values by plotting the cumulative sums of the deviations of the sample values from a target value. For example, suppose that samples of size $n \geq 1$ are collected, and $\bar{x}_j$ is the average of the jth sample. Then if μ_0 is the target for the process mean, the cumulative sum control chart is formed by plotting the quantity

$$C_i = \sum_{j=1}^{i} \left(\bar{x}_j - \mu_0 \right) \tag{9.1}$$

against the sample number i. C_i is called the cumulative sum up to and including the ith sample. Because they combine information from *several* samples, cumulative sum charts are more effective than Shewhart charts for detecting small process shifts. Furthermore, they are particularly effective with samples of size $n = 1$. This makes the cumulative sum control chart a good candidate for use in the chemical and process industries where rational subgroups are frequently of size 1, and in discrete parts manufacturing with automatic measurement of each part and on-line process monitoring directly at the work center.

Cumulative sum control charts were first proposed by Page (1954) and have been studied by many authors; in particular, see Ewan (1963), Page (1961), Gan (1991), Lucas (1976), Hawkins (1981, 1993a), and Woodall and Adams (1993). The book by Hawkins and Olwell (1998) is highly recommended. In this section, we concentrate on the cumulative sum chart for the process mean. It is possible to devise cumulative sum procedures for other variables, such as Poisson and binomial variables for modeling nonconformities and fraction nonconforming. We will show subsequently how the cusum can be used for monitoring process variability.

We note that if the process remains in control at the target value μ_0, the cumulative sum defined in equation (9.1) is a random walk with mean zero. However, if the mean shifts upward to some value $\mu_1 > \mu_0$, say, then an upward or positive drift will develop in the cumulative sum C_i. Conversely, if the mean shifts downward to some $\mu_1 < \mu_0$, then a downward or negative drift in C_i will develop. Therefore, if a significant trend develops in the plotted points either upward or downward, we should consider this as evidence that the process mean has shifted, and a search for some assignable cause should be performed.

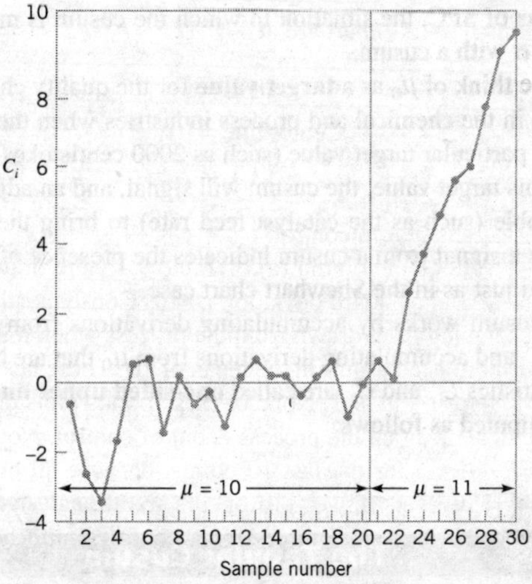

FIGURE 9.2 Plot of the cumulative sum from column (c) of Table 9.1.

This theory can be easily demonstrated by using the data in column (a) of Table 9.1 again. To apply the cusum in equation (9.1) to these observations, we would take $\bar{x} = x_i$ (since our sample size is $n = 1$) and let the target value $\mu_0 = 10$. Therefore, the cusum becomes

$$\begin{aligned} C_i &= \sum_{j=1}^{i} (x_j - 10) \\ &= (x_i - 10) + \sum_{j=1}^{i-1} (x_j - 10) \\ &= (x_i - 10) + C_{i-1} \end{aligned}$$

Column (b) of Table 9.1 contains the differences $x_i - 10$, and the cumulative sums are computed in column (c). The starting value for the cusum, C_0, is taken to be zero. Figure 9.2 plots the cusum from column (c) of Table 9.1. Note that for the first 20 observations where $\mu = 10$, the cusum tends to drift slowly, in this case maintaining values near zero. However, in the last 10 observations, where the mean has shifted to $\mu = 11$, a strong upward trend develops.

Of course, the cusum plot in Fig. 9.2 is not a control chart because it lacks statistical control limits. There are two ways to represent cusums, the **tabular** (or **algorithmic**) **cusum,** and the **V-mask form of the cusum.** Of the two representations, the tabular cusum is preferable. We now present the construction and use of the tabular cusum. We will also briefly discuss the V-mask procedure and indicate why it is not the best representation of a cusum.

9.1.2 The Tabular or Algorithmic Cusum for Monitoring the Process Mean

We now show how a tabular cusum may be constructed for monitoring the mean of a process. Cusums may be constructed both for individual observations and for the averages of rational subgroups. The case of individual observations occurs very often in practice, so that situation will be treated first. Later we will see how to modify these results for rational subgroups.

Let x_i be the ith observation on the process. When the process is in control, x_i has a normal distribution with mean μ_0 and standard deviation σ. We assume that either σ is known or that a reliable estimate is available. These assumptions are very consistent with phase II applications of SPC, the situation in which the cusum is most useful. Later we will discuss monitoring σ with a cusum.

Sometimes we think of μ_0 as a **target value** for the quality characteristic x. This viewpoint is often taken in the chemical and process industries when the objective is to control x (viscosity, say) to a particular target value (such as 2000 centistokes at 100°C). If the process drifts or shifts off this target value, the cusum will signal, and an adjustment is made to some manipulatable variable (such as the catalyst feed rate) to bring the process back on target. Also, in some cases a signal from a cusum indicates the presence of an assignable cause that must be investigated just as in the Shewhart chart case.

The tabular cusum works by accumulating derivations from μ_0 that are above target with one statistic C^+ and accumulating derivations from μ_0 that are below target with another statistic C^-. The statistics C^+ and C^- are called **one-sided upper and lower cusums,** respectively. They are computed as follows:

The Tabular Cusum

$$C_i^+ = \max\left[0, x_i - (\mu_0 + K) + C_{i-1}^+\right] \tag{9.2}$$

$$C_i^- = \max\left[0, (\mu_0 - K) - x_i + C_{i-1}^-\right] \tag{9.3}$$

where the starting values are $C_0^+ = C_0^- = 0$.

In equations (9.2) and (9.3), K is usually called the **reference value** (or the **allowance,** or the **slack value**), and it is often chosen about halfway between the target μ_0 and the out-of-control value of the mean μ_1 that we are interested in detecting quickly.

Thus, if the shift is expressed in standard deviation units as $\mu_1 = \mu_0 + \delta\sigma$ (or $\delta = |\mu_1 - \mu_0|/\sigma$), then K is one-half the magnitude of the shift or

$$K = \frac{\delta}{2}\sigma = \frac{|\mu_1 - \mu_0|}{2} \tag{9.4}$$

Note that C_i^+ and C_i^- accumulate deviations from the target value μ_0 that are greater than K, with both quantities reset to zero on becoming negative. If either C_i^+ or C_i^- exceed the **decision interval** H, the process is considered to be out of control.

We have briefly mentioned how to choose K, but how does one choose H? Actually, the proper selection of these two parameters is quite important, as it has substantial impact on the performance of the cusum. We will talk more about this later, but a reasonable value for H is five times the process standard deviation σ.

EXAMPLE 9.1 A Tabular Cusum

Set up the tabular cusum using the data from Table 9.1.

SOLUTION

Recall that the target value is $\mu_0 = 10$, the subgroup size is $n = 1$, the process standard deviation is $\sigma = 1$, and suppose that the magnitude of the shift we are interested in detecting is $1.0\sigma = 1.0(1.0) = 1.0$. Therefore, the out-of-control value of the process mean is $\mu_1 = 10 + 1 = 11$. We will use a tabular cusum with $K = \frac{1}{2}$ (because the shift size is 1.0σ and $\sigma = 1$) and $H = 5$

■ **TABLE 9.2**
The Tabular Cusum for Example 9.1

		(a)			(b)		
Period i	x_i	$x_i - 10.5$	C_i^+	N^+	$9.5 - x_i$	C_i^-	N^-
1	9.45	−1.05	0	0	0.05	0.05	1
2	7.99	−2.51	0	0	1.51	1.56	2
3	9.29	−1.21	0	0	0.21	1.77	3
4	11.66	1.16	1.16	1	−2.16	0	0
5	12.16	1.66	2.82	2	−2.66	0	0
6	10.18	−0.32	2.50	3	−0.68	0	0
7	8.04	−2.46	0.04	4	1.46	1.46	1
8	11.46	0.96	1.00	5	−1.96	0	0
9	9.20	−1.3	0	0	0.30	0.30	1
10	10.34	−0.16	0	0	−0.84	0	0
11	9.03	−1.47	0	0	0.47	0.47	1
12	11.47	0.97	0.97	1	−1.97	0	0
13	10.51	0.01	0.98	2	−1.01	0	0
14	9.40	−1.10	0	0	0.10	0.10	1
15	10.08	−0.42	0	0	−0.58	0	0
16	9.37	−1.13	0	0	0.13	0.13	1
17	10.62	0.12	0.12	1	−1.12	0	0
18	10.31	−0.19	0	0	−0.81	0	0
19	8.52	−1.98	0	0	0.98	0.98	1
20	10.84	0.34	0.34	1	−1.34	0	0
21	10.90	0.40	0.74	2	−1.40	0	0
22	9.33	−1.17	0	0	0.17	0.17	1
23	12.29	1.79	1.79	1	−2.79	0	0
24	11.50	1.00	2.79	2	−2.00	0	0
25	10.60	0.10	2.89	3	−1.10	0	0
26	11.08	0.58	3.47	4	−1.58	0	0
27	10.38	−0.12	3.35	5	−0.88	0	0
28	11.62	1.12	4.47	6	−2.12	0	0
29	11.31	0.81	5.28	7	−1.81	0	0
30	10.52	0.02	5.30	8	−1.02	0	0

(because the recommended value of the decision interval is $H = 5\sigma = 5(1) = 5$).

Table 9.2 presents the tabular cusum scheme. To illustrate the calculations, consider period 1. The equations for C_i^+ and C_i^- are

$$C_1^+ = \max\left[0, x_1 - 10.5 + C_0^+\right]$$

and

$$C_1^- = \max\left[0, 9.5 - x_1 + C_0^-\right]$$

since $K = 0.5$ and $\mu_0 = 10$. Now $x_1 = 9.45$, so since $C_0^+ = C_0^- = 0$,

$$C_1^+ = \max[0, 9.45 - 10.5 + 0] = 0$$

and

$$C_1^- = \max[0, 9.5 - 9.45 + 0] = 0.05$$

For period 2, we would use

$$\begin{aligned} C_2^+ &= \max\left[0, x_2 - 10.5 + C_1^+\right] \\ &= \max\left[0, x_2 - 10.5 + 0\right] \end{aligned}$$

and

$$\begin{aligned} C_2^- &= \max\left[0, 9.5 - x_2 + C_1^-\right] \\ &= \max\left[0, 9.5 - x_2 + 0.05\right] \end{aligned}$$

Since $x_2 = 7.99$, we obtain

$$C_2^+ = \max[0, 7.99 - 10.5 + 0] = 0$$

(*continued*)

and

$$C_2^- = \max[0, 9.5 - 7.99 + 0.05] = 1.56$$

Panels (a) and (b) of Table 9.2 summarize the remaining calculations. The quantities N^+ and N^- in Table 9.2 indicate the number of consecutive periods that the cusums C_i^+ or C_i^- have been nonzero.

The cusum calculations in Table 9.2 show that the upper-side cusum at period 29 is $C_{29}^+ = 5.28$. Since this is the first period at which $C_i^+ > H = 5$, we would conclude that the process is out of control at that point. The tabular cusum also indicates when the shift probably occurred. The counter N^+ records the number of consecutive periods since the upper-side cusum C_i^+ rose above the value of zero. Since $N^+ = 7$ at period 29, we would conclude that the process was last in control at period $29 - 7 = 22$, so the shift likely occurred between periods 22 and 23.

It is useful to present a graphical display for the tabular cusum. These charts are sometimes called **cusum status charts.** They are constructed by plotting C_i^+ and C_i^- versus the sample number. Figure 9.3*a* shows the cusum status chart for the data in Example 9.1. Each vertical bar represents the value of C_i^+ and C_i^- in period *i*. With the decision interval plotted on the chart, the cusum status chart resembles a Shewhart control chart. We have also plotted the observations x_i for each period on the cusum status chart as the solid dots. This frequently helps the user of the control chart to visualize the actual process performance that has led to a particular value of the cusum. Some computer software packages have implemented the cusum status chart. Figure 9.3*b* shows the Minitab version. In Minitab, the lower cusum is defined as

$$C_i^- = \min\left(0, x_i - \mu_0 + k + C_{i-1}^-\right)$$

This results in a lower cusum that is always ≤ 0 [it is the negative of the lower cusum value from equation (9.3)]. Note in Figure 9.3*b* that the values of the lower cusum range from 0 to −5.

The action taken following an out-of-control signal on a cusum control scheme is identical to that with any control chart; one should search for the assignable cause, take any corrective action required, and then reinitialize the cusum at zero. The cusum is particularly helpful in determining when the assignable cause has occurred; as we noted in the previous example, just count backward from the out-of-control signal to the time period when the cusum lifted above zero to find the first period following the process shift. The counters N^+ and N^- are used in this capacity.

In situations where an adjustment to some manipulatable variable is required in order to bring the process back to the target value μ_0, it may be helpful to have an estimate of the new process mean following the shift. This can be computed from

$$\hat{\mu} = \begin{cases} \mu_0 + K + \dfrac{C_i^+}{N^+}, & \text{if } C_i^+ > H \\ \mu_0 - K - \dfrac{C_i^-}{N^-}, & \text{if } C_i^- > H \end{cases} \tag{9.5}$$

To illustrate the use of equation (9.5), consider the cusum in period 29 with $C_{29}^+ = 5.28$. From equation (9.5), we would estimate the new process average as

$$\begin{aligned} \hat{\mu} &= \mu_0 + K + \frac{C_{29}^+}{N^+} \\ &= 10.0 + 0.5 + \frac{5.28}{7} \\ &= 11.25 \end{aligned}$$

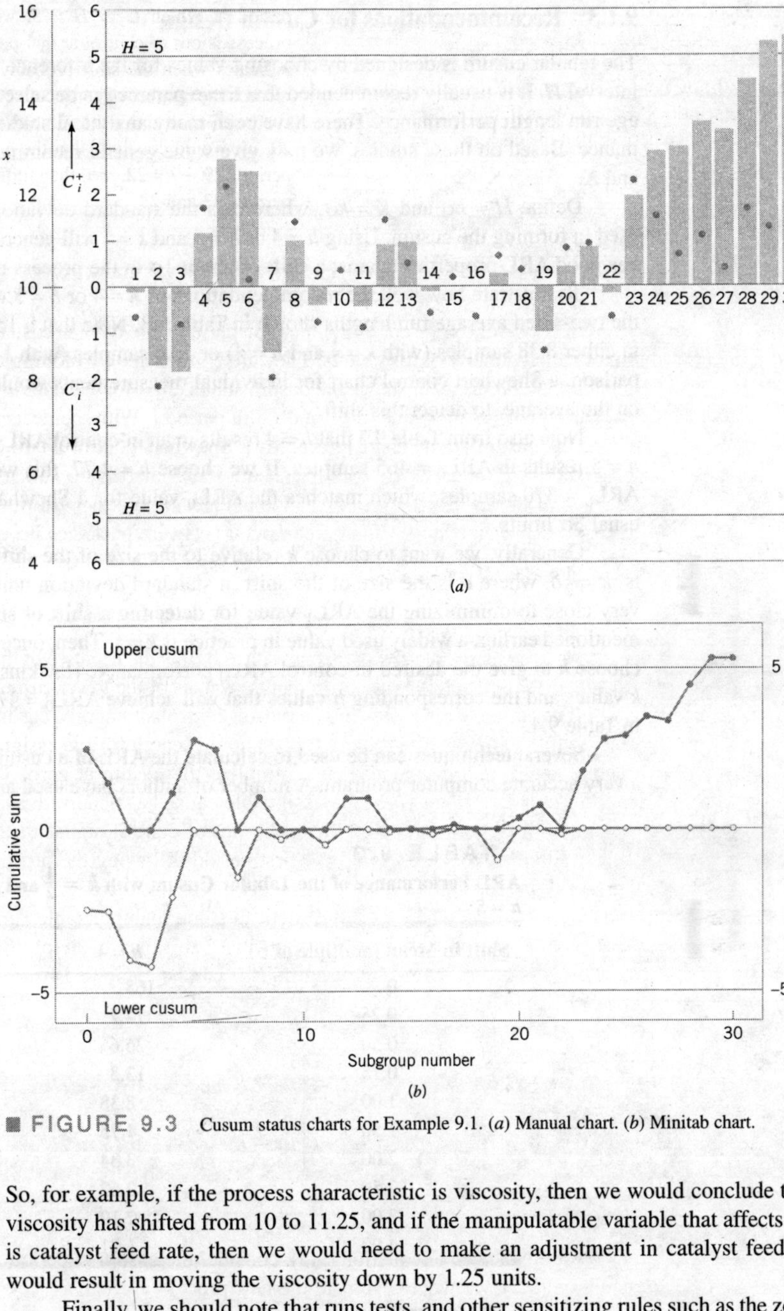

■ FIGURE 9.3 Cusum status charts for Example 9.1. (*a*) Manual chart. (*b*) Minitab chart.

So, for example, if the process characteristic is viscosity, then we would conclude that mean viscosity has shifted from 10 to 11.25, and if the manipulatable variable that affects viscosity is catalyst feed rate, then we would need to make an adjustment in catalyst feed rate that would result in moving the viscosity down by 1.25 units.

Finally, we should note that runs tests, and other sensitizing rules such as the zone rules, cannot be safely applied to the cusum, because successive values of C_i^+ and C_i^- are not independent. In fact, the cusum can be thought of as a weighted average, where the weights are stochastic or random. For example, consider the cusum shown in Table 9.2. The cusum at period 30 is $C_{30}^+ = 5.30$. This can be thought of as a weighted average in which we give equal weight to the last $N^+ = 8$ observations and weight zero to all other observations.

9.1.3 Recommendations for Cusum Design

The tabular cusum is designed by choosing values for the reference value K and the decision interval H. It is usually recommended that these parameters be selected to provide good average run length performance. There have been many analytical studies of cusum ARL performance. Based on these studies, we may give some general recommendations for selecting H and K.

Define $H = h\sigma$ and $K = k\sigma$, where σ is the standard deviation of the sample variable used in forming the cusum. Using $h = 4$ or $h = 5$ and $k = \frac{1}{2}$ will generally provide a cusum that has good ARL properties against a shift of about 1σ in the process mean.

To illustrate how well the recommendations of $h = 4$ or $h = 5$ with $k = \frac{1}{2}$ work, consider the two-sided average run lengths shown in Table 9.3. Note that a 1σ shift would be detected in either 8.38 samples (with $k = \frac{1}{2}$ and $h = 4$) or 10.4 samples (with $k = \frac{1}{2}$ and $h = 5$). By comparison, a Shewhart control chart for individual measurements would require 43.96 samples, on the average, to detect this shift.

Note also from Table 9.3 that $h = 4$ results in an in-control $ARL_0 = 168$ samples, whereas $h = 5$ results in $ARL_0 = 465$ samples. If we choose $h = 4.77$, this will provide a cusum with $ARL_0 = 370$ samples, which matches the ARL_0 value for a Shewhart control chart with the usual 3σ limits.

Generally, we want to choose k relative to the size of the shift we want to detect; that is, $k = \frac{1}{2}\delta$, where δ is the size of the shift in standard deviation units. This approach comes very close to minimizing the ARL_1 value for detecting a shift of size δ for fixed ARL_0. As mentioned earlier, a widely used value in practice is $k = \frac{1}{2}$. Then, once k is selected, you should choose h to give the desired in-control ARL_0 performance. Hawkins (1993a) gives a table of k values and the corresponding h values that will achieve $ARL_0 = 370$. These are reproduced in Table 9.4.

Several techniques can be used to calculate the ARL of a cusum. Vance (1986) provides a very accurate computer program. A number of authors have used an approach to calculating

■ **TABLE 9.3**

ARL Performance of the Tabular Cusum with $k = \frac{1}{2}$ and $h = 4$ or $h = 5$

Shift in Mean (multiple of σ)	$h = 4$	$h = 5$
0	168	465
0.25	74.2	139
0.50	26.6	38.0
0.75	13.3	17.0
1.00	8.38	10.4
1.50	4.75	5.75
2.00	3.34	4.01
2.50	2.62	3.11
3.00	2.19	2.57
4.00	1.71	2.01

■ **TABLE 9.4**

Values of k and the Corresponding Values of h That Give $ARL_0 = 370$ for the Two-Sided Tabular Cusum [from Hawkins (1993a)]

k	0.25	0.5	0.75	1.0	1.25	1.5
h	8.01	4.77	3.34	2.52	1.99	1.61

ARLs due to Brook and Evans (1972) that is based on approximating transitions from the in-control to the out-of-control state with a Markov chain.[1] Hawkins (1992) has provided a simple but very accurate ARL calculation procedure based on an approximating equation. His approximation requires a table of constants to apply and is accurate to within 1%–3% of the true ARL value. Woodall and Adams (1993) recommend the ARL approximation given by Siegmund (1985) because of its simplicity. For a **one-sided cusum** (that is, C_i^+ or C_i^-) with parameters h and k, Siegmund's approximation is

$$\text{ARL} = \frac{\exp(-2\Delta b) + 2\Delta b - 1}{2\Delta^2} \tag{9.6}$$

for $\Delta \neq 0$, where $\Delta = \delta^* - k$ for the upper one-sided cusum C_i^+, $\Delta = -\delta^* - k$ for the lower one-sided cusum C_i^-, $b = h + 1.166$, and $\delta^* = (\mu_1 - \mu_0)/\sigma$. If $\Delta = 0$, one can use $\text{ARL} = b^2$.

The quantity δ^* represents the shift in the mean, in the units of σ, for which the ARL is to be calculated. Therefore, if $\delta^* = 0$, we would calculate ARL_0 from equation (9.6), whereas if $\delta^* \neq 0$, we would calculate the value of ARL_1 corresponding to a shift of size δ^*. To obtain the ARL of the two-sided cusum from the ARLs of the two one-sided statistics—say, ARL^+ and ARL^-—use

$$\frac{1}{\text{ARL}} = \frac{1}{\text{ARL}^+} + \frac{1}{\text{ARL}^-} \tag{9.7}$$

To illustrate, consider the two-sided cusum with $k = \frac{1}{2}$ and $h = 5$. To find ARL_0 we would first calculate the ARL_0 values for the two-sided schemes—say, ARL_0^+ and ARL_0^-. Set $\delta^* = 0$; then $\Delta = \delta^* - k = 0 - \frac{1}{2} = -\frac{1}{2}$, $b = h + 1.166 = 5 + 1.166 = 6.166$, and from equation (9.6)

$$\text{ARL}_0^+ \simeq \frac{\exp\left[-2\left(-\frac{1}{2}\right)(6.166)\right] + 2\left(-\frac{1}{2}\right)(6.166) - 1}{2\left(-\frac{1}{2}\right)^2} = 938.2$$

By symmetry, we have $\text{ARL}_0^- = \text{ARL}_0^+$, and so from equation (9.7), the in-control ARL for the two-sided cusum is

$$\frac{1}{\text{ARL}_0} = \frac{1}{938.2} + \frac{1}{938.2}$$

or

$$\text{ARL}_0 = 469.1$$

This is very close to the true ARL_0 value of 465 shown in Table 9.3. If the mean shifts by 2σ, then $\delta^* = 2$, $\Delta = 1.5$ for the upper one-sided cusum, $\Delta = -2.5$ for the lower one-sided cusum, and from equations (9.6) and (9.7) we can calculate the approximate ARL_1 of the two-sided cusum as $\text{ARL}_1 = 3.89$. The exact value shown in Table 9.3 is 4.01.

[1]The Brook and Evans Markov chain approach is discussed in the supplemental text material for this chapter. Cusum ARLs can also be determined from integral equations. This approach is also discussed in the supplemental material for this chapter.

One could use Siegmund's approximation and trial-and-error arithmetic to give a control limit that would have any desired ARL. Alternatively, numerical root-finding methods would also work well. Woodall and Adams (1993) give an excellent discussion of this approach.

9.1.4 The Standardized Cusum

Many users of the cusum prefer to standardize the variable x_i before performing the calculations. Let

$$y_i = \frac{x_i - \mu_0}{\sigma} \tag{9.8}$$

be the standardized value of x_i. Then the standardized cusums are defined as follows.

The Standardized Two-Sided Cusum

$$C_i^+ = \max\left[0, y_i - k + C_{i-1}^+\right] \tag{9.9}$$

$$C_i^- = \max\left[0, -k - y_i + C_{i-1}^-\right] \tag{9.10}$$

There are two advantages to standardizing the cusum. First, many cusum charts can now have the same values of k and h, and the choices of these parameters are not scale dependent (that is, they do not depend on σ). Second, a standardized cusum leads naturally to a cusum for controlling variability, as we will see in Section 9.1.8.

9.1.5 Improving Cusum Responsiveness for Large Shifts

We have observed that the cusum control chart is very effective in detecting small shifts. However, the cusum control chart is not as effective as the Shewhart chart in detecting large shifts. An approach to improving the ability of the cusum control chart to detect large process shifts is to use a **combined cusum-Shewhart procedure** for on-line control. Adding the Shewhart control is a very simple modification of the cumulative sum control procedure. The Shewhart control limits should be located approximately 3.5 standard deviations from the center line or target value μ_0. An out-of-control signal on either (or both) charts constitutes an action signal. Lucas (1982) gives a good discussion of this technique. Column (a) of Table 9.5 presents the ARLs of the basic cusum with $k = \frac{1}{2}$ and $h = 5$. Column (b) of Table 9.5 presents the ARLs of the cusum with Shewhart limits added to the individual measurements. As suggested above, the Shewhart limits are at 3.5σ. Note from examining these ARL values that the addition of the Shewhart limits has improved the ability of the procedure to detect larger shifts and has only slightly decreased the in-control ARL_0. We conclude that a combined cusum-Shewhart procedure is an effective way to improve cusum responsiveness to large shifts.

9.1.6 The Fast Initial Response or Headstart Feature

This procedure was devised by Lucas and Crosier (1982) to improve the sensitivity of a cusum at process start-up. Increased sensitivity at process start-up would be desirable if the corrective action did not reset the mean to the target value. The **fast initial response (FIR)** or **headstart** essentially just sets the starting values C_0^+ and C_0^- equal to some nonzero value, typically $H/2$. This is called a 50% headstart.

To illustrate the headstart procedure, consider the data in Table 9.6. These data have a target value of 100, $K = 3$, and $H = 12$. We will use a 50% headstart value of $C_0^+ = C_0^- =$

■ **TABLE 9.5**
ARL Values for Some Modifications of the Basic Cusum with $k = \frac{1}{2}$ and $h = 5$ (If subgroups of size $n > 1$ are used, then $\sigma = \sigma_{\bar{x}} = \sigma/\sqrt{n}$)

Shift in Mean (multiple of σ)	(a) Basic Cusum	(b) Cusum-Shewhart (Shewhart limits at 3.5σ)	(c) Cusum with FIR	(d) FIR Cusum-Shewhart (Shewhart limits at 3.5σ)
0	465	391	430	360
0.25	139	130.9	122	113.9
0.50	38.0	37.20	28.7	28.1
0.75	17.0	16.80	11.2	11.2
1.00	10.4	10.20	6.35	6.32
1.50	5.75	5.58	3.37	3.37
2.00	4.01	3.77	2.36	2.36
2.50	3.11	2.77	1.86	1.86
3.00	2.57	2.10	1.54	1.54
4.00	2.01	1.34	1.16	1.16

■ **TABLE 9.6**
A Cusum with a Headstart, Process Mean Equal to 100

	(a)				(b)		
Period i	x_i	$x_i - 103$	C_i^+	N^+	$97 - x_i$	C_i^-	N^-
1	102	−1	5	1	−5	1	1
2	97	−6	0	0	0	1	2
3	104	1	1	1	−7	0	0
4	93	−6	0	0	4	4	1
5	100	−3	0	0	−3	1	2
6	105	2	2	1	−8	0	0
7	96	−7	0	0	1	1	1
8	98	−5	0	0	−1	0	0
9	105	2	2	1	−8	0	0
10	99	−4	0	0	−2	0	0

$H/2 = 6$. The first 10 samples are in control with mean equal to the target value of 100. Since $x_1 = 102$, the cusums for the first period will be

$$C_i^+ = \max\left[0, x_1 - 103 + C_0^+\right]$$
$$= \max[0, 102 - 103 + 6] = 5$$
$$C_i^- = \max\left[0, 97 - x_1 + C_0^-\right]$$
$$= \max[0, 97 - 102 + 6] = 1$$

Note that the starting cusum value is the headstart $H/2 = 6$. In addition, we see from panels (a) and (b) of Table 9.6 that both cusums decline rapidly to zero from the starting value. In fact, from period 2 onward C_1^+ is unaffected by the headstart, and from period 3 onward C_1^- is unaffected by the headstart. This has occurred because the process is in control at the target value of 100, and several consecutive observations near the target value were observed.

■ TABLE 9.7
A Cusum with a Headstart, Process Mean Equal to 105

		(a)			(b)		
Period i	x_i	$x_i - 103$	C_i^+	N^+	$97 - x_i$	C_i^-	N^-
1	107	4	10	1	−10	0	0
2	102	−1	9	2	−5	0	0
3	109	6	15	3	−12	0	0
4	98	−5	10	4	−1	0	0
5	105	2	12	5	−8	0	0
6	110	7	19	6	−13	0	0
7	101	−2	17	7	−4	0	0
8	103	0	17	8	−6	0	0
9	110	7	24	9	−13	0	0
10	104	1	25	10	−7	0	0

Now suppose the process had been out of control at process start-up, with mean 105. Table 9.7 presents the data that would have been produced by this process and the resulting cusums. Note that the third sample causes C_3^+ to exceed the limit $H = 12$. If no headstart had been used, we would have started with $C_0^+ = 0$, and the cusum would not exceed H until sample number 6.

This example demonstrates the benefits of a headstart. If the process starts in control at the target value, the cusums will quickly drop to zero and the headstart will have little effect on the performance of the cusum procedure. Figure 9.4 illustrates this property of the headstart using the data from Table 9.1. The cusum chart was produced using Minitab. However, if the process starts at some level different from the target value, the headstart will allow the cusum to detect it more quickly, resulting in shorter out-of-control ARL values.

Column (c) of Table 9.5 presents the ARL performance of the basic cusum with the headstart or FIR feature. The ARLs were calculated using a 50% headstart. Note that the ARL values for the FIR cusum are valid for the case when the process is out of control at the time the cusums are reset. When the process is in control, the headstart value quickly drops to zero.

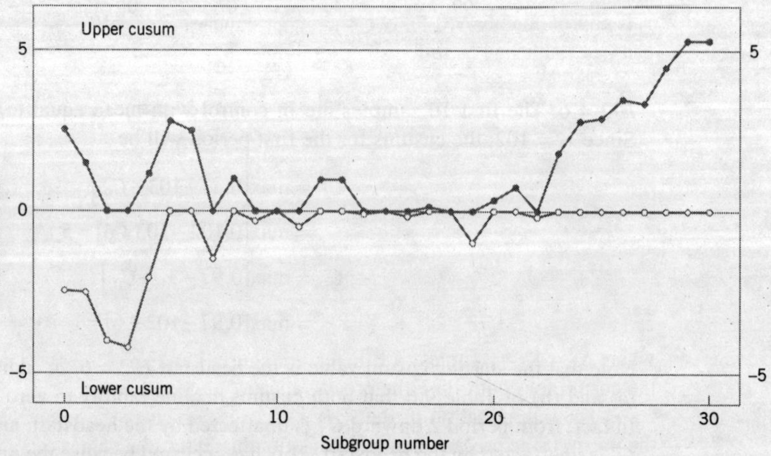

■ FIGURE 9.4 A Minitab cusum status chart for the data in Table 9.1 illustrating the fast initial response or headstart feature.

Thus, if the process is in control when the cusum is reset but shifts out of control later, the more appropriate ARL for such a case should be read from column (a)—that is, the cusum without the FIR feature.

9.1.7 One-Sided Cusums

We have focused primarily on the two-sided cusum. Note that the tabular procedure is constructed by running two one-sided procedures, C_i^+ and C_i^-. There are situations in which only a single one-sided cusum procedure is useful.

For example, consider a chemical process for which the critical quality characteristic is the product viscosity. If viscosity drops below the target (μ_0 = 2000 centistokes at 100°C, say), there is no significant problem, but any increase in viscosity should be detected quickly. A one-sided upper cusum would be an ideal process-monitoring scheme. Siegmund's procedure [equation (9.6)] could be used to calculate the ARLs for the one-sided scheme.

It is also possible to design cusums that have different sensitivity on the upper and lower side. This could be useful in situations where shifts in either direction are of interest, but shifts above the target (say) are more critical than shifts below the target.

9.1.8 A Cusum for Monitoring Process Variability

It is possible to construct cusum control charts for monitoring process variability. Since cusums are usually employed with individual observations, the procedure due to Hawkins (1981) is potentially useful. As before, let x_i be the normally distributed process measurement with mean or target value μ_0 and standard deviation σ. The standardized value of x_i is $y_i = (x_i - \mu_0)/\sigma$. Hawkins (1981, 1993a) suggests creating a new standardized quantity

$$v_i = \frac{\sqrt{|y_i|} - 0.822}{0.349} \tag{9.11}$$

He suggests that the v_i are sensitive to variance changes rather than mean changes. In fact, the statistic v_i is sensitive to both mean and variance changes. Since the in-control distribution of v_i is approximately $N(0,1)$, two one-sided standardized scale (i.e., standard deviation) cusums can be established as follows.

The Scale Cusum

$$S_i^+ = \max\left[0, v_i - k + S_{i-1}^+\right] \tag{9.12}$$

$$S_i^- = \max\left[0, -k - v_i + S_{i-1}^-\right] \tag{9.13}$$

where $S_0^+ = S_0^- = 0$ (unless a FIR feature is used) and the values of k and h are selected as in the cusum for controlling the process mean.

The interpretation of the scale cusum is similar to the interpretation of the cusum for the mean. If the process standard deviation increases, the values of S_i^+ will increase and eventually exceed h, whereas if the standard deviation decreases, the values of S_i^- will increase and eventually exceed h.

Although one could maintain separate cusum status charts for the mean and standard deviation, Hawkins (1993a) suggests plotting them on the same graph. He also provides several excellent examples and further discussion of this procedure. Study of his examples will be of value in improving your ability to detect changes in process variability from the scale cusum. If the scale cusum signals, one would suspect a change in variance, but if both cusums signal, one would suspect a shift in the mean.

9.1.9 Rational Subgroups

Although we have given the development of the tabular cusum for the case of individual observations ($n = 1$), it is easily extended to the case of averages of rational subgroups where the sample size $n > 1$. Simply replace x_i by $\bar{x}_i$ (the sample or subgroup average) in the above formulas, and replace σ with $\sigma_{\bar{x}} = \sigma/\sqrt{n}$.

With Shewhart charts, the use of averages of rational subgroups substantially improves control chart performance. However, this does not always happen with the cusum. If, for example, you have a choice of taking a sample of size $n = 1$ every half hour or a sample consisting of a rational subgroup of size $n = 5$ every 2.5 hours (not that both choices have the same sampling intensity), the cusum will often work best with the choice of $n = 1$ every half hour. For more discussion of this, see Hawkins and Olwell (1998). Only if there is some significant economy of scale or some other valid reason for taking samples of size greater than unity should one consider using $n > 1$ with the cusum.

One practical reason for using rational subgroups of size $n > 1$ is that we could now set up a cusum on the sample **variance** and use it to monitor **process variability.** Cusums for variances are discussed in detail by Hawkins and Olwell (1998); the paper by Chang and Gan (1995) is also recommended. We assume that the observations are normally distributed and that the in-control and out-of-control values are σ_0^2 and σ_1^2, respectively.

Let S_i^2 be the sample variance of the ith subgroup. The cusum for a normal variance is

$$C_i^- = \max\left(0, C_{i-1}^- + S_i^2 - k\right) \tag{9.14}$$

$$C_i^+ = \max\left(0, C_{i-1}^+ + S_i^2 + k\right) \tag{9.15}$$

where $k = [2\ln(\sigma_0/\sigma_1)\sigma_0^2\sigma_1^2/(\sigma_0^2 - \sigma_1^2)]$ with $C_0^- = C_0^+ = 0$. A headstart or FIR feature can also be used with this cusum. Hawkins and Olwell (1998) have a Website with software that supports their book [(the cusum Website of the School of Statistics at the University of Minnesota (www.stat.umn.edu)]. The software provided at this Website can be used for designing this cusum; that is, obtaining the required value of H for a specified target value of ARL_0.

9.1.10 Cusums for Other Sample Statistics

We have concentrated on cusums for sample averages. However, it is possible to develop cusums for other sample statistics such as the ranges and standard deviations of rational subgroups, fractions nonconforming, and defects. These are well-developed procedures and have proven optimality properties for detecting step changes in the parameters. Some of these cusums are discussed in the papers by Lowry, Champ, and Woodall (1995), Gan (1993), Lucas (1985), and White, Keats, and Stanley (1997). The book by Hawkins and Olwell (1998) is an excellent reference.

One variation of the cusum is extremely useful when working with count data and the count rate is very low. In this case, it is frequently more effective to form a cusum using the time between events (TBE). The most common situation encountered in practice is to use the TBE cusum to detect an *increase* in the count rate. This is equivalent to detecting a *decrease* in the time between these events. When the number of counts is generated from a

Poisson distribution, the time between these events will follow an exponential distribution. An appropriate TBE cusum scheme is

$$C_i^- = \max\left[0, K - T_i + C_{i-1}^-\right] \tag{9.16}$$

where K is the reference value and T_i is the time that has elapsed since that last observed count. Lucas (1985) and Bourke (1991) discuss the choice of K and H for this procedure. Borror, Keats, and Montgomery (2003) have examined the robustness of the TBE cusum to the exponential distribution and report that moderate departures from the exponential do not affect its performance.

An alternative and very effective procedure would be to transform the time between observed counts to an approximately normally distributed random variable, as discussed in Section 7.3.5, and use the cusum for monitoring the mean of a normal distribution in Section 9.1.2 instead of equation (9.16).

9.1.11 The V-Mask Procedure

An alternative procedure to the use of a tabular cusum is the V-mask control scheme proposed by Barnard (1959). The V-mask is applied to successive values of the cusum statistic

$$C_i = \sum_{j=1}^{i} y_j = y_i + C_{i-1}$$

where y_i is the standardized observation $y_i = (x_i - \mu_0)/\sigma$. A typical V-mask is shown in Fig. 9.5.

The decision procedure consists of placing the V-mask on the cumulative sum control chart with the point O on the last value of C_i and the line OP parallel to the horizontal axis. If all the previous cumulative sums, $C_1, C_2, \ldots, C_i$ lie within the two arms of the V-mask, the process is in control. However, if any of the cumulative sums lie outside the arms of the mask, the process is considered to be out of control. In actual use, the V-mask would be applied to each new point on the cusum chart as soon as it was plotted, and the arms are assumed to extend backward to the origin. The performance of the V-mask is determined by the lead distance d and the angle θ shown in Fig. 9.5.

The tabular cusum and the V-mask scheme are equivalent if

$$k = A \tan\theta \tag{9.17}$$

and

$$h = A\,d\tan(\theta) = dk \tag{9.18}$$

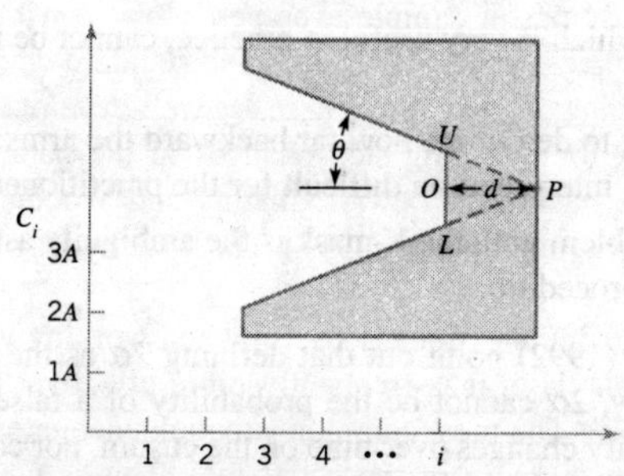

■ FIGURE 9.5 A typical V-mask.

In these two equations, A is the horizontal distance on the V-mask plot between successive points in terms of unit distance on the vertical scale. Refer to Fig. 9.5. For example, to construct a V-mask equivalent to the tabular cusum scheme used in Example 9.1, where $k = \frac{1}{2}$ and $h = 5$, we would select $A = 1$ (say), and then equations (9.17) and (9.18) would be solved as follows:

$$k = A \tan \theta$$

$$\frac{1}{2} = (1) \tan \theta$$

or

$$\theta = 26.57°$$

and

$$h = dk$$

$$5 = d\left(\frac{1}{2}\right)$$

or

$$d = 10$$

That is, the lead distance of the V-mask would be 10 horizontal plotting positions, and the angle opening on the V-mask would be 26.57°.

Johnson (1961) [also see Johnson and Leone (1962a, b, c)] has suggested a method for designing the V-mask; that is, selecting d and θ. He recommends the V-mask parameters

$$\theta = \tan^{-1}\left(\frac{\delta}{2A}\right) \tag{9.19}$$

and

$$d = \left(\frac{2}{\delta^2}\right) \ln\left(\frac{1-\beta}{\alpha}\right) \tag{9.20}$$

where 2α is the greatest allowable probability of a signal when the process mean is on target (a false alarm) and β is the probability of not detecting a shift of size δ. If β is small, which is usually the case, then

$$d \simeq -2\frac{\ln(\alpha)}{\delta} \tag{9.21}$$

We strongly advise **against using the V-mask procedure.** Some of the disadvantages and problems associated with this scheme are as follows:

1. The headstart feature, which is very useful in practice, cannot be implemented with the V-mask.
2. It is sometimes difficult to determine how far backward the arms of the V-mask should extend, thereby making interpretation difficult for the practitioner.
3. Perhaps the biggest problem with the V-mask is the ambiguity associated with α and β in the Johnson design procedure.

Adams, Lowry, and Woodall (1992) point out that defining 2α as the probability of a false alarm is incorrect. Essentially, 2α cannot be the probability of a false alarm on any single sample, because this probability changes over time on the cusum, nor can 2α be the probability of eventually obtaining a false alarm (this probability is, of course, 1). In fact, 2α must be

■ **TABLE 9.8**
Actual Values of ARL_0 for a V-Mask Scheme Designed Using Johnson's Method [Adapted from Table 2 in Woodall and Adams (1993)]

Shift to Be Detected, δ	Values of α [Desired Value of $ARL_0 = 1/(2\alpha)$] 0.00135 (370)	0.001 (500)
1.0	2350.6	3184.5
2.0	1804.5	2435.8
3.0	2194.8	2975.4

the long-run proportion of observations resulting in false alarms. If this is so, then the in-control ARL should be $ARL_0 = 1/(2\alpha)$. However, Johnson's design method produces values of ARL_0 that are substantially larger than $1/(2\alpha)$.

Table 9.8 shows values of ARL_0 for a V-mask scheme designed using Johnson's method. Note that the actual values of ARL_0 are about five times the desired value used in the design procedure. The schemes will also be much less sensitive to shifts in the process mean. Consequently, the use of the V-mask scheme is not a good idea. Unfortunately, it is the default cusum in some SPC software packages.

9.1.12 The Self-Starting Cusum

The cusum is typically used as a phase II procedure; that is, it is applied to monitor a process that has already been through the phase I process and most of the large assignable causes have been removed. In phase II, we typically assume that the process parameters are reasonably well estimated. In practice, this turns out to be a fairly important assumption, as using estimates of the parameters instead of the true values has an effect on the average run length performance of the control chart [this was discussed in Chapter 4; also see the review paper by Jensen et al. (2006)]. Control charts that are designed to detect small shifts are particularly sensitive to this assumption, including the cusum. A Shewhart control chart with the Western Electric rules also would be very sensitive to the estimates of the process parameters. One solution to this is to use a large sample of phase I data to estimate the parameters.

An alternative approach for the cusum is to use a **self-starting cusum** procedure due to Hawkins (1987). The self-starting cusum for the mean of a normally distributed random variable is easy to implement. It can be applied immediately without any need for a phase I sample to estimate the process parameters, in this case the mean μ and the variance σ^2.

Let $\bar{x}_n$ be the average of the first n observations and let $w_n = \sum_{i=1}^{n} (x_i - \bar{x}_n)^2$ be the sum of squared deviations from the average of those observations. Convenient computing formulas to update these quantities after each new observation are

$$\bar{x}_n = \bar{x}_{n-1} + \frac{x_n - \bar{x}_{n-1}}{n}$$

$$w_n = w_{n-1} + \frac{(n-1)(x_n - \bar{x}_{n-1})^2}{n}$$

The sample variance of the first n observations is $s_n^2 = w_n/(n-1)$. Standardize each successive new process observation using

$$T_n = \frac{x_n - \bar{x}_{n-1}}{s_{n-1}}$$

for the case where n is greater than or equal to 3. If the observations are normally distributed, the distribution of $\sqrt{\frac{n-1}{n}}T_n$ is a t distribution with $n-1$ degrees of freedom. The cumulative distribution of T_n is

$$P(T_n \le t) = F_{n-2}\left(t\sqrt{\frac{n-1}{n}}\right)$$

where F_n is the cumulative t distribution with $n-1$ degrees of freedom. It turns out that if the tail area for any continuous random variable is converted to a normal ordinate we obtain a new random variable that is distributed exactly as a standard normal random variable. That is, if Φ^{-1} is the inverse normal cumulative distribution, then the transformation

$$U_n = \Phi^{-1}[F_{n-2}(a_n T_n)] \quad \text{where } a_n = \sqrt{\frac{n-1}{n}}$$

converts the cusum quantity T_n into a standard normal random variable. It turns out that the values of U_n are statistically independent (this isn't obvious, because successive values of U_n share the same data points), so one can plot all values of U_n for $n \ge 3$ on a N(0, 1) cusum. This nicely avoids the problem of using a large sample of phase I data to estimate the process parameters for a conventional cusum.

To illustrate the procedure, consider the data from Table 9.1. The first eight of these observations are shown in Table 9.9. The columns to the right of the data are the running average, the running sum of squared deviations from the average, the running standard deviation, the standardized value of each observation, the t distribution value that corresponds to it, the t distribution tail area, and finally the equivalent inverse normal value. The values of U_n can be handled as any data for a cusum. For example, they could be entered into a tabular cusum and plotted on a cusum status chart.

There is a difference in practical usage of a self-starting cusum in comparison to an ordinary cusum surrounding the out-of-control situation. In a standard or ordinary cusum, the cusum moves upward indefinitely following an upward shift in the mean until the assignable cause is discovered. However, in a self-starting cusum the plotted statistic will begin moving upward following the shift, but as the shifted values are entered into the calculations of the running average and running standard deviation, they move the running mean closer to the new shifted value of the mean and the running standard deviation gets larger. Consequently, if the process is not adjusted and the cusum reset, the self-starting cusum will turn back downward. Therefore, the users of a self-starting cusum should to take investigative and corrective action immediately following an out-of-control signal. When restarting, it is also necessary to remove the out-of-control data from the running average and running standard deviation. Outliers can also impact the self-starting cusum, principally by inflating the running standard

■ **TABLE 9.9**

Calculations for a Self-Starting Cusum

n	x_n	$\bar{x}_n$	w_n	S_n	T_n	a_nT_n	$F_{n-2}(a_nT_n)$	U_n
1	9.45	9.45	0	—	—	—	—	—
2	7.99	8.72	1.07	1.03	—	—	—	—
3	9.29	8.91	1.25	0.80	0.55	0.45	0.6346	0.34406
4	11.66	9.60	6.92	1.52	3.44	2.98	0.9517	1.66157
5	12.16	10.11	12.16	1.75	1.68	1.50	0.8847	1.19881
6	10.18	10.12	12.16	1.56	0.04	0.04	0.5152	0.03811
7	8.04	9.82	15.87	1.63	−1.33	−1.23	0.1324	−1.11512
8	11.46	10.03	18.22	1.62	1.01	0.94	0.8107	0.88048

deviation. Maintaining a Shewhart control chart on the observations can give protection against this problem. Refer to Hawkins and Olwell (1998) for more suggestions and discussion.

9.2 The Exponentially Weighted Moving Average Control Chart

The exponentially weighted moving average (EWMA) control chart is also a good alternative to the Shewhart control chart when we are interested in detecting small shifts. The performance of the EWMA control chart is approximately equivalent to that of the cumulative sum control chart, and in some ways it is easier to set up and operate. As with the cusum, the EWMA is typically used with individual observations, and so, consequently, we will discuss that case first. We will also give the results for rational subgroups of size $n > 1$.

9.2.1 The Exponentially Weighted Moving Average Control Chart for Monitoring the Process Mean

The EWMA control chart was introduced by Roberts (1959). See also Crowder (1987a, 1989) and Lucas and Saccucci (1990) for good discussions of the EWMA. The exponentially weighted moving average is defined as

$$z_i = \lambda x_i + (1-\lambda)z_{i-1} \tag{9.22}$$

where $0 < \lambda \leq 1$ is a constant and the starting value (required with the first sample at $i = 1$) is the process target, so that

$$z_0 = \mu_0$$

Sometimes the average of preliminary data is used as the starting value of the EWMA, so that $z_0 = \bar{x}$.

To demonstrate that the EWMA z_i is a weighted average of all previous sample means, we may substitute for z_{i-1} on the right-hand side of equation (9.22) to obtain

$$\begin{aligned} z_i &= \lambda x_i + (1-\lambda)\left[\lambda x_{i-1} + (1-\lambda)z_{i-2}\right] \\ &= \lambda x_i + \lambda(1-\lambda)x_{i-1} + (1-\lambda)^2 z_{i-2} \end{aligned}$$

Continuing to substitute recursively for z_{i-j}, $j = 2, 3, \ldots, t$, we obtain

$$z_i = \lambda \sum_{j=0}^{i-1} (1-\lambda)^j x_{i-j} + (1-\lambda)^i z_0 \tag{9.23}$$

The weights $\lambda(1-\lambda)^j$ decrease geometrically with the age of the sample mean. Furthermore, the weights sum to unity, since

$$\lambda \sum_{j=0}^{i-1} (1-\lambda)^j = \lambda\left[\frac{1-(1-\lambda)^i}{1-(1-\lambda)}\right] = 1-(1-\lambda)^i$$

If $\lambda = 0.2$, then the weight assigned to the current sample mean is 0.2 and the weights given to the preceding means are 0.16, 0.128, 0.1024, and so forth. A comparison of these weights with those of a five-period moving average is shown in Fig. 9.6. Because these weights decline geometrically when connected by a smooth curve, the EWMA is sometimes called a **geometric moving average (GMA).** The EWMA is used extensively in time series modeling and in forecasting [see Box, Jenkins, and Reinsel (1994) and Montgomery, Johnson, and Gardiner (1990)]. Since the EWMA can be viewed as a weighted average of all past and current

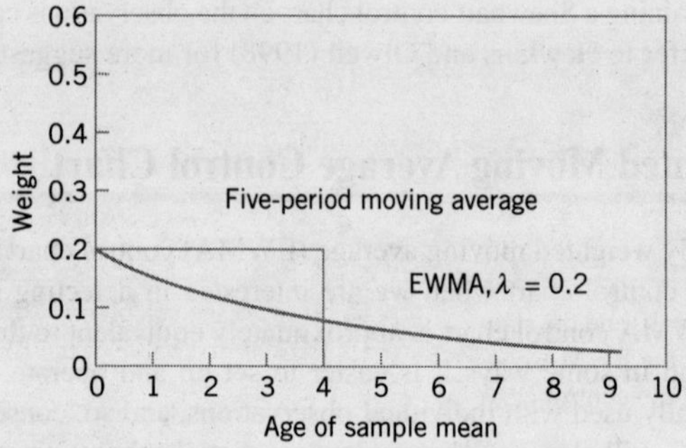

■ **FIGURE 9.6** Weights of past sample means.

observations, it is very insensitive to the normality assumption. It is therefore an ideal control chart to use with individual observations.

If the observations x_i are independent random variables with variance σ^2, then the variance of z_i is

$$\sigma_{z_i}^2 = \sigma^2\left(\frac{\lambda}{2-\lambda}\right)\left[1-(1-\lambda)^{2i}\right] \tag{9.24}$$

Therefore, the EWMA control chart would be constructed by plotting z_i versus the sample number i (or time). The center line and control limits for the EWMA control chart are as follows.

The EWMA Control Chart

$$\text{UCL} = \mu_0 + L\sigma\sqrt{\frac{\lambda}{(2-\lambda)}\left[1-(1-\lambda)^{2i}\right]} \tag{9.25}$$

$$\text{Center line} = \mu_0$$

$$\text{LCL} = \mu_0 - L\sigma\sqrt{\frac{\lambda}{(2-\lambda)}\left[1-(1-\lambda)^{2i}\right]} \tag{9.26}$$

In equations (9.25) and (9.26), the factor L is the width of the control limits. We will discuss the choice of the parameters L and λ shortly.

Note that the term $[1 - (1 - \lambda)^{2i}]$ in equations (9.25) and (9.26) approaches unity as i gets larger. This means that after the EWMA control chart has been running for several time periods, the control limits will approach steady-state values given by

$$\text{UCL} = \mu_0 + L\sigma\sqrt{\frac{\lambda}{(2-\lambda)}} \tag{9.27}$$

and

$$\text{LCL} = \mu_0 - L\sigma\sqrt{\frac{\lambda}{(2-\lambda)}} \tag{9.28}$$

However, we strongly recommend using the exact control limits in equations (9.25) and (9.26) for small values of i. This will greatly improve the performance of the control chart in detecting an off-target process immediately after the EWMA is started up.

EXAMPLE 9.2 Constructing an EWMA Control Chart

Set up an EWMA control chart with $\lambda = 0.10$ and $L = 2.7$ to the data in Table 9.1.

SOLUTION

Recall that the target value of the mean is $\mu_0 = 10$ and the standard deviation is $\sigma = 1$. The calculations for the EWMA control chart are summarized in Table 9.10, and the control chart (from Minitab) is shown in Fig. 9.7.

To illustrate the calculations, consider the first observation, $x_1 = 9.45$. The first value of the EWMA is

$$\begin{aligned} z_1 &= \lambda x_1 + (1-\lambda)z_0 \\ &= 0.1(9.45) + 0.9(10) \\ &= 9.945 \end{aligned}$$

■ **TABLE 9.10**
EWMA Calculations for Example 9.2

Subgroup, i	* = Beyond Limits x_i	EWMA, z_i	Subgroup, i	* = Beyond Limits x_i	EWMA, z_i
1	9.45	9.945	16	9.37	9.98426
2	7.99	9.7495	17	10.62	10.0478
3	9.29	9.70355	18	10.31	10.074
4	11.66	9.8992	19	8.52	9.91864
5	12.16	10.1253	20	10.84	10.0108
6	10.18	10.1307	21	10.9	10.0997
7	8.04	9.92167	22	9.33	10.0227
8	11.46	10.0755	23	12.29	10.2495
9	9.2	9.98796	24	11.5	10.3745
10	10.34	10.0232	25	10.6	10.3971
11	9.03	9.92384	26	11.08	10.4654
12	11.47	10.0785	27	10.38	10.4568
13	10.51	10.1216	28	11.62	10.5731
14	9.4	10.0495	29	11.31	10.6468*
15	10.08	10.0525	30	10.52	10.6341*

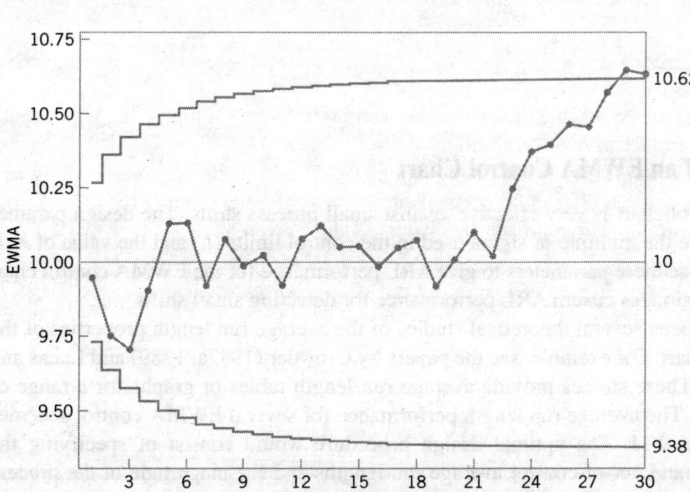

■ **FIGURE 9.7** The EWMA control chart for Example 9.2.

(continued)

Therefore, $z_1 = 9.945$ is the first value plotted on the control chart in Fig. 9.7. The second value of the EWMA is

$$\begin{aligned} z_2 &= \lambda x_2 + (1-\lambda)z_1 \\ &= 0.1(7.99) + 0.9(9.945) \\ &= 9.7495 \end{aligned}$$

The other values of the EWMA statistic are computed similarly.

The control limits in Fig. 9.7 are found using equations (9.25) and (9.26). For period $i = 1$,

$$\begin{aligned} \text{UCL} &= \mu_0 + L\sigma\sqrt{\frac{\lambda}{(2-\lambda)}\left[1-(1-\lambda)^{2i}\right]} \\ &= 10 + 2.7(1)\sqrt{\frac{0.1}{(2-0.1)}\left[1-(1-0.1)^{2(1)}\right]} \\ &= 10.27 \end{aligned}$$

and

$$\begin{aligned} \text{LCL} &= \mu_0 - L\sigma\sqrt{\frac{\lambda}{(2-\lambda)}\left[1-(1-\lambda)^{2i}\right]} \\ &= 10 - 2.7(1)\sqrt{\frac{0.1}{(2-0.1)}\left[1-(1-0.1)^{2(1)}\right]} \\ &= 9.73 \end{aligned}$$

For period 2, the limits are

$$\begin{aligned} \text{UCL} &= \mu_0 + L\sigma\sqrt{\frac{\lambda}{(2-\lambda)}\left[1-(1-\lambda)^{2i}\right]} \\ &= 10 + 2.7(1)\sqrt{\frac{0.1}{(2-0.1)}\left[1-(1-0.1)^{2(2)}\right]} \\ &= 10.36 \end{aligned}$$

and

$$\begin{aligned} \text{LCL} &= \mu_0 - L\sigma\sqrt{\frac{\lambda}{(2-\lambda)}\left[1-(1-\lambda)^{2i}\right]} \\ &= 10 - 2.7(1)\sqrt{\frac{0.1}{(2-0.1)}\left[1-(1-0.1)^{2(2)}\right]} \\ &= 9.64 \end{aligned}$$

Note from Fig. 9.7 that the control limits increase in width as i increases from $i = 1, 2, \ldots,$ until they stabilize at the steady-state values given by equations (9.27) and (9.28)

$$\begin{aligned} \text{UCL} &= \mu_0 + L\sigma\sqrt{\frac{\lambda}{(2-\lambda)}} \\ &= 10 + 2.7(1)\sqrt{\frac{0.1}{(2-0.1)}} \\ &= 10.62 \end{aligned}$$

and

$$\begin{aligned} \text{LCL} &= \mu_0 - L\sigma\sqrt{\frac{\lambda}{(2-\lambda)}} \\ &= 10 - 2.7(1)\sqrt{\frac{0.1}{(2-0.1)}} \\ &= 9.38 \end{aligned}$$

The EWMA control chart in Fig. 9.7 signals at observation 28, so we would conclude that the process is out of control.

9.2.2 Design of an EWMA Control Chart

The EWMA control chart is very effective against small process shifts. The design parameters of the chart are the multiple of sigma used in the control limits (L) and the value of λ. It is possible to choose these parameters to give ARL performance for the EWMA control chart that closely approximates cusum ARL performance for detecting small shifts.

There have been several theoretical studies of the average run length properties of the EWMA control chart. For example, see the papers by Crowder (1987a, 1989) and Lucas and Saccucci (1990). These studies provide average run length tables or graphs for a range of values of λ and L. The average run length performance for several EWMA control schemes is shown in Table 9.11. The optimal design procedure would consist of specifying the desired in-control and out-of-control average run lengths and the magnitude of the process shift that is anticipated, and then to select the combination of λ and L that provide the desired ARL performance.

TABLE 9.11
Average Run Lengths for Several EWMA Control Schemes [Adapted from Lucas and Saccucci (1990)]

Shift in Mean (multiple of σ)	$L = 3.054$ $\lambda = 0.40$	2.998 0.25	2.962 0.20	2.814 0.10	2.615 0.05
0	500	500	500	500	500
0.25	224	170	150	106	84.1
0.50	71.2	48.2	41.8	31.3	28.8
0.75	28.4	20.1	18.2	15.9	16.4
1.00	14.3	11.1	10.5	10.3	11.4
1.50	5.9	5.5	5.5	6.1	7.1
2.00	3.5	3.6	3.7	4.4	5.2
2.50	2.5	2.7	2.9	3.4	4.2
3.00	2.0	2.3	2.4	2.9	3.5
4.00	1.4	1.7	1.9	2.2	2.7

In general, we have found that values of λ in the interval $0.05 \le \lambda \le 0.25$ work well in practice, with $\lambda = 0.05$, $\lambda = 0.10$, and $\lambda = 0.20$ being popular choices. A good rule of thumb is to use smaller values of λ to detect smaller shifts. We have also found that $L = 3$ (the usual three-sigma limits) works reasonably well, particularly with the larger value of λ, although when λ is small—say, $\lambda \le 0.1$—there is an advantage in reducing the width of the limits by using a value of L between about 2.6 and 2.8. Recall that in Example 9.2, we used $\lambda = 0.1$ and $L = 2.7$. We would expect this choice of parameters to result in an in-control ARL of $ARL_0 \simeq 500$ and an ARL for detecting a shift of one standard deviation in the mean of $ARL_1 = 10.3$. Thus this design is approximately equivalent to the cusum with $h = 5$ and $k = \frac{1}{2}$.

Hunter (1989) has also studied the EWMA and suggested choosing λ so that the weight given to current and previous observations matches as closely as possible the weights given to these observations by a Shewhart chart with the Western Electric rules. This results in a recommended value of $\lambda = 0.4$. If $L = 3.054$, then Table 9.11 indicates that this chart would have $ARL_0 = 500$ and for detecting a shift of one standard deviation in the process mean, the $ARL_1 = 14.3$.

There is one potential concern about an EWMA with a small value of λ. If the value of the EWMA is on one side of the center line when a shift in the mean in the opposite direction occurs, it could take the EWMA several periods to react to the shift, because the small λ does not weight the new data very heavily. This is called the **inertia effect.** It can reduce the effectiveness of the EWMA in shift detection.

Woodall and Mahmoud (2005) have investigated the inertial properties of several different types of control charts. They define the **signal resistance of a control chart** to be the largest standardized deviation of the sample mean from the target or in-control value not leading to an immediate out-of-control signal. For a Shewhart $\bar{x}$ chart, the signal resistance is $SR(\bar{x}) = L$, the multiplier used to obtain the control limits. Thus the signal resistance is constant. For the EWMA control chart, the signal resistance is

$$SR(EWMA) = \frac{L\sqrt{\dfrac{\lambda}{2-\lambda}} - (1-\lambda)w}{\lambda}$$

where w is the value of the EWMA statistic. For the EWMA, the maximum value of the signal resistance averaged over all values of the EWMA statistic is $L\sqrt{(2-\lambda)/\lambda}$, if the chart has the asymptotic limits. These results apply for any sample size, as they are given in terms of shifts expressed as multiples of the standard error.

Clearly the signal resistance of the EWMA control chart depends on the value chosen for λ, with smaller values leading to larger values of the maximum signal resistance. This is in a sense unfortunate, because we almost always want to use the EWMA with a small value of λ as this results in good ARL performance in detecting small shifts. As we will see in Section 9.2.3, small values of λ are also desirable because they make the EWMA chart quite insensitive to normality of the process data. Woodall and Mahmoud (2005) recommend always using a Shewhart chart in conjunction with an EWMA (especially if λ is small) as one way to counteract the signal resistance.

Like the cusum, the EWMA performs well against small shifts but does not react to large shifts as quickly as the Shewhart chart. A good way to further improve the sensitivity of the procedure to large shifts without sacrificing the ability to detect small shifts quickly is to combine a Shewhart chart with the EWMA. These combined Shewhart-EWMA control procedures are effective against both large and small shifts. When using such schemes, we have found it helpful to use slightly wider than usual limits on the Shewhart chart (say, 3.25-sigma, or even 3.5-sigma). It is also possible to plot *both* x_i (or $\overline{x}_i$) and the EWMA statistic z_i on the same control chart along with both the Shewhart and EWMA limits. This produces one chart for the combined control procedure that operators quickly become adept at interpreting. When the plots are computer generated, different colors or plotting symbols can be used for the two sets of control limits and statistics.

9.2.3 Robustness of the EWMA to Non-normality

When discussing the Shewhart control chart for individuals in Chapter 6, we observed that the individuals chart was very sensitive to non-normality in the sense that the actual in-control ARL (ARL_0) would be considerably less than the "advertised" or expected value based on the assumption of a normal distribution. Borror, Montgomery, and Runger (1999) compared the ARL performance of the Shewhart individuals chart and the EWMA control chart for the case of non-normal distributions. Specifically, they used the gamma distribution to represent the case of skewed distributions and the *t* distribution to represent symmetric distributions with heavier tails than the normal.

The ARL_0 of the Shewhart individuals chart and several EWMA control charts for these non-normal distributions are given in Tables 9.12 and 9.13. Two aspects of the information in these tables are very striking. First, even moderately non-normal distributions have the effect of greatly reducing the in-control ARL of the Shewhart individuals chart. This will, of course, dramatically increase the rate of false alarms. Second, an EWMA with $\lambda = 0.05$ or $\lambda = 0.10$ and an appropriately chosen control limit will perform very well against both normal and non-normal distributions. With $\lambda = 0.05$ and $L = 2.492$ the ARL_0 for the EWMA is within approx-

■ **TABLE 9.12**
In-Control ARLs for the EWMA and the Individuals Control Charts for Various Gamma Distributions

	EWMA			Shewhart
λ	**0.05**	**0.1**	**0.2**	**1**
L	**2.492**	**2.703**	**2.86**	**3.00**
Normal	370.4	370.8	370.5	370.4
Gam(4, 1)	372	341	259	97
Gam(3, 1)	372	332	238	85
Gam(2, 1)	372	315	208	71
Gam(1, 1)	369	274	163	55
Gam(0.5, 1)	357	229	131	45

TABLE 9.13
In-Control ARLs for the EWMA and the Individuals Control Charts for Various t Distributions

	EWMA			Shewhart
λ	**0.05**	**0.1**	**0.2**	**1**
L	**2.492**	**2.703**	**2.86**	**3.00**
Normal	370.4	370.8	370.5	370.4
t_{50}	369	365	353	283
t_{40}	369	363	348	266
t_{30}	368	361	341	242
t_{20}	367	355	325	204
t_{15}	365	349	310	176
t_{10}	361	335	280	137
t_8	358	324	259	117
t_6	351	305	229	96
t_4	343	274	188	76

imately 8% of the advertised normal theory in-control ARL_0 of 370, except in the most extreme cases. Furthermore, the shift detection properties of the EWMA are uniformly superior to the Shewhart chart for individuals.

Based on this information, we would recommend a properly designed EWMA as a control chart for individual measurements in a wide range of applications, particularly phase II process monitoring. It is almost a perfectly nonparametric (distribution-free) procedure.

9.2.4 Rational Subgroups

The EWMA control chart is often used with individual measurements. However, if rational subgroups of size $n > 1$ are taken, then simply replace x_i with $\bar{x}_i$ and σ with $\sigma_{\bar{x}} = \sigma/\sqrt{n}$ in the previous equations.

9.2.5 Extensions of the EWMA

There have been numerous extensions and variations of the basic EWMA control chart. In this section, we describe a few of these procedures.

Fast Initial Response Feature. It is possible to add the fast initial response (FIR) or headstart feature to the EWMA. As with the cusum, the advantage of the procedure would be to more quickly detect a process that is off target at start-up.

Two approaches have been suggested. Rhoads, Montgomery, and Mastrangelo (1996) set up two one-sided EWMA charts and start them off at values midway between the target and the control limit. Both one-sided charts are assumed to have the time-varying limits (readers are asked to develop a one-sided EWMA procedure in Exercise 9.35).

Steiner (1999) uses a single control chart but narrows the time-varying limits even further for the first few sample points. He uses an exponentially decreasing adjustment to further narrow the limits, so that the control limits are located a distance

$$\pm L\sigma\left\{\left(1-(1-f)^{1+a(t-1)}\right)\sqrt{\frac{\lambda}{2-\lambda}\left[1-(1-\lambda)^{2t}\right]}\right\}$$

around the target. The constants f and a are to be determined. Steiner suggests choosing a so that the FIR has little effect after about 20 observations. This leads to choosing $a =$

$[-2/\log(1-f)-1]/19$. For example, if $f = 0.5$, then $a = 0.3$. The choice of $f = 0.5$ is attractive because it mimics the 50% headstart often used with cusums.

Both of these procedures perform very well in reducing the ARL to detect an off-target process at start-up. The Steiner procedure is easier to implement in practice.

Monitoring Variability. MacGregor and Harris (1993) discuss the use of EWMA-based statistics for monitoring the process standard deviation. Let x_i be normally distributed with mean μ and standard deviation σ. The **exponentially weighted mean square error (EWMS)** is defined as

$$S_i^2 = \lambda(x_i - \mu)^2 + (1-\lambda)S_{i-1}^2 \tag{9.29}$$

It can be shown that $E(S_i^2) = \sigma^2$ (for large i) and if the observations are independent and normally distributed, then S_i^2/σ^2 has an approximate chi-square distribution with $v = (2-\lambda)/\lambda$ degrees of freedom. Therefore, if σ_0 represents the in-control or target value of the process standard deviation, we could plot $\sqrt{S_i^2}$ on an exponentially weighted root mean square (EWRMS) control chart with control limits given by

$$\text{UCL} = \sigma_0\sqrt{\frac{\chi^2_{v,\alpha/2}}{v}} \tag{9.30}$$

and

$$\text{LCL} = \sigma_0\sqrt{\frac{\chi^2_{v,1-(\alpha/2)}}{v}} \tag{9.31}$$

MacGregor and Harris (1993) point out that the EWMS statistic can be sensitive to shifts in both the process mean and the standard deviation. They suggest replacing μ in equation (9.27) with an estimate $\hat{\mu}_i$ at each point in time. A logical estimate of μ turns out to be the ordinary EWMA z_i. They derive control limits for the resulting exponentially weighted moving variance (EWMV)

$$S_i^2 = \lambda(x_i - z_i)^2 + (1-\lambda)S_{i-1}^2 \tag{9.32}$$

Another approach to monitoring the process standard deviation with an EWMA is in Crowder and Hamilton (1992).

The EWMA for Poisson Data. Just as the cusum can be used as the basis of an effective control chart for Poisson counts, so can a suitably designed EWMA. Borror, Champ, and Rigdon (1998) describe the procedure, show how to design the control chart, and provide an example. If x_i is a count, then the basic EWMA recursion remains unchanged:

$$z_i = \lambda x_i + (1-\lambda)z_{i-1}$$

with $z_0 = \mu_0$ the in-control or target count rate. The control chart parameters are as follows:

$$\begin{aligned} \text{UCL} &= \mu_0 + A_U\sqrt{\frac{\lambda\mu_0}{2-\lambda}\left[1-(1-\lambda)^{2i}\right]} \\ \text{Center line} &= \mu_0 \\ \text{LCL} &= \mu_0 - A_L\sqrt{\frac{\lambda\mu_0}{2-\lambda}\left[1-(1-\lambda)^{2i}\right]} \end{aligned} \tag{9.33}$$

where A_U and A_L are the upper and lower control limit factors. In many applications we would choose $A_U = A_L = A$. Borror, Champ, and Rigdon (1998) give graphs of the ARL performance of the Poisson EWMA control chart as a function of λ and A and for various in-control or target count rates μ_0. Once μ_0 is determined and a value is specified for λ, these charts can be used to select the value of A that results in the desired in-control ARL_0. The authors also show that this control chart has considerably better ability to detect assignable causes than the Shewhart c chart. The Poisson EWMA should be used much more widely in practice.

The EWMA as a Predictor of Process Level. Although we have discussed the EWMA primarily as a statistical process-monitoring tool, it actually has a much broader interpretation. From an SPC viewpoint, the EWMA is roughly equivalent to the cusum in its ability to *monitor* a process and detect the presence of assignable causes that result in a process shift. However, the EWMA provides a **forecast** of where the process mean will be at the next time period. That is, z_i is actually a forecast of the value of the process mean μ at time $i + 1$. Thus, the EWMA could be used as the basis for a dynamic process-control algorithm.

In computer-integrated manufacturing where sensors are used to measure every unit manufactured, a forecast of the process mean based on previous behavior would be very useful. If the forecast of the mean is different from target by a critical amount, then either the operator or some electromechanical control system can make the necessary process adjustment. If the operator makes the adjustment, then he or she must exercise caution and not make adjustments too frequently because this will actually cause process variability to increase. The control limits on the EWMA chart can be used to signal *when* an adjustment is necessary, and the difference between the target and the forecast of the mean μ_{i+1} can be used to determine *how much* adjustment is necessary.

The EWMA can be modified to enhance its ability to forecast the mean. Suppose that the process mean trends or drifts steadily away from the target. The forecasting performance of the EWMA can be improved in this case. First, note that the usual EWMA can be written as

$$\begin{aligned} z_i &= \lambda x_i + (1-\lambda) z_{i-1} \\ &= z_{i-1} + \lambda(x_i - z_{i-1}) \end{aligned}$$

and if we view z_{i-1} as a forecast of the process mean in period i, we can think of $x_i - z_{i-1}$ as the forecast error e_i for period i. Therefore,

$$z_i = z_{i-1} + \lambda e_i \tag{9.34}$$

Thus, the EWMA for period i is equal to the EWMA for period $i - 1$ plus a fraction λ of the forecast error for the mean in period i. Now add a second term to this last equation to give

$$z_i = z_{i-1} + \lambda_1 e_i + \lambda_2 \sum_{j=1}^{i} e_j \tag{9.35}$$

where λ_1 and λ_2 are constants that weight the error at time i and the *sum* of the errors accumulated to time i. If we let $\nabla e_i = e_i - e_{i-1}$ be the first difference of the errors, then we can arrive at a final modification of the EWMA:

$$z_i = z_{i-1} + \lambda_1 e_i + \lambda_2 \sum_{j=1}^{i} e_j + \lambda_3 \nabla e_i \tag{9.36}$$

Note that in this empirical control equation the EWMA in period i (which is the forecast of the process mean in period $i + 1$) equals the current estimate of the mean (z_{i-1} estimates μ_i), plus a term proportional to the error, plus a term related to the sum of the errors, plus a term related to the first difference of the errors. These three terms can be thought of as **proportional, integral,** and **differential** adjustments. The parameters λ_1, λ_2, and λ_3 would be chosen to give the best forecasting performance.

Because the EWMA statistic z_i can be viewed as a **forecast** of the mean of the process at time $i + 1$, we often plot the EWMA statistic one time period ahead. That is, we actually plot z_i at time period $i + 1$ on the control chart. This allows the analyst to visually see how much difference there is between the current observation and the estimate of the current mean of the process. In statistical process-control applications where the mean may "wander" over time, this approach has considerable appeal.

9.3 The Moving Average Control Chart

Both the cusum and the EWMA are **time-weighted** control charts. The EWMA chart uses a weighted average as the chart statistic. Occasionally, another type of time-weighted control chart based on a simple, unweighted **moving average** may be of interest.

Suppose that individual observations have been collected, and let $x_1, x_2, \ldots$ denote these observations. The moving average of span w at time i is defined as

$$M_i = \frac{x_i + x_{i-1} + \cdots + x_{i-w+1}}{w} \tag{9.37}$$

That is, at time period i, the oldest observation in the moving average set is dropped and the newest one added to the set. The variance of the moving average M_i is

$$V(M_i) = \frac{1}{w^2} \sum_{j=i-w+1}^{i} V(x_j) = \frac{1}{w^2} \sum_{j=i-w+1}^{i} \sigma^2 = \frac{\sigma^2}{w} \tag{9.38}$$

Therefore, if μ_0 denotes the target value of the mean used as the center line of the control chart, then the three-sigma control limits for M_i are

$$\text{UCL} = \mu_0 + \frac{3\sigma}{\sqrt{w}} \tag{9.39}$$

and

$$\text{LCL} = \mu_0 - \frac{3\sigma}{\sqrt{w}} \tag{9.40}$$

The control procedure would consist of calculating the new moving average M_i as each observation x_i becomes available, plotting M_i on a control chart with upper and lower control limits given by equations (9.39) and (9.40), and concluding that the process is out of control if M_i exceeds the control limits. In general, the magnitude of the shift of interest and w are inversely related; smaller shifts would be guarded against more effectively by longer-span moving averages, at the expense of quick response to large shifts.

EXAMPLE 9.3 A Moving Average Control Chart

Set up a moving average control chart for the data in Table 9.1, using $w = 5$.

SOLUTION

The observations x_i for periods $1 \le i \le 30$ are shown in Table 9.14. The statistic plotted on the moving average control chart will be

$$M_i = \frac{x_i + x_{i-1} + \cdots + x_{i-4}}{5}$$

for periods $i \ge 5$. For time periods $i < 5$ the average of the observations for periods $1, 2, \ldots, i$ is plotted. The values of these moving averages are shown in Table 9.14.

■ **TABLE 9.14**
Moving Average Chart for Example 9.3

Observation, i	x_i	M_i	Observation, i	x_i	M_i
1	9.45	9.45	16	9.37	10.166
2	7.99	8.72	17	10.62	9.996
3	9.29	8.91	18	10.31	9.956
4	11.66	9.5975	19	8.52	9.78
5	12.16	10.11	20	10.84	9.932
6	10.18	10.256	21	10.9	10.238
7	8.04	10.266	22	9.33	9.98
8	11.46	10.7	23	12.29	10.376
9	9.2	10.208	24	11.5	10.972
10	10.34	9.844	25	10.6	10.924
11	9.03	9.614	26	11.08	10.96
12	11.47	10.3	27	10.38	11.17
13	10.51	10.11	28	11.62	11.036
14	9.4	10.15	29	11.31	10.998
15	10.08	10.098	30	10.52	10.982

The control limits for the moving average control chart may be easily obtained from equations (9.39) and (9.40). Since we know that $\sigma = 1.0$, then

$$\text{UCL} = \mu_0 + \frac{3\sigma}{\sqrt{w}} = 10 + \frac{3(1.0)}{\sqrt{5}} = 11.34$$

and

$$\text{LCL} = \mu_0 - \frac{3\sigma}{\sqrt{w}} = 10 - \frac{3(1.0)}{\sqrt{5}} = 8.66$$

The control limits for M_i apply for periods $i \geq 5$. For periods $0 < i < 5$, the control limits are given by $\mu_0 \pm 3\sigma/\sqrt{i}$. An alternative procedure that avoids using special control limits for periods $i < w$ is to use an ordinary Shewhart chart until at least w sample means have been obtained.

The moving average control chart is shown in Fig. 9.8. No points exceed the control limits. Note that for the initial periods $i < w$ the control limits are wider than their final steady-state value. Moving averages that are less than w periods apart are highly correlated, which often complicates interpreting patterns on the control chart. This is easily seen by examining Fig. 9.8.

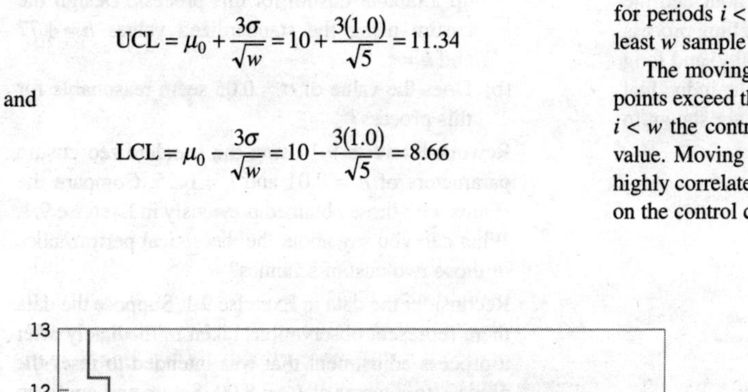

■ **FIGURE 9.8** Moving average control chart with $w = 5$, Example 9.3.

The moving average control chart is more effective than the Shewhart chart in detecting small process shifts. However, it is generally not as effective against small shifts as either the cusum or the EWMA. The moving average control chart is considered by some to be simpler to implement than the cusum. This author prefers the EWMA to the moving average control chart.

Important Terms and Concepts

ARL calculations for the cusum
Average run length
Combined cusum-Shewhart procedures
Cusum control chart
Cusum status chart
Decision interval
Design of a cusum
Design of an EWMA control chart
EWMA control chart
Fast initial response (FIR) or headstart feature for a cusum
Fast initial response (FIR) or headstart feature for an EWMA
Moving average control chart
One-sided cusums
Poisson EWMA
Reference value
Robustness of the EWMA to normality
Scale cusum
Self-starting cusum
Signal resistance of a control chart
Standardized cusum
Tabular or algorithmic cusum
V-mask form of the cusum

Exercises

9.1. A machine is used to fill cans with motor oil additive. A single sample can is selected every hour and the weight of the can is obtained. Since the filling process is automated, it has very stable variability, and long experience indicates that $\sigma = 0.05$ oz. The individual observations for 24 hours of operation are shown in Table 9E.1.

(a) Assuming that the process target is 8.02 oz, set up a tabular cusum for this process. Design the cusum using the standardized values $h = 4.77$ and $k = \frac{1}{2}$.

(b) Does the value of $\sigma = 0.05$ seem reasonable for this process?

■ TABLE 9E.1
Fill Data for Exercise 9.1

Sample Number	x	Sample Number	x
1	8.00	13	8.05
2	8.01	14	8.04
3	8.02	15	8.03
4	8.01	16	8.05
5	8.00	17	8.06
6	8.01	18	8.04
7	8.06	19	8.05
8	8.07	20	8.06
9	8.01	21	8.04
10	8.04	22	8.02
11	8.02	23	8.03
12	8.01	24	8.05

9.2. Rework Exercise 9.1 using the standardized cusum parameters of $h = 8.01$ and $k = 0.25$. Compare the results with those obtained previously in Exercise 9.1. What can you say about the theoretical performance of those two cusum schemes?

9.3. Reconsider the data in Exercise 9.1. Suppose the data there represent observations taken immediately after a process adjustment that was intended to reset the process to a target of $\mu_0 = 8.00$. Set up and apply an FIR cusum to monitor this process.

9.4. The data in Table 9E.2 represent individual observations on molecular weight taken hourly from a chemical process.

The target value of molecular weight is 1050 and the process standard deviation is thought to be about $\sigma = 25$.

(a) Set up a tabular cusum for the mean of this process. Design the cusum to quickly detect a shift of about 1.0σ in the process mean.

(b) Is the estimate of σ used in part (a) of this problem reasonable?

9.5. Rework Exercise 9.4 using a standardized cusum.

TABLE 9E.2
Molecular Weight

Observation Number	x	Observation Number	x
1	1045	11	1139
2	1055	12	1169
3	1037	13	1151
4	1064	14	1128
5	1095	15	1238
6	1008	16	1125
7	1050	17	1163
8	1087	18	1188
9	1125	19	1146
10	1146	20	1167

9.6. (a) Add a headstart feature to the cusum in Exercise 9.4.
(b) Use a combined Shewhart-cusum scheme on the data in Exercise 9.4. Interpret the results of both charts.

9.7. Set up a tabular cusum scheme for the flow width data used in Example 6.1 (see Tables 6.1 and 6.2). When the procedure is applied to all 45 samples, does the cusum react more quickly than the $\bar{x}$ chart to the shift in the process mean? Use $\sigma = 0.14$ in setting up the cusum, and design the procedure to quickly detect a shift of about 1σ.

9.8. Bath concentrations are measured hourly in a chemical process. Data (in ppm) for the last 32 hours are shown in Table 9E.3 (read down from left).
The process target is $\mu_0 = 175$ ppm.
(a) Estimate the process standard deviation.
(b) Construct a tabular cusum for this process using standardized values of $h = 5$ and $k = \frac{1}{2}$.

9.9. Viscosity measurements on a polymer are made every 10 minutes by an on-line viscometer. Thirty-six observations are shown in Table 9E.4 (read down from left). The target viscosity for this process is $\mu_0 = 3200$.

TABLE 9E.3
Bath Concentration

160	186	190	206
158	195	189	210
150	179	185	216
151	184	182	212
153	175	181	211
154	192	180	202
158	186	183	205
162	197	186	197

TABLE 9E.4
Polymer Viscosity

3169	3205	3185	3188
3173	3203	3187	3183
3162	3209	3192	3175
3154	3208	3199	3174
3139	3211	3197	3171
3145	3214	3193	3180
3160	3215	3190	3179
3172	3209	3183	3175
3175	3203	3197	3174

(a) Estimate the process standard deviation.
(b) Construct a tabular cusum for this process using standardized values of $h = 8.01$ and $k = 0.25$.
(c) Discuss the choice of h and k in part (b) of this problem on cusum performance.

9.10. The data in Table 9E.5 are temperature readings from a chemical process in °C, taken every two minutes. (Read the observations down, from left.)
The target value for the mean is $\mu_0 = 950$.
(a) Estimate the process standard deviation.
(b) Set up and apply a tabular cusum for this process, using standardized values $h = 5$ and $k = \frac{1}{2}$. Interpret this chart.

9.11. Apply the scale cusum discussed in Section 9.1.8 to the concentration data in Exercise 9.8.

9.12. Apply the scale cusum discussed in Section 9.1.8 to the data in Exercise 9.4.

9.13. Consider the velocity of light data introduced in Exercises 6.56 and 6.55. Use only the 20 observations in Exercise 6.56 to set up a cusum with target value 734.5. Plot all 40 observations from both Exercises 6.56 and 6.55 on this cusum. What conclusions can you draw?

TABLE 9E.5
Chemical Process Temperature Data

953	985	949	937	959	948	958	952
945	973	941	946	939	937	955	931
972	955	966	954	948	955	947	928
945	950	966	935	958	927	941	937
975	948	934	941	963	940	938	950
970	957	937	933	973	962	945	970
959	940	946	960	949	963	963	933
973	933	952	968	942	943	967	960
940	965	935	959	965	950	969	934
936	973	941	956	962	938	981	927

9.14. Consider a standardized two-sided cusum with $k = 0.2$ and $h = 8$. Use Siegmund's procedure to evaluate the in-control ARL performance of this scheme. Find ARL_1 for $\delta^* = 0.5$.

9.15. Consider the viscosity data in Exercise 9.9. Suppose that the target value of viscosity is $\mu_0 = 3150$ and that it is only important to detect disturbances in the process that result in increased viscosity. Set up and apply an appropriate one-sided cusum for this process.

9.16. Consider a process with $\mu_0 = 10$ and $\sigma = 1$. Set up the following EWMA control charts:
(a) $\lambda = 0.1, L = 3$
(b) $\lambda = 0.2, L = 3$
(c) $\lambda = 0.4, L = 3$
Discuss the effect of λ on the behavior of the control limits.

9.17. Reconsider the data in Exercise 9.1. Set up an EWMA control chart with $\lambda = 0.2$ and $L = 3$ for this process. Interpret the results.

9.18. Reconstruct the control chart in Exercise 9.17 using $\lambda = 0.1$ and $L = 2.7$. Compare this chart with the one constructed in Exercise 9.17.

9.19. Rework Exercise 9.4 using an EWMA control chart with $\lambda = 0.1$ and $L = 2.7$. Compare your results to those obtained with the cusum.

9.20. Rework Exercise 9.13 using an EWMA with $\lambda = 0.10$.

9.21. Reconsider the data in Exercise 9.9. Set up and apply an EWMA control chart to these data using $\lambda = 0.1$ and $L = 2.7$.

9.22. Reconsider the data in Exercise 9.8. Set up and apply an EWMA control chart to these data using $\lambda = 0.05$ and $L = 2.6$.

9.23. Reconsider the data in Exercise 9.10. Apply an EWMA control chart to these data using $\lambda = 0.1$ and $L = 2.7$.

9.24. Show that if the process is in control at the level μ, the exponentially weighted moving average is an unbiased estimator of the process mean.

9.25. Derive the variance of the exponentially weighted moving average z_i.

9.26. Analyze the data in Exercise 9.1 using a moving average control chart with $w = 5$. Compare the results obtained with the cumulative sum control chart in Exercise 9.1.

9.27. Analyze the data in Exercise 9.4 using a moving average control chart with $w = 6$. Compare the results obtained with the cumulative sum control chart in Exercise 9.4.

9.28. **Equivalence of moving average and exponentially weighted moving average control charts.** Show that if $\lambda = 2/(w + 1)$ for the EWMA control chart, then this chart is equivalent to a w-period moving average control chart in the sense that the control limits are identical in the steady state.

9.29. **Continuation of Exercise 9.28.** Show that if $\lambda = 2/(w + 1)$, then the average "ages" of the data used in computing the statistics z_i and M_i are identical.

9.30. Show how to modify the control limits for the moving average control chart if rational subgroups of size $n > 1$ are observed every period, and the objective of the control chart is to monitor the process mean.

9.31. An EWMA control chart uses $\lambda = 0.4$. How wide will the limits be on the Shewhart control chart, expressed as a multiple of the width of the steady-state EWMA limits?

9.32. A Shewhart $\bar{x}$ chart has center line at 10 with UCL = 16 and LCL = 4. Suppose you wish to supplement this chart with an EWMA control chart using $\lambda = 0.1$ and the same control limit width in σ-units as employed on the $\bar{x}$ chart. What are the values of the steady-state upper and lower control limits on the EWMA chart?

9.33. Consider the valve failure data in Example 7.6. Set up a cusum chart for monitoring the time between events using the transformed variable approach illustrated in that example. Use standardized values of $h = 5$ and $k = \frac{1}{2}$.

9.34. Set up an appropriate EWMA control chart for the valve failure data in Example 7.6. Use the transformed variable approach illustrated in that example.

9.35. Discuss how you could set up one-sided EWMA control charts.

9.36. Consider the valve failure data in Example 7.6. Set up a one-sided cusum chart for monitoring and detecting an increase in failure rate of the valve. Assume that the target value of the mean time between failures is 700 hr.

10 Advanced Control Charting Techniques

Chapter Outline

The supplemental material is on the textbook Web site www.wiley.com/college/montgomery.

Chapter Overview and Learning Objectives

The widespread successful use of the basic SPC methods described in Part III and the cusum and EWMA control charts in the previous chapter have led to the development of many new techniques and procedures over the past 20 years. This chapter is an overview of some of the more useful recent developments. We begin with a discussion of SPC methods for short production runs and concentrate on how conventional control charts can be modified for this situation. Although there are other techniques that can be applied to the short-run scenario, this approach seems to be most widely used in practice. We then discuss modified and acceptance control charts. These techniques find some application in situations where process capability is high, such as the six-sigma manufacturing environment. Multiple-stream processes are encountered in many industries. An example is container filling on a multiple-head machine. We present the group control chart (a classical method for the multiple-stream process) and another procedure based on control charts for monitoring the specific types of assignable causes associated with these systems. We also discuss techniques for monitoring processes with autocorrelated data, a topic of considerable importance in the chemical and process industries. Other chapter topics include a discussion of formal consideration of process economics in designing a monitoring scheme, adaptive control charts in which the sample size or time between samples (or both) may be modified based on the current value of the sample statistic, the Cuscore monitoring procedure, changepoints as the framework for a process-monitoring procedure, profile monitoring, the use of control charts in health care, methods for tool wear, fill control problems, and control charts for sample statistics other than the conventional ones considered in previous chapters. In many cases we give only a brief summary of the topic and provide references to more complete descriptions.

After careful study of this chapter you should be able to do the following:

1. Set up and use $\bar{x}$ and R control charts for short production runs
2. Know how to calculate modified limits for the Shewhart $\bar{x}$ control chart
3. Know how to set up and use an acceptance control chart
4. Use group control charts for multiple-stream processes, and understand the alternative procedures that are available
5. Understand the sources and effects of autocorrelation on standard control charts
6. Know how to use model-based residuals control charts for autocorrelated data
7. Know how to use the batch means control chart for autocorrelated data
8. Know what the Cuscore control chart can be used for

9. Know how changepoint methods relate to statistical process monitoring techniques
10. Understand the practical reason behind the use of adaptive control charts
11. Understand the basis of economic principles of control chart design
12. Know how control charts can be used for monitoring processes whose output is a profile

10.1 Statistical Process Control for Short Production Runs

Statistical process-control methods have found wide application in almost every type of business. Some of the most interesting applications occur in job-shop manufacturing systems, or generally in any type of system characterized by **short production runs.** Some of the SPC methods for these situations are straightforward adaptations of the standard concepts and require no new methodology. In fact, Example 6.8 illustrated one of the basic techniques of control charting used in the short-run environment—using deviation from the nominal dimension as the variable on the control chart. In this section, we present a summary of several techniques that have proven successful in the short production run situation.

10.1.1 $\bar{x}$ and R Charts for Short Production Runs

The simplest technique for using $\bar{x}$ and R charts in the short production run situation was introduced previously in Example 6.8; namely, use deviation from nominal instead of the measured variable control chart. This is sometimes called the **deviation from normal (DNOM) control chart.** To illustrate the procedure, consider the data in Table 10.1. The first four samples represent hole diameters in a particular part (say, part A). Panel (a) of this table shows the actual diameters in millimeters. For this part, the nominal diameter is $T_A = 50$ mm. Thus, if M_i represents the ith actual sample measurement in millimeters, then

$$x_i = M_i - T_A$$

would be the deviation from nominal. Panel (b) of Table 10.1 shows the deviations from nominal x_i, as well as the $\bar{x}$ and R values for each sample. Now consider the last six samples in

■ TABLE 10.1
Data for Short-Run $\bar{x}$ and R Charts (deviation from nominal approach)

		(a) Measurements			(b) Deviation from Nominal				
Sample Number	Part Number	M_1	M_2	M_3	x_1	x_2	x_3	$\bar{x}$	R
1	A	50	51	52	0	1	2	1.00	2
2	A	49	50	51	−1	0	1	0.00	2
3	A	48	49	52	−2	−1	2	−0.33	4
4	A	49	53	51	−1	3	1	1.00	4
5	B	24	27	26	−1	2	1	0.67	3
6	B	25	27	24	0	2	−1	0.33	3
7	B	27	26	23	2	1	−2	0.33	4
8	B	25	24	23	0	−1	−2	−1.00	2
9	B	24	25	25	−1	0	0	−0.33	1
10	B	26	24	25	1	−1	0	0.00	2
								$\bar{\bar{x}} = 0.17$	$\bar{R} = 2.7$

Table 10.1. These hole diameters are from a different part number, B, for which the nominal dimension is $T_B = 25$ mm. Panel (b) of Table 10.1 presents the deviations from nominal and the averages and ranges of the deviations from nominal for the part B data.

The control charts for $\bar{x}$ and R using deviation from nominal are shown in Fig. 10.1. Note that control limits have been calculated using the data from all 10 samples. In practice, we would recommend waiting until approximately 20 samples are available before calculating control limits. However, for purposes of illustration we have calculated the limits based on 10 samples to show that, when using deviation from nominal as the variable on the chart, it is not necessary to have a long production run for each part number. It is also customary to use a dashed vertical line to separate different products or part numbers and to identify clearly which section of the chart pertains to each part number, as shown in Fig. 10.1.

Three important points should be made relative to the DNOM approach:

1. An assumption is that the process standard deviation is approximately the same for all parts. If this assumption is invalid, use a *standardized* $\bar{x}$ and R chart (see the next subsection).
2. This procedure works best when the sample size is constant for all part numbers.
3. Deviation from nominal control charts have intuitive appeal when the nominal specification is the desired target value for the process.

This last point deserves some additional discussion. In some situations the process should not (or cannot) be centered at the nominal dimension. For example, when the part has one-sided specifications, frequently a nominal dimension will not be specified. (For an example, see the data on bottle bursting strength in Chapter 8.) In cases where either no nominal is given or a nominal is not the desired process target, then in constructing the control chart, use the historical process average ($\bar{\bar{x}}$) instead of the nominal dimension. In some cases it will be necessary to compare the historical average to a desired process target to determine whether the

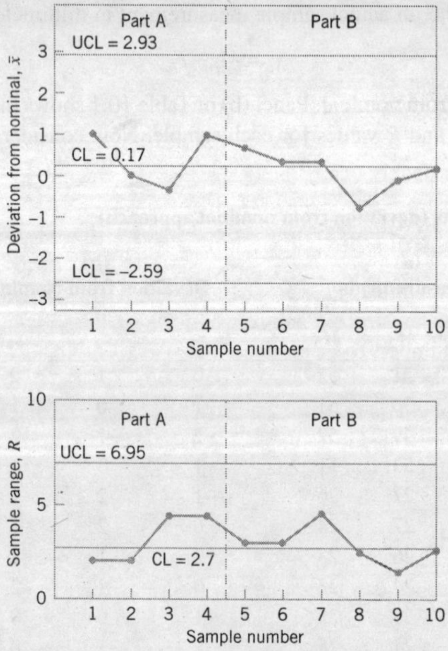

■ FIGURE 10.1 Deviation from nominal $\bar{x}$ and R charts.

true process mean is different from the target. Standard hypothesis testing procedures can be used to perform this task.

Standardized $\bar{x}$ and R Charts. If the process standard deviations are different for different part numbers, the deviation from nominal (or the deviation from process target) control charts described above will not work effectively. However, **standardized $\bar{x}$ and R charts** will handle this situation easily. Consider the jth part number. Let $-\bar{R}_j$ and T_j be the average range and nominal value of x for this part number. Then for all the samples from this part number, plot

$$R_i^s = \frac{R_i}{\bar{R}_j} \tag{10.1}$$

on a standardized R chart with control limits at LCL = D_3 and UCL = D_4, and plot

$$\bar{x}_i^s = \frac{\bar{M}_i - T_j}{\bar{R}_j} \tag{10.2}$$

on a standardized $\bar{x}$ chart with control limits at LCL = $-A_2$ and UCL = $+A_2$. Note that the center line of the standardized $\bar{x}$ chart is zero because $\bar{M}_i$ is the average of the *original* measurements for subgroups of the jth part number. We point out that for this to be meaningful, there must be some logical justification for "pooling" parts on the same chart.

The target values $\bar{R}_j$ and T_j for each part number can be determined by using specifications for T_j and taking $\bar{R}_j$ from prior history (often in the form of a control chart, or by converting an estimate of σ into $\bar{R}_j$ by the relationship $\bar{R}_j = Sd_2/c_4$). For new parts, it is a common practice to utilize prior experience on similar parts to set the targets.

Farnum (1992) has presented a generalized approach to the DNOM procedure that can incorporate a variety of assumptions about process variability. The standardized control chart approach discussed above is a special case of his method. His method would allow construction of DNOM charts in the case where the coefficient of variation (σ/μ) is approximately constant. This situation probably occurs fairly often in practice.

10.1.2 Attributes Control Charts for Short Production Runs

Dealing with attributes data in the short production run environment is extremely simple; the proper method is to use a standardized control chart for the attribute of interest. This method will allow different part numbers to be plotted on the same chart and will automatically compensate for variable sample size.

Standardized control charts for attributes were discussed in Chapter 7. For convenience, the relevant formulas are presented in Table 10.2. All standardized attributes control charts have the center line at zero, and the upper and lower control limits are at +3 and −3, respectively.

10.1.3 Other Methods

A variety of other approaches can be applied to the short-run production environment. For example, the cusum and EWMA control charts discussed in Chapter 9 have potential application to short production runs, because they have shorter average run-length performance than Shewhart-type charts, particularly in detecting small shifts. Since most production runs in the short-run environment will not, by definition, consist of many units, the rapid shift

■ TABLE 10.2
Standardized Attributes Control Charts Suitable for Short Production Runs

Attribute	Target Value	Standard Deviation	Statistic to Plot on the Control Chart
$\hat{p}_i$	$\overline{p}$	$\sqrt{\dfrac{\overline{p}(1-\overline{p})}{n}}$	$Z_i = \dfrac{\hat{p}_i - \overline{p}}{\sqrt{\overline{p}(1-\overline{p})/n}}$
$n\hat{p}_i$	$n\overline{p}$	$\sqrt{n\overline{p}(1-\overline{p})}$	$Z_i = \dfrac{n\hat{p}_i - n\overline{p}}{\sqrt{n\overline{p}(1-\overline{p})}}$
c_i	$\overline{c}$	$\sqrt{\overline{c}}$	$Z_i = \dfrac{c_i - \overline{c}}{\sqrt{\overline{c}}}$
u_i	$\overline{u}$	$\sqrt{\overline{u}/n}$	$Z_i = \dfrac{u_i - \overline{u}}{\sqrt{\overline{u}/n}}$

detection capability of those charts would be useful. Furthermore, cusum and EWMA control charts are very effective with subgroups of size one, another potential advantage in the short-run situation.

The "self-starting" version of the cusum [see Hawkins and Olwell, Chapter 9 (1998)] is also a useful procedure for the short-run environment. The self-starting approach uses regular process measurements for both establishing or calibrating the cusum and for process monitoring. Thus it avoids the phase I parameter estimation phase. It also produces the Shewhart control statistics as a by-product of the process.

The number of subgroups used in calculating the trial control limits for Shewhart charts impacts the false alarm rate of the chart; in particular, when a small number of subgroups are used, the false alarm rate is inflated. Hillier (1969) studied this problem and presented a table of factors to use in setting limits for $\overline{x}$ and R charts based in a small number of subgroups for the case of $n = 5$ [see also Wang and Hillier (1970)]. Quesenberry (1993) has investigated a similar problem for both $\overline{x}$ and individuals control charts. Since control limits in the short-run environment will typically be calculated from a relatively small number of subgroups, these papers present techniques of some interest.

Quesenberry (1991a, b, c) has presented procedures for short-run SPC using a transformation that is different from the standardization approach discussed above. He refers to these as *Q-charts*, and notes that they can be used for both short or long production runs. The *Q*-chart idea was first suggested by Hawkins (1987). Del Castillo and Montgomery (1994) have investigated the average run-length performance of the *Q*-chart for variables and show that in some cases the **average run length (ARL)** performance is inadequate. They suggest some modifications to the *Q*-chart procedure and some alternate methods based on the EWMA and a related technique called the Kalman filter that have better ARL performance than the *Q*-chart. Crowder (1992) has also reported a short-run procedure based on the Kalman filter. In a subsequent series of papers, Quesenberry (1995a, b, c, d) reports some refinements to the use of *Q*-charts that also enhance their performance in detecting process shifts. He also suggests that the probability that a shift is detected within a specified number of samples following its occurrence is a more appropriate measure of the performance of a short-run SPC procedure than its average run length. The interested reader should refer to the July and October 1995 issues of the *Journal of Quality Technology* that contain these papers and a discussion of *Q*-charts by several authorities. These papers and the discussion include a number of useful additional references.

10.2 Modified and Acceptance Control Charts

In most situations in which control charts are used, the focus is on statistical monitoring or control of the process, reduction of variability, and continuous process improvement. When a high level of process capability has been achieved, it is sometimes useful to relax the level of surveillance provided by the standard control chart. One method for doing this with $\bar{x}$ charts uses **modified** (or **reject**) **control limits,** and the second uses the **acceptance control chart.**

10.2.1 Modified Control Limits for the $\bar{x}$ Chart

Modified control limits are generally used in situations where the natural variability or "spread" of the process is considerably smaller than the spread in the specification limits; that is, C_p or C_{pk} is much greater than 1. This situation occurs occasionally in practice. In fact, this should be the natural eventual result of a successful variability reduction effort—reduction of process variability with a corresponding increase in the process capability ratio. The six-sigma approach to variability reduction focuses on improving processes until the minimum value of C_{pk} is 2.0.

Suppose, for example, that the specification limits on the fill volume of a carbonated beverage container are LSL = 10.00 oz and USL = 10.20 oz, but as the result of a program of engineering and operating refinements, the filling machine can operate with a standard deviation of fill volume of approximately $\sigma = 0.01$ oz. Therefore, the distance USL − LSL is approximately twenty-sigma, or much greater than the six-sigma natural tolerance limits on the process, and the process capability ratio is PCR = (USL − LSL)/6σ = 0.20/[6(0.01)] = 3.33. This is clearly a six-sigma process.

In situations where six-sigma is much smaller than the spread in the specifications (USL–LSL), the process mean can sometimes be allowed to vary over an interval without appreciably affecting the overall performance of the process.[1] For example, see Fig. 10.2. When this situation occurs, we can use a **modified control chart** for $\bar{x}$ instead of the usual $\bar{x}$ chart. The modified $\bar{x}$ control chart is concerned only with detecting whether the true process mean μ is located such that the process is producing a fraction nonconforming in excess of some specified value δ. In effect, μ is allowed to vary over an interval—say, $\mu_L \le \mu \le \mu_U$—where μ_L and μ_U are chosen as the smallest and largest permissible values of μ, respectively, consistent with producing a fraction nonconforming of at most δ. We will assume that the process variability σ is in control. Good general discussions of the modified control chart are in Hill (1956) and Duncan (1986). As noted in Duncan (1986), the procedure is sometimes used when a process is subject to tool wear (see Section 10.7.1).

To specify the control limits for a modified $\bar{x}$ chart, we will assume that the process output is normally distributed. For the process fraction nonconforming to be less than δ, we must require that the true process mean is in the interval. Consequently, we see from Fig. 10.3a that we must have

$$\mu_L = \text{LSL} + Z_\delta \sigma$$

and

$$\mu_U = \text{USL} - Z_\delta \sigma$$

---

[1]In the original Motorola definition of a six-sigma process, the process mean was assumed to drift about, wandering as far as 1.5σ from the desired target. If this is the actual behavior of the process and this type of behavior is acceptable, then modified control charts are a useful alternative to standard charts. There are also many cases where the mean should not be allowed to vary even if C_p or C_{pk} is large. The conventional control charts should be used in such situations.

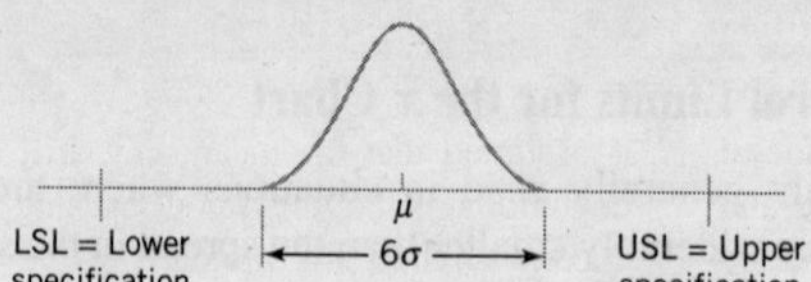

■ FIGURE 10.2 A process with the spread of the natural tolerance limits less than the spread of the specification limits, or $6\sigma <$ USL − LSL.

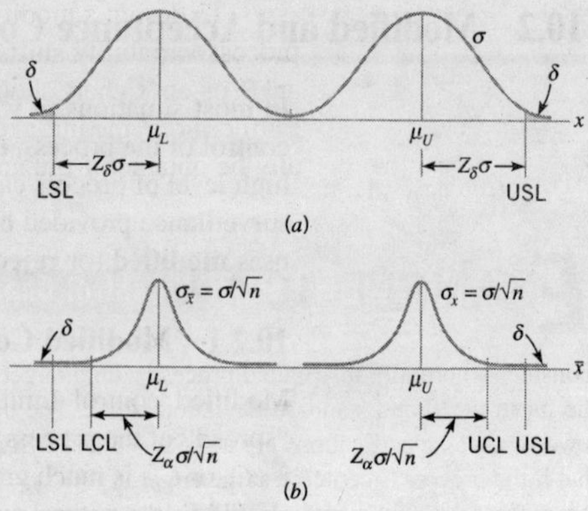

■ FIGURE 10.3 Control limits on a modified control chart. (*a*) Distribution of process output. (*b*) Distribution of the sample mean $\bar{x}$.

where Z_δ is the upper $100(1-\delta)$ percentage point of the standard normal distribution. Now if we specify a type I error of α, the upper and lower control limits are

$$\begin{aligned} \mathrm{UCL} &= \mu_U + \frac{Z_\alpha \sigma}{\sqrt{n}} \\ &= \mathrm{USL} - Z_\delta \sigma + \frac{Z_\alpha \sigma}{\sqrt{n}} \\ &= \mathrm{USL} - \left(Z_\delta - \frac{Z_\alpha}{\sqrt{n}} \right) \sigma \end{aligned} \tag{10.3a}$$

and

$$\begin{aligned} \mathrm{LCL} &= \mu_L - \frac{Z_\alpha \sigma}{\sqrt{n}} \\ &= \mathrm{LSL} + Z_\delta \sigma - \frac{Z_\alpha \sigma}{\sqrt{n}} \\ &= \mathrm{LSL} + \left(Z_\delta - \frac{Z_\alpha}{\sqrt{n}} \right) \sigma \end{aligned} \tag{10.3b}$$

respectively. The control limits are shown on the distribution of $\bar{x}$ in Fig. 10.3*b*. Instead of specifying a type I error, one may use the following:

$$\mathrm{UCL} = \mathrm{USL} - \left(Z_\delta - \frac{3}{\sqrt{n}} \right) \sigma \tag{10.4a}$$

and

$$\mathrm{LCL} = \mathrm{LSL} + \left(Z_\delta - \frac{3}{\sqrt{n}} \right) \sigma \tag{10.4b}$$

Two-sigma limits are sometimes recommended for the modified control chart, based on an argument that the tighter control limits afford better protection (smaller β-risk) against critical shifts in the mean at little loss in the α-risk. A discussion of this subject is in Freund (1957). Note that the modified control chart is equivalent to testing the hypothesis that the process mean lies in the interval $\mu_L \le \mu \le \mu_U$.

To design a modified control chart, we must have a good estimate of σ available. If the process variability shifts, then the modified control limits are not appropriate. Consequently, an R or an s chart should always be used in conjunction with the modified control chart. Furthermore, the initial estimate of σ required to set up the modified control chart would usually be obtained from an R or an s chart.

EXAMPLE 10.1 A Control Chart for a Six-Sigma Process

Consider a normally distributed process with a target value of the mean of 20 and standard deviation $\sigma = 2$. The upper and lower process specifications are at LSL = 8 and USL = 32, so that if the process is centered at the target, $C_p = C_{pk} = 2.0$. This is a process with six-sigma capability. In a six-sigma process it is assumed that the mean may drift as much as 1.5 standard deviations off target without causing serious problems. Set up a control chart for monitoring the mean of this six-sigma process with a sample size of $n = 4$.

SOLUTION

Figure 10.4*a* shows this six-sigma process and Fig. 10.4*b* illustrates the control limit calculation. Notice that we can use equation (10.4) with Z_δ replaced by 4.5. Therefore, the upper and lower control limits become

$$\begin{aligned}\text{UCL} &= \text{USL} - \left(4.5 - \frac{3}{\sqrt{4}}\right)\sigma \\ &= 32 - (4.5 - 1.5)2 \\ &= 26\end{aligned}$$

and

$$\begin{aligned}\text{LCL} &= \text{LSL} + \left(4.5 - \frac{3}{\sqrt{4}}\right)\sigma \\ &= 8 + (4.5 - 1.5)2 \\ &= 14\end{aligned}$$

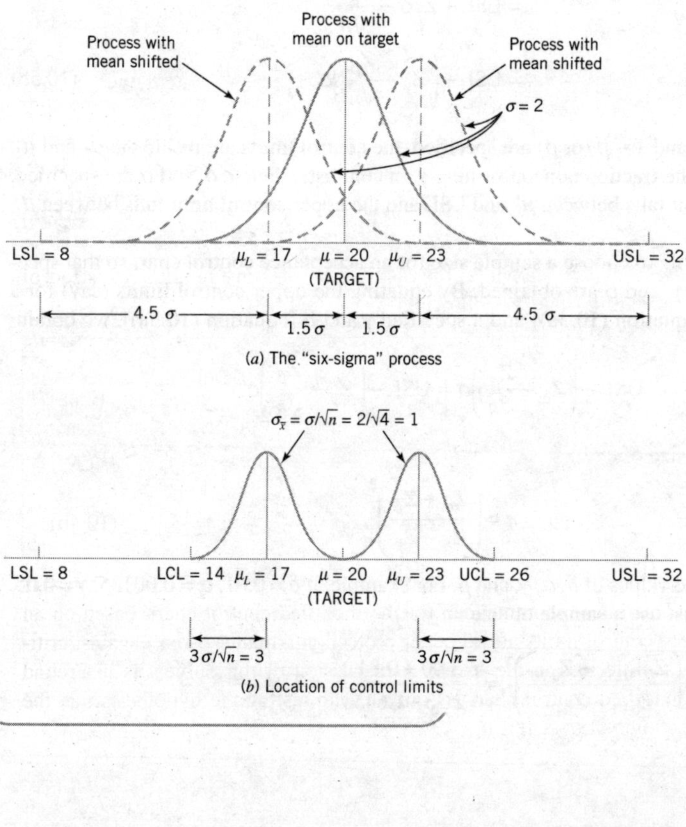

FIGURE 10.4 Control limits for a six-sigma process.

10.2.2 Acceptance Control Charts

The second approach to using an $\bar{x}$ chart to monitor the fraction of nonconforming units, or the fraction of units exceeding specifications, is called the acceptance control chart. In the modified control chart design of Section 10.2.1, the chart was based on a specified sample size n, a process fraction nonconforming δ, and type I error probability α. Thus, we interpret δ as a process fraction nonconforming that we will accept with probability $1 - \alpha$. Freund (1957) developed the **acceptance control chart** to take into account both the risk of rejecting a process operating at a satisfactory level (type I error or α-risk) and the risk of accepting a process that is operating at an unsatisfactory level (type II error or β-risk).

There are two ways to design the control chart. In the first approach, we design the control chart based on a specified n and a process fraction nonconforming γ that we would like to reject with probability $1 - \beta$. In this case, the control limits for the chart are

$$\begin{aligned} \text{UCL} &= \mu_U - \frac{Z_\beta \sigma}{\sqrt{n}} \\ &= \text{USL} - Z_\gamma \sigma - \frac{Z_\beta \sigma}{\sqrt{n}} \\ &= \text{USL} - \left(Z_\gamma + \frac{Z_\beta}{\sqrt{n}} \right)\sigma \end{aligned} \tag{10.5a}$$

and

$$\begin{aligned} \text{LCL} &= \mu_L + \frac{Z_\beta \sigma}{\sqrt{n}} \\ &= \text{LSL} + Z_\gamma \sigma + \frac{Z_\beta \sigma}{\sqrt{n}} \\ &= \text{LSL} + \left(Z_\gamma + \frac{Z_\beta}{\sqrt{n}} \right)\sigma \end{aligned} \tag{10.5b}$$

Note that when n, γ, and $1 - \beta$ (or β) are specified, the control limits are inside the μ_L and μ_U values that produce the fraction nonconforming γ. In contrast, when n, δ, and α are specified, the lower control limit falls between μ_L and LSL and the upper control limit falls between μ_U and USL.

It is also possible to choose a sample size for an acceptance control chart so that specified values of δ, α, γ, and β are obtained. By equating the upper control limits (say) for a specified δ and α [equation (10.3a)] and a specified γ and β [equation (10.5a)], we obtain

$$\text{USL} - \left(Z_\delta - \frac{Z_\alpha}{\sqrt{n}} \right)\sigma = \text{USL} - \left(Z_\gamma + \frac{Z_\beta}{\sqrt{n}} \right)\sigma$$

Therefore, a sample size of

$$n = \left(\frac{Z_\alpha + Z_\beta}{Z_\delta - Z_\gamma} \right)^2$$

will yield the required values of δ, α, γ, and β. For example, if $\delta = 0.01$, $\alpha = 0.00135$, $\gamma = 0.05$, and $\beta = 0.20$, we must use a sample of size

$$n = \left(\frac{Z_{0.00135} + Z_{0.20}}{Z_{0.01} - Z_{0.05}} \right)^2 = \left(\frac{3.00 + 0.84}{2.33 - 1.645} \right)^2 = 31.43 \simeq 32$$

on the acceptance control chart. Obviously, to use this approach, n must not be seriously restricted by cost or other factors such as rational subgrouping considerations.

10.3 Control Charts for Multiple-Stream Processes

10.3.1 Multiple-Stream Processes

A **multiple-stream process (MSP)** is a process with data at a point in time consisting of measurements from several individual sources or streams. When the process is in control, the sources or streams are assumed to be identical. Another characteristic of the MSP is that we can monitor and adjust each of the streams individually or in small groups.

The MSP occurs often in practice. For example, a machine may have several heads, with each head producing (we hope) identical units of product. In such situations several possible control procedures may be followed. One possibility is to use separate control charts on each stream. This approach usually results in a prohibitively large number of control charts. If the output streams are highly correlated—say, nearly perfectly correlated—then control charts on only one stream may be adequate. The most common situation is that the streams are only moderately correlated, so monitoring only one of the streams is not appropriate. There are at least two types of situations involving the occurrence of assignable causes in the MSP.

1. The output of one stream (or a few streams) has shifted off target.
2. The output of all streams has shifted off target.

In the first case, we are trying to detect an assignable cause that affects only one stream (or at most a few streams), whereas in the second, we are looking for an assignable cause that impacts *all* streams (such as would result from a change in raw materials).

The standard control chart for the MSP is the group control chart, introduced by Boyd (1950). We will also discuss other approaches to monitoring the MSP. Throughout this section we assume that the process has s streams and that the output quality characteristic from each stream is normally distributed.

10.3.2 Group Control Charts

The **group control chart (GCC)** was introduced by Boyd (1950) and remains the basic procedure for monitoring an MSP. To illustrate the methods of construction and use, suppose that the process has $s = 6$ streams and that each stream has the same target value and inherent variability. Variables measurement is made on the items produced, and the distribution of the measurement is well approximated by the normal. To establish a group control chart, the sampling is performed as if separate control charts were to be set up on each stream. Suppose, for purposes of illustration, that a sample size of $n = 4$ is used. This means that 4 units will be taken from each of the $s = 6$ streams over a short period of time. This will be repeated until about 20 such groups of samples have been taken. At this point we would have $20 \times 6 = 120$ averages of $n = 4$ observations each and 120 corresponding ranges. These averages and ranges would be averaged to produce a grand average $\bar{\bar{x}}$ and an average range $\bar{R}$. The limits on the group control charts would be at

$$\text{UCL} = \bar{\bar{x}} + A_2\bar{R}$$

$$\text{LCL} = \bar{\bar{x}} - A_2\bar{R}$$

for the $\bar{x}$ chart and at

$$\text{UCL} = D_4\bar{R}$$

$$\text{LCL} = D_3\bar{R}$$

for the R chart, with $A_2 = 0.729$, $D_3 = 0$, and $D_4 = 2.282$. Note that the sample size $n = 4$ determines the control chart constants.

When the group control chart is used to control the process, we plot only the largest and smallest of the $s = 6$ means observed at any time period on the $\bar{x}$ chart. If these means are inside the control limits, then all other means will also lie inside the limits. Similarly, only the largest range will be plotted on the range chart. Each plotted point is identified on the chart by the number of the stream that produced it. The process is out of control if a point exceeds a three-sigma limit. Runs tests cannot be applied to these charts, because the conventional runs tests were not developed to test averages or ranges that are the extremes of a group of averages or ranges.

It is useful to examine the stream numbers on the chart. In general, if a stream consistently gives the largest (or smallest) value several times in a row, that may constitute evidence that this stream is different from the others. If the process has s streams and if r is the number of consecutive times that a particular stream is the largest (or smallest) value, then the one-sided in-control average run length for this event is given by Nelson (1986) as

$$\text{ARL}(1)_0 = \frac{s^r - 1}{s - 1} \tag{10.6}$$

if all streams are identical. To illustrate the use of this equation, if $s = 6$ and $r = 4$, then

$$\text{ARL}(1)_0 = \frac{6^4 - 1}{6 - 1} = 259$$

That is, if the process is in control, we will expect to see the same stream producing an extreme value on the group control chart four times in a row only once every 259 samples.

One way to select the value of r to detect the presence of one stream that is different from the others is to use equation (10.6) to find an ARL that is roughly consistent with the ARL of a conventional control chart. The ARL for an in-control process for a single point beyond the upper control limit (say) is 740. Thus, using $r = 4$ for a six-stream process results in an ARL that is too short and that will give too many false alarms. A better choice is $r = 5$, since

$$\text{ARL}(1)_0 = \frac{6^5 - 1}{6 - 1} = 1555$$

Thus, if we have six streams and if the same stream produces an extreme value on the control chart in five consecutive samples, then we have strong evidence that this stream is different from the others.

Using equation (10.6), we can generate some general guidelines for choosing r given the number of streams s. Suitable pairs (s, r) would include (3, 7), (4, 6), (5–6, 5), and (7–10, 4). All of these combinations would give reasonable values of the one-sided ARL when the process is in control.

The two-sided in-control average run length $\text{ARL}(2)_0$ is defined as the expected number of trials until r consecutive largest or r consecutive smallest means come from the same stream while the MSP is in control. Mortell and Runger (1995) and Nelson and Stephenson (1996) used the *Markov chain approach* of Brook and Evans (1972) to compute $\text{ARL}(2)_0$ numerically. A closed-form expression is not possible for $\text{ARL}(2)_0$, but Nelson and Stephenson (1996) give a lower bound on $\text{ARL}(2)_0$ as

$$\text{ARL}(2)_0 = \frac{s^r - 1}{2(r - 1)} \tag{10.7}$$

This approximation agrees closely with the numerical computations from the Markov chain approach.

There are some drawbacks connected with the GCC. These may be summarized as follows:

1. At each point in time where samples are taken, all s streams must be sampled. When s is small, this may be a satisfactory approach. However, some high-speed filling and packaging machines may have $100 \le s \le 200$ streams. The GCC is not practical for these situations.
2. There is no information about nonextreme streams at each trial, thus, we cannot utilize past values to form an EWMA or a cusum statistic to improve on the GCC performance.
3. The supplementary run tests fail if more than one stream shifts simultaneously (all up or all down) to the same off-target level, because the shifted streams will most likely alternate having the extreme value, and no single stream shift can be identified.
4. The selection of the run or pattern length r for a specific problem with s streams is a discrete process, and the difference in ARL_0 for $r = r^*$ or $r = r^* + 1$ choice can be substantial, as observed by Mortell and Runger (1995). This problem is evident in the original run rule devised by Nelson (1986), but can be alleviated somewhat by using the modified run rules in Nelson and Stephenson (1996), which are based on an $r - 1$ out of r in a row approach. In fact, it can be easily shown that the difference in the ARL_0 between $r = r^*$ and $r = r^* + 1$ choices equals s^{r^*}, which becomes very large for problems with large numbers of streams.
5. Although using an $r - 1$ out of r in a row run rule allows some flexibility in the choice of the critical value $r = r^*$ and ARL_0, it adds some complexity since it is no longer a simple counting procedure.

10.3.3 Other Approaches

Mortell and Runger (1995) proposed the following model for the MSP to accommodate the practical case of dependent (cross-correlated) streams:

$$x_{tjk} = \mu + A_t + \varepsilon_{tjk} \tag{10.8}$$

where x_{tjk} is the kth measurement on the jth stream at time t, $A_t \sim N(0,\sigma_a^2)$ represents the difference of the mean over all the streams at time t from the MSP target μ, and ε_{tjk} is a $N(0, \sigma^2)$ random variable that represents the difference of the kth measurements on the jth stream from the process mean over all streams at time t. In this representation of MSP data, the total variation is allocated into two sources: σ_a^2 accounting for the variation over time common to all streams, and σ^2 accounting for the variation between the streams at specific time t. From this model, the cross correlation between any pair of streams is given by $\rho = \sigma_a^2/(\sigma_a^2 + \sigma^2)$.

Mortell and Runger proposed monitoring the average at time t of the means across all streams with an individuals control chart to detect an overall assignable cause. Also, they proposed monitoring the range of the stream's means at time t denoted by $R_t = \max(\bar{x}_{tj}) - \min(\bar{x}_{tj})$ or the maximum ***residual*** at time t given by $\max(\bar{x}_{tj}) - \bar{x}_t$, with any individuals control chart to detect a relative assignable cause affecting one or a few streams. These proposed **control charts on residuals** are better than the GCC, especially when the variation in the process means over time is greater than the between-stream variability (i.e., when $\sigma_a > \sigma$). Mortell and Runger compared the performance of these proposed charts with the runs test of the GCC by Nelson (1986) using simulations of various MSPs and concluded that the cusum chart on the range outperforms the Shewhart and EWMA on either the range or the maximum residual. On the other hand, little difference in performance exists between the runs test of Nelson (1986) and the proposed cusum chart, but it is preferred because of the flexibility in the choice of in-control ARL.

Runger, Alt, and Montgomery (1996a) related control charts for the MSP with correlated data to principal components analysis. (See Chapter 11 for information on principal components.) The first control chart monitors the major principal component variable, which equals the mean of the streams at any time t. The second control chart is based on the Hotelling T^2 statistic (see Chapter 11) of the last $p - 1$ principal components, which is shown to be equivalent to the s^2 chart; thus it is sensitive to relative assignable causes that affect the uniformity across the streams.

Lanning (1998) studied the use of "fractional" and "adaptive" sampling in the multiple-stream process with a large number of identical and independent streams, where simultaneous monitoring of all streams is impractical. In his procedures, only a fraction of the s streams are sampled at each time period, and this fraction is increased when there are indications that an out-of-control condition may be present. (Adaptive sampling schemes are introduced in Section 10.5.) He used the average time to signal (ATS) to compare performance of the competing charts, and focused on the scenarios where assignable causes tend to impact all or most of the process streams together. He concluded that the adaptive fraction approach gives better ATS results than the fixed fraction scheme, and often yields satisfactory results compared to a complete sampling situation. An application of his methodology to a multiple-head filling machine with many filling valves is described in Lanning, Montgomery, and Runger (2002–03).

10.4 SPC with Autocorrelated Process Data

10.4.1 Sources and Effects of Autocorrelation in Process Data

The standard assumptions that are usually cited in justifying the use of control charts are that the data generated by the process when it is in control are normally and independently distributed with mean μ and standard deviation σ. Both μ and σ are considered fixed and unknown. An out-of-control condition is a change or shift in μ or σ (or both) to some different value. Therefore, we could say that when the process is in control the quality characteristic at time t, x_t, is represented by the model

$$x_t = \mu + \varepsilon_t \quad t = 1, 2, \ldots \tag{10.9}$$

where ε_t is normally and independently distributed with mean zero and standard deviation σ. This is often called the **Shewhart process model.**

When these assumptions are satisfied, one may apply conventional control charts and draw conclusions about the state of statistical control of the process. Furthermore, the statistical properties of the control chart, such as the false alarm rate with three-sigma control limits, or the average run length, can be easily determined and used to provide guidance for chart interpretation. Even in situations in which the normality assumption is violated to a slight or moderate degree, these control charts will still work reasonably well.

The most important of the assumptions made concerning control charts is that of independence of the observations, for conventional control charts do not work well if the quality characteristic exhibits even low levels of correlation over time. Specifically, these control charts will give misleading results in the form of too many false alarms if the data are positively correlated. This point has been made by numerous authors, including Berthouex, Hunter, and Pallesen (1978), Alwan and Roberts (1988), Montgomery and Friedman (1989), Alwan (1992), Harris and Ross (1991), Montgomery and Mastrangelo (1991), and Maragah and Woodall (1992).

Unfortunately, the assumption of uncorrelated or independent observations is not even approximately satisfied in some manufacturing processes. Examples include chemical processes

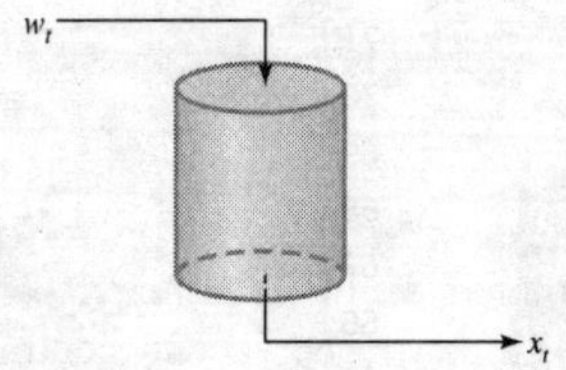

■ FIGURE 10.5 A tank with volume V and input and output material streams.

where consecutive measurements on process or product characteristics are often highly correlated, or automated test and inspection procedures, where every quality characteristic is measured on every unit in time order of production. An example of correlated process data was given in Fig. 5.6*b*. Basically, all manufacturing processes are driven by inertial elements, and when the interval between samples becomes small relative to these forces, the observations on the process will be correlated over time.

It is easy to give an analytical demonstration of this phenomenon. Figure 10.5 shows a simple system consisting of a tank with volume V, with the input and output material streams having flow rate f. Let w_t be the concentration of a certain material in the input stream at time t and x_t be the corresponding concentration in the output stream at time t. Assuming homogeneity within the tank, the relationship between x_t and w_t is

$$x_t = w_t - T\frac{dx_t}{dt}$$

where $T = V/f$ is often called the **time constant** of the system. If the input stream experiences a step change of w_0 at time $t = 0$ (say), then the output concentration at time t is

$$x_t = w_0\left(1 - e^{-t/T}\right)$$

Now in practice, we do not observe x_t continuously, but only at small, equally spaced intervals of time Δt. In this case,

$$\begin{aligned} x_t &= x_{t-1} + \left(w_t - x_{t-1}\right)\left(1 - e^{-\Delta t/T}\right) \\ &= aw_t + (1-a)x_{t-1} \end{aligned}$$

where $a = 1 - e^{-\Delta t/T}$

The properties of the output stream concentration x_t depend on those of the input stream concentration w_t and the sampling interval Δt. If we assume that the w_t are uncorrelated random variables, then the correlation between successive values of x_t (or the autocorrelation between x_t and x_{t-1}) is given by

$$\rho = 1 - a = e^{-\Delta t/T}$$

Note that if Δt is much greater than T, $\rho = 0$. That is, if the interval between samples Δt in the output stream is long—much longer than the time constant T—the observations on output concentration will be uncorrelated. However, if $\Delta t \le T$, this will not be the case. For example, if

$$\begin{aligned} \Delta t/T &= 1 & \rho &= 0.37 \\ \Delta t/T &= 0.5 & \rho &= 0.61 \\ \Delta t/T &= 0.25 & \rho &= 0.78 \\ \Delta t/T &= 0.10 & \rho &= 0.90 \end{aligned}$$

Clearly if we sample at least once per time constant there will be significant autocorrelation present in the observations. For instance, sampling four times per time constant ($\Delta t/T = 0.25$)

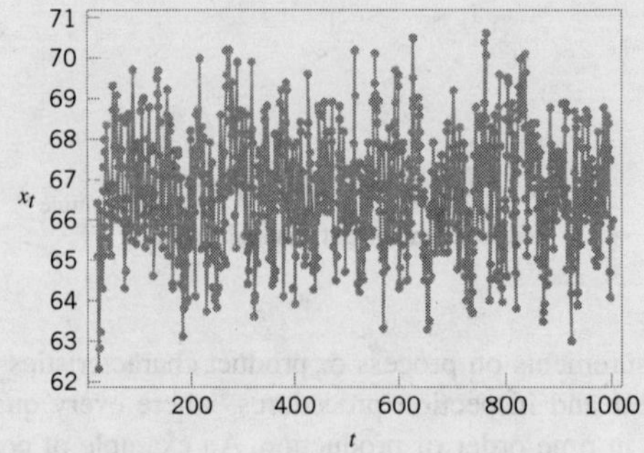

■ FIGURE 10.6 A process variable with autocorrelation.

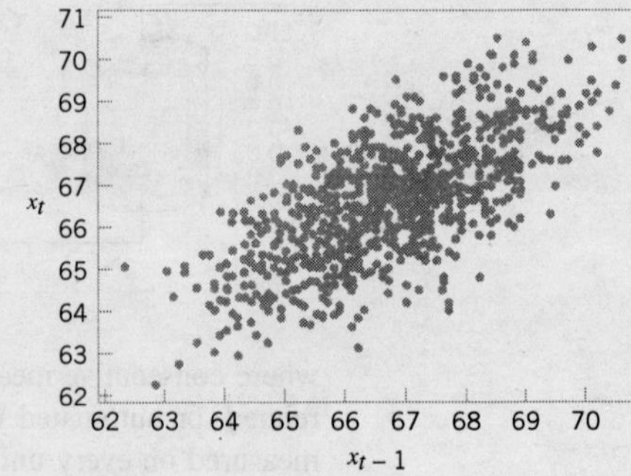

■ FIGURE 10.7 Scatter plot of x_t versus x_{t-1}.

results in autocorrelation between x_t and x_{t-1} of $\rho = 0.78$. Autocorrelation between successive observations as small as 0.25 can cause a substantial increase in the false alarm rate of a control chart, so clearly this is an important issue to consider in control chart implementation.

We can also give an empirical demonstration of this phenomena. Figure 10.6 is a plot of 1000 observations on a process quality characteristic x_t. Close examination of this plot will reveal that the behavior of the variable is nonrandom in the sense that a value of x_t that is above the long-term average (about 66) tends to be followed by other values above the average, whereas a value below the average tends to be followed by other similar values. This is also reflected in Fig. 10.7, a scatter plot of x_t (the observation at time t) versus x_{t-1} (the observation one period earlier). Note that the observations cluster around a straight line with a positive slope. That is, a relatively low observation on x at time $t-1$ tends to be followed by another low value at time t, whereas a relatively large observation at time $t-1$ tends to be followed by another large value at time t. This type of behavior is indicative of **positive autocorrelation** in the observations.

It is also possible to measure the level of autocorrelation analytically. The autocorrelation over a series of time-oriented observations (called a ***time series***) is measured by the **autocorrelation function**

$$\rho_k = \frac{\text{Cov}(x_t, x_{t-k})}{V(x_t)} \qquad k = 0, 1, \ldots$$

where $\text{Cov}(x_t, x_{t-k})$ is the covariance of observations that are k time periods apart, and we have assumed that the observations have constant variance given by $V(x_t)$. We usually estimate the values of ρ_k with the **sample autocorrelation function:**

$$r_k = \frac{\sum_{t=1}^{n-k}(x_t - \bar{x})(x_{t-k} - \bar{x})}{\sum_{t=1}^{n}(x_t - \bar{x})^2} \qquad k = 0, 1, \ldots, K \tag{10.10}$$

As a general rule, we usually need to compute values of r_k for a few values of k, $k \le n/4$. Many software programs for statistical data analysis can perform these calculations.

The sample autocorrelation function for the data in Fig. 10.6 is shown in Fig. 10.8. This sample autocorrelation function was constructed using Minitab. The dashed lines on the graph are two standard deviation limits on the autocorrelation parameter ρ_k at lag k. They are useful in detecting non-zero autocorrelations; in effect, if a sample autocorrelation exceeds its

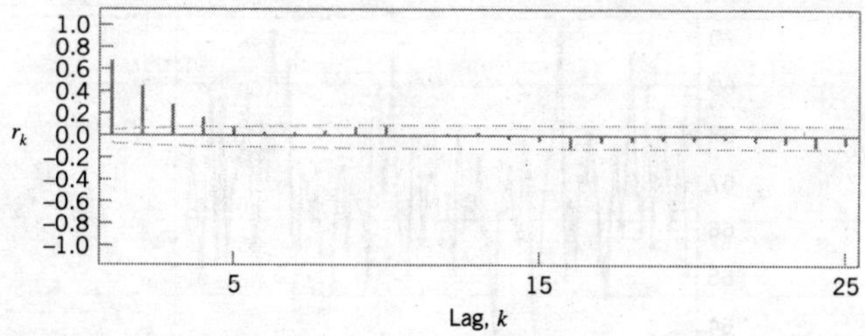

■ FIGURE 10.8 Sample autocorrelation function for the data in Fig. 10.6.

two standard deviation limit, the corresponding autocorrelation parameter ρ_k is likely nonzero. Note that the autocorrelation at lag 1 is $r_1 \simeq 0.7$. This is certainly large enough to severely distort control chart performance.

Figure 10.9 presents control charts for the data in Fig. 10.6, constructed by Minitab. Note that both the individuals chart and the EWMA exhibit many out-of-control points.

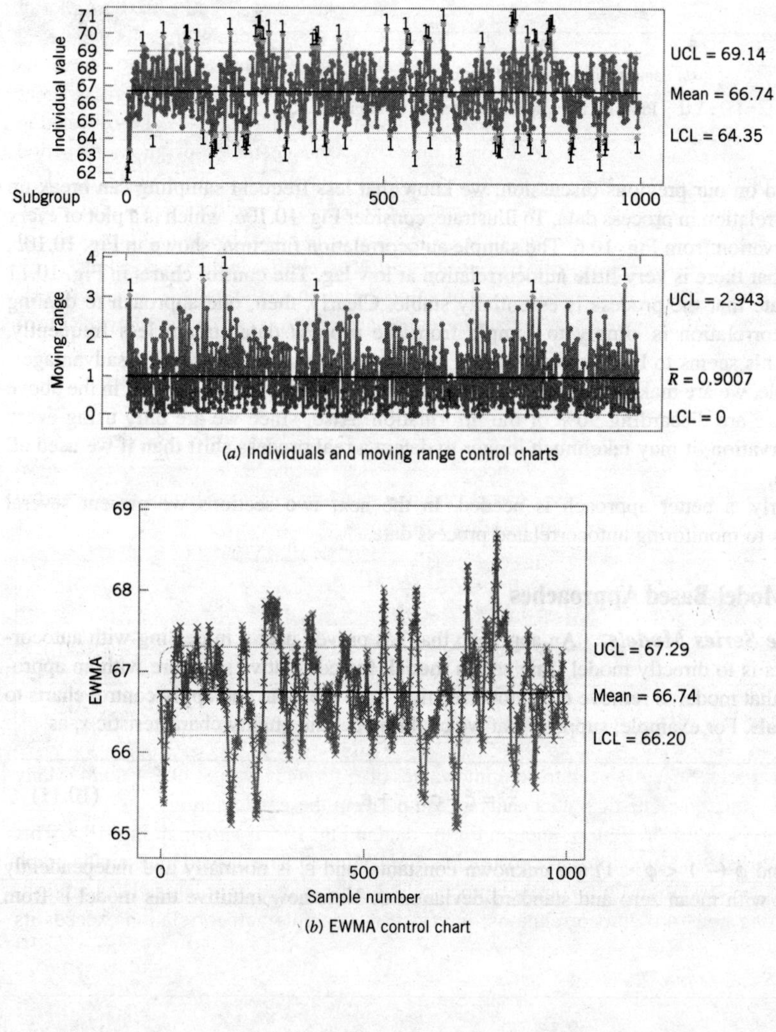

■ FIGURE 10.9 Control charts (Minitab) for the data in Fig. 10.6.

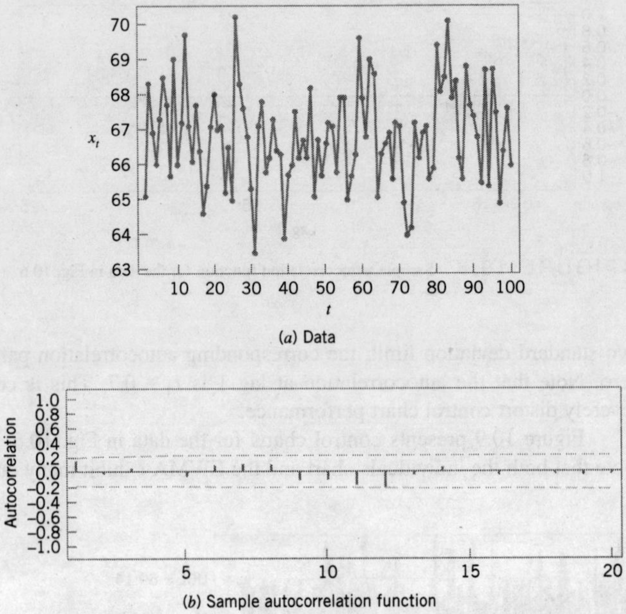

■ **FIGURE 10.10** Plots for every tenth observation from Fig. 10.6.

Based on our previous discussion, we know that less frequent sampling can break up the autocorrelation in process data. To illustrate, consider Fig. 10.10*a*, which is a plot of every tenth observation from Fig. 10.6. The sample autocorrelation function, shown in Fig. 10.10*b*, indicates that there is very little autocorrelation at low lag. The control charts in Fig. 10.11 now indicate that the process is essentially stable. Clearly, then, one approach to dealing with autocorrelation is simply to sample from the process data stream less frequently. Although this seems to be an easy solution, on reconsideration it has some disadvantages. For example, we are making very inefficient use of the available data. Literally, in the above example, we are discarding 90% of the information! Also, since we are only using every tenth observation, it may take much longer to detect a real process shift than if we used all of the data.

Clearly, a better approach is needed. In the next two sections we present several approaches to monitoring autocorrelated process data.

10.4.2 Model-Based Approaches

Time Series Models. An approach that has proved useful in dealing with autocorrelated data is to directly model **time series model,** the correlative structure with an appropriate use that model to remove the autocorrelation from the data, and apply control charts to the **residuals.** For example, suppose that we could model the quality characteristic x_t as

$$x_t = \xi + \phi x_{t-1} + \varepsilon_t \tag{10.11}$$

where ξ and ϕ $(-1 < \phi < 1)$ are unknown constants, and ε_t is normally and independently distributed with mean zero and standard deviation σ. Note how intuitive this model is from

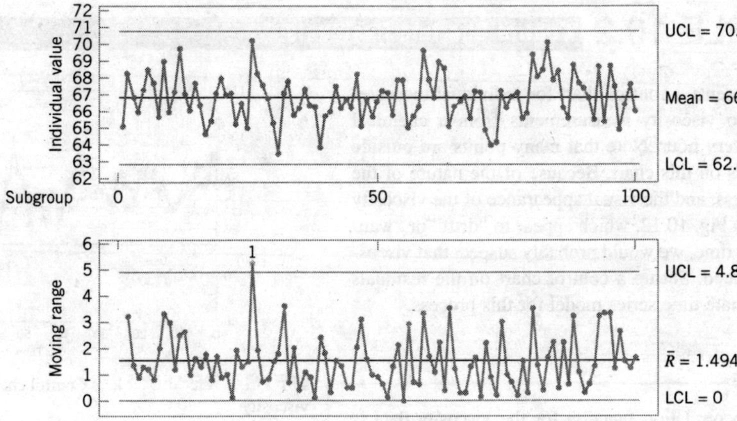

(*a*) Individuals and moving range control charts

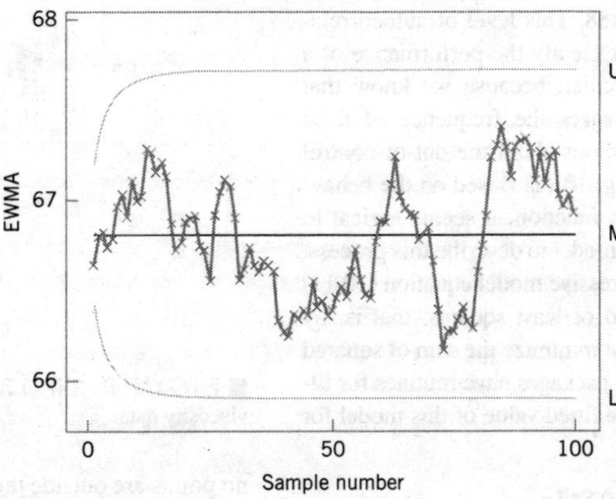

(*b*) EWMA control chart

■ **FIGURE 10.11** Control charts (Minitab) for the data in Fig. 10.10*a*.

examining Figs. 10.6, 10.7, and 10.8. Equation (10.11) is called a **first-order autoregressive model;** the observations x_t from such a model have mean $\xi/(1 - \phi)$, standard deviation $\sigma/(1 - \phi^2)^{1/2}$, and the observations that are k periods apart (x_t and x_{t-k}) have correlation coefficient ϕ^k. That is, the autocorrelation function should decay exponentially just as the sample autocorrelation function did in Fig. 10.8. Suppose that $\hat{\phi}$ is an estimate of ϕ, obtained from analysis of sample data from the process, and $\hat{x}_t$ is the fitted value of x_t. Then the residuals

$$e_t = x_t - \hat{x}_t$$

are approximately normally and independently distributed with mean zero and constant variance. Conventional control charts could now be applied to the sequence of residuals. Points out of control or unusual patterns on such charts would indicate that the parameter ϕ or ξ had changed, implying that the original variable x_t was out of control. For details of identifying and fitting time series models such as this one, see Montgomery, Johnson, and Gardiner (1990) and Box, Jenkins, and Reinsel (1994).

EXAMPLE 10.2 Control Charting Residuals

Figure 10.12 presents a control chart for individual measurements applied to viscosity measurements from a chemical process taken every hour. Note that many points are outside the control limits on this chart. Because of the nature of the production process, and the visual appearance of the viscosity measurements in Fig. 10.12, which appear to "drift" or "wander" slowly over time, we would probably suspect that viscosity is autocorrelated. Set up a control chart on the residuals from on appropriate time series model for this process.

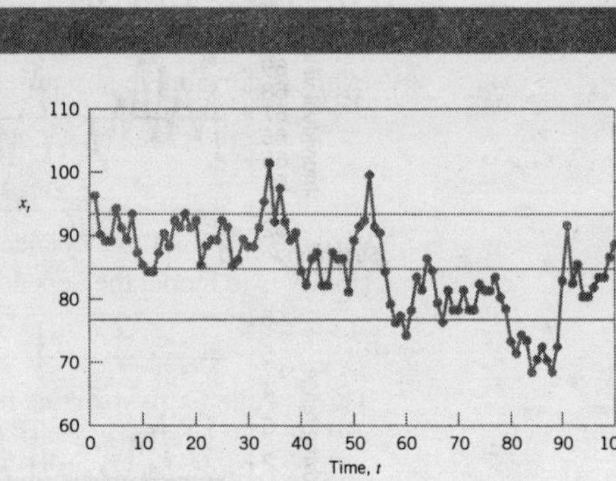

■ **FIGURE 10.12** Control chart for individuals applied to viscosity.

SOLUTION

The sample autocorrelation function for the viscosity data is shown in Fig. 10.13. Note that there is a strong positive correlation at lag 1; that is, observations that are one period apart are positively correlated with $r_1 = 0.88$. This level of autocorrelation is sufficiently high to distort greatly the performance of a Shewhart control chart. In particular, because we know that positive correlation greatly increases the frequence of false alarms, we should be very suspicious about the out-of-control signals on the control chart in Fig. 10.12. Based on the behavior of the sample autocorrelation function, it seems logical to use the first-order autoregressive model to describe this process.

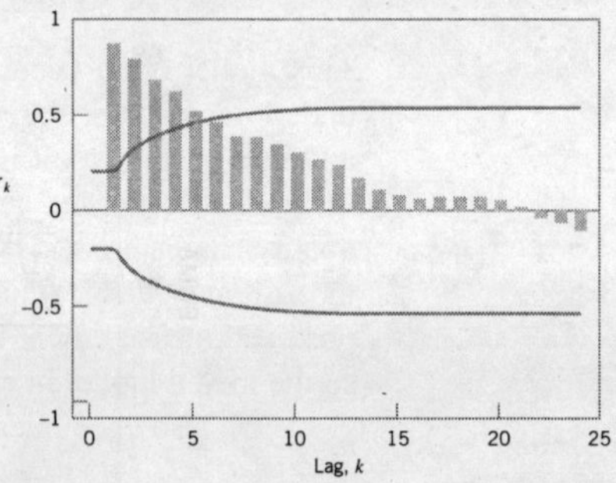

■ **FIGURE 10.13** Sample autocorrelation function for the viscosity data.

The parameters in the autoregressive model equation (10.11) may be estimated by the method of least squares; that is, by choosing the values of ξ and ϕ that minimize the sum of squared errors ε_t. Many statistics software packages have routines for fitting these time series models. The fitted value of this model for the viscosity data is

$$x_t = 13.04 + 0.847x_{t-1}$$

We may think of this as an alternative to the Shewhart model for this process.

Figure 10.14 is an individuals control chart of the residuals from the fitted first-order autoregressive model. Note that now no points are outside the control limits, although around period 90 two points are near the upper control limit. In contrast to the control chart on the individual measurements on Fig. 10.12, we would conclude that this process is in a reasonable state of statistical control.

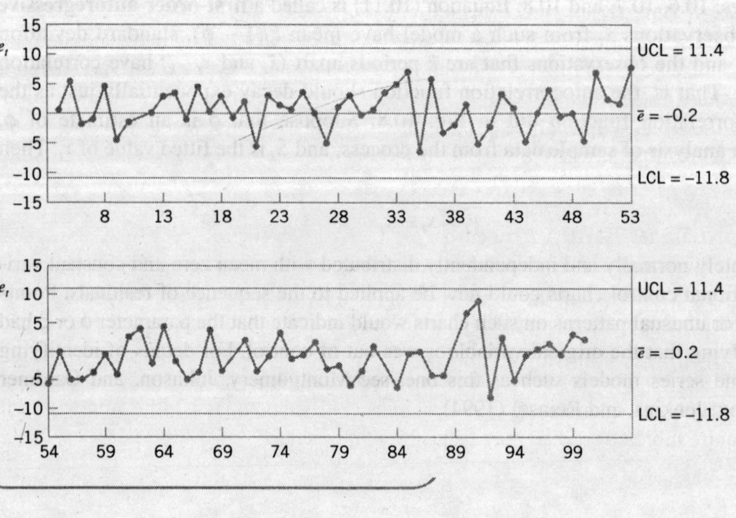

■ **FIGURE 10.14** Control chart for individuals applied to the residuals from the model $x_t = 13.04 + 0.847x_{t-1}$.

Other Time Series Models. The first-order autoregressive model used in the viscosity example [equation (10.11)] is not the only possible model for time-oriented data that exhibits correlative structure. An obvious extension to equation (10.11) is

$$x_t = \xi + \phi_1 x_{t-1} + \phi_2 x_{t-2} + \varepsilon_t \tag{10.12}$$

which is a **second-order autoregressive model.** In general, in autoregressive-type models, the variable x_t is directly dependent on previous observations x_{t-1}, x_{t-2}, and so forth. Another possibility is to model the dependency through the random component ε_t. A simple way to do this is

$$x_t = \mu + \varepsilon_t - \theta\varepsilon_{t-1} \tag{10.13}$$

This is called a **first-order moving average model.** In this model, the correlation between x_t and x_{t-1} is $\rho_1 = -\theta/(1+\theta^2)$ and is zero at all other lags. Thus, the correlative structure in x_t only extends backwards one time period.

Sometimes combinations of autoregressive and moving average terms are useful. A **first-order mixed model** is

$$x_t = \xi + \phi x_{t-1} + \varepsilon_t - \theta\varepsilon_{t-1} \tag{10.14}$$

This model often occurs in the chemical and process industries. The reason is that if the underlying process variable x_t is first-order autoregressive and a random error component is added to x_t, the result is the mixed model in equation (10.14). In the chemical and process industries first-order autoregressive process behavior is fairly common. Furthermore, the quality characteristic is often measured in a laboratory (or by an on-line instrument) that has measurement error, which we can usually think of as random or uncorrelated. The reported or observed measurement then consists of an autoregressive component plus random variation, so the mixed model in equation (10.14) is required as the process model.

We also encounter the **first-order integrated moving average** model

$$x_t = x_{t-1} + \varepsilon_t - \theta\varepsilon_{t-1} \tag{10.15}$$

in some applications. Whereas the previous models are used to describe stationary behavior (that is, x_t wanders around a "fixed" mean), the model in equation (10.15) describes nonstationary behavior (the variable x_t "drifts" as if there is no fixed value of the process mean). This model often arises in chemical and process plants when x_t is an "uncontrolled" process output; that is, when no control actions are taken to keep the variable close to a target value.

The models we have been discussing in equations (10.11) through (10.15) are members of a class of time series models called **autoregressive integrated moving average (ARIMA)** models. Montgomery, Johnson, and Gardiner (1990) and Box, Jenkins, and Reinsel (1994) discuss these models in detail. Although these models appear very different than the Shewhart model [equation (9.9)], they are actually relatively similar and include the Shewhart model as a special case. Note that if we let $\phi = 0$ in equation (10.11), the Shewhart model results. Similarly, if we let $\theta = 0$ in equation (10.13), the Shewhart model results.

An Approximate EWMA Procedure for Correlated Data. The time series modeling approach illustrated in the viscosity example can be awkward in practice. Typically, we apply control charts to several process variables and developing an explicit time series model for each variable of interest is potentially time-consuming. Some authors have developed automatic time series model building to partially alleviate this difficulty. [See Yourstone and Montgomery (1989) and the references therein.] However, unless the time series model itself is of intrinsic value in explaining process dynamics (as it sometimes is), this approach will frequently require more effort than may be justified in practice.

Montgomery and Mastrangelo (1991) have suggested an approximate procedure based on the EWMA. They utilize the fact that the EWMA can be used in certain situations where the data are autocorrelated. Suppose that the process can be modeled by the integrated moving average model in equation (10.15). It can be easily shown that the EWMA with $\lambda = 1 - \theta$ is the optimal one-step-ahead forecast for this process. That is, if $\hat{x}_{t+1}(t)$ is the forecast for the observation in period $t + 1$ made at the end of period t, then

$$\hat{x}_{t+1}(t) = z_t$$

where $z_t = \lambda x_t + (1 - \lambda)z_{t-1}$ is the EWMA. The sequence of one-step-ahead prediction errors

$$e_t = x_t - \hat{x}_t(t-1) \tag{10.16}$$

is independently and identically distributed with mean zero. Therefore, control charts could be applied to these one-step-ahead prediction errors. The parameter λ (or equivalently, θ) would be found by minimizing the sum of squares of the errors e_t.

Now suppose that the process is not modeled exactly by equation (10.15). In general, if the observations from the process are positively autocorrelated and the process mean does not drift too quickly, the EWMA with an appropriate value for λ will provide an excellent one-step-ahead predictor. The forecasting and time series analysis field has used this result for many years; for examples, see Montgomery, Johnson, and Gardiner (1990). Consequently, we would expect many processes that obey first-order dynamics (that is, they follow a slow "drift") to be well represented by the EWMA.

Consequently, under the conditions just described, we may use the EWMA as the basis of a statistical process-monitoring procedure that is an approximation of the exact time series model approach. The procedure would consist of plotting one-step-ahead EWMA prediction errors (or model residuals) on a control chart. This chart could be accompanied by a run chart of the original observations on which the EWMA forecast is superimposed. Our experience indicates that both charts are usually necessary, as operational personnel feel that the control chart of residuals sometimes does not provide a direct frame of reference to the process. The run chart of original observations allows process dynamics to be visualized.

Figure 10.15 is a graph of the sum of squares of the EWMA prediction errors versus λ for the viscosity data. The minimum squared prediction error occurs at $\lambda = 0.825$. Figure 10.16 presents a control chart for individuals applied to the EWMA prediction errors. This chart is slightly different from the control chart of the exact autoregressive model residuals shown in

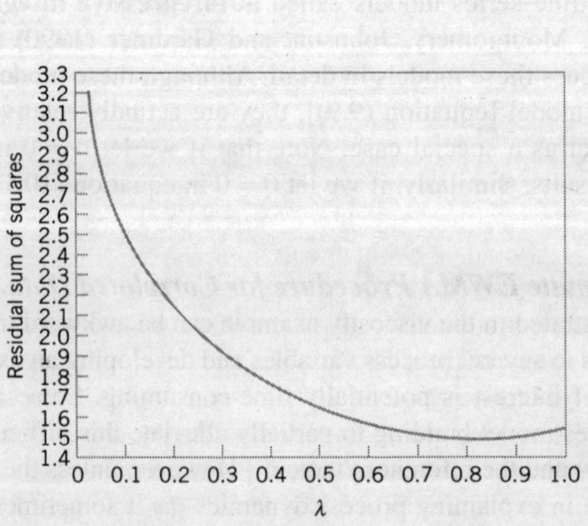

■ FIGURE 10.15 Residual sum of squares versus λ.

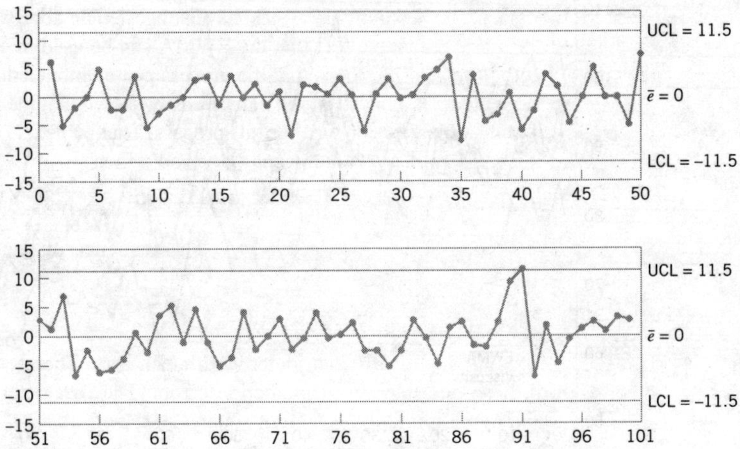

■ FIGURE 10.16 EWMA prediction errors with $\lambda = 0.825$ and Shewhart limits.

Fig. 10.14, but not significantly so. Both indicate a process that is reasonably stable, with a period around $t = 90$ where an assignable cause may be present.

Montgomery and Mastrangelo (1991) point out that it is possible to combine information about the state of statistical control and process dynamics on a single control chart. Assume that the one-step-ahead prediction errors (or model residuals) e_t are normally distributed. Then the usual three-sigma control limits on the control chart on these errors satisfy the following probability statement

$$P[-3\sigma \le e_t \le 3\sigma] = 0.9973$$

where σ is the standard deviation of the errors or residuals e_t. We may rewrite this as

$$P[-3\sigma \le x_t - \hat{x}_t(t-1) \le 3\sigma] = 0.9973$$

or

$$P[\hat{x}_t(t-1) - 3\sigma \le x_t \le \hat{x}_t(t-1) + 3\sigma] = 0.9973 \tag{10.17}$$

Equation (10.17) suggests that if the EWMA is a suitable one-step-ahead predictor, then one could use z_t as the center line on a control chart for period $t + 1$ with upper and lower control limits at

$$\text{UCL}_{t+1} = z_t + 3\sigma \tag{10.18a}$$

and

$$\text{LCL}_{t+1} = z_t - 3\sigma \tag{10.18b}$$

and the observation x_{t+1} would be compared to these limits to test for statistical control. We can think of this as a **moving center-line EWMA control chart.** As mentioned above, in many cases this would be preferable from an interpretation standpoint to a control chart of residuals and a separate chart of the EWMA as it combines information about process dynamics and statistical control on one chart.

Figure 10.17 is the moving center-line EWMA control chart for the viscosity data, with $\lambda = 0.825$. It conveys the same information about statistical control as the residual or EWMA prediction error control chart in Fig. 10.16, but operating personnel often feel more comfortable with this display.

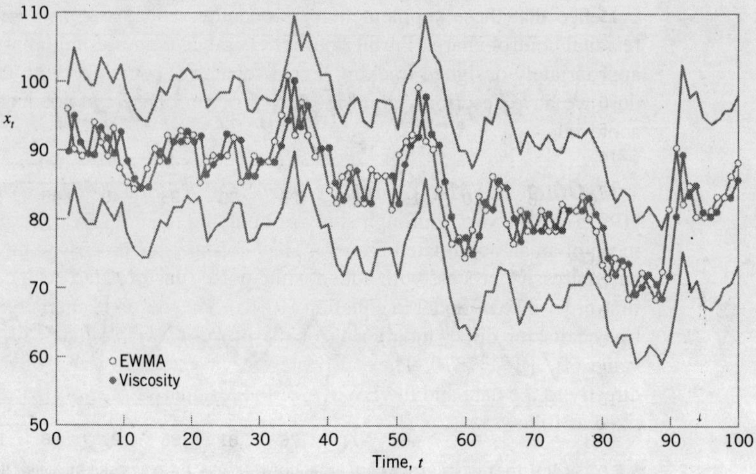

■ FIGURE 10.17 Moving center-line EWMA control chart applied to the viscosity data ($\lambda = 0.825$).

Estimation and Monitoring of σ. The standard deviation of the one-step-ahead errors or model residuals σ may be estimated in several ways. If λ is chosen as suggested above over a record of n observations, then dividing the sum of squared prediction errors for the optimal λ by n will produce an estimate of σ^2. This is the method used in many time-series analysis computer programs.

Another approach is to compute the estimate of σ as typically done in forecasting systems. The mean absolute deviation (MAD) could be used in this regard. The MAD is computed by applying an EWMA to the absolute value of the prediction error

$$\Delta_t = \alpha|e_t| + (1-\alpha)\Delta_{t-1} \quad 0 < \alpha \le 1$$

Since the MAD of a normal distribution is related to the standard deviation by $\sigma = 1.25\Delta$ [see Montgomery, Johnson, and Gardiner (1990)], we could estimate the standard deviation of the prediction errors at time t by

$$\hat{\sigma}_t \simeq 1.25\Delta_t \tag{10.19}$$

Another approach is to directly calculate a smoothed variance

$$\hat{\sigma}_t^2 = \alpha e_t^2 + (1-\alpha)\hat{\sigma}_{t-1}^2 \quad 0 < \alpha \le 1 \tag{10.20}$$

MacGregor and Harris (1993) discuss the use of exponentially weighted moving variance estimates in monitoring the variability of a process. They show how to find control limits for these quantities for both correlated and uncorrelated data.

The Sensitivity of Residual Control Charts. Several authors have pointed out that residual control charts are not sensitive to small process shifts [see Wardell, Moskowitz, and Plante (1994)]. To improve sensitivity, we would recommend using cusum or EWMA control charts on residuals instead of Shewhart charts. Tseng and Adams (1994) note that because the EWMA is not an optimal forecasting scheme for most processes [except the model in equation (10.15)], it will not completely account for the autocorrelation, and this can affect the statistical performance of control charts based on EWMA residuals or prediction errors. Montgomery and Mastrangelo (1991) suggest the use of supplementary procedures called **tracking signals** combined with the control chart for residuals. There is evidence that these supplementary procedures enhance considerably the performance of residual control charts. Furthermore, Mastrangelo and Montgomery (1995) show that if an appropriately designed tracking signal scheme is combined with the EWMA-based procedure we have described, good in-control performance and adequate shift detection can be achieved.

Other EWMA Control Charts for Autocorrelated Data. Lu and Reynolds (1999a) give a very thorough study of applying the EWMA control chart to monitoring the mean of an autocorrelated process. They consider the process to be modeled by a first-order autoregressive process with added white noise (uncorrelated error). This is equivalent to the first-order mixed model in equation (10.13). They provide charts for designing EWMA control charts for direct monitoring of the process variable that will give an in-control ARL value of $ARL_0 = 370$. They also present an extensive study of both the EWMA applied directly to the data and the EWMA of the residuals. Some of their findings may be summarized as follows:

1. When there is significant autocorrelation in process data and this autocorrelation is an inherent part of the process, traditional methods of estimating process parameters and constructing control charts should not be used. Instead, one should model the autocorrelation so that reliable control charts can be constructed.
2. A large data set should be used in the process of fitting a model for the process observations and estimating the parameters of this model. If a control chart must be constructed using a small data set, then signals from this chart should be interpreted with caution and the process of model fitting and parameter estimation should be repeated as soon as additional data become available. That is, the control limits for the chart are relatively sensitive to poor estimates of the process parameters.
3. For the low to moderate levels of correlation, a Shewhart chart of the observations will be much better at detecting a shift in the process mean than a Shewhart chart of the residuals. Unless interest is only in detecting large shifts, an EWMA chart will be better than a Shewhart chart. An EWMA chart of the residuals will be better than an EWMA chart of the observations for large shifts, and the EWMA of the observations will be a little better for small shifts.

In a subsequent paper, Lu and Reynolds (1999b) present control charts for monitoring both the mean and variance of autocorrelated process data. Several types of control charts and combinations of control charts are studied. Some of these are control charts of the original observations with control limits that are adjusted to account for the autocorrelation and others are control charts of residuals from a time series model. Although there is no combination that emerges as best overall, an EWMA control chart of the observations and a Shewhart chart of residuals is a good combination for many practical situations.

Know Your Process! When autocorrelation is observed, we must be careful to ensure that the autocorrelation is really an inherent part of the process and not the result of some assignable cause. For example, consider the data in Fig. 10.18*a* for which the sample autocorrelation function is shown in Fig. 10.18*b*. The sample autocorrelation function gives a clear indication of positive autocorrelation in the data. Closer inspection of the data, however, reveals that there may have been an assignable cause around time $t = 50$ that resulted in a shift in the mean from 100 to about 105, and another shift may have occurred around time $t = 100$ resulting in a shift in the mean to about 95.

When these potential shifts are accounted for, the apparent autocorrelation may vanish. For example, Fig. 10.19 presents the sample autocorrelation functions for observations

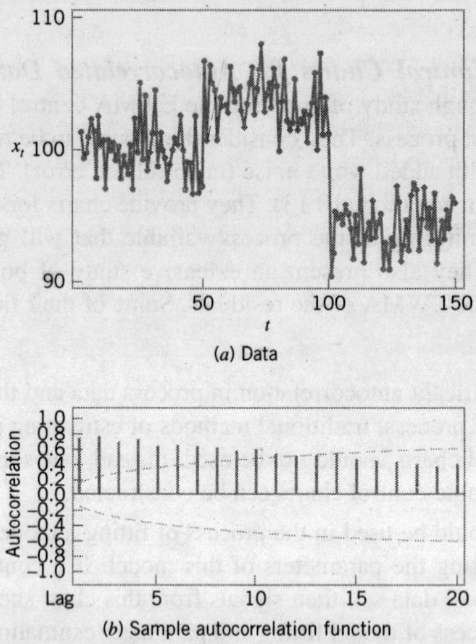

■ **FIGURE 10.18** Data with apparent positive autocorrelation.

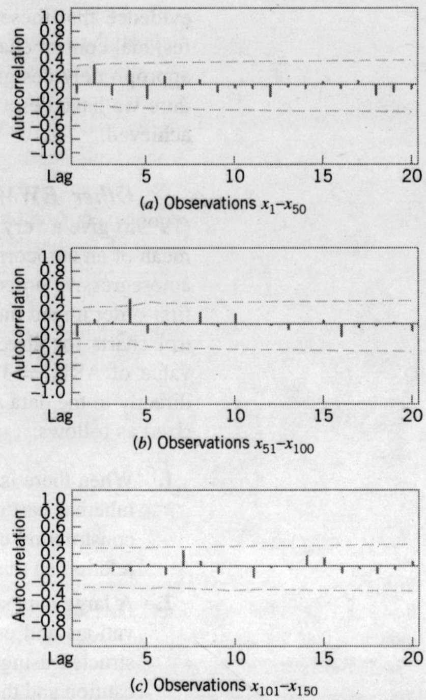

■ **FIGURE 10.19** Sample autocorrelation functions after the process shifts are removed.

$x_1 - x_{50}$, $x_{51} - x_{100}$, and $x_{101} - x_{150}$. There is no evidence of autocorrelation in any of the three groups of data. Therefore, the autocorrelation in the original data is likely due to assignable causes and is not an inherent characteristic of the process.

10.4.3 A Model-Free Approach

The Batch Means Control Chart. Runger and Willemain (1996) proposed a control chart based on unweighted batch means for monitoring autocorrelated process data. The batch means approach has been used extensively in the analysis of the output from computer simulation models, another area where highly autocorrelated data often occur. The **unweighted batch means (UBM) control chart** breaks successive groups of sequential observations into batches, with equal weights assigned to every point in the batch. Let the jth unweighted batch mean be

$$\bar{x}_j = \frac{1}{b} \sum_{i=1}^{b} x_{(j-1)b+i} \qquad j = 1, 2, \ldots \tag{10.21}$$

The important implication of equation (10.21) is that although one has to determine an appropriate batch size b, it is not necessary to construct an ARIMA model of the data. This approach is quite standard in simulation output analysis, which also focuses on inference for long time series with high autocorrelation.

Runger and Willemain (1996) showed that the batch means can be plotted and analyzed on a standard individuals control chart. Distinct from residuals plots, UBM charts retain the basic simplicity of averaging observations to form a point in a control chart. With UBMs, the control chart averaging is used to dilute the autocorrelation of the data.

Procedures for determining an appropriate batch size have been developed by researchers in the simulation area. These procedures are empirical and do not depend on identifying and estimating a time series model. Of course, a time series model can guide the process of selecting the batch size and also provide analytical insights.

Runger and Willemain (1996) provided a detailed analysis of batch sizes for AR(1) models. They recommend that the batch size be selected so as to reduce the lag 1 autocorrelation of the batch means to approximately 0.10. They suggest starting with $b = 1$ and doubling b until the lag 1 autocorrelation of the batch means is sufficiently small. This parallels the logic of the Shewhart chart in that larger batches are more effective for detecting smaller shifts; smaller batches respond more quickly to larger shifts.

EXAMPLE 10.3 A Batch Means Control Chart

Construct a batch means control chart using the data in Fig. 10.6.

SOLUTION

In Fig. 10.20*a* we give a plot of batch means computed using $b = 10$. The sample autocorrelation function in Fig. 10.20*b* indicates that the autocorrelation has been reduced dramatically by the batch means approach. The control charts for the batch means are shown in Fig. 10.21. The general indication is that the process is stable.

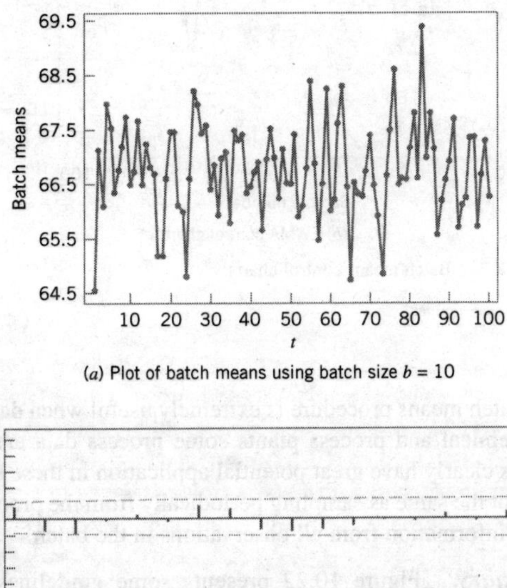

(*a*) Plot of batch means using batch size $b = 10$

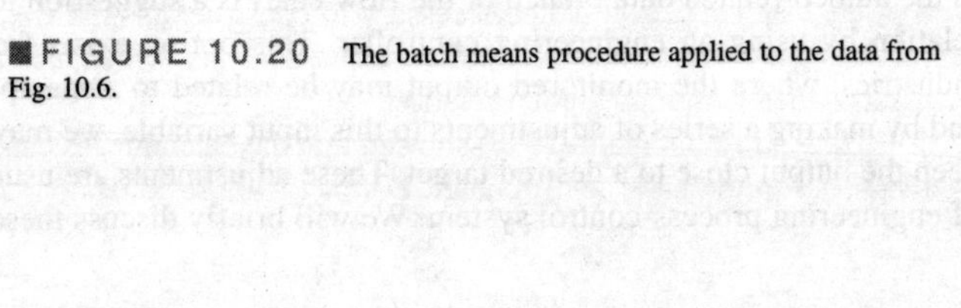

(*b*) Sample autocorrelation function

■ FIGURE 10.20 The batch means procedure applied to the data from Fig. 10.6.

(continued)

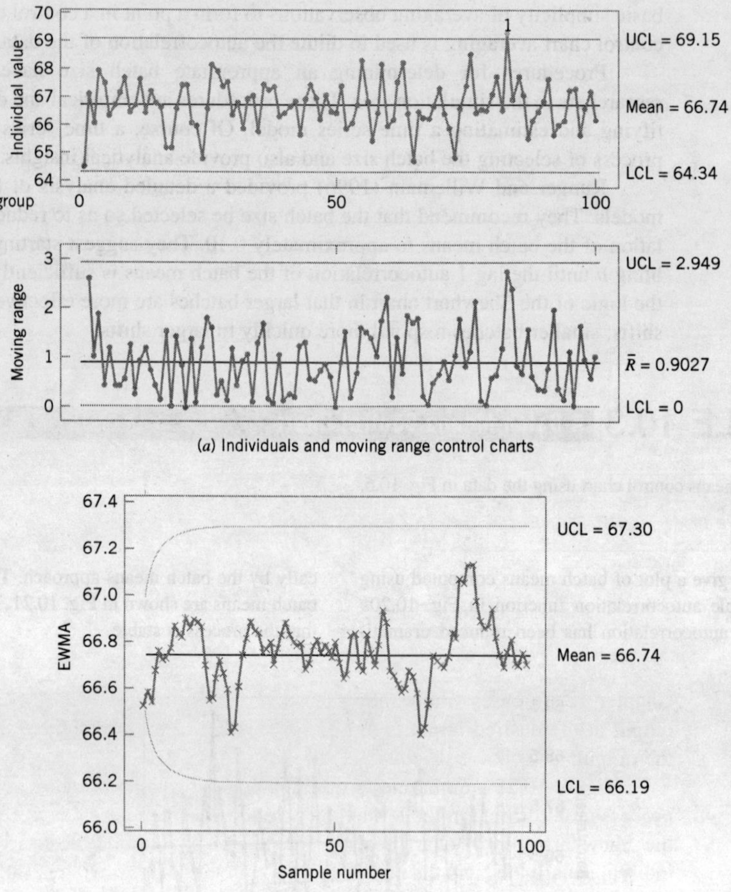

■ FIGURE 10.21 Batch means control charts.

The batch means procedure is extremely useful when data become available very often. In many chemical and process plants some process data are observed every few seconds. Batch means clearly have great potential application in these situations. Also, note that batch means are not the same as sampling periodically from the process, because the averaging procedure uses information from all observations in the batch.

Summary. Figure 10.22 presents some guidelines for using univariate control charts to monitor processes with both correlated and uncorrelated data. The correlated data branch of the flow chart assumes that the sample size is $n = 1$. Note that one of the options in the autocorrelated data branch of the flow chart is a suggestion to eliminate the autocorrelation by using an engineering controller. This option exists frequently in the process industries, where the monitored output may be related to a manipulatable input variable, and by making a series of adjustments to this input variable, we may be able to consistently keep the output close to a desired target. These adjustments are usually made by some type of engineering process-control system. We will briefly discuss these types of controllers in

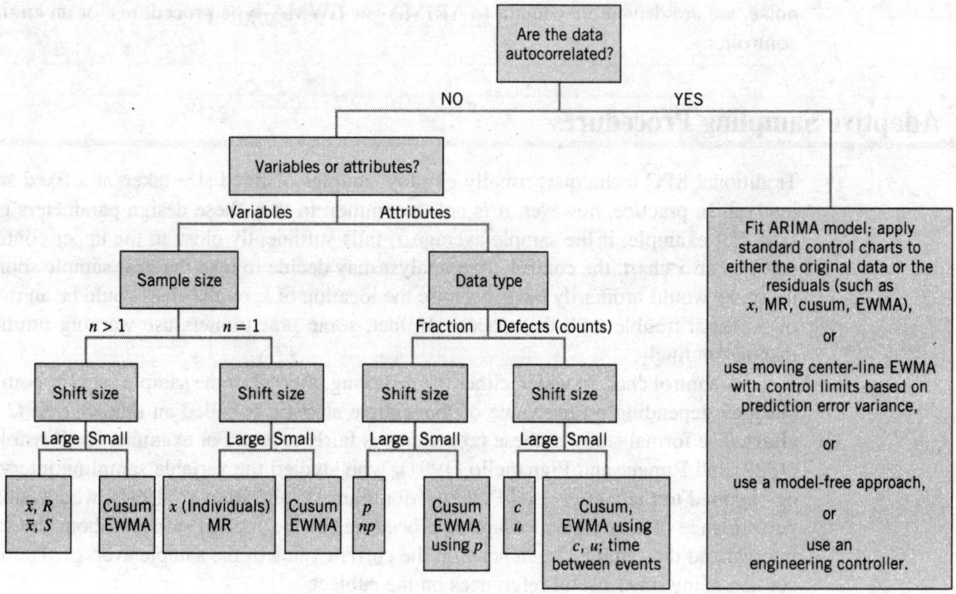

■ **FIGURE 10.22** Some guidelines for univariate control chart selection.

Chapter 12. In cases where they can be successfully employed, the effect of keeping the output at the desired target is often to eliminate (or greatly reduce) the autocorrelation in the output.

Figure 10.23 summarizes some situations in which various procedures are useful for process monitoring. On the left axis we find that as the interval between samples increases, the Shewhart control chart becomes an appropriate choice because the larger sampling interval usually negates the effects of autocorrelation. As the interval between samples gets smaller, autocorrelation plays a much more important role, which leads to the ARIMA or EWMA approach. On the right axis we find that as the cost of process adjustment increases, we are driven to the Shewhart chart for process monitoring. On the other hand, if adjustment cost is low, we are driven to some type of engineering process-control system, which we will discuss in the next section. Finally, on the vertical axis, we see that as the variability due to random causes or noise dominates any motion in the mean, the Shewhart chart becomes more appropriate. However, if the motion in the mean is large relative to random

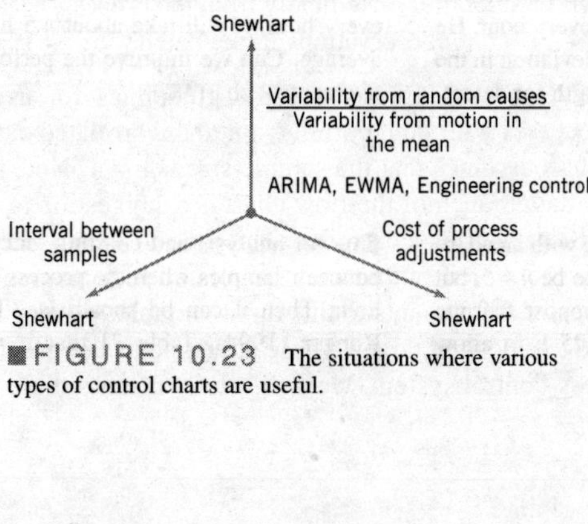

■ **FIGURE 10.23** The situations where various types of control charts are useful.

noise, we are driven once again to ARIMA- or EWMA-type procedures, or an engineering controller.

10.5 Adaptive Sampling Procedures

Traditional SPC techniques usually employ samples of fixed size taken at a fixed sampling interval. In practice, however, it is not uncommon to vary these design parameters on occasion. For example, if the sample average $\bar{x}_i$ falls sufficiently close to the upper control limit (say) on an $\bar{x}$ chart, the control chart analyst may decide to take the next sample sooner than he or she would ordinarily have, because the location of $\bar{x}_i$ on the chart could be an indication of potential trouble with the process. In fact, some practitioners use warning limits in this manner routinely.

A control chart in which either the sampling interval or the sample size (or both) can be changed depending on the value of the sample statistic is called an **adaptive SPC control chart.** The formal study of these procedures is fairly recent. For example, see Reynolds et al. (1988) and Runger and Pignatiello (1991), who studied the variable sampling interval strategy applied to the $\bar{x}$ chart, and Prabhu, Montgomery, and Runger (1994), who evaluated the performance of a combined adaptive procedure for the $\bar{x}$ chart in which both the sampling interval and the sample size depend on the current value of the sample average. These papers contain many other useful references on the subject.

The general approach used by these authors is to divide the region between the upper and lower control limits into zones, such that

$$\text{LCL} \le -w \le \text{CL} \le w \le \text{UCL}$$

If the sample statistic falls between $-w$ and w, then the standard sampling interval (and possibly sample size) is used for the next sample. However, if $w < \bar{x}_i < \text{UCL}$ or if $\text{LCL} < \bar{x}_i < -w_b$ then a shorter sampling interval (and possibly a larger sample size) is used for the next sample. It can be shown that these procedures greatly enhance control chart performance in that they reduce the average time to signal (ATS) particularly for small process shifts, when compared to an ordinary nonadaptive control chart that has a sample size and sampling interval equal to the average of those quantities for the adaptive chart when the process is in control. Prabhu, Montgomery, and Runger (1995) have given a FORTRAN program for evaluating the ATS for several different adaptive versions of the $\bar{x}$ chart.

EXAMPLE 10.4 An $\bar{x}$ Control Chart with a Variable Sampling Interval

An engineer is currently monitoring a process with an $\bar{x}$ chart using a sample size of five, with samples taken every hour. He is interested in detecting a shift of one standard deviation in the mean. It is easy to show that the average run length for detecting this shift is 4.5 samples. Therefore, if samples are taken every hour, it will take about 4.5 h to detect this shift on the average. Can we improve the performance by using an adaptive control chart?

SOLUTION

Suppose that we try to improve this performance with an adaptive control chart. We still want the sample size to be $n = 5$, but the time between samples could be variable. Suppose that the shortest time allowable between samples is 0.25 h to allow time for analysis and charting, but we want the average time between samples when the process is in control to still be one hour. Then it can be shown [see Prabhu, Montgomery, and Runger (1994), Table 7] that if we set the warning limit

$w = 0.67\sigma_{\bar{x}}$ and choose the shortest and longest times between samples as $t_1 = 0.25$ h and $t_2 = 1.75$ h, respectively, the average time to signal can be reduced to 2.26 h. In this scheme, if $-0.67\sigma_{\bar{x}} \le \bar{x} \le 0.67\sigma_{\bar{x}}$, the time until the next sample is 1.75 h, whereas if the sample average $0.67\sigma_{\bar{x}} < \bar{x} < \text{UCL} = 3\sigma_{\bar{x}}$ or LCL $= -3\sigma_{\bar{x}} < \bar{x} < -0.67\,\sigma_{\bar{x}}$, the next sample is taken at 0.25 h. This adaptive scheme essentially reduces the ATS by 50%.

It is possible to do even better if one is willing to adapt both the sample size and the sampling interval. This chart will require that we plot a standardized value

$$z_i = \frac{\bar{x}_i - \mu_0}{\sigma_0 / \sqrt{n(i)}}$$

where μ_0 and σ_0 are the in-control values of μ and σ, and $n(i)$ is the sample size taken at the ith sample. Now if we want the average sample size to be five and the average interval between samples to be 1 h when the process is in control but both chart parameters can be variable, we have what Prabhu, Montgomery, and Runger (1994) called the combined adaptive $\bar{x}$ chart. If we use $n_1 = 3$, $n_2 = 8$, $t_1 = 0.25$, $t_2 = 1.50$, and $w = 0.84$, then the average time to signal for a one-sigma shift in the mean is 1.72 h [see Prabhu, Montgomery, and Runger (1994), Table 7]. In this scheme, if $-0.84 \le z_i \le 0.84$, use $n_1 = 3$ and $t_2 = 1.5$ h for the next sample, whereas if $0.84 < z_i < 3$ or if $-3 < z_i < -0.84$, use $n_2 = 8$ and $t_1 = 0.25$ h for the next sample.

Adaptive sampling procedures have considerable potential for application, if some flexibility exists with respect to the frequency and size of samples. If only one chart parameter can be adapted, we have found that more improvement in performance usually results from varying the sample size than from varying the sampling interval. The Supplemental Text Material contains more information about adaptive control charting methods.

10.6 Economic Design of Control Charts

10.6.1 Designing a Control Chart

Control charts are widely used to establish and maintain statistical control of a process. They are also effective devices for estimating process parameters, particularly in process capability studies. The use of a control chart requires that the engineer or analyst select a sample size, a sampling frequency or interval between samples, and the control limits for the chart. Selection of these three parameters is usually called the ***design*** of the control chart.

Traditionally, control charts have been designed with respect to statistical criteria only. This usually involves selecting the sample size and control limits such that the average run length of the chart to detect a particular shift in the quality characteristic and the average run length of the procedure when the process is in control are equal to specified values. The frequency of sampling is rarely treated analytically, and usually the practitioner is advised to consider such factors as the production rate, the expected frequency of shifts to an out-of-control state, and the possible consequences of such process shifts in selecting the sampling interval. The use of statistical criteria and practical experience has led, in many cases, to general guidelines for the design of control charts. Many of these guidelines, as well as the approach used in developing them, have been discussed for specific types of control charts in previous chapters.

The design of a control chart has economic consequences in that the costs of sampling and testing, costs associated with investigating out-of-control signals and possibly correcting assignable causes, and costs of allowing nonconforming units to reach the consumer are all affected by the choice of the control chart parameters. Therefore, it is logical to consider the design of a control chart from an economic viewpoint. In recent years, considerable research has been devoted to **economic models of control charts.** This section will present several models for the optimal economic design of control charts. Some of the practical implications of these models will also be discussed.

10.6.2 Process Characteristics

To formulate an economic model for the design of a control chart, it is necessary to make certain assumptions about the behavior of the process. The assumptions summarized next are relatively standard in that most economic models incorporate them to some degree. In later sections we see how these assumptions are used in building specific models, and we discuss their relative importance.

The process is assumed to be characterized by a single in-control state. For example, if the process has one measurable quality characteristic, then the in-control state will correspond to the mean of this quality characteristic when no assignable causes are present. Similarly, when the quality characteristic is an attribute, the in-control state will be represented by the fraction nonconforming (say) produced by the process when no assignable causes are present. The process may have, in general, $s \geq 1$ out-of-control states. Each out-of-control state is usually associated with a particular type of assignable cause.

Determining the nature of the transitions between the in-control and out-of-control states requires certain assumptions. It is customary to assume that assignable causes occur during an interval of time according to a Poisson process. This implies that the length of time the process remains in the in-control state, given that it begins in control, is an exponential random variable. This assumption allows considerable simplification in the development of economic models, and in some situations results in a Markov chain model structure. The nature in which process shifts occur is sometimes called the **process-failure mechanism.** This can be a very critical assumption. We also observe that the assumption of discrete states and the nature of the failure mechanism imply that process transitions between states are instantaneous. Processes that "drift" slowly from an in-control state—as, for example, in the case of tool wear—have received little analytical attention.

It is also usually assumed that the process is not self-correcting. That is, once a transition to an out-of-control state has occurred, the process can be returned to the in-control condition only by management intervention following an appropriate out-of-control signal on the control chart. In some cases, however, transitions between different out-of-control states are allowed, provided the transitions are always consistent with further quality deterioration.

10.6.3 Cost Parameters

Three categories of costs are customarily considered in the economic design of control charts: the costs of sampling and testing, the costs associated with investigating an out-of-control signal and with the repair or correction of any assignable causes found, and the costs associated with the production of nonconforming items.

The costs of sampling and testing include the out-of-pocket expenses of inspectors' and technicians' salaries and wages, the costs of any necessary test equipment, and, in the case of destructive testing, the unit costs of the items sampled. Usually, the cost of sampling and testing is assumed to consist of both fixed and variable components—say, a_1 and a_2, respectively—such that the total cost of sampling and testing is

$$a_1 + a_2 n$$

Because of the difficulty of obtaining and evaluating cost information, use of more complex relationships is probably inappropriate.

The costs of investigating and possibly correcting the process following an out-of-control signal have been treated in several ways. Some authors have suggested that the costs of investigating false alarms will differ from the costs of correcting assignable causes; consequently, these two situations must be represented in the model by different cost coefficients. Furthermore, the cost of repairing or correcting the process could depend on the type of assignable cause present. Thus, in models having s out-of-control states, $s + 1$ cost coefficients might be necessary to model the search and adjustment procedures associated with out-of-control signals. Usually, these cost coefficients would be chosen so that larger process shifts incurred larger costs of repair or adjustment. Other authors have argued that this level of modeling detail is unnecessary because in many cases small shifts are difficult to find but easy to correct, whereas large shifts are easy to find but difficult to correct. Hence, one loses little accuracy by using a single cost coefficient to represent the *average* costs of investigating and possibly correcting out-of-control signals.

The costs associated with producing nonconforming items consist of typical *failure* costs—that is, the costs of rework or scrap for internal failures, or replacement or repair costs for units covered by warranties in the case of external failures. With external failures, there may also be secondary effects from the production of nonconforming items if the customer's dissatisfaction with the product causes an alteration in future purchases of the product or other products manufactured by the company. Finally, there may be losses resulting from product liability claims against the company. Most authors model these costs with a single, average cost coefficient, expressed on either a per unit time or per item basis.

Economic models are generally formulated using a total cost function, which expresses the relationships between the control chart design parameters and the three types of costs discussed above. The production, monitoring, and adjustment process may be thought of as a series of independent cycles over time. Each cycle begins with the production process in the in-control state and continues until process monitoring via the control chart results in an out-of-control signal. Following an adjustment in which the process is returned to the in-control state, a new cycle begins. Let $E(T)$ be the *expected length* (that is, the *long-term average length*, or *mean length*) of a cycle, and let $E(C)$ be the *expected total cost incurred* during a cycle. Then the expected cost per unit time is

$$E(A) = \frac{E(C)}{E(T)} \tag{10.22}$$

Optimization techniques are then applied to equation (10.22) to determine the economically optimal control chart design. Minor variations in equation (10.22) have appeared in the literature. For example, some authors have elected to replace $E(T)$ in equation (10.22) by the expected number of units produced during the cycle, resulting in the expected cost expressed on a per item rather than a per unit time basis. In other studies, a somewhat different definition of a cycle is used, depending on whether the process is shut down or allowed to continue operation while out-of-control signals are investigated.

The general model structure in equation (10.22) has a disturbing appearance. Note that C and T are dependent random variables, yet we have represented the expected value of their ratio $E(A)$ by the ratio of expectations $E(C)/E(T)$. Now it is well known that the expected value of a ratio is not equal to the ratio of expected values (even for independent random variables), so some further explanation of the structure of equation (10.22) seems warranted. The sequence of production–monitoring–adjustment, with accumulation of costs over the cycle, can be represented by a particular type of stochastic process called a *renewal reward process*. Stochastic processes of this type have the property that their average time cost is given by the ratio of the expected reward per cycle to the expected cycle length, as shown in equation (10.22).

10.6.4 Early Work and Semieconomic Designs

A fundamental paper in the area of cost modeling of quality control systems was published by Girshick and Rubin (1952). They consider a process model in which a machine producing items characterized by a measurable quality characteristic x can be in one of four states. States 1 and 2 are production states, and, in state i, the output quality characteristic is described by the probability density function $f_i(x)$, $i = 1, 2$. State 1 is the "in-control" state. While in state 1, there is a constant probability of a shift state 2. The process is not self-correcting; repair is necessary to return the process to state 1. States $j = 3$ and $j = 4$ are repair states, if we assume that the machine was previously in state $j - 2$. In state $j = 3, 4$, n_j units of time are required for repair, where a time unit is defined as the time to produce one unit of product. Girshick and Rubin treat both 100% inspection and periodic inspection rules. The economic criterion is to maximize the expected income from the process. The optimal control rules are difficult to derive, as they depend on the solution to complex integral equations. Consequently, the model's use in practice has been very limited.

Although it has had little or no practical application, Girshick and Rubin's work is of significant theoretical value. They were the first researchers to propose the expected cost (or income) per unit time criterion [equation (10.22)], and rigorously show its appropriateness for this problem. Later analysts' use of this criterion [equation (10.22)] rests directly on its development by Girshick and Rubin. Other researchers have investigated generalized formulations of the Girshick-Rubin model, including Bather (1963), Ross (1971), Savage (1962), and White (1974). Again, their results are primarily of theoretical interest, as they do not lead to process control rules easily implemented by practitioners.

Economic design of conventional Shewhart control charts was investigated by several early researchers. Most of their work could be classified as semieconomic design procedures, in that either the proposed model did not consider all relevant costs or no formal optimization techniques were applied to the cost function. Weiler (1952) suggested that for an $\bar{x}$ chart, the optimum sample size should minimize the total amount of inspection required to detect a specified shift. If the shift is from an in-control state μ_0 to an out-of-control state $\mu_1 = \mu_0 + \delta\sigma$, then Weiler shows that the optimal sample size is

$$n = \frac{12.0}{\delta^2} \quad \text{when } \pm 3.09\text{-sigma control limits are used}$$

$$n = \frac{11.1}{\delta^2} \quad \text{when } \pm 3\text{-sigma control limits are used}$$

$$n = \frac{6.65}{\delta^2} \quad \text{when } \pm 2.58\text{-sigma control limits are used}$$

$$n = \frac{4.4}{\delta^2} \quad \text{when } \pm 2.33\text{-sigma control limits are used}$$

Note that Weiler did not formally consider costs; the implication is that minimizing total inspection will minimize total costs.

Taylor (1965) has shown that control procedures based on taking a sample of constant size at fixed intervals of time is nonoptimal. He suggests that sample size and sampling frequency should be determined at each point in time based on the posterior probability that the process is in an out-of-control state. Dynamic programming-type methods are utilized extensively in the development. In a subsequent paper, Taylor (1967) derives the optimal control rule for a two-state process with a normally distributed quality characteristic. Although Taylor's work has indicated their nonoptimality, fixed sample size–fixed sampling interval control rules are widely used in practice because of their administrative simplicity. Consequently, most researchers have concentrated on the optimal economic design of such procedures.

10.6.5 An Economic Model of the $\bar{x}$ Control Chart

Much of the research in the development of economic models of control charts has been devoted to the $\bar{x}$ chart. The interest of analysts in this control chart follows directly from its widespread use in practice. In this section, we discuss one of the economic models that has been widely studied.

In 1956, Duncan proposed an economic model for the optimum economic design of the $\bar{x}$ control chart. His paper was the first to deal with a fully economic model of a Shewhart-type control chart and to incorporate formal optimization methodology into determining the control chart parameters. Duncan's paper was the stimulus for much of the subsequent research in this area.

Duncan drew on the earlier work of Girshick and Rubin (1952) in that he utilized a design criterion that maximized the expected net income per unit of time from the process. In the development of the cost model, Duncan assumed that the process is characterized by an in-control state μ_0 and that a single assignable cause of magnitude δ, which occurs at random, results in a shift in the mean from μ_0 to either $\mu_0 + \delta\sigma$ or $\mu_0 - \delta\sigma$. The process is monitored by an $\bar{x}$ chart with center line μ_0 and upper and lower control limits $\mu_0 \pm k(\sigma/\sqrt{n})$. Samples are to be taken at intervals of h hours. When one point exceeds the control limits, a search for the assignable cause is initiated. During the search for the assignable cause, the process is allowed to continue in operation. Furthermore, it is assumed that the cost of adjustment or repairs (if necessary) is not charged against the net income from the process. The parameters μ_0, δ, and σ are assumed known, whereas n, k, and h are to be determined.

The assignable cause is assumed to occur according to a Poisson process with an intensity of λ occurrences per hour. That is, assuming that the process begins in the in-control state, the time interval that the process remains in control is an exponential random variable with mean $1/\lambda$ h. Therefore, given the occurrence of the assignable cause between the jth and $(j+1)$st samples, the expected time of occurrence within this interval is

$$\tau = \frac{\int_{jh}^{(j+1)h} e^{-\lambda t}\lambda(t-jh)dt}{\int_{jh}^{(j+1)h} e^{-\lambda t}\lambda dt} = \frac{1-(1+\lambda h)e^{-\lambda h}}{\lambda\left(1-e^{-\lambda h}\right)} \tag{10.23}$$

When the assignable cause occurs, the probability that it will be detected on any subsequent sample is

$$1-\beta = \int_{-\infty}^{-k-\delta\sqrt{n}} \phi(z)dz + \int_{k-\delta\sqrt{n}}^{\infty} \phi(z)dz \tag{10.24}$$

where $\phi(z) = (2\pi)^{-1/2}\exp(-z^2/2)$ is the standard normal density. The quantity $1-\beta$ is the power of the test, and β is the type II error probability. The probability of a false alarm is

$$\alpha = 2\int_{k}^{\infty} \phi(z)dz \tag{10.25}$$

A production cycle is defined as the interval of time from the start of production (the process is assumed to start in the in-control state) following an adjustment to the detection and elimination of the assignable cause. The cycle consists of four periods: (1) the in-control period, (2) the out-of-control period, (3) the time to take a sample and interpret the results, and (4) the time to find the assignable cause. The expected length of the in-control period is $1/\lambda$. Noting the number of samples required to produce an out-of-control signal given that the process is actually out of control is a geometric random variable with mean $1/(1-\beta)$, we conclude that the expected length of the out-of-control period is $h/(1-\beta)-\tau$. The time required to take a sample and interpret the results is a constant g proportional to the sample size, so that gn is the length of this segment of the cycle. The time required to find the assignable cause following an action signal is a constant D. Therefore, the expected length of a cycle is

$$E(T)=\frac{1}{\lambda}+\frac{h}{1-\beta}-\tau+gn+D \tag{10.26}$$

The net income per hour of operation in the in-control state is V_0, and the net income per hour of operation in the out-of-control state is V_1. The cost of taking a sample of size n is assumed to be of the form a_1+a_2n; that is, a_1 and a_2 represent, respectively, the fixed and variable components of sampling cost. The expected number of samples taken within a cycle is the expected cycle length divided by the interval between samples, or $E(T)/h$. The cost of finding an assignable cause is a_3, and the cost of investigating a false alarm is a_3'. The expected number of false alarms generated during a cycle is α times the expected number of samples taken before the shift, or

$$\alpha\sum_{j=0}^{\infty}\int_{jh}^{(j+1)h} je^{-\lambda t}\,dt=\frac{\alpha e^{-\lambda h}}{1-e^{-\lambda h}} \tag{10.27}$$

Therefore, the expected net income per cycle is

$$\begin{aligned}E(C)=V_0\frac{1}{\lambda}+V_1\left(\frac{h}{1-\beta}-\tau+gn+D\right)-a_3-\frac{a_3'e^{-\lambda h}}{1-e^{-\lambda h}}\\-\left(a_1+a_2n\right)\frac{E(T)}{h}\end{aligned} \tag{10.28}$$

The expected net income per hour is found by dividing the expected net income per cycle [equation (10.28)] by the expected cycle length [equation (10.26)], resulting in

$$\begin{aligned}E(A)&=\frac{E(C)}{E(T)}\\&=\frac{V_0(1/\lambda)+V_1\left[h/(1-\beta)-\tau+gn+D\right]-a_3-a_3'\alpha e^{-\lambda h}\Big/\left(1-e^{-\lambda/h}\right)}{1/\lambda+h/(1-\beta)-\tau+gn+D}\\&\quad-\frac{a_1+a_2n}{h}\end{aligned} \tag{10.29}$$

Let $a_4=V_0-V_1$; that is, a_4 represents the hourly penalty cost associated with production in the out-of-control state. Then equation (10.29) may be rewritten as

$$\begin{aligned}E(A)=V_0-\frac{a_1+a_2n}{h}\\-\frac{a_4\left[h/(1-\beta)-\tau+gn+D\right]+a_3+a_3'\alpha e^{-\lambda h}\Big/\left(1-e^{-\lambda/h}\right)}{1/\lambda+h/(1-\beta)-\tau+gn+D}\end{aligned} \tag{10.30}$$

or

$$E(A) = V_0 - E(L)$$

where

$$E(L) = \frac{a_1 + a_2 n}{h} + \frac{a_4\left[h/(1-\beta) - \tau + gn + D\right] + a_3 + a_3' \alpha e^{-\lambda h} \Big/ \left(1 - e^{-\lambda/h}\right)}{1/\lambda + h/(1-\beta) - \tau + gn + D} \tag{10.31}$$

The expression $E(L)$ represents the expected loss per hour incurred by the process. $E(L)$ is a function of the control chart parameters n, k, and h. Clearly, maximizing the expected net income per hour is equivalent to minimizing $E(L)$.

Duncan introduces several approximations to develop an optimization procedure for this model.[2] The optimization procedure suggested is based on solving numerical approximations to the system for first partial derivatives of $E(L)$ with respect to n, k, and h. An iterative procedure is required to solve for the optimal n and k. A closed-form solution for h is given using the optimal values of n and k.

Several authors have reported optimization methods for Duncan's model. Chiu and Wetherill (1974) have developed a simple, approximate procedure for optimizing Duncan's model. Their procedure utilizes a constraint on the power of the test $(1 - \beta)$. The recommended values are either $1 - \beta = 0.90$ or $1 - \beta = 0.95$. Tables are provided to generate the optimum design subject to this constraint. This procedure usually produces a design close to the true optimum. We also note that $E(L)$ could be easily minimized by using an unconstrained optimization or search technique coupled with a digital computer program for repeated evaluations of the cost function. This is the approach to optimization most frequently used. Montgomery (1982) has given a FORTRAN program for the optimization of Duncan's model.

[2]Several numerical approximations are also introduced in the actual structure of the model. Approximations used are for $\tau = h/2 - \lambda h^2/12$, and for the expected number of false alarms $\alpha e^{-\lambda h}/(1 - e^{-\lambda h}) = \alpha/\lambda h$.

EXAMPLE 10.5 Economically Optimal $\bar{x}$ Charts

A manufacturer produces nonreturnable glass bottles for packaging a carbonated soft-drink beverage. The wall thickness of the bottles is an important quality characteristic. If the wall is too thin, internal pressure generated during filling will cause the bottle to burst. The manufacturer has used $\bar{x}$ and R charts for process surveillance for some time. These control charts have been designed with respect to statistical criteria. However, in an effort to reduce costs, the manufacturer wishes to design an economically optimum $\bar{x}$ chart for the process. Analyze the situation and set up the control chart.

SOLUTION

Based on an analysis of quality control technicians' salaries and the costs of test equipment, it is estimated that the fixed cost of taking a sample is \$1. The variable cost of sampling is estimated to be \$0.10 per bottle, and it takes approximately 1 min (0.0167h) to measure and record the wall thickness of a bottle.

(continued)

The process is subject to several different types of assignable causes. However, on the average, when the process goes out of control, the magnitude of the shift is approximately two standard deviations. Process shifts occur at random with a frequency of about one every 20 h of operation. Thus, the exponential distribution with parameter $\lambda = 0.05$ is a reasonable model of the run length in control. The average time required to investigate an out-of-control signal is 1 h. The cost of investigating an action signal that results in the elimination of an assignable cause is \$25, whereas the cost of investigating a false alarm is \$50.

The bottles are sold to a soft-drink bottler. If the walls are too thin, an excessive number of bottles will burst when they are filled. When this happens, the bottler's standard practice is to backcharge the manufacturer for the costs of cleanup and lost production. Based on this practice, the manufacturer estimates that the penalty cost of operating in the out-of-control state for one hour is \$100.

The expected cost per hour associated with the use of an $\bar{x}$ chart for this process is given by equation (10-31), with $a_1 = \$1$, $a_2 = \$0.10$, $a_3 = \$25$, $a_3' = \$50$, $a_4 = \$100$, $\lambda = 0.05$, $\delta = 2.0$, $g = 0.0167$, and $D = 1.0$. Montgomery's computer program referenced earlier is used to optimize this problem. The output from this program, using the values of the model parameters given above, is shown in Fig. 10.24. The program calculates the optimal control limit width k and sampling frequency h for several values of n and computes the value of the cost function equation (10.31). The corresponding α-risk and power for each combination of n, k, and h are also provided. The optimal control chart design may be found by inspecting the values of the cost function to find the minimum. From Fig. 10.24, we note that the minimum cost is \$10.38 per hour, and the economically optimal $\bar{x}$ chart would use samples of size $n = 5$, the control limits would be located at $\pm k\sigma$, with $k = 2.99$, and samples would be taken at intervals of $h = 0.76$ h (approximately every 45 min). The α risk for this control chart is $\alpha = 0.0028$, and the power of the test is $1 - \beta = 0.9308$.

After studying the optimal $\bar{x}$ chart design, the bottle manufacturer suspects that the penalty cost of operating out of control (a_4) may not have been precisely estimated. At worst, a_4 may have been underestimated by about 50%. Therefore, they decide to rerun the computer program with $a_4 = \$150$ to investigate the effect of misspecifying this parameter. The results of this additional run are shown in Fig. 10.25. We see that the optimal solution is now $n = 5$, $k = 2.99$, and $h = 0.62$, and the cost per hour is \$13.88. Note that the optimal sample size and control limit width are unchanged. The primary effect of increasing a_4 by 50% is to reduce the optimal sampling frequency from 0.76 h to 0.62 h (i.e., from 45 min to 37 min). Based on this analysis, the manufacturer decides to adopt a sampling frequency of 45 min because of its administrative convenience.

n	Optimum k	Optimum h	Alpha	Power	Cost
1	2.30	.45	.0214	.3821	14.71
2	2.51	.57	.0117	.6211	11.91
3	2.68	.66	.0074	.7835	10.90
4	2.84	.71	.0045	.8770	10.51
5	2.99	.76	.0028	.9308	10.38
6	3.13	.79	.0017	.9616	10.39
7	3.27	.82	.0011	.9784	10.48
8	3.40	.85	.0007	.9880	10.60
9	3.53	.87	.0004	.9932	10.75
10	3.66	.89	.0003	.9961	10.90
11	3.78	.92	.0002	.9978	11.06
12	3.90	.94	.0001	.9988	11.23
13	4.02	.96	.0001	.9993	11.39
14	4.14	.98	.0000	.9996	11.56
15	4.25	1.00	.0000	.9998	11.72

■ FIGURE 10.24 Optimum solution to Example 10.5.

n	Optimum k	Optimum h	Alpha	Power	Cost
1	2.31	.37	.0209	.3783	19.17
2	2.52	.46	.0117	.6211	15.71
3	2.68	.54	.0074	.7835	14.48
4	2.84	.58	.0045	.8770	14.01
5	2.99	.62	.0028	.9308	13.88
6	3.13	.65	.0017	.9616	13.91
7	3.27	.67	.0011	.9784	14.04
8	3.40	.69	.0007	.9880	14.21
9	3.53	.71	.0004	.9932	14.41
10	3.66	.73	.0003	.9961	14.62
11	3.78	.75	.0002	.9978	14.84
12	3.90	.77	.0001	.9988	15.06
13	4.02	.78	.0001	.9993	15.28
14	4.14	.80	.0000	.9996	15.50

■ FIGURE 10.25 Optimum $\bar{x}$ chart design for Example 10.5 with $a_4 = \$150$.

From analysis of numerical problems such as those in Example 10.5, it is possible to draw several general conclusions about the optimum economic design of the $\bar{x}$ control chart. Some of these conclusions are illustrated next.

1. The optimum sample size is largely determined by the magnitude of the shift δ. In general, relatively large shifts—say, $\delta \geq 2$—often result in relatively small optimum sample size—say, $2 \leq n \leq 10$. Smaller shifts require much larger samples, with $1 \leq \delta \leq 2$ frequently producing optimum sample sizes in the range $10 \leq n \leq 20$. Very small shifts—say, $\delta \leq 0.5$—may require sample sizes as large as $n \geq 40$.
2. The hourly penalty cost for production in the out-of-control state a_4 mainly affects the interval between samples h. Larger values of a_4 imply smaller values of h (more frequent sampling), and smaller values of a_4 imply larger values of h (less frequent sampling). The effect of increasing a_4 is illustrated in Figs. 10.24 and 10.25 for the data in Example 10.5.
3. The costs associated with looking for assignable causes (a_3 and a_3') mainly affect the width of the control limits. They also have a slight effect on the sample size n. Generally, as the cost of investigating action signals increases, the incidence of false alarms is decreased (i.e., reduce α).
4. Variation in the costs of sampling affects all three design parameters. Increasing the fixed cost of sampling increases the interval between samples. It also usually results in slightly larger samples.
5. Changes in the mean number of occurrences of the assignable cause per hour primarily affect the interval between samples.
6. The optimum economic design is relatively insensitive to errors in estimating the cost coefficients. That is, the cost surface is relatively flat in the vicinity of the optimum. We typically find that the cost surface is steeper near the origin, so that it would be preferable to overestimate the optimum n slightly rather than underestimate it. The optimum economic design is relatively sensitive to errors in estimating the magnitude of the shift (δ), the in-control state (μ_0), and the process standard deviation (σ).

7. One should exercise caution in using arbitrarily designed $\bar{x}$ control charts. Duncan (1956) has compared the optimum economic design with the arbitrary design $n = 5$, $k = 3.00$, and $h = 1$ for several sets of system parameters. Depending on the values of the system parameters, very large economic penalties may result from the use of the arbitrary design.

10.6.6 Other Work

The economic design of control charts is a rich area for research into the performance of control charts. Essentially, cost is simply another metric in which we can evaluate the performance of a control scheme. There is substantial literature in this field; see the review papers by Montgomery (1980), Svoboda (1991), Ho and Case (1994), and Keats et al. (1997) for discussion of most of the key work. A particularly useful paper by Lorenzen and Vance (1986) generalized Duncan's original model so that it was directly applicable to most types of control charts.

Woodall (1986, 1987) has criticized the economic design of control charts, noting that in many economic designs the type I error of the control chart is considerably higher than it usually would be in a statistical design, and that this will lead to more false alarms—an undesirable situation. The occurrence of excessive false alarms is always a problem, as managers will be reluctant to shut down a process if the control scheme has a history of many false alarms. Furthermore, if the type I error is high, then this could lead to excessive process adjustment, which often increases the variability of the quality characteristic. Woodall also notes that economic models assign a cost to passing defective items, which would include liability claims and customer dissatisfaction costs, among other components, and this is counter to Deming's philosophy that these costs cannot be measured and that customer satisfaction is necessary to staying in business.

Some of these concerns can be overcome. An economic design should always be evaluated for statistical properties, such as type I and type II error probabilities, average run lengths, and so forth. If any of these properties are at undesirable levels, this may indicate that inappropriate costs have been assigned, or that a constrained solution is necessary. It is recommended to optimize the cost function with suitable constraints on type I error, type II error, average run length, or other statistical properties. Saniga (1989) has reported such a study relating to the joint economic statistical design of $\bar{x}$ and R charts. Saniga uses constraints on type I error, power, and the average time to signal for the charts. His economic statistical designs have higher costs than the pure economic designs, but give superior protection over a wider range of process shifts and also have statistical properties that are as good as control charts designed entirely from statistical considerations. We strongly recommend that Saniga's approach be used in practice.

Saniga and Shirland (1977) and Chiu and Wetherill (1975) report that very few practitioners have implemented economic models for the design of control charts. This is somewhat surprising, as most quality engineers claim that a major objective in the use of statistical process-control procedures is to reduce costs. There are at least two reasons for the lack of practical implementation of this methodology. First, the mathematical models and their associated optimization schemes are relatively complex and are often presented in a manner that is difficult for the practitioner to understand and use. The availability of computer programs for these models and the development of simplified optimization procedures and methods for handling constraints is increasing. The availability of microcomputers and the ease with which these applications may be implemented on them should alleviate this problem. A second problem is the difficulty in estimating costs and other model parameters. Fortunately, costs do not have to be estimated with high precision, although other model components, such as the magnitude of the shift, require relatively accurate determination. Sensitivity analysis of the specific model could help the practitioner decide which parameters are critical in the problem.

10.7 Cuscore Charts

This book has focused on Shewhart control charts because of their widespread usefulness in process monitoring (particularly in phase I), and other techniques such as the cusum and EWMA control charts that also find important applications. The statistics plotted on these control charts can all be developed from a very general procedure based on efficient score statistics [due to Fisher (1925)]. This process results in what are called **Cuscore statistics,** and the corresponding control charts are called **Cuscore control charts.** A Cuscore control chart can be devised to be sensitive to very specific types of departures from the standard operating conditions for the process, or the in-control state. In this section we give an overview of Cuscore charts; for more details and some applications, see Box and Ramirez (1992), Box and Luceño (1997), Ramirez (1998), Luceño (1999), and Runger and Testik (2003).

The general form of the Cuscore statistic is

$$Q = \sum e_{t0} r_t \tag{10.32}$$

where e_{t0} are the residuals from an in-control model for the process and r_t is a **detector** that measures the rate of change of the in-control residuals when the process goes out of control. To illustrate the terminology, consider the Shewhart process model first given in equation (10.9):

$$x_t = \mu + \varepsilon_t \tag{10.33}$$

Assume that the process is in control. Once we observe the data for a particular period the model error term ε_t becomes a residual, say

$$e_{t0} = x_t - \mu$$

The zero in the residual subscript indicates that it is a residual from the in-control process. Now suppose that when the assignable cause occurs, it results in a step change of magnitude δ in the mean. Therefore, the new model is

$$x_t = \mu + \delta + \varepsilon_t \tag{10.34}$$

and the new residuals are

$$e_t = x_t - \mu - \delta$$

In this example, the introduction of δ into the signal produces a linear change in the residuals, and for linear models like this the detector is always of the form

$$r_t = \frac{e_{t0} - e_t}{\delta} \tag{10.35}$$

Therefore, for the step change, the detector is

$$r_t = \frac{e_{t0} - e_t}{\delta} = \frac{x_t - \mu - (x_t - \mu - \delta)}{\delta} = 1$$

and the Cuscore statistic in equation (10.32) is

$$Q = \sum e_{t0} r_t = \sum (x_t - \mu)1 = \sum (x_t - \mu)$$

This is the familiar cusum statistic from Chapter 9. That is, the Cuscore chart for detecting a step change in the process is the cumulative sum control chart.

It can be shown that if the assignable cause results in a single spike of magnitude δ in the process, the Cuscore control chart reduces to the Shewhart control chart. Furthermore, if the assignable cause results in a level change that only lasts w periods, the Cuscore procedure is the ordinary moving average control chart of span w described in Section 9.3. Finally, if the assignable cause results in an exponential increase in the signal, the EWMA control chart (with smoothing parameter exactly equal to the parameter in the exponential function) is the Cuscore control chart.

Because they can be tuned to detect specific signals, Cuscore charts are most effectively used as supplementary process monitoring devices in processes where, in addition to the usual nonspecific types of disturbances, it is feared that a very specific type of problem occasionally occurs. For example, consider a process in which a certain catalyst is employed. Because the catalyst depletes with time, periodically new catalyst must be added to the process. Let's say this is usually done every week. However, in addition to the usual assignable causes that may occur, process engineering personnel are concerned that the catalyst may begin to wear out earlier than expected. As the catalyst depletes, a very slow linear trend will be observed in the process output, but if the catalyst is wearing out too soon, the slope of this trend line will increase quickly. Now a drift or trend can be detected by the EWMA chart that is used for general process monitoring, but a Cuscore designed to detect this change in trend can be designed to augment the EWMA. The process model for the in-control process is

$$x_t = \mu + \beta t + \varepsilon_t$$

and the residuals are

$$e_{t0} = x_t - \mu - \beta t$$

If the catalyst begins to wear out too soon, the slope changes, as in

$$x_t = \mu + \beta t + \delta t + \varepsilon_t$$

and the new residuals are

$$e_t = x_t - \mu - \beta t - \delta t$$

The detector portion of the Cuscore is

$$r_t = \frac{e_{t0} - e_t}{\delta} = \frac{x_t - \mu - \beta t - (x_t - \mu - \beta t - \delta t)}{\delta} = t$$

Therefore, the Cuscore statistic for monitoring this process is

$$Q = \sum e_{t0} r_t = \sum (x_t - \mu - \beta t) t$$

It is possible to obtain Cuscore statistics for monitoring processes and detecting almost any type of signal in almost any type of noise (not just white noise, or uncorrelated observations, as we have been illustrating here). For additional details and examples, see Box and Luceño (1997).

Runger and Testik (2003) observe that a more familiar way to write the Cuscore statistic is

$$C_t = \max\left[C_{t-1} + (x_t - \mu + k_t) f(t, \delta, \tau); 0\right], \quad t = 1, 2, \ldots$$

where now μ is the in-control mean of the observations, $f(t,\delta,\tau)$ is the specific signal generated by the assignable cause which occurs at time τ, δ is a parameter that reflects the nature and magnitude of the process shift, and k_t is a reference value or handicap. The control chart is obtained by plotting C_t versus t. A decision interval H is used to test for the presence of the out-of-control signal in the data. Specifically, if C_t exceeds H the Cuscore chart signals. One must specify H and k_t to operationalize the chart. Usually the reference value is chosen proportional to the signal value $f(t,\delta,\tau)$, such as $0.5\,f(t,\delta,\tau)$. To obtain the best performance with a Cuscore control chart, the time that the assignable cause occurs, τ, must be known. Luceño (1999) used reinitialization and restart procedures with the Cuscore chart to overcome this problem. He also studied the ARL and run length distribution for a number of different forms of the Cuscore chart.

Runger and Testik (2003) also discuss a competitor to the Cuscore chart based on a generalized likelihood ratio (GLR) approach. This procedure is closely related to the changepoint model discussed in the next section. The advantage of their GLR control chart is that the procedure is very robust to the time that the assignable cause occurs. It also generally outperforms the Cuscore chart in detecting assignable causes. GLR control charts are very computationally intensive because there are no simple recursive formulations available; however, the increasing capability of desktop computers and the development of windowing algorithms that work with a moving window of the most recent w observations will certainly lead to increasing use of GLR-based process monitoring procedures.

10.8 The Changepoint Model for Process Monitoring

Control charts are used to monitor processes looking for assignable causes that result in changes in the process output, such as sustained shifts in parameter values. Shewhart control charts and EWMA and cusum control charts are widely used in practice for these types of problems. There is another approach that can be useful for detecting process upsets, the **changepoint model.** This approach focuses on finding the point in time where the underlying model generating a series of observations has changed in some fashion. Most of the work on changepoints has concentrated on detecting a sustained shift in the mean of the process, and that is the case that we will discuss here.

Suppose that the output of a process is modeled by two normal distributions with the same variance, say

$$x_t \sim N\left(\mu_0,\sigma^2\right), t = 1,2,\ldots,\tau$$

$$x_t \sim N\left(\mu_1,\sigma^2\right), t = \tau+1,\tau+2,\ldots,n \qquad (10.36)$$

The in-control distribution is $N(\mu_0,\sigma^2)$ up to a point in time τ (called the changepoint), beyond which the mean shifts to a new level $\mu_1 \neq \mu_0$, and in subsequent periods the process follows the $N(\mu_1,\sigma^2)$ distribution. There are two aspects of the changepoint approach to process monitoring; determining if there has been a change in the process, and estimating τ, the time of the change. Hawkins, Qiu, and Kang (2003) is a very readable introduction to the changepoint model and they provide a list of useful references.

There are several important variations of the changepoint model for detecting sustained shifts in the mean. The first of these is the case where all of the parameters in equation (10.36) μ_0, μ_1, and σ^2 are known. The cusum chart is the appropriate procedure for this setting. An EWMA would also be appropriate, as it can be designed to be approximately equivalent in performance to the cusum. Another situation would be the case in which only some of the parameters are known. Typically, we assume that μ_0 and σ^2 are known, but the out-of-control value of the mean μ_1 is unknown. Our usual approach to this case is to design the cusum for a value of μ_1 that reflects the smallest value of the out-of-control mean that is thought to be likely to occur. Likelihood ratio methods can also be used to address this case. Hawkins, Qiu, and Kang (2003) point out that the "known" values of μ_0 and σ^2 are typically estimated from a sequence of observations taken when the process is thought to be in control, or from a phase I study. Errors in estimating these parameters are reflected in distortions in the average run lengths of the control charts. Even relatively modest errors in estimating the unknown parameters (on the order of one standard error) can significantly impact the ARLs of the cusum and EWMA control charts. Now this does not prevent the control chart from being useful, but it is a cause of concern that the performance of the procedure cannot be characterized accurately.

The most interesting variation of the changepoint model occurs when none of the parameters is known. If there is a single changepoint, it turns out that the appropriate statistic for this problem is the familiar two-sample t statistic for comparing two means, which can be written as

$$t_{jn} = \sqrt{\frac{j(n-j)}{n}}\,\frac{\bar{x}_{jn} - \bar{x}^*_{jn}}{\hat{\sigma}_{jn}} \tag{10.37}$$

where $\bar{x}_{jn}$ is the average of the first j observations, $\bar{x}^*_{jn}$ is the average of the last $n-j$ observations, $\hat{\sigma}^2_{jn}$ is the usual pooled estimate of variance, and $1 \le j \le n-1$. To test for a changepoint, calculate the maximum absolute value of t_{jn} over all $1 \le j \le n-1$ and compare to a critical value, say h_n. If the critical value is exceeded, then there has been a change in the process. The j giving the maximum is the estimate of the changepoint τ, and $\bar{x}_{jn}$ and $\bar{x}^*_{jn}$ are the estimates of μ_0 and μ_1, respectively. Finding the appropriate critical value for this procedure h_n is not easy. Hawkins, Qiu, and Kang (2003) provide some references and guidance for the phase I case (the length of the data is fixed at n). They also report the results of a study to determine critical values appropriate for phase II (where n would increase without bound). The critical values can be found from a table in their paper or computed from numerical approximations that they provide.

The performance of the changepoint procedure is very good, comparing favorably to the cusum. Specifically, it is slightly inferior to a cusum that is tuned perfectly to the exact shift in mean that actually occurs, but nearly optimal for a wide range of shifts. Because of this good performance, changepoint methods should be given wider attention in process monitoring problems.

10.9 Profile Monitoring

A recent development of considerable practical value is methodology for **profile monitoring.** Profiles occur when a critical-to-quality characteristic is functionally dependent on one or more explanatory, or independent, variables. Thus, instead of observing a single measurement on each unit or product we observe a set of values over a range which, when plotted, takes the shape of a curve. That is, there is a response variable y and one or more explanatory variables $x_1, x_2, \ldots, x_k$ and the situation is like regression analysis (refer to Chapter 3). Figure 10.26 provides three illustrations. In Figure 10.26*a* the torque if produced by an automobile engine is related to the engine speed in RPM. In Figure 10.26*b* the measured pressure for a mass flow controller is expressed as a function of the set point x for flow. In Figure 10.26*c* the vertical density of particle board is shown as a function of depth [from Walker and Wright (2002)]. Profiles can be thought of as multivariate vectors, but use of the standard multivariate charts

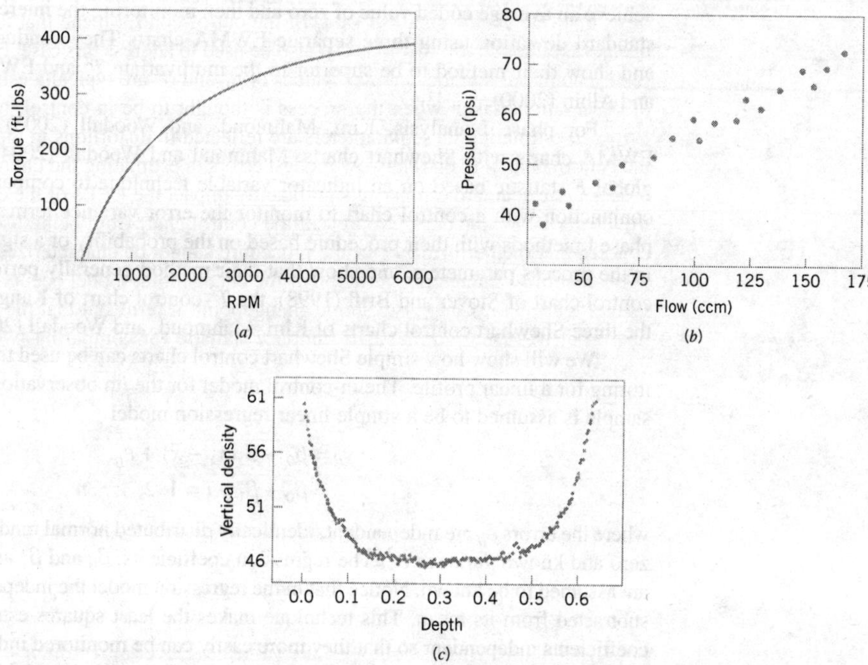

FIGURE 10.26 Profile data. (*a*) Torque versus rpm. (*b*) Pressure versus flow. (*c*) Vertical density versus depth.

such as the ones we discuss in Chapter 11 is usually not appropriate. Profile monitoring has extensive applications in calibration to ascertain performance of the measurement method and to verify that it remained unchanged over time. It has also been used to determine optimum calibration frequency and to avoid errors due to "overcalibration" [see Croarkin and Varner (1982)]. Profiles occur in many other areas, such as performance testing where the response is a performance curve over a range of an independent variable such as frequency or speed. Jin and Shi (2001) refer to profiles as waveform signals and cite examples of force and torque signals collected from online sensors. The review paper by Woodall, Spitzer, Montgomery, and Gupta (2004) provides additional examples of profiles and discusses several monitoring methods, in addition to identifying some weaknesses in existing methods and proposing research directions. Other recent papers on various aspects of monitoring profiles are Gupta, Montgomery, and Woodall (2006); Kim, Mahmoud, and Woodall (2003); Staudhammer, Maness, and Kozak (2007); Wang and Tsung (2005); Woodall (2007); Zou, Zhang, and Wang (2006); and Mahmoud, Parker, Woodall, and Hawkins (2007).

Most of the literature on profile monitoring deals with the phase II analysis of linear profiles, that is, monitoring the process or product when the underlying in-control model parameters are assumed to be known. Stover and Brill (1998) use the Hotelling T^2 control chart discussed in Chapter 11) and a univariate chart based on the first principal component of the vectors of the estimated regression parameters to determine the response stability of a calibration instrument and the optimum calibration frequency. Kang and Albin (2000) suggest using a Hotelling T^2 control chart or a combination of an EWMA and R chart based on residuals for monitoring phase II linear profiles. They recommend the use of similar methods for phase I. Kim, Mahmoud, and Woodall (2003) propose transforming the x-values to achieve an average coded value of zero and then monitoring the intercept, slope, and process standard deviation using three separate EWMA charts They conduct performance studies and show their method to be superior to the multivariate T^2 and EWMA–R charts of Kang and Albin (2000).

For phase I analysis, Kim, Mahmoud, and Woodall (2003) suggest replacing the EWMA charts with Shewhart charts. Mahmoud and Woodall (2004) propose the use of a global F statistic based on an indicator variable technique to compare k regression lines in conjunction with a control chart to monitor the error variance term. They compare various phase I methods with their procedure based on the probability of a signal under various shifts in the process parameters, and show that their method generally performs better than the T^2 control chart of Stover and Brill (1998), the T^2 control chart of Kang and Albin (2000), and the three Shewhart control charts of Kim, Mahmoud, and Woodall (2003).

We will show how simple Shewhart control charts can be used to conduct phase II monitoring for a linear profile. The in-control model for the ith observation within the jth random sample is assumed to be a simple linear regression model

$$\begin{aligned} y_{ij} &= \beta_0 + \beta_1(x_1 - \bar{x}) + \varepsilon_{ij}, \\ &= \beta_0 + \beta_1 x_i \; i = 1, 2, \ldots, n \end{aligned}$$

where the errors ε_{ij} are independent, identically distributed normal random variables with mean zero and known variance σ^2. The regression coefficients, β_0 and β_1 and the error variance σ^2 are assumed to be known. Notice that in the regression model the independent variable has been subtracted from its mean. This technique makes the least squares estimates of the regression coefficients independent so that they more easily can be monitored individually using separate control charts. As new samples come available, the regression model is fit to the data producing estimates of the model parameters for that sample. The control limits for the intercept, slope, and error variance computed from new samples of data are as follows:

$$\begin{aligned} \text{UCL} &= \beta_0 + Z_{\alpha/2}\sqrt{\frac{\sigma^2}{n}} \\ \text{Center line} &= \beta_0 \\ \text{LCL} &= \beta_0 - Z_{\alpha/2}\sqrt{\frac{\sigma^2}{n}}. \end{aligned} \tag{10.38}$$

The control limits for monitoring the slope are

$$\begin{aligned} \text{UCL} &= \beta_1 + Z_{\alpha/2}\sqrt{\frac{\sigma^2}{S_{xx}}} \\ \text{Center line} &= \beta_1 \\ \text{LCL} &= \beta_1 - Z_{\alpha/2}\sqrt{\frac{\sigma^2}{S_{xx}}}, \end{aligned} \tag{10.39}$$

where S_{xx} is defined as $\Sigma_{i=1}^{n}(x_i - \bar{x})^2$ (refer to Montgomery et al. 2001: 15–17). Finally, the control limits for monitoring the error variance are

$$\begin{aligned} \text{UCL} &= \frac{\sigma^2}{n-2}\chi^2_{\alpha/2,\,(n-2)} \\ \text{Center line} &= \sigma^2 \\ \text{LCL} &= \frac{\sigma^2}{n-2}\chi^2_{(1-\alpha/2),\,(n-2)}, \end{aligned} \tag{10.40}$$

where $\chi^2_{\alpha/2,\,(n-2)}$ and $\chi^2_{(1-\alpha/2),\,(n-2)}$ are the upper and lower $\alpha/2$ percentage points of the chi-square distribution with $n - 2$ degrees of freedom [see Montgomery, Peck, and Vining (2006) for details]. The value of $\alpha_{overall}$ is calculated using the equation $\alpha_{overall} = 1 - (1 - \alpha)^3$ and the in-control ARL is computed by taking the reciprocal of $\alpha_{overall}$. The value of α can be chosen to obtain a desired ARL value.

We will use the data presented in the *NIST/SEMATECH e-Handbook of Statistical Methods* to illustrate the method. The dataset consists of line widths of photo masks reference standards on 10 units (40 measurements) used for monitoring linear calibration profiles of an optical imaging system. The line widths are used to estimate the parameters of the linear calibration profile, $\hat{y}_{ij} = 0.2817 + +0.9767x'_i$ with a residual standard deviation of 0.06826 micrometers. This is the phase I profile. A monitoring scheme is established to monitor measurements on units for upper, middle, and lower end of the relevant measurement range from the estimated phase I profile. The dataset is provided in Table 10.3 and plotted in Fig. 10.27. In the plot, the in-control line is the established phase I profile. On careful observation of the measurements for the fourth sample, the plotted values seem to be slightly offset from the in-control line. We employ both the Shewhart control charts defined in equations (10.38), (10.39), and (10.40) to monitor the phase II line width data. The control charts are as shown in Fig. 10.28. In the control charts, the three horizontal lines indicate the upper control limit, the center line, and the lower control limit, respectively. The numerical values for these quantities are (4.62, 4.49, 4.37), (1.01, 0.98, 0.94), and (0.0087, 0.0046, 0.002), respectively. To achieve the overall in-control ARL of 200, the value of α for the control charts was adjusted to be 0.00167. Note that the measurements on the fourth day are out of control. The error variance values on the fifth and sixth days are below the lower control limit with the values 0.0018 and 0.0000, respectively.

TABLE 10.3
Line-Width Measurements

Day	Position	x	y
1	L	0.76	1.12
1	M	3.29	3.49
1	U	8.89	9.11
2	L	0.76	0.99
2	M	3.29	3.53
2	U	8.89	8.89
3	L	0.76	1.05
3	M	3.29	3.46
3	U	8.89	9.02
4	L	0.76	0.76
4	M	3.29	3.75
4	U	8.89	9.3
5	L	0.76	0.96
5	M	3.29	3.53
5	U	8.89	9.05
6	L	0.76	1.03
6	M	3.29	3.52
6	U	8.89	9.02

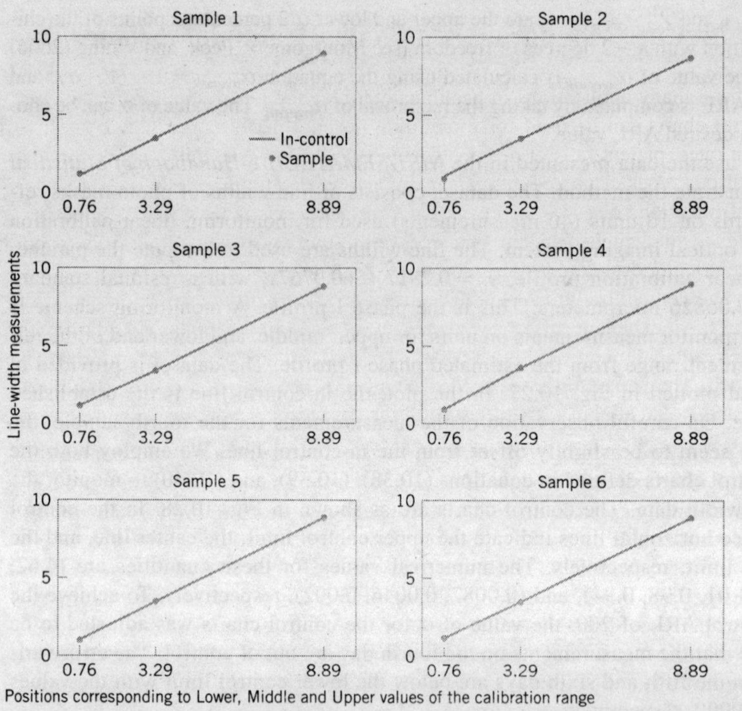

■ FIGURE 10.27 Plot of the line-width measurements.

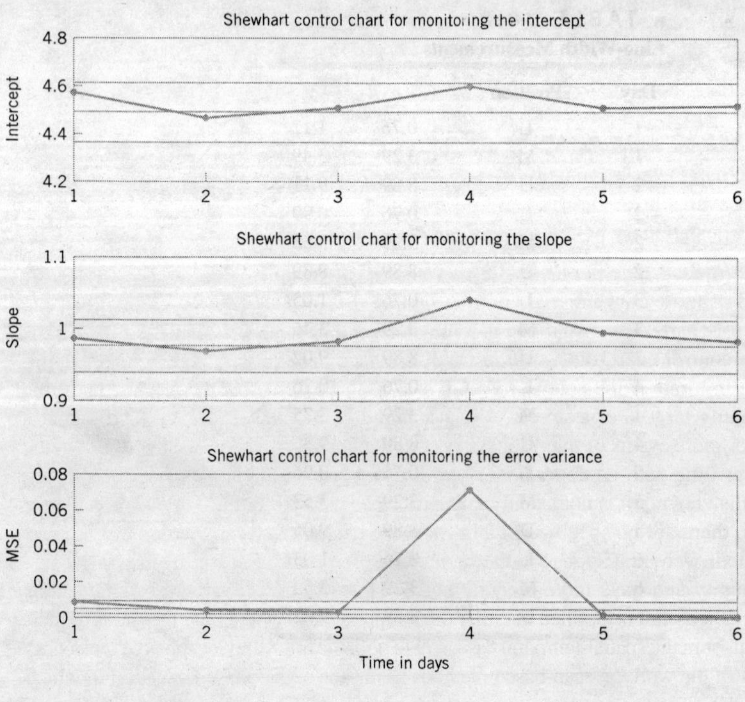

■ FIGURE 10.28 Shewhart control charts for monitoring the parameters of the calibration line.

10.10 Control Charts in Health Care Monitoring and Public Health Surveillance

Control charts have many applications in health care and public health monitoring and surveillance. Control charts can be used for monitoring hospital performance with respect to patient infection rates, patient falls or accidents, emergency room waiting times, or surgical outcomes for various types of procedures. There are also applications for monitoring potential outbreaks of infectious diseases, and even bioterrorism events. This is often called *syndromic surveillance,* in which data are obtained from sources such as emergency room records, over-the-counter drug and prescription sales, visits to physicians, and other sources, in an attempt to supplement traditional sentinel surveillance for natural disease outbreaks or bioterrorist attacks. An excellent review paper on control chart applications in public health surveillance and health care monitoring is Woodall (2006). The book by Winkel and Zhang is also recommended. The papers by Fienberg and Shmueli (2005), Buckeridge et al. (2005), Fricker (2007), and Rolka et al. (2007) offer useful insight on syndromic surveillance.

Health Care Applications of Control Charts. There are some important differences between the industrial and business settings where statistical process control and control charts are traditionally applied and the health care and disease-monitoring environments. One of these is data. Attribute data are much more widely encountered in the health care environment than in the industrial and business world. For example, in surveillance for outbreaks of a particular disease, the incidence rate, or number of cases in the population of interest per unit of time, is typically monitored. Furthermore, disease outbreaks are very likely to be transitory, with more gradual increases and decreases as opposed to the distinct shifts usually encountered in industrial applications. In the health care and public health environment, one-sided methods tend to be employed to allow a focus on detecting increases in rates, which are of primary concern. Two-sided methods are more typically used in business and industry. Some of the techniques used in health care monitoring and disease surveillance were developed independently of the industrial statistical process-control field. There have been few comparative studies of the methods unique to health care monitoring and disease surveillance and often the performance measures used are different from those employed in industrial APC. Often the data monitored in these environments is nonstationary, or has some built-in patterns that are part of the process. An example would be influenza outbreaks, which are largely confined to the winter and late spring months. In some public health surveillance applications, the parameter estimates and measures of uncertainty are updated as new observations become available or the baseline performance is adjusted. These are methods to account for the nonstationary nature of the monitored data.

Scan Methods. The public health surveillance community often uses scan statistic methods instead of more conventional control charting methods such as the cumulative sum or EWMA control chart. A scan statistic is a moving window approach that is similar to the moving average control chart, discussed in Chapter 9 (see Section 9.3). A scan method signals an increase in a rate if the count of events in the most recent specified number of time periods is unusually large. For example, a scan method would signal an increased rate at a given time if m or more events of interest have occurred in the most recent n trials. A plot of the scan statistic over time with an upper control limit could be considered as a control charting technique, but this viewpoint is not usually taken in the health care or the disease surveillance filed. In general, there are no specific guidelines on the design of a scan method.

Scan methods were first applied to the surveillance of chronic diseases by the cancer surveillance community and have more recently been adapted to the surveillance of infectious diseases. Scan methods can be applied in either the temporal case, where only the times of incidences are known, or in the spatial-temporal case, where both the times and locations of incidences are known. Most of the work on scan-based methods has been for the phase I situation in which a set of historical data is analyzed. Comprehensive reviews of many scan-based procedures are in Balakrishnan and Koutras (2002) and Glaz et al. (2001). Also see Kulldorff (1997), (2001), (2003), (2005), Sonesson and Bock (2003), and Naus and Wallenstein (2006).

An important feature of health care monitoring is the human element of the process. Differences between the people in the system are likely to be great, and these differences have great potential impact on the outcomes. For example, when evaluating hospital performance and physician care, we have to take into account that the patients will vary (from patient to patient, from hospital to hospital, from physician to physician) with regard to their general state of health and other demographics and factors. Risk-adjusted control charts can be devised to deal with this situation. Grigg and Farewell (2004) give a review of risk-adjusted monitoring. Grigg and Spiegelhalter (2007) recently proposed a risk-adjusted EWMA method. Risk adjusted control charts are also discussed by Winkel and Zhang (2007).

10.11 Overview of Other Procedures

There are many other process monitoring and control techniques in addition to those presented previously. This section gives a brief overview of some of these methods, along with some basic references. The selection of topics is far from exhaustive but does reflect a collection of ideas that have found practical application.

10.11.1 Tool Wear

Many production processes are subject to tool wear. When tool wear occurs, we usually find that the process variability at any one point in time is considerably less than the allowable variability over the entire life of the tool. Furthermore, as the tool wears out, there will generally be an upward drift or trend in the mean caused by the worn tool producing larger dimensions. In such cases, the distance between specification limits is generally much greater than, say, 6σ. Consequently, the modified control chart concept can be applied to the tool-wear problem. The procedure is illustrated in Fig. 10.29.

The initial setting for the tool is at some multiple of σ_x above the lower specification limit—say, $3\sigma_x$—and the maximum permissible process average is at the same multiple of σ_x below the upper specification limit. If the rate of wear is known or can be estimated from the data, we can construct a set of slanting control limits about the tool-wear trend line. If the sample values of $\bar{x}$ fall within these limits, the tool wear is in control. When the trend line exceeds the maximum permissible process average, the process should be reset or the tool replaced.

Control charts for tool wear are discussed in more detail by Duncan (1986) and Manuele (1945). The regression control chart [see Mandel (1969)] can also be adapted to the tool-wear problem. Quesenberry (1988) points out that these approaches essentially assume that resetting the process is expensive and that they attempt to minimize the number of adjustments made to keep the parts within specifications rather than reducing overall variability. Quesenberry develops a two-part tool-wear compensator that centers the process periodically and protects against assignable causes, as well as adjusting for the estimated mean tool wear since the previous adjustment.

10.11.2 Control Charts Based on Other Sample Statistics

Some authors have suggested the use of sample statistics other than the average and range (or standard deviation) for construction of control charts. For example, Ferrell (1953) proposed that subgroup midranges and ranges be used, with control limits determined by the median midrange and the median range. The author noted that ease of computation would be

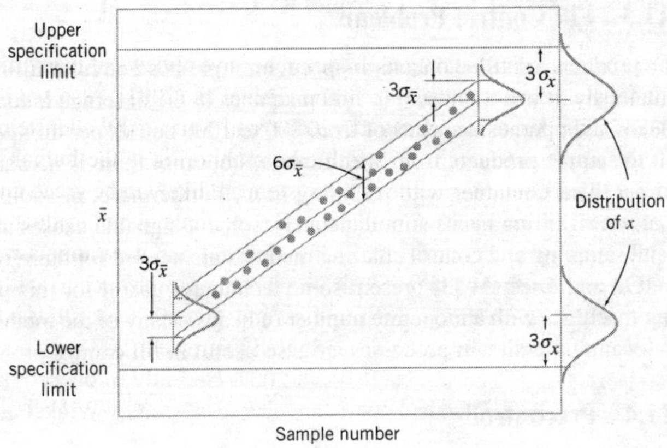

■ FIGURE 10.29 Control chart for tool wear.

a feature of such control charts and that they would do a better job of detecting "outlier" points than conventional control charts. The median has been used frequently instead of $\bar{x}$ as a center line on charts of individuals when the underlying distribution is skewed. Similarly, medians of R and s have been proposed as the center lines of those charts so that the asymmetrical distribution of these statistics will not influence the number of runs above and below the center line.

The recent interest in robust statistical methods has generated some application of these ideas to control charts. Generally speaking, the presence of assignable causes produces outlier values that stretch or extend the control limits, thereby reducing the sensitivity of the control chart. One approach to this problem has been to develop control charts using statistics that are themselves outlier-resistant. Examples include the median and midrange control charts [see Clifford (1959)] and plotting subgroup boxplots [(see Inglewitz and Hoaglin (1987) and White and Schroeder (1987)]. These procedures are typically not as effective in assignable-cause or outlier detection as are conventional $\bar{x}$ and R (or S) charts.

A better approach is to plot a sample statistic that is sensitive to assignable causes ($\bar{x}$ and R or s), but to base the control limits on some outlier-resistant method. The paper by Ferrell (1953) mentioned above is an example of this approach, as is plotting $\bar{x}$ and R on charts with control limits determined by the trimmed mean of the sample means and the trimmed mean of the ranges, as suggested by Langenberg and Inglewitz (1986).

Rocke (1989) has reported that plotting an outlier-sensitive statistic on a control chart with control limits determined using an outlier-resistant method works well in practice. The suggested procedures in Ferrell (1953), Langenberg and Inglewitz (1986), and his own method are very effective in detecting assignable causes. Interestingly enough, Rocke also notes that the widely used two-stage method of setting control limits, wherein the initial limits are treated as trial control limits, the samples that plot outside these trial limits are then removed, and a final set of limits are then calculated, performs nearly as well as the more complex robust methods. In other words, the use of this two-stage method creates a robust control chart.

In addition to issues of robustness, other authors have suggested control charts for other sample statistics for process-specific reasons. For example, when pairs of measurements are made on each unit or when comparison with a standard unit is desired, one may plot the difference $x_{1j} - x_{2j}$ on a **difference control chart** [see Grubbs (1946) and the supplemental text material]. In some cases, the largest and smallest sample values may be of interest. These charts have been developed by Howell (1949).

10.11.3 Fill Control Problems

Many products are filled on a high-speed, multiple-head circular filling machine that operates continuously. It is not unusual to find machines in the beverage industry that have from 40 to 72 heads and operate at speeds of from 800 to 1000 bottles per minute. In such cases, it is difficult to sample products from specific heads because there is no automatic method of identifying a filled container with its filling head. Furthermore, in addition to assignable causes that affect all filling heads simultaneously, some assignable causes affect only certain heads. Special sampling and control charting methods are needed for these types of fill control problems. Ott and Snee (1973) present some techniques useful for this problem, particularly for filling machines with a moderate number of heads. Many of the methods described in Section 10.3 for multiple-stream processes are also useful in fill control problems.

10.11.4 Precontrol

Precontrol is a technique that is used to detect shifts or upsets in the process that may result in the production of nonconforming units. The technique differs from statistical process control in that conventional control charts are designed to detect shifts in process parameters that are statistically significant, and precontrol requires no plotting of graphs and no computations. Precontrol uses the normal distribution in determining changes in the process mean or standard deviation that could result in increased production of nonconforming units. Only three units are required to give control information.

To demonstrate the procedure, suppose that the quality characteristic is normally distributed and that the natural tolerance limits ($\mu \pm 3\sigma$) exactly coincide with the specification limits. Furthermore, the process average μ is halfway between the specifications, so that the process is producing 0.27% fallout. Construct two precontrol limits (called upper and lower PC lines), each of which is one-fourth the distance in from the modified limit, as in Fig. 10.30. Since the distribution of the quality characteristic is normal, approximately 86% of the process output will lie inside the PC lines, and approximately 7% will lie in each of the regions between the PC line and specification limit. This means that only about one item in 14 will fall outside a PC line if the process mean and standard deviation are on the target values.

If the probability is one-fourteenth that one unit falls outside a PC line, the probability that two consecutive units fall outside a PC line is $\left(\frac{1}{14}\right)\left(\frac{1}{14}\right) = \frac{1}{196} \simeq \frac{1}{200}$. That is, if the process is operating correctly, the probability of finding two consecutive units outside of a given PC line is only about $\frac{1}{200}$. When two such consecutive units are found, it is likely that the process has shifted to an out-of-control state. Similarly, it is unlikely to find the first unit beyond one PC line and the next beyond the other PC line. In this case, we suspect that process variability has increased.

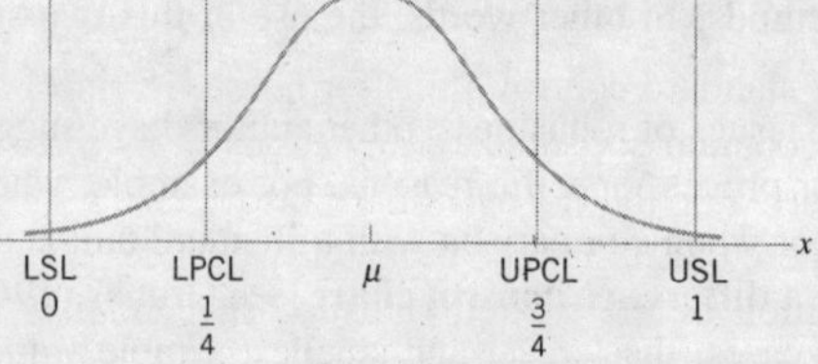

■ FIGURE 10.30 Location of precontrol lines.

A set of rules follow that describe the operation of precontrol. These rules assume that 1% to 3% nonconforming production is acceptable and that the process capability ratio is at least 1.15.

1. Start the process. If the first item is outside specifications, reset and start again.
2. If an item is inside specifications but outside a PC line, check the next item.
3. If the second item is outside the same PC line, reset the process.
4. If the second item is inside the PC line, continue. The process is reset only when two consecutive items are outside a given PC line.
5. If one item is outside a PC line and the next item is outside the other PC line, the process variability is out of control.
6. When five consecutive units are inside the PC lines, shift to frequency gauging.
7. When frequency gauging, do not adjust process until an item exceeds a PC line. Then examine the next consecutive item, and proceed as in step 4.
8. When the process is reset, five consecutive items must fall inside the PC lines before frequency gauging can be resumed.
9. If the operator samples from the process more than 25 times without having to reset the process, reduce the gauging frequency so that more units are manufactured between samples. If we must reset before 25 samples are taken, increase the gauging frequency. An average of 25 samples to a reset indicates that the sampling frequency is satisfactory.

Precontrol is closely related to a technique called **narrow-limit gauging** (or **compressed-limit gauging**), in which inspection procedures are determined using tightened limits located so as to meet established risks of accepting nonconforming product. Narrow-limit gauging is discussed in more general terms by Ott (1975).

Although precontrol has the advantage of simplicity, it should not be used indiscriminately. The procedure has serious drawbacks. First, because no control chart is usually constructed, all the aspects of pattern recognition associated with the control chart cannot be used. Thus, the diagnostic information about the process contained in the pattern of points on the control chart, along with the logbook aspect of the chart, is lost. Second, the small sample sizes greatly reduce the ability of the procedure to detect even moderate-to-large shifts. Third, precontrol does not provide information that is helpful in bringing the process into control or that would be helpful in reducing variability (which is the goal of statistical process control). Finally, the assumption of an in-control process and adequate process capability is extremely important. Precontrol should only be considered in manufacturing processes where the process capability ratio is much greater than one (perhaps at least two or three), and where a near-zero defects environment has been achieved. Ledolter and Swersey (1997) in a comprehensive analysis of precontrol also observe that its use will likely lead to unnecessary tampering with the process; this can actually increase variability. This author believes that precontrol is a poor substitute for standard control charts and would never recommend it in practice.

10.11.5 Tolerance Interval Control Charts

The usual intent of standard control limits for phase II control charts based on normal distribution is that they contain six standard deviations of the distribution of the statistic that is plotted on the chart. For the normal distribution, this is the familiar quantity $0.9973 = 1 - 2(0.00135)$, where 0.00135 is the probability outside each control limit or the area in the tail of the distribution of the plotted statistic. Standard control limits do not satisfy this because while a normal distribution is assumed, many plotted statistics do not follow the normal distribution. The sample range R and sample standard deviation s are good examples. The random variables R and s have skewed distributions that lead to zero lower control limits when the subgroup size is six or less for the R chart and five or less for the s chart. Using probability limits would avoid this problem. However, there is another problem. The phase II control limits also depend on the parameters of the distribution that are estimated using the data that was collected and analyzed in phase I.

Hamada (2003) proposes the use of beta-content tolerance intervals as the basis for control limits to more precisely control the probability content of the control limits. He develops these control limits for the $\bar{x}$, R, and s charts, and he provides tables of the constants necessary for their construction and use. His constants control the probability content in each tail at 0.000135, but the formulas provided allow different probability values and potentially different probability contents in each tail. A useful benefit of his approach is that nonzero lower control limits arise naturally for the R and s charts, affording an opportunity to detect downward shifts in process variability more easily.

10.11.6 Monitoring Processes with Censored Data

There are many situations where a process is monitored and the data that is collected is **censored.** For example, Steiner and MacKay (2000) describe manufacturing material used in making automobile interiors. In this process, a vinyl outer layer is bonded to a foam backing; to check the bond strength, a sample of the material is cut and the force required to break the bond is measured. A predetermined maximum force is applied, and most samples do not fail. Therefore, the bond strength measurements are censored data.

When the censoring proportion is not large, say, under 50%, it is fairly standard practice to ignore the censoring. When the censoring proportion is high, say above 95%, it is often possible to use an *np* control chart to monitor the number of censored observations. However, there are many situations where the proportion of censored observations is between 50% and 95% and these conventional approaches do not apply. Steiner and MacKay (2000) develop conditional expected value (CEV) weight control charts for this problem. To develop the charts, they assume that the measured quantity x is normally distributed with mean and standard deviation μ and σ, respectively. The censoring level is C; that is, the measurement value is not observed exactly if x exceeds C. The probability of censoring is

$$p_c = 1 - \Phi\left(\frac{C-\mu}{\sigma}\right) = Q(C)$$

where Φ is the standard normal cumulative distribution function and $Q(C)$ is called the **survivor function** of the distribution. Their CEV control charts simply replace each censored observation with its conditional expected value. Then the subgroup averages and standard deviations are calculated and plotted in the usual manner. The conditional expected value of a censored observation is

$$w_c = E(x|x > C) = \mu + \sigma\left(\frac{\phi(z_c)}{\Phi(z_c)}\right)$$

where $\phi(z_c)$ is the standard normal density function, and $z_c = (C - \mu)/\sigma$. Therefore, the actual data used to construct the control charts is

$$w = \begin{cases} x, & \text{if } x \le C \\ w_c, & \text{if } x > C \end{cases}$$

The control limits for the CEV control charts depend on the sample size and the censoring proportion p_c. The relationship is complex, and does not lead to a simple rule such as the use of three-sigma limits. Instead, graphs provided by Steiner and Mackay (2000) that are based on simulation must be used to determine the control limits. Furthermore, in application the mean and standard deviation μ and σ must be estimated. This is done in phase I using preliminary process data. An iterative maximum likelihood procedure is provided by the authors for doing this.

10.11.7 Nonparametric Control Charts

The performance of most control charts depends on the assumption of a particular probability distribution as a model for the process data. The normal distribution is usually assumed, and almost all of the performance analysis reported in the literature assumes that the observations are drawn from a normal distribution. However, much process data is *not* normally distributed and so the robustness of control charts to this assumption has long been an issue in SPC. The robustness of the Shewhart $\bar{x}$ chart to normality has been studied very thoroughly (refer to Section 6.2.5). Researchers have found that some control charts are significantly affected by nonnormality; for example, the Shewhart control chart for individuals.

Because nonnormality can affect control chart performance, some authors have developed nonparametric control charts that do not depend on normality or any other specific distributional assumption. Most nonparametric statistical process-control (NSPC) techniques depend on ranks. Procedures have been developed that are alternatives to many of the standard Shewhart charts, the cusum, and the EWMA. The empirical reference distribution control charts of Willemain and Runger (1996), which are based on order statistics from a large reference sample, are also a form of nonparametric control chart. There has also been some work done on multivariate NSPC. A good review of much of the literature in this area is in Chakraborti, Van Der Laan, and Bakir (2001). There is little evidence that these NSPC techniques have gained any real acceptance in practice. As we have noted previously, a properly designed univariate (and as we will subsequently see, a multivariate) EWMA control chart is very robust to the assumption of normality, and performs quite well for both heavy-tailed symmetric distributions and skewed distributions. Because the univariate EWMA is widely available in standard statistics packages, and the multivariate EWMA discussed in Chapter 11 is also very easy to implement, these charts would seem to be good alternatives to NSPC in many situations.

Important Terms and Concepts

Acceptance control charts
Adaptive (SPC) control charts
Autocorrelation function
Autoregressive integrated moving average (ARIMA) models
Autocorrelated process data
Average run length
Changepoint model for process monitoring
Control charts on residuals
Cuscore statistics and control charts
Deviation from nominal (DNOM) control charts
Economic models of control charts
First-order autoregressive model
First-order integrated moving average model
First-order mixed model
First-order moving average model
Group control charts (GCC)
Health care applications of control charts
Impact of autocorrelation on control charts
Modified control charts
Multiple-stream processes
Positive autocorrelation
Profile monitoring
Sample autocorrelation function
Second-order autoregressive model
Shewhart process model
Standardized $\bar{x}$ and R control charts
Time series model
Unweighted batch means (UBM) control charts

Exercises

10.1. Discuss how you would use a cusum in the short production run situation. What advantages would it have relative to a Shewhart chart, such as a DNOM version of the $\bar{x}$ chart?

10.2. Use the data in Table 10E.1 to set up appropriate short-run $\bar{x}$ and R charts, assuming that the standard deviations of the measured characteristic for each part type are not the same. The normal dimensions for each part are $T_A = 100$, $T_B = 200$, and $T_C = 2000$.

10.3. Use the data in Table 10E.2 to set up short-run $\bar{x}$ and R charts using the DNOM approach. The nominal dimensions for each part are $T_A = 100$, $T_B = 60$, $T_C = 75$, and $T_D = 50$.

10.4. A machine has four heads. Samples of $n = 3$ units are selected from each head, and the $\bar{x}$ and R values for an important quality characteristic are computed. The data are shown in Table 10E.3. Set up group control charts for this process.

10.5. Printed circuit boards used in several different avionics devices are 100% tested for defects. The batch size for each board type is relatively small, and management wishes to establish SPC using a

■ **TABLE 10E.1**
Data for Exercise 10.2

Sample Number	Part Type	M_1	M_2	M_3	M_3
1	A	120	95	100	110
2	A	115	123	99	102
3	A	116	105	114	108
4	A	120	116	100	96
5	A	112	100	98	107
6	A	98	110	116	105
7	B	230	210	190	216
8	B	225	198	236	190
9	B	218	230	199	195
10	B	210	225	200	215
11	B	190	218	212	225
12	C	2150	2230	1900	1925
13	C	2200	2116	2000	1950
14	C	1900	2000	2115	1990
15	C	1968	2250	2160	2100
16	C	2500	2225	2475	2390
17	C	2000	1900	2230	1960
18	C	1960	1980	2100	2150
19	C	2320	2150	1900	1940
20	C	2162	1950	2050	2125

■ **TABLE 10E.2**
Data for Exercise 10.3

Sample Number	Part Type	M_1	M_2	M_3
1	A	105	102	103
2	A	101	98	100
3	A	103	100	99
4	A	101	104	97
5	A	106	102	100
6	B	57	60	59
7	B	61	64	63
8	B	60	58	62
9	C	73	75	77
10	C	78	75	76
11	C	77	75	74
12	C	75	72	79
13	C	74	75	77
14	C	73	76	75
15	D	50	51	49
16	D	46	50	50
17	D	51	46	50
18	D	49	50	53
19	D	50	52	51
20	D	53	51	50

■ **TABLE 10E.3**
Data for Exercise 10.4

	Head							
Sample	1		2		3		4	
Number	$\bar{x}$	R	$\bar{x}$	R	$\bar{x}$	R	$\bar{x}$	R
1	53	2	54	1	56	2	55	3
2	51	1	55	2	54	4	54	4
3	54	2	52	5	53	3	57	2
4	55	3	54	3	52	1	51	5
5	54	1	50	2	51	2	53	1
6	53	2	51	1	54	2	52	2
7	51	1	53	2	58	5	54	1
8	52	2	54	4	51	2	55	2
9	50	2	52	3	52	1	51	3
10	51	1	55	1	53	3	53	5
11	52	3	57	2	52	4	55	1
12	51	2	55	1	54	2	58	2
13	54	4	58	2	51	1	53	1
14	53	1	54	4	50	3	54	2
15	55	2	52	3	54	2	52	6
16	54	4	51	1	53	2	58	5
17	53	3	50	2	57	1	53	1
18	52	1	49	1	52	1	49	2
19	51	2	53	3	51	2	50	3
20	52	4	52	2	50	3	52	2

■ **TABLE 10E.4**
Defect Data for Exercise 10.5

Production Day	Part Number	Total Number of Defects	Production Day	Part Number	Total Number of Defects
245	1261	16	251	4610	10
	1261	10		4610	0
	1261	15		1261	20
246	1261	8		1261	21
	1261	11	252	1261	15
	1385	24		1261	8
	1385	21		1261	10
247	1385	28		1130	64
	1385	35		1130	75
	1261	10		1130	53
248	1261	8	253	1055	16
	8611	47		1055	15
	8611	45		1055	10
249	8611	53	254	1055	12
	8611	41		8611	47
	1385	21		8611	60
250	1385	25	255	8611	51
	1385	29		8611	57
	1385	30		4610	0
	4610	6		4610	4
	4610	8			

short-run version of the c chart. Defect data from the last two weeks of production are shown in Table 10E.4. What chart would you recommend? Set up the chart and examine the process for control.

10.6. Consider the group control charts constructed in Exercise 10.4. Suppose the next 10 samples are in Table 10E.5.
Plot the new data on the control charts and discuss your findings.

■ **TABLE 10E.5**
Data for Exercise 10E.6

	Head							
	1		2		3		4	
Sample Number	$\bar{x}$	R	$\bar{x}$	R	$\bar{x}$	R	$\bar{x}$	R
21	50	3	54	1	57	2	55	5
22	51	1	53	2	54	4	54	3
23	53	2	52	4	55	3	57	1
24	54	4	54	3	53	1	56	2
25	50	2	51	1	52	2	58	4
26	51	2	55	5	54	5	54	3
27	53	1	50	2	51	4	60	1
28	54	3	51	4	54	3	61	4
29	52	2	52	1	53	2	62	3
30	52	1	53	3	50	4	60	1

10.7. Reconsider the data in Exercises 10.4 and 10.6. Suppose the process measurements are individual data values, not subgroup averages.
(a) Use observations 1–20 in Exercise 10.4 to construct appropriate group control charts.
(b) Plot observations 21–30 from Exercise 10.6 on the charts from part (a). Discuss your findings.
(c) Using observations 1–20, construct an individuals chart using the average of the readings on all four heads as an individual measurement and an s control chart using the individual measurements on each head. Discuss how these charts function relative to the group control chart.
(d) Plot observations 21–30 on the control charts from part (c). Discuss your findings.

10.8. A sample of five units is taken from a process every half hour. It is known that the process standard deviation is in control with $\sigma = 2.0$. The $\bar{x}$ values for the last 20 samples are shown in Table 10E.6. Specifications on the product are 40 ± 8.
(a) Set up a modified control chart on this process. Use three-sigma limits on the chart and assume that the largest fraction nonconforming that is tolerable is 0.1%.
(b) Reconstruct the chart in part (a) using two-sigma limits. Is there any difference in the analysis of the data?
(c) Suppose that if the true process fraction nonconforming is 5%, we would like to detect this condition with probability 0.95. Construct the corresponding acceptance control chart.

10.9. The $\bar{x}$ and R values for 20 samples of size five are shown in Table 10E.7. Specifications on this product have been established as 0.550 ± 0.02.
(a) Construct a modified control chart with three-sigma limits, assuming that if the true process

■ **TABLE 10E.6**
Data for Exercise 10.8

Sample Number	$\bar{x}$	Sample Number	$\bar{x}$
1	41.5	11	40.6
2	42.7	12	39.4
3	40.5	13	38.6
4	39.8	14	42.5
5	41.6	15	41.8
6	44.7	16	40.7
7	39.6	17	42.8
8	40.2	18	43.4
9	41.4	19	42.0
10	43.9	20	41.9

■ TABLE 10E.7
Data for Exercise 10.9

Sample Number	$\bar{x}$	R
1	0.549	0.0025
2	0.548	0.0021
3	0.548	0.0023
4	0.551	0.0029
5	0.553	0.0018
6	0.552	0.0017
7	0.550	0.0020
8	0.551	0.0024
9	0.553	0.0022
10	0.556	0.0028
11	0.547	0.0020
12	0.545	0.0030
13	0.549	0.0031
14	0.552	0.0022
15	0.550	0.0023
16	0.548	0.0021
17	0.556	0.0019
18	0.546	0.0018
19	0.550	0.0021
20	0.551	0.0022

fraction nonconforming is as large as 1%, the process is unacceptable.

(b) Suppose that if the true process fraction nonconforming is as large as 1%, we would like an acceptance control chart to detect this out-of-control condition with probability 0.90. Construct this acceptance control chart, and compare it to the chart obtained in part (a).

10.10. A manufacturing process operates with an in-control fraction of nonconforming production of at most 0.1%, which management is willing to accept 95% of the time; however, if the fraction nonconforming increases to 2% or more, management wishes to detect this shift with probability 0.90. Design an appropriate acceptance control chart for this process.

10.11. An $\bar{x}$ chart is to be established to control a quality characteristic assumed to be normally distributed with a standard deviation of 4. Specifications on the quality characteristic are 800 ± 20. The control chart is to be designed so that if the fraction nonconforming is 1%, the probability of a point falling inside the control limits will be 0.90. The sample size is $n = 4$. What are the control limits and center line for the chart?

10.12. An $\bar{x}$ chart is to be designed for a quality characteristic assumed to be normal with a standard deviation of 4. Specifications on the product quality characteristics are 50 ± 20. The control chart is to be designed so that if the fraction nonconforming is 1%, the probability of a point falling inside the control limits will be 0.995. The sample size is $n = 4$. What are the control limits and center line for the chart?

10.13. Specifications on a bearing diameter are established at 8.0 ± 0.01 cm. Samples of size $n = 8$ are used, and a control chart for s shows statistical control, with the best current estimate of the population standard deviation $S = 0.001$. If the fraction of nonconforming product that is barely acceptable is 0.135%, find the three-sigma limits on the modified control chart for this process.

10.14. Consider a modified control chart with center line at $\mu = 0$, and $\sigma = 1.0$ (known). If $n = 5$, the tolerable fraction nonconforming is $\delta = 0.00135$, and the control limits are at three-sigma, sketch the OC curve for the chart. On the same set of axes, sketch the OC curve corresponding to the chart with two-sigma limits.

10.15. A normally distributed quality characteristic is controlled by $\bar{x}$ and R charts having the following parameters ($n = 4$, both charts are in control):

R Chart	$\bar{x}$ Chart
UCL = 18.795	UCL = 626.00
Center line = 8.236	Center line = 620.00
LCL = 0	LCL = 614.00

(a) What is the estimated standard deviation of the quality characteristic x?

(b) If specifications are 610 ± 15, what is your estimate of the fraction of nonconforming material produced by this process when it is in control at the given level?

(c) Suppose you wish to establish a modified $\bar{x}$ chart to substitute for the original $\bar{x}$ chart. The process mean is to be controlled so that the fraction nonconforming is less than 0.005. The probability of type I error is to be 0.01. What control limits do you recommend?

10.16. The data shown in Table 10E.8 are concentration readings from a chemical process, made every 30 minutes (read down, then across from left to right).

(a) Calculate the sample autocorrelation function and provide an interpretation.

(b) Construct an individuals control chart with the standard deviation estimated using the moving range method. Provide an interpretation of this control chart.

TABLE 10E.8

Chemical Process Concentration Readings

204	190	208	207	200
202	196	209	204	202
201	199	209	201	202
202	203	206	197	207
197	199	200	189	206
201	207	203	189	211
198	204	202	196	205
188	207	195	193	210
195	209	196	193	210
189	205	203	198	198
195	202	196	194	194
192	200	197	198	192
196	208	197	199	189
194	214	203	204	188
196	205	205	200	189
199	211	194	203	194
197	212	199	200	194
197	214	201	197	198
192	210	198	196	196
195	208	202	202	200

(c) Fit a first-order autoregressive model $x_t = \xi + \phi x_{t-1} + \varepsilon_t$ to the data. Set up an individuals control chart on the residuals from this model. Interpret this chart.

(d) Are the residuals from the model in part (c) uncorrelated? Does this have any impact on your interpretation of the control chart from part (c)?

10.17. Consider the concentration data in Exercise 10.16. Construct a cusum chart in the residuals from the model you fit in part (c) of that exercise.

10.18. Consider the concentration data in Exercise 10.16. Construct an EWMA control chart in the residuals from the model you fit in part (c) of that exercise.

10.19. Set up a moving center line EWMA control chart for the concentration data in Exercise 10.16. Compare it to the residuals control chart in Exercise 10.16, part (c).

10.20. The data in Table 10E.9 are molecular weight measurements made every two hours on a polymer (read down, then across from left to right).

(a) Calculate the sample autocorrelation function and provide an interpretation.

(b) Construct an individuals control chart with the standard deviation estimated using the moving range method. How would you interpret the chart? Are you comfortable with this interpretation?

TABLE 10E.9

Molecular Weight Measurements on a Polymer

2048	2039	2051	2002	2029
2025	2015	2056	1967	2019
2017	2021	2018	1994	2016
1995	2010	2030	2001	2010
1983	2012	2023	2013	2000
1943	2003	2036	2016	2009
1940	1979	2019	2019	1990
1947	2006	2000	2036	1986
1972	2042	1986	2015	1947
1983	2000	1952	2032	1958
1935	2002	1988	2016	1983
1948	2010	2016	2000	2010
1966	1975	2002	1988	2000
1954	1983	2004	2010	2015
1970	2021	2018	2015	2032

(c) Fit a first-order autoregressive model $x_t = \xi + \phi x_{t-1} + \varepsilon_t$ to the molecular weight data. Set up an individuals control chart on the residuals from this model. Interpret this control chart.

10.21. Consider the molecular weight data in Exercise 10.20. Construct a cusum control chart on the residuals from the model you fit to the data in part (c) of that exercise.

10.22. Consider the molecular weight data in Exercise 10.20. Construct an EWMA control chart on the residuals from the model you fit to the data in part (c) of that exercise.

10.23. Set up a moving center-line EWMA control chart for the molecular weight data in Exercise 10.20. Compare it to the residual control chart in Exercise 10.20, part (c).

10.24. The viscosity of a chemical product is read every two minutes. Some data from this process are shown in Table 10E.10 (read down, then across from left to right).

(a) Is there a serious problem with autocorrelation in these data?

(b) Set up a control chart for individuals with a moving range used to estimate process variability. What conclusion can you draw from this chart?

(c) Design a cusum control scheme for this process, assuming that the observations are uncorrelated. How does the cusum perform?

(d) Set up an EWMA control chart with $\lambda = 0.15$ for the process. How does this chart perform?

(e) Set up a moving center line EWMA scheme for these data.

■ TABLE 10E.10
Chemical Product Viscosity

29.330	33.220	27.990	24.280
19.980	30.150	24.130	22.690
25.760	27.080	29.200	26.600
29.000	33.660	34.300	28.860
31.030	36.580	26.410	28.270
32.680	29.040	28.780	28.170
33.560	28.080	21.280	28.580
27.500	30.280	21.710	30.760
26.750	29.350	21.470	30.620
30.550	33.600	24.710	20.840
28.940	30.290	33.610	16.560
28.500	20.110	36.540	25.230
28.190	17.510	35.700	31.790
26.130	23.710	33.680	32.520
27.790	24.220	29.290	30.280
27.630	32.430	25.120	26.140
29.890	32.440	27.230	19.030
28.180	29.390	30.610	24.340
26.650	23.450	29.060	31.530
30.010	23.620	28.480	31.950
30.800	28.120	32.010	31.680
30.450	29.940	31.890	29.100
36.610	30.560	31.720	23.150
31.400	32.300	29.090	26.740
30.830	31.580	31.920	32.440

(f) Suppose that a reasonable model for the viscosity data is an AR (2) model. How could this model be used to assist in the development of a statistical process-control procedure for viscosity? Set up an appropriate control chart and use it to assess the current state of statistical control.

10.25. (a) Discuss the use of the moving range method to estimate the process standard deviation when the data are positively autocorrelated.

(b) Discuss the use of the sample variance s^2 with positively autocorrelated data. Specifically, if the observations at lag ρ_i have autocorrelation ρ_i, is s^2 still an unbiased estimator for σ^2?

(c) Does your answer in part (b) imply that s^2 would really be a good way (in practice) to estimate σ^2 in constructing a control chart for autocorrelated data?

10.26. A control chart for tool wear. A sample of five units of product is taken from a production process every hour. The results in Table 10E.11 are obtained. Assume that the specifications on this quality characteristic are at 1.0015 and 1.0035. Set up the R chart on this process. Set up a control chart to monitor the tool wear.

■ TABLE 10E.11
Tool Wear Data

Sample Number	$\bar{x}$	R
1	1.0020	0.0008
2	1.0022	0.0009
3	1.0025	0.0006
4	1.0028	0.0007
5	1.0029	0.0005
6	1.0032	0.0006
	Tool Reset	
7	1.0018	0.0005
8	1.0021	0.0006
9	1.0024	0.0005
10	1.0026	0.0008
11	1.0029	0.0005
12	1.0031	0.0007

10.27. Consider the cost information given in Exercise 10.30. Suppose that the process model represented by equation (10.31) is appropriate. It requires 2 h to investigate a false alarm, the profit per hour of operating in the in-control state is \$500, and it costs \$25 to eliminate the assignable cause. Evaluate the cost of the arbitrary control chart design $n = 5$, $k = 3$, and $h = 1$.

10.28. An $\bar{x}$ chart is used to maintain current control of a process. The cost parameters are a_1 = \$2, a_2 = \$0.50, a_3 = \$50, a_3' = \$75, and a_4 = \$200. A single assignable cause occurs, with magnitude $\delta = 1$, and the run length of the process in control is exponentially distributed with mean 100 h. It requires 0.05 h to sample and test, and 1 h to locate the assignable cause.

(a) Evaluate the cost of the arbitrary $\bar{x}$ chart design $n = 5$, $k = 3$, and $h = 0.5$.

(b) Find the economically optimum design.

10.29. An $\bar{x}$ chart is used to maintain current control of a process. The cost parameters are a_1 = \$0.50, a_2 = \$0.10, a_3 = \$25, a_3' = \$50, and a_4 = \$100. A single assignable cause of magnitude $\delta = 2$ occurs, and the duration of the process in control is an exponential random variable with mean 100 h. Sampling and testing require 0.05 h, and it takes 2 h to locate the assignable cause. Assume that equation (10.31) is the appropriate process model.

(a) Evaluate the cost of the arbitrary control chart design $n = 5$, $k = 3$, and $h = 1$.

(b) Evaluate the cost of the arbitrary control chart design $n = 5$, $k = 3$, and $h = 0.5$.

(c) Determine the economically optimum design.

10.30. An $\bar{x}$ chart is used to maintain current control of a process. A single assignable cause of magnitude 2σ occurs, and the time that the process remains in control is an exponential random variable with mean 100 h. Suppose that sampling costs are \$0.50 per sample and \$0.10 per unit, it costs \$5 to investigate a false alarm, \$2.50 to find the assignable cause, and \$100 is the penalty cost per hour to operate in the out-of-control state. The time required to collect and evaluate a sample is 0.05 h, and it takes 2 h to locate the assignable cause. Assume that the process is allowed to continue operating during searches for the assignable cause.

(a) What is the cost associated with the arbitrary control chart design $n = 5$, $k = 3$, and $h = 1$?

(b) Find the control chart design that minimizes the cost function given by equation (10.31).

11 Multivariate SPC

Chapter Outline

The supplemental material is on the textbook Website www.wiley.com/college/montgomery.

Chapter Overview and Learning Objectives

In previous chapters we have addressed process monitoring and control primarily from the univariate perspective; that is, we have assumed that there is only one process output variable or quality characteristic of interest. In practice, however, many if not most process monitoring and control scenarios involve several related variables. Although applying univariate control charts to each individual variable is a possible solution, we will see that this is inefficient and can lead to erroneous conclusions. Multivariate methods that consider the variables jointly are required.

This chapter presents control charts that can be regarded as the multivariate extensions of some of the univariate charts of previous chapters. The Hotelling T^2 chart is the analog of the Shewhart $\bar{x}$ chart. We will also discuss a multivariate version of the EWMA control chart, and some methods for monitoring variability in the multivariate case. These multivariate control charts work well when the number of process variables is not too large—say, 10 or fewer. As the number of variables grows, however, traditional multivariate control charts lose efficiency with regard to shift detection. A popular approach in these situations is to reduce the dimensionality of the problem. We show how this can be done with principal components.

After careful study of this chapter, you should be able to do the following:

1. Understand why applying several univariate control charts simultaneously to a set of related quality characteristics may be an unsatisfactory monitoring procedure
2. Know how the multivariate normal distribution is used as a model for multivariate process data
3. Know how to estimate the mean vector and covariance matrix from a sample of multivariate observations
4. Know how to set up and use a chi-square control chart
5. Know how to set up and use the Hotelling T^2 control chart
6. Know how to set up and use the multivariate exponentially weighted moving average (MEWMA) control chart
7. Know how to use multivariate control charts for individual observations
8. Know how to find the phase I and phase II limits for multivariate control charts
9. Use control charts for monitoring multivariate variability
10. Understand the basis of the regression adjustment procedure and know how to apply regression adjustment in process monitoring
11. Understand the basis of principal components and know how to apply principal components in process monitoring

11.1 The Multivariate Quality-Control Problem

There are many situations in which the **simultaneous monitoring** or control of two or more related quality characteristics is necessary. For example, suppose that a bearing has both an inner diameter (x_1) and an outer diameter (x_2) that together determine the usefulness of the part. Suppose that x_1 and x_2 have independent normal distributions. Because both quality characteristics are measurements, they could be monitored by applying the usual $\bar{x}$ chart to each characteristic, as illustrated in Fig. 11.1. The process is considered to be in control only if the sample means $\bar{x}_1$ and $\bar{x}_2$ fall within their respective control limits. This is equivalent to the pair of means $(\bar{x}_1, \bar{x}_2)$ plotting within the shaded region in Fig. 11.2.

Monitoring these two quality characteristics independently can be very misleading. For example, note from Fig. 11.2 that one observation appears somewhat unusual with respect to the others. That point would be inside the control limits on both of the univariate $\bar{x}$ charts for x_1 and x_2, yet when we examine the two variables **simultaneously,** the unusual behavior of the point is fairly obvious. Furthermore, note that the probability that either $\bar{x}_1$ or $\bar{x}_2$ exceeds three-sigma control limits is 0.0027. However, the joint probability that both variables exceed their control limits simultaneously when they are both in control is (0.0027)(0.0027) = 0.00000729, which is considerably smaller than 0.0027. Furthermore, the probability that both $\bar{x}_1$ and $\bar{x}_2$ will simultaneously plot inside the control limits when the process is really in control is (0.9973)(0.9973) = 0.99460729. Therefore, the use of two independent $\bar{x}$ charts has distorted the simultaneous monitoring of $\bar{x}_1$ and $\bar{x}_2$, in that the type I error and the probability of a point correctly plotting in control are not equal to their advertised levels for the

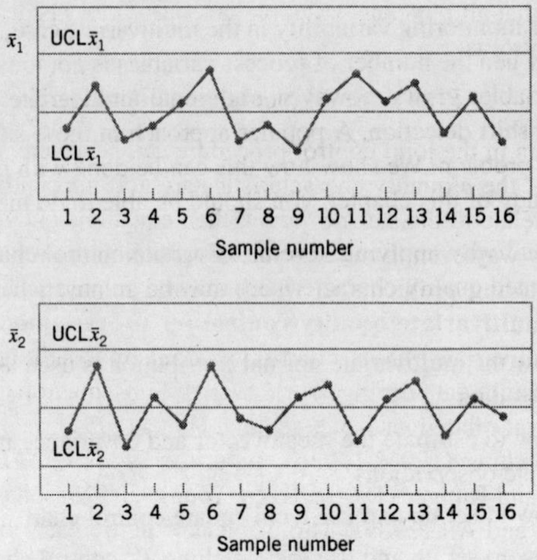

■ FIGURE 11.1 **Control charts for inner ($\bar{x}_1$) and outer ($\bar{x}_2$) bearing diameters.**

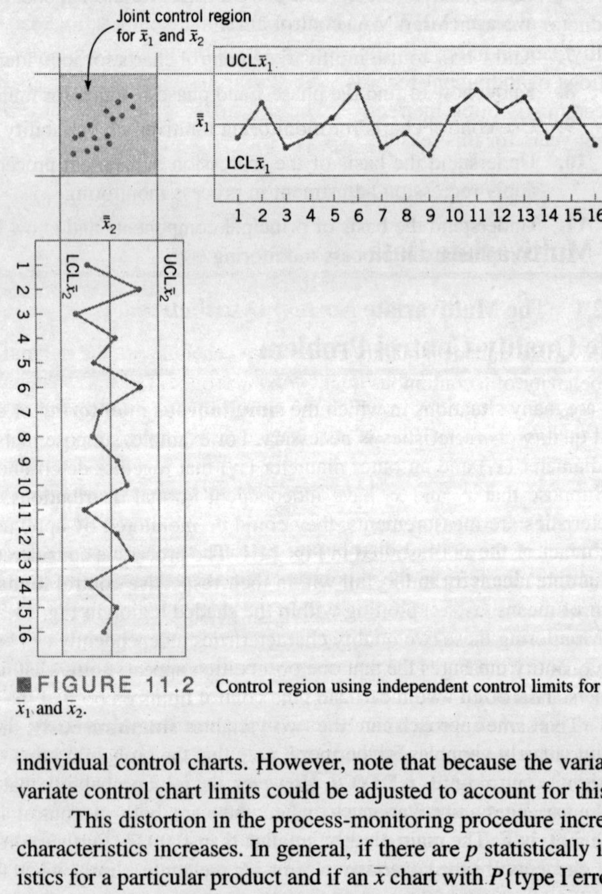

■ FIGURE 11.2 **Control region using independent control limits for $\bar{x}_1$ and $\bar{x}_2$.**

individual control charts. However, note that because the variables are independent the univariate control chart limits could be adjusted to account for this.

This distortion in the process-monitoring procedure increases as the number of quality characteristics increases. In general, if there are p statistically independent quality characteristics for a particular product and if an $\bar{x}$ chart with $P\{\text{type I error}\} = \alpha$ is maintained on each, then the true probability of type I error for the joint control procedure is

$$\alpha' = 1 - (1-\alpha)^p \tag{11.1}$$

and the probability that all p means will simultaneously plot inside their control limits when the process is in control is

$$P\{\text{all } p \text{ means plot in control}\} = (1-\alpha)^p \tag{11.2}$$

Clearly, the distortion in the joint control procedure can be severe, even for moderate values of p. Furthermore, if the p quality characteristics are not independent, which usually would be the case if they relate to the same product, then equations (11.1) and (11.2) do not hold, and we have no easy way even to measure the distortion in the joint control procedure.

Process-monitoring problems in which several related variables are of interest are sometimes called **multivariate quality-control** (or **process-monitoring) problems.** The original work in multivariate quality control was done by Hotelling (1947), who applied his procedures to bombsight data during World War II. Subsequent papers dealing with control procedures for several related variables include Hicks (1955), Jackson (1956, 1959, 1985), Crosier (1988), Hawkins (1991, 1993b), Lowry et al. (1992), Lowry and Montgomery (1995), Pignatiello and Runger (1990), Tracy, Young, and Mason (1992), Montgomery and Wadsworth (1972), and Alt (1985). This subject is particularly important today, as automatic inspection procedures make it relatively easy to measure many parameters on each unit of product manufactured. For example, many chemical and process plants and semiconductor manufacturers routinely maintain manufacturing databases with process and quality data on hundreds of variables. Often the total size of these databases is measured in millions of individual records. Monitoring or analysis of these data with univariate SPC procedures is often ineffective. The use of multivariate methods has increased greatly in recent years for this reason.

11.2 Description of Multivariate Data

11.2.1 The Multivariate Normal Distribution

In univariate statistical quality control, we generally use the **normal distribution** to describe the behavior of a continuous quality characteristic. The univariate normal probability density function is

$$f(x) = \frac{1}{\sqrt{2\pi\sigma^2}} e^{-\frac{1}{2}\left(\frac{x-\mu}{\sigma}\right)^2} \qquad -\infty < x < \infty \tag{11.3}$$

The mean of the normal distribution is μ and the variance is σ^2. Note that (apart from the minus sign) the term in the exponent of the normal distribution can be written as follows:

$$(x-\mu)\left(\sigma^2\right)^{-1}(x-\mu) \tag{11.4}$$

This quantity measures the squared standardized distance from x to the mean μ, where by the term "standardized" we mean that the distance is expressed in standard deviation units.

This same approach can be used in the **multivariate normal distribution** case. Suppose that we have p variables, given by $x_1, x_2, \ldots, x_p$. Arrange these variables in a p-component vector $\mathbf{x}' = [x_1, x_2, \ldots, x_p]$. Let $\boldsymbol{\mu}' = [\mu_1, \mu_2, \ldots, \mu_p]$ be the vector of the means of the x's, and let the variances and covariances of the random variables in $\mathbf{x}$ be contained in a $p \times p$ **covariance matrix Σ.** The main diagonal elements of Σ are the variances of the x's and the off-diagonal elements are the covariances. Now the squared standardized (generalized) distance from $\mathbf{x}$ to $\boldsymbol{\mu}$ is

$$(\mathbf{x}-\boldsymbol{\mu})'\Sigma^{-1}(\mathbf{x}-\boldsymbol{\mu}) \tag{11.5}$$

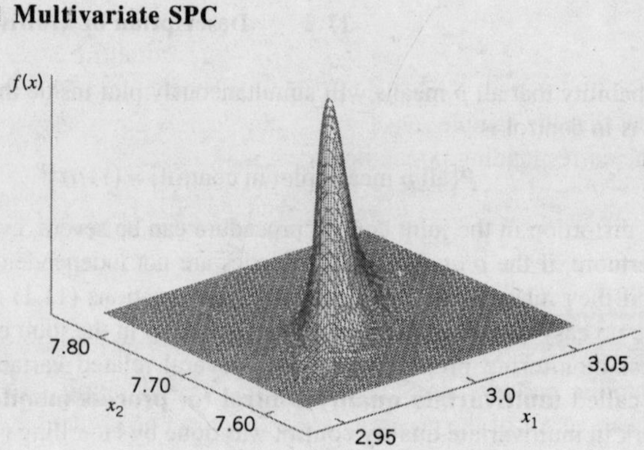

■ **FIGURE 11.3** A multivariate normal distribution with $p = 2$ variables (bivariate normal).

The multivariate normal density function is obtained simply by replacing the standardized distance in equation (11.4) by the multivariate generalized distance in equation (11.5) and changing the constant term $1/\sqrt{2\pi\sigma^2}$ to a more general form that makes the area under the probability density function unity regardless of the value of p. Therefore, the **multivariate normal** probability density function is

$$f(\mathbf{x}) = \frac{1}{(2\pi)^{p/2}|\boldsymbol{\Sigma}|^{1/2}} e^{-\frac{1}{2}(\mathbf{x}-\boldsymbol{\mu})'\boldsymbol{\Sigma}^{-1}(\mathbf{x}-\boldsymbol{\mu})} \tag{11.6}$$

where $-\infty < x_j < \infty$, $j = 1, 2, \ldots, p$.

A multivariate normal distribution for $p = 2$ variables (called a **bivariate normal**) is shown in Fig. 11.3. Note that the density function is a surface. The correlation coefficient between the two variables in this example is 0.8, and this causes the probability to concentrate closely along a line.

11.2.2 The Sample Mean Vector and Covariance Matrix

Suppose that we have a random sample from a multivariate normal distribution—say,

$$\mathbf{x}_1, \mathbf{x}_2, \ldots, \mathbf{x}_n$$

where the ith sample vector contains observations on each of the p variables $x_{i1}, x_{i2}, \ldots, x_{ip}$. Then the **sample mean vector** is

$$\overline{\mathbf{x}} = \frac{1}{n}\sum_{i=1}^{n}\mathbf{x}_i \tag{11.7}$$

and the **sample covariance matrix** is

$$\mathbf{S} = \frac{1}{n-1}\sum_{i=1}^{n}(\mathbf{x}_i - \overline{\mathbf{x}})(\mathbf{x}_i - \overline{\mathbf{x}})' \tag{11.8}$$

That is, the sample variances on the main diagonal of the matrix **S** are computed as

$$s_j^2 = \frac{1}{n-1}\sum_{i=1}^{n}\left(x_{ij} - \overline{x}_j\right)^2 \tag{11.9}$$

and the sample covariances are

$$s_{jk} = \frac{1}{n-1}\sum_{i=1}^{n}\left(x_{ij} - \overline{x}_j\right)\left(x_{ik} - \overline{x}_k\right) \tag{11.10}$$

We can show that the sample mean vector and sample covariance matrix are unbiased estimators of the corresponding population quantities; that is,

$$E(\bar{\mathbf{x}}) = \boldsymbol{\mu} \quad \text{and} \quad E(\mathbf{S}) = \boldsymbol{\Sigma}$$

11.3 The Hotelling T^2 Control Chart

The most familiar multivariate SPC procedure is the **Hotelling T^2 control chart** for monitoring the mean vector of the process. It is a direct analog of the univariate Shewhart $\bar{x}$ chart. We present two versions of the Hotelling T^2 chart: one for subgrouped data, and another for individual observations.

11.3.1 Subgrouped Data

Suppose that two quality characteristics x_1 and x_2 are jointly distributed according to the bivariate normal distribution (see Fig. 11.3). Let μ_1 and μ_2 be the mean values of the quality characteristics, and let σ_1 and σ_2 be the standard deviations of x_1 and x_2, respectively. The covariance between x_1 and x_2 is denoted by σ_{12}. We assume that σ_1, σ_2, and σ_{12} are known. If $\bar{x}_1$ and $\bar{x}_2$ are the sample averages of the two quality characteristics computed from a sample of size n, then the statistic

$$\chi_0^2 = \frac{n}{\sigma_1^2\sigma_2^2 - \sigma_{12}^2}\left[\sigma_2^2(\bar{x}_1 - \mu_1)^2 + \sigma_1^2(\bar{x}_2 - \mu_2)^2 - 2\sigma_{12}(\bar{x}_1 - \mu_1)(\bar{x}_2 - \mu_2)\right] \tag{11.11}$$

will have a chi-square distribution with 2 degrees of freedom. This equation can be used as the basis of a control chart for the process means μ_1 and μ_2. If the process means remain at the values μ_1 and μ_2, then values of χ_0^2 should be less than the upper control limit $\text{UCL} = \chi^2_{\alpha,2}$ where $\chi^2_{\alpha,2}$ is the upper α percentage point of the chi-square distribution with 2 degrees of freedom. If at least one of the means shifts to some new (out-of-control) value, then the probability that the statistic χ_0^2 exceeds the upper control limit increases.

The process-monitoring procedure may be represented graphically. Consider the case in which the two random variables x_1 and x_2 are independent; that is, $\sigma_{12} = 0$. If $\sigma_{12} = 0$, then equation (11.11) defines an ellipse centered at (μ_1, μ_2) with principal axes parallel to the $\bar{x}_1$, $\bar{x}_2$ axes, as shown in Fig. 11.4. Taking χ_0^2 in equation (11.11) equal to $\chi^2_{\alpha,2}$ implies that a pair of sample averages $(\bar{x}_2, \bar{x}_1)$ yielding a value of χ_0^2 plotting inside the ellipse indicates that the process is in control, whereas if the corresponding value of χ_0^2 plots outside the ellipse the process is out of control. Figure 11.4 is often called a **control ellipse.**

In the case where the two quality characteristics are dependent, then $\sigma_{12} \neq 0$, and the corresponding control ellipse is shown in Fig. 11.5. When the two variables are dependent, the principal axes of the ellipse are no longer parallel to the $\bar{x}_1$, $\bar{x}_2$ axes. Also, note that sample point number 11 plots outside the control ellipse, indicating that an assignable cause is present, yet point 11 is inside the control limits on both of the individual control charts for $\bar{x}_1$ and $\bar{x}_2$. Thus there is nothing apparently unusual about point 11 when the variables are viewed individually, yet the customer who received that shipment of material would quite likely observe very different performance in the product. It is nearly impossible to detect an assignable cause resulting in a point such as this one by maintaining individual control charts.

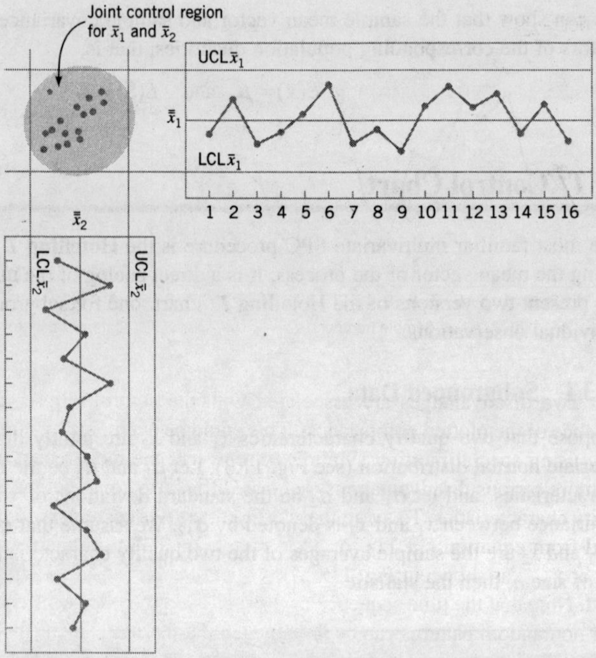

■ FIGURE 11.4 A control ellipse for two independent variables.

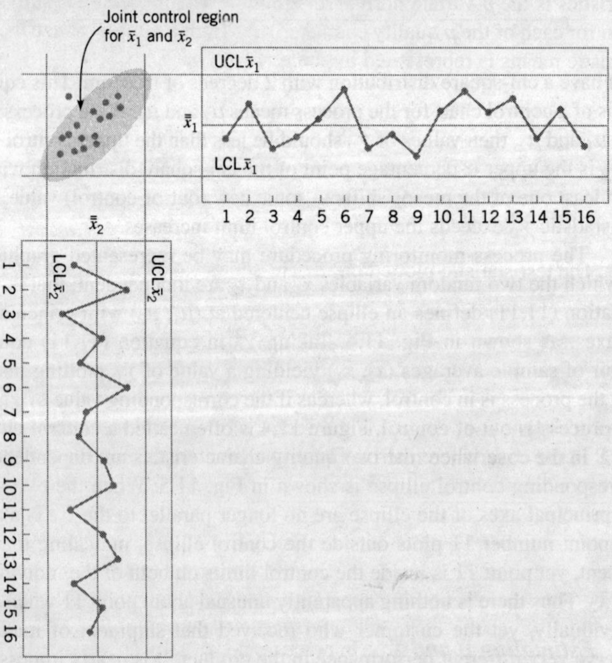

■ FIGURE 11.5 A control ellipse for two dependent variables.

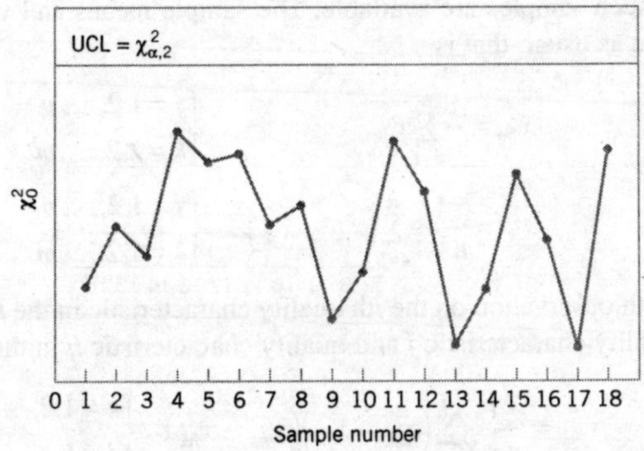

FIGURE 11.6 A chi-square control chart for $p = 2$ quality characteristics.

Two disadvantages are associated with the control ellipse. The first is that the time sequence of the plotted points is lost. This could be overcome by numbering the plotted points or by using special plotting symbols to represent the most recent observations. The second and more serious disadvantage is that it is difficult to construct the ellipse for more than two quality characteristics. To avoid these difficulties, it is customary to plot the values of χ^2_0 computed from equation (11.11) for each sample on a control chart with only an upper control limit at $\chi^2_{\alpha,\,2}$, as shown in Fig. 11.6. This control chart is usually called the **chi-square control chart.** Note that the time sequence of the data is preserved by this control chart, so that runs or other nonrandom patterns can be investigated. Furthermore, it has the additional advantage that the "state" of the process is characterized by a single number (the value of the statistic χ^2_0). This is particularly helpful when there are two or more quality characteristics of interest.

It is possible to extend these results to the case where p related quality characteristics are controlled jointly. It is assumed that the joint probability distribution of the p quality characteristics is the p-variate normal distribution. The procedure requires computing the sample mean for each of the p quality characteristics from a sample of size n. This set of quality characteristic means is represented by the $p \times 1$ vector

$$\overline{\mathbf{x}} = \begin{bmatrix} \overline{x}_1 \\ \overline{x}_2 \\ \vdots \\ \overline{x}_p \end{bmatrix}$$

The test statistic plotted on the chi-square control chart for each sample is

$$\chi^2_0 = n(\overline{\mathbf{x}} - \boldsymbol{\mu})' \boldsymbol{\Sigma}^{-1} (\overline{\mathbf{x}} - \boldsymbol{\mu}) \tag{11.12}$$

where $\boldsymbol{\mu}' = [\mu_1, \mu_2, \ldots, \mu_p]$ is the vector of in-control means for each quality characteristic and $\boldsymbol{\Sigma}$ is the covariance matrix. The upper limit on the control chart is

$$\text{UCL} = \chi^2_{\alpha,p} \tag{11.13}$$

Estimating $\boldsymbol{\mu}$ and $\boldsymbol{\Sigma}$. In practice, it is usually necessary to estimate $\boldsymbol{\mu}$ and $\boldsymbol{\Sigma}$ from the analysis of preliminary samples of size n, taken when the process is assumed to be in control.

Suppose that m such samples are available. The sample means and variances are calculated from each sample as usual; that is,

$$\bar{x}_{jk} = \frac{1}{n}\sum_{i=1}^{n} x_{ijk} \qquad \begin{cases} j = 1,2,\ldots,p \\ k = 1,2,\ldots,m \end{cases} \tag{11.14}$$

$$s_{jk}^2 = \frac{1}{n-1}\sum_{i=1}^{n}\left(x_{ijk} - \bar{x}_{jk}\right)^2 \qquad \begin{cases} j = 1,2,\ldots,p \\ k = 1,2,\ldots,m \end{cases} \tag{11.15}$$

where x_{ijk} is the ith observation on the jth quality characteristic in the kth sample. The covariance between quality characteristic j and quality characteristic h in the kth sample is

$$s_{jhk} = \frac{1}{n-1}\sum_{i=1}^{n}\left(x_{ijk} - \bar{x}_{jk}\right)\left(x_{ihk} - \bar{x}_{hk}\right) \qquad \begin{cases} k = 1,2,\ldots,m \\ j \neq h \end{cases} \tag{11.16}$$

The statistics $\bar{x}_{jk}$, s_{jk}^2, and s_{jhk} are then averaged over all m samples to obtain

$$\bar{\bar{x}}_j = \frac{1}{m}\sum_{k=1}^{m} \bar{x}_{jk} \qquad j = 1,2,\ldots,p \tag{11.17a}$$

$$\bar{s}_j^2 = \frac{1}{m}\sum_{k=1}^{m} s_{jk}^2 \qquad j = 1,2,\ldots,p \tag{11.17b}$$

and

$$\bar{s}_{jh} = \frac{1}{m}\sum_{k=1}^{m} s_{jhk} \qquad j \neq h \tag{11.17c}$$

The $\{\bar{\bar{x}}_j\}$ are the elements of the vector $\bar{\bar{\mathbf{x}}}$, and the $p \times p$ average of sample covariance matrices $\mathbf{S}$ is formed as

$$\mathbf{S} = \begin{bmatrix} \bar{s}_1^2 & \bar{s}_{12} & \bar{s}_{13} & \cdots & \bar{s}_{1p} \\ & \bar{s}_2^2 & \bar{s}_{23} & \cdots & \bar{s}_{2p} \\ & & \bar{s}_3^2 & & \vdots \\ & & & \ddots & \bar{s}_p^2 \end{bmatrix} \tag{11.18}$$

The average of the sample covariance matrices $\mathbf{S}$ is an unbiased estimate of $\mathbf{\Sigma}$ when the process is in control.

The T^2 Control Chart. Now suppose that $\mathbf{S}$ from equation (11.18) is used to estimate Σ and that the vector $\bar{\bar{\mathbf{x}}}$ is taken as the in-control value of the mean vector of the process. If we replace $\boldsymbol{\mu}$ with $\bar{\bar{\mathbf{x}}}$ and $\mathbf{\Sigma}$ with $\mathbf{S}$ in equation (11.12), the test statistic now becomes

$$T^2 = n\left(\bar{\mathbf{x}} - \bar{\bar{\mathbf{x}}}\right)'\mathbf{S}^{-1}\left(\bar{\mathbf{x}} - \bar{\bar{\mathbf{x}}}\right) \tag{11.19}$$

In this form, the procedure is usually called the **Hotelling T^2 control chart.** This is a **directionally invariant** control chart; that is, its ability to detect a shift in the mean vector only depends on the magnitude of the shift, and not in its direction.

Alt (1985) has pointed out that in multivariate quality control applications one must be careful to select the control limits for Hotelling's T^2 statistic [equation (11.19)] based on how the chart is being used. Recall that there are two distinct phases of control chart usage. **Phase I** is the use of the charts for establishing control; that is, testing whether the process was in control when the m preliminary subgroups were drawn and the sample statistics $\bar{\bar{\mathbf{x}}}$ and $\mathbf{S}$ computed. The objective in phase I is to obtain an in-control set of observations so that control limits can be established for phase II, which is the monitoring of future production. Phase I analysis is sometimes called a **retrospective analysis.**

The phase I control limits for the T^2 control chart are given by

$$\text{UCL} = \frac{p(m-1)(n-1)}{mn-m-p+1} F_{\alpha,p,mn-m-p+1}$$
$$\text{LCL} = 0 \tag{11.20}$$

In **phase II,** when the chart is used for monitoring future production, the control limits are as follows:

$$\text{UCL} = \frac{p(m+1)(n-1)}{mn-m-p+1} F_{\alpha,p,mn-m-p+1}$$
$$\text{LCL} = 0 \tag{11.21}$$

Note that the UCL in equation (11.21) is just the UCL in equation (11.20) multiplied by $(m+1)/(m-1)$.

When $\boldsymbol{\mu}$ and $\boldsymbol{\Sigma}$ are estimated from a large number of preliminary samples, it is customary to use $\text{UCL} = \chi^2_{\alpha,p}$ as the upper control limit in both phase I and phase II. Retrospective analysis of the preliminary samples to test for statistical control and establish control limits also occurs in the univariate control chart setting. For the $\bar{x}$ chart, it is typically assumed that if we use $m \geq 20$ or 25 preliminary samples, the distinction between phase I and phase II limits is usually unnecessary, because the phase I and phase II limits will nearly coincide. In a recent review paper, Jensen et al. (2006) point out that even larger sample sizes are required to ensure that the phase II **average run length (ARL)** performance will actually be close to the anticipated values. They recommend using as many phase I samples as possible to estimate the phase II limits. With multivariate control charts, we must be very careful.

Lowry and Montgomery (1995) show that in many situations a large number of preliminary samples would be required before the exact phase II control limits are well approximated by the chi-square limits. These authors present tables indicating the recommended minimum value of m for sample sizes of $n = 3$, 5, and 10 and for $p = 2$, 3, 4, 5, 10, and 20 quality characteristics. The recommended values of m are always greater than 20 preliminary samples, and often more than 50 samples. Jensen et al. (2006) observe that these recommended sample sizes are probably too small. Sample sizes of at least 200 are desirable when estimating the phase II limits.

EXAMPLE 11.1 The T^2 Control Chart

The tensile strength and diameter of a textile fiber are two important quality characteristics that are to be jointly controlled. The quality engineer has decided to use $n = 10$ fiber specimens in each sample. He has taken 20 preliminary samples, and on the basis of these data he concludes that $\bar{\bar{x}}_1 = 115.59$ psi, $\bar{\bar{x}}_2 = 1.06$ ($\times 10^{-2}$) inch, $\bar{s}_1^2 = 1.23$, $\bar{s}_2^2 = 0.83$, and $\bar{s}_{12} = 0.79$. Set up the T^2 control chart.

(continued)

SOLUTION

The statistic he will use for process-control purposes is

$$T^2 = \frac{10}{(1.23)(0.83)-(0.79)^2}\left[0.83(\bar{x}_1-115.59)^2+1.23(\bar{x}_2-1.06)^2 -2(0.79)(\bar{x}_1-115.59)(\bar{x}_2-1.06)\right]$$

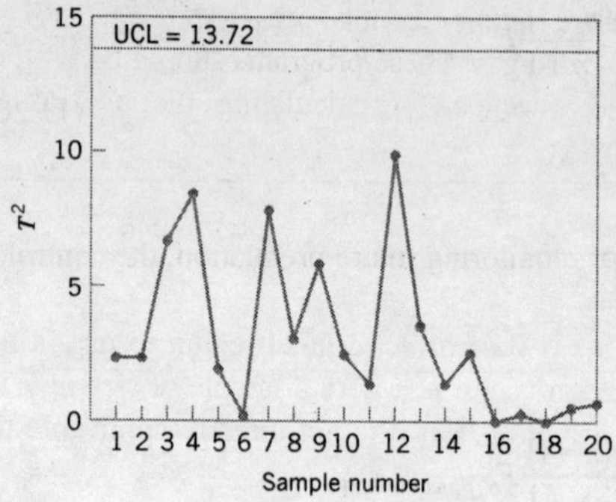

■ **FIGURE 11.7** The Hotelling T^2 control chart for tensile strength and diameter, Example 11.1.

The data used in this analysis and the summary statistics are in Table 11.1, panels (a) and (b).

Figure 11.7 presents the Hotelling T^2 control chart for this example. We will consider this to be phase I, establishing statistical control in the preliminary samples, and calculate the upper control limit from equation (11.20). If $\alpha = 0.001$, then the UCL is

$$\begin{aligned}\text{UCL} &= \frac{p(m-1)(n-1)}{mn-m-p+1}F_{\alpha,p,mn-m-p+1}\\ &= \frac{2(19)(9)}{20(10)-20-2+1}F_{0.001,2,20(10)-20-2+1}\\ &= \frac{342}{179}F_{0.001,2,179}\\ &= (1.91)7.18\\ &= 13.72\end{aligned}$$

This control limit is shown on the chart in Fig. 11.7. Notice that no points exceed this limit, so we would conclude that the process is in control. Phase II control limits could be calculated

■ **TABLE 11.1**
Data for Example 11.1

Sample Number k	(a) Means: Tensile Strength ($\bar{x}_{1k}$)	Diameter ($\bar{x}_{2k}$)	(b) Variances and Covariances: s^2_{1k}	s^2_{2k}	s_{12k}	(c) Control Chart Statistics: T^2_k	$\lvert S_k \rvert$
1	115.25	1.04	1.25	0.87	0.80	2.16	0.45
2	115.91	1.06	1.26	0.85	0.81	2.14	0.41
3	115.05	1.09	1.30	0.90	0.82	6.77	0.50
4	116.21	1.05	1.02	0.85	0.81	8.29	0.21
5	115.90	1.07	1.16	0.73	0.80	1.89	0.21
6	115.55	1.06	1.01	0.80	0.76	0.03	0.23
7	114.98	1.05	1.25	0.78	0.75	7.54	0.41
8	115.25	1.10	1.40	0.83	0.80	3.01	0.52
9	116.15	1.09	1.19	0.87	0.83	5.92	0.35
10	115.92	1.05	1.17	0.86	0.95	2.41	0.10
11	115.75	0.99	1.45	0.79	0.78	1.13	0.54
12	114.90	1.06	1.24	0.82	0.81	9.96	0.36
13	116.01	1.05	1.26	0.55	0.72	3.86	0.17
14	115.83	1.07	1.17	0.76	0.75	1.11	0.33
15	115.29	1.11	1.23	0.89	0.82	2.56	0.42
16	115.63	1.04	1.24	0.91	0.83	0.08	0.44
17	115.47	1.03	1.20	0.95	0.70	0.19	0.65
18	115.58	1.05	1.18	0.83	0.79	0.00	0.36
19	115.72	1.06	1.31	0.89	0.76	0.35	0.59
20	115.40	1.04	1.29	0.85	0.68	0.62	0.63
Averages	$\bar{\bar{x}}_1 = 115.59$	$\bar{\bar{x}}_2 = 1.06$	$\bar{s}^2_1 = 1.23$	$\bar{s}^2_2 = 0.83$	$\bar{s}_{12} = 0.79$		

from equation (11.21). If $\alpha = 0.001$, the upper control limit is UCL = 15.16. If we had used the approximate chi-square control limit, we would have obtained $\chi^2_{0.001,2} = 13.816$, which is reasonably close to the correct limit for phase I but somewhat too small for phase II. The amount of data used here to estimate the phase II limits is very small, and if subsequent samples continue to exhibit control, the new data should be used to revise the control limits.

The widespread interest in multivariate quality control has led to including the Hotelling T^2 control chart in some software packages. These programs should be used carefully, as they sometimes use an incorrect formula for calculating the control limit. Specifically, some packages use:

$$\text{UCL} = \frac{p(m-1)}{m-p} F_{\alpha,p,m-p}$$

This control limit is obviously incorrect. This is the correct critical region to use in multivariate statistical hypothesis testing on the mean vector $\boldsymbol{\mu}$, where a sample of size m is taken at random from a p-dimensional normal distribution, but it is not directly applicable to the control chart for either phase I or phase II problems.

Interpretation of Out-of-Control Signals. One difficulty encountered with any multivariate control chart is practical **interpretation** of an out-of-control signal. Specifically, which of the p variables (or which *subset* of them) is responsible for the signal? This question is not always easy to answer. The standard practice is to plot **univariate** $\bar{x}$ charts on the individual variables $x_1, x_2, \ldots, x_p$. However, this approach may not be successful, for reasons discussed previously. Alt (1985) suggests using $\bar{x}$ charts with Bonferroni-type control limits [i.e., replace $Z_{\alpha/2}$ in the $\bar{x}$ chart control limit calculation with $Z_{\alpha/(2p)}$]. This approach reduces the number of false alarms associated with using many simultaneous univariate control charts. Hayter and Tsui (1994) extend this idea by giving a procedure for exact simultaneous confidence intervals. Their procedure can also be used in situations where the normality assumption is not valid. Jackson (1980) recommends using control charts based on the p principal components (which are linear combinations of the original variables). Principal components are discussed in Section 11.7. The disadvantage of this approach is that the principal components do not always provide a clear interpretation of the situation with respect to the original variables. However, they are often effective in diagnosing an out-of-control signal, particularly in cases where the principal components do have an interpretation in terms of the original variables.

Another very useful approach to diagnosis of an out-of-control signal is to decompose the T^2 statistic into components that reflect the contribution of each individual variable. If T^2 is the current value of the statistic, and $T^2_{(i)}$ is the value of the statistic for all process variables except the ith one, then Runger, Alt, and Montgomery (1996b) show that

$$d_i = T^2 - T^2_{(i)} \tag{11.22}$$

is an indicator of the relative contribution of the ith variable to the overall statistic. When an out-of-control signal is generated, we recommend computing the values of d_i $(i = 1, 2, \ldots, p)$ and focusing attention on the variables for which d_i are relatively large. This procedure has an additional advantage in that the calculations can be performed using standard software packages.

To illustrate this procedure, consider the following example from Runger, Alt, and Montgomery (1996a). There are $p = 3$ quality characteristics and the covariance matrix is known. Assume that all three variables have been scaled as follows:

$$y_{ij} = \frac{x_{ij} - \mu_j}{\sqrt{(m-1)\sigma_j^2}}$$

This scaling results in each process variable having mean zero and variance one. Therefore, the covariance matrix $\mathbf{\Sigma}$ is in **correlation form;** that is, the main diagonal elements are all one and the off-diagonal elements are the pairwise correlation between the process variables (the x's). In our example,

$$\Sigma = \begin{bmatrix} 1 & 0.9 & 0.9 \\ 0.9 & 1 & 0.9 \\ 0.9 & 0.9 & 1 \end{bmatrix}$$

The in-control value of the process mean is $\boldsymbol{\mu}' = [0, 0, 0]$. Consider the following display:

Observation Vector $\mathbf{y}'$	Control Chart Statistic $T_0^2(=\chi_0^2)$	$d_i = T^2 - T_{(i)}^2$ d_1	d_2	d_3
(2, 0, 0)	27.14	27.14	6.09	6.09
(1, 1, −1)	26.79	6.79	6.79	25.73
(1, −1, 0)	20.00	14.74	14.74	0
(0.5, 0.5, 1)	15.00	3.69	3.68	14.74

Since $\mathbf{\Sigma}$ is known, we can calculate the upper control limit for the chart from a chi-square distribution. We will choose $\chi^2_{0.005,3} = 12.84$ as the upper control limit. Clearly all four observation vectors in the above display would generate an out-of-control signal. Runger, Alt, and Montgomery (1996b) suggest that an approximate cutoff for the magnitude of an individual d_i is $\chi^2_{\alpha,1}$. Selecting $\alpha = 0.01$, we would find $\chi^2_{0.01,1} = 6.63$, so any d_i exceeding this value would be considered a large contributor. The decomposition statistics d_i computed above give clear guidance regarding *which* variables in the observation vector have shifted.

Other diagnostics have been suggested in the literature. For example, Murphy (1987) and Chua and Montgomery (1992) have developed procedures based on discriminant analysis, a statistical procedure for classifying observations into groups. Tracy, Mason, and Young (1996) also use decompositions of T^2 for diagnostic purposes, but their procedure requires more extensive computations and uses more elaborate decompositions than equation (11.22).

11.3.2 Individual Observations

In some industrial settings the subgroup size is naturally $n = 1$. This situation occurs frequently in the chemical and process industries. Since these industries frequently have multiple quality characteristics that must be monitored, multivariate control charts with $n = 1$ would be of interest there.

Suppose that m samples, each of size $n = 1$, are available and that p is the number of quality characteristics observed in each sample. Let $\overline{\mathbf{x}}$ and $\mathbf{S}$ be the sample mean vector and covariance matrix, respectively, of these observations. The Hotelling T^2 statistic in equation (11.19) becomes

$$T^2 = (\mathbf{x} - \overline{\mathbf{x}})' \mathbf{S}^{-1} (\mathbf{x} - \overline{\mathbf{x}}) \qquad (11.23)$$

The phase II control limits for this statistic are

$$\text{UCL} = \frac{p(m+1)(m-1)}{m^2 - mp} F_{\alpha,p,m-p}$$
$$\text{LCL} = 0 \tag{11.24}$$

When the number of preliminary samples m is large—say, $m > 100$—many practitioners use an approximate control limit, either

$$\text{UCL} = \frac{p(m-1)}{m-p} F_{\alpha,p,m-p} \tag{11.25}$$

or

$$\text{UCL} = \chi^2_{\alpha,p} \tag{11.26}$$

For $m > 100$, equation (11.25) is a reasonable approximation. The chi-square limit in equation (11.26) is only appropriate if the covariance matrix is known, but it is widely used as an approximation. Lowry and Montgomery (1995) show that the chi-square limit should be used with caution. If p is large—say, $p \geq 10$—then at least 250 samples must be taken ($m \geq 250$) before the chi-square upper control limit is a reasonable approximation to the correct value.

Tracy, Young, and Mason (1992) point out that if $n = 1$, the phase I limits should be based on a beta distribution. This would lead to phase I limits defined as

$$\text{UCL} = \frac{(m-1)^2}{m} \beta_{\alpha,p/2,(m-p-1)/2}$$
$$\text{LCL} = 0 \tag{11.27}$$

where $\beta_{\alpha,p/2,(m-p-1)/2}$ is the upper α percentage point of a beta distribution with parameters $p/2$ and $(m-p-1)/2$. Approximations to the phase I limits based on the F and chi-square distributions are likely to be inaccurate.

A significant issue in the case of individual observations is estimating the covariance matrix $\mathbf{\Sigma}$. Sullivan and Woodall (1995) give an excellent discussion and analysis of this problem, and compare several estimators. Also see Vargas (2003) and Williams, Woodall, Birch, and Sullivan (2006). One of these is the "usual" estimator obtained by simply pooling all m observations—say,

$$\mathbf{S}_1 = \frac{1}{m-1} \sum_{i=1}^{m} (\mathbf{x}_i - \bar{\mathbf{x}})(\mathbf{x}_i - \bar{\mathbf{x}})'$$

Just as in the univariate case with $n = 1$, we would expect that $\mathbf{S}_1$ would be sensitive to outliers or out-of-control observations in the original sample of n observations. The second estimator [originally suggested by Holmes and Mergen (1993)] uses the difference between successive pairs of observations:

$$\mathbf{v}_i = \mathbf{x}_{i+1} - \mathbf{x}_i \quad i = 1, 2, \ldots, m-1 \tag{11.28}$$

Now arrange these vectors into a matrix **V**, where

$$\mathbf{V} = \begin{bmatrix} \mathbf{v}_1' \\ \mathbf{v}_2' \\ \vdots \\ \mathbf{v}_{m-1}' \end{bmatrix}$$

The estimator for $\boldsymbol{\Sigma}$ is one-half the sample covariance matrix of these differences:

$$\mathbf{S}_2 = \frac{1}{2}\frac{\mathbf{V}'\mathbf{V}}{(m-1)} \tag{11.29}$$

(Sullivan and Woodall originally denoted this estimator $\mathbf{S}_5$.)

Table 11.2 shows the example from Sullivan and Woodall (1995), in which they apply the T^2 chart procedure to the Holmes and Mergen (1993) data. There are 56 observations on the composition of "grit," where L, M, and S denote the percentages classified as large, medium, and small, respectively. Only the first two components were used because all those

■ **TABLE 11.2**

Example from Sullivan and Woodall (1995) Using the Data from Holmes and Mergen (1993) and the T^2 Statistics Using Estimators $\mathbf{S}_1$ and $\mathbf{S}_2$

i	$L = x_{i,1}$	$M = x_{i,2}$	$S = x_{i,3}$	$T^2_{1,i}$	$T^2_{2,i}$	i	$L = x_{i,1}$	$M = x_{i,2}$	$S = x_{i,3}$	$T^2_{1,i}$	$T^2_{2,i}$
1	5.4	93.6	1.0	4.496	6.439	29	7.4	83.6	9.0	1.594	3.261
2	3.2	92.6	4.2	1.739	4.227	30	6.8	84.8	8.4	0.912	1.743
3	5.2	91.7	3.1	1.460	2.200	31	6.3	87.1	6.6	0.110	0.266
4	3.5	86.9	9.6	4.933	7.643	32	6.1	87.2	6.7	0.077	0.166
5	2.9	90.4	6.7	2.690	5.565	33	6.6	87.3	6.1	0.255	0.564
6	4.6	92.1	3.3	1.272	2.258	34	6.2	84.8	9.0	1.358	2.069
7	4.4	91.5	4.1	0.797	1.676	35	6.5	87.4	6.1	0.203	0.448
8	5.0	90.3	4.7	0.337	0.645	36	6.0	86.8	7.2	0.193	0.317
9	8.4	85.1	6.5	2.088	4.797	37	4.8	88.8	6.4	0.297	0.590
10	4.2	89.7	6.1	0.666	1.471	38	4.9	89.8	5.3	0.197	0.464
11	3.8	92.5	3.7	1.368	3.057	39	5.8	86.9	7.3	0.242	0.353
12	4.3	91.8	3.9	0.951	1.986	40	7.2	83.8	9.0	1.494	2.928
13	3.7	91.7	4.6	1.105	2.688	41	5.6	89.2	5.2	0.136	0.198
14	3.8	90.3	5.9	1.019	2.317	42	6.9	84.5	8.6	1.079	2.062
15	2.6	94.5	2.9	3.099	7.262	43	7.4	84.4	8.2	1.096	2.477
16	2.7	94.5	2.8	3.036	7.025	44	8.9	84.3	6.8	2.854	6.666
17	7.9	88.7	3.4	3.803	6.189	45	10.9	82.2	6.9	7.677	17.666
18	6.6	84.6	8.8	1.167	1.997	46	8.2	89.8	2.0	6.677	10.321
19	4.0	90.7	5.3	0.751	1.824	47	6.7	90.4	2.9	2.708	3.869
20	2.5	90.2	7.3	3.966	7.811	48	5.9	90.1	4.0	0.888	1.235
21	3.8	92.7	3.5	1.486	3.247	49	8.7	83.6	7.7	2.424	5.914
22	2.8	91.5	5.7	2.357	5.403	50	6.4	88.0	5.6	0.261	0.470
23	2.9	91.8	5.3	2.094	4.959	51	8.4	84.7	6.9	1.995	4.731
24	3.3	90.6	6.1	1.721	3.800	52	9.6	80.6	9.8	4.732	11.259
25	7.2	87.3	5.5	0.914	1.791	53	5.1	93.0	1.9	2.891	4.303
26	7.3	79.0	13.7	9.226	14.372	54	5.0	91.4	3.6	0.989	1.609
27	7.0	82.6	10.4	2.940	4.904	55	5.0	86.2	8.8	1.770	2.495
28	6.0	83.5	10.5	3.310	4.771	56	5.9	87.2	6.9	0.102	0.166

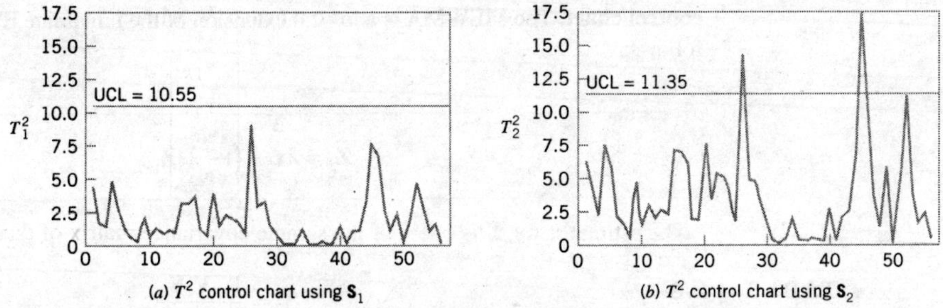

■ FIGURE 11.8 T^2 control charts for the data in Table 11.2.

percentages add to 100%. The mean vector for these data is $\bar{\mathbf{x}}' = [5.682, 88.22]$. The two sample covariance matrices are

$$\mathbf{S}_1 = \begin{bmatrix} 3.770 & -5.495 \\ -5.495 & 13.53 \end{bmatrix} \text{ and } \mathbf{S}_2 = \begin{bmatrix} 1.562 & -2.093 \\ -2.093 & 6.721 \end{bmatrix}$$

Figure 11.8 shows the T^2 control charts from this example. Sullivan and Woodall (1995) used simulation methods to find exact control limits for this data set (the false alarm probability is 0.155). Williams et al. (2006) observe that the asymptotic (large-sample) distribution of the T^2 statistic using $\mathbf{S}_2$ is χ^2_p. They also discuss approximating distributions. However, using simulation to find control limits is a reasonable approach. Note that only the control chart in Fig. 11.8*b* is based on $\mathbf{S}_2$ signals. It turns out that if we consider only samples 1–24, the sample mean vector is

$$\bar{\mathbf{x}}'_{1\text{-}24} = [4.23, 90.8]$$

and if we consider only the last 32 observations the sample mean vector is

$$\bar{\mathbf{x}}'_{25\text{-}56} = [6.77, 86.3]$$

These are statistically significantly different, whereas the "within" covariance matrices are not significantly different. There is an apparent shift in the mean vector following sample 24, and this was correctly detected by the control chart based on $\mathbf{S}_2$.

11.4 The Multivariate EWMA Control Chart

The chi-square and T^2 charts described in the previous section are Shewhart-type control charts. That is, they use information only from the current sample, so consequently, they are relatively insensitive to small and moderate shifts in the mean vector. As we noted, the T^2 chart can be used in both phase I and phase II situations. Cumulative sum (cusum) and EWMA control charts were developed to provide more sensitivity to small shifts in the univariate case, and they can be extended to multivariate quality control problems.[1] As in the univariate case, the multivariate version of these charts are a phase II procedure.

Crosier (1988) and Pignatiello and Runger (1990) have proposed several multivariate cusum procedures. Lowry et al. (1992) have developed a **multivariate EWMA (MEWMA)**

[1]The supplementary material for this chapter discusses the multivariate cusum control chart.

control chart. The MEWMA is a logical extension of the univariate EWMA and is defined as follows:

$$\mathbf{Z}_i = \lambda \mathbf{x}_i + (1-\lambda)\mathbf{Z}_{i-1} \tag{11.30}$$

■ TABLE 11.3
Average Run Lengths (zero state) for the MEWMA Control Chart [from Prabhu and Runger (1997)]

		λ							
p	δ	0.05	0.10	0.20	0.30	0.40	0.50	0.60	0.80
		H = 7.35	8.64	9.65	10.08	10.31	10.44	10.52	10.58
2	0.0	199.93	199.98	199.91	199.82	199.83	200.16	200.04	200.20
	0.5	26.61	28.07	35.17	44.10	53.82	64.07	74.50	95.88
	1.0	11.23	10.15	10.20	11.36	13.26	15.88	19.24	28.65
	1.5	7.14	6.11	5.49	5.48	5.78	6.36	7.25	10.28
	2.0	5.28	4.42	3.78	3.56	3.53	3.62	3.84	4.79
	3.0	3.56	2.93	2.42	2.20	2.05	1.95	1.90	1.91
		H = 11.22	12.73	13.87	14.34	14.58	14.71	14.78	14.85
4	0.0	199.84	200.12	199.94	199.91	199.96	200.05	199.99	200.05
	0.5	32.29	35.11	46.30	59.28	72.43	85.28	97.56	120.27
	1.0	13.48	12.17	12.67	14.81	18.12	22.54	28.06	42.58
	1.5	8.54	7.22	6.53	6.68	7.31	8.40	10.03	15.40
	2.0	6.31	5.19	4.41	4.20	4.24	4.48	4.93	6.75
	3.0	4.23	3.41	2.77	2.50	2.36	2.27	2.24	2.37
		H = 14.60	16.27	17.51	18.01	18.26	18.39	18.47	18.54
6	0.0	200.11	200.03	200.11	200.18	199.81	200.01	199.87	200.17
	0.5	36.39	40.38	54.71	70.30	85.10	99.01	111.65	133.91
	1.0	15.08	13.66	14.63	17.71	22.27	28.22	35.44	53.51
	1.5	9.54	8.01	7.32	7.65	8.60	10.20	12.53	20.05
	2.0	7.05	5.74	4.88	4.68	4.80	5.20	5.89	8.60
	3.0	4.72	3.76	3.03	2.72	2.58	2.51	2.51	2.77
		H = 20.72	22.67	24.07	24.62	24.89	25.03	25.11	25.17
10	0.0	199.91	199.95	200.08	200.01	199.98	199.84	200.12	200.00
	0.5	42.49	48.52	67.25	85.68	102.05	116.25	128.82	148.96
	1.0	17.48	15.98	17.92	22.72	29.47	37.81	47.54	69.71
	1.5	11.04	9.23	8.58	9.28	10.91	13.49	17.17	28.33
	2.0	8.15	6.57	5.60	5.47	5.77	6.48	7.68	12.15
	3.0	5.45	4.28	3.43	3.07	2.93	2.90	2.97	3.54
		H = 27.82	30.03	31.59	32.19	32.48	32.63	32.71	32.79
15	0.0	199.95	199.89	200.08	200.03	199.96	199.91	199.93	200.16
	0.5	48.20	56.19	78.41	98.54	115.36	129.36	141.10	159.55
	1.0	19.77	18.28	21.40	28.06	36.96	47.44	59.03	83.86
	1.5	12.46	10.41	9.89	11.08	13.53	17.26	22.38	37.07
	2.0	9.20	7.36	6.32	6.30	6.84	7.97	9.80	16.36
	3.0	6.16	4.78	3.80	3.43	3.29	3.31	3.49	4.49

where $0 \le \lambda \le 1$ and $\mathbf{Z}_0 = \mathbf{0}$. The quantity plotted on the control chart is

$$T_i^2 = \mathbf{Z}_i' \mathbf{\Sigma}_{\mathbf{Z}_i}^{-1} \mathbf{Z}_i \tag{11.31}$$

where the covariance matrix is

$$\mathbf{\Sigma}_{\mathbf{Z}_i} = \frac{\lambda}{2-\lambda}\left[1-(1-\lambda)^{2i}\right]\mathbf{\Sigma} \tag{11.32}$$

which is analogous to the variance of the univariate EWMA.

Prabhu and Runger (1997) have provided a thorough analysis of the average run length performance of the MEWMA control chart, using a modification of the Brook and Evans (1972) Markov chain approach. They give tables and charts to guide selection of the upper control limit—say, UCL = H—for the MEWMA. Tables 11.3 and 11.4 contain this information. Table 11.3 contains ARL performance for MEWMA for various values of λ for $p = 2$, 4, 6, 10, and 15 quality characteristics. The control limit H was chosen to give an in-control $\text{ARL}_0 = 200$. The ARLs in this table are all zero-state ARLs; that is, we assume that the process is in control when the chart is initiated. The shift size is reported in terms of a quantity

$$\delta = \left(\mu' \Sigma^{-1} \mu\right)^{1/2} \tag{11.33}$$

usually called the **noncentrality parameter.** Basically, large values of δ correspond to bigger shifts in the mean. The value $\delta = 0$ is the in-control state (this is true because the control chart can be constructed using "standardized" data). Note that for a given shift size, ARLs generally tend to increase as λ increases, except for very large values of δ (or large shifts).

■ **TABLE 11.4**
Optimal MEWMA Control Charts [From Prabhu and Runger (1997)]

		$p = 4$		$p = 10$		$p = 20$	
δ	$\text{ARL}_0 =$	500	1000	500	1000	500	1000
0.5	λ	0.04	0.03	0.03	0.025	0.03	0.025
	H	13.37	14.68	22.69	24.70	37.09	39.63
	$\text{ARL}_{\min}$	42.22	49.86	55.94	66.15	70.20	83.77
1.0	λ	0.105	0.09	0.085	0.075	0.075	0.065
	H	15.26	16.79	25.42	27.38	40.09	42.47
	$\text{ARL}_{\min}$	14.60	16.52	19.29	21.74	24.51	27.65
1.5	λ	0.18	0.18	0.16	0.14	0.14	0.12
	H	16.03	17.71	26.58	28.46	41.54	43.80
	$\text{ARL}_{\min}$	7.65	8.50	10.01	11.07	12.70	14.01
2.0	λ	0.28	0.26	0.24	0.22	0.20	0.18
	H	16.49	18.06	27.11	29.02	42.15	44.45
	$\text{ARL}_{\min}$	4.82	5.30	6.25	6.84	7.88	8.60
3.0	λ	0.52	0.46	0.42	0.40	0.36	0.34
	H	16.84	18.37	27.55	29.45	42.80	45.08
	$\text{ARL}_{\min}$	2.55	2.77	3.24	3.50	4.04	4.35

Note: ARL_0 and $\text{ARL}_{\min}$ are zero-state average run lengths.

Since the MEWMA with $\lambda = 1$ is equivalent to the T^2 (or chi-square) control chart, the MEWMA is more sensitive to smaller shifts. This is analogous to the univariate case. Because the MEWMA is a **directionally invariant** procedure, all that we need to characterize its performance for any shift in the mean vector is the corresponding value of δ.

Table 11.4 presents "optimum" MEWMA chart designs for various shifts (δ) and in-control target values of ARL_0 of either 500 or 1000. ARL_{min} is the minimum value of ARL_1 achieved for the value of λ specified.

To illustrate the design of a MEWMA control chart, suppose that $p = 6$ and the covariance matrix is

$$\mathbf{\Sigma} = \begin{bmatrix} 1 & 0.7 & 0.9 & 0.3 & 0.2 & 0.3 \\ 0.7 & 1 & 0.8 & 0.1 & 0.4 & 0.2 \\ 0.9 & 0.8 & 1 & 0.1 & 0.2 & 0.1 \\ 0.3 & 0.1 & 0.1 & 1 & 0.2 & 0.1 \\ 0.2 & 0.4 & 0.2 & 0.2 & 1 & 0.1 \\ 0.3 & 0.2 & 0.1 & 0.1 & 0.1 & 1 \end{bmatrix}$$

Note that $\mathbf{\Sigma}$ is in **correlation** form. Suppose that we are interested in a process shift from $\boldsymbol{\mu}' = \mathbf{0}$ to

$$\boldsymbol{\mu}' = [1,1,1,1,1,1]$$

This is essentially a one-sigma upward shift in all $p = 6$ variables. For this shift, $\delta = (\boldsymbol{\mu}'\mathbf{\Sigma}^{-1}\boldsymbol{\mu})^{1/2} = 1.86$. Table 11.3 suggests that $\lambda = 0.2$ and $H = 17.51$ would give an in-control $ARL_0 = 200$ and the ARL_1 would be between 4.88 and 7.32. It turns out that if the mean shifts by any constant multiple—say, k—of the original vector $\boldsymbol{\mu}$, then δ changes to $k\delta$. Therefore, ARL performance is easy to evaluate. For example, if $k = 1.5$, then the new δ is $\delta = 1.5(1.86) = 2.79$, and the ARL_1 would be between 3.03 and 4.88.

MEWMA control charts provide a very useful procedure. They are relatively easy to apply and design rules for the chart are well documented. Molnau et al. (2001) give a computer program for calculating ARLs for the MEWMA. This could be a useful way to supplement the design information in the paper by Prabhu and Runger (1997). Scranton et al. (1996) show how the ARL performance of the MEWMA control chart can be further improved by applying it to only the important principal components of the monitored variables. (Principal components are discussed in Section 11.7.1.) Reynolds and Cho (2006) develop MEWMA procedures for simultaneous monitoring of the mean vector and covariance matrix. Economic models of the MEWMA are discussed by Linderman and Love (2000a, b) and Molnau, Montgomery, and Runger (2001). MEWMA control charts, like their univariate counterparts, are robust to the assumption of normality, if properly designed. Stoumbos and Sullivan (2002) and Testik, Runger, and Borror (2003) report that small values of the parameter λ result in a MEWMA that is very insensitive to the form of the underlying multivariate distribution of the process data. Small values of λ also provide very good performance in detecting small shifts, and they would seem to be a good general choice for the MEWMA. A comprehensive discussion of design strategies for the MEWMA control chart is in Testik and Borror (2004).

Hawkins, Choi, and Lee (2007) have recently proposed a modification of the MEWMA control chart in which the use of a single smoothing constant λ is generalized to a **smoothing matrix** which has non-zero diagonal elements. The MEWMA scheme in equation (11.30) becomes

$$\mathbf{Z}_i = \mathbf{R}\mathbf{x}_i + (\mathbf{I} - \mathbf{R})\mathbf{Z}_{i-1}$$

The authors restrict the elements of **R** so that the diagonal elements are equal, and they also suggest that the off-diagonals (say r_{off}) be equal and smaller in magnitude than the diagonal elements (say r_{on}). They propose choosing $r_{off} = cr_{on}$, with $|c| < 1$. Then *the full smoothing matrix MEWMA* or *FEWMA* is characterized by the parameters λ and c with the diagonal and off-diagonal elements defined as

$$r_{on} = \frac{\lambda}{1 + (p + 1)c} \quad \text{and} \quad r_{off} = \frac{c\lambda}{1 + (p - 1)c}$$

The FEWMA is not a directionally invariant procedure, as are the Hotelling T^2 and MEWMA control charts. That is, they are more sensitive to shifts is certain directions than in others. The exact performance of the FEWMA depends on the covariance matrix of the process data and the direction of the shift in the mean vector. There is a computer program to assist in designing the FEWMA to obtain specific ARL performance (see www.stat.umn.edu/hawkins). The authors show that the FEWMA can improve MEWMA performance particularly in cases where the process starts up in an out-of-control state.

11.5 Regression Adjustment

The Hotelling T^2 (and chi-square) control chart is based on the general idea of testing the hypothesis that the mean vector of a multivariate normal distribution is equal to a constant vector against the alternative hypothesis that the mean vector is not equal to that constant. In fact, it is an optimal test statistic for that hypothesis. However, it is not necessarily an optimal control-charting procedure for detecting mean shifts. The MEWMA can be designed to have faster detection capability (smaller values of the ARL_1). Furthermore, the Hotelling T^2 is not optimal for more structured shifts in the mean, such as shifts in only a few of the process variables. It also turns out that the Hotelling T^2, and any method that uses the *quadratic form* structure of the Hotelling T^2 test statistic (such as the MEWMA), will be sensitive to shifts in the variance as well as to shifts in the mean. Consequently, various researchers have developed methods to monitor multivariate processes that do not depend on the Hotelling T^2 statistic.

Hawkins (1991) has developed a procedure called **regression adjustment** that is potentially very useful. The scheme essentially consists of plotting univariate control charts of the *residuals* from each variable obtained when that variable is regressed on all the others. **Residual control charts** are very applicable to individual measurements, which occurs frequently in practice with multivariate data. Implementation is straightforward, since it requires only a least squares regression computer program to process the data prior to constructing the control charts. Hawkins shows that the ARL performance of this scheme is very competitive with other methods, but depends on the types of control charts applied to the residuals.

A very important application of regression adjustment occurs when the process has a distinct hierarchy of variables, such as a set of *input* process variables (say, the x's) and a set of *output* variables (say, the y's). Sometimes we call this situation a **cascade process** [Hawkins (1993b)]. Table 11.5 shows 40 observations from a cascade process, where there are nine input variables and two output variables. We will demonstrate the regression adjustment approach using only one of the output variables, y_1. Figure 11.9 is a control chart for individuals and a moving range control chart for the 40 observations on the output variable y_1. Note that there are seven out-of-control points on the individuals control chart. Using standard least squares regression techniques, we can fit the following regression model for y_1 to the process variables $x_1, x_2, \ldots, x_9$:

$$\hat{y}_1 = 826 + 0.474x_1 + 1.41x_2 - 0.117x_3 - 0.0824x_4 - 2.39x_5 - 1.30x_6 + 2.18x_7$$
$$+ 2.98x_8 + 113x_9$$

■ **TABLE 11.5**
Cascade Process Data

Observation	x_1	x_2	x_3	x_4	x_5	x_6	x_7	x_8	x_9	y_1	Residuals	y_2
1	12.78	0.15	91	56	1.54	7.38	1.75	5.89	1.11	951.5	0.81498	87
2	14.97	0.1	90	49	1.54	7.14	1.71	5.91	1.109	952.2	−0.31685	88
3	15.43	0.07	90	41	1.47	7.33	1.64	5.92	1.104	952.3	−0.28369	86
4	14.95	0.12	89	43	1.54	7.21	1.93	5.71	1.103	951.8	−0.45924	89
5	16.17	0.1	83	42	1.67	7.23	1.86	5.63	1.103	952.3	−0.56512	86
6	17.25	0.07	84	54	1.49	7.15	1.68	5.8	1.099	952.2	−0.22592	91
7	16.57	0.12	89	61	1.64	7.23	1.82	5.88	1.096	950.2	−0.55431	99
8	19.31	0.08	99	60	1.46	7.74	1.69	6.13	1.092	950.5	−0.18874	100
9	18.75	0.04	99	52	1.89	7.57	2.02	6.27	1.084	950.6	0.15245	103
10	16.99	0.09	98	57	1.66	7.51	1.82	6.38	1.086	949.8	−0.33580	107
11	18.2	0.13	98	49	1.66	7.27	1.92	6.3	1.089	951.2	−0.85525	98
12	16.2	0.16	97	52	2.16	7.21	2.34	6.07	1.089	950.6	0.47027	96
13	14.72	0.12	82	61	1.49	7.33	1.72	6.01	1.092	948.9	−1.74107	93
14	14.42	0.13	81	63	1.16	7.5	1.5	6.11	1.094	951.7	0.62057	91
15	11.02	0.1	83	56	1.56	7.14	1.73	6.14	1.102	951.5	0.72583	91
16	9.82	0.1	86	53	1.26	7.32	1.54	6.15	1.112	951.3	−0.03421	93
17	11.41	0.12	87	49	1.29	7.22	1.57	6.13	1.114	952.9	0.28093	91
18	14.74	0.1	81	42	1.55	7.17	1.77	6.28	1.114	953.9	−1.87257	94
19	14.5	0.08	84	53	1.57	7.23	1.69	6.28	1.109	953.3	−0.20805	96
20	14.71	0.09	89	46	1.45	7.23	1.67	6.12	1.108	952.6	−0.66749	94
21	15.26	0.13	91	47	1.74	7.28	1.98	6.19	1.105	952.3	−0.75390	99
22	17.3	0.12	95	47	1.57	7.18	1.86	6.06	1.098	952.6	−0.03479	95
23	17.62	0.06	95	42	2.05	7.15	2.14	6.15	1.096	952.9	0.24439	92
24	18.21	0.06	93	41	1.46	7.28	1.61	6.11	1.096	953.9	0.67889	87
25	14.38	0.1	90	46	1.42	7.29	1.73	6.13	1.1	954.2	1.94313	89
26	12.13	0.14	87	50	1.76	7.21	1.9	6.31	1.112	951.9	−0.92344	98
27	12.72	0.1	90	47	1.52	7.25	1.79	6.25	1.112	952.3	−0.74707	95
28	17.42	0.1	89	51	1.33	7.38	1.51	6.01	1.111	953.7	−0.21053	88
29	17.63	0.11	87	45	1.51	7.42	1.68	6.11	1.103	954.7	0.66802	86
30	16.17	0.05	83	57	1.41	7.35	1.62	6.14	1.105	954.6	1.35076	84
31	16.88	0.16	86	58	2.1	7.15	2.28	6.42	1.105	954.8	0.61137	91
32	13.87	0.16	85	46	2.1	7.11	2.16	6.44	1.106	954.4	0.56960	92
33	14.56	0.05	84	41	1.34	7.14	1.51	6.24	1.113	955	−0.09131	88
34	15.35	0.12	83	40	1.52	7.08	1.81	6	1.114	956.5	1.03785	83
35	15.91	0.12	81	45	1.76	7.26	1.9	6.07	1.116	955.3	−0.07282	83
36	14.32	0.11	85	47	1.58	7.15	1.72	6.02	1.113	954.2	0.53440	86
37	15.43	0.13	86	43	1.46	7.15	1.73	6.11	1.115	955.4	0.16379	85
38	14.47	0.08	85	54	1.62	7.1	1.78	6.15	1.118	953.8	−0.37110	88
39	14.74	0.07	84	52	1.47	7.24	1.66	5.89	1.112	953.2	0.17177	83
40	16.28	0.13	86	49	1.72	7.05	1.89	5.91	1.109	954.2	0.47427	85

The residuals are found simply by subtracting the fitted value from this equation from each corresponding observation on y_1. These residuals are shown in the next-to-last column of Table 11.5.

Figure 11.10 shows a control chart for individuals and a moving range control chart for the 40 residuals from this procedure. Note that there is now only one out-of-control point on the moving range chart, and the overall impression of process stability is rather different than was

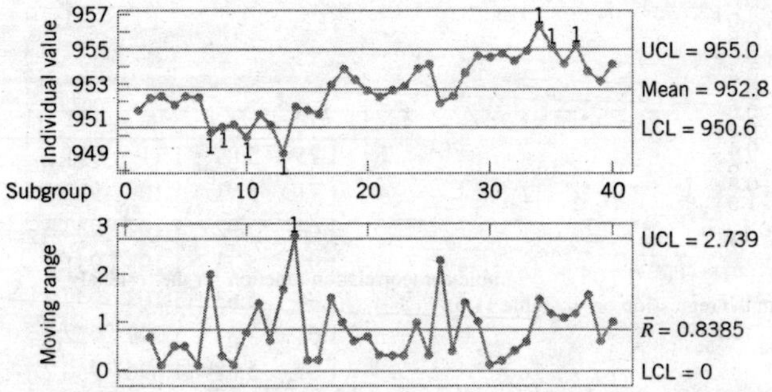

■ FIGURE 11.9 Individuals and moving range control charts for y_1 from Table 11.5.

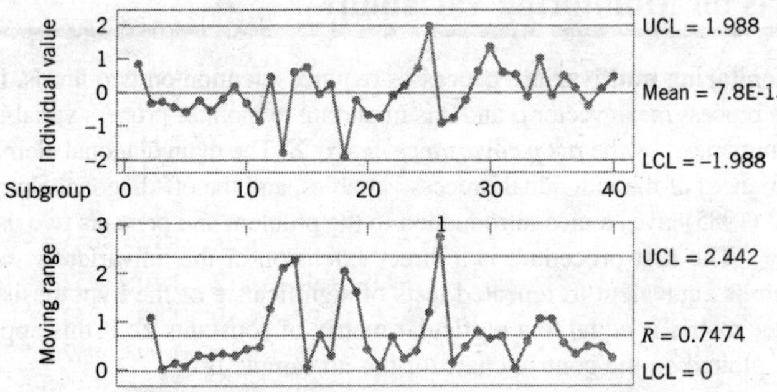

■ FIGURE 11.10 Individuals and moving range control charts for the residuals of the regression on y_1, Table 11.5.

obtained from the control charts for y_1 alone, without the effects of the process variables taken into account.

Regression adjustment has another nice feature. If the proper set of variables is included in the regression model, the residuals from the model will typically be uncorrelated, even though the original variable of interest y_1 exhibited correlation. To illustrate, Figure 11.11 is the sample autocorrelation function for y_1. Note that there is considerable autocorrelation at low lags in this variable. This is very typical behavior for data from a chemical or process plant. The sample autocorrelation function for the residuals is shown in Fig. 11.12. There is no evidence of autocorrelation in the residuals. Because of this nice feature, the regression

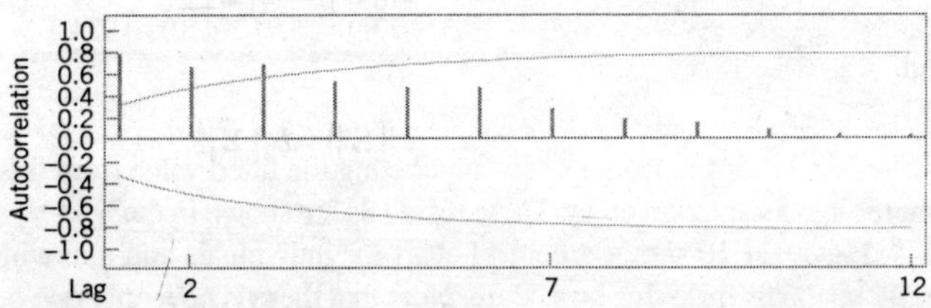

■ FIGURE 11.11 Sample autocorrelation function for y_1 from Table 11.5.

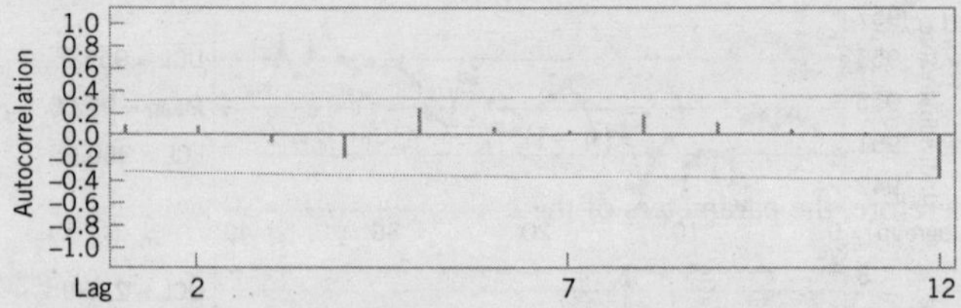

■ FIGURE 11.12 Sample autocorrelation function for the residuals from the regression on y_1, Table 11.5.

adjustment procedure has many possible applications in chemical and process plants where there are often cascade processes with several inputs but only a few outputs, and where many of the variables are highly autocorrelated.

11.6 Control Charts for Monitoring Variability

Monitoring multivariate processes requires attention on two levels. It is important to monitor the process mean vector $\boldsymbol{\mu}$ and it is important to monitor process variability. Process variability is summarized by the $p \times p$ *covariance matrix* $\boldsymbol{\Sigma}$. The main diagonal elements of this matrix are the variances of the individual process variables, and the off-diagonal elements are the covariances. Alt (1985) gives a nice introduction to the problem and presents two useful procedures.

The first procedure is a direct extension of the univariate s^2 control chart. The procedure is equivalent to repeated tests of significance of the hypothesis that the process covariance matrix is equal to a particular matrix of constants $\boldsymbol{\Sigma}$. If this approach is used, the statistic plotted on the control chart for the ith sample is

$$W_i = -pn + pn\ln(n) - n\ln\left(|\mathbf{A}_i|/|\boldsymbol{\Sigma}|\right) + \mathrm{tr}\left(\boldsymbol{\Sigma}^{-1}\mathbf{A}_i\right) \tag{11.34}$$

where $\mathbf{A}_i = (n-1)\mathbf{S}_i$, $\mathbf{S}_i$ is the sample covariance matrix for sample i, and tr is the trace operator. (The trace of a matrix is the sum of the main diagonal elements.) If the value of W_i plots above the upper control limit $\mathrm{UCL} = \chi^2_{\alpha, p(p+1)/2}$, the process is out of control.

The second approach is based on the sample *generalized* variance, $|\mathbf{S}|$. This statistic, which is the determinant of the sample covariance matrix, is a widely used measure of multivariate dispersion. Montgomery and Wadsworth (1972) used an asymptotic normal approximation to develop a control chart for $|\mathbf{S}|$. Another method would be to use the mean and variance of $|\mathbf{S}|$—that is, $E(|\mathbf{S}|)$ and $V(|\mathbf{S}|)$—and the property that most of the probability distribution of $|\mathbf{S}|$ is contained in the interval $E|\mathbf{S}| \pm 3\sqrt{V(|\mathbf{S}|)}$. It can be shown that

$$E(|\mathbf{S}|) = b_1|\boldsymbol{\Sigma}| \tag{11.35}$$

and

$$V(|\mathbf{S}|) = b_2|\boldsymbol{\Sigma}|^2$$

where

$$b_1 = \frac{1}{(n-1)^p}\prod_{i=1}^{p}(n-i)$$

and

$$b_2 = \frac{1}{(n-1)^{2p}} \prod_{i=1}^{p} (n-i) \left[\prod_{j=1}^{p} (n-j+2) - \prod_{j=1}^{p} (n-j) \right]$$

Therefore, the parameters of the control chart for $|\mathbf{S}|$ would be

$$\begin{aligned} \text{UCL} &= |\boldsymbol{\Sigma}|\left(b_1 + 3b_2^{1/2}\right) \\ \text{CL} &= b_1|\boldsymbol{\Sigma}| \\ \text{LCL} &= |\boldsymbol{\Sigma}|\left(b_1 - 3b_2^{1/2}\right) \end{aligned} \tag{11.36}$$

The lower control limit in equation (11.36) is replaced with zero if the calculated value is less than zero.

In practice, $\boldsymbol{\Sigma}$ usually will be estimated by a sample covariance matrix **S**, based on the analysis of preliminary samples. If this is the case, we should replace $|\boldsymbol{\Sigma}|$ in equation (11.36) by $|\mathbf{S}|/b_1$, since equation (11.35) has shown that $|\mathbf{S}|/b_1$ is an unbiased estimator of $|\boldsymbol{\Sigma}|$.

EXAMPLE 11.2 Monitoring Variability

Use the data in Example 11.1 and construct a control chart for the generalized variance.

SOLUTION

Based on the 20 preliminary samples in Table 11.1, the sample covariance matrix is

$$\mathbf{S} = \begin{bmatrix} 1.23 & 0.79 \\ 0.79 & 0.83 \end{bmatrix}$$

so

$$|\mathbf{S}| = 0.3968$$

The constants b_1 and b_2 are (recall that $n = 10$)

$$b_1 = \frac{1}{81}(9)(8) = 0.8889$$

$$b_2 = \frac{1}{6561}(9)(8)[(11)(10) - (9)(8)] = 0.4170$$

Therefore, replacing $|\boldsymbol{\Sigma}|$ in equation (11.36) by $|\mathbf{S}|/b_1 = 0.3968/0.8889 = 0.4464$, we find that the control chart parameters are

$$\text{UCL} = (|\mathbf{S}|/b_1)\left(b_1 + 3b_2^{1/2}\right) = 0.4464\left[0.8889 + 3(0.4170)^{1/2}\right] = 1.26$$

$$\text{CL} = |\mathbf{S}| = 0.3968$$

$$\text{LCL} = (|\mathbf{S}|/b_1)\left(b_1 - 3b_2^{1/2}\right) = 0.4464\left[0.8889 - 3(0.4170)^{1/2}\right] = -0.47 = 0$$

Figure 11.13 presents the control chart. The values of $|\mathbf{S}_i|$ for each sample are shown in the last column of panel (c) of Table 11.1.

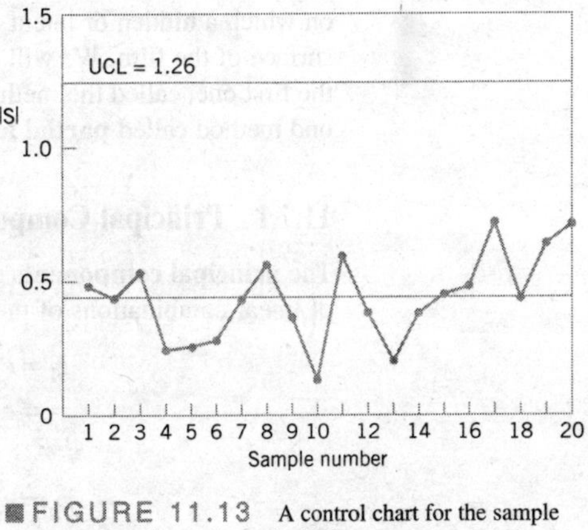

■ FIGURE 11.13 A control chart for the sample generalized variance, Example 11.2.

Although the sample generalized variance is a widely used measure of multivariate dispersion, remember that it is a relatively simplistic scalar representation of a complex multivariable problem, and it is easy to be fooled if all we look at is $|\mathbf{S}|$. For example, consider the three covariance matrices:

$$\mathbf{S}_1 = \begin{bmatrix} 1 & 0 \\ 0 & 1 \end{bmatrix}, \ \mathbf{S}_2 = \begin{bmatrix} 2.32 & 0.40 \\ 0.40 & 0.50 \end{bmatrix}, \text{ and } \mathbf{S}_3 = \begin{bmatrix} 1.68 & -0.40 \\ -0.40 & 0.50 \end{bmatrix}$$

Now $|\mathbf{S}_1| = |\mathbf{S}_2| = |\mathbf{S}_3| = 1$, yet the three matrices convey considerably different information about process variability and the correlation between the two variables. It is probably a good idea to use univariate control charts for variability in conjunction with the control chart for $|\mathbf{S}|$.

11.7 Latent Structure Methods

Conventional multivariate control-charting procedures are reasonably effective as long as p (the number of process variables to be monitored) is not very large. However, as p increases, the average run-length performance to detect a specified shift in the mean of these variables for multivariate control charts also increases, because the shift is "diluted" in the p-dimensional space of the process variables. To illustrate this, consider the ARLs of the MEWMA control chart in Table 11.3. Suppose we choose $\lambda = 0.1$ and the magnitude of the shift is $\delta = 1.0$. Now in this table $\text{ARL}_0 = 200$ regardless of p, the number of parameters. However, note that as p increases, ARL_1 also increases. For $p = 2$, $\text{ARL}_1 = 10.15$, for $p = 6$, $\text{ARL}_1 = 13.66$, and for $p = 15$, $\text{ARL}_1 = 18.28$. Consequently, other methods are sometimes useful for process monitoring, particularly in situations where it is suspected that the variability in the process is not equally distributed among all p variables. That is, most of the "motion" of the process is in a relatively small subset of the original process variables.

Methods for discovering the subdimensions in which the process moves about are sometimes called **latent structure methods,** because of the analogy with photographic film on which a hidden or latent image is stored as a result of light interacting with the chemical surface of the film. We will discuss two of these methods, devoting most of our attention to the first one, called the method of **principal components.** We will also briefly discuss a second method called **partial least squares.**

11.7.1 Principal Components

The **principal components** of a set of process variables $x_1, x_2, \ldots, x_p$ are just a particular set of linear combinations of these variables—say,

$$\begin{aligned} z_1 &= c_{11}x_1 + c_{12}x_2 + \cdots + c_{1p}x_p \\ z_2 &= c_{21}x_1 + c_{22}x_2 + \cdots + c_{2p}x_p \\ &\vdots \\ z_p &= c_{p1}x_1 + c_{p2}x_2 + \cdots + c_{pp}x_p \end{aligned} \tag{11.37}$$

where the c_{ij}'s are constants to be determined. Geometrically, the principal component variables $z_1, z_2, \ldots, z_p$ are the axes of a new coordinate system obtained by rotating the axes of the *original* system (the x's). The new axes represent the directions of maximum variability.

To illustrate, consider the two situations shown in Fig. 11.14. In Fig. 11.14*a*, there are two original variables x_1 and x_2, and two principal components z_1 and z_2. Note that the first

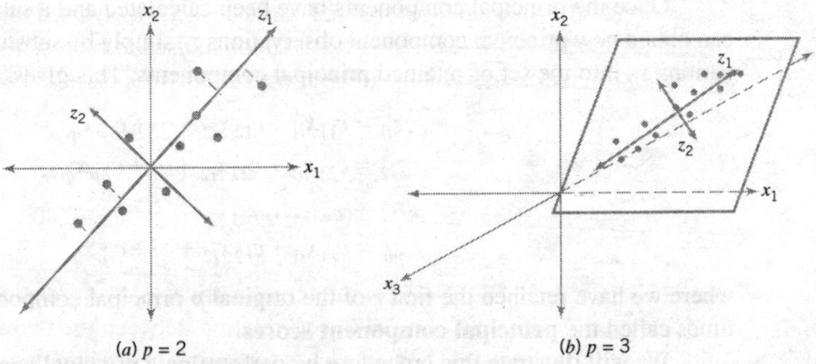

FIGURE 11.14 Principal components for $p = 2$ and $p = 3$ process variables.

principal component z_1 accounts for most of the variability in the two original variables. Figure 11.14*b* illustrates three original process variables. Most of the variability or "motion" in these two variables is in a plane, so only two principal components have been used to describe them. In this picture, once again z_1 accounts for most of the variability, but a nontrivial amount is also accounted for by the second principal component z_2. This is, in fact, the basic intent of principal components: Find the new set of orthogonal directions that define the maximum variability in the original data, and, hopefully, this will lead to a description of the process requiring considerably fewer than the original p variables. The information contained in the complete set of all p principal components is exactly equivalent to the information in the complete set of all original process variables, but hopefully we can use far fewer than p principal components to obtain a satisfactory description.

It turns out that finding the c_{ij}'s that define the principal components is fairly easy. Let the random variables $x_1, x_2, \ldots, x_p$ be represented by a vector $\mathbf{x}$ with covariance matrix $\mathbf{\Sigma}$, and let the **eigenvalues** of $\mathbf{\Sigma}$ be $\lambda_1 \geq \lambda_2 \geq \cdots \geq \lambda_p \geq 0$. Then the constants c_{ij} are simply the elements of the ith **eigenvector** associated with the eigenvalue λ_i. Basically, if we let $\mathbf{C}$ be the matrix whose columns are the eigenvectors, then

$$\mathbf{C}'\mathbf{\Sigma}\mathbf{C} = \mathbf{\Lambda}$$

where $\mathbf{\Lambda}$ is a $p \times p$ diagonal matrix with main diagonal elements equal to the eigenvalues $\lambda_1 \geq \lambda_2 \geq \cdots \geq \lambda_p \geq 0$. Many software packages will compute eigenvalues and eigenvectors and perform the principal components analysis.

The variance of the ith principal component is the ith eigenvalue λ_i. Consequently, the proportion of variability in the original data explained by the ith principal component is given by the ratio

$$\frac{\lambda_i}{\lambda_1 + \lambda_2 + \cdots + \lambda_p}$$

Therefore, one can easily see how much variability is explained by retaining just a few (say, r) of the p principal components simply by computing the sum of the eigenvalues for those r components and comparing that total to the sum of all p eigenvalues. It is a fairly typical practice to compute principal components using variables that have been standardized so that they have mean zero and unit variance. Then the covariance matrix $\mathbf{\Sigma}$ is in the form of a correlation matrix. The reason for this is that the original process variables are often expressed in different scales and as a result they can have very different magnitudes. Consequently, a variable may seem to contribute a lot to the total variability of the system just because its scale of measurement has larger magnitudes than the other variables. Standardization solves this problem nicely.

Once the principal components have been calculated and a subset of them selected, we can obtain new principal component observations z_{ij} simply by substituting the original observations x_{ij} into the set of retained principal components. This gives, for example,

$$
\begin{aligned}
z_{i1} &= c_{11}x_{i1} + c_{12}x_{i2} + \cdots + c_{1p}x_{ip} \\
z_{i2} &= c_{21}x_{i1} + c_{22}x_{i2} + \cdots + c_{2p}x_{ip} \\
&\vdots \\
z_{ir} &= c_{r1}x_{i1} + c_{r2}x_{i2} + \cdots + c_{rp}x_{ip}
\end{aligned}
\tag{11.38}
$$

where we have retained the first r of the original p principal components. The z_{ij}'s are sometimes called the **principal component scores.**

We will illustrate this procedure by performing a principal components analysis (PCA) using the data on the $p = 4$ variables x_1, x_2, x_3, and x_4 in Table 11.6, which are process variables

■ **TABLE 11.6**
Chemical Process Data

Observation	x_1	x_2	x_3	x_4	z_1	z_2
Original Data						
1	10	20.7	13.6	15.5	0.291681	–0.6034
2	10.5	19.9	18.1	14.8	0.294281	0.491533
3	9.7	20	16.1	16.5	0.197337	0.640937
4	9.8	20.2	19.1	17.1	0.839022	1.469579
5	11.7	21.5	19.8	18.3	3.204876	0.879172
6	11	20.9	10.3	13.8	0.203271	–2.29514
7	8.7	18.8	16.9	16.8	–0.99211	1.670464
8	9.5	19.3	15.3	12.2	–1.70241	–0.36089
9	10.1	19.4	16.2	15.8	–0.14246	0.560808
10	9.5	19.6	13.6	14.5	–0.99498	–0.31493
11	10.5	20.3	17	16.5	0.944697	0.504711
12	9.2	19	11.5	16.3	–1.2195	–0.09129
13	11.3	21.6	14	18.7	2.608666	–0.42176
14	10	19.8	14	15.9	–0.12378	–0.08767
15	8.5	19.2	17.4	15.8	–1.10423	1.472593
16	9.7	20.1	10	16.6	–0.27825	–0.94763
17	8.3	18.4	12.5	14.2	–2.65608	0.135288
18	11.9	21.8	14.1	16.2	2.36528	–1.30494
19	10.3	20.5	15.6	15.1	0.411311	–0.21893
20	8.9	19	8.5	14.7	–2.14662	–1.17849
New Data						
21	9.9	20	15.4	15.9	0.074196	0.239359
22	8.7	19	9.9	16.8	–1.51756	–0.21121
23	11.5	21.8	19.3	12.1	1.408476	–0.87591
24	15.9	24.6	14.7	15.3	6.298001	–3.67398
25	12.6	23.9	17.1	14.2	3.802025	–1.99584
26	14.9	25	16.3	16.6	6.490673	–2.73143
27	9.9	23.7	11.9	18.1	2.738829	–1.37617
28	12.8	26.3	13.5	13.7	4.958747	–3.94851
29	13.1	26.1	10.9	16.8	5.678092	–3.85838
30	9.8	25.8	14.8	15	3.369657	–2.10878

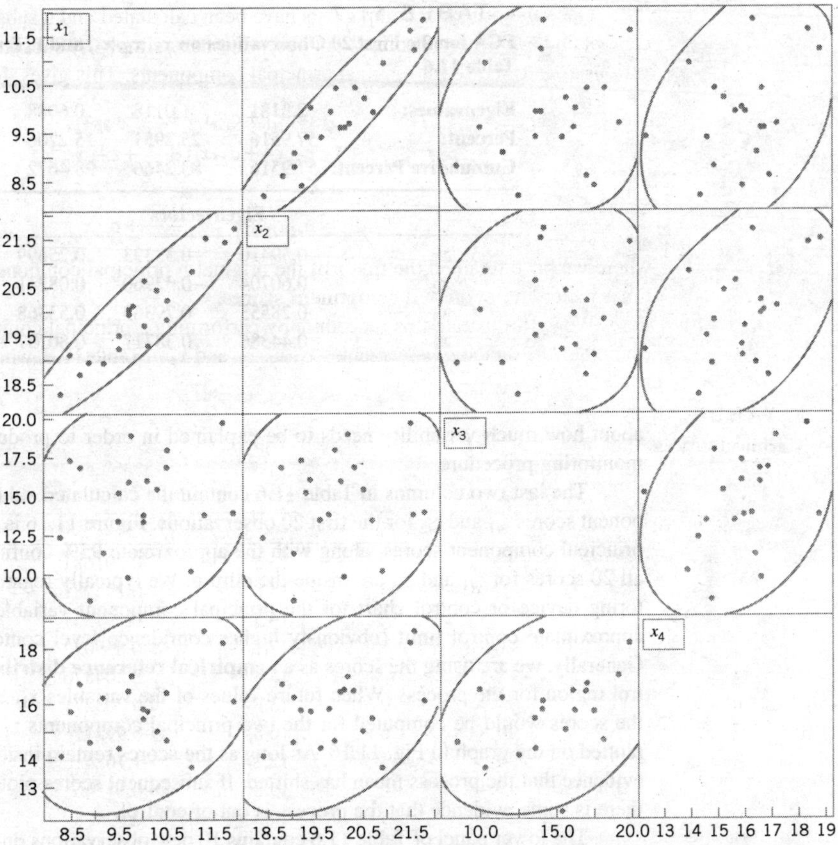

FIGURE 11.15 Matrix of scatter plots for the first 20 observations on x_1, x_2, x_3, and x_4 from Table 11.6.

from a chemical process. The first 20 observations in the upper panel of this table are first plotted against each other in a pairwise manner in Fig. 11.15. This display is usually called a **matrix of scatter plots,** and it indicates that the first two variables are highly correlated, whereas the other two variables exhibit only moderate correlation. The ellipses in Fig. 11.15 are approximate 95% confidence contours based on the assumption of a normal distribution. The sample covariance matrix of the first 20 observations on the x's, in correlation form, is

$$\mathbf{\Sigma} = \begin{bmatrix} 1.0000 & 0.9302 & 0.2060 & 0.3595 \\ 0.9302 & 1.0000 & 0.1669 & 0.4502 \\ 0.2060 & 0.1669 & 1.0000 & 0.3439 \\ 0.3595 & 0.4502 & 0.3439 & 1.0000 \end{bmatrix}$$

Note that the correlation coefficient between x_1 and x_2 is 0.9302, which confirms the visual impression obtained from the matrix of scatter plots.

Table 11.7 presents the results of a PCA (Minitab was used to perform the calculations) on the first 20 observations, showing the eigenvalues and eigenvectors, as well as the percentage and the cumulative percentage of the variability explained by each principal component. By using only the first two principal components, we can account for over 83% of the variability in the original four variables. Generally, we will want to retain enough components to explain a reasonable proportion of the total process variability, but there are no firm guidelines

■ TABLE 11.7
PCA for the First 20 Observations on x_1, x_2, x_3, and x_4 from Table 11.6

Eigenvalues:	2.3181	1.0118	0.6088	0.0613
Percent:	57.9516	25.2951	15.2206	1.5328
Cumulative Percent:	57.9516	83.2466	98.4672	100.0000
		Eigenvectors		
x_1	0.59410	−0.33393	0.25699	0.68519
x_2	0.60704	−0.32960	0.08341	−0.71826
x_3	0.28553	0.79369	0.53368	−0.06092
x_4	0.44386	0.38717	−0.80137	0.10440

about how much variability needs to be explained in order to produce an effective process-monitoring procedure.

The last two columns in Table 11.6 contain the calculated values of the principal component scores z_{i1} and z_{i2} for the first 20 observations. Figure 11.16 is a scatter plot of these 20 principal component scores, along with the approximate 95% confidence contour. Note that all 20 scores for z_{i1} and z_{i2} are inside the ellipse. We typically regard this display as a monitoring device or control chart for the principal component variables, and the ellipse is an approximate control limit (obviously higher confidence level contours could be selected). Generally, we are using the scores as an **empirical reference distribution** to establish a control region for the process. When future values of the variables $x_1, x_2, \ldots, x_p$ are observed, the scores would be computed for the two principal components z_1 and z_2 and these scores plotted on the graph in Fig. 11.16. As long as the scores remain inside the ellipse, there is no evidence that the process mean has shifted. If subsequent scores plot outside the ellipse, then there is some evidence that the process is out of control.

The lower panel of Table 11.6 contains 10 new observations on the process variables $x_1, x_2, \ldots, x_p$ that were not used in computing the principal components. The **principal component scores** for these new observations are also shown in the table, and the scores are plotted on the control chart in Fig. 11.17. A different plotting symbol (×) has been used to assist

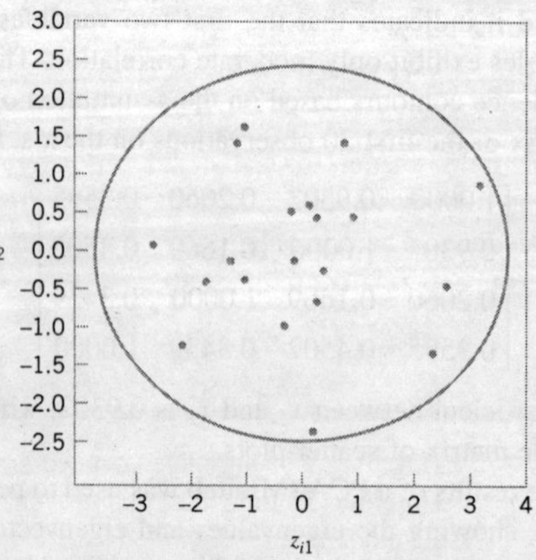

■ FIGURE 11.16 Scatter plot of the first 20 principal component scores z_{i1} and z_{i2} from Table 11.6, with 95% confidence ellipse.

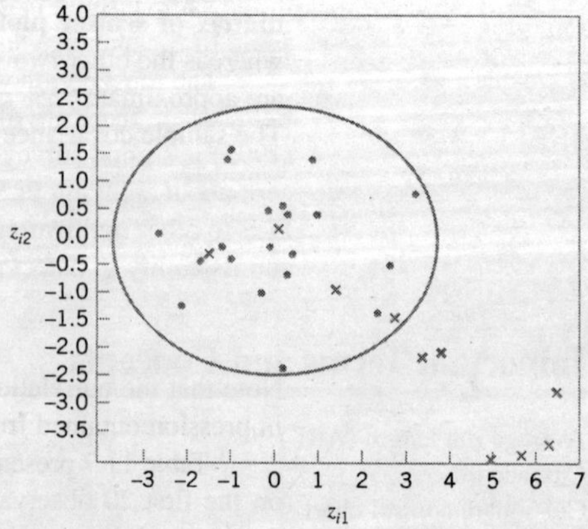

■ FIGURE 11.17 Principal components trajectory chart, showing the last 10 observations from Table 11.6.

in identifying the scores from the new points. Although the first few new scores are inside the ellipse, it is clear that beginning with observation 24 or 25 there has been a shift in the process. Control charts such as Fig. 11.17 based on principal component scores are often called principal component **trajectory plots.** Mastrangelo, Runger, and Montgomery (1996) also give an example of this procedure.

If more than two principal components need to be retained, then pairwise scatter plots of the principal component scores would be used analogously to Fig. 11.17. However, if more than $r = 3$ or 4 components are retained, interpretation and use of the charts becomes cumbersome. Furthermore, interpretation of the principal components can be difficult, because they are not the original set of process variables but instead linear combinations of them. Sometimes principal components have a relatively simple interpretation and that can assist the analyst in using the trajectory chart. For instance, in our example the constants in the first principal component are all about the same size and have the same sign, so the first principal component can be thought of as an analog of the average of all $p = 4$ original variables. Similarly, the second component is roughly equivalent to the difference between the averages of the first two and the last two process variables. It's not always that easy.

A potentially useful alternative to the trajectory plot is to collect the r retained principal component scores into a vector and apply the MEWMA control chart to them. Practical experience with this approach has been very promising, and the ARL of the MEWMA control chart to detect a shift will be much less using the set of retained principal components than it would have been if all p original process variables were used. Scranton et al. (1996) give more details of this technique.

Finally, note that control charts and trajectory plots based on PCA will be most effective in detecting shifts in the directions defined by the principal components. Shifts in other directions, particularly directions orthogonal to the retained principal component directions, may be very hard to detect. One possible solution to this would be to use a MEWMA control chart to monitor all the remaining principal components $z_{r+1}, z_{r+2}, \ldots, z_p$.

11.7.2 Partial Least Squares

The method of **partial least squares (PLS)** is somewhat related to PCS, except that, like the regression adjustment procedure, it classifies the variables into x's (or inputs) and y's (or outputs). The goal is to create a set of weighted averages of the x's and y's that can be used for prediction of the y's or linear combinations of the y's. The procedure maximizes covariance in the same fashion that the principal component directions maximize variance. Minitab has some PLS capability.

The most common applications of partial least squares today are in the **chemometrics** field, where there are often many variables, both process and response. Frank and Friedman (1993) is a good survey of this field, written for statisticians and engineers. A potential concern about applying PLS is that there has not been any extensive performance comparison of PLS to other multivariate procedures. There is only antidotal evidence about its performance and its ability to detect process upsets relative to other approaches.

Important Terms and Concepts

Average run length (ARL)
Cascade process
Chi-square control chart
Control ellipse
Covariance matrix
Hotelling T^2 control chart
Hotelling T^2 subgrouped data control chart
Hotelling T^2 individuals control chart
Latent structure methods
Matrix of scatter plots
Monitoring multivariate variability
Multivariate EWMA control chart

- Multivariate normal distribution
- Multivariate quality control process monitoring
- Partial least squares (PLS)
- Phase I control limits
- Phase II control limits
- Principal component scores
- Principal components
- Principal components analysis (PCA)
- Regression adjustment
- Residual control chart
- Sample covariance matrix
- Sample mean vector
- Trajectory plots

Exercises

11.1. A product has three quality characteristics. The nominal values of these quality characteristics and their sample covariance matrix have been determined from the analysis of 30 preliminary samples of size $n = 10$ as follows:

$$\bar{\bar{\mathbf{x}}} = \begin{bmatrix} 3.0 \\ 3.5 \\ 2.8 \end{bmatrix} \quad \mathbf{S} = \begin{bmatrix} 1.40 & 1.02 & 1.05 \\ 1.02 & 1.35 & 0.98 \\ 1.05 & 0.98 & 1.20 \end{bmatrix}$$

The sample means for each quality characteristic for 15 additional samples of size $n = 10$ are shown in Table 11E.1. Is the process in statistical control?

11.2. The data shown in Table 11E.2 come from a production process with two observable quality characteristics, x_1 and x_2. The data are sample means of each quality characteristic, based on samples of size $n = 25$.

■ **TABLE 11E.1**
Data for Exercise 11.1

Sample Number	$\bar{x}_1$	$\bar{x}_2$	$\bar{x}_3$
1	3.1	3.7	3.0
2	3.3	3.9	3.1
3	2.6	3.0	2.4
4	2.8	3.0	2.5
5	3.0	3.3	2.8
6	4.0	4.6	3.5
7	3.8	4.2	3.0
8	3.0	3.3	2.7
9	2.4	3.0	2.2
10	2.0	2.6	1.8
11	3.2	3.9	3.0
12	3.7	4.0	3.0
13	4.1	4.7	3.2
14	3.8	4.0	2.9
15	3.2	3.6	2.8

■ **TABLE 11E.2**
Data for Exercise 11.2

Sample Number	$\bar{x}_1$	$\bar{x}_2$
1	58	32
2	60	33
3	50	27
4	54	31
5	63	38
6	53	30
7	42	20
8	55	31
9	46	25
10	50	29
11	49	27
12	57	30
13	58	33
14	75	45
15	55	27

Assume that mean values of the quality characteristics and the covariance matrix were computed from 50 preliminary samples:

$$\bar{\bar{\mathbf{x}}} = \begin{bmatrix} 55 \\ 30 \end{bmatrix} \quad \mathbf{S} = \begin{bmatrix} 200 & 130 \\ 130 & 120 \end{bmatrix}$$

Construct a T^2 control chart using these data. Use the phase II limits.

11.3. Reconsider the situation in Exercise 11.1. Suppose that the sample mean vector and sample covariance matrix provided were the actual population parameters. What control limit would be appropriate for phase II of the control chart? Apply this limit to the data and discuss any differences in results that you find in comparison to the original choice of control limit.

11.4. Reconsider the situation in Exercise 11.2. Suppose that the sample mean vector and sample covariance matrix provided were the actual population parameters. What control limit would be appropriate for phase II for the control chart? Apply this limit to the data and discuss any differences in results that you find in comparison to the original choice of control limit.

11.5. Consider a T^2 control chart for monitoring $p = 10$ quality characteristics. Suppose that the subgroup size is $n = 3$ and there are 25 preliminary samples available to estimate the sample covariance matrix. Calculate both the phase I and the phase II control limits (use $\alpha = 0.01$).

11.6. Consider a T^2 control chart for monitoring $p = 10$ quality characteristics. Suppose that the subgroup size is $n = 3$ and there are 25 preliminary samples available to estimate the sample covariance matrix.

(a) Find the phase II control limits assuming that $\alpha = 0.005$.

(b) Compare the control limits from part (a) to the chi-square control limit. What is the magnitude of the difference in the two control limits?

(c) How many preliminary samples would have to be taken to ensure that the chi-square control limit is within 1% of the exact phase II control limit?

11.7. Rework Exercise 11.6, assuming that the subgroup size is $n = 5$.

11.8. Consider a T^2 control chart for monitoring $p = 6$ quality characteristics. Suppose that the subgroup size is $n = 3$ and there are 30 preliminary samples available to estimate the sample covariance matrix.

(a) Find the phase II control limits assuming that $\alpha = 0.005$.

(b) Compare the control limits from part (a) to the chi-square control limit. What is the magnitude of the difference in the two control limits?

(c) How many preliminary samples would have to be taken to ensure that the exact phase II control limit is within 1% of the chi-square control limit?

11.9. Rework Exercise 11.8, assuming that the subgroup size is $n = 5$.

11.10. Suppose that we have $p = 3$ quality characteristics, and in correlation form all three variables have variance unity and all pairwise correlation coefficients are 0.8. The in-control value of the process mean vector is $\boldsymbol{\mu}' = [0, 0, 0]$.

(a) Write out the covariance matrix $\boldsymbol{\Sigma}$.

(b) What is the chi-square control limit for the chart, assuming that $\alpha = 0.05$?

(c) Suppose that a sample of observations results in the standardized observation vector $\mathbf{y}' = [1, 2, 0]$. Calculate the value of the T^2 statistic. Is an out-of-control signal generated?

(d) Calculate the diagnostic quantities d_i, $i = 1, 2, 3$ from equation (11.22). Does this information assist in identifying which process variables have shifted?

(e) Suppose that a sample of observations results in the standardized observation vector $\mathbf{y}' = [2, 2, 1]$. Calculate the value of the T^2 statistic. Is an out-of-control signal generated?

(f) For the case in (e), calculate the diagnostic quantities d_i, $i = 1, 2, 3$ from equation (11.22). Does this information assist in identifying which process variables have shifted?

11.11. Suppose that we have $p = 4$ quality characteristics, and in correlation form all four variables have variance unity and all pairwise correlation coefficients are 0.7. The in-control value of the process mean vector is $\boldsymbol{\mu}' = [0, 0, 0, 0]$.

(a) Write out the covariance matrix $\boldsymbol{\Sigma}$.

(b) What is the chi-square control limit for the chart, assuming that $\alpha = 0.01$?

(c) Suppose that a sample of observations results in the standardized observation vector $\mathbf{y}' = [3.5, 3.5, 3.5, 3.5]$. Calculate the value of the T^2 statistic. Is an out-of-control signal generated?

(d) Calculate the diagnostic quantities d_i, $i = 1, 2, 3, 4$ from equation (11.22). Does this information assist in identifying which process variables have shifted?

(e) Suppose that a sample of observations results in the standardized observation vector $\mathbf{y}' = [2.5, 2, -1, 0]$. Calculate the value of the T^2 statistic. Is an out-of-control signal generated?

(f) For the case in (e), calculate the diagnostic quantities d_i, $i = 1, 2, 3, 4$ from equation (11.22). Does this information assist in identifying which process variables have shifted?

11.12. Consider the first three process variables in Table 11.5. Calculate an estimate of the sample covariance matrix using both estimators $\mathbf{S}_1$ and $\mathbf{S}_2$ discussed in Section 11.3.2.

11.13. Consider all 30 observations on the first two process variables in Table 11.6. Calculate an estimate of the sample covariance matrix using both estimators $\mathbf{S}_1$ and $\mathbf{S}_2$ discussed in Section 11.3.2. Are the estimates very different? Discuss your findings.

11.14. Suppose that there are $p = 4$ quality characteristics, and in correlation form all four variables have variance unity and that all pairwise correlation coefficients are 0.9. The in-control value of the process mean vector is $\boldsymbol{\mu}' = [0, 0, 0, 0]$, and we want to design an MEWMA control chart to provide good protection against a shift to a new mean vector of $\mathbf{y}' = [1, 1, 1, 1]$. Suppose that an in-control ARL_0 of 500 is desired. What value of λ and what upper control limit would you recommend? Approximately, what is the ARL_1 for detecting the shift in the mean vector?

11.15. Suppose that there are $p = 4$ quality characteristics, and in correlation form all four variables have variance unity and all pairwise correlation coefficients are 0.75. The in-control value of the process mean vector is $\mu' = [0, 0, 0, 0]$, and we want to design an MEWMA control chart to provide good protection against a shift to a new mean vector of $\mathbf{y}' = [1, 1, 1, 1]$. If an in-control ARL_0 of 200 is satisfactory, what value of λ and what upper control limit should be used? Approximately, what is the ARL_1 for detecting the shift in the mean vector?

11.16. Consider the cascade process data in Table 11.5.

(a) Set up an individuals control chart on y_2.

(b) Fit a regression model to y_2, and set up an individuals control chart on the residuals. Comment on the differences between this chart and the one in part (a).

(c) Calculate the sample autocorrelation functions on y_2 and on the residuals from the regression model in part (b). Discuss your findings.

11.17. Consider the cascade process data in Table 11.5. In fitting regression models to both y_1 and y_2 you will find that not all of the process variables are required to obtain a satisfactory regression model for the output variables. Remove the nonsignificant variables from these equations and obtain subset regression models for both y_1 and y_2. Then construct individuals control charts for both sets of residuals. Compare them to the residual control charts in the text (Fig. 11.11) and from Exercise 11.16. Are there any substantial differences between the charts from the two different approaches to fitting the regression models?

11.18. Continuation of Exercise 11.17. Using the residuals from the regression models in Exercise 11.17, set up EWMA control charts. Compare these EWMA control charts to the Shewhart charts for individuals constructed previously. What are the potential advantages of the EWMA control chart in this situation?

11.19. Consider the $p = 9$ process variables in Table 11.5.

(a) Perform a PCA on the first 30 observations. Be sure to work with the standardized variables.

(b) How much variability is explained if only the first $r = 3$ principal components are retained?

(c) Construct an appropriate set of pairwise plots of the first $r = 3$ principal component scores.

(d) Now consider the last 10 observations. Obtain the principal component scores and plot them on the chart in part (c). Does the process seem to be in control?

11.20. Consider the $p = 4$ process variables in Table 11.6. After applying the PCA procedure to the first 20 observations data (see Table 11.7), suppose that the first three principal components are retained.

(a) Obtain the principal component scores. (Hint: Remember that you must work in standardized variables.)

(b) Construct an appropriate set of pairwise plots of the principal component scores.

(c) Calculate the principal component scores for the last 10 observations. Plot the scores on the charts from part (b) and interpret the results.

12 Process Adjustment and Process Monitoring

Chapter Outline

Chapter Overview and Learning Objectives

Throughout this book we have stressed the importance of process control and variability reduction as essential ingredients of modern manufacturing strategy. There are two statistically based approaches for addressing this problem. The first of these is statistical process monitoring by control charts, or statistical process control (SPC). The focus of SPC is on identifying assignable causes so that they can be removed, thereby leading to permanent process improvement or reduction in variability. The second approach is based on adjusting the process using information about its current level or deviation from a desired target. This approach is often called feedback adjustment, and it is a form of **engineering process control** or **EPC**. Feedback adjustment regulates the process to account for sources of variability that cannot be removed by the SPC approach.

This chapter introduces simple methods of feedback adjustment and shows how these techniques can be easily implemented in processes where there is a manipulatable variable that affects the process output. We also show how simple SPC schemes can be combined or integrated with EPC.

After careful study of this chapter you should be able to do the following:

1. Explain the origins of process monitoring and process adjustment
2. Explain the different statistical frameworks of SPC and EPC
3. Explain how an integral controller works
4. Understand how EPC transfers variability from the process output into a manipulatable variable

5. Know how to set up and use a manual adjustment chart
6. Understand the basis of the bounded adjustment chart
7. Understand the basis of proportional integral (PI) and proportional integral derivative (PID) controllers
8. Know how to combine SPC and EPC by applying a control chart to the output quality characteristic

12.1 Process Monitoring and Process Regulation

Reduction of variability is an important part of improving process performance in all industries. Statistical process control is an effective tool for reduction of variability through the ability of the control chart to detect assignable causes. When the assignable causes are removed, process variability is reduced and process performance is improved.

SPC has had a long history of successful use in **discrete parts manufacturing.** In continuous processes, such as those found in the chemical and process industries, another approach is often used to reduce variability. This approach is based on **process compensation and regulation,** in which some **manipulatable process variable** is **adjusted** with the objective of keeping the process output on target (or equivalently, minimizing the variability of the output around this target). These process compensation or regulation schemes are widely known as **engineering process control (EPC),** stochastic control, or feedback or feedforward control depending on the nature of the adjustments.

SPC is always applied in a situation where we assume that it is possible to bring the process into a state of statistical control. By "statistical control," we mean that we observe only stable random variation around the process target. Furthermore, SPC also assumes that once the process is in this in-control state, it will tend to stay there for a relatively long period of time without continual ongoing adjustment. Now certainly if we eliminate assignable causes such as differences due to operators and variations in raw materials, it is often possible to obtain this in-control state. However, in some industrial settings, despite our best effort, the process may still have a tendency to **drift** or **wander** away from the target. This may occur because of phenomena such as continuous variation in input materials or effects of environmental or process variables, or it may be due entirely to unknown forces that impact the process. Process regulation through EPC assumes that there is another variable that can be adjusted to compensate for the drift in process output, and that a series of regular adjustments to this manipulatable variable will keep the process output close to the desired target.

There is considerable interest in combining or **integrating SPC and EPC** in an effort to provide an improved procedure—that is, an enhancement to EPC that would enable assignable-cause-type disturbances to be detected. For additional background and discussion, see Box and Kramer (1992); MacGregor (1987); Vander Weil, Tucker, Faltin, and Doganaksoy (1992); MacGregor and Harris (1990); Montgomery, Keats, Runger, and Messina (1994); Box, Jenkins, and Reinsel (1994); Box and Luceño (1997); and Del Castillo (2002).

It is natural to question the need for integrating EPC and SPC. Historically, these techniques have developed in somewhat different environments. SPC is often part of an organization's strategic thrust to improve quality, and it is usually a top-down, management driven, high-visibility activity, with emphasis on people, methods, and procedures. EPC on the other hand, is more tactical in nature with its origins in the process-engineering organization, and its primary focus is on the process. The statistical framework of SPC is similar to that of **hypothesis testing,** whereas the statistical framework of EPC is **parameter estimation**—that is, estimating how much disturbance there is in the system forcing the process off target and then making an adjustment to cancel its effect. What these two procedures share is a common objective: **reduction of variability.** EPC assumes that there is a specific dynamic model that links the process input and output. If that model is correct, then the EPC process adjustment rules will minimize variation around the output target. However, when certain types of external disturbances or assignable causes occur that are outside the framework of this dynamic model, then the compensation rules will not completely account for this upset. As a result, variability will be increased. By applying SPC in a specific way, these assignable causes can be detected and the combined EPC/SPC procedure will be more effective than EPC alone.

12.2 Process Control by Feedback Adjustment

12.2.1 A Simple Adjustment Scheme: Integral Control

In this section we consider a simple situation involving a process in which feedback adjustment is appropriate and highly effective. The process output characteristic of interest at time period t is y_t, and we wish to keep y_t as close as possible to a target T. This process has a manipulatable variable x, and a change in x will produce all of its effect on y within one period; that is,

$$y_{t+1} - T = gx_t \tag{12.1}$$

where g is a constant usually called the **process gain.** The gain is like a regression coefficient, in that it relates the magnitude of a change in x_t to a change in y_t. Now, if no adjustment is made, the process drifts away from the target according to

$$y_{t+1} - T = N_{t+1} \tag{12.2}$$

where N_{t+1} is a **disturbance.** The disturbance in equation (12.2) is usually represented by an appropriate time-series model, often an autoregressive integrated moving average (ARIMA) model of the type discussed in Chapter 10, Section 10.4. Such a model is required because the uncontrolled output is usually autocorrelated (see the material in Section 10.4 about SPC with autocorrelated data).

Suppose that the disturbance can be predicted adequately using an EWMA:

$$\begin{aligned}\hat{N}_{t+1} &= \hat{N}_t + \lambda\left(N_t - \hat{N}_t\right)\\ &= \hat{N}_t + \lambda e_t\end{aligned} \tag{12.3}$$

where $e_t = N_t - \hat{N}_t$ is the prediction error at time period t and $0 < \lambda \leq 1$ is the weighting factor for the EWMA. This assumption is equivalent to assuming that the uncontrolled process is drifting according to the integrated moving average model in equation (10.15) with parameter $\theta = 1 - \lambda$. At time t, the adjusted process is

$$y_{t+1} - T = N_{t+1} + gx_t$$

This equation says that at time $t + 1$ the output deviation from target will depend on the disturbance in period $t + 1$ plus the level x_t to which we set the manipulatable variable in period t, or the **setpoint** in period t. Obviously, we should set x_t so as to exactly cancel out the disturbance. However, we can't do this, because N_{t+1} is unknown in period t. We can, however, forecast N_{t+1} by $\hat{N}_{t+1}$ using equation (12.3). Then we obtain

$$y_{t+1} - T = e_{t+1} + \hat{N}_{t+1} + gx_t \tag{12.4}$$

since $e_{t+1} = N_{t+1} - \hat{N}_{t+1}$.

From equation (12.4), it is clear that if we set $gx_t = -\hat{N}_{t+1}$ or the setpoint $x_t = -(1/g)\hat{N}_{t+1}$, then the adjustment should cancel out the disturbance, and in period $t + 1$ the output deviation from target should be $y_{t+1} - T = e_{t+1}$, where e_{t+1} is the prediction error in period t; that is, $e_{t+1} = N_{t+1} - \hat{N}_{t+1}$. The actual adjustment to the manipulatable variable made at time t is

$$x_t - x_{t-1} = -\frac{1}{g}\left(\hat{N}_{t+1} - \hat{N}_t\right) \tag{12.5}$$

Now the difference in the two EWMA predictions $\hat{N}_{t+1} - \hat{N}_t$ can be rewritten as

$$\begin{aligned}\hat{N}_{t+1} - \hat{N}_t &= \lambda N_t + (1-\lambda)\hat{N}_t - \hat{N}_t \\ &= \lambda N_t - \lambda \hat{N}_t \\ &= \lambda\left(N_t - \hat{N}_t\right) \\ &= \lambda e_t\end{aligned}$$

and since the actual error at time t, e_t, is simply the difference between the output and the target, we can write

$$\hat{N}_{t+1} - \hat{N}_t = \lambda(y_t - T)$$

Therefore, the adjustment to be made to the manipulatable variable at time period t [equation (12.5)] becomes

$$x_t - x_{t-1} = -\frac{\lambda}{g}(y_t - T) = -\frac{\lambda}{g}e_t \tag{12.6}$$

The actual **setpoint** for the manipulatable variable at the end of period t is simply the sum of all the adjustments through time t, or

$$x_t = \sum_{j=1}^{t}\left(x_j - x_{j-1}\right) = -\frac{\lambda}{g}\sum_{j=1}^{t} e_j \tag{12.7}$$

This type of process adjustment scheme is called **integral control.** It is a pure feedback control scheme that sets the level of the manipulatable variable equal to a weighted sum of all current and previous process deviations from target. It can be shown that if the deterministic part of the process model [equation (12.1)] is correct, and if the disturbance N_t is predicted perfectly apart from random error by an EWMA, then this is an optimal control rule in the sense that it minimizes the mean-square error of the process output deviations from the target T. For an excellent discussion of this procedure, see Box (1991–1992) and Box and Luceño (1997).

EXAMPLE 12.1 An Example of Integral Control

Figure 12.1 shows 100 observations on the number average molecular weight of a polymer, taken every four hours. It is desired to maintain the molecular weight as close as possible to the target value $T = 2000$. Note that, despite our best efforts to bring the process into a state of statistical control, the molecular weight tends to wander away from the target. Individuals and moving range control charts are shown in Fig. 12.2, indicating the lack of statistical stability in the process. Note that the engineers have used the target value $T = 2000$ as the center line for the individuals chart. The actual sample average and standard deviation of molecular weight for these 100 observations is $\bar{x} = 2008$ and $s = 19.4$.

In this process, the drifting behavior of the molecular weight is likely caused by unknown and uncontrollable disturbances in the incoming material feedstock and other inertial forces, but it can be compensated for by making adjustments to the setpoint of the catalyst feed rate x. A change in the setpoint of the feed rate will have all of its effect on molecular weight within one period, so an integral control procedure such as the one discussed previously will be appropriate.

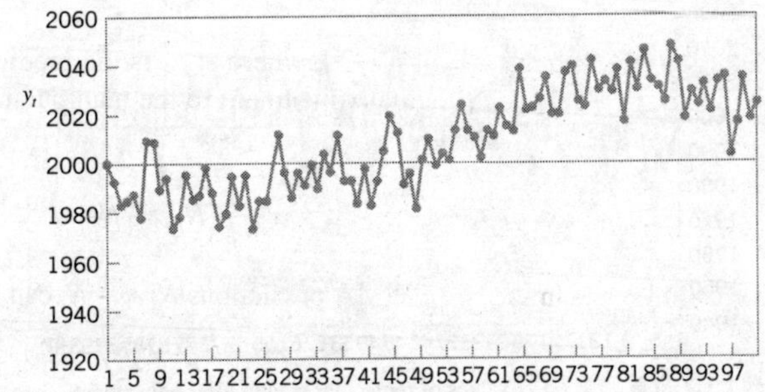

Figure 12.1 Molecular weight of a polymer, target value T = 2000 (uncontrolled process).

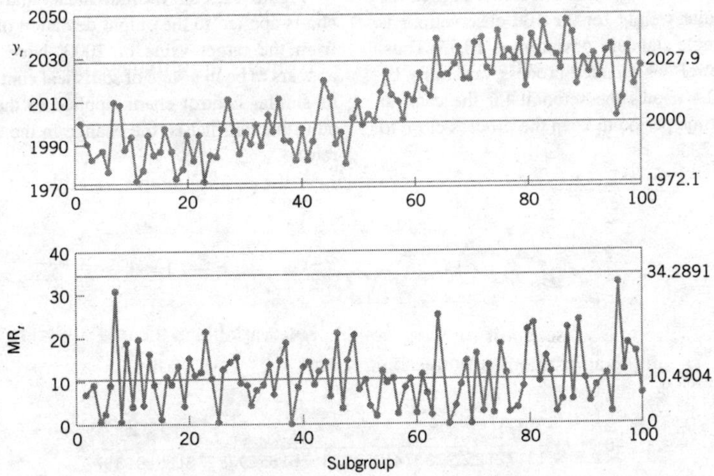

Figure 12.2 Control charts for individuals and moving range applied to the polymer molecular weight data.

Suppose that the gain in the system is 1.2:1; that is, an increase in the feed rate of 1 unit increases the molecular weight by 1.2 units. Now for our example, the adjusted process would be

$$y_t - 2000 = N_{t+1} + 1.2x_t$$

We will forecast the disturbances with an EWMA having $\lambda = 0.2$. This is an arbitrary choice for λ. It is possible to use estimation techniques to obtain a precise value for λ, but as we will see, often a value for λ between 0.2 and 0.4 works very well. Now the one-period-ahead forecast for the disturbance N_{t+1} is

$$\begin{aligned}\hat{N}_{t+1} &= \hat{N}_t + \lambda e_t \\ &= \hat{N}_t + 0.2\left(N_t - \hat{N}_t\right) \\ &= 0.2N_t + 0.8\hat{N}_t \\ &= 0.2\left(y_t - 2000\right) + 0.8\hat{N}_t\end{aligned}$$

Consequently, the setpoint for catalyst feed rate at the end of period t would be

$$gx_t = -\hat{N}_{t+1}$$

or

$$1.2x_t = -\left[0.2\left(y_t - 2000\right) + 0.8\hat{N}_t\right]$$

The adjustment made to the catalyst feed rate is

$$\begin{aligned}x_t - x_{t-1} &= -\frac{\lambda}{g}\left(y_t - 2000\right) \\ &= -\frac{0.2}{1.2}\left(y_t - 2000\right) \\ &= -\frac{1}{6}\left(y_t - 2000\right)\end{aligned}$$

Figure 12.3 plots the values of molecular weight after the adjustments are made to the catalyst feed rate. Note that the

(continued)

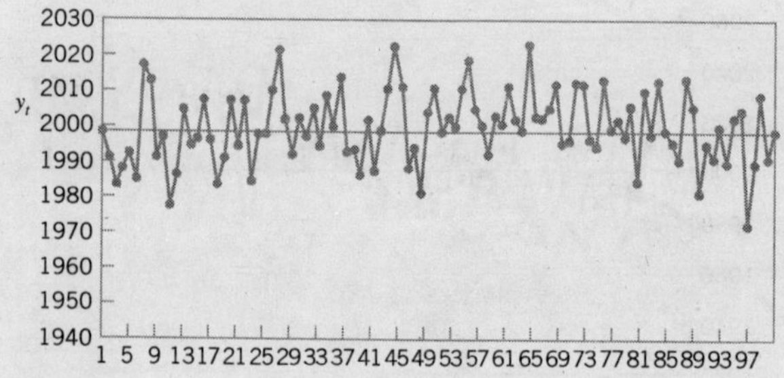

■ **Figure 12.3** Values of molecular weight after adjustment.

process is much closer to the target value of 2000. In fact, the sample average molecular weight for the 100 observations is now 2001, and the sample standard deviation is 10.35. Thus, the use of integral control has reduced process variability by nearly 50%. Figure 12.4 shows the setpoint for the catalyst feed rate used in each time period to keep the process close to the target value of $T = 2000$.

Figure 12.5 shows individuals and moving range control charts applied to the output deviation of the molecular weight from the target value of 2000. Note that now the process appears to be in a state of statistical control. Figure 12.6 is a set of similar control charts applied to the sequence of process adjustments (that is, the change in the setpoint value for feed rate).

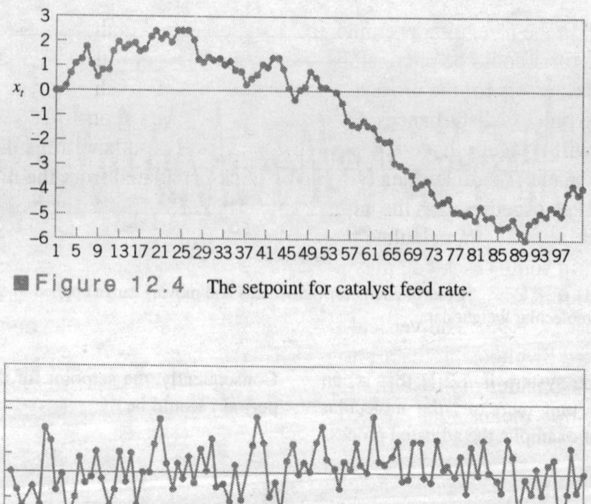

■ **Figure 12.4** The setpoint for catalyst feed rate.

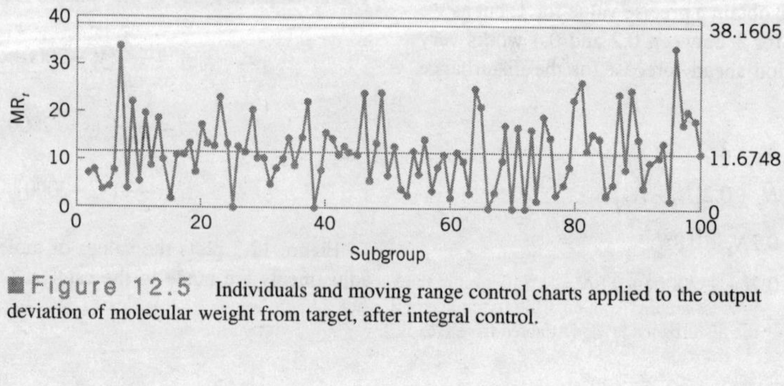

■ **Figure 12.5** Individuals and moving range control charts applied to the output deviation of molecular weight from target, after integral control.

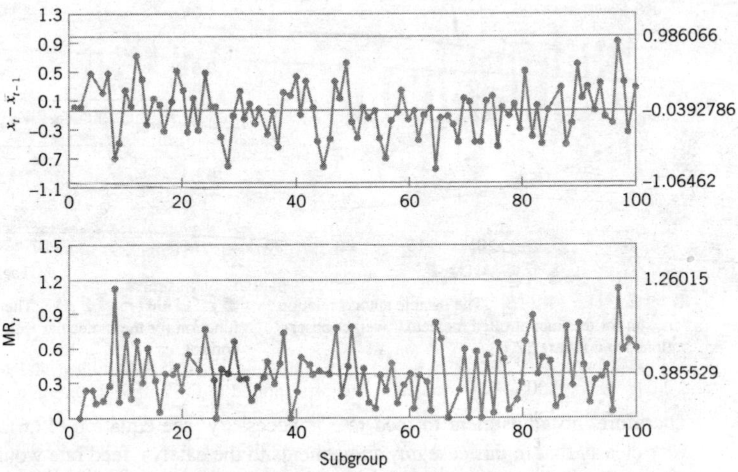

■ **Figure 12.6** Individuals and moving range control charts for the sequence of adjustments to the catalyst feed rate.

In the foregoing example, the value of λ used in the EWMA was $\lambda = 0.2$. An "optimal" value for λ could be obtained by finding the value of λ that minimizes the sum of the squared forecast errors for the process disturbance. To perform this calculation, you will need a record of the process disturbances. Usually, you will have to construct this from past history. That is, you will typically have a history of the actual output and a history of whatever adjustments were made. The disturbance would be back-calculated from the historical deviation from target taken together with the adjustments. This will usually give you a disturbance series of sufficient accuracy to calculate the correct value for λ.

In some cases you may not be able to do this easily, and it may be necessary to choose λ arbitrarily. Figure 12.7 shows the effect of choosing λ arbitrarily when the true optimum value of λ is λ_0. The vertical scale $(\sigma_\lambda^2/\sigma_{\lambda_0}^2)$ shows how much the variance of the output is inflated by choosing the arbitrary λ instead of λ_0.

Consider the case in Fig. 12.7 where $\lambda_0 = 0$. Now, since λ in the EWMA is equal to zero, this means that the process is in statistical control and it will not drift off target.

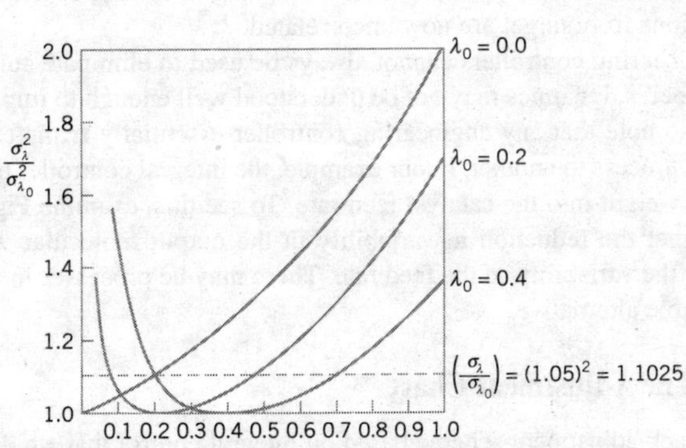

■ **FIGURE 12.7** Inflation in the variance of the adjusted process arising from an arbitrary choice of λ when the true value of λ in the disturbance is λ_0. [Adapted from Box (1991–1992), with permission.]

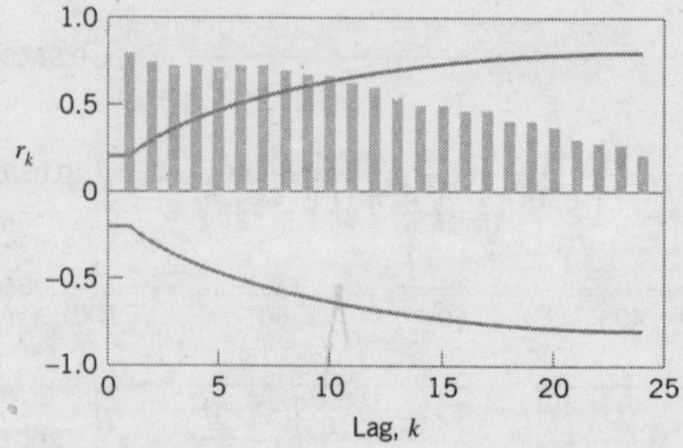

■ FIGURE 12.8 The sample autocorrelation function for the uncontrolled molecular weight observations from Figure 12.1.

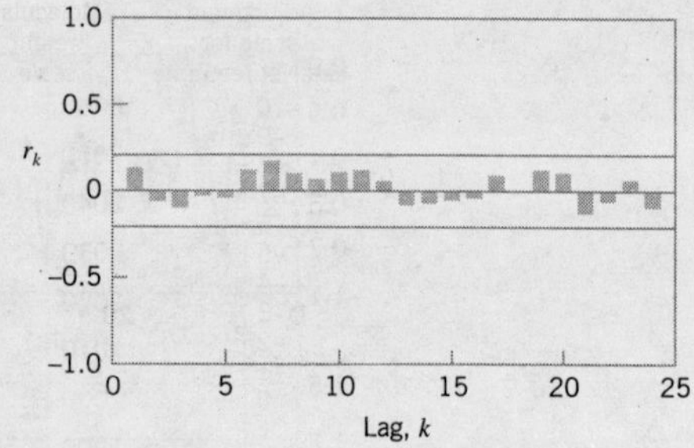

■ FIGURE 12.9 The sample autocorrelation function for the molecular weight variable after integral control.

Therefore, no adjustment to feed rate is necessary; see equation (12.6). Figure 12.7 shows very clearly that in this case *any* adjustments to the catalyst feed rate would increase the variance of the output. This is what Deming means by "tampering with the process." The worst case would occur with $\lambda = 1$, where the output variance would be doubled. Of course, $\lambda = 1$ implies that we are making an adjustment that (apart from the gain g) is exactly equal to the current deviation from target, something *no* rational control engineer would contemplate. Note, however, that a smaller value of λ ($\lambda \le 0.2$, say) would not inflate the variance very much. Alternatively, if the true value of λ_0 driving the disturbance is *not* zero, meaning that the process drifts off target yet *no* adjustment is made, the output process variance will increase a lot. From the figure, we see that if you use a value of λ in the 0.2–0.4 range, that almost no matter what the *true* value of λ_0 is that drives the disturbances, the increase in output variance will be at most about 5% over what the true minimum variance would be if λ_0 were known exactly. Therefore, an educated guess about the value of λ in the 0.2–0.4 range will often work very well in practice.

We noted in Section 10.4 that one possible way to deal with autocorrelated data was to use an engineering controller to remove the autocorrelation. We can demonstrate that in the previous example.

Figure 12.8 is the sample autocorrelation function of the uncontrolled molecular weight measurements from Fig. 12.1. Obviously, the original unadjusted process observations exhibit strong autocorrelation. Figure 12.9 is the sample autocorrelation function of the output molecular weight deviations from target after the integral control adjustments. Note that the output deviations from target are now uncorrelated.

Engineering controllers cannot always be used to eliminate autocorrelation. For example, the process dynamics may not be understood well enough to implement an effective controller. Also note that any engineering controller essentially **transfers variability** from one part of the process to another. In our example, the integral controller transfers variability from molecular weight into the catalyst feed rate. To see this, examine Figs. 12.1, 12.3, and 12.4, and note that the reduction in variability in the output molecular weight was achieved by increasing the variability of the feed rate. There may be processes in which this is not always an acceptable alternative.

12.2.2 The Adjustment Chart

The feedback adjustment scheme based on integral control that we described in the previous section can be implemented so that the adjustments are made automatically. Usually this involves some combination of sensors or measuring devices, a logic device or computer, and actuators to physically make the adjustments to the manipulatable variable x. When EPC or

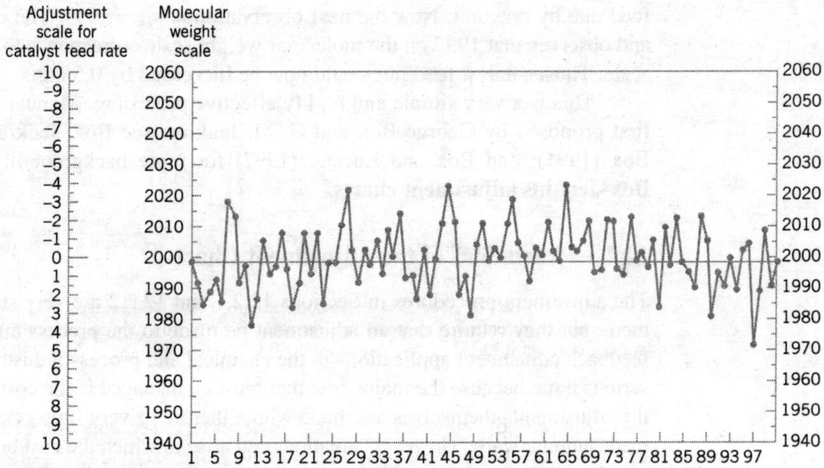

■ FIGURE 12.10 The adjustment chart for molecular weight.

feedback adjustment is implemented in this manner, it is often called **automatic process control (APC).**

In many processes, feedback adjustments can be made manually. Operating personnel routinely observe the current output deviation from target, compute the amount of adjustment to apply using equation (12.6), and then bring x_t to its new setpoint. When adjustments are made manually by operating personnel, a variation of Fig. 12.3 called the **manual adjustment chart** is very useful.

Figure 12.10 is the manual adjustment chart corresponding to Fig. 12.3. Note that there is now a second scale, called the adjustment scale, on the vertical axis. Note also that the divisions on the adjustment scale are arranged so that one unit of adjustment exactly equals six units on the molecular weight scale. Furthermore, the units on the adjustment scale that correspond to molecular weight values above the target of 2000 are negative, whereas the units on the adjustment scale that correspond to molecular weight values below the target of 2000 are positive. The reason for this is that the specific adjustment equation that is used for the molecular weight variable is

$$x_t - x_{t-1} = -\frac{1}{6}(y_t - 2000)$$

or

$$\text{adjustment to catalyst feed rate} = -\frac{1}{6}(\text{deviation of molecular weight from 2000})$$

That is, a **six-unit** change in molecular weight from its target of 2000 corresponds to a **one-unit** change in the catalyst feed rate. Furthermore, if the molecular weight is **above** the target, the catalyst feed rate must be **reduced** to drive molecular weight toward the target value, whereas if the molecular weight is **below** the target, the catalyst feed rate must be **increased** to drive molecular weight toward the target.

The adjustment chart is extremely easy for operating personnel to use. For example, consider Fig. 12.10 and, specifically, observation y_{13} as molecular weight. As soon as y_{13} = 2006 is observed and plotted on the chart, the operator simply reads off the corresponding value of −1 on the adjustment scale. This is the amount by which the operator should change the current setting of the catalyst feed rate. That is, the operator should **reduce** the catalyst feed rate by one unit. Now the next observation is $y_{14} = 1997$. The operator plots this point and observes that 1997 on the molecular weight scale corresponds to +0.5 on the adjustment scale. Thus, catalyst feed rate could now be **increased** by 0.5 units.

This is a very simple and highly effective procedure. Manual adjustment charts were first proposed by George Box and G. M. Jenkins [see Box, Jenkins, and Reinsel (1994); Box (1991); and Box and Luceño (1997) for more background]. They are often called **Box–Jenkins adjustment charts.**

12.2.3 Variations of the Adjustment Chart

The adjustment procedures in Sections 12.2.1 and 12.2.2 are very straightforward to implement, but they require that an adjustment be made to the process after each observation. In feedback adjustment applications in the chemical and process industries, this is not usually a serious issue because the major cost that must be managed is the cost of being off target, and the adjustments themselves are made with either no or very little cost. Indeed, they are often made automatically. However, situations can arise in which the cost or convenience of making an adjustment is a concern. For example, in discrete parts manufacturing it may be necessary to actually stop the process to make an adjustment. Consequently, it may be of interest to make some modification to the feedback adjustment procedure so that less frequent adjustments will be made.

There are several ways to do this. One of the simplest is the **bounded adjustment chart,** a variation of the procedure in Section 12.2.2 in which an adjustment will be made only in periods for which the EWMA forecast is outside one of the bounds given by $\pm L$. The boundary value L is usually determined from engineering judgment, taking the costs of being off target and the cost of making the adjustment into account. Box and Luceño (1997) discuss this situation in detail and, in particular, how costs can be used specifically for determining L.

We will use the data in Table 12.1 to illustrate the bounded adjustment chart. Column 1 of this table presents the unadjusted values of an important output characteristic from a chemical process. The values are reported as deviations from the actual target, so the target for this variable—say, y_t—is zero. Figure 12.11 plots these output data, along with an EWMA prediction made using $\lambda = 0.2$. Note that the variable does not stay very close to the desired target. The average of these 50 observations is 17.2 and the sum of the squared deviations from target is 21,468. The standard deviation of these observations is approximately 11.6.

There is a manipulatable variable in this process, and the relationship between the output and this variable is given by

$$y_t - T = 0.8x_t$$

That is, the process gain $g = 0.8$. The EWMA in Fig. 12.11 uses $\lambda = 0.2$. This value was chosen arbitrarily, but remember from our discussion in Section 12.2.1 that the procedure is relatively insensitive to this parameter.

Suppose that we decide to set $L = 10$. This means that we will only make an adjustment to the process when the EWMA exceeds $L = 10$ or $-L = -10$. Economics and the ease of making adjustments are typically factors in selecting L, but here we did it a slightly different way. Note that the standard deviation of the unadjusted process is approximately 11.6, so the standard deviation of the EWMA in Fig. 12.11 is approximately

$$\hat{\sigma}_{\text{EWMA}} = \sqrt{\frac{\lambda}{2-\lambda}}\,\hat{\sigma}_{\text{unadjusted process}} = \sqrt{\frac{0.2}{2-0.2}}11.6 = 3.87$$

Therefore, using $L = 10$ is roughly equivalent to using control limits on the EWMA that are about $2.6\sigma_{\text{EWMA}}$ in width. (Recall from Chapter 9 that we often use control limits on an EWMA that are slightly less than three-sigma.)

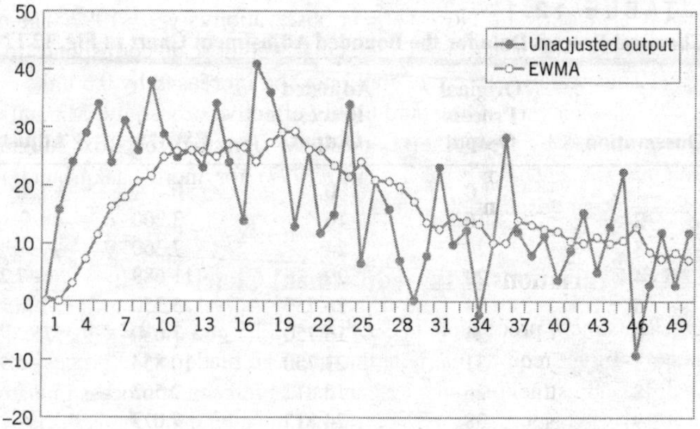

FIGURE 12.11 The unadjusted process data from Table 12.1 and an EWMA with $\lambda = 0.2$.

The computations for the EWMA are given in Table 12.1. Note that the EWMA is started off at zero, and the first period in which it exceeds $L = 10$ is period 4. The output deviation from target in period 4 is +29, so the adjustment would be calculated as usual in integral control as

$$x_t - x_{t-1} = -\frac{\lambda}{g}(y_t - T)$$

or

$$x_4 - x_3 = -\frac{0.2}{0.8}(y_4 - 0) = -\frac{1}{4}(29) = -7.250$$

That is, we would change the manipulatable variable from its previous setting in period 3 by −7.250 units. The full effect of this adjustment then would be felt in the next period, 5. The EWMA would be reset to zero at the end of period 4 and the forecasting procedure started afresh. The next adjustment occurs in period 7, where an additional −5.938 units of adjustment are made. The last column records the cumulative effect of all adjustments.

Note that only five adjustments are made over the 50 observations. Figure 12.12 is a plot of the original unadjusted output variable, the adjusted output, the EWMA forecasts, and the actual process adjustments. The variability in the adjusted output around the target has been reduced considerably; the sum of squared deviations from target is 9780 and the average deviation from target is 1.76. This is a reduction of over 50% in the output deviation from the target, achieved with only five adjustments to the process.

Bounded adjustment charts are often very good substitutes for making an adjustment every period. They usually result in slightly degraded performance when compared to the "always adjust" scheme, but usually the degradation is small.

Another variation of the adjustment chart encountered in practice is the **rounded adjustment chart.** This procedure is sometimes used to assist operating personnel in making simple adjustments. The adjustment scale is "rounded" to perhaps four or five zones on either side of the target, with each zone corresponding to adjustments that are easy to make (such as change the manipulatable variable by 1 unit, 2 units, and so forth). Often the central zone corresponds to making no adjustment. In this case, adjustments would not necessarily be made every period. See Box and Luceño (1997) for more discussion of these charts.

■ **TABLE 12.1**
Chemical Process Data for the Bounded Adjustment Chart in Fig. 12.12

Observation	Original Process Output	Adjusted Process Output	EWMA	Adjustment	Cumulative Adjustment or Setpoint
1	0	0	0		0
2	16	16	3.200		0
3	24	24	7.360		0
4	29	29	11.688	−7.250	−7.250
5	34	26.750	5.350		−7.250
6	24	16.750	7.630		−7.250
7	31	23.750	10.854	−5.938	−13.188
8	26	12.812	2.562		−13.188
9	38	24.812	7.013		−13.188
10	29	15.812	8.773		−13.188
11	25	11.812	9.381		−13.188
12	26	12.812	10.067	−3.203	−16.391
13	23	6.609	1.322		−16.391
14	34	17.609	4.579		−16.391
15	24	7.609	5.185		−16.391
16	14	−2.391	3.670		−16.391
17	41	24.609	7.858		−16.391
18	36	19.609	10.208	−4.904	−21.293
19	29	7.707	1.541		−21.293
20	13	−8.293	−0.425		−21.293
21	26	4.707	0.601		−21.293
22	12	−9.293	−1.378		−21.293
23	15	−6.293	−2.361		−21.293
24	34	12.707	0.653		−21.293
25	7	−14.293	−2.336		−21.293
26	20	−1.293	−2.128		−21.293
27	16	−5.293	−2.761		−21.293
28	7	−14.293	−5.067		−21.293
29	0	−21.293	−8.312		−21.293
30	8	−13.293	−9.308		−21.293
31	23	1.707	−7.105		−21.293
32	10	−11.293	−7.943		−21.293
33	12	−9.293	−8.213		−21.293
34	−2	−23.293	−11.229	5.823	−15.470
35	10	−5.470	−1.094		−15.470
36	28	12.530	1.631		−15.470
37	12	−3.470	0.611		−15.470
38	8	−7.470	−1.005		−15.470
39	11	−4.470	−1.698		−15.470
40	4	−11.470	−3.653		−15.470
41	9	−6.470	−4.216		− 15.470
42	15	−0.470	−3.467		−15.470
43	5	−10.470	−4.867		−15.470
44	13	−2.470	−4.388		−15.470
45	22	6.530	−2.204		−15.470
46	−9	−24.470	−6.657		−15.470
47	3	−12.470	−7.820		−15.470
48	12	−3.470	−6.950		−15.470
49	3	−12.470	−8.054		−15.470
50	12	−3.470	−7.137		−15.470

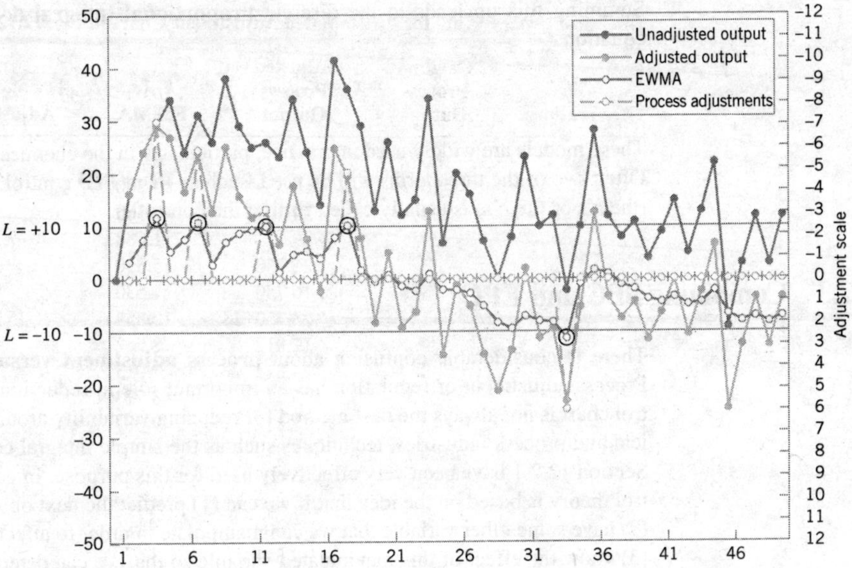

■ FIGURE 12.12 Bounded adjustment chart showing the original unadjusted output, the adjusted output, the EWMA, and the actual process adjustments. The circled EWMAs indicate points where adjustments are made.

12.2.4 Other Types of Feedback Controllers

We have considered a feedback controller for which the process adjustment rule is

$$g(x_t - x_{t-1}) = -\lambda e_t \tag{12.8}$$

where e_t is the output deviation from target and λ is the EWMA parameter. By summing this equation we arrived at

$$x_t = -\frac{\lambda}{g}\sum_{i=1}^{t} e_i \tag{12.9}$$

where x_t is the level or setpoint of the manipulatable variable at time t. This is, of course, an integral control adjustment rule.

Now suppose that to make reasonable adjustments to the process we feel it is necessary to consider the last *two* errors, e_t and e_{t-1}. Suppose we write the adjustment equation in terms of two constants c_1 and c_2,

$$g(x_t - x_{t-1}) = c_1 e_t + c_2 e_{t-1} \tag{12.10}$$

If this expression is summed, the setpoint becomes

$$x_t = k_P e_t + k_I \sum_{i=1}^{t} e_i \tag{12.11}$$

where $k_P = -(c_2/g)$ and $k_I = (c_1 + c_2)/g$. Note that the setpoint control equation contains a term calling for "proportional" control actions as well as the familiar integral action term. The two constants k_P and k_I are the proportional and integral action parameters, respectively. This is a discrete **proportional integral (PI) control** equation.

Now suppose that the adjustment depends on the last *three* errors:

$$g(x_t - x_{t-1}) = c_1 e_t + c_2 e_{t-1} + c_3 e_{t-2} \tag{12.12}$$

Summing this up leads to the discrete **proportional integral derivative (PID) control** equation

$$x_t = k_P e_t + k_I \sum_{i=1}^{t} e_i + k_D (e_t - e_{t-1}) \tag{12.13}$$

These models are widely used in practice, particularly in the chemical and process industries. Often two of the three terms will be used, such as **PI** or **PID** control. Choosing the constants (the k's or the c's) is usually called **tuning** the controller.

12.3 Combining SPC and EPC

There is considerable confusion about **process adjustment versus process monitoring.** Process adjustment or regulation has an important role in reduction of variability; the control chart is not always the best method for reducing variability around a target. In the chemical and process industries, techniques such as the simple integral control rule illustrated in Section 12.2.1 have been very effectively used for this purpose. In general, engineering control theory is based on the idea that if we can (1) predict the next observation on the process, (2) have some other variable that we can manipulate in order to affect the process output, and (3) know the effect of this manipulated variable so that we can determine how much control action to apply, then we can make the adjustment in the manipulated variable at time t that is most likely to produce an on-target value of the process output in period $t + 1$. Clearly, this requires good knowledge of the relationship between the output or controlled variable and the manipulated variable, as well as an understanding of process dynamics. We must also be able to easily change the manipulated variable. In fact, if the cost of taking control action is negligible, then the variability in the process output is minimized by taking control action every period. Note that this is in sharp contrast with SPC, where "control action" or a process adjustment is taken only when there is statistical evidence that the process is out of control. This statistical evidence is usually a point outside the limits of a control chart.

There are many processes where some type of feedback-control scheme would be preferable to a control chart. For example, consider the process of driving a car, with the objective of keeping it in the center of the right-hand lane (or equivalently, minimizing variation around the center of the right-hand lane). The driver can easily see the road ahead, and process adjustments (corrections to the steering wheel position) can be made at any time at negligible cost. Consequently, if the driver knew the relationship between the output variable (car position) and the manipulated variable (steering wheel adjustment), he would likely prefer to use a feedback-control scheme to control car position, rather than a statistical control chart. (Driving a car with a Shewhart control chart may be an interesting idea, but the author doesn't want to be in the car during the experiment.)

On the other hand, EPC makes no attempt to identify an assignable cause that may impact the process. The elimination of assignable causes can result in significant process improvement. All EPC schemes do is react to process upsets; they do not make any effort to remove the assignable causes. Consequently, in processes where feedback control is used there may be substantial improvement if control charts are also used for **statistical process monitoring** (as opposed to *control;* the control actions are based on the engineering scheme). Some authors refer to systems where both EPC and an SPC system for process monitoring have been implemented as **algorithmic SPC;** see Vander Weil et al. (1992).

The control chart should be applied to either the control error (the difference between the controlled variable and the target) or to the sequence of adjustments to the manipulated variable. Combinations of these two basic approaches are also possible. For example, the control error and the adjustments (or the output characteristic and the adjustable variable)

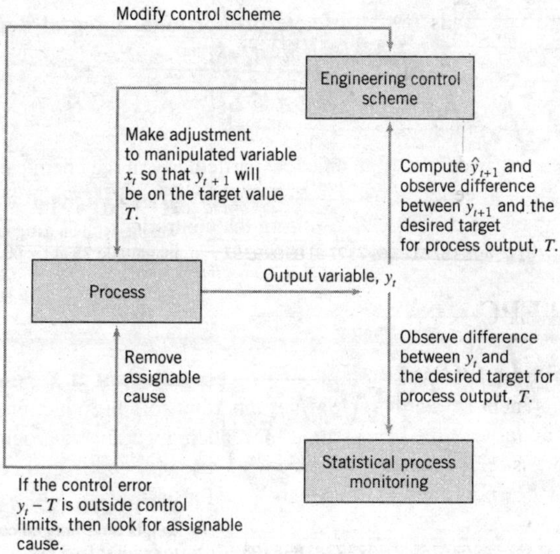

■ **FIGURE 12.13** Engineering process control and statistical process monitoring.

could be jointly monitored using a multivariate control chart. Points that lie outside the control limits on these charts would identify periods where the control errors are large or where large changes to the manipulated variable are being made. These periods would likely be good opportunities to search for assignable causes. Montgomery et al. (1994) have demonstrated the effectiveness of such a system. Other very useful references and discussion are in Del Castillo (2002). Figure 12.13 illustrates how such a combination of EPC and statistical process monitoring might be employed.

EXAMPLE 12.2 Integrating SPC and EPC

Figure 12.14 shows the molecular weight measurements from Fig. 12.1 in Example 12.1, except that now an assignable cause has impacted the process starting at period $t = 60$. The effect of this assignable cause is to increase the molecular weight by 25 units, and this results in adding variability to the process; the sample average and standard deviation of molecular weight are $\bar{x} = 2019$ and $s = 30.4$ (compared to $\bar{x} = 2008$ and $s = 19.4$ when there was no assignable cause present). Figure 12.15 shows the molecular weight after adjustments to the catalyst feed rate by the integral control rule in Example 12.1 are applied. Figure 12.16 shows the setpoints for feed rate. Process performance has improved, as the sample average and standard deviation are now $\bar{x} = 1992$ and $s = 15.4$. Clearly the assignable cause is still adding to process variability, because when there was no assignable cause in the system, $\bar{x} = 2001$ and $s = 10.35$ after the adjustments.

Figure 12.17 presents individuals and moving range control charts applied to the output molecular weight deviation from the target value $T = 2000$, after the integral control adjustments. An out-of-control signal is generated at period $t = 80$, indicating that an assignable cause is present. An EWMA or cusum control chart on the output deviation from target would generally detect the assignable cause more quickly. Figure 12.18 is an EWMA with $\lambda = 0.1$, and it signals the assignable cause at period $t = 70$.

Suppose that we detected and eliminated the assignable cause at period $t = 70$. Figure 12.19 is the resulting sequence of output molecular weight values. The sample average and standard deviation are now $\bar{x} = 1998$ and $s = 10.8$, so we see that coupling a control chart on the output deviation from target with the integral controller has improved the performance of the process when assignable causes are present.

(continued)

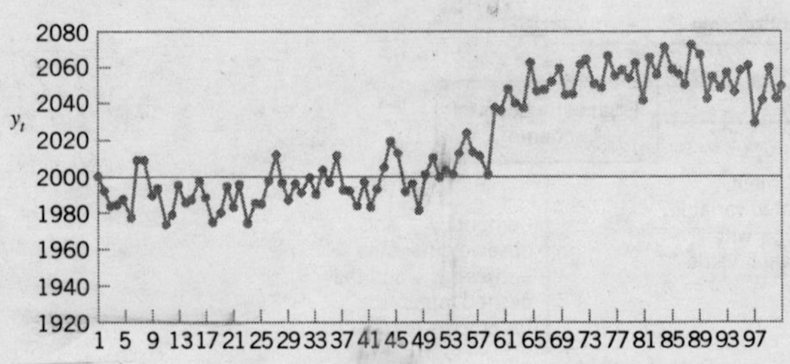

■ **Figure 12.14** Molecular weight, with an assignable cause of magnitude 25 at t = 60.

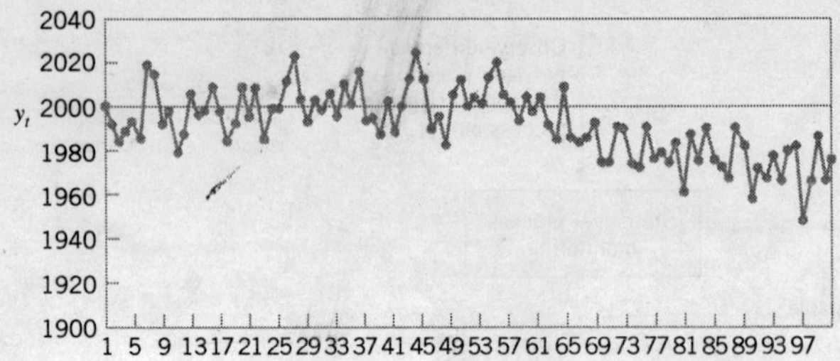

■ **Figure 12.15** Molecular weight after integral control adjustments to catalyst feed rate.

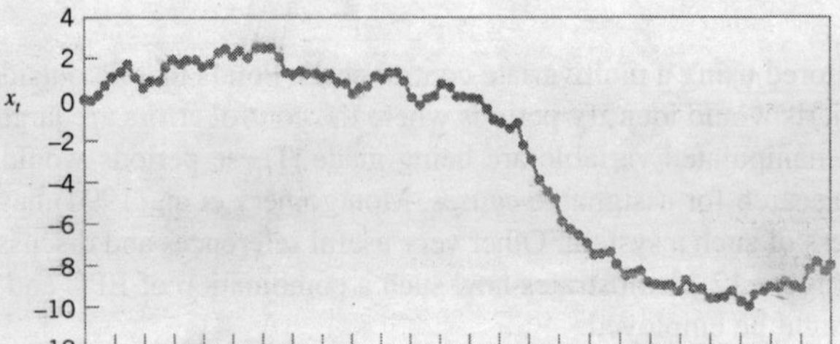

■ **Figure 12.16** Setpoint values for catalyst feed rate, Example 12.2.

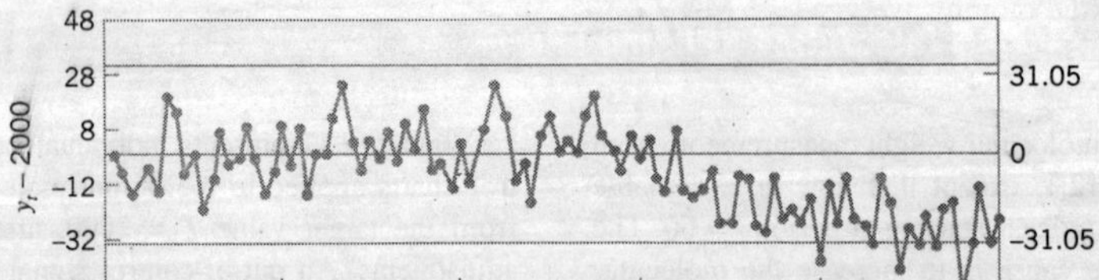

■ **Figure 12.17** Individuals and moving range control charts applied to the output deviation from target, Example 12.2.

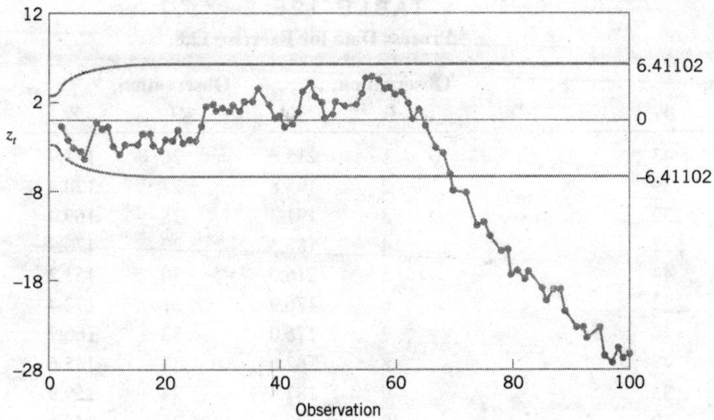

Figure 12.18 EWMA control chart with $\lambda = 0.1$ applied to the output deviation from target, Example 12.2.

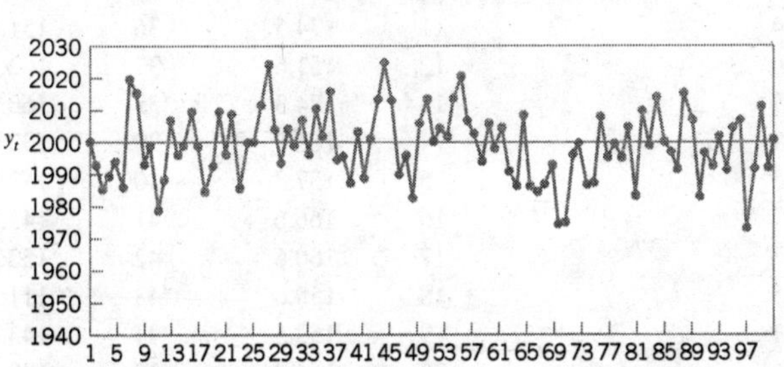

Figure 12.19 Molecular weight after adjustments to catalyst feed rate with the assignable cause removed following period $\tau = 70$.

Important Terms and Concepts

Automatic process control (APC)
Bounded adjustment chart
Engineering process control (EPC)
Exponentially weighted moving average (EWMA)
Integral control
Integrating SPC and EPC
Manipulatable process variable
Manual adjustment chart
Process adjustment versus process monitoring
Process gain
Proportional integral (PI) control
Proportional integral (PID) derivative control
Setpoint
Statistical process control (SPC)
Statistical process monitoring

Exercises

12.1. Consider the data in Table 12.1. Suppose that an adjustment is made to the output variable after every observation. Compare the performance of this chart to the one in Table 12.1 and Fig. 12.12.

12.2. Consider the data in Table 12.1. Construct a bounded adjustment chart using $\lambda = 0.4$ and $L = 10$. Compare the performance of this chart to the one in Table 12.1 and Fig. 12.12.

12.3. Consider the data in Table 12.1. Construct a bounded adjustment chart using $\lambda = 0.3$ and $L = 10$. Compare the performance of this chart to the one in Table 12.1 and Fig. 12.12.

12.4. If y_t are the observations and z_t is the EWMA, show that the following relationships are true.

(a) $z_t - z_{t-1} = \lambda(y_t - z_{t-1})$

(b) $e_t - (1 - \lambda)e_{t-1} = y_t - y_{t-1}$

12.5. **The Variogram.** Consider the variance of observations that are m periods apart; that is, $V_m = V(y_{t+m} - y_t)$. A graph of V_m/V_1 versus m is called a variogram. It is a nice way to check a data series for nonstationary

■ **TABLE 12E.1**
Process Data for Exercise 12.6.

Observation, t	y_t	Observation, t	y_t
1	50	26	43
2	58	27	39
3	54	28	32
4	45	29	37
5	56	30	44
6	56	31	52
7	66	32	42
8	55	33	47
9	69	34	33
10	56	35	49
11	63	36	34
12	54	37	40
13	67	38	27
14	55	39	29
15	56	40	35
16	65	41	27
17	65	42	33
18	61	43	25
19	57	44	21
20	61	45	16
21	64	46	24
22	43	47	18
23	44	48	20
24	45	49	23
25	39	50	26

■ **TABLE 12E.2**
Process Data for Exercise 12.8.

Observation, t	y_t	Observation, t	y_t
1	215.8	26	171.9
2	195.8	27	170.4
3	191.3	28	169.4
4	185.3	29	170.9
5	216.0	30	157.2
6	176.9	31	172.4
7	176.0	32	160.7
8	162.6	33	145.6
9	187.5	34	159.9
10	180.5	35	148.6
11	174.5	36	151.1
12	151.6	37	162.1
13	174.3	38	160.0
14	166.5	39	132.9
15	157.3	40	152.8
16	166.6	41	143.7
17	160.6	42	152.3
18	155.6	43	111.3
19	152.5	44	143.6
20	164.9	45	129.9
21	159.0	46	122.9
22	174.2	47	126.2
23	143.6	48	133.2
24	163.1	49	145.0
25	189.7	50	129.5

(drifting mean) behavior. If a data series is completely uncorrelated (white noise) the variogram will always produce a plot that stays near unity. If the data series is autocorrelated but stationary, the plot of the variogram will increase for a while, but as m increases the plot of V_m/V_1 will gradually stabilize and not increase any further. The plot of V_m/V_1 versus m will increase without bound for nonstationary data. Apply this technique to the data in Table 12.1. Is there an indication of nonstationary behavior? Calculate the sample autocorrelation function for the data. Compare the interpretation of both graphs.

12.6. Consider the observations in Table 12E.1. The target value for this process is 50.

(a) Set up an integral controller for this process. Assume that the gain for the adjustment variable is $g = 1.6$ and assume that $\lambda = 0.2$ in the EWMA forecasting procedure will provide adequate one-step-ahead predictions.

(b) How much reduction in variability around the target does the integral controller achieve?

(c) Rework parts (a) and (b) assuming that $\lambda = 0.4$. What change does this make in the variability around the target in comparison to that achieved with $\lambda = 0.2$?

12.7. Use the data in Exercise 12.6 to construct a bounded adjustment chart. Use $\lambda = 0.2$ and set $L = 4$. How does the bounded adjustment chart perform relative to the integral control adjustment procedure in part (a) of Exercise 12.6?

12.8. Consider the observations shown in Table 12E.2. The target value for this process is 200.

(a) Set up an integral controller for this process. Assume that the gain for the adjustment variable is $g = 1.2$ and assume that $\lambda = 0.2$ in the EWMA forecasting procedure will provide adequate one-step-ahead predictions.

(b) How much reduction in variability around the target does the integral controller achieve?

(c) Rework parts (a) and (b) assuming that $\lambda = 0.4$. What change does this make in the variability around the target in comparison to that achieved with $\lambda = 0.2$?

12.9. Use the data in Exercise 12.8 to construct a bounded adjustment chart. Use $\lambda = 0.2$ and set $L = 12$. How does the bounded adjustment chart perform relative to the integral control adjustment procedure in part (a) of Exercise 12.8?

12.10. Rework Exercise 12.9 using $\lambda = 0.4$ and $L = 15$. What differences in the results are obtained?

PART 5

Process Design and Improvement with Designed Experiments

Quality and productivity improvement are most effective when they are an integral part of the product realization process. In particular, the formal introduction of **experimental design** methodology at the earliest stage of the development cycle, where new products are designed, existing product designs improved, and manufacturing processes optimized, is often the key to overall product success. This principle has been established in many different industries, including electronics and semiconductors, aerospace, automotive, medical devices, food and pharmaceuticals, and the chemical and process industries. Designed experiments play a crucial role in the DMAIC process, mostly in the improve step. Statistical design of experiments often is cited as the most important of the six-sigma tool kit, and it is a critical part of design for six-sigma (DFSS). The effective use of sound statistical experimental design methodology can lead to products that are easier to manufacture, have higher reliability, and have enhanced field performance. Experimental design can also greatly enhance process development and improvements activities. Designed experiments, and how to use than in these types of applications, are the primary focus of this section.

Factorial and **fractional factorial designs** are introduced in Chapter 13 with particular emphasis on the two-level design system; that is, the 2^k factorial design and the fractions thereof. These designs are particularly useful for screening the variables in a process to determine those that are most important. Chapter 14 introduces **response surface methods,** a collection of techniques useful for process and system optimization. This chapter also discusses **process robustness studies,** an approach to reducing the variability in process or product performance by minimizing the effects on the output transmitted by variables that are difficult to control during routine process operation. Finally, we present an overview of evolutionary operation, an experimental-design-based process-monitoring scheme.

Throughout Part 5 we use the analysis of variance as the basis for analyzing data from designed experiments. It is possible to introduce experimental design without using analysis of variance methods, but this author believes that it is a mistake to do so, primarily because students will encounter the analysis of variance in virtually every computer program they use, either in the classroom, or in professional practice. We also illustrate software packages supporting designed experiments.

The material in this section is not a substitute for a full course in experimental design. Those interested in applying experimental design to process improvement will need additional background, but this presentation illustrates some of the many applications of this powerful tool. In many industries, the effective use of statistical experimental design is the key to higher yields, reduced variability, reduced development lead times, better products, and satisfied customers.

13 Basic Experimental Design for Process Improvement

CHAPTER OUTLINE

The supplemental material is on the textbook Website www.wiley.com/college/montgomery.

Chapter Overview and Learning Objectives

Most experiments for process design and improvement involve several variables. Factorial experimental designs, and their variations, are used in such situations. This chapter gives an introduction to factorial designs, emphasizing their applications for process and quality improvement. Designed experiments are widely used in the DMAIC process, and are extremely important in the improve step. They also play a leading role in design for six-sigma (DFSS). We concentrate on experimental designs where all the factors have two levels, and show how fractional versions of these designs can be used with great effectiveness in industrial experimentation. Important topics include the analysis of factorial experimental designs and the use of graphical methods in interpretation of the results. Both the interaction graph and a response surface plot are shown to be very useful in interpretation of results.

After careful study of this chapter you should be able to do the following:

1. Explain how designed experiments can be used to improve product design and improve process performance
2. Explain how designed experiments can be used to reduce the cycle time required to develop new products and processes
3. Understand how main effects and interactions of factors can be estimated
4. Understand the factorial design concept
5. Know how to use the analysis of variance (ANOVA) to analyze data from factorial designs
6. Know how residuals are used for model adequacy checking for factorial designs
7. Know how to use the 2^k system of factorial designs
8. Know how to construct and interpret contour plots and response surface plots
9. Know how to add center points to a 2^k factorial design to test for curvature and provide an estimate of pure experimental error
10. Understand how the blocking principal can be used in a factorial design to eliminate the effects of a nuisance factor
11. Know how to use the 2^{k-p} system of fractional factorial designs

13.1 What Is Experimental Design?

As indicated in Chapter 1, a designed experiment is a test or series of tests in which purposeful changes are made to the input variables of a process so that we may observe and identify corresponding changes in the output response. The process, as shown in Fig. 13.1, can be visualized as some combination of machines, methods, and people that transforms an input material into an output product. This output product has one or more observable quality characteristics or responses. Some of the process variables $x_1, x_2, \ldots, x_p$ are **controllable,** whereas others $z_1, z_2, \ldots, z_q$ are **uncontrollable** (although they may be controllable for purposes of the test). Sometimes these uncontrollable factors are called **noise** factors. The objectives of the experiment may include

1. Determining which variables are most influential on the response, y.
2. Determining where to set the influential x's so that y is near the nominal requirement.
3. Determining where to set the influential x's so that variability in y is small.
4. Determining where to set the influential x's so that the effects of the uncontrollable variables z are minimized.

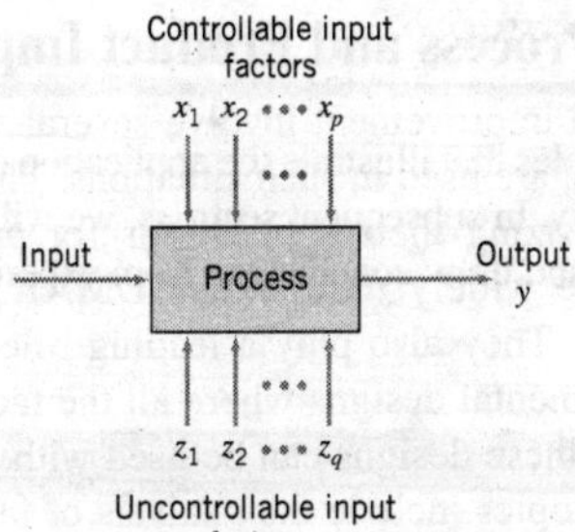

■ FIGURE 13.1 General model of a process.

Thus, experimental design methods may be used either in process development or process troubleshooting to improve process performance or to obtain a process that is **robust** or **insensitive** to external sources of variability.

Statistical process-control methods and experimental design, two very powerful tools for the improvement and optimization of processes, are closely interrelated. For example, if a process is in statistical control but still has poor capability, then to improve process capability it will be necessary to reduce variability. Designed experiments may offer a more effective way to do this than SPC. Essentially, SPC is a **passive** statistical method: We watch the process and wait for some information that will lead to a useful change. However, if the process is in control, passive observation may not produce much useful information. On the other hand, experimental design is an **active** statistical method: We will actually perform a series of tests on the process or system, making changes in the inputs and observing the corresponding changes in the outputs, and this will produce information that can lead to process improvement.

Experimental design methods can also be very useful in establishing statistical control of a process. For example, suppose that a control chart indicates that the process is out of control, and the process has many controllable input variables. Unless we know *which* input variables are the important ones, it may be very difficult to bring the process under control. Experimental design methods can be used to identify these influential process variables.

Experimental design is a critically important engineering tool for improving a manufacturing process. It also has extensive application in the development of new processes. Application of these techniques early in process development can result in

1. Improved yield
2. Reduced variability and closer conformance to the nominal
3. Reduced development time
4. Reduced overall costs

Experimental design methods can also play a major role in **engineering design** activities, where new **products** are developed and existing ones improved. Designed experiments are widely used in design for six-sigma (DFSS) activities. Some applications of statistical experimental design in engineering design include

1. Evaluation and comparison of basic design configurations
2. Evaluation of material alternatives
3. Determination of key product design parameters that impact performance

Use of experimental design in these areas can result in improved manufacturability of the product, enhanced field performance and reliability, lower product cost, and shorter product development time.

13.2 Examples of Designed Experiments in Process and Product Improvement

In this section, we present several examples that illustrate the application of designed experiments in improving process and product quality. In subsequent sections, we will demonstrate the statistical methods used to analyze the data and draw conclusions from experiments such as these.

EXAMPLE 13.1 Characterizing a Process

An engineer has applied SPC to a process for soldering electronic components to printed circuit boards. Through the use of *u* charts and Pareto analysis he has established statistical control of the flow solder process and has reduced the average number of defective solder joints per board to around 1%. However, since the average board contains over 2000 solder joints, even 1% defective presents far too many solder joints requiring rework. The engineer would like to reduce defect levels even further; however, since the process is in statistical control, it is not obvious what machine adjustments will be necessary.

The flow solder machine has several variables that can be controlled. They include

1. Solder temperature
2. Preheat temperature
3. Conveyor speed
4. Flux type
5. Flux specific gravity
6. Solder wave depth
7. Conveyor angle

In addition to these controllable factors, several others cannot be easily controlled during routine manufacturing, although they could be controlled for purposes of a test. They are

1. Thickness of the printed circuit board
2. Types of components used on the board
3. Layout of the components on the board
4. Operator
5. Production rate

In this situation, the engineer is interested in **characterizing** the flow solder machine; that is, he wants to determine which factors (both controllable and uncontrollable) affect the occurrence of defects on the printed circuit boards. To accomplish this task he can design an experiment that will enable him to estimate the magnitude and direction of the factor effects. That is, how much does the response variable (defects per unit) change when each factor is changed, and does changing the factors *together* produce different results than are obtained from individual factor adjustments? A factorial experiment will be required to do this. Sometimes we call this kind of factorial experiment a **screening experiment.**

The information from this screening or characterization experiment will be used to identify the critical process factors and to determine the direction of adjustment for these factors to further reduce the number of defects per unit. The experiment may also provide information about which factors should be more carefully controlled during routine manufacturing to prevent high defect levels and erratic process performance. Thus, one result of the experiment could be the application of control charts to one or more *process* variables (such as solder temperature) in addition to the *u* chart on process output. Over time, if the process is sufficiently improved, it may be possible to base most of the process-control plan on controlling process input variables instead of control charting the output.

EXAMPLE 13.2 Optimizing a Process

In a characterization experiment, we are usually interested in determining which process variables affect the response. A logical next step is to **optimize**—that is, to determine the region in the important factors that lead to the best possible response. For example, if the response is yield, we will look for a region of maximum yield, and if the response is variability in a critical product dimension, we will look for a region of minimum variability.

Suppose we are interested in improving the yield of a chemical process. Let's say that we know from the results of a characterization experiment that the two most important process variables that influence yield are operating temperature and reaction time. The process currently runs at 155° F and 1.7 h of reaction time, producing yields around 75%. Figure 13.2 shows a view of the time-temperature region from above. In this graph the lines of constant yield are connected to form **response contours,** and we have shown the contour lines for 60, 70, 80, 90, and 95% yield.

To locate the optimum, it is necessary to perform an experiment that varies time and temperature together. This type of experiment is called a **factorial experiment;** an example of a

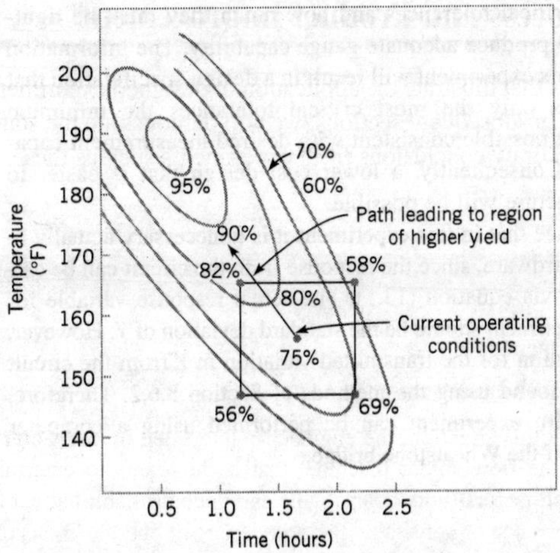

factorial experiment with both time and temperature run at two levels is shown in Fig. 13.2. The responses observed at the four corners of the square indicate that we should move in the general direction of increased temperature and decreased reaction time to increase yield. A few additional runs could be performed in this direction, which would be sufficient to locate the region of maximum yield. Once we are in the region of the optimum, a more elaborate experiment could be performed to give a very precise estimate of the optimum operating conditions. This type of experiment, called a **response surface experiment,** is discussed in Chapter 14.

FIGURE 13.2 Contour plot of yield as a function of reaction time and reaction temperature, illustrating an optimization experiment.

EXAMPLE 13.3 A Product Design Example

Designed experiments can often be applied in the product design process. To illustrate, suppose that a group of engineers are designing a door hinge for an automobile. The quality characteristic of interest is the check effort, or the holding ability of the door latch that prevents the door from swinging closed when the vehicle is parked on a hill. The check mechanism consists of a spring and a roller. When the door is opened, the roller travels through an arc causing the leaf spring to be compressed. To close the door, the spring must be forced aside, which creates the check effort. The engineering team believes the check effort is a function of the following factors:

1. Roller travel distance
2. Spring height pivot to base
3. Horizontal distance from pivot to spring
4. Free height of the reinforcement spring
5. Free height of the main spring

The engineers build a prototype hinge mechanism in which all these factors can be varied over certain ranges. Once appropriate levels for these five factors are identified, an experiment can be designed consisting of various combinations of the factor levels, and the prototype hinge can be tested at these combinations. This will produce information concerning which factors are most influential on latch check effort, and through use of this information the design can be improved.

EXAMPLE 13.4 Determining System and Component Tolerances

The Wheatstone bridge shown in Fig. 13.3 is a device used for measuring an unknown resistance, Y. The adjustable resistor B is manipulated until a particular current flow is obtained through the ammeter (usually $X = 0$). Then the unknown resistance is calculated as

$$Y = \frac{BD}{C} - \frac{X^2}{C^2E}[A(D+C)+D(B+C)][B(C+D)+F(B+C)] \tag{13.1}$$

The engineer wants to design the circuit so that overall gauge capability is good; that is, he would like the standard deviation of measurement error to be small. He has decided that $A = 20\ \Omega$, $C = 2\ \Omega$, $D = 50\ \Omega$, $E = 1.5\ \Omega$, and $F = 2\ \Omega$ is the best choice of the design parameters as far as gauge capability is concerned, but the overall measurement error is still too high. This is likely due to the tolerances that have been specified on the circuit components. These tolerances are $\pm 1\%$ for each resistor A, B, C, D, and F, and $\pm 5\%$ for the

(continued)

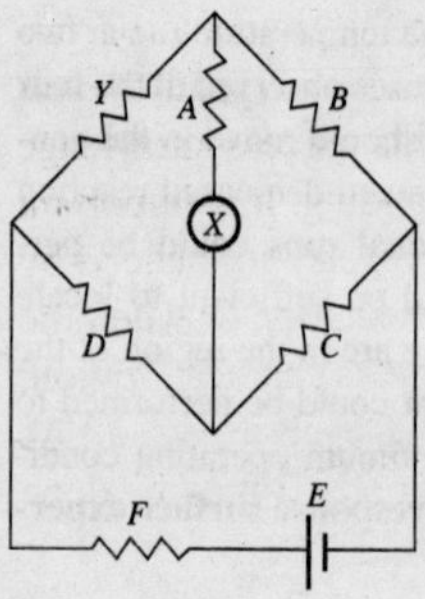

■ FIGURE 13.3 A Wheatstone bridge.

power supply E. These tolerance bands can be used to define appropriate factor levels, and an experiment can be performed to determine which circuit components have the most critical tolerances and how much they must be tightened to produce adequate gauge capability. The information from this experiment will result in a design specification that tightens only the most critical tolerances the minimum amount possible consistent with desired measurement capability. Consequently, a lower cost design that is easier to manufacture will be possible.

Notice that in this experiment it is unnecessary actually to build hardware, since the response from the circuit can be calculated via equation (13.1). The actual response variable for the experiment should be the standard deviation of Y. However, an equation for the transmitted variation in Y from the circuit can be found using the methods of Section 8.6.2. Therefore, the entire experiment can be performed using a computer model of the Wheatstone bridge.

13.3 Guidelines for Designing Experiments

Designed experiments are a powerful approach to improving a process. To use this approach, it is necessary that everyone involved in the experiment have a clear idea in advance of the objective of the experiment, exactly what factors are to be studied, how the experiment is to be conducted, and at least a qualitative understanding of how the data will be analyzed. Montgomery (2005) gives an outline of the recommended procedure, reproduced in Fig. 13.4. We now briefly amplify each point in this checklist.

1. Recognition of and statement of the problem. In practice, it is often difficult to realize that a problem requiring formal designed experiments exists, so it may not be easy to develop a clear and generally accepted statement of the problem. However, it is absolutely essential to fully develop all ideas about the problem and about the specific objectives of the experiment. Usually, it is important to solicit input from all concerned parties—engineering, quality, marketing, the customer, management, and the operators (who usually have much insight that is all too often ignored). A clear statement of the problem and the objectives of the experiment often contributes substantially to better process understanding and eventual solution of the problem.

Pre-experimental planning	1. Recognition of and statement of the problem	
	2. Choice of factors and levels	often done simultaneously, or in reverse order
	3. Selection of the response variable	
	4. Choice of experimental design	
	5. Performing the experiment	
	6. Data analysis	
	7. Conclusions and recommendations	

■ FIGURE 13.4 Procedure for designing an experiment.

2. Choice of factors and levels. The experimenter must choose the factors to be varied in the experiment, the ranges over which these factors will be varied, and the specific levels at which runs will be made. Process knowledge is required to do this. This process knowledge is usually a combination of practical experience and theoretical understanding. It is important to investigate all factors that may be of importance and to avoid being overly influenced by past experience, particularly when we are in the early stages of experimentation or when the process is not very mature. When the objective is factor screening or process characterization, it is usually best to keep the number of factor levels low. (Most often two levels are used.) As noted in Fig. 13.4, steps 2 and 3 are often carried out simultaneously, or step 3 may be done first in some applications.

3. Selection of the response variable. In selecting the response variable, the experimenter should be certain that the variable really provides useful information about the process under study. Most often the average or standard deviation (or both) of the measured characteristic will be the response variable. Multiple responses are not unusual. Gauge capability is also an important factor. If gauge capability is poor, then only relatively large factor effects will be detected by the experiment, or additional replication will be required.

4. Choice of experimental design. If the first three steps are done correctly, this step is relatively easy. Choice of design involves consideration of sample size (number of replicates), selection of a suitable run order for the experimental trials, and whether or not blocking or other randomization restrictions are involved. This chapter and Chapter 14 illustrate some of the more important types of experimental designs.

5. Performing the experiment. When running the experiment, it is vital to carefully monitor the process to ensure that everything is being done according to plan. Errors in experimental procedure at this stage will usually destroy experimental validity. Up-front planning is crucial to success. It is easy to underestimate the logistical and planning aspects of running a designed experiment in a complex manufacturing environment.

6. Data analysis. Statistical methods should be used to analyze the data so that results and conclusions are objective rather than judgmental. If the experiment has been designed correctly and if it has been performed according to the design, then the type of statistical method required is not elaborate. Many excellent software packages are available to assist in the data analysis, and simple graphical methods play an important role in data interpretation. Residual analysis and model validity checking are also important.

7. Conclusions and recommendations. Once the data have been analyzed, the experiment must draw *practical* conclusions about the results and recommend a course of action. Graphical methods are often useful in this stage, particularly in presenting the results to others. Follow-up runs and confirmation testing should also be performed to validate the conclusions from the experiment.

Steps 1 to 3 are usually called **pre-experimental planning.** It is vital that these steps be performed as well as possible if the experiment is to be successful. Coleman and Montgomery (1993) discuss this in detail and offer more guidance in pre-experimental planning, including worksheets to assist the experimenter in obtaining and documenting the required information. Section S13.1 of the supplemental text material contains additional useful material on planning experiments.

Throughout this entire process, it is important to keep in mind that experimentation is an important part of the learning process, where we tentatively formulate hypotheses about a system, perform experiments to investigate these hypotheses, and on the basis of the results formulate new hypotheses, and so on. This suggests that experimentation is **iterative**. It is usually a major mistake to design a single, large comprehensive experiment at the start of a study. A successful experiment requires knowledge of the important factors, the ranges over which these factors should be varied, the appropriate number of levels to use, and the proper units of measurement for these variables. Generally, we do not know perfectly the answers to these questions, but we learn about them as we go along. As an experimental program progresses, we often drop some variables, add others, change the region of exploration for some factors, or add new response variables. Consequently, we usually experiment **sequentially,** and as a general rule, no more than about 25% of the available resources should be invested in the first experiment. This will ensure that sufficient resources are available to accomplish the final objective of the experiment.

13.4 Factorial Experiments

When there are several factors of interest in an experiment, a **factorial design** should be used. In such designs factors are varied together. Specifically, by a factorial experiment we mean that in each complete trial or replicate of the experiment all possible combinations of the levels of the factors are investigated. Thus, if there are two factors *A* and *B* with *a* levels of factor *A* and *b* levels of factor *B*, then each replicate contains all *ab* possible combinations.

The effect of a factor is defined as the change in response produced by a change in the level of the factor. This is called a **main effect** because it refers to the primary factors in the study. For example, consider the data in Fig. 13.5. In this factorial design, both the factors *A* and *B* have two levels, denoted by "−" and "+." These two levels are called "low" and "high," respectively. The main effect of factor *A* is the difference between the average response at the high level of *A* and the average response at the low level of *A*, or

$$A = \bar{y}_{A^+} - \bar{y}_{A^-} = \frac{30+40}{2} - \frac{10+20}{2} = 20$$

That is, changing factor *A* from the low level (−) to the high level (+) causes an average response increase of 20 units. Similarly, the main effect of *B* is

$$B = \bar{y}_{B^+} - \bar{y}_{B^-} = \frac{20+40}{2} - \frac{10+30}{2} = 10$$

In some experiments, the difference in response between the levels of one factor is not the same at all levels of the other factors. When this occurs, there is an **interaction** between the factors. For example, consider the data in Fig. 13.6. At the low level of factor *B*, the *A* effect is

$$A = 30 - 10 = 20$$

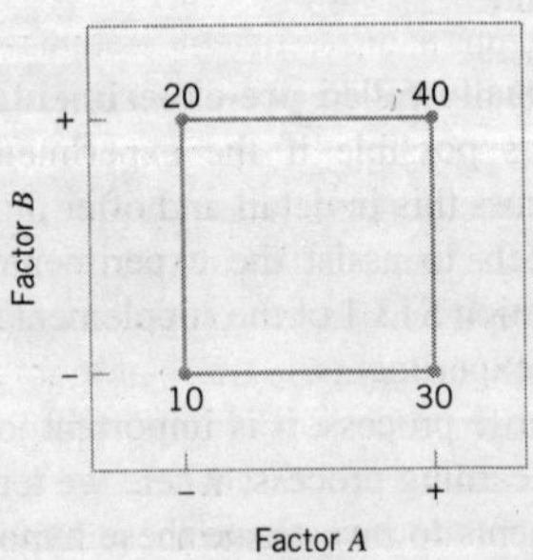

■ FIGURE 13.5 A factorial experiment with two factors.

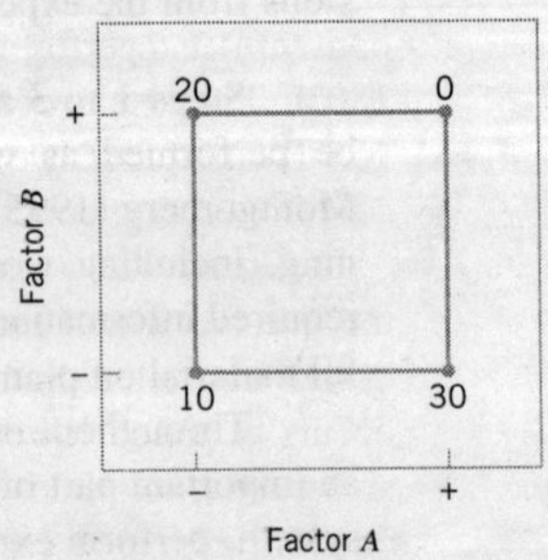

■ FIGURE 13.6 A factorial experiment with interaction.

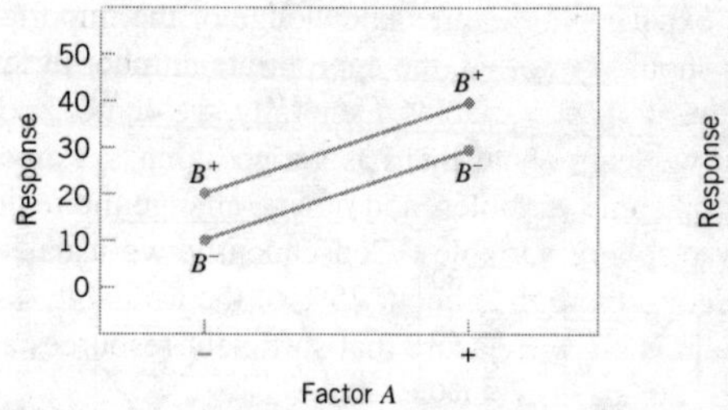

■ FIGURE 13.7 Factorial experiment, no interaction.

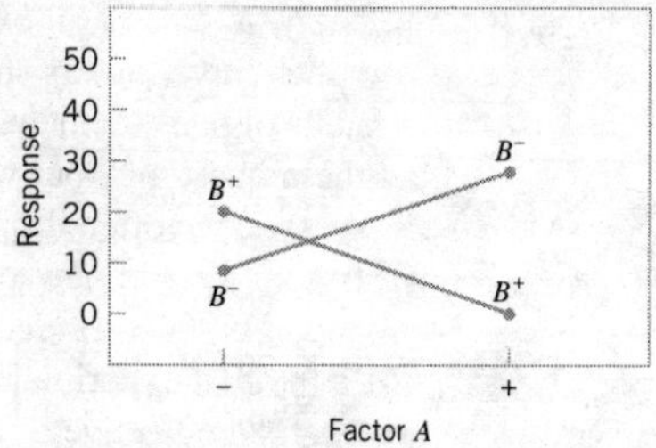

■ FIGURE 13.8 Factorial experiment with interaction.

and at the high level of factor B, the A effect is

$$A = 0 - 20 = -20$$

Since the effect of A depends on the level chosen for factor B, there is interaction between A and B.

When an interaction is large, the corresponding main effects have little meaning. For example, by using the data in Fig. 13.6, we find the main effect of A as

$$A = \frac{30+0}{2} - \frac{10+20}{2} = 0$$

and we would be tempted to conclude that there is no A effect. However, when we examine the main effect of A at *different levels of factor B*, we see that this is not the case. The effect of factor A depends on the levels of factor B. Thus, knowledge of the AB interaction is more useful than knowledge of the main effect. A significant interaction can mask the significance of main effects.

The concept of interaction can be illustrated graphically. Figure 13.7 plots the data in Fig. 13.5 against the levels of A for both levels of B. Note that the B^- and B^+ lines are roughly parallel, indicating that factors A and B do not interact. Figure 13.8 plots the data in Fig. 13.6. In Fig. 13.8, the B^- and B^+ lines are not parallel, indicating the interaction between factors A and B. Such graphical displays are often useful in presenting the results of experiments.

An alternative to the factorial design that is (unfortunately) used in practice is to change the factors one at a time rather than to vary them simultaneously. To illustrate the one-factor-at-a-time procedure, consider the optimization experiment described earlier in Example 13.2. The engineer is interested in finding the values of temperature and time that maximize yield. Suppose that we fix temperature at 155°F (the current operating level) and perform five runs at different levels of time—say, 0.5 h, 1.0 h, 1.5 h, 2.0 h, and 2.5 h. The results of this series of runs are shown in Fig. 13.9. This figure indicates that maximum yield is achieved at about 1.7 h of reaction time. To optimize temperature, the engineer fixes time at 1.7 h (the apparent optimum) and performs five runs at different temperatures—say, 140°F, 150°F, 160°F, 170°F, and 180°F. The results of this set of runs are plotted in Fig. 13.10. Maximum yield occurs at about 155°F. Therefore, we would conclude that running the process at 155°F and 1.7 h is the best set of operating conditions, resulting in yields around 75%.

Figure 13.11 displays the contour plot of yield as a function of temperature and time with the one-factor-at-a-time experiment shown on the contours. Clearly, the one-factor-at-a-time design has failed dramatically here, as the true optimum is at least 20 yield points higher and occurs at much lower reaction times and higher temperatures. The failure to discover the shorter reaction times is particularly important because it could have significant impact on production volume or capacity, production planning, manufacturing cost, and total productivity.

The one-factor-at-a-time method has failed here because it fails to detect the interaction between temperature and time. Factorial experiments are the only way to detect interactions.

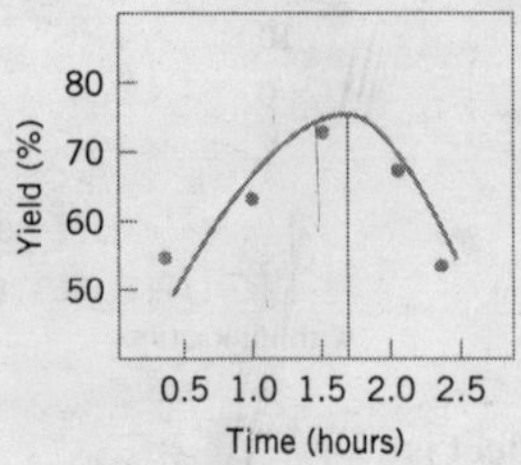

■ FIGURE 13.9 Yield versus reaction time with temperature constant at 155°F.

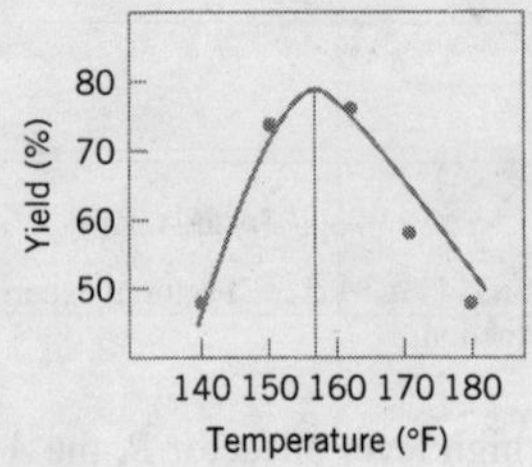

■ FIGURE 13.10 Yield versus temperature with reaction time constant at 1.7 h.

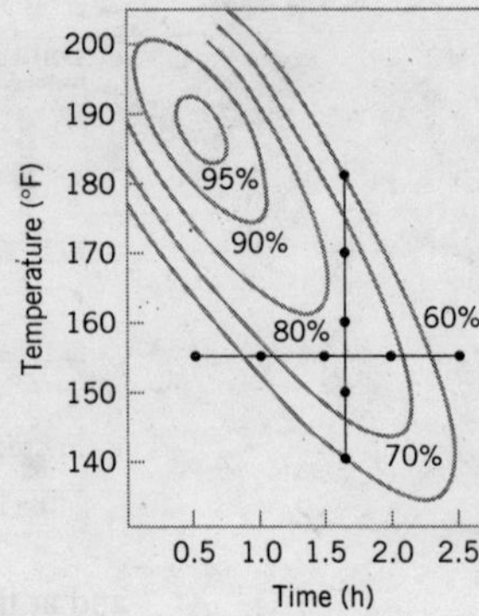

■ FIGURE 13.11 Optimization experiment using the one-factor-at-a-time method.

Furthermore, the one-factor-at-a-time method is inefficient; it will require more experimentation than a factorial, and as we have just seen, there is no assurance that it will produce the correct results. The experiment shown in Fig. 13.2 that produced the information pointing to the region of the optimum is a simple example of a factorial experiment.

13.4.1 An Example

Aircraft primer paints are applied to aluminum surfaces by two methods—dipping and spraying. The purpose of the primer is to improve paint adhesion; some parts can be primed using either application method. A team using the DMAIC approach has identified three different primers that can be used with both application methods. Three specimens were painted with each primer using each application method, a finish paint was applied, and the adhesion force was measured. The 18 runs from this experiment were run in random order. The resulting data are shown in Table 13.1. The circled numbers in the cells are the cell totals. The objective of the experiment was to determine which combination of primer paint and application method produced the highest adhesion force. It would be desirable if at least one of the primers produced high adhesion force *regardless* of application method, as this would add some flexibility to the manufacturing process.

13.4.2 Statistical Analysis

The analysis of variance (ANOVA) described in Chapter 4 can be extended to handle the two-factor factorial experiment. Let the two factors be denoted A and B, with a levels of factor A and

■ TABLE 13.1
Adhesion Force Data

	Application Method				
Primer Type	**Dipping**		**Spraying**		$y_{i..}$
1	4.0, 4.5, 4.3	(12.8)	5.4, 4.9, 5.6	(15.9)	28.7
2	5.6, 4.9, 5.4	(15.9)	5.8, 6.1, 6.3	(18.2)	34.1
3	3.8, 3.7, 4.0	(11.5)	5.5, 5.0, 5.0	(15.5)	27.0
$y_{.j.}$	40.2		49.6		$89.8 = y_{...}$

■ **TABLE 13.2**
Data for a Two-Factor Factorial Design

		Factor B			
		1	2	...	b
	1	$y_{111}, y_{112}, \ldots, y_{11n}$	$y_{121}, y_{122}, \ldots, y_{12n}$	...	$y_{1b1}, y_{1b2}, \ldots, y_{1bn}$
Factor A	2	$y_{211}, y_{212}, \ldots, y_{21n}$	$y_{221}, y_{222}, \ldots, y_{22n}$	...	$y_{2b1}, y_{2b2}, \ldots, y_{2bn}$
	⋮	⋮	⋮	⋮	⋮
	a	$y_{a11}, y_{a12}, \ldots, y_{a1n}$	$y_{a21}, y_{a22}, \ldots, y_{a2n}$	...	$y_{ab1}, y_{ab2}, \ldots, y_{abn}$

b levels of *B*. If the experiment is replicated *n* times, the data layout will look like Table 13.2. In general, the observation in the *ij*th cell in the *k*th replicate is y_{ijk}. In collecting the data, the *abn* observations would be run in *random* order. Thus, like the single-factor experiment studied in Chapter 4, the two-factor factorial is a **completely randomized design.** Both factors are assumed to be fixed effects.

The observations from a two-factor factorial experiment may be described by the model

$$y_{ijk} = \mu + \tau_i + \beta_j + (\tau\beta)_{ij} + \varepsilon_{ijk} \quad \begin{cases} i = 1, 2, \ldots, a \\ j = 1, 2, \ldots, b \\ k = 1, 2, \ldots, n \end{cases} \tag{13.2}$$

where μ is the overall mean effect, τ_i is the effect of the *i*th level of factor *A*, β_j is the effect of the *j*th level of factor *B*, $(\tau\beta)_{ij}$ is the effect of the interaction between *A* and *B*, and ε_{ijk} is an NID(0, σ^2) random error component. We are interested in testing the hypotheses of no significant factor *A* effect, no significant factor *B* effect, and no significant *AB* interaction.

Let $y_{i..}$ denote the total of the observations at the *i*th level of factor *A*, $y_{.j.}$ denote the total of the observations at the *j*th level of factor *B*, $y_{ij.}$ denote the total of the observations in the *ij*th cell of Table 13.2, and $y_{...}$ denote the grand total of all the observations.

Define $\bar{y}_{i..}$, $\bar{y}_{.j.}$, $\bar{y}_{ij.}$, and $\bar{y}_{...}$ as the corresponding row, column, cell, and grand averages. That is,

$$\begin{aligned} y_{i..} &= \sum_{j=1}^{b}\sum_{k=1}^{n} y_{ijk} & \bar{y}_{i..} &= \frac{y_{i..}}{bn} & & i = 1, 2, \ldots, a \\ y_{.j.} &= \sum_{i=1}^{a}\sum_{k=1}^{n} y_{ijk} & \bar{y}_{.j.} &= \frac{y_{.j.}}{an} & & j = 1, 2, \ldots, b \\ y_{ij.} &= \sum_{k=1}^{n} y_{ijk} & \bar{y}_{ij.} &= \frac{y_{ij.}}{n} & & i = 1, 2, \ldots, a \quad j = 1, 2, \ldots, b \\ y_{...} &= \sum_{i=1}^{a}\sum_{j=1}^{b}\sum_{k=1}^{n} y_{ijk} & \bar{y}_{...} &= \frac{y_{...}}{abn} \end{aligned} \tag{13.3}$$

The analysis of variance decomposes the total corrected sum of squares

$$SS_T = \sum_{i=1}^{a}\sum_{j=1}^{b}\sum_{k=1}^{n}\left(y_{ijk} - \bar{y}_{...}\right)^2$$

as follows:

$$\sum_{i=1}^{a}\sum_{j=1}^{b}\sum_{k=1}^{n}\left(y_{ijk} - \bar{y}_{...}\right)^2 = bn\sum_{i=1}^{a}\left(\bar{y}_{i..} - \bar{y}_{...}\right)^2 + an\sum_{j=1}^{b}\left(\bar{y}_{.j.} - \bar{y}_{...}\right)^2$$
$$+ n\sum_{i=1}^{a}\sum_{j=1}^{b}\left(\bar{y}_{ij.} - \bar{y}_{i..} - \bar{y}_{.j.} + \bar{y}_{...}\right)^2$$
$$+ \sum_{i=1}^{a}\sum_{j=1}^{b}\sum_{k=1}^{n}\left(y_{ijk} - \bar{y}_{ij.}\right)^2$$

or symbolically,

$$SS_T = SS_A + SS_B + SS_{AB} + SS_E \tag{13.4}$$

The corresponding degree of freedom decomposition is

$$abn - 1 = (a-1) + (b-1) + (a-1)(b-1) + ab(n-1) \tag{13.5}$$

This decomposition is usually summarized in an analysis of variance table such as the one shown in Table 13.3.

To test for no row factor effects, no column factor effects, and no interaction effects, we would divide the corresponding mean square by mean square error. Each of these ratios will follow an F distribution, with numerator degrees of freedom equal to the number of degrees of freedom for the numerator mean square and $ab(n - 1)$ denominator degrees of freedom, when the null hypothesis of no factor effect is true. We would reject the corresponding

■ **TABLE 13.3**
The ANOVA Table for a Two-Factor Factorial, Fixed Effects Model

Source of Variation	Sum of Squares	Degrees of Freedom	Mean Square	F_0
A	SS_A	$a-1$	$MS_A = \dfrac{SS_A}{a-1}$	$F_0 = \dfrac{MS_A}{MS_E}$
B	SS_B	$b-1$	$MS_B = \dfrac{SS_B}{b-1}$	$F_0 = \dfrac{MS_B}{MS_E}$
Interaction	SS_{AB}	$a-1\ \ b-1$	$MS_{AB} = \dfrac{SS_{AB}}{a-1\ \ b-1}$	$F_0 = \dfrac{MS_{AB}}{MS_E}$
Error	SS_E	$ab\ n-1$	$MS_E = \dfrac{SS_E}{ab\ n-1}$	
Total	SS_T	$abn-1$		

hypothesis if the computed F exceeded the tabular value at an appropriate significance level, or alternatively, if the P-value were smaller than the specified significance level.

The ANOVA is usually performed with computer software, although simple computing formulas for the sums of squares may be obtained easily. The computing formulas for these sums of squares follow.

$$SS_T = \sum_{i=1}^{a}\sum_{j=1}^{b}\sum_{k=1}^{n} y_{ijk}^2 - \frac{y_{...}^2}{abn} \tag{13.6}$$

Main effects

$$SS_A = \sum_{i=1}^{a} \frac{y_{i..}^2}{bn} - \frac{y_{...}^2}{abn} \tag{13.7}$$

$$SS_B = \sum_{j=1}^{b} \frac{y_{.j.}^2}{an} - \frac{y_{...}^2}{abn} \tag{13.8}$$

Interaction

$$SS_{AB} = \sum_{i=1}^{a}\sum_{j=1}^{b} \frac{y_{ij.}^2}{n} - \frac{y_{...}^2}{abn} - SS_A - SS_B \tag{13.9}$$

Error

$$SS_E = SS_T - SS_A - SS_B - SS_{AB} \tag{13.10}$$

EXAMPLE 13.5 The Aircraft Primer Paint Problem

Use the ANOVA described above to analyze the aircraft primer paint experiment described in Section 13.4.1.

SOLUTION

The sums of squares required are

$$SS_T = \sum_{i=1}^{a}\sum_{j=1}^{b}\sum_{k=1}^{n} y_{ijk}^2 - \frac{y_{...}^2}{abn}$$

$$= (4.0)^2 + (4.5)^2 + \cdots + (5.0)^2 - \frac{(89.8)^2}{18} = 10.72$$

$$SS_{\text{primers}} = \sum_{i=1}^{a} \frac{y_{i..}^2}{bn} - \frac{y_{...}^2}{abn}$$

$$= \frac{(28.7)^2 + (34.1)^2 + (27.0)^2}{6} - \frac{(89.8)^2}{18} = 4.58$$

$$SS_{\text{methods}} = \sum_{j=1}^{b} \frac{y_{.j.}^2}{an} - \frac{y_{...}^2}{abn}$$

$$= \frac{(40.2)^2 + (49.6)^2}{9} - \frac{(89.8)^2}{18} = 4.91$$

$$SS_{\text{interaction}} = \sum_{i=1}^{a}\sum_{j=1}^{b} \frac{y_{ij.}^2}{n} - \frac{y_{...}^2}{abn} - SS_{\text{primers}} - SS_{\text{methods}}$$

$$= \frac{(12.8)^2 + (15.9)^2 + (11.5)^2 + (15.9)^2 + (18.2)^2 + (15.5)^2}{3} - \frac{(89.8)^2}{18} - 4.58 - 4.91 = 0.24$$

and

$$SS_E = SS_T - SS_{\text{primers}} - SS_{\text{methods}} - SS_{\text{interaction}}$$

$$= 10.72 - 4.58 - 4.91 - 0.24 = 0.99$$

The ANOVA is summarized in Table 13.4. Note that the P-values for **both** main effects are very small, indicating that the type of primer used and the application method significantly affect adhesion force. Since the P-value for the interaction effect F-ratio is relatively large, we would conclude that there

(continued)

■ **TABLE 13.4**
ANOVA for Example 13.5

Source of Variation	Sum of Squares	Degrees of Freedom	Mean Square	F_0	*P*-value
Primer types	4.58	2	2.290	27.93	1.93×10^{-4}
Application methods	4.91	1	4.910	59.88	5.28×10^{-6}
Interaction	0.24	2	0.120	1.46	0.269
Error	0.99	12	0.082		
Total	10.72	17			

is no interaction between primer type and application method. As an alternative to using the *P*-values, we could compare the computed *F*-ratios to a 5% (say) upper critical value of the *F* distribution. Since $F_{0.05,2,12} = 3.89$ and $F_{0.05,1,12} = 4.75$, we conclude that primer type and application method affect adhesion force. Furthermore, since $1.5 < F_{0.05,2,12}$, there is no indication of interaction between these factors.

In practice, ANOVA computations are performed on a computer using a statistics software package. Table 13.5 is the analysis of variance from Minitab. Note the similarity of this display to Table 13.4. Because the computer carries more decimal places than we did in the manual calculations, the *F*-ratios in Tables 13.4 and 13.5 are slightly different. The *P*-value for each *F*-ratio is called "significance level" in Table 13.5, and when a *P*-value is less than 0.001, Minitab reports it as 0.000.

A graph of the adhesion force cell averages $\{\bar{y}_{ij.}\}$ versus the levels of primer type for each application method is shown in Fig. 13.12. This interaction graph was constructed by Minitab. The absence of interaction is evident in the parallelism of the two lines. Furthermore, since a large response indicates greater adhesion force, we conclude that spraying is a superior application method and that primer type 2 is most effective. Therefore, if we wish to operate the process so as to attain maximum adhesion force, we should use primer type 2 and spray all parts.

■ **TABLE 13.5**
ANOVA Output from Minitab, Example 13.5

```
Two-way ANOVA: Force versus Primer, Method
Analysis of Variance for Force
Source        DF       SS        MS          F        P
Primer         2    4.5811    2.2906     27.86    0.000
Method         1    4.9089    4.9089     59.70    0.000
Interaction    2    0.2411    0.1206      1.47    0.269
Error         12    0.9867    0.0822
Total         17   10.7178
                        Individual 95% CI
Primer      Mean   ------+---------+---------+---------+--------
1           4.78            (----*----)
2           5.68                                        (----*----)
3           4.50   (----*----)
                   ------+---------+---------+---------+--------
                       4.50      5.00      5.50      6.00
                        Individual 95% CI
Method      Mean   ---------+---------+---------+---------+-----
Dip        4.467   (-----*-----)
Spray      5.511                        (-----*-----)
                   ---------+---------+---------+---------+-----
                        4.550     4.900     5.250     5.600
```

Confidence intervals on each mean calculated using MS_E as an estimate of σ^2 and applying the standard confidence interval procedure for the mean of a normal distribution with unknown variance.

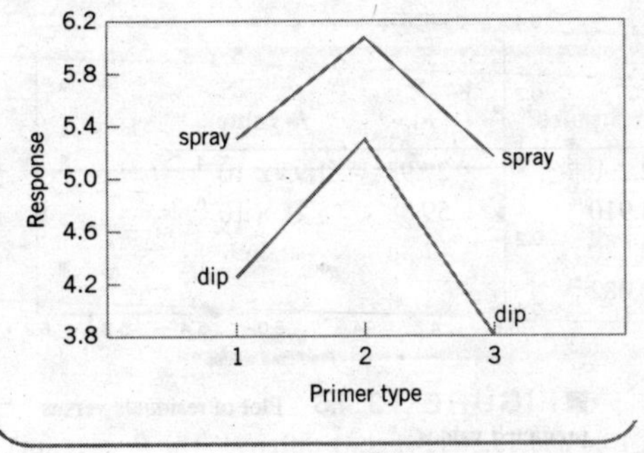

■ FIGURE 13.12 Graph of average adhesion force versus primer types for Example 13.5.

13.4.3 Residual Analysis

Just as in the single-factor experiments discussed in Chapter 4, the **residuals** from a factorial experiment play an important role in assessing model adequacy. The residuals from a two-factor factorial are

$$\begin{aligned} e_{ijk} &= y_{ijk} - \hat{y}_{ijk} \\ &= y_{ijk} - \bar{y}_{ij.} \end{aligned}$$

That is, the residuals are simply the difference between the observations and the corresponding cell averages.

Table 13.6 presents the residuals for the aircraft primer paint data in Example 13.5. The normal probability plot of these residuals is shown in Fig. 13.13. This plot has tails that do not fall exactly along a straight line passing through the center of the plot, indicating some small problems with the normality assumption, but the departure from normality is not serious. Figures 13.14 and 13.15 plot the residuals versus the levels of primer types and application methods, respectively. There is some indication that primer type 3 results in slightly

■ TABLE 13.6
Residuals for the Aircraft Primer Paint Experiment

Primer Type	**Application Method**	
	Dipping	Spraying
1	−0.26, 0.23, 0.03	0.10, −0.40, 0.30
2	0.30, −0.40, 0.10	−0.26, 0.03, 0.23
3	−0.03, −0.13, 0.16	0.34, −0.17, −0.17

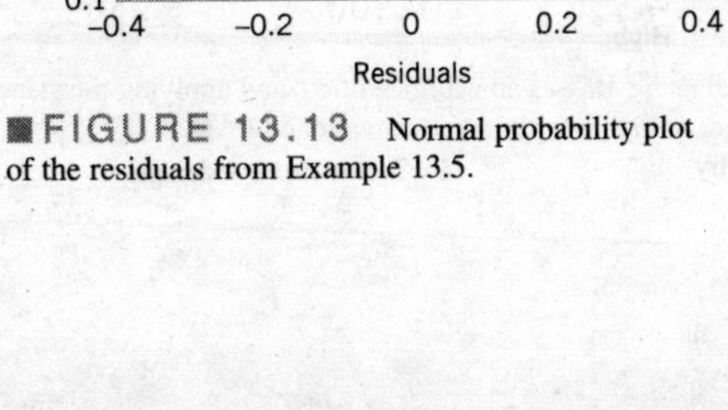

■ FIGURE 13.13 Normal probability plot of the residuals from Example 13.5.

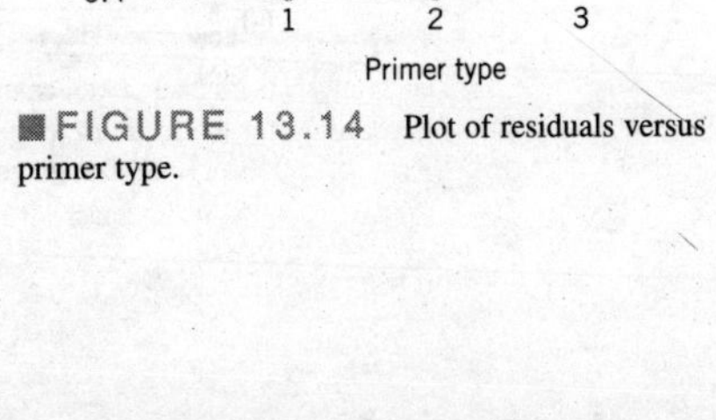

■ FIGURE 13.14 Plot of residuals versus primer type.

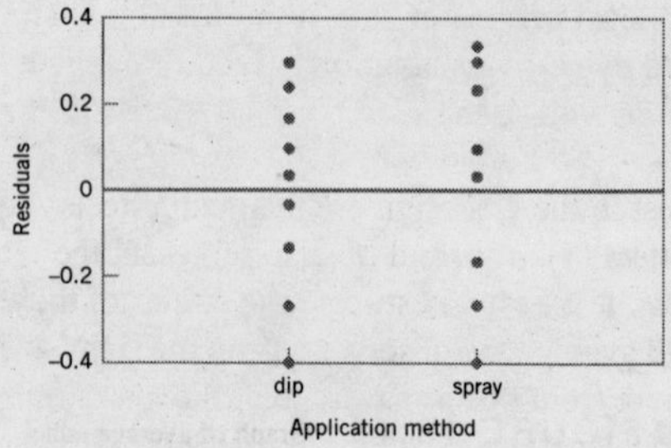

■ FIGURE 13.15 Plot of residuals versus application method.

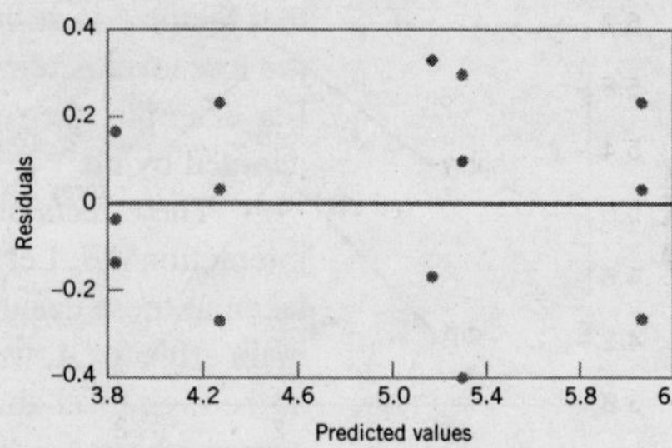

■ FIGURE 13.16 Plot of residuals versus predicted values.

lower variability in adhesion force than the other two primers. The graph of residuals versus fitted values in Fig. 13.16 does not reveal any unusual or diagnostic pattern.

13.5 The 2^k Factorial Design

Certain special types of factorial designs are very useful in process development and improvement. One of these is a factorial design with k factors, each at two levels. Because each complete replicate of the design has 2^k runs, the arrangement is called a **2^k factorial design.** These designs have a greatly simplified analysis, and they also form the basis of many other useful designs.

13.5.1 The 2^2 Design

The simplest type of 2^k design is the 2^2—that is, two factors A and B, each at two levels. We usually think of these levels as the "low" or "−" and "high" or "+" levels of the factor. The geometry of the 2^2 design is shown in Fig. 13.17*a*. Note that the design can be represented geometrically as a square with the $2^2 = 4$ runs forming the corners of the square. Figure 13.17*b* shows the four runs in a tabular format often called the **test matrix** or the **design matrix.** Each run of the test matrix is on the corners of the square and the − and + signs in each row show the settings for the variables A and B for that run.

Another notation is used to represent the runs. In general, a run is represented by a series of lowercase letters. If a letter is present, then the corresponding factor is set at the high level in that run; if it is absent, the factor is run at its low level. For example, run a indicates

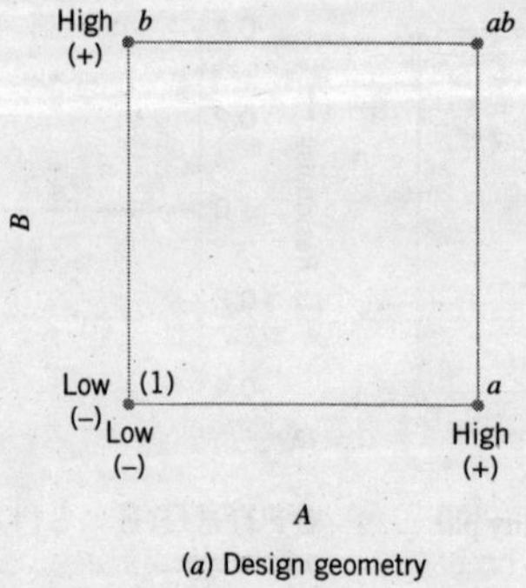

(*a*) Design geometry

A	B
−	−
+	−
−	+
+	+

(*b*) Test matrix

■ FIGURE 13.17 The 2^2 factorial design.

that factor A is at the high level and factor B is at the low level. The run with both factors at the low level is represented by (1). This notation is used throughout the family of 2^k designs. For example, the run in a 2^4 with A and C at the high level and B and D at the low level is denoted by ac.

The effects of interest in the 2^2 design are the main effects A and B and the two-factor interaction AB. Let the letters (1), a, b, and ab also represent the totals of all n observations taken at these design points. It is easy to estimate the effects of these factors. To estimate the main effect of A, we would average the observations on the right side of the square when A is at the high level and subtract from this the average of the observations on the left side of the square where A is at the low level, or

$$\begin{aligned} A &= \bar{y}_{A^+} - \bar{y}_{A^-} \\ &= \frac{a+ab}{2n} - \frac{b+(1)}{2n} \\ &= \frac{1}{2n}[a+ab-b-(1)] \end{aligned} \tag{13.11}$$

Similarly, the main effect of B is found by averaging the observations on the top of the square where B is at the high level and subtracting the average of the observations on the bottom of the square where B is at the low level:

$$\begin{aligned} B &= \bar{y}_{B^+} - \bar{y}_{B^-} \\ &= \frac{b+ab}{2n} - \frac{a+(1)}{2n} \\ &= \frac{1}{2n}[b+ab-a-(1)] \end{aligned} \tag{13.12}$$

Finally, the AB interaction is estimated by taking the difference in the diagonal averages in Fig. 13.17, or

$$\begin{aligned} AB &= \frac{ab+(1)}{2n} - \frac{a+b}{2n} \\ &= \frac{1}{2n}[ab+(1)-a-b] \end{aligned} \tag{13.13}$$

The quantities in brackets in equations (13.11), (13.12), and (13.13) are called **contrasts.** For example, the A contrast is

$$\text{Contrast}_A = a + ab - b - (1)$$

In these equations, the contrast coefficients are always either + 1 or − 1. A table of plus and minus signs, such as Table 13.7, can be used to determine the sign on each run for a particular

■ **TABLE 13.7**
Signs for Effects in the 2^2 Design

Run		Factorial Effect			
		I	*A*	*B*	*AB*
1	(1)	+	−	−	+
2	*a*	+	+	−	−
3	*b*	+	−	+	−
4	*ab*	+	+	+	+

contrast. The column headings for the table are the main effects *A* and *B*, the *AB* interaction, and *I*, which represents the total. The row headings are the runs. Note that the signs in the *AB* column are the product of signs from columns *A* and *B*. To generate a contrast from this table, multiply the signs in the appropriate column of Table 13.7 by the runs listed in the rows and add.

To obtain the sums of squares for *A*, *B*, and *AB*, we use the following result.

$$SS = \frac{(\text{contrast})^2}{n\sum(\text{contrast coefficients})^2} \tag{13.14}$$

Therefore, the sums of squares for *A*, *B*, and *AB* are

$$\begin{aligned} SS_A &= \frac{[a + ab - b - (1)]^2}{4n} \\ SS_B &= \frac{[b + ab - a - (1)]^2}{4n} \\ SS_{AB} &= \frac{[ab + (1) - a - b]^2}{4n} \end{aligned} \tag{13.15}$$

The analysis of variance is completed by computing the total sum of squares SS_T (with $4n - 1$ degrees of freedom) as usual, and obtaining the error sum of squares SS_E [with $4(n - 1)$ degrees of freedom] by subtraction.

EXAMPLE 13.6 The Router Experiment

A router is used to cut registration notches in printed circuit boards. The average notch dimension is satisfactory, and the process is in statistical control (see the $\bar{x}$ and *R* control charts in Fig. 13.18), but there is too much variability in the process. This excess variability leads to problems in board assembly. The components are inserted into the board using automatic equipment, and the variability in notch dimension causes improper board registration. As a result, the auto-insertion equipment does not work properly. How would you improve this process?

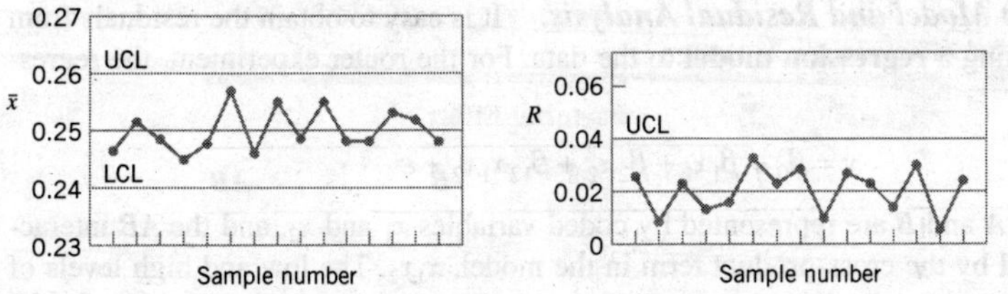

■ FIGURE 13.18 $\bar{x}$ and R control charts on notch dimension, Example 13.6.

SOLUTION

Since the process is in statistical control, the quality improvement team assigned to this project decided to use a designed experiment to study the process. The team considered two factors: bit size (*A*) and speed (*B*). Two levels were chosen for each factor (bit size *A* at $\frac{1}{16}''$ and $\frac{1}{8}''$ and speed *B* at 40 rpm and 80 rpm), and a 2^2 design was set up. Since variation in notch dimension was difficult to measure directly, the team decided to measure it indirectly. Sixteen test boards were instrumented with accelerometers that allowed vibration on the (*X*, *Y*, *Z*) coordinate axes to be measured. The resultant vector of these three components was used as the response variable. Since vibration at the surface of the board when it is cut is directly related to variability in notch dimension, reducing vibration levels will also reduce the variability in notch dimension.

Four boards were tested at each of the four runs in the experiment, and the resulting data are shown in Table 13-8.

■ **TABLE 13.8**
Data from the Router Experiment

Run		Factors A	Factors B	Vibration				Total
1	(1)	−	−	18.2	18.9	12.9	14.4	64.4
2	*a*	+	−	27.2	24.0	22.4	22.5	96.1
3	*b*	−	+	15.9	14.5	15.1	14.2	59.7
4	*ab*	+	+	41.0	43.9	36.3	39.9	161.1

Using equations (13.11), (13.12), and (13.13), we can compute the factor effect estimates as follows:

$$A = \frac{1}{2n}[a + ab - b - (1)]$$
$$= \frac{1}{2(4)}[96.1 + 161.1 - 59.7 - 64.4] = \frac{133.1}{8} = 16.64$$

$$B = \frac{1}{2n}[b + ab - a - (1)]$$
$$= \frac{1}{2(4)}[59.7 + 161.1 - 96.1 - 64.4] = \frac{60.3}{8} = 7.54$$

$$AB = \frac{1}{2n}[ab + (1) - a - b]$$
$$= \frac{1}{2(4)}[161.1 + 64.4 - 96.1 - 59.7] = \frac{69.7}{8} = 8.71$$

All the numerical effect estimates seem large. For example, when we change factor *A* from the low level to the high level (bit size from $\frac{1}{16}''$ to $\frac{1}{8}''$), the average vibration level increases by 16.64 cps.

The magnitude of these effects may be confirmed with the analysis of variance, which is summarized in Table 13.9. The sums of squares in this table for main effects and interaction were computed using equation (13.15). The analysis of variance confirms our conclusions that were obtained by initially examining the magnitude and direction of the factor effects; both bit size and speed are important, and there is interaction between two variables.

■ **TABLE 13.9**
Analysis of Variance for the Router Experiment

Source of Variation	Sum of Squares	Degrees of Freedom	Mean Square	F_0	*P*-value
Bit size (*A*)	1107.226	1	1107.226	185.25	1.17×10^{-8}
Speed (*B*)	227.256	1	227.256	38.03	4.82×10^{-5}
AB	303.631	1	303.631	50.80	1.20×10^{-5}
Error	71.723	12	5.977		
Total	1709.836	15			

Regression Model and Residual Analysis. It is easy to obtain the residuals from a 2^k design by fitting a **regression model** to the data. For the router experiment, the regression model is

$$y = \beta_0 + \beta_1 x_1 + \beta_2 x_2 + \beta_{12} x_1 x_2 + \varepsilon$$

where the factors A and B are represented by coded variables x_1 and x_2, and the AB interaction is represented by the cross-product term in the model, x_1x_2. The low and high levels of each factor are assigned the values $x_j = -1$ and $x_j = +1$, respectively. The coefficients β_0, β_1, β_2, and β_{12} are called **regression coefficients,** and ε is a random error term, similar to the error term in an analysis of variance model.

The fitted regression model is

$$\hat{y} = 23.83 + \left(\frac{16.64}{2}\right)x_1 + \left(\frac{7.54}{2}\right)x_2 + \left(\frac{8.71}{2}\right)x_1x_2$$

where the estimate of the intercept $\hat{\beta}_0$ is the grand average of all 16 observations ($\bar{y}$) and the estimates of the other regression coefficients $\hat{\beta}_j$ are one-half the effect estimate for the corresponding factor. [Each regression coefficient estimate is one-half the effect estimate because regression coefficients measure the effect of a unit change in x_j on the mean of y, and the effect estimate is based on a two-unit change (from −1 to +1).]

This model can be used to obtain the predicted values of vibration level at any point in the region of experimentation, including the four points in the design. For example, consider the point with the small bit ($x_1 = -1$) and low speed ($x_2 = -1$). The predicted vibration level is

$$\hat{y} = 23.83 + \left(\frac{16.64}{2}\right)(-1) + \left(\frac{7.54}{2}\right)(-1) + \left(\frac{8.71}{2}\right)(-1)(-1) = 16.1$$

The four residuals corresponding to the observations at this design point are found by taking the difference between the actual observation and the predicted value as follows:

$$e_1 = 18.2 - 16.1 = 2.1 \quad e_3 = 12.9 - 16.1 = -3.2$$
$$e_2 = 18.9 - 16.1 = 2.8 \quad e_4 = 14.4 - 16.1 = -1.7$$

The residuals at the other three runs would be computed similarly.

Figures 13.19 and 13.20 present the normal probability plot and the plot of residuals versus the fitted values, respectively. The normal probability plot is satisfactory, as is the plot of residuals versus $\hat{y}$, although this latter plot does give some indication that there may be less variability in the data at the point of lowest predicted vibration level.

Practical Interpretation of Example 13.6. Since both factors A (bit size) and B (speed) have large, positive effects, we could reduce vibration levels by running both factors

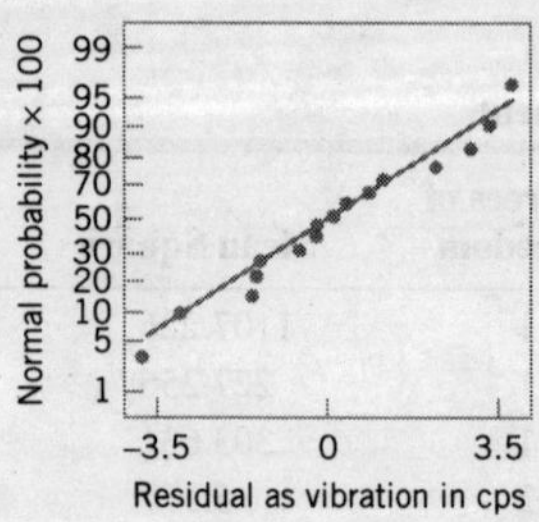

■ FIGURE 13.19 Normal probability plot, Example 13.6.

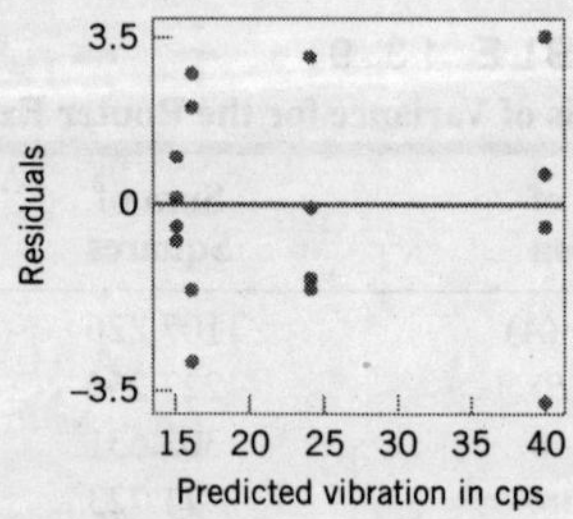

■ FIGURE 13.20 Plot of residuals versus $\hat{y}$, Example 13.6.

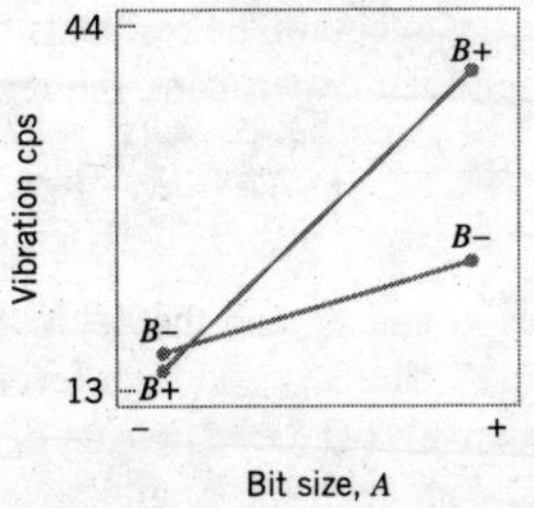

■ FIGURE 13.21 *AB* interaction plot.

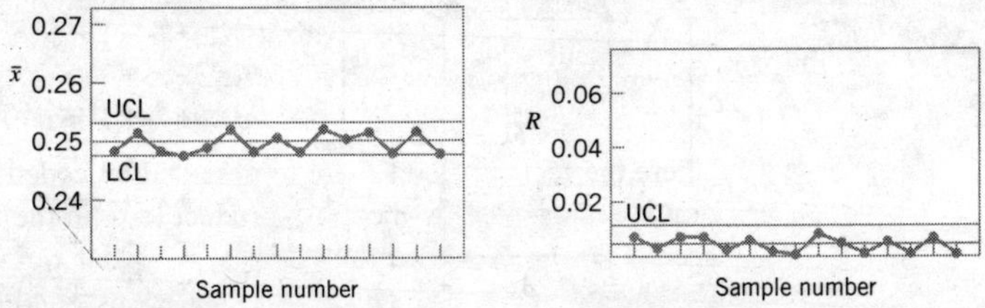

■ FIGURE 13.22 $\bar{x}$ and *R* charts for the router process after the experiment.

at the low level. However, with both bit size and speed at low level, the production rate could be unacceptably low. The *AB* interaction provides a solution to this potential dilemma. Figure 13.21 presents the two-factor *AB* interaction plot. Note that the large positive effect of speed occurs primarily when bit size is at the high level. If we use the small bit, then either speed level will provide lower vibration levels. If we run with speed high and use the small bit, the production rate will be satisfactory.

When manufacturing implemented this set of operating conditions, the result was a dramatic reduction in variability in the registration notch dimension. The process remained in statistical control, as the control charts in Fig. 13.22 imply, and the reduced variability dramatically improved the performance of the auto-insertion process.

Analysis Procedure for Factorial Experiments. Table 13.10 summarizes the sequence of steps that is usually employed to analyze factorial experiments. These steps were followed in the analysis of the router experiment in Example 13.6. Recall that our first activity, after the experiment was run, was to estimate the effect of the factors bit size, speed, and the two-factor interaction. The preliminary model that we used in the analysis was the two-factor factorial model with interaction. Generally, in any factorial experiment with replication, we will almost always use the full factorial model as the preliminary model. We tested for significance of factor effects by using the analysis of variance. Since the residual analysis was satisfactory, and both main effects and the interaction term were significant, there was no need to refine the model. Therefore, we were able to interpret the results in terms of the original full factorial model, using the two-factor interaction graph in Fig. 13.21. Sometimes refining the model includes deleting terms from the final model that are not significant, or taking other actions that may be indicated from the residual analysis.

Several statistics software packages include special routines for the analysis of two-level factorial designs. Many of these packages follow an analysis process similar to the one we have outlined. We will illustrate this analysis procedure again several times in this chapter.

13.5.2 The 2^k Design for $k \geq 3$ Factors

The methods presented in the previous section for factorial designs with $k = 2$ factors each at two levels can be easily extended to more than two factors. For example, consider $k = 3$

■ TABLE 13.10
Analysis Procedure for Factorial Designs

1. Estimate the factor effects	4. Analyze residuals
2. Form preliminary model	5. Refine model, if necessary
3. Test for significance of factor effects	6. Interpret results

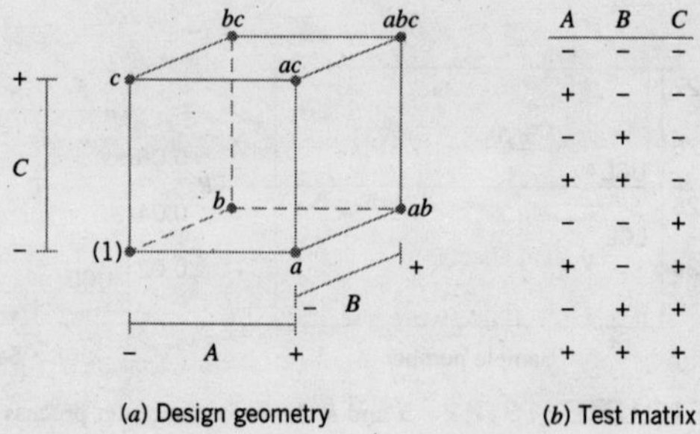

■ FIGURE 13.23 The 2^3 factorial design.

factors, each at two levels. This design is a 2^3 factorial design, and it has eight factor-level combinations. Geometrically, the design is a cube as shown in Fig. 13.23*a*, with the eight runs forming the corners of the cube. Figure 13.23*b* shows the **test design matrix.** This design allows three main effects to be estimated (*A*, *B*, and *C*) along with three two-factor interactions (*AB*, *AC*, and *BC*) and a three-factor interaction (*ABC*). Thus, the full factorial model could be written symbolically as

$$y = \mu + A + B + C + AB + AC + BC + ABC + \varepsilon$$

where μ is an overall mean, ε is a random error term assumed to be NID(0, σ^2), and the uppercase letters represent the main effects and interactions of the factors [note that we could have used Greek letters for the main effects and interactions, as in equation (13.2)].

The main effects can be estimated easily. Remember that the lowercase letters (1), *a*, *b*, *ab*, *c*, *ac*, *bc*, and *abc* represent the total of all *n* replicates at each of the eight runs in the design. Referring to the cube in Fig. 13.23, we would estimate the main effect of *A* by averaging the four runs on the right side of the cube where *A* is at the high level and subtracting from that quantity the average of the four runs on the left side of the cube where *A* is at the low level. This gives

$$A = \bar{y}_{A^+} - \bar{y}_{A^-} = \frac{1}{4n}\left[a + ab + ac + abc - b - c - bc - (1)\right] \tag{13.16}$$

In a similar manner, the effect of *B* is the average difference of the four runs in the back face of the cube and the four in the front, or

$$B = \bar{y}_{B^+} - \bar{y}_{B^-} = \frac{1}{4n}\left[b + ab + bc + abc - a - c - ac - (1)\right] \tag{13.17}$$

and the effect of *C* is the average difference between the four runs in the top face of the cube and the four in the bottom, or

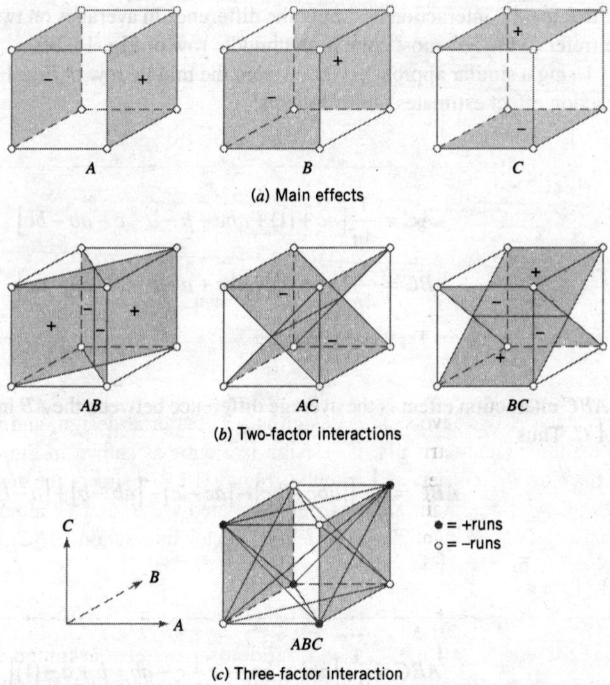

■ FIGURE 13.24 Geometric presentation of contrasts corresponding to the main effects and interaction in the 2^3 design.

$$C = \bar{y}_{C^+} - \bar{y}_{C^-} = \frac{1}{4n}[c + ac + bc + abc - a - b - ab - (1)] \tag{13.18}$$

The top row of Fig. 13.24 shows how the main effects of the three factors are computed.

Now consider the two-factor interaction *AB*. When *C* is at the low level, *AB* is simply the average difference in the *A* effect at the two levels of *B*, or

$$AB(C\text{ low}) = \frac{1}{2n}[ab - b] - \frac{1}{2n}[a - (1)]$$

Similarly, when *C* is at the high level, the *AB* interaction is

$$AB(C\text{ high}) = \frac{1}{2n}[abc - bc] - \frac{1}{2n}[ac - c]$$

The *AB* interaction is the average of these two components, or

$$AB = \frac{1}{4n}[ab + (1) + abc + c - b - a - bc - ac] \tag{13.19}$$

Note that the AB interaction is simply the difference in averages on two diagonal planes in the cube (refer to the left-most cube in the middle row of Fig. 13.24).

Using a similar approach, we see from the middle row of Fig. 13.24 that the AC and BC interaction effect estimates are as follows:

$$AC = \frac{1}{4n}\left[ac + (1) + abc + b - a - c - ab - bc\right] \tag{13.20}$$

$$BC = \frac{1}{4n}\left[bc + (1) + abc + a - b - c - ab - ac\right] \tag{13.21}$$

The ABC interaction effect is the average difference between the AB interaction at the two levels of C. Thus

$$ABC = \frac{1}{4n}\left\{\left[abc - bc\right] - \left[ac - c\right] - \left[ab - b\right] + \left[a - (1)\right]\right\}$$

or

$$ABC = \frac{1}{4n}\left[abc - bc - ac + c - ab + b + a - (1)\right] \tag{13.22}$$

This effect estimate is illustrated in the bottom row of Fig. 13.24.

The quantities in brackets in equations (13.16) through (13.22) are contrasts in the eight factor-level combinations. These contrasts can be obtained from a table of plus and minus signs for the 2^3 design, shown in Table 13.11. Signs for the main effects (columns A, B, and C) are obtained by associating a plus with the high level and a minus with the low level. Once the signs for the main effects have been established, the signs for the remaining columns are found by multiplying the appropriate preceding columns, row by row. For example, the signs in column AB are the product of the signs in columns A and B.

■ **TABLE 13.11**
Signs for Effects in the 2^3 Design

Treatment Combination	Factorial Effect							
	I	*A*	*B*	*AB*	*C*	*AC*	*BC*	*ABC*
(1)	+	−	−	+	−	+	+	−
a	+	+	−	−	−	−	+	+
b	+	−	+	−	−	+	−	+
ab	+	+	+	+	−	−	−	−
c	+	−	−	+	+	−	−	+
ac	+	+	−	−	+	+	−	−
bc	+	−	+	−	+	−	+	−
abc	+	+	+	+	+	+	+	+

Table 13.11 has several interesting properties:

1. Except for the identity column I, each column has an equal number of plus and minus signs.
2. The sum of products of signs in any two columns is zero; that is, the columns in the table are *orthogonal*.
3. Multiplying any column by column I leaves the column unchanged; that is, I is an *identity element*.
4. The product of any two columns yields a column in the table; for example, $A \times B = AB$, and $AB \times ABC = A^2B^2C = C$, since any column multiplied by itself is the identity column.

The estimate of any main effect or interaction is determined by multiplying the factor-level combinations in the first column of the table by the signs in the corresponding main effect or interaction column, adding the result to produce a contrast, and then dividing the contrast by one-half the total number of runs in the experiment. Expressed mathematically,

$$\text{Effect} = \frac{\text{Contrast}}{n2^{k-1}} \tag{13.23}$$

The sum of squares for any effect is

$$SS = \frac{(\text{Contrast})^2}{n2^k} \tag{13.24}$$

EXAMPLE 13.7 A 2^3 Factorial Design

An experiment was performed to investigate the surface finish of a metal part. The experiment is a 2^3 factorial design in the factors feed rate (A), depth of cut (B), and tool angle (C), with $n = 2$ replicates. Table 13.12 presents the observed surface-finish data for this experiment, and the design is shown graphically in Fig. 13.25. Analyze and interpret the data from this experiment.

■ **TABLE 13.12**
Surface-Finish Data for Example 13.7

Run		Design Factors A	B	C	Surface Finish	Totals
1	(1)	−1	−1	−1	9, 7	16
2	*a*	1	−1	−1	10, 12	22
3	*b*	−1	1	−1	9, 11	20
4	*ab*	1	1	−1	12, 15	27
5	*c*	−1	−1	1	11, 10	21
6	*ac*	1	−1	1	10, 13	23
7	*bc*	−1	1	1	10, 8	18
8	*abc*	1	1	1	16, 14	30

(*continued*)

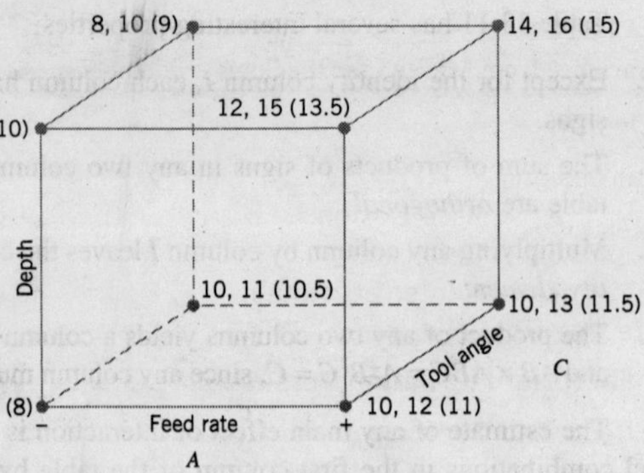

■ FIGURE 13.25 2^3 design for the surface-finish experiment in Example 13.7 (the numbers in parentheses are the average responses at each design point).

SOLUTION

The main effects may be estimated using equations (13.16) through (13.22). The effect of A, for example, is

$$A = \frac{1}{4n}[a + ab + ac + abc - b - c - bc - (1)]$$
$$= \frac{1}{4(2)}[22 + 27 + 23 + 30 - 20 - 21 - 18 - 16]$$
$$= \frac{1}{8}[27] = 3.375$$

and the sum of squares for A is found using equation (13.24):

$$SS_A = \frac{(\text{Contrast}_A)^2}{n2^k}$$
$$= \frac{(27)^2}{2(8)} = 45.5625$$

It is easy to verify that the other effect estimates and sums of squares are

$$B = 1.625 \qquad SS_B = 10.5625$$
$$C = 0.875 \qquad SS_C = 3.0625$$
$$AB = 1.375 \qquad SS_{AB} = 7.5625$$
$$AC = 0.125 \qquad SS_{AC} = 0.0625$$
$$BC = -0.625 \qquad SS_{BC} = 1.5625$$
$$ABC = 1.125 \qquad SS_{ABC} = 5.0625$$

From examining the magnitude of the effects, feed rate (factor A) is clearly dominant, followed by depth of cut (B) and the AB interaction, although the interaction effect is relatively small. The analysis of variance for the full factorial model is summarized in Table 13.13. Based on the P-values, it is clear that the feed rate (A) is highly significant.

■ TABLE 13.13
Analysis of Variance for the Surface-Finish Experiment

Source of Variation	Sum of Squares	Degrees of Freedom	Mean Square	F_0	P-value
A	45.5625	1	45.5625	18.69	2.54×10^{-3}
B	10.5625	1	10.5625	4.33	0.07
C	3.0625	1	3.0625	1.26	0.29
AB	7.5625	1	7.5625	3.10	0.12
AC	0.0625	1	0.0625	0.03	0.88
BC	1.5625	1	1.5625	0.64	0.45
ABC	5.0625	1	5.0625	2.08	0.19
Error	19.5000	8	2.4375		
Total	92.9375	15			

■ TABLE 13.14
Analysis of Variance from Minitab for the Surface-Finish Experiment

Factorial Design

Full Factorial Design

Factors:	3	Base Design:	3, 8
Runs:	16	Replicates:	2
Blocks:	none	Center pts (total):	0

All terms are free from aliasing

Fractional Factorial Fit: Finish versus A, B, C

Estimated Effects and Coefficients for Finish (coded units)

Term	Effect	Coef	SE Coef	T	P
Constant		11.0625	0.3903	28.34	0.000
A	3.3750	1.6875	0.3903	4.32	0.003
B	1.6250	0.8125	0.3903	2.08	0.071
C	0.8750	0.4375	0.3903	1.12	0.295
A*B	1.3750	0.6875	0.3903	1.76	0.116
A*C	0.1250	0.0625	0.3903	0.16	0.877
B*C	−0.6250	−0.3125	0.3903	−0.80	0.446
A*B*C	1.1250	0.5625	0.3903	1.44	0.188

Analysis of Variance for Finish (coded units)

Source	DF	Seq SS	Adj SS	Adj MS	F	P
Main Effects	3	59.187	59.187	19.729	8.09	0.008
2-Way Interactions	3	9.187	9.187	3.062	1.26	0.352
3-Way Interactions	1	5.062	5.062	5.062	2.08	0.188
Residual Error	8	19.500	19.500	2.437		
Pure Error	8	19.500	19.500	2.438		
Total	15	92.937				

Many computer programs analyze the 2^k factorial design. Table 13.14 is the output from Minitab. Although at first glance the two tables seem somewhat different, they actually provide the same information. The analysis of variance displayed in the lower portion of Table 13.14 presents F-ratios computed on important groups of model terms; main effects, two-way interactions, and the three-way interaction. The mean square for each group of model terms was obtained by combining the sums of squares for each model component and dividing by the number of degrees of freedom associated with that group of model terms.

A t-test is used to test the significance of each individual term in the model. These t-tests are shown in the upper portion of Table 13.14. Note that a "coefficient estimate" is given for each variable in the full factorial model. These are actually the estimates of the coefficients in the regression model that would be used to predict surface finish in terms of the variables in the full factorial model. Each t-value is computed according to

$$t_0 = \frac{\hat{\beta}}{s.e.\left(\hat{\beta}\right)}$$

where $\hat{\beta}$ is the coefficient estimate and $s.e.\ (\hat{\beta})$ is the estimated standard error of the coefficient. For a 2^k factorial design, the estimated standard error of the coefficient is

$$s.e.\left(\hat{\beta}\right) = \sqrt{\frac{\hat{\sigma}^2}{n2^k}}$$

We use the error or residual mean square from the analysis of variance as the estimate $\hat{\sigma}^2$. In our example,

$$s.e.\left(\hat{\beta}\right) = \sqrt{\frac{2.4375}{2\left(2^3\right)}} = 0.390312$$

as shown in Table 13.14. It is easy to verify that dividing any coefficient estimate by its estimated standard error produces the t-value for testing whether the corresponding regression coefficient is zero.

The t-tests in Table 13.14 are equivalent to the ANOVA F-tests in Table 13.13. You may have suspected this already, since the P-values in the two tables are identical to two decimal places. Furthermore, note that the square of any t-value in Table 13.14 produces the corresponding F-ratio value in Table 13.13.

(continued)

In general, the square of a t random variable with v degrees of freedom results in an F random variable with one numerator degree of freedom and v denominator degrees of freedom. This explains the equivalence of the two procedures used to conduct the analysis of variance for the surface-finish experiment data.

Based on the ANOVA results, we conclude that the full factorial model in all these factors is unnecessary, and that a reduced model including fewer variables is more appropriate. The main effects of A and B both have relatively small P-values (< 0.10), and this AB interaction is the next most important effect (P-value $\cong 0.12$). The regression model that we would use to represent this process is

$$y = \beta_0 + \beta_1 x_1 + \beta_2 x_2 + \beta_{12} x_1 x_2 + \varepsilon$$

where x_1 represents factor A, x_2 represents factor B, and $x_1 x_2$ represents the AB interaction. The regression coefficients $\hat{\beta}_1$, $\hat{\beta}_2$, and $\hat{\beta}_{12}$ are one-half the corresponding effect estimates and $\hat{\beta}_0$ is the grand average. Thus

$$\begin{aligned}\hat{y} &= 11.0625 + \left(\frac{3.375}{2}\right)x_1 + \left(\frac{1.625}{2}\right)x_2 + \left(\frac{1.375}{2}\right)x_1 x_2 \\ &= 11.0625 + 1.6875x_1 + 0.8125x_2 + 0.6875x_1 x_2\end{aligned}$$

Note that we can read the values of $\hat{\beta}_0$, $\hat{\beta}_1$, $\hat{\beta}_2$, and $\hat{\beta}_{12}$ directly from the "coefficient" column of Table 13.14.

This regression model can be used to predict surface finish at any point in the original experimental region. For example, consider the point where all three variables are at the low level. At this point, $x_1 = x_2 = -1$, and the predicted value is

$$\hat{y} = 11.0625 + 1.6875(-1) + 0.8125(-1) + 0.6875(-1)(-1) = 9.25$$

Figure 13.26 shows the predicted values at each point in the original experimental design.

The residuals can be obtained as the difference between the observed and predicted values of surface finish at each design point. For the point where all three factors A, B, and C are at the low level, the observed values of surface finish are 9 and 7, so the residuals are $9 - 9.25 = -0.25$ and $7 - 9.25 = -2.25$.

A normal probability plot of the residuals is shown in Fig. 13.27. Since the residuals lie approximately along a straight line, we do not suspect any severe nonnormality in the data. There are also no indications of outliers. It would also be helpful to plot the residuals versus the predicted values and against each of the factors A, B, and C. These plots do not indicate any potential model problems.

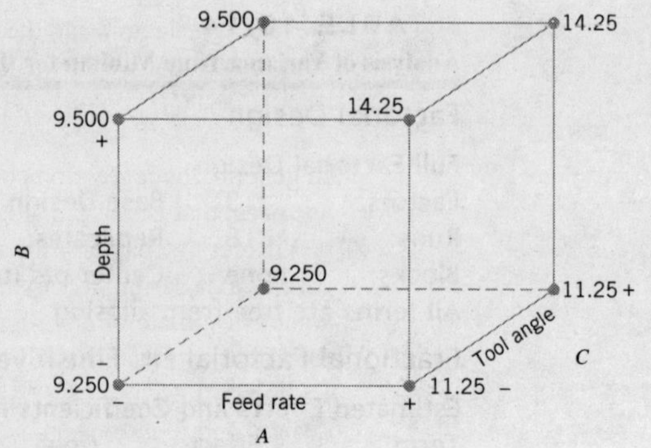

■ FIGURE 13.26 Predicted values of surface finish at each point in the original design, Example 13.7.

Finally, we can provide a practical interpretation of the results of our experiment. Both main effects A and B are positive, and since small values of the surface finish response are desirable, this would suggest that both A (feed rate) and B (depth of cut) should be run at the low level. However, the model has an interaction term, and the effect of this interaction should be taken into account when drawing conclusions. We could do this by examining an interaction plot, as in Example 13.6 (see Fig. 13.21). Alternatively, the cube plot of predicted responses in Fig. 13.26 can also be used for model interpretation. This figure indicates that the lowest values of predicted surface finish will be obtained when A and B are at the low level.

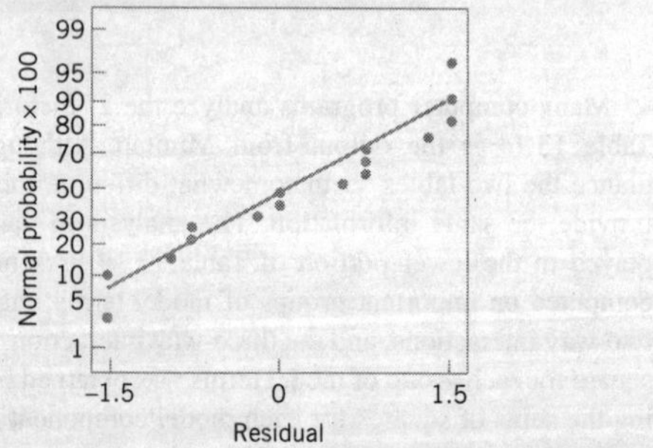

■ FIGURE 13.27 Normal probability plot of residuals, Example 13.7.

Some Comments on the Regression Model. In the two previous examples, we used a **regression model** to summarize the results of the experiment. In general, a regression model is an equation of the form

$$y = \beta_0 + \beta_1 x_1 + \beta_2 x_2 + \cdots \beta_k x_k + \varepsilon \tag{13.25}$$

where y is the response variable, the x's are a set of regressor or predictor variables, the β's are the regression coefficients, and ε is an error term, assumed to be NID$(0, \sigma^2)$. In our examples, we had $k = 2$ factors and the models had an interaction term, so the specific form of the regression model that we fit was

$$y = \beta_0 + \beta_1 x_1 + \beta_2 x_2 + \beta_{12} x_1 x_2 + \varepsilon$$

In general, the regression coefficients in these models are estimated using the **method of least squares;** that is, the $\hat{\beta}$'s are chosen so as to minimize the sum of the squares of the errors (the ε's). Refer to Chapter 4 for an introduction to least squares regression. However, in the special case of a 2^k design, it is extremely easy to find the least squares estimates of the β's. The least squares estimate of any regression coefficient β is simply one-half of the corresponding factor effect estimate. Recall that we have used this result to obtain the regression models in Examples 13.6 and 13.7. Also, please remember that this result only works for a 2^k factorial design, and it assumes that the x's are coded variables over the range $-1 \le x \le +1$ that represent the design factors.

It is very useful to express the results of a designed experiment in terms of a **model,** which will be a valuable aid in interpreting the experiment. Recall that we used the cube plot of predicted values from the model in Fig. 13.27 to find appropriate settings for feed rate and depth of cut in Example 13.7. More general graphical displays can also be useful. For example, consider the model for surface finish in terms of feed rate (x_1) and depth of cut (x_2) without the interaction term

$$\hat{y} = 11.0625 + 1.6875 x_1 + 0.8125 x_2$$

Note that the model was obtained simply by deleting the interaction term from the original model. This can only be done if the variables in the experimental design are **orthogonal,** as they are in a 2^k design. Figure 13.28 plots the predicted value of surface finish ($\hat{y}$) in terms of the two process variables x_1 and x_2. Figure 13.28*a* is a three-dimensional plot showing the plane of predicted response values generated by the regression model. This type of display is called a **response surface plot,** and the regression model used to generate the graph is often called a **first-order response surface model.** The graph in Fig. 13.28*b* is a two-dimensional **contour plot** obtained by looking down on the three-dimensional response surface plot and connecting points of constant surface finish (response) in the x_1–x_2 plane. The lines of constant response are straight lines because the response surface is first-order; that is, it contains only the main effects x_1 and x_2.

In Example 13.7, we actually fit a first-order model with interaction:

$$\hat{y} = 11.0625 + 1.6875 x_1 + 0.8125 x_2 + 0.6875 x_1 x_2$$

Figure 13.29*a* is the three-dimensional response surface plot for this model and Fig. 13.29*b* is the contour plot. Note that the effect of adding the interaction term to the model is to introduce **curvature** into the response surface; in effect, the plane is "twisted" by the interaction effect.

Inspection of a response surface makes interpretation of the results of an experiment very simple. For example, note from Fig. 13.29 that if we wish to minimize the surface-finish response, we need to run x_1 and x_2 at (or near) their low levels. We reached the same conclusion by inspection of the cube plot in Fig. 13.26. However, suppose we needed to obtain a particular value of surface finish, say 10.25 (the surface might need to be this rough so that a coating will adhere properly). Figure 13.29*b* indicates that there are many combinations of x_1 and x_2 that will allow the process to operate on the contour line $\hat{y} = 10.25$. The experimenter might select a set of operating conditions that maximized x_1 subject to x_1 and x_2 giving a predicted response on or near to the contour $\hat{y} = 10.25$, as this would satisfy the surface-finish objective while simultaneously making the feed rate as large as possible, which would maximize the production rate.

Response surface models have many uses. In Chapter 14 we will give an overview of some aspects of response surfaces and how they can be used for process improvement and optimization. However, note how useful the response surface was, even in this simple example. This is why we tell experimenters that **the objective of every designed experiment is a quantitative model of the process.**

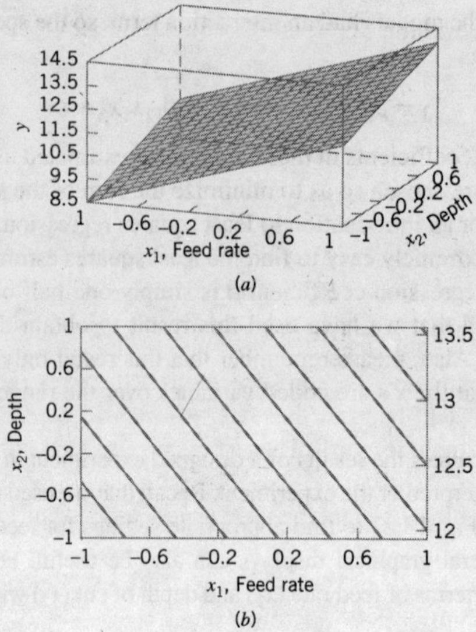

■ FIGURE 13.28 (*a*) Response surface for the model $\hat{y} = 11.0625 + 1.6875x_1 + 0.8125x_2$. (*b*) The contour plot.

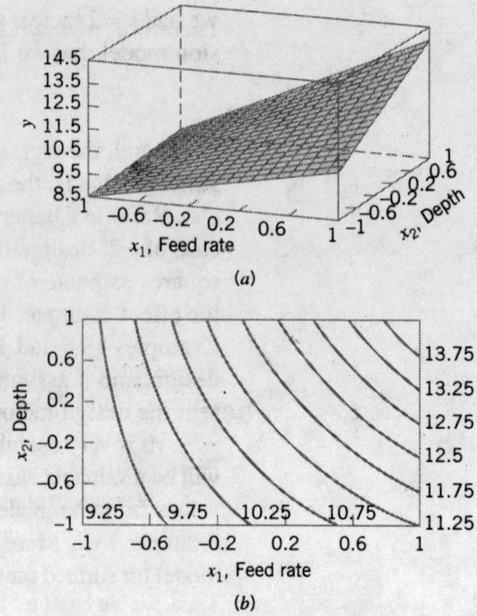

■ FIGURE 13.29 (*a*) Response surface for the model $\hat{y} = 11.0625 + 1.6875x_1 + 0.8125x_2 + 0.6875x_1x_2$. (*b*) The contour plot.

Projection of 2^k Designs. Any 2^k design will collapse or project into another two-level factorial design in fewer variables if one or more of the original factors are dropped. Usually this will provide additional insight into the remaining factors. For example, consider the surface-finish experiment. Since factor C and all its interactions are negligible, we could eliminate factor C from the design. The result is to collapse the cube in Fig. 13.25 into a square in the A-B plane; however, each of the four runs in the new design has four replicates. In general, if we delete h factors so that $r = k - h$ factors remain, the original 2^k design with n replicates will project into a 2^r design with $n2^h$ replicates.

Other Methods for Judging the Significance of Effects. The analysis of variance is a formal way to determine which effects are nonzero. Two other methods are useful. In the first method, we can calculate the standard errors of the effects and compare the magnitude of the effects to their standard errors. The second method uses normal probability plots to assess the importance of the effects.

The standard error of any effect estimate in a 2^k design is given by

$$s.e.\,(\text{Effect}) = \sqrt{\frac{\hat{\sigma}^2}{n2^{k-2}}} \tag{13.26}$$

where $\hat{\sigma}^2$ is an estimate of the experimental error variance σ^2. We usually take the error (or residual) mean square from the analysis of variance as the estimate $\hat{\sigma}^2$ of σ^2.

As an illustration for the surface-finish experiment, we find that $MS_E = \hat{\sigma}^2 = 2.4375$, and the standard error of each effect is

$$\begin{aligned} s.e.\,(\text{Effect}) &= \sqrt{\frac{\hat{\sigma}^2}{n2^{k-2}}} \\ &= \sqrt{\frac{2.4375}{(2)2^{3-2}}} \\ &= 0.78 \end{aligned}$$

Therefore, two standard deviation limits on the effect estimates are

$$A: \; 3.375 \pm 1.56$$
$$B: \; 1.625 \pm 1.56$$
$$C: \; 0.875 \pm 1.56$$
$$AB: \; 1.375 \pm 1.56$$
$$AC: \; 0.125 \pm 1.56$$
$$BC: \; -0.625 \pm 1.56$$
$$ABC: \; 1.125 \pm 1.56$$

These intervals are approximate 95% confidence intervals. They indicate that the two main effects A and B are important but that the other effects are not, since the intervals for all effects except A and B include zero. These conclusions are similar to those found in Example 13.7.

Normal probability plots can also be used to judge the significance of effects. We will illustrate that method in the next section.

13.5.3 A Single Replicate of the 2^k Design

As the number of factors in a factorial experiment grows, the number of effects that can be estimated also grows. For example, a 2^4 experiment has 4 main effects, 6 two-factor interactions, 4 three-factor interactions, and 1 four-factor interaction, whereas a 2^6 experiment has 6 main effects, 15 two-factor interactions, 20 three-factor interactions, 15 four-factor interactions, 6 five-factor interactions, and 1 six-factor interaction. In most situations the **sparsity of effects principle** applies; that is, the system is usually dominated by the main effects and low-order interactions. Three-factor and higher interactions are usually negligible. Therefore, when the number of factors is moderately large—say, $k \geq 4$ or 5—a common practice is to run only a single replicate of the 2^k design and then pool or combine the higher-order interactions as an estimate of error.

EXAMPLE 13.8 Characterizing a Plasma Etching Process

An article in *Solid State Technology* ("Orthogonal Design for Process Optimization and Its Application in Plasma Etching," May 1987, pp. 127–132) describes the application of factorial designs in developing a nitride etch process on a single-wafer plasma etcher. The process uses C_2F_6 as the reactant gas. It is possible to vary the gas flow, the power applied to the cathode, the pressure in the reactor chamber, and the spacing between the anode and the cathode (gap). Several response variables would usually be of interest in this process, but in this example we will concentrate on etch rate for silicon nitride. Perform an appropriate experiment to characterize the performance of this etching process with respect to the four process variables.

SOLUTION

The authors used a single replicate of a 2^4 design to investigate this process. Since it is unlikely that the three-factor and four-factor interactions are significant, we will tentatively plan to combine them as an estimate of error. The factor levels used in the design are shown here:

Design Factor Level	Gap A (cm)	Pressure B (m Torr)	C_2F_6 Flow C (SCCM)	Power D (W)
Low (−)	0.80	450	125	275
High (+)	1.20	550	200	325

Table 13.15 presents the data from the 16 runs of the 2^4 design. The design is shown geometrically in Fig. 13.30. Table 13.16 is the table of plus and minus signs for the 2^4 design. The signs in the columns of this table can be used to estimate the

(continued)

■ **TABLE 13.15**
The 2^4 Design for the Plasma Etch Experiment

Run	*A* (Gap)	*B* (Pressure)	*C* (C_2F_6 flow)	*D* (Power)	Etch Rate (Å/min)
1	−1	−1	−1	−1	550
2	1	−1	−1	−1	669
3	−1	1	−1	−1	604
4	1	1	−1	−1	650
5	−1	−1	1	−1	633
6	1	−1	1	−1	642
7	−1	1	1	−1	601
8	1	1	1	−1	635
9	−1	−1	−1	1	1037
10	1	−1	−1	1	749
11	−1	1	−1	1	1052
12	1	1	−1	1	868
13	−1	−1	1	1	1075
14	1	−1	1	1	860
15	−1	1	1	1	1063
16	1	1	1	1	729

factor effects. To illustrate, the estimate of the effect of gap on factor *A* is

$$A = \frac{1}{8}[a + ab + ac + abc + ad + abd + acd + abcd - (1) - b$$
$$-c - d - bc - bd - cd - bcd]$$
$$= \frac{1}{8}[669 + 650 + 642 + 635 + 749 + 868 + 860 + 729 - 550$$
$$-604 - 633 - 601 - 1037 - 1052 - 1075 - 1063]$$
$$= -101.625$$

Thus, the effect of increasing the gap between the anode and the cathode from 0.80 cm to 1.20 cm is to decrease the etch rate by 101.625 angstroms per minute. It is easy to verify that the complete set of effect estimates is

$A =$	−101.625	$AD =$	−153.625
$B =$	−1.625	$BD =$	−0.625
$AB =$	−7.875	$ABD =$	4.125
$C =$	7.375	$CD =$	−2.125
$AC =$	−24.875	$ACD =$	5.625
$BC =$	−43.875	$BCD =$	−25.375
$ABC =$	−15.625	$ABCD =$	−40.125
$D =$	306.125		

A very helpful method in judging the significance of factors in a 2^k experiment is to construct a **normal probability plot** of the effect estimates. If none of the effects is significant, then the estimates will behave like a random sample drawn from a normal distribution with zero mean, and the plotted effects will lie approximately along a straight line. Those effects that do not plot on the line are significant factors.

The normal probability plot of effect estimates from the plasma etch experiment is shown in Fig. 13.31. Clearly, the main effects of *A* and *D* and the *AD* interaction are significant, as they fall far from the line passing through the other points. The analysis of variance summarized in Table 13.17 confirms these

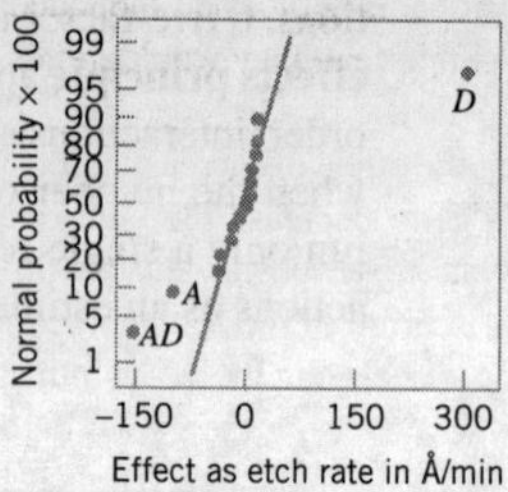

■ **FIGURE 13.31** Normal probability plot of effects, Example 13.8.

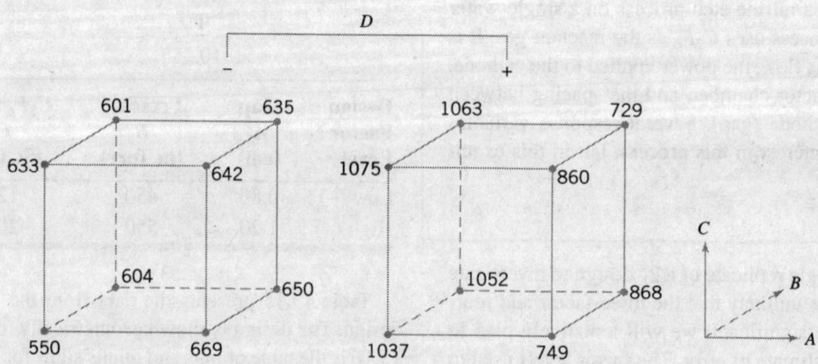

■ **FIGURE 13.30** The 2^4 design for Example 13.8. The etch rate response is shown at the corners of the cubes.

■ TABLE 13.16
Contrast Constants for the 2^4 Design

Run		A	B	AB	C	AC	BC	ABC	D	AD	BD	ABD	CD	ACD	BCD	ABCD
1	(1)	−	−	+	−	+	+	−	−	+	+	−	+	−	−	+
2	*a*	+	−	−	−	−	+	+	−	−	+	+	+	+	−	−
3	*b*	−	+	−	−	+	−	+	−	+	−	+	+	−	+	−
4	*ab*	+	+	+	−	−	−	−	−	−	−	−	+	+	+	+
5	*c*	−	−	+	+	−	−	+	−	+	+	−	−	+	+	−
6	*ac*	+	−	−	+	+	−	−	−	−	+	+	−	−	+	+
7	*bc*	−	+	−	+	−	+	−	−	+	−	+	−	+	−	+
8	*abc*	+	+	+	+	+	+	+	−	−	−	−	−	−	−	−
9	*d*	−	−	+	−	+	+	−	+	−	−	+	−	+	+	−
10	*ad*	+	−	−	−	−	+	+	+	+	−	−	−	−	+	+
11	*bd*	−	+	−	−	+	−	+	+	−	+	−	−	+	−	+
12	*abd*	+	+	+	−	−	−	−	+	+	+	+	−	−	−	−
13	*cd*	−	−	+	+	−	−	+	+	−	−	+	+	−	−	+
14	*acd*	+	−	−	+	+	−	−	+	+	−	−	+	+	−	−
15	*bcd*	−	+	−	+	−	+	−	+	−	+	−	+	−	+	−
16	*abcd*	+	+	+	+	+	+	+	+	+	+	+	+	+	+	+

findings. Note that in the analysis of variance we have pooled the three- and four-factor interactions to form the error mean square. If the normal probability plot had indicated that any of these interactions were important, they would not be included in the error term.

Since $A = -101.625$, the effect of increasing the gap between the cathode and anode is to decrease the etch rate. However, $D = 306.125$, so applying higher power levels will increase the etch rate. Figure 13.32 is a plot of the *AD* interaction. This plot indicates that the effect of changing the gap width at low power settings is small, but that increasing the gap at high power settings dramatically reduces the etch rate. High etch rates are obtained at high power settings and narrow gap widths.

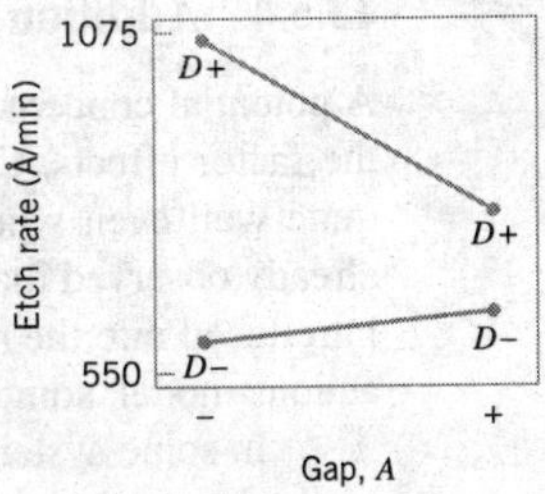

■ FIGURE 13.32 *AD* interaction in the plasma etch experiment.

■ TABLE 13.17
Analysis of Variance for the Plasma Etch Experiment

Source of Variation	Sum of Squares	Degrees of Freedom	Mean Square	F_0
A	41,310.563	1	41,310.563	20.28
B	10.563	1	10.563	< 1
C	217.563	1	217.563	< 1
D	374,850.063	1	374,850.063	183.99
AB	248.063	1	248.063	< 1
AC	2,475.063	1	2,475.063	1.21
AD	94,402.563	1	99,402.563	46.34
BC	7,700.063	1	7,700.063	3.78
BD	1.563	1	1.563	< 1
CD	18.063	1	18.063	< 1
Error	10,186.815	5	2,037.363	
Total	531,420.938	15		

(continued)

The regression model for this experiment is

$$\hat{y} = 776.0625 - \left(\frac{101.625}{2}\right)x_1 + \left(\frac{306.125}{2}\right)x_4 - \left(\frac{153.625}{2}\right)x_1x_4$$

For example, when both A and D are at the low level, the predicted value from this model is

$$\hat{y} = 776.0625 - \left(\frac{101.625}{2}\right)(-1) + \left(\frac{306.125}{2}\right)(-1) - \left(\frac{153.625}{2}\right)(-1)(-1) = 597$$

The four residuals at this run are

$$e_1 = 550 - 597 = -47$$
$$e_2 = 604 - 597 = 7$$
$$e_3 = 633 - 597 = 36$$
$$e_4 = 601 - 597 = 4$$

The residuals at the other three runs, (A high, D low), (A low, D high), and (A high, D high), are obtained similarly. A normal probability plot of the residuals is shown in Fig. 13.33. The plot is satisfactory.

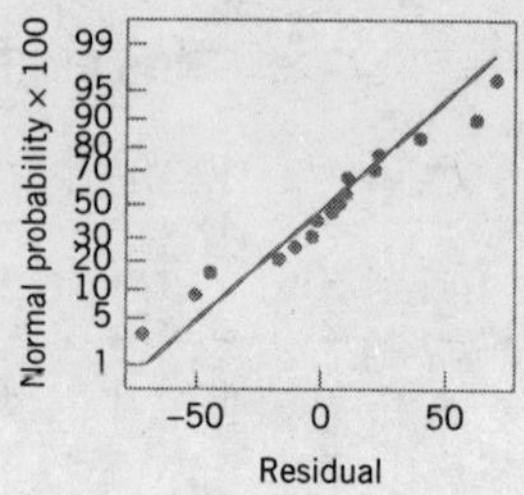

■ FIGURE 13.33
Normal probability plot of residuals, Example 13.8.

13.5.4 Addition of Center Points to the 2^k Design

A potential concern in the use of two-level factorial designs is the assumption of linearity in the factor effects. Of course, perfect linearity is unnecessary, and the 2^k system will work quite well even when the linearity assumption holds only approximately. In fact, we have already observed that when an interaction term is added to a main-effects model, curvature is introduced into the response surface. Since a 2^k design will support a main effects plus interactions model, some protection against curvature is already inherent in the design.

In some systems or processes, it will be necessary to incorporate **second-order effects** to obtain an adequate model. Consider the case of $k = 2$ factors. A model that includes second-order effects is

$$y = \beta_0 + \beta_1 x_1 + \beta_2 x_2 + \beta_{12} x_1 x_2 + \beta_{11} x_1^2 + \beta_{22} x_2^2 + \varepsilon \qquad (13.27)$$

where the coefficients β_{11} and β_{22} measure pure quadratic effects. Equation (13.27) is a **second-order response surface model.** This model cannot be fitted using a 2^2 design, because to fit a quadratic model, all factors must be run at at least three levels. It is important, however, to be able to determine whether the pure quadratic terms in equation (13.27) are needed.

There is a method of adding one point to a 2^k factorial design that will provide some protection against pure quadratic effects (in the sense that one can test to determine if the quadratic terms are necessary). Furthermore, if this point is replicated, then an independent estimate of experimental error can be obtained. The method consists of adding **center points** to the 2^k design. These center points consist of n_C replicates run at the point $x_i = 0$ ($i = 1, 2, \ldots, k$). One important reason for adding the replicate runs at the design center is that center points do not impact the usual effect estimates in a 2^k design. We assume that the k factors are quantitative; otherwise, a "middle" or center level of the factor would not exist.

To illustrate the approach, consider a 2^2 design with one observation at each of the factorial points (−, −), (+, −), (−, +), and (+, +) and n_C observations at the center points

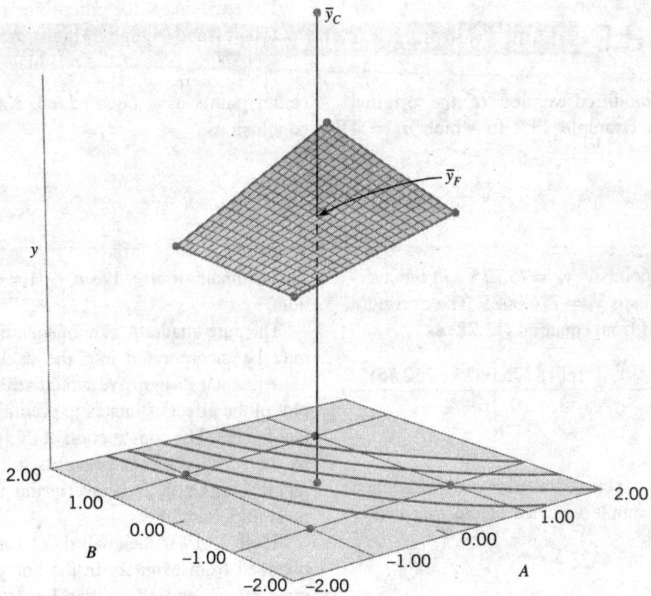

■ FIGURE 13.34 A 2^2 design with center points.

(0, 0). Figure 13.34 illustrates the situation. Let $\bar{y}_F$ be the average of the four runs at the four factorial points, and let $\bar{y}_C$ be the average of the n_C runs at the center point. If the difference $\bar{y}_F - \bar{y}_C$ is small, then the center points lie on or near the plane passing through the factorial points, and there is no curvature. On the other hand, if $\bar{y}_F - \bar{y}_C$ is large, then curvature is present. A single-degree-of-freedom sum of squares for pure quadratic curvature is given by

$$SS_{\text{pure quadratic}} = \frac{n_F n_C (\bar{y}_F - \bar{y}_C)^2}{n_F + n_C} \tag{13.28}$$

where, in general, n_F is the number of factorial design points. This quantity may be compared to the error mean square to test for curvature.[1] More specifically, when points are added to the center of the 2^k design, then the model we may entertain is

$$y = \beta_0 + \sum_{j=1}^{k} \beta_j x_j + \sum_{i<j}\sum \beta_{ij} x_i x_j + \sum_{j=1}^{k} \beta_{jj} x_j^2 + \varepsilon$$

where the β_{jj} are pure quadratic effects. The test for curvature actually tests the hypotheses

$$H_0\colon \sum_{j=1}^{k} \beta_{jj} = 0$$

$$H_1\colon \sum_{j=1}^{k} \beta_{jj} \neq 0$$

Furthermore, if the factorial points in the design are unreplicated, we may use the n_C center points to construct an estimate of error with $n_C - 1$ degrees of freedom.

[1] A t-test can also be used; see Section S13.2 of the supplemental text material for this chapter.

EXAMPLE 13.9 Adding Center Points to a 2^k Design

Table 13.18 presents a modified version of the original unreplicated 2^4 design in Example 13.8 to which $n_C = 4$ center points have been added. Analyze the data and draw conclusions.

SOLUTION

The average of the center points is $\bar{y}_C = 752.75$ and the average of the 16 factorial points is $\bar{y}_F = 776.0625$. The curvature sum of squares is computed from equation (13.28) as

$$SS_{\text{pure quadratic}} = \frac{n_F n_C(\bar{y}_F - \bar{y}_C)^2}{n_F + n_C} = \frac{16(4)(776.0625 - 752.75)^2}{16+4}$$
$$= 1739.1$$

Furthermore, an estimate of experimental error can be obtained by simply calculating the sample variance of the four center points as follows:

$$\hat{\sigma}^2 = \frac{\sum_{i=17}^{20}(y_i - 752.75)^2}{3} = \frac{3122.7}{3} = 1040.92$$

This estimate of error has $n_C - 1 = 4 - 1 = 3$ degrees of freedom.

The pure quadratic sum of squares and the estimate of error may be incorporated into the analysis of variance for this experimental design. We would still use a normal probability plot of the effect estimates to preliminarily identify the important factors. The construction of this plot would not be affected by the addition of center points in the design, we would still identify A (Gap), D (Power), and the AD interaction as the most important effect.

Table 13.19 is the analysis of variance for this experiment obtained from Minitab. In the analysis, we included all four main effects and all six two-factor interactions in the model (just as we did in Example 13.8; see also Table 13.17). Note also that the pure quadratic sum of squares from equation

■ **TABLE 13.18**
The 2^4 Design for the Plasma Etch Experiment

Run	*A* (Gap)	*B* (Pressure)	*C* (C_2F_6 flow)	*D* (Power)	Etch Rate (Å/min)
1	−1	−1	−1	−1	550
2	1	−1	−1	−1	669
3	−1	1	−1	−1	604
4	1	1	−1	−1	650
5	−1	−1	1	−1	633
6	1	−1	1	−1	642
7	−1	1	1	−1	601
8	1	1	1	−1	635
9	−1	−1	−1	1	1037
10	1	−1	−1	1	749
11	−1	1	−1	1	1052
12	1	1	−1	1	868
13	−1	−1	1	1	1075
14	1	−1	1	1	860
15	−1	1	1	1	1063
16	1	1	1	1	729
17	0	0	0	0	706
18	0	0	0	0	764
19	0	0	0	0	780
20	0	0	0	0	761

■ TABLE 13.19
Analysis of Variance Output from Minitab for Example 13.9

Estimated Effects and Coefficients for Etch Rate (coded units)

Term	Effect	Coef	SE Coef	T	P
Constant		776.06	10.20	76.11	0.000
A	-101.62	-50.81	10.20	-4.98	0.001
B	-1.63	-0.81	10.20	-0.08	0.938
C	7.37	3.69	10.20	0.36	0.727
D	306.12	153.06	10.20	15.01	0.000
A*B	-7.88	-3.94	10.20	-0.39	0.709
A*C	-24.88	-12.44	10.20	-1.22	0.257
A*D	-153.63	-76.81	10.20	-7.53	0.000
B*C	-43.87	-21.94	10.20	-2.15	0.064
B*D	-0.63	-0.31	10.20	-0.03	0.976
C*D	-2.13	-1.06	10.20	-0.10	0.920
Ct Pt		-23.31	22.80	-1.02	0.337

Analysis of Variance for Etch (coded units)

Source	DF	Seq SS	Adj SS	Adj MS	F	P
Main Effects	4	416389	416389	104097	62.57	0.000
2-Way Interactions	6	104845	104845	17474	10.50	0.002
Curvature	1	1739	1739	1739	1.05	0.337
Residual Error	8	13310	13310	1664		
Lack of Fit	5	10187	10187	2037	1.96	0.308
Pure Error	3	3123	3123	1041		
Total	19	536283				

13.28 is called the "curvature" sum of squares, and the estimate of error calculated from the $n_C = 4$ center points is called the "pure error" sum of squares in Table 13.19. The "lack-of-fit" sum of squares in Table 13.19 is actually the total of the sums of squares for the three-factor and four-factor interactions. The F-test for lack of fit is computed as

$$F_0 = \frac{MS_{\text{lack of fit}}}{MS_{\text{pure error}}} = \frac{2037}{1041} = 1.96$$

and is not significant, indicating that none of the higher-order interaction terms is important. This computer program combines the pure error and lack-of-fit sum of squares to form a residual sum of squares with eight degrees of freedom. This residual sum of squares is used to test for pure quadratic curvature with

$$F_0 = \frac{MS_{\text{curvature}}}{MS_{\text{residual}}} = \frac{1739}{1664} = 1.05$$

The P-value in Table 13.19 associated with this F-ratio indicates that there is no evidence of pure quadratic curvature.

The upper portion of Table 13.19 shows the regression coefficient for each model effect, the corresponding t-value, and the P-value. Clearly the main effects of A and D and the AD interaction are the three largest effects.

13.5.5 Blocking and Confounding in the 2^k Design

It is often impossible to run all of the observations in a 2^k factorial design under constant or homogeneous conditions. For example, it might not be possible to conduct all the tests on one shift or use material from a single batch. When this problem occurs, **blocking** is an excellent technique for eliminating the unwanted variation that could be caused by the nonhomogeneous conditions. If the design is replicated, and if the block is of sufficient size, then one approach is to run each replicate in one **block** (set of homogeneous conditions). For example, consider a 2^3 design that is to be replicated twice. Suppose that it takes about 1 h to complete each run. Then by running the eight runs from replicate one on one day and the eight runs from the second replicate on another day, any time effect, or difference between how the process works on the two days, can be eliminated. Thus, the two days became the two blocks in the design. The average difference between the responses on the two days is the block effect. For more introductory material about blocking and how it is used to eliminate the effect of a nuisance factor, see Section S13.3 of the supplemental material for this chapter.

Sometimes we cannot run a complete replicate of a factorial design under homogeneous experimental conditions. **Confounding** is a design technique for running a factorial experiment in blocks, where the block size is smaller than the number of runs in one complete replicate. The technique causes certain interactions to be indistinguishable from or **confounded with blocks.** We will illustrate confounding in the 2^k factorial design in 2^p blocks, where $p < k$.

Consider a 2^2 design. Suppose that each of the $2^2 = 4$ runs require 4 h of laboratory analysis. Thus, two days are required to perform the experiment. If days are considered as blocks, then we must assign two of the four runs to each day.

Consider the design shown in Fig. 13.35. Note that block 1 contains the runs (1) and *ab* and that block 2 contains *a* and *b*. The contrasts for estimating the main effects *A* and *B* are

$$\text{Contrast}_A = ab + a - b - (1)$$

$$\text{Contrast}_B = ab + b - a - (1)$$

These contrasts are unaffected by blocking since in each contrast there is one plus and one minus run from each block. That is, any difference between block 1 and block 2 will cancel out. The contrast for the *AB* interaction is

$$\text{Contrast}_{AB} = ab + (1) - a - b$$

Since the two runs with the plus sign, *ab* and (1), are in block 1 and the two with the minus sign, *a* and *b*, are in block 2, the block effect and *AB* interaction are identical. That is, *AB* is confounded with blocks.

The reason for this is apparent from the table of plus and minus signs for the 2^2 design, shown in Table 13.7. From this table, we see that all runs that have a plus on *AB* are assigned to block 1, and all runs that have a minus sign on *AB* are assigned to block 2.

This scheme can be used to confound any 2^k design in two blocks. As a second example, consider a 2^3 design, run in two blocks. Suppose we wish to confound the three-factor interaction *ABC* with blocks. From the table of plus and minus signs, shown in Table 13.11, we assign the runs that are minus on *ABC* to block 1 and those that are plus on *ABC* to block 2. The resulting design is shown in Fig. 13.36.

For more information on confounding, refer to Montgomery (2005, Chapter 8). This book contains guidelines for selecting factors to confound with blocks so that main effects

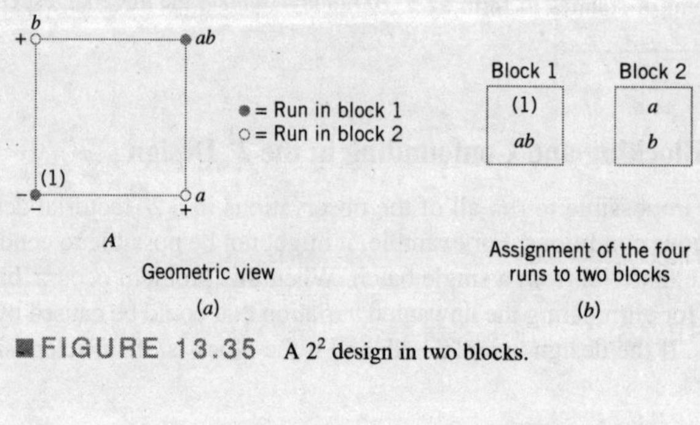

■ FIGURE 13.35 A 2^2 design in two blocks.

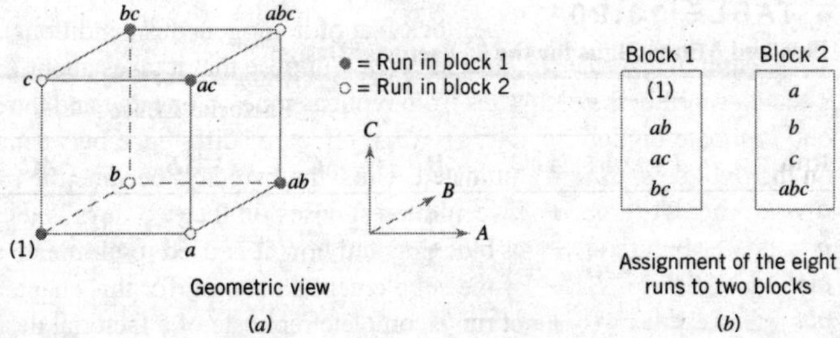

■ FIGURE 13.36 The 2^3 design in two blocks with ABC confounded.

and low-order interactions are not confounded. In particular, the book contains a table of suggested confounding schemes for designs with up to seven factors and a range of block sizes, some as small as two runs.

13.6 Fractional Replication of the 2^k Design

As the number of factors in a 2^k design increases, the number of runs required increases rapidly. For example, a 2^5 requires 32 runs. In this design, only 5 degrees of freedom correspond to main effects and 10 degrees of freedom correspond to two-factor interactions. If we can assume that certain high-order interactions are negligible, then a fractional factorial design involving fewer than the complete set of 2^k runs can be used to obtain information on the main effects and low-order interactions. In this section, we will introduce fractional replication of the 2^k design. For a more complete treatment, see Montgomery (2005, Chapter 8).

13.6.1 The One-Half Fraction of the 2^k Design

A one-half fraction of the 2^k design contains 2^{k-1} runs and is often called a 2^{k-1} fractional factorial design. As an example, consider the 2^{3-1} design—that is, a one-half fraction of the 2^3. The table of plus and minus signs for the 2^3 design is shown in Table 13.20. Suppose we select the four runs a, b, c, and abc as our one-half fraction. These runs are shown in the top half of Table 13.20. The design is shown geometrically in Fig. 13.37*a*.

Note that the 2^{3-1} design is formed by selecting only those runs that yield a plus on the ABC effect. Thus, ABC is called the **generator** of this particular fraction. Furthermore, the identity element I is also plus for the four runs, so we call

$$I = ABC$$

the **defining relation** for the design.

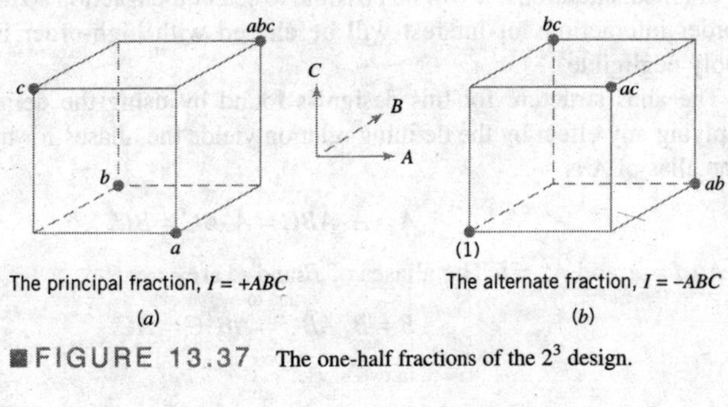

■ FIGURE 13.37 The one-half fractions of the 2^3 design.

■ **TABLE 13.20**
Plus and Minus Signs for the 2^3 Factorial Design

	Factorial Effect							
Run	I	A	B	C	AB	AC	BC	ABC
a	+	+	−	−	−	−	+	+
b	+	−	+	−	−	+	−	+
c	+	−	−	+	+	−	−	+
abc	+	+	+	+	+	+	+	+
ab	+	+	+	−	+	−	−	−
ac	+	+	−	+	−	+	−	−
bc	+	−	+	+	−	−	+	−
(1)	+	−	−	−	+	+	+	−

The runs in the 2^{3-1} designs yield three degrees of freedom associated with the main effects. From Table 13.20, we obtain the estimates of the main effects as

$$A = \frac{1}{2}[a - b - c + abc]$$

$$B = \frac{1}{2}[-a + b - c + abc]$$

$$C = \frac{1}{2}[-a - b + c + abc]$$

It is also easy to verify that the estimates of the two-factor interactions are

$$BC = \frac{1}{2}[a - b - c + abc]$$

$$AC = \frac{1}{2}[-a + b - c + abc]$$

$$AB = \frac{1}{2}[-a - b + c + abc]$$

Thus, the linear combination of observations in column A—say, $[A]$—estimates $A + BC$. Similarly, $[B]$ estimates $B + AC$, and $[C]$ estimates $C + AB$. Two or more effects that have this property are called **aliases.** In our 2^{3-1} design, A and BC are aliases, B and AC are aliases, and C and AB are aliases. Aliasing is the direct result of fractional replication. In many practical situations, it will be possible to select the fraction so that the main effects and low-order interactions of interest will be aliased with high-order interactions (which are probably negligible).

The alias structure for this design is found by using the defining relation $I = ABC$. Multiplying any effect by the defining relation yields the aliases for that effect. In our example, the alias of A is

$$A = A \cdot ABC = A^2BC = BC$$

since $A \cdot I = A$ and $A^2 = I$. The aliases of B and C are

$$B = B \cdot ABC = AB^2C = AC$$

and

$$C = C \cdot ABC = ABC^2 = AB$$

Now suppose that we had chosen the other one-half fraction, that is, the runs in Table 13.20 associated with minus on ABC. This design is shown geometrically in Fig. 13.37*b*. The defining relation for this design is $I = -ABC$. The aliases are $A = -BC$, $B = -AC$, and $C = -AB$. Thus, the effects A, B, and C with this particular fraction really estimate $A - BC$, $B - AC$, and $C - AB$. In practice, it usually does not matter which one-half fraction we select. The fraction with the plus sign in the defining relation is usually called the **principal fraction;** the other fraction is usually called the **alternate fraction.**

Sometimes we use **sequences** of fractional factorial designs to estimate effects. For example, suppose we had run the principal fraction of the 2^{3-1} design. From this design we have the following effect estimates:

$$[A] = A + BC$$
$$[B] = B + AC$$
$$[C] = C + AB$$

Suppose we are willing to assume at this point that the two-factor interactions are negligible. If they are, then the 2^{3-1} design has produced estimates of the three main effects A, B, and C. However, if after running the principal fraction we are uncertain about the interactions, it is possible to estimate them by running the alternate fraction. The alternate fraction produces the following effect estimates:

$$[A]' = A - BC$$
$$[B]' = B - AC$$
$$[C]' = C - AC$$

If we combine the estimates from the two fractions, we obtain the following:

Effect, *i*	$\frac{1}{2}([i]+[i]')$	$\frac{1}{2}([i]-[i]')$
$i = A$	$\frac{1}{2}(A + BC + A - BC) = A$	$\frac{1}{2}[A + BC - (A - BC)] = BC$
$i = B$	$\frac{1}{2}(B + AC + B - AC) = B$	$\frac{1}{2}[B + AC - (B - AC)] = AC$
$i = C$	$\frac{1}{2}(C + AB + C - AB) = C$	$\frac{1}{2}[C + AB - (C - AB)] = AB$

Thus, by combining a sequence of two fractional factorial designs, we can isolate both the main effects and the two-factor interactions. This property makes the fractional factorial design highly useful in experimental problems because we can run sequences of small, efficient experiments, combine information across *several* experiments, and take advantage of learning about the process we are experimenting with as we go along.

A 2^{k-1} design may be constructed by writing down the treatment combinations for a full factorial in $k - 1$ factors and then adding the kth factor by identifying its plus and minus levels with the plus and minus signs of the highest-order interaction $\pm ABC \cdots (K - 1)$. Therefore, a 2^{3-1} fractional factorial is obtained by writing down the full 2^2 factorial and then equating factor C to the $\pm AB$ interaction. Thus, to generate the principal fraction, we would use $C = +AB$ as follows:

Full 2^2		$2^{3-1}, I = ABC$		
A	B	A	B	$C = AB$
−	−	−	−	+
+	−	+	−	−
−	+	−	+	−
+	+	+	+	+

To generate the alternate fraction we would equate the last column to $C = -AB$.

EXAMPLE 13.10 A One-Half Fraction for the Plasma Etch Experiment

To illustrate the use of a one-half fraction, consider the plasma etch experiment described in Example 13.8. Suppose we decide to use a 2^{4-1} design with $I = ABCD$ to investigate the four factors gap (A), pressure (B), C_2F_6 flow rate (C), and power setting (D). Set up this design and analyze it using only the data from the full factorial that corresponds to the runs in the fraction.

SOLUTION

This design would be constructed by writing down a 2^3 in the factors A, B, and C and then setting $D = ABC$. The design and the resulting etch rates are shown in Table 13.21. The design is shown geometrically in Fig. 13.38.

In this design, the main effects are aliased with the three-factor interactions; note that the alias of A is

$$A \cdot I = A \cdot ABCD$$
$$A = A^2BCD$$
$$A = BCD$$

Similarly,

$$B = ACD$$
$$C = ABD$$
$$D = ABC$$

■ TABLE 13.21
The 2^{4-1} Design with Defining Relation $I = ABCD$

Run		A	B	C	$D = ABC$	Etch Rate
1	(1)	−	−	−	−	550
2	ad	+	−	−	+	749
3	bd	−	+	−	+	1052
4	ab	+	+	−	−	650
5	cd	−	−	+	+	1075
6	ac	+	−	+	−	642
7	bc	−	+	+	−	601
8	$abcd$	+	+	+	+	729

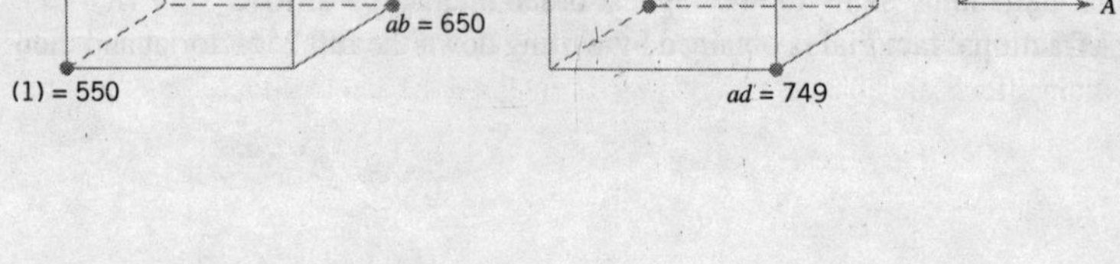

■ FIGURE 13.38 The 2^{4-1} design for Example 13.10.

The two-factor interactions are aliased with each other. For example, the alias of AB is CD:

$$AB \cdot I = AB \cdot ABCD$$
$$AB = A^2B^2CD$$
$$AB = CD$$

The other aliases are

$$AC = BD$$
$$AD = BC$$

The estimates of the main effects (and their aliases) are found using the four columns of signs in Table 13.21. For example, from column A we obtain

$$[A] = A + BCD = \frac{1}{4}(-550 + 749 - 1052 + 650 - 1075 + 642 - 601 + 729) = -127.00$$

The other columns produce

$$[B] = B + ACD = 4.00$$
$$[C] = C + ABD = 11.50$$

and

$$[D] = D + ABC = 290.5$$

Clearly, $[A]$ and $[D]$ are large, and if we believe that the three-factor interactions are negligible, then the main effects A (gap) and D (power setting) significantly affect the etch rate.

The interactions are estimated by forming the AB, AC, and AD columns and adding them to the table. The signs in the AB column are +, −, −, +, +, −, −, +, and this column produces the estimate

$$[AB] = AB + CD = \frac{1}{4}(550 - 749 - 1052 + 650 + 1075 - 642 - 601 + 729) = -10.00$$

From the AC and AD columns we find

$$[AC] = AC + BD = -25.50$$
$$[AD] = AD + BD = -197.50$$

The $[AD]$ estimate is large; the most straightforward interpretation of the results is that this is the A and D interaction. Thus, the results obtained from the 2^{4-1} design agree with the full factorial results in Example 13.8.

Normal Probability Plots and Residuals. The normal probability plot is very useful in assessing the significance of effects from a fractional factorial, especially when many effects are to be estimated. Residuals can be obtained from a fractional factorial by the regression model method shown previously. These residuals should be plotted against the predicted values, against the levels of the factors, and on normal probability paper as we have discussed before, both to assess the validity of the underlying model assumptions and to gain additional insight into the experimental situation.

Projection of the 2^{k-1} Design. If one or more factors from a one-half fraction of a 2^k can be dropped, the design will project into a full factorial design. For example, Fig. 13.39 presents a 2^{3-1} design. Note that this design will project into a full factorial in any two of the three original factors. Thus, if we think that at most two of the three factors are important, the 2^{3-1} design is an excellent design for identifying the significant factors. Sometimes experiments that seek to identify a relatively few significant factors from a larger number of factors are called **screening experiments.** This projection property is highly useful in factor screening because it allows negligible factors to be eliminated, resulting in a stronger experiment in the active factors that remain.

In the 2^{4-1} design used in the plasma etch experiment in Example 13.10, we found that two of the four factors (B and C) could be dropped. If we eliminate these two factors, the remaining columns in Table 13.21 form a 2^2 design in the factors A and D, with two replicates. This design is shown in Fig. 13.40.

Design Resolution. The concept of design resolution is a useful way to catalog fractional factorial designs according to the alias patterns they produce. Designs of resolution III, IV, and V are particularly important. The definitions of these terms and an example of each follow.

1. **Resolution III designs.** In these designs, no main effects are aliased with any other main effect, but main effects are aliased with two-factor interactions and two-factor interactions

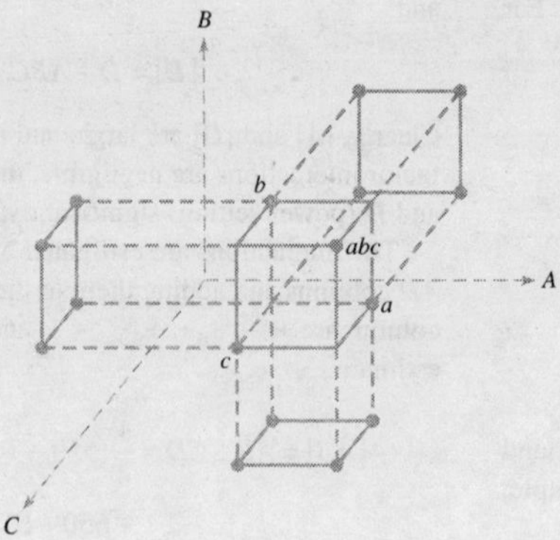

■ FIGURE 13.39 Projection of a 2^{3-1} design into three 2^2 designs.

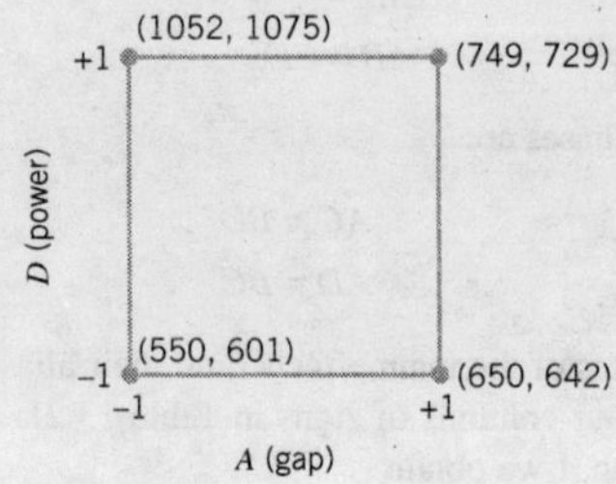

■ FIGURE 13.40 The 2^2 design obtained by dropping factors B and C from the plasma etch experiment.

may be aliased with each other. The 2^{3-1} design with $I = ABC$ is of resolution III. We usually employ a subscript Roman numeral to indicate design resolution; thus, this one-half fraction is a 2^{3-1}_{III} design.

2. **Resolution IV designs.** In these designs, no main effect is aliased with any other main effect or two-factor interaction, but two-factor interactions are aliased with each other. The 2^{4-1} design with $I = ABCD$ used in Example 13.10 is of resolution IV (2^{4-1}_{IV}).
3. **Resolution V designs.** In these designs, no main effect or two-factor interaction is aliased with any other main effect or two-factor interaction, but two-factor interactions are aliased with three-factor interactions. A 2^{5-1} design with $I = ABCDE$ is of resolution V (2^{5-1}_{V}).

Resolution III and IV designs are particularly useful in factor screening experiments. The resolution IV design provides very good information about main effects and will provide some information about two-factor interactions.

13.6.2 Smaller Fractions: The 2^{k-p} Fractional Factorial Design

Although the 2^{k-1} design is valuable in reducing the number of runs required for an experiment, we frequently find that smaller fractions will provide almost as much useful information at even greater economy. In general, a 2^k design may be run in a $\frac{1}{2^p}$ fraction called a 2^{k-p} fractional factorial design. Thus, a $\frac{1}{4}$ fraction is called a 2^{k-2} fractional factorial design, a $\frac{1}{8}$ fraction is called a 2^{k-3} design, a $\frac{1}{16}$ fraction is called a 2^{k-4} design, and so on.

To illustrate a $\frac{1}{4}$ fraction, consider an experiment with six factors and suppose that the engineer is interested primarily in main effects but would also like to get some information about the two-factor interactions. A 2^{6-1} design would require 32 runs and would have 31 degrees of freedom for estimation of effects. Since there are only 6 main effects and 15 two-factor interactions, the one-half fraction is inefficient—it requires too many runs. Suppose we consider a $\frac{1}{4}$ fraction, or a 2^{6-2} design. This design contains 16 runs and with 15 degrees of freedom will allow estimation of all six main effects, with some capability for examination of the two-factor interactions. To generate this design we would write down a 2^4 design in the factors A, B, C, and D, and then add two columns for E and F. Refer to Table 13.22. To find the new columns, we would select the two design generators $I = ABCE$ and $I = BCDF$. Thus, column E would be found from $E = ABC$ and column F would be $F = BCD$. Thus, columns $ABCE$ and $BCDF$ are equal to the identity column. However, we know that the product of any

TABLE 13.22

Construction of the 2^{6-2} Design with Generators $I = ABCE$ and $I = BCDF$

Run	A	B	C	D	$E = ABC$	$F = BCD$
1	−	−	−	−	−	−
2	+	−	−	−	+	−
3	−	+	−	−	+	+
4	+	+	−	−	−	+
5	−	−	+	−	+	+
6	+	−	+	−	−	+
7	−	+	+	−	−	−
8	+	+	+	−	+	−
9	−	−	−	+	−	+
10	+	−	−	+	+	+
11	−	+	−	+	+	−
12	+	+	−	+	−	−
13	−	−	+	+	+	−
14	+	−	+	+	−	−
15	−	+	+	+	−	+
16	+	+	+	+	+	+

two columns in the table of plus and minus signs for a 2^k is just another column in the table; therefore, the product of $ABCE$ and $BCDF$ or $ABCE\,(BCDF) = AB^2C^2DEF = ADEF$ is also an identity column. Consequently, the **complete defining relation** for the 2^{6-2} design is

$$I = ABCE = BCDF = ADEF$$

To find the alias of any effect, simply multiply the effect by each word in the above defining relation. The complete alias structure is shown here.

$$A = BCE = DEF = ABCDF \qquad AB = CE = ACDF = BDEF$$
$$B = ACE = CDF = ABDEF \qquad AC = BE = ABDF = CDEF$$
$$C = ABE = BDF = ACDEF \qquad AD = EF = BCDE = ABCF$$
$$D = BCF = AEF = ABCDE \qquad AE = BC = DF = ABCDEF$$
$$E = ABC = ADF = BCDEF \qquad AF = DE = BCEF = ABCD$$
$$F = BCD = ADE = ABCEF \qquad BD = CF = ACDE = ABEF$$
$$ABD = CDE = ACF = BEF \qquad BF = CD = ACEF = ABDE$$
$$ACD = BDE = ABF = CEF$$

Note that this is a resolution IV design; the main effects are aliased with three-factor and higher interactions, and two-factor interactions are aliased with each other. This design would provide very good information on the main effects and give some idea about the strength of the two-factor interactions.

Selection of Design Generators. In the foregoing example, we selected $I = ABCD$ and $I = BCDF$ as the generators to construct the 2^{6-2} fractional factorial design. This choice is not arbitrary; some generators will produce designs with more attractive alias structures than other generators. For a given number of factors and number of runs we wish to make, we want to select the generators so that the design has the highest possible resolution. Montgomery (2005) presents a set of designs of maximum resolution for 2^{k-p} designs with $p \leq 10$ factors. A portion of this table is reproduced in Table 13.23. In this table, each choice

■ **TABLE 13.23**

Selected 2^{k-p} Fractional Factorial Designs (from *Design and Analysis of Experiments*, 6th ed., by D. C. Montgomery, John Wiley, 2005)

Number of Factors, k	Fraction	Number of Runs	Design Generators
3	2^{3-1}_{III}	4	$C = \pm AB$
4	2^{4-1}_{IV}	8	$D = \pm ABC$
5	2^{5-1}_{V}	16	$E = \pm ABCD$
	2^{5-2}_{III}	8	$D = \pm AB$
			$E = \pm AC$
6	2^{6-1}_{VI}	32	$F = \pm ABCDE$
	2^{6-2}_{IV}	16	$E = \pm ABC$
			$F = \pm BCD$
	2^{6-3}_{III}	8	$D = \pm AB$
			$E = \pm AC$
			$F = \pm BC$
7	2^{7-1}_{VIII}	64	$G = \pm ABCDEF$
	2^{7-2}_{IV}	32	$F = \pm ABCD$
			$G = \pm ABDE$
	2^{7-3}_{IV}	16	$E = \pm ABC$
			$F = \pm BCD$
			$G = \pm ACD$
	2^{7-4}_{III}	8	$D = \pm AB$
			$E = \pm AC$
			$F = \pm BC$
			$G = \pm ABC$
8	2^{8-2}_{V}	64	$G = \pm ABCD$
			$H = \pm ABEF$
	2^{8-3}_{IV}	32	$F = \pm ABC$
			$G = \pm ABD$
			$H = \pm BCDE$
	2^{8-4}_{IV}	16	$E = \pm BCD$
			$F = \pm ACD$
			$G = \pm ABC$
			$H = \pm ABD$
9	2^{9-2}_{VI}	128	$H = \pm ACDFG$
			$J = \pm BCEFG$
	2^{9-3}_{IV}	64	$G = \pm ABCD$
			$H = \pm ACEF$
			$J = \pm CDEF$
	2^{9-4}_{IV}	32	$F = \pm BCDE$
			$G = \pm ACDE$
			$H = \pm ABDE$
			$J = \pm ABCE$
	2^{9-5}_{III}	16	$E = \pm ABC$
			$F = \pm BCD$
			$G = \pm ACD$
			$H = \pm ABD$
			$J = \pm ABCD$
10	2^{10-3}_{V}	128	$H = \pm ABCG$
			$J = \pm BCDE$
			$K = \pm ACDF$
	2^{10-4}_{IV}	64	$G = \pm BCDF$
			$H = \pm ACDF$
			$J = \pm ABDE$
			$K = \pm ABCE$
	2^{10-5}_{IV}	32	$F = \pm ABCD$
			$G = \pm ABCE$
			$H = \pm ABDE$
			$J = \pm ACDE$
			$K = \pm BCDE$
	2^{10-6}_{III}	16	$E = \pm ABC$
			$F = \pm BCD$
			$G = \pm ACD$
			$H = \pm ABD$
			$J = \pm ABCD$
			$K = \pm AB$

of generator is shown with a ± sign. If all generators are selected with a positive sign (as above), the principal fraction will result; selection of one or more negative signs for a set of generators will produce an alternate fraction.

EXAMPLE 13.11 A 2^{7-4} Fractional Factorial Design

Parts manufactured in an injection-molding process are experiencing excessive shrinkage, which is causing problems in assembly operations upstream from the injection-molding area. A quality-improvement team has decided to use a designed experiment to study the injection-molding process so that shrinkage can be reduced. The team decides to investigate seven factors: mold temperature (A), screw speed (B), holding time (C), cycle time (D), moisture content (E), gate size (F), and holding pressure (G). Each is examined at two levels, with the objective of learning how each factor affects shrinkage, as well as about how the factors interact. Set up an appropriate 16-run fractional factorial design.

SOLUTION

Table 13.23 indicates that the appropriate design is a 2_{IV}^{7-3} design, with generators $I = ABCE$, $I = BCDF$, and $I = ACDG$. The design is shown in Table 13.24 and the alias structure for the design is shown in Table 13.25. The last column of Table 13.24 gives the observed shrinkage ×10 for the test part produced at each of the 16 runs in the design.

A normal probability plot of the effect estimates from this experiment is shown in Fig. 13.41. The only large effects are $A = 13.8750$ (mold temperature), $B = 35.6250$ (screw speed), and the AB interaction ($AB = 11.8750$). In light of the alias relationships in Table 13.25, it seems reasonable to tentatively adopt those conclusions. The AB interaction plot in Fig. 13.42 shows that the process is very insensitive to temperature if screw speed is at the low level, but is very temperature-sensitive if screw speed is at the high level. With screw speed at the low level, the process should operate with average shrinkage around 10%, regardless of the temperature level chosen.

Based on this initial analysis, the team decided to set both mold temperature and screw speed at the low level. This set of conditions will reduce *mean* parts shrinkage to around 10%. However, the variability in shrinkage from part to part is still a potential problem. In effect, the mean shrinkage can be reduced effectively to nearly zero by appropriate modification of the tool; but the part-to-part variability in shrinkage over a production run could still cause problems in assembly, even if the average shrinkage over the run were nearly zero. One way to address this issue is to see whether any of the process variables affect *variability* in parts shrinkage.

■ **TABLE 13.24**
2_{IV}^{7-3} Design for the Injection-Molding Experiment, Example 13.11

Run	A	B	C	D	$E\ (=ABC)$	$F\ (=BCD)$	$G\ (=ACD)$	Observed Shrinkage (×10)
1	−	−	−	−	−	−	−	6
2	+	−	−	−	+	−	+	10
3	−	+	−	−	+	+	−	32
4	+	+	−	−	−	+	+	60
5	−	−	+	−	+	+	+	4
6	+	−	+	−	−	+	−	15
7	−	+	+	−	−	−	+	26
8	+	+	+	−	+	−	−	60
9	−	−	−	+	−	+	+	8
10	+	−	−	+	+	+	−	12
11	−	+	−	+	+	−	+	34
12	+	+	−	+	−	−	−	60
13	−	−	+	+	+	−	−	16
14	+	−	+	+	−	−	+	5
15	−	+	+	+	−	+	−	37
16	+	+	+	+	+	+	+	52

■ **TABLE 13.25**
Aliases for the 2_{IV}^{7-3} Design Used in Example 13.11

$A = BCE = DEF = CDG = BFG$	$AB = CE = FG$
$B = ACE = CDF = DEG = AFG$	$AC = BE = DG$
$C = ABE = BDF = ADG = EFG$	$AD = EF = CF$
$D = BCF = AEF = ACG = BEG$	$AE = BC = DF$
$E = ABC = ADF = BDG = CFG$	$AF = DE = BG$
$F = BCD = ADE = ABG = CEG$	$AG = CD = BF$
$G = ACD = BDE = ABF = CEF$	$BD = CF = EG$
$ABD = CDE = ACF = BEF = BCG = AEG = DFG$	

(continued)

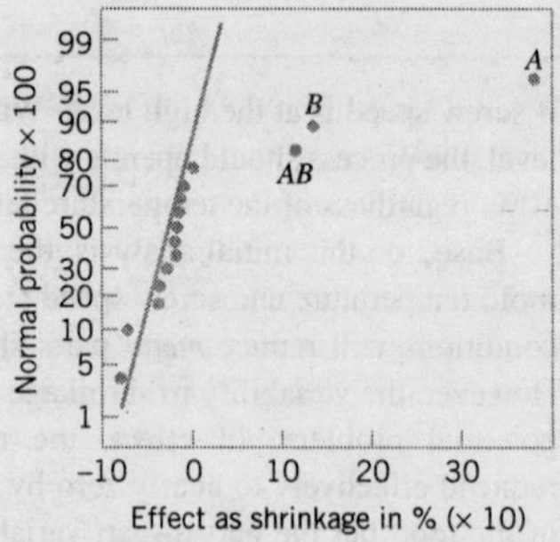

■ FIGURE 13.41 Normal probability plot of effects, Example 13.11.

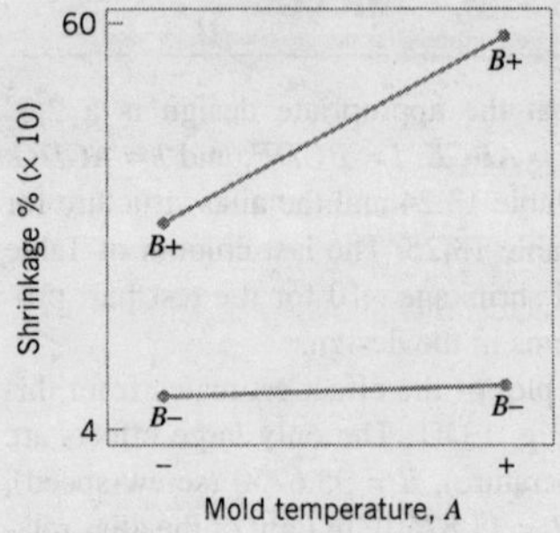

■ FIGURE 13.42 *AB* or mold temperature–screw speed interaction plot, Example 13.11.

Figure 13.43 presents the normal probability plot of the residuals. This plot appears satisfactory. The plots of residuals versus each variable were then constructed. One of these plots, that for residuals versus factor *C* (holding time), is shown in Fig. 13.44. The plot reveals that there is much less scatter in the residuals at low holding time than at high holding time. Now the residuals were obtained by first fitting a model for predicted shrinkage

$$\hat{y} = 27.3125 + 6.9375x_1 + 17.8125x_2 + 5.9375x_1x_2$$

where x_1, x_2, and x_1x_2 are coded variables that correspond to the factors *A*, *B*, and the *AB* interaction, respectively. The residuals are then

$$e = y - \hat{y}$$

The regression model used to produce the residuals essentially removes the *location* effects of *A*, *B*, and *AB* from the data; the residuals therefore contain information about unexplained variability. Figure 13.44 indicates that there is a *pattern* in that variability and that variability in parts shrinkage may be smaller when holding time is at the low level. Note that this analysis assumes that the model for the location effects is a good one, and that it adequately models the mean of the process over the factor space.

Figure 13.45 shows the data from this experiment projected onto a cube in the factors *A*, *B*, and *C*. The average observed shrinkage and the range of observed shrinkage are shown at each corner of the cube. From inspection of this graph, we see that running the process with screw speed (*B*) at the low level is the key to reducing average parts shrinkage. If *B* is low, virtually any combination of temperature (*A*) and holding time (*C*) will result in low values of average parts shrinkage. However, from examining the ranges of the shrinkage values at each corner of the cube, it is immediately clear that holding time (*C*) at the low level is the only reasonable choice if we wish to keep the part-to-part variability in shrinkage low during a production run.

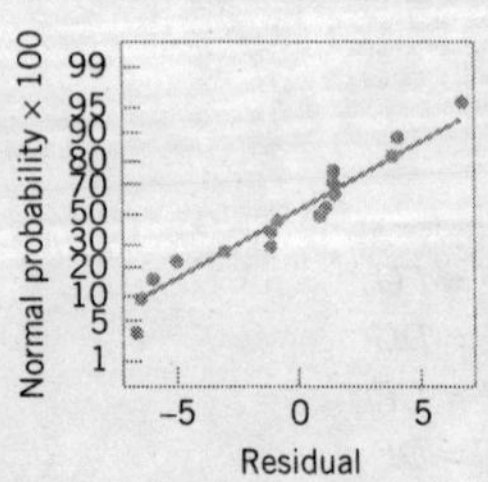

■ FIGURE 13.43 Normal probability plot of residuals, Example 13.11.

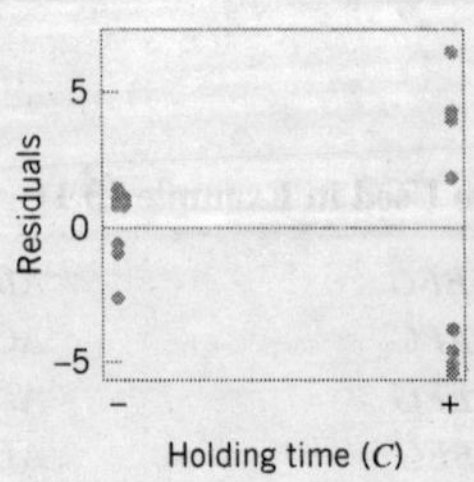

■ FIGURE 13.44 Residuals versus holding time (*C*), Example 13.11.

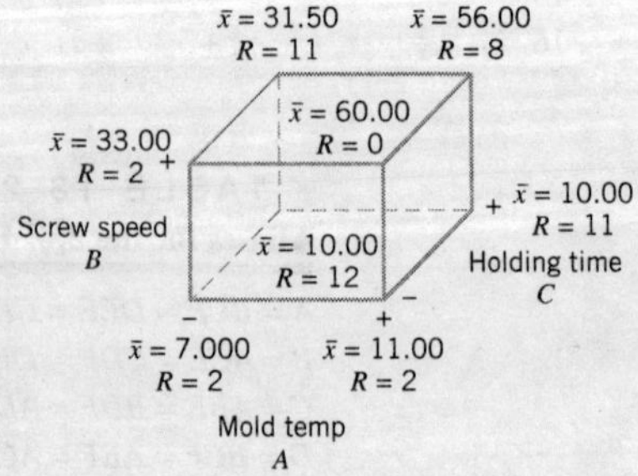

■ FIGURE 13.45 Average and range of shrinkage in factors *A*, *B*, *C*, Example 13.11

Important Terms and Concepts

2^k factorial designs
2^{k-p} fractional factorial designs
Aliasing
Analysis of variance (ANOVA)
Analysis procedure for factorial designs
Blocking
Center points in 2^k and 2^{k-p} factorial designs
Completely randomized design
Confounding
Contour plot
Controllable process variables
Curvature in the response function
Defining relation for a fractional factorial design
Factorial design
Fractional factorial design
Generators for a fractional factorial design
Guidelines for planning experiments
Interaction
Main effect of a factor
Normal probability plot of effects
Orthogonal design
Pre-experimental planning
Projection of 2^k and 2^{k-p} factorial designs
Regression model representation of experimental results
Residual analysis
Residuals
Resolution of a fractional factorial design
Response surface
Screening experiments
Sequential experimentation
Sparsity of effects principle
Two-factor interaction

Exercises

13.1. A process engineer is trying to improve the life of a cutting tool. He has run a 2^3 experiment using cutting speed (A), metal hardness (B), and cutting angle (C) as the factors. The data from two replicates are shown in Table 13E.1.
(a) Do any of the three factors affect tool life?
(b) What combination of factor levels produces the longest tool life?
(c) Is there a combination of cutting speed and cutting angle that always gives good results regardless of metal hardness?

TABLE 13E.1
Data for the Experiment in Exercise 13.1.

	Replicate	
Run	**I**	**II**
(1)	221	311
a	325	435
b	354	348
ab	552	472
c	440	453
ac	406	377
bc	605	500
abc	392	419

13.2. Find the residuals from the tool life experiment in Exercise 13.1. Construct a normal probability plot of the residuals. Plot the residuals versus the predicted values. Comment on the plots.

13.3. An article in *Industrial Quality Control* (1956, pp. 5–8) describes an experiment to investigate the effect of glass type and phosphor type on the brightness of a television tube. The response measured is the current necessary (in microamps) to obtain a specified brightness level. The data are shown in Table 13E.2. Analyze the data and draw conclusions.

TABLE 13E.2
Data for Exercise 13.3.

	Phosphor Type		
Glass Type	**1**	**2**	**3**
1	280	300	290
	290	310	285
	285	295	290
2	230	260	220
	235	240	225
	240	235	230

TABLE 13E.3
Taste-Text Experiment for Exercise 13.4.

Treatment Combination	Replicate I	Replicate II
(1)	188	195
a	172	180
b	179	187
ab	185	178
c	175	180
ac	183	178
bc	190	180
abc	175	168
d	200	193
ad	170	178
bd	189	181
abd	183	188
cd	201	188
acd	181	173
bcd	189	182
abcd	178	182

13.4. Four factors are thought to possibly influence the taste of a soft-drink beverage: type of sweetener (A), ratio of syrup to water (B), carbonation level (C), and temperature (D). Each factor can be run at two levels, producing a 2^4 design. At each run in the design, samples of the beverage are given to a test panel consisting of 20 people. Each tester assigns a point score from 1 to 10 to the beverage. Total score is the response variable, and the objective is to find a formulation that maximizes total score. Two replicates of this design are run, and the results are shown in Table 13E.3. Analyze the data and draw conclusions.

13.5. Consider the experiment in Exercise 13.4. Plot the residuals against the levels of factors A, B, C, and D. Also construct a normal probability plot of the residuals. Comment on these plots.

13.6. Find the standard error of the effects for the experiment in Exercise 13.4. Using the standard errors as a guide, what factors appear significant?

13.7. Suppose that only one replicate of the 2^4 design in Exercise 13.4 could be run, and we could only conduct eight tests each day. Set up a design that would block out the day effect. Show specifically which runs would be made on each day.

13.8. Suppose that only the data from replicate I in Exercise 13.4 were available. Analyze the data and draw appropriate conclusions.

13.9. A 2^4 factorial design has been run in a pilot plant to investigate the effect of four factors on the molecular weight of a polymer. The data from this experiment are as follows (values are coded by dividing by 10).

(1) = 88	d = 86
a = 80	ad = 81
b = 89	bd = 85
ab = 87	abd = 86
c = 86	cd = 85
ac = 81	acd = 79
bc = 82	bcd = 84
abc = 80	$abcd$ = 81

(a) Construct a normal probability plot of the effects. Which effects are active?
(b) Construct an appropriate model. Fit this model and test for significant effects.
(c) Analyze the residuals from this model by constructing a normal probability plot of the residuals and plotting the residuals versus the predicted values of y.

13.10. Show how a 2^5 experiment could be set up in two blocks of 16 runs each. Specifically, which runs would be made in each block?

13.11. R. D. Snee ("Experimenting with a Large Number of Variables," in *Experiments in Industry: Design, Analysis and Interpretation of Results*, by R. D. Snee, L. B. Hare, and J. B. Trout, editors, ASQC, 1985) describes an experiment in which a 2^{5-1} design with $I = ABCDE$ was used to investigate the effects of five factors on the color of a chemical product. The factors were A = solvent/reactant, B = catalyst/reactant, C = temperature, D = reactant purity, and E = reactant pH. The results obtained are as follows:

e = −0.63	d = 6.79
a = 2.51	ade = 6.47
b = 2.68	bde = 3.45
abe = 1.66	abd = 5.68
c = 2.06	cde = 5.22
ace = 1.22	acd = 4.38
bce = −2.09	bcd = 4.30
abc = 1.93	$abcde$ = 4.05

(a) Prepare a normal probability plot of the effects. Which effects seem active? Fit a model using these effects.
(b) Calculate the residuals for the model you fit in part (a). Construct a normal probability plot of

the residuals and plot the residuals versus the fitted values. Comment on the plots.

(c) If any factors are negligible, collapse the 2^{5-1} design into a full factorial in the active factors. Comment on the resulting design and interpret the results.

13.12. Reconsider the data in Exercise 13.9. Suppose that four center points were added to this experiment. The molecular weights at the center point are 90, 87, 86, and 93.

(a) Analyze the data as you did in Exercise 13.9, but include a test for curvature.

(b) If curvature is significant in an experiment such as this one, describe what strategy you would pursue next to improve your model of the process.

13.13. An article in *Industrial and Engineering Chemistry* ("More on Planning Experiments to Increase Research Efficiency," 1970, pp. 60–65) uses a 2^{5-2} design to investigate the effect of A = condensation temperature, B = amount of material 1, C = solvent volume, D = condensation time, and E = amount of material 2, on yield. The results obtained are as follows:

$e = 23.2$	$cd = 23.8$
$ab = 15.5$	$ace = 23.4$
$ad = 16.9$	$bde = 16.8$
$bc = 16.2$	$abcde = 18.1$

(a) Verify that the design generators used were $I = ACE$ and $I = BDE$.

(b) Write down the complete defining relation and the aliases from this design.

(c) Estimate the main effects.

(d) Prepare an analysis of variance table. Verify that the AB and AD interactions are available to use as error.

(e) Plot the residuals versus the fitted values. Also construct a normal probability plot of the residuals. Comment on the results.

13.14. An engineer has performed an experiment to study the effect of four factors on the surface roughness of a machined part. The factors (and their levels) are A = tool angle (12, 15), B = cutting fluid viscosity (300, 400), C = feed rate (10, 15 in/min), and D = cutting fluid cooler used (no, yes). The data from this experiment (with the factors coded to the usual +1, −1 levels) are shown in Table 13E.4.

(a) Estimate the factor effects. Plot the effect estimates on a normal probability plot and select a tentative model.

(b) Fit the model identified in part (a) and analyze the residuals. Is there any indication of model inadequacy?

TABLE 13E.4
Surface Roughness Experiment for Exercise 13.14

Run	A	B	C	D	Surface Roughness
1	−	−	−	−	0.00340
2	+	−	−	−	0.00362
3	−	+	−	−	0.00301
4	+	+	−	−	0.00182
5	−	−	+	−	0.00280
6	+	−	+	−	0.00290
7	−	+	+	−	0.00252
8	+	+	+	−	0.00160
9	−	−	−	+	0.00336
10	+	−	−	+	0.00344
11	−	+	−	+	0.00308
12	+	+	−	+	0.00184
13	−	−	+	+	0.00269
14	+	−	+	+	0.00284
15	−	+	+	+	0.00253
16	+	+	+	+	0.00163

(c) Repeat the analysis from parts (a) and (b) using $1/y$ as the response variable. Is there an indication that the transformation has been useful?

(d) Fit the model in terms of the coded variables that you think can be used to provide the best predictions of the surface roughness. Convert this prediction equation into a model in the natural variables.

13.15. An article by L. B. Hare ("In the Soup: A Case Study to Identify Contributors to Filling Variability." *Journal of Quality Technology*, vol. 20, pp. 36–43) describes a factorial experiment used to study the filling variability of dry soup mix packages. The factors are A = number of mixing ports through which the vegetable oil was added (1, 2), B = temperature surrounding the mixer (cooled, ambient), C = mixing time (60, 80 sec), D = batch weight (1500, 2000 lb), and E = number of days of delay between mixing and packaging (1, 7). Between 125 and 150 packages of soup were sampled over an eight-hour period for each run in the design, and the standard deviation of package weight was used as the response variable. The design and resulting data are shown in Table 13E.5 (see next page).

(a) What is the generator for this design?

(b) What is the resolution of this design?

(c) Estimate the factor effects. Which effects are large?

(d) Does a residual analysis indicate any problems with the underlying assumptions?

(e) Draw conclusions about this filling process.

■ **TABLE 13E.5**
Soup-Filling Experiment for Exercise 13.15.

	A	*B*	*C*	*D*	*E*	*v*
Std Order	Mixer Ports	Temp	Time	Batch Weight	Delay	Std Dev
1	–	–	–	–	–	1.13
2	+	–	–	–	+	1.25
3	–	+	–	–	+	0.97
4	+	+	–	–	–	1.70
5	–	–	+	–	+	1.47
6	+	–	+	–	–	1.28
7	–	+	+	–	–	1.18
8	+	+	+	–	+	0.98
9	–	–	–	+	+	0.78
10	+	–	–	+	–	1.36
11	–	+	–	+	–	1.85
12	+	+	–	+	+	0.62
13	–	–	+	+	–	1.09
14	+	–	+	+	+	1.10
15	–	+	+	+	+	0.76
16	+	+	+	+	–	2.10

13.16. A 2^{4-1} design has been used to investigate the effect of four factors on the resistivity of a silicon wafer. The data from this experiment are shown in Table 13E.6.

(a) Estimate the factor effects. Plot the effect estimates on a normal probability scale.

(b) Identify a tentative model for this process. Fit the model and test for curvature.

(c) Plot the residuals from the model in part (b) versus the predicted resistivity. Is there any indication on this plot of model inadequacy?

■ **TABLE 13E.6**
Resistivity Experiment for Exercise 13.16.

Run	*A*	*B*	*C*	*D*	Resistivity
1	–	–	–	–	33.2
2	+	–	–	+	4.6
3	–	+	–	+	31.2
4	+	+	–	–	9.6
5	–	–	+	+	40.6
6	+	–	+	–	162.4
7	–	+	+	–	39.4
8	+	+	+	+	158.6
9	0	0	0	0	63.4
10	0	0	0	0	62.6
11	0	0	0	0	58.7
12	0	0	0	0	60.9

(d) Construct a normal probability plot of the residuals. Is there any reason to doubt the validity of the normality assumption?

13.17. A nickel-titanium alloy is used to make components for jet turbine aircraft engines. Cracking is a potentially serious problem in the final part because it can lead to nonrecoverable failure. A test is run at the parts producer to determine the effect of four factors on cracks. The four factors are pouring temperature (*A*), titanium content (*B*), heat treatment method (*C*), and amount of grain refiner used (*D*). Two replicates of a 2^4 design are run, and the length of crack (in mm $\times 10^{-2}$) induced in a sample coupon subjected to a standard test is measured. The data are shown in the Table 13E.7.

(a) Estimate the factor effects. Which factor effects appear to be large?

(b) Conduct an analysis of variance. Do any of the factors affect cracking? Use $\alpha = 0.05$.

(c) Write down a regression model that can be used to predict crack length as a function of the significant main effects and interactions you have identified in part (b).

(d) Analyze the residuals from this experiment.

(e) Is there an indication that any of the factors affect the variability in cracking?

(f) What recommendations would you make regarding process operations? Use interaction and/or main effect plots to assist in drawing conclusions.

■ **TABLE 13E.7**
Crack Experiment for Exercise 13.17.

A	*B*	*C*	*D*	Treatment Combination	Replicate I	Replicate II
–	–	–	–	(1)	7.037	6.376
+	–	–	–	*a*	14.707	15.219
–	+	–	–	*b*	11.635	12.089
+	+	–	–	*ab*	17.273	17.815
–	–	+	–	*c*	10.403	10.151
+	–	+	–	*ac*	4.368	4.098
–	+	+	–	*bc*	9.360	9.253
+	+	+	–	*abc*	13.440	12.923
–	–	–	+	*d*	8.561	8.951
+	–	–	+	*ad*	16.867	17.052
–	+	–	+	*bd*	13.876	13.658
+	+	–	+	*abd*	19.824	19.639
–	–	+	+	*cd*	11.846	12.337
+	–	+	+	*acd*	6.125	5.904
–	+	+	+	*bcd*	11.190	10.935
+	+	+	+	*abcd*	15.653	15.053

13.18. Reconsider the crack experiment from Exercise 13.17. Suppose that the two crack length measurements were made on two cracks that formed in the same test coupon at each set of test conditions. Are the two observations replicates? How do you think this data should be analyzed?

13.19. **Continuation of Exercise 13.17.** One of the variables in the experiment described in Exercise 13.17, heat treatment method (C), is a categorical variable. Assume that the remaining factors are continuous.

(a) Write two regression models for predicting crack length, one for each level of the heat treatment method variable. What differences, if any, do you notice in these two equations?

(b) Generate appropriate response surface contour plots for the two regression models in part (a).

(c) What set of conditions would you recommend for the factors A, B, and D if you use heat treatment method $C = +$?

(d) Repeat part (c) assuming that you wish to use heat treatment method $C = -$.

14 Process Optimization

Chapter Outline

The supplemental material is on the textbook Website www.wiley.com/college/montgomery.

Chapter Overview and Learning Objectives

In Chapter 13 we focused on factorial and fractional factorial designs. These designs are very useful for **factor screening**—that is, identifying the most important factors that affect the performance of a process. Sometimes this is called **process characterization.** Once the appropriate subset of process variables are identified, the next step is usually **process optimization,** or finding the set of operating conditions for the process variables that result in the best process performance. This chapter gives a brief account of how designed experiments can be used in process optimization.

We discuss and illustrate **response surface methodology,** an approach to optimization developed in the early 1950s and initially applied in the chemical and process industries. This is probably the most widely used and successful optimization technique based on designed experiments. Then we discuss how designed experiments can be used in **process robustness**

studies. These are activities in which process engineering personnel try to reduce the variability in the output of a process by setting controllable factors to levels that minimize the variability transmitted into the responses of interest by other factors that are difficult to control during routine operation. We also present an example of **evolutionary operation,** an approach to maintaining optimum performance that is, in effect, an on-line or in-process application of the factorial design concepts of Chapter 13.

After careful study of this chapter you should be able to do the following:

1. Know how to use the response surface approach to optimizing processes
2. Know how to apply the method of steepest ascent
3. Know how to analyze a second-order response surface model
4. Know how to determine optimum operating conditions for a process
5. Know how to set up and conduct an experiment using a central composite design
6. Understand the difference between controllable process variables and noise variables
7. Understand the advantages of a combined array design for a process robustness study
8. Know how to use the response model approach to conduct a process robustness study
9. Know how evolutionary operation (EVOP) is used to maintain a process that is subject to drift near its optimum operating conditions

14.1 Response Surface Methods and Designs

Response surface methodology (RSM) is a collection of mathematical and statistical techniques that are useful for modeling and analysis in applications where a response of interest is influenced by several variables and the objective is to **optimize this response.** The general RSM approach was developed in the early 1950s and was initially applied in the chemical industry with considerable success. Over the past 20 years RSM has found extensive application in a wide variety of industrial settings, far beyond its origins in chemical processes, including semiconductor and electronics manufacturing, machining, metal cutting, and joining processes, among many others. Many statistics software packages have included the experimental designs and optimization techniques that make up the basics of RSM as standard features. For a recent comprehensive presentation of RSM, see Myers and Montgomery (2002).

To illustrate the general idea of RSM, suppose that a chemical engineer wishes to find the levels of reaction temperature (x_1) and reaction time (x_2) that maximize the yield (y) of a process. The process yield is a function of the levels of temperature and time—say,

$$y = f(x_1, x_2) + \varepsilon$$

where ε represents the noise or error observed in the response y. If we denote the expected value of the response by $E(y) = f(x_1, x_2)$, then the surface represented by

$$E(y) = f(x_1, x_2)$$

is called a **response surface.** Recall that we introduced the idea of a response surface in Chapter 13, where we presented an example of a response surface generated from a model that arose from a factorial design.

We may represent the response surface graphically as shown in Fig. 14.1, where $E(y)$ is plotted versus the levels of x_1 and x_2. Note that the response is represented as a surface plot in three-dimensional space. To help visualize the shape of a response surface, we often plot the contours of the response surface as shown in Fig. 14.2. In the **contour plot,** lines of constant

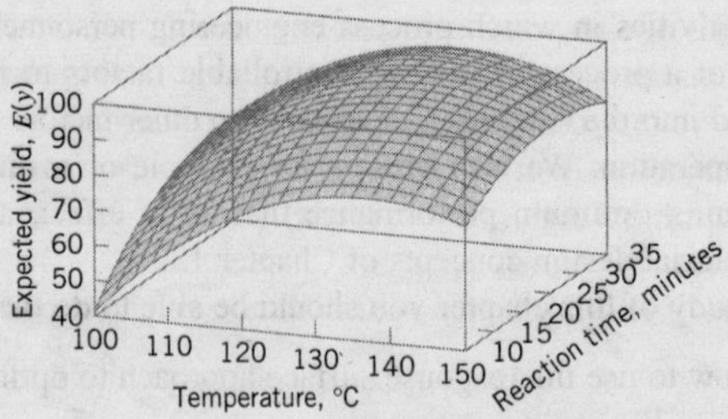

■ FIGURE 14.1 A three-dimensional response surface showing the expected yield as a function of reaction temperature and reaction time.

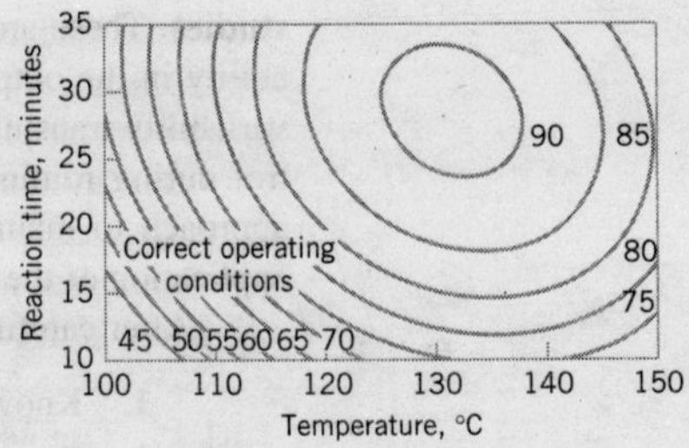

■ FIGURE 14.2 A contour plot of the yield response surface in Fig. 14.1.

response are drawn in the x_1, x_2 plane. Each contour corresponds to a particular height of the response surface. The contour plot is helpful in studying the levels of x_1, x_2 that result in changes in the shape or height of the response surface.

In most RSM problems, the form of the relationship between the response and the independent variables is unknown. Thus, the first step in RSM is to find a suitable approximation for the true relationship between y and the independent variables. Usually, a low-order polynomial in some region of the independent variables is employed. If the response is well modeled by a linear function of the independent variables, then the approximating function is the **first-order model**

$$y = \beta_0 + \beta_1 x_1 + \beta_2 x_2 + \cdots \beta_k x_k + \varepsilon \tag{14.1}$$

If there is curvature in the system, then a polynomial of higher degree must be used, such as the **second-order model**

$$y = \beta_0 + \sum_{i=1}^{k} \beta_i x_i + \sum_{i=1}^{k} \beta_{ii} x_i^2 + \sum_{i<j=2}\sum^{k} \beta_{ij} x_i x_j + \varepsilon \tag{14.2}$$

Many RSM problems utilize one or both of these approximating polynomials. Of course, it is unlikely that a polynomial model will be a reasonable approximation of the true functional relationship over the entire space of the independent variables, but for a relatively small region they usually work quite well.

The method of least squares (see Chapter 4) is used to estimate the parameters in the approximating polynomials. That is, the estimates of the β's in equations (14.1) and (14.2) are those values of the parameters that minimize the sum of squares of the model errors. The response surface analysis is then done in terms of the fitted surface. If the fitted surface is an adequate approximation of the true response function, then analysis of the fitted surface will be approximately equivalent to analysis of the actual system.

RSM is a **sequential procedure.** Often, when we are at a point on the response surface that is remote from the optimum, such as the current operating conditions in Fig. 14.2, there is little curvature in the system and the first-order model will be appropriate. Our objective here is to lead the experimenter rapidly and efficiently to the general vicinity of the optimum. Once the region of the optimum has been found, a more elaborate model such as the second-order model may be employed, and an analysis may be performed to locate the optimum. From Fig. 14.2, we see that the analysis of a response surface can be thought of as "climbing a hill," where the top of the hill represents the point of maximum response. If the true optimum is a point of minimum response, then we may think of "descending into a valley."

The eventual objective of RSM is to determine the optimum operating conditions for the system or to determine a region of the factor space in which operating specifications are satisfied. Also, note that the word "optimum" in RSM is used in a special sense. The "hill climbing" procedures of RSM guarantee convergence to a local optimum only.

14.1.1 The Method of Steepest Ascent

Frequently, the initial estimate of the optimum operating conditions for the system will be far away from the actual optimum. In such circumstances, the objective of the experimenter is to move rapidly to the general vicinity of the optimum. We wish to use a simple and economically efficient experimental procedure. When we are remote from the optimum, we usually assume that a first-order model is an adequate approximation to the true surface in a small region of the x's.

The **method of steepest ascent** is a procedure for moving sequentially along the path of steepest ascent—that is, in the direction of the maximum increase in the response. Of course, if **minimization** is desired, then we would call this procedure the **method of steepest descent.** The fitted first-order model is

$$\hat{y} = \hat{\beta}_0 + \sum_{i=1}^{k} \hat{\beta}_i x_i \tag{14.3}$$

and the first-order response surface—that is, the contours of $\hat{y}$—is a series of parallel straight lines such as shown in Fig. 14.3. The direction of steepest ascent is the direction in which $\hat{y}$ increases most rapidly. This direction is normal to the fitted response surface contours. We usually take as the **path of steepest ascent** the line through the center of the region of interest and normal to the fitted surface contours. Thus, the steps along the path are proportional to the magnitudes of the regression coefficients $\{\hat{\beta}_i\}$. The experimenter determines the actual amount of movement along this path based on process knowledge or other practical considerations.

Experiments are conducted along the path of steepest ascent until no further increase in response is observed or until the desired response region is reached. Then a new first-order model may be fitted, a new direction of steepest ascent determined, and, if necessary, further experiments conducted in that direction until the experimenter feels that the process is near the optimum.

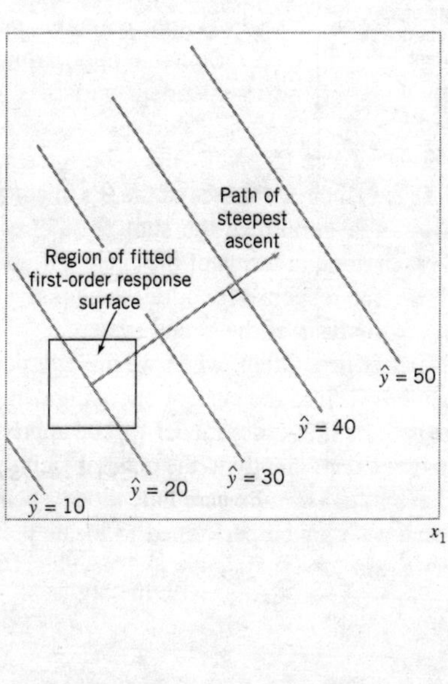

■ FIGURE 14.3 First-order response surface and path of steepest ascent.

EXAMPLE 14.1 An Application of Steepest Ascent

In Example 13.8, we described an experiment on a plasma etching process in which four factors were investigated to study their effect on the etch rate in a semiconductor water-etching application. We found that two of the four factors, the gap (x_1) and the power (x_4), significantly affected etch rate. Recall from that example that if we fit a model using only these main effects we obtain

$$\hat{y} = 776.0625 - 50.8125x_1 + 153.0625x_4$$

as a prediction equation for the etch rate.

Figure 14.4 shows the contour plot from this model, over the original region of experimentation—that is, for gaps between 0.8 and 1.2 cm and power between 275 and 325 W. Note that within the original region of experimentation, the maximum etch rate that can be obtained is approximately 980 Å/m. The engineers would like to run this process at an etch rate of 1100–1150 Å/m. Use the method of steepest ascent to move away from the original region of experimentation to increase the etch rate.

SOLUTION

From examining the plot in Fig. 14.4 (or the fitted model) we see that to move away from the design center—the point ($x_1 = 0$, $x_2 = 0$)—along the path of steepest ascent, we would move −50.8125 units in the x_1 direction for every 153.0625 units in the x_4 direction. Thus the path of steepest ascent passes through the point ($x_1 = 0$, $x_2 = 0$) and has slope 153.0625/(−50.8125) ≅ −3. The engineer decides to use 25 W of power as the basic step size. Now, 25 W of power is equivalent to a step in the coded variable x_4 of $\Delta x_4 = 1$. Therefore, the steps along the path of steepest ascent are $\Delta x_4 = 1$ and $\Delta x_1 = \Delta x_4/(-3) = -0.33$. A change of $\Delta x_1 = -0.33$ in the coded variable x_1 is equivalent to about −0.067 cm in the original variable gap. Therefore, the engineer will move along the path of steepest ascent by increasing power by 25 W and decreasing gap by −0.067 cm. An actual observation on etch rate will be obtained by running the process at each point.

Figure 14.4 shows three points along this path of steepest ascent and the etch rates actually observed from the process at those points. At points *A*, *B*, and *C*, the observed etch rates increase steadily. At point *C*, the observed etch rate is 1163 Å/m. Therefore, the steepest ascent procedure would terminate in the vicinity of power = 375 W and gap = 0.8 cm with an observed etch rate of 1163 Å/m. This region is very close to the desired operating region for the process.

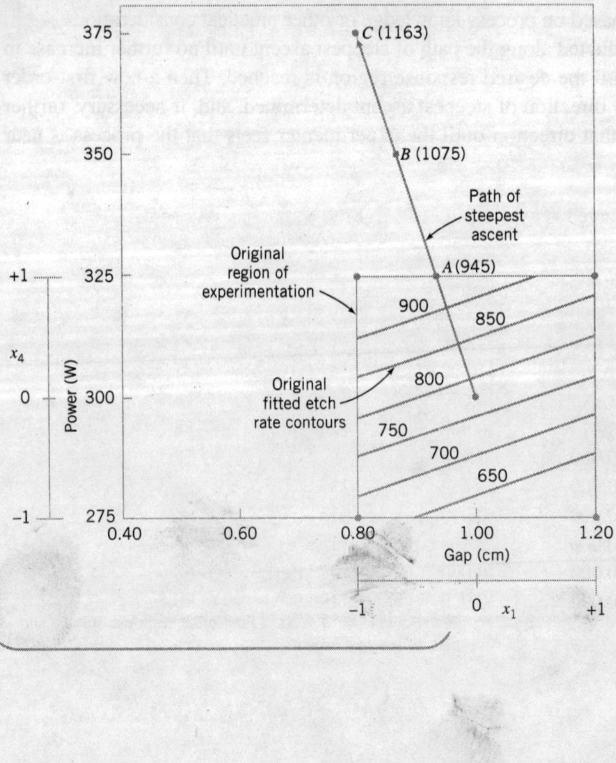

■ FIGURE 14.4 Steepest ascent experiment for Example 14.1.

14.1.2 Analysis of a Second-Order Response Surface

When the experimenter is relatively close to the optimum, a second-order model is usually required to approximate the response because of curvature in the true response surface. The fitted second-order response surface model is

$$\hat{y} = \hat{\beta}_0 + \sum_{i=1}^{k} \hat{\beta}_i x_i + \sum_{i=1}^{k} \hat{\beta}_{ii} x_i^2 + \sum_{i<j}\sum \hat{\beta}_{ij} x_i x_j$$

where $\hat{\beta}$ denotes the least squares estimate of β. In the next example, we illustrate how a fitted second-order model can be used to find the optimum operating conditions for a process, and how to describe the behavior of the response function.

EXAMPLE 14.2 Continuation of Example 14.1

Recall that in applying the method of steepest ascent to the plasma etching process in Example 14.1 we had found a region near gap = 0.8 cm and power = 375 W, which would apparently give etch rates near the desired target of between 1100 and 1150 Å/m. The experimenters decided to explore this region more closely by running an experiment that would support a second-order response surface model. Table 14.1 and Fig. 14.5 show the experimental design, centered at gap = 0.8 cm and power = 375 W, which consists of a 2^2 factorial design with four center points and four runs located along the coordinate axes called axial runs. The resulting design is called a **central composite design,** and it is widely used in practice for fitting second-order response surfaces.

Two response variables were measured during this phase of the study: etch rate (in Å/m) and etch uniformity (this is the standard deviation of the thickness of the layer of material applied to the surface of the wafer after it has been etched to a particular average (thickness). Determine optimal operating conditions for this process.

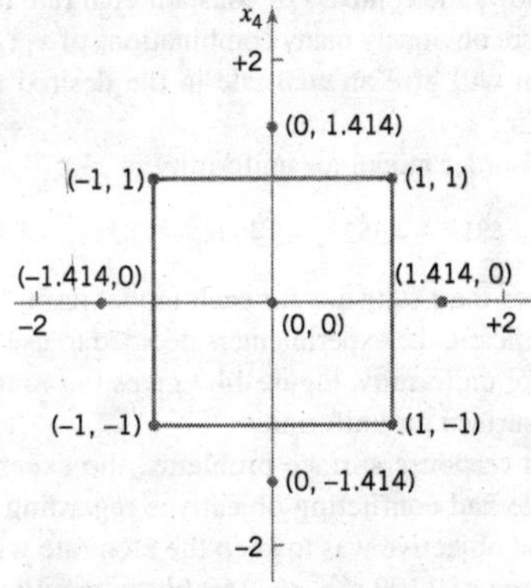

FIGURE 14.5 Central composite design in the coded variables for Example 14.2.

TABLE 14.1
Central Composite Design of Example 14.2

Observation	Gap (cm)	Power (W)	Coded x_1	Variables x_4	Etch Rate y_1(Å/m)	Uniformity y_2(Å/m)
1	0.600	350.0	−1.000	−1.000	1054.0	79.6
2	1.000	350.0	1.000	−1.000	936.0	81.3
3	0.600	400.0	−1.000	1.000	1179.0	78.5
4	1.000	400.0	1.000	1.000	1417.0	97.7
5	0.517	375.0	−1.414	0.000	1049.0	76.4
6	1.083	375.0	1.414	0.000	1287.0	88.1
7	0.800	339.6	0.000	−1.414	927.0	78.5
8	0.800	410.4	0.000	1.414	1345.0	92.3
9	0.800	375.0	0.000	0.000	1151.0	90.1
10	0.800	375.0	0.000	0.000	1150.0	88.3
11	0.800	375.0	0.000	0.000	1177.0	88.6
12	0.800	375.0	0.000	0.000	1196.0	90.1

(continued)

SOLUTION

Minitab can be used to analyze the data from this experiment. The Minitab output is in Table 14.2.

The second-order model fit to the etch rate response is

$$\hat{y}_1 = 1168.50 + 57.07x_1 + 149.64x_4 - 1.62x_1^2 - 17.63x_4^2 + 89.00x_1x_4$$

However, we note from the t-test statistics in Table 14.2 that the quadratic terms x_1^2 and x_4^2 are not statistically significant. Therefore, the experimenters decided to model etch rate with a first-order model with interaction:

$$\hat{y}_1 = 1155.7 + 57.1x_1 + 149.7x_4 + 89x_1x_4$$

Figure 14.6 shows the contours of constant etch rate from this model. There are obviously many combinations of x_1 (gap) and x_4 (power) that will give an etch rate in the desired range of 1100–1150 Å/m.

The second-order model for uniformity is

$$\hat{y}_2 = 89.275 + 4.681x_1 + 4.352x_4 - 3.400x_1^2 - 1.825x_4^2 + 4.375x_1x_4$$

Table 14.2 gives the t-statistics for each model term. Since all terms are significant, the experimenters decided to use the quadratic model for uniformity. Figure 14.7 gives the contour plot and response surface for uniformity.

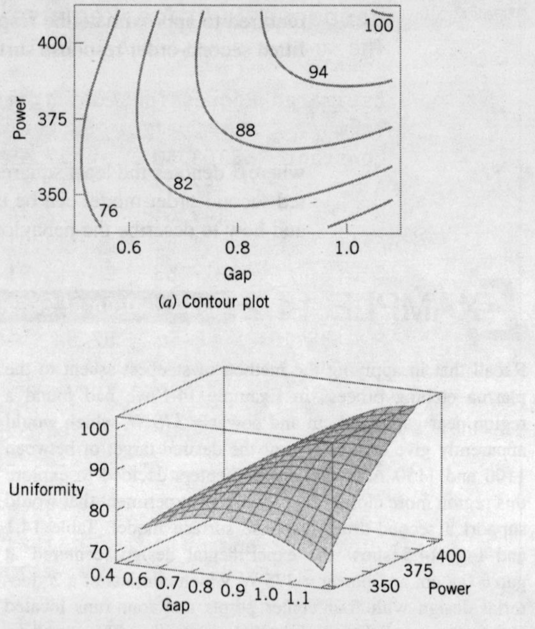

(a) Contour plot

(b) Three-dimensional response surface

■ FIGURE 14.7 Plots of the uniformity response, Example 14.2.

As in most response surface problems, the experimenter in this example had conflicting objectives regarding the two responses. One objective was to keep the etch rate within the acceptable range of $1100 \le y_1 \le 1150$ but to simultaneously minimize the uniformity. Specifically, the uniformity must not exceed $y_2 = 80$, or many of the wafers will be defective in subsequent processing operations. When there are only a few independent variables, an easy way to solve this problem is to overlay the response surfaces to find the optimum. Figure 14.8 presents the overlay plot of both responses, with the contours of $\hat{y}_1 = 100$, $\hat{y}_1 = 150$, and $\hat{y}_2 = 80$ shown. The shaded areas on this plot identify infeasible combinations of gap and power. The graph indicates that several combinations of gap and power should result in acceptable process performance.

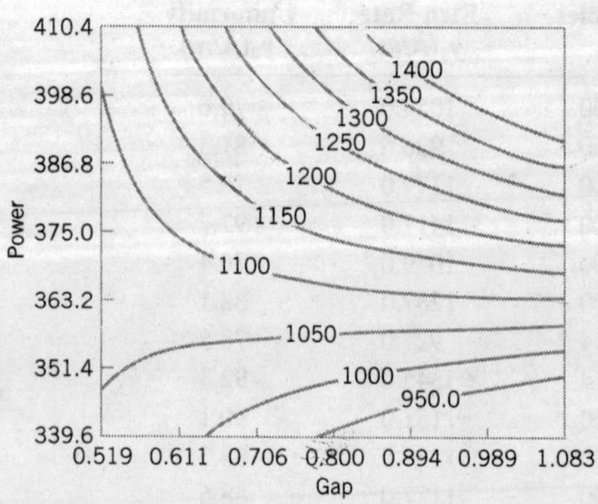

■ FIGURE 14.6 Contours of constant predicted etch rate, Example 14.2.

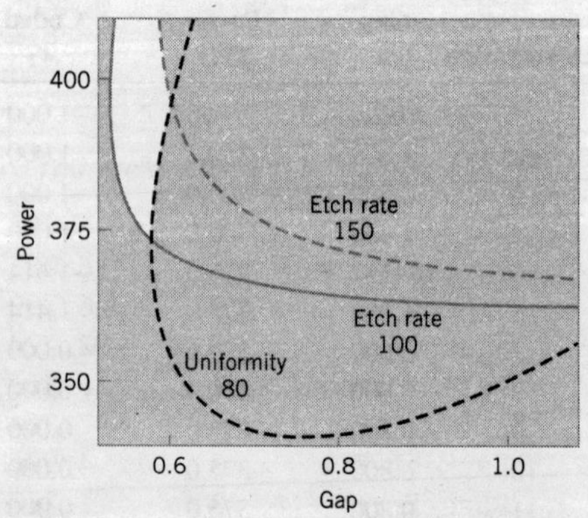

■ FIGURE 14.8 Overlay of the etch rate and uniformity response surfaces in Example 14.2 showing the region of the optimum (unshaded region).

■ TABLE 14.2
Minitab Analysis of the Central Composite Design in Example 14.2

```
Response Surface Regression: Etch Rate versus A, B
The analysis was done using coded units.

Estimated Regression Coefficients for Etch Rate
Term          Coef    SE Coef        T       P
Constant   1168.50      17.59   66.417   0.000
A            57.07      12.44    4.588   0.004
B           149.64      12.44   12.029   0.000
A*A          -1.62      13.91   -0.117   0.911
B*B         -17.63      13.91   -1.267   0.252
A*B          89.00      17.59    5.059   0.002
S = 35.19   R-Sq = 97.0%    R-Sq(adj) = 94.5%
Analysis of Variance for Etch Rate
Source          DF    Seq SS   Adj SS   Adj MS       F       P
Regression       5    238898   238898    47780   38.59   0.000
 Linear          2    205202   205202   102601   82.87   0.000
 Square          2      2012     2012     1006    0.81   0.487
 Interaction     1     31684    31684    31684   25.59   0.002
Residual Error   6      7429     7429     1238
 Lack-of-Fit     3      5952     5952     1984    4.03   0.141
 Pure Error      3      1477     1477      492
Total           11    246327
Response Surface Regression: Uniformity versus A, B
The analysis was done using coded units.

Estimated Regression Coefficients for Uniformity
Term          Coef    SE Coef        T       P
Constant    89.275     0.5688  156.963   0.000
A            4.681     0.4022   11.639   0.000
B            4.352     0.4022   10.821   0.000
A*A         -3.400     0.4496   -7.561   0.000
B*B         -1.825     0.4496   -4.059   0.007
A*B          4.375     0.5688    7.692   0.000
S = 1.138       R - Sq = 98.4%     R - Sq(adj) = 97.1%

Analysis of Variance for Uniformity

Source          DF    Seq SS    Adj SS    Adj MS        F       P
Regression       5   486.085   486.085    97.217    75.13   0.000
 Linear          2   326.799   326.799   163.399   126.28   0.000
 Square          2    82.724    82.724    41.362    31.97   0.001
 Interaction     1    76.563    76.563    76.563    59.17   0.000
Residual Error   6     7.764     7.764     1.294
 Lack-of-Fit     3     4.996     4.996     1.665     1.81   0.320
 Pure Error      3     2.768     2.768     0.923
Total           11   493.849
```

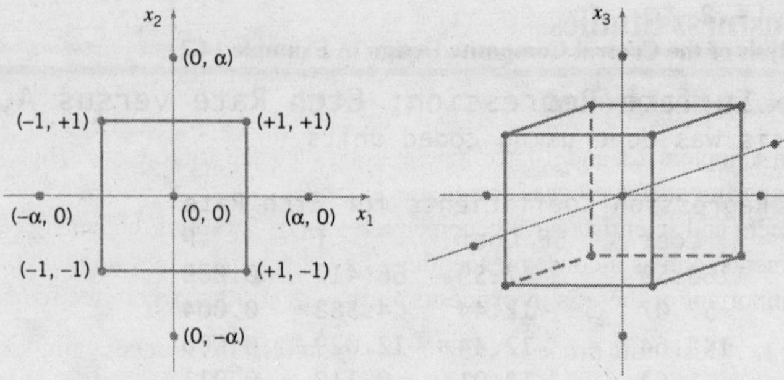

■ **FIGURE 14.9** Central composite designs for $k = 2$ and $k = 3$.

Example 14.2 illustrates the use of a **central composite design (CCD)** for fitting a second-order response surface model. These designs are widely used in practice because they are relatively efficient with respect to the number of runs required. In general, a CCD in k factors requires 2^k factorial runs, $2k$ axial runs, and at least one center point (3 to 5 center points are typically used). Designs for $k = 2$ and $k = 3$ factors are shown in Fig. 14.9.

The central composite design may be made **rotatable design** by proper choice of the axial spacing α in Fig. 14.9. If the design is rotatable, the standard deviation of predicted response $\hat{y}$ is constant at all points that are the same distance from the center of the design. For rotatability, choose $\alpha = (F)^{1/4}$, where F is the number of points in the factorial part of the design (usually $F = 2^k$). For the case of $k = 2$ factors, $\alpha = (2^2)^{1/4} = 1.414$, as was used in the design in Example 14.2. Figure 14.10 presents a contour plot and a surface plot of the standard deviation of prediction for the quadratic model used for the uniformity response. Note that the contours are concentric circles, implying that uniformity is predicted with equal precision for all points that are the same distance from the center of the design. Also, note that the precision of response estimation decreases with increasing distance from the design center.

The central composite design is the most widely used design for fitting a second-order response surface model. However, there are many other useful designs. Section S14.1 of the supplemental material for this chapter contains more details of designs for fitting response surfaces.

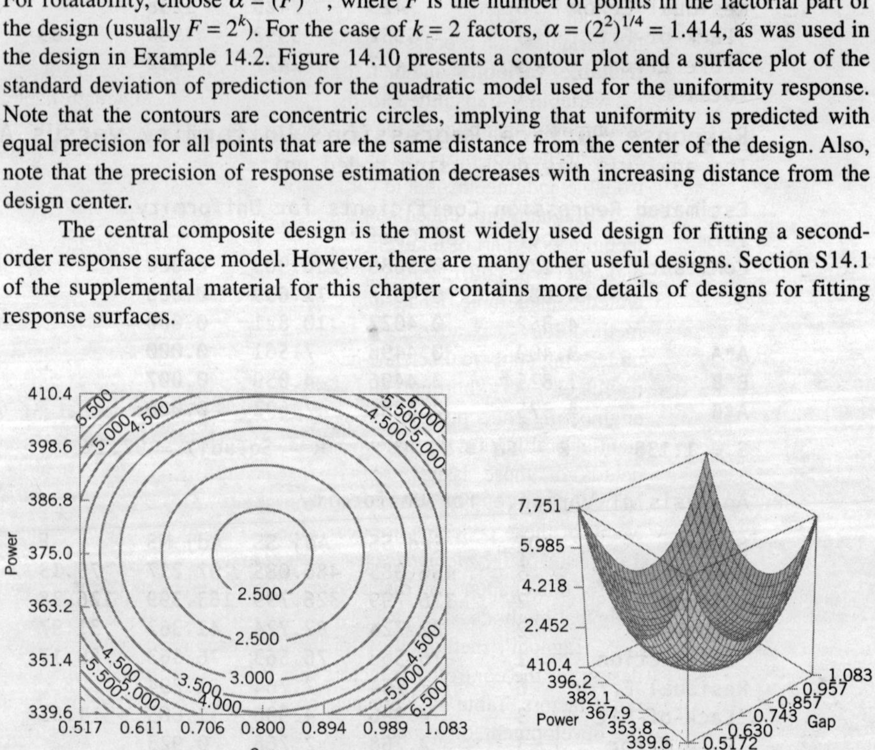

(*a*) Contours of constant standard deviation of $\hat{y}_2$ (*b*) Surface plot

■ **FIGURE 14.10** Plots of constant standard deviation of predicted uniformity (y_2), Example 14.2.

14.2 Process Robustness Studies

14.2.1 Background

In Chapters 13 and 14 we have emphasized the importance of using statistically designed experiments for process design, development, and improvement. Over the past 30 years, engineers and scientists have become increasingly aware of the benefits of using designed experiments, and as a consequence, there have been many new application areas. One of the most important of these is in **process robustness studies,** where the focus is on the following:

1. Designing processes so that the manufactured product will be as close as possible to the desired target specifications even though some process variables (such as temperature), environmental factors (such as relative humidity), or raw material characteristics are impossible to control precisely.
2. Determining the operating conditions for a process so that critical product characteristics are as close as possible to the desired target value and the variability around this target is minimized. Examples of this type of problem occur frequently. For instance, in semiconductor manufacturing we would like the oxide thickness on a wafer to be as close as possible to the target mean thickness, and we would also like the variability in thickness across the wafer (a measure of uniformity) to be as small as possible.

In the early 1980s, a Japanese engineer, Genichi Taguchi, introduced an approach to solving these types of problems, which he referred to as the **robust parameter design (RPD)** problem [see Taguchi and Wu (1980), Taguchi (1986)]. His approach was based on classifying the variables in a process as either **control** (or **controllable**) **variables** and **noise** (or **uncontrollable**) **variables,** and then finding the settings for the controllable variables that minimized the variability transmitted to the response from the uncontrollable variables. We make the assumption that although the noise factors are uncontrollable in the full-scale system, they can be controlled for purposes of an experiment. Refer to Fig. 13.1 for a graphical view of controllable and uncontrollable variables in the general context of a designed experiment.

Taguchi introduced some novel statistical methods and some variations on established techniques as part of his RPD procedure. He made use of highly fractionated factorial designs and other types of fractional designs obtained from orthogonal arrays. His methodology generated considerable debate and controversy. Part of the controversy arose because Taguchi's methodology was advocated in the West initially (and primarily) by consultants, and the underlying statistical science had not been adequately peer-reviewed. By the late 1980s, the results of a very thorough and comprehensive peer review indicated that although Taguchi's engineering concepts and the overall objective of RPD were well founded, there were substantial problems with his experimental strategy and methods of data analysis. For specific details of these issues, see Box, Bisgaard, and Fung (1988); Hunter (1985, 1987); Montgomery (1999); Myers and Montgomery (2002); and Pignatiello and Ramberg (1991). Many of these concerns are also summarized in the extensive panel discussion in the May 1992 issue of *Technometrics* [see Nair et al. (1992)]. Section S14.2 of the supplemental material for this chapter also discusses and illustrates many of the problems underlying Taguchi's technical methods.

Taguchi's methodology for the RPD problem revolves around the use of an orthogonal design for the controllable factors that is "crossed" with a separate orthogonal design for the noise factors. Table 14.3 presents an example from Byrne and Taguchi (1987) that involved the development of a method to assemble an elastometric connector to a nylon tube that would deliver the required pull-off force. There are four controllable factors, each at three levels (A = interference, B = connector wall thickness, C = insertion depth, D = percent adhesive), and three noise or uncontrollable factors, each at two levels (E = conditioning time,

■ TABLE 14.3
Taguchi Parameter Design with Both Inner and Outer Arrays [Byrne and Taguchi (1987)]

					(b) Outer Array							
				E	1	1	1	1	2	2	2	2
				F	1	1	2	2	1	1	2	2
				G	1	2	1	2	1	2	1	2
(a) Inner Array												
Run	***A***	***B***	***C***	***D***								
1	1	1	1	1	15.6	9.5	16.9	19.9	19.6	19.6	20.0	19.1
2	1	2	2	2	15.0	16.2	19.4	19.2	19.7	19.8	24.2	21.9
3	1	3	3	3	16.3	16.7	19.1	15.6	22.6	18.2	23.3	20.4
4	2	1	2	3	18.3	17.4	18.9	18.6	21.0	18.9	23.2	24.7
5	2	2	3	1	19.7	18.6	19.4	25.1	25.6	21.4	27.5	25.3
6	2	3	1	2	16.2	16.3	20.0	19.8	14.7	19.6	22.5	24.7
7	3	1	3	2	16.4	19.1	18.4	23.6	16.8	18.6	24.3	21.6
8	3	2	1	3	14.2	15.6	15.1	16.8	17.8	19.6	23.2	24.2
9	3	3	2	1	16.1	19.9	19.3	17.3	23.1	22.7	22.6	28.6

F = conditioning temperature, *G* = conditioning relative humidity). Panel (a) of Table 14.3 contains the design for the controllable factors. Note that the design is a three-level fractional factorial; specifically, it is a 3^{4-2} design. Taguchi calls this the **inner array design.** Panel (b) of Table 14.3 contains a 2^3 design for the noise factors, which Taguchi calls the **outer array design.** Each run in the inner array is performed for all treatment combinations in the outer array, producing the 72 observations on pull-off force shown in the table. This type of design is called a **crossed array design.**

Taguchi suggested that we summarize the data from a crossed array experiment with two statistics: the average of each observation in the inner array across all runs in the outer array, and a summary statistic that attempted to combine information about the mean and variance, called the **signal-to-noise ratio.** These signal-to-noise ratios are purportedly defined so that a maximum value of the ratio minimizes variability transmitted from the noise variables. Then an analysis is performed to determine which settings of the controllable factors result in (1) the mean as close as possible to the desired target and (2) a maximum value of the signal-to-noise ratio.

Examination of Table 14.3 reveals a major problem with the Taguchi design strategy; namely, the crossed array approach will lead to a very large experiment. In our example, there are only seven factors, yet the design has 72 runs. Furthermore, the inner array design is a 3^{4-2} resolution III design [see Montgomery (2005), Chapter 9, for discussion of this design], so in spite of the large number of runs, we cannot obtain *any* information about interactions among the controllable variables. Indeed, even information about the main effects is potentially tainted, because the main effects are heavily aliased with the two-factor interactions. It also turns out that the Taguchi signal-to-noise ratios are problematic; maximizing the ratio does not necessarily minimize variability. Refer to the supplemental text material for more details.

An important point about the crossed array design is that it *does* provide information about controllable factor × noise factor interactions. These interactions are crucial to the solution of an RPD problem. For example, consider the two-factor interaction graphs in Fig. 14.11, where *x* is the controllable factor and *z* is the noise factor. In Fig. 14.11*a*, there is no $x \times z$ interaction; therefore, there is no setting for the controllable variable *x* that will affect the

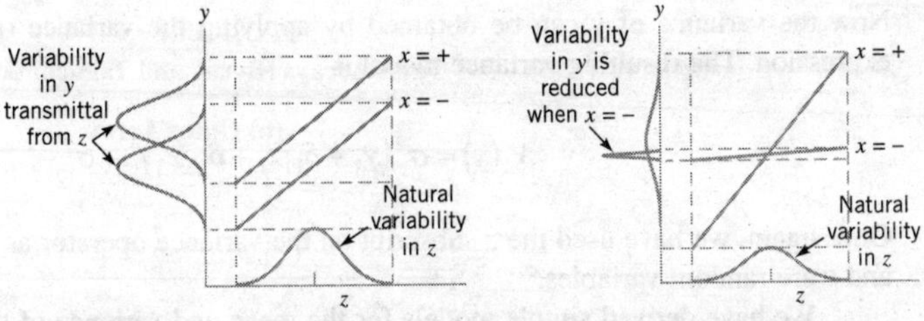

■ FIGURE 14.11 The role of the control × noise interaction in robust design.

variability transmitted to the response by the variability in z. However, in Fig. 14.11b there is a strong $x \times z$ interaction. Note that when x is set to its low level there is much less variability in the response variable than when x is at the high level. Thus, unless there is at least one controllable factor × noise factor interaction, there is no robust design problem. As we will see in the next section, focusing on identifying and modeling these interactions is one of the keys to a more efficient and effective approach to investigating process robustness.

14.2.2 The Response Surface Approach to Process Robustness Studies

As noted in the previous section, interactions between controllable and noise factors are the key to a process robustness study. Therefore, it is logical to utilize a **model** for the response that includes both controllable and noise factors and their interactions. To illustrate, suppose that we have two controllable factors x_1 and x_2 and a single noise factor z_1. We assume that both control and noise factors are expressed as the usual coded variables (that is, they are centered at zero and have lower and upper limits at ± 1). If we wish to consider a first-order model involving the controllable variables, then a logical model is

$$y = \beta_0 + \beta_1 x_1 + \beta_2 x_2 + \beta_{12} x_1 x_2 + \gamma_1 z_1 + \delta_{11} x_1 z_1 + \delta_{21} x_2 z_1 + \varepsilon \tag{14.4}$$

Note that this model has the main effects of both controllable factors, the main effect of the noise variable, and both interactions between the controllable and noise variables. This type of model incorporating both controllable and noise variables is often called a **response model.** Unless at least one of the regression coefficients δ_{11} and δ_{21} is nonzero, there will be no robust design problem.

An important advantage of the response model approach is that both the controllable factors and the noise factors can be placed in a single experimental design; that is, the inner and outer array structure of the Taguchi approach can be avoided. We usually call the design containing both controllable and noise factors a **combined array design.**

As mentioned previously, we assume that noise variables are random variables, although they are controllable for purposes of an experiment. Specifically, we assume that the noise variables are expressed in coded units, that they have expected value zero, variance σ_z^2, and that if there are several noise variables, they have zero covariances. Under these assumptions, it is easy to find a model for the mean response just by taking the expected value of y in equation (14.4). This yields

$$E_z(y) = \beta_0 + \beta_1 x_1 + \beta_2 x_2 + \beta_{12} x_1 x_2$$

where the z subscript on the expectation operator is a reminder to take the expected value with respect to *both* random variables in equation (14.4), z_1 and ε. To find a model for the variance of the response y, first rewrite equation (14.4) as follows:

$$y = \beta_0 + \beta_1 x_1 + \beta_2 x_2 + \beta_{12} x_1 x_2 + (\gamma_1 + \delta_{11} x_1 + \delta_{22} x_2) z_1 + \varepsilon$$

Now the variance of y can be obtained by applying the variance operator across this last expression. The resulting variance model is

$$V_z(y) = \sigma_z^2(\gamma_1 + \delta_{11}x_1 + \delta_{22}x_2)^2 + \sigma^2$$

Once again, we have used the z subscript on the variance operator as a reminder that *both* z_1 and ε are random variables.

We have derived simple models for the mean and variance of the response variable of interest. Note the following:

1. The mean and variance models involve **only the controllable variables.** This means that we can potentially set the controllable variables to achieve a target value of the mean and minimize the variability transmitted by the noise variable.
2. Although the variance model involves only the controllable variables, it also involves the *interaction regression coefficients* between the controllable and noise variables. This is how the noise variable influences the response.
3. The variance model is a **quadratic function** of the controllable variables.
4. The variance model (apart from σ^2) is simply the square of the **slope** of the fitted response model in the direction of the noise variable.

To use these models operationally, we would:

1. Perform an experiment and fit an appropriate response model such as equation (14.4).
2. Replace the unknown regression coefficients in the mean and variance models with their least squares estimates from the response model and replace σ^2 in the variance model by the residual mean square found when fitting the response model.
3. Simultaneously optimize the mean and variance models. Often this can be done graphically. For more discussion of other optimization methods, refer to Myers and Montgomery (2002).

It is very easy to generalize these results. Suppose that there are k controllable variables $\mathbf{x}' = [x_1, x_2, \ldots, x_k]$, and r noise variables $\mathbf{z}' = [z_1, z_2, \ldots, z_r]$. We will write the general response model involving these variables as

$$y(\mathbf{x}, \mathbf{z}) = f(\mathbf{x}) + h(\mathbf{x}, \mathbf{z}) + \varepsilon \tag{14.5}$$

where $f(\mathbf{x})$ is the portion of the model that involves only the controllable variables and $h(\mathbf{x}, \mathbf{z})$ are the terms involving the main effects of the noise factors and the interactions between the controllable and noise factors. Typically, the structure for $h(\mathbf{x}, \mathbf{z})$ is

$$h(\mathbf{x}, \mathbf{z}) = \sum_{i=1}^{r} \gamma_i z_i + \sum_{i=1}^{k}\sum_{j=1}^{r} \delta_{ij} x_i z_j$$

The structure for $f(\mathbf{x})$ will depend on what type of model for the controllable variables the experimenter thinks is appropriate. The logical choices are the first-order model with interaction and the second-order model. If we assume that the noise variables have mean zero, variance σ_z^2, and have zero covariances, and that the noise variables and the random errors ε have zero covariances, then the mean model for the response is simply

$$E_z[y(\mathbf{x}, \mathbf{z})] = f(\mathbf{x}) \tag{14.6}$$

To find the variance model, we will use the transmission of error approach from Section 8.7.2. This involves first expanding equation (14.5) around $\mathbf{z} = \mathbf{0}$ in a first-order Taylor series:

$$y(\mathbf{x},\mathbf{z}) \cong f(\mathbf{x}) + \sum_{i=1}^{r} \frac{\partial h(\mathbf{x},\mathbf{z})}{\partial z_i}(z_i - 0) + R + \varepsilon$$

where R is the remainder. If we ignore the remainder and apply the variance operator to this last expression, the variance model for the response is

$$V_z[y(\mathbf{x},\mathbf{z})] = \sigma_z^2 \sum_{i=1}^{r} \left(\frac{\partial h(\mathbf{x},\mathbf{z})}{\partial z_i} \right)^2 + \sigma^2 \tag{14.7}$$

Myers and Montgomery (2002) give a slightly more general form for equation (14.7) based on applying a conditional variance operator directly to the response model in equation (14.5).

EXAMPLE 14.3 Robust Design

To illustrate a process robustness study, consider an experiment [described in detail in Montgomery (2005)] in which four factors were studied in a 2^4 factorial design to investigate their effect on the filtration rate of a chemical product. We will assume that factor A, temperature, is hard to control in the full-scale process but it can be controlled during the experiment (which was performed in a pilot plant). The other three factors, pressure (B), concentration (C), and stirring rate (D), are easy to control. Thus the noise factor z_1 is temperature and the controllable variables x_1, x_2, and x_3 are pressure, concentration, and stirring rate, respectively. The experimenters conducted the (unreplicated) 2^4 design shown in Table 14.4. Since both the controllable factors and the noise factor are in the same design, the 2^4 factorial design used in this experiment is an example of a **combined array design.** We want to determine operating conditions that maximize the filtration rate and minimize the variability transmitted from the noise variable temperature.

TABLE 14.4
Pilot Plant Filtration Rate Experiment

Run Number	Factor A	B	C	D	Run Label	Filtration Rate (gal/h)
1	−	−	−	−	(1)	45
2	+	−	−	−	*a*	71
3	−	+	−	−	*b*	48
4	+	+	−	−	*ab*	65
5	−	−	+	−	*c*	68
6	+	−	+	−	*ac*	60
7	−	+	+	−	*bc*	80
8	+	+	+	−	*abc*	65
9	−	−	−	+	*d*	43
10	+	−	−	+	*ad*	100
11	−	+	−	+	*bd*	45
12	+	+	−	+	*abd*	104
13	−	−	+	+	*cd*	75
14	+	−	+	+	*acd*	86
15	−	+	+	+	*bcd*	70
16	+	+	+	+	*abcd*	96

(continued)

SOLUTION

Using the methods for analysing a 2^k factorial design from Chapter 13, the response model is

$$\hat{y}(\mathbf{x}, z_1) = 70.06 + \left(\frac{21.625}{2}\right)z_1 + \left(\frac{9.875}{2}\right)x_2 + \left(\frac{14.625}{2}\right)x_3$$

$$-\left(\frac{18.125}{2}\right)x_2 z_1 + \left(\frac{16.625}{2}\right)x_3 z_1$$

$$= 70.06 + 10.81z_1 + 4.94x_2 + 7.31x_3 - 9.06x_2 z_1 + 8.31x_3 z_1$$

Using equations (14.6) and (14.7), we can find the mean and variance models as

$$E_z[y(\mathbf{x}, z_1)] = 70.06 + 4.94x_2 + 7.31x_3$$

and

$$V_z[y(\mathbf{x}, z_1)] = \sigma_z^2(10.81 - 9.06x_2 + 8.31x_3)^2 + \sigma^2$$

$$= \sigma_z^2(116.91 + 82.08x_2^2 + 69.06x_3^2 - 195.88x_2 + 179.66x_3 - 150.58x_2x_3) + \sigma^2$$

respectively. Now assume that the low and high levels of the noise variable temperature have been run at one standard deviation either side of its typical or average value, so that $\sigma_z^2 = 1$, and use $\hat{\sigma} = 19.51$ (this is the residual mean square obtained by fitting the response model). Therefore, the variance model becomes

$$V_z[y(\mathbf{x}, z_1)] = 136.42 - 195.88x_2 + 179.66x_3 - 150.58x_2x_3 + 82.08x_2^2 + 69.06x_3^2$$

Figure 14.12 presents a contour plot of the response contours from the mean model. To construct this plot, we held the noise factor (temperature) at zero and the nonsignificant controllable factor (pressure) at zero. Note that mean filtration rate increases as both concentration and stirring rate increase. The square root of $V_z[y(\mathbf{x}, \mathbf{z})]$ is plotted in Fig. 14.13. Note that both a contour plot and a three-dimensional response surface plot are given. This plot was also constructed by setting the noise factor temperature and the nonsignificant controllable factor to zero.

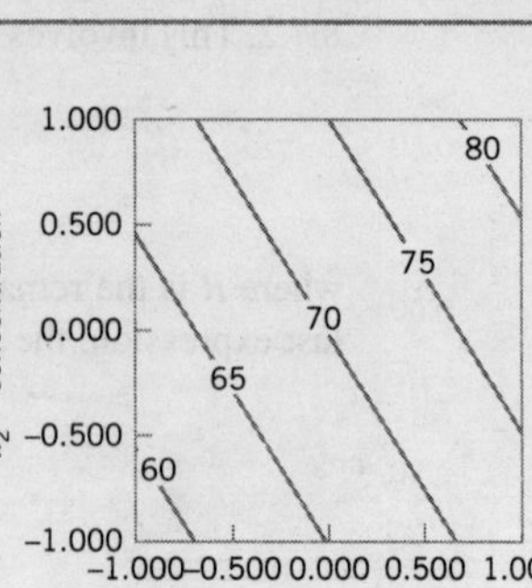

■ **FIGURE 14.12** Contours of constant mean filtration rate, Example 14.3, with z_1 = temperature = 0.

Suppose that the experimenter wants to maintain mean filtration rate above 75 and minimize the variability around this value. Figure 14.14 shows an overlay plot of the contours of mean filtration rate and the square root of $V_z[y(\mathbf{x}, \mathbf{z})]$ as a function of concentration and stirring rate, the significant controllable variables. To achieve the desired objectives, it will be necessary to hold concentration at the high level and stirring rate very near the middle level.

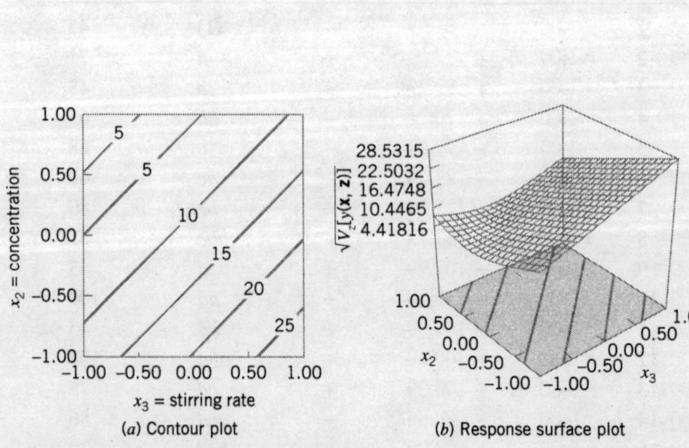

■ **FIGURE 14.13** Contour plot and response surface of $\sqrt{V_z[y(\mathbf{x}, \mathbf{z})]}$ for Example 14.3, with z_1 = temperature = 0.

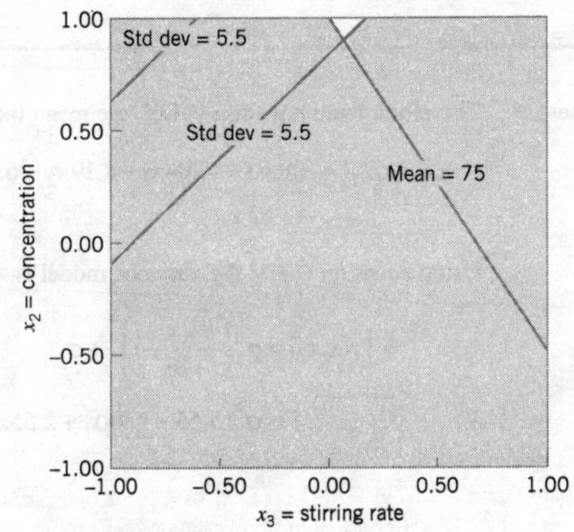

■ **FIGURE 14.14** Overlay plot of mean and standard deviation for filtration rate, Example 13.3, with z_1 = temperature = 0.

Example 14.3 illustrates the use of a first-order model with interaction as the model for the controllable factors, $f(\mathbf{x})$. In Example 14.4, we present a second-order model.

EXAMPLE 14.4 Robust Manufacturing

A process robustness study was conducted in a semiconductor manufacturing plant involving two controllable variables x_1 and x_2 and a single noise factor z. Table 14.5 shows the experiment that was performed, and Fig. 14.15 gives a graphical view of the design. Note that the experimental design is a "modified" central composite design in which the axial runs in the z direction have been eliminated. It is possible to delete these runs because no quadratic term (z^2) in the noise variable is included in the model. The objective is to find operating conditions that give a mean response between 90 and 100, while making the variability transmitted from the noise variable as small as possible.

■ **TABLE 14.5**
The Modified Central Composite Design for the Process Robustness Study in Example 13-4

Run	x_1	x_2	z	y
1	−1.00	−1.00	−1.00	73.93
2	1.00	−1.00	−1.00	81.99
3	−1.00	1.00	−1.00	77.03
4	1.00	1.00	−1.00	99.29
5	−1.00	−1.00	1.00	70.21
6	1.00	−1.00	1.00	97.72
7	−1.00	1.00	1.00	83.20
8	1.00	1.00	1.00	125.50
9	−1.68	0.00	0.00	64.75
10	1.68	0.00	0.00	102.90
11	0.00	−1.68	0.00	70.20
12	0.00	1.68	0.00	100.30
13	0.00	0.00	0.00	100.50
14	0.00	0.00	0.00	100.00
15	0.00	0.00	0.00	98.86
16	0.00	0.00	0.00	103.90

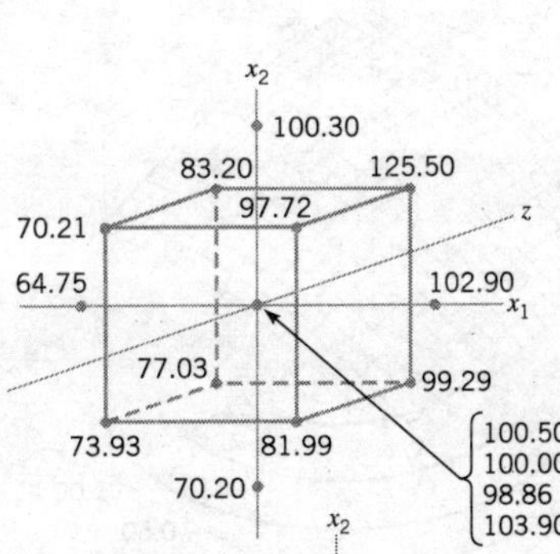

■ **FIGURE 14.15** The Modified central composite design in Example 14.4.

(*continued*)

SOLUTION

Using equation (14.5), the response model for this process robustness study is

$$y(\mathbf{x},\mathbf{z}) = f(\mathbf{x}) + h(\mathbf{x},\mathbf{z}) + \varepsilon$$
$$= \beta_0 + \beta_1 x_1 + \beta_2 x_2 + \beta_{11}x_1^2 + \beta_{22}x_2^2 + \beta_{12}x_1x_2 + \gamma_1 z + \delta_{11}x_1 z + \delta_{21}x_2 z + \varepsilon$$

The least squares fit is

$$\hat{y}(\mathbf{x},\mathbf{z}) = 100.63 + 12.04x_1 + 8.19x_2 - 6.11x_1^2 - 5.61x_2^2 + 3.62x_1x_2 + 5.55z + 4.94x_1z + 2.55x_2z$$

Therefore, from equation (14.6), the mean model is

$$E_z[y(\mathbf{x},\mathbf{z})] = 100.63 + 12.04x_1 + 8.19x_2 - 6.11x_1^2 - 5.61x_2^2 + 3.62x_1x_2$$

Using equation (14.7) the variance model is

$$V_z[y(\mathbf{x},\mathbf{z})] = \sigma_z^2\left(\frac{\partial h(\mathbf{x},\mathbf{z})}{\partial z}\right)^2 + \sigma^2$$
$$= \sigma_z^2(5.55 + 4.94x_1 + 2.55x_2)^2 + \sigma^2$$

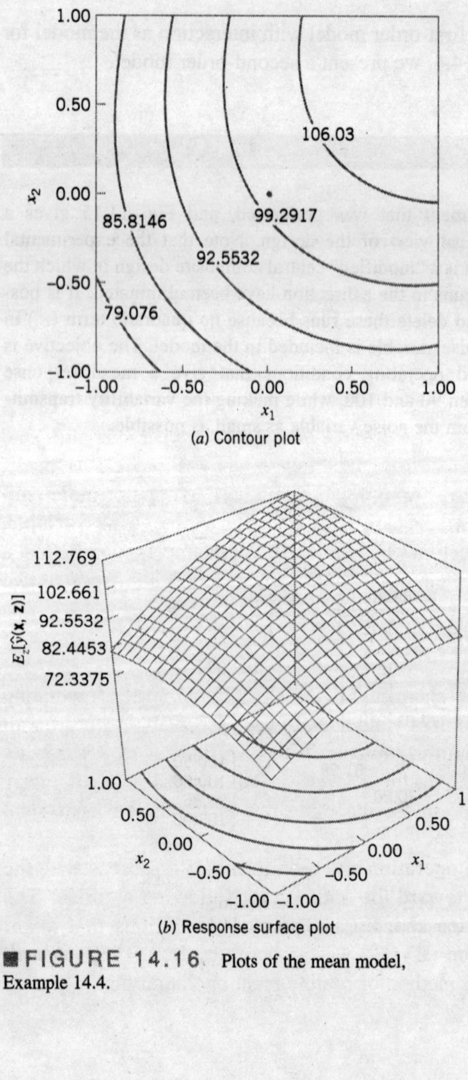

■ FIGURE 14.16. Plots of the mean model, Example 14.4.

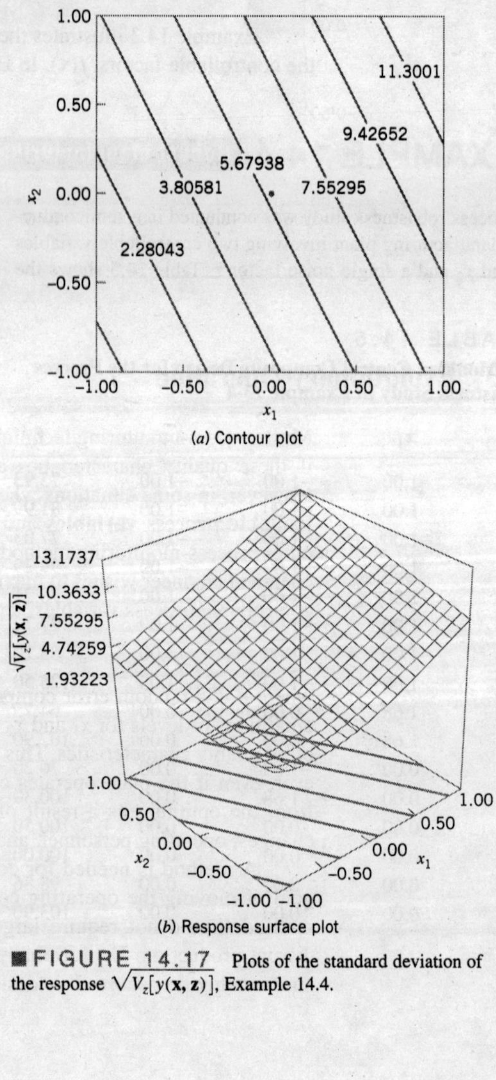

■ FIGURE 14.17. Plots of the standard deviation of the response $\sqrt{V_z[y(\mathbf{x},\mathbf{z})]}$, Example 14.4.

We will assume (as in the previous example) that $\sigma_z^2 = 1$ and since the residual mean square from fitting the response model is $MS_E = 3.73$, we will use $\hat{\sigma}^2 = MS_E = 3.73$. Therefore, the variance model is

$$V_z[y(\mathbf{x},\mathbf{z})] = (5.55 + 4.94x_1 + 2.55x_2)^2 + 3.73$$

Figures 14.16 and 14.17 show response surface contour plots and three-dimensional surface plots of the mean model and the standard deviation $\sqrt{V_z[y(\mathbf{x}, \mathbf{z})]}$, respectively.

The objective of the experimenters in this process robustness study was to find a set of operating conditions that would result in a mean response between 90 and 100 with low variability. Figure 14.18 is an overlay of the contours 90 and 100 from the mean model with the contour of constant standard deviation of 4. The unshaded region of this plot indicates operating conditions on x_1 and x_2, where the requirements for the mean response are satisfied and the response standard deviation does not exceed 4.

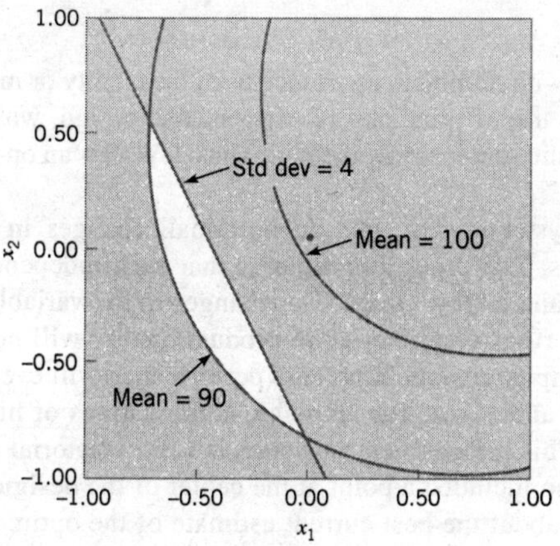

■ FIGURE 14.18 Overlay of the mean and standard deviation contours, Example 14.4.

14.3 Evolutionary Operation

Most process-monitoring techniques measure one or more output quality characteristics, and if these quality characteristics are satisfactory, no modification of the process is made. However, in some situations where there is a strong relationship between one or more **controllable process variables** and the observed quality characteristic or **response variable,** other process-monitoring methods can sometimes be employed. For example, suppose that a chemical engineer wishes to maximize the yield of the process. The yield is a function of two controllable process variables, temperature (x_1) and time (x_2)—say,

$$y = f(x_1, x_2) + \varepsilon$$

where ε is a random error component. The chemical engineer has found a set of operating conditions or levels for x_1 and x_2 that maximizes yield and provides acceptable values for all other quality characteristics. This process optimization may have been done using RSM; however, even if the plant operates continuously at these levels, it will eventually "drift" away from the optimum as a result of variations in the incoming raw materials, environmental changes, operating personnel, and the like.

A method is needed for continuous operation and monitoring of a process with the goal of moving the operating conditions toward the optimum or following a "drift." The method should not require large or sudden changes in operating conditions that might disrupt production. **Evolutionary operation (EVOP)** was proposed by Box (1957) as such an operating procedure. It is designed as a method of routine plant operation that is carried

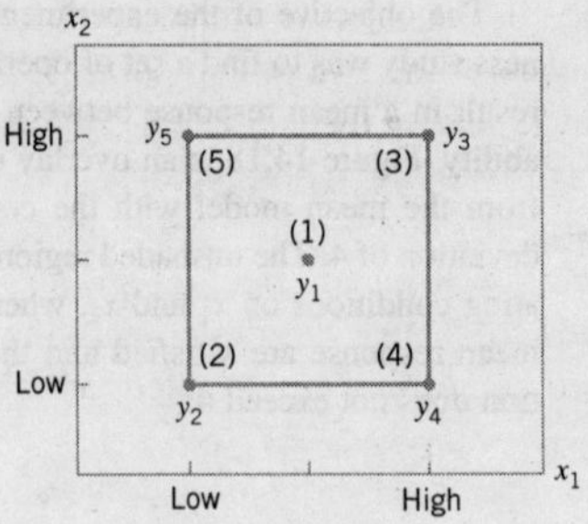

■ FIGURE 14.19 2^2 factorial design.

out by operating personnel with minimum assistance from the quality or manufacturing engineering staff. EVOP makes use of principles of experimental design, which usually is considered to be an off-line quality-engineering method. Thus, EVOP is an on-line application of designed experiments.

EVOP consists of systematically introducing small changes in the levels of the process operating variables. The procedure requires that each independent process variable be assigned a "high" and a "low" level. The changes in the variables are assumed to be small enough so that serious disturbances in product quality will not occur, yet large enough so that potential improvements in process performance will eventually be discovered. For two variables x_1 and x_2, the four possible combinations of high and low levels are shown in Fig. 14.19. This arrangement of points is the 2^2 factorial design introduced in Chapter 13. We have also included a point at the center of the design. Typically, the 2^2 design would be centered about the best current estimate of the optimum operating conditions.

The points in the 2^2 design are numbered 1, 2, 3, 4, and 5. Let y_1, y_2, y_3, y_4, and y_5 be the observed values of the dependent or response variable corresponding to these points. After one observation has been run at each point in the design, an **EVOP cycle** is said to have been completed. Recall that the main effect of a factor is defined as the average change in response produced by a change from the low level to the high level of the factor. Thus, the effect of x_1 is the average difference between the responses on the right-hand side of the design in Fig. 14.19 and the responses on the left-hand side, or

$$x_1\text{effect} = \frac{1}{2}\left[(y_3 + y_4) - (y_2 + y_5)\right]$$
$$= \frac{1}{2}\left[y_3 + y_4 - y_2 - y_5\right] \tag{14.8}$$

Similarly, the effect of x_2 is found by computing the average difference in the responses on the top of the design in Fig. 14.19 and the responses on the bottom; that is,

$$x_2\text{effect} = \frac{1}{2}\left[(y_3 + y_5) - (y_2 + y_4)\right]$$
$$= \frac{1}{2}\left[y_3 + y_5 - y_2 - y_4\right] \tag{14.9}$$

If the change from the low to the high level of x_1 produces an effect that is different at the two levels of x_2, then there is interaction between x_1 and x_2. The interaction effect is

$$x_1 \times x_2\text{interaction} = \frac{1}{2}\left[y_2 + y_3 - y_4 - y_5\right] \tag{14.10}$$

or simply the average difference between the diagonal totals in Fig. 14.19. After n cycles, there will be n observations at each of the five design points. The effects of x_1, x_2, and their interaction are then computed by replacing the individual observations y_i, in equations (14.8), (14.9), and (14.10) by the averages $\bar{y}_i$ of the n observations at each point.

After several cycles have been completed, one or more process variables, or their interaction, may appear to have a significant effect on the response variable y. When this occurs, a decision may be made to change the basic operating conditions to improve the process output. When improved conditions are detected, an **EVOP phase** is said to have been completed.

In testing the significance of process variables and interactions, an estimate of experimental error is required. This is calculated from the cycle data. By comparing the response at the center point with the 2^k points in the factorial portion, we may check on the presence of curvature in the response function; that is, if the process is really centered at the maximum (say), then the response at the center should be significantly greater than the responses at the 2^k peripheral points.

In theory, EVOP can be applied to an arbitrary number of process variables. In practice, only two or three variables are usually considered at a time. Example 14.5 shows the procedure for two variables. Box and Draper (1969) give a discussion of the three-variable case, including necessary forms and worksheets. Myers and Montgomery (2002) show how EVOP calculations can be easily performed in statistical software packages for factorial designs.

EXAMPLE 14.5 Two-Variable EVOP

Consider a chemical process whose yield is a function of temperature (x_1) and pressure (x_2). The current operating conditions are $x_1 = 250°F$ and $x_2 = 145$ psi. The EVOP procedure uses the 2^2 design plus the center point shown in Fig. 14.20. The cycle is completed by running each design point in numerical order (1, 2, 3, 4, 5). The yields in the first cycle are shown in Fig. 14.20. Set up the EVOP procedure.

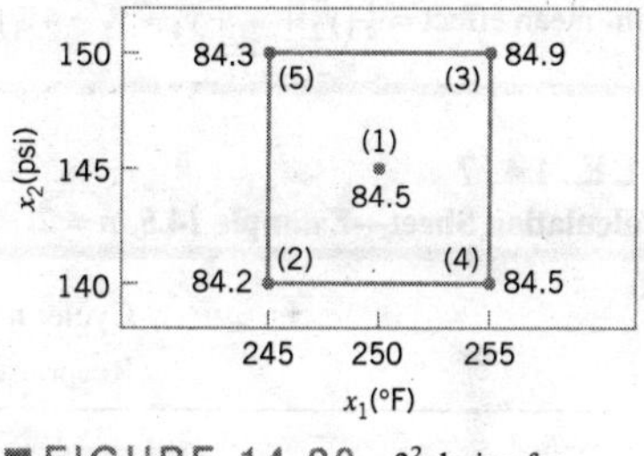

■ FIGURE 14.20 2^2 design for Example 14.5.

SOLUTION

The yields from the first cycle are entered in the EVOP calculation sheet shown in Table 14.6. At the end of the first cycle, no estimate of the standard deviation can be made. The calculation of the main effects of temperature and pressure and their interaction are shown in the bottom half of Table 14.6.

A second cycle is then run, and the yield data are entered in another EVOP calculation sheet shown in Table 14.7. At the end of the second cycle, the experimental error can be estimated and the estimates of the effects compared to approximate 95% (two standard deviation) limits. Note that the range refers to the range of the differences in row (iv); thus, the range is +1.0 − (−1.0) = 2.0. Since none of the effects in Table 14.7 exceeds their error limits, the true effect is probably zero, and no changes in operating conditions are contemplated.

The results of a third cycle are shown in Table 14.8. The effect of pressure now exceeds its error limit, and the temperature effect is equal to the error limit. A change in operating conditions is now probably justified.

In light of the results, it seems reasonable to begin a new EVOP phase about point (3). Thus, $x_1 = 225°F$ and $x_2 = 150$ psi would become the center of the 2^2 design in the second phase.

An important aspect of EVOP is feeding the information generated back to the process operators and supervisors. This is accomplished by a prominently displayed EVOP information board. The information board for this example at the end of cycle three is shown in Table 14.9.

(continued)

■ **TABLE 14.6**

EVOP Calculation Sheet—Example 14.5, n = 1

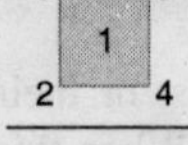

Cycle: n = 1
Response: Yield

Phase 1
Date: 6-14-07

Operating Conditions	(1)	(2)	(3)	(4)	(5)	Calculation of Standard Deviation
(i) Previous cycle sum						Previous sum $S =$
(ii) Previous cycle average						Previous average $S =$
(iii) New observations	84.5	84.2	84.9	84.5	84.3	New $S = \text{range} \times f_{5,n} =$
(iv) Differences [(ii) − (iii)]						Range of (iv) =
(v) New sums [(i) + (iii)]	84.5	84.2	84.9	84.5	84.3	New sum $S =$
(vi) New averages [$\bar{y}_i = (v)/n$]	84.5	84.2	84.9	84.5	84.3	New average $S = \dfrac{\text{new sum } S}{n-1}$

(Columns (1)–(5): Calculation of Averages)

Calculation of Effects

Temperature effect $= \frac{1}{2}(\bar{y}_3 + \bar{y}_4 - \bar{y}_2 - \bar{y}_5) = 0.45$

Pressure effect $= \frac{1}{2}(\bar{y}_3 + \bar{y}_5 - \bar{y}_2 - \bar{y}_4) = 0.25$

$T \times P$ interaction effect $= \frac{1}{2}(\bar{y}_2 + \bar{y}_3 - \bar{y}_4 - \bar{y}_5) = 0.15$

Change-in-mean effect $= \frac{1}{5}(\bar{y}_2 + \bar{y}_3 + \bar{y}_4 + \bar{y}_5 - 4\bar{y}_1) = -0.02$

Calculation of Error Limits

For new average $\frac{2}{\sqrt{n}} S =$

For new effects $\frac{2}{\sqrt{n}} S =$

For change in mean $\frac{1.78}{\sqrt{n}} S =$

■ **TABLE 14.7**

EVOP Calculation Sheet—Example 14.5, n = 2

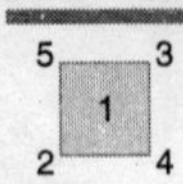

Cycle: n = 2
Response: Yield

Phase 1
Date: 6-14-07

Operating Conditions	(1)	(2)	(3)	(4)	(5)	Calculation of Standard Deviation
(i) Previous cycle sum	84.5	84.2	84.9	84.5	84.3	Previous sum $S =$
(ii) Previous cycle average	84.5	84.2	84.9	84.5	84.3	Previous average $S =$
(iii) New observations	84.9	84.6	85.9	83.5	84.0	New $S = \text{range} \times f_{5,n} = 0.60$
(iv) Differences [(ii) − (iii)]	−0.4	−0.4	−1.0	+1.0	0.3	Range of (iv) = 2.0
(v) New sums [(i) + (iii)]	169.4	168.8	170.8	168.0	168.3	New sum $S = 0.60$
(vi) New averages [$\bar{y}_i = (v)/n$]	84.70	84.40	85.40	84.00	84.15	New average $S = \dfrac{\text{New sum } S}{n-1} = 0.60$

(Columns (1)–(5): Calculation of Averages)

Temperature effect $= \frac{1}{2}(\bar{y}_3 + \bar{y}_4 - \bar{y}_2 - \bar{y}_5) = 0.43$ — For new average $\frac{2}{\sqrt{n}} S = 0.85$

Pressure effect $= \frac{1}{2}(\bar{y}_3 + \bar{y}_5 - \bar{y}_2 - \bar{y}_4) = 0.58$ — For new effects $\frac{2}{\sqrt{n}} S = 0.85$

$T \times P$ interaction effect $= \frac{1}{2}(\bar{y}_2 + \bar{y}_3 - \bar{y}_4 - \bar{y}_5) = 0.83$

Change-in-mean effect $= \frac{1}{5}(\bar{y}_2 + \bar{y}_3 + \bar{y}_4 + \bar{y}_5 - 4\bar{y}_1) = -0.17$ — For change in mean $\frac{1.78}{\sqrt{n}} S = 0.76$

■ **TABLE 14.8**
EVOP Calculation Sheet—Example 14.5, n = 3

Cycle: n = 3
Response: Yield

Phase 1
Date: 6-14-07

Calculation of Averages

Operating Conditions	(1)	(2)	(3)	(4)	(5)
(i) Previous cycle sum	169.4	168.8	170.8	168.0	168.3
(ii) Previous cycle average	84.70	84.40	85.40	84.00	84.15
(iii) New observations	85.0	84.0	86.6	84.9	85.2
(iv) Differences [(ii) − (iii)]	−0.30	+0.40	−1.20	−0.90	−1.05
(v) New sums [(i) + (iii)]	254.4	252.8	257.4	252.9	253.5
(vi) New averages[$\bar{y}$ = (v)/n]	84.80	84.27	85.80	84.30	84.50

Calculation of Standard Deviation

Previous sum $S = 0.60$
Previous average $S = 0.60$
New $S = \text{range} \times f_{5,n} = 0.56$
Range of (iv) = 1.60
New sum $S = 1.16$
New average $S = \dfrac{\text{New sum } S}{n-1} = 0.58$

Calculation of Effects

Temperature effect $= \frac{1}{2}(\bar{y}_3 + \bar{y}_4 - \bar{y}_2 - \bar{y}_5) = 0.67$

Pressure effect $= \frac{1}{2}(\bar{y}_3 + \bar{y}_5 - \bar{y}_2 - \bar{y}_4) = 0.87$

$T \times P$ interaction effect $= \frac{1}{2}(\bar{y}_2 + \bar{y}_3 - \bar{y}_4 - \bar{y}_5) = 0.64$

Change-in-mean effect $= \frac{1}{5}(\bar{y}_2 + \bar{y}_3 + \bar{y}_4 + \bar{y}_5 - 4\bar{y}_1) = -0.07$

Calculation of Error Limits

For new average $\dfrac{2}{\sqrt{n}} S = 0.67$

For new effects $\dfrac{2}{\sqrt{n}} S = 0.67$

For change in mean $\dfrac{1.78}{\sqrt{n}} S = 0.60$

■ **TABLE 14.9**
EVOP Information Board—Cycle Three

Response: Percent yield
Requirement: Maximize

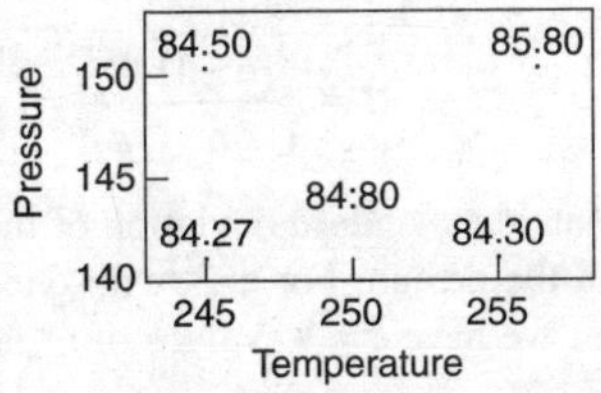

Effects with 95% Error Limits		Error Limits for Averages: ± 0.67
Temperature	0.67	±0.67
Pressure	0.87	±0.67
$T \times P$	0.64	±0.67
Change in mean	0.07	±0.60

Standard deviation: 0.58

■ TABLE 14.10
Values of $f_{k,n}$

$n =$	2	3	4	5	6	7	8	9	10
$k = 5$	0.30	0.35	0.37	0.38	0.39	0.40	0.40	0.40	0.41
9	0.24	0.27	0.29	0.30	0.31	0.31	0.31	0.32	0.32
10	0.23	0.26	0.28	0.29	0.30	0.30	0.30	0.31	0.31

Most of the quantities on the EVOP calculation sheet follow directly from the analysis of the 2^k factorial design. For example, the variance of any effect such as $\frac{1}{2}(\bar{y}_3 + \bar{y}_5 - \bar{y}_2 - \bar{y}_4)$ is simply

$$V\left[\frac{1}{2}(\bar{y}_3 + \bar{y}_5 - \bar{y}_2 - \bar{y}_4)\right] = \frac{1}{4}\left(\sigma^2_{\bar{y}_3} + \sigma^2_{\bar{y}_5} + \sigma^2_{\bar{y}_2} + \sigma^2_{\bar{y}_4}\right)$$

$$= \frac{1}{4}\left(4\sigma^2_{\bar{y}}\right) = \frac{\sigma^2}{n}$$

where σ^2 is the variance of the observations (y). Thus, two standard deviation (corresponding to approximately 95%) error limits on any effect would be $\pm 2\sigma/\sqrt{n}$. The variance of the change in mean is

$$V(\text{CIM}) = V\left[\frac{1}{5}(\bar{y}_2 + \bar{y}_3 + \bar{y}_4 + \bar{y}_5 - 4\bar{y}_1)\right]$$

$$= \frac{1}{25}\left(4\sigma^2_{\bar{y}} + 16\sigma^2_{\bar{y}}\right) = \frac{20}{25}\frac{\sigma^2}{n}$$

Thus, two standard deviation error limits on the CIM are $\pm 2\sigma\sqrt{(20/25)n} = \pm 1.78\sigma/\sqrt{n}$. For more information on the 2^k factorial design, see Chapter 13 and Montgomery (2005).

The standard deviation σ is estimated by the range method. Let $y_i(n)$ denote the observation at the ith design point in cycle n, and $\bar{y}_i(n)$ the corresponding average of $y_i(n)$ after n cycles. The quantities in row (iv) of the EVOP calculation sheet are the differences $y_i(n) - \bar{y}_i(n-1)$. The variance of these differences is $V[y_i(n) - \bar{y}_i(n-1)] \equiv \sigma^2[n/(n-1)]$. The range of the differences—say, R_D—is related to the estimate of the distribution of the differences by $\hat{\sigma}_D = R_D/d_2$. Now $R_D/d_2 = \hat{\sigma}\sqrt{n/(n-1)}$, so

$$\hat{\sigma} = \sqrt{\frac{(n-1)}{n}}\frac{R_D}{d_2} = \left(f_{k,n}\right)R_D \equiv S$$

can be used to estimate the standard deviation of the observations, where k denotes the number of points used in the design. For a 2^2 with one center point we have $k = 5$, and for a 2^3 with one center point we have $k = 9$. Values of $f_{k,n}$ are given in Table 14.10.

Important Terms and Concepts

Central composite design
Combined array design
Contour plot
Controllable variable
Crossed array design
Evolutionary operation (EVOP)
EVOP cycle
EVOP phase
First-order model
Inner array design
Method of steepest ascent
Noise variable
Outer array design
Path of steepest ascent

Process robustness study
Response model
Response surface
Response surface methodology (RSM)
Robust parameter design (RPD)
Rotatable design
Second-order model
Sequential experimentation
Taylor series
Transmission of error

Exercises

14.1. Consider the first-order model

$$\hat{y} = 50 + 2x_1 - 15x_2 + 3x_3$$

where $-1 \le x_i \le +1$, $i = 1, 2, 3$. Find the direction of steepest ascent.

14.2. Consider the first-order model

$$\hat{y} = 75 + 10x_1 + 6x_2$$

(a) Sketch the contours of constant predicted response over the range $-1 \le x_i \le +1$, $i = 1, 2$.
(b) Find the direction of steepest ascent.

14.3. In their book *Empirical Model Building and Response Surfaces* (John Wiley, 1987), G. E. P. Box and N. R. Draper describe an experiment with three factors. The data shown in Table 14E.1 are a variation of the original experiment on p. 247 of their book. Suppose that these data were collected in a semiconductor manufacturing process.
(a) The response y_1 is the average of three readings on resistivity for a single wafer. Fit a quadratic model to this response.
(b) The response y_2 is the standard deviation of the three resistivity measurements. Fit a first-order model to this response.
(c) Where would you recommend that we set x_1, x_2, and x_3 if the objective is to hold mean resistivity at 500 and minimize the standard deviation?

14.4. The data shown in the Table 14E.5 (see next page) were collected in an experiment to optimize crystal growth as a function of three variables x_1, x_2, and x_3. Large values of y (yield in grams) are desirable. Fit a second-order model and analyze the fitted surface. Under what set of conditions is maximum growth achieved?

14.5. A second-order response surface model in two variables is

$$\hat{y} = 69.0 + 1.6x_1 + 1.1x_2 - 1x_1^2 - 1.2x_2^2 + 0.3x_1x_2$$

(a) Generate a two-dimensional contour plot for this model over the region $-2 \le x_i \le +2$, $i = 1, 2$, and select the values of x_1 and x_2 that maximize $\hat{y}$.
(b) Find the two equations given by

$$\frac{\partial \hat{y}}{\partial x_1} = 0 \text{ and } \frac{\partial \hat{y}}{\partial x_2} = 0$$

Show that the solution to these equations for the optimum conditions x_1 and x_2 are the same as those found graphically in part (a).

■ **TABLE 14E.1**
The Experiment for Exercise 14.3

x_1	x_2	x_3	y_1	y_2
−1	−1	−1	24.00	12.49
0	−1	−1	120.33	8.39
1	−1	−1	213.67	42.83
−1	0	−1	86.00	3.46
0	0	−1	136.63	80.41
1	0	−1	340.67	16.17
−1	1	−1	112.33	27.57
0	1	−1	256.33	4.62
1	1	−1	271.67	23.63
−1	−1	0	81.00	0.00
0	−1	0	101.67	17.67
1	−1	0	357.00	32.91
−1	0	0	171.33	15.01
0	0	0	372.00	0.00
1	0	0	501.67	92.50
−1	1	0	264.00	63.50
0	1	0	427.00	88.61
1	1	0	730.67	21.08
−1	−1	1	220.67	133.82
0	−1	1	239.67	23.46
1	−1	1	422.00	18.52
−1	0	1	199.00	29.44
0	0	1	485.33	44.67
1	0	1	673.67	158.21
−1	1	1	176.67	55.51
0	1	1	501.00	138.94
1	1	1	1010.00	142.45

■ TABLE 14E.2
Crystal Growth Experiment for Exercise 14.4

x_1	x_2	x_3	y
−1	−1	−1	66
−1	−1	1	70
−1	1	−1	78
−1	1	1	60
1	−1	−1	80
1	−1	1	70
1	1	−1	100
1	1	1	75
−1.682	0	0	65
1.682	0	0	82
0	−1.682	0	68
0	1.682	0	63
0	0	−1.682	100
0	0	1.682	80
0	0	0	83
0	0	0	90
0	0	0	87
0	0	0	88
0	0	0	91
0	0	0	85

■ TABLE 14E.3
The Spring Experiment for Exercise 14.6

A	*B*	*C*	*D*	*E*			
−	−	−	−	−	7.78,	7.78,	7.81
+	−	−	+	−	8.15,	8.18,	7.88
−	+	−	+	−	7.50,	7.56,	7.50
+	+	−	−	−	7.59,	7.56,	7.75
−	−	+	+	−	7.54,	8.00,	7.88
+	−	+	−	−	7.69,	8.09,	8.06
−	+	+	−	−	7.56,	7.52,	7.44
+	+	+	+	−	7.56,	7.81,	7.69
−	−	−	−	+	7.50,	7.25,	7.12
+	−	−	+	+	7.88,	7.88,	7.44
−	+	−	+	+	7.50,	7.56,	7.50
+	+	−	−	+	7.63,	7.75,	7.56
−	−	+	+	+	7.32,	7.44,	7.44
+	−	+	−	+	7.56,	7.69,	7.62
−	+	+	−	+	7.18,	7.18,	7.25
+	+	+	+	+	7.81,	7.50,	7.59

14.6. An article by J. J. Pignatiello, Jr. and J. S. Ramberg in the *Journal of Quality Technology* (Vol. 17, 1985, pp. 198–206) describes the use of a replicated fractional factorial to investigate the effect of five factors on the free height of leaf springs used in an automotive application. The factors are *A* = furnace temperature, *B* = heating time, *C* = transfer time, *D* = hold down time, and *E* = quench oil temperature. The data are shown in Table 14E.3.

(a) Write out the alias structure for this design. What is the resolution of this design?

(b) Analyze the data. What factors influence mean free height?

(c) Calculate the range and standard deviation of free height for each run. Is there any indication that any of these factors affects variability in free height?

(d) Analyze the residuals from this experiment and comment on your findings.

(e) Is this the best possible design for five factors in 16 runs? Specifically, can you find a fractional design for five factors in 16 runs with higher resolution than this one?

14.7. Consider the leaf spring experiment in Exercise 14.6. Rework this problem, assuming that factors *A*, *B*, and *C* are easy to control but factors *D* and *E* are hard to control.

14.8. Consider the leaf spring experiment in Exercise 14.6. Suppose that factor *E* (quench oil temperature) is very difficult to control during manufacturing. We want to have the mean spring height as close to 7.50 as possible with minimum variability. Where would you set factors *A*, *B*, *C*, and *D* to reduce variability in free height as much as possible regardless of the quench oil temperature used?

14.9. Reconsider the crystal growth experiment from Exercise 14.4. Suppose that $x_3 = z$ is now a noise variable, and that the modified experimental design shown in Table 14E.4 has been conducted. The experimenters want the growth rate to be as large as possible, but they also want the variability transmitted from z to be small. Under what set of conditions is growth greater than 90 with minimum variability achieved?

14.10. An experiment was run to study the effect of two factors, time and temperature, on the inorganic impurity levels in paper pulp. The results of this experiment are shown in Table 14E.5:

(a) What type of experimental design has been used in this study? Is the design rotatable?

■ TABLE 14E.4
Crystal Growth Experiment for Exercise 14.9

x_1	x_2	z	y
−1	−1	−1	66
−1	−1	1	70
−1	1	−1	78
−1	1	1	60
1	−1	−1	80
1	−1	1	70
1	1	−1	100
1	1	1	75
−1.682	0	0	65
1.682	0	0	82
0	−1.682	0	68
0	1.682	0	63
0	0	0	83
0	0	0	90
0	0	0	87
0	0	0	88
0	0	0	91
0	0	0	85

■ TABLE 14E.5
The Experiment for Exercise 14.10

x_1	x_2	y
−1	−1	210
1	−1	95
−1	1	218
1	1	100
−1.5	0	225
1.5	0	50
0	−1.5	175
0	1.5	180
0	0	145
0	0	175
0	0	158
0	0	166

(b) Fit a quadratic model to the response, using the method of least squares.

(c) Construct the fitted impurity response surface. What values of x_1 and x_2 would you recommend if you wanted to minimize the impurity level?

■ TABLE 14E.6
Chemical Process Experiment for Exercise 14.11

x_1	x_2	y
−1	−1	54
−1	1	45
1	−1	32
1	1	47
−1.414	0	50
1.414	0	53
0	−1.414	47
0	1.414	51
0	0	41
0	0	39
0	0	44
0	0	42
0	0	40

(d) Suppose that

$$x_1 = \frac{\text{temp} - 750}{50} \qquad x_2 = \frac{\text{time} - 30}{15}$$

where temperature is in °C and time is in hours. Find the optimum operating conditions in terms of the natural variables temperature and time.

14.11. The data in Table 14E.6 were collected by a chemical engineer. The response y is filtration time, x_1 is temperature, and x_2 is pressure. Fit a second-order model.

(a) What operating conditions would you recommend if the objective is to minimize the filtration time?

(b) What operating conditions would you recommend if the objective is to operate the process at a mean filtration rate very close to 46?

14.12. An article in *Rubber Chemistry and Technology* (Vol. 47, 1974, pp. 825–836) describes an experiment that studies the relationship of the Mooney viscosity of rubber to several variables, including silica filler (parts per hundred) and oil filler (parts per hundred). Some of the data from this experiment are shown in Table 14E.7 (see next page), where

$$x_1 = \frac{\text{silica} - 60}{15} \qquad x_2 = \frac{\text{oil} - 21}{1.5}$$

(a) What type of experimental design has been used? Is it rotatable?

(b) Fit a quadratic model to these data. What values of x_1 and x_2 will maximize the Mooney viscosity?

■ TABLE 14E.2
The Viscosity Experiment for Exercise 14.5

Coded Levels		
x_1	x_2	y
−1	−1	13.71
1	−1	14.15
−1	1	12.87
1	1	13.53
−1.4	0	12.99
1.4	0	13.89
0	−1.4	14.16
0	1.4	12.90
0	0	13.75
0	0	13.66
0	0	13.86
0	0	13.63
0	0	13.74

14.13. Consider the response model in equation (14.5). Suppose that in the response model we allow for a complete second-order model in the noise factors so that

$$h(\mathbf{x},\mathbf{z}) = \sum_{i=1}^{r}\gamma_i z_i + \sum_{i=1}^{k}\sum_{j=1}^{r}\delta_{ij}x_i z_j + \sum_{i<j=2}\sum^{r}\lambda_{ij}z_i z_j + \sum_{i=1}^{r}\theta_i z_i^2$$

What effect does this have on the variance model?

14.14. Consider the response model in equation (14.5) and the transmission of error approach to finding the variance model [equation (14.7)]. Suppose that in the response model we use

$$h(\mathbf{x},\mathbf{z}) = \sum_{i=1}^{r}\gamma_i z_i + \sum_{i=1}^{k}\sum_{j=1}^{r}\delta_{ij}x_i z_j + \sum_{i<j=2}\sum^{r}\lambda_{ij}z_i z_j$$

What effect does including the interaction terms between the noise variables have on the variance model?

PART 6

Acceptance Sampling

Inspection of raw materials, semifinished products, or finished products is one aspect of quality assurance. When inspection is for the purpose of acceptance or rejection of a product, based on adherence to a standard, the type of inspection procedure employed is usually called acceptance sampling. This section presents two chapters that deal with the design and use of sampling plans, schemes, and systems. The primary focus is on lot-by-lot acceptance sampling.

Chapter 15 presents lot-by-lot acceptance-sampling plans for attributes. Included in the chapter is a discussion of MIL STD 105E and its civilian counterpart ANSI/ASQC Z1.4. Variables sampling plans are presented in Chapter 16, including MIL STD 414 and its civilian counterpart ANSI/ASQC Z1.9, along with a survey of several additional topics in acceptance sampling, including chain-sampling plans, sampling plans for continuous production, and skip-lot sampling plans.

The underlying philosophy here is that acceptance sampling is not a substitute for adequate process monitoring and control and use of other statistical methods to drive variability reduction. The successful use of these techniques at the early stages of manufacturing, including the supplier or supplier base, can greatly reduce and in some cases eliminate the need for extensive sampling inspection.

15 Basic Acceptance Sampling Procedures

Chapter Outline

The supplemental material is on the textbook Website www.wiley.com/college/montgomery.

Chapter Overview and Learning Objectives

This chapter presents lot-by-lot acceptance-sampling plans for attributes. Key topics include the design and operation of single-sampling plans, the use of the operating characteristic curve, and the concepts of rectifying inspection, average outgoing quality, and average total inspection. Similar concepts are briefly introduced for types of sampling plans where more than one sample may be taken to determine the disposition of a lot (double, multiple, and sequential sampling). Two systems of standard sampling plans are also presented, the military standard plans known as MIL STD 105E and the Dodge–Romig plans. These plans are designed around different philosophies: MIL STD 105E has an acceptable quality level focus, whereas the Dodge–Romig plans are oriented around either the lot tolerance percent defective or the average outgoing quality limit perspective.

After careful study of this chapter you should be able to do the following:

1. Understand the role of acceptance sampling in modern quality control systems
2. Understand the advantages and disadvantages of sampling
3. Understand the difference between attributes and variables sampling plans, and the major types of acceptance-sampling procedures
4. Know how single-, double-, and sequential-sampling plans are used
5. Understand the importance of random sampling
6. Know how to determine the OC curve for a single-sampling plan for attributes
7. Understand the effects of the sampling plan parameters on sampling plan performance
8. Know how to design single-sampling, double-sampling, and sequential-sampling plans for attributes
9. Know how rectifying inspection is used
10. Understand the structure and use of MIL STD 105E and its civilian counterpart plans
11. Understand the structure and use of the Dodge–Romig system of sampling plans

15.1 The Acceptance-Sampling Problem

As we observed in Chapter 1, acceptance sampling is concerned with inspection and decision making regarding products, one of the oldest aspects of quality assurance. In the 1930s and 1940s, acceptance sampling was one of the major components of the field of statistical quality control, and was used primarily for incoming or receiving inspection. In more recent years, it has become typical to work with suppliers to improve their process performance through the use of SPC and designed experiments, and not to rely as much on acceptance sampling as a primary quality assurance tool.

A typical application of acceptance sampling is as follows: A company receives a shipment of product from a supplier. This product is often a component or raw material used in the company's manufacturing process. A sample is taken from the lot, and some quality characteristic of the units in the sample is inspected. On the basis of the information in this sample, a decision is made regarding **lot disposition.** Usually, this decision is either to accept or to reject the lot. Sometimes we refer to this decision as **lot sentencing.** Accepted lots are put into production; rejected lots may be returned to the supplier or may be subjected to some other **lot disposition action.**

Although it is customary to think of acceptance sampling as a receiving inspection activity, there are other uses of sampling methods. For example, frequently a manufacturer will sample and inspect its own product at various stages of production. Lots that are accepted are sent forward for further processing, and rejected lots may be reworked or scrapped.

Three aspects of sampling are important:

1. It is the purpose of acceptance sampling to sentence lots, not to estimate the lot quality. Most acceptance-sampling plans are not designed for estimation purposes.

2. Acceptance-sampling plans do not provide any *direct* form of quality control. Acceptance sampling simply accepts and rejects lots. Even if all lots are of the same quality, sampling will accept some lots and reject others, the accepted lots being no better than the rejected ones. Process controls are used to control and systematically improve quality, but acceptance sampling is not.
3. The most effective use of acceptance sampling is *not* to "inspect quality into the product," but rather as an audit tool to ensure that the output of a process conforms to requirements.

Generally, there are three approaches to lot sentencing: (1) accept with no inspection; (2) 100% inspection—that is, inspect every item in the lot, removing all defective[1] units found (defectives may be returned to the supplier, reworked, replaced with known good items, or discarded); and (3) acceptance sampling. The no-inspection alternative is useful in situations where either the supplier's process is so good that defective units are almost never encountered or where there is no economic justification to look for defective units. For example, if the supplier's process capability ratio is 3 or 4, acceptance sampling is unlikely to discover any defective units. We generally use 100% inspection in situations where the component is extremely critical and passing any defectives would result in an unacceptably high failure cost at subsequent stages, or where the supplier's process capability is inadequate to meet specifications. Acceptance sampling is most likely to be useful in the following situations:

1. When testing is destructive
2. When the cost of 100% inspection is extremely high
3. When 100% inspection is not technologically feasible or would require so much calendar time that production scheduling would be seriously impacted
4. When there are many items to be inspected and the inspection error rate is sufficiently high that 100% inspection might cause a higher percentage of defective units to be passed than would occur with the use of a sampling plan
5. When the supplier has an excellent quality history, and some reduction in inspection from 100% is desired, but the supplier's process capability is sufficiently low as to make no inspection an unsatisfactory alternative
6. When there are potentially serious product liability risks, and although the supplier's process is satisfactory, a program for continuously monitoring the product is necessary

15.1.1 Advantages and Disadvantages of Sampling

When acceptance sampling is contrasted with 100% inspection, it has the following advantages:

1. It is usually less expensive because there is less inspection.
2. There is less handling of the product, hence reduced damage.
3. It is applicable to destructive testing.
4. Fewer personnel are involved in inspection activities.
5. It often greatly reduces the amount of inspection error.
6. The rejection of entire lots as opposed to the simple return of defectives often provides a stronger motivation to the supplier for quality improvements.

[1]In previous chapters, the terms "nonconforming" and "nonconformity" were used instead of defective and defect. This is because the popular meanings of defective and defect differ from their technical meanings and have caused considerable misunderstanding, particularly in product liability litigation. In the field of sampling inspection, however, "defective" and "defect" continue to be used in their technical sense—that is, nonconformance to requirements.

Acceptance sampling also has several disadvantages, however. These include the following:

1. There are risks of accepting "bad" lots and rejecting "good" lots.
2. Less information is usually generated about the product or about the process that manufactured the product.
3. Acceptance sampling requires planning and documentation of the acceptance-sampling procedure whereas 100% inspection does not.

Although this last point is often mentioned as a disadvantage of acceptance sampling, proper design of an acceptance-sampling plan usually requires study of the actual level of quality required by the consumer. This resulting knowledge is often a useful input into the overall quality planning and engineering process. Thus, in many applications, it may not be a significant disadvantage.

We have pointed out that acceptance sampling is a middle ground between the extremes of 100% inspection and no inspection. It often provides a methodology for moving between these extremes as sufficient information is obtained on the control of the manufacturing process that produces the product. Although there is no direct control of quality in the application of an acceptance-sampling plan to an isolated lot, when that plan is applied to a stream of lots from a supplier, it becomes a means of providing protection for both the producer of the lot and the consumer. It also provides for an accumulation of quality history regarding the process that produces the lot, and it may provide feedback that is useful in process control, such as determining when process controls at the supplier's plant are not adequate. Finally, it may place economic or psychological pressure on the supplier to improve the production process.

15.1.2 Types of Sampling Plans

There are a number of different ways to classify acceptance-sampling plans. One major classification is by variables and attributes. **Variables,** of course, are quality characteristics that are measured on a numerical scale. **Attributes** are quality characteristics that are expressed on a "go, no-go" basis. This chapter deals with lot-by-lot acceptance-sampling plans for attributes. Variables sampling plans are the subject of Chapter 16, along with a brief discussion of several special acceptance-sampling procedures.

A **single-sampling plan** is a lot-sentencing procedure in which one sample of n units is selected at random from the lot, and the disposition of the lot is determined based on the information contained in that sample. For example, a single-sampling plan for attributes would consist of a sample size n and an acceptance number c. The procedure would operate as follows: Select n items at random from the lot. If there are c or fewer defectives in the sample, accept the lot, and if there are more than c defective items in the sample, reject the lot. We investigate this type of sampling plan extensively in Section 15.2.

Double-sampling plans are somewhat more complicated. Following an initial sample, a decision based on the information in that sample is made either to (1) accept the lot, (2) reject the lot, or (3) take a second sample. If the second sample is taken, the information from both the first and second sample is combined in order to reach a decision whether to accept or reject the lot. Double-sampling plans are discussed in Section 15.3.

A **multiple-sampling plan** is an extension of the double-sampling concept, in that more than two samples may be required in order to reach a decision regarding the disposition of the lot. Sample sizes in multiple sampling are usually smaller than they are in either single or double sampling. The ultimate extension of multiple sampling is **sequential sampling,** in which units are selected from the lot one at a time, and following inspection of each unit, a decision is made either to accept the lot, reject the lot, or select another unit. Multiple- and sequential-sampling plans are also discussed in Section 15.3.

Single-, double-, multiple-, and sequential-sampling plans can be designed so that they produce equivalent results. That is, these procedures can be designed so that a lot of specified quality has exactly the same probability of acceptance under all four types of sampling plans. Consequently, when selecting the type of sampling procedure, one must consider factors such as the administrative efficiency, the type of information produced by the plan, the average amount of inspection required by the procedure, and the impact that a given procedure may have on the material flow in the manufacturing organization. These issues are discussed in more detail in Section 15.3.

15.1.3 Lot Formation

How the lot is formed can influence the effectiveness of the acceptance-sampling plan. There are a number of important considerations in forming lots for inspection. Some of these are as follows:

1. **Lots should be homogeneous.** The units in the lot should be produced by the same machines, the same operators, and from common raw materials, at approximately the same time. When lots are nonhomogeneous, such as when the output of two different production lines is mixed, the acceptance-sampling scheme may not function as effectively as it could. Nonhomogeneous lots also make it more difficult to take corrective action to eliminate the source of defective products.
2. **Larger lots are preferred over smaller ones.** It is usually more economically efficient to inspect large lots than small ones.
3. **Lots should be conformable to the materials-handling systems used in both the supplier and consumer facilities.** In addition, the items in the lots should be packaged so as to minimize shipping and handling risks, and so as to make selection of the units in the sample relatively easy.

15.1.4 Random Sampling

The units selected for inspection from the lot should be chosen at random, and they should be representative of all the items in the lot. The random-sampling concept is extremely important in acceptance sampling. Unless random samples are used, bias will be introduced. For example, the supplier may ensure that the units packaged on the top of the lot are of extremely good quality, knowing that the inspector will select the sample from the top layer. "Salting" a lot in this manner is not a common practice, but if it occurs and nonrandom-sampling methods are used, the effectiveness of the inspection process is destroyed.

The technique often suggested for drawing a random sample is to first assign a number to each item in the lot. Then n random numbers are drawn, where the range of these numbers is from 1 to the maximum number of units in the lot. This sequence of random numbers determines which units in the lot will constitute the sample. If products have serial or other code numbers, these numbers can be used to avoid the process of actually assigning numbers to each unit. Another possibility would be to use a three-digit random number to represent the length, width, and depth in a container.

In situations where we cannot assign a number to each unit, utilize serial or code numbers, or randomly determine the location of the sample unit, some other technique must be employed to ensure that the sample is random or representative. Sometimes the inspector may **stratify** the lot. This consists of dividing the lot into strata or layers and then subdividing each strata into cubes, as shown in Fig. 15.1. Units are then selected from within each cube. Although this stratification of the lot is usually an imaginary activity performed by the inspector and does not necessarily ensure random samples, at least it ensures that units are selected from all locations in the lot.

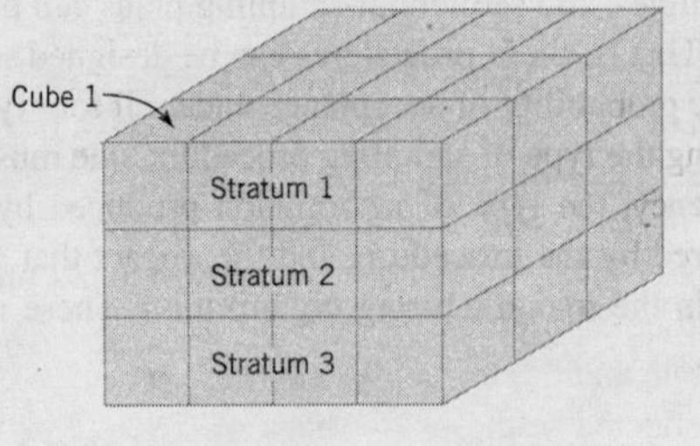

■ FIGURE 15.1 Stratifying a lot.

We cannot overemphasize the importance of random sampling. If judgment methods are used to select the sample, the statistical basis of the acceptance-sampling procedure is lost.

15.1.5 Guidelines for Using Acceptance Sampling

An acceptance-sampling plan is a statement of the sample size to be used and the associated acceptance or rejection criteria for sentencing individual lots. A sampling scheme is defined as a set of procedures consisting of acceptance-sampling plans in which lot sizes, sample sizes, and acceptance or rejection criteria along with the amount of 100% inspection and sampling are related. Finally, a sampling system is a unified collection of one or more acceptance-sampling schemes. In this chapter, we see examples of sampling plans, sampling schemes, and sampling systems.

The major types of acceptance-sampling procedures and their applications are shown in Table 15.1. In general, the selection of an acceptance-sampling procedure depends on both the objective of the sampling organization and the history of the organization whose product is sampled. Furthermore, the application of sampling methodology is not static; that is, there is a natural evolution from one level of sampling effort to another. For example, if we are dealing with a supplier who enjoys an excellent quality history, we might begin with an attributes sampling plan. As our experience with the supplier grows, and its good-quality reputation is proved by the results of our sampling activities, we might transition to a sampling procedure that requires much less inspection, such as skip-lot sampling. Finally, after extensive experience with the supplier, and if its process capability is extremely good, we might stop all acceptance-sampling activities on the product. In another situation, where we have little knowledge of or experience with the supplier's quality-assurance efforts, we might begin with attributes sampling using a plan that assures us that the quality of accepted lots is no worse

■ TABLE 15.1
Acceptance-Sampling Procedures

Objective	Attributes Procedure	Variables Procedure
Assure quality levels for consumer/producer	Select plan for specific OC curve	Select plan for specific OC curve
Maintain quality at a target	AQL system; MIL STD 105E, ANSI/ASQC Z1.4	AQL system; MIL STD 414, ANSI/ASQC Z1.9
Assure average outgoing quality level	AOQL system; Dodge–Romig plans	AOQL system
Reduce inspection, with small sample sizes, good-quality history	Chain sampling	Narrow-limit gauging
Reduce inspection after good-quality history	Skip-lot sampling; double sampling	Skip-lot sampling; double sampling
Assure quality no worse than target	LTPD plan; Dodge–Romig plans	LTPD plan; hypothesis testing

than a specified target value. If this plan proves successful, and if the supplier's performance is satisfactory, we might transition from attributes to variables inspection, particularly as we learn more about the nature of the supplier's process. Finally, we might use the information gathered in variables sampling plans in conjunction with efforts directly at the supplier's manufacturing facility to assist in the installation of process controls. A successful program of process controls at the supplier level might improve the supplier's process capability to the point where inspection could be discontinued.

These examples illustrate that there is a life cycle of application of acceptance-sampling techniques. This was also reflected in the phase diagram, Fig. 1.7, which presented the percentage of application of various quality-assurance techniques as a function of the maturity of the business organization. Typically, we find that organizations with relatively new quality-assurance efforts place a great deal of reliance on acceptance sampling. As their maturity grows and the quality organization develops, they begin to rely less on acceptance sampling and more on statistical process control and experimental design.

Manufacturers try to improve the quality of their products by reducing the number of suppliers from whom they buy their components, and by working more closely with the ones they retain. Once again, the key tool in this effort to improve quality is statistical process control. Acceptance sampling can be an important ingredient of any quality-assurance program; however, remember that it is an activity that you try to avoid doing. It is much more cost effective to use statistically based process monitoring at the appropriate stage of the manufacturing process. Sampling methods can in some cases be a tool that you employ along the road to that ultimate goal.

15.2 Single-Sampling Plans for Attributes

15.2.1 Definition of a Single-Sampling Plan

Suppose that a lot of size N has been submitted for inspection. A **single-sampling plan** is defined by the sample size n and the acceptance number c. Thus, if the lot size is $N = 10{,}000$, then the sampling plan

$$n = 89$$
$$c = 2$$

means that from a lot of size 10,000 a random sample of $n = 89$ units is inspected and the number of nonconforming or defective items d observed. If the number of observed defectives d is less than or equal to $c = 2$, the lot will be accepted. If the number of observed defectives d is greater than 2, the lot will be rejected. Since the quality characteristic inspected is an attribute, each unit in the sample is judged to be either conforming or nonconforming. One or several attributes can be inspected in the same sample; generally, a unit that is nonconforming to specifications on one or more attributes is said to be a defective unit. This procedure is called a single-sampling plan because the lot is sentenced based on the information contained in one sample of size n.

15.2.2 The OC Curve

An important measure of the performance of an acceptance-sampling plan is the **operating-characteristic (OC) curve.** This curve plots the probability of accepting the lot versus the lot fraction defective. Thus, the OC curve displays the discriminatory power of the sampling plan. That is, it shows the probability that a lot submitted with a certain fraction defective will be either accepted or rejected. The OC curve of the sampling plan $n = 89$, $c = 2$ is shown in

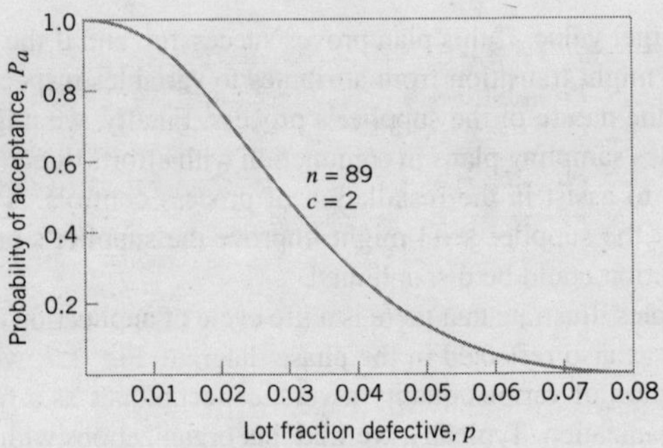

■ **FIGURE 15.2** OC curve of the single-sampling plan $n = 89$, $c = 2$.

Fig. 15.2. It is easy to demonstrate how the points on this curve are obtained. Suppose that the lot size N is large (theoretically infinite). Under this condition, the distribution of the number of defectives d in a random sample of n items is binomial with parameters n and p, where p is the fraction of defective items in the lot. An equivalent way to conceptualize this is to draw lots of N items at random from a theoretically infinite process, and then to draw random samples of n from these lots. Sampling from the lot in this manner is the equivalent of sampling directly from the process. The probability of observing exactly d defectives is

$$P\{d \text{ defectives}\} = f(d) = \frac{n!}{d!(n-d)!} p^d (1-p)^{n-d} \tag{15.1}$$

The probability of acceptance is simply the probability that d is less than or equal to c, or

$$P_a = P\{d \le c\} = \sum_{d=0}^{c} \frac{n!}{d!(n-d)!} p^d (1-p)^{n-d} \tag{15.2}$$

For example, if the lot fraction defective is $p = 0.01$, $n = 89$, and $c = 2$, then

$$\begin{aligned} P_a = P\{d \le 2\} &= \sum_{d=0}^{2} \frac{89!}{d!(89-d)!} (0.01)^d (0.99)^{89-d} \\ &= \frac{89!}{0!89!}(0.01)^0(0.99)^{89} + \frac{89!}{1!88!}(0.01)^1(0.99)^{88} + \frac{89!}{2!(87)!}(0.01)^2(0.99)^{87} \\ &= 0.9397 \end{aligned}$$

The OC curve is developed by evaluating equation (15.2) for various values of p. Table 15.2 displays the calculated value of several points on the curve.

The OC curve shows the **discriminatory power** of the sampling plan. For example, in the sampling plan $n = 89$, $c = 2$, if the lots are 2% defective, the probability of acceptance is approximately 0.74. This means that if 100 lots from a process that manufactures 2% defective product are submitted to this sampling plan, we will expect to accept 74 of the lots and reject 26 of them.

Effect of n and c on OC Curves. A sampling plan that discriminated perfectly between good and bad lots would have an OC curve that looks like Fig. 15.3. The OC curve runs horizontally at a probability of acceptance $P_a = 1.00$ until a level of lot quality that is considered "bad" is reached, at which point the curve drops vertically to a probability of acceptance $P_a = 0.00$, and then the curve runs horizontally again for all lot fraction defectives

■ TABLE 15.2
Probabilities of Acceptance for the Single-Sampling Plan $n = 89$, $c = 2$

Fraction Defective, p	Probability of Acceptance, P_a
0.005	0.9897
0.010	0.9397
0.020	0.7366
0.030	0.4985
0.040	0.3042
0.050	0.1721
0.060	0.0919
0.070	0.0468
0.080	0.0230
0.090	0.0109

greater than the undesirable level. If such a sampling plan could be employed, all lots of "bad" quality would be rejected, and all lots of "good" quality would be accepted.

Unfortunately, the **ideal OC curve** in Fig. 15.3 can almost never be obtained in practice. In theory, it could be realized by 100% inspection, if the inspection were error-free. The ideal OC curve shape can be approached, however, by increasing the sample size. Figure 15.4 shows that the OC curve becomes more like the idealized OC curve shape as the sample size increases. (Note that the acceptance number c is kept proportional to n.) Thus, the precision with which a sampling plan differentiates between good and bad lots increases with the size of the sample. The greater is the slope of the OC curve, the greater is the discriminatory power.

Figure 15.5 shows how the OC curve changes as the acceptance number changes. Generally, changing the acceptance number does not dramatically change the slope of the OC curve. As the acceptance number is decreased, the OC curve is shifted to the left. Plans with smaller values of c provide discrimination at lower levels of lot fraction defective than do plans with larger values of c.

Specific Points on the OC Curve. Frequently, the quality engineer's interest focuses on certain points on the OC curve. The supplier or consumer is usually interested in knowing what level of lot or process quality would yield a high probability of acceptance. For example, the supplier might be interested in the 0.95 probability of acceptance point. This would indicate the level of process fallout that could be experienced and still have a 95% chance that the lots would be accepted. Conversely, the consumer might be interested in the other end of the OC curve. That is, what level of lot or process quality will yield a low probability of acceptance?

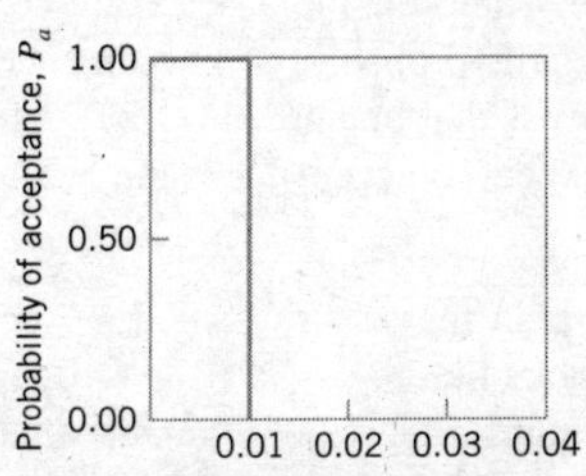

■ FIGURE 15.3 Ideal OC curve.

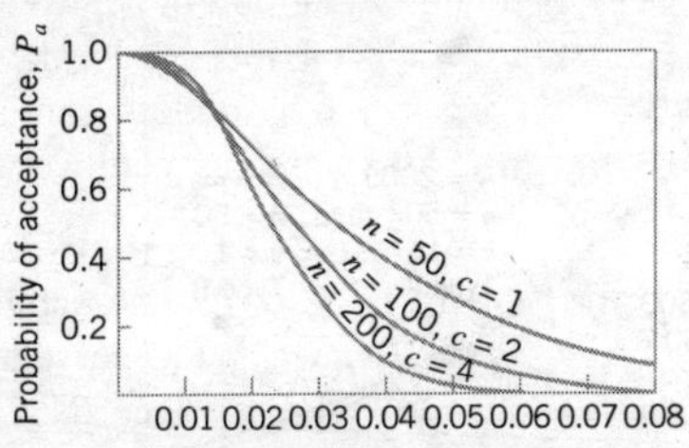

■ FIGURE 15.4 OC curves for different sample sizes.

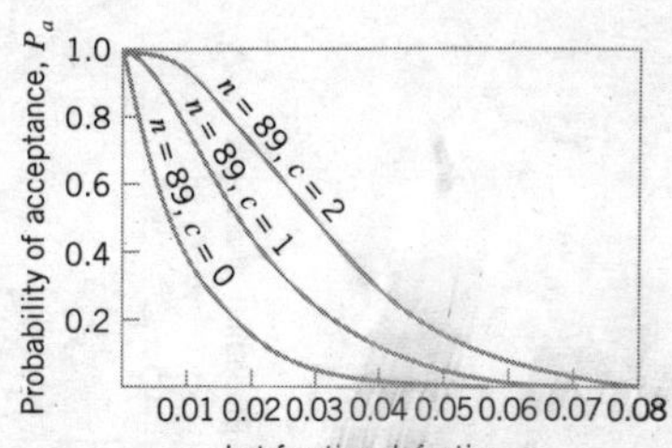

■ FIGURE 15.5 The effect of changing the acceptance number on the OC curve.

A consumer often establishes a sampling plan for a continuing supply of components or raw material with reference to an **acceptable quality level (AQL).** The AQL represents the poorest level of quality for the supplier's process that the consumer would consider to be acceptable as a process average. Note that the AQL is a property of the supplier's manufacturing process; it is not a property of the sampling plan. The consumer will often design the sampling procedure so that the OC curve gives a high probability of acceptance at the AQL. Furthermore, the AQL is not usually intended to be a specification on the product, nor is it a target value for the supplier's production process. It is simply a standard against which to judge the lots. It is hoped that the supplier's process will operate at a fallout level that is considerably better than the AQL.

The consumer will also be interested in the other end of the OC curve—that is, in the protection that is obtained for individual lots of poor quality. In such a situation, the consumer may establish a **lot tolerance percent defective (LTPD).** The LTPD is the poorest level of quality that the consumer is willing to accept in an individual lot. Note that the lot tolerance percent defective is not a characteristic of the sampling plan, but is a level of lot quality specified by the consumer. Alternate names for the LTPD are the **rejectable quality level (RQL)** and the **limiting quality level (LQL).** It is possible to design acceptance-sampling plans that give specified probabilities of acceptance at the LTPD point. Subsequently, we will see how to design sampling plans that have specified performance at the AQL and LTPD points.

Type-A and Type-B OC Curves. The OC curves that were constructed in the previous examples are called **type-B OC curves.** In the construction of the OC curve it was assumed that the samples came from a large lot or that we were sampling from a stream of lots selected at random from a process. In this situation, the **binomial distribution** is the exact probability distribution for calculating the probability of lot acceptance. Such an OC curve is referred to as a type-B OC curve.

The **type-A OC curve** is used to calculate probabilities of acceptance for an isolated lot of finite size. Suppose that the lot size is N, the sample size is n, and the acceptance number is c. The exact sampling distribution of the number of defective items in the sample is the **hypergeometric distribution.**

Figure 15.6 shows the type-A OC curve for a single-sampling plan with $n = 50$, $c = 1$, where the lot size is $N = 500$. The probabilities of acceptance defining the OC curve were calculated using the hypergeometric distribution. Also shown on this graph is the type-A OC curve for $N = 2000$, $n = 50$, and $c = 1$. Note that the two OC curves are very similar. Generally, as the size of the lot increases, the lot size has a decreasing impact on the OC curve. In fact, if the lot size is at least 10 times the sample size ($n/N \leq 0.10$), the type-A and type-B OC curves are virtually indistinguishable. As an illustration, the type-B OC curve for the sampling plan $n = 50$, $c = 1$ is also shown in Fig. 15.6. Note that it is identical to the type-A OC curve based on a lot size of $N = 2000$.

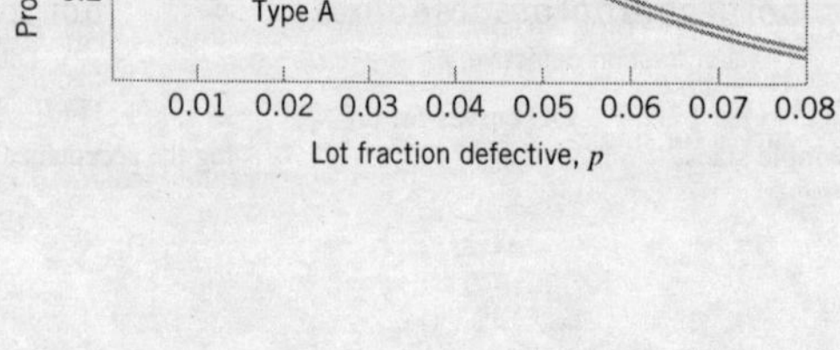

■ **FIGURE 15.6** Type-A and type-B OC curves.

The type-A OC curve will always lie below the type-B OC curve. That is, if a type-B OC curve is used as an approximation for a type-A curve, the probabilities of acceptance calculated for the type-B curve will always be higher than they would have been if the type-A curve had been used instead. However, this difference is only significant when the lot size is small relative to the sample size. Unless otherwise stated, all discussion of OC curves in this text is in terms of the type-B OC curve.

Other Aspects of OC Curve Behavior. Two approaches to designing sampling plans that are encountered in practice have certain implications for the behavior of the OC curve. Since not all of these implications are positive, it is worthwhile to briefly mention these two approaches to sampling plan design. These approaches are the use of sampling plans with zero acceptance numbers ($c = 0$) and the use of sample sizes that are a fixed percentage of the lot size.

Figure 15.7 shows several OC curves for acceptance-sampling plans with $c = 0$. By comparing Fig. 15.7 with Fig. 15.5, it is easy to see that plans with zero acceptance numbers have OC curves that have a very different shape than the OC curves of sampling plans for which $c > 0$. Generally, sampling plans with $c = 0$ have OC curves that are convex throughout their range. As a result of this shape, the probability of acceptance begins to drop very rapidly, even for small values of the lot fraction defective. This is extremely hard on the supplier, and in some circumstances, it may be extremely uneconomical for the consumer. For example, consider the sampling plans in Fig. 15.5. Suppose the acceptable quality level is 1%. This implies that we would like to accept lots that are 1% defective or better. Note that if sampling plan $n = 89$, $c = 1$ is used, the probability of lot acceptance at the AQL is about 0.78. On the other hand, if the plan $n = 89$, $c = 0$ is used, the probability of acceptance at the AQL is approximately 0.41. That is, nearly 60% of the lots of AQL quality will be rejected if we use an acceptance number of zero. If rejected lots are returned to the supplier, then a large number of lots will be unnecessarily returned, perhaps creating production delays at the consumer's manufacturing site. If the consumer screens or 100% inspects all rejected lots, a large number of lots that are of acceptable quality will be screened. This is, at best, an inefficient use of sampling resources. In Chapter 16, we suggest an alternative approach to using zero acceptance numbers called **chain-sampling plans.** Under certain circumstances, chain sampling works considerably better than acceptance-sampling plans with $c = 0$. Also refer to Section S15.1 of the supplemental material for a discussion of **lot-sensitive compliance sampling,** another technique that utilizes zero acceptance numbers.

Figure 15.8 presents the OC curves for sampling plans in which the sample size is a fixed percentage of the lot size. The principal disadvantage of this approach is that the different

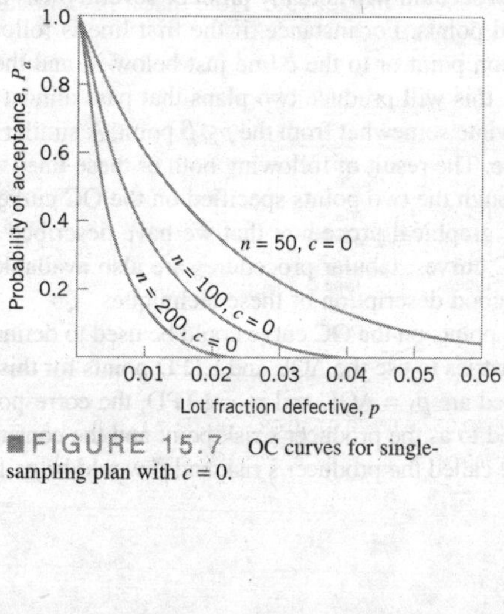

■ FIGURE 15.7 OC curves for single-sampling plan with $c = 0$.

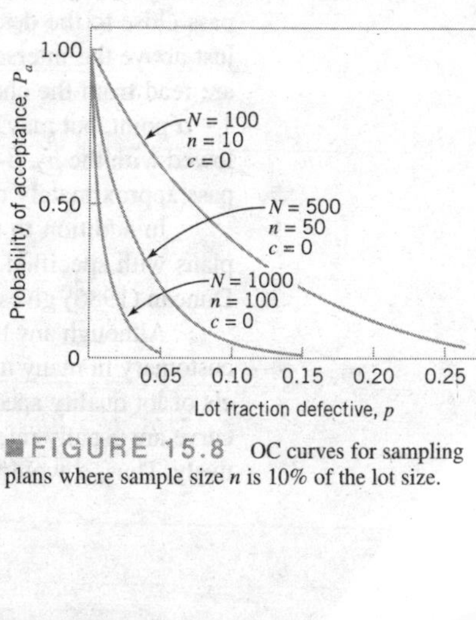

■ FIGURE 15.8 OC curves for sampling plans where sample size n is 10% of the lot size.

sample sizes offer different levels of protection. It is illogical for the level of protection that the consumer enjoys for a critical part or component to vary as the size of the lot varies. Although sampling procedures such as this one were in wide use before the statistical principles of acceptance sampling were generally known, their use has (unfortunately) not entirely disappeared.

15.2.3 Designing a Single-Sampling Plan with a Specified OC Curve

A common approach to the design of an acceptance-sampling plan is to require that the OC curve pass through two designated points. Note that one point is not enough to fully specify the sampling plan; however, two points are sufficient. In general, it does not matter which two points are specified.

Suppose that we wish to construct a sampling plan such that the probability of acceptance is $1-\alpha$ for lots with fraction defective p_1, and the probability of acceptance is β for lots with fraction defective p_2. Assuming that binomial sampling (with type-B OC curves) is appropriate, we see that the sample size n and acceptance number c are the solution to

$$1-\alpha = \sum_{d=0}^{c} \frac{n!}{d!(n-d)!} p_1^d (1-p_1)^{n-d}$$

$$\beta = \sum_{d=0}^{c} \frac{n!}{d!(n-d)!} p_2^d (1-p_2)^{n-d} \tag{15.3}$$

Equation (15.3) was obtained by writing out the two points on the OC curve using the binomial distribution. The two simultaneous equations in equation (15.3) are nonlinear, and there is no simple, direct solution.

The nomograph in Fig. 15.9 can be used for solving these equations. The procedure for using the nomograph is very simple. Two lines are drawn on the nomograph, one connecting p_1 and $1-\alpha$, and the other connecting p_2 and β. The intersection of these two lines gives the region of the nomograph in which the desired sampling plan is located. To illustrate the use of the nomograph, suppose we wish to construct a sampling plan for which $p_1 = 0.01$, $\alpha = 0.05$, $p_2 = 0.06$, and $\beta = 0.10$. Locating the intersection of the lines connecting ($p_1 = 0.01$, $1-\alpha = 0.95$) and ($p_2 = 0.06$, $\beta = 0.10$) on the nomograph indicates that the plan $n = 89$, $c = 2$ is very close to passing through these two points on the OC curve. Obviously, since n and c must be integers, this procedure will actually produce several plans that have OC curves that pass close to the desired points. For instance, if the first line is followed either to the c-line just above the intersection point or to the c-line just below it, and the alternate sample sizes are read from the chart, this will produce two plans that pass almost exactly through the p_1, $1-\alpha$ point, but may deviate somewhat from the p_2, β point. A similar procedure could be followed with the p_2, β-line. The result of following both of these lines would be four plans that pass approximately through the two points specified on the OC curve.

In addition to the graphical procedure that we have described for designing sampling plans with specified OC curves, tabular procedures are also available for the same purpose. Duncan (1986) gives a good description of these techniques.

Although any two points on the OC curve could be used to define the sampling plan, it is customary in many industries to use the AQL and LTPD points for this purpose. When the levels of lot quality specified are $p_1 = \text{AQL}$ and $p_2 = \text{LTPD}$, the corresponding points on the OC curve are usually referred to as the producer's risk point and the consumer's risk point, respectively. Thus, α would be called the producer's risk and β would be called the consumer's risk.

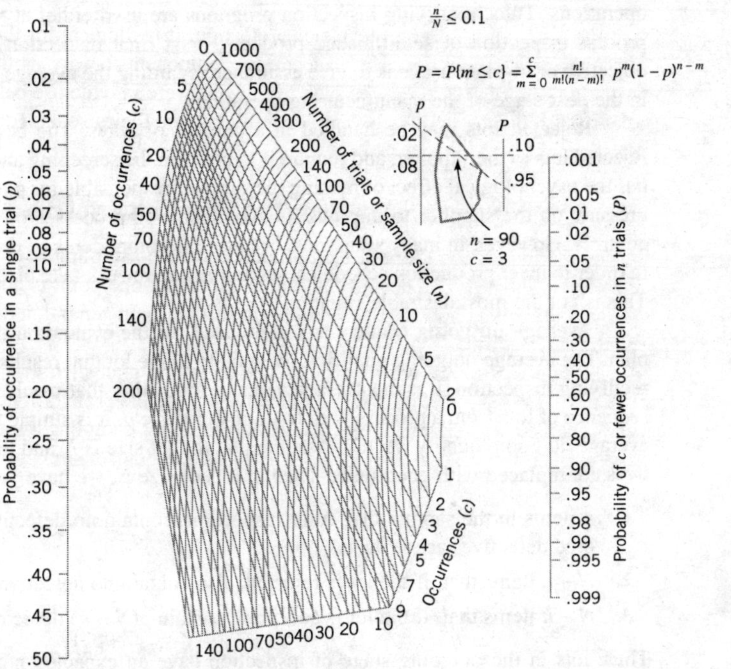

■ FIGURE 15.9 Binomial nomograph.

15.2.4 Rectifying Inspection

Acceptance-sampling programs usually require corrective action when lots are rejected. This generally takes the form of 100% inspection or **screening** of rejected lots, with all discovered defective items either removed for subsequent rework or return to the supplier, or replaced from a stock of known good items. Such sampling programs are called **rectifying inspection programs,** because the inspection activity affects the final quality of the outgoing product. This is illustrated in Fig. 15.10. Suppose that incoming lots to the inspection activity have fraction defective p_0. Some of these lots will be accepted, and others will be rejected. The rejected lots will be screened, and their final fraction defective will be zero. However, accepted lots have fraction defective p_0. Consequently, the outgoing lots from the inspection activity are a mixture of lots with fraction defective p_0 and fraction defective zero, so the average fraction defective in the stream of outgoing lots is p_1, which is less than p_0. Thus, a rectifying inspection program serves to "correct" lot quality.

Rectifying inspection programs are used in situations where the manufacturer wishes to know the average level of quality that is likely to result at a given stage of the manufacturing

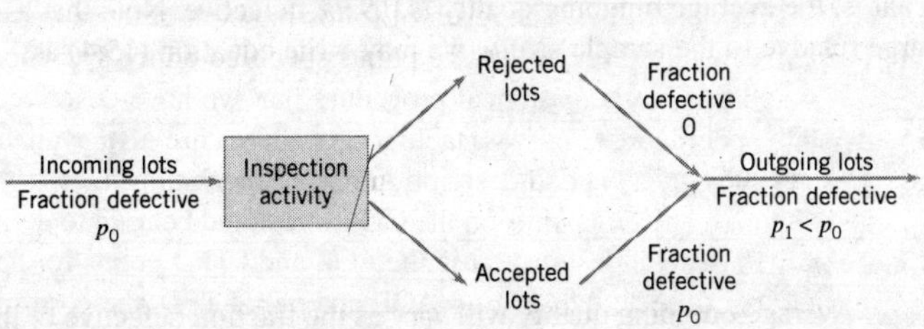

■ FIGURE 15.10 Rectifying inspection.

operations. Thus, rectifying inspection programs are used either at receiving inspection, in-process inspection of semifinished products, or at final inspection of finished goods. The objective of in-plant usage is to give assurance regarding the average quality of material used in the next stage of the manufacturing operations.

Rejected lots may be handled in a number of ways. The best approach is to **return** rejected lots to the supplier, and require it to perform the screening and rework activities. This has the psychological effect of making the supplier responsible for poor quality and may exert pressure on the supplier to improve its manufacturing processes or to install better process controls. However, in many situations, because the components or raw materials are required in order to meet production schedules, screening and rework take place at the consumer level. This is not the most desirable situation.

Average outgoing quality is widely used for the evaluation of a rectifying sampling plan. The average outgoing quality is the quality in the lot that results from the application of rectifying inspection. It is the average value of lot quality that would be obtained over a long sequence of lots from a process with fraction defective p. It is simple to develop a formula for average outgoing quality (AOQ). Assume that the lot size is N and that all discovered defectives are replaced with good units. Then in lots of size N, we have

1. n items in the sample that, after inspection, contain no defectives, because all discovered defectives are replaced
2. $N - n$ items that, if the lot is rejected, also contain no defectives
3. $N - n$ items that, if the lot is accepted, contain $p(N - n)$ defectives

Thus, lots in the outgoing stage of inspection have an expected number of defective units equal to $P_a p(N - n)$, which we may express as an *average fraction defective,* called the **average outgoing quality** or

$$\text{AOQ} = \frac{P_a p(N-n)}{N} \tag{15.4}$$

To illustrate the use of equation (15.4), suppose that $N = 10{,}000$, $n = 89$, and $c = 2$, and that the incoming lots are of quality $p = 0.01$. Now at $p = 0.01$, we have $P_a = 0.9397$, and the AOQ is

$$\begin{aligned} \text{AOQ} &= \frac{P_a p(N-n)}{N} \\ &= \frac{(0.9397)(0.01)(10{,}000-89)}{10{,}000} \\ &= 0.0093 \end{aligned}$$

That is, the average outgoing quality is 0.93% defective. Note that as the lot size N becomes large relative to the sample size n, we may write equation (15.4) as

$$\text{AOQ} \simeq P_a p \tag{15.5}$$

Average outgoing quality will vary as the fraction defective of the incoming lots varies. The curve that plots average outgoing quality against incoming lot quality is called an *AOQ*

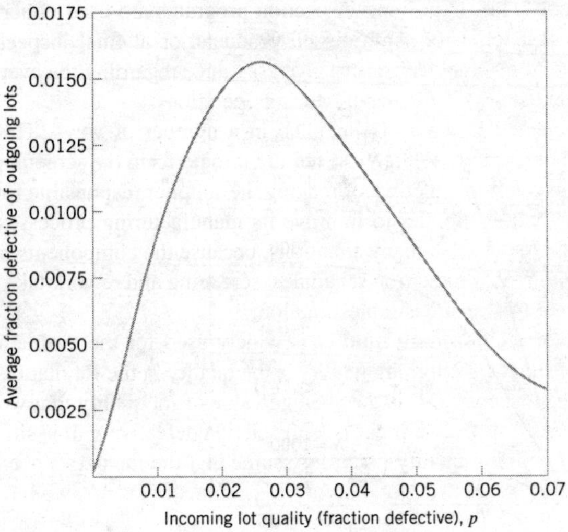

FIGURE 15.11 Average outgoing quality curve for $n = 89$, $c = 2$.

curve. The AOQ curve for the sampling plan $n = 89$, $c = 2$ is shown in Fig. 15.11. From examining this curve we note that when the incoming quality is very good, the average outgoing quality is also very good. In contrast, when the incoming lot quality is very bad, most of the lots are rejected and screened, which leads to a very good level of quality in the outgoing lots. In between these extremes, the AOQ curve rises, passes through a maximum, and descends. The maximum ordinate on the AOQ curve represents the worst possible average quality that would result from the rectifying inspection program, and this point is called the **average outgoing quality limit (AOQL).** From examining Fig. 15.11, the AOQL is seen to be approximately 0.0155. That is, no matter how bad the fraction defective is in the incoming lots, the outgoing lots will never have a worse quality level on the average than 1.55% defective. Let us emphasize that this AOQL is an *average level of quality, across a large stream of lots*. It does not give assurance that an isolated lot will have quality no worse than 1.55% defective.

Another important measure relative to rectifying inspection is the total amount of inspection required by the sampling program. If the lots contain no defective items, no lots will be rejected, and the amount of inspection per lot will be the sample size n. If the items are all defective, every lot will be submitted to 100% inspection, and the amount of inspection per lot will be the lot size N. If the lot quality is $0 < p < 1$, the average amount of inspection per lot will vary between the sample size n and the lot size N. If the lot is of quality p and the probability of lot acceptance is P_a, then the **average total inspection** per lot will be

$$\text{ATI} = n + (1 - P_a)(N - n) \tag{15.6}$$

To illustrate the use of equation (15.6), consider our previous example with $N = 10{,}000$, $n = 89$, $c = 2$, and $p = 0.01$. Then, since $P_a = 0.9397$, we have

$$\begin{aligned}\text{ATI} &= n + (1 - P_a)(N - n)\\ &= 89 + (1 - 0.9397)(10{,}000 - 89)\\ &= 687\end{aligned}$$

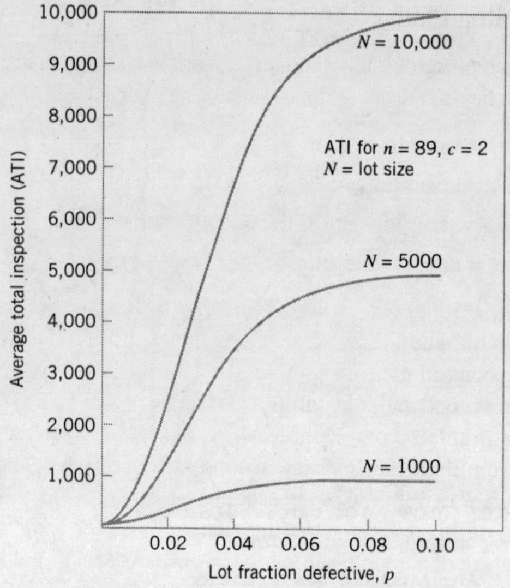

■ **FIGURE 15.12** Average total inspection (ATI) curves for sampling plan $n = 89$, $c = 2$, for lot sizes of 1000, 5000, and 10,000.

Remember that this is an average number of units inspected over *many* lots with fraction defective $p = 0.01$.

It is possible to draw a curve of average total inspection as a function of lot quality. Average total inspection curves for the sampling plan $n = 89$, $c = 2$, for lot sizes of 1000, 5000, and 10,000, are shown in Fig. 15.12.

The AOQL of a rectifying inspection plan is a very important characteristic. It is possible to design rectifying inspection programs that have specified values of AOQL. However, specification of the AOQL is not sufficient to determine a unique sampling plan. Therefore, it is relatively common practice to choose the sampling plan that has a specified AOQL and, in addition, yields a minimum ATI at a particular level of lot quality. The level of lot quality usually chosen is the most likely level of incoming lot quality, which is generally called the *process average*. The procedure for generating these plans is relatively straightforward and is illustrated in Duncan (1986). Generally, it is unnecessary to go through this procedure, because tables of sampling plans that minimize ATI for a given AOQL and a specified process average p have been developed by Dodge and Romig. We describe the use of these tables in Section 15.5.

It is also possible to design a rectifying inspection program that gives a specified level of protection at the LTPD point and that minimizes the average total inspection for a specified process average p. The Dodge–Romig sampling inspection tables also provide these LTPD plans. Section 15.5 discusses the use of the Dodge–Romig tables to find plans that offer specified LTPD protection.

15.3 Double, Multiple, and Sequential Sampling

A number of extensions of single-sampling plans for attributes are useful. These include **double-sampling plans, multiple-sampling plans,** and **sequential-sampling plans.** This section discusses the design and application of these sampling plans.

15.3.1 Double-Sampling Plans

A double-sampling plan is a procedure in which, under certain circumstances, a second sample is required before the lot can be sentenced. A double-sampling plan is defined by four parameters:[2]

n_1 = sample size on the first sample
c_1 = acceptance number of the first sample
n_2 = sample size on the second sample
c_2 = acceptance number for both sample

As an example, suppose $n_1 = 50$, $c_1 = 1$, $n_2 = 100$, and $c_2 = 3$. Thus, a random sample of $n_1 = 50$ items is selected from the lot, and the number of defectives in the sample, d_1, is observed. If $d_1 \leq c_1 = 1$, the lot is accepted on the first sample. If $d_1 > c_2 = 3$, the lot is rejected on the first sample. If $c_1 < d_1 \leq c_2$, a second random sample of size $n_2 = 100$ is drawn from the lot, and the number of defectives in this second sample, d_2, is observed. Now the combined number of observed defectives from both the first and second sample, $d_1 + d_2$, is used to determine the lot sentence. If $d_1 + d_2 \leq c_2 = 3$, the lot is accepted. However, if $d_1 + d_2 > c_2 = 3$, the lot is rejected. The operation of this double-sampling plan is illustrated graphically in Fig. 15.13.

The principal advantage of a double-sampling plan with respect to single-sampling is that it may reduce the total amount of required inspection. Suppose that the first sample taken under a double-sampling plan is smaller than the sample that would be required using a single-sampling plan that offers the consumer the same protection. In all cases, then, in which a lot is accepted or rejected on the first sample, the cost of inspection will be lower for double-sampling than it would be for single-sampling. It is also possible to reject a lot without complete inspection of the second sample. (This is called *curtailment* on the second sample.) Consequently, the use of double-sampling can often result in lower total inspection costs. Furthermore, in some situations, a double-sampling plan has the psychological advantage of giving a lot a second chance. This may have some appeal to the supplier. However, there is no real advantage to double sampling in this regard, because single- and double-sampling plans can be chosen so that they have the same OC curves. Thus, both plans would offer the same risks of accepting or rejecting lots of specified quality.

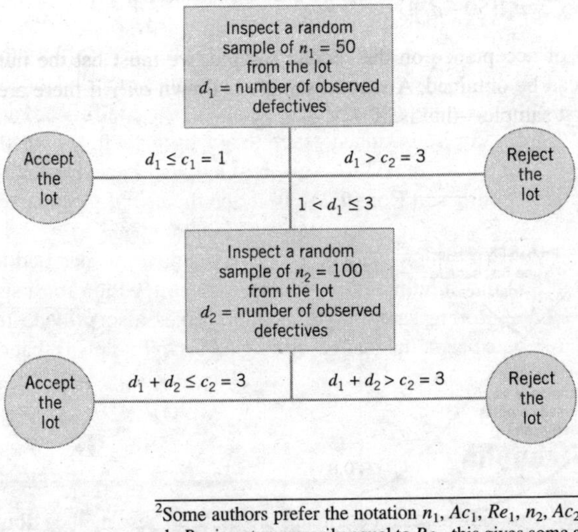

■ FIGURE 15.13 Operation of the double-sampling plan, $n_1 = 50$, $c_1 = 1$, $n_2 = 100$, $c_2 = 3$.

[2]Some authors prefer the notation n_1, Ac_1, Re_1, n_2, Ac_2, $Re_2 = Ac_2 + 1$. Since the rejection number on the first sample Re_1 is not necessarily equal to Re_2, this gives some additional flexibility in designing double-sampling plans. MIL STD 105E and ANSI/ASQC Z1.4 currently use this notation. However, because assuming that $Re_1 = Re_2$ does not significantly affect the plans obtained, we have chosen to discuss this slightly simpler system.

Double-sampling has two potential disadvantages. First, unless curtailment is used on the second sample, under some circumstances double-sampling may require more total inspection than would be required in a single-sampling plan that offers the same protection. Thus, unless double-sampling is used carefully, its potential economic advantage may be lost. The second disadvantage of double sampling is that it is administratively more complex, which may increase the opportunity for the occurrence of inspection errors. Furthermore, there may be problems in storing and handling raw materials or component parts for which one sample has been taken, but that are awaiting a second sample before a final lot dispositioning decision can be made.

The OC Curve. The performance of a double-sampling plan can be conveniently summarized by means of its operating-characteristic (OC) curve. The OC curve for a double-sampling plan is somewhat more involved than the OC curve for single sampling. In this section, we describe the construction of type-B OC curves for double sampling. A double-sampling plan has a primary OC curve that gives the probability of acceptance as a function of lot or process quality. It also has supplementary OC curves that show the probability of lot acceptance and rejection on the first sample. The OC curve for the probability of rejection on the first sample is simply the OC curve for the single-sampling plan $n = n_1$ and $c = c_2$. Primary and supplementary OC curves for the plan $n_1 = 50$, $c_1 = 1$, $n_2 = 100$, $c_2 = 3$ are shown in Fig. 15.14.

We now illustrate the computation of the OC curve for the plan $n_1 = 50$, $c_1 = 1$, $n_2 = 100$, $c_2 = 3$. If P_a denotes the probability of acceptance on the combined samples, and P_a^{I} and P_a^{II} denote the probability of acceptance on the first and second samples, respectively, then

$$P_a = P_a^{\mathrm{I}} + P_a^{\mathrm{II}}$$

P_a^{I} is just the probability that we will observe $d_1 \le c_1 = 1$ defectives out of a random sample of $n_1 = 50$ items. Thus

$$P_a^{\mathrm{I}} = \sum_{d_1=0}^{1} \frac{50!}{d_1!(50-d_1)!} p^{d_1}(1-p)^{50-d_1}$$

If $p = 0.05$ is the fraction defective in the incoming lot, then

$$P_a^{\mathrm{I}} = \sum_{d_1=0}^{1} \frac{50!}{d_1!(50-d_1)!}(0.05)^{d_1}(0.95)^{50-d_1} = 0.279$$

To obtain the probability of acceptance on the second sample, we must list the number of ways the second sample can be obtained. A second sample is drawn *only* if there are two or three defectives on the first sample—that is, if $c_1 < d_1 \le c_2$.

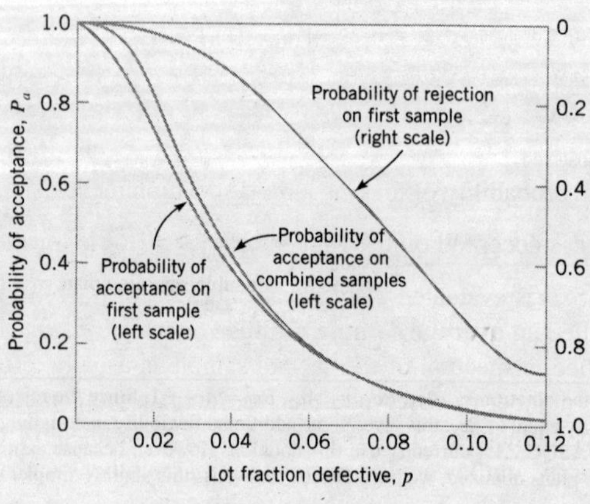

■ **FIGURE 15.14** OC curves for the double-sampling plan, $n_1 = 50$, $c_1 = 1$, $n_2 = 100$, $c_2 = 3$.

1. $d_1 = 2$ *and* $d_2 = 0$ or 1; that is, we find two defectives on the first sample and one or less defectives on the second sample. The probability of this is

$$P\{d_1 = 2, d_2 \le 1\} = P\{d_1 = 2\} \cdot P\{d_2 \le 1\}$$
$$= \frac{50!}{2!48!}(0.05)^2(0.95)^{48} \sum_{d_2=0}^{1} \frac{100!}{d_2!(100-d_2)!}(0.05)^{d_2}(0.95)^{100-d_2}$$
$$= (0.261)(0.037) = 0.0097$$

2. $d_1 = 3$ *and* $d_2 = 0$; that is, we find three defectives on the first sample and no defectives on the second sample. The probability of this is

$$P\{d_1 = 3, d_2 = 0\} = P\{d_1 = 3\} \cdot P\{d_2 = 0\}$$
$$= \frac{50!}{3!(47)!}(0.05)^3(0.95)^{47} \frac{100!}{0!100!}(0.05)^0(0.95)^{100}$$
$$= (0.220)(0.0059) = 0.001$$

Thus, the probability of acceptance on the second sample is

$$P_a^{\text{II}} = P\{d_1 = 2, d_2 \le 1\} + P\{d_1 = 3, d_2 = 0\}$$
$$= 0.0097 + 0.001 = 0.0107$$

The probability of acceptance of a lot that has fraction defective $p = 0.05$ is therefore

$$P_a = P_a^{\text{I}} + P_a^{\text{II}}$$
$$= 0.279 + 0.0107 = 0.2897$$

Other points on the OC curve are calculated similarly.

The Average Sample Number Curve. The average sample number curve of a double-sampling plan is also usually of interest to the quality engineer. In single-sampling, the size of the sample inspected from the lot is always constant, whereas in double-sampling, the size of the sample selected depends on whether or not the second sample is necessary. The probability of drawing a second sample varies with the fraction defective in the incoming lot. With complete inspection of the second sample, the average sample size in double-sampling is equal to the size of the first sample times the probability that there will only be one sample, plus the size of the combined samples times the probability that a second sample will be necessary. Therefore, a general formula for the average sample number in double-sampling, if we assume complete inspection of the second sample, is

$$\begin{aligned} \text{ASN} &= n_1 P_{\text{I}} + (n_1 + n_2)(1 - P_{\text{I}}) \\ &= n_1 + n_2(1 - P_{\text{I}}) \end{aligned} \tag{15.7}$$

where P_{I} is the probability of making a lot-dispositioning decision on the *first* sample. This is

$$P_{\text{I}} = P\{\text{lot is accepted on the first sample}\} + P\{\text{lot is rejected on the first sample}\}$$

If equation (15.7) is evaluated for various values of lot fraction defective p, the plot of ASN versus p is called an **average sample number curve.**

In practice, inspection of the second sample is usually terminated and the lot rejected as soon as the number of observed defective items in the combined sample exceeds the second acceptance number c_2. This is referred to as curtailment of the second sample. The use of curtailed inspection lowers the average sample number required in double-sampling. It is not recommended that curtailment be used in single-sampling, or in the first sample of double-sampling, because it is usually desirable to have complete inspection of a fixed sample size in order to secure an unbiased estimate of the quality of the material supplied by the supplier. If curtailed inspection is used in single-sampling or on the first sample of double-sampling, the estimate of lot or process fallout obtained from these data is biased. For instance, suppose that the acceptance number is one. If the first two items in the sample are defective, and the inspection process is curtailed, the estimate of lot or process fraction defective is 100%. Based on this information, even nonstatistically trained managers or engineers will be very reluctant to believe that the lot is really 100% defective.

The ASN curve formula for a double-sampling plan with curtailment on the second sample is

$$\text{ASN} = n_1 + \sum_{j=c_1+1}^{c_2} P(n_1, j)\left[n_2 P_L(n_2, c_2 - j) + \frac{c_2 - j + 1}{p} P_M(n_2 + 1, c_2 - j + 2)\right] \quad (15.8)$$

In equation (15.8), $P(n_1, j)$ is the probability of observing exactly j defectives in a sample of size n_1, $P_L(n_2, c_2 - j)$ is the probability of observing $c_2 - j$ or fewer defectives in a sample of size n_2, and $P_M(n_2 + 1, c_2 - j + 2)$ is the probability of observing $c_2 - j + 2$ defectives in a sample of size $n_2 + 1$.

Figure 15.15 compares the average sample number curves for complete and curtailed inspection for the double-sampling plan $n_1 = 60$, $c_1 = 2$, $n_2 = 120$, $c_3 = 3$, and the average sample number that would be used in single-sampling with $n = 89$, $c = 2$. Obviously, the sample size in the single-sampling plan is always constant. This double-sampling plan has been selected because it has an OC curve that is nearly identical to the OC curve for the single-sampling plan. That is, both plans offer equivalent protection to the producer and the consumer. Note from inspection of Fig. 15.15 that the ASN curve for double-sampling without curtailment on the second sample is not lower than the sample size used in single-sampling throughout the entire range of lot fraction defective. If lots are of very good quality, they will usually be accepted on the first sample, whereas if lots are of very bad quality, they will usually be rejected on the first sample. This gives an ASN for double sampling that is smaller than the sample size used

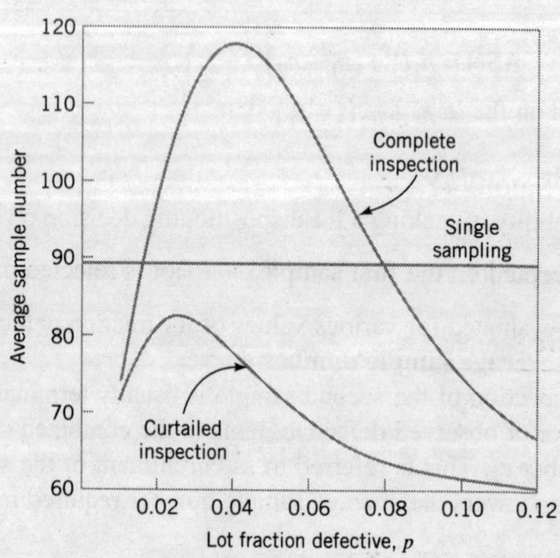

■ FIGURE 15.15 Average sample number curves for single and double sampling.

in single-sampling for lots that are either very good or very bad. However, if lots are of intermediate quality, the second sample will be required in a large number of cases before a lot disposition decision can be made. In this range of lot quality, the ASN performance of double-sampling is worse than single-sampling.

This example points out that it is important to use double-sampling very carefully. Unless care is exercised to ensure that lot or process quality is in the range where double-sampling is most effective, then the economic advantages of double-sampling relative to single-sampling may be lost. It is a good idea to maintain a running estimate of the supplier's lot or process fallout, so that if it shifts into a range where double-sampling is not economically effective, a change to single-sampling (or some other appropriate strategy) can be made. Another way to do this would be to record the proportion of times that the second sample is required in order to make a decision.

Figure 15.15 also shows the ASN curve using curtailment on the second sample. Note that if curtailment is used, the average sample number curve for double sampling always lies below the sample size used in single-sampling.

Designing Double-Sampling Plans with Specified $p_1, 1-\alpha, p_2$, and β. It is often necessary to be able to design a double-sampling plan that has a specified OC curve. Let $(p_1, 1-\alpha)$ and (p_2, β) be the two points of interest on the OC curve. If, in addition, we impose another relationship on the parameters of the sampling plan, then a simple procedure can be used to obtain such plans. The most common constraint is to require that n_2 is a multiple of n_1. Refer to Duncan (1986) for a discussion of these techniques.

Rectifying Inspection. When rectifying inspection is performed with double-sampling, the AOQ curve is given by

$$\text{AOQ} = \frac{\left[P_a^{\text{I}}(N-n_1) + P_a^{\text{II}}(N-n_1-n_2)\right]p}{N} \tag{15.9}$$

assuming that all defective items discovered, either in sampling or 100% inspection, are replaced with good ones. The average total inspection curve is given by

$$\text{ATI} = n_1 P_a^{\text{I}} + (n_1+n_2)P_a^{\text{II}} + N(1-P_a) \tag{15.10}$$

Remember that $P_a = P_a^{\text{I}} + P_a^{\text{II}}$ is the probability of final lot acceptance and that the acceptance probabilities depend on the level of lot or process quality p.

15.3.2 Multiple-Sampling Plans

A multiple-sampling plan is an extension of double-sampling in that more than two samples can be required to sentence a lot. An example of a multiple-sampling plan with five stages follows.

Cumulative-Sample Size	Acceptance Number	Rejection Number
20	0	3
40	1	4
60	3	5
80	5	7
100	8	9

This plan will operate as follows: If, at the completion of any stage of sampling, the number of defective items is less than or equal to the acceptance number, the lot is accepted. If, during any stage, the number of defective items equals or exceeds the rejection number, the lot is rejected; otherwise the next sample is taken. The multiple-sampling procedure continues until the fifth sample is taken, at which time a lot disposition decision must be made. The first sample is usually inspected 100%, although subsequent samples are usually subject to curtailment.

The construction of OC curves for multiple-sampling is a straightforward extension of the approach used in double-sampling. Similarly, it is also possible to compute the average sample number curve of multiple-sampling plans. One may also design a multiple-sampling plan for specified values of p_1, $1-\alpha$, p_2, and β. For an extensive discussion of these techniques, see Duncan (1986).

The principal advantage of multiple-sampling plans is that the samples required at each stage are usually smaller than those in single- or-double-sampling; thus, some economic efficiency is connected with the use of the procedure. However, multiple-sampling is much more complex to administer.

15.3.3 Sequential-Sampling Plans

Sequential-sampling is an extension of the double-sampling and multiple-sampling concept. In sequential-sampling, we take a sequence of samples from the lot and allow the number of samples to be determined entirely by the results of the sampling process. In practice, sequential-sampling can theoretically continue indefinitely, until the lot is inspected 100%. In practice, sequential-sampling plans are usually truncated after the number inspected is equal to three times the number that would have been inspected using a corresponding single-sampling plan. If the sample size selected at each stage is greater than one, the process is usually called *group* sequential-sampling. If the sample size inspected at each stage is one, the procedure is usually called **item-by-item sequential-sampling.**

Item-by-item sequential-sampling is based on the sequential probability ratio test (SPRT), developed by Wald (1947). The operation of an item-by-item sequential-sampling plan is illustrated in Fig. 15.16. The cumulative observed number of defectives is plotted on the chart. For each point, the abscissa is the total number of items selected up to that time, and the ordinate is the total number of observed defectives. If the plotted points stay within the boundaries of the acceptance and rejection lines, another sample must be drawn. As soon as a point falls on or above the upper line, the lot is rejected. When a sample point falls on or below the lower line, the lot is accepted. The equations for the two limit lines for specified values of p_1, $1-\alpha$, p_2, and β are

$$X_A = -h_1 + sn \quad \text{(acceptance line)} \tag{15.11a}$$

$$X_R = h_2 + sn \quad \text{(rejection line)} \tag{15.11b}$$

where

$$h_1 = \left(\log \frac{1-\alpha}{\beta}\right)\Big/k \tag{15.12}$$

$$h_2 = \left(\log \frac{1-\beta}{\alpha}\right)\Big/k \tag{15.13}$$

$$k = \log \frac{p_2(1-p_1)}{p_1(1-p_2)} \tag{15.14}$$

$$s = \log\left[(1-p_1)/(1-p_2)\right]/k \tag{15.15}$$

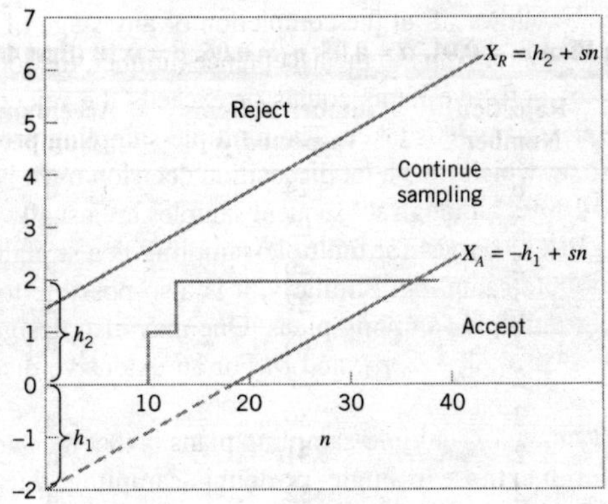

■ FIGURE 15.16 Graphical performance of sequential sampling.

To illustrate the use of these equations, suppose we wish to find a sequential-sampling plan for which $p_1 = 0.01$, $\alpha = 0.05$, $p_2 = 0.06$, and $\beta = 0.10$. Thus,

$$k = \log \frac{p_2(1-p_1)}{p_1(1-p_2)}$$

$$= \log \frac{(0.06)(0.99)}{(0.01)(0.94)} = 0.80066$$

$$h_1 = \left(\log \frac{1-\alpha}{\beta}\right) \Big/ k$$

$$= \left(\log \frac{0.95}{0.10}\right) \Big/ 0.80066 = 1.22$$

$$h_2 = \left(\log \frac{1-\beta}{\alpha}\right) \Big/ k$$

$$= \left(\log \frac{0.90}{0.05}\right) \Big/ 0.80066 = 1.57$$

$$s = \log\left[(1-p_1)/(1-p_2)\right] \big/ k$$

$$= \left[\log(0.99/0.94)\right] \big/ 0.80066 = 0.028$$

Therefore, the limit lines are

$$X_A = -1.22 + 0.028n \qquad \text{(accept)}$$

and

$$X_R = 1.57 + 0.028n \qquad \text{(reject)}$$

Instead of using a graph to determine the lot disposition, the sequential-sampling plan can be displayed in a table such as Table 15.3. The entries in the table are found by substituting values of n into the equations for the acceptance and rejection lines and calculating acceptance and rejection numbers. For example, the calculations for $n = 45$ are

$$X_A = -1.22 + 0.028n$$

$$= -1.22 + 0.028(45) = 0.04 \qquad \text{(accept)}$$

$$X_R = 1.57 + 0.028n$$

$$= 1.57 + 0.028(45) = 2.83 \qquad \text{(reject)}$$

■ TABLE 15.3

Item-by-Item Sequential-Sampling Plan $p_1 = 0.01, \alpha = 0.05, p_2 = 0.06, \beta = 0.10$ (first 46 units only)

Number of Items Inspected, *n*	Acceptance Number	Rejection Number	Number of Items Inspected, *n*	Acceptance Number	Rejection Number
1	a	b	24	a	3
2	a	2	25	a	3
3	a	2	26	a	3
4	a	2	27	a	3
5	a	2	28	a	3
6	a	2	29	a	3
7	a	2	30	a	3
8	a	2	31	a	3
9	a	2	32	a	3
10	a	2	33	a	3
11	a	2	34	a	3
12	a	2	35	a	3
13	a	2	36	a	3
14	a	2	37	a	3
15	a	2	38	a	3
16	a	3	39	a	3
17	a	3	40	a	3
18	a	3	41	a	3
19	a	3	42	a	3
20	a	3	43	a	3
21	a	3	44	0	3
22	a	3	45	0	3
23	a	3	46	0	3

"a" means acceptance not possible.
"b" means rejection not possible.

Acceptance and rejection numbers must be integers, so the acceptance number is the next integer less than or equal to X_A, and the rejection number is the next integer greater than or equal to X_R. Thus, for $n = 45$, the acceptance number is 0 and the rejection number is 3. Note that the lot cannot be accepted until at least 44 units have been tested. Table 15.3 shows only the first 46 units. Usually, the plan would be truncated after the inspection of 267 units, which is three times the sample size required for an equivalent single-sampling plan.

The OC Curve and ASN Curve for Sequential Sampling. The OC curve for sequential-sampling can be easily obtained. Two points on the curve are $(p_1, 1 - \alpha)$ and (p_2, β). A third point, near the middle of the curve, is $p = s$ and $P_a = h_2/(h_1 + h_2)$.

The average sample number taken under sequential-sampling is

$$\text{ASN} = P_a\left(\frac{A}{C}\right) + (1 - P_a)\frac{B}{C} \tag{15.16}$$

where

$$A = \log\frac{\beta}{1-\alpha}$$

$$B = \log\frac{1-\beta}{\alpha}$$

and

$$C = p\log\left(\frac{p_2}{p_1}\right) + (1-p)\log\left(\frac{1-p_2}{1-p_1}\right)$$

Rectifying Inspection. The average outgoing quality (AOQ) for sequential-sampling is given approximately by

$$AOQ \simeq P_a p \tag{15.17}$$

The average total inspection is also easily obtained. Note that the amount of sampling is A/C when a lot is accepted and N when it is rejected. Therefore, the average total inspection is

$$ATI = P_a\left(\frac{A}{C}\right) + (1-P_a)N \tag{15.18}$$

15.4 Military Standard 105E (ANSI/ASQC Z1.4, ISO 2859)

15.4.1 Description of the Standard

Standard sampling procedures for inspection by attributes were developed during World War II. MIL STD 105E is the most widely used acceptance-sampling system for attributes in the world today. The original version of the standard, MIL STD 105A, was issued in 1950. Since then, there have been four revisions; the latest version, MIL STD 105E, was issued in 1989.

The sampling plans discussed in previous sections of this chapter are individual sampling plans. A sampling scheme is an overall strategy specifying the way in which sampling plans are to be used. MIL STD 105E is a collection of sampling schemes; therefore, it is an acceptance-sampling system. Our discussion will focus primarily on MIL STD 105E; however, there is a derivative civilian standard, ANSI/ASQC Z1.4, which is quite similar to the military standard. The standard was also adopted by the International Organization for Standardization as ISO 2859.

The standard provides for three types of sampling: single-sampling, double-sampling, and multiple-sampling. For each type of sampling plan, a provision is made for either normal inspection, tightened inspection, or reduced inspection. Normal inspection is used at the start of the inspection activity. Tightened inspection is instituted when the supplier's recent quality history has deteriorated. Acceptance requirements for lots under tightened inspection are more stringent than under normal inspection. Reduced inspection is instituted when the supplier's recent quality history has been exceptionally good. The sample size generally used under reduced inspection is less than that under normal inspection.

The primary focal point of MIL STD 105E is the acceptable quality level (AQL). The standard is indexed with respect to a series of AQLs. When the standard is used for percent defective plans, the AQLs range from 0.10% to 10%. For defects per units plans, there are an additional ten AQLs running up to 1000 defects per 100 units. It should be noted that for the smaller AQL levels, the same sampling plan can be used to control either a fraction defective or a number of defects per unit. The AQLs are arranged in a progression, each AQL being approximately 1.585 times the preceding one.

The AQL is generally specified in the contract or by the authority responsible for sampling. Different AQLs may be designated for different types of defects. For example, the standard differentiates critical defects, major defects, and minor defects. It is relatively common practice to choose an AQL of 1% for major defects and an AQL of 2.5% for minor defects. No critical defects would be acceptable.

The sample size used in MIL STD 105E is determined by the lot size and by the choice of inspection level. Three general levels of inspection are provided. Level II is designated as normal. Level I requires about one-half the amount of inspection as Level II and may be used when less discrimination is needed. Level III requires about twice as much inspection as Level II and should be used when more discrimination is needed. There are also four special inspection levels, S-1, S-2, S-3, and S-4. The special inspection levels use very small samples, and should be employed only when the small sample sizes are necessary and when greater sampling risks can or must be tolerated.

For a specified AQL and inspection level and a given lot size, MIL STD 105E provides a normal sampling plan that is to be used as long as the supplier is producing the product at AQL quality or better. It also provides a procedure for switching to tightened and reduced inspection whenever there is an indication that the supplier's quality has changed. The switching procedures between normal, tightened, and reduced inspection are illustrated graphically in Fig. 15.17 and are described next.

1. **Normal to tightened.** When normal inspection is in effect, tightened inspection is instituted when two out of five consecutive lots have been rejected on original submission.
2. **Tightened to normal.** When tightened inspection is in effect, normal inspection is instituted when five consecutive lots or batches are accepted on original inspection.
3. **Normal to reduced.** When normal inspection is in effect, reduced inspection is instituted provided all four of the following conditions are satisfied.
   - **a.** The preceding ten lots have been on normal inspection, and none of the lots has been rejected on original inspection.
   - **b.** The total number of defectives in the samples from the preceding ten lots is less than or equal to the applicable limit number specified in the standard.
   - **c.** Production is at a steady rate; that is, no difficulty such as machine breakdowns, material shortages, or other problems have recently occurred.
   - **d.** Reduced inspection is considered desirable by the authority responsible for sampling.

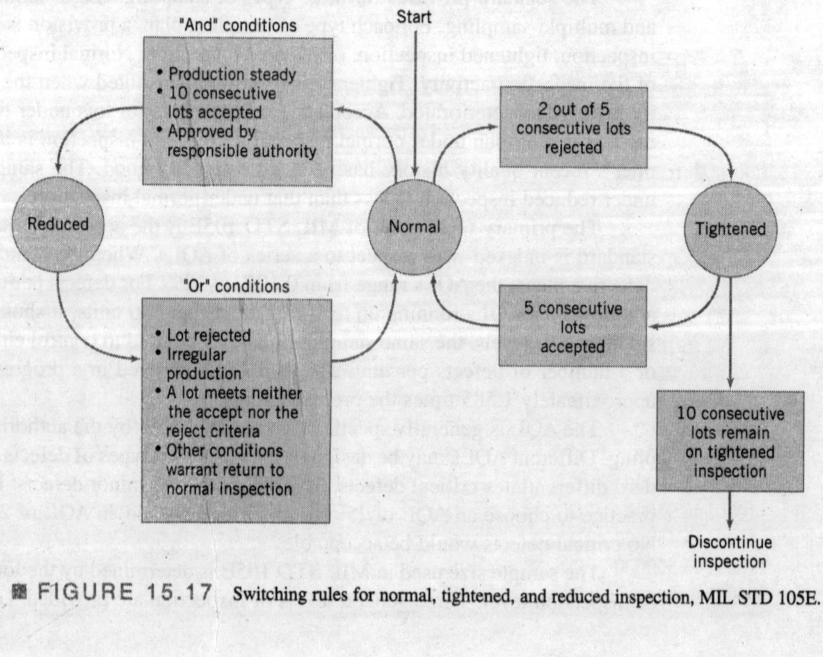

■ FIGURE 15.17 Switching rules for normal, tightened, and reduced inspection, MIL STD 105E.

4. **Reduced to normal.** When reduced inspection is in effect, normal inspection is instituted when any of the following four conditions occur.
   a. A lot or batch is rejected.
   b. When the sampling procedure terminates with neither acceptance nor rejection criteria having been met, the lot or batch will be accepted, but normal inspection is reinstituted starting with the next lot.
   c. Production is irregular or delayed.
   d. Other conditions warrant that normal inspection be instituted.
5. **Discontinuance of inspection.** In the event that ten consecutive lots remain on tightened inspection, inspection under the provision of MIL STD 105E should be terminated, and action should be taken at the supplier level to improve the quality of submitted lots.

15.4.2 Procedure

A step-by-step procedure for using MIL STD 105E is as follows:

1. Choose the AQL.
2. Choose the inspection level.
3. Determine the lot size.
4. Find the appropriate sample size code letter from Table 15.4.
5. Determine the appropriate type of sampling plan to use (single, double, multiple).
6. Enter the appropriate table to find the type of plan to be used.
7. Determine the corresponding normal and reduced inspection plans to be used when required.

Table 15.4 presents the sample size code letters for MIL STD 105E. Tables 15.5, 15.6, and 15.7 present the single-sampling plans for normal inspection, tightened inspection, and reduced inspection, respectively. The standard also contains tables for double-sampling plans and multiple-sampling plans for normal, tightened, and reduced inspection.

■ **TABLE 15.4**
Sample Size Code Letters (MIL STD 105E, Table 1)

	Special Inspection Levels				General Inspection Levels		
Lot or Batch Size	S-1	S-2	S-3	S-4	I	II	III
2 to 8	A	A	A	A	A	A	B
9 to 15	A	A	A	A	A	B	C
16 to 25	A	A	B	B	B	C	D
26 to 50	A	B	B	C	C	D	E
51 to 90	B	B	C	C	C	E	F
91 to 150	B	B	C	D	D	F	G
151 to 280	B	C	D	E	E	G	H
281 to 500	B	C	D	E	F	H	J
501 to 1200	C	C	E	F	G	J	K
1201 to 3200	C	D	E	G	H	K	L
3201 to 10000	C	D	F	G	J	L	M
10001 to 35000	C	D	F	H	K	M	N
35001 to 150000	D	E	G	J	L	N	P
150001 to 500000	D	E	G	J	M	P	Q
500001 and over	D	E	H	K	N	Q	R

■ TABLE 15.5

Master Table for Normal Inspection for Single-Sampling (U.S. Dept. of Defense MIL STD 105E, Table II-A)

Sample Size Code Letter	Sample Size	0.010	0.015	0.025	0.040	0.065	0.10	0.15	0.25	0.40	0.65	1.0	1.5	2.5	4.0	6.5	10	15	25	40	65	100	150	250	400	650	1000
		Acceptable Quality Levels (normal inspection)																									
		Ac Re	Ac Re	Ac Re	Ac Re	Ac Re	Ac Re	Ac Re	Ac Re	Ac Re	Ac Re	Ac Re	Ac Re	Ac Re	Ac Re	Ac Re	Ac Re	Ac Re	Ac Re	Ac Re	Ac Re	Ac Re	Ac Re	Ac Re	Ac Re	Ac Re	Ac Re
A	2	↓	↓	↓	↓	↓	↓	↓	↓	↓	↓	↓	↓	↓	↓	0 1	↓	↓	1 2	2 3	3 4	5 6	7 8	10 11	14 15	21 22	30 31
B	3	↓	↓	↓	↓	↓	↓	↓	↓	↓	↓	↓	↓	↓	0 1	↑	↓	1 2	2 3	3 4	5 6	7 8	10 11	14 15	21 22	30 31	44 45
C	5	↓	↓	↓	↓	↓	↓	↓	↓	↓	↓	↓	↓	0 1	↑	↓	1 2	2 3	3 4	5 6	7 8	10 11	14 15	21 22	30 31	44 45	↑
D	8	↓	↓	↓	↓	↓	↓	↓	↓	↓	↓	↓	0 1	↑	↓	1 2	2 3	3 4	5 6	7 8	10 11	14 15	21 22	30 31	44 45	↑	↑
E	13	↓	↓	↓	↓	↓	↓	↓	↓	↓	↓	0 1	↑	↓	1 2	2 3	3 4	5 6	7 8	10 11	14 15	21 22	30 31	44 45	↑	↑	↑
F	20	↓	↓	↓	↓	↓	↓	↓	↓	↓	0 1	↑	↓	1 2	2 3	3 4	5 6	7 8	10 11	14 15	21 22	↑	↑	↑	↑	↑	↑
G	32	↓	↓	↓	↓	↓	↓	↓	↓	0 1	↑	↓	1 2	2 3	3 4	5 6	7 8	10 11	14 15	21 22	↑	↑	↑	↑	↑	↑	↑
H	50	↓	↓	↓	↓	↓	↓	↓	0 1	↑	↓	1 2	2 3	3 4	5 6	7 8	10 11	14 15	21 22	↑	↑	↑	↑	↑	↑	↑	↑
J	80	↓	↓	↓	↓	↓	↓	0 1	↑	↓	1 2	2 3	3 4	5 6	7 8	10 11	14 15	21 22	↑	↑	↑	↑	↑	↑	↑	↑	↑
K	125	↓	↓	↓	↓	↓	0 1	↑	↓	1 2	2 3	3 4	5 6	7 8	10 11	14 15	21 22	↑	↑	↑	↑	↑	↑	↑	↑	↑	↑
L	200	↓	↓	↓	↓	0 1	↑	↓	1 2	2 3	3 4	5 6	7 8	10 11	14 15	21 22	↑	↑	↑	↑	↑	↑	↑	↑	↑	↑	↑
M	315	↓	↓	↓	0 1	↑	↓	1 2	2 3	3 4	5 6	7 8	10 11	14 15	21 22	↑	↑	↑	↑	↑	↑	↑	↑	↑	↑	↑	↑
N	500	↓	↓	0 1	↑	↓	1 2	2 3	3 4	5 6	7 8	10 11	14 15	21 22	↑	↑	↑	↑	↑	↑	↑	↑	↑	↑	↑	↑	↑
P	800	↓	0 1	↑	↓	1 2	2 3	3 4	5 6	7 8	10 11	14 15	21 22	↑	↑	↑	↑	↑	↑	↑	↑	↑	↑	↑	↑	↑	↑
Q	1250	0 1	↑	↓	1 2	2 3	3 4	5 6	7 8	10 11	14 15	21 22	↑	↑	↑	↑	↑	↑	↑	↑	↑	↑	↑	↑	↑	↑	↑
R	2000	↑	↑	1 2	2 3	3 4	5 6	7 8	10 11	14 15	21 22	↑	↑	↑	↑	↑	↑	↑	↑	↑	↑	↑	↑	↑	↑	↑	↑

↓ = Use first sampling plan below arrow. If sample size equals, or exceeds, lot or batch size, do 100% inspection.

↑ = Use first sampling plan above arrow.

Ac = Acceptance number.

Re = Rejection number.

■ TABLE 15.6

Master Table for Tightened Inspection—Single-Sampling (U.S. Dept. of Defense MIL STD 105E, Table II-B)

Sample Size Code Letter	Sample Size	Acceptable Quality Levels (tightened inspection)																									
		0.010	0.015	0.025	0.040	0.065	0.10	0.15	0.25	0.40	0.65	1.0	1.5	2.5	4.0	6.5	10	15	25	40	65	100	150	250	400	650	1000
		Ac Re	Ac Re	Ac Re	Ac Re	Ac Re	Ac Re	Ac Re	Ac Re	Ac Re	Ac Re	Ac Re	Ac Re	Ac Re	Ac Re	Ac Re	Ac Re	Ac Re	Ac Re	Ac Re	Ac Re	Ac Re	Ac Re	Ac Re	Ac Re	Ac Re	Ac Re
A	2	↓	↓	↓	↓	↓	↓	↓	↓	↓	↓	↓	↓	↓	↓	↓	↓	↓	↓	1 2	2 3	3 4	5 6	8 9	12 13	18 19	27 28
B	3	↓	↓	↓	↓	↓	↓	↓	↓	↓	↓	↓	↓	↓	↓	0 1	↓	↓	1 2	2 3	3 4	5 6	8 9	12 13	18 19	27 28	41 42
C	5	↓	↓	↓	↓	↓	↓	↓	↓	↓	↓	↓	↓	↓	0 1	↓	↓	1 2	2 3	3 4	5 6	8 9	12 13	18 19	27 28	41 42	↑
D	8	↓	↓	↓	↓	↓	↓	↓	↓	↓	↓	↓	↓	0 1	↓	↓	1 2	2 3	3 4	5 6	8 9	12 13	18 19	27 28	41 42	↑	↑
E	13	↓	↓	↓	↓	↓	↓	↓	↓	↓	↓	↓	0 1	↓	↓	1 2	2 3	3 4	5 6	8 9	12 13	18 19	27 28	41 42	↑	↑	↑
F	20	↓	↓	↓	↓	↓	↓	↓	↓	↓	↓	0 1	↓	↓	1 2	2 3	3 4	5 6	8 9	12 13	18 19	↑	↑	↑	↑	↑	↑
G	32	↓	↓	↓	↓	↓	↓	↓	↓	↓	0 1	↓	↓	1 2	2 3	3 4	5 6	8 9	12 13	18 19	↑	↑	↑	↑	↑	↑	↑
H	50	↓	↓	↓	↓	↓	↓	↓	↓	0 1	↓	↓	1 2	2 3	3 4	5 6	8 9	12 13	18 19	↑	↑	↑	↑	↑	↑	↑	↑
J	80	↓	↓	↓	↓	↓	↓	↓	0 1	↓	↓	1 2	2 3	3 4	5 6	8 9	12 13	18 19	↑	↑	↑	↑	↑	↑	↑	↑	↑
K	125	↓	↓	↓	↓	↓	↓	0 1	↓	↓	1 2	2 3	3 4	5 6	8 9	12 13	18 19	↑	↑	↑	↑	↑	↑	↑	↑	↑	↑
L	200	↓	↓	↓	↓	↓	0 1	↓	↓	1 2	2 3	3 4	5 6	8 9	12 13	18 19	↑	↑	↑	↑	↑	↑	↑	↑	↑	↑	↑
M	315	↓	↓	↓	↓	0 1	↓	↓	1 2	2 3	3 4	5 6	8 9	12 13	18 19	↑	↑	↑	↑	↑	↑	↑	↑	↑	↑	↑	↑
N	500	↓	↓	↓	0 1	↓	↓	1 2	2 3	3 4	5 6	8 9	12 11	18 19	↑	↑	↑	↑	↑	↑	↑	↑	↑	↑	↑	↑	↑
P	800	↓	↓	0 1	↓	↓	1 2	2 3	3 4	5 6	8 9	12 13	18 19	↑	↑	↑	↑	↑	↑	↑	↑	↑	↑	↑	↑	↑	↑
Q	1250	↓	0 1	↓	↓	1 2	2 3	3 4	5 6	8 9	12 13	18 19	↑	↑	↑	↑	↑	↑	↑	↑	↑	↑	↑	↑	↑	↑	↑
R	2000	0 1	↑	↓	1 2	2 3	3 4	5 6	8 9	12 13	18 19	↑	↑	↑	↑	↑	↑	↑	↑	↑	↑	↑	↑	↑	↑	↑	↑
S	3150			1 2																							

↓ = Use first sampling plan below arrow. If sample size equals, or exceeds, lot or batch size, do 100% inspection.

↑ = Use first sampling plan above arrow.

Ac = Acceptance number.

Re = Rejection number.

■ TABLE 15.7
Master Table for Reduced Inspection—Single-Sampling (U.S. Dept. of Defense MIL STD 105E, Table II-C)

Acceptable Quality Levels (reduced inspection)† — each cell gives Ac Re

Sample Size Code Letter	Sample Size	0.010	0.015	0.025	0.040	0.065	0.10	0.15	0.25	0.40	0.65	1.0	1.5	2.5	4.0	6.5	10	15	25	40	65	100	150	250	400	650	1000
		Ac Re	Ac Re	Ac Re	Ac Re	Ac Re	Ac Re	Ac Re	Ac Re	Ac Re	Ac Re	Ac Re	Ac Re	Ac Re	Ac Re	Ac Re	Ac Re	Ac Re	Ac Re	Ac Re	Ac Re	Ac Re	Ac Re	Ac Re	Ac Re	Ac Re	Ac Re
A	2	↓	↓	↓	↓	↓	↓	↓	↓	↓	↓	↓	↓	↓	↓	0 1	↓	↓	1 2	2 3	3 4	5 6	7 8	10 11	14 15	21 22	30 31
B	2	↓	↓	↓	↓	↓	↓	↓	↓	↓	↓	↓	↓	↓	0 1	↑	↓	0 2	1 3	2 4	3 5	5 6	7 8	10 11	14 15	21 22	30 31
C	2	↓	↓	↓	↓	↓	↓	↓	↓	↓	↓	↓	↓	0 1	↑	↓	0 2	1 3	1 4	2 5	3 6	5 8	7 10	10 13	14 17	21 24	↑
D	3	↓	↓	↓	↓	↓	↓	↓	↓	↓	↓	↓	0 1	↑	↓	0 2	1 3	1 4	2 5	3 6	5 8	7 10	10 13	14 17	21 24	↑	↑
E	5	↓	↓	↓	↓	↓	↓	↓	↓	↓	↓	0 1	↑	↓	0 2	1 3	1 4	2 5	3 6	5 8	7 10	10 13	14 17	21 24	↑	↑	↑
F	8	↓	↓	↓	↓	↓	↓	↓	↓	↓	0 1	↑	↓	0 2	1 3	1 4	2 5	3 6	5 8	7 10	10 13	↑	↑	↑	↑	↑	↑
G	13	↓	↓	↓	↓	↓	↓	↓	↓	0 1	↑	↓	0 2	1 3	1 4	2 5	3 6	5 8	7 10	10 13	↑	↑	↑	↑	↑	↑	↑
H	20	↓	↓	↓	↓	↓	↓	↓	0 1	↑	↓	0 2	1 3	1 4	2 5	3 6	5 8	7 10	10 13	↑	↑	↑	↑	↑	↑	↑	↑
J	32	↓	↓	↓	↓	↓	↓	0 1	↑	↓	0 2	1 3	1 4	2 5	3 6	5 8	7 10	10 13	↑	↑	↑	↑	↑	↑	↑	↑	↑
K	50	↓	↓	↓	↓	↓	0 1	↑	↓	0 2	1 3	1 4	2 5	3 6	5 8	7 10	10 13	↑	↑	↑	↑	↑	↑	↑	↑	↑	↑
L	80	↓	↓	↓	↓	0 1	↑	↓	0 2	1 3	1 4	2 5	3 6	5 8	7 10	10 13	↑	↑	↑	↑	↑	↑	↑	↑	↑	↑	↑
M	125	↓	↓	↓	0 1	↑	↓	0 2	1 3	1 4	2 5	3 6	5 8	7 10	10 13	↑	↑	↑	↑	↑	↑	↑	↑	↑	↑	↑	↑
N	200	↓	↓	0 1	↑	↓	0 2	1 3	1 4	2 5	3 6	5 8	7 10	10 13	↑	↑	↑	↑	↑	↑	↑	↑	↑	↑	↑	↑	↑
P	315	↓	0 1	↑	↓	0 2	1 3	1 4	2 5	3 6	5 8	7 10	10 13	↑	↑	↑	↑	↑	↑	↑	↑	↑	↑	↑	↑	↑	↑
Q	500	0 1	↑	↓	0 2	1 3	1 4	2 5	3 6	5 8	7 10	10 13	↑	↑	↑	↑	↑	↑	↑	↑	↑	↑	↑	↑	↑	↑	↑
R	800	↑	↑	0 2	1 3	1 4	2 5	3 6	5 8	7 10	10 13	↑	↑	↑	↑	↑	↑	↑	↑	↑	↑	↑	↑	↑	↑	↑	↑

↓ = Use first sampling plan below arrow. If sample size equals, or exceeds, lot or batch size, do 100% inspection.

↑ = Use first sampling plan above arrow.

Ac = Acceptance number.

Re = Rejection number.

† = If the acceptance number has been exceeded, but the rejection number has not been reached, accept the lot, but reinstate normal inspection.

To illustrate the use of MIL STD 105E, suppose that a product is submitted in lots of size $N = 2000$. The acceptable quality level is 0.65%. We will use the standard to generate normal, tightened, and reduced single-sampling plans for this situation. For lots of size 2000 under general inspection level II, Table 15.4 indicates that the appropriate sample size code letter is K. Therefore, from Table 15.5, for single-sampling plans under normal inspection, the normal inspection plan is $n = 125$, $c = 2$. Table 15.6 indicates that the corresponding tightened inspection plan is $n = 125$, $c = 1$. Note that in switching from normal to tightened inspection, the sample size remains the same, but the acceptance number is reduced by one. This general strategy is used throughout MIL STD 105E for a transition to tightened inspection. If the normal inspection acceptance number is 1, 2, or 3, the acceptance number for the corresponding tightened inspection plan is reduced by one. If the normal inspection acceptance number is 5, 7, 10, or 14, the reduction in acceptance number for tightened inspection is two. For a normal acceptance number of 21, the reduction is three. Table 15.7 indicates that under reduced inspection, the sample size for this example would be $n = 50$, the acceptance number would be $c = 1$, and the rejection number would be $r = 3$. Thus, if two defectives were encountered, the lot would be accepted, but the next lot would be inspected under normal inspection.

In examining the tables, note that if a vertical arrow is encountered, the first sampling plan above or below the arrow should be used. When this occurs, the sample size code letter and the sample size change. For example, if a single-sampling plan is indexed by an AQL of 1.5% and a sample size code letter of F, the code letter changes to G and the sample size changes from 20 to 32.

15.4.3 Discussion

MIL STD 105E presents the OC curves for single-sampling plans. These are all type-B OC curves. The OC curves for the matching double- and multiple-sampling plans are roughly comparable with those for the corresponding single-sampling plans. Figure 15.18 presents an example of these curves for code letter K. The OC curves presented in the standard are for the initial sampling plan only. They are not the OC curves for the overall inspection program,[3] including shifts to and from tightened or reduced inspection.

Average sample number curves for double and multiple sampling are given, assuming that no curtailment is used. These curves are useful in evaluating the average sample sizes that may be expected to occur under the various sampling plans for a given lot or process quality.

There are several points about MIL STD 105E that should be emphasized. These include the following. First, MIL STD 105E is AQL-oriented. It focuses attention on the producer's risk end of the OC curve. The only control over the discriminatory power of the sampling plan (i.e., the steepness of the OC curve) is through the choice of inspection level.

Second, the sample sizes selected for use in MIL STD 105E are 2, 3, 5, 8, 13, 20, 32, 50, 80, 125, 200, 315, 500, 800, 1250, and 2000. Thus, not all sample sizes are possible. Note that there are some rather significant gaps, such as between 125 and 200, and between 200 and 315.

Third, the sample sizes in MIL STD 105E are related to the lot sizes. To see the nature of this relationship, calculate the midpoint of each lot size range, and plot the logarithm of the sample size for that lot size range against the logarithm of the lot size range midpoint. Such a plot will follow roughly a straight line up to $n = 80$, and thereafter another straight

[3]ANSI/ASQC Z1.4 presents the scheme performance of the standard, giving scheme OC curves and the corresponding percentage points.

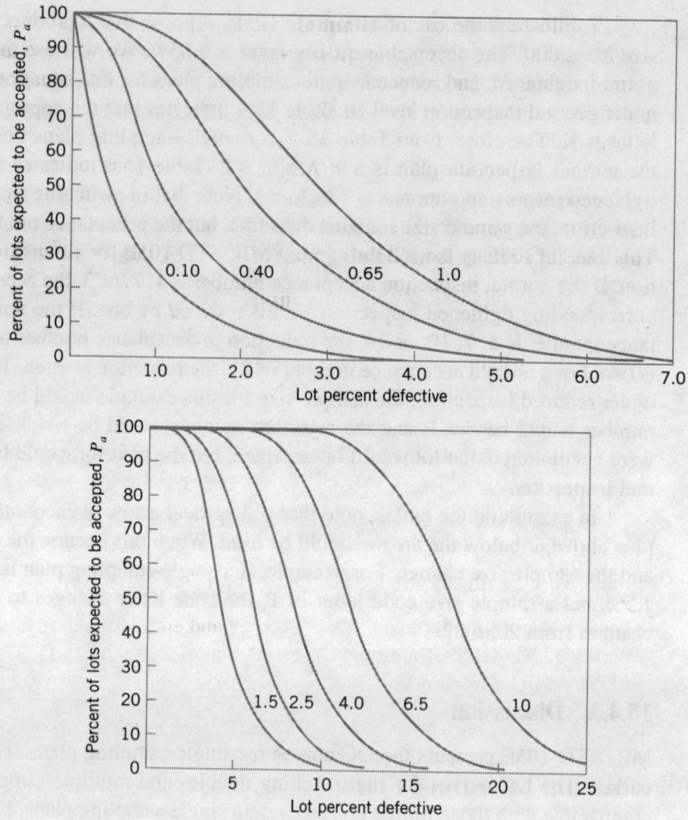

■ FIGURE 15.18 OC curves for sample size code letter K, MIL STD 105E.

line with a shallower slope. Thus, the sample size will increase as the lot size increases. However, the ratio of sample size to lot size will decrease rapidly. This gives significant economy in inspection costs per unit when the supplier submits large lots. For a given AQL, the effect of this increase in sample size as the lot size increases is to increase the probability of acceptance for submitted lots of AQL quality. The probability of acceptance at a given AQL will vary with increasing sample size from about 0.91 to about 0.99. This feature of the standard was and still is subject to some controversy. The argument in favor of the approach in MIL STD 105E is that rejection of a large lot has more serious consequences for the supplier than rejection of a small lot, and if the probability of acceptance at the AQL increases with sample size, this reduces the risk of false rejection of a large lot. Furthermore, the large sample also gives a more discriminating OC curve, which means that the protection that the consumer receives against accepting an isolated bad lot will also be increased.

Fourth, the switching rules from normal to tightened inspection and from tightened to normal inspection are also subject to some criticism. In particular, some engineers dislike the switching rules because there is often a considerable amount of misswitching from normal to tightened or normal to reduced inspection when the process is actually producing lots of AQL quality. Also, there is a significant probability that production would even be discontinued, even though there has been no actual quality deterioration.

Fifth, a **flagrant** and **common abuse** of MIL STD 105E is failure to use the switching rules at all. When this is done, it results in ineffective and deceptive inspection and a substantial increase in the consumer's risk. It is not recommended that MIL STD 105E be implemented without use of the switching rules from normal to tightened and normal to reduced inspection.

A civilian standard, ANSI/ASQC Z1.4 or ISO 2859, is the counterpart of MIL STD 105E. It seems appropriate to conclude our discussion of MIL STD 105E with a comparison of the military and civilian standards. ANSI/ASQC Z1.4 was adopted in 1981 and differs from MIL STD 105E in the following five ways:

1. The terminology "nonconformity," "nonconformance," and "percent nonconforming" is used.
2. The switching rules were changed slightly to provide an option for reduced inspection without the use of limit numbers.
3. Several tables that show measures of scheme performance (*including* the switching rules) were introduced. Some of these performance measures include AOQL, limiting quality for which $P_a = 0.10$ and $P_a = 0.05$, ASN, and operating-characteristic curves.
4. A section was added describing proper use of individual sampling plans when extracted from the system.
5. A figure illustrating the switching rules was added.

These revisions modernize the terminology and emphasize the system concept of the civilian standard. All tables, numbers, and procedures used in MIL STD 105E are retained in ANSI/ASQC Z1.4 and ISO 2859.

15.5 The Dodge–Romig Sampling Plans

H. F. Dodge and H. G. Romig developed a set of sampling inspection tables for lot-by-lot inspection of product by attributes using two types of sampling plans: plans for lot tolerance percent defective (LTPD) protection and plans that provide a specified average outgoing quality limit (AOQL). For each of these approaches to sampling plan design, there are tables for single- and double-sampling.

Sampling plans that emphasize LTPD protection, such as the Dodge–Romig plans, are often preferred to AQL-oriented sampling plans, such as those in MIL STD 105E, particularly for critical components and parts. Many manufacturers believe that they have relied too much on AQLs in the past, and they are now emphasizing other measures of performance, such as defective parts per million (ppm). Consider the following:

AQL	Defective Parts per Million
10%	100,000
1%	10,000
0.1%	1,000
0.01%	100
0.001%	10
0.0001%	1

Thus, even very small AQLs imply large numbers of defective ppm. In complex products, the effect of this can be devastating. For example, suppose that a printed circuit board contains 100 elements, each manufactured by a process operating at 0.5% defective. If the AQLs for these elements are 0.5% and if all elements on the printed circuit board must operate for the card to function properly, then the probability that a board works is

$$P(\text{function properly}) = (0.995)^{100} = 0.6058$$

Thus, there is an obvious need for sampling plans that emphasize LTPD protection, even when the process average fallout is low. The Dodge–Romig plans are often useful in these situations.

The Dodge–Romig AOQL plans are designed so that the average total inspection for a given AOQL and a specified process average p will be minimized. Similarly, the LTPD plans are designed so that the average total inspection is a minimum. This makes the Dodge–Romig plans very useful for in-plant inspection of semifinished product.

The Dodge–Romig plans apply only to programs that submit rejected lots to 100% inspection. Unless rectifying inspection is used, the AOQL concept is meaningless. Furthermore, to use the plans, we must know the process average—that is, the average fraction nonconforming of the incoming product. When a supplier is relatively new, we usually do not know its process fallout. Sometimes this may be estimated from a preliminary sample or from data provided by the supplier. Alternatively, the largest possible process average in the table can be used until enough information has been generated to provide a more accurate estimate of the supplier's process fallout. Obtaining a more accurate estimate of the incoming fraction nonconforming or process average will allow a more appropriate sampling plan to be adopted. It is not uncommon to find that sampling inspection begins with one plan, and after sufficient information is generated to reestimate the supplier's process fallout, a new plan is adopted. We discuss estimation of the process average in more detail in Section 15.5.3.

15.5.1 AOQL Plans

The Dodge–Romig (1959) tables give AOQL sampling plans for AOQL values of 0.1%, 0.25%, 0.5%, 0.75%, 1%, 1.5%, 2%, 2.5%, 3%, 4%, 5%, 7%, and 10%. For each of these AOQL values, six classes of values for the process average are specified. Tables are provided for both single- and double-sampling. These plans have been designed so that the average total inspection at the given AOQL and process average is approximately a minimum.

An example of the Dodge–Romig sampling plans is shown in Table 15.8.[4] To illustrate the use of the Dodge–Romig AOQL tables, suppose that we are inspecting LSI memory elements for a personal computer and that the elements are shipped in lots of size $N = 5000$. The supplier's process average fallout is 1% nonconforming. We wish to find a single-sampling plan with an AOQL = 3%. From Table 15.8, we find that the plan is

$$n = 65 \quad c = 3$$

Table 15.8 also indicates that the LTPD for this sampling plan is 10.3%. This is the point on the OC curve for which $P_a = 0.10$. Therefore, the sampling plan $n = 65$, $c = 3$ gives an AOQL of 3% nonconforming and provides assurance that 90% of incoming lots that are as bad as 10.3% defective will be rejected. Assuming that incoming quality is equal to the process average and

[4]Tables 15.8 and 15.9 are adapted from H. F. Dodge and H. G. Romig, *Sampling Inspection Tables, Single and Double Sampling*, 2nd ed., John Wiley, New York, 1959, with the permission of the publisher.

■ **TABLE 15.8**

Dodge–Romig Inspection Table—Single-Sampling Plans for AOQL = 3.0%

	Process Average																	
	0–0.06%			0.07–0.60%			0.61–1.20%			1.21–1.80%			1.81–2.40%			2.41–3.00%		
Lot Size	*n*	*c*	LTPD %	*n*	*c*	LTPD %	*n*	*c*	LTPD %	*n*	*c*	LTPD %	*n*	*c*	LTPD %	*n*	*c*	LTPD %
1–10	All	0	—	All	0	—	All	0	—	All	0	—	All	0	—	All	0	—
11–50	10	0	19.0	10	0	19.0	10	0	19.0	10	0	19.0	10	0	19.0	10	0	19.0
51–100	11	0	18.0	11	0	18.0	11	0	18.0	11	0	18.0	11	0	18.0	22	1	16.4
101–200	12	0	17.0	12	0	17.0	12	0	17.0	25	1	15.1	25	1	15.1	25	1	15.1
201–300	12	0	17.0	12	0	17.0	26	1	14.6	26	1	14.6	26	1	14.6	40	2	12.8
301–400	12	0	17.1	12	0	17.1	26	1	14.7	26	1	14.7	41	2	12.7	41	2	12.7
401–500	12	0	17.2	27	1	14.1	27	1	14.1	42	2	12.4	42	2	12.4	42	2	12.4
501–600	12	0	17.3	27	1	14.2	27	1	14.2	42	2	12.4	42	2	12.4	60	3	10.8
601–800	12	0	17.3	27	1	14.2	27	1	14.2	43	2	12.1	60	3	10.9	60	3	10.9
801–1000	12	0	17.4	27	1	14.2	44	2	11.8	44	2	11.8	60	3	11.0	80	4	9.8
1,001–2,000	12	0	17.5	28	1	13.8	45	2	11.7	65	3	10.2	80	4	9.8	100	5	9.1
2,001–3,000	12	0	17.5	28	1	13.8	45	2	11.7	65	3	10.2	100	5	9.1	140	7	8.2
3,001–4,000	12	0	17.5	28	1	13.8	65	3	10.3	85	4	9.5	125	6	8.4	165	8	7.8
4,001–5,000	28	1	13.8	28	1	13.8	65	3	10.3	85	4	9.5	125	6	8.4	210	10	7.4
5,001–7,000	28	1	13.8	45	2	11.8	65	3	10.3	105	5	8.8	145	7	8.1	235	11	7.1
7,001–10,000	28	1	13.9	46	2	11.6	65	3	10.3	105	5	8.8	170	8	7.6	280	13	6.8
10,001–20,000	28	1	13.9	46	2	11.7	85	4	9.5	125	6	8.4	215	10	7.2	380	17	6.2
20,001–50,000	28	1	13.9	65	3	10.3	105	5	8.8	170	8	7.6	310	14	6.5	560	24	5.7
50,001–100,000	28	1	13.9	65	3	10.3	125	6	8.4	215	10	7.2	385	17	6.2	690	29	5.4

■ **TABLE 15.9**

Dodge–Romig Single-Sampling Table for Lot Tolerance Percent Defective (LTPD) = 1.0%

	Process Average																	
	0–0.01%			0.011%–0.10%			0.11–0.20%			0.21–0.30%			0.31–0.40%			0.41–0.50%		
			AOQL			AOQL			AOQL			AOQL			AOQL			AOQL
Lot Size	*n*	*c*	%	*n*	*c*	%	*n*	*c*	%	*n*	*c*	%	*n*	*c*	%	*n*	*c*	%
1–120	All	0	0	All	0	0	All	0	0	All	0	0	All	0	0	All	0	0
121–150	120	0	0.06	120	0	0.06	120	0	0.06	120	0	0.06	120	0	0.06	120	0	0.06
151–200	140	0	0.08	140	0	0.08	140	0	0.08	140	0	0.08	140	0	0.08	140	0	0.08
201–300	165	0	0.10	165	0	0.10	165	0	0.10	165	0	0.10	165	0	0.10	165	0	0.10
301–400	175	0	0.12	175	0	0.12	175	0	0.12	175	0	0.12	175	0	0.12	175	0	0.12
401–500	180	0	0.13	180	0	0.13	180	0	0.13	180	0	0.13	180	0	0.13	180	0	0.13
501–600	190	0	0.13	190	0	0.13	190	0	0.13	190	0	0.13	190	0	0.13	305	1	0.14
601–800	200	0	0.14	200	0	0.14	200	0	0.14	330	1	0.15	330	1	0.15	330	1	0.15
801–1000	205	0	0.14	205	0	0.14	205	0	0.14	335	1	0.17	335	1	0.17	335	1	0.17
1,001–2,000	220	0	0.15	220	0	0.15	360	1	0.19	490	2	0.21	490	2	0.21	610	3	0.22
2,001–3,000	220	0	0.15	375	1	0.20	505	2	0.23	630	3	0.24	745	4	0.26	870	5	0.26
3,001–4,000	225	0	0.15	380	1	0.20	510	2	0.23	645	3	0.25	880	5	0.28	1,000	6	0.29
4,001–5,000	225	0	0.16	380	1	0.20	520	2	0.24	770	4	0.28	895	5	0.29	1,120	7	0.31
5,001–7,000	230	0	0.16	385	1	0.21	655	3	0.27	780	4	0.29	1,020	6	0.32	1,260	8	0.34
7,001–10,000	230	0	0.16	520	2	0.25	660	3	0.28	910	5	0.32	1,150	7	0.34	1,500	10	0.37
10,001–20,000	390	1	0.21	525	2	0.26	785	4	0.31	1,040	6	0.35	1,400	9	0.39	1,980	14	0.43
20,001–50,000	390	1	0.21	530	2	0.26	920	5	0.34	1,300	8	0.39	1,890	13	0.44	2,570	19	0.48
50,001–100,000	390	1	0.21	670	3	0.29	1,040	6	0.36	1,420	9	0.41	2,120	15	0.47	3,150	23	0.50

that the probability of lot acceptance at this level of quality is $P_a = 0.9957$, we find that the average total inspection for this plan is

$$\begin{aligned}\text{ATI} &= n + (1 - P_a)(N - n) \\ &= 65 + (1 - 0.9957)(5000 - 65) = 86.22\end{aligned}$$

Thus, we will inspect approximately 86 units, on the average, in order to sentence a lot.

15.5.2 LTPD Plans

The Dodge–Romig LTPD tables are designed so that the probability of lot acceptance at the LTPD is 0.1. Tables are provided for LTPD values of 0.5%, 1%, 2%, 3%, 4%, 5%, 7%, and 10%. Table 15.9 for an LTPD of 1% is representative of these Dodge–Romig tables.

To illustrate the use of these tables, suppose that LSI memory elements for a personal computer are shipped from the supplier in lots of size $N = 5000$. The supplier's process average fallout is 0.25% nonconforming, and we wish to use a single-sampling plan with an LTPD of 1%. From inspection of Table 15-9, the sampling plan that should be used is

$$n = 770 \qquad c = 4$$

If we assume that rejected lots are screened 100% and that defective items are replaced with good ones, the AOQL for this plan is approximately 0.28%.

Note from inspection of the Dodge–Romig LTPD tables that values of the process average cover the interval from zero to one-half the LTPD. Provision for larger process averages is unnecessary, since 100% inspection is more economically efficient than inspection-sampling when the process average exceeds one-half the desired LTPD.

15.5.3 Estimation of Process Average

As we have observed, selection of a Dodge–Romig plan depends on knowledge of the supplier's process average fallout or percent nonconforming. An estimate of the process average can be obtained using a fraction defective control chart, based on the first 25 lots submitted by the supplier. If double-sampling is used, only the results from the first sample should be included in the computations. Any lot fraction defective that exceeds the upper control limit will be discarded, provided it has an assignable cause, and a new process average is calculated. Until results from 25 lots have been accumulated, the recommended procedure is to use the largest process average in the appropriate table.

Important Terms and Concepts

100% inspection
Acceptable quality level (AQL)
Acceptance-sampling plan
ANSI/ASQC Z1.4, ISO 2859
AOQL plans
Attributes data
Average outgoing quality
Average outgoing quality limit
Average sample number curve
Average total inspection
Dodge–Romig sampling plans
Double-sampling plan
Ideal OC curve
Lot disposition actions
Lot sentencing
Lot tolerance percent defective (LTPD)
LTPD plans
MIL STD 105E
Multiple-sampling plan
Normal, tightened, and reduced inspection
Operating-characteristic (OC) curve
Random sampling
Rectifying inspection
Sample size code letters

Sequential-sampling plan
Single-sampling plan
Switching rules in MIL STD 105E
Type-A and Type-B OC curves
Variables data

Exercises

15.1. Suppose that a product is shipped in lots of size $N = 5000$. The receiving inspection procedure used is singlesampling with $n = 50$ and $c = 1$.
(a) Draw the type-A OC curve for the plan.
(b) Draw the type-B OC curve for this plan and compare it to the type-A OC curve found in part (a).
(c) Which curve is appropriate for this situation?

15.2. Draw the type-B OC curve for the single-sampling plan $n = 100$, $c = 2$.

15.3. Draw the type-B OC curve for the single-sampling plan $n = 50$, $c = 1$.

15.4. Find a single-sampling plan for which $p_1 = 0.05$, $\alpha = 0.05$, $p_2 = 0.15$, and $\beta = 0.10$.

15.5. Find a single-sampling plan for which $p_1 = 0.01$, $\alpha = 0.05$, $p_2 = 0.10$, and $\beta = 0.10$.

15.6. Find a single-sampling plan for which $p_1 = 0.02$, $\alpha = 0.01$, $p_2 = 0.06$, and $\beta = 0.10$.

15.7. Suppose that a single-sampling plan with $n = 150$ and $c = 2$ is being used for receiving inspection where the supplier ships the product in lots of size $N = 3000$.
(a) Draw the OC curve for this plan.
(b) Draw the AOQ curve and find the AOQL.
(c) Draw the ATI curve for this plan.

15.8. A company uses a sample size equal to the square root of the lot size. If 1% or less of the items in the sample are defective, the lot is accepted; otherwise, it is rejected. Submitted lots vary in size from 1000 to 5000 units. Comment on the effectiveness of this procedure.

15.9. A company uses the following acceptance-sampling procedure. A sample equal to 10% of the lot is taken. If 2% or less of the items in the sample are defective, the lot is accepted; otherwise, it is rejected. If submitted lots vary in size from 5000 to 10,000 units, what can you say about the protection by this plan? If 0.05 is the desired LTPD, does this scheme offer reasonable protection to the consumer?

15.10. Consider the single-sampling plan found in Exercise 15-5. Suppose that lots of $N = 2000$ are submitted. Draw the ATI curve for this plan. Draw the AOQ curve and find the AOQL.

15.11. (a) Derive an item-by-item sequential-sampling plan for which $p_1 = 0.02$, $\alpha = 0.05$, $p_2 = 0.15$, and $\beta = 0.10$.
(b) Draw the OC curve for this plan.

15.12. Suppose that a supplier ships components in lots of size 5000. A single-sampling plan with $n = 50$ and $c = 2$ is being used for receiving inspection. Rejected lots are screened, and all defective items are reworked and returned to the lot.
(a) Draw the OC curve for this plan.
(b) Find the level of lot quality that will be rejected 90% of the time.
(c) Management has objected to the use of the above sampling procedure and wants to use a plan with an acceptance number $c = 0$, arguing that this is more consistent with their zero-defects program. What do you think of this?
(d) Design a single-sampling plan with $c = 0$ that will give a 0.90 probability of rejection of lots having the quality level found in part (b). Note that the two plans are now matched at the LTPD point. Draw the OC curve for this plan and compare it to the one for $n = 50$, $c = 2$ in part (a).
(e) Suppose that incoming lots are 0.5% nonconforming. What is the probability of rejecting these lots under both plans? Calculate the ATI at this point for both plans. Which plan do you prefer? Why?

15.13. Draw the primary and supplementary OC curves for a double-sampling plan with $n_1 = 50$, $c_1 = 2$, $n_2 = 100$, $c_2 = 6$. If the incoming lots have fraction nonconforming $p = 0.05$, what is the probability of acceptance on the first sample? What is the probability of final acceptance? Calculate the probability of rejection on the first sample.

15.14. A supplier ships a component in lots of size $N = 3000$. The AQL has been established for this product at 1%. Find the normal, tightened, and reduced single-sampling plans for this situation from MIL STD 105E, assuming that general inspection level II is appropriate.

15.15. Repeat Exercise 15.14, using general inspection level I. Discuss the differences in the various sampling plans.

15.16. Consider rectifying inspection for single-sampling. Develop an AOQ equation assuming that all defective items are removed but *not* replaced with good ones.

15.17. MIL STD 105E is being used to inspect incoming lots of size $N = 5000$. Single sampling, general inspection level II, and an AQL of 0.65% are being used.

(a) Find the normal, tightened, and reduced inspection plans.

(b) Draw the OC curves of the normal, tightened, and reduced inspection plans on the same graph.

15.18. A supplier ships a product in lots of size $N = 8000$. We wish to have an AOQL of 3%, and we are going to use single sampling. We do not know the supplier's process fallout but suspect that it is at most 1% defective.

(a) Find the appropriate Dodge–Romig plan.

(b) Find the ATI for this plan, assuming that incoming lots are 1% defective.

(c) Suppose that our estimate of the supplier's process average is incorrect and that it is really 0.25% defective. What sampling plan should we have used? What reduction in ATI would have been realized if we had used the correct plan?

15.19. We wish to find a single-sampling plan for a situation where lots are shipped from a supplier. The supplier's process operates at a fallout level of 0.50% defective. We want the AOQL from the inspection activity to be 3%.

(a) Find the appropriate Dodge–Romig plan.

(b) Draw the OC curve and the ATI curve for this plan. How much inspection will be necessary, on the average, if the supplier's process operates close to the average fallout level?

(c) What is the LTPD protection for this plan?

15.20. A product is shipped in lots of size $N = 2000$. Find a Dodge–Romig single-sampling plan for which the LTPD = 1%, assuming that the process average is 0.25% defective. Draw the OC curve and the ATI curve for this plan. What is the AOQL for this sampling plan?

16 Additional Sampling Procedures

Chapter Outline

Chapter Overview and Learning Objectives

This chapter summarizes several useful acceptance-sampling techniques, including variables sampling plans, which can be used as alternatives to attribute plans when measurement data are available. We also briefly discuss chain sampling, continuous sampling, and skip-lot sampling.

After careful study of this chapter you should be able to do the following:

1. Understand the difference between attributes and variables sampling plans
2. Understand the advantages and disadvantages of variables sampling
3. Understand the two major types of variables sampling plans
4. Know how to design a variables sampling plan with a specified OC

5. Understand the structure and use of MIL STD 414 and its civilian counterpart plans
6. Understand the differences between the MIL STD 414 and ANSI/ASQC Z1.9 sampling plans
7. Understand how chain sampling plans are designed and used
8. Understand how continuous sampling plans are designed and used
9. Understand how skip-lot sampling plans are designed and used

16.1 Acceptance Sampling by Variables

16.1.1 Advantages and Disadvantages of Variables Sampling

The primary advantage of variables sampling plans is that the same operating-characteristic curve can be obtained with a smaller sample size than would be required by an attributes sampling plan. Thus, a variables acceptance-sampling plan that has the same protection as an attributes acceptance-sampling plan would require less sampling. The measurements data required by a variables sampling plan would probably cost more per observation than the collection of attributes data. However, the reduction in sample size obtained may more than offset this increased cost. For example, suppose that an attributes sampling plan requires a sample of size 100 items, but the equivalent variables sampling plan requires a sample size of only 65. If the cost of measurement data is less than 1.61 times the cost of measuring the observations on an attributes scale, the variables sampling plan will be more economically efficient, considering sampling costs only. When destructive testing is employed, variables sampling is particularly useful in reducing the costs of inspection.

A second advantage is that measurement data usually provide more information about the manufacturing process or the lot than do attributes data. Generally, numerical measurements of quality characteristics are more useful than simple classification of the item as defective or nondefective.

A final point to be emphasized is that when acceptable quality levels are very small, the sample sizes required by attributes sampling plans are very large. Under these circumstances, there may be significant advantages in switching to variables measurement. Thus, as many manufacturers begin to emphasize allowable numbers of defective parts per million, variables sampling becomes very attractive.

Variables sampling plans have several disadvantages. Perhaps the primary disadvantage is that the distribution of the quality characteristic must be known. Furthermore, most standard variables acceptance-sampling plans assume that the distribution of the quality characteristic is normal. If the distribution of the quality characteristic is not normal, and a plan based on the normal assumption is employed, serious departures from the advertised risks of accepting or rejecting lots of given quality may be experienced. We discuss this point more completely in Section 16.1.3. The second disadvantage of variables sampling is that a separate sampling plan must be employed for each quality characteristic that is being inspected. For example, if an item is inspected for four quality characteristics, it is necessary to have four separate variables inspection sampling plans; under attributes sampling, one attributes sampling plan could be employed. Finally, it is possible that the use of a variables sampling plan will lead to rejection of a lot even though the actual sample inspected does not contain any defective items. Although this does not happen very often, when it does occur it usually causes considerable unhappiness in both the suppliers' and the consumers' organizations, particularly if rejection of the lot has caused a manufacturing facility to shut down or operate on a reduced production schedule.

16.1.2 Types of Sampling Plans Available

There are two general types of variables sampling procedures: plans that control the lot or process fraction defective (or nonconforming) and plans that control a lot or process parameter (usually the mean). Sections 16.2 and 16.3 present variables sampling plans to control the process fraction defective. Variables sampling plans for the process mean are presented in Section 16.4.

Consider a variables sampling plan to control the lot or process fraction nonconforming. Since the quality characteristic is a variable, there will exist either a lower specification limit (LSL), an upper specification limit (USL), or both, that define the acceptable values of this parameter. Figure 16.1 illustrates the situation in which the quality characteristic x is normally distributed and there is a lower specification limit on this parameter. The symbol p represents the fraction defective in the lot. Note that the fraction defective is a function of the lot or process mean μ and the lot or process standard deviation σ.

Suppose that the standard deviation σ is known. Under this condition, we may wish to sample from the lot to determine whether or not the value of the mean is such that the fraction defective p is acceptable. As described next, we may organize the calculations in the variables sampling plan in two ways.

Procedure 1. Take a random sample of n items from the lot and compute the statistic

$$Z_{\text{LSL}} = \frac{\bar{x} - \text{LSL}}{\sigma} \tag{16.1}$$

Note that Z_{LSL} in equation (16.1) simply expresses the distance between the sample average $\bar{x}$ and the lower specification limit in standard deviation units. The larger is the value of Z_{LSL}, the farther the sample average $\bar{x}$ is from the lower specification limit, and consequently, the smaller is the lot fraction defective p. If there is a critical value of p of interest that should not be exceeded with stated probability, we can translate this value of p into a **critical distance**—say, k—for Z_{LSL}. Thus, if $Z_{\text{LSL}} \geq k$, we would accept the lot because the sample data imply that the lot mean is sufficiently far above the LSL to ensure that the lot fraction nonconforming is satisfactory. However, if $Z_{\text{LSL}} < k$, the mean is too close to the LSL, and the lot should be rejected.

Procedure 2. Take a random sample of n items from the lot and compute Z_{LSL} using equation (16.1). Use Z_{LSL} to estimate the fraction defective of the lot or process as the area under the standard normal curve below Z_{LSL}. (Actually, using $Q_{\text{LSL}} = Z_{\text{LSL}} \sqrt{n/(n-1)}$ as a standard normal variable is slightly better, because it gives a better estimate of p.) Let $\hat{p}$ be the estimate of p so obtained. If the estimate $\hat{p}$ exceeds a specified maximum value M, reject the lot; otherwise, accept it.

The two procedures can be designed so that they give equivalent results. When there is only a single specification limit (LSL or USL), either procedure may be used. Obviously, in the case of an upper specification limit, we would compute

$$Z_{\text{USL}} = \frac{\text{USL} - \bar{x}}{\sigma} \tag{16.2}$$

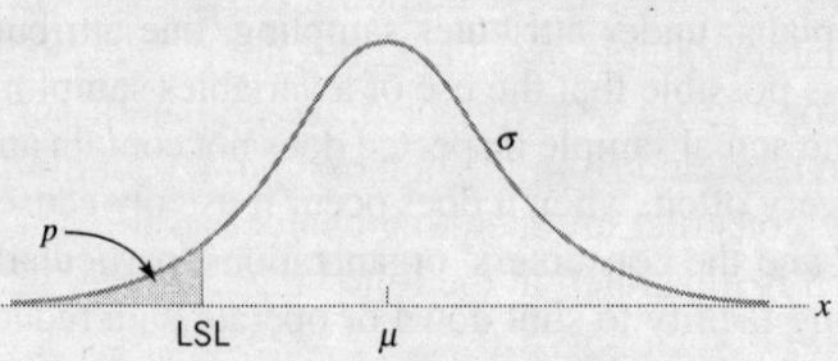

■ FIGURE 16.1 Relationship of the lot or process fraction defective p to the mean and standard deviation of a normal distribution.

instead of using equation (16.1). When there are both lower and upper specifications, the *M* method, Procedure 2, should be used.

When the standard deviation σ is unknown, it is estimated by the sample standard deviation s, and σ in equations (16.1) and (16.2) is replaced by s. It is also possible to design plans based on the sample range R instead of s. However, these plans are not discussed in this chapter because using the sample standard deviation will lead to smaller sample sizes. Plans based on R were once in wide use because R is easier to compute by hand than is s, but computation is not a problem today.

16.1.3 Caution in the Use of Variables Sampling

We have remarked that the distribution of the quality characteristic must be of known form to use variables sampling. Furthermore, the usual assumption is that the parameter of interest follows the **normal distribution.** This assumption is critical because all variables sampling plans require that there be some method of converting a sample mean and standard deviation into a lot or process fraction defective. If the parameter of interest is not normally distributed, estimates of the fraction defective based on the sample mean and sample standard deviation will not be the same as if the parameter were normally distributed. The difference between these estimated fraction defectives may be large when we are dealing with very small fractions defective. For example, if the mean of a normal distribution lies three standard deviations below a single upper specification limit, the lot will contain no more than 0.135% defective. On the other hand, if the quality characteristic in the lot or process is very nonnormal, and the mean lies three standard deviations below the specification limit, it is entirely possible that 1% or more of the items in the lot might be defective.

It is possible to use variables sampling plans when the parameter of interest does not have a normal distribution. Provided that the form of the distribution is known, or that there is a method of determining the fraction defective from the sample average and sample standard deviation (or other appropriate sample statistics), it is possible to devise a procedure for applying a variables sampling plan. For example, Duncan (1986) presents a procedure for using a variables sampling plan when the distribution of the quality characteristic can be described by a Pearson type III distribution. A general discussion of variables sampling in the nonnormal case is, however, beyond the scope of this book.

16.2 Designing a Variables Sampling Plan with a Specified OC Curve

It is easy to design a variables sampling plan using Procedure 1, the *k*-method, that has a specified OC curve. Let $(p_1, 1 - \alpha)$, (p_2, β) be the two points on the OC curve of interest. Note that p_1 and p_2 may be the levels of lot or process fraction nonconforming that correspond to acceptable and rejectable levels of quality, respectively.

The nomograph shown in Fig. 16.2 enables the quality engineer to find the required sample size n and the critical value k to meet a set of given conditions $p_1, 1 - \alpha, p_2, \beta$ for both the σ known and the σ unknown cases. The nomograph contains separate scales for sample size for these two cases. The greater uncertainty in the case where the standard deviation is unknown requires a larger sample size than does the σ known case, but the same value of k is used. In addition, for a given sampling plan, the probability of acceptance for any value of fraction defective can be found from the nomograph. By plotting several of these points, the quality engineer may construct an operating-characteristic curve of the sampling plan. The use of this nomograph is illustrated in the following example.

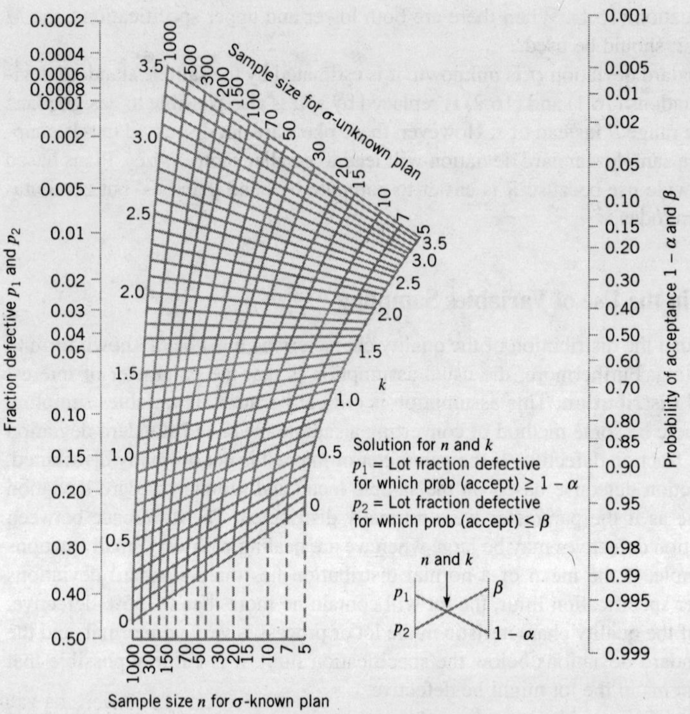

■ FIGURE 16.2 Nomograph for designing variables sampling plans.

EXAMPLE 16.1 A Variables Sampling Plan

A soft-drink bottler buys nonreturnable bottles from a supplier. The bottler has established a lower specification on the bursting strength of the bottles at 225 psi. If 1% or less of the bottles burst below this limit, the bottler wishes to accept the lot with probability 0.95 ($p_1 = 0.01$, $1 - \alpha = 0.95$), whereas if 6% or more of the bottles burst below this limit, the bottler would like to reject the lot with probability 0.90 ($p_2 = 0.06$, $\beta = 0.10$). Find the sampling plan.

SOLUTION

To find the sampling plan, draw a line connecting the point 0.01 on the fraction defective scale in Figure 16.2 to the point 0.95 on the probability of acceptance scale. Then draw a similar line connecting the points $p_2 = 0.06$ and $P_a = 0.10$. At the intersection of these lines, we read $k = 1.9$. Suppose that σ is unknown. Following the curved line from the intersection point to the upper sample size scale gives $n = 40$. Therefore, the procedure is to take a random sample of $n = 40$ bottles, observe the bursting strengths, compute $\bar{x}$ and s, then calculate

$$Z_{LSL} = \frac{\bar{x} - LSL}{s}$$

and to accept the lot if

$$Z_{LSL} \geq k = 1.9$$

If σ is known, drop vertically from the intersection point to the σ-known scale. This would indicate a sample size of $n = 15$. Thus, if the standard deviation is known, a considerable reduction in sample size is possible.

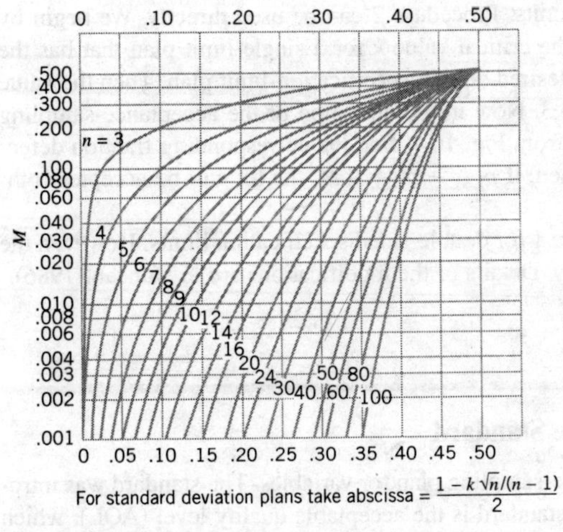

■ FIGURE 16.3 Chart for determining the maximum allowable fraction defective M. (From A. J. Duncan, *Quality Control and Industrial Statistics,* 5th ed., Irwin, Homewood, IL., 1986, with the permission of the publisher.)

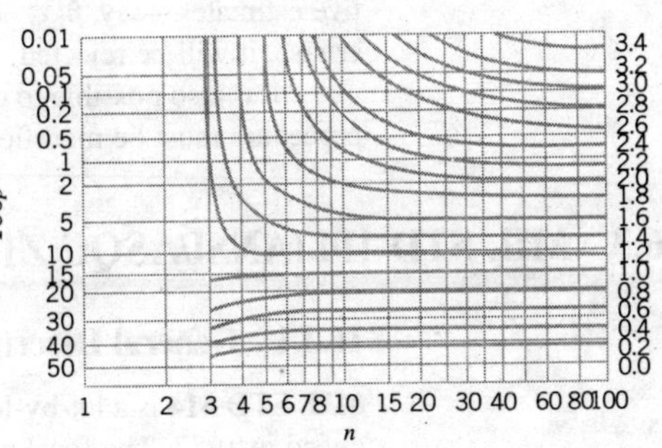

■ FIGURE 16.4 Chart for determining $\hat{p}$ from Z. (From A. J. Duncan, *Quality Control and Industrial Statistics,* 5th ed., Irwin, Homewood, IL., 1986, with the permission of the publisher.)

It is also possible to design a variables acceptance-sampling plan from the nomograph using Procedure 2 (the M-method). To do so, an additional step is necessary. Figure 16.3 presents a chart for determining the maximum allowable fraction defective M. Once the values of n and k have been determined for the appropriate sampling plan from Fig. 16.2, a value of M can be read directly from Fig. 16.3. To use Procedure 2, it is necessary to convert the value of Z_{LSL} or Z_{USL} into an estimated fraction defective. Figure 16.4 can be used for this purpose. The following example illustrates how a single-sampling plan for variables with a one-sided specification limit using Procedure 2 can be designed.

EXAMPLE 16.2 Variables Sampling with a One-Sided Specification

Consider the situation described in Example 16.1. Design a sampling plan using Procedure 2.

SOLUTION

Since we know that $n = 40$ and $k = 1.9$, we enter Fig. 16.3 with $n = 40$ and abscissa value

$$\frac{1 - \frac{k\sqrt{n}}{(n-1)}}{2} = \frac{1 - \frac{1.9\sqrt{40}}{39}}{2} = 0.35$$

This indicates that $M = 0.030$. Now suppose that a sample of $n = 40$ is taken, and we observe $\bar{x} = 255$ and $s = 15$. The value of Z_{LSL} is

$$Z_{LSL} = \frac{\bar{x} - \text{LSL}}{s} = \frac{255 - 225}{15} = 2$$

From Fig. 16.4 we read $\hat{p} = 0.020$. Since $\hat{p} = 0.020$ is less than $M = 0.030$, we will accept the lot.

When there are double-specification limits, Procedure 2 can be used directly. We begin by first obtaining the sample size n and the critical value k for a single-limit plan that has the same values of p_1, p_2, α, and β as the desired double-specification-limit plan. Then the value of M is obtained directly from Fig. 16.3. Now in the operation of the acceptance-sampling plan, we compute Z_{LSL} and Z_{USL} and, from Fig. 16.4, find the corresponding fraction defective estimates—say, $\hat{p}_{LSL}$ and $\hat{p}_{USL}$. Then, if $\hat{p}_{LSL} + \hat{p}_{USL} \le M$, the lot will be accepted; otherwise, it will be rejected.

It is also possible to use Procedure 1 for double-sided specification limits. However, the procedure must be modified extensively. Details of the modifications are in Duncan (1986).

16.3 MIL STD 414 (ANSI/ASQC Z1.9)

16.3.1 General Description of the Standard

MIL STD 414 is a lot-by-lot acceptance-sampling plan for variables. The standard was introduced in 1957. The focal point of this standard is the acceptable quality level (AQL), which ranges from 0.04% to 15%. There are five general levels of inspection, and level IV is designated as "normal." Inspection level V gives a steeper OC curve than level IV. When reduced sampling costs are necessary and when greater risks can or must be tolerated, lower inspection levels can be used. As with the attributes standard, MIL STD 105E, sample size code letters are used, but the same code letter does not imply the same sample size in both standards. In addition, the lot size classes are different in both standards. Sample sizes are a function of the lot size and the inspection level. Provision is made for normal, tightened, and reduced inspection. All the sampling plans and procedures in the standard assume that the quality characteristic of interest is normally distributed.

Figure 16.5 presents the organization of the standard. Note that acceptance-sampling plans can be designed for cases where the lot or process variability is either known or unknown, and where there are either single-specification limits or double-specification limits on the quality characteristic. In the case of single-specification limits, either Procedure 1 or Procedure 2 may be used. If there are double-specification limits, then Procedure 2 must be used. If the process or lot variability is known and stable, the variability known plans are the most economically efficient. When lot or process variability is unknown, either the standard deviation or the range of the sample may be used in operating the sampling plan. The range method requires a larger sample size, and we do not generally recommend its use.

MIL STD 414 is divided into four sections. Section A is a general description of the sampling plans, including definitions, sample size code letters, and OC curves for the various

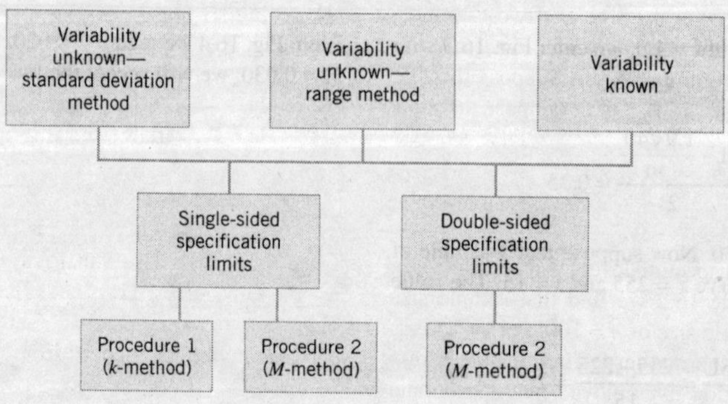

■ FIGURE 16.5 Organization of MIL STD 414.

■ TABLE 16.1
Sample Size Code Letters (MIL STD 414, Table A.2)

Lot Size	Inspection Levels I	II	III	IV	V
3 to 8	B	B	B	B	C
9 to 15	B	B	B	B	D
16 to 25	B	B	B	C	E
26 to 40	B	B	B	D	F
41 to 65	B	B	C	E	G
66 to 110	B	B	D	F	H
111 to 180	B	C	E	G	I
181 to 300	B	D	F	H	J
301 to 500	C	E	G	I	K
501 to 800	D	F	H	J	L
801 to 1,300	E	G	I	K	L
1,301 to 3,200	F	H	J	L	M
3,201 to 8,000	G	I	L	M	N
8,001 to 22,000	H	J	M	N	O
22,001 to 110,000	I	K	N	O	P
110,001 to 550,000	I	K	O	P	Q
550,001 and over	I	K	P	Q	Q

sampling plans. Section B of the standard gives variables sampling plans based on the sample standard deviation for the case in which the process or lot variability is unknown. Section C presents variables sampling plans based on the sample range method. Section D gives variables sampling plans for the case where the process standard deviation is known.

16.3.2 Use of the Tables

Two typical tables from MIL STD 414 are reproduced as Tables 16.1 and 16.2. The following example illustrates the use of these tables.

EXAMPLE 16.3 Using MIL STD 414

Consider the soft-drink bottler in the previous two examples who is purchasing bottles from a supplier. The lower specification limit on bursting strength is 225 psi. Suppose that the AQL at this specification limit is 1%. Let us suppose that bottles are shipped in lots of size 100,000. Find a variables sampling plan that uses Procedure 1 from MIL STD 414. Assume that the lot standard deviation is unknown.

SOLUTION

From Table 16.1, if we use inspection level IV, the sample size code letter is O. From Table 16.2 we find that sample size code letter O implies a sample size of $n = 100$. For an acceptable quality level of 1%, on normal inspection, the value of k is 2.00. If tightened inspection is employed, the appropriate value of k is 2.14. Note that normal and tightened inspection use the same tables. The AQL values for normal inspection are indexed at the top of the table, and the AQL values for tightened inspection are indexed from the bottom of the table.

TABLE 16.2

Master Table for Normal and Tightened Inspection for Plans Based on Variability Unknown (Standard Deviation Method) (Single-Specification Limit—Form 1)(MIL STD 414, Table B.1)

Sample Size Code Letter	Sample Size	Acceptable Quality Levels (normal inspection)													
		.04	.065	.10	.15	.25	.40	.65	1.00	1.50	2.50	4.00	6.50	10.00	15.00
		k	*k*	*k*	*k*	*k*	*k*	*k*	*k*	*k*	*k*	*k*	*k*	*k*	*k*
B	3	↓	↓	↓	↓	↓	↓	↓	↓	↓	1.12	.958	.765	.566	.341
C	4	↓	↓	↓	↓	↓	↓	↓	1.45	1.34	1.17	1.01	.814	.617	.393
D	5	↓	↓	↓	↓	↓	↓	1.65	1.53	1.40	1.24	1.07	.874	.675	.455
E	7	↓	↓	↓	↓	2.00	1.88	1.75	1.62	1.50	1.33	1.15	.955	.755	.536
F	10	↓	↓	↓	2.24	2.11	1.98	1.84	1.72	1.58	1.41	1.23	1.03	.828	.611
G	15	2.64	2.53	2.42	2.32	2.20	2.06	1.91	1.79	1.65	1.47	1.30	1.09	.886	.664
H	20	2.69	2.58	2.47	2.36	2.24	2.11	1.96	1.82	1.69	1.51	1.33	1.12	.917	.695
I	25	2.72	2.61	2.50	2.40	2.26	2.14	1.98	1.85	1.72	1.53	1.35	1.14	.936	.712
J	30	2.73	2.61	2.51	2.41	2.28	2.15	2.00	1.86	1.73	1.55	1.36	1.15	.946	.723
K	35	2.77	2.65	2.54	2.45	2.31	2.18	2.03	1.89	1.76	1.57	1.39	1.18	.969	.745
L	40	2.77	2.66	2.55	2.44	2.31	2.18	2.03	1.89	1.76	1.58	1.39	1.18	.971	.746
M	50	2.83	2.71	2.60	2.50	2.35	2.22	2.08	1.93	1.80	1.61	1.42	1.21	1.00	.774
N	75	2.90	2.77	2.66	2.55	2.41	2.27	2.12	1.98	1.84	1.65	1.46	1.24	1.03	.804
O	100	2.92	2.80	2.69	2.58	2.43	2.29	2.14	2.00	1.86	1.67	1.48	1.26	1.05	.819
P	150	2.96	2.84	2.73	2.61	2.47	2.33	2.18	2.03	1.89	1.70	1.51	1.29	1.07	.841
Q	200	2.97	2.85	2.73	2.62	2.47	2.33	2.18	2.04	1.89	1.70	1.51	1.29	1.07	.845
		.065	.10	.15	.25	.40	.65	1.00	1.50	2.50	4.00	6.50	10.00	15.00	
		Acceptable Quality Levels (tightened inspection)													

All AQL values are in percent defective.

↓ Use first sampling plan below arrow, that is, both sample size as well as *k* value. When sample size equals or exceeds lot size, every item in the lot must be inspected.

MIL STD 414 contains a provision for a shift to tightened or reduced inspection when this is warranted. The process average is used as the basis for determining when such a shift is made. The process average is taken as the average of the sample estimates of percent defective computed for lots submitted on original inspection. Usually, the process average is computed using information from the preceding ten lots. Full details of the switching procedures are described in the standard and in a technical memorandum on MIL STD 414, published by the United States Department of the Navy, Bureau of Ordnance.

Estimation of the fraction defective is required in using Procedure 2 of MIL STD 414. It is also required in implementing the switching rules between normal, tightened, and reduced inspection. In the standard, three tables are provided for estimating the fraction defective.

When starting to use MIL STD 414, one can choose between the known standard deviation and unknown standard deviation procedures. When there is no basis for knowledge of σ, obviously the unknown standard deviation plan must be used. However, it is a good idea to maintain either an R or s chart on the results of each lot so that some information on the state of statistical control of the scatter in the manufacturing process can be collected. If this control chart indicates statistical control, it will be possible to switch to a known σ plan. Such a switch will reduce the required sample size. Even if the process were not perfectly controlled, the control chart could provide information leading to a conservative estimate of σ for use in a known σ plan. When a known σ plan is used, it is also necessary to maintain a control chart on either R or s as a continuous check on the assumption of stable and known process variability.

MIL STD 414 contains a special procedure for application of mixed variables/attributes acceptance-sampling plans. If the lot does not meet the acceptability criterion of the variables plan, an attributes single-sampling plan, using tightened inspection and the same AQL, is obtained from MIL STD 105E. A lot can be accepted by either of the plans in sequence, but must be rejected by both the variables and attributes plan.

16.3.3 Discussion of MIL STD 414 and ANSI/ASQC Z1.9

In 1980, the American National Standards Institute and the American Society for Quality Control released an updated civilian version of MIL STD 414 known as ANSI/ASQC Z1.9. MIL STD 414 was originally structured to give protection essentially equivalent to that provided by MIL STD 105A (1950). When MIL STD 105D was adopted in 1963, this new standard contained substantially revised tables and procedures that led to differences in protection between it and MIL STD 414. Consequently, it is not possible to move directly from an attributes sampling plan in the current MIL STD 105E to a corresponding variables plan in MIL STD 414 if the assurance of continued protection is desired for certain lot sizes and AQLs.

The civilian counterpart of MIL STD 414, ANSI/ASQC Z1.9, restores this original match. That is, ANSI/ASQC Z1.9 is directly compatible with MIL STD 105E (and its equivalent civilian counterpart ANSI/ASQC Z1.4). This equivalence was obtained by incorporating the following revisions in ANSI/ASQC Z1.9:

1. Lot size ranges were adjusted to correspond to MIL STD 105D.
2. The code letters assigned to the various lot size ranges were arranged to make protection equal to that of MIL STD 105E.
3. AQLs of 0.04, 0.065, and 15 were deleted.
4. The original inspection levels I, II, III, IV, and V were relabeled S3, S4, I, II, III, respectively.
5. The original switching rules were replaced by those of MIL STD 105E, with slight revisions.

In addition, to modernize terminology, the word *nonconformity* was substituted for defect, *nonconformance* was substituted for defective, and *percent nonconforming* was substituted for percent defective. The operating-characteristic curves were recomputed and replotted, and a number of editorial changes were made to the descriptive material of the standard to match MIL STD 105E as closely as possible. Finally, an appendix was included showing the match between ANSI/ASQC Z1.9, MIL STD 105E, and the corresponding civilian version ANSI Z1.4. This appendix also provided selected percentage points from the OC curves of these standards and their differences.

As of this writing, the Department of Defense has not officially adopted ANSI/ASQC Z1.9 and continues to use MIL STD 414. Both standards will probably be used for the immediate future. The principal advantage of the ANSI/ASQC Z1.9 standard is that it is possible to start inspection by using an attributes sampling scheme from MIL STD 105E or ANSI/ASQC Z1.4, collect sufficient information to use variables inspection, and then switch to the variables scheme, while maintaining the same AQL-code letter combination. It would then be possible to switch back to the attributes scheme if the assumption of the variables scheme appeared not to be satisfied. It is also possible to take advantage of the information gained in coordinated attributes and variables inspection to move in a logical manner from inspection sampling to statistical process control.

As in MIL STD 414, ANSI/ASQC Z1.9 assumes that the quality characteristic is normally distributed. This is an important assumption that we have commented on previously. We have suggested that a test for normality should be incorporated as part of the standard. One way this can be done is to plot a control chart for $\bar{x}$ and S (or $\bar{x}$ and R) from the variables data from each lot. After a sufficient number of observations have been obtained, a test for normality can be employed by plotting the individual measurements on normal probability paper or by conducting one of the specialized statistical tests for normality. It is recommended that a relatively large sample size be used in this statistical test. At least 100 observations should be collected before the test for normality is made, and it is our belief that the sample size should increase inversely with AQL. If the assumption of normality is badly violated, either a special variables sampling procedure must be developed, or we must return to attributes inspection.

An additional advantage of applying a control chart to the result of each lot is that if the process variability has been in control for at least 30 samples, it will be possible to switch to a known standard deviation plan, thereby allowing a substantial reduction in sample size. Although this can be instituted in any combined program of attributes and variables inspection, it is easy to do so using the ANSI/ASQC standards, because of the design equivalence between the attributes and variables procedures.

16.4 Other Variables Sampling Procedures

16.4.1 Sampling by Variables to Give Assurance Regarding the Lot or Process Mean

Variables sampling plans can also be used to give assurance regarding the **average** quality of a material, instead of the fraction defective. Sampling plans such as this are most likely to be employed in the sampling of bulk materials that come in bags, drums, or other containers. However, they can also be applied to discrete parts and to other variables, such as energy loss in power transformers. The general approach employed in this type of variables sampling is statistical hypothesis testing. We now present an example of the procedure.

EXAMPLE 16.4 Sampling to Provide Assurance Regarding Average Quality

A manufacturer of wood paneling samples the substrate blanks bought from an offshore supplier to determine their formaldehyde emission level. As long as the mean emission level is less than 0.3 ppm, the lot is satisfactory. We want to design a variables sampling procedure that will give lots that have a mean emission level of 0.3 ppm a 0.95 probability of acceptance, and lots that have a mean emission level of 0.4 ppm a 0.10 probability of acceptance. The largest probable value of the standard deviation of emission level is known from past experience to be $\sigma = 0.10$ ppm.

SOLUTION

Let $\bar{x}_A$ be the value of the sample average above which the lot will be accepted. Then, we know that

$$\frac{\bar{x}_A - 0.30}{\sigma/\sqrt{n}} = \frac{\bar{x}_A - 0.30}{0.10/\sqrt{n}}$$

is distributed as a standard normal variable. If lots of this type have a 0.95 probability of acceptance, then

$$\frac{\bar{x}_A - 0.30}{0.10/\sqrt{n}} = +1.645$$

Similarly, if lots that have a mean emission level of 0.40 ppm are to have a 0.10 probability of acceptance, then

$$\frac{\bar{x}_A - 0.40}{0.10/\sqrt{n}} = -1.282$$

These two equations may be solved for n and $\bar{x}_A$, giving $n = 9$ and $\bar{x}_A = 0.356$. It is also possible to design the sampling plan using an OC curve method.

We may also design variables acceptance-sampling procedures such as this one for the case where the standard deviation is unknown. Similarly, we may derive lot-by-lot variables acceptance-sampling plans to give assurance regarding the standard deviation of a lot or process. The standard techniques of statistical hypothesis testing on means and variances can be used to obtain sampling procedures that have specified OC curves. For an extensive discussion of designing these procedures, refer to Montgomery and Runger (2007).

16.4.2 Sequential Sampling by Variables

Just as sequential sampling proves useful in attributes inspection, it can also be applied in variables inspection. The usual assumptions are that the quality characteristic is normally distributed and that the standard deviation of the lot or process is known. The item-by-item sequential sampling plan by variables plots the cumulative sum of the measurements on the quality characteristic. Limit lines for accepting the lot, rejecting the lot, and continuing sampling are constructed much as they are in the case of attributes inspection. Duncan (1986) provides a good discussion of the design of these plans.

16.5 Chain Sampling

For situations in which testing is destructive or very expensive, sampling plans with small sample sizes are usually selected. These small sample size plans often have acceptance numbers of zero. Plans with zero acceptance numbers are often undesirable, however, in that their OC curves are convex throughout. This means that the probability of lot acceptance begins to drop very rapidly as the lot fraction defective becomes greater than zero. This is often unfair to the producer, and in situations where rectifying inspection is used, it can require the consumer to screen a large number of lots that are essentially of acceptable quality. Figures 15.5

and 15.7 in Chapter 15 present OC curves of sampling plans that have acceptance numbers of zero and acceptance numbers that are greater than zero.

Dodge (1955) suggested an alternate procedure, known as **chain sampling,** that might be a substitute for ordinary single-sampling plans with zero acceptance numbers in certain circumstances. Chain-sampling plans make use of the cumulative results of several preceding lots. The general procedure is as follows:

1. For each lot, select the sample of size n and observe the number of defectives.
2. If the sample has zero defectives, accept the lot; if the sample has two or more defectives, reject the lot; and if the sample has one defective, accept the lot provided there have been no defectives in the previous i lots.

Thus, for a chain-sampling plan given by $n = 5$, $i = 3$, a lot would be accepted if there were no defectives in the sample of five, or if there were one defective in the sample of five and no defectives had been observed in the samples from the previous three lots. This type of plan is known as a ChSP-1 plan.

The effect of chain sampling is to alter the shape of the OC curve near the origin so that it has a more desirable shape. That is, it is more difficult to reject lots with very small fraction defectives with a ChSP-1 plan than it is with ordinary single sampling. Figure 16.6 shows OC curves for ChSP-1 plans with $n = 5$, $c = 0$, and $i = 1$, 2, 3, and 5. The curve for $i = 1$ is dotted, and it is not a preferred choice. In practice, values of i usually vary between three and five, since the OC curves of such plans approximate the single-sampling plan OC curve. The points on the OC curve of a ChSP-1 plan are given by the equation

$$P_a = P(0,n) + P(1,n)\left[P(0,n)\right]^i \tag{16.3}$$

where $P(0, n)$ and $P(1, n)$ are the probabilities of obtaining 0 and 1 defectives, respectively, out of a random sample of size n. To illustrate the computations, consider the ChSP-1 plan with $n = 5$, $c = 0$, and $i = 3$. For $p = 0.10$, we have

$$P(0,n) = \frac{n!}{d!(n-d)!}p^d(1-p)^{n-d} = \frac{5!}{0!5!}(0.10)^0(0.90)^5 = 0.590$$

$$P(1,n) = \frac{n!}{d!(n-d)!}p^d(1-p)^{n-d} = \frac{5!}{1!(5-1)!}(0.10)^1(0.90)^4 = 0.328$$

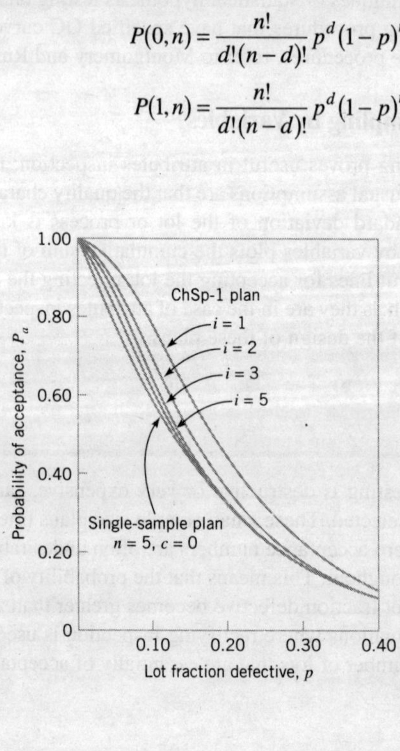

■ **FIGURE 16.6** OC curves for ChSP-1 plan with $n = 5$, $c = 0$, and $i = 1$, 2, 3, 5. (Reproduced with permission from H. F. Dodge. "Chain Sampling Inspection Plans," *Industrial Quality Control*, Vol. 11, No. 4, 1955.)

and

$$\begin{aligned}P_a &= P(0,n) + P(1,n)[P(0,n)]^i \\ &= 0.590 + (0.328)(0.590)^3 \\ &= 0.657\end{aligned}$$

The proper use of chain sampling requires that the following conditions be met:

1. The lot should be one of a series in a continuing stream of lots, from a process in which there is repetitive production under the same conditions, and in which the lots of products are offered for acceptance in substantially the order of production.
2. Lots should usually be expected to be of essentially the same quality.
3. The sampling agency should have no reason to believe that the current lot is of poorer quality than those immediately preceding.
4. There should be a good record of quality performance on the part of the supplier.
5. The sampling agency must have confidence in the supplier, in that the supplier will not take advantage of its good record and occasionally send a bad lot when such a lot would have the best chance of acceptance.

16.6 Continuous Sampling

All the sampling plans discussed previously are lot-by-lot plans. With these plans, there is an explicit assumption that the product is formed into lots, and the purpose of the sampling plan is to sentence the individual lots. However, many manufacturing operations, particularly complex assembly processes, do not result in the natural formation of lots. For example, manufacturing of many electronics products, such as personal computers, is performed on a conveyorized assembly line.

When production is continuous, two approaches may be used to form lots. The first procedure allows the accumulation of production at given points in the assembly process. This has the disadvantage of creating in-process inventory at various points, which requires additional space, may constitute a safety hazard, and is a generally inefficient approach to managing an assembly line. The second procedure arbitrarily marks off a given segment of production as a "lot." The disadvantage of this approach is that if a lot is ultimately rejected and 100% inspection of the lot is subsequently required, it may be necessary to recall products from manufacturing operations that are further downstream. This may require disassembly or at least partial destruction of semifinished items.

For these reasons, special sampling plans for continuous production have been developed. **Continuous-sampling plans** consist of alternating sequences of sampling inspection and screening (100% inspection). The plans usually begin with 100% inspection, and when a stated number of units is found to be free of defects (the number of units i is usually called the **clearance number**), sampling inspection is instituted. Sampling inspection continues until a specified number of defective units is found, at which time 100% inspection is resumed. Continuous-sampling plans are rectifying inspection plans, in that the quality of the product is improved by the partial screening.

16.6.1 CSP-1

Continuous-sampling plans were first proposed by Harold F. Dodge (1943). Dodge's initial plan is called CSP-1. At the start of the plan, all units are inspected 100%. As soon as the

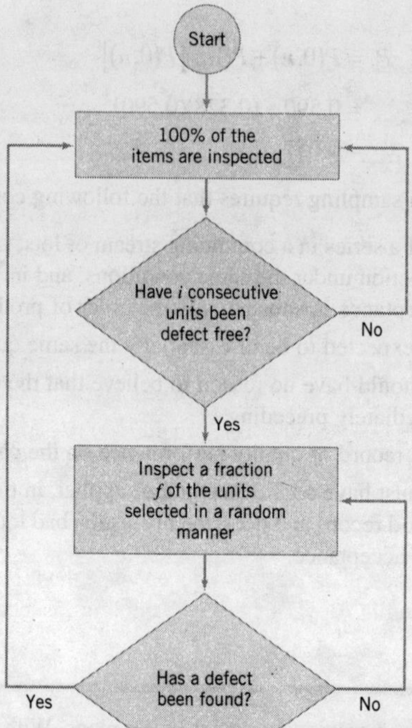

■ **FIGURE 16.7** Procedure for CSP-1 plans.

clearance number has been reached—that is, as soon as i consecutive units of product are found to be free of defects—100% inspection is discontinued, and only a fraction (f) of the units are inspected. These sample units are selected one at a time at random from the flow of production. If a sample unit is found to be defective, 100% inspection is resumed. All defective units found are either reworked or replaced with good ones. The procedure for CSP-1 is shown in Fig. 16.7.

A CSP-1 plan has an overall AOQL. The value of the AOQL depends on the values of the clearance number i and the sampling fraction f. The same AOQL can be obtained by different combinations of i and f. Table 16.3 presents various values of i and f for CSP-1 that will lead to a stipulated AOQL. Note in the table that an AOQL of 0.79% could be obtained using a sampling plan with $i = 59$ and $f = \frac{1}{3}$, or with $i = 113$ and $f = \frac{1}{7}$.

The choice of i and f is usually based on practical considerations in the manufacturing process. For example, i and f may be influenced by the workload of the inspectors and operators in the system. It is a fairly common practice to use quality-assurance inspectors to do the sampling inspection, and place the burden of 100% inspection on manufacturing. As a general rule, however, it is not a good idea to choose values of f smaller than 1/200 because the protection against bad quality in a continuous run of production then becomes very poor.

The average number of units inspected in a 100% screening sequence following the occurrence of a defect is equal to

$$u = \frac{1 - q^i}{pq^i} \tag{16.4}$$

■ TABLE 16.3
Values of *i* for CSP-1 Plans

	AOQL (%)															
f	**0.018**	**0.033**	**0.046**	**0.074**	**0.113**	**0.143**	**0.198**	**0.33**	**0.53**	**0.79**	**1.22**	**1.90**	**2.90**	**4.94**	**7.12**	**11.46**
1/2	1,540	840	600	375	245	194	140	84	53	36	23	15	10	6	5	3
1/3	2,550	1,390	1,000	620	405	321	232	140	87	59	38	25	16	10	7	5
1/4	3,340	1,820	1,310	810	530	420	303	182	113	76	49	32	21	13	9	6
1/5	3,960	2,160	1,550	965	630	498	360	217	135	91	58	38	25	15	11	7
1/7	4,950	2,700	1,940	1,205	790	623	450	270	168	113	73	47	31	18	13	8
1/10	6,050	3,300	2,370	1,470	965	762	550	335	207	138	89	57	38	22	16	10
1/15	7,390	4,030	2,890	1,800	1,180	930	672	410	255	170	108	70	46	27	19	12
1/25	9,110	4,970	3,570	2,215	1,450	1,147	828	500	315	210	134	86	57	33	23	14
1/50	11,730	6,400	4,590	2,855	1,870	1,477	1,067	640	400	270	175	110	72	42	29	18
1/100	14,320	7,810	5,600	3,485	2,305	1,820	1,302	790	500	330	215	135	89	52	36	22
1/200	17,420	9,500	6,810	4,235	2,760	2,178	1,583	950	590	400	255	165	106	62	43	26

where $q = 1 - p$, and p is the fraction defective produced when the process is operating in control. The average number of units passed under the sampling inspection procedure before a defective unit is found is

$$v = \frac{1}{fp} \tag{16.5}$$

The average fraction of total manufactured units inspected in the long run is

$$\text{AFI} = \frac{u + fv}{u + v} \tag{16.6}$$

The average fraction of manufactured units passed under the sampling procedure is

$$P_a = \frac{v}{u + v} \tag{16.7}$$

When P_a is plotted as a function of p, we obtain an operating-characteristic curve for a continuous-sampling plan. Note that whereas an OC curve for a lot-by-lot acceptance-sampling plan gives the percentage of lots that would be passed under sampling inspection, the OC curve for a continuous-sampling plan gives the percentage of units passed under sampling inspection. Graphs of operating-characteristic curves for several values of f and i for CSP-1 plans are shown in Fig. 16.8. Note that for moderate-to-small values of f, i has much more effect on the shape of the curve than does f.

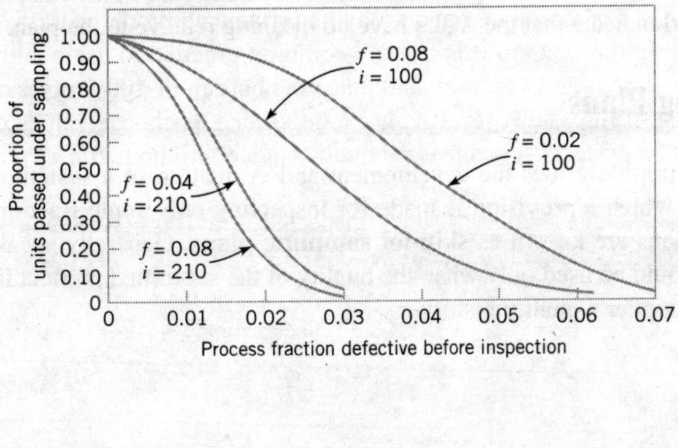

■ **FIGURE 16.8** Operating-characteristic curves for various continuous sampling plans, CSP-1. (Adapted with permission from A. J. Duncan, *Quality Control and Industrial Statistics*, 5th ed., Irwin, Homewood, IL, 1986.)

16.6.2 Other Continuous-Sampling Plans

There have been a number of variations of the original Dodge CSP-1 plan. One variation was designed to meet the objection that the occurrence of a single isolated defective unit sometimes does not warrant return to 100% inspection. This is particularly true when dealing with minor defects. To meet this objection, Dodge and Torrey (1951) proposed CSP-2 and CSP-3. Under CSP-2, 100% inspection will not be reinstated when production is under sampling inspection until two defective sample units have been found within a space of K sample units of each other. It is common practice to choose K equal to the clearance number i. CSP-2 plans are indexed by specific AOQLs that may be obtained by different combinations of i and f. CSP-3 is very similar to CSP-2, but is designed to give additional protection against spotty production. It requires that after a defective unit has been found in sampling inspection, the immediately following four units should be inspected. If any of these four units is defective, 100% inspection is immediately reinstituted. If no defectives are found, the plan continues as under CSP-2.

Another common objection to continuous-sampling plans is the abrupt transition between sampling inspection and 100% inspection. Lieberman and Solomon (1955) have designed multilevel continuous-sampling plans to overcome this objection. Multilevel continuous-sampling plans begin with 100% inspection, as does CSP-1, and then switch to inspecting a fraction f of the production as soon as the clearance number i has been reached. However, when under sampling inspection at rate f, a run of i consecutive sample units is found free of defects, then sampling continues at the rate f^2. If a further run of i consecutive units is found to be free of defects, then sampling may continue at the rate f^3. This reduction in sampling frequency may be continued as far as the sampling agency wishes. If at any time sampling inspection reveals a defective unit, return is immediately made to the next lower level of sampling. This type of multilevel continuous-sampling plan greatly reduces the inspection effort when the manufacturing process is operating very well, and increases it during periods of poor production. This transition in inspection intensity is also accomplished without abrupt changes in the inspection load.

Much of the work on continuous-sampling plans has been incorporated into MIL STD 1235C. The standard provides for five different types of continuous-sampling plans. Tables to assist the analyst in designing sampling plans are presented in the standard. CSP-1 and CSP-2 are a part of MIL STD 1235C. In addition, there are two other single-level continuous-sampling procedures, CSP-F and CSP-V. The fifth plan in the standard is CSP-T, a multilevel continuous-sampling plan.

The sampling plans in MIL STD 1235C are indexed by sampling frequency code letter and AOQL. They are also indexed by the AQLs of MIL STD 105E. This aspect of MIL STD 1235C has sparked considerable controversy. CSP plans are not AQL plans and do not have AQLs naturally associated with them. MIL STD 105E, which does focus on the AQL, is designed for manufacturing situations in which lotting is a natural aspect of production, and provides a set of decision rules for sentencing lots so that certain AQL protection is obtained. CSP plans are designed for situations in which production is continuous and lotting is not a natural aspect of the manufacturing situations. In MIL STD 1235C, the sampling plan tables are footnoted and indicate that the AQLs have no meaning relative to the plan, and are only an index.

16.7 Skip-Lot Sampling Plans

This section describes the development and evaluation of a system of lot-by-lot inspection plans in which a provision is made for inspecting only some fraction of the submitted lots. These plans are known as **skip-lot sampling plans.** Generally speaking, skip-lot sampling plans should be used only when the quality of the submitted product is good as demonstrated by the supplier's quality history.

Dodge (1956) initially presented skip-lot sampling plans as an extension of CSP-type continuous-sampling plans. In effect, a skip-lot sampling plan is the application of continuous sampling to lots rather than to individual units of production on an assembly line. The version of skip-lot sampling initially proposed by Dodge required a single determination or analysis to ascertain the lot's acceptability or unacceptability. These plans are called SkSP-1. Skip-lot sampling plans designated SkSP-2 follow the next logical step; that is, each lot to be sentenced is sampled according to a particular attribute lot inspection plan. Perry (1973) gives a good discussion of these plans.

A skip-lot sampling plan of type SkSP-2 uses a specified lot inspection plan called the "reference-sampling plan," together with the following rules:

1. Begin with normal inspection, using the reference plan. At this stage of operation, every lot is inspected.
2. When i consecutive lots are accepted on normal inspection, switch to skipping inspection. In skipping inspection, a fraction f of the lots is inspected.
3. When a lot is rejected on skipping inspection, return to normal inspection.

The parameters f and i are the parameters of the skip-lot sampling plan SkSP-2. In general, the clearance number i is a positive integer, and the sampling fraction f lies in the interval $0 < f < 1$. When the sampling fraction $f = 1$, the skip-lot sampling plan reduces to the original reference-sampling plan. Let P denote the probability of acceptance of a lot from the reference-sampling plan. Then, $P_a(f, i)$ is the probability of acceptance for the skip-lot sampling plan SkSP-2, where

$$P_a(f,i) = \frac{fP + (1-f)P^i}{f + (1-f)P^i} \tag{16.8}$$

It can be shown that for $f_2 < f_1$, a given value of the clearance number i, and a specified reference-sampling plan,

$$P_a(f_1,i) \le P_a(f_2,i) \tag{16.9}$$

Furthermore, for integer clearance numbers $i < j$, a fixed value of f, and a given reference-sampling plan,

$$P_a(f,j) \le P_a(f,i) \tag{16.10}$$

These properties of a skip-lot sampling plan are shown in Figs. 16.9 and 16.10 for the reference-sampling plan $n = 20$, $c = 1$. The OC curve of the reference-sampling plan is also shown on these graphs.

A very important property of a skip-lot sampling plan is the average amount of inspection required. In general, skip-lot sampling plans are used where it is necessary to reduce the average amount of inspection required. The average sample number of a skip-lot sampling plan is

$$\text{ASN}(SkSP) = \text{ASN}(R)F \tag{16.11}$$

where F is the average fraction of submitted lots that are sampled and ASN(R) is the average sample number of the reference-sampling plan. It can be shown that

$$F = \frac{f}{(1-f)P^i + f} \tag{16.12}$$

Thus, since $0 < F < 1$, it follows that

$$\text{ASN}(SkSP) < \text{ASN}(R) \tag{16.13}$$

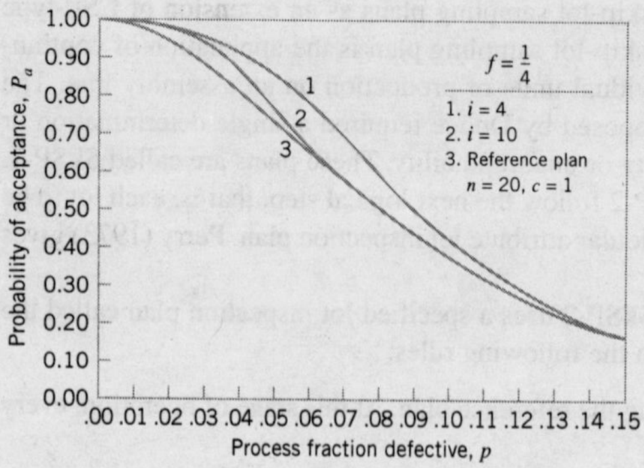

■ FIGURE 16.9 OC curves for SkSP-2 skip-lot plans: single-sampling reference plan, same f, different i. (From R. L. Perry, "Skip-Lot Sampling Plans," *Journal of Quality Technology*, Vol. 5, 1973, with permission of the American Society for Quality Control.)

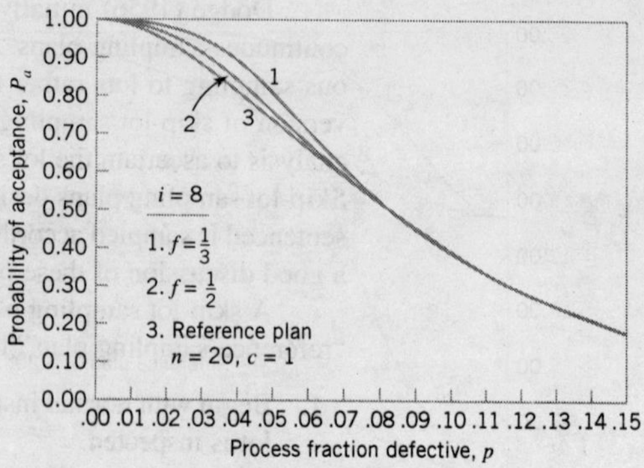

■ FIGURE 16.10 OC curves for SkSP-2 skip-lot plans: single-sampling reference plan, same i, different f. (From R. L. Perry, "Skip-Lot Sampling Plans," *Journal of Quality Technology*, Vol. 5, 1973, with permission of the American Society for Quality Control.)

Therefore, skip-lot sampling yields a reduction in the **average sample number (ASN).** For situations in which the quality of incoming lots is very high, this reduction in inspection effort can be significant.

To illustrate the average sample number behavior of a skip-lot sampling plan, consider a reference-sampling plan of $n = 20$ and $c = 1$. Since the average sample number for a single-sampling plan is ASN $= n$, we have

$$\text{ASN}(SkSP) = n(F)$$

Figure 16.11 presents the ASN curve for the reference-sampling plan $n = 20$, $c = 1$ and the following skip-lot sampling plans:

1. $f = \frac{1}{3}, \; i = 4$
2. $f = \frac{1}{3}, \; i = 14$
3. $f = \frac{2}{3}, \; i = 4$
4. $f = \frac{2}{3}, \; i = 14$

From examining Fig. 16.11, we note that for small values of incoming lot fraction defective, the reductions in average sample number are very substantial for the skip-lot sampling plans evaluated. If the incoming lot quality is very good, consistently close to zero fraction nonconforming, say, then a small value of f, perhaps $\frac{1}{4}$ or $\frac{1}{5}$, could be used. If incoming quality is slightly worse, then an appropriate value of f might be $\frac{1}{2}$.

Skip-lot sampling plans are an effective acceptance-sampling procedure and may be useful as a system of reduced inspection. Their effectiveness is partially good when the quality of submitted lots is very good. However, one should be careful to use skip-lot sampling plans only for situations in which there is a sufficient history of supplier quality to ensure that the quality of submitted lots is very good. Furthermore, if the supplier's process is highly erratic and there is a great deal of variability from lot to lot, skip-lot sampling plans are inappropriate. They seem to work best when the supplier's processes are in a state of statistical control and when the process capability is adequate to ensure virtually defect-free production.

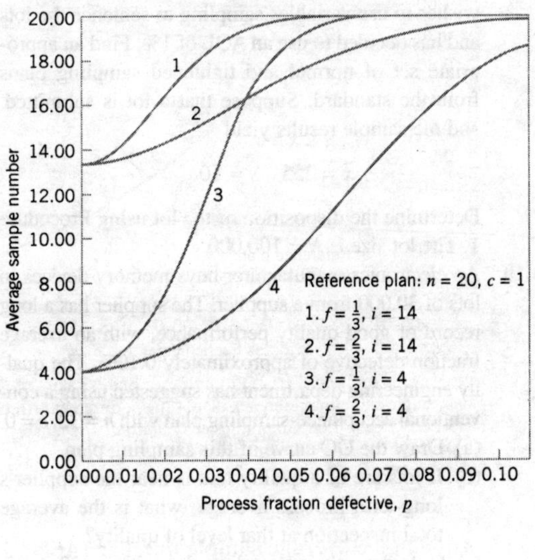

FIGURE 16.11 Average sample number (ASN) curves for SkSP 2 skip-lot plans with single-sampling reference plan. (From R. L. Perry, "Skip-Lot Sampling Plans," *Journal of Quality Technology*, Vol. 5, 1973, with permission of the American Society for Quality Control.)

Important Terms and Concepts

Acceptable quality level (AQL)
ANSI/ASQC Z1.9
Average outgoing quality limit (AOQL)
Average sample number (ASN)
Chain sampling
Clearance number
Continuous sampling plans
MIL STD 414
Normal, tightened, and reduced inspection
Operating-characteristic (OC) curve
Sample size code letters
Skip-lot sampling plans
Switching between normal, tightened, and reduced inspection
The normal distribution in variables sampling
Variables data
Zero-acceptance-number plans

Exercises

16.1. A belt that is used in a drive mechanism in a copier machine is required to have a minimum tensile strength of LSL = 150 lb. It is known from long experience that $\sigma = 5$ lb for this particular belt. Find a variables sampling plan so that $p_1 = 0.005$, $p_2 = 0.02$, $\alpha = 0.05$, and $\beta = 0.10$. Assume that Procedure 1 is to be used.

16.2. The density of a plastic part used in a cellular telephone is required to be at least 0.70 g/cm^3. The parts are supplied in large lots, and a variables sampling plan is to be used to sentence the lots. It is desired to have $p_1 = 0.02$, $p_2 = 0.10$, $\alpha = 0.10$, and $\beta = 0.05$. The variability of the manufacturing process is unknown but will be estimated by the sample standard deviation.

(a) Find an appropriate variables sampling plan, using Procedure 1.

(b) Suppose that a sample of the appropriate size was taken, and $\bar{x} = 0.73$, $s = 1.05 \times 10^{-2}$. Should the lot be accepted or rejected?

(c) Sketch the OC curve for this sampling plan. Find the probability of accepting lots that are 5% defective.

16.3. Describe how rectifying inspection can be used with variables sampling. What are the appropriate equations for the AOQ and the ATI, assuming single sampling and requiring that all defective items found in either sampling or 100% inspection are replaced by good ones?

16.4. A lot of 500 items is submitted for inspection. Suppose that we wish to find a plan from MIL STD 414, using inspection level II. If the AQL is 4%, find the Procedure 1 sampling plan from the standard.

16.5. An inspector for a military agency desires a variables sampling plan for use with an AQL of 1.5%, assuming that lots are of size 7000. If the standard deviation of the lot or process is unknown, derive a sampling plan using Procedure 1 from MIL STD 414.

16.6. How does the sample size found in Exercise 16.5 compare with what would have been used under MIL STD 105E?

16.7. A standard of 0.3 ppm has been established for formaldehyde emission levels in wood products. Suppose that the standard deviation of emissions in an individual board is $\sigma = 0.10$ ppm. Any lot that contains 1% of its items above 0.3 ppm is considered acceptable. Any lot that has 8% or more of its items above 0.3 ppm is considered unacceptable. Good lots are to be accepted with probability 0.95, and bad lots are to be rejected with probability 0.90.

(a) Derive a variables sampling plan for this situation.

(b) Using the 1% nonconformance level as an AQL, and assuming that lots consist of 5000 panels, find an appropriate set of sampling plans from MIL STD 414, assuming σ unknown. Compare the sample sizes and the protection that both producer and consumer obtain from this plan with the plan derived in part (a).

(c) Find an attributes sampling plan that has the same OC curve as the variables sampling plan derived in part (a). Compare the sample sizes required for equivalent protection. Under what circumstances would variables sampling be more economically efficient?

(d) Using the 1% nonconforming as an AQL, find an attributes sampling plan from MIL STD 105E. Compare the sample sizes and the protection obtained from this plan with the plans derived in parts (a), (b), and (c).

16.8. A chemical ingredient is packed in metal containers. A large shipment of these containers has been delivered to a manufacturing facility. The mean bulk density of this ingredient should not be less than 0.15 g/cm^3. Suppose that lots of this quality are to have a 0.95 probability of acceptance. If the mean bulk density is as low as 0.1450, the probability of acceptance of the lot should be 0.10. Suppose we know that the standard deviation of bulk density is approximately 0.005 g/cm^3. Obtain a variables sampling plan that could be used to sentence the lots.

16.9. A soft-drink bottler purchases nonreturnable glass bottles from a supplier. The lower specification on bursting strength in the bottles is 225 psi. The bottler wishes to use variables sampling to sentence the lots and has decided to use an AQL of 1%. Find an appropriate set of normal and tightened sampling plans from the standard. Suppose that a lot is submitted, and the sample results yield

$$\bar{x} = 255 \quad s = 10$$

Determine the disposition of the lot using Procedure 1. The lot size is $N = 100{,}000$.

16.10. An electronics manufacturer buys memory devices in lots of 30,000 from a supplier. The supplier has a long record of good quality performance, with an average fraction defective of approximately 0.10%. The quality engineering department has suggested using a conventional acceptance-sampling plan with $n = 32$, $c = 0$.

(a) Draw the OC curve of this sampling plan.

(b) If lots are of a quality that is near the supplier's long-term process average, what is the average total inspection at that level of quality?

(c) Consider a chain-sampling plan with $n = 32$, $c = 0$, and $i = 3$. Contrast the performance of this plan with the conventional sampling plan $n = 32$, $c = 0$.

(d) How would the performance of this chain-sampling plan change if we substituted $i = 4$ in part (c)?

16.11. A ChSP-1 plan has $n = 4$, $c = 0$, and $i = 3$. Draw the OC curve for this plan.

16.12. Consider a single-sampling plan with $n = 25$, $c = 0$. Draw the OC curve for this plan. Now consider chainsampling plans with $n = 25$, $c = 0$, and $i = 1, 2, 5, 7$. Sketch the OC curves for these chain-sampling plans on the same axis. Discuss the behavior of chain sampling in this situation compared to the conventional single-sampling plan with $c = 0$.

16.13. Suppose that CSP-1 is used for a manufacturing process where it is desired to maintain an AOQL of 1.90%. Specify two CSP-1 plans that would meet this AOQL target.

16.14. Compare the plans developed in Exercise 16.13 in terms of average fraction inspected and their operating-characteristic curves. Which plan would you prefer if $p = 0.0375$?

16.15. Suppose that a manufacturing process operates in continuous production, such that continuous sampling plans could be applied. Determine three different CSP-1 sampling plans that could be used for an AOQL of 0.198%.

16.16. For the sampling plans developed in Exercise 16.15, compare the plans' performance in terms of average fraction inspected, given that the process is in control at an average fallout level of 0.15%. Compare the plans in terms of their operating-characteristic curves.

Appendix

APPENDIX I

Summary of Common Probability Distributions Often Used in Statistical Quality Control

Name	Probability Distribution	Mean	Variance
Discrete			
Uniform	$\frac{1}{b-a},\ a \le b$	$\frac{(b+a)}{2}$	$\frac{(b-a+1)^2-1}{12}$
Binomial	$\binom{n}{x} p^x (1-p)^{n-x}$, $x = 0, 1, \ldots, n, 0 \le p \le 1$	np	$np(1-p)$
Pascal (negative binomial)	$\binom{x-1}{r-1} p^r (1-p)^{x-r}$, $x = r, r+1, r+2, \ldots$	$\frac{r}{p}$	$\frac{r(1-p)}{p^2}$
Geometric	$(1-p)^{x-1} p$, $x = 1, 2, \ldots, 0 \le p \le 1$	$\frac{1}{p}$	$\frac{(1-p)}{p^2}$
Hypergeometric	$\frac{\binom{D}{x}\binom{N-D}{n-x}}{\binom{N}{n}}$, $x = 0, 1, \ldots, \min(D, n), D \le N$, $n \le N$	np, where $p = \frac{D}{N}$	$np(1-p)\left(\frac{N-n}{N-1}\right)$
Poisson	$\frac{e^{-\lambda}\lambda^x}{x!}, x = 0, 1, 2, \ldots, \lambda > 0$	λ	λ
Continuous			
Uniform	$\frac{1}{b-a}, a \le x \le b$	$\frac{(b+a)}{2}$	$\frac{(b-a)^2}{12}$
Normal	$\frac{1}{\sqrt{2\pi}\sigma} e^{-\frac{1}{2}\left(\frac{x-\mu}{\sigma}\right)^2}$, $-\infty < x < \infty, -\infty < \mu < \infty, \sigma > 0$	μ	σ^2
Exponential	$\lambda e^{-\lambda x}, x \ge 0 \quad \lambda > 0$	$1/\lambda$	$1/\lambda^2$
Gamma	$\frac{\lambda x^{r-1} e^{-\lambda x}}{\Gamma(r)},\ x > 0,\ r > 0,\ \lambda > 0$	r/λ	r/λ^2
Erlang	$\frac{\lambda^r x^{r-1} e^{-\lambda x}}{(r-1)!},\ x > 0,\ r = 1, 2, \ldots$	r/λ	r/λ^2
Weibull	$\frac{\beta}{\theta}\left(\frac{x}{\theta}\right)^{\beta-1} e^{-(x/\theta)^\beta}$, $x > 0,\ \beta > 0,\ \theta > 0$	$\theta\Gamma\left(1+\frac{1}{\beta}\right)$	$\theta^2\Gamma\left(1+\frac{2}{\beta}\right) - \theta^2\left[\Gamma\left(1+\frac{1}{\beta}\right)\right]^2$

APPENDIX II
Cumulative Standard Normal Distribution

$$\Phi(z) = \int_{-\infty}^{z} \frac{1}{\sqrt{2\pi}} e^{-u^2/2} du$$

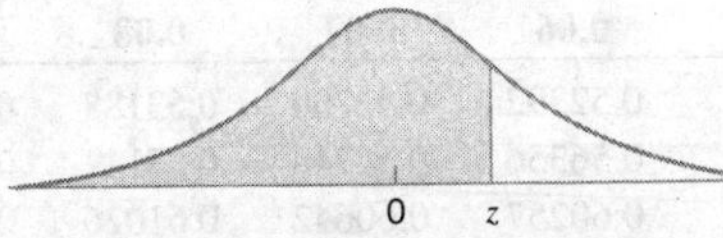

z	0.00	0.01	0.02	0.03	0.04	z
0.0	0.50000	0.50399	0.50798	0.51197	0.51595	0.0
0.1	0.53983	0.54379	0.54776	0.55172	0.55567	0.1
0.2	0.57926	0.58317	0.58706	0.59095	0.59483	0.2
0.3	0.61791	0.62172	0.62551	0.62930	0.63307	0.3
0.4	0.65542	0.65910	0.62276	0.66640	0.67003	0.4
0.5	0.69146	0.69497	0.69847	0.70194	0.70540	0.5
0.6	0.72575	0.72907	0.73237	0.73565	0.73891	0.6
0.7	0.75803	0.76115	0.76424	0.76730	0.77035	0.7
0.8	0.78814	0.79103	0.79389	0.79673	0.79954	0.8
0.9	0.81594	0.81859	0.82121	0.82381	0.82639	0.9
1.0	0.84134	0.84375	0.84613	0.84849	0.85083	1.0
1.1	0.86433	0.86650	0.86864	0.87076	0.87285	1.1
1.2	0.88493	0.88686	0.88877	0.89065	0.89251	1.2
1.3	0.90320	0.90490	0.90658	0.90824	0.90988	1.3
1.4	0.91924	0.92073	0.92219	0.92364	0.92506	1.4
1.5	0.93319	0.93448	0.93574	0.93699	0.93822	1.5
1.6	0.94520	0.94630	0.94738	0.94845	0.94950	1.6
1.7	0.95543	0.95637	0.95728	0.95818	0.95907	1.7
1.8	0.96407	0.96485	0.96562	0.96637	0.96711	1.8
1.9	0.97128	0.97193	0.97257	0.97320	0.97381	1.9
2.0	0.97725	0.97778	0.97831	0.97882	0.97932	2.0
2.1	0.98214	0.98257	0.98300	0.98341	0.98382	2.1
2.2	0.98610	0.98645	0.98679	0.98713	0.98745	2.2
2.3	0.98928	0.98956	0.98983	0.99010	0.99036	2.3
2.4	0.99180	0.99202	0.99224	0.99245	0.99266	2.4
2.5	0.99379	0.99396	0.99413	0.99430	0.99446	2.5
2.6	0.99534	0.99547	0.99560	0.99573	0.99585	2.6
2.7	0.99653	0.99664	0.99674	0.99683	0.99693	2.7
2.8	0.99744	0.99752	0.99760	0.99767	0.99774	2.8
2.9	0.99813	0.99819	0.99825	0.99831	0.99836	2.9
3.0	0.99865	0.99869	0.99874	0.99878	0.99882	3.0
3.1	0.99903	0.99906	0.99910	0.99913	0.99916	3.1
3.2	0.99931	0.99934	0.99936	0.99938	0.99940	3.2
3.3	0.99952	0.99953	0.99955	0.99957	0.99958	3.3
3.4	0.99966	0.99968	0.99969	0.99970	0.99971	3.4
3.5	0.99977	0.99978	0.99978	0.99979	0.99980	3.5
3.6	0.99984	0.99985	0.99985	0.99986	0.99986	3.6
3.7	0.99989	0.99990	0.99990	0.99990	0.99991	3.7
3.8	0.99993	0.99993	0.99993	0.99994	0.99994	3.8
3.9	0.99995	0.99995	0.99996	0.99996	0.99996	3.9

■ APPENDIX II

Cumulative Standard Normal Distribution (*continued*)

$$\Phi(z) = \int_{-\infty}^{z} \frac{1}{\sqrt{2\pi}} e^{-u^2/2} du$$

z	**0.05**	**0.06**	**0.07**	**0.08**	**0.09**	z
0.0	0.51994	0.52392	0.52790	0.53188	0.53586	0.0
0.1	0.55962	0.56356	0.56749	0.57142	0.57534	0.1
0.2	0.59871	0.60257	0.60642	0.61026	0.61409	0.2
0.3	0.63683	0.64058	0.64431	0.64803	0.65173	0.3
0.4	0.67364	0.67724	0.68082	0.68438	0.68793	0.4
0.5	0.70884	0.71226	0.71566	0.71904	0.72240	0.5
0.6	0.74215	0.74537	0.74857	0.75175	0.75490	0.6
0.7	0.77337	0.77637	0.77935	0.78230	0.78523	0.7
0.8	0.80234	0.80510	0.80785	0.81057	0.81327	0.8
0.9	0.82894	0.83147	0.83397	0.83646	0.83891	0.9
1.0	0.85314	0.85543	0.85769	0.85993	0.86214	1.0
1.1	0.87493	0.87697	0.87900	0.88100	0.88297	1.1
1.2	0.89435	0.89616	0.89796	0.89973	0.90147	1.2
1.3	0.91149	0.91308	0.91465	0.91621	0.91773	1.3
1.4	0.92647	0.92785	0.92922	0.93056	0.93189	1.4
1.5	0.93943	0.94062	0.94179	0.94295	0.94408	1.5
1.6	0.95053	0.95154	0.95254	0.95352	0.95448	1.6
1.7	0.95994	0.96080	0.96164	0.96246	0.96327	1.7
1.8	0.96784	0.96856	0.96926	0.96995	0.97062	1.8
1.9	0.97441	0.97500	0.97558	0.97615	0.97670	1.9
2.0	0.97982	0.98030	0.98077	0.98124	0.98169	2.0
2.1	0.98422	0.98461	0.98500	0.98537	0.98574	2.1
2.2	0.98778	0.98809	0.98840	0.98870	0.98899	2.2
2.3	0.99061	0.99086	0.99111	0.99134	0.99158	2.3
2.4	0.99286	0.99305	0.99324	0.99343	0.99361	2.4
2.5	0.99461	0.99477	0.99492	0.99506	0.99520	2.5
2.6	0.99598	0.99609	0.99621	0.99632	0.99643	2.6
2.7	0.99702	0.99711	0.99720	0.99728	0.99736	2.7
2.8	0.99781	0.99788	0.99795	0.99801	0.99807	2.8
2.9	0.99841	0.99846	0.99851	0.99856	0.99861	2.9
3.0	0.99886	0.99889	0.99893	0.99897	0.99900	3.0
3.1	0.99918	0.99921	0.99924	0.99926	0.99929	3.1
3.2	0.99942	0.99944	0.99946	0.99948	0.99950	3.2
3.3	0.99960	0.99961	0.99962	0.99964	0.99965	3.3
3.4	0.99972	0.99973	0.99974	0.99975	0.99976	3.4
3.5	0.99981	0.99981	0.99982	0.99983	0.99983	3.5
3.6	0.99987	0.99987	0.99988	0.99988	0.99989	3.6
3.7	0.99991	0.99992	0.99992	0.99992	0.99992	3.7
3.8	0.99994	0.99994	0.99995	0.99995	0.99995	3.8
3.9	0.99996	0.99996	0.99996	0.99997	0.99997	3.9

▪ APPENDIX III

Percentage Points of the χ^2 Distribution[a]

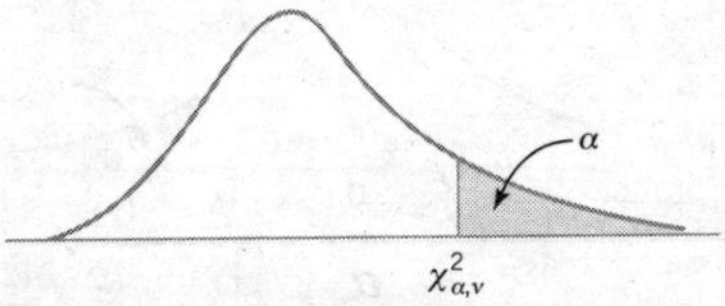

ν	0.995	0.990	0.975	0.950	0.500	0.050	0.025	0.010	0.005
1	0.00 +	0.00 +	0.00 +	0.00 +	0.45	3.84	5.02	6.63	7.88
2	0.01	0.02	0.05	0.10	1.39	5.99	7.38	9.21	10.60
3	0.07	0.11	0.22	0.35	2.37	7.81	9.35	11.34	12.84
4	0.21	0.30	0.48	0.71	3.36	9.49	11.14	13.28	14.86
5	0.41	0.55	0.83	1.15	4.35	11.07	12.38	15.09	16.75
6	0.68	0.87	1.24	1.64	5.35	12.59	14.45	16.81	18.55
7	0.99	1.24	1.69	2.17	6.35	14.07	16.01	18.48	20.28
8	1.34	1.65	2.18	2.73	7.34	15.51	17.53	20.09	21.96
9	1.73	2.09	2.70	3.33	8.34	16.92	19.02	21.67	23.59
10	2.16	2.56	3.25	3.94	9.34	18.31	20.48	23.21	25.19
11	2.60	3.05	3.82	4.57	10.34	19.68	21.92	24.72	26.76
12	3.07	3.57	4.40	5.23	11.34	21.03	23.34	26.22	28.30
13	3.57	4.11	5.01	5.89	12.34	22.36	24.74	27.69	29.82
14	4.07	4.66	5.63	6.57	13.34	23.68	26.12	29.14	31.32
15	4.60	5.23	6.27	7.26	14.34	25.00	27.49	30.58	32.80
16	5.14	5.81	6.91	7.96	15.34	26.30	28.85	32.00	34.27
17	5.70	6.41	7.56	8.67	16.34	27.59	30.19	33.41	35.72
18	6.26	7.01	8.23	9.39	17.34	28.87	31.53	34.81	37.16
19	6.884	7.63	8.91	10.12	18.34	30.14	32.85	36.19	38.58
20	7.43	8.26	9.59	10.85	19.34	31.41	34.17	37.57	40.00
25	10.52	11.52	13.12	14.61	24.34	37.65	40.65	44.31	46.93
30	13.79	14.95	16.79	18.49	29.34	43.77	46.98	50.89	53.67
40	20.71	22.16	24.43	26.51	39.34	55.76	59.34	63.69	66.77
50	27.99	29.71	32.36	34.76	49.33	67.50	71.42	76.15	79.49
60	35.53	37.48	40.48	43.19	59.33	79.08	83.30	88.38	91.95
70	43.28	45.44	48.76	51.74	69.33	90.53	95.02	100.42	104.22
80	51.17	53.54	57.15	60.39	79.33	101.88	106.63	112.33	116.32
90	59.20	61.75	65.65	69.13	89.33	113.14	118.14	124.12	128.30
100	67.33	70.06	74.22	77.93	99.33	124.34	129.56	135.81	140.17

ν = degrees of freedom.

[a]Adapted with permission from *Biometrika Tables for Statisticians,* Vol. 1, 3rd ed., by E. S. Pearson and H. O. Hartley, Cambridge University Press, Cambridge, 1966.

APPENDIX IV

Percentage Points of the t Distribution[a]

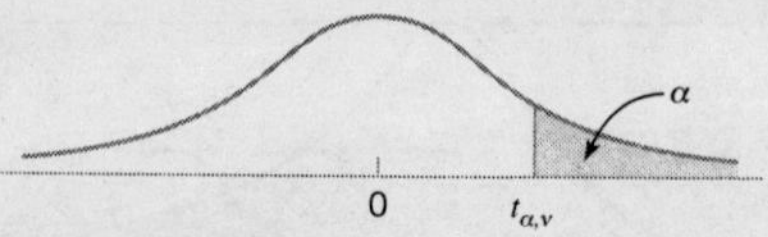

	α									
v	**0.40**	**0.25**	**0.10**	**0.05**	**0.025**	**0.01**	**0.005**	**0.0025**	**0.001**	**0.0005**
1	0.325	1.000	3.078	6.314	12.706	31.821	63.657	127.32	318.31	636.62
2	0.289	0.816	1.886	2.920	4.303	6.965	9.925	14.089	23.326	31.598
3	0.277	0.765	1.638	2.353	3.182	4.541	5.841	7.453	10.213	12.924
4	0.271	0.741	1.533	2.132	2.776	3.747	4.604	5.598	7.173	8.610
5	0.267	0.727	1.476	2.015	2.571	3.365	4.032	4.773	5.893	6.869
6	0.265	0.727	1.440	1.943	2.447	3.143	3.707	4.317	5.208	5.959
7	0.263	0.711	1.415	1.895	2.365	2.998	3.49	4.019	4.785	5.408
8	0.262	0.706	1.397	1.860	2.306	2.896	3.355	3.833	4.501	5.041
9	0.261	0.703	1.383	1.833	2.262	2.821	3.250	3.690	4.297	4.781
10	0.260	0.700	1.372	1.812	2.228	2.764	3.169	3.581	4.144	4.587
11	0.260	0.697	1.363	1.796	2.20	2.718	3.106	3.497	4.025	4.437
12	0.259	0.695	1.356	1.782	2.179	2.681	3.055	3.428	3.930	4.318
13	0.259	0.694	1.350	1.771	2.160	2.650	3.012	3.372	3.852	4.221
14	0.258	0.692	1.345	1.761	2.145	2.624	2.977	3.326	3.787	4.140
15	0.258	0.691	1.341	1.753	2.131	2.602	2.947	3.286	3.733	4.073
16	0.258	0.690	1.337	1.746	2.120	2.583	2.921	3.252	3.686	4.015
17	0.257	0.689	1.333	1.740	2.110	2.567	2.898	3.222	3.646	3.965
18	0.257	0.688	1.330	1.734	2.101	2.552	2.878	3.197	3.610	3.992
19	0.257	0.688	1.328	1.729	2.093	2.539	2.861	3.174	3.579	3.883
20	0.257	0.687	1.325	1.725	2.086	2.528	2.845	3.153	3.552	3.850
21	0.257	0.686	1.323	1.721	2.080	2.518	2.831	3.135	3.527	3.819
22	0.256	0.686	1.321	1.717	2.074	2.508	2.819	3.119	3.505	3.792
23	0.256	0.685	1.319	1.714	2.069	2.500	2.807	3.104	3.485	3.767
24	0.256	0.685	1.318	1.711	2.064	2.492	2.797	3.091	3.467	3.745
25	0.256	0.684	1.316	1.708	2.060	2.485	2.787	3.078	3.450	3.725
26	0.256	0.684	1.315	1.706	2.056	2.479	2.779	3.067	3.435	3.707
27	0.256	0.684	1.314	1.703	2.052	2.473	2.771	3.057	3.421	3.690
28	0.256	0.683	1.313	1.701	2.048	2.467	2.763	3.047	3.408	3.674
29	0.256	0.683	1.311	1.699	2.045	2.462	2.756	3.038	3.396	3.659
30	0.256	0.683	1.310	1.697	2.042	2.457	2.750	3.030	3.385	3.646
40	0.255	0.681	1.303	1.684	2.021	2.423	2.704	2.971	3.307	3.551
60	0.254	0.679	1.296	1.671	2.000	2.390	2.660	2.915	3.232	3.460
120	0.254	0.677	1.289	1.658	1.980	2.358	2.617	2.860	3.160	3.373
∞	0.253	0.674	1.282	1.645	1.960	2.326	2.576	2.807	3.090	3.291

v = degrees of freedom.

[a]Adapted with permission from *Biometrika Tables for Statisticians,* Vol. 1, 3rd ed., by E. S. Pearson and H. O. Hartley, Cambridge University Press, Cambridge, 1966.

■ APPENDIX V

Percentage Points of the *F* Distribution

$F_{0.25, v_1, v_2}$

v_2 \ v_1	1	2	3	4	5	6	7	8	9	10	12	15	20	24	30	40	60	120	∞
1	5.83	7.50	8.20	8.58	8.82	8.98	9.10	9.19	9.26	9.32	9.41	9.49	9.58	9.63	9.67	9.71	9.76	9.80	9.85
2	2.57	3.00	3.15	3.23	3.28	3.31	3.34	3.35	3.37	3.38	3.39	3.41	3.43	3.43	3.44	3.45	3.46	3.47	3.48
3	2.02	2.28	2.36	2.39	2.41	2.42	2.43	2.44	2.44	2.44	2.45	2.46	2.46	2.47	2.47	2.47	2.47	2.47	2.47
4	1.81	2.00	2.05	2.06	2.07	2.08	2.08	2.08	2.08	2.08	2.08	2.08	2.08	2.08	2.08	2.08	2.08	2.08	2.08
5	1.69	1.85	1.88	1.89	1.89	1.89	1.89	1.89	1.89	1.89	1.89	1.89	1.88	1.88	1.88	1.88	1.87	1.87	1.87
6	1.62	1.76	1.78	1.79	1.79	1.78	1.78	1.78	1.77	1.77	1.77	1.76	1.76	1.75	1.75	1.75	1.74	1.74	1.74
7	1.57	1.70	1.72	1.72	1.71	1.71	1.70	1.70	1.70	1.69	1.68	1.68	1.67	1.67	1.66	1.66	1.65	1.65	1.65
8	1.54	1.66	1.67	1.66	1.66	1.65	1.64	1.64	1.63	1.63	1.62	1.62	1.61	1.60	1.60	1.59	1.59	1.58	1.58
9	1.51	1.62	1.63	1.63	1.62	1.61	1.60	1.60	1.59	1.59	1.58	1.57	1.56	1.56	1.55	1.54	1.54	1.53	1.53
10	1.49	1.60	1.60	1.59	1.59	1.58	1.57	1.56	1.56	1.55	1.54	1.53	1.52	1.52	1.51	1.51	1.50	1.49	1.48
11	1.47	1.58	1.58	1.57	1.56	1.55	1.54	1.53	1.53	1.52	1.51	1.50	1.49	1.49	1.48	1.47	1.47	1.46	1.45
12	1.46	1.56	1.56	1.55	1.54	1.53	1.52	1.51	1.51	1.50	1.49	1.48	1.47	1.46	1.45	1.45	1.44	1.43	1.42
13	1.45	1.55	1.55	1.53	1.52	1.51	1.50	1.49	1.49	1.48	1.47	1.46	1.45	1.44	1.43	1.42	1.42	1.41	1.40
14	1.44	1.53	1.53	1.52	1.51	1.50	1.49	1.48	1.47	1.46	1.45	1.44	1.43	1.42	1.41	1.41	1.40	1.39	1.38
15	1.43	1.52	1.52	1.51	1.49	1.48	1.47	1.46	1.46	1.45	1.44	1.43	1.41	1.41	1.40	1.39	1.38	1.37	1.36
16	1.42	1.51	1.51	1.50	1.48	1.47	1.46	1.45	1.44	1.44	1.43	1.41	1.40	1.39	1.38	1.37	1.36	1.35	1.34
17	1.42	1.51	1.50	1.49	1.47	1.46	1.45	1.44	1.43	1.43	1.41	1.40	1.39	1.38	1.37	1.36	1.35	1.34	1.33
18	1.41	1.50	1.49	1.48	1.46	1.45	1.44	1.43	1.42	1.42	1.40	1.39	1.38	1.37	1.36	1.35	1.34	1.33	1.32
19	1.41	1.49	1.49	1.47	1.46	1.44	1.43	1.42	1.41	1.41	1.40	1.38	1.37	1.36	1.35	1.34	1.33	1.32	1.30
20	1.40	1.49	1.48	1.47	1.45	1.44	1.43	1.42	1.41	1.40	1.39	1.37	1.36	1.35	1.34	1.33	1.32	1.31	1.29
21	1.40	1.48	1.48	1.46	1.44	1.43	1.42	1.41	1.40	1.39	1.38	1.37	1.35	1.34	1.33	1.32	1.31	1.30	1.28
22	1.40	1.48	1.47	1.45	1.44	1.42	1.41	1.40	1.39	1.39	1.37	1.36	1.34	1.33	1.32	1.31	1.30	1.29	1.28
23	1.39	1.47	1.47	1.45	1.43	1.42	1.41	1.40	1.39	1.38	1.37	1.35	1.34	1.33	1.32	1.31	1.30	1.28	1.27
24	1.39	1.47	1.46	1.44	1.43	1.41	1.40	1.39	1.38	1.38	1.36	1.35	1.33	1.32	1.31	1.30	1.29	1.28	1.26
25	1.39	1.47	1.46	1.44	1.42	1.41	1.40	1.39	1.38	1.37	1.36	1.34	1.33	1.32	1.31	1.29	1.28	1.27	1.25
26	1.38	1.46	1.45	1.44	1.42	1.41	1.39	1.38	1.37	1.37	1.35	1.34	1.32	1.31	1.30	1.29	1.28	1.26	1.25
27	1.38	1.46	1.45	1.43	1.42	1.40	1.39	1.38	1.37	1.36	1.35	1.33	1.32	1.31	1.30	1.28	1.27	1.26	1.24
28	1.38	1.46	1.45	1.43	1.41	1.40	1.39	1.38	1.37	1.36	1.34	1.33	1.31	1.30	1.29	1.28	1.27	1.25	1.24
29	1.38	1.45	1.45	1.43	1.41	1.40	1.38	1.37	1.36	1.35	1.34	1.32	1.31	1.30	1.29	1.27	1.26	1.25	1.23
30	1.38	1.45	1.44	1.42	1.41	1.39	1.38	1.37	1.36	1.35	1.34	1.32	1.30	1.29	1.28	1.27	1.26	1.24	1.23
40	1.36	1.44	1.42	1.40	1.39	1.37	1.36	1.35	1.34	1.33	1.31	1.30	1.28	1.26	1.25	1.24	1.22	1.21	1.19
60	1.35	1.42	1.41	1.38	1.37	1.35	1.33	1.32	1.31	1.30	1.29	1.27	1.25	1.24	1.22	1.21	1.19	1.17	1.15
120	1.34	1.40	1.39	1.37	1.35	1.33	1.31	1.30	1.29	1.28	1.26	1.24	1.22	1.21	1.19	1.18	1.16	1.13	1.10
∞	1.32	1.39	1.37	1.35	1.33	1.31	1.29	1.28	1.27	1.25	1.24	1.22	1.19	1.18	1.16	1.14	1.12	1.08	1.00

Columns: Degrees of freedom for the numerator (v_1); rows: Degrees of freedom for the denominator (v_2).

Note: $F_{0.75, v_1, v_2} = 1/F_{0.25, v_2, v_1}$.

Source: Adapted with permission from *Biometrika Tables for Statisticians,* Vol. 1, 3rd ed., by E. S. Pearson and H. O. Hartley, Cambridge University Press, Cambridge, 1966.

■ APPENDIX V

Percentage Points of the *F* Distribution (*Continued*)

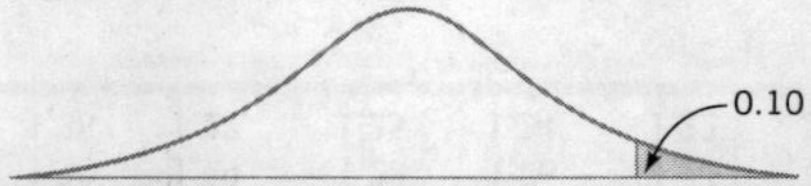

$F_{0.10, \nu_1, \nu_2}$

ν_2 \ ν_1	1	2	3	4	5	6	7	8	9	10	12	15	20	24	30	40	60	120	∞
	Degrees of freedom for the numerator (n_1)																		
1	39.86	49.50	53.59	55.83	57.24	58.20	58.91	59.44	59.86	60.19	60.71	61.22	61.74	62.00	62.26	62.53	62.79	63.06	63.33
2	8.53	9.00	9.16	9.24	9.29	9.33	9.35	9.37	9.38	9.39	9.41	9.42	9.44	9.45	9.46	9.47	9.47	9.48	9.49
3	5.54	5.46	5.39	5.34	5.31	5.28	5.27	5.25	5.24	5.23	5.22	5.20	5.18	5.18	5.17	5.16	5.15	5.14	5.13
4	4.54	4.32	4.19	4.11	4.05	4.01	3.98	3.95	3.94	3.92	3.90	3.87	3.84	3.83	3.82	3.80	3.79	3.78	3.76
5	4.06	3.78	3.62	3.52	3.45	3.40	3.37	3.34	3.32	3.30	3.27	3.24	3.21	3.19	3.17	3.16	3.14	3.12	3.10
6	3.78	3.46	3.29	3.18	3.11	3.05	3.01	2.98	2.96	2.94	2.90	2.87	2.84	2.82	2.80	2.78	2.76	2.74	2.72
7	3.59	3.26	3.07	2.96	2.88	2.83	2.78	2.75	2.72	2.70	2.67	2.63	2.59	2.58	2.56	2.54	2.51	2.49	2.47
8	3.46	3.11	2.92	2.81	2.73	2.67	2.62	2.59	2.56	2.54	2.50	2.46	2.42	2.40	2.38	2.36	2.34	2.32	2.29
9	3.36	3.01	2.81	2.69	2.61	2.55	2.51	2.47	2.44	2.42	2.38	2.34	2.30	2.28	2.25	2.23	2.21	2.18	2.16
10	3.29	2.92	2.73	2.61	2.52	2.46	2.41	2.38	2.35	2.32	2.28	2.24	2.20	2.18	2.16	2.13	2.11	2.08	2.06
11	3.23	2.86	2.66	2.54	2.45	2.39	2.34	2.30	2.27	2.25	2.21	2.17	2.12	2.10	2.08	2.05	2.03	2.00	1.97
12	3.18	2.81	2.61	2.48	2.39	2.33	2.28	2.24	2.21	2.19	2.15	2.10	2.06	2.04	2.01	1.99	1.96	1.93	1.90
13	3.14	2.76	2.56	2.43	2.35	2.28	2.23	2.20	2.16	2.14	2.10	2.05	2.01	1.98	1.96	1.93	1.90	1.88	1.85
14	3.10	2.73	2.52	2.39	2.31	2.24	2.19	2.15	2.12	2.10	2.05	2.01	1.96	1.94	1.91	1.89	1.86	1.83	1.80
15	3.07	2.70	2.49	2.36	2.27	2.21	2.16	2.12	2.09	2.06	2.02	1.97	1.92	1.90	1.87	1.85	1.82	1.79	1.76
16	3.05	2.67	2.46	2.33	2.24	2.18	2.13	2.09	2.06	2.03	1.99	1.94	1.89	1.86	1.84	1.81	1.78	1.75	1.72
17	3.03	2.64	2.44	2.31	2.22	2.15	2.10	2.06	2.03	2.00	1.96	1.91	1.86	1.84	1.81	1.78	1.75	1.72	1.69
18	3.01	2.62	2.42	2.29	2.20	2.13	2.08	2.04	2.00	1.98	1.93	1.89	1.84	1.81	1.78	1.75	1.72	1.69	1.66
19	2.99	2.61	2.40	2.27	2.18	2.11	2.06	2.02	1.98	1.96	1.91	1.86	1.81	1.79	1.76	1.73	1.70	1.67	1.63
20	2.97	2.59	2.38	2.25	2.16	2.09	2.04	2.00	1.96	1.94	1.89	1.84	1.79	1.77	1.74	1.71	1.68	1.64	1.61
21	2.96	2.57	2.36	2.23	2.14	2.08	2.02	1.98	1.95	1.92	1.87	1.83	1.78	1.75	1.72	1.69	1.66	1.62	1.59
22	2.95	2.56	2.35	2.22	2.13	2.06	2.01	1.97	1.93	1.90	1.86	1.81	1.76	1.73	1.70	1.67	1.64	1.60	1.57
23	2.94	2.55	2.34	2.21	2.11	2.05	1.99	1.95	1.92	1.89	1.84	1.80	1.74	1.72	1.69	1.66	1.62	1.59	1.55
24	2.93	2.54	2.33	2.19	2.10	2.04	1.98	1.94	1.91	1.88	1.83	1.78	1.73	1.70	1.67	1.64	1.61	1.57	1.53
25	2.92	2.53	2.32	2.18	2.09	2.02	1.97	1.93	1.89	1.87	1.82	1.77	1.72	1.69	1.66	1.63	1.59	1.56	1.52
26	2.91	2.52	2.31	2.17	2.08	2.01	1.96	1.92	1.88	1.86	1.81	1.76	1.71	1.68	1.65	1.61	1.58	1.54	1.50
27	2.90	2.51	2.30	2.17	2.07	2.00	1.95	1.91	1.87	1.85	1.80	1.75	1.70	1.67	1.64	1.60	1.57	1.53	1.49
28	2.89	2.50	2.29	2.16	2.06	2.00	1.94	1.90	1.87	1.84	1.79	1.74	1.69	1.66	1.63	1.59	1.56	1.52	1.48
29	2.89	2.50	2.28	2.15	2.06	1.99	1.93	1.89	1.86	1.83	1.78	1.73	1.68	1.65	1.62	1.58	1.55	1.51	1.47
30	2.88	2.49	2.28	2.14	2.03	1.98	1.93	1.88	1.85	1.82	1.77	1.72	1.67	1.64	1.61	1.57	1.54	1.50	1.46
40	2.84	2.44	2.23	2.09	2.00	1.93	1.87	1.83	1.79	1.76	1.71	1.66	1.61	1.57	1.54	1.51	1.47	1.42	1.38
60	2.79	2.39	2.18	2.04	1.95	1.87	1.82	1.77	1.74	1.71	1.66	1.60	1.54	1.51	1.48	1.44	1.40	1.35	1.29
120	2.75	2.35	2.13	1.99	1.90	1.82	1.77	1.72	1.68	1.65	1.60	1.55	1.48	1.45	1.41	1.37	1.32	1.26	1.19
∞	2.71	2.30	2.08	1.94	1.85	1.77	1.72	1.67	1.63	1.60	1.55	1.49	1.42	1.38	1.34	1.30	1.24	1.17	1.00

Degrees of freedom for the denominator (ν_2)

Note: $F_{0.90, \nu_1, \nu_2} = 1/F_{0.10, \nu_2, \nu_1}$.

■ **APPENDIX V**

(Continued)

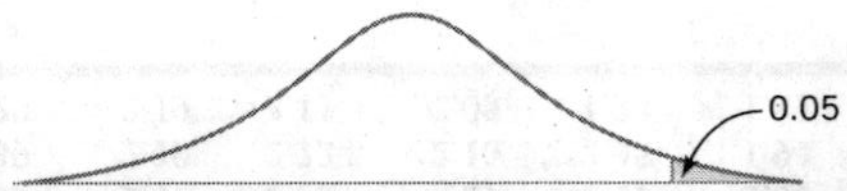

$F_{0.05, v_1, v_2}$

v_2 \ v_1	1	2	3	4	5	6	7	8	9	10	12	15	20	24	30	40	60	120	∞
1	161.4	199.5	215.7	224.6	230.2	234.0	236.8	238.9	240.5	241.9	243.9	245.9	248.0	249.1	250.1	251.1	252.2	253.3	254.3
2	18.51	19.00	19.16	19.25	19.30	19.33	19.35	19.37	19.38	19.40	19.41	19.43	19.45	19.45	19.46	19.47	19.48	19.49	19.50
3	10.13	9.55	9.28	9.12	9.01	8.94	8.89	8.85	8.81	8.79	8.74	8.70	8.66	8.64	8.62	8.59	8.57	8.55	8.53
4	7.71	6.94	6.59	6.39	6.26	6.16	6.09	6.04	6.00	5.96	5.91	5.86	5.80	5.77	5.75	5.72	5.69	5.66	5.63
5	6.61	5.79	5.41	5.19	5.05	4.95	4.88	4.82	4.77	4.74	4.68	4.62	4.56	4.53	4.50	4.46	4.43	4.40	4.36
6	5.99	5.14	4.76	4.53	4.39	4.28	4.21	4.15	4.10	4.06	4.00	3.94	3.87	3.84	3.81	3.77	3.74	3.70	3.67
7	5.59	4.74	4.35	4.12	3.97	3.87	3.79	3.73	3.68	3.64	3.57	3.51	3.44	3.41	3.38	3.34	3.30	3.27	3.23
8	5.32	4.46	4.07	3.84	3.69	3.58	3.50	3.44	3.39	3.35	3.28	3.22	3.15	3.12	3.08	3.04	3.01	2.97	2.93
9	5.12	4.26	3.86	3.63	3.48	3.37	3.29	3.23	3.18	3.14	3.07	3.01	2.94	2.90	2.86	2.83	2.79	2.75	2.71
10	4.96	4.10	3.71	3.48	3.33	3.22	3.14	3.07	3.02	2.98	2.91	2.85	2.77	2.74	2.70	2.66	2.62	2.58	2.54
11	4.84	3.98	3.59	3.36	3.20	3.09	3.01	2.95	2.90	2.85	2.79	2.72	2.65	2.61	2.57	2.53	2.49	2.45	2.40
12	4.75	3.89	3.49	3.26	3.11	3.00	2.91	2.85	2.80	2.75	2.69	2.62	2.54	2.51	2.47	2.43	2.38	2.34	2.30
13	4.67	3.81	3.41	3.18	3.03	2.92	2.83	2.77	2.71	2.67	2.60	2.53	2.46	2.42	2.38	2.34	2.30	2.25	2.21
14	4.60	3.74	3.34	3.11	2.96	2.85	2.76	2.70	2.65	2.60	2.53	2.46	2.39	2.35	2.31	2.27	2.22	2.18	2.13
15	4.54	3.68	3.29	3.06	2.90	2.79	2.71	2.64	2.59	2.54	2.48	2.40	2.33	2.29	2.25	2.20	2.16	2.11	2.07
16	4.49	3.63	3.24	3.01	2.85	2.74	2.66	2.59	2.54	2.49	2.42	2.35	2.28	2.24	2.19	2.15	2.11	2.06	2.01
17	4.45	3.59	3.20	2.96	2.81	2.70	2.61	2.55	2.49	2.45	2.38	2.31	2.23	2.19	2.15	2.10	2.06	2.01	1.96
18	4.41	3.55	3.16	2.93	2.77	2.66	2.58	2.51	2.46	2.41	2.34	2.27	2.19	2.15	2.11	2.06	2.02	1.97	1.92
19	4.38	3.52	3.13	2.90	2.74	2.63	2.54	2.48	2.42	2.38	2.31	2.23	2.16	2.11	2.07	2.03	1.98	1.93	1.88
20	4.35	3.49	3.10	2.87	2.71	2.60	2.51	2.45	2.39	2.35	2.28	2.20	2.12	2.08	2.04	1.99	1.95	1.90	1.84
21	4.32	3.47	3.07	2.84	2.68	2.57	2.49	2.42	2.37	2.32	2.25	2.18	2.10	2.05	2.01	1.96	1.92	1.87	1.81
22	4.30	3.44	3.05	2.82	2.66	2.55	2.46	2.40	2.34	2.30	2.23	2.15	2.07	2.03	1.98	1.94	1.89	1.84	1.78
23	4.28	3.42	3.03	2.80	2.64	2.53	2.44	2.37	2.32	2.27	2.20	2.13	2.05	2.01	1.96	1.91	1.86	1.81	1.76
24	4.26	3.40	3.01	2.78	2.62	2.51	2.42	2.36	2.30	2.25	2.18	2.11	2.03	1.98	1.94	1.89	1.84	1.79	1.73
25	4.24	3.39	2.99	2.76	2.60	2.49	2.40	2.34	2.28	2.24	2.16	2.09	2.01	1.96	1.92	1.87	1.82	1.77	1.71
26	4.23	3.37	2.98	2.74	2.59	2.47	2.39	2.32	2.27	2.22	2.15	2.07	1.99	1.95	1.90	1.85	1.80	1.75	1.69
27	4.21	3.35	2.96	2.73	2.57	2.46	2.37	2.31	2.25	2.20	2.13	2.06	1.97	1.93	1.88	1.84	1.79	1.73	1.67
28	4.20	3.34	2.95	2.71	2.56	2.45	2.36	2.29	2.24	2.19	2.12	2.04	1.96	1.91	1.87	1.82	1.77	1.71	1.65
29	4.18	3.33	2.93	2.70	2.55	2.43	2.35	2.28	2.22	2.18	2.10	2.03	1.94	1.90	1.85	1.81	1.75	1.70	1.64
30	4.17	3.32	2.92	2.69	2.53	2.42	2.33	2.27	2.21	2.16	2.09	2.01	1.93	1.89	1.84	1.79	1.74	1.68	1.62
40	4.08	3.23	2.84	2.61	2.45	2.34	2.25	2.18	2.12	2.08	2.00	1.92	1.84	1.79	1.74	1.69	1.64	1.58	1.51
60	4.00	3.15	2.76	2.53	2.37	2.25	2.17	2.10	2.04	1.99	1.92	1.84	1.75	1.70	1.65	1.59	1.53	1.47	1.39
120	3.92	3.07	2.68	2.45	2.29	2.17	2.09	2.02	1.96	1.91	1.83	1.75	1.66	1.61	1.55	1.55	1.43	1.35	1.25
∞	3.84	3.00	2.60	2.37	2.21	2.10	2.01	1.94	1.88	1.83	1.75	1.67	1.57	1.52	1.46	1.39	1.32	1.22	1.00

Degrees of freedom for the numerator (v_1); Degrees of freedom for the denominator (v_2)

Note: $F_{0.95, v_1, v_2} = 1/F_{0.05, v_2, v_1}$.

■ APPENDIX V

Percentage Points of the *F* Distribution (*Continued*)

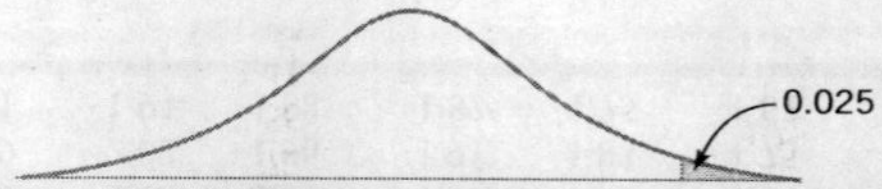

$F_{0.025, v_1, v_2}$

v_2 \ v_1 (Degrees of freedom for the numerator (v_1))	1	2	3	4	5	6	7	8	9	10	12	15	20	24	30	40	60	120	∞
1	647.8	799.5	864.2	899.6	921.8	937.1	948.2	956.7	963.3	968.6	976.7	984.9	993.1	997.2	1001.0	1006.0	1010.0	1014.0	1018.0
2	38.51	39.00	39.17	39.25	39.30	39.33	39.36	39.37	39.39	39.40	39.41	39.43	39.45	39.46	39.46	39.47	39.48	39.49	39.50
3	17.44	16.04	15.44	15.10	14.88	14.73	14.62	14.54	14.47	14.42	14.34	14.25	14.17	14.12	14.08	14.04	13.99	13.95	13.90
4	12.22	10.65	9.98	9.60	9.36	9.20	9.07	8.98	8.90	8.84	8.75	8.66	8.56	8.51	8.46	8.41	8.36	8.31	8.26
5	10.01	8.43	7.76	7.39	7.15	6.98	6.85	6.76	6.68	6.62	6.52	6.43	6.33	6.28	6.23	6.18	6.12	6.07	6.02
6	8.81	7.26	6.60	6.23	5.99	5.82	5.70	5.60	5.52	5.46	5.37	5.27	5.17	5.12	5.07	5.01	4.96	4.90	4.85
7	8.07	6.54	5.89	5.52	5.29	5.12	4.99	4.90	4.82	4.76	4.67	4.57	4.47	4.42	4.36	4.31	4.25	4.20	4.14
8	7.57	6.06	5.42	5.05	4.82	4.65	4.53	4.43	4.36	4.30	4.20	4.10	4.00	3.95	3.89	3.84	3.78	3.73	3.67
9	7.21	5.71	5.08	4.72	4.48	4.32	4.20	4.10	4.03	3.96	3.87	3.77	3.67	3.61	3.56	3.51	3.45	3.39	3.33
10	6.94	5.46	4.83	4.47	4.24	4.07	3.95	3.85	3.78	3.72	3.62	3.52	3.42	3.37	3.31	3.26	3.20	3.14	3.08
11	6.72	5.26	4.63	4.28	4.04	3.88	3.76	3.66	3.59	3.53	3.43	3.33	3.23	3.17	3.12	3.06	3.00	2.94	2.88
12	6.55	5.10	4.47	4.12	3.89	3.73	3.61	3.51	3.44	3.37	3.28	3.18	3.07	3.02	2.96	2.91	2.85	2.79	2.72
13	6.41	4.97	4.35	4.00	3.77	3.60	3.48	3.39	3.31	3.25	3.15	3.05	2.95	2.89	2.84	2.78	2.72	2.66	2.60
14	6.30	4.86	4.24	3.89	3.66	3.50	3.38	3.29	3.21	3.15	3.05	2.95	2.84	2.79	2.73	2.67	2.61	2.55	2.49
15	6.20	4.77	4.15	3.80	3.58	3.41	3.29	3.20	3.12	3.06	2.96	2.86	2.76	2.70	2.64	2.59	2.52	2.46	2.40
16	6.12	4.69	4.08	3.73	3.50	3.34	3.22	3.12	3.05	2.99	2.89	2.79	2.68	2.63	2.57	2.51	2.45	2.38	2.32
17	6.04	4.62	4.01	3.66	3.44	3.28	3.16	3.06	2.98	2.92	2.82	2.72	2.62	2.56	2.50	2.44	2.38	2.32	2.25
18	5.98	4.56	3.95	3.61	3.38	3.22	3.10	3.01	2.93	2.87	2.77	2.67	2.56	2.50	2.44	2.38	2.32	2.26	2.19
19	5.92	4.51	3.90	3.56	3.33	3.17	3.05	2.96	2.88	2.82	2.72	2.62	2.51	2.45	2.39	2.33	2.27	2.20	2.13
20	5.87	4.46	3.86	3.51	3.29	3.13	3.01	2.91	2.84	2.77	2.68	2.57	2.46	2.41	2.35	2.29	2.22	2.16	2.09
21	5.83	4.42	3.82	3.48	3.25	3.09	2.97	2.87	2.80	2.73	2.64	2.53	2.42	2.37	2.31	2.25	2.18	2.11	2.04
22	5.79	4.38	3.78	3.44	3.22	3.05	2.93	2.84	2.76	2.70	2.60	2.50	2.39	2.33	2.27	2.21	2.14	2.08	2.00
23	5.75	4.35	3.75	3.41	3.18	3.02	2.90	2.81	2.73	2.67	2.57	2.47	2.36	2.30	2.24	2.18	2.11	2.04	1.97
24	5.72	4.32	3.72	3.38	3.15	2.99	2.87	2.78	2.70	2.64	2.54	2.44	2.33	2.27	2.21	2.15	2.08	2.01	1.94
25	5.69	4.29	3.69	3.35	3.13	2.97	2.85	2.75	2.68	2.61	2.51	2.41	2.30	2.24	2.18	2.12	2.05	1.98	1.91
26	5.66	4.27	3.67	3.33	3.10	2.94	2.82	2.73	2.65	2.59	2.49	2.39	2.28	2.22	2.16	2.09	2.03	1.95	1.88
27	5.63	4.24	3.65	3.31	3.08	2.92	2.80	2.71	2.63	2.57	2.47	2.36	2.25	2.19	2.13	2.07	2.00	1.93	1.85
28	5.61	4.22	3.63	3.29	3.06	2.90	2.78	2.69	2.61	2.55	2.45	2.34	2.23	2.17	2.11	2.05	1.98	1.91	1.83
29	5.59	4.20	3.61	3.27	3.04	2.88	2.76	2.67	2.59	2.53	2.43	2.32	2.21	2.15	2.09	2.03	1.96	1.89	1.81
30	5.57	4.18	3.59	3.25	3.03	2.87	2.75	2.65	2.57	2.51	2.41	2.31	2.20	2.14	2.07	2.01	1.94	1.87	1.79
40	5.42	4.05	3.46	3.13	2.90	2.74	2.62	2.53	2.45	2.39	2.29	2.18	2.07	2.01	1.94	1.88	1.80	1.72	1.64
60	5.29	3.93	3.34	3.01	2.79	2.63	2.51	2.41	2.33	2.27	2.17	2.06	1.94	1.88	1.82	1.74	1.67	1.58	1.48
120	5.15	3.80	3.23	2.89	2.67	2.52	2.39	2.30	2.22	2.16	2.05	1.94	1.82	1.76	1.69	1.61	1.53	1.43	1.31
∞	5.02	3.69	3.12	2.79	2.57	2.41	2.29	2.19	2.11	2.05	1.94	1.83	1.71	1.64	1.57	1.48	1.39	1.27	1.00

Degrees of freedom for the denominator (v_2)

Note: $F_{0.975, v_1, v_2} = 1/F_{0.025, v_2, v_1}$.

■ **APPENDIX V**

(Continued)

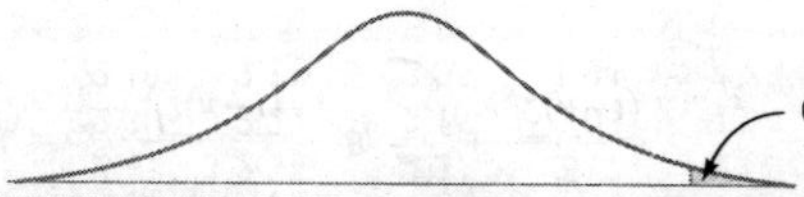

$F_{0.01, \nu_1, \nu_2}$

ν_2 \ ν_1	1	2	3	4	5	6	7	8	9	10	12	15	20	24	30	40	60	120	∞
1	4052.0	4999.5	5403.0	5625.0	5764.0	5859.0	5928.0	5982.0	6022.0	6056.0	6106.0	6157.0	6209.0	6235.0	6261.0	6287.0	6313.0	6339.0	6366.0
2	98.50	99.00	99.17	99.25	99.30	99.33	99.36	99.37	99.39	99.40	99.42	99.43	99.45	99.46	99.47	99.47	99.48	99.49	99.50
3	34.12	30.82	29.46	28.71	28.24	27.91	27.67	27.49	27.35	27.23	27.05	26.87	26.69	26.00	26.50	26.41	26.32	26.22	26.13
4	21.20	18.00	16.69	15.98	15.52	15.21	14.98	14.80	14.66	14.55	14.37	14.20	14.02	13.93	13.84	13.75	13.65	13.56	13.46
5	16.26	13.27	12.06	11.39	10.97	10.67	10.46	10.29	10.16	10.05	9.89	9.72	9.55	9.47	9.38	9.29	9.20	9.11	9.02
6	13.75	10.92	9.78	9.15	8.75	8.47	8.26	8.10	7.98	7.87	7.72	7.56	7.40	7.31	7.23	7.14	7.06	6.97	6.88
7	12.25	9.55	8.45	7.85	7.46	7.19	6.99	6.84	6.72	6.62	6.47	6.31	6.16	6.07	5.99	5.91	5.82	5.74	5.65
8	11.26	8.65	7.59	7.01	6.63	6.37	6.18	6.03	5.91	5.81	5.67	5.52	5.36	5.28	5.20	5.12	5.03	4.95	4.86
9	10.56	8.02	6.99	6.42	6.06	5.80	5.61	5.47	5.35	5.26	5.11	4.96	4.81	4.73	4.65	4.57	4.48	4.40	4.31
10	10.04	7.56	6.55	5.99	5.64	5.39	5.20	5.06	4.94	4.85	4.71	4.56	4.41	4.33	4.25	4.17	4.08	4.00	3.91
11	9.65	7.21	6.22	5.67	5.32	5.07	4.89	4.74	4.63	4.54	4.40	4.25	4.10	4.02	3.94	3.86	3.78	3.69	3.60
12	9.33	6.93	5.95	5.41	5.06	4.82	4.64	4.50	4.39	4.30	4.16	4.01	3.86	3.78	3.70	3.62	3.54	3.45	3.36
13	9.07	6.70	5.74	5.21	4.86	4.62	4.44	4.30	4.19	4.10	3.96	3.82	3.66	3.59	3.51	3.43	3.34	3.25	3.17
14	8.86	6.51	5.56	5.04	4.69	4.46	4.28	4.14	4.03	3.94	3.80	3.66	3.51	3.43	3.35	3.27	3.18	3.09	3.00
15	8.68	6.36	5.42	4.89	4.36	4.32	4.14	4.00	3.89	3.80	3.67	3.52	3.37	3.29	3.21	3.13	3.05	2.96	2.87
16	8.53	6.23	5.29	4.77	4.44	4.20	4.03	3.89	3.78	3.69	3.55	3.41	3.26	3.18	3.10	3.02	2.93	2.84	2.75
17	8.40	6.11	5.18	4.67	4.34	4.10	3.93	3.79	3.68	3.59	3.46	3.31	3.16	3.08	3.00	2.92	2.83	2.75	2.65
18	8.29	6.01	5.09	4.58	4.25	4.01	3.84	3.71	3.60	3.51	3.37	3.23	3.08	3.00	2.92	2.84	2.75	2.66	2.57
19	8.18	5.93	5.01	4.50	4.17	3.94	3.77	3.63	3.52	3.43	3.30	3.15	3.00	2.92	2.84	2.76	2.67	2.58	2.59
20	8.10	5.85	4.94	4.43	4.10	3.87	3.70	3.56	3.46	3.37	3.23	3.09	2.94	2.86	2.78	2.69	2.61	2.52	2.42
21	8.02	5.78	4.87	4.37	4.04	3.81	3.64	3.51	3.40	3.31	3.17	3.03	2.88	2.80	2.72	2.64	2.55	2.46	2.36
22	7.95	5.72	4.82	4.31	3.99	3.76	3.59	3.45	3.35	3.26	3.12	2.98	2.83	2.75	2.67	2.58	2.50	2.40	2.31
23	7.88	5.66	4.76	4.26	3.94	3.71	3.54	3.41	3.30	3.21	3.07	2.93	2.78	2.70	2.62	2.54	2.45	2.35	2.26
24	7.82	5.61	4.72	4.22	3.90	3.67	3.50	3.36	3.26	3.17	3.03	2.89	2.74	2.66	2.58	2.49	2.40	2.31	2.21
25	7.77	5.57	4.68	4.18	3.85	3.63	3.46	3.32	3.22	3.13	2.99	2.85	2.70	2.62	2.54	2.45	2.36	2.27	2.17
26	7.72	5.53	4.64	4.14	3.82	3.59	3.42	3.29	3.18	3.09	2.96	2.81	2.66	2.58	2.50	2.42	2.33	2.23	2.13
27	7.68	5.49	4.60	4.11	3.78	3.56	3.39	3.26	3.15	3.06	2.93	2.78	2.63	2.55	2.47	2.38	2.29	2.20	2.10
28	7.64	5.45	4.57	4.07	3.75	3.53	3.36	3.23	3.12	3.03	2.90	2.75	2.60	2.52	2.44	2.35	2.26	2.17	2.06
29	7.60	5.42	4.54	4.04	3.73	3.50	3.33	3.20	3.09	3.00	2.87	2.73	2.57	2.49	2.41	2.33	2.23	2.14	2.03
30	7.56	5.39	4.51	4.02	3.70	3.47	3.30	3.17	3.07	2.98	2.84	2.70	2.55	2.47	2.39	2.30	2.21	2.11	2.01
40	7.31	5.18	4.31	3.83	3.51	3.29	3.12	2.99	2.89	2.80	2.66	2.52	2.37	2.29	2.20	2.11	2.02	1.92	1.80
60	7.08	4.98	4.13	3.65	3.34	3.12	2.95	2.82	2.72	2.63	2.50	2.35	2.20	2.12	2.03	1.94	1.84	1.73	1.60
120	6.85	4.79	3.95	3.48	3.17	2.96	2.79	2.66	2.56	2.47	2.34	2.19	2.03	1.95	1.86	1.76	1.66	1.53	1.38
∞	6.63	4.61	3.78	3.32	3.02	2.80	2.64	2.51	2.41	2.32	2.18	2.04	1.88	1.79	1.70	1.59	1.47	1.32	1.00

Columns: Degrees of freedom for the numerator (ν_1); rows: Degrees of freedom for the denominator (ν_2)

Note: $F_{0.99, \nu_1, \nu_2} = 1/F_{0.01, \nu_2, \nu_1}$.

APPENDIX VI

Factors for Constructing Variables Control Charts

Observations in Sample, n	Chart for Averages: Factors for Control Limits			Chart for Averages: Factors for Center Line		Chart for Standard Deviations: Factors for Control Limits				Chart for Ranges: Factors for Center Line		Chart for Ranges: Factors for Control Limits				
	A	A_2	A_3	c_4	$1/c_4$	B_3	B_4	B_5	B_6	d_2	$1/d_2$	d_3	D_1	D_2	D_3	D_4
2	2.121	1.880	2.659	0.7979	1.2533	0	3.267	0	2.606	1.128	0.8865	0.853	0	3.686	0	3.267
3	1.732	1.023	1.954	0.8862	1.1284	0	2.568	0	2.276	1.693	0.5907	0.888	0	4.358	0	2.574
4	1.500	0.729	1.628	0.9213	1.0854	0	2.266	0	2.088	2.059	0.4857	0.880	0	4.698	0	2.282
5	1.342	0.577	1.427	0.9400	1.0638	0	2.089	0	1.964	2.326	0.4299	0.864	0	4.918	0	2.114
6	1.225	0.483	1.287	0.9515	1.0510	0.030	1.970	0.029	1.874	2.534	0.3946	0.848	0	5.078	0	2.004
7	1.134	0.419	1.182	0.9594	1.0423	0.118	1.882	0.113	1.806	2.704	0.3698	0.833	0.204	5.204	0.076	1.924
8	1.061	0.373	1.099	0.9650	1.0363	0.185	1.815	0.179	1.751	2.847	0.3512	0.820	0.388	5.306	0.136	1.864
9	1.000	0.337	1.032	0.9693	1.0317	0.239	1.761	0.232	1.707	2.970	0.3367	0.808	0.547	5.393	0.184	1.816
10	0.949	0.308	0.975	0.9727	1.0281	0.284	1.716	0.276	1.669	3.078	0.3249	0.797	0.687	5.469	0.223	1.777
11	0.905	0.285	0.927	0.9754	1.0252	0.321	1.679	0.313	1.637	3.173	0.3152	0.787	0.811	5.535	0.256	1.744
12	0.866	0.266	0.886	0.9776	1.0229	0.354	1.646	0.346	1.610	3.258	0.3069	0.778	0.922	5.594	0.283	1.717
13	0.832	0.249	0.850	0.9794	1.0210	0.382	1.618	0.374	1.585	3.336	0.2998	0.770	1.025	5.647	0.307	1.693
14	0.802	0.235	0.817	0.9810	1.0194	0.406	1.594	0.399	1.563	3.407	0.2935	0.763	1.118	5.696	0.328	1.672
15	0.775	0.223	0.789	0.9823	1.0180	0.428	1.572	0.421	1.544	3.472	0.2880	0.756	1.203	5.741	0.347	1.653
16	0.750	0.212	0.763	0.9835	1.0168	0.448	1.552	0.440	1.526	3.532	0.2831	0.750	1.282	5.782	0.363	1.637
17	0.728	0.203	0.739	0.9845	1.0157	0.466	1.534	0.458	1.511	3.588	0.2787	0.744	1.356	5.820	0.378	1.622
18	0.707	0.194	0.718	0.9854	1.0148	0.482	1.518	0.475	1.496	3.640	0.2747	0.739	1.424	5.856	0.391	1.608
19	0.688	0.187	0.698	0.9862	1.0140	0.497	1.503	0.490	1.483	3.689	0.2711	0.734	1.487	5.891	0.403	1.597
20	0.671	0.180	0.680	0.9869	1.0133	0.510	1.490	0.504	1.470	3.735	0.2677	0.729	1.549	5.921	0.415	1.585
21	0.655	0.173	0.663	0.9876	1.0126	0.523	1.477	0.516	1.459	3.778	0.2647	0.724	1.605	5.951	0.425	1.575
22	0.640	0.167	0.647	0.9882	1.0119	0.534	1.466	0.528	1.448	3.819	0.2618	0.720	1.659	5.979	0.434	1.566
23	0.626	0.162	0.633	0.9887	1.0114	0.545	1.455	0.539	1.438	3.858	0.2592	0.716	1.710	6.006	0.443	1.557
24	0.612	0.157	0.619	0.9892	1.0109	0.555	1.445	0.549	1.429	3.895	0.2567	0.712	1.759	6.031	0.451	1.548
25	0.600	0.153	0.606	0.9896	1.0105	0.565	1.435	0.559	1.420	3.931	0.2544	0.708	1.806	6.056	0.459	1.541

For $n > 25$.

$$A = \frac{3}{\sqrt{n}} \qquad A_3 = \frac{3}{c_4\sqrt{n}} \qquad c_4 \cong \frac{4(n-1)}{4n-3}$$

$$B_3 = 1 - \frac{3}{c_4\sqrt{2(n-1)}} \qquad B_4 = 1 + \frac{3}{c_4\sqrt{2(n-1)}}$$

$$B_5 = c_4 - \frac{3}{\sqrt{2(n-1)}} \qquad B_6 = c_4 + \frac{3}{\sqrt{2(n-1)}}$$

APPENDIX VII

Factors for Two-Sided Normal Tolerance Limits

	90% Confidence That Percentage of Population Between Limits Is			95% Confidence That Percentage of Population Between Limits Is			99% Confidence That Percentage of Population Between Limits Is		
n	90%	95%	99%	90%	95%	99%	90%	95%	99%
2	15.98	18.80	24.17	32.02	37.67	48.43	160.2	188.5	242.3
3	5.847	6.919	8.974	8.380	9.916	12.86	18.93	22.40	29.06
4	4.166	4.943	6.440	5.369	6.370	8.299	9.398	11.15	14.53
5	3.494	4.152	5.423	4.275	5.079	6.634	6.612	7.855	10.26
6	3.131	3.723	4.870	3.712	4.414	5.775	5.337	6.345	8.301
7	2.902	3.452	4.521	3.369	4.007	5.248	4.613	5.448	7.187
8	2.743	3.264	4.278	3.136	3.732	4.891	4.147	4.936	6.468
9	2.626	3.125	4.098	2.967	3.532	4.631	3.822	4.550	5.966
10	2.535	3.018	3.959	2.829	3.379	4.433	3.582	4.265	5.594
11	2.463	2.933	3.849	2.737	3.259	4.277	3.397	4.045	5.308
12	2.404	2.863	3.758	2.655	3.162	4.150	3.250	3.870	5.079
13	2.355	2.805	3.682	2.587	3.081	4.044	3.130	3.727	4.893
14	2.314	2.756	3.618	2.529	3.012	3.955	3.029	3.608	4.737
15	2.278	2.713	3.562	2.480	2.954	3.878	2.945	3.507	4.605
16	2.246	2.676	3.514	2.437	2.903	3.812	2.872	3.421	4.492
17	2.219	2.643	3.471	2.400	2.858	3.754	2.808	3.345	4.393
18	2.194	2.614	3.433	2.366	2.819	3.702	2.753	3.279	4.307
19	2.172	2.588	3.399	2.337	2.784	3.656	2.703	3.221	[illegible]
20	2.152	2.564	3.368	2.310	2.752	3.615	2.659	3.168	4.161
21	2.135	2.543	3.340	2.286	2.723	3.577	2.620	3.121	4.100
22	2.118	2.524	3.315	2.264	2.697	3.543	2.584	3.078	4.044
23	2.103	2.506	3.292	2.244	2.673	3.512	2.551	3.040	3.993
24	2.089	2.489	3.270	2.225	2.651	3.483	2.522	3.004	3.947
25	2.077	2.474	3.251	2.208	2.631	3.457	2.494	2.972	3.904
26	2.065	2.460	3.232	2.193	2.612	3.432	2.469	2.941	3.865
27	2.054	2.447	3.215	2.178	2.595	3.409	2.446	2.914	3.828
28	2.044	2.435	3.199	2.164	2.579	3.388	2.424	2.888	3.794
29	2.034	2.424	3.184	2.152	2.554	3.368	2.404	2.864	3.763
30	2.025	2.413	3.170	2.140	2.549	3.350	2.385	2.841	3.733
35	1.988	2.368	3.112	2.090	2.490	3.272	2.306	2.748	3.611
40	1.959	2.334	3.066	2.052	2.445	3.213	2.247	2.677	3.518
50	1.916	2.284	3.001	1.996	2.379	3.126	2.162	2.576	3.385
60	1.887	2.248	2.955	1.958	2.333	3.066	2.103	2.506	3.293
80	1.848	2.202	2.894	1.907	2.272	2.986	2.026	2.414	3.173
100	1.822	2.172	2.854	1.874	2.233	2.934	1.977	2.355	3.096
200	1.764	2.102	2.762	1.798	2.143	2.816	1.865	2.222	2.921
500	1.717	2.046	2.689	1.737	2.070	2.721	1.777	2.117	2.783
1000	1.695	2.019	2.654	1.709	2.036	2.676	1.736	2.068	2.718
∞	1.645	1.960	2.576	1.645	1.960	2.576	1.645	1.960	2.576

APPENDIX VIII

Factors for One-Sided Normal Tolerance Limits

	90% Confidence That Percentage of Population Below (Above) Limits Is			95% Confidence That Percentage of Population Below (Above) Limits Is			99% Confidence That Percentage of Population Below (Above) Limits Is		
n	90%	95%	99%	90%	95%	99%	90%	95%	99%
3	4.258	5.310	7.340	6.158	7.655	10.552			
4	3.187	3.957	5.437	4.163	5.145	7.042			
5	2.742	3.400	4.666	3.407	4.202	5.741			
6	2.494	3.091	4.242	3.006	3.707	5.062	4.408	5.409	7.334
7	2.333	2.894	3.972	2.755	3.399	4.641	3.856	4.730	6.411
8	2.219	2.755	3.783	2.582	3.188	4.353	3.496	4.287	5.811
9	2.133	2.649	3.641	2.454	3.031	4.143	3.242	3.971	5.389
10	2.065	2.568	3.532	2.355	2.911	3.981	3.048	3.739	5.075
11	2.012	2.503	3.444	2.275	2.815	3.852	2.897	3.557	4.828
12	1.966	2.448	3.371	2.210	2.736	3.747	2.773	3.410	4.633
13	1.928	2.403	3.310	2.155	2.670	3.659	2.677	3.290	4.472
14	1.895	2.363	3.257	2.108	2.614	3.585	2.592	3.189	4.336
15	1.866	2.329	3.212	2.068	2.566	3.520	2.521	3.102	4.224
16	1.842	2.299	3.172	2.032	2.523	3.463	2.458	3.028	4.124
17	1.820	2.272	3.136	2.001	2.486	3.415	2.405	2.962	4.038
18	1.800	2.249	3.106	1.974	2.453	3.370	2.357	2.906	3.961
19	1.781	2.228	3.078	1.949	2.423	3.331	2.315	2.855	3.893
20	1.765	2.208	3.052	1.926	2.396	3.295	2.275	2.807	3.832
21	1.750	2.190	3.028	1.905	2.371	3.262	2.241	2.768	3.776
22	1.736	2.174	3.007	1.887	2.350	3.233	2.208	2.729	3.727
23	1.724	2.159	2.987	1.869	2.329	3.206	2.179	2.693	3.680
24	1.712	2.145	2.969	1.853	2.309	3.181	2.154	2.663	3.638
25	1.702	2.132	2.952	1.838	2.292	3.158	2.129	2.632	3.601
30	1.657	2.080	2.884	1.778	2.220	3.064	2.029	2.516	3.446
35	1.623	2.041	2.833	1.732	2.166	2.994	1.957	2.431	3.334
40	1.598	2.010	2.793	1.697	2.126	2.941	1.902	2.365	3.250
45	1.577	1.986	2.762	1.669	2.092	2.897	1.857	2.313	3.181
50	1.560	1.965	2.735	1.646	2.065	2.863	1.821	2.296	3.124

Bibliography

Adams, B. M., C. Lowry, and W. H. Woodall (1992). "The Use (and Misuse) of False Alarm Probabilities in Control Chart Design," in *Frontiers in Statistical Quality Control 4,* H. J. Lenz, G. B. Wetherill, and P.-Th. Wilrich, (eds.) Physica-Verlag, Heidelberg, pp. 155–158.

Alt, F. B. (1985). "Multivariate Quality Control," in *Encyclopedia of Statistical Sciences,* Vol. 6, N. L. Johnson and S. Kotz, (eds.) Wiley, New York.

Alwan, L. C. (1992). "Effects of Autocorrelation on Control Charts," *Communications in Statistics—Theory and Methods,* Vol. 21, (4), pp. 1025–1049.

Alwan, L. C., and H. V. Roberts (1988). "Time Series Modeling for Statistical Process Control," *Journal of Business and Economic Statistics,* Vol. 6(1), pp. 87–95.

Automotive Industry Action Group (1985). *Measurement Systems Analysis,* 2nd ed., Detroit, MI.

Automotive Industry Action Group (2002). *Measurement Systems Analysis,* 3rd ed., Detroit, MI.

Balakrishnan, N. and M. V. Koutras (2002). *Runs and Scans with Applications,* John Wiley & Sons, New York.

Barnard, G. A. (1959). "Control Charts and Stochastic Processes," *Journal of the Royal Statistical Society,* (B), Vol. 21(2), pp. 239–271.

Bather, J. A. (1963). "Control Charts and the Minimization of Costs," *Journal of the Royal Statistical Society,* (B), Vol. 25(1), pp. 49–80.

Berthouex, P. M., W. G. Hunter, and L. Pallesen (1978). "Monitoring Sewage Treatment Plants: Some Quality Control Aspects," *Journal of Quality Technology,* Vol. 10(4), pp. 139–149.

Bisgaard, S., W. G. Hunter, and L. Pallesen (1984). "Economic Selection of Quality of Manufactured Product," *Technometrics,* Vol. 26(1), pp. 9–18.

Bissell, A. F. (1990). "How Reliable Is Your Capability Index?" *Applied Statistics,* Vol. 39(3), pp. 331–340.

Borror, C. M., and C. M. Champ (2001). "Phase I Control Charts for Independent Bernoulli Data," *Quality and Reliability Engineering International,* Vol. 17(5), pp. 391–396.

Borror, C. M., C. W. Champ, and S. E. Rigdon (1998). "Poisson EWMA Control Charts," *Journal of Quality Technology,* Vol. 30(4), pp. 352–361.

Borror, C. M., J. B. Keats, and D. C. Montgomery (2003). "Robustness of the Time Between Events CUSUM," *International Journal of Production Research,* Vol. 41(5), pp. 3435–3444.

Borror, C. M., D. C. Montgomery, and G. C. Runger (1997). "Confidence Intervals for Variance Components from Gauge Capability Studies," *Quality and Reliability Engineering International,* Vol. 13(6), pp. 361–369.

Borror, C. M., D. C. Montgomery, and G. C. Runger (1999). "Robustness of the EWMA Control Chart to Nonnormality," *Journal of Quality Technology,* Vol. 31(3), pp. 309–316.

Bourke, P. O. (1991). "Detecting a Shift in the Fraction Nonconforming Using Run-Length Control Chart with 100% Inspection," *Journal of Quality Technology,* Vol. 23(3), pp. 225–238.

Bowker, A. H., and G. J. Lieberman (1972). *Engineering Statistics,* 2nd ed., Prentice-Hall, Englewood Cliffs, NJ.

Box, G. E. P. (1957). "Evolutionary Operation: A Method for Increasing Industrial Productivity," *Applied Statistics,* Vol. 6(2), pp. 81–101.

Box, G. E. P. (1991). "The Bounded Adjustment Chart," *Quality Engineering,* Vol. 4(2), pp. 331–338.

Box, G. E. P. (1991–1992). "Feedback Control by Manual Adjustment," *Quality Engineering,* Vol. 4(1) pp. 143–151.

Box, G. E. P., S. Bisgaard, and C. Fung (1988). "An Explanation and Critique of Taguchi's Contributions to Quality Engineering." *Quality and Reliability Engineering International,* Vol. 4(2), pp. 123–131.

Box, G. E. P., and N. R. Draper (1969). *Evolutionary Operation,* Wiley, New York.

Box, G. E. P., and N. R. Draper (1986). *Empirical Model Building and Response Surfaces,* Wiley, New York.

Box, G. E. P., G. M. Jenkins, and G. C. Reinsel (1994). *Time Series Analysis, Forecasting, and Control,* 3rd ed. Prentice-Hall, Englewood Cliffs, NJ.

Box, G. E. P., and T. Kramer (1992). "Statistical Process Monitoring and Feedback Adjustment: A Discussion," *Technometrics,* Vol. 34. (3), 251–267

Box, G. E. P., and A. Luceño (1997). *Statistical Control by Monitoring and Feedback Adjustment,* Wiley, New York.

Box, G. E. P., and J. G. Ramirez (1992). "Cumulative Score Charts," *Quality and Reliability Engineering International,* Vol. 8(1), pp. 17–27.

Boyd, D. F. (1950). "Applying the Group Control Chart for $\bar{x}$ and *R*," *Industrial Quality Control,* Vol. 7(3), pp. 22–25.

Boyles, R. A. (1991). "The Taguchi Capability Index," *Journal of Quality Technology,* Vol. 23(2), pp. 107–126.

Boyles, R. A. (2000). "Phase I Analysis for Autocorrelated Processes," *Journal of Quality Technology,* Vol. 32(4), pp. 395–409.

Boyles, R. A. (2001). "Gauge Capability for Pass-Fail Inspection," *Technometrics,* Vol. 43(2), pp. 223–229.

Brook, D., and D. A. Evans (1972). "An Approach to the Probability Distribution of CUSUM Run Length," *Biometrika,* Vol. 59(3), pp. 539–549.

Bryce, G. R., M. A. Gaudard, and B. L. Joiner (1997–1998). "Estimating the Standard Deviation for Individuals Charts," *Quality Engineering,* Vol. 10(2), pp. 331–341.

Buckeridge, D. L., H. Burkom, M. Campbell, W. R. Hogan, and A. W. Moore (2005). "Algorithms for Rapid Outbreak Detection: A Research Synthesis," *Journal of Biomedical Informatics,* Vol. 38, pp. 99–113.

Burdick, R. K., C. M. Borror, and D. C. Montgomery (2003). "A Review of Methods for Measurement Systems Capability Analysis," *Journal of Quality Technology,* Vol. 35(4), pp. 342–354. Available at www.asq.org/pub/jqt.

Burdick, R. K., and G. A. Larsen (1997). "Confidence Intervals on Measures of Variability in Gauge R & R Studies," *Journal of Quality Technology,* Vol. 29(2), pp. 261–273.

Burdick, R. K., C. M. Borror, and D. C. Montgomery (2005). *Design and Analysis of Gauge R&R Studies: Making Decisions with Confidence Intervals in Random and Mixed ANOVA Models,* ASA-SIAM Series on Statistics and Applied Probability, SIAM, Philadelphia, PA, and ASA, Alexandria, VA.

Burdick, R. K., Y.-J. Park, D. C. Montgomery, and C. M. Borror (2005), "Confidence Intervals for Misclassification Rates in a Gauge R&R Study," *Journal of Quality Technology,* Vol. 37(4), pp. 294–303.

Burr, I. J. (1967). "The Effect of Nonnormality on Constants for $\bar{x}$ and R Charts," *Industrial Quality Control,* Vol. 23(11), pp. 563–569.

Byrne, D. M., and S. Taguchi (1987). "The Taguchi Approach to Robust Parameter Design," *40th Annual Quality Progress Transactions* December, pp. 19–26, Milwaukee, Wisconsin.

Champ, C. M., and S.-P. Chou (2003). "Comparison of Standard and Individual Limits Phase I Shewhart, $\bar{X}$, R, and S Charts," *Quality and Reliability Engineering International,* Vol. 19(1), pp. 161–170.

Champ, C. W., and W. H. Woodall (1987). "Exact Results for Shewhart Control Charts with Supplementary Runs Rules," *Technometrics,* Vol. 29(4), pp. 393–399.

Chan, L. K., S. W. Cheng, and F. A. Spiring (1988). "A New Measure of Process Capability: C_{pm}," *Journal of Quality Technology,* Vol. 20(3), pp. 160–175.

Chan, L. K., K. P. Hapuarachchi, and B. D. Macpherson (1988). "Robustness of $\bar{x}$ and R Charts," *IEEE Transactions on Reliability,* Vol. 37(3), pp. 117–123.

Chang, T. C., and F. F. Gan (1995). "A Cumulative Sum Control Chart for Monitoring Process Variance," *Journal of Quality Technology,* Vol. 27(2), pp. 109–119.

Chakraborti, S., P. Van Der Laan, and S. T. Bakir (2001). "Nonparametric Control Charts: An Overview and Some Results," *Journal of Quality Technology,* Vol. 33(3), pp. 304–315.

Chiu, W. K., and G. B. Wetherill (1974). "A Simplified Scheme for the Economic Design of $\bar{x}$-Charts," *Journal of Quality Technology,* Vol. 6(2), pp. 63–69.

Chiu, W. K., and G. B. Wetherill (1975). "Quality Control Practices," *International Journal of Production Research,* Vol. 13(2), pp. 175–182.

Chrysler, Ford, and GM (1995). *Measurement Systems Analysis Reference Manual,* AIAG, Detroit, MI.

Chua, M., and D. C. Montgomery (1992). "Investigation and Characterization of a Control Scheme for Multivariate Quality Control," *Quality and Reliability Engineering International,* Vol. 8(1) pp. 37–44.

Clements, J. A. (1989). Process Capability Calculations for Non-Normal Distributions," *Quality Progress,* Vol. 22(2), pp. 95–100.

Clifford, P. C. (1959). "Control Charts Without Calculations," *Industrial Quality Control,* Vol. 15(11), pp. 40–44.

Coleman, D. E., and D. C. Montgomery (1993). "A Systematic Method for Planning for a Designed Industrial Experiment" (with discussion), *Technometrics,* Vol. 35(1), pp. 1–12.

Cornell, J. A., and A. I. Khuri (1996). *Response Surfaces,* 2nd ed., Dekker, New York.

Cowden, D. J. (1957). *Statistical Methods in Quality Control,* Prentice-Hall, Englewood Cliffs, NJ.

Croarkin, C. and R. Varner (1982). "Measurement Assurance for Dimensional Measurements on Integrated-Circuit Photomasks," NBS Technical Note 1164, U.S. Department of Commerce, Washington, DC.

Crosier, R. B. (1988). "Multivariate Generalizations of Cumulative Sum Quality Control Schemes," *Technometrics,* Vol. 30(3), pp. 291–303.

Crowder, S. V. (1987a). "A Simple Method for Studying Run-Length Distributions of Exponentially Weighted Moving Average Charts," *Technometrics,* Vol. 29(4), pp. 401–407.

Crowder, S. V. (1987b). "Computation of ARL for Combined Individual Measurement and Moving Range Charts," *Journal of Quality Technology,* Vol. 19(1), pp. 98–102.

Crowder, S. V. (1989). "Design of Exponentially Weighted Moving Average Schemes," *Journal of Quality Technology,* Vol. 21(2), pp. 155–162.

Crowder, S. V. (1992). "An SPC Model for Short Production Runs: Minimizing Expected Costs," *Technometrics,* Vol. 34(1), pp. 64–73.

Crowder, S. V., and M. Hamilton (1992). "An EWMA for Monitoring a Process Standard Deviation," *Journal of Quality Technology,* Vol. 24(1), pp. 12–21.

Cruthis, E. N., and S. E. Rigdon (1992–1993). "Comparing Two Estimates of the Variance to Determine the Stability of a Process," *Quality Engineering,* Vol. 5(1), pp. 67–74.

Davis, R. B., and W. H. Woodall (1988), "Performance of the Control Chart Trend Rule Under Linear Shift," *Journal of Quality Technology,* Vol. 20(4), pp. 260–262.

Del Castillo, E., and D. C. Montgomery (1994). "Short-Run Statistical Process Control: *Q*-Chart Enhancements and Alternative Methods," *Quality and Reliability Engineering International,* Vol. 10(1), pp. 87–97.

Del Castillo. E. (2002), *Statistical Process Adjustment for Quality Control,* John Wiley & Sons, New York.

De Mast, J. and W. N. Van Wieringen (2004). "Measurement System Analysis for Bounded Ordinal Data," *Quality and Reliability Engineering International,* Vol. 20, pp. 383–395.

De Mast, J. and W. N. Van Wieringen (2007). "Measurement Systems for Categorical Measurements: Agreement and Kappa-Type Indices," *Journal of Quality Technology,* Vol. 39, pp. 191–202.

Dodge, H. F. (1943). "A Sampling Plan for Continuous Production," *Annals of Mathematical Statistics,* Vol. 14(3), pp. 264–279.

Dodge, H. F. (1955). "Chain Sampling Inspection Plans," *Industrial Quality Control,* Vol. 11(4), pp. 10–13.

Dodge, H. F. (1956). "Skip-Lot Sampling Plan," *Industrial Quality Control,* Vol. 11(5), pp. 3–5.

Dodge, H. F., and H. G. Romig (1959). *Sampling Inspection Tables, Single and Double Sampling,* 2nd ed., Wiley, New York.

Dodge, H. F., and M. N. Torrey (1951). "Additional Continuous Sampling Inspection Plans," *Industrial Quality Control,* Vol. 7(1), pp. 5–9.

Duncan, A. J. (1956). "The Economic Design of $\bar{x}$-Charts Used to Maintain Current Control of a Process," *Journal of the American Statistical Association,* Vol. 51(274), pp. 228–242.

Duncan, A. J. (1986). *Quality Control and Industrial Statistics,* 5th ed., Irwin, Homewood, IL.

Duncan, A. J. (1978). "The Economic Design of *p*-Charts to Maintain Current Control of a Process: Some Numerical Results," *Technometrics,* Vol. 20(3), pp. 235–244.

English, J. R., and G. D. Taylor (1993). "Process Capability Analysis: A Robustness Study," *International Journal of Production Research,* Vol. 31(7), pp. 1621–1635.

Ewan, W. D. (1963). "When and How to Use Cu-Sum Charts," *Technometrics,* Vol. 5(1), pp. 1–22.

Farnum, N. R. (1992). "Control Charts for Short Runs: Nonconstant Process and Measurement Error," *Journal of Quality Technology,* Vol. 24(2), pp. 138–144.

Fienberg, S. E., and G. Shmueli (2005). "Statistical Issues and Challenges Associated with the Rapid Detection of Terrorist Outbreaks," *Statistics in Medicine,* Vol. 24, pp. 513–529.

Ferrell, E. B. (1953). "Control Charts Using Midranges and Medians," *Industrial Quality Control,* Vol. 9(5), pp. 30–34.

Fisher, R. A. (1925). "Theory of Statistical Estimation," *Proceedings of the Cambridge Philosophical Society,* Vol. 22, pp. 700–725.

Freund, R. A. (1957). "Acceptance Control Charts," *Industrial Quality Control,* Vol. 14(4), pp. 13–23.

Fricker, R. D., Jr. (2007). "Directionally Sensitive Multivariate Statistical Process Control Procedures with Application to Syndromic Surveillance," *Advances in Disease Surveillance,* Vol. 3, pp. 1–17.

Gan, F. F. (1991). "An Optimal Design of CUSUM Quality Control Charts," *Journal of Quality Technology,* Vol. 23(4), pp. 279–286.

Gan, F. F. (1993). "An Optimal Design of CUSUM Control Charts for Binomial Counts," *Journal of Applied Statistics,* Vol. 20, pp. 445–460.

Gardiner, J. S. (1987). *Detecting Small Shifts in Quality Levels in a Near-Zero Defect Environment for Integrated Circuits,* Ph.D. Dissertation, Department of Mechanical Engineering, University of Washington, Seattle, WA.

Gardiner, J. S., and D. C. Montgomery (1987). "Using Statistical Control Charts for Software Quality Control," *Quality and Reliability Engineering International,* Vol. 3(1), pp. 15–20.

Garvin, D. A. (1987). "Competing in the Eight Dimensions of Quality," *Harvard Business Review,* Sept.–Oct., 87(6), pp. 101–109.

George, M. L. (2002). *Lean Six Sigma,* McGraw-Hill, New York.

Girshick, M. A., and H. Rubin (1952). "A Bayesian Approach to a Quality Control Model," *Annals of Mathematical Statistics,* Vol. 23(1), pp. 114–125.

Glaz, J., J. Naus, and S. Wallenstein (2001). *Scan Statistics,* Springer, New York.

Grant, E. L., and R. S. Leavenworth (1980). *Statistical Quality Control,* 5th ed., McGraw-Hill, New York.

Grigg, O., and V. Farewell (2004). "An Overview of Risk-Adjusted Charts," *Journal of the Royal Statistical Society,* Series A, Vol. 167, pp. 523–539.

Grigg, O., and D. Spiegelhalter (2007). "A Simple Risk-Adjusted Exponentially Weighted Moving Average," *Journal of the American Statistical Association,* Vol. 102, pp. 140–152.

Grubbs, F. E. (1946). "The Difference Control Chart with an Example of Its Use," *Industrial Quality Control,* Vol. 3(1), pp. 22–25.

Guenther, W. C. (1972). "Tolerance Intervals for Univariate Distributions," *Naval Research Logistics Quarterly,* Vol. 19(2), pp. 309–334.

Gupta, S., D. C. Montgomery, and W. H. Woodall (2006), "Performance Evaluation of Two Methods for Online Monitoring of Linear Calibration Profiles," *International Journal of Production Research,* Vol. 44, pp. 1927–1942.

Hahn, G. J., and S. S. Shapiro (1967). *Statistical Models in Engineering,* Wiley, New York.

Hamada. M. (2003). "Tolerance Interval Control Limits for the $\overline{x}$, *R*, and *S* Charts," *Quality Engineering,* Vol. 15(3), pp. 471–487.

Harris, T. J., and W. H. Ross (1991). "Statistical Process Control Procedures for Correlated Observations," *Canadian Journal of Chemical Engineering,* Vol. 69(Feb), pp. 48–57.

Hawkins, D. M. (1981). "A CUSUM for a Scale Parameter," *Journal of Quality Technology,* Vol. 13(4), pp. 228–235.

Hawkins, D. M. (1991). "Multivariate Quality Control Based on Regression Adjusted Variables," *Technometrics,* Vol. 33(1), pp. 61–75.

Hawkins, D. M. (1992). "A Fast, Accurate Approximation of Average Run Lengths of CUSUM Control Charts," *Journal of Quality Technology,* Vol. 24(1), pp. 37–43.

Hawkins, D. M. (1993a). "Cumulative Sum Control Charting: An Underutilized SPC Tool," *Quality Engineering,* Vol. 5(3), pp. 463–477.

Hawkins, D. M. (1993b). "Regression Adjustment for Variables in Multivariate Quality Control," *Journal of Quality Technology,* Vol. 25(3), pp. 170–182.

Hawkins, D. M. (1987). "Self-starting Cusums for Location and Scale," *The Statistician,* Vol. 36, pp. 299–315.

Hawkins, D. M., S. Choi, and S. Lee (2007). "A General Multivariate Exponentially Weighted Moving-Average Control Chart," *Journal of Quality Technoloyg,* Vol. 39, pp. 118–125.

Hawkins, D. M., and D. H. Olwell (1998). *Cumulative Sum Charts and Charting for Quality Improvement,* Springer Verlag, New York, NY.

Hawkins, D. M., P. Qiu, and C. W. Kang (2003). "The Changepoint Model for Statistical Process Control," *Journal of Quality Technology,* Vol. 35(4), pp. 355–366. Available at www.asq.org/pub/jqt.

Hayter, A. J., and K.-L. Tsui (1994). "Identification and Quantification in Multivariate Quality Control Problems," *Journal of Quality Technology,* Vol. 26(3), pp. 197–208.

Hicks, C. R. (1955). "Some Applications of Hotelling's T^2," *Industrial Quality Control,* Vol. 11(9), pp. 23–29.

Hill, D. (1956). "Modified Control Limits," *Applied Statistics,* Vol. 5(1), pp. 12–19.

Hillier, F. S. (1969). "$\bar{x}$ and R Chart Control Limits Based on a Small Number of Subgroups," *Journal of Quality Technology,* Vol. 1(1), pp. 17–25.

Hines, W. W., D. C. Montgomery, D. M. Goldsman, and C. M. Borror (2004). *Probability and Statistics in Engineering,* 4th ed., Wiley, New York.

Ho, C., and K. E. Case (1994). "Economic Design of Control Charts: A Literature Review for 1981–1991," *Journal of Quality Technology,* Vol. 26(1), pp. 39–53.

Holmes, D. S., and A. E. Mergen (1993). "Improving the Performance of the T^2 Control Chart," *Quality Engineering,* Vol. 5(4), pp. 619–625.

Hotelling, H. (1947). "Multivariate Quality Control," *Techniques of Statistical Analysis,* Eisenhart, Hastay, and Wallis (eds.), McGraw-Hill, New York.

Houf, R. F., and D. B. Berman (1988). "Statistical Analysis of Power Module Thermal Test Equipment Performance," *IEEE Transactions on Components, Hybrids, and Manufacturing Technology,* Vol. 11(4), pp. 516–520.

Howell, J. M. (1949). "Control Charting Largest and Smallest Value," *Annals of Mathematical Statistics,* Vol. 20(2), pp. 305–309.

Hunter, J. S. (1985). "Statistical Design Applied to Product Design," *Journal of Quality Technology,* Vol. 17(4), pp. 210–221.

Hunter, J. S. (1986). "The Exponentially Weighted Moving Average," *Journal of Quality Technology,* Vol. 18(4), pp. 203–210.

Hunter, J. S. (1987). "Signal-To-Noise Ratio Debate," Letter to the Editor, *Quality Progress,* May 1987, pp. 7–9.

Hunter, J. S. (1989). "A One-Point Plot Equivalent to the Shewhart Chart with Western Electric Rules," *Quality Engineering,* Vol. 2(1), pp. 13–19.

Hunter, J. S. (1997). "The Box-Jenkins Manual Bounded Adjustment Chart," *Annual Quality Progress Proceedings,* Orlando, FL, Vol 51(0), pp. 158–169.

Hunter, W. G., and C. P. Kartha (1977). "Determining the Most Profitable Target Value for a Production Process," *Journal of Quality Technology,* Vol. 9(4), pp. 176–181.

Iglewitz, B., and D. Hoaglin (1987). "Use of Boxplots for Process Evaluation," *Journal of Quality Technology,* Vol. 19(4) pp. 180–190.

Jackson, J. E. (1956). "Quality Control Methods for Two Related Variables," *Industrial Quality Control,* Vol. 12(7), pp. 4–8.

Jackson, J. E. (1959). "Quality Control Methods for Several Related Variables," *Technometrics,* Vol. 1(4), pp. 359–377.

Jackson, J. E. (1972). "All Count Distributions Are Not Alike," *Journal of Quality Technology,* Vol. 4(2), pp. 86–92.

Jackson, J. E. (1980). "Principal Components and Factor Analysis: Part I—Principal Components," *Journal of Quality Technology,* Vol. 12(4), pp. 201–213.

Jackson, J. E. (1985). "Multivariate Quality Control," *Communications in Statistics—Theory and Methods,* Vol. 14(110), pp. 2657–2688.

Jensen, W. A., L. A. Jones-Farmer, C. W. Champ, and W. H. Woodall (2006). "Effects of Parameter Estimation on Control Chart Properties: A Literature Review," *Journal of Quality Technology,* Vol. 38, pp. 95–108.

Jin, J. and J. Shi (2001). "Automatic Feature Extraction of Waveform Signals for In-process Diagnostic Performance Improvement," *Journal of Intelligent Manufacturing,* Vol. 12, pp. 257–268.

Johnson, N. L. (1961). "A Simple Theoretical Approach to Cumulative Sum Control Charts," *Journal of the American Statistical Association,* Vol. 56(296), pp. 835–840.

Johnson, N. L., and S. Kotz (1969). *Discrete Distributions,* Houghton Mifflin, Boston.

Johnson, N. L., and F. C. Leone (1962a). "Cumulative Sum Control Charts—Mathematical Principles Applied to Their Construction and Use," Part I, *Industrial Quality Control,* Vol. 19(2), pp. 15–21.

Johnson, N. L., and F. C. Leone (1962b). "Cumulative Sum Control Charts—Mathematical Principles Applied to Their Construction and Use," Part II, *Industrial Quality Control,* Vol. 19(2), pp. 22–28.

Johnson, N. L., and F. C. Leone (1962c). "Cumulative Sum Control Charts—Mathematical Principles Applied to Their Construction and Use," Part III, *Industrial Quality Control,* Vol. 19(2), pp. 29–36.

Jones, L. A., W. H. Woodall, and M. D. Conerly (1999). "Exact Properties of Demerit Control Charts," *Journal of Quality Technology,* Vol. 31(2), pp. 221–230.

Jones, M. C., and J. A. Rice (1992). "Displaying the Important Features of Large Collections of Similar Curves," *The American Statistician,* Vol. 46, pp. 140–145.

Juran, J. M., and F. M. Gryna, Jr. (1980). *Quality Planning and Analysis,* 2nd ed., McGraw-Hill, New York.

Kaminski, F. C., J. C. Benneyan, R. D. Davis (1992) and R. J. Burke (1992), "Statistical Control Charts Based on a Geometric Distribution," *Journal of Quality Technology,* Vol. 24, pp. 63–69.

Kane, V. E. (1986). "Process Capability Indices," *Journal of Quality Technology,* Vol. 18(1), pp. 41–52.

Kang, L., and S. L. Albin (2000). "On-Line Monitoring When the Process Yields a Linear Profile," *Journal of Quality Technology,* Vol. 32(4), pp. 418–426. Available at www.asq.org/pub/jqt.

Keats, J. B., E. Del Castillo, E. von Collani, and E. M. Saniga (1997). Economic Modeling for Statistical Process Control," *Journal of Quality Technology,* Vol. 29(2), pp. 144–147.

Kim, K., M. A. Mahmoud, and W. H. Woodall (2003). "On the Monitoring of Linear Profiles," *Journal of Quality Technology,* Vol. 35(3), pp. 317–328.

Kittlitz, R. J. (1999). "Transforming the Exponential for SPC Applications," *Journal of Quality Technology,* Vol. 31(3), pp. 301–308.

Kotz, S., and N. L. Johnson (2002). "Process Capability Indices: A Review 1992–2000" (with Discussion), *Journal of Quality Technology,* Vol. 34(1), pp. 2–19. Available at www.asq.org/pub/jqt.

Kotz, S., and C. R. Lovelace (1998). *Process Capability Indices in Theory and Practice,* Arnold, London.

Kovach, J. (2007). "Designing Effective Six Sigma Experiments for Service Process Improvement Projects," *International Journal of Six Sigma and Competitive Advantage,* Vol. 3, No. 1, pp. 72–90.

Kulldorff, M. (1997). "A Spatial Scan Statistic," *Communications in Statistics—Theory and Methods,* Vol. 26, pp. 1481–1496.

Kulldorff, M. (2001). "Prospective Time Periodic Geographical Disease Surveillance Using a Scan Statistic," *Journal of the Royal Statistical Society,* Series A, Vol. 164, pp. 61–72.

Kulldorff, M. (2003). Information Management Services, Inc. *SaTScan*™ Version 3.1: Software for the Spatial and Space-Time Scan Statistics. Available at www.satscan.org.

Kulldorff, M. (2005). "Scan Statistics for Geographical Disease Surveillance: An Overview," Chapter 7 in *Spatial & Syndromic Surveillance,* by A. B. Lawson and K. Kleinman, John Wiley & Sons, New York, pp. 115–132.

Kushler, R. H., and P. Hurley (1992). "Confidence Bounds for Capability Indices," *Journal of Quality Technology,* Vol. 24(4), pp. 188–195.

Langenberg, P., and B. Inglewitz (1986). "Trimmed Mean $\bar{x}$ and R Charts," *Journal of Quality Technology,* Vol. 18(3), pp. 152–161.

Lanning, J. W. (1998). *Methods for Monitoring Fractionally Sampled Multiple Stream Processes,* Ph.D. Dissertation, Department of Industrial Engineering, Arizona State University, Tempe, AZ.

Lanning, J. W., D. C. Montgomery, and G. C. Runger (2002–2003). "Monitoring a Multiple-Stream Filling Operation Using Fractional Samples," *Quality Engineering,* Vol. 15(2), pp. 183–195.

Ledolter, J., and A. Swersey (1997). "An Evaluation of Pre-Control," *Journal of Quality Technology,* Vol. 29(2), pp. 163–171.

Lieberman, G. J., and G. J. Resnikoff (1955). "Sampling Plans for Inspection by Variables," *Journal of the American Statistical Association,* Vol. 50(270), pp. 457–516.

Lieberman, G. J., and H. Solomon (1955). "Multi-Level Continuous Sampling Plans," *Annals of Mathematical Statistics,* Vol. 26(4), pp. 686–704.

Linderman, K., and T. E. Love (2000a). "Economic and Economic Statistical Design for MEWMA Control Charts," *Journal of Quality Technology,* Vol. 32(4), pp. 410–417. Available at www.asq.org/pub/jqt.

Linderman, K., and T. E. Love (2000b). "Implementing Economic and Economic Statistical Design for MEWMA Control Charts," *Journal of Quality Technology,* Vol. 32(4), pp. 457–463. Available at www.asq.org/pub/jqt.

Lorenzen, T. J., and L. C. Vance (1986). "The Economic Design of Control Charts: A Unified Approach," *Technometrics,* Vol. 28(1), pp. 3–10.

Lowry, C. A., C. W. Champ, and W. H. Woodall (1995). "The Performance of Control Charts for Monitoring Process Variation," *Communications in Statistics—Simulation and Computation,* Vol. 24(2), pp. 409–431.

Lowry, C. A., and D. C. Montgomery (1995). "A Review of Multivariate Control Charts," *IIE Transactions,* Vol. 27(6), pp. 800–810.

Lowry, C. A., W. H. Woodall, C. W. Champ, and S. E. Rigdon (1992). "A Multivariate Exponentially Weighted Moving Average Control Chart," *Technometrics,* Vol. 34(1), pp. 46–53.

Lu, C.-W., and M. R. Reynolds, Jr. (1999a). "EWMA Control Charts for Monitoring the Mean of Autocorrelated Processes," *Journal of Quality Technology,* Vol. 31(2), pp. 189–206.

Lu, C.-W., and M. R. Reynolds, Jr. (1999b). "Control Charts for Monitoring the Mean and Variance of Autocorrelated Processes," *Journal of Quality Technology,* Vol. 31(3), pp. 259–274.

Lucas, J. M. (1973). "A Modified V-Mask Control Scheme," *Technometrics,* Vol. 15(4), pp. 833–847.

Lucas, J. M. (1976). "The Design and Use of V-mask Control Schemes," *Journal of Quality Technology,* Vol. 8(1), pp. 1–12.

Lucas, J. M. (1982). "Combined Shewhart-CUSUM Quality Control Schemes," *Journal of Quality Technology,* Vol. 14(2), pp. 51–59.

Lucas, J. M. (1985). "Counted Data CUSUM's," *Technometrics,* Vol. 27(3), pp. 129–144.

Lucas, J. M., and R. B. Crosier (1982). "Fast Initial Response for CUSUM Quality Control Schemes," *Technometrics,* Vol. 24(3), pp. 199–205.

Lucas, J. M., and M. S. Saccucci (1990). "Exponentially Weighted Moving Average Control Schemes: Properties and Enhancements," *Technometrics,* Vol. 32(1), pp. 1–29.

Luceño, A. (1996). "A Process Capability Ratio with Reliable Confidence Intervals," *Communications in Statistics—Simulation and Computation,* Vol. 25(1), pp. 235–246.

Luceño, A. (1999). "Average Run Lengths and Run Length Probability Distributions for Cuscore Charts to Control Normal Mean," *Computational Statistics and Data Analysis,* Vol. 32, pp. 177–195.

MacGregor, J. F. (1987). "Interfaces Between Process Control and On-Line Statistical Process Control," *A.I.Ch.E. Cast Newsletter,* 9–19.

MacGregor, J. F., and T. J. Harris (1993). "The Exponentially Weighted Moving Variance," *Journal of Quality Technology,* Vol. 25(2), pp. 106–118.

MacGregor, J. F., and T. J. Harris (1990). "Discussion of: "EWMA Control Schemes: Properties and Enhancement," by Lucas and Sacucci," *Technometrics,* Vol. 32(9), pp. 23–26.

Mahmoud, M. A., P. A. Parker, W. H. Woodall, and D. M. Hawkins (2007). "A Change Point Method for Linear Profile Data," *Quality & Reliability Engineering International,* Vol. 23, pp. 247–268.

Mandel, J. (1969). "The Regression Control Chart," *Journal of Quality Technology,* Vol. 1(1), pp. 1–9.

Manuele, J. (1945). "Control Chart for Determining Tool Wear," *Industrial Quality Control,* Vol. 1(6), pp. 7–10.

Maragah, H. D., and W. H. Woodall (1992). "The Effect of Autocorrelation on the Retrospective $\bar{x}$ -chart," *Journal of Statistical Computation and Simulation,* Vol. 40(1), pp. 29–42.

Mason, R. L., N. D. Tracy, and J. C. Young (1995). "Decomposition of T^2 for Multivariate Control Chart Interpretation," *Journal of Quality Technology,* Vol. 27(2), pp. 109–119.

Mastrangelo, C. M., and D. C. Montgomery (1995). "SPC with Correlated Observations for the Chemical and Process Industries," *Quality and Reliability Engineering International,* Vol. 11(2), pp. 79–89.

Mastrangelo, C. M., G. C. Runger, and D. C. Montgomery (1996). "Statistical Process Monitoring with Principal Components," *Quality and Reliability Engineering International,* Vol. 12(3), pp. 203–210.

Mazza, J. (2000). "Cost Reduction for Document Processing in Major Litigations," presented at the 54th Annual Quality Congress, Charlotte, NC.

Molina, E. C. (1942). *Poisson's Exponential Binomial Limit,* Van Nostrand Reinhold, New York.

Molnau, W. E., D. C. Montgomery, and G. C. Runger (2001). "Statistically Constrained Economic Design of the Multivariate Exponentially Weighted Moving Average Control Chart," *Quality and Reliability Engineering International,* Vol. 17(1), pp. 39–49.

Molnau, W. E., G. C. Runger, D. C. Montgomery, K. R. Skinner, E. N. Loredo, and S. S. Prabhu (2001). "A Program for ARL Calculation for Multivariate EWMA Control Charts," *Journal of Quality Technology,* Vol. 33(4), pp. 515–521.

Montgomery, D. C. (1980). "The Economic Design of Control Charts: A Review and Literature Survey," *Journal of Quality Technology,* Vol. 12(2), pp. 75–87.

Montgomery, D. C. (1982). "Economic Design of an $\bar{x}$ Control Chart," *Journal of Quality Technology,* Vol. 14.(1), pp. 40–43.

Montgomery, D. C. (1999). "Experimental Design for Product and Process Design and Development" (with commentary), *Journal of the Royal Statistical Society Series D (The Statistician),* Vol. 48(2), pp. 159–177.

Montgomery, D. C. (2005). *Design and Analysis of Experiments,* 6th ed., Wiley, New York.

Montgomery, D. C., and J. J. Friedman (1989). "Statistical Process Control in a Computer-Integrated Manufacturing Environment," *Statistical Process Control in Automated Manufacturing,* J. B. Keats and N. F. Hubele, (eds.) Dekker, Series in Quality and Reliability, New York.

Montgomery, D. C., L. A. Johnson, and J. S. Gardiner (1990). *Forecasting and Time Series Analysis,* 2nd ed., McGraw-Hill, New York.

Montgomery, D. C., J. B. Keats, G. C. Runger, and W. S. Messina (1994). "Integrating Statistical Process Control and Engineering Process Control," *Journal of Quality Technology,* Vol. 26(2), pp. 79–87.

Montgomery, D. C., and C. M. Mastrangelo (1991). "Some Statistical Process Control Methods for Aurocorrelated Data" (with discussion), *Journal of Quality Technology,* Vol. 23(3), pp. 179–204.

Montgomery, D. C., E. A. Peck, and G. G. Vining (2006). *Introduction to Linear Regression Analysis,* 4th ed., Wiley, New York.

Montgomery, D. C., and G. C. Runger (1993a). "Gauge Capability and Designed Experiments: Part I: Basic Methods," *Quality Engineering,* Vol. 6(1), pp. 115–135.

Montgomery, D. C., and G. C. Runger (1993b). "Gauge Capability Analysis and Designed Experiments: Part II: Experimental Design Models and Variance Component Estimation," *Quality Engineering,* Vol. 6(2), pp. 289–305.

Montgomery, D. C., and G. C. Runger (2007). *Applied Statistics and Probability for Engineers,* 4th ed., Wiley, New York.

Montgomery, D. C., and H. M. Wadsworth, Jr. (1972). "Some Techniques for Multivariate Quality Control Applications," *ASQC Technical Conference Transactions,* Washington, DC, May, pp. 427–435.

Montgomery, D. C., and W. H. Woodall, eds. (1997). "A Discussion of Statistically-Based Process Monitoring and Control," *Journal of Quality Technology,* Vol. 29(2), pp. 121–162.

Mortell, R. R., and G. C. Runger (1995). "Statistical Process Control of Multiple Stream Processes," *Journal of Quality Technology,* Vol. 27(1), pp. 1–12.

Murphy, B. J. (1987). "Screening Out-of-Control Variables with T^2 Multivariate Quality Control Procedures," *The Statistician,* Vol. 36(5), pp. 571–583.

Myers, R. H., and D. C. Montgomery (2002). *Response Surface Methodology: Process and Product Optimization Using Designed Experiments,* 2nd ed., Wiley, New York.

Nair, V. N., editor (1992). "Taguchi's Parameter Design: A Panel Discussion," *Technometrics,* Vol. 34(2) pp. 127–161.

Naus, J., and S. Wallenstein (2006). "Temporal Surveillance Using Scan Statistics," *Statistics in Medicine,* Vol. 25, pp. 311–324.

Nelson, L. S. (1978). "Best Target Value for a Production Process," *Journal of Quality Technology,* Vol. 10(2), pp. 88–89.

Nelson, L. S. (1984). "The Shewhart Control Chart—Tests for Special Causes," *Journal of Quality Technology,* Vol. 16(4), pp. 237–239.

Nelson, L. S. (1986). "Control Chart for Multiple Stream Processes," *Journal of Quality Technology,* Vol. 18(4), pp. 255–256.

Nelson, L. S. (1994). "A Control Chart for Parts-per-Million Nonconforming Items," *Journal of Quality Technology,* Vol. 26(3), pp. 239–240.

Nelson, P. R., and P. L. Stephenson (1996). "Runs Tests for Group Control Charts," *Communications in Statistics—Theory and Methods,* Vol. 25(11), pp. 2739–2765.

NIST/SEMATECH e-Handbook of Statistical Methods. Available at www.itl.nist.gov/div898/handbook/mpc/section3/mpc37.htm.

Ott, E. R. (1975). *Process Quality Control,* McGraw-Hill, New York.

Ott, E. R., and R. D. Snee (1973). "Identifying Useful Differences in a Multiple-Head Machine," *Journal of Quality Technology,* Vol. 5(2), pp. 47–57.

Page, E. S. (1954). "Continuous Inspection Schemes," *Biometrics,* Vol. 41(1), pp. 100–115.

Page, E. S. (1961). "Cumulative Sum Control Charts," *Technometrics,* Vol. 3(1), pp. 1–9.

Page, E. S. (1963). "Controlling the Standard Deviation by Cusums and Warning Lines," *Technometrics,* Vol. 5(3), pp. 307–316.

Pearn, W. L., S. Kotz, and N. L. Johnson (1992). "Distributional and Inferential Properties of Process Capability Indices," *Journal of Quality Technology,* Vol. 24(4), pp. 216–231.

Perry, R. L. (1973). "Skip-Lot Sampling Plans," *Journal of Quality Technology,* Vol. 5(3), pp. 123–130.

Pignatiello, J. J., Jr., and J. S. Ramberg (1991). "Top Ten Triumphs and Tragedies of Genichi Taguchi," *Quality Engineering,* Vol. 4(2), pp. 211–225.

Pignatiello, J. J., Jr., and G. C. Runger (1990). "Comparison of Multivariate CUSUM Charts," *Journal of Quality Technology,* Vol. 22(3), pp. 173–186.

Pignatiello, J. J., Jr., and G. C. Runger (1991). "Adaptive Sampling for Process Control," *Journal of Quality Technology,* Vol. 22(3), pp. 135–155.

Pignatiello, J. J., Jr., and T. R. Samuel (2001). "Estimation of the Change Point of a Normal Process Mean in SPC Applications," *Journal of Quality Technology,* Vol. 33(1), pp. 82–95.

Prabhu, S. S., D. C. Montgomery, and G. C. Runger (1994). "A Combined Adaptive Sample Size and Sampling Interval $\bar{x}$ Control Scheme," *Journal of Quality Technology,* Vol. 26(3), pp. 164–176.

Prabhu, S. S., D. C. Montgomery, and G. C. Runger (1995). "A Design Tool to Evaluate Average Time to Signal Properties of Adaptive $\bar{x}$ Charts," *Journal of Quality Technology,* Vol. 27(1), pp. 74–76.

Prabhu, S. S., and G. C. Runger (1997). "Designing a Multivariate EWMA Control Chart," *Journal of Quality Technology,* Vol. 29(1), pp. 8–15.

Quesenberry, C. P. (1988). "An SPC Approach to Compensating a Tool-Wear Process," *Journal of Quality Technology,* Vol. 20(4), pp. 220–229.

Quesenberry, C. P. (1991a). "SPC *Q* Charts for Start-Up Processes and Short or Long Runs," *Journal of Quality Technology,* Vol. 23(3), pp. 213–224.

Quesenberry, C. P. (1991b). "SPC *Q* Charts for a Binomial Parameter *p*: Short or Long Runs," *Journal of Quality Technology,* Vol. 23(3), pp. 239–246.

Quesenberry, C. P. (1991c). "SPC *Q* Charts for a Poisson Parameter λ: Short or Long Runs," *Journal of Quality Technology,* Vol. 23(4), pp. 296–303.

Quesenberry, C. P. (1993). "The Effect of Sample Size on Estimated Limits for $\bar{x}$ and x Control Charts," *Journal of Quality Technology,* Vol. 25(4), pp. 237–247.

Quesenberry, C. P. (1995a). "On Properties of *Q* Charts for Variables," *Journal of Quality Technology,* Vol. 27(3), pp. 184–203.

Quesenberry, C. P. (1995b). "On Properties of Binomial *Q*-charts for Attributes," *Journal of Quality Technology,* Vol. 27(3), pp. 204–213.

Quesenberry, C. P. (1995c). "Geometric *Q* Charts for High Quality Processes," *Journal of Quality Technology,* Vol. 27(4), pp. 304–315.

Quesenberry, C. P. (1995d). "On Properties of Poisson *Q* Charts for Attributes" (with discussion), *Journal of Quality Technology,* Vol. 27(4), pp. 293–303.

Ramírez J. G. (1998). "Monitoring Clean Room Air Using Cuscore Charts," *Quality and Reliability Engineering International,* Vol. 14(3), pp. 281–289.

Reynolds, M. R., Jr., R. W. Amin, J. C. Arnold, and J. A. Nachlas (1988). "$\bar{x}$ Charts with Variable Sampling Intervals," *Technometrics,* Vol. 30(2), pp. 181–192.

Reynolds, M. R., Jr. and G.-Y. Cho (2006). "Multivariate Control Charts for Monitoring the Mean Vector and Covariance Matrix," *Journal of Quality Technology,* Vol. 38, pp. 230–253.

Rhoads, T. R., D. C. Montgomery, and C. M. Mastrangelo (1996). "Fast Initial Response Scheme for the EWMA Control Chart," *Quality Engineering,* Vol. 9(2), pp. 317–327.

Roberts, S. W. (1958). "Properties of Control Chart Zone Tests," *Bell System Technical Journal,* Vol. 37, pp. 83–114.

Roberts, S. W. (1959). "Control Chart Tests Based on Geometric Moving Averages," *Technometrics,* Vol. 42(1), pp. 97–102.

Rocke, D. M. (1989). "Robust Control Charts," *Technometrics,* Vol. 31(2), pp. 173–184.

Rodriguez, R. N. (1992). "Recent Developments in Process Capability Analysis," *Journal of Quality Technology,* Vol. 24(4), pp. 176–187.

Rolka, H., H. Burkom, G. F. Cooper, M. Kulldorff, D. Madigan, and W. K. Wong (2007). "Issues in Applied Statistics for Public Health Bioterrorism Surveillance Using Multiple Data Streams: Some Research Needs," *Statistics in Medicine,* Vol. 26, pp. 1834–1856.

Ross, S. M. (1971). "Quality Control Under Markovian Deterioration," *Management Science,* Vol. 17(9), pp. 587–596.

Runger, G. C., and T. R. Willemain (1996). "Batch Means Control Charts for Autocorrelated Data," *IIE Transactions,* Vol. 28(6), pp. 483–487.

Runger, G. C., F. B. Alt, and D. C. Montgomery (1996a). "Controlling Multiple Stream Processes with Principal Components," *International Journal of Production Research,* Vol. 34(11), pp. 2991–2999.

Runger, G. C., F. B. Alt, and D. C. Montgomery (1996b). "Contributors to a Multivariate Statistical Process Control Signal," *Communications in Statistics—Theory and Methods,* Vol. 25(10), pp. 2203–2213.

Runger, G. C., and M. C. Testik (2003). "Control Charts for Monitoring Fault Signatures: Cuscore Versus GLR," *Quality and Reliability Engineering International,* Vol. 19(4), pp. 387–396.

Saniga, E. M. (1989). "Economic Statistical Control Chart Design with an Application to $\overline{x}$ and R Charts," *Technometrics,* Vol. 31(3), pp. 313–320.

Saniga, E. M., and L. E. Shirland (1977). "Quality Control in Practice—A Survey," *Quality Progress,* Vol. 10(5), pp. 30–33.

Savage, I. R. (1962). "Surveillance Problems," *Naval Research Logistics Quarterly,* Vol. 9(384), pp. 187–209.

Schilling, E. G., and P. R. Nelson (1976). "The Effect of Nonnormality on the Control Limits of $\overline{x}$ Charts," *Journal of Quality Technology,* Vol. 8(4), pp. 183–188.

Schmidt, S. R., and J. R. Boudot (1989). "A Monte Carlo Simulation Study Comparing Effectiveness of Signal-to-Noise Ratios and Other Methods for Identifying Dispersion Effects," presented at the 1989 Rocky Mountain Quality Conference.

Scranton, R., G. C. Runger, J. B. Keats, and D. C. Montgomery (1996). "Efficient Shift Detection Using Exponentially Weighted Moving Average Control Charts and Principal Components," *Quality and Reliability Engineering International,* Vol. 12(3), pp. 165–172.

Shapiro, S. S. (1980). *How to Test Normality and Other Distributional Assumptions,* Vol 3, The ASQC Basic References in Quality Control: Statistical Techniques, ASQC, Milwaukee, WI.

Sheaffer, R. L., and R. S. Leavenworth (1976). "The Negative Binomial Model for Counts in Units of Varying Size," *Journal of Quality Technology,* Vol. 8(3), pp. 158–163.

Siegmund, D. (1985). *Sequential Analysis: Tests and Confidence Intervals,* Springer-Verlag, New York.

Snee, R. D. and R. W. Hoerl (2005). *Six Sigma Beyond the Factory Floor,* Pearson Prentice Hall, Upper Saddle River, NJ.

Sonesson, C. and D. Bock (2003). "A Review and Discussion of Prospective Statistical Surveillance in Public Health," *Journal of the Royal Statistical Society,* Series A, Vol. 166, pp. 5–21.

Somerville, S. E., and D. C. Montgomery (1996). "Process Capability Indices and Nonnormal Distributions," *Quality Engineering,* Vol. 9(2), pp. 305–316.

Spiring, F., B. Leung, S. Cheng, and A. Yeung (2003). "A Bibliography of Process Capability Papers," *Quality and Reliability Engineering International,* Vol. 19(5), pp. 445–460.

Staudhammer, C., T. C. Maness, and R. A. Kozak (2007). "Profile Charts for Monitoring Lumber Manufacturing Using Laser Range Sensor Data," *Journal of Quality Technology,* Vol. 39, pp. 224–240.

Steiner, S. H. (1999). "EWMA Control Charts with Time-Varying Control Limits and Fast Initial Response," *Journal of Quality Technology,* Vol. 31(1), pp. 75–86.

Steiner, S. H., and R. J. MacKay (2000). "Monitoring Processes with Highly Censored Data," *Journal of Quality Technology,* Vol. 32(3), pp. 199–208.

Stephens, K. S. (1979). *How to Perform Continuous Sampling (CSP),* Vol. 2, The ASQC Basic References in Quality Control: Statistical Techniques, ASQC, Milwaukee, WI.

Stover, F. S. and R. V. Brill (1998). "Statistical Quality Control Applied to Ion Chromatography Calibrations," *Journal of Chromatography A,* Vol. 804, pp. 37–43.

Stoumbos, Z. G, and J. H. Sullivan (2002). Robustness to Non-normality of the Multivariate EWMA Control Chart," *Journal of Quality Technology,* Vol. 34(3), pp. 260–276.

Stover, F. S., and R. V. Brill (1998). "Statistical Quality Control Applied to Ion Chromatography Calibrations," *Journal of Chromatography,* A 804, pp. 37–43.

Sullivan, J. H., and W. H. Woodall (1995). "A Comparison of Multivariate Quality Control Charts for Individual Observations," *Journal of Quality Technology,* Vol. 28(4), pp. 398–408.

Svoboda, L. (1991). "Economic Design of Control Charts: A Review and Literature Survey (1979–1989)," in *Statistical Process Control in Manufacturing,* J. B. Keats and D. C. Montgomery, (eds.) Dekker, New York.

Taguchi, G. (1986). *Introduction to Quality Engineering,* Asian Productivity Organization, UNIPUB, White Plains, NY.

Taguchi, G., and Y. Wu (1980). *Introduction to Off-Line Quality Control,* Japan Quality Control Organization, Nagoya, Japan.

Taylor, H. M. (1965). "Markovian Sequential Replacement Processes," *Annals of Mathematical Statistics,* Vol. 36(1), pp. 13–21.

Taylor, H. M. (1967). "Statistical Control of a Gaussian Process," *Technometrics,* Vol. 9(1), pp. 29–41.

Taylor, H. M. (1968). "The Economic Design of Cumulative Sum Control Charts," *Technometrics,* Vol. 10(3), pp. 479–488.

Testik, M. C., G. C. Runger, and C. M. Borror (2003). "Robustness Properties of Multivariate EWMA Control Charts," *Quality and Reliability Engineering International,* Vol. 19(1), pp. 31–38.

Testik, M. C., and C. M. Borror (2004). "Design Strategies for the Multivariate EWMA Control Chart," *Quality and Reliability Engineering International,* Vol. 20, pp. 571–577.

Tracy, N. D., J. C. Young, and R. L. Mason (1992). "Multivariate Control Charts for Individual Observations," *Journal of Quality Technology,* Vol. 24(2), pp. 88–95.

Tseng, S., and B. M. Adams (1994). "Monitoring Autocorrelated Processes with an Exponentially Weighted Moving Average Forecast," *Journal of Statistical Computation and Simulation,* Vol. 50(3–4), pp. 187–195.

Tsui, K. and S. Weerahandi (1989). "Generalized *p*-values in Significance Testing of Hypotheses in the Presence of Nuisance Parameters," *Journal of the American Statistical Association,* Vol. 84, pp. 602–607.

United States Department of Defense (1957). *Sampling Procedures and Tables for Inspection by Variables for Percent Defective,* MIL STD 414, U.S. Government Printing Office, Washington, DC.

United States Department of Defense (1989). *Sampling Procedures and Tables for Inspection by Attributes,* MIL STD 105E, U.S. Government Printing Office, Washington, DC.

Vance, L. C. (1986). "Average Run Lengths of Cumulative Sum Control Charts for Controlling Normal Means," *Journal of Quality Technology,* Vol. 18(3), pp. 189–193.

Vander Weil, S., W. T. Tucker, F. W. Faltin, and N. Doganaksoy (1992). "Algorithmic Statistical Process Control: Concepts and an Application," *Technometrics,* Vol. 34(3), pp. 286–288.

Van Wieringen, W. N. (2003). *Statistical Models for the Precision of Categorical Measurement Systems.* Ph. D. thesis, University of Amsterdam.

Wadsworth, H. M., K. S. Stephens, and A. B. Godfrey (2002). *Modern Methods for Quality Control and Improvement,* 2nd ed., Wiley, New York.

Wald, A. (1947). *Sequential Analysis,* Wiley, New York.

Walker, E., J. W. Philpot, and J. Clement (1991). "False Signal Rates for the Shewhart Control Chart with Supplementary Runs Tests," *Journal of Quality Technology,* Vol. 23(3), pp. 247–252.

Walker, E., and S. P. Wright (2002). "Comparing Curves Using Additive Models," *Journal of Quality Technology,* Vol. 34(1), pp. 118–129.

Wang, C.–H., and F. S. Hillier (1970). "Mean and Variance Control Chart Limits Based on a Small Number of Subgroups," *Journal of Quality Technology,* Vol. 2(1), pp. 9–16.

Wang, K. B. and F. Tsung (2005). "Using Profile Monitoring Techniques for a Data-Rich Environment with Huge Sample Size," *Quality and Reliability Engineering International,* Vol. 21, pp. 677–688.

Wardell, D. G., H. Moskowitz, and R. D. Plante (1994). "Run Length Distributions of Special-Cause Control Charts for Correlated Processes," *Technometrics,* Vol. 36(1), pp. 3–18.

Weerahandi, S. (1993). "Generalized Confidence Intervals," *Journal of the American Statistical Association,* Vol. 88, pp. 899–905.

Weiler, H. (1952). "On the Most Economical Sample Size for Controlling the Mean of a Population," *Annals of Mathematical Statistics,* Vol. 23(2), pp. 247–254.

Western Electric (1956). *Statistical Quality Control Handbook,* Western Electric Corporation, Indianapolis, IN.

Wetherill, G. B., and D. W. Brown (1991). *Statistical Process Control: Theory and Practice,* Chapman and Hall, New York.

White, C. C. (1974). "A Markov Quality Control Process Subject to Partial Observation," *Management Science,* Vol. 23(8), pp. 843–852.

White, C. H., J. B. Keats, and J. Stanley (1997). "Poison Cusum Versus *c* Chart for Defect Data," *Quality Engineering,* Vol. 9(4), pp. 673–679.

White, E. M., and R. Schroeder (1987). "A Simultaneous Control Chart," *Journal of Quality Technology,* Vol. 19(1), pp. 1–10.

Willemain, T. R., and G. C. Runger (1996). "Designing Control Charts Based on an Empirical Reference Distribution," *Journal of Quality Technology,* Vol. 28(1), pp. 31–38.

Williams, J. D., W. H. Woodall, J. B. Birch, and J. H. Sullivan (2006). "Distribution of Hotelling's T^2 Statistic Based on the Successive Difference Estimator," *Journal of Quality Technology,* Vol. 38, pp. 217–229.

Winkel, P., and N. F. Zhang (2007). *Statistical Development of Quality in Medicine,* John Wiley and Sons, New York.

Woodall, W. H. (1986). "Weakness of the Economic Design of Control Charts," Letter to the Editor, *Technometrics,* Vol. 28(4), pp. 408–409.

Woodall, W. H. (1987). "Conflicts Between Deming's Philosophy and the Economic Design of Control Charts," in *Frontiers in Statistical Quality Control,* 3rd ed., H. J. Lenz, G. B. Wetherill, and P.–T. Wilrich, Physica-Verlag, Vienna, pp. 242–248.

Woodall, W. H. (1997). "Control Charts Based on Attribute Data: Bibliography and Review," *Journal of Quality Technology,* Vol. 29(2), pp. 172–183.

Woodall, W. H. (2000). "Controversies and Contradictions in Statistical Process Control," *Journal of Quality Technology,* Vol. 20(4), pp. 515–521. Available at www.asq.org/pub/jqt.

Woodall, W. H. (2007). "Profile Monitoring," entry in *Encyclopedia of Statistics in Quality and Reliability* edited by Fabrizio Ruggeri, Frederick Faltin, and Ron Kenett, John Wiley & Sons, New York.

Woodall, W. H., and B. M. Adams (1993). "The Statistical Design of CUSUM Charts," *Quality Engineering,* Vol. 5(4), pp. 559–570.

Woodall, W. H., and D. C. Montgomery (1999). "Research Issues and Ideas in Statistical Process Control," *Journal of Quality Technology,* Vol. 31(4), pp. 376–386.

Woodall, W. H., and D. C. Montgomery (2000–2001). "Using Ranges to Estimate Variability," *Quality Engineering,* Vol. 13(2), pp. 211–217.

Woodall, W. H., D. J. Spitzner, D. C. Montgomery, and S. Gupta (2004). "Using Control Charts to Monitor Process and Product Quality Profiles," *Journal of Quality Technology,* Vol. 36, pp. 309–320.

Woodall, W. H. (2006). "Use of Control Charts in Health Care Monitoring and Public Health Surveillance" (with discussion), *Journal of Quality Technology,* Vol. 38, pp. 89–104. Available at www.asq.org/pub/jqt.

Woodall, W. H. and M. A. Mahmoud (2005), "The Inertial Properties of Quality Control Charts," *Technometrics,* Vol. 47, pp. 425–436.

Yourstone, S. A., and D. C. Montgomery (1989). "Development of a Real-Time Statistical Process-Control Algorithm," *Quality and Reliability Engineering International,* Vol. 5(4), pp. 309–317.

Yourstone, S., and W. Zimmer (1992). "Non-normality and the Design of Control Charts for Averages," *Decision Sciences,* Vol. 23(5), pp. 1099–1113.

Zhang, N. F., G. A. Stenback, and D. M. Wardrop (1990). "Interval Estimation of Process Capability Index C_{pk}," *Communications in Statistics—Theory and Methods,* Vol. 19(12), pp. 4455–4470.

Zou, C., Y. Zhang, and Z. Wang (2006). "A Control Chart Based on a Change-Point Model for Monitoring Profiles," *IIE Transactions,* Vol. 38, pp. 1093–1103.

Answers to Selected Exercises

CHAPTER 3

3.1. (a) $\bar{x} = 121.25$. (b) $s = 22.63$.

3.2. (a) $\bar{x} = 952.9$. (b) $s = 3.7$.

3.4. (a) $\bar{x} = 16.029$. (b) $s = 0.0202$.

3.6. (a) $\bar{x} = 89.476$. (b) $s = 4.158$.

3.13. Both the normal and lognormal distributions appear to be reasonable models for the data.

3.14. The lognormal distribution appears to be a reasonable model for the concentration data.

3.22. *sample space*: {2, 3, 4, 5, 6, 7, 8, 9, 10, 11, 12}

$$p(x) = \begin{cases} 1/36; x=2 & 2/36; x=3 \\ 3/36; x=4 & 4/36; x=5 \\ 5/36; x=6 & 6/36; x=7 \\ 5/36; x=8 & 4/36; x=9 \\ 3/36; x=10 & 2/36; x=11 \\ 1/36; x=12 & 0; \text{otherwise} \end{cases}$$

3.24. (a) Approximately 11.8%. (b) Decrease profit by \$5.90/calculator.

3.25. (a) $k = 0.05$. (b) $\mu = 1.867$, $\sigma^2 = 0.615$.
(c) $F(x) = \{0.383; x=1 \quad 0.750; x=2 \quad 1.000; x=3$

3.26. (a) 0.0196. (b) 0.0198.
(c) Cutting occurrence rate reduces probability from 0.0198 to 0.0100.

3.27. Decision rule means 22% of samples will have one or more nonconforming units.

3.30. 0.921

3.32. (a) 0.633. (b) 0.659. Approximation is not satisfactory.
(c) $n/N = 0.033$. Approximation is satisfactory. (d) $n = 11$

3.34. $\Pr\{x \geq 1\} = 0.00001$

3.36. $\mu = 1/p$

3.37. $\Pr\{x > 1000\} = 0.0021$

3.39. $\Pr\{x \leq 35\} = 0.159$. Number failing minimum spec is 7950.
$\Pr\{x > 48\} = 0.055$. Number failing maximum spec is 2750.

3.41. Process is centered at target, so shifting process mean in either direction increases nonconformities. Process variance must be reduced to 0.015^2 to have at least 999 of 1000 conform to specification.

CHAPTER 4

4.2. (a) $t_0 = 1.952$. Reject H_0.
(b) $25.06 \leq \mu \leq 26.94$.

4.4. (a) $Z_0 = 6.78$. Reject H_0.
(b) $P = 0$. (c) $8.2525 \leq \mu \leq 8.2545$.

4.7. $n = 246$

4.8. (a) $t_0 = -6.971$. Reject H_0.
(b) $9.727 \leq \mu \leq 10.792$
(c) $\chi_0^2 = 14.970$. Do not reject H_0.
(d) $0.738 \leq \sigma \leq 1.546$
(e) $\sigma \leq 1.436$

4.9. (a) $t_0 = -0.77$. Do not reject H_0.
(b) $-6.7 \leq (\mu_1 - \mu_2) \leq 3.1$.
(c) $0.21 \leq \sigma_1^2/\sigma_2^2 \leq 3.34$

4.12. (a) $t_0 = 0.11$. Do not reject H_0.
(c) $-0.127 \leq (\mu_1 - \mu_2) \leq 0.141$
(d) $F_0 = 0.8464$. Do not reject H_0.
(e) $0.165 \leq \sigma_1^2/\sigma_2^2 \leq 4.821$
(f) $0.007 \leq \sigma^2 \leq 0.065$

4.13. (a) $F_0 = 1.0987$. Do not reject H_0.
(b) $t_0 = 1.461$. Do not reject H_0.

4.14. $t_0 = -1.10$. There is no difference between mean measurements.

4.15. (a) $Z_0 = 4.0387$. Reject H_0. (b) $P = 0.00006$.
(c) $p \leq 0.155$.

4.20. (a) $\chi_0^2 = 42.75$. Do not reject H_0.
(b) $1.14 \le \sigma \le 2.19$.

4.22. $n = [(Z_{\alpha/2} + Z_\beta)\sigma/\delta]^2$

4.25. $Z_0 = 0.3162$. Do not reject H_0.

4.27. (a) $F_0 = 30.85$, $P = 0.000$.

4.28. (a) $F_0 = 1.45$, $P = 0.258$.

4.30. (a) $F_0 = 1.87$, $P = 0.214$.

4.32. (a) $F_0 = 3.59$, $P = 0.053$.

CHAPTER 5

5.9. There is a nonrandom, cyclic pattern.

5.10. Pattern is random.

5.18. Points 16, 17, and 18 are 2 of 3 beyond 2 sigma of centerline. Points 5, 6, 7, 8, and 9 are of 5 at 1 sigma or beyond of centerline.

5.20. Points 17, 18, 19, and 20 are outside lower 1-sigma area.

CHAPTER 6

6.1. (a) $\bar{x}$ chart: CL = 10.9, UCL = 50.35, LCL = −28.55
R chart: CL = 54.1, UCL = 123.5, LCL = 0
Process is in statistical control.
(b) $\bar{\sigma}_x = 23.3$. (c) $\hat{C}_P = 1.43$.

6.3. (a) Samples 12 and 15 exceed $\bar{x}$ UCL.
(b) $\bar{p} = 0.00050$.

6.6. $\bar{x}$ chart: CL = 10.33, UCL = 14.73, LCL = 5.92
s chart: CL = 2.703, UCL = 6.125, LCL = 0

6.7. (a) $\bar{x}$ chart: CL = −0.003, UCL = 1.037, LCL = −1.043
s chart: CL = 1.066, UCL = 1.830, LCL = 0.302
(b) R chart: CL = 3.2, UCL = 5.686, LCL = 0.714
(c) s^2 chart: CL = 1.2057, UCL = 3.6297, LCL = 0.1663

6.9. $\bar{x}$ chart: CL = 80, UCL = 89.49, LCL = 70.51
s chart: CL = 9.727, UCL = 16.69, LCL = 2.76

6.10. (a) chart: CL = 74.00118, UCL = 74.01458, LCL = 73.98777
R chart: CL = 0.02324, UCL = 0.04914, LCL = 0 (b) No. (c) $\hat{C}_P = 1.668$.

6.12. (a) $\bar{x}$ chart: CL = 34.00, UCL = 37.50, LCL = 30.50
R chart: CL = 3.42, UCL = 8.81, LCL = 0
(b) Detect shift more quickly.
(c) $\bar{x}$ chart: CL = 34.00, UCL = 36.14, LCL = 31.86
R chart: CL = 5.75, UCL = 10.72, LCL = 0.78

6.13. (a) $\bar{x}$ chart: CL = 79.53, UCL = 84.58, LCL = 74.49
R chart: CL = 8.75, UCL = 18.49, LCL = 0
Process is in statistical control.
(b) Several subgroups exceed UCL on R chart.

6.15. (a) $\bar{x}$ chart: CL = 20, UCL = 22.34, LCL = 17.66
s chart: CL = 1.44, UCL = 3.26, LCL = 0
(b) LNTL = 15.3, UNTL = 24.7
(c) $\hat{C}_P = 0.85$
(d) $\hat{p}_{\text{rework}} = 0.0275$, $\hat{p}_{\text{scrap}} = 0.00069$, Total = 2.949%
(e) $\hat{p}_{\text{rework}} = 0.00523$, $\hat{p}_{\text{scrap}} = 0.00523$, Total = 1.046%

6.17. (a) $\hat{\sigma}_x = 1.60$
(b) $\bar{x}$ chart: UCL = 22.14, LCL = 17.86
s chart: UCL = 3.13, LCL = 0
(c) Pr{in control} = 0.57926

6.19. (a) $\bar{x}$ chart: CL = 223, UCL = 237.37, LCL = 208.63
R chart: CL = 34.29, UCL = 65.97, LCL = 2.61
(b) $\hat{\mu} = 223$; $\hat{\sigma}_x = 12.68$
(c) $\hat{C}_P = 0.92$. (d) $\hat{p} = 0.00578$

6.21. $\hat{C}_P = 0.8338$

6.24. The process continues to be in a state of statistical control.

6.26. (a) $\bar{x}$ chart: CL = 449.68, UCL = 462.22, LCL = 437.15
s chart: CL = 17.44, UCL = 7.70, LCL = 0

6.27. (a) $\bar{\bar{x}} = 20.26$, $\text{UCL}_{\bar{x}} = 23.03$, $\text{LCL}_{\bar{x}} = 17.49$; $\bar{R} = 4.8$, $\text{UCL}_R = 10.152$, $\text{LCL}_R = 0$
(b) $\hat{p} = 0.0195$

6.30. Pr{detecting shift on 1st sample} = 0.37

6.32. (a) $\bar{x}$ Recalculating limits without samples 1, 12, and 13:
$\bar{x}$ chart: CL = 1.45, UCL = 5.46, LCL = (2.57
R chart: CL = 6.95, UCL = 14.71, LCL = 0
(b) Samples 1, 12, 13, 16, 17, 18, and 20 are out-of-control, for a total 7 of the 25 samples, with runs of points both above and below the centerline. This suggests that the process is inherently unstable, and that the sources of variation need to be identified and removed.

6.33. (a) $\overline{R} = 45.0$, $UCL_R = 90.18$, $LCL_R = 0$
(b) $\hat{\mu} = 429.0$, $\hat{\sigma}_x = 17.758$
(c) $\hat{C}_p = 0.751$; $\hat{p} = 0.0533$
(d) To minimize fraction nonconforming the mean should be located at the nominal dimension (440) for a constant variance.

6.35. (a) $UCL_{\overline{x}} = 108, LCL_{\overline{x}} = 92$.
(b) $UCL_{\overline{x}} = 111.228, LCL_{\overline{x}} = 88.772$.

6.37. (a) $\overline{\overline{x}} = 90, UCL_{\overline{x}} = 91.676, LCL_{\overline{x}} = 88.324$; $\overline{R} = 4, UCL_R = 7.696, LCL_R = 0.304$.
(b) $\hat{\sigma}_x = 1.479$.
(c) $\overline{s} = 1.419$, $UCL_s = 2.671$, $LCL_s = 0.167$.

6.40. (a) $CL_s = 9.213, UCL_s = 20.88, LCL_s = 0$.
(b) $UCL_{\overline{x}} = 209.8, LCL_{\overline{x}} = 190.2$.

6.42. $ARL_1 = 2.986$

6.43. Pr{detect shift on 1st sample} = 0.1587

6.45. $\overline{\overline{x}} = 16.1052$; $\hat{\sigma}_x = 0.021055$; $\overline{MR2} = 0.02375$. Assumption of normally distributed coffee can weights is valid. %underfilled = 0.0003%.

6.46. (a) $\hat{\mu} = 706.00$; $\hat{\sigma}_x = 1.827$.
(b) $UNTL = 711.48, LNTL = 700.52$.
(c) $\hat{p} = 0.1006$.
(d) Pr{detect on 1st sample} = 0.9920
(e) Pr{detect by 3rd sample}

6.48. (a) $\alpha = 0.0026$. (b) $\hat{C}_P = 0.667$.
(c) Pr{not detect on 1st sample} = 0.5000.
(d) $UCL_{\overline{x}} = 362.576, LCL_{\overline{x}} = 357.424$.

6.50. (a) Viscosity measurements appear to follow a normal distribution.
(b) The process appears to be in statistical control, with no out-of-control points, runs, trends, or other patterns.
(c) $\hat{\mu} = 2928.9$; $\hat{\sigma}_x = 131.346$; $\overline{MR2} = 148.158$

6.53. (a) The process is in statistical control. The normality assumption is reasonable.
(b) It is clear that the process is out of control during this period of operation.
(c) The process has been returned to a state of statistical control.

6.54. (a) The data are not normally distributed. The distribution of the natural-log transformed uniformity measurements is approximately normally distributed.
(b) $\overline{x}$ chart: CL = 2.653, UCL = 3.586, LCL = 1.720
R chart: CL = 0.351, UCL = 1.146, LCL = 0

6.56. The measurements are approximately normally distributed. The out-of-control signal on the moving range chart indicates a significantly large difference between successive measurements (7 and 8). Consider the process to be in a state of statistical process control.

6.57. x chart: $\overline{x} = 16.11$, $UCL_x = 16.17$, $LCL_x = 16.04$
MR chart: $\overline{MR2} = 0.02365$, $UCL_{MR2} = 0.07726$, $LCL_{MR2} = 0$

6.58. x chart: $\overline{x} = 2929$, $UCL_x = 3338$, $LCL_x = 2520$
MR chart: $\overline{MR2} = 153.7$, $UCL_{MR2} = 502.2$, $LCL_{MR2} = 0$

6.59. (a) $\hat{\sigma}_x = 1.157$. (b) $\hat{\sigma}_x = 1.682$. (c) $\hat{\sigma}_x = 1.137$
(d) $\hat{\sigma}_{x,\text{ span }3} = 1.210$, $\hat{\sigma}_{x,\text{ span }4} = 1.262$, ..., $\hat{\sigma}_{x,\text{ span }19} = 1.406$, $\hat{\sigma}_{x,\text{ span }20} = 1.435$

6.62. (a) $\overline{x}$ chart: CL = 11.76, UCL = 11.79, LCL = 11.72
R chart (within): CL = 0.06109, UCL = 0.1292, LCL = 0
(c) I chart: CL = 11.76, UCL = 11.87, LCL = 11.65
MR2 chart (between): CL = 0.04161, UCL = 0.1360, LCL = 0

6.64. (b) R chart (within): CL = 0.06725, UCL = 0.1422, LCL = 0
(c) I chart: CL = 2.074, UCL = 2.159, LCL = 1.989
MR2 chart (between): CL = 0.03210, UCL = 0.1049, LCL = 0
(d) Need lot average, moving range between lot averages, and range within a lot.
I chart: CL = 2.074, UCL = 2.133, LCL = 2.015
MR2 chart (between): CL = 0.02205, UCL = 0.07205, LCL = 0
R chart (within): CL = 0.1335, UCL = 0.2372, LCL = 0.02978

CHAPTER 7

7.1. For $n = 80$, $UCL_i = 0.1397$, $LCL_i = 0$. Process is in statistical control.

7.3. $\overline{p} = 0.0585$, UCL = 0.1289, LCL = 0. Sample 12 exceeds UCL. Without sample 12: $\overline{p} = 0.0537$, UCL = 0.1213, LCL = 0.

7.6. $\overline{p} = 0.10$, UCL = 0.2125, LCL = 0
$p = 0.212$ to make $\beta = 0.50$. $n \geq 82$ to give positive LCL.

7.7. Pr{detect shift on 1st sample} = 0.278,
Pr{detect shift by 3rd sample} = 0.624

7.10. $n = 81$

7.13. (a) Less sample 3: $n\overline{p} = 14.78$, UCL = 27.421, LCL = 4.13
(b) Pr{detect shift on 1st sample} = 0.813

7.14. (a) $n\overline{p} = 40$, UCL = 58, LCL = 22.
(b) Pr{detect shift on 1st sample} = 0.583.

7.15. (a) $\overline{p} = 0.07$, UCL = 0.108, LCL = 0.032
(b) Pr{detect shift on 1st sample} = 0.297
(c) Pr{detect shift on 1st or 2nd sample} = 0.506

7.17. ARL1 = 1.715 ≈– 2

7.19. $n \geq 892$

7.21. (a) CL = = 0.0221
for n = 100: UCL = 0.0622, LCL = 0
for n = 150: UCL = 0.0581, LCL = 0
for n = 200: UCL = 0.0533, LCL = 0
for n = 250: UCL = 0.0500, LCL = 0
(b) $Z_i = (\hat{p}_i - 0.0221)\Big/\sqrt{0.0221(1-0.0221)/n_i}$

7.23. $Z_i = (\hat{p}_i - 0.0221)\Big/\sqrt{0.0216 / n_i}$

7.25. (a) $n \geq 397$. (b) $n = 44$.

7.26. (a) $L = 2.83$. (b) $n\overline{p} = 20$, UCL = 32.36, LCL = 7.64.
(c) Pr{detect shift on 1st sample} = 0.140.

7.29. $Z_i = (\hat{p}_i - 0.06)\Big/\sqrt{0.0564 / n_i}$

7.30. $n\overline{p} = 2.505$, UCL = 7.213, LCL = 0

7.32. Variable u: CL = 0.7007; $\text{UCL}_i = 0.7007 + 3\sqrt{0.7007/n_i}$; $\text{LCL}_i = 0.7007 - 3\sqrt{0.7007/n_i}$
Averaged u: CL = 0.701, UCL = 1.249, LCL = 0.1527

7.34. $Z_i = (u_i - 0.7007)\Big/\sqrt{0.7007 / n_i}$

7.35. $\overline{c} = 8.59$, UCL = 17.384, LCL = 0. Process is not in statistical control.

7.37. (a) c chart: CL = 15.43, UCL = 27.21, LCL = 3.65
(b) u chart: CL = 15.42, UCL = 27.20, LCL = 3.64

7.40. $\overline{u} = 7$; $\text{UCL}_i = 7 + 3\sqrt{7 / n_i}$; $\text{LCL}_i = 7 - 3\sqrt{7 / n_i}$

7.41. (a) c chart: CL = 9, UCL = 18, LCL = 0
(b) u chart: CL = 4, UCL = 7, LCL = 1

7.42. (a) c chart: CL = 4, UCL = 10, LCL = 0
(b) u chart: CL = 1, UCL = 2.5, LCL = 0

7.44. $\overline{c} = 7.6$, UCL = 13.00, LCL = 2.20

7.48. $\overline{u} = 4$, UCL = 9

7.49. $\overline{c} = 8.5$, UCL = 13.98, LCL = 3.02

7.52. (a) $\overline{c} = 0.533$, UCL = 1.993, LCL = 0.
(b) $\alpha = 0.104$.
(c) $\beta = 0.271$. (d) $\text{ARL}_1 = 1.372 \approx 2$.

7.53. $n > L^2 / \overline{c}$

7.54. (a) $\overline{c} = 4$, UCL = 10, LCL = 0. (b) $\alpha = 0.03$.

7.59. The variable NYRSB can be thought of as an "inspection unit," representing an identical "area of opportunity" for each "sample." The "process characteristic" to be controlled is the rate of CAT scans. A u chart which monitors the average number of CAT scans per NYRSB is appropriate.

CHAPTER 8

8.1. $\hat{C}_p = 5.48$, $\hat{C}_{pk} = 4.34$, $\hat{C}_{pkm} = 0.43$

8.4. Process A: $\hat{C}_p = \hat{C}_{pk} = \hat{C}_{pm} = 1.045$, = 0.001726
Process B: $\hat{C}_p = 3.133$, $\hat{C}_{pk} = 1.566$, $\hat{C}_{pm} = 0.652$, $\hat{p} = 0.000001$

8.7. (a) $\hat{C}_p = 2.98$. (b) $\hat{C}_{pk} = 1.49$.
(c) $\hat{p}_{\text{actual}} = 0.000004$, $\hat{p}_{\text{potential}} = 0.000000$.

8.8. (a) $\hat{C}_p = 0.75$. (b) $\hat{C}_{pk} = 0.71$.
(c) $\hat{C}_{pkm} = 0.70$.
(d) $\hat{p}_{\text{Actual}} = 0.025348$, $\hat{p}_{\text{Potential}} = 0.024220$

8.10. No. Data is not normally distributed.

8.11. $6\hat{\sigma} = 0.05514$

8.12. $6\hat{\sigma} = 0.1350$

8.14. (a) $6\hat{\sigma} = 73.2$. (b) $C_{pu} = 0.58$, $\hat{p} = 0.041047$.

8.15. $1.26 \leq C_p$, $\alpha = 0.12$

8.17. (a) $\hat{C}_{pk} = 0.42$
(b) $0.2957 \leq C_{pk} \leq 0.5443$

8.20. (a) $6\hat{\sigma}_{\text{gauge}} = 8.154$. (b) R chart indicates operator has difficulty using gauge.

8.22. (a) R chart indicates operator has no difficulty making consistent measurements. (b) $\hat{\sigma}^2_{\text{total}} = 4.717$, $\hat{\sigma}^2_{\text{product}} = 1.695$. (c) 62.5%. (d) $P/T = 0.272$.

8.23. $\hat{\sigma}_{\text{process}} = 4$

8.29. $\hat{p} = 0.4330$

8.31. $\hat{\mu}_{\text{Weight}} = 48$, $\hat{\sigma}_{\text{Weight}} = 0.04252$

8.33. $C \sim N(0.006, 0.000005)$. Pr{positive clearance} = 0.9964.

8.34. $\mu_I \cong \mu_E / (\mu_{R_1} + \mu_{R_2})$

$$\sigma_I^2 \cong \sigma_E^2 / (\mu_{R_1} + \mu_{R_2})^2 + \left(\mu_E^2 / (\mu_{R_1} + \mu_{R_2})^2\right)$$

$(\sigma_{R_1}^2 + \sigma_{R_2}^2)$

8.36. UTL = 323.55

8.40. (a) $0.1257 \le x \le 0.1271$. (b) $0.1263 \le \bar{x} \le 0.1265$.

CHAPTER 9

9.2. Process is in control. $ARL_0 = 370.84$

9.4. (a) $K = 12.5$, $H = 125$. Process is out of control on upper side after observation 7. (b) $\hat{\sigma} = 34.43$

9.6. (a) $K = 12.5$, $H = 62.5$. Process is out of control on upper side after observation 7. (b) Process is out of control on lower side at sample 6 and upper at sample 15.

9.9. (a) $\hat{\sigma} = 5.95$. (b) Process is out of control on lower side at start, then upper after observation 9.

9.10. (a) $\hat{\sigma} = 12.16$. (b) Process is out of control on upper side after reading 2.

9.12. Process is out of control on upper side after observation 7.

9.13. $K = 54.35$, $H = 543.5$. Process is out of control virtually from the first sample.

9.14. $ARL_0 = 215.23$, $ARL_1 = 25.02$

9.17. EWMA chart: CL = 8.02, UCL = 8.07, LCL = 7.97. Process is in control.

9.19. EWMA chart: CL = 1050, UCL = 1065.49, LCL = 1034.51.
Process exceeds upper control limit at sample 10.

9.21. EWMA chart: CL = 3200, UCL = 3203.69, LCL = 3196.31.
Process is out of control from the first sample.

9.22. EWMA chart: CL = 175, UCL = 177.3, LCL = 172.70.
Process is out of control.

9.23. EWMA chart: CL = 950, UCL = 957.53, LCL = 942.47.
Process is out of control at samples 8, 12, and 13.

9.24. MA chart: CL = 1050, UCL = 1080.62, LCL = 1019.38.
Process is out of control at sample 10.

9.26. MA chart: CL = 8.02, UCL = 8.087, LCL = 7.953. Process is in control.

9.31. $k = 0.5L$

CHAPTER 10

10.3. $\bar{x}$ chart: CL = 0.55, UCL = 4.44, LCL = −3.34
R chart: CL = 3.8, UCL = 9.78, LCL = 0

10.4. $\bar{x}$ chart: CL = 52.988, UCL = 55.379, LCL = 50.596
R chart: CL = 2.338, UCL = 6.017, LCL = 0

10.7. (a) $\bar{x}$ chart: CL = 52.988, UCL = 58.727, LCL = 47.248
R chart: CL = 2.158, UCL = 7.050, LCL = 0
(c) $\bar{x}$ chart: CL = 52.988, UCL = 55.159, LCL = 49.816
s chart: CL = 1.948, UCL = 4.415, LCL = 0

10.8. (a) UCL = 44.503, LCL = 35.497
(b) UCL = 43.609, LCL = 36.391
(c) UCL = 43.239, LCL = 36.761

10.12. $\bar{x}$ chart: CL = 50, UCL = 65.848, LCL = 34.152

10.15. (a) $\hat{\sigma} = 4.000$. (b) $\hat{p} = 0.1056$. (c) UCL = 619.35, LCL = 600.65.

10.17. $\mu_0 = 0$, $\delta = 1\sigma$, $k = 0.5$, $h = 5$, UCL = 22.79, LCL = 22.79, no FIR.
No observations exceed the control limits.

10.19. $\alpha = 0.1$, $\lambda = 0.7055$, = 3.227.
Observations 8, 56 and 90 exceed control limits.

10.21. $\mu_0 = 0$, $\delta = 1\sigma$, $k = 0.5$, $h = 5$, UCL = 97.9, LCL = 97.9, no FIR.
No observations exceed the control limit.

10.23. $\alpha = 0.1$, $\lambda = 0.9238$, $\hat{\sigma} = 15.93$.
Observation 16 exceeds UCL.

10.24. (a) $r_1 = 0.49$
(b) I chart: CL = 28.57, UCL = 37.11, LCL = 20.03
(c) $\mu_0 = 28.569$, $\delta = 1\sigma$, $k = 0.5$, $h = 5$, UCL = 14.24, LCL = 14.24, no FIR. Several observations are out of control on both lower and upper sides.
(d) EWMA chart: $\lambda = 0.15$, $L = 2.7$, CL = 28.569, UCL = 30.759, LCL = 26.380
(e) Moving CL EWMA chart: $\alpha = 0.1$, $\lambda = 0.150$, $= 2.85$. A few observations are beyond the lower control limit.
(f) $\xi = 20.5017$, $\phi_1 = 0.7193$, $\phi_2 = -0.4349$. Set up an I and MR chart for residuals. I chart: CL = −0.04, UCL = 9.60, LCL = −9.68

10.28. (a) $E(L)$ = \$16.17/hr. (b) $E(L)$ = \$10.39762/hr.

10.29. (a) $E(L)$ = \$4.12/hr. (b) $E(L)$ = \$4.98/hr.
(c) $n = 5$, $k_{opt} = 3.080$, $h_{opt} = 1.368$, $\alpha = 0.00207$, $1 - \beta = 0.918$, $E(L)$ = \$4.01392/hr

CHAPTER 11

11.1. $UCL_{\text{Phase 2}} = 13.186$

11.2. $UCL_{\text{Phase 2}} = 14.186$, $LCL_{\text{Phase 2}} = 0$

11.5. Assume $\alpha = 0.01$. $UCL_{\text{Phase 1}} = 32.638$, $UCL_{\text{Phase 2}} = 35.360$

11.6. (a) $UCL_{\text{Phase 2}} = 39.326$.
(b) $UCL_{\text{chi-square}} = 25.188$. (c) $m = 988$.

11.8. (a) $UCL_{\text{Phase 2}} = 23.882$, $LCL_{\text{Phase 2}} = 0$.
(b) $UCL_{\text{chi-square}} = 18.548$.

11.10. (a) $\mathbf{\Sigma} = \begin{bmatrix} 1 & 0.8 & 0.8 \\ 0.8 & 1 & 0.8 \\ 0.8 & 0.8 & 1 \end{bmatrix}$
(b) $UCL_{\text{chi-square}} = 7.815$.
(c) $T^2 = 11.154$. (d) $d_1 = 0.043$, $d_2 = 8.376$, $d_3 = 6.154$.
(e) $T^2 = 21.800$. (f) $d_1 = 16.800$, $d_2 = 16.800$, $d_3 = 17.356$.

11.12. $\mathbf{\Sigma} = \begin{bmatrix} 4.440 & -0.016 & 5.395 \\ -0.016 & 0.001 & -0.014 \\ 5.395 & -0.014 & 27.599 \end{bmatrix}$

11.15. $\lambda = 0.1$ with UCL = H = 12.73, ARL_1 is between 7.22 and 12.17.

11.17. Significant variables for y_1 are x_1, x_3, x_4, x_8, and x_9.
Control limits for y_1 model I chart: CL = 0, UCL = 2.105, LCL = −2.105
Control limits for y_1 model MR chart: CL = 0.791, UCL = 2.586, LCL = 0
Significant variables for y_2 are x_1, x_3, x_4, x_8, and x_9.
Control limits for y_2 model I chart: CL = 0, UCL = 6.52, LCL = −6.52
Control limits for y_2 model MR chart: CL = 2.45, UCL = 8.02, LCL = 0

11.20. (a) $\mathbf{z}_1$ = {0.29168, 0.29428, 0.19734, 0.83902, 3.20488, 0.20327, −0.99211, −1.70241, −0.14246, −0.99498, 0.94470, −1.21950, 2.60867, −0.12378, −1.10423, −0.27825, −2.65608, 2.36528, 0.41131, −2.14662}

CHAPTER 12

12.2. Process is adjusted at observations 3, 4, 7, and 29.

12.5. $m = 1$, $Var_1 = 147.11$, $Var_1/Var_1 = 1.000$
$m = 2$, $Var_2 = 175.72$, $Var_2/Var_1 = 1.195$
$m = 3$, $Var_3 = 147.47$, $Var_3/Var_1 = 1.002$
$m = 4$, $Var_4 = 179.02$, $Var_4/Var_1 = 1.217$
$m = 5$, $Var_5 = 136.60$, $Var_5/Var_1 = 0.929$, . . .
Variogram stabilizes near 1.5
$r_1 = 0.44$, $r_2 = 0.33$, $r_3 = 0.44$, $r_4 = 0.32$, $r_5 = 0.30$, . . .
Sample ACF slowly decays.

12.6. (b) Average is closer to target (44.4 vs. 46.262), and variance is smaller (223.51 vs. 78.32).
(c) Average is closer to target (47.833) and variance is smaller (56.40).

12.9. In each control scheme, adjustments are made after each observation following observation 2. There is no difference in results; variance for each procedure is the same.

CHAPTER 13

13.1. Glass effect: $F_0 = 273.79$, P value = 0.000
Phosphor effect: $F_0 = 8.84$, P value = 0.004
Glass × Phosphor interaction: $F_0 = 1.26$, P value = 0.318

13.2. Normality assumption is reasonable. Constant variance assumption is reasonable.

13.5. Plots of residuals versus factors A and C show unequal scatter. Residuals versus predicted indicates that variance not constant. Residuals are approximately normally distributed.

13.8. Largest effect is factor A.

13.10. Block 1: (1), *ab, ac, bc, ad, bd, cd, ae, be, ce, de, abcd, abce, abde, acde, bcde*
Block 2: *a, b, c, d, e, abc, abd, acd, bcd, abe, ace, bce, ade, bde, cde, abcde*

13.12. (a) Main Effects: $F_0 = 1.70$, P value = 0.234
2-Way Interactions: $F_0 = 0.46$, P value = 0.822
Curvature: $F_0 = 16.60$, P value = 0.004
Lack of fit: $F_0 = 0.25$, P value = 0.915

13.13. (b) $I = ACE = BDE = ABCD$, $A = CE = BCD = ABDE$, $B = DE = ACD = ABCE$, $C = AE = ABD = BCDE$, $D = BE = ABC = ACDE$, $E = AC = BD = BCDE$, $AB = CD = ADE = BCE$, $AD = BC = ABE = CDE$
(c) A = –1.525, B = –5.175, C = 2.275, D = –0.675, E = 2.275, AB = 1.825, AD = –1.275
(d) With only main effect B: $F_0 = 8.88$, P value = 0.025.
(e) Residuals plots are satisfactory.

13.16. (a) A = 47.7, B = –0.50, C = 80.6, D = –2.40, AB = 1.10, AC = 72.80, AD = –2.00
(b) Model with C, AC, A:
Main Effects: $F_0 = 1710.43$, P value = 0.000
2-Way Interactions: $F_0 = 2066.89$, P value = 0.000
Curvature: $F_0 = 1.11$, P value = 0.327

CHAPTER 14

14.2. (b) $\Delta x = 1$, $\Delta x_2 = 0.6$

14.6. (a) The design is resolution IV with $A = BCD$, $B = ACD$, $C = ABD$, $D = ABC$, $E = ABCDE$, $AB = CD$, $AC = BD$, $AD = BC$, $AE = BCDE$, $BE = ACDE$, $CE = ABDE$, $DE = ABCE$, $ABE = CDE$, $ACE = BDE$, $ADE = BCE$.
(b) Factors A, B, D, E and interaction BE affect mean free height.
(c) Factors A, B, D and interactions CE and ADE affect standard deviation of free height.
(e) A 2^{5-1}, resolution V design can be generated with $E = \pm ABCD$.

14.7. Mean Free Height = 7.63 + 0.12A – 0.081B
Variance of Free Height = $(0.046)^2 + (-0.12 + 0.077B)^2 + 0.02$
One solution with mean Free Height ≅ 7.50 and minimum standard deviation of Free Height is A = –0.42 and B = 0.99.

14.10. (a) CCD with $k = 2$ and $\alpha = 1.5$. The design is not rotatable.
(b) $y = 160.868 - 58.294x_1 + 2.412x_2 - 10.855x_1^2 + 6.923x_2^2 - 0.750x_1x_2$
(c) $x_1 = +1.5$, $x_2 = -0.22$
(d) Temp = 825, Time = 26.7

14.11. (a) Recommended operating conditions are temperature = +1.4109 and pressure = 1.4142, to achieve predicted filtration time of 36.7.
(b) Recommended operating conditions are temperature = +1.3415 and pressure = 0.0785, to achieve predicted filtration time of 46.0.

14.12. (a) CCD with $k = 2$ and $\alpha = 1.4$. The design is rotatable.
(b) $y = 13.727 + 0.298x_1 - 0.407x_2 - 0.125x_1^2 - 0.079x_2^2 + 0.055x_1x_2$
From the plots and the optimizer, setting x_1 in a range from 0 to +1.4 and setting x_2 between –1 and –1.4 will maximize viscosity.

CHAPTER 15

15.1. (a) Two points on OC curve are $P_a\{d = 35\}$ = 0.95271 and $P_a\{d = 375\}$ = 0.10133.
(b) Two points on OC curve are $P_a\{p = 0.0070\}$ = 0.9519 and $P_a\{p = 0.0750\}$ = 0.1025.
(c) Difference in curves is small. Either is appropriate.

15.3. Two points on OC curve are $P_a\{p = 0.007\}$ = 0.95190 and $P_a\{p = 0.080\}$ = 0.08271.

15.4. $n = 80$, $c = 7$

15.9. Different sample sizes offer different levels of protection. Consumer is protected from an LTPD = 0.05 by $P_a\{N = 5000\}$ = 0.00046 or $P_a\{N = 10{,}000\}$ = 0.00000, but pays for high probability of rejecting acceptable lots (i.e., for $p = 0.025$, $P_a\{N = 5000\}$ = 0.294 while $P_a\{N = 10{,}000\}$ = 0.182).

15.10. AOQL = 0.0234

15.12. (a) Two points on OC curve are $P_a\{p = 0.016\}$= 0.95397 and $P_a\{p = 0.105\}$= 0.09255.
(b) $p = 0.103$
(d) $n = 20$, $c = 0$. This OC curve is much steeper.

(e) For $c = 2$, Pr{reject} = 0.00206, ATI = 60. For $c = 0$, Pr{reject} = 0.09539, ATI = 495

15.15. Normal: sample size code letter = H, $n = 50$, Ac = 1, Re = 2
Tightened: sample size code letter = J, $n = 80$, Ac = 1, Re = 2
Reduced: sample size code letter = H, $n = 20$, Ac = 0, Re = 2

15.16. AOQ = $[P_a \times p \times (N-n)] / [N - P_a \times (n\,p) - (1-P_a) \times (N\,p)]$

15.17. (a) Sample size code letter = L
Normal: $n = 200$, Ac = 3, Re = 4
Tightened: $n = 200$, Ac = 2, Re = 3
Reduced: $n = 80$, Ac = 1, Re = 4

15.19. (a) Minimum cost sampling effort that meets quality requirements is $50{,}001 \le N \le 100{,}000$, $n = 65$, $c = 3$. (b) ATI = 82

CHAPTER 16

16.2. (a) $n = 35$, $k = 1.7$. (b) $Z_{LSL} = 2.857 > 1.7$, so accept lot.
(c) From nomograph, $P_a\{p = 0.05\} \approx 0.38$

16.3. AOQ = $P_a \times p \times (N-n)/N$, → ATI = $n + (1-P_a) \times (N-n)$

16.6. From MIL-STD-105E, $n = 200$ for normal and tightened and $n = 80$ for reduced. Sample sizes required by MIL-STD-414 are considerably smaller than those for MIL-STD-105E.

16.7. (a) From nomograph for variables: $n = 30$, $k = 1.8$
(b) Assume inspection level IV. Sample size code letter = M
Normal: $n = 50$, $M = 1.00$
Tightened: $n = 50$, $M = 1.71$
Reduced: $n = 20$, $M = 4.09$
σ known permits smaller sample sizes than σ unknown.
(c) From nomograph for attributes: $n = 60$, $c = 2$
Variables sampling is more economic when σ is known.
(d) Assume inspection level II. Sample size code letter = L
Normal: $n = 200$, Ac = 5, Re = 6
Tightened: $n = 200$, Ac = 3, Re = 4
Reduced: $n = 80$, Ac = 2, Re = 5
Much larger samples are required for this plan than others.

16.9. Assume inspection level IV. Sample size code letter = O, $n = 100$, $k_{\text{normal}} = 2.00$, $k_{\text{tightened}} = 2.14$. $Z_{LSL} = 3.000 > 2.00$, so accept lot.

16.10. (a) Three points on OC curve are $P_a\{p = 0.001\} = 0.9685$, $P_a\{p = 0.015\} = 0.9531$, and $P_a\{p = 0.070\} = 0.0981$.
(b) ATI = 976
(c) $P_a\{p = 0.001\} = 0.9967$, ATI = 131
(d) $P_a\{p = 0.001\} = 0.9958$, ATI = 158

16.14. For $f = 1/5$, $i = 38$: AFI = 0.5165, $P_a\{p = 0.0375\} = 0.6043$
For $f = 1/25$, $i = 86$: AFI = 0.5272, $P_a\{p = 0.0375\} = 0.4925$

16.16. For $f = 1/2$, $i = 140$: $u = 155.915$, $v = 1333.3$, AFI = 0.5523, $P_a\{p = 0.0015\} = 0.8953$
For $f = 1/10$, $i = 550$: $u = 855.530$, $v = 6666.7$, AFI = 0.2024, $P_a\{p = 0.0015\} = 0.8863$
For $f = 1/100$, $i = 1302$: $u = 4040.00$, $v = 66666.7$, AFI = 0.0666, $P_a\{p = 0.0015\} = 0.9429$

Index

Other Wiley books by Douglas C. Montgomery

Website: www.wiley.com/college/montgomery

Engineering Statistics, Fourth Edition
by D.C. Montgomery, G.C. Runger, and N.F. Hubele
Introduction to engineering statistics, with topical coverage appropriate for a one-semester course. A modest mathematical level, and an applied approach.

Applied Statistics and Probability for Engineers, Fourth Edition
by D.C. Montgomery and G.C. Runger
Introduction to engineering statistics, with topical coverage appropriate for either a one- or two-semester course. An applied approach to solving real-world engineering problems.

Probability and Statistics in Engineering, Fourth Edition
by W.W. Hines, D.C. Montgomery, D.M. Goldsman, and C.M. Borror
Website: www.wiley.com/college/hines
For a first two-semester course in applied probability and statistics for undergraduate students, or a one-semester refresher for graduate students, covering probability from the start.

Design and Analysis of Experiments, Sixth Edition
by Douglas C. Montgomery
An introduction to the design and analysis of experiments, with the modest prerequisite of a first course in statistical methods.

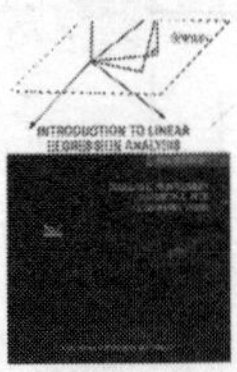

Introduction to Linear Regression Analysis, Fourth Edition
by D.C. Montgomery, E.A. Peck, and G.G. Vining
A comprehensive and thoroughly up-to-date look at regression analysis, still the most widely used technique in statistics today.

Response Surface Methodology: Process and Product Optimization Using Designed Experiments, Second Edition
by R.H. Myers and D.C. Montgomery
Website: www.wiley.com/college/myers
The exploration and optimization of response surfaces, for graduate courses in experimental design, and for applied statisticians, engineers, and chemical and physical scientists.

Generalized Linear Models: With Applications in Engineering and the Sciences
by R.H. Myers, D.C. Montgomery, and G.G. Vining
Website: www.wiley.com/college/myers
An introductory text or reference on Generalized Linear Models (GLMs). The range of theoretical topics and applications appeals both to students and practicing professionals.

Introduction to Time Series Analysis and Forecasting
by Douglas C. Montgomery, Cheryl L. Jennings, Murat Kulahci
Methods for modeling and analyzing time series data, to draw inferences about the data and generate forecasts useful to the decision maker. Minitab and SAS are used to illustrate how the methods are implemented in practice. For advanced undergrad/first-year graduate, with a prerequisite of basic statistical methods. Portions of the book require calculus and matrix algebra.

Quality Improvement Tools

Process Flow Diagram

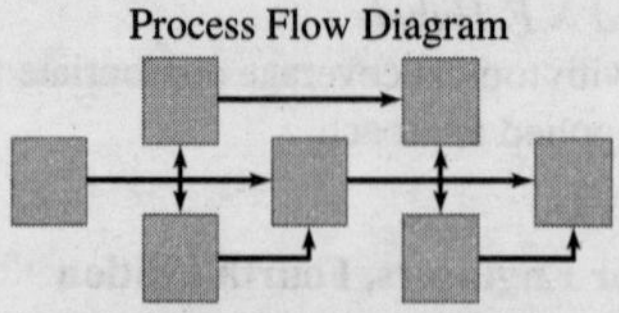

- Expresses detailed knowledge of the process
- Identifies process flow and interaction among the process steps
- Identifies potential control points

Cause-and-Effect (Fishbone) Diagram

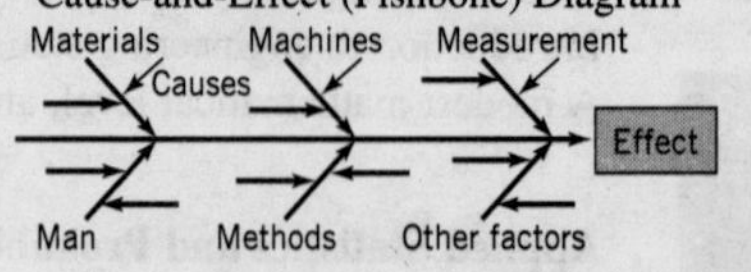

- All contributing factors and their relationships are displayed
- Identifies problem areas where data can be collected and analyzed

Control Chart

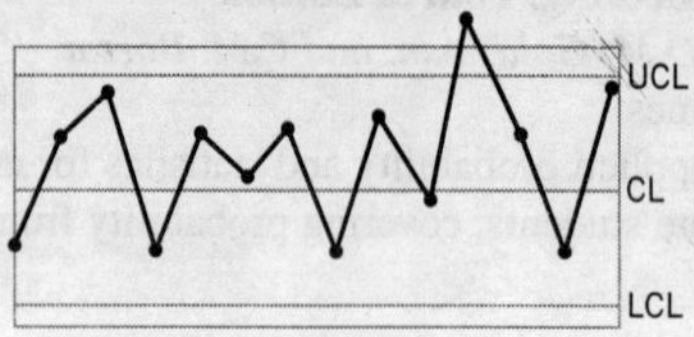

- Helps reduce variability
- Monitors performance over time
- Allows process corrections to prevent rejections
- Trends and out-of-control conditions are immediately detected

Check Sheet

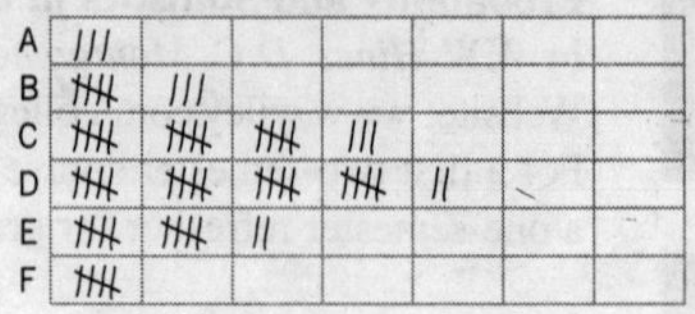

- Simplifies data collection and analysis
- Spots problem areas by frequency of location, type, or cause

Pareto Diagram

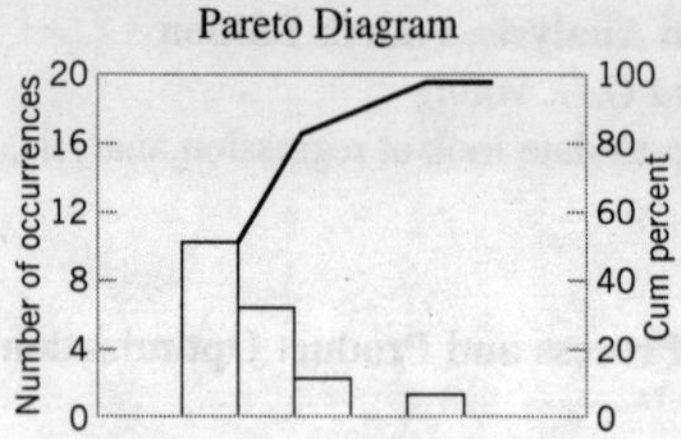

- Identifies most significant problems to be worked first
- Historically 80% of the problems are due to 20% of the factors
- Shows the vital few

Scatter Plot

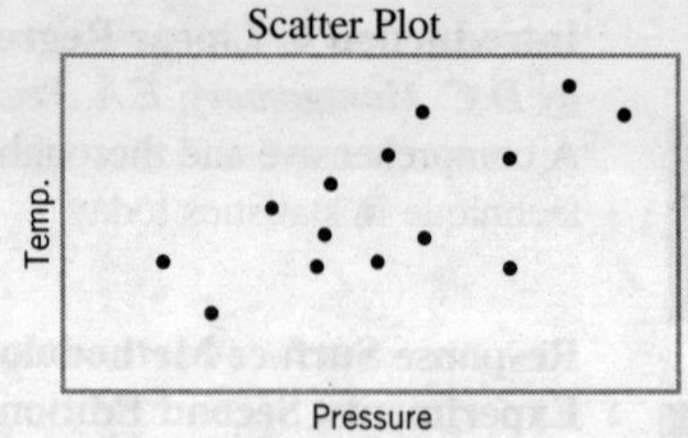

- Identifies the relationship between two variables
- A positive, negative, or no relationship can be easily detected

Design of Experiments (DOX)

- Useful in process development and troubleshooting
- Identifies magnitude and direction of important process variable effects
- Greatly reduces the number of runs required with a process experiment
- Identifies interaction among process variables
- Useful in engineering design and development
- Focuses on optimizing system performance

Histogram

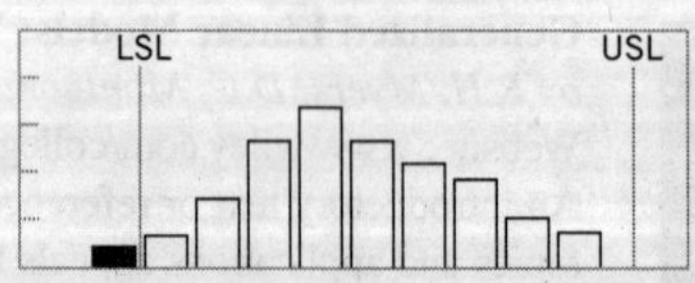

- The shape shows the nature of the distribution of the data
- The central tendency (average) and variability are easily seen
- Specification limits can be used to display the capability of the process

England's Dark DREAMING

THE BOOK OF

England's Dark DREAMING

A Series of Drawings on the Subject of

THE MATTER OF ENGLAND

and

THE WORLD TURNED UPSIDE DOWN

Including an additional essay investigating the related subject of DEEP ENGLAND

by the Artist

PAUL WATSON

with a Foreword by

DAVID SOUTHWELL of HOOKLAND

The Lazarus Corporation, Brighton

First Published in Great Britain in 2018
by the Lazarus Corporation
Brighton, United Kingdom.
www.lazaruscorporation.co.uk

ISBN 978-0-9934736-1-6

Contents

Foreword

by David Southwell

"This is the essence of England: in the field waits an unearthing that tells of a time before the English."

— C.L. Nolan, from his 1933 BBC National Programme talk *England, A Peculiarly Persistent Lie*.

When the county becomes drought pale, the ghost lines appear. Iron Age villages. Lost hill figures. The land as a book whose invisible ink is revealed. The withering trauma of heat bringing revelation, exposing a map of connective tissue to past. The soil giving up its stories. A rising of mystery through place.

That was the summer of my sixth year. It is my summer now. It the essence of the book you hold within your hands.

Paul has produced a work of an England under stress and an unearthing. A folkloric pushing through the layers of memory, through layers of occulted history, to the inform today's psychic static. He charts the growth of dark vines through the sun-bullied cracks of the once green lawn that now disrupt the deep dream of England. You hold the equivalent of the rude music that breaks the May Day dawn. The old ways given permission, given manifestation, to shatter the sleepy peace of place that never truly existed.

It is entirely apposite that this book has come to surface through Paul's harrowing of the fields of English dreaming. The unearthing is one of the most prevalent and powerful tropes in the folk horror mode of Gothic. There in the strange skull discovered whilst ploughing in *Blood On Satan's Claw*, there in the bone whistle of M.R. James' *Oh, Whistle, And I'll Come To You, My Lad*. There even in *Quatermass And The Pit*. In what some like to call English eerie, the past always works its way to discovery. When it breaks ground, the ancient, hidden forces behind fable are unleashed. Trust me, when you have read it, you will see how beautifully the book fits into the English tradition of digging stuff up that disturbs the structures of class and power.

I have been incredibly lucky to see this book emerge, not just online in weekly revelation of the latest drawing session, not just in various iterations of its core essay, but through discussion with Paul himself. Across wooden tables scarred by decades of pub life, holding potential for archaeological developments in cigarette burn dating and graffiti sigil interpretation, he talked me through his and its journey. One figure being joined by another on the road till the long march is that of a crowd. One voice of the land becoming two, becoming a dozen and eventually a choir singing ancient songs to the noise of the modern world.

Paul has let me walk alongside this project, even at points when the destination was not clear to him. For this work has been an unearthing for him as well. Breaking ground, discovering fragments. Clues causing him to carve deeper in the ghost soil. Working like a crazed archaeologist moving from pottery shards thrown up by ploughing to an eventual plunging down to Saxon burial or Bell-Beaker hoard. Seen him scrape away at land wight loam, pull away clumps of mythic dirt to give us this treasure.

I remember December 2016, the moment in the *Bree Louise* — now erased by that most modern of monsters which leaves a ruin-wake as it moves across the country, HS2 — when Paul put down his pint of porter. Almost as if explaining the drawings for both out benefit, said: "It's a telling of the land by its spirits. It's a new entry in the Matter of Britain." I grasped then the shape and importance of the project, but it is only in the unity of the whole in *England's Dark Dreaming* that you can finally understand the harsh beauty, the power of what he has unearthed.

One promise I will make on behalf of what you are about to read is that it possesses dark gravity. The drawings will pull ideas from their previously safe orbits, drag stories towards them. It may even play havoc with your emotional tides. It will certainly alter the trajectory of objects travelling across your inner mythscape. There is no benefit in me providing here the narrative that the series of twenty-four drawings pull from me. You will find it in Hookland, which has continually been powered by their energy.

While I hesitate to call what I write about landscape punk, what I create in Hookland as my artistic practice[1], in Paul's practice I see someone who walks the same territory. We tramp towns and downs, backwoods and backstreets. We listen to the spirits of place, we listen to the what-if sci-fi futures of our childhoods echoing backwards to the now. Folklore for both us is not just trapping, but a mouth for mystery, for place itself. We poke sticks into pools and puddles knowing that not all monsters are myth. Walking we scuff the ghost soil, release the stories held within landscape. And yes, we both often produce work in a Gothic mode. In Paul's case, gloriously and gracefully so.

In times of radical cultural and economic change, Romanticism also rises.

It may start with Paleo diet regimes, rejections of modernity. It may begin with a swathe of environment writing as a middle-class commodity that simultaneously fetishes and insulates them from having a direct experience with place. However, in times of trouble, the glorification of the past and nature are wide and wild disease. Unfortunately, it is especially prone to be caught by those in the areas of conservation and nationalism, where the infection may eventually turn to the feverish wankery of excluding blood and soil narratives[2].

When the Romanticism becomes illness, burning through our collective dreamscape, antibodies are released. The Gothic is one them. Tapping on the shoulder, pointing out that those old ways come with a tithe of blood. Reminding that nature often delivers starvation seasons, long hungers; blind and casual death at its extremes. Gothic as the cooling shadow where the confusion of fever dream is broken. I am of the belief that the current revival in folk horror, and the recent outstanding work by John Harrigan, Melissa Harrison, Stephen Prince, Layla Legard, and Paul himself, is part of this process.

For part of what Paul has unearthed with this project are the antibodies inherent in myth and the land itself. Unleash the primal lusts of woodwose and flesh may be torn. Mab's faërie Otherworld enfolding our reality is clearly a country of sharp and wicked teeth. Call and response of cup and ring may mean blood on stone. The reaping of harvest always requires sacrifice — the scything of the Neck — and as any magician will tell you, crossroad spirits always demand paying.

In the shadow of Paul's work, there is no escaping the brutal truths of our collective mythscape. Facing these truths is necessary at the moment. Falsehood is the only currency of Deep England, its leaders are dealers in seductive lies, planting seeds that risk the most poisonous of dark harvests. I make no claims to intellectual strength, I am a bear of little brains, but I do know this, *England's Dark Dreaming* gives a mouth to mythic infrastructure of England. One day, this book may be the gallery show, complete with documentary, that it so clearly deserves to be.

Whatever iterations its future holds, it will remain an essential entry in the Matter of England, a vital telling of the land itself.

— David Southwell

1. I am from Essex, where that degree of self-poncery is frowned upon.

2. As was demonstrated in June 2018, even some of the fiercest writing talents of the nation are not immune to this terrible symptom.

David Southwell is the author of a number of books that have been translated into a dozen languages. He currently writes about Landscape Punk and is putting together the Hookland Edition of *The Phoenix Guide to Strange England, County by County* on Twitter at @HooklandGuide

Introduction

England's Dark Dreaming has dominated my artistic practice for the past two years. The series consists of 24 charcoal drawings, each one metre high and seventy centimetres wide, the figures depicted more-or-less lifesize. Each drawing emerged from one-or-more of nearly thirty three-hour life-drawing sessions with one of nine different life models scheduled specifically for this project. Each drawing was then worked on further for several hours, until the individual piece was finished.

The series was not conceived fully-formed, but rather evolved and developed through the two years of its life, reacting to events in the outside world as they happened.

Alongside creating the artwork I was also researching all the related concepts of the dream England which informed the series. Sometimes I'd write up my notes and publish them on my blog - the expanded *Deep England* essay included in this book is one such example which was particularly well-received and generated significant discussion online.

Throughout these two years of work I've been posting snapshots of the drawings — in various stages of completion — on Twitter (@lazcorp), and then posting the finished drawings on my website as each was completed. The positive reaction they've generated has been fantastic, humbling, and uplifting.

The decision to publish the series in book format was therefore straightforward: it allows the people who have enjoyed the series unfolding since 2016 (or who have discovered it since) to own good quality reproductions of the finished drawings, and it allows me to earn some money from all my hard work. One day perhaps the *England's Dark Dreaming* drawings will be exhibited in a gallery where people can see them in the flesh at their full size, but until then this book is the definitive experience, and will always be the definitive record of them.

To conclude this introduction, I'd like to take this opportunity to thank the life models who worked with me to create these drawings, without whom none of this would have been possible: Sharon, Tom, Rachel, Carole, Rowy, Katie, Gracie, Mark, and Priss.

Paul Watson
Brighton, July 2018
www.lazaruscorporation.co.uk

About England's Dark Dreaming

In April 2015 I wrote a blogpost in which I drew comparisons between our current times and the social and political upheaval around the time of the English Revolution (upheavals separate to the armed conflict of the civil war itself):

> "The whole of Britain (not just England) seems to be in a similar mode of radicalism and revaluing at the moment, albeit that blogs and online articles have replaced pamphlets and broadsheets, and this time they're talking about landscape, rewilding, psychogeography, archaeology, myth, and hauntology as well as politics and government. The British political landscape has also changed over the past few years: the recent seven-party televised election debates replacing the three-party debates of 2010, the rise of Scottish Nationalism and last year's close referendum on Scottish Independence (and the inevitable prospect of a second referendum at some point in the future), talk about devolution of central government power to local governments in England as well as Scotland and Wales that might actually happen (although maybe I'm being too optimistic there), and the Snowden leaks that prompted people to re-evaluate the reach of government into private life. I should say that I'm not expecting Britain or England to erupt into civil war or revolution, but I think the similarities in the upsurge of radical rethinking and revaluing is notable, and non-violent change seems afoot."

The post was written in the final days of the Conservative/Liberal Democrat coalition government of 2010-2015 whose austerity policies slashed the budgets that protected and supported the poorest and most vulnerable, and whose Immigration Act (2014) led to the Windrush scandal in 2018. Since writing that post we've seen the emergence of new left-wing radicalism in the Labour Party and, at the other end of the spectrum, the extending reach of far-right politics into the mainstream, reflected in the UKIP bubble, which deflated rapidly when the Conservative Party made a dramatic shift to the right to secure the hard-right vote.

We've also seen continued austerity and hostility to immigrants from Conservative governments under Cameron (2015-2016) and May (2016-), and the Brexit referendum, in which the country was split in many ways: old against young, Wales and England (with some notable exceptions, particularly in London and the South East) against Scotland and Northern Ireland, and many more ways depending on which demographic you're looking at: education level, socio-economic class, etc. The Brexit result also triggered a rise in racist attacks (both verbal and physical violence) as the far-right look to expand on what they see as a referendum mandate for violence and open displays of hatred.

This is a country which is just starting to experience again (and still only at a relatively small scale compared to things that are happening elsewhere in the world) the trauma of wide-scale socio-political upheaval at societal, familial, and personal levels. That this trauma coincides with a growing concern about land and place is therefore unsurprising. And it's therefore also unsurprising that my artistic practice should reflect this socio-political upheaval by utilising myth and folklore, which are older, deeper, stories about the land and our place in it.

The *England's Dark Dreaming* series of drawings, which I began in 2016 and finished in 2018, draws on all of this: current commentary, past dreams, political activism, calls to the past, cries to the future, ancient myths, future legends. Darkness, shadows, politics, gestural marks, folklore and myth, weird mystery, and the mysterious weird, all scrawled in burnt and blackened wood. However, despite those references to folklore and myth, *England's Dark Dreaming* probably owes more to Derek Jarman's *The Last of England* than it does to *Le Morte d'Arthur*. Using mythic archetypes allows me to make allusions that would otherwise be unwieldy to include, although they do introduce the potential downside that the viewer concentrates only on the archetype rather than on the references they embody.

There's a temptation in dark times to retreat into a fantasy of the past, and my use of folklore and myth may lead some people to conclude that this is what I'm doing, but this was not the aim of this series. *England's Dark Dreaming* concerns itself — although neither wholly nor blatantly — with contemporary politics: the rise of the far-right, their language always laden with anger, violence, threat, talk of "traitors" and locking up people who speak out against them. It's my reaction, realised in the Gothic mode, against a country where calmness, truth, and reason have been discarded in favour of the sophistry and screaming of the far-right.

The series is not dominated by political comment, though. It was not intended as a series of political cartoons or sloganeering, but rather as something that I hope has weaved several themes into a more complex whole. The political is inseparable from the landscape so the work can be thought of as a palimpsest, the layers of folklore, land, and the movements of history all visible in its surface.

The drawings should not be read as adjacent panels in a comic strip - there is no simple narrative step from one to the next. That said, the projection of a narrative onto a numbered series of figurative drawings is unavoidable. To use the analogy of comic books — for those familiar of contemporary comics — the drawings are probably best understood as the covers of a series of twenty four comics, each highlighting the main character or action extracted from a single comic without giving a full narrative account of the narrative journey from one comic to the next. For those unfamiliar with contemporary comics, they can be imagined as the twenty-four frontispieces for a series of twenty-four volumes of a very long novel.

The problem with the analogies above — comic covers or frontispieces — suggests that the drawings illustrate, and are secondary to, a primary text. There is no primary text, there is no additional narrative that is only revealed via these windows into it: the drawings stand alone. Anyone looking at the drawings will, of course, project their own narrative onto the pieces in the series, and into the spaces between them.

I mentioned above that the drawings are "realised in the Gothic mode" and this is something I want to expand on a bit. In her 2006 book *Contemporary Gothic* Catherine Spooner makes the argument that the Gothic is not a fixed genre or classification that excludes other classifications, but rather a mode in which a piece of art can be made.

This non-exclusory relationship to the Gothic feels to me like a more accurate explanation of the relationship of the *England's Dark Dreaming* drawings to the Gothic: a series of drawings, created from life-drawings, using mythic and folkloric elements for socio-political commentary, in the Gothic mode.

There are, of course, as many definitions of the word "Gothic" as there are people writing about it (and it seems to be a growing area of academic study).

I grew up in the 1980s and 1990s clad in black (and the occasional paisley shirt) and listening to the Sisters of Mercy, Joy Division, Bauhaus, the Fields of the Nephilim, and so on. As such my view of the Gothic is very much coloured by the music/subculture side of things, and even then from within a very specific time period and English region. I don't want you thinking of Dracula capes and a coffin obsession when I'm thinking of the Joy Division's *Day of the Lords* or the Sisters of Mercy's *Reptile House* EP.

The trouble with the term Gothic is the myriad of different meanings it has to different people - and that's after you exclude the barbaric tribes rampaging in the Roman Empire in the 5th Century, the architecture of the High and Late Middle Ages, and the Victorian novels.

In a blogpost in August 2017 I loosely defined what I meant by "the Gothic" in relation to *England's Dark Dreaming* as:

1. A dark mix of emotion and energy,
2. A knowing tension between performative identities expressed through drawing styles and the poses, props, and lighting of the figures, and the quest for authentic (and sometimes anguished) self-expression, and
3. An impression of impending descent into disintergration.

It's a pick-and-mix definition borrowed from various scholarly studies, but that's as close as I'll probably get to a working definition as far as it applies to my own artwork.

Later in 2017, and half in jest, I coined the term "Albionic Gothic" in a tweet to describe not just *England's Dark Dreaming*, but also the work of others who are working in a similar vein, such as the *Hookland* writing of David Southwell and *Armageddon Gospels*, the 2018 film written by John Harrigan for Foolish People. There are clear differences between our respective artworks, not least the chosen medium, but they all touch on similar themes using the same mode. It's not just a touch of the "English Eerie", but also the fascination with the history and mythology of England.

And this reference back to English history brings me back to where I started talking about comparisons between our current times and the social and political upheaval around the time of the English Civil War. These comparisons have, for me, been increasingly clear, especially on re-reading Christopher Hill's 1972 book *The World Turned Upside Down: Radical ideas during the English Revolution*. This should go some way to explaining the decision to create the cover of this book in the general style of a pamphlet from the time of the English Revolution.

However *England's Dark Dreaming* is no manifesto, but a documentary of the troubles of the past two years, viewed through a filter of mythology and folkore.

Paul Watson,
Brighton, June 2018.

The Drawings

1. The Beginning (2016)
2. Separation (2016)
3. Ritual, Part I (2016)
4. In the Woods (2016)
5. A Chronic Poison (2016)
6. Ritual, Part II (2017)
7. The Glorification of Ignorance (2017)
8. Antenora, after Doré (2017)
9. Come Unto The Corn (2017)
10. Mab (2017)
11. Heel to Haunch/Transformation (2017)
12. Ritual, Part III (2017)
13. The Procession, Part I (2017)
14. At the Crossroads (2017)
15. Ritual, Part IV (2017)
16. Healing Hand (2017)
17. The Procession, Part II (2017)
18. May Queen (2018)
19. The Green Man (2018)
20. Spirit of Albion, Memory of the Land (2018)
21. The Procession, Part III (2018)
22. The Birth of Albion from the Shadow of the Forest (2018)
23. The Green Man, II (2018)
24. Departure/The Midnight Shore (2018)

1. The Beginning

2016, charcoal on paper, 100 × 70cm / 39.3 × 27.5"

The two figures depicted in this first drawing are the two main characters that are depicted periodically across the series of twenty-four drawings.

The pose of the two figures is a distorted echo of the Long Man of Wilmington chalk hill figure in Sussex. The hill carving of a single figure holding two staffs transformed into two figures holding a staff each. It's not certain when this hill figure was cut into the landscape, but recent archaeological work has suggested it is relatively modern (16th or 17th century) rather than being an ancient hill figure like others in Britain. The parallel staffs also form an entrance way, the outline of a door, through which the figures are stepping into the series of drawings.

The two figures are at the start of their journey across England's myth-landscape. They are presented as "Guardians of a loveless isle" and "gloomy browed", as in David Bowie's 1970 song *The Supermen.*

The figures, drawn from slightly below eye-level so that they look down on the viewer, also reference the legends of the island of Albion as a land of giants.

2. Separation

2016, charcoal on paper, 100 × 70cm / 39.3 × 27.5"

The two main characters appear at a point of division, the pivotal point before conflict.

3. Ritual, Part I

2016, charcoal on paper, 100 × 70cm / 39.3 × 27.5"

This is the first of an embedded mini-series of four "Ritual" drawings.

4. In the Woods

2016, charcoal on paper, 100 × 70cm / 39.3 × 27.5"

This is the first appearance of a somewhat mysterious character. She reappears with dark hair as a version of Hekate in *At the Crossroads* and *The Procession, Part II* before returning to her original state in *Departure/The Midnight Shore.*

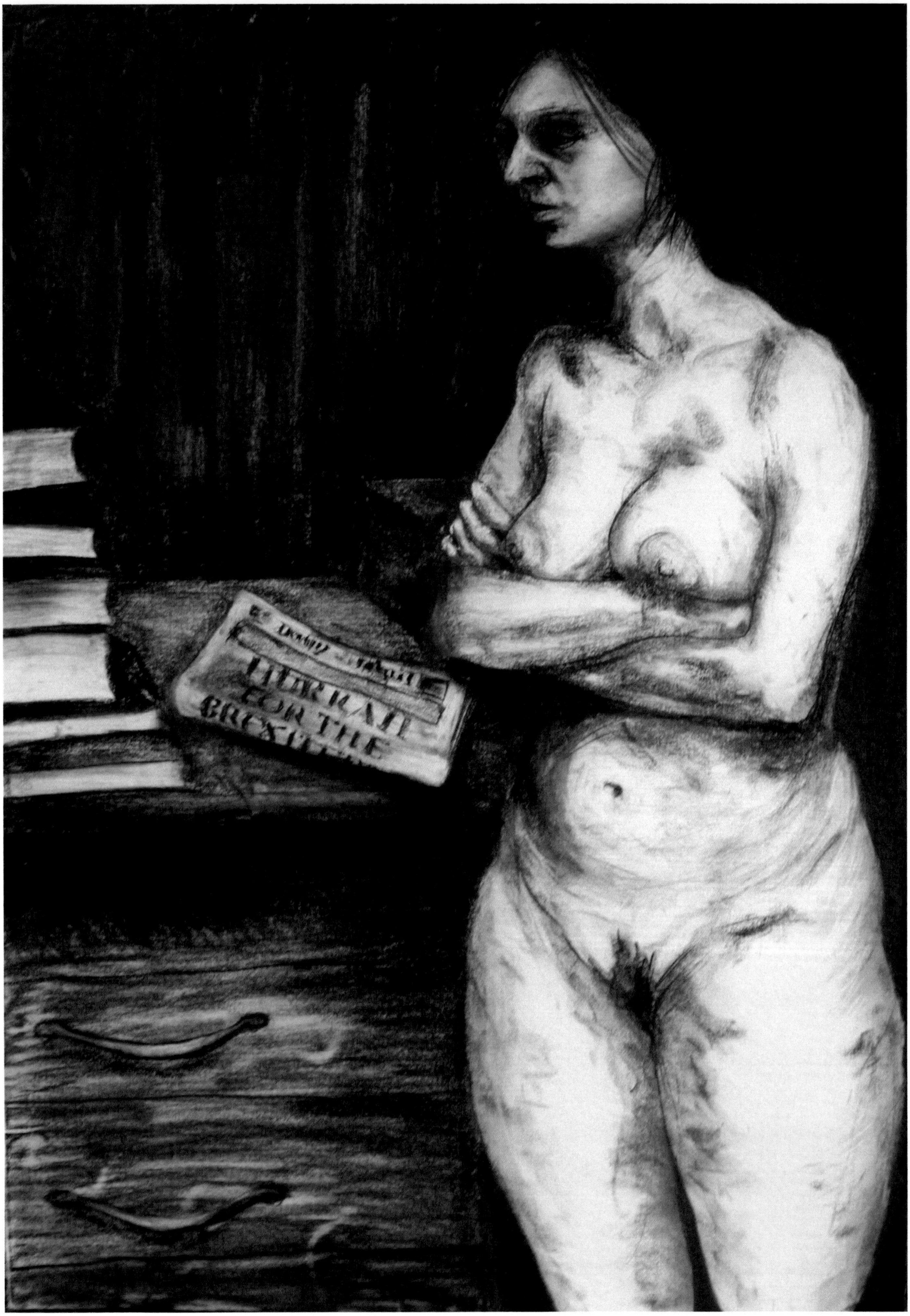
HURRAH
FOR THE

5. A Chronic Poison

2016, charcoal on paper, 100 × 70cm / 39.3 × 27.5"

The "Hurrah for the Brexiteers" headline on the copy of the Daily Mail 'newspaper' on the table beside the figure should require no explanation for those familiar with the Daily Mail's infamous past (and present).

6. Ritual, Part II

2017, charcoal on paper, 100 × 70cm / 39.3 × 27.5"

This is the second of the mini-series of "Ritual" drawings, reversing the view from "Ritual, Part I."

7. The Glorification of Ignorance

2017, charcoal on paper, 100 × 70cm / 39.3 × 27.5"

This drawing probably least requires any explanation or commentary.

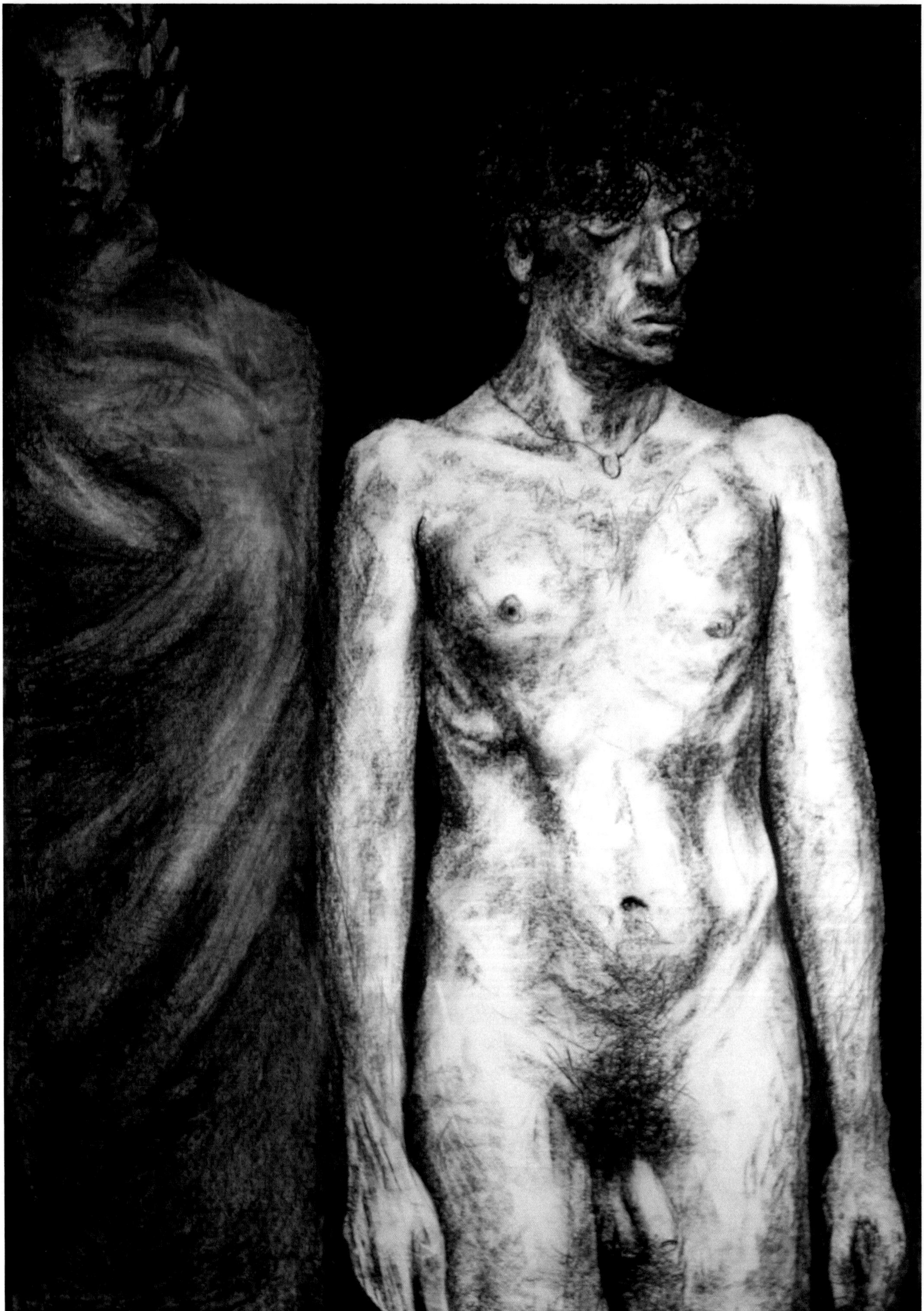

8. Antenora, after Doré

2017, charcoal on paper, 100 × 70cm / 39.3 × 27.5"

In Dante's *Divine Comedy* Antenora is the second zone of Cocytus (the ninth and lowest circle of hell) reserved for traitors to their country. The drawing is based on Gustave Doré's engraving for Canto XXXII of the *Divine Comedy*, showing Dante and Virgil standing on the surface of a frozen lake where traitors are buried up to their necks in the ice.

As mentioned in the introductory text to this series, this was drawn in a climate where the more extreme right-wing press have been using inflammatory language, describing their opponents as "enemies of the people" (Daily Mail front page, Nov 4, 2016), "saboteurs" (Daily Mail front page, Apr 19, 2017), and "traitors" (Daily Mail front page, Dec 14, 2017). This violent vocabulary is mirrored across social media.

That deliberately divisive language would be used by the character in the previous drawing, *The Glorification of Ignorance*, but this drawing is less violent and more somber, a reflection on what these words actually mean.

Cocytus (Canto XXXII) by Gustave Doré (1857). Public Domain.

9. Come Unto the Corn

2017, charcoal and gold/silver leaf on paper, 100 × 70cm / 39.3 × 27.5"

This is the only drawing in this series that explicitly references some of my earlier artwork (a drawing and a photograph of the same name, both from a few months before I began this series, shown below). The drawing is named after a 2015 song by spook-folk band *The Hare and the Moon.*

The figure bears a sheaf of corn and a sickle and wears a corn mask, and has a mythic role related to the Harvest and all its connotations of blood, death, and sacrifice (and rebirth) as in the traditional British folk song *John Barleycorn.*

As a minor point for non-British readers, in British English "corn" refers to wheat (and sometimes barley or oats), whereas in American English "corn" refers to maize. The artist resolutely draws in British English.

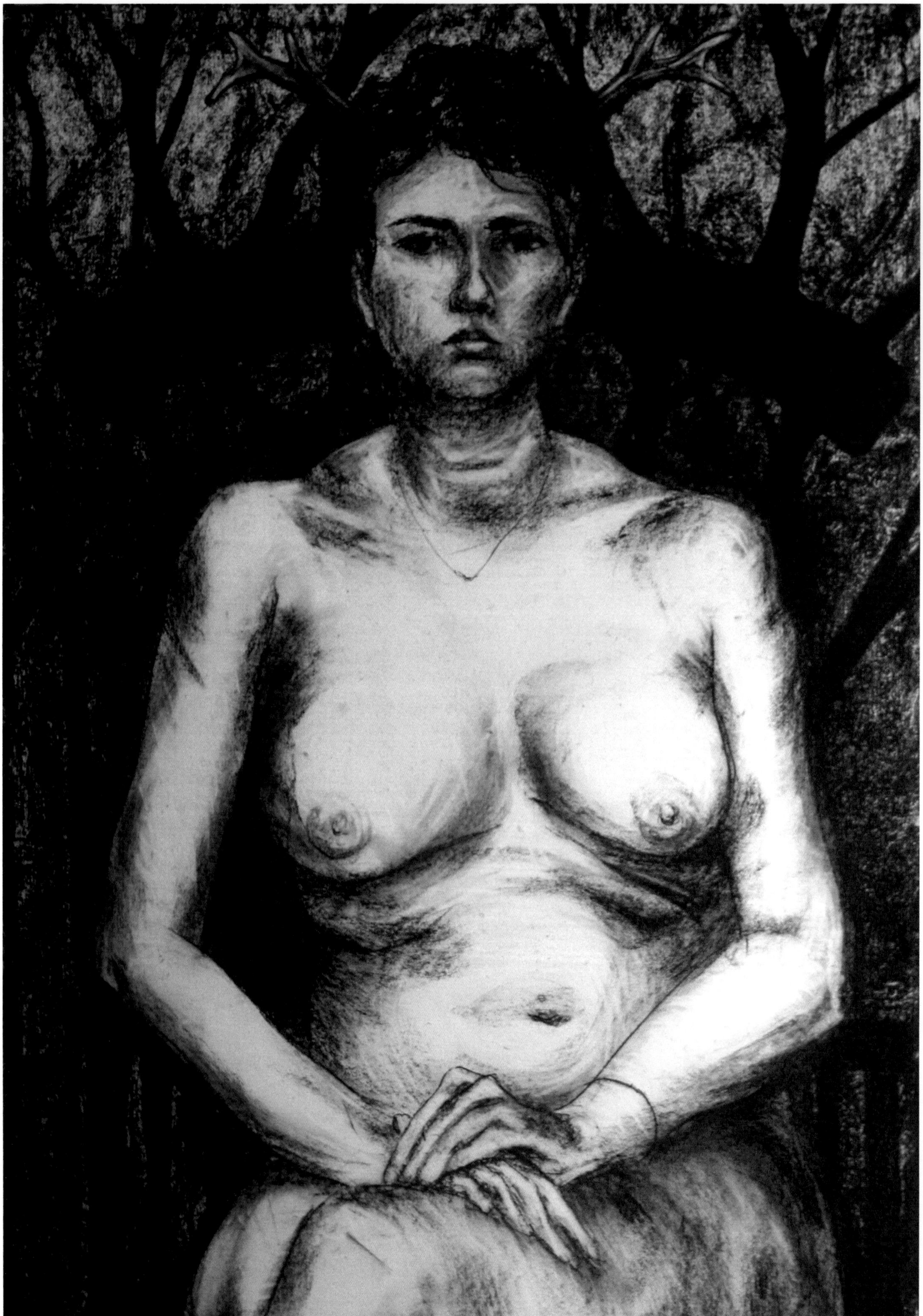

10. Mab

2017, charcoal on paper, 100 × 70cm / 39.3 × 27.5"

Queen Mab is an English folkloric figure particularly connected to dreams. She is described in Shakespeare's *Romeo and Juliet* as "the fairies' midwife."

Mab here is antlered, denoting power (similar to the symbolism of the horns on Michelangelo's *Moses*) rather than evil, as well as connecting her to the animal world.

11. Heel to Haunch/Transformation

2017, charcoal on paper, 100 × 70cm / 39.3 × 27.5"

Barely lit, the main male character crouches on the floor, his face hidden in shadows.

12. Ritual, Part III

2017, charcoal on paper, 100 × 70cm / 39.3 × 27.5"

This is the third of the mini-series of "Ritual" drawings. The character is now outside in a cornfield, bearing a sickle (the attributes of the corn and the sickle link this drawing to the earlier *Come Unto the Corn* drawing).

13. The Procession, Part I

2017, charcoal on paper, 100 × 70cm / 39.3 × 27.5"

This is the first in an embedded mini-series of “Procession” drawings.

Two figures dominate the foreground, the one on the left is the main male character. The female figure is not represented in any other drawing in this series.

In the mid-ground, between the two foreground figures, a third figure is just visible in near-silhouette, wearing an antlered headdress similar to that found at the Mesolithic site at Star Carr in North Yorkshire. This mysterious figure is also part of the Procession.

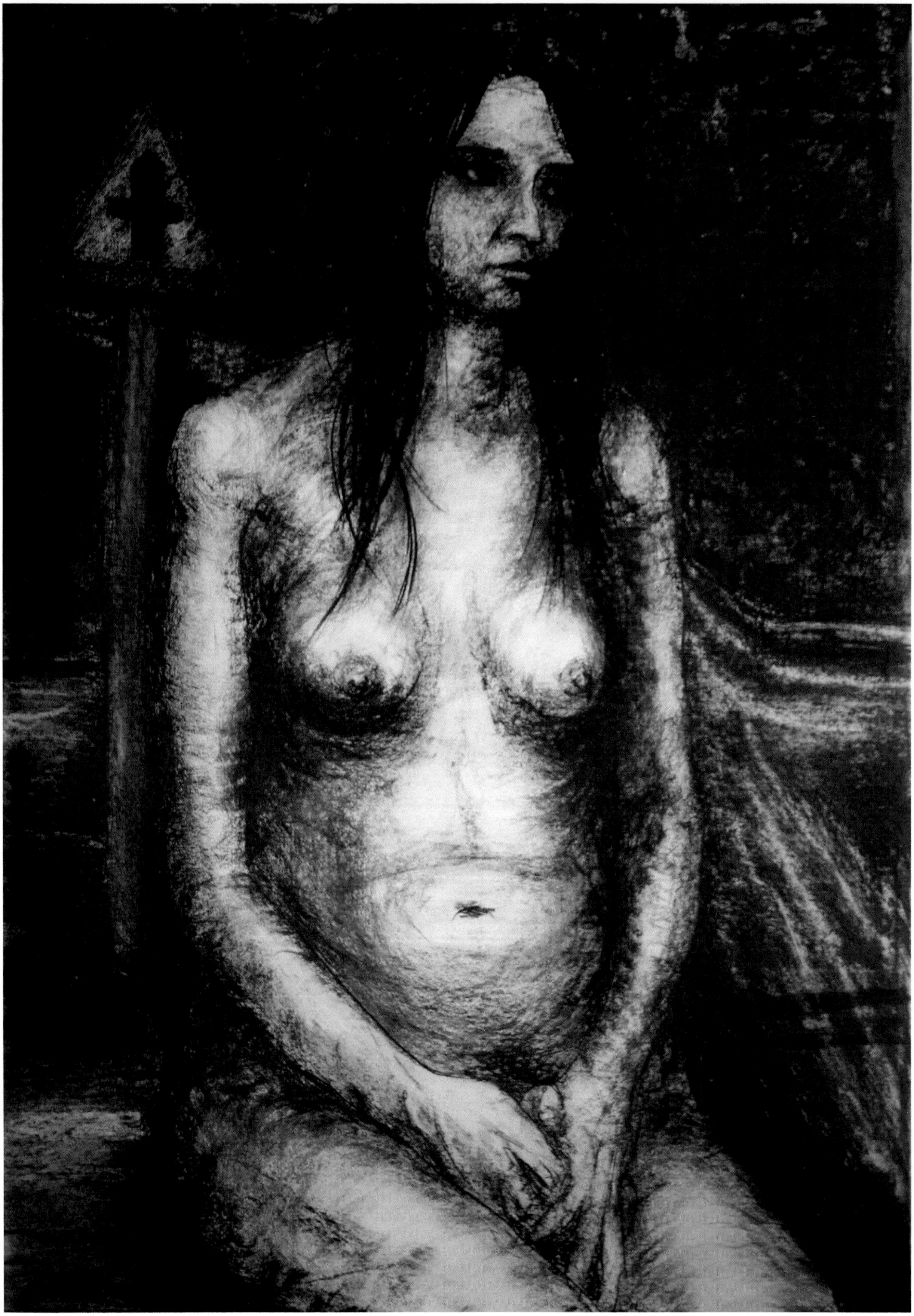

14. At the Crossroads

2017, charcoal on paper, 100 × 70cm / 39.3 × 27.5"

The Ancient Greek goddess Hekate is connected with crossroads as well as with magic (her most famous priestess, Medea, has been the subject of some of my earlier artwork), and the figure in this drawing can be seen in part as an interpretation of that mythological character.

The character in this drawing was first portrayed with fair hair in the earlier drawing *In the Woods*. Now she has transformed into Hekate, taking on a more mythic role. She reappears in *The Procession, Part II* and finally, returning to her original state in *Departure/The Midnight Shore*.

Crossroads are places of decision and changes of direction. They represent liminality and so frequently appear in folklore and superstition.

The atemporality of the series is briefly thrown by the inclusion of a contemporary roadsign and traces of headlights on the roads in the background.

15. Ritual, Part IV

2017, charcoal on paper, 100 × 70cm / 39.3 × 27.5"

This is the fourth and final drawing of the mini-series of "Ritual" drawings.

The "cave paintings" in the drawing are mostly stencilled hands, which tend to be from the Paleolithic, but there are also two Cup-and-Ring marks which is a design that dates from the Early Neolithic (carved rather than painted) and can be found in several places in Britain.

In comparison to *Ritual, Part III*, where the blade of the sickle infers death or violence, in this drawing the ritual has taken a less violent and more creative direction.

16. Healing Hand

2017, charcoal on paper, 100 × 70cm / 39.3 × 27.5"

This drawing is clearly linked through the background with the preceding drawing, *Ritual, Part IV*.

This is the second drawing that references the song *This Corrosion* by the Sisters of Mercy in its title (the other being *Heel to Haunch/Transformation*). Both drawings depict the same character, the main male character of the series.

17. The Procession, Part II

2017, charcoal on paper, 100 × 70cm / 39.3 × 27.5"

This is the second of the mini-series of "Procession" drawings.

The two figures are the Hekate character from *At the Crossroads* and the recurring main female character of the series. In front of them is a figure wearing antlers.

17. The Procession, Part II

2017, charcoal on paper, 100 × 70cm / 39.3 × 27.5"

This is the second of the mini-series of "Procession" drawings.

The two figures are the Hekate character from *At the Crossroads* and the recurring main female character of the series. In front of them is a figure wearing antlers.

18. May Queen

2018, charcoal on paper, 100 × 70cm / 39.3 × 27.5"

The May Queen is a personification of Spring, celebrated at May Day, the beginning of Spring. In some folklore sources the May Queen is killed at the end of the May Day festivals, a necessary sacrifice to ensure a more fruitful future.

19. The Green Man

2018, charcoal on paper, 100 × 70cm / 39.3 × 27.5"

Green Men appear frequently as architectural ornaments on churches and other buildings across Europe from the 5th century onwards, human faces either wreathed in leaves or with branches sprouting from the mouth. There's no historical evidence of what they were meant to signify, but popular imagination links them to nature spirits, fertility symbols, and woodwose (wild men of the woods, which were common figures in Medieval European stories and art).

For the purposes of this series he can be read as a combination between tree spirit and woodwose, representing the antithesis of human civilization.

20. Spirit of Albion, Memory of the Land

2018, charcoal on paper, 100 × 70cm / 39.3 × 27.5"

In the months before this drawing was planned a DNA analysis of a Mesolithic human male fossil in Somerset nicknamed 'Cheddar Man' found that the man had "dark or dark to black skin, blue/green eyes and dark brown possibly black hair". As such, it made perfect sense to me to have the spirit of England be a reflection of those earliest continual inhabitants.

21. The Procession, Part III

2018, charcoal on paper, 100 × 70cm / 39.3 × 27.5"

This is the third and final drawing in the mini-series of "Procession" drawings. The two figures are the May Queen and the Green Man. This brings the procession to a conclusion.

22. The Birth of Albion from the Shadow of the Forest

2018, charcoal on paper, 100 × 70cm / 39.3 × 27.5"

A second appearance by the Spirit of Albion, the *genius loci* of the island of Britain.

23. The Green Man, II

2018, charcoal on paper, 100 × 70cm / 39.3 × 27.5"

In his third and final appearance the Green Man appears seated or enthroned.

24. Departure/The Midnight Shore

2018, charcoal on paper, 100 × 70cm / 39.3 × 27.5"

This final drawing in the series breaks the developed format of the rest of the series by having the only clearly visible figure in the mid-ground rather than the foreground, the foreground figure being little more than a silhouette.

The figure with her back turned to the viewer first appeared in *In the Woods*. She took on an aspect of Hekate in *At the Crossroads* and *The Procession, Part II* before finally returning to her original form here.

The foreground figure, in darkness, is the main female character of the series.

Deep England - an essay

A shorter version of this article was originally published at www.lazaruscorporation.co.uk/blogs/artists-notebook/posts/deep-england

On some days, when the veil between worlds is at its thinnest, it is said that you can glimpse the mythical land of Deep England, particularly if you read the Daily Mail, the Daily Express, or the Daily Telegraph too much.

Invariably rural and white, Deep England manages simultaneously to be Medieval, Georgian, Victorian, and interwar - where ruddy-faced yeoman farmers tug their forelocks at the local squire while their wives practice traditional rural crafts to the sound of church bells and the smack of leather on willow. In his essay *Skewing the Picture*[1] China Miéville refers to it as the picturesque (although it's a very English version of the picturesque):

> "You know the picturesque when you see it. Higgledy-piggledy, a winding country path, overhanging hedgerow, tumbledown cottages."

As part of the conclusion to his 1924 speech[2] *What England means to me* Conservative Prime Minister Stanley Baldwin proclaimed:

> "The sounds of England, the tinkle of the hammer on the anvil in the country smithy, the corncrake on a dewy morning, the sound of the scythe against the whetstone, and the sight of a plough team coming over the brow of a hill, the sign that has been seen in England since England was a land, and may be seen in England long after the Empire has perished and every works in England has ceased to function, for centuries the one eternal sight of England."

Baldwin, of course, only wanted to *hear* the sounds of the blacksmith and *watch* the plough team, not to have to take part in any back-breaking manual labour. Deep England is something to be enjoyed from one step back, by those who don't actually have to do any hard physical work. This is a recurring theme that is a key to understanding how Deep England is used, which I'll return to later - it is not a simple celebration of the English countryside, or of 'traditional ways' that we are in danger of losing.

Decades late Conservative Prime Minister John Major conjured up Deep England again in his 1993 speech to the Conservative Group for Europe (which probably now consists of three people and a stray dog) when he declared:

> "Fifty years on from now, Britain will still be the country of long shadows on county grounds, warm beer, invincible green suburbs, dog lovers and pools fillers and, as George Orwell said,

"There is little sign of the British Fascists becoming a danger, but they may quite well become a nuisance. But nothing Lord Rothermere can say will help them so much as dictatorship-talk from the Left."

Presumably the uncredited writer in the Spectator back in 1934 later realised that fascists can't be accommodated or appeased. We shouldn't sneer at this pre-war writer because we have the benefit of already knowing how the following years turned out.

English Array was dissolved around the beginning of the Second World War. Wallop and another member of English Array (and former member of the Kindred of the Kibbo Kift) Rolf Gardiner, went on to found the organisation Kinship in Husbandry in 1941, which also included Jorian Jenks, member of, and agricultural advisor to, the British Union of Fascists[10].

Gardiner and Jenks went on to join the Soil Association (founded in 1945/46) which at the time had an openly far-right agenda, and Jenks was the Editorial Secretary of the Association's journal *Mother Earth*. Following Jenks' death in 1963, and with a new president, the Soil Association swung towards a more centre-left agenda having successfully purged itself of all fascist leanings.

The sixties and seventies saw the Hippy-Folk Rock and Green movements try to mould the Deep England myth. While generally left-wing, there were some extremist conservative — and possibly fascist — elements within the early Green movement.

In 1997 the Countryside Alliance was formed, ostensibly to campaign on a wide range of countryside issues, but for all practical concerns its focus was — and remains — as a pro-Bloodsports lobby group. It was notably visible around the years leading up to the passing of the Hunting Act 2004 that banned hunting wild mammals with dogs, hare coursing, and other bloodsports. It organised an unsuccessful pro-Bloodsports march against the Hunting Act in 2002, a march which the far-right British National Party also urged its members to attend and support.

As I said earlier, social myths such as Deep England are persuasive, enticing, and deeply ingrained. As a national myth it probably won't go away, but it can be remade. Myths are, according to Joseph Campbell, society's dreams. And by that definition they are collectively-owned and therefore collectively-mutable. Unlike *Star Wars*, there is no unalterable "canon" that cannot be changed.

In the mid-twentieth century no imagined scene of Deep England would have been complete without a fox hunt. However social attitudes changed over time, culminating with the Hunting Act 2004 which banned fox hunting and hare coursing (although there are many allegations that criminals continue with illegal bloodsports). A recent opinion poll showed 85% of people now against fox hunting[11] — an all-time high — with even higher numbers against deer hunting, hare coursing, badger baiting, and dog fighting.

But interest in (and access to) the English countryside has never been solely the domain of the upper- and upper-middle-classes, nor the right-wing. The Woodcraft Folk have been mentioned above, J.B. Priestley evoked a left-wing version of Deep England in a number of his short propaganda radio shows during the Second World War which were very popular[12], and as Calder notes:

> "Hiking and rambling were popular with the working classes: the Ramblers' Association was in fact left-wing, and organised demonstrations to keep open rights of way. But even manual workers seem, when seeking in the countryside an escape from everyday conditions, to have ignored its primary function. Men and women laboured in the countryside to produce food."

As I have been writing this essay the Guardian newspaper has published an article by Alex Preston[13], *If our landscape truly belongs to us all, we must stop romanticising it*, which makes some very good points about how the current Conservative government's environmental policies, on the surface based on sound ecological principles, feel like they have a covert political instinct behind them.

And of course that covert political instinct is another attempt to shape or constrain the myth of Deep England. Preston's Guardian article includes an interview with author Melissa Harrison, in which she poses a very apt question:

> "When it comes to the fetishisation of place that happened in the 1930s, and is happening again now, it's vital to ask: who does this vision serve and who does it exclude?"

And indeed this is one of the

'Old maids bicycling to holy communion through the morning mist' and, if we get our way, Shakespeare will still be read even in school."

Major's embedded Orwell quote comes from his 1941 essay *England Your England*, and is probably the only part of Orwell's essay that a Conservative Prime Minister would dare to quote publically - well, apart from some pretty appalling non-English national stereotypes which would probably go down well at their next party conference given the increasing dominance of the more extreme right in the Tory party lately.

In his speech Major referred to Britain, but he's actually talking about a dream of England, and not just any part of England, but Deep England. In his 1991 book *The Myth of the Blitz* Angus Calder defined the boundaries of this dream:

"There was a Green and Pleasant heartland, 'Deep England', which stretched from Hardy's Wessex to Tennyson's Lincolnshire, from Kipling's Sussex to Elgar's Worcestershire. It excluded, self-evidently, the 'Black Country' of the industrial Midlands and the north with its factories and windswept moors. It included those areas of the Home Counties around London which had not been invaded by suburban development. Parts of Kent, for instance, were 'deeper' than anywhere, but areas of the country closer to London were commuter territory."

Deep England is Tolkien's Shire (without the Nazgûl), Midsomer (without the Murders), and a hundred other locales, none of them real.

It is the subtle subversion of the unwritten-but-instinctively-known trappings of the myth of Deep England that gives us what Robert Macfarlane called "the English Eerie"[3]; China Miéville, in his essay mentioned above, calls it the "bad picturesque" or the "pictureskew"; Stephen Prince, in his book *A Year in the Country: Wandering through Spectral Fields* refers to "otherly pastoralism" or "the undercurrents and flipside of the bucolic countryside dream"; and the writer David Southwell simply calls it "Ghost Soil" which manifests in "Hookland"[4].

And while Deep England doesn't exist, and has never existed, it is a powerfully enticing auto-stereotype, but for many — particularly many who live in urban and suburban areas, and especially, but not exclusively, on the political right wing — it is a vision of *how things were and should always be.*

This is not to say that your dreams of living in a "characterful" house on the outskirts of an English village — with a spacious kitchen-diner with a range and Butler sink, cosy living room with a multi-fuel-burning stove in the inglenook fireplace, master bedroom with ensuite and dressing room, and enough land to have a veg patch and maybe keep some chickens — has turned you into a frothing member of the Tory/UKIP grassroots. Honestly, if you add a studio, that's probably my dream house too. The BBC is not peddling *Escape to the Country* as a gateway drug leading to racism and the far right.

In his 2001 BBC Proms Lecture[5] *Deep and True? Reflections on the Cultural Life of the English Countryside* — and in the wake of the Foot and Mouth outbreak — Patrick Wright spoke of the English countryside in its mythic role:

> "I think this is also an appropriate time to reflect on the cultural dimension of the countryside. Not so much the way we farm it, but the way we have imagined it as something closely connected to our sense of identity, both locally and in a more national sense. The countryside, then, as a repository of values that neither farmers nor scientific conservationists may immediately recognise as belonging on their turf: ideas like innocence, beauty, peace, tradition, nature and, of course, nationhood too."

This concept of Deep England is so prevalent, so enticing, because it has been so constantly fed to us over the past hundred years. It has become a deeply-ingrained myth, even by those who know it is a myth.

And of course there are problems with this myth of Deep England. Deep problems.

In 2011 Brian True-May, the producer of *Midsomer Murders*, was suspended after saying[6] that "We just don't have ethnic minorities involved. Because it wouldn't be the English village with them…it just wouldn't work. Suddenly we might be in Slough…We're the last bastion of Englishness and I want to keep it that way."

He continued to dig himself deeper into a hole while muttering something about political correctness. A few days later, after what sounds suspiciously to me like a non-apology ("Brian apologises if his remarks gave unintended offence"), he was reinstated as producer, then stepped down at the end of that year's series[7].

I can only presume it was one of those complicated dances involving HR, PR, and lawyers that happens behind-the-scenes when you reach a certain level in British society, that ensures that no one on any side is publically seen to be held to account for their actions while still getting rid of the person who should have been, but without any unseemly fuss or lawsuits. The following series apparently saw more racial diversity introduced into the show.

The problem isn't just about a producer of *Midsomer Murders*, though. The myth of Deep England is, as I mentioned at the beginning of this piece, invariably and exclusively white. True-May's comment that racial diversity wouldn't work in *Midsomer Murders*, and the use of the phrase last bastion of Englishness suggest that racial diversity is an existential threat to the myth of Deep England. A bastion, after all, is a part of a fortification meant to keep people out.

Deep England is also rigidly class-structured, with everyone contently knowing "their place", and those who dream the myth certainly never picture themselves as farm labourers doing manual work for minimum wage. In Deep England, as under New Labour in the late nineties, it seems that we're all middle class now. The myth is about the dream of rural English life, not agriculture. As Calder (1991) describes, for both the conservatives and the avant-garde among the British propagandists in the 1940s:

> "The decline of rural crafts in the face of mass production struck a nerve; less so the pauperised condition of farm labour."

The Guardian took a swipe at the myth of Deep England[8] in April 2017, but couldn't bring themselves to stick the knife in too deeply because, well, that just wouldn't be cricket. But their argument that the Deep England myth was a driver for Brexit is certainly true.

The history of the Far Right's involvement with the myth of Deep England goes back much further than Brexit, though.

In 1920 the Kindred of the Kibbo Kift was formed by John Hargrave as an alternative to the Scouts and Guides (which Hargrave and others saw as overly militaristic), with a stronger focus on camping and woodland/rural crafts and, notably, some strange costumes. Five years later the left wing elements of the the Kibbo Kift broke away to form the Woodcraft Folk due to what they saw as Hargrave's increasingly authoritarian control of the organisation.

It seems they weren't wrong - by the early 1930s Hargrave decided that the Kindred of the Kibbo Kift would drop all woodland crafts, adopt paramilitary uniforms, and become the Social Credit Party (it eventually disbanded in 1951 after little or no political success).

Incidentally the Woodcraft Folk still continues as an alternative to the Scouts and Guides, fostering craft skills. Labour leader Jeremy Corbyn is an active supporter of the Woodcraft Folk, and wrote the introduction for a book on the history of the organisation in 2016 and former Green Party leader Natalie Bennett spoke in a debate at one of their "District Fellows" camps in 2013.

English Mistery was a Conservative fringe group founded in 1930 in favour of bringing back the feudal system (no, seriously, it did). It split in 1936 and an even more pro-Nazi successor group with a "back to the land" agenda called English Array was formed by English Mistery member and former Conservative MP Gerard Wallop (Lord Lymington and, later, 9th Earl of Portsmouth).

If Conservative MPs and the English aristocracy openly supporting fascism sounds slightly unbelievable then remember that it was at a time when the Daily Mail openly supported fascism at home and abroad - the paper's owner Lord Rothermere was a friend of both Hitler and Mussolini, and the Daily Mail published articles supporting Hitler's Blackshirts as well as Oswald Mosley and the British Union of Fascists. In 1934 the Spectator condemned[9] the Daily Mail's infamous "*Hurrah for the Blackshirts*" article with a quote that some would argue could still be relevant today.

> "But the Blackshirts, like the Daily Mail, appeal to people unaccustomed to thinking. The average Daily Mail reader is a potential Blackshirt ready made."

The Spectator unfortunately continued with the all-too-familiar call to accommodate the fascists and not insult them by calling them out on their fascism:

central questions in Harrison's latest (and highly recommended) novel *All Among the Barley*.

Harrison also explored the enticing dangers of the myth in her article[14] *A postcard from Deep England* for the website *Caught By The River*:

> "'I've moved into an advert for butter,' I find myself joking to friends, 'or perhaps an Enid Blyton book'. Certainly, this is Deep England, that beguiling but exclusionary wellspring of English imagination and identity that's starting to be explored by some of the writers and artists I know. I feel its siren call, and always have done: it's been there in everything I write, not least *All Among the Barley*, which explores its power explicitly. But I am wary of it, too – and of the dangers of nostalgia more generally, whether the collective false memory of a white English Eden that never really existed, or for the 'happy highways' of our own lost childhoods, that cannot come again."

I don't think that the myth of Deep England, the fetishisation of place (or of a place that has never existed except in myth), is going to go away - it's too deeply embedded. But as the change in public opinion over bloodsports shows, the collective myth of Deep England has been changed for the vast majority of society, in one aspect at least, over the past 20-30 years. This means it can be changed in its other aspects.

Myths constantly change as society changes, but the change feeds both ways. A change in society will feed into the myth, but also a change in the way the myth of Deep England is invoked — in art, in literature, in films and television shows — will feed back into society. That's just one of many reasons why diverse representation matters in the arts, and why I have been deliberately seeking out people of colour to life model for my artwork.

And since myths act as templates within a society for how to conduct yourself and what standards to uphold, a social mythscape that is exclusively white implicitly suggests that racism is acceptable. A myth that uncritically presents the class system or sexism indicates to society that class discrimination or sexism are acceptable. And the same applies for sexualities, gender identities, and so on.

This is why such minor-sounding changes send the far-right into rabid rage. A Muslim woman winning *the Great British Bake Off*; a female actor playing *Doctor Who* - why would these tiny things provoke such a huge response from the far right? Why do they immediately trigger numerous dog-whistle articles in the Daily Mail?

It's because they incrementally reshape the social myth. Each change is a precedent, a small alteration in the shared social myth that both controls us and that we control. These aren't shouts of rage from the far right, they're howls of fear and loss, wounds from yet another irrevocable progressive change in the myth they thought that they owned and which served them.

References

1. http://chinamieville.net/post/173542023303/skewing-the-picture
2. http://spinnet.humanities.uva.nl/images/2013-05/baldwin1924.pdf
3. https://www.theguardian.com/books/2015/apr/10/eeriness-english-countryside-robert-macfarlane
4. https://twitter.com/HooklandGuide
5. http://www.patrickwright.net/wp-content/uploads/pwright-proms-lecture-2001.pdf
6. http://www.bbc.co.uk/news/uk-12741847
7. https://www.theguardian.com/media/2011/mar/23/midsomer-murders-brian-true-may-english
8. https://www.theguardian.com/politics/shortcuts/2017/apr/11/deep-england-brexit-britain
9. http://archive.spectator.co.uk/article/19th-january-1934/6/lord-rothermeres-hurrah-for-the-blackshirts-articl
10. For more on this and a wealth of other information see David Matless' book *Landscape and Englishness*
11. https://www.ipsos.com/ipsos-mori/en-uk/attitudes-hunting-2017
12. Some of which can be heard in this broadcast:
https://www.bbc.co.uk/programmes/b00sf0tg
13. https://www.theguardian.com/commentisfree/2018/jan/14/landscape-belongs-to-us-all-stop-romanticising-it-michael-gove
14. https://www.caughtbytheriver.net/2018/05/a-postcard-from-deep-england-melissa-harrison/

Afterword

What next? A two-year project such as *England's Dark Dreaming* is all-consuming during its creation — the constant work and planning and research all focused solely on this one project — and when finally finished leaves the creator in the unfamiliar territory of being free to go off in any direction they want. The honest answer is: I don't know what's next (yet).

England's Dark Dreaming has taught me a lot about my artistic practice, and also about England and Englishness - none of which is ever covered in the periodic vacuous newspaper articles about Englishness. I have learned so much from this project, not just in terms of technique and skills, but also about myself and how I think about, and respond to, all of the news and information that we are confronted with on a daily basis.

In the research and reading I have done for this project I have once again been reminded me of the importance of the late Mark Fisher's work, not just his defining work on hauntology (a term whose definition for many has been erroneously reduced to "a 70s retro future aesthetic") and politics, but also his later work on the Weird and the Eerie, published posthumously in 2016. His deep understanding and analysis of contemporary culture continues to be sorely missed.

I have been interested in the rise of academic research into the Gothic which I have referred to earlier in this book, particularly the scholarly research into the contemporary works that are being produced in this mode. For too long the Gothic was seen as an discrete genre rather than a mode in which any type of artwork could be made, regardless of genre or subject matter. At the moment much of the academic work is along the lines of "The Gothic in [insert name of film/book]" which I suppose is necessary groundwork, but once these foundations are laid then I hope to see some deeper analysis and insight of the type that Mark Fisher was so good at.

I've been inspired and enthused by various artists working with similar themes and motifs, in particular David Southwell's *Hookland* work and actor/director/screenwriter John Harrigan's work on the Foolish People film *Armageddon Gospels*. I'm delighted to say that David is a personal friend who I've had many a pint with discussing our respective work and all things related (sometimes very tenuously related), and I've also had the privilege of meeting John and discussing both his work and my own work with him. I met both David and John through social media, so it can't be wholly as bad as the media makes out. Being able to talk with other artists working with the same themes and ideas — regardless of the medium they work in, or the country they live in — has enabled this project to grow and develop over these past two years.

And the soundtrack to my work over these past two years? On the one hand there's Layla and Phil Legard's Hawthonn, the Hare and the Moon, William Wright, Sharron Kraus, A Year in the Country, the Rowan Amber Mill, Inkubus Sukkubus, and Lutine. And on the other hand there's the old favourites: the Sisters of Mercy, David Bowie, P.J. Harvey, the Psychedelic Furs, and Flesh for Lulu. These seemingly disparate sounds combine and coalesce in my mind, and if you can imagine a mixtape with all of these musicians then that is my personal soundtrack to *England's Dark Dreaming*.

But I still haven't answered my question of "what next?" To be honest, I don't know. A couple of weeks rest then I'll start putting something together. *England's Dark Dreaming* wasn't predetermined and planned out from the start, it evolved.

And so will the next one.

Paul Watson
Brighton, August 2018
Twitter: @lazcorp
www.lazaruscorporation.co.uk